Focus Company and Contrast Company Used in Each Chapter

Chapter Title	Focus Company	Focus Company Logo	Focus Company Industry	Contrast Company
9. Profit Planning and Activity-Based Budgeting	Cozycamp.ca	cozycamp.ca	Manufacturer of backpacking tents, with heavy reliance on Internet sales	Canadian Fitness Cooperative (fitness club)
10. Standard Costing and Flexible Budgeting	DCdesserts.com	DC desserts	Producer of fresh fancy desserts, with complete reliance on e-commerce for both sales and purchasing	Tri-Cities Auto Rentals (auto rental company)
11. Cost Management Tools	Canadian Pacific Bank	CANADIAN PACIFIC BANK	Chartered bank, headquartered in Vancouver	Handico (cordless phone manufacturer)
12. Responsibility Accounting, Investment Centres, and Transfer Pricing	Aloha Hotels and Resorts	Aloha HOTELS & RESORTS	Hotel chain	Suncoast Food Centres (retail grocery chain)
13. Decision Making: Relevant Costs and Benefits	Worldwide Airways	Worldwide Airways	Airline company	International Chocolate Company (chocolate manufacturer)
14. Target Costing and Cost Analysis for Pricing Decisions	Sydney Sailing Supplies	SYDNEY SAILING SUPPLIES	Manufacturer of sailboats in Sydney, Australia	Marine Services Division (marina contractor)
15. Capital Expenditure Decisions (Online)	City of Mountainview	CITY OF MOUNTAINVIEW	City government	High Country Department Stores (retailer)
16. Allocation of Support Activity Costs and Joint Costs (Online)	Riverside Clinic	RIVERSIDE CLINIC	Health care provider	International Chocolate Company (chocolate manufacturer)

Managerial Accounting

Creating Value in a Dynamic Business Environment

CANADIAN
EDITION

Ronald W. Hilton
Cornell University

Michael Favere-Marchesi
Simon Fraser University

McGraw-Hill Ryerson
Connect. Learn. Succeed.

McGraw-Hill
Ryerson
Connect. Learn. Succeed.™

Managerial Accounting: Creating Value in a Dynamic Business Environment
Canadian Edition

ISBN-13: 978-0-07-096824-0
ISBN-10: 0-07-096824-1

1 2 3 4 5 6 7 8 9 10 WCD 1 9 8 7 6 5 4 3 2 1 0

Printed and bound in the United States of America.

Care has been taken to trace ownership of copyright material contained in this text; however, the publisher will welcome any information that enables them to rectify any reference or credit for subsequent editions.

Vice-President and Editor-in-Chief: *Joanna Cotton*
Executive Sponsoring Editor: *Rhondda McNabb*
Executive Marketing Manager: *Joy Armitage Taylor*
Developmental Editors: *Denise Foote & Leslie Mutic*
Editorial Associate: *Christine Lomas*
Supervising Editor: *Jessica Barnoski*
Copy Editor: *Rodney Rawlings*
Team Lead, Production: *Jennifer Hall*
Cover Design: *Michelle Losier*
Cover Images: Main cover image: © *Grafissimo/iStockphoto;* Skiing image: © *Erin Riley/Getty Images;* Airplane image: © *Stockbyte/Superstock;* Theatre image: © *Siri Stafford/Getty Images;* Resort image: © *Chris Caldicott/Getty Images;* Canoe image: © *Bill Curtsinger/Getty Images*
Interior Design: *Michelle Losier*
Page Layout: *Aptara, Inc.*
Printer: *World Color Press, Inc.*

Library and Archives Canada Cataloguing in Publication

Hilton, Ronald W.
    Managerial accounting : creating value in a dynamic business environment / Ronald W. Hilton, Michael Favere-Marchesi.—1st Canadian ed.

Includes bibliographical references and index.
ISBN 978-0-07-096824-0

    1. Managerial accounting—Textbooks.
I. Favere-Marchesi, Michael II. Title.

HF5657.4.H55 2009   658.15'11   C2009-903664-9

To my wife, Meg, and our sons, Brad and Tim.

—Ronald W. Hilton

To my son, Michael Justin.

—Michael Favere-Marchesi

ABOUT THE AUTHORS

Ronald W. Hilton is a Professor of Accounting at Cornell University. With bachelor's and master's degrees in accounting from The Pennsylvania State University, he received his Ph.D. from The Ohio State University.

A Cornell faculty member since 1977, Professor Hilton has also taught accounting at Ohio State and the University of Florida, where he held the position of Walter J. Matherly Professor of Accounting. Prior to pursuing his doctoral studies, Hilton worked for Peat, Marwick, Mitchell, and Company and served as an officer in the United States Air Force.

Professor Hilton is a member of the Institute of Management Accountants and has been active in the American Accounting Association. He has served as associate editor of the *Accounting Review* and as a member of its editorial board. Hilton also has served on the editorial board of the *Journal of Management Accounting Research.* He has been a member of the resident faculties of both the Doctoral Consortium and the New Faculty Consortium sponsored by the American Accounting Association.

With wide-ranging research interests, Hilton has published articles in many journals, including the *Journal of Accounting Research*, the *Accounting Review*, *Management Science*, *Decision Sciences*, the *Journal of Economic Behavior and Organization*, *Contemporary Accounting Research,* and the *Journal of Mathematical Psychology.* He also has published a monograph in the *AAA Studies in Accounting Research* series, and he is a co-author of *Cost Management: Strategies for Business Decisions*, *Budgeting: Profit Planning and Control*, and *Cost Accounting: Concepts and Managerial Applications.* Professor Hilton's current research interests focus on contemporary cost management systems and international issues in managerial accounting. In recent years, he has toured manufacturing facilities and consulted with practising managerial accountants in North America, Europe, Asia, and Australia.

Michael Favere-Marchesi is an Associate Professor of Accounting at Simon Fraser University. With bachelor's and master's degrees in accounting from Brigham Young University, he received his Ph.D. from the University of Southern California.

A Simon Fraser faculty member since 2000, Professor Favere-Marchesi has also taught accounting at the University of Southern California, the Monterey Institute of International Studies, HEC Paris, the University of Mannheim, the Helsinki School of Economics, Chulalongkorn University, and the National Institute of Development Administration (Thailand). Prior to pursuing his doctoral studies, Professor Favere-Marchesi worked for Arthur Andersen and Mattel. He is also a reserve officer in the United States Navy.

Professor Favere-Marchesi is a licensed Certified Public Accountant (California) and a Certified Internal Auditor. He is a member of the American Accounting Association and the Canadian Academic Accounting Association. He is also a member of the American Institute of Certified Public Accountants, and served both on its Board of Examiners and as Chair of its International Qualification Examination committee. He has served as reviewer of *Auditing: A Journal of Practice and Theory, Behavioral Research in Accounting,* the *International Journal of Accounting, Advances in Accounting Behavioral Research,* the *Journal of Accounting and Public Policy*, and *OR Spectrum: Quantitative Approaches in Management.*

With wide-ranging research interests, Professor Favere-Marchesi has published articles in several journals, including *Accounting Horizons, Auditing: A Journal of Practice and Theory, Behavioral Research in Accounting, Advances in Accounting,* the *International Journal of Accounting*, and *Advances in Accounting Behavioral Research.* Professor Favere-Marchesi's current research interests focus on audit judgment and decision making, audit review, fraudulent financial reporting, audit quality, and international audit environment.

Brief Contents

Contents

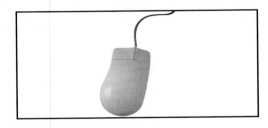

Note: Entries printed in blue denote topics that emphasize contemporary issues in managerial accounting and cost management.

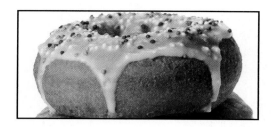

How does Hilton *Managerial Accounting* expose students to a range of businesses?

Managerial Accounting.

The world of business is changing dramatically. As a result, the role of managerial accounting is much different than it was even a decade ago. Today, managerial accountants serve as internal business consultants, working side-by-side in cross-functional teams with managers from all areas of the organization. For a thorough understanding of managerial accounting, students should not only be able to produce accounting information, but also understand how managers are likely to use and react to the information in a range of businesses.

The goal of *Managerial Accounting* is to acquaint students of business with the fundamental tools of management accounting and to promote their understanding of the dramatic ways in which the field is changing. The emphasis throughout the text is on using accounting information to help manage an organization.

Hilton *Managerial Accounting* is recognized for being:

Relevant.

Focus Companies provide a powerful strategy for fostering learning, and the integration of Focus Companies throughout the text is unmatched by any other managerial accounting book. Each chapter introduces important managerial accounting topics within the context of a realistic company. Students see the immediate impact of managerial accounting decisions on companies and gain exposure to different types of organizations.

Balanced.

Managerial Accounting offers the most balanced coverage of manufacturing and service sector companies. Recognizing that students will work in a great variety of business environments and will benefit from exposure to diverse types of companies, *Managerial Accounting* uses a wide variety of examples from retail, service, manufacturing, and nonprofit organizations.

Contemporary.

Managerial Accounting continues to be the leader in presenting the most contemporary coverage of managerial accounting topics. The traditional tools of managerial accounting such as product costing and budgeting have been updated with current approaches. New topics such as environmental cost management and responsibility accounting have been added.

Flexible.

Managerial Accounting is written in a modular format allowing topics to be covered in the order you want. For example, Chapter 8 covers absorption and variable costing. Many instructors like to cover this topic early in the course. So, Chapter 8 is written so that it can be assigned right after Chapter 3. A table showing the text's flexibility is in the Instructor's Resource Manual.

How does Hilton help students learn managerial accounting in the context of business?

FOCUS COMPANIES

Students need to see the relevance of managerial accounting information in order to actively engage in learning the material. The authors have found that by using Focus Companies to illustrate concepts, they can help students immediately see the significance of the material and get excited about the content. *Managerial Accounting's* integration of Focus Companies throughout the text is unmatched by any other managerial accounting textbook. Each chapter introduces important managerial topics within the context of a realistic company.

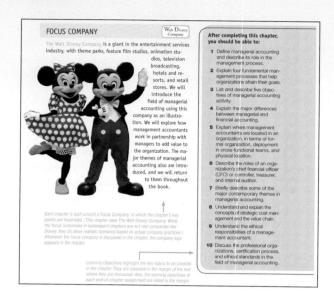

FOCUS COMPANY   [Walt Disney Company]

The Walt Disney Company is a giant in the entertainment services industry, with theme parks, feature film studios, animation studios, television broadcasting, hotels and resorts, and retail stores. We will introduce the field of managerial accounting using this company as an illustration. We will explore how management accountants work in partnership with managers to add value to the organization. The major themes of managerial accounting also are introduced, and we will return to them throughout the book.

Each chapter is built around a Focus Company, in which the chapter's key points are illustrated. (This chapter uses The Walt Disney Company. While the focus companies in subsequent chapters are not real companies like Disney, they do allow realistic scenarios based on actual company practices.) Whenever the focus company is discussed in the chapter, the company logo appears in the margin.

Learning Objectives highlight the key topics to be covered in the chapter. They are repeated in the margin of the text where they are discussed. Also, the learning objectives of each end-of-chapter assignment are listed in the margin.

After completing this chapter, you should be able to:

1 Define managerial accounting and describe its role in the management process.

2 Explain four fundamental management processes that help organizations attain their goals.

3 List and describe five objectives of managerial accounting activity.

4 Explain the major differences between managerial and financial accounting.

5 Explain where management accountants are located in an organization, in terms of formal organization, deployment in cross-functional teams, and physical location.

6 Describe the roles of an organization's chief financial officer (CFO) or controller, treasurer, and internal auditor.

7 Briefly describe some of the major contemporary themes in managerial accounting.

8 Understand and explain the concepts of strategic cost management and the value chain.

9 Understand the ethical responsibilities of a management accountant.

10 Discuss the professional organizations, certification process, and ethical standards in the field of managerial accounting.

Whenever the Focus Company is presented in the chapter, its logo is shown so the student sees its application to the text topic.

IN CONTRAST

In contrast to the entertainment services setting of The Walt Disney Company, we will turn our attention to Gap, Inc. This major clothing retailer has over 3,000 stores around the world, which sell Gap, Banana Republic, and Old Navy. We will explore Gap's value chain, which is the set of linked, value-creating activities, ranging from securing basic raw materials and energy to the ultimate delivery of products and services. As a retailer, Gap focuses on apparel design, marketing, and sales. All manufacturing of its clothing lines is contracted out to garment manufacturers around the world.

Each chapter also includes a Contrast Company. In most cases, the contrast company will present a key chapter topic in an industry different from that of the focus company. In this chapter, the focus company (Walt Disney) is an entertainment services company, whereas the contrast company (Gap) is a fashion retailer.

CONTRAST COMPANIES

A Contrast Company is also introduced in each chapter. In most cases, these highlight an industry different from that of the Focus Company. This feature allows even greater emphasis on service-sector firms and other non-manufacturing environments. The complete list of Focus Companies and Contrast Companies is featured on the front endpapers.

Real-World Examples

The text provides a variety of thought-provoking, real-world examples to focus students on managerial accounting as an essential part of the management process. Featured organizations include FedEx, WestJet Airlines, TD Canada Trust, Amazon.ca, Gap, and many others. These companies are highlighted in blue in the text.

Organization Chart

Notice that a company's top management group usually consists of the board of directors, chairman and chief executive officer (CEO), vice-chairman, and chief of corporate operations.

Line and Staff Positions   The other positions in an organization chart are of two types: line positions and staff positions. Managers in **line positions** are *directly* involved in the provision of goods or services. For example, Disney's line positions include the chairman and president of Disney Consumer Products, the chairman and president of Walt Disney Feature Animation, and the chairman and president of Walt Disney Attractions, which is the division responsible for the company's theme parks in Florida, California, and Japan. Also in line positions would be the thousands of managers in the various operating units of the divisions. For example, the general manager of Disney's Animal Kingdom, the manager of food and beverage services at the Magic

---

In Their Own Words

Quotes from both practising managers and managerial accountants are included in the margins throughout the text. These actual quotes show how the field of management accounting is changing, emphasize how the concepts are actually used, and demonstrate that management accountants are key players in most companies' management teams.

Professional Organizations

To keep up with new developments in their field, management accountants often belong to one or more professional organizations. Many management accountants belong to the Canadian Institute of Chartered Accountants, the Certified General Accountants Association of Canada, or the Society of Management Accountants of Canada. The latter publishes a journal, entitled *CMA Management*, and also supports research on managerial accounting topics through the CMA Canada Research Foundation.

The primary professional association for management accountants in the United States is the Institute of Management Accountants. Great Britain's main professional organization is the Institute of Chartered Management Accountants, and Australia's organization is the Institute of Chartered Accountants in Australia. In all, over 75 countries have professional organizations for their practising accountants.

> "You've got to know how to talk to people, express yourself. And that's oral and written. You also have to be able to understand a lot of different areas, not necessarily just accounting. You've got to understand the business itself." (1)
>
> Qwest

Management Accounting Practice

The managerial accounting practices of well-known, real-world organizations are highlighted in these boxes. They stimulate student interest and provide a springboard for classroom discussion.

MASS CUSTOMIZATION

Management Accounting Practice

Dell Inc.

"There is no better way to make, sell, and deliver PCs than the way Dell Inc. does it, and nobody executes that model better than Dell." The company's machines are made to order and delivered directly to customers, who get the exact machines they want cheaper than they can get them from Dell's competition. "Dell has some 24 facilities in and around Austin and employs more than 18,000 local workers. Dell is improving its earnings and gaining market share even in tough economic times. Nevertheless, Michael Dell, the company's restless founder, is constantly looking for ways to improve the company's operations."[2] In one year alone, Dell cut $1 billion out of its costs—half from manufacturing—and Dell executives vowed to cut another $1 billion.

"Visit the Topfer Manufacturing Center in Austin, and it's hard to conceive how Dell could be any more efficient. Workers already scuttle about in the 200,000-square-foot plant like ants on a hot plate. Gathered in cramped six-person 'cells,' they assemble computers from batches of parts that arrive via a computer-directed conveyor system overhead. If a worker encounters a problem, that batch can instantly be shifted to another cell, avoiding the stoppages that plague conventional assembly lines. Dell is constantly tinker-

---

Focus on Ethics

Focus on Ethics boxes pose an ethical dilemma, then ask tough questions that underscore the importance of ethical management. Some of these are based on real-world incidents, while others are fictional but based on well-established anecdotal evidence.

Focus on Ethics

WAS WORLDCOM'S CONTROLLER JUST FOLLOWING ORDERS?

Through a series of mergers and acquisitions, WorldCom, Inc. grew to become North America's second-largest long-distance telecommunications company. WorldCom's core communication services included network data transmission over public and private networks. Trouble arose for WorldCom because of the immense overcapacity in the telecommunications industry due to overly optimistic growth projections during the Internet boom. The combination of overcapacity, decreased demand, and high fixed costs still poses a serious problem for many of the major players in the industry.

In June 2002, the company disclosed that it had overstated earnings for 2001 and the first quarter of 2002 to the tune of $3.8 billion. The overstatement arose because the company incorrectly classified period expenses as capital expenditures. This manoeuvre had two major effects on the company's financial statements: the company's assets were artificially inflated and the capitalization allowed the company to spread the recognition of its

alleged accounting scandal. The auditing company maintained that the details of the fraud were kept from them by senior management. WorldCom's controller and chief financial officer (CFO), who was a former KPMG employee, were fired after the alleged accounting frauds were revealed. WorldCom's CEO maintained that he knew nothing of the accounting decisions made by the CFO, but many observers question how almost $8 billion in expenses could slip by senior management.[14]

According to an Associated Press article that ran on September 27, 2002, "the former controller of WorldCom, Inc. pleaded guilty to securities fraud charges, saying he was instructed by 'senior management' to falsify records. His plea was the first admission of guilt to fall from the largest corporate accounting scandal in U.S. history."[15] Subsequently, WorldCom's CFO pleaded guilty to his part in the accounting scandal.[16] In March of 2005, the company's CEO was convicted by a jury of nine criminal counts in the accounting fraud, including conspiracy and securities fraud.[17]

The CFO and controller were the top two financial

How can my students use Hilton to master the concepts of managerial accounting?

Managerial Accounting is known for its comprehensive and reliable end-of-chapter material.

Review Problems present both a problem and a complete solution allowing students to review the entire problem-solving process.

Review Problems on Cost Classifications

Problem 1

Several costs incurred by Myrtle Beach Golf Equipment, Inc. are listed below. For each cost, indicate which of the following classifications best describe the cost. More than one classification may apply to the same cost item. For example, a cost may be both a variable cost and a product cost.

Cost Classifications
a. Variable
b. Fixed
c. Period
d. Product
e. Administrative
f. Selling
g. Manufacturing
h. Research and development
i. Direct material
j. Direct labour
k. Manufacturing overhead

Cost Items

Key Terms are bolded in the text and repeated at the end of the chapter with page references. The book's Web site at the Online Learning Centre, at www.mcgrawhill.ca/olc/hilton, also includes a complete Glossary for these Key Terms.

Key Terms

For each term's definition refer to the indicated page, or turn to the glossary at the end of the text.

activity, 38	direct cost, 43	inventoriable cost, 28	raw material, 31
average cost per unit, 47	direct-labour cost, 34	manufacturing overhead, 34	schedule of cost of goods manufactured, 36
controllable cost, 43	direct material, 34	marginal cost, 46	
conversion costs, 36	expense, 27	mass customization, 32	schedule of cost of goods sold, 36
cost, 27	finished goods, 31	operating expenses, 29	service departments (or support departments), 35
cost driver, 39	fixed costs, 40	opportunity cost, 44	
cost object, 43	idle time, 35	out-of-pocket costs, 44	sunk costs, 45
cost of goods manufactured, 36	incremental cost, 46	overtime premium, 35	uncontrollable cost, 43
	indirect cost, 43	period costs, 28	variable cost, 39
cost of goods sold, 27	indirect labour, 35	prime costs, 36	work in process, 31
differential cost, 46	indirect material, 34	product cost, 27	

End-of-Chapter Assignment Material Each chapter includes an extensive selection of assignment material, including Review Questions, Exercises, Problems, and Cases. Our problem and case material facilitates class discussions.

Review Questions

2–1. Distinguish between product costs and period costs.
2–2. Why are product costs also called inventoriable costs?
2–3. What is the most important difference between a manufacturing firm and a service industry firm, with regard to the classification of costs as product costs or period costs?
2–4. List, describe, and give an example of each of the five different types of production processes.
2–5. "The words *mass* and *customization* in the term *mass customization* seem contradictory." Do you agree or disagree? Explain.
2–6. Why is the cost of idle time treated as manufacturing overhead?
2–7. Explain why an overtime premium is included in man-

2–17. Which of the following costs are likely to be controllable by the chief of nursing in a hospital?
    a. Cost of medication administered
    b. Cost of overtime paid to nurses due to scheduling errors
    c. Cost of depreciation of hospital beds
2–18. Distinguish between out-of-pocket costs and opportunity costs.
2–19. Define the terms *sunk cost* and *differential cost.*
2–20. Distinguish between marginal and average costs.
2–21. Think about the process of registering for classes at your college or university. What additional information would you like to have before you register? How would it help you? What sort of information might create

Excel® Spreadsheets

Spreadsheet applications are essential to contemporary accounting practice. Students must recognize the power of spreadsheets and know how accounting data are presented in them. Excel® applications are discussed where appropriate in the text.

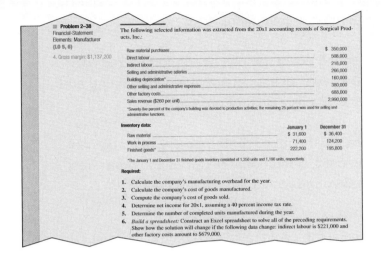

Several exercises and problems in each chapter include an optional requirement for students to **Build a Spreadsheet** to develop the solution.

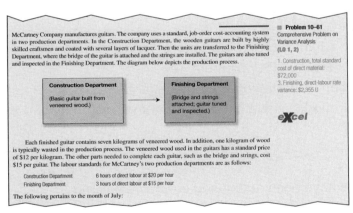

Many problems can be solved using the Excel spreadsheet templates contained on the text's Web site. An Excel® logo appears in the margin next to these problems for easy identification.

Icons identify key business areas in the problems and cases in each chapter:

 Ethical Issues

 Group Work

 Internet Research

 International Issues

 Business Communication

 Excel Template

New to the Canadian Edition

Major Revisions and Reorganizations

Based on input from users and reviewers, the activity-based costing and activity-based management coverage has been heavily revised, reorganized, and condensed into a single chapter. Chapter 5, "Activity-Based Costing and Management," covers all aspects of ABC and ABM in a single comprehensive Focus Company illustration.

Similarly, standard costing and flexible budgeting coverage has been reorganized and condensed into a single chapter. Chapter 10 covers all aspects of standard costing and groups all cost variances into a single Focus Company illustration.

Chapter 11, "Cost Management Tools," regroups the most contemporary management tools and techniques such as balanced scorecard, operational performance measures, kaizen costing, quality cost reporting, and environmental cost management.

Online Chapters and Supplements

Additional chapters and supplements on special topics are available on the Online Learning Centre (OLC). These bonus chapters and supplements include:

- Capital Expenditure Decisions (Chapter 15)
- Allocation of Support Activity Costs and Joint Costs (Chapter 16)
- Process Costing: The First-In, First-Out Method (Supplement 4A)
- Process Costing in Sequential Production Departments (Supplement 4B)
- Hybrid Product-Costing Systems: Operation Costing in Batch Manufacturing Processes (Supplement 4C)

Management Accounting Practice

New Management Accounting Practice boxes have been added and several real-world examples have been updated to give a Canadian flavour to the examples.

Emphasis on the Service Sector

A greater effort has been made to point out the relevance of managerial accounting concepts and tools in service-sector settings. Many examples are given throughout the text of real-world service-sector firms using managerial accounting information.

End-of-Chapter Assignment Material

Several new problems have been added, and virtually all of the exercises, problems, and cases contain new data.

Chapter-by-Chapter Changes

Chapter 1: A Management Accounting Practice box explains how new technology is making it easier for Canadian companies to conduct business. All three Canadian professional designations are discussed, and the Focus on Ethics section relates to the Code of Professional Ethics of CMA Ontario. Because of its wide appeal, The Walt Disney Company is the Focus Company, and the Contrast Company is Gap, an apparel retailer. References are made in this chapter to several Canadian firms, such as Canadian Direct Insurance, London Drugs, and WestJet Airlines.

Chapter 2: The Focus Company is Comet Computer Company, a manufacturer, and the Contrast Company is Midas, an automotive service company. References are made in this chapter to several Canadian firms, such as Fairmont Hotels & Resorts, Manulife Insurance, TD Canada Trust, and Tim Hortons.

Chapter 3: The Focus Company is Rocky Mountain Outfitters, a manufacturer of canoes and small boats, and the Contrast Company is Metro Advertising Agency, an advertising services company. References are made in this chapter to several Canadian firms, such as Air Canada and Bank of Montreal. Discussion of radio frequency identification systems includes a reference to Bell Canada and CN, the Canadian National Railway Company. A review problem on job-order costing in included.

Chapter 4: The Focus Company is the Alberta division of MVP Sports Equipment Company, a manufacturer, and the Contrast Company is MVP's Ontario division. A Management Accounting Practice box describes the British Columbia wine industry. Three online supplements are associated with this chapter: Process Costing: The First-In, First-Out Method; Process Costing in Sequential Production Departments; and Hybrid Product-Costing Systems: Operation Costing in Batch Manufacturing Processes.

Chapter 5: The Focus Company is Patio Grill Company, a manufacturer of gas barbeque grills, and the Contrast Company is the Toronto General Hospital's Ambulatory Care Clinic, a health-care provider. This chapter covers activity-based costing and activity-based management. References are made in this chapter to several Canadian firms, such as TELUS and BMO Financial Group. An appendix to this chapter covers JIT inventory and production management.

Chapter 6: The Focus Company is Tasty Donuts, a restaurant chain, and the Contrast Company is Cosmos Communications Technology, a manufacturer of communications satellites. References are made in this chapter to several Canadian firms, such as WestJet Airlines and Chapters. The coverage of regression analysis reflects less emphasis on manual calculations and more focus on the use of Excel® regression commands.

Chapter 7: The Focus Company is Toronto Contemporary Theatre, a nonprofit theatre organization, and the Contrast Company is AccuTime, a manufacturer of digital clocks. References are made in this chapter to several Canadian firms, such as CBC, Toronto Maple Leafs, and WestJet Airlines.

Chapter 8: Only one company is used in this shorter chapter to illustrate absorption and variable costing. Quikmath.com is a manufacturer of hand-held calculators. A review problem is included to help students understand the two costing methods. The placement of this chapter is appropriate following CVP analysis that emphasizes contribution margin, and this chapter may easily be skipped for instructors who prefer not to cover this topic.

Chapter 9: The Focus Company is CozyCamp.ca, a manufacturer of camping equipment, with online sales, and the Contrast Company is Canadian Fitness Cooperative, a fitness club. Introduction of activity-based budgeting ties with the materials in Chapter 5. A Management Accounting Practice box makes reference to the budget administration at a Canadian university.

Chapter 10: The Focus Company is DCdesserts.com, a producer of fresh fancy desserts with emphasis on e-commerce, and the Contrast Company is Tri-Cities Auto Rentals, a car-rental service company. This chapter covers all aspects of standard costing, and includes variance analysis for direct material, direct labour, and variable and fixed manufacturing overhead, with a related discussion of flexible budgeting. Included in two appendices are the preparation of journal entries in a standard costing system and a discussion of sales variances.

Chapter 11: The Focus Company is the Canadian Pacific Bank, a financial-services bank, and the Contrast Company is Handico, a manufacturer of cordless phones. References are made in this chapter to several Canadian firms, such as CIBC, Toronto's Hospital for Sick Children, Rogers Wireless Communications, and Scotia Bank. This chapter regroups various cost management tools and starts with a discussion of the balanced scorecard and operational performance measures. It describes concepts of kaizen costing, benchmarking, reengineering, and the theory of constraints. It also discusses quality cost reporting and environmental cost management.

Chapter 12: The Focus Company is Aloha Hotels and Resorts, a hotel and resort chain, and the Contrast Company is Suncoast Food Centres, a grocery retailer. References are made in this chapter to some Canadian firms, such as Royal Bank of Canada, and a governmental agency (CRA). Introduction of activity-based responsibility accounting ties with the materials in Chapter 5. This chapter covers segmented reporting, performances measures (ROI, residual income, and EVA), and transfer pricing between segments of an enterprise.

Chapter 13: The Focus Company is Worldwide Airways, an international airline, and the Contrast Company is International Chocolate Company, a chocolate producer. An appendix to this chapter describes the use of linear programming in product-mix decisions.

Chapter 14: The Focus Company is Sydney Sailing Supplies, a manufacturer of sailing supplies and equipment, and the Contrast Company is the Marine Services Division of Sydney Sailing Supplies. References are made in this chapter to several Canadian firms, such as Bell Canada, TELUS, and Fido. This chapter assumes students have covered basic economic principles in a microeconomic course and focuses on pricing decisions.

Chapter 15 (Online): The Focus organization is the City of Mountainview, a city government, and the Contrast Company is High Country Department Stores, a retailer. This online chapter covers discounted-cash-flow analysis (net present-value method and internal-rate-of-return method) and alternative methods (payback method and accounting-rate-of-return method). Income tax issues related to CCA are covered at the end of the chapter and can be easily omitted for instructors who prefer to eliminate this more complex topic.

Chapter 16 (Online): The Focus organization is Riverside Clinic, a health-care provider, and the Contrast Company is International Chocolate Company, a chocolate producer. This online chapter covers the allocation of support activity costs and joint costs.

Enriched Learning with Technology

Lyryx Assessment for Managerial Accounting

Lyryx Assessment for Managerial Accounting is a Web-based teaching and learning tool that has captured the attention of post-secondary institutions across the country. Lyryx Assessment is a leading-edge online assessment system that delivers significant benefits to both students and instructors.

After registering their course with us, instructors can create Labs of their choice by selecting problems from our test bank and setting deadlines. Instructors have access to all the students' marks and can view their best Labs. At any time, instructors can download the class grades for their own programs to analyze individual and class performance.

The assessment takes the form of a homework assignment called a Lab. The Labs are algorithmically generated and automatically graded, so students get instant scores and feedback—no need to wait until the next class to find out how well they did!

If students are doing their managerial accounting practice and homework, they will improve their performance in the course. Recent research regarding the use of Lyryx has shown when Labs are tied to assessment, even if worth only a small percentage of the total grade for the course, students *will* do their homework—*and more than once. The result is improved student success in managerial accounting!*

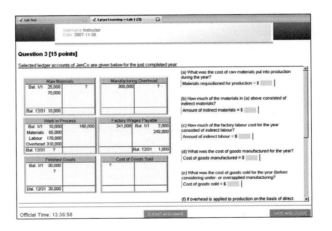

Please contact your *i*Learning Sales Specialist

for additional information on Lyryx Assessment for Managerial Accounting.

Connect Accounting

McGraw-Hill Ryerson's ***Connect Accounting*** is a Web-based assignment and assessment platform that gives students the means to better connect with their coursework, with their instructors, and with the important concepts they will need to know for success now and in the future.

In partnership with Youthography, a Canadian youth research company, and hundreds of students from across Canada, McGraw-Hill Ryerson conducted extensive student research on student study habits, behaviours, and attitudes—we asked questions and listened . . . and we heard some things we didn't expect. We had two goals: to help faculty be more efficient in and out of the classroom by providing a study tool that would help them improve student engagement and to help students learn their course material and get better grades. Through this research, we gained a better understanding of how students study—and how we could make vast improvements to our current online study tools. The result is a study tool that students overwhelming said is better and there's *nothing else like it out there.* **Connect** really is the first study tool built by students for students. Getting better grades really is only a click away!

Study Plan
An innovative tool that helps students customize their own learning experience. Students can diagnose their knowledge with a pre and post test, identify the areas where they are weak, search contents of the entire learning package for content specific to the topic they're studying and add these resources to their study plan. Students told us the act of creating a study plan is how they actually study and that having the opportunity to have everything in one place, with the ability to search, customize and prioritize the class resources, was critical. No other publisher provides this type of tool and students told us without a doubt, the "Study Plan" feature is the most valuable tool they have used to help them study.

eText
Now students can search the textbook online, too! When struggling with a concept or reviewing for an exam, students can conduct key word searches to quickly find the content they need.

Homework Assessment
Connect Accounting assessment activities don't stop with students. Instructors can deliver assignments, quizzes, and tests online. They can edit existing questions and add new ones; track individual student performance—by question, assignment, or in relation to the class overall—with detailed grade reports; integrate grade reports easily with Learning Management Systems such as WebCT and Blackboard; and much more.

Please contact your *i*Learning Sales Specialist for additional information on *Connect Accounting*.

Online Learning Centre
(www.mcgrawhill.ca/olc/hilton)
The Student Centre of this Web site includes additional online content and an interactive student component with Excel® templates (for selected problems as identified in the text by the appropriate icon), self-study multiple-choice questions, and more.

What Other Resources are Available to Instructors?

COMPREHENSIVE SUPPORT

Hilton offers a complete, integrated supplements package. All available on the Instructor area of the Online Learning Centre (www.mcgrawhill.ca/olc/hilton), the instructor supplements include:

- **Instructor's Manual:** This comprehensive manual includes chapter outlines, summaries, and teaching overviews.
- **Solutions Manual:** This manual, prepared by the author, contains complete solutions to all the text's end-of-chapter review questions, exercises, problems, and cases.
- **Computerized Test Bank:** This test bank contains multiple-choice questions, essay, and short problems. Each test item is coded for level of difficulty and learning objective.
- **PowerPoint® Presentations:** These slides cover key concepts found in each chapter using outlines, summaries, and visuals.

SUPERIOR SERVICE

Your Integrated Learning Sales Specialist is a McGraw-Hill Ryerson representative who has the experience, product knowledge, training, and support to help you assess and integrate any of our products, technology, and services into your course for optimum teaching and learning performance. Whether it's using our test bank software, helping your students improve their grades, or putting your entire course online, your *i*Learning Sales Specialist is there to help you do it. Contact your local *i*Learning Sales Specialist today to learn how to maximize all of McGraw-Hill Ryerson's resources!

*i*LEARNING SERVICES PROGRAM

McGraw-Hill Ryerson offers a unique *i*Services package designed for Canadian faculty. Our mission is to equip providers of higher education with superior tools and resources required for excellence in teaching. For additional information visit www.mcgrawhill.ca/highereducation/iservices.

COURSESMART

CourseSmart brings together thousands of textbooks across hundreds of courses in an e-textbook format providing unique benefits to students and faculty. By purchasing an e-textbook, students can save up to 50 percent off the cost of a print textbook, reduce their impact on the environment, and gain access to powerful Web tools for learning including full-text search, notes and highlighting, and e-mail tools for sharing notes between classmates. For faculty, CourseSmart provides instant access to review and compare textbooks and course materials in their discipline area without the time, cost, and environmental impact of mailing print exam copies. For further details contact your *i*Learning Sales Specialist or go to www.coursesmart.com.

PRIMIS

Through McGraw-Hill Ryerson's custom publishing division, **Primis**, instructors are able to select cases to accompany *Managerial Accounting* in a number of ways. Create your own case set, or browse the selection of cases that correspond to the chapter material. Contact your McGraw-Hill Ryerson *i*Learning Sales specialist for more information.

Acknowledgments

I am grateful . . .

I would like to express my appreciation to people who have provided assistance in the development of this textbook. First, my gratitude goes to the thousands of accounting students I have had the privilege to teach over many years. Their enthusiasm, comments, and questions have challenged me to clarify my thinking about many topics in managerial accounting.

Second, I express my sincere thanks to the following professors who provided extensive reviews for this first Canadian edition:

REVIEWERS

Marcia Annisette, *York University*

Robert Bergquist, *Nipissing University*

Brent Bertrand, *University of Toronto*

Ann Bigelow, *University of Western Ontario*

Lynn Carty, *Wilfrid Laurier University*

Liang Chen, *University of Toronto Scarborough*

Elliott Currie, *University of Guelph*

Dennis Dober, *College of the North Atlantic*

Gerry Dupont, *Carleton University*

Clinton Free, *Queen's University*

David Hoffman, *Seneca College*

Sylvia Hsu, *York University*

Marg Johnson, *Thompson Rivers University*

Ferdinand Jones, *University of Ontario Institute of Technology*

Anita Lakra, *University of Calgary*

D. L. Losell, *University of Toronto*

Abbe Nielsen, *Langara College*

Pamela Quon, *Athabasca University*

Todd Rose, *Memorial University of Newfoundland*

Naqi Sayed, *Lakehead University*

Ken Sutley, *Grant MacEwan College*

Shu-Lun Wong, *Memorial University*

I also want to thank Susan Cohlmeyer and Elliott Currie and for their thorough checking of the text and solutions manual for accuracy and completeness.

The supplements are a great deal of work to prepare. I appreciate the efforts of those who prepared them, since these valuable aids make teaching the course easier for everyone who uses the text.

I acknowledge the Institute of Management Accountants for permission to use problems from Certified Management Accountant (CMA) examinations. I also acknowledge the American Institute of Certified Public Accountants for permission to use problems from the Uniform CPA Examinations, Questions, and Unofficial Answers. I am indebted to Professors Roland Minch, David Solomons, and Michael Maher for allowing the use of their case materials in the text. The source for the actual company information in Chapters 1 and 2 regarding The Walt Disney Company, Caterpillar, Wal-Mart, and WestJet Airlines was the companies' published annual reports.

Finally, I wish to express my gratitude to the fine people at McGraw-Hill Ryerson who so professionally guided this book through the publication process. In particular, I wish to acknowledge Denise Foote, Leslie Mutic, Rhondda McNabb, Jessica Barnoski, and Rodney Rawlings.

Michael Favere-Marchesi

Chapter One

The Changing Role of Managerial Accounting

FOCUS COMPANY

Walt Disney Company

The Walt Disney Company is a giant in the entertainment services industry, with theme parks, feature film studios, animation studios, television broadcasting, hotels and resorts, and retail stores. We will introduce the field of managerial accounting using this company as an illustration. We will explore how management accountants work in partnership with managers to add value to the organization. The major themes of managerial accounting also are introduced, and we will return to them throughout the book.

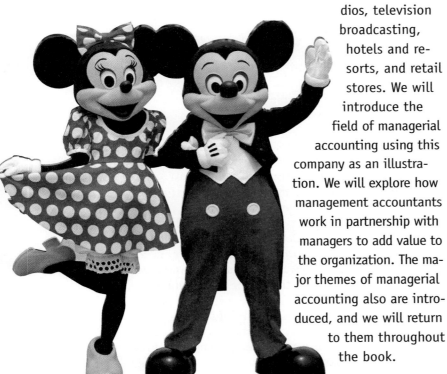

Each chapter is built around a Focus Company, in which the chapter's key points are illustrated. (This chapter uses The Walt Disney Company. While the focus companies in subsequent chapters are not real companies like Disney, they do allow realistic scenarios based on actual company practices.) Whenever the focus company is discussed in the chapter, the company logo appears in the margin.

Learning Objectives highlight the key topics to be covered in the chapter. They are repeated in the margin of the text where they are discussed. Also, the learning objectives of each end-of-chapter assignment are listed in the margin.

After completing this chapter, you should be able to:

1 Define managerial accounting and describe its role in the management process.

2 Explain four fundamental management processes that help organizations attain their goals.

3 List and describe five objectives of managerial accounting activity.

4 Explain the major differences between managerial and financial accounting.

5 Explain where management accountants are located in an organization, in terms of formal organization, deployment in cross-functional teams, and physical location.

6 Describe the roles of an organization's chief financial officer (CFO) or controller, treasurer, and internal auditor.

7 Briefly describe some of the major contemporary themes in managerial accounting.

8 Understand and explain the concepts of strategic cost management and the value chain.

9 Understand the ethical responsibilities of a management accountant.

10 Discuss the professional organizations, certification process, and ethical standards in the field of managerial accounting.

IN CONTRAST

In contrast to the entertainment services setting of The Walt Disney Company, we will turn our attention to Gap, Inc. This major clothing retailer has over 3,000 stores around the world, which sell Gap, Banana Republic, and Old Navy. We will explore Gap's value chain, which is the set of linked, value-creating activities, ranging from securing basic raw materials and energy to the ultimate delivery of products and services. As a retailer, Gap focuses on apparel design, marketing, and sales. All manufacturing of its clothing lines is contracted out to garment manufacturers around the world.

Each chapter also includes a Contrast Company. In most cases, the contrast company will present a key chapter topic in an industry different from that of the focus company. In this chapter, the focus company (Walt Disney) is an entertainment services company, whereas the contrast company (Gap) is a fashion retailer.

In Their Own Words
These quotes are from practising management accountants or line managers. The quotes show how various managerial accounting concepts are actually used and how management accountants are key players in most companies.

Learning Objective 1

Define managerial accounting and describe its role in the management process.

Many different kinds of organizations affect our daily lives. Manufacturers, retailers, service industry firms, agribusiness companies, nonprofit organizations, and government agencies provide us with a vast array of goods and services. All of these organizations have two things in common. First, they all have a set of *goals* or objectives. An airline, such as British Airways or WestJet Airlines, might specify profitability and customer service as its goals. The Vancouver Police Department's goals would include public safety and security coupled with cost minimization. Second, in pursuing an organization's goals, managers need *information*. The information needs of management range across financial, production, marketing, legal, and environmental issues. Generally, the larger the organization, the greater management's need for information.

Managerial accounting is the process of identifying, measuring, analyzing, interpreting, and communicating information in pursuit of an organization's goals. It is an integral part of the management process, and management accountants are important strategic partners in an organization's management team.

In this chapter, we will explore the role of managerial accounting within the overall management process. In the remaining chapters, we will expand our study by exploring the many concepts and tools used in managerial accounting.

A Business Partnership with Management

"We are looked upon as business advisors, more than just accountants, and that has a lot to do with the additional analysis and the forward-looking goals we are setting." (1a)[1]

Caterpillar

The role of managerial accounting is very different now from what it was even a decade ago. In the past, management accountants operated in a strictly staff capacity, usually physically separated from the managers for whom they provided reports and information. Today, management accountants serve as internal business consultants, working side-by-side in cross-functional teams with managers from all areas of the organization. Rather than isolate management accountants in a separate accounting department, companies now tend to locate them in the operating departments where they are working with other managers to make decisions and resolve operational problems. Management accountants take on leadership roles on their teams and are sought out for the valuable information they provide. The role of the accountant in leading-edge companies "has been transformed from number cruncher and financial historian to being business partner and trusted advisor."[2]

An organization's management team, on which management accountants play an integral role, seeks to create value for the organization by managing resources, activities, and people to achieve the organization's goals effectively.

Managing Resources, Activities, and People

The owners, directors, or trustees of an organization set its goals, often with the help of management. For example, The Walt Disney Company's goals are set by its board of directors, who are elected by the company's stockholders. The overall goal of the company, according to a recent annual report, may be expressed as a commitment to creative excellence and guest service coupled with strict financial discipline in order to maximize value to the company's shareholders.[3]

In pursuing its goals, an organization acquires *resources*, hires *people*, and then engages in an organized set of *activities*. It is up to the management team to make the best use of the organization's resources, activities, and people in achieving the organization's goals. The day-to-day work of the management team comprises four activities:

- Decision making
- Planning
- Directing operational activities
- Controlling

Walt Disney Company

Learning Objective 2

Explain four fundamental management processes that help organizations attain their goals.

Decision Making

Several years ago, Disney's board of directors decided as one of the company's growth objectives to expand its theme park operations in Florida. It was not immediately clear, however, what would be the best way to accomplish that goal. Would it be best to expand one of the company's three existing theme parks—the Magic Kingdom, Epcot, or Disney-MGM Studios? Or should the company branch out in an entirely new direction with a brand-new theme park attraction? How would each of these alternative courses of action mesh with the company's other goals of bringing the best in creative entertainment to its customers and maintaining sound financial discipline? Disney's top management team had to *make a decision* about the best way to expand the company's Florida operations, which entailed *choosing among the available alternatives*.

Planning

Disney's top management team decided to expand the company's Florida operations by building an entirely new theme park named Disney's Animal Kingdom. Created and designed by Walt Disney's Imagineering Division, this 500-acre theme park would offer guests wide-ranging adventures and tell the fascinating stories of all animals—ancient and present-day, real and imagined. Now the detailed planning phase began. How would the Animal Kingdom's many attractions designed by the Imagineering Division be laid out and organized? What food and beverage operations would be appropriate? How many employees would be needed on a day-to-day basis? What supplies would be required to run the park? How much would electricity and other utilities cost? How much would running the park during a typical year cost? Finally, how should the park's admission be priced given predicted patronage? Disney's management team had to *plan* for running the Animal Kingdom, which meant *developing a detailed financial and operational description of anticipated operations*.

"The accounting people are expected to do things that are much more strategic and much more forward looking than [they] have been expected to do in the past." (1b)
Caterpillar

Directing Operational Activities

Now the theme park has been built, equipped, and staffed. How many cashiers should be on duty on Saturday morning? How much food should be ordered each day? How much cash will be needed to meet the payroll, pay the utility bills, and buy maintenance supplies next month? All of these questions fall under the general heading of *directing operational activities*, which means *running the organization on a day-to-day basis*.

Controlling

The theme park has operated for several years now. Is the company's goal being accomplished? More specifically, have the theme park's operations adhered to the plans developed by management for achieving the goal? In seeking to answer these questions, management is engaged in *control*, which means *ensuring that the organization operates in the intended manner and achieves its goals*.

Adding Value to the Organization

Managers need information for all of the managerial activities described in the preceding section. That information comes from a variety of sources, including economists, financial experts, marketing and production personnel, and the organization's managerial accounting system.

Objectives of Managerial Accounting Activity

Learning Objective 3

List and describe five objectives of managerial accounting activity.

Management accountants add value to an organization by pursuing five major objectives:

1. Providing information for decision making and planning, and proactively participating as part of the management team in the decision-making and planning processes
2. Assisting managers in directing and controlling operational activities
3. Motivating managers and other employees toward the organization's goals
4. Measuring and evaluating the performance of activities, subunits, managers, and other employees within the organization
5. Assessing the organization's competitive position, and working with other managers to ensure the organization's long-run competitiveness in its industry

Today managerial accounting analysis is considered so crucial in managing an enterprise that in most cases management accountants are integral members of the management team. Far from playing a passive role as information providers, management accountants take a proactive role in both the strategic and day-to-day decisions that confront an enterprise.

Although much of the information provided by the managerial accounting system is financial, there is a strong trend toward the presentation of substantial nonfinancial data as well. Management accountants supply all kinds of information to management and act as strategic business partners in support of management's role in decision making and managing the organization's activities. As we will see in subsequent chapters, contemporary managerial accounting systems are focusing more and more on the activities that occur on all levels of the organization. Measuring, managing, and continuously improving operational activities are critical to an organization's success.

To illustrate the objectives of managerial accounting activity, let us continue with the example of Disney's Animal Kingdom.

"In five years [we will become] even more strategic. Really understanding the ins and outs of all the organizations, and really trying to be visionary—understanding what is happening to our business." (1c)

Hewlett-Packard

Providing Information for Decision Making and Planning, and Proactively Participating as Part of the Management Team in the Decision-Making and Planning Processes For virtually all major decisions, Disney's management team would rely largely on managerial accounting information. For example, the *decision* to establish the new theme park would be influenced heavily by estimates of the costs of building the Animal Kingdom and maintaining it throughout its life. The theme park's managers would also rely on managerial accounting data in formulating plans for the park's operations. Prominent in those *plans* would be a budget detailing the projected revenues and costs of providing entertainment.

While Disney's top management contemplated its decision about the theme park, the company's management accountants could not simply gather information and then sit on the sidelines. The management accountants were key participants in the management team as decisions were made and plans formulated for the theme park's operations.

"What we're seeing is less transactional and more decision support type of work. More analytical, more . . . option analysis. Looking at the whole spectrum of options in helping management make decisions." (1d)
Boeing

Assisting Managers in Directing and Controlling Operational Activities Directing and controlling day-to-day operations require a variety of data about the process of providing entertainment services. For example, in *directing* operational activities, the park's management team would need data about customer food-service demand patterns in order to make sure appropriate staffing was provided in the theme park's various food venues. In *controlling* operations, management would compare actual costs incurred with those specified in the budget.

Managerial accounting information often assists management through its **attention-directing function**. Managerial accounting reports rarely solve a decision problem. However, managerial accounting information often directs managers' attention to an issue that requires their skills. To illustrate, suppose Disney's Animal Kingdom incurred electricity costs that significantly exceeded the budget. This fact does not explain why the budget was exceeded, nor does it tell management what action to take, but it does direct management's attention to the situation. Suppose that upon further investigation, the accounting records reveal that the local electric rates have increased substantially. This information will help management in framing the decision problem. Should steps be taken to conserve electricity? Should the park's hours be curtailed? Perhaps management should consider switching to a lower-cost method of air conditioning.

Motivating Managers and Other Employees toward the Organization's Goals Organizations have goals. However, organizations comprise people who have goals of their own. The goals of individuals are diverse, and they do not always match those of the organization. A key purpose of managerial accounting is to motivate managers and other employees to direct their efforts toward achieving the organization's goals. One means of achieving this purpose is through budgeting. In establishing a budget for Disney's Animal Kingdom, top management indicates how resources are to be allocated and what activities are to be emphasized. When actual operations do not conform to the budget, the theme park's managers will be asked to explain the reasons for the deviation.

One way in which employees can be motivated toward the organization's goals is through employee **empowerment**, which is the concept of encouraging and authorizing workers to take the initiative to improve operations, reduce costs, and improve product quality and customer service. At The Walt Disney Company's theme parks, for example, employees are routinely asked for suggestions about ways to improve service to the parks' millions of visitors.

Measuring the Performance of Activities, Subunits, Managers, and Other Employees within the Organization One means of motivating people toward the organization's goals is to measure their performance in achieving those goals. Such measurements then can be used as the basis for rewarding performance through positive feedback, promotions, and pay raises. For example, most large corporations compensate their executives, in part, on the basis of the profit achieved by the subunits they manage. In other companies, executives are rewarded on the basis of operational measures, such as product quality, sales, or on-time delivery. At Disney's Animal Kingdom, for example, management might be rewarded, in part, on the basis of growth in attendance at the theme park.

In addition to measuring the performance of people, the managerial accounting system measures the performance of an organization's subunits, such as divisions, product lines, geographical territories, and departments. These measurements help the subunits' managers obtain the highest possible performance level in their units. Such measurements also help top management decide whether a particular subunit is a viable economic investment. For example, it may turn out that a particular attraction at Disney's Animal Kingdom is too costly an activity to continue, despite the efforts of a skilled management team.

> "You want to be on the team. You want to be the business consultant. You want to be thought of as a value-adding department versus just someone who closes the books." (1e)
>
> **Qwest**

Assessing the Organization's Competitive Position, and Working with Other Managers to Ensure the Organization's Long-Run Competitiveness in Its Industry   Nowadays the business environment is changing very rapidly. These changes are reflected in global competition, rapidly advancing technology, and improved communication systems, such as the Internet. The activities that make an enterprise successful today may no longer be sufficient next year. A crucial role of managerial accounting is to continually assess how an organization stacks up against the competition, with an eye toward continuously improving. Among the questions asked in assessing an organization's competitive position are the following:

- How well is the organization doing in its internal operations and business processes?
- How well is the organization doing in the eyes of its customers? Are their needs being served as well as possible?
- How well is the organization doing from the standpoint of innovation, learning, and continuously improving operations? Is the organization a trendsetter that embraces new products, new services, and new technology? Or is it falling behind?
- How well is the organization doing financially? Is the enterprise viable as a continuing entity?

Managerial versus Financial Accounting

Take another look at the major objectives of managerial accounting activity. Notice that the focus in each of these objectives is on *managers*. Thus, the focus of *managerial accounting* is on the needs of managers *within* the organization, rather than interested parties outside the organization.

Financial accounting is the use of accounting information for reporting to parties outside the organization. The annual report distributed by McDonald's Corporation to its stockholders is an example of the output from a financial accounting system. Users of financial accounting information include current and prospective stockholders, lenders, investment analysts, unions, consumer groups, and government agencies.

There are many similarities between managerial accounting information and financial accounting information, because they both draw upon data from an organization's *accounting system*. This is the system of procedures, personnel, and computers used to accumulate and store financial data in the organization. One part of the overall accounting system is the **cost accounting system**, which accumulates cost data for use in both managerial and financial accounting. For example, production

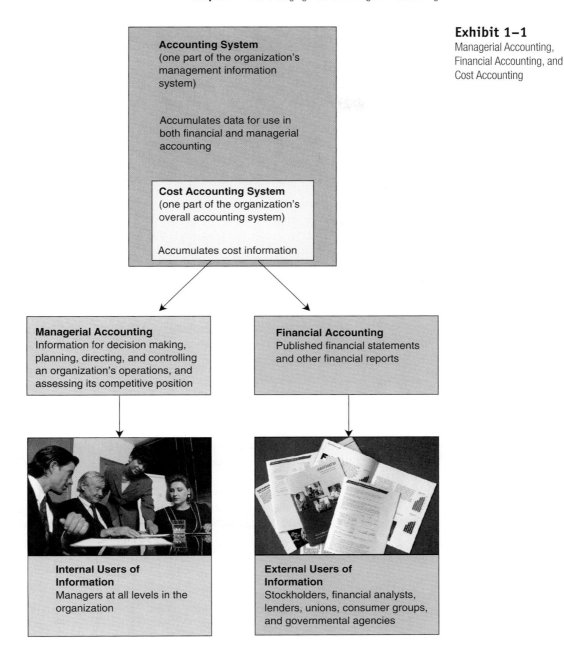

Exhibit 1–1
Managerial Accounting,
Financial Accounting, and
Cost Accounting

cost data typically are used in helping managers set prices, which is a managerial accounting use. However, production cost data also are used to value inventory on a manufacturer's balance sheet, which is a financial accounting use.

Exhibit 1–1 depicts the relationships among an organization's accounting system, cost accounting system, managerial accounting, and financial accounting. Although similarities do exist between managerial and financial accounting, the differences are even greater. Exhibit 1–2 lists the most important differences.

Managerial Accounting in Different Types of Organizations

All organizations need information, whether they are profit-seeking or nonprofit enterprises and regardless of the activities they pursue. As a result, managerial

Exhibit 1–2
Differences between
Managerial and Financial
Accounting

	Managerial Accounting	**Financial Accounting**
Users of Information	Managers, *within the organization.*	Interested parties, *outside the organization.*
Regulation	*Not required* and *unregulated,* since it is intended only for management.	*Required* and must conform to generally accepted accounting principles. *Regulated by* the Accounting Standards Board of the Canadian Institute of Chartered Accountants (CICA), and, to a lesser degree, by Canada's provincial and territorial securities regulators.
Source of Data	The organization's *accounting system, plus various other sources,* such as rates of defective products manufactured, physical quantities of material and labour used in production, occupancy rates in hotels and hospitals, and average takeoff delays in airlines.	Almost exclusively drawn from the organization's *accounting system,* which accumulates financial information.
Nature of Reports and Procedures	*Reports often focus on subunits* within the organization, such as departments, divisions, geographical regions, or product lines. Based on a combination of historical data, estimates, and projections of future events.	*Reports focus on the enterprise in its entirety.* Based almost exclusively on historical transaction data.

accounting information is vital in all organizations. American Express, the City of Montreal, the Department of National Defence, Fairmont Hotels & Resorts, Ford, Manulife Insurance, The United Way, WestJet Airlines, and York University all have management accountants who provide information to management. Moreover, the five basic purposes of managerial accounting activity are relevant in each of these organizations.

Where Are Management Accountants Located in an Organization?

Learning Objective 5

Explain where management accountants are located in an organization, in terms of formal organization, deployment in cross-functional teams, and physical location.

This question can be interpreted in three different ways:

- Where are management accountants located in an organization chart?
- How are management accountants deployed?
- In what physical location do management accountants actually do their work?

Organization Chart

Notice that a company's top management group usually consists of the board of directors, chairman and chief executive officer (CEO), vice-chairman, and chief of corporate operations.

"[Management accountants] need to be strongly partnered with the line management. They need to be proactive. They need to have a broad sense of business. It's not strictly accounting. It's looking at the full spectrum and range of business." (1f)

Boeing

Line and Staff Positions   The other positions in an organization chart are of two types: line positions and staff positions. Managers in **line positions** are *directly* involved in the provision of goods or services. For example, Disney's line positions include the chairman and president of Disney Consumer Products, the chairman and president of Walt Disney Feature Animation, and the chairman and president of Walt Disney Attractions, which is the division responsible for the company's theme parks in Florida, California, and Japan. Also in line positions would be the thousands of managers in the various operating units of the divisions. For example, the general manager of Disney's Animal Kingdom, the manager of food and beverage services at the Magic

Kingdom, and the manager of the Disney Store at the West Edmonton Mall in Alberta would all be in line positions.

Managers in **staff positions** supervise activities that support Disney's strategy, but they are only *indirectly* involved in operational activities. Disney's staff positions include the general counsel, the executive VP for government relations, and the chief financial officer (CFO), among others.

CFO or Controller   In many organizations, the designation given to the top managerial *and* financial accountant is the **chief financial officer (CFO)**. In other organizations, this individual is called the **controller** (or sometimes the **comptroller**, particularly in nonprofit or governmental organizations).

Learning Objective 6

Describe the roles of an organization's chief financial officer (CFO) or controller, treasurer, and internal auditor.

The CFO or controller usually is responsible for supervising the personnel in the accounting department and for preparing the information and reports used in both managerial and financial accounting. As the organization's chief management accountant, the CFO or controller often interprets accounting information for line managers and participates as an integral member of the management team. Most controllers are involved in planning and decision making at all levels and across all functional areas of the enterprise. This broad role has enabled many management accountants to rise to the top of their organizations. Former accountants have served as CEO in such companies as BC Hydro, London Drugs, Manulife Financial, and Research In Motion.

In addition to the CFO or controller for the entire corporation, most companies, including The Walt Disney Company, have divisional controllers. Thus, Disney's organization chart would show a controller for ABC, Inc., Disneyland Paris, Walt Disney Studios, and so forth.

Treasurer   The **treasurer** typically is responsible for raising capital and safeguarding the organization's assets. In addition, the treasurer is responsible for the organization's assets, the management of its investments, its credit policy, and its insurance coverage.

Internal Auditor   Most large corporations and many governmental agencies have an internal auditor. An organization's **internal auditor** is often responsible for reviewing the accounting procedures, records, and reports in both the controller's and the treasurer's areas of responsibility. The auditor then expresses an opinion to top management regarding the effectiveness of the organization's accounting system. In some organizations, the internal auditor also makes a broad performance evaluation of middle and lower management.

"Actually, most of the people . . . are decentralized and actually are co-located with the people that they support. That's our approach and we're moving more and more toward that and less and less toward a central group that provides information." (1g)

Boeing

Cross-Functional Deployment

On a formal organization chart, accountants generally are in a staff capacity, as explained in the preceding section. However, management accountants are increasingly being *deployed* in cross-functional management teams. Management accountants work with executives from top management, marketing and sales personnel, design engineers, operations managers, legal experts, quality-control personnel, and virtually every other specialized type of employee in an organization. Managerial teams are formed to make decisions, engage in planning exercises, or address operational problems from many perspectives. Since financial and other managerial accounting issues are often critically important in addressing business problems, management accountants routinely play a major role in these cross-functional teams.

Physical Location

Finally, where do management accountants actually do their work? The answer is "just about everywhere." Managerial accountants are not sequestered in some remote corner of the business. To the contrary, they are located in every part of an enterprise, from corporate headquarters to the locations where goods and services are being produced. At Disney, for example, management accountants would be present on location when a feature film is being produced, near the ABC newsroom when decisions are made about deploying journalistic resources, and in the various Disney hotels, such as the Disney Ambassador Hotel in Tokyo.

Major Themes in Managerial Accounting

Learning Objective 7

Briefly describe some of the major contemporary themes in managerial accounting.

Several major themes influence virtually all aspects of contemporary managerial accounting. We will briefly introduce these themes now, and they will be apparent throughout the text.

Information and Incentives

The need for information is the driving force behind managerial accounting. However, managerial accounting information often serves two functions: a *decision-facilitating* function and a *decision-influencing* function. Information usually is supplied to a decision maker to assist that manager in choosing an alternative. Often, that information is also intended to influence the manager's decision. That is, to provide an incentive to choose one alternative over another.

To illustrate, let us consider The Walt Disney Company's annual budget. Although the budget is prepared under the direction of the CFO, it must be approved by the chairman of the board and CEO and, ultimately, by the board of directors. As part of the budget approval process, the CEO and the board of directors will make important decisions that determine how the company's resources will be allocated. Throughout the year, the decisions of management will be facilitated by the information contained in the budget. Management decisions also will be influenced by the budget, since at year-end actual expenditures will be compared with the budgeted amounts. Explanations will then be requested for any significant deviations.

Behavioural Issues

The reactions of both individuals and groups to managerial accounting information will significantly affect the course of events in an organization. How will the general manager of Disney's Animal Kingdom react to a budget? How will data regarding the cost of providing entertainment services affect the way the theme park's management prices those services? How much detail should be included in the quarterly accounting reports to the general manager? If too much detail is provided, will the manager be overloaded with information and distracted from the main points?

All of these questions involve the behavioural tendencies of people and their cognitive limitations in using information. The better a management accountant's understanding of human behaviour is, the more effective he or she will be as a provider of information.

Costs and Benefits

Like other goods and services, information can be produced, purchased, and used. It can be of high or low quality, timely or late, appropriate for its intended use or utterly irrelevant. As is true of all goods and services, information entails both costs and benefits. The costs of providing managerial accounting information to the managers in Disney's Animal Kingdom include the cost of compensation for the theme park's controller and Accounting Department personnel, the cost of purchasing and operating computers, and the cost of the time spent by the information users to read, understand, and utilize the information. The benefits include improved decisions, more effective planning, greater efficiency of operations, and better direction and control of operations.

Thus, there are both costs and benefits associated with managerial accounting information. The desirability of any particular managerial accounting technique or information must be determined in light of both its costs and benefits. We will reinforce this cost–benefit trade-off throughout the text by pointing out areas where managerial accounting information could be improved, but only at too great a cost.

Evolution and Adaptation in Managerial Accounting

Compared to financial accounting, managerial accounting is a young discipline. As a result, managerial accounting concepts and tools are still evolving as new ways are found to provide information that assists management. Moreover, the business environment is changing rapidly. For managerial accounting to be as useful a tool in the future as it has been in the recent past, managerial accounting information must adapt to reflect those changes. Several changes in the business environment that are especially pertinent to managerial accounting are discussed briefly here. The effect of these changes on various topics in managerial accounting will be explored in subsequent chapters.

E-Business Most of us have gone online to order a book from Amazon.ca, an airline reservation from Expedia.ca, or possibly a computer from Dell.ca. Perhaps what we're less aware of, though, is the depth of the e-commerce impact throughout the spectrum of the business environment. Just as we can order books or computers online in *consumer-to-business* e-commerce channels, businesses can order raw materials and supplies using *business-to-business* networks. *Supply-chain management*, which encompasses the coordination of order generation, order taking, order fulfillment, and distribution of products and services, is increasingly an electronic, online process.[4] *E-commerce* may be defined as buying and selling over digital media.[5] E-business is a broader concept. In addition to encompassing e-commerce, *e-business* includes the business processes that form the engine for modern business.

How does the e-business phenomenon affect the practice of managerial accounting? Just as management accountants participate as business partners in decisions about a company's product mix or its investment in robotic equipment, they also are active participants in decisions to go online with a company's business processes. The cost management opportunities presented by e-business are sometimes astounding in magnitude. Michael Dell built Dell Inc. into a computer giant with the simple philosophy of managing the supply chain to minimize inventory and fill customer orders in record time. Moreover, management accountants are not only quantifying the cost-management benefits of e-business, they are rapidly moving toward *e-accounting* themselves. Management accountants are harnessing the power of online communications to streamline the procedures of managerial accounting. For example, *e-budgeting* is now used by hundreds of companies to quickly and effectively transmit the information needed to construct a budget from business units around the globe.

Service versus Manufacturing Firms The service sector occupies a growing role in the Canadian economy. Moreover, several key service industries have been deregulated by the government—for example, telecommunications, financial services, and airlines. As more and more companies provide financial, medical, communication, transportation, consulting, and hospitality services, managerial accounting techniques must be adapted to meet the needs of managers in those industries. The key difference between service and manufacturing firms is that most services are consumed as they are produced. Most services cannot be inventoried like manufactured goods. Service organizations also tend to be more labour-intensive than manufacturing firms. Many of the techniques developed for measuring costs and performance in manufacturing companies have been adapted successfully to service industry firms. Throughout the text, you will notice that roughly two-thirds of the illustrations of managerial accounting techniques involve service industry firms and nonprofit organizations.

Emergence of New Industries   Scientific discoveries are opening up whole new industries that were not even contemplated a short time ago. Such discoveries as hybrid automobiles, genetic engineering, and superconductivity have spawned business activities in which managers face new challenges. Management accountants also face new challenges as they seek to provide relevant information in these new high-tech industries.

Globalization   Today the marketplace is truly a global one. A firm is just as likely to be in competition with a company from Japan or Germany as from across town. Intense international competition is forcing companies to strive for excellence in product quality and service more than ever before.

Moreover, new economic arrangements and potential trade agreements are constantly in the news, as national economies become more and more intertwined. Organizations such as the European Union (EU) and the World Trade Organization (WTO), as well as international agreements like the North American Free Trade Agreement (NAFTA), all have the potential to dramatically change international commerce.

A *multinational* company is an organization that has operational subunits, such as manufacturing plants or sales facilities, in two or more countries. Multinational firms face several challenges that do not confront domestic companies. Political systems, accounting rules for external reporting, legal systems, income tax systems, and cultural norms vary widely among countries. Managers of multinationals must be aware of these differences to successfully carry out operations across international boundaries. Monetary systems also differ among countries, and multinationals must continually monitor the fluctuating values of foreign currencies. The price at which one country's currency can be converted into that of another country is called an *exchange rate.* The exchange rates can fluctuate daily as various forces shape the world economy. Managers of multinationals would consider the risk of changes in exchange rates as they sign contracts, buy and sell goods, and conduct business operations in many countries.

Focus on the Customer   To succeed in this era, businesses of all types must continually focus on their customers. Managers are increasingly aware of their product's value to the customer, which is the customer's perceived difference between the benefits the customer receives and the sacrifice the customer incurs to receive the product. The value of a product or service to the customer is affected by such diverse attributes as product price, quality, functionality, user-friendliness, customer service, warranty, and maintenance costs. In response to this heightened customer focus, managerial accounting systems now often measure various attributes of customer value.

Computer-Integrated Manufacturing   Manufacturing processes have evolved from labour-intensive methods to more automated processes, in which most of the work is accomplished by machines. This trend continues today, as *computer-integrated-manufacturing* (or *CIM*) systems become more common. A CIM process is fully automated, with computers controlling the entire production process. In CIM systems, the types of costs incurred by the manufacturer are quite different from those in traditional manufacturing environments.

Product Life Cycles and Diversity   One impact of highly automated manufacturing systems has been to enable manufacturers to produce an ever-more diverse set of products. Moreover, the rate at which technology is changing means that the life cycles of most products are becoming shorter. In the computer industry, for example, product models are used only a few years before they are replaced by more powerful versions. To be competitive, manufacturers must keep up with the rapidly changing marketplace. Managers must have timely information about production costs and other product characteristics in order to respond quickly and effectively to the competition.

Time-Based Competition   *Response time*, *lead time*, *on time*, and *downtime* are among the many time-based phrases that dot the conversations of today's managers. Why are

M anagement
A ccounting
P ractice

Canadian Direct
Insurance,
London Drugs,
Viewtrak Technologies,
and PropertyGuys.com

THE INTERNET AS A LIFELINE

In a tough economic environment, the Internet can be a lifeline. "Companies in a sales squeeze are looking to the Net as a tool for cutting costs, generating new revenue streams, trimming inventories, and serving customers and employees more efficiently." Here are some examples of how companies are using the Web to their advantage.

Canadian Direct Insurance

"Canadian Direct Insurance improved the delivery of their products by using 'eDelivery,' a secure way of retrieving insurance documents from their website. When quoting or purchasing a policy online at canadiandirect.com, customers are able to view and print their insurance documents online. Policy holders also have the option or renewing and paying for their policy online. These costs savings have allowed Canadian Direct Insurance to offer premiums that are substantially lower than many of its competitors."

London Drugs

"London Drugs operate 68 retail stores situated across British Columbia, Alberta, Saskatchewan and Manitoba. Customers can go on line for prescription refills, to place photo finishing orders, to purchase travel insurance, and buy on line any merchandise carried in the stores."

Viewtrak Technologies

"Viewtrak Technologies, Edmonton, has created a web-based software system that enables cattle breeders, producers, processors and distributors to track an animal's production information from birth to death. As prescribed in recent federal legislation, the software tracks and records information about animal's genetics, feed, production inputs, and environment. Viewtrak.com is an integrated food source management system that provides agricultural producers with the information they need to streamline production and boost earnings in the wake of the BSE crisis. As animals move along the supply chain, access to the information is provided to each stakeholder."

PropertyGuys.com

"PropertyGuys.com harnessed the power of the Internet to rival the multiple listing web-based service provided by the Canadian Real Estate Association. The Canadian private sale company offers do-it-yourself home sellers the option to list their property, deal directly with interested parties, and gain international exposure on a website receiving 30 million hits a month, for a fee that is substantially lower than that commanded by real estate agents."[6]

managers so concerned with time? In the global competitive environment, time has become a crucial element in many companies' strategies for success. By reducing the time it takes to develop a new product and getting the product on the market more quickly, a company can gain an important advantage over its competitors. Thus, the *time to market* becomes a critical objective for many companies. Reducing the time elapsed from the new product concept stage to having the product in Wal-Mart requires careful time management at each stage of a product's development. The product must be designed with the customer's needs in mind and with a view toward manufacturability. Delays between product development stages must be reduced or eliminated. The production process must be efficient and product quality must be high. A cross-functional approach to management is crucial in managing the time to market. Managerial accounting information is critical for the cross-functional management team. Information about the trade-offs between time and cost in all phases of a product's development is particularly important. For example, how much more would it cost to get a new product to market six months earlier? Can these cost increases be reflected in the product's price? How much higher would sales be if our company beats the competition by six more months? The answers to these and similar questions are increasingly important to managers as they are ever more likely to find themselves competing against time.

Information and Communication Technology   Although large mainframe computers still perform certain kinds of tasks, businesses now make heavy use of personal computers. In most offices, virtually every employee has a personal computer for such tasks as word processing, data analysis, report generation, presentation preparation, and communication. These PCs are usually linked together in a network that enables employees to electronically transfer files and reports, share data, and communicate via e-mail. Often called an *intranet*, these networked PCs are invaluable tools in the era of cross-functional management teams. Moreover, these intranets are not confined to the walls of a building, as the World Wide Web or *Internet* allows computer-to-computer interface anywhere in the world.

> "The pace of change in technology is becoming much faster, and accounting and finance people are very heavy users of technology, more so than a lot of the other functions." (1h)
>
> **Hewlett-Packard**

Managerial accounting analyses are done on PCs using a variety of software products. Spreadsheet programs, such as Excel®, are in wide use for data analysis.[7] Software packages specifically designed for accounting applications are also widely available. Many businesses are adopting integrated business software packages, such as Systems Applications and Products in Data Processing (SAP) and PeopleSoft, that handle a broad range of computing needs, such as customer and supplier databases, personnel and payroll functions, production scheduling and management, inventory records, and financial and managerial accounting functions. Management accountants often play significant roles in selecting software for their organizations or designing in-house software to meet the organization's unique needs.

Other innovations also have served to speed communications and link business parties around the world. Global cellular phone technology now enables voice and e-mail communications from the most remote locations. The global positioning satellite system (GPS) now enables trucking, railroad, shipping, and rental car companies to more easily track vehicles. This virtual explosion in data availability has enabled managerial accounting systems to provide information that would have been impossible to supply only a few years ago.

Just-in-Time Inventory Management   In traditional manufacturing settings, inventories of raw materials and parts, partially completed components, and finished goods were kept as a reserve against the possibility of running out of a needed item. However, large reserve inventories consume valuable resources and generate hidden costs. Consequently, many companies have completely changed their approach to production and inventory management. These manufacturers have adopted a strategy for controlling the flow of manufacturing in a multistage production process. In a

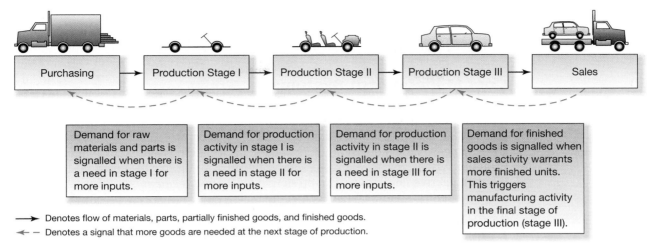

| Demand for raw materials and parts is signalled when there is a need in stage I for more inputs. | Demand for production activity in stage I is signalled when there is a need in stage II for more inputs. | Demand for production activity in stage II is signalled when there is a need in stage III for more inputs. | Demand for finished goods is signalled when sales activity warrants more finished units. This triggers manufacturing activity in the final stage of production (stage III). |

⟶ Denotes flow of materials, parts, partially finished goods, and finished goods.
⟵ – Denotes a signal that more goods are needed at the next stage of production.

Exhibit 1–3
Just-in-Time (JIT) Production and Inventory Management System

just-in-time (JIT) production system, raw materials and parts are purchased or produced just in time to be used at each stage of the production process. This approach to inventory and production management brings considerable cost savings from reduced inventory levels.

The key to the JIT system is the "pull" approach to controlling manufacturing. To visualize this approach, look at Exhibit 1–3, which displays a simple diagram of a multistage production process. The flow of manufacturing activity is depicted by the solid arrows running across the page from one stage of production to the next. However, the signal that triggers more production activity in each stage comes from the *next* stage of production. These signals, depicted by the dashed-line arrows, run from right to left. We begin with sales at the right-hand side of the Exhibit. When sales activity warrants more production of finished goods, the goods are "pulled" from production stage III by sending a signal that more goods are needed. Similarly, when production employees in stage III need more inputs, they send a signal back to stage II. This triggers production activity in stage II. Working our way back to the beginning of the process, purchases of raw materials and parts are triggered by a signal that they are needed in stage I. This pull system of production management, which characterizes the JIT approach, results in a smooth flow of production and significantly reduced inventory levels. The upshot is considerable cost savings for the manufacturer.

Further details of the JIT production system and other changes in the manufacturing environment will be covered in subsequent chapters. The impact of these changes will be a recurrent theme in this book.

Total Quality Management   One implication of a just-in-time inventory philosophy is the need to emphasize product quality. If a component is to be produced just in time for the next production stage, it must be "just right" for its intended purpose. One flawed component can shut down the entire production line, entailing considerable cost. Therefore, management accountants have become involved increasingly in monitoring product quality and measuring the costs of maintaining quality. This information helps companies maintain programs of **total quality management**, or **TQM**. This refers to the broad set of management and control processes designed to focus the entire organization and all of its employees on providing products or services that do the best possible job of satisfying the customer.

Continuous Improvement   Global competition is forcing companies to continuously improve their operations. **Continuous improvement** is the constant effort to eliminate waste, reduce response time, simplify the design of both products and processes, and improve quality and customer service. Management accountants are contributing to the continuous improvement programs of many organizations through the development of cost management systems, which are discussed next.

Cost Management Systems

The explosion in technology we are experiencing, coupled with increasing worldwide competition, is forcing managers to produce high-quality goods and services, provide outstanding customer service, and do so at the lowest possible cost. These demands are placing ever-greater requirements on the information provided by managerial accounting systems. Many companies have moved away from a historical cost accounting perspective and toward a proactive *cost management* perspective. A **cost management system** is a management planning and control system with the following objectives:

- To measure the cost of the resources consumed in performing the organization's significant *activities*.
- To identify and eliminate **non-value-added costs**. These are the costs of *activities* that can be eliminated with no deterioration of product quality, performance, or perceived value.
- To determine the efficiency and effectiveness of all major *activities* performed in the enterprise.
- To identify and evaluate new *activities* that can improve the future performance of the organization.

Notice the emphasis of a cost management system on the organization's activities. This emphasis, sometimes called **activity accounting**, is crucial to the goal of producing quality goods and services at the lowest possible cost. In keeping with the focus on activities, management accountants have developed a system for determining the cost of producing goods or services called **activity-based costing (ABC)**. In an ABC system, the costs of the organization's significant activities are accumulated and then assigned to goods or services in accordance with how resources are used in the production of those goods and services. An ABC system helps management to understand the causal linkages between activities and costs.

Using an activity-based costing system to improve the operations of an organization is called **activity-based management** or **ABM**. We will have considerably more to say about activity-based costing, activity-based management, and the role of cost management systems throughout the text.

Strategic Cost Management and the Value Chain

Learning Objective 8

Understand and explain the concepts of strategic cost management and the value chain.

How are the goods and services that we all consume created? Usually many activities are involved in securing basic raw materials and turning them into valuable products or services. The set of linked, value-creating activities, ranging from securing basic raw materials and energy to the ultimate delivery of products and services, is called the **value chain**. Although there may be only one organization involved in a particular value chain, usually there are many. Mayo Clinic's value chain, for example, would include not only the hospital but also the suppliers of pharmaceutical products and medical supplies, the manufacturers of diagnostic equipment, the private-practice physicians whose patients use the Mayo Clinic, and the ambulance services that transport patients to the hospital.

The value chain for Walt Disney Studios would include upstream contributions such as screenwriting, film studio construction and maintenance, set design and construction, costume design and production, travel arrangements for shooting scenes on location, lighting technicians, film crews, and acting talent. Once the film has been

Securing raw materials, energy, and other resources

Research and development

Product design

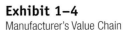

Exhibit 1–4
Manufacturer's Value Chain

Gap's value chain consists of myriad activities, from securing raw materials through distribution and sales.

GAP

Production

Marketing

Distribution and sales

produced, the downstream contributions include advertising personnel; TV, radio, and print media; film distributors; theatre companies such as Cineplex Entertainment LP; DVD producers; video rental stores such as Rogers Video; and DVD retailers such as Best Buy.

The major steps in the value chain for Gap, Inc. are depicted in Exhibit 1–4. Gap is a major clothing retailer with over 3,000 stores worldwide. As Exhibit 1–4 shows, major steps in Gap's value chain include the following:

GAP

- Securing raw material, energy, and other resources
- Research and development
- Product design
- Production
- Marketing
- Distribution and sales

What is the role of Gap, Inc. in this value chain? As the company's Web site explains, "We're not a manufacturer. To produce our clothes, we contract with garment manufacturers around the world." What Gap does is design its clothing lines, outsource the manufacturing, market the products, distribute them to retail stores where they are sold, and provide customer service. Quoting again from Gap's site, "From a design concept born in New York by our product designers, to an in-store display in one of our more than 3,000 stores around the world, each Gap, Banana Republic, and Old Navy product goes through a multistage process before reaching our customers." That multistage process is the company's value chain.

In order for any organization to most effectively achieve its goals, it is important for its managers to understand the *entire* value chain in which their organization participates. This understanding can help managers ask, and answer, important questions about their organization's strategy. Should the company concentrate on only a narrow link in the value chain, such as design or retailing? Or should it expand its operational scope to include securing the raw materials or manufacturing the product? Are there opportunities to form beneficial linkages with suppliers, which come earlier in the value chain? Or with customers?

These questions involve fundamental, strategic issues about how an organization can best meet its goals. Although many factors affect such decisions, one important factor concerns the costs incurred in creating value in each link in the value chain. In order for a company to achieve a sustainable competitive advantage, it must either (1) perform one or more activities in the value chain at the same quality level as its competitors, but at a lower cost, or (2) perform its value chain activities at a higher quality level than its competitors, but at no greater cost. Understanding the value chain, and the factors that cause costs to be incurred in each activity in the value chain, is a crucial step in the development of a firm's strategy. These cost-causing factors are called **cost drivers**, and we will have much more to say about them throughout the text. The overall recognition of the importance of cost relationships among the activities in the value chain, and the process of managing those cost relationships to the firm's advantage, is called **strategic cost management**. Issues in strategic cost management will arise in a variety of contexts as we pursue our study of managerial accounting.

Theory of Constraints   Along with a value-chain analysis, managers should carefully examine the chain of linked activities with a view toward identifying the constraints that prevent their organization from reaching a higher level of achievement. Sometimes called the **theory of constraints**, this approach seeks to find the most cost-effective ways to alleviate an organization's most limiting constraints. When binding constraints are relaxed, the organization can reach a higher level of goal attainment. For example, suppose a delay occurred in the design process for Gap's line of summer clothing because too few designers were assigned to the project. This might result in a delay in contracting for the manufacturing of the summer line, which might ultimately delay the delivery of the products to Gap's many retail outlets. In this context, the design process is a *bottleneck operation*, meaning that it slows down the progress of Gap's products through the retailer's value chain. By assigning even one or two more designers to the summer clothing line, the delay could perhaps have been avoided.

The Ethical Climate of Business and the Role of the Accountant

Learning Objective **9**

Understand the ethical responsibilities of a management accountant.

Who among us is not shocked and dismayed by the seemingly endless stream of corporate scandals that we have experienced over the past few years? The headlines keep on coming—AOL, Bristol-Myers Squib, LiveEnt, Enron, Global Crossing, KPMG, Nortel, Tyco, Worldcom, Xerox—the list goes on. Many of the cases involve mismanagement, some are characterized by ethical lapses, and in some instances there is criminal behaviour. Who is to blame? According to most observers, there is plenty of blame to go around: greedy corporate executives, managers who make overreaching business deals, lack of oversight by various companies' boards of directors (particularly the boards' audit committees), shoddy work by external auditors, lack of sufficient probing by financial analysts and the financial press, and some accountants who have been all too willing to push the envelope on aggressive accounting to (or beyond) the edge. Billions of dollars have been lost in employee pension funds, several investment portfolios, and the private investment accounts of the public. It will no doubt take many years to sort out the mess. Companies have gone bankrupt; fortunes have been lost; careers have been ruined; and more of the same is yet to come. Several financial executives have filed guilty pleas on felony charges. Others have been convicted by juries. Some are serving time in prison. Six members of the audit subcommittee of Enron's board resigned. Some observers have wondered if the confidence of the investing public can ever be regained.

One important lesson from these scandals is that not only is unethical behaviour in business wrong in a moral sense, but it also can be disastrous from the standpoint of the economy. We cannot have businesspeople lying, stealing, perpetrating frauds, and making up accounting rules as they go without seriously disrupting business. Thus, ethical behaviour by businesspeople in general, and accountants in particular, is not a luxury or a discretionary "good thing to do"; it is an absolute necessity to the smooth functioning of the economy.

Most of the purely accounting issues in these cases involve financial accounting (external reporting) rather than managerial accounting (internal reporting). In most companies, however, many of the same individuals are involved in both types of accounting. In the Enron case, for example, which is perhaps the most notorious of all, investigators allege that a massive fraud was perpetrated on the investing public by creating so-called related parties with names like Raptor for the sole purpose of hiding debt and overstating earnings. Yet the same alleged fraud must have been perpetrated on many at Enron itself. Surely not all of the company's thousands of employees knew of these accounting schemes. So ultimately, what may have been largely financial (external) accounting misstatements, almost certainly resulted in misstated managerial (internal) accounting reports as well.[8]

For many in the accounting profession, the scandals have served as a wakeup call to concentrate more on ethical issues in practising and teaching accounting.[9] To this end, a significant *ethical issue in managerial accounting* will be addressed at the end of most chapters. The goal of these "Focus on Ethics" pieces is to raise the consciousness of students that legitimate ethical issues do arise in the daily practice of managerial accounting. In the last section of this chapter, we will turn our attention to managerial accounting as a profession. In the context of that discussion, the Focus on Ethics piece for this chapter will be a summary of The Society of Management Accountants of Ontario's code of professional ethics.

Managerial Accounting as a Career

Management accountants serve a crucial function in virtually any enterprise. As the providers of information, they are often in touch with the heartbeat of the organization. In most businesses, management accountants interact frequently with sales personnel, finance specialists, production people, and managers at all levels. To perform their duties effectively, management accountants must be knowledgeable not only in accounting but in the other major business disciplines as well. Moreover, strong oral and written communication skills are becoming increasingly important for success as a management accountant.

Learning Objective **10**

Discuss the professional organizations, certification process, and ethical standards in the field of managerial accounting.

Professional Organizations

To keep up with new developments in their field, management accountants often belong to one or more professional organizations. Many management accountants belong to the Canadian Institute of Chartered Accountants, the Certified General Accountants Association of Canada, or the Society of Management Accountants of Canada. The latter publishes a journal, entitled *CMA Management*, and also supports research on managerial accounting topics through the CMA Canada Research Foundation.

The primary professional association for management accountants in the United States is the Institute of Management Accountants. Great Britain's main professional organization is the Institute of Chartered Management Accountants, and Australia's organization is the Institute of Chartered Accountants in Australia. In all, over 75 countries have professional organizations for their practising accountants.

> "You've got to know how to talk to people, express yourself. And that's oral and written. You also have to be able to understand a lot of different areas, not necessarily just accounting. You've got to understand the business itself." (1i)
> **Qwest**

Professional Designations

In keeping with the importance of their role and the specialized knowledge they must have, management accountants can earn a professional designation such as Chartered

Accountant (CA), Certified General Accountant (CGA), or Certified Management Accountant (**CMA**). For example, the requirements for becoming a **certified management accountant** include meeting specified educational requirements, passing the CMA entrance examination, and completing a two-year Strategic Leadership Program while gaining practical experience in a management accounting environment. In the United States, the IMA administers the CMA program. Great Britain and many other countries also have professional certification programs for their management accountants.

Professional Ethics

As professionals, management accountants have an obligation to themselves, their colleagues, and their organizations to adhere to high standards of ethical conduct. In recognition of this obligation, the provincial and territorial Societies/Orders of Management Accountants have developed ethical standards for its members, who are practitioners of managerial accounting and financial management. The standards of The Society of Management Accountants of Ontario (CMA Ontario), given below, are representative. *Note:* Various problems and cases at the end of each chapter in this text include ethical issues to be resolved. In addressing those issues, readers will need to refer to these ethical standards.

Focus on Ethics These scenarios discuss ethical issues and underscore the importance of ethical behaviour in managerial accounting.

Focus on Ethics

CODE OF PROFESSIONAL ETHICS (CMA ONTARIO)

All Members will adhere to the following "Code of Professional Ethics" of the Society:

(a) A Member will act at all times with:

   (i)   responsibility for and fidelity to public needs;

   (ii) fairness and loyalty to such Member's associates, clients and employers; and

   (iii) competence through devotion to high ideals of personal honour and professional integrity.

(b) A Member will:

   (i)   maintain at all times independence of thought and action;

   (ii) not express an opinion on financial reports or statements without first assessing her or his relationship with her or his client to determine whether such Member might expect her or his opinion to be considered independent, objective and unbiased by one who has knowledge of all the facts; and

   (iii) when preparing financial reports or statements or expressing an opinion on financial reports or statements, disclose all material facts known to such Member in order not to make such financial reports or statements misleading, acquire sufficient information to warrant an expression of opinion and report all material misstatements or departures from generally accepted accounting principles.

(c) A Member will:

   (i)   not disclose or use any confidential information concerning the affairs of such Member's employer or client unless acting in the course of his or her duties or except when such information is required to be disclosed in the course of any defence of himself or herself or any associate or employee in any lawsuit or other legal proceeding or against alleged professional misconduct by order of lawful authority of the Board or any committee of the Society in the proper exercise of their duties but only to the extent necessary for such purpose;

   (ii) inform his or her employer or client of any business connections or interests of which such Member's employer or client would reasonably expect to be informed;

   (iii) not, in the course of exercising his or her duties on behalf of such Member's employer or client, hold, receive, bargain for or acquire any fee, remuneration or benefit without such employer's or client's knowledge and consent; and

(iv) take all reasonable steps, in arranging any engagement as a consultant, to establish a clear understanding of the scope and objectives of the work before it is commenced and will furnish the client with an estimate of cost, preferably before the engagement is commenced, but in any event as soon as possible thereafter.

(d) A Member will:

(i) conduct himself or herself toward other Members with courtesy and good faith;

(ii) not commit an act discreditable to the profession;

(iii) not engage in or counsel any business or occupation which, in the opinion of the Society, is incompatible with the professional ethics of a management accountant;

(iv) not accept any engagement to review the work of another Member for the same employer except with the knowledge of that Member, or except where the connection of that Member with the work has been terminated, unless the Member reviews the work of others as a normal part of his or her responsibilities;

(v) not attempt to gain an advantage over other Members by paying or accepting a commission in securing management accounting or public accounting work;

(vi) uphold the principle of adequate compensation for management accounting and public accounting work; and

(vii) not act maliciously or in any other way which may adversely reflect on the public or professional reputation or business of another Member.

(e) A Member will:

(i) at all times maintain the standards of competence expressed by the Board from time to time;

(ii) disseminate the knowledge upon which the profession of management accounting is based to others within the profession and generally promote the advancement of the profession;

(iii) undertake only such work as he or she is competent to perform by virtue of his or her training and experience and will, where it would be in the best interests of an employer or client, engage, or advise the employer or client to engage, other specialists;

(iv) expose before the proper tribunals of the Society any incompetent, unethical, illegal or unfair conduct or practice of a Member which involves the reputation, dignity or honour of the Society; and

(v) endeavour to ensure that a professional partnership or company, with which such Member is associated as a partner, principal, director, officer, associate or employee, abides by the Code of Professional Ethics and the rules of professional conduct established by the Society.

(CMA Ontario. See www.cmaontario.org.)

Chapter Summary

All organizations have goals, and their managers need information as they strive to attain those goals. Information is needed for the management functions of decision making, planning, directing operations, and controlling. Managerial accounting is the process of identifying, measuring, analyzing, interpreting, and communicating information in pursuit of an organization's goals. Managerial accounting is an integral part of the management process, and management accountants are important strategic partners in an organization's management team.

Managerial accounting is an important part of any organization's management information system. The five objectives of managerial accounting activity are (1) providing information for decision making and planning, and proactively participating as part of the management team in the decision-making and planning processes; (2) assisting managers in directing and controlling operations; (3) motivating managers and other employees toward the organization's goals; (4) measuring the performance of activities, subunits, managers, and other employees within the organization; and (5) assessing the organization's competitive position and working with other managers to ensure the organization's long-run competitiveness in its industry.

Managerial accounting differs from financial accounting in several ways. The users of managerial accounting information are managers inside the organization. Managerial accounting information is not mandatory, is unregulated, and draws on data from the accounting system as well as other data sources.

The users of financial accounting information are interested parties outside the organization, such as investors and creditors. Financial accounting information is required for publicly held companies, is regulated by the Accounting Standards Board of the Canadian Institute of Chartered Accountants (CICA), and is based in great part on historical transaction data.

In a formal organization chart, management accountants are in a staff capacity. However, management accountants are increasingly being deployed as members of cross-functional teams, which address a variety of managerial decisions and business issues. More than ever before, management accountants are physically located throughout an enterprise alongside the managers with whom they work closely.

Managerial accounting continually evolves and adapts as the business environment changes. The growth of international competition and dramatic changes in technology are placing ever-greater demands on the information provided by managerial accounting systems. Many organizations have moved away from a historical cost accounting perspective and toward a proactive cost management perspective. Under this approach, the management accountant is part of a cross-functional management team that seeks to create value for the organization by managing resources, activities, and people to achieve the organization's goals.

An organization's value chain is the set of linked, value-creating activities, ranging from securing basic raw materials and energy to the ultimate delivery of products and services. Understanding the value chain is a crucial step in the development of an organization's strategy. The overall recognition of the importance of cost relationships among the activities in the value chain, and the process of managing those cost relationships to the organization's advantage, is called strategic cost management.

Managerial accounting is a profession with a designation process and a code of professional ethics. Management accountants are highly trained professionals, who can contribute significantly to the success of any enterprise.

Key Terms

For each term's definition refer to the indicated page, or turn to the glossary at the end of the text.

activity accounting 16	chief financial officer (CFO), 9	financial accounting, 6	strategic cost management, 18
activity-based costing (ABC) 16	continuous improvement, 15	internal auditor, 9	theory of constraints, 18
activity-based management (ABM) 16	controller (or comptroller), 9	just-in-time (JIT) production system, 15	total quality management (TQM), 15
attention-directing function, 5	cost accounting system, 6	line positions, 8	treasurer, 9
certified management accountant (CMA), 20	cost driver, 18	managerial accounting, 2	value chain, 16
	cost management system, 16	non-value-added costs, 16	
	empowerment, 5	staff positions, 9	

Review Questions

1–1.   According to some estimates, the volume of electronic commerce transactions exceeds $3 trillion. Business-to-business transactions account for almost half of this amount. What changes do you believe are in store for managerial accounting as a result of the explosion in e-commerce?

1–2.   List two plausible goals for each of these organizations: Amazon.ca, Canadian Red Cross, General Motors, Wal-Mart, the City of Toronto, and Hertz.

1–3.   List and define the four basic management activities.

1–4.   Give examples of each of the four primary management activities in the context of a national fast-food chain such as Burger King.

1–5.   Give examples of how each of the objectives of managerial accounting activity would be important in an airline company such as WestJet Airlines.

1–6.   List and describe four important differences between managerial and financial accounting.

1–7.   Distinguish between cost accounting and managerial accounting.

1–8.   Distinguish between line and staff positions. Give two examples of each in a university setting.

1–9.   Distinguish between the following two accounting positions: controller and treasurer.

1–10.   What does the following statement by a management accountant at Caterpillar imply about where in the organization the management accountants are located? "[We] are a partner with all of the other functions in the business here." (Reference 1a at end of the text.)

1–11.   What is meant by the following statement? "Managerial accounting often serves an attention-directing role."

1–12.   What is the chief difference between manufacturing and service industry firms?

1–13.   Define the following terms: just-in-time, computer-integrated manufacturing, cost management system, empowerment, and total quality management.

1–14. Explain the difference between e-business and e-commerce.

1–15. Define and explain the term *CMA*.

1–16. Briefly explain what is meant by each of the following ethical principles for management accountants: competence, confidentiality, integrity, and credibility.

1–17. What is meant by the term *non-value-added costs*?

1–18. Managerial accounting is an important part of any enterprise's management information system. Name two other information systems that supply information to management.

1–19. Can managerial accounting play an important role in a nonprofit organization? Explain your answer.

1–20. A large manufacturer of electronic machinery stated the following as one of its goals: "The company should become the low-cost producer in its industry." How can managerial accounting help the company achieve this goal?

1–21. What do you think it means to be a professional? In your view, are management accountants professionals?

1–22. Name several activities in the value chain of (*a*) a manufacturer of cotton shirts and (*b*) an airline.

1–23. Define the term *strategic cost management*.

Exercises

Use the Internet to access the Web site for one of the following companies, or any other company of your choosing.

Air Canada	www.aircanada.com
Coca-Cola	www.cocacola.com
Deere and Company	www.deere.com
IBM	www.ibm.com
Sears	www.sears.com

Required: Find the management discussion and analysis portion of the firm's most recent online annual report. Then briefly discuss how managerial accounting can contribute to the company's financial goals.

Use the Internet to access the Web site for one of the following companies, or any other company of your choosing.

Avis Rent-a-Car	www.avis.ca
Expedia.ca	www.expedia.ca
Holland America Cruise Lines	www.hollandamerica.com
Levi Strauss & Company	www.levistrauss.com
Nokia	www.nokia.com
Cineplex Entertainment	www.cineplex.com

Required: After perusing the company's Web site, work as a group to list several key activities you believe would be in the company's value chain.

■ **Exercise 1–24**
Contributions of Managerial Accounting; Use of Internet
(LO 1, 3, 5)

This icon indicates use of the Internet.

■ **Exercise 1–25**
Value Chain; Use of Internet
(LO 8)

This icon indicates group work.

The pen icon indicates a written response is needed.

Problems

Dave Nelson recently retired at age 48, courtesy of a very healthy stock market and numerous stock options he had been granted while president of e-Shops.com, an Internet startup company. He soon moved to Montana to follow his dream of living in the mountains and Big-Sky country. Nelson, always the entrepreneur, began a sporting-goods store shortly after relocating. The single store soon grew to a chain of four outlets throughout the sparsely populated state. As Nelson put it, "I can't believe how fast we've expanded. It's basically uncontrolled growth—growth that has occurred in spite of what we've done."

Although business has been profitable, the chain did have its share of problems. Store traffic was somewhat seasonal, with a slowdown occurring as winter approached. Nelson therefore added ski equipment and accessories to his product line. The need to finance required inventories, which seemed to be bulging, left cash balances at very low levels, occasionally giving rise to short-term bank loans.

■ **Problem 1–26**
Managing a Retail Business; Cross-Functional Teams; E-Commerce
(LO 5, 6, 7)

The flag icon indicates an international issue.

Part of Nelson's operation focused on canoe building and whitewater rafting trips. Reports from the company's financial accounting system seemed to indicate that these operations were losing money because of increasing costs, although Nelson could not be sure. "The traditional income statement is not too useful in assessing the problem," he noted. "Also, my gut feeling is that we are not dealing with the best suppliers in terms of quality of goods, delivery reliability, and prices." Additional complications were caused by an increasingly competitive marketplace, with many former customers now buying merchandise and booking river excursions via the Internet, through catalogues received in the mail, or through businesses that advertised heavily in outdoor magazines.

Nelson's background is marketing, and he appeared somewhat puzzled on how to proceed. The company's chief financial officer (CFO) would be an obvious asset in terms of addressing these problems. Unfortunately, she knew her numbers but lacked key knowledge of general business operations. The same could be said for other executives who managed somewhat in "silos," becoming experts in a narrow facet of the company but, in general, lacking a big-picture outlook for the firm.

Required:

1. Explain how the CFO and managerial accounting could assist Nelson in addressing the company's problems.
2. Would a cross-functional team be useful here? Briefly discuss.
3. Does e-commerce appear to be a viable option for the firm? Explain, citing the difference between business-to-consumer and business-to-business channels. Which of the two channels, if either, would you recommend? Why?

■ **Problem 1–27**
Role of the Divisional
Controller; Retailer
(LO 4, 6, 9, 10)

*The balance icon indicates
an ethical issue.*

Urban Elite Apparel designs women's apparel and sells it through retail outlets across the country. All of the company's clothing lines are manufactured by contract manufacturers around the world. A division manager is responsible for each of the company's retail divisions. Each division's controller, assigned by the corporate controller's office, manages the division's accounting system and provides analysis of financial information for the division manager. The division manager evaluates the performance of the division controller and makes recommendations for salary increases and promotions. However, the final responsibility for promotion evaluation and salary increases rests with the corporate controller.

Each of Urban Elite Apparel's divisions is responsible for product design, sales, pricing, operating expenses, and profit. However, corporate management exercises tight control over divisional financial operations. For example, all capital expenditure above a modest amount must be approved by corporate management. The method of financial reporting from the division to corporate headquarters provides further evidence of the degree of financial control. The division manager and the division controller submit to corporate headquarters separate and independent commentary on the financial results of the division. Corporate management states that the division controller is there to provide an independent view of the division's operations, not as a spy.

Required:

1. Discuss the arrangements for line and staff reporting in Urban Elite Apparel.
2. The division controller for Urban Elite Apparel has a "dual reporting" responsibility. The division controller is responsible both to the division manager, who makes recommendations on salary and promotion, *and* to the corporate controller, who has the final say in such matters.
    a. Identify and discuss the factors that make the division controller's role difficult in this type of situation.
    b. Discuss the effect of the dual reporting relationship on the motivation of the divisional controller.

(CMA, adapted)

Case

Progressive Applications Corporation, a developer and distributor of business applications software, has been in business for five years. The company's main products include programs used for list management, billing, and accounting for the mail order shopping business. Progressive's sales have increased steadily to the current level of $25 million per year. The company has 250 employees.

Andrea Nolan joined Progressive approximately one year ago as accounting manager. Nolan's duties include supervision of the company's accounting operations and preparation of the company's financial statements. In the past six months Progressive's sales have ceased to rise and have actually declined in the two most recent months. This unexpected downturn has resulted in cash shortages. Compounding these problems, Progressive has had to delay the introduction of a new product line due to delays in documentation preparation.

Progressive contracts most of its printing requirements to Web Graphic Inc., a small company owned by Rob Borman. Borman has dedicated a major portion of his printing capacity to Progressive's requirements because Progressive's contracts represent approximately 50 percent of Web Graphic's business. Nolan has known Borman for many years; as a matter of fact, she learned of Progressive's need for an accounting manager through Borman.

While preparing Progressive's most recent financial statements, Nolan became concerned about the company's ability to maintain steady payments to its suppliers; she estimated that payments to all vendors, normally made within 30 days, could exceed 75 days. Nolan is particularly concerned about payments to Web Graphic; she knows that Progressive had recently placed a large order with that company for the printing of the new product documentation, and she knows that Web Graphic will soon be placing an order for the special paper required for Progressive's documentation. Nolan is considering telling Borman about Progressive's cash problems; however, she is aware that a delay in the printing of the documentation would jeopardize Progressive's new product.

Required:

1. As a group, describe Nolan's ethical responsibilities in this situation.

2. Independent of your answer to requirement (1), assume that Nolan learns that Borman of Web Graphic has decided to postpone the special paper order required for Progressive's printing job; Nolan believes Borman must have heard rumours about Progressive's financial problems from some other source, because she has not talked to Borman. Should Nolan tell the appropriate Progressive officials that Borman has postponed the paper order? Explain your answer.

3. Independently of your answers to the first two requirements, assume that Borman has decided to postpone the special paper order because he has learned of Progressive's financial problems from some source other than Nolan. In addition, Nolan realizes that Jim Grason, Progressive's purchasing manager, knows of her friendship with Borman. Now Nolan is concerned that Grason may suspect she told Borman of Progressive's financial problems when Grason finds out Borman has postponed the order. Describe the steps Nolan should take to resolve this situation.

(CMA, adapted)

Chapter Two

Basic Cost Management Concepts

The Comet Computer Company produces computers in its Mississauga, Ontario plant. Most of the company's sales are made online through its Web site at cometcomp.com. This manufacturer is a mass customizer, which means that its products combine standardized components in different ways to produce custom-made computers to order. In this chapter, we will explore the many different issues involved in understanding the costs of running any business.

After completing this chapter, you should be able to:

1 Explain what is meant by the word "cost."

2 Distinguish among product costs, period costs, and expenses.

3 Describe the role of costs on published financial statements.

4 List five types of manufacturing operations and describe mass customization.

5 Give examples of three types of manufacturing costs.

6 Prepare a schedule of cost of goods manufactured, a schedule of cost of goods sold, and an income statement for a manufacturer.

7 Understand the importance of identifying an organization's cost drivers.

8 Describe the behaviour of variable and fixed costs, in total and on a per-unit basis.

9 Distinguish among direct, indirect, controllable, and uncontrollable costs.

10 Define and give examples of an opportunity cost, an out-of-pocket cost, a sunk cost, a differential cost, a marginal cost, and an average cost.

IN CONTRAST

In contrast to the manufacturing setting of the Comet Computer Company, we explore the cost issues covered in the chapter in the context of Midas, Inc. One of the world's largest automotive service companies, Midas has more than 2,500 company-owned or franchised automotive service locations on four continents. Midas' management, like that of any other company, must understand its costs in order to be successful in a competitive business environment.

The process of management involves formulating strategy, planning, control, decision making, and directing operational activities. Managers can perform each of these functions more effectively with managerial accounting information. Much of this information focuses on the costs incurred in the organization. For example, in *formulating its overall strategy*, WestJet Airlines' management team considered the cost savings that result from being a low-cost airline. In *planning* WestJet's routes and flight schedules, managers must consider aircraft fuel costs, salaries of flight crews, and airport landing fees. *Controlling* the costs of manufacturing heavy equipment requires that Caterpillar's managerial accountants carefully measure and manage production costs. In *making decisions* about locating a new store, Wal-Mart managers need information about the cost of building, maintaining, equipping, and staffing the store. Finally, to *direct operational activities*, managers in all three of these companies need information about the cost of salaries, utilities, security, and a host of other goods and services.

The Meaning of Cost

Each of the examples in the preceding paragraph focuses on costs of one type or another. An important first step in studying managerial accounting is to gain an understanding of the various types of costs incurred by organizations and how those costs are actively managed.

At the most basic level, a **cost** may be defined as the sacrifice made, usually measured by the resources given up, to achieve a particular purpose. If we look more carefully, though, we find that the word cost can have different meanings depending on the context in which it is used. Cost data that are classified and recorded in a particular way for one purpose may be inappropriate for another use. For example, the costs incurred in producing gasoline last year are important in measuring Petro-Canada's income for the year. However, those costs may not be useful in planning the company's refinery operations for the next year if the cost of oil has changed significantly or if the methods of producing gasoline have improved.

The important point is that different cost concepts and classifications are used for different purposes. Understanding these concepts and classifications enables the managerial accountant to provide appropriate cost data to the managers who need it. The purpose of this chapter is to enable the users of this textbook to gain a firm grasp of the cost terminology used in managerial accounting, which will be used throughout the book.

Product Costs, Period Costs, and Expenses

An important issue in both managerial and financial accounting is the timing with which the costs of acquiring assets or services are recognized as expenses. An **expense** is defined as the cost incurred when an asset is used up or sold for the purpose of generating revenue. The terms *product cost* and *period cost* are used to describe the timing with which various expenses are recognized.

A **product cost** is a cost assigned to goods that were either purchased or manufactured for resale. The product cost is used to value the inventory of manufactured goods or merchandise until the goods are sold. In the period of the sale, the product costs are recognized as an expense called **cost of goods sold**. The product cost of merchandise inventory acquired by a retailer or wholesaler for resale consists of the purchase cost of the inventory plus any shipping charges. The product cost of manufactured inventory includes all of the costs incurred in its manufacture. For example, the labour cost of a production employee at Comet Computer Company is included as

> **Learning Objective 1**
>
> Explain what is meant by the word "cost."

> "We are expected to say, 'Here are the costs, and this is why the costs are what they are, and this is how they compare to other things, and here are some suggestions where we could possible improve.'" (2a)
> **Caterpillar**

> **Learning Objective 2**
>
> Distinguish among product costs, period costs, and expenses.

Exhibit 2–1
Product Costs and Cost of
Goods Sold

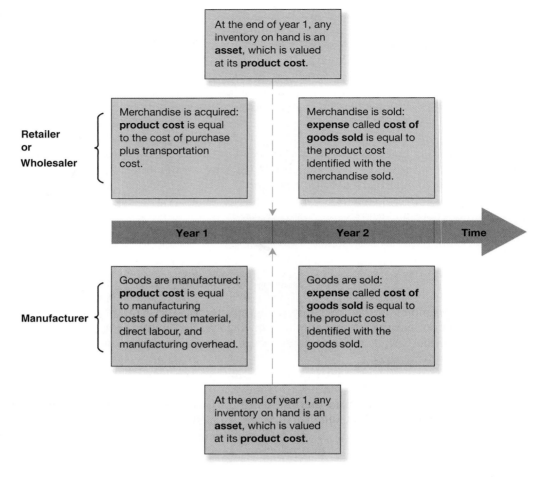

a product cost of the computers manufactured. Exhibit 2–1 illustrates the relationship between product costs and cost-of-goods-sold expense.

Another term for product cost is **inventoriable cost**, since a product cost is stored as the cost of inventory until the goods are sold. In addition to retailers, wholesalers, and manufacturers, the concept of product cost is relevant to other producers of inventoriable goods. Agricultural firms, lumber companies, and mining firms are examples of nonmanufacturers that produce inventoriable goods. Apples, timber, coal, and other such goods are inventoried at their product cost until the time period during which they are sold.

All costs that are not product costs are called **period costs**. These costs are identified with the period of time in which they are incurred rather than with units of purchased or produced goods. Period costs are recognized as expenses during the time period in which they are incurred. All research, selling, and administrative costs are treated as period costs. This is true in manufacturing, retail, and service industry firms.

Research costs include costs of developing new products and services. For example, the costs of running laboratories are all classified as research costs. Selling costs include salaries, commissions, and travel costs of sales personnel and the costs of advertising and promotion. *Administrative costs* refer to all costs of running the organization as a whole. The salaries of top-management personnel and the costs of the accounting, legal, and public relations activities are examples of administrative costs.

Exhibit 2–2 illustrates the nature of period costs.

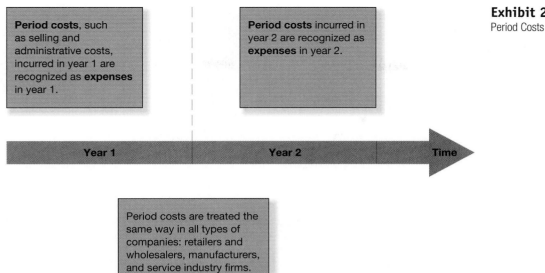

Exhibit 2–2
Period Costs

Costs on Financial Statements

The distinction between product costs and period costs is emphasized by examining financial statements from three different types of firms.

Learning Objective 3

Describe the role of costs on published financial statements.

Income Statement

Exhibit 2–3 displays recent income statements, in highly summarized form, from Caterpillar, Inc., Wal-Mart Stores, Inc., and WestJet Airlines Ltd. These companies are from three different industries. Caterpillar is a heavy equipment manufacturer. Wal-Mart Stores is a large retail firm with 4,022 locations throughout the United States and 2,757 locations internationally, including 309 stores across Canada. Representing the service industry is WestJet Airlines, a major airline based in Western Canada.

Selling and administrative costs are period costs on all three income statements shown in Exhibit 2–3. For example, Caterpillar lists $4.578 billion of selling, general, and administrative expenses.

For Caterpillar, the costs of manufactured inventory are product costs. All costs incurred in manufacturing finished products are stored in inventory until the time period when the products are sold. Then the product costs of the inventory sold become cost of goods sold, an expense, on the income statement.

Product costs for Wal-Mart include all costs of acquiring merchandise inventory for resale. These product costs are stored in inventory until the time period during which the merchandise is sold. Then these costs become cost of goods sold.

There are no inventoried product costs at WestJet Airlines. Although this firm does engage in the production of air transportation services, its service output is consumed as soon as it is produced. Service industry firms, such as WestJet Airlines, TD Canada Trust, Fairmont Hotels & Resorts, Manulife Insurance, and Tim Hortons, generally refer to the costs of producing services as **operating expenses**. Operating expenses are treated as period costs and are expensed during the period in which they

"What we should become in the future is a business partner who helps people understand what the financials are saying and helps them design their businesses." (2b)

Qwest

Exhibit 2–3
Income Statements from
Three Different Industries
(all figures in thousands of
dollars)

CATERPILLAR, INC.
Statement of Income for a Recent Year

Value
measured ⟶
by product
costs

Sales revenue	$ 51,324,000
Less: Cost of goods sold	38,415,000
Gross profit	12,909,000
Less: Operating costs:	
Selling, general, and administrative expenses	4,399,000
Research and development expenses	1,728,000
Depreciation	1,980,000
Total operating costs	8,107,000
Operating income	4,802,000
Add: Nonoperating income	336,000
Less: Nonoperating expenses	628,000
Income before taxes	4,510,000
Provision for income taxes	(953,000)
Net income	$ 3,557,000

WAL-MART STORES, INC.
Statement of Income for a Recent Year

Value
measured ⟶
by product
costs

Sales revenue	$405,607,000
Less: Cost of goods sold	306,158,000
Gross profit	99,449,000
Less: Selling, general, and administrative expenses	76,651,000
Operating income	22,798,000
Less: Interest expense	1,900,000
Income before income taxes	20,898,000
Provision for income taxes	(7,145,000)
Minority interest	(499,000)
Income from discontinued operations, net of tax	146,000
Net income	$ 13,400,000

WESTJET AIRLINES LTD.
Statement of Income for a Recent Year

Revenues:	
Guest revenues	$ 2,301,301
Charter and other revenues	248,205
	2,549,506
Expenses:	
Aircraft fuel	803,293
Airport operations	342,922
Flight operations and navigational charges	280,920
Marketing, general, and administration	211,979
Sales and distribution	170,605
Depreciation and amortization	136,485
Inflight	105,849
Aircraft leasing	86,050
Maintenance	85,093
Employee profit share	33,435
	2,256,631
Earnings from operations	292,875

(continued)

Non-operating income (expenses):	
Interest income..	25,485
Interest expense	(76,078)
Gain (loss) on foreign exchange	30,587
Gain (loss) on disposal of property and equipment	(701)
Loss on derivatives	(17,331)
	(38,038)
Earnings before income taxes	254,837
Income tax expense	(76,702)
Net earnings	$ 178,135

are incurred. WestJet Airlines includes costs such as flight operations, aircraft fuel, and aircraft maintenance in operating expenses for the period.

Balance Sheet

Since retailers, wholesalers, and manufacturers sell inventoriable products, their balance sheets are also affected by product costs. Exhibit 2–4 displays the current-assets section from recent balance sheets of Caterpillar and Wal-Mart. Included in the current-assets section of each of these balance sheets is inventory. Manufacturers, such as Caterpillar, have three types of inventory. **Raw-material** inventory includes all materials before they are placed into production. **Work-in-process** inventory refers to manufactured products that are only partially completed at the date when the balance sheet is prepared. **Finished-goods** inventory refers to manufactured goods that are complete and ready for sale. The values of the work-in-process and finished-goods inventories are measured by their product costs.

On the Wal-Mart balance sheet, the cost of acquiring merchandise is listed as the value of the merchandise inventories.

> "Now the accountants are not only the interpreters. They drive management toward the proper response to what the numbers are telling us." (2c)
>
> **ITT Automotive**

CATERPILLAR, INC.
Partial Balance Sheet at the End of a Recent Year

Current assets:	
Cash and cash equivalents...	$ 2,736,000
Accounts receivable (net)	18,128,000
Inventories	8,781,000
Other current assets	1,998,000
Total current assets	$31,633,000

Value measured by product costs → (points to Inventories)

WAL-MART STORES, INC.
Partial Balance Sheet at the End of a Recent Year

Current assets:	
Cash and cash equivalents	$ 5,488,000
Receivables (net)	1,715,000
Inventories	29,447,000
Prepaid expenses and other current assets	1,841,000
Total current assets	$38,491,000

Value measured by product costs → (points to Inventories)

Exhibit 2–4

Partial Balance Sheets for a Manufacturer and a Retailer (all figures in thousands of dollars)

CATERPILLAR®

WAL★MART
ALWAYS LOW PRICES. ALWAYS WAL-MART.
Always

Manufacturing Operations and Costs

Learning Objective 4

List five types of manufacturing operations and describe mass customization.

Although there are tens of thousands of manufacturing firms, their basic production processes can be classified into five generic types. The nature of the manufacturing process can affect the manufacturing costs incurred. Therefore, the management team is in a better position to manage these costs if the relationship of the production process to the types of costs incurred is understood. Exhibit 2–5 defines and describes the five generic manufacturing processes.[1]

We will study the role of managerial accounting and cost management in four of these manufacturing processes. This chapter will focus on mass customization operations, similar to that used by Dell Inc. Chapter 3 will examine managerial accounting techniques used in job-shop and batch-processing operations. Chapter 4 will focus on the cost accumulation and cost management processes in a continuous-flow manufacturing environment.

Mass-Customization Operations

In a **mass-customization** manufacturing environment, many standardized components are combined in different ways to produce custom-made products to customer order. Dell Inc. is a prime example of mass customizers. Such companies are characterized by high production volume and often use a direct-sales approach, in which the consumer orders directly from the manufacturer often via the Internet.

Exhibit 2–5
Types of Production
Processes

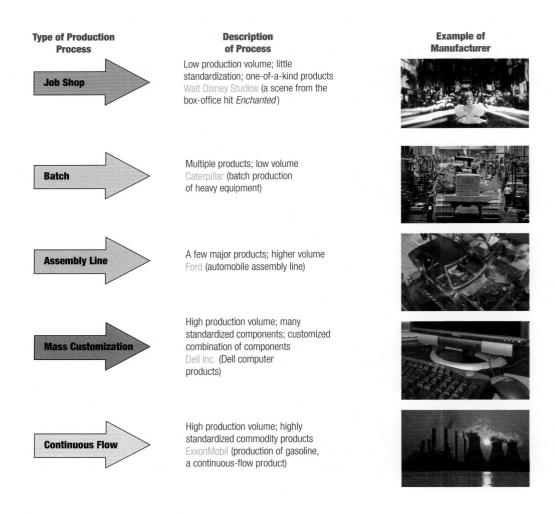

Type of Production Process	Description of Process	Example of Manufacturer
Job Shop	Low production volume; little standardization; one-of-a-kind products Walt Disney Studios (a scene from the box-office hit *Enchanted*)	
Batch	Multiple products; low volume Caterpillar (batch production of heavy equipment)	
Assembly Line	A few major products; higher volume Ford (automobile assembly line)	
Mass Customization	High production volume; many standardized components; customized combination of components Dell Inc. (Dell computer products)	
Continuous Flow	High production volume; highly standardized commodity products ExxonMobil (production of gasoline, a continuous-flow product)	

MASS CUSTOMIZATION

"There is no better way to make, sell, and deliver PCs than the way Dell Inc. does it, and nobody executes that model better than Dell." The company's machines are made to order and delivered directly to customers, who get the exact machines they want cheaper than they can get them from Dell's competition. "Dell has some 24 facilities in and around Austin and employs more than 18,000 local workers. Dell is improving its earnings and gaining market share even in tough economic times. Nevertheless, Michael Dell, the company's restless founder, is constantly looking for ways to improve the company's operations."[2] In one year alone, Dell cut $1 billion out of its costs—half from manufacturing—and Dell executives vowed to cut another $1 billion.

"Visit the Topfer Manufacturing Center in Austin, and it's hard to conceive how Dell could be any more efficient. Workers already scuttle about in the 200,000-square-foot plant like ants on a hot plate. Gathered in cramped six-person 'cells,' they assemble computers from batches of parts that arrive via a computer-directed conveyor system overhead. If a worker encounters a problem, that batch can instantly be shifted to another cell, avoiding the stoppages that plague conventional assembly lines. Dell is constantly tinkering with factory layout and product design to move computers through at a higher velocity. So far they've done extraordinarily well. Dell has increased production by one-third over two years while cutting manufacturing space in half. Workers in the six-person cells assemble 18 units an hour, double the pace of a couple of years ago.

"Can Dell keep it up? The manager of the Topfer factory explains how. He points to places where Dell can shave off a few seconds of assembly time or move completed products out the door a couple of minutes faster. A robot is being tested to pack computers into cartons, eliminating a human-staffed line doing the same thing, freeing up space for more assembly cells. Elsewhere Dell plans to combine the tasks of downloading software and testing computers, eliminating a step—and valuable seconds of worker time. Subtle changes in product design simplify assembly or reduce the number of people needed to complete a product. Other gains are harder to quantify. Dell builds each unit to order, for example, so flexibility is essential. Every change on the factory floor that allows workers to adapt to sudden shifts in demand reduces the excess capacity of people and plant space Dell must maintain to get products out on time. Dell's purchasing managers are working equally hard with suppliers to watch parts inventories on an hour-by-hour basis, making sure Dell has just enough parts to meet expected demand without clogging the system with excess inventory."[3]

In spite of the ups and downs of the computer technology industry, most observers believe that Dell's business model will continue to be successful. However, the company has recently acknowledged that it needs to upgrade its tech support services in order to better serve its customers.[4]

To illustrate a mass-customization environment, let's focus on Comet Computer Corporation, a manufacturer of computers and peripheral devices.[5] Comet purchases computer parts such as motherboards, computer chips, and power units and then assembles these parts into customized personal computers to customer specifications. A finished computer is then packaged with the monitor, keyboard, printer, and cables ordered by the customer, all of which are purchased by Comet.

The direct-sales model, which was popularized by Dell Inc., is used. Ninety percent of Comet's orders are placed on the company's Web site at cometcomp.com, and 10 percent are taken on a toll-free phone number. No sales are made through retail channels.

Comet's production process is triggered when a customer places an order, either on the company's Web site or through its toll-free phone line. The customer specifies every aspect of the desired computer system, including the type of processor and amount of memory in the hard drive, the size of the monitor and type of printer, and finally any preinstalled software. Either a Web or a phone sales representative transmits the order electronically to the appropriate production cell module.[6] A production cell module, or *mod*, is responsible for manufacturing a particular product line, such as a desktop computer, laptop, or server. When the order is received in the appropriate mod, the assembly process begins. Memory and processor chips are installed in the motherboard, which is then mounted on the chassis. Then such components as the CD-ROM drive, hard drive, and power supply are placed into the chassis. After all of the components are mounted, the computer's hood (cover) is installed, and the finished unit moves to a test and inspection mod. After the unit checks out for reliability, it goes to the software installation mod, where the software ordered by the customer is preinstalled. From the software mod, the unit goes to the shipping mod, where it is boxed and prepared for shipping. Comet strives to ship every customer order within six days.

Before we discuss Comet's production process further, let's turn our attention to the types of manufacturing costs incurred by Comet and other manufacturers.

> "[Management accountants] will be more analytical . . . and more of a partner with the operational side of the business." (2d)
>
> **ITT Automotive**

Manufacturing Costs

Learning Objective 5

Give examples of three types of manufacturing costs.

To assist managers in planning, decision making, and cost management, managerial accountants classify costs by the functional area of the organization to which costs relate. Some examples of functional areas are manufacturing, marketing, administration, and research and development. Manufacturing costs are further classified into the following three categories: direct material, direct labour, and manufacturing overhead.

Direct Material   Raw material consumed in the manufacturing process is physically incorporated in the finished product, and can be traced to products conveniently is called **direct material**. Examples include the sheet metal in a Subaru automobile and the semiconductors in a Comet computer.

Some confusion arises by the seemingly interchangeable use of the terms *raw material* and *direct material*. However, there is a difference in the meaning of these terms. Before material is entered into the production process, it is called *raw material*. *After* it enters production, it becomes *direct material*.

Direct Labour   The cost of salaries, wages, and fringe benefits for personnel who work directly on the manufactured products is classified as **direct-labour cost**. Examples include the wages of personnel who assemble Comet computers and who operate the equipment in a Petro-Canada refinery.

The cost of fringe benefits for direct-labour personnel, such as employer-paid extended health care premiums and the employer's pension contributions, also should be classified as direct-labour costs.

Manufacturing Overhead   All other manufacturing costs are classified as **manufacturing overhead**, which includes three types of costs: indirect material, indirect labour, and other manufacturing costs.

Indirect Material   The cost of materials that are required for the production process but do not become an integral part of the finished product are classified as **indirect material** costs. An example is the cost of drill bits used in a metal-fabrication department at Ford Motor Company. The drill bits wear out and are discarded, but they do not become part of the product. Materials that do become an integral part of the finished product but are insignificant in cost are also often classified as indirect material. Materials such as glue or paint may be so inexpensive that it is not worth tracing their costs to specific products as direct materials.

Indirect Labour   The costs of personnel who do not work directly on the product, but whose services are necessary for the manufacturing process, are classified as **indirect labour**. Such personnel include production department supervisors, custodial employees, and security guards.

Other Manufacturing Costs   All other manufacturing costs that are neither material nor labour costs are classified as manufacturing overhead. These costs include depreciation of plant and equipment, property taxes, insurance, and utilities such as electricity, as well as the costs of operating service departments. **Service departments** or **support departments** are those that do not work directly on manufacturing products but are necessary for the manufacturing process to occur. Examples include equipment-maintenance departments and computer-aided-design (CAD) departments. In some manufacturing firms, departments are referred to as *work centres*.

Other manufacturing overhead costs include overtime premiums and the cost of idle time. An **overtime premium** is the extra compensation paid to an employee who works beyond the time normally scheduled. Suppose a technician who assembles Comet computers earns $16 per hour. The technician works 48 hours during a week instead of the scheduled time of 40 hours. The overtime pay scale is time-and-a-half, or 150 percent of the regular wage. The technician's compensation for the week is classified as follows:

> "If you just simply have [an employee] performing an [assembly] operation, that's direct labor. But when you put in a robot to do the job, which we're all doing, then you've got to have an engineer to make sure the [robot] is programmed right. So now it becomes indirect labor." (2e)
> **Chrysler**

Direct-labour cost ($16 × 48)	$768
Overhead (overtime premium: ½ × $16 × 8)	64
Total compensation paid	$832

Only the *extra* compensation of $8 per hour is classified as overtime premium. The regular wage of $16 per hour is treated as direct labour, even for the eight overtime hours.

Idle time is time that is not spent productively by an employee due to such events as equipment breakdowns or new setups of production runs. Such idle time is an unavoidable feature of most manufacturing processes. The cost of an employee's idle time is classified as overhead so that it may be spread across all production jobs, rather than being associated with a particular production job. Suppose that during one 40-hour shift, a machine breakdown resulted in idle time of 1½ hours and a power failure idled workers for an additional ½ hour. If an employee earns $14 per hour, the employee's wages for the week will be classified as follows:

Direct-labour cost ($14 × 38)	$532
Overhead (idle time $14 × 2)	28
Total compensation paid	$560

Both overtime premiums and the cost of idle time should be classified as manufacturing overhead, rather than associated with a particular production job, because the particular job on which idle time or overtime may occur tends to be selected at random. Suppose several production jobs are scheduled during an eight-hour shift, and the last job remains unfinished at the end of the shift. The overtime to finish the last job is necessitated by all of the jobs scheduled during the shift, not just the last one. Similarly, if a power failure occurs during one of several production jobs, the idle time that results is not due to the job that happens to be in process at the time.

The power failure is a random event, and the resulting cost should be treated as a cost of all of the department's production.

To summarize, manufacturing costs include direct material, direct labour, and manufacturing overhead. Direct labour and overhead are often called **conversion costs**, since they are the costs of "converting" raw material into finished products. Direct material and direct labour are often referred to as **prime costs**.

Manufacturing Cost Flows

> "In my mind, cost accountants are going to be business analysts." (2f)
>
> **Boeing**

Direct material, direct labour, and manufacturing overhead are the three types of production costs incurred by manufacturers. These costs are product costs because they are stored in inventory until the time period when the manufacturer's products are sold. Manufacturers have product-costing systems to keep track of the flow of these costs from the time production begins until finished products are sold. This flow of manufacturing costs is depicted in Exhibit 2–6. As direct material is consumed in production, its cost is added to work-in-process inventory. Similarly, the costs of direct labour and manufacturing overhead are accumulated in work in process.

When products are finished, their costs are transferred from work-in-process inventory to finished-goods inventory. The total cost of direct material, direct labour, and manufacturing overhead transferred from work-in-process inventory to finished-goods inventory is called the **cost of goods manufactured**. The costs then are stored in finished goods until the time period when the products are sold. At that time, the product costs are transferred from finished goods to cost of goods sold, which is an expense of the period when the sale is made. Exhibit 2–6 concentrates on the conceptual basis of a product-costing system. The detailed procedures and accounts used to keep track of product costs are covered in Chapters 3 and 4.

Learning Objective 6

Prepare a schedule of cost of goods manufactured, a schedule of cost of goods sold, and an income statement for a manufacturer.

Manufacturers generally prepare a **schedule of cost of goods manufactured** and a **schedule of cost of goods sold** to summarize the flow of manufacturing costs during an accounting period. These schedules are intended for internal use by management and are generally not made available to the public. Exhibit 2–7 shows these two schedules along with an income statement for Comet Computer Corporation. Notice the extremely low inventories of raw material, finished goods, and work in process in these schedules. With annual sales of $700 million, Comet's year-end inventory of raw material is only $5,020,000, which is less than 1 percent of sales. Work-in-process inventory ($100,000) and finished-goods inventory ($190,000) are even lower. These low inventories, relative to sales volume, are characteristic of mass customizers using the direct-sales approach.

Exhibit 2–6
Flow of Manufacturing Costs

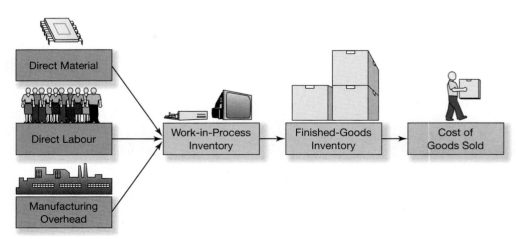

Product costs . . .   . . . are stored in inventory . . .   . . . until the products are sold.

Production Costs in Service Firms and Nonprofit Organizations

Service firms and many nonprofit organizations are also engaged in production. What distinguishes these organizations from manufacturers is that a service is consumed as it is produced, whereas a manufactured product can be stored in inventory. Such businesses as Fairmont Hotels & Resorts, TD Canada Trust, WestJet, and the Toronto Maple Leafs are in the business of producing services. Similarly, nonprofit organizations

COMET COMPUTER CORPORATION
Schedule of Cost of Goods Manufactured
For the Year Ended December 31, 20x2
(in thousands)

Direct material:		
Raw-material inventory, January 1	$ 6,000	
Add: Purchases of raw material	134,000	
Raw material available for use	$140,000	
Deduct: Raw-material inventory, December 31	5,020	
Raw material used		$134,980
Direct labour		50,000
Manufacturing overhead:		
Indirect material	$ 10,000	
Indirect labour	40,000	
Depreciation on factory	90,000	
Depreciation on equipment	70,000	
Utilities	15,000	
Insurance	5,000	
Total manufacturing overhead		230,000
Total manufacturing costs		$414,980
Add: Work-in-process inventory, January 1		120
Subtotal		$415,100
Deduct: Work-in-process inventory, December 31		100
Cost of goods manufactured*		$415,000

*Formula used to compute cost of goods manufactured: Beg. inventory of WIP + Total manufacturing costs − End. inventory of WIP = Cost of goods manufactured.

COMET COMPUTER CORPORATION
Schedule of Cost of Goods Sold
For the Year Ended December 31, 20x2
(in thousands)

Finished-goods inventory, January 1	$ 200
Add: Cost of goods manufactured*	415,000
Cost of goods available for sale	$415,200
Finished-goods inventory, December 31	190
Cost of goods sold†	$415,010

*From the Schedule of Cost of Goods Manufactured.

†Formula used to compute cost of goods sold: Beg. inventory of FG + Cost of goods manufactured − End. inventory of FG = Cost of goods sold.

Exhibit 2–7
Manufacturing Cost Schedules

Cometcomp.com

(continued)

Exhibit 2–7
(concluded)

Cometcomp.com

COMET COMPUTER CORPORATION Income Statement For the Year Ended December 31, 20x2 (in thousands)	
Sales revenue	$700,000
Less: Cost of goods sold*	415,010
Gross margin	$284,990
Selling and administrative expenses	174,490
Income before taxes	$110,500
Income tax expense	30,000
Net Income	$ 80,500

*From the Schedule of Cost of Goods Sold.

such as the Royal Winnipeg Ballet School and the Canadian Red Cross also are engaged in service production. While less commonly observed in service firms, the same cost classifications used in manufacturing companies can be applied. For example, WestJet produces air transportation services. Direct material includes such costs as jet fuel, aircraft parts, and food and beverages. Direct labour includes the salaries of the flight crew and the wages of aircraft-maintenance personnel. Overhead costs include depreciation of baggage-handling equipment, insurance, and airport landing fees.

The process of recording and classifying costs is important in service firms and nonprofit organizations for the same reasons as in manufacturing firms. Cost analysis is used in pricing banking and insurance services, locating travel and car-rental agencies, setting enrolment targets in universities, and determining cost reimbursements in hospitals. As such organizations occupy an ever-growing role in our economy, applying managerial accounting to their activities will take on ever-greater importance.

Basic Cost Management: Different Costs for Different Purposes

An understanding of cost concepts is absolutely critical to cost management. Moreover, different perspectives on costs are important in different managerial situations. The phrase *different costs for different purposes* is often used to convey the notion that different characteristics of costs can be important to understand in a variety of managerial circumstances. In this section, we will briefly discuss the work of several cross-functional management teams at Comet Computer Corporation, each of which is focusing on a particular management challenge. Through our discussion of these cost management teams' work, we will explore some of the key cost terms and concepts used in managerial accounting and cost management.

The Cost Driver Team

Learning Objective 7

Understand the importance of identifying an organization's cost drivers.

One of the most important cost classifications involves the way a cost changes in relation to changes in the activity of the organization. **Activity** refers to a measure of the organization's output of products or services. The number of automobiles manufactured by Ford, the number of days of patient care provided by Vancouver General Hospital, and the number of insurance claims settled by Canadian Direct Insurance are all measures of activity. The activities that cause costs to be incurred are also called *cost drivers*.

One of Comet Computer Corporation's cost management teams was formed to examine the various costs incurred by Comet. The team consisted of an engineer, a production manager, a purchasing manager, and a managerial accountant. After identifying the various costs incurred by Comet, the team was charged to go on to identify the cost drivers upon which various types of costs depend.[7] A **cost driver** is a characteristic of an activity or event that causes costs to be incurred by that activity or event. In most organizations, different types of costs respond to widely differing cost drivers. For example, in a manufacturing firm, the cost of assembly labour would be driven by the quantity of products manufactured as well as the number of parts in each product. In contrast, the cost of machine-setup labour would be driven by the number of production runs. The cost of material-handling labour would be driven by material-related factors such as the quantity and cost of raw material used, the number of parts in various products, and the number of raw-material shipments received.

Cost drivers in the airline industry are complex. The capacity of an airplane and its passenger load drive costs, but so do a variety of other factors related to the airline's operations.

In identifying a cost driver, the managerial accountant should consider the extent to which a cost or pool of costs varies in accordance with the cost driver. The higher the correlation between the cost and the cost driver, the more accurate will be the resulting understanding of cost behaviour. Another important consideration is the cost of measuring the cost driver. Thus, there is a cost-benefit trade-off in the identification of cost drivers. As the number of cost drivers used in explaining an organization's cost behaviour increases, the accuracy of the resulting information will increase. However, the cost of the information will increase also. The concept of a cost driver will be an important aspect of many of the topics discussed in subsequent chapters.

Variable and Fixed Costs

After identifying costs and cost drivers for Comet Computer Corporation's operations, the cost driver team went on to examine the relationship of various costs to the activities performed. Such a relationship is referred to as *cost behaviour* and will be the focus of Chapter 6. At this juncture, though, let's look at two types of cost behaviour identified at Comet: *variable* and *fixed costs*.

Learning Objective 8

Describe the behaviour of variable and fixed costs, in total and on a per-unit basis.

Variable Costs A **variable cost** changes in total in direct proportion to a change in the level of activity (or cost driver). If activity increases by 20 percent, total variable cost increases by 20 percent also. For example, the cost of sheet metal used by Ford will increase by approximately 5 percent if automobile production increases by 5 percent. The cost of napkins and other paper products used at a Tim Hortons will increase by roughly 10 percent if the restaurant's patronage increases by 10 percent.

At Comet Computer Corporation, the cost management team identified direct material as a variable cost. One purchased component, a power bus assembly, costs $100 per computer manufactured. The cost behaviour for this direct material cost is graphed and tabulated in Exhibit 2–8.

Panel A of Exhibit 2–8 displays a graph of this variable cost. As this graph shows, *total* variable cost increases proportionately with activity. When activity doubles, from 10 to 20 units, total variable cost doubles, from $1,000 to $2,000. However, the variable cost *per unit* remains the same as activity changes. The variable cost associated with each unit of activity is $100, whether it is the first unit, the fourth, or the eighteenth. The table in panel B of Exhibit 2–8 illustrates this point.

To summarize, as activity changes, total variable cost increases or decreases proportionately with the activity change, but unit variable cost remains the same.

Exhibit 2–8

Variable Cost

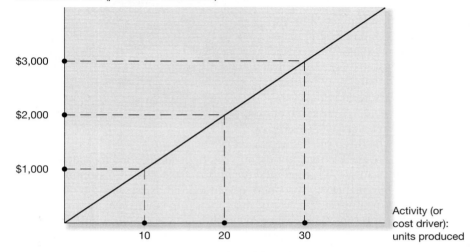

A. Graph of Total Variable Cost

Total variable cost (power bus assemblies)

B. Tabulation of Variable Cost

Activity (or cost driver)	Variable Cost per Unit	Total Variable Cost
1	$100	$ 100
4	100	400
18	100	1,800
30	100	3,000

Fixed Costs   A **fixed cost** remains unchanged in total as the level of activity (or cost driver) varies. If activity increases or decreases by 20 percent, total fixed cost remains the same. Examples of fixed costs include depreciation of plant and equipment at a Ford factory, the cost of property taxes at a Fairmont Hotel, and the salary of a pilot employed by WestJet.

Comet Computer Corporation's cost driver team identified the salary of the manager of Web sales operations as a fixed cost. Her $150,000 annual salary does not vary with the number of units produced or sold.

This fixed cost is graphed in panel A of Exhibit 2–9.

From the graph in Exhibit 2–9, it is apparent that *total* fixed cost remains unchanged as activity changes. When activity triples, from 10 to 30 units, total fixed cost remains constant at $150,000. However, the fixed cost *per unit* does change as activity changes. If the activity level is only 1 unit, then the fixed cost per unit is $150,000 per unit ($150,000 ÷ 1). If the activity level is 10 units, then the fixed cost per unit declines to $15,000 per unit ($150,000 ÷ 10). The behaviour of total fixed cost and unit fixed cost is illustrated by the table in panel B of Exhibit 2–9.

Another way of viewing the change in unit fixed cost as activity changes is in a graph, as shown in panel C of Exhibit 2–9. Unit fixed cost declines steadily as activity increases. Notice that the decrease in unit fixed cost when activity changes from 1 to 2 units is much larger than the decrease in unit fixed cost when activity changes from 10 to 11 units or from 20 to 21 units. Thus, the amount of the change in unit fixed cost declines as the activity level increases.

To summarize, as the activity level increases, total fixed cost remains constant but unit fixed cost declines. As you will see in subsequent chapters, it is vital in managerial accounting to thoroughly understand the behaviour of both total fixed costs and unit fixed costs.

A. Graph of Total Fixed Cost

Total fixed cost (Web sales manager's salary)

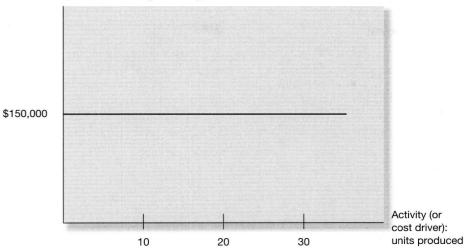

Exhibit 2–9
Fixed Cost

Cometcomp.com

B. Tabulation of Fixed Cost

Activity (or cost driver)	Fixed Cost per Unit	Total Fixed Cost
1	$150,000	$150,000
2	75,000	150,000
5	30,000	150,000
10	15,000	150,000
11	13,636*	150,000
20	7,500	150,000
21	7,143*	150,000
30	5,000	150,000

*Rounded.

C. Graph of Unit Fixed Cost

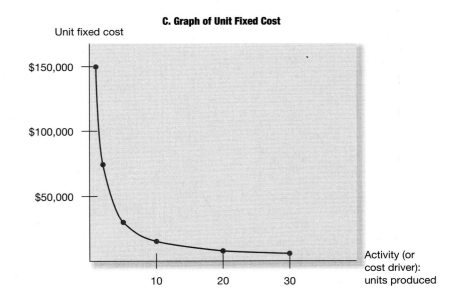

The Cost Management and Control Team

An important objective of managerial accounting is to assist managers in managing and controlling costs. Sometimes cost management is facilitated by tracing costs to the department or work centre in which the cost was incurred. Such tracing of costs to departments is known as *responsibility accounting*.

Comet Computer Corporation formed a cost management and control team to refine the company's responsibility accounting system. The team consisted of an engineer, the production scheduling manager, the assistant manager of quality control, the manager of human resources, and a managerial accountant. The ultimate objective of the team was to develop a responsibility accounting system that would assist management in managing and controlling costs as well as reducing costs whenever

Management **A**ccounting **P**ractice

Southwest, Continental, American, United, Delta, JetBlue, Frontier, and Air-Tran

AIRLINE INDUSTRY: COST STRUCTURE, COST DRIVERS, AND A SHIFTING BUSINESS MODEL

"American business has changed its flying habits, possibly forever. The bottom line: business travel is being 'Wal-Marted' by low-cost operators. Just as Wal-Mart Stores did in retailing, the discounters of the air—Southwest Airlines and others such as JetBlue Airways—are proving that even some of the most finicky corporate fliers can't resist a bargain.

"Low-cost carriers now account for nearly 20 percent of U.S. domestic air capacity. A second force behind the fundamental shift in airline economics is the Internet, which has given travelers, travel agents, and corporate travel managers powerful tools to find and take advantage of deeply discounted fares.

"The shift is dire news for the big airlines, the full-service retailers of flight. The carriers, which are bleeding red ink, have massive fixed costs that aren't easy to scale back. Most of them have built expensive hub-and-spoke route systems and signed costly labor contracts that they had hoped to finance by charging high-margin business fares. But now, there is 'a low-fare network in this country that did not exist previously.' A senior vice president at Continental Airlines told a recent aviation conference, 'We've finally reached the point, perhaps, where [its] penetration may be fatal' to the major carriers' high-cost business models.

"Some carriers, including American Airlines and United Airlines, are now rethinking their entire operations, even considering whether they should cut back their high-cost route systems." At American, "a special task force is hunting for immediate money-saving ideas and another is studying longer-range restructuring." It won't be easy, however, for major airlines to cut their costs. "Consider the current advantages low-fare carriers have over full-service rivals. They tend to have younger fleets, which require less maintenance, and younger labor forces that aren't tied to complicated, inefficient labor contracts. That's why labor costs are equivalent to just 25 percent of revenue at discounters Air-Tran Airways, Frontier Airlines, and Jet Blue and 30 percent at Southwest. At United and Delta, labor costs exceed 40 percent of revenue. Moreover, low-fare carriers typically stick to one airplane model, thus minimizing maintenance, operating, and training costs." Many of the biggest carriers still fly six or seven types of aircraft.[8]

The bottom line is that the airline industry is undergoing a sea change in its business model, and it is driven by the very different cost structures that characterize the largest carriers as against their smaller discount competitors. The discounters are more flexible and have proportionately lower fixed costs. An understanding of the cost drivers in the industry will be crucial to the survival of the big airlines.

possible. We will study cost management systems and cost reduction in considerable detail in Chapter 5 and responsibility accounting is covered in Chapter 12. For now, let's focus on a couple of cost concepts that are useful in these areas of managerial accounting.

Direct and Indirect Costs   An entity, such as a particular product, service, or department, to which a cost is assigned is called a **cost object**. A cost that can be traced to a particular cost object is called a **direct cost** of that cost object.

> Learning Objective **9**
>
> Distinguish among direct, indirect, controllable, and uncontrollable costs.

For example, the salary of an auto mechanic is a direct cost of the automotive service department in a Canadian Tire store. The cost of paint used in the painting department of a Ford plant is a direct cost of the painting department.

A cost that is not directly traceable to a particular cost object is called an **indirect cost** of that cost object. For example, the costs of national advertising for Fairmont Hotels & Resorts are indirect costs of each of the hotel and resort properties. The salary of a Ford plant manager is an indirect cost of each of the plant's production departments. The plant manager's duties are important to the smooth functioning of each of the plant's departments, but there is no way to trace a portion of the plant manager's salary cost to each department.

> "The flight crew's salaries on a flight, say from Atlanta to St. Louis, would be considered a direct cost of that flight. The salaries of the flight scheduling folks, on the other hand, would be an indirect cost of any given flight." (2g)
>
> **Delta Air Lines**

Whether a cost is a direct cost or an indirect cost of a department often depends on which department is under consideration. A cost can be a direct cost of one department or subunit in the organization but an indirect cost of other departments. While the salary of a Ford Company plant manager is an *indirect* cost of the plant's departments, the manager's salary is a *direct* cost of the plant.

Comet Computer Corporation's cost management and control team determined that many of the company's costs were traceable to various departments or to specific activities of those departments. In the purchasing department, for example, costs were traced not just to the department, but also to the specific activities of identifying vendors, qualifying vendors, securing design specifications from the engineering design department, negotiating prices, placing orders, expediting orders, receiving materials and components, inspecting materials, and releasing materials to the material-handling operation.

An important objective of a cost management system is to trace as many costs as possible directly to the activities that cause them to be incurred. Sometimes called *activity accounting*, this process is vital to management's objective of eliminating *non-value-added costs*. These are costs of activities that can be eliminated without deterioration of product quality, performance, or perceived value. (We will study the elimination of non-value-added costs in greater detail in Chapter 5.)

Controllable and Uncontrollable Costs   Another cost classification that can be helpful in cost control involves the controllability of a cost item by a particular manager. If a manager can control or heavily influence the level of a cost, then that cost is classified as a **controllable cost** of that manager. Costs that a manager cannot influence significantly are classified as **uncontrollable costs** of that manager. Many costs are not completely under the control of any individual. In classifying costs as controllable or uncontrollable, managerial accountants generally focus on a manager's ability to influence costs. The question is not "Who controls the cost?" but "Who is in the best position to influence the level of a cost item?" Exhibit 2–10 lists several cost items along with their typical classification as controllable or uncontrollable.

Comet Computer's cost management and control team was able to designate many of Comet's costs as controllable or uncontrollable by various managers. Take the cost of raw materials and components: the team determined that the *quantity* of materials used was largely controllable by the production supervisor, but the *price* of the materials was influenced more by the purchasing manager.

Exhibit 2–10
Controllable and
Uncontrollable Costs

Cost Item	Manager	Classification
Cost of raw material used to produce computer chips in an Intel factory	Supervisor of the production department for computer chips	Controllable (The production supervisor can exercise some control over the quantity of material used by ensuring that waste and defective units are minimized.)
Cost of food used in a Subway restaurant	Restaurant manager	Controllable (The restaurant manager exercises some control over the quantity of food used by scheduling production to ensure that excess food is not produced and wasted.)
Cost of national advertising for the Avis car rental company	Manager of the Avis rental agency at the Vancouver airport	Uncontrollable
Cost of national accounting and data processing operations for Future Shop	Manager of a Future Shop store in Coquitlam, B.C.	Uncontrollable

The Outsourcing Action Team

Another of Comet Computer Corporation's interdisciplinary management teams was formed to take a close look at which of the raw materials and components used in Comet's products should be manufactured by Comet and which ones should be outsourced (purchased from outside vendors).[9] This team consisted of the assistant manager of purchasing, a product design engineer, a product group sales manager, and a managerial accountant. As the team pursued its assignment, its members soon found that they were once again dealing with several different cost concepts.

In addition to accounting cost classifications, such as product costs and period costs, the team's members also found themselves using economic concepts in classifying costs. Such concepts are often useful in helping managerial accountants decide what cost information is relevant to the decisions faced by the organization's managers. Several of the most important economic cost concepts are discussed next.

Learning Objective 10

Define and give examples of an opportunity cost, an out-of-pocket cost, a sunk cost, a differential cost, a marginal cost, and an average cost.

Opportunity Costs   An **opportunity cost** is defined as the benefit sacrificed when the choice of one action precludes taking an alternative action. If beef and fish are the available choices for dinner, the opportunity cost of eating beef is the forgone pleasure associated with eating fish.

Opportunity costs arise in many business decisions. For example, suppose a sport equipment manufacturer receives a special order for basketballs from the recreation department of a large city. If the firm accepts the order, it will not have enough productive capacity (labour and machine time) to produce its usual output of basketballs for sale to a large chain of sporting-goods stores. The opportunity cost of accepting the order is the forgone benefit from the basketball production that cannot be achieved. This forgone benefit is measured by the potential revenue from the basketball sales minus the cost of manufacturing the basketballs.

Opportunity costs also arise in personal decisions. The opportunity cost of a student's college education includes the salary that is forgone as a result of not taking a full-time job during the student's years in college.

From an economic perspective, a dollar of opportunity cost associated with an action should be treated as equivalent to a dollar of out-of-pocket cost. **Out-of-pocket costs** are those that require the payment of cash or other assets as a result of their incurrence. The out-of-pocket costs associated with the basketball order consist of the manufacturing costs required to produce the basketballs. In making the decision to accept or reject the order, the firm's management should consider *both* the out-of-pocket cost and the opportunity cost of the order.

Studies by behavioural scientists and economists have shown that many people have a tendency to ignore or downplay the importance of opportunity costs. For example, in one study people were asked if they would pay $500 for two tickets to the Super Bowl.[10] Most people responded that they would not. However, many of the same people said that they would not sell the Super Bowl tickets for $500 if they were given the tickets free of charge. These people refused to incur the $500 *out-of-pocket cost* of buying the Super Bowl tickets. However, they were willing to incur the $500 *opportunity cost* of going to the game rather than sell the tickets. In each case, a couple that attends the game ends up $500 poorer than a couple that does not attend the game.

Behaviour such as that illustrated in the Super Bowl example is economically inconsistent. Ignoring or downplaying the importance of opportunity costs can result in inconsistent and faulty business decisions.

Comet Computer's outsourcing action team found that the opportunity cost of using constrained production resources (such as space, machine time, and employee time) to produce a computer component in-house was an important factor to consider in deciding whether to outsource the component.[11]

Sunk Costs   **Sunk costs** are costs that have been incurred in the past. Consequently, they do not affect future costs and cannot be changed by any current or future action. Examples of such costs include the acquisition cost of equipment previously purchased and the manufacturing cost of inventory on hand. Regardless of the current usefulness of the equipment or the inventory, the costs of acquiring them cannot be changed by any prospective action. Hence, these costs are irrelevant to all future decisions.

Suppose, for example, that a university's parking department purchased a desktop computer to assist in the vehicle registration process. A year has passed, the computer's warranty has expired, and the computer is not working well. An investigation reveals that this brand of computer is very sensitive to humidity and temperature changes. The parking department is located in an old building with poor heating and no air conditioning. As a result, the computer works only intermittently, repair bills have been high, and the office staff is fed up. The office manager requests that the department director junk the computer and instruct the staff to return to the old manual registration system. The director responds by insisting, "We can't afford to junk the computer! We paid $3,400 for it."

This illustration is a typical example of the inappropriate attention paid to sunk costs. The $3,400 paid for the computer is sunk. No future decision about the computer or the office's procedures can affect that cost. Future decisions should be based on future costs, such as the computer repair bills or the costs of upgrading the building's heating and air-conditioning systems.

Although it is incorrect, from an economic perspective, to allow sunk costs to affect future decisions, people often do so. It is human nature to attempt to justify past decisions. When there is a perceived need to demonstrate competence, either to themselves or to others, managers may seek to justify their decisions. The response of the parking department director that "We can't afford to junk the computer!" may represent the director's need to justify the past decision to purchase the computer. It is important for managerial accountants to be aware of such behavioural tendencies. Such an awareness enables the accountant to prepare the most relevant data for managers' decisions and, sometimes, to assist the managers in using the information.

Comet Computer's outsourcing action team encountered a sunk cost as it considered outsourcing production of a component called a monitor interface unit (MIU). The team discovered that the robot used to insert components into the MIU was difficult to maintain and expensive to operate. Nevertheless, the department supervisor was inclined to keep the robot and continue in-house production of the MIU, because, as he put it, "Comet paid an arm and a leg for this robot." The team was able to demonstrate that the robot's acquisition cost was a sunk cost and was irrelevant to the outsourcing decision. We will explore sunk costs in more detail in Chapter 13.

Differential Costs   A **differential cost** is the amount by which the cost differs under two alternative actions. Suppose, for example, that a county government is considering two competing sites for a new landfill. If the northern site is chosen, the annual cost of transporting refuse to the site is projected at $85,000. If the southern site is selected, annual transportation charges are expected to be $70,000. The annual differential cost of transporting refuse is calculated as follows:

Annual cost of transporting refuse to northern site	$85,000
Annual cost of transporting refuse to southern site	70,000
Annual differential cost	$15,000

The increase in cost from one alternative to another is called an **incremental cost**. In the landfill example, the annual incremental cost of refuse transportation is $15,000 if the site is moved from the southern location to the northern location. Differential or incremental costs are found in a variety of economic decisions. The additional cost incurred by a travel agency in locating a new office in the suburbs is the incremental cost of the new business location. The difference in the total cost incurred by the travel agency with or without the suburban location is the differential cost of the decision whether to establish the new office. Decisions about establishing new airline routes, adding additional shifts in a manufacturing firm, or increasing the nursing staff in a hospital all involve differential costs.

At Comet Computer, the outsourcing action team estimated that the differential cost between outsourcing the production of the MIU (monitor interface unit) and producing it in-house would be $200,000 annually in favour of outsourcing, on the basis of current projections of annual production.

Marginal Costs and Average Costs   A special case of the differential-cost concept is the **marginal cost**, which is the extra cost incurred when one additional unit is produced. The additional cost incurred by Comet Computer when one additional high-performance laptop computer is made is the marginal cost of manufacturing the computer. The table in Exhibit 2–11 shows how marginal cost can change across different ranges of production quantities.

Marginal costs typically differ across different ranges of production quantities because the efficiency of the production process changes. At Comet Computer, the marginal cost of producing a laptop computer declines as output increases. It is much more efficient for the company to manufacture 101 computers than to make only one.

It is important to distinguish between *marginal costs* and *average costs*. In the Comet Computer example, the marginal cost of the second computer is $1,900.

Exhibit 2–11
Marginal Cost of Producing Laptop Computers at Comet Computer Corporation

Cømet

Number of Laptop Computers Produced	Total Cost of Producing Laptops	Marginal Cost of Producing a Laptop
1	$ 2,000	Difference is $1,900 ⟶ Marginal cost of 2nd laptop is $1,900.
2	3,900	
10	18,000	Difference is $1,690 ⟶ Marginal cost of 11th laptop is $1,690.
11	19,690	
100	150,000	Difference is $995 ⟶ Marginal cost of 101st laptop is $995.
101	150,995	

However, the average cost per unit when two laptops are manufactured is $3,900 divided by 2, or $1,950. Similarly, the marginal cost of the eleventh laptop is $1,690, but the average cost per unit when 11 laptops are produced is $1,790 (calculated by dividing $19,690 by 11). What is the marginal cost of the 101st laptop computer? The average cost per unit when 101 laptops are manufactured?[12]

To summarize, the marginal cost of production is the extra cost incurred when one more unit is produced. The **average cost per unit** is the total cost, for whatever quantity is manufactured, divided by the number of units manufactured. Marginal costs and average costs arise in a variety of economic situations. A University of Toronto administrator might be interested in the marginal cost of educating one additional student, and a Ford executive might want to know the marginal cost of producing one more Ford truck. A Greyhound route manager might be interested in the average cost per mile on the Vancouver to Calgary route.

Costs and Benefits of Information

Many different cost concepts have been explored in this chapter. An important task of the managerial accountant is to determine which of these cost concepts is most appropriate in each situation. Then the accountant strives to *communicate* the cost information to the user in the most effective manner possible. The accountant attempts to structure the organization's accounting information system to record data that will be useful for a variety of purposes. The benefits of measuring and classifying costs in a particular way are realized through the improvements in planning, control, and decision making that the information facilitates.

Another important task of the managerial accountant is to weigh the benefits of providing information against the costs of generating, communicating, and using that information. Some accountants, eager to show that they have not overlooked anything, tend to provide too much information. But when managers receive more data than they can utilize effectively, *information overload* occurs. Struggling to process large amounts of information, managers may be unable to recognize the most important facts. In deciding how much and what type of information to provide, managerial accountants should consider these human limitations.

> "If you can't communicate information to the individual, then the information is . . . lost. So, your communication skills are very important." (2h)
> **Abbott Labs**

Costs in the Service Industry

MĪDAS

The cost terms and concepts that we have studied in this chapter are just as relevant in the service industry as in a manufacturing firm like Comet Computer Corporation. Here we will explore those cost issues in the context of a well-known automotive service company.

Midas, Inc. is one of the world's largest providers of automotive service, including exhaust system, brakes, steering, suspension, and routine maintenance services. There are more than 1,800 franchised and company-owned Midas locations in Canada and the United States, and over 700 licensed and franchised locations in 17 other countries on four continents. In recent years, Midas has undergone some significant changes. First, the company intentionally transitioned from an under-car repair specialist to a full-service automotive repair and maintenance provider. Second, Midas has sold its exhaust system manufacturing business to concentrate fully on automotive service provision. To this end, Midas has established relationships with automobile parts vendors who distribute their products directly to Midas auto service shops.

A typical Midas automotive maintenance and repair shop has approximately 370 square

Midas is one of the world's largest providers of automotive maintenance service.

metres and six service bays. A company-owned shop usually is staffed with a manager, an assistant manager, and three to four automotive service technicians. Midas supports the franchise dealer network with 30 district managers and six regional managers. Each district manager covers approximately 58 franchised Midas shops and assists franchisees with operations, retail initiatives, training, and monitoring of the franchise agreement.[13]

Now let's think about a typical Midas-owned auto service shop to explore the various cost issues we have studied in a service-industry environment.

Product and Period Costs   Midas purchases auto parts and supplies, such as exhaust pipes, brake pads, oil filters, and engine oil, from vendors. These costs are stored in inventory as *product costs* (or *inventoriable costs*) until the time period when they are consumed in the repair process. At that time, these *product costs* become part of *cost of goods sold*, an *expense*. All of Midas' other costs are *period costs*, and they are expensed as *operating expenses* during the period they are incurred. Examples of these period costs include employee salaries and wages, utilities, and depreciation on equipment and facilities.

Variable and Fixed Costs   The costs incurred in the Midas service shop that vary directly with activity are *variable costs*. For example, the cost of lubricant, engine oil, and oil filters is a variable cost, because it varies in proportion to the number of lube-oil-filter (LOF) jobs the shop provides. Thus, a likely *cost driver* for this cost would be the number of LOF jobs performed. In contrast, any costs that do not tend to vary with service activity are *fixed costs*. Examples include the Midas shop's managerial salaries, depreciation on equipment and facilities, insurance, and property taxes.

Direct and Indirect Costs   Consider a typical service and repair job. The customer has requested a routine lube-oil-filter job and an exhaust system repair, which requires a new muffler. The *direct costs* of this service and repair job (the *cost object*) include the parts and supplies used (lubricant, engine oil, oil filter, and a new muffler) and the wages of the automotive service technician for the time spent on this job. The many *indirect costs* of this service job include the shop manager's salary, the depreciation on the building, and national media advertising purchased nationwide by Midas, Inc.

Now consider a different cost object—this Midas shop. For this cost object, the shop manager's salary is a direct cost of the Midas shop. However, the Midas CEO's salary is an indirect cost of this particular shop.

Controllable and Uncontrollable Costs   Costs that are *controllable* by the manager of this Midas auto shop include local advertising, assuming the shop manager is responsible for such local ad buys. A cost that is partially controllable by the manager might include heating costs. Although the manager has little control over electricity or heating oil prices, the manager can ensure that the shop's heating system is properly maintained and the windows and doors have the proper weather stripping. Many of the shop's costs are largely *uncontrollable* by the shop manager. The depreciation, insurance, and property taxes on the building, for example, are the result of decisions made higher up in the Midas organization.

Opportunity, Out-of-Pocket, and Sunk Costs   These cost types all are represented in the Midas auto service business. Suppose the Midas shop manager decides to shut down one of the service bays on a particular day to inspect and maintain the lift and other equipment. Any customer business that is lost that day due to a shortage of service bays would be an *opportunity cost* of the shutdown decision. (Note that such an opportunity cost does not necessarily mean the shutdown decision was a poor one. The opportunity cost of any lost business could well be exceeded by the additional operating costs that could be incurred if the service bay was not properly maintained.) The wages paid to service technicians and utility costs are examples of *out-of-pocket costs*. The money spent last year to replace an auto lift is an example of a *sunk cost*.

Differential, Marginal, and Average Costs Suppose the Midas shop owns a small van to make short runs to pick up auto parts needed on short notice. The van needs to be replaced, and two vehicles are under consideration. The difference in the cost of these two alternative vehicles is a *differential cost* of the vehicle replacement decision. The cost of performing one additional LOF job in a given time period is the *marginal cost* of that type of service. The total cost of all LOF jobs in a time period, divided by the number of jobs, is the average cost of an LOF job.

To summarize, although manufacturers, like Bombardier, Magna International, or Research In Motion, and service firms, like WestJet Airlines, Fairmont Hotels & Resorts, or Midas, are in very different businesses, they all must understand their costs in order to be successful in a competitive environment.

Focus on Ethics

WAS WORLDCOM'S CONTROLLER JUST FOLLOWING ORDERS?

Through a series of mergers and acquisitions, WorldCom, Inc. grew to become North America's second-largest long-distance telecommunications company. WorldCom's core communication services included network data transmission over public and private networks. Trouble arose for WorldCom because of the immense overcapacity in the telecommunications industry due to overly optimistic growth projections during the Internet boom. The combination of overcapacity, decreased demand, and high fixed costs still poses a serious problem for many of the major players in the industry.

In June 2002, the company disclosed that it had overstated earnings for 2001 and the first quarter of 2002 to the tune of $3.8 billion. The overstatement arose because the company incorrectly classified period expenses as capital expenditures. This manoeuvre had two major effects on the company's financial statements: the company's assets were artificially inflated and the capitalization allowed the company to spread the recognition of its expenses into the future, which increased net income in the current period. The expenses in question related to line costs—the fees that WorldCom pays outside providers for access to their communications networks. In addition, the company announced in July 2002 that it had also manipulated reserve accounts, which affected another $3.8 billion in earnings in 1999 and 2000.

The problems at WorldCom were discovered during an internal audit and brought to the attention of the company's new auditors, KPMG. Arthur Andersen served as WorldCom's auditors during the period covered by the alleged accounting scandal. The auditing company maintained that the details of the fraud were kept from them by senior management. WorldCom's controller and chief financial officer (CFO), who was a former KPMG employee, were fired after the alleged accounting frauds were revealed. WorldCom's CEO maintained that he knew nothing of the accounting decisions made by the CFO, but many observers question how almost $8 billion in expenses could slip by senior management.[14]

According to an Associated Press article that ran on September 27, 2002, "the former controller of WorldCom, Inc. pleaded guilty to securities fraud charges, saying he was instructed by 'senior management' to falsify records. His plea was the first admission of guilt to fall from the largest corporate accounting scandal in U.S. history."[15] Subsequently, WorldCom's CFO pleaded guilty to his part in the accounting scandal.[16] In March of 2005, the company's CEO was convicted by a jury of nine criminal counts in the accounting fraud, including conspiracy and securities fraud.[17]

The CFO and controller were the top two financial and managerial accountants in the WorldCom organization. They were ultimately responsible for all of the company's financial and managerial accounting reports. (Note that this case also involves the alleged intentional misclassification of period costs.)

What ethical issues are involved here? What do you make of the controller's assertion that he was just following orders given by senior management? What steps should WorldCom's controller have taken? (Review the Code of Professional Ethics from the Ontario Society of CMAs on page 20.)

Chapter Summary

The term *cost* is familiar to everyone. We all discuss the cost of a sweater, a movie ticket, or a semester's tuition. Yet, as we have seen in this chapter, the word cost can have a variety of meanings in different situations. Managerial accountants often find it useful to classify costs in different ways for different purposes. An understanding of cost terms, concepts, and classifications is fundamental in any study of managerial accounting.

Several cost management terms are defined and illustrated in the chapter. A cost driver is any activity or event that causes costs to be incurred. Fixed and variable costs are defined by the behaviour of total cost as the organization's activity level changes. Direct and indirect costs refer to the ability of the accountant to trace costs to various departments in the organization. The terms *controllable* and *uncontrollable* are used to describe the extent to which a manager can influence a cost. Costs are classified into such functional categories as manufacturing costs, selling costs, and administrative costs. Manufacturing costs are further subdivided into direct-material, direct-labour, and manufacturing-overhead costs. The terms product cost and period cost refer to the timing with which costs become expenses.

There are five basic types of manufacturing operations: job shop, batch, assembly line, mass customization, and continuous flow. In a mass-customization production environment, many standardized components are used to manufacture customized products to customer order. The direct-sales method often is used, with a large portion of sales orders often taken over the Internet. Raw material and parts inventories, work-in-process inventories, and finished-goods inventories are very low. Cost driver analysis, cost management, and outsourcing decisions are very important in this production environment.

Economic concepts are also important in describing costs. An opportunity cost is the benefit forgone because the choice of one action precludes another action. Sunk costs are costs incurred in the past that cannot be altered by a current or future decision. The term *differential cost* or *incremental cost* refers to the difference in the costs incurred under two alternative actions. Marginal cost is defined as the cost of producing one additional unit. Finally, the average cost per unit is the total cost for whatever quantity is produced, divided by the number of units produced.

These cost terms are an integral part of the specialized language of business, and they are every bit as relevant in service-industry firms as in manufacturers. The manager of any organization must understand costs in order to be successful in a competitive environment.

Review Problems on Cost Classifications

Problem 1

Several costs incurred by Myrtle Beach Golf Equipment, Inc. are listed below. For each cost, indicate which of the following classifications best describe the cost. More than one classification may apply to the same cost item. For example, a cost may be both a variable cost and a product cost.

Cost Classifications

a.   Variable

b.   Fixed

c.   Period

d.   Product

e.   Administrative

f.   Selling

g.   Manufacturing

h.   Research and development

i.   Direct material

j.   Direct labour

k.   Manufacturing overhead

Cost Items

1.   Metal used in golf clubs

2.   Salary of the plant manager

3.   Cost of natural gas used to heat factory

4.   Commissions paid to sales personnel

5. Wages paid to employees who assemble golf bags

6. Salary of an engineer who is working on a prototype of a new solar-powered golf cart

7. Depreciation on the computer used by the company president's secretary

Problem 2

Listed below are several costs incurred in the loan department of Suwanee Bank and Trust Company. For each cost, indicate which of the following classifications best describe the cost. More than one classification may apply to the same cost item.

Cost Classifications

a. Controllable by the loan department manager

b. Uncontrollable by the loan department manager

c. Direct cost of the loan department

d. Indirect cost of the loan department

e. Differential cost

f. Marginal cost

g. Opportunity cost

h. Sunk cost

i. Out-of-pocket cost

Cost Items

1. Salary of the loan department manager

2. Cost of office supplies used in the loan department

3. Cost of the department's personal computers purchased by the loan department manager last year

4. Cost of general advertising by the bank, which is allocated to the loan department

5. Revenue that the loan department would have generated for the bank if a branch loan office had been located downtown instead of in the suburb

6. Difference in the cost incurred by the bank when one additional loan application is processed

Solutions to Review Problems
Problem 1

1. a, d, g, i	**2.** b, d, g, k	**3.** a, d, g, k	**4.** a, c, f	**5.** a, d, g, j
6. b, c, h	**7.** b, c, e			

Problem 2

1. b, c, i	**2.** a, c, i	**3.** a, c, h	**4.** b, d, i	**5.** g	**6.** e, f

Key Terms

For each term's definition refer to the indicated page, or turn to the glossary at the end of the text.

activity, 38	direct cost, 43	inventoriable cost, 28	raw material, 31
average cost per unit, 47	direct-labour cost, 34	manufacturing overhead, 34	schedule of cost of goods manufactured, 36
controllable cost, 43	direct material, 34	marginal cost, 46	
conversion costs, 36	expense, 27	mass customization, 32	schedule of cost of goods sold, 36
cost, 27	finished goods, 31	operating expenses, 29	
cost driver, 39	fixed costs, 40	opportunity cost, 44	service departments (*or* support departments), 35
cost object, 43	idle time, 35	out-of-pocket costs, 44	
cost of goods manufactured, 36	incremental cost, 46	overtime premium, 35	sunk costs, 45
	indirect cost, 43	period costs, 28	uncontrollable cost, 43
cost of goods sold, 27	indirect labour, 35	prime costs, 36	variable cost, 39
differential cost, 46	indirect material, 34	product cost, 27	work in process, 31

Review Questions

2–1. Distinguish between product costs and period costs.

2–2. Why are product costs also called inventoriable costs?

2–3. What is the most important difference between a manufacturing firm and a service industry firm, with regard to the classification of costs as product costs or period costs?

2–4. List, describe, and give an example of each of the five different types of production processes.

2–5. "The words *mass* and *customization* in the term *mass customization* seem contradictory." Do you agree or disagree? Explain.

2–6. Why is the cost of idle time treated as manufacturing overhead?

2–7. Explain why an overtime premium is included in manufacturing overhead.

2–8. What is meant by the phrase "different costs for different purposes"?

2–9. Give examples to illustrate how a city could use cost information in planning, controlling costs, and making decisions.

2–10. Distinguish between fixed costs and variable costs.

2–11. How does the fixed cost per unit change as the level of activity (or cost driver) increases? Why?

2–12. How does the variable cost per unit change as the level of activity (or cost driver) increases? Why?

2–13. Distinguish between volume-based and operations-based cost drivers in the airline industry.

2–14. Would each of the following characteristics be a volume-based or an operations-based cost driver in a college: (*a*) number of students, (*b*) number of disciplines offered for study, and (*c*) urban versus rural location?

2–15. List three direct costs of the food and beverage department in a hotel. List three indirect costs of the department.

2–16. List three costs that are likely to be controllable by a city's airport manager. List three costs that are likely to be uncontrollable by the manager.

2–17. Which of the following costs are likely to be controllable by the chief of nursing in a hospital?

   a. Cost of medication administered

   b. Cost of overtime paid to nurses due to scheduling errors

   c. Cost of depreciation of hospital beds

2–18. Distinguish between out-of-pocket costs and opportunity costs.

2–19. Define the terms *sunk cost* and *differential cost*.

2–20. Distinguish between marginal and average costs.

2–21. Think about the process of registering for classes at your college or university. What additional information would you like to have before you register? How would it help you? What sort of information might create information overload for you?

2–22. Two years ago, the manager of a large department store purchased new barcode scanners costing $39,000. A salesperson recently tried to sell the manager a new computer-integrated checkout system for the store. The new system would save the store a substantial amount of money each year. The recently purchased scanners could be sold in the second-hand market for $19,000. The store manager refused to listen to the salesperson, saying, "I just bought those scanners. I can't get rid of them until I get my money's worth out of them."

     What type of cost is the cost of purchasing the old bar code scanners? What common behavioural tendency is the manager exhibiting?

2–23. Indicate whether each of the following costs is a direct cost or an indirect cost of the restaurant in a hotel.

   a. Cost of food served

   b. Chef's salary and fringe benefits

   c. Part of the cost of maintaining the grounds around the hotel, which is allocated to the restaurant

   d. Part of the cost of advertising the hotel, which is allocated to the restaurant

Exercises

■ **Exercise 2–24**
Cost of Goods Manufactured and Sold; Missing Data
(LO 6)

For each case below, find the missing amount.

	Case I	Case II	Case III
Beginning inventory of finished goods	?	$ 18,000	$ 3,500
Cost of goods manufactured during period	$104,750	$142,500	?
Ending inventory of finished goods	24,500	12,000	10,500
Cost of goods sold	101,250	?	152,000

■ **Exercise 2–25**
Idle Time
(LO 5)

A foundry employee worked a normal 40-hour shift, but four hours were idle due to a small fire in the plant. The employee earns $16 per hour.

Required:

1. Calculate the employee's total compensation for the week.
2. How much of this compensation is a direct-labour cost? How much is overhead?

A loom operator in a textiles factory earns $17 per hour. The employee earns $22 for overtime hours. The operator worked 43 hours during the first week of May, instead of the usual 40 hours.

Required:

1. Compute the loom operator's compensation for the week.
2. Calculate the employee's total overtime premium for the week.
3. How much of the employee's total compensation for the week is direct-labour cost? How much is overhead?

■ **Exercise 2–26**
Overtime Cost
(LO 5)

Find Dell Inc.'s Web site on the Internet, www.dell.com.

Required:　Read on the company's Web site about how Dell operates and serves its customers. Then briefly explain whether you believe mass customization to be the best type of manufacturing process for Dell.

■ **Exercise 2–27**
Mass Customization; Use of Internet
(LO 4)

Consider the following costs that were incurred during the current year:

1. Advertising costs of Coca-Cola
2. Straight-line depreciation on factory machinery of Bombardier Corporation
3. Wages of assembly-line personnel of Whirlpool Canada
4. Delivery costs on customer shipments of Chapman's ice cream
5. Newsprint consumed in printing *The Globe and Mail*
6. Plant insurance costs of Research In Motion
7. Glass costs incurred in light-bulb manufacturing of Sylvania
8. Tire costs incurred by Ford Motor Company
9. Sales commissions paid to the sales force of Dell Inc.
10. Wood glue consumed in the manufacture of Palliser furniture
11. Hourly wages of refinery security guards employed by Petro-Canada
12. The salary of a financial vice-president of Sony Canada

■ **Exercise 2–28**
Cost Classifications
(LO 2, 8, 9)

Required:　Evaluate each of the preceding and determine whether the cost is (*a*) a product cost or a period cost, (*b*) variable or fixed in terms of behaviour, and (*c*) for the product costs only, whether the cost is properly classified as direct material, direct labour, or manufacturing overhead. Item 8 is done as an example:

Tire costs: Product cost, variable, direct material

Alhambra Aluminum Company, a manufacturer of recyclable soda cans, had the following inventory balances at the beginning and end of 20x1.

■ **Exercise 2–29**
Schedules of Cost of Goods Manufactured and Sold; Income Statement
(LO 6)

Inventory Classification	January 1, 20x1	December 31, 20x1
Raw material	$ 55,000	$ 75,000
Work in process	110,000	125,000
Finished goods	160,000	155,000

During 20x1, the company purchased $240,000 of raw material and spent $420,000 on direct labour. Manufacturing overhead costs were as follows:

Indirect material	$ 12,000
Indirect labour	22,000
Depreciation on plant and equipment	110,000
Utilities	23,000
Other	35,000

Sales revenue was $1,210,000 for the year. Selling and administrative expenses for the year amounted to $105,000. The firm's tax rate is 35 percent.

Required:

1. Prepare a schedule of cost of goods manufactured.
2. Prepare a schedule of cost of goods sold.
3. Prepare an income statement.
4. **Build a spreadsheet:** Construct an Excel spreadsheet to solve all of the preceding requirements. Show how both cost schedules and the income statement will change if the following data change: direct labour is $410,000 and utilities cost $24,000.

■ **Exercise 2–30**
Fixed and Variable Costs; Automobile Service; Missing Data
(LO 1, 8)

Mighty Muffler, Inc. operates an automobile service facility that specializes in replacing mufflers on compact cars. The following table shows the costs incurred during a month when 600 mufflers were replaced.

	Muffler Replacements		
	600	700	800
Total costs:			
Fixed costs	a	$56,000	b
Variable costs	c	28,000	d
Total costs	e	$84,000	f
Cost per muffler replacement:			
Fixed cost	g	h	i
Variable cost	j	k	l
Total cost per muffler replacement	m	n	o

Required: Fill in the missing amounts, labelled (a) through (o), in the table.

■ **Exercise 2–31**
Fixed, Variable, Marginal, and Average Costs; Hotel
(LO 1, 8, 10)

A hotel pays the phone company $200 per month plus $.15 for each call made. During January, 7,000 calls were made. In February, 8,000 calls were made.

Required:

1. Calculate the hotel's phone bills for January and February.
2. Calculate the cost per phone call in January and in February.
3. Separate the January phone bill into its fixed and variable components.
4. What is the marginal cost of one additional phone call in January?
5. What was the average cost of a phone call in January?

■ **Exercise 2–32**
Economic Characteristics of Costs
(LO 1, 10)

Thomas Cleverly purchased a vacant lot outside of London for £17,200, because he heard that a shopping mall was going to be built on the other side of the road. He figured that he could make a bundle by putting in a fast-food outlet on the site. As it turned out, the rumour was false. A sanitary landfill was located on the other side of the road, and the land was worthless. (£ denotes the British monetary unit, pounds sterling. Although the Euro is generally used in European markets, day-to-day business in the United Kingdom is still conducted in pounds sterling.)

Required: What type of cost is the £17,200 that Martin paid for the vacant lot?

■ **Exercise 2–33**
Differential Cost
(LO 1, 10)

Global Communications, Inc. manufactures communications satellites used in TV signal transmission. The firm currently purchases one component for its satellites from a European firm. A Global Communications engineering team has found a way to use the company's own component, part number A200, instead of the European component. However, the Global Communications component must be modified at a cost of $650 per part. The European component costs $9,100 per part. Global Communications' part number A200 costs $4,900 before it is modified. Global Communications currently uses 15 of the European components per year.

Required: Calculate the annual differential cost between Global Communications' two production alternatives.

The British Columbia Ministry of Education owns a computer system, which its employees use for word processing and keeping track of education statistics. The premier's office recently began using this computer also. As a result of the increased usage, the demands on the computer soon exceeded its capacity. The director of Management Services for the Ministry of Education was soon forced to lease several personal computers to meet the computing needs of her employees. The annual cost of leasing the equipment is $12,500.

■ **Exercise 2–34**
Computing Costs;
Government Agency
(LO 1, 9, 10)

Required:

1. Is this $12,500 an opportunity cost? Why or why not?
2. Should this cost be associated with the premier's office or the Ministry of Education? Why?

Suppose you paid $75 for a ticket to see your city's hockey team compete in a championship game. Someone offered to buy your ticket for $100, but you decided to go to the game.

■ **Exercise 2–35**
Economic Characteristics of
Costs
(LO 1, 10)

Required:

1. What was your economic cost to see the game?
2. What type of cost is this?

List the costs that would likely be included in each of the following marginal-cost calculations:

■ **Exercise 2–36**
Marginal Costs
(LO 10)

1. The marginal cost of adding a flight from Toronto to Vancouver
2. The marginal cost of keeping a travel agency open one additional hour on Saturdays
3. The marginal cost of manufacturing one additional pair of water skis
4. The marginal cost of one additional passenger on a flight
5. The marginal cost of serving one additional customer in a restaurant

Problems

Consider the following cost items:

■ **Problem 2–37**
Content of Financial
Statements and Reports;
Mass Customization
(LO 3, 4)

1. Current year's depreciation on a ship owned by a cruise line
2. The cost of chemicals and paper used during the period by a producer of film products
3. Assembly-line wage cost incurred by a bicycle manufacturer
4. Year-end production in process of a computer manufacturer
5. The cost of products sold to customers of a department store
6. The cost of products sold to distributors of a carpet manufacturer
7. Salaries of players on a professional hockey team
8. Year-end completed goods of a clothing manufacturer
9. Executive compensation costs of a mass-market retailer
10. Advertising costs for an electronics manufacturer
11. Costs incurred during the period to insure a manufacturing plant against fire and flood losses

Required:

1. Evaluate the costs just cited, and determine whether the associated dollar amounts would be found on the firm's balance sheet, income statement, or schedule of cost of goods manufactured. (*Note:* In some cases, more than one answer will apply.)
2. What major asset will normally be insignificant for service enterprises and relatively substantial for retailers, wholesalers, and manufacturers? Briefly discuss.
3. Briefly explain the major differences between income statements of service enterprises versus those of retailers, wholesalers, and manufacturers.

4. Picture the operations of a firm such as Comet Computer, one that is involved in direct sales and mass customization of products. What would be the major difference in the balance sheet of this type of organization versus the balance sheet of a company that engages in more traditional manufacturing activities, that is, producing goods and waiting for customer orders to arrive?

■ Problem 2–38
Financial-Statement
Elements: Manufacturer
(LO 5, 6)

4. Gross margin: $1,137,200

POST

The following selected information was extracted from the 20x1 accounting records of Surgical Products, Inc.:

Raw material purchases	$ 350,000
Direct labour	508,000
Indirect labour	218,000
Selling and administrative salaries	266,000
Building depreciation*	160,000
Other selling and administrative expenses	380,000
Other factory costs	688,000
Sales revenue ($260 per unit)	2,990,000

*Seventy-five percent of the company's building was devoted to production activities; the remaining 25 percent was used for selling and administrative functions.

Inventory data:

	January 1	December 31
Raw material	$ 31,600	$ 36,400
Work in process	71,400	124,200
Finished goods*	222,200	195,800

*The January 1 and December 31 finished-goods inventory consisted of 1,350 units and 1,190 units, respectively.

Required:

1. Calculate the company's manufacturing overhead for the year.
2. Calculate the company's cost of goods manufactured.
3. Compute the company's cost of goods sold.
4. Determine net income for 20x1, assuming a 40 percent income tax rate.
5. Determine the number of completed units manufactured during the year.
6. *Build a spreadsheet:* Construct an Excel spreadsheet to solve all of the preceding requirements. Show how the solution will change if the following data change: indirect labour is $221,000 and other factory costs amount to $679,000.

■ Problem 2–39
Inventory Estimates;
Partial Data
(LO 5, 6)

Cost of goods manufactured:
$357,000

On May 10, after the close of business, Smith & Sons had a devastating fire that destroyed the company's work-in-process and finished-goods inventories. Fortunately, all raw materials escaped damage, because materials owned by the firm were stored in another warehouse. The following information is available:

Sales revenue through May 10	$495,000
Income before taxes through May 10	102,000
Direct labour through May 10	180,000
Cost of goods available for sale, May 10	412,500
Work-in-process inventory, January 1	31,500
Finished-goods inventory, January 1	55,500

The firm's accountants determined that the cost of direct materials used normally averages 25 percent of prime costs (i.e., direct material plus direct labour). In addition, manufacturing overhead is 50 percent of the firm's total production costs. The gross margin is 30 percent of sales.

Required: The company is in the process of negotiating a settlement with its insurance company. Prepare an estimate of the cost of work-in-process and finished-goods inventories that were destroyed by the fire.

Mason Corporation began operations at the beginning of the current year. One of the company's products, a refrigeration element, sells for $265 per unit. Information related to the current year's activities follows.

Variable costs per unit:	
Direct material	$40
Direct labour	74
Manufacturing overhead	96
Annual fixed costs:	
Manufacturing overhead	$1,200,000
Selling and administrative	1,720,000
Sales and production activity:	
Sales (units)	20,000
Production (units)	24,000

Mason carries its finished-goods inventory at the average unit cost of production and is subject to a 40 percent income tax rate. There was no work in process at year-end.

Required:

1. Determine the cost of the December 31 finished-goods inventory.
2. Compute Mason's net income for the current year ended December 31.
3. If next year's production decreases to 22,500 units and general cost behaviour patterns do not change, what is the likely effect on:
   a. The direct-labour cost of $74 per unit? Why?
   b. The fixed manufacturing overhead cost of $1,200,000? Why?
   c. The fixed selling and administrative cost of $1,720,000? Why?
   d. The average unit cost of production? Why?

Problem 2–40
Financial-Statement Elements; Cost Behaviour
(LO 5, 6, 8)

2. Gross margin: $2,200,000

Determine the missing amounts in each of the following independent cases.

Problem 2–41
Incomplete Data; Manufacturing Costs
(LO 2, 5)

Case A: Cost of goods available for sale: $1,150,000

	Case A	Case B	Case C
Sales	$?	$?	$240,000
Beginning inventory, raw material	?	60,000	7,500
Ending inventory, raw material	180,000	?	15,000
Purchases of raw material	200,000	255,000	?
Direct material used	140,000	285,000	?
Direct labour	?	300,000	62,500
Manufacturing overhead	500,000	?	80,000
Total manufacturing costs	1,040,000	1,035,000	170,000
Beginning inventory, work in process	70,000	60,000	?
Ending inventory, work in process	?	105,000	2,500
Cost of goods manufactured	1,050,000	?	175,000
Beginning inventory, finished goods	100,000	120,000	?
Cost of goods available for sale	?	?	185,000
Ending inventory, finished goods	?	?	12,500
Cost of goods sold	1,090,000	990,000	?
Gross margin	510,000	510,000	?
Selling and administrative expenses	?	225,000	?
Income before taxes	300,000	?	45,000
Income tax expense	80,000	135,000	?
Net income	?	?	27,500

■ **Problem 2–42**
Cost Terminology
(LO 2, 5, 10)

1(b) Total manufacturing
overhead: $267,000

The following cost data for the year just ended pertain to Sentiments, Inc., a greeting card manufacturer:

Service department costs*	$ 50,000
Direct labour: Wages	242,500
Direct labour: Fringe benefits	47,500
Indirect labour: Fringe benefits	15,000
Fringe benefits for production supervisor	4,500
Total overtime premiums paid	27,500
Cost of idle time: Production employees†	20,000
Administrative costs	75,000
Rental of office space for sales personnel§	7,500
Sales commissions	2,500
Product promotion costs	5,000
Direct material	1,050,000
Advertising expense	49,500
Depreciation on factory building	57,500
Cost of finished goods inventory at year-end	57,500
Indirect labour: Wages	70,000
Production supervisor's salary	22,500

*All services are provided to manufacturing departments.

†Cost of idle time is an overhead item; it is not included in the direct-labour wages given above.

§The rental of sales space was made necessary when the sales offices were converted to storage space for raw material.

Required:

1. Compute each of the following costs for the year just ended: (*a*) total prime costs, (*b*) total manufacturing overhead costs, (*c*) total conversion costs, (*d*) total product costs, and (*e*) total period costs.
2. One of the costs listed above is an opportunity cost. Identify this cost, and explain why it is an opportunity cost.

■ **Problem 2–43**
Schedules of Cost of Goods
Manufactured and Sold;
Income Statement
(LO 1, 3, 5, 6)

1. Total manufacturing costs:
$300,000

The following data refer to Laredo Luggage Company for the year 20x2:

Sales revenue	$475,000
Work-in-process inventory, December 31	15,000
Work-in-process inventory, January 1	20,000
Selling and administrative expenses	75,000
Income tax expense	45,000
Purchases of raw material	90,000
Raw-material inventory, December 31	12,500
Raw-material inventory, January 1	20,000
Direct labour	100,000
Utilities: Plant	20,000
Depreciation: Plant and equipment	30,000
Finished-goods inventory, December 31	25,000
Finished-goods inventory, January 1	10,000
Indirect material	5,000
Indirect labour	7,500
Other manufacturing overhead	40,000

Required:

1. Prepare the company's schedule of cost of goods manufactured for the year.
2. Prepare the company's schedule of cost of goods sold for the year.
3. Prepare the company's income statement for the year.
4. *Build a spreadsheet:* Construct an Excel spreadsheet to solve all of the preceding requirements. Show how both cost schedules and the income statement will change if raw-material purchases amounted to $92,000 and indirect labour was $9,000.

Highlander Cutlery manufactures kitchen knives. One of the employees, whose job is to cut out wooden knife handles, worked 49 hours during a week in January. The employee earns $14 per hour for a 40-hour week. For additional hours, the employee is paid an overtime rate of $19 per hour. The employee's time was spent as follows:

■ **Problem 2–44**
Direct and Indirect Labour
(LO 3, 5)

2. Direct labour: $574

Regular duties involving cutting out knife handles	41 hours
General shop cleanup duties	6 hours
Idle time due to power outage	2 hours

Required:

1. Calculate the total cost of the employee's wages during the week described above.
2. Determine the portion of this cost to be classified in each of the following categories:

   a. Direct labour
   b. Manufacturing overhead (idle time)
   c. Manufacturing overhead (overtime premium)
   d. Manufacturing overhead (indirect labour)

Cape Cod Shirt Shop manufactures T-shirts and decorates them with custom designs for retail sale on the premises. Several costs incurred by the company are listed below. For each cost, indicate which of the following classifications best describe the cost. More than one classification may apply to the same cost item.

■ **Problem 2–45**
Cost Classifications
(LO 5, 8, 9)

Cost Classifications

a. Variable
b. Fixed
c. Period
d. Product
e. Administrative
f. Selling
g. Manufacturing
h. Research and development
i. Direct material
j. Direct labour
k. Manufacturing overhead

Cost Items

1. Wages of T-shirt designers and painters
2. Salaries of sales personnel
3. Depreciation on sewing machines
4. Rent on the building. Part of the building's first floor is used to make and paint T-shirts. Part of it is used for the retail sales shop. The second floor is used for administrative offices and storage of raw material and finished goods.
5. Cost of daily advertisements in local media
6. Salaries of designers who experiment with new fabrics, paints, and T-shirt designs
7. Cost of hiring a pilot to fly along the beach pulling a banner advertising the shop
8. Salary of the owner's secretary
9. Cost of repairing the gas furnace
10. Cost of health insurance for the production employees
11. Cost of fabric used in T-shirts
12. Wages of shirtmakers
13. Cost of new sign in front of retail T-shirt shop
14. Wages of the employee who repairs the firm's sewing machines
15. Cost of electricity used in the sewing department

■ **Problem 2–46**
Overtime Premiums and
Fringe Benefit Costs; Airline
(LO 1, 5, 9)

Central Mountain Air operates scheduled and flights to over 17 British Columbia and Alberta communities. Due to a political convention held in Vancouver, the airline added several extra flights during a two-week period. Additional cabin crews were hired on a temporary basis. However, rather than hiring additional flight attendants, the airline used its current attendants on overtime. Monica Gaines worked the following schedule on August 10. All of Gaines's flights on that day were extra flights that the airline would not normally fly.

Regular time:	2 round-trip flights between Vancouver and Ft. St. John (8 hours)
Overtime:	1 one-way flight from Vancouver to Ft. Nelson (3 hours)

Gaines earns $14 per hour plus time and a half for overtime. Fringe benefits cost the airline $4 per hour for any hour worked, regardless of whether it is a regular or overtime hour.

Required:

1. Compute the direct cost of compensating Gaines for her services on the flight from Vancouver to Ft. Nelson.
2. Compute the cost of Gaines' services that is an indirect cost.
3. How should the cost computed in requirement (2) be treated for cost accounting purposes?
4. Gaines ended her workday on August 10 in Ft. Nelson. However, her next scheduled flight departed Vancouver at 11:00 a.m. on August 11. This required Gaines to "dead-head" back to Vancouver on an early-morning flight. This means she travelled from Ft. Nelson to Vancouver as a passenger, rather than as a working flight attendant. Since the morning flight from Ft. Nelson to Vancouver was full, Gaines displaced a paying customer. The revenue lost by the airline was $87. What type of cost is the $87? To what flight, if any, is it chargeable? Why?

■ **Problem 2–47**
Variable Costs; Graphical
and Tabular Analyses
(LO 8)

2. 50 kilograms, total cost:
$800

Richmond Sheet Metal, Inc. incurs a variable cost of $16 per kilogram for raw material to produce a special alloy used in manufacturing aircraft.

Required:

1. Draw a graph of the firm's raw material cost, showing the total cost at the following production levels: 50,000 kilograms, 100,000 kilograms, and 150,000 kilograms.
2. Prepare a table that shows the unit cost and total cost of raw material at the following production levels: 1 kilograms, 50 kilograms, and 5,000 kilograms.

■ **Problem 2–48**
Fixed Costs; Graphical and
Tabular Analyses
(LO 8)

2. 50,000 litres, unit fixed
cost: $10 per litre

Thermal Technology, Inc. manufactures a special chemical used to coat certain electrical components that will be exposed to high heat in various applications. The company's annual fixed production cost is $500,000.

Required:

1. Draw a graph of the company's fixed production cost showing the total cost at the following production levels of the chemical: 50,000 litres, 100,000 litres, 150,000 litres, and 200,000 litres.
2. Prepare a table that shows the unit cost and the total cost for the firm's fixed production costs at the following production levels: 1 litre, 50 litres, 50,000 litres, and 200,000 litres.
3. Prepare a graph that shows the unit cost for the company's fixed production cost at the following production levels: 50,000 litres, 100,000 litres, 150,000 litres, and 200,000 litres.

■ **Problem 2–49**
Direct, Indirect, Controllable,
and Uncontrollable Costs
(LO 1, 9)

For each of the following costs, indicate whether the amount is a direct or indirect cost of the equipment maintenance department. Also indicate whether each cost is at least partially controllable by the department supervisor.

1. Cost of electricity used in the maintenance department
2. Depreciation on the building space occupied by the maintenance department
3. Idle time of maintenance department employees
4. Cost of plant manager's salary, which is allocated to the maintenance department
5. Cost of property taxes allocated to the maintenance department

Indicate for each of the following costs whether it is a product cost or a period cost.

1. Cost of grapes purchased by a winery
2. Depreciation on pizza ovens in a pizza restaurant
3. Cost of plant manager's salary in a computer production facility
4. Wages of security personnel in a department store
5. Cost of utilities in a manufacturing facility
6. Wages of aircraft mechanics employed by an airline
7. Wages of drill-press operators in a manufacturing plant
8. Cost of food in a microwaveable dinner
9. Cost incurred by a department store chain to transport merchandise to its stores

■ **Problem 2–50**
Product Costs and
Period Costs
(LO 1, 2)

Toledo Toy Company incurred the following costs during 20x4. The company sold all of its products manufactured during the year.

Direct material	$4,500,000
Direct labour	3,300,000
Manufacturing overhead:	
Utilities (primarily electricity)	210,000
Depreciation on plant and equipment	345,000
Insurance	240,000
Supervisory salaries	450,000
Property taxes	315,000
Selling costs:	
Advertising	292,000
Sales commissions	135,000
Administrative costs:	
Salaries of top management and staff	558,000
Office supplies	60,000
Depreciation on building and equipment	120,000

■ **Problem 2–51**
Fixed and Variable Costs;
Forecasting
(LO 7, 8)

20x5 direct labour forecast:
$4,290,000

During 20x4, the company operated at about half of its capacity, due to a slowdown in the economy. Prospects for 20x5 are slightly better. Jared Lowes, the marketing manager, forecasts a 30 percent growth in sales over the 20x4 level.

Required: Categorize each of the costs listed above as to whether it is most likely variable or fixed. Forecast the 20x5 cost amount for each of the cost items listed above.

The following terms are used to describe various economic characteristics of costs.

a. Opportunity cost
b. Out-of-pocket cost
c. Sunk cost
d. Differential cost
e. Marginal cost
f. Average cost

■ **Problem 2–52**
Economic Characteristics
of Costs
(LO 10)

Required: Choose one of the terms listed above to characterize each of the amounts described below.

1. The management of a high-rise office building uses 3,100 square metres of space in the building for its own management functions. This space could be rented for $335,000. What economic term describes this $335,000 in lost rental revenue?
2. The cost of building an automated assembly line in a factory is $700,000. The cost of building a manually operated assembly line is $475,000. What economic term is used to describe the difference between these two amounts?
3. Referring to the preceding question, what economic term is used to describe the $700,000 cost of building the automated assembly line?
4. What economic term describes the cost incurred by a mass customizer such as Dell Inc. to produce one more unit in its most popular line of laptop computers?

5. The cost of feeding 400 children in a public school cafeteria is $740 per day, or $1.85 per child per day. What economic term describes this $1.85 cost?

6. What economic term describes the cost of including one extra child in a day-care centre?

7. What economic term describes the cost of merchandise inventory purchased two years ago, which is now obsolete?

■ **Problem 2–53**
Cost Classifications; Hotel
(LO 9, 10)

Several costs incurred by Bayview Hotel and Restaurant are given in the following list. For each cost, indicate which of the following classifications best describe the cost. More than one classification may apply to the same cost item.

Cost Classifications

a. Direct cost of the food and beverage department

b. Indirect cost of the food and beverage department

c. Controllable by the kitchen manager

d. Uncontrollable by the kitchen manager

e. Controllable by the hotel general manager

f. Uncontrollable by the hotel general manager

g. Differential cost

h. Marginal cost

i. Opportunity cost

j. Sunk cost

k. Out-of-pocket cost

Cost Items

1. The wages earned by table-service personnel

2. The salary of the kitchen manager

3. The cost of the refrigerator purchased 14 months ago. The unit was covered by a warranty for 12 months, during which time it worked perfectly. It stopped working after 14 months, despite an original estimate that it would last five years.

4. The hotel has two options for obtaining fresh pies, cakes, and pastries. The goodies can be purchased from a local bakery for approximately $1,550 per month, or they can be made in the hotel's kitchen. To make the pastries on the premises, the hotel will have to hire a part-time pastry chef. This will cost $500 per month. The cost of ingredients will amount to roughly $850 per month. Thus, the savings from making the goods in the hotel's kitchen amount to $200 per month.

5. The cost of dishes broken by kitchen employees

6. The cost of leasing a computer used for reservations, payroll, and general hotel accounting

7. The cost of a pool service that cleans and maintains the hotel's swimming pool

8. The wages of the hotel's maintenance employees, who spent nine hours (at $13.50 per hour) repairing the dishwasher in the kitchen

9. The cost of general advertising by the hotel, which is allocated to the food and beverage department

10. The cost of food used in the kitchen

11. The difference in the total cost incurred by the hotel when one additional guest is registered

12. The cost of space (depreciation) occupied by the kitchen

13. The cost of space (depreciation) occupied by a sauna next to the pool, space that could otherwise have been used for a magazine- and book shop

14. The profit that would have been earned in a magazine-and-book shop, if the hotel had one

15. The discount on room rates given as a special offer for a "Labour Day Getaway Special"

Refer to Exhibit 2–3, and answer the following questions.

Required:

1. List the major differences between the income statements shown for Caterpillar, Inc., Wal-Mart Stores, Inc., and WestJet Airlines Ltd.
2. Explain how cost-accounting data were used to prepare these income statements.
3. On the income statement for WestJet Airlines, where would the ticket agents' salaries be shown? Where would the costs of the computer equipment used to keep track of reservations be included on the statement?
4. On the income statement for Wal-Mart Stores, Inc., where would the cost of newspaper advertising be shown? How about the cost of merchandise?
5. Refer to the income statement for Caterpillar, Inc. Where would the salary of the brand manager who plans advertising for Caterpillar equipment be shown? How about the salary of a production employee? Where would the cost of the raw materials used in the company's products be included on the statement?

Problem 2–54
Interpretation of Accounting Reports
(LO 1, 3)

Roberta Coy makes custom mooring covers for boats. Each mooring cover is hand sewn to fit a particular boat. If covers are made for two or more identical boats, each successive cover generally requires less time to make. Coy has been approached by a local boat dealer to make mooring covers for all of the boats sold by the dealer. Coy has developed the following cost schedule for mooring covers made to fit outboard power boats.

Problem 2–55
Marginal Costs and Average Costs
(LO 10)

4. Average cost: $637.50

Mooring Covers Made	Total Cost of Covers
1	$ 675
2	1,275
3	1,815
4	2,310
5	2,775

Required: Compute the following:

1. Marginal cost of second mooring cover
2. Marginal cost of fourth mooring cover
3. Marginal cost of fifth mooring cover
4. Average cost if two mooring covers are made
5. Average cost if four mooring covers are made
6. Average cost if five mooring covers are made

BC Parks, an agency of the B.C. Ministry of Environment, is responsible for maintaining the province's parks and forest lands, and generally overseeing the protection of the environment. Several costs incurred by the agency are listed below. For each cost, indicate which of the following classifications best describe the cost. More than one classification may apply to the same cost item.

Problem 2–56
Cost Classifications; Government Agency
(LO 3, 8, 9, 10)

Cost Classifications

a. Variable
b. Fixed
c. Controllable by the BC Parks director
d. Uncontrollable by the BC Parks director
e. Differential cost
f. Marginal cost
g. Opportunity cost
h. Sunk cost
i. Out-of-pocket cost
j. Direct cost of the agency

   k. Indirect cost of the agency

   l. Direct cost of providing a particular service

   m. Indirect cost of providing a particular service

Cost Items

   1. Cost of maintaining recreational trails in the various provincial parks

   2. The difference between (*a*) the cost of maintaining recreational trails in the various provincial parks and (*b*) the cost of contracting out the maintenance of recreational trails

   3. Cost of producing literature that describes the agency's role in environmental protection and is mailed free, upon request, to schools, local governments, libraries, and private citizens

   4. Cost of sending the agency's hydro engineers to inspect one additional dam for stability and safety

   5. Cost of operating the provincial computer services department, a portion of which is allocated to the Ministry of Environment

   6. Cost of administrative supplies used in the agency's head office

   7. Cost of providing a toll-free number for the province's residents to report environmental problems

   8. Cost of replacing batteries in sophisticated monitoring equipment used to evaluate the effects of acid rain on the province's lakes

   9. Cost of a ranger's salary, when the ranger is giving a talk about environmental protection to elementary-school children

  10. Cost of direct-mailing to 1 million residents a brochure explaining the benefits of voluntarily recycling cans and bottles

  11. The cost of producing a TV show to be aired on public television whose purpose is to educate people on how to spot and properly dispose of hazardous waste

  12. Cost of the automobiles used by BC Parks' rangers, which were purchased by the province and which would otherwise have been used by the another ministry

  13. Cost of live-trapping and moving beaver that were creating a nuisance in recreational lakes

  14. The agency director's salary

  15. Cost of containing naturally caused forest fires, which are threatening private property

---

Problem 2–57
Unit Costs; Profit-Maximizing
Output
(LO 8)

The controller for Canandaigua Vineyards, Inc. has predicted the following costs at various levels of wine output.

	Wine Output (.75-litre bottles)		
	10,000 Bottles	**15,000 Bottles**	**20,000 Bottles**
Variable production costs	$ 44,400	$ 66,600	$ 88,800
Fixed production costs	120,000	120,000	120,000
Fixed selling and administrative costs	48,000	48,000	48,000
Total	$212,400	$234,600	$256,800

   The company's marketing manager has predicted the following prices for the firm's fine wines at various levels of sales.

	Wine Sales		
	10,000 Bottles	**15,000 Bottles**	**20,000 Bottles**
Sales price per .75-litre bottle	$21.60	$18.00	$14.40

Required:

   1. Calculate the unit costs of wine production at each level of output. At what level of output is the unit cost minimized?

   2. Calculate the company's profit at each level of production. Assume that the company will sell all of its output. At what production level is profit maximized?

3. Which of the three output levels is best for the company?

4. Why does the unit cost of wine decrease as the output level increases?

Langley Industries currently manufactures 40,000 units of part JR63 every month for use in production of several of its products. The facilities now used to produce part JR63 have a fixed monthly cost of $165,000 and a capacity to produce 74,000 units per month. If the company were to buy part JR63 from an outside supplier, the facilities would be idle, but its fixed costs would continue at $45,000. The variable production costs of part JR63 are $12 per unit.

Problem 2–58
Variable and Fixed Costs;
Make or Buy a Component
(LO 8, 10)

Required:

1. If Langley Industries continues to use 40,000 units of part JR63 each month, it would realize a net benefit by purchasing part JR63 from an outside supplier only if the supplier's unit price is less than what amount?

2. If Langley Industries is able to obtain part JR63 from an outside supplier at a unit purchase price of $14, what is the monthly usage at which it will be indifferent between purchasing and making part JR63?

(CMA, adapted)

Cases

CompTech, Inc. manufactures printers for use with home computing systems. The firm currently manufactures both the electronic components for its printers and the plastic cases in which the devices are enclosed. Jim Cassanitti, the production manager, recently received a proposal from Universal Plastics Corporation to manufacture the cases for CompTech's printers. If the cases are purchased outside, CompTech will be able to close down its Printer Case Department. To help decide whether to accept the bid from Universal Plastics Corporation, Cassanitti asked CompTech's controller to prepare an analysis of the costs that would be saved if the Printer Case Department were closed. Included in the controller's list of annual cost savings were the following items:

Case 2–59
Economic Characteristics of
Costs; Closing a Department;
Ethics
(LO 1, 9, 10)

Building rental (The Printer Case Department occupies one-sixth of the factory building, which CompTech rents for $180,600 per year.)	$30,100
Salary of the Printer Case Department supervisor	$48,000

In a lunchtime conversation with the controller, Cassanitti learned that CompTech was currently renting space in a warehouse for $41,000. The space is used to store completed printers. If the Printer Case Department were discontinued, the entire storage operation could be moved into the factory building and occupy the space vacated by the closed department. Cassanitti also learned that the supervisor of the Printer Case Department would be retained by CompTech even if the department were closed. The supervisor would be assigned the job of managing the assembly department, whose supervisor recently gave notice of his retirement. All of CompTech's department supervisors earn the same salary.

Required:

1. You have been hired as a consultant by Cassanitti to advise him in his decision. Write a memo to Cassanitti commenting on the costs of space and supervisory salaries included in the controller's cost analysis. Explain in your memo about the "real" costs of the space occupied by the Printer Case Department and the supervisor's salary. What types of costs are these?

2. Independently of your response to requirement (1), suppose that CompTech's controller had been approached by his friend Jack Westford, the assistant supervisor of the Printer Case Department. Westford is worried that he will be laid off if the Printer Case Department is closed down.

    Westford has asked his friend to understate the cost savings from closing the department, in order to slant the production manager's decision toward keeping the department in operation. Comment on the controller's ethical responsibilities.

■ **Case 2–60**
Understanding Cost Concepts
(LO 7, 8, 10)

You just started a summer internship with the successful management consulting firm of Kirk, Spock, and McCoy. Your first day on the job was a busy one, as the following problems were presented to you.

Required: Supply the requested comments in each of the following independent situations.

1. Alderon Enterprises is evaluating a special order it has received for a ceramic fixture to be used in aircraft engines. Alderon has recently been operating at less than full capacity, so the firm's management will accept the order if the price offered exceeds the costs that will be incurred in producing it. You have been asked for advice on how to determine the cost of two raw materials that would be required to produce the order.

   a. The special order will require 900 litres of endor, a highly perishable material that is purchased as needed. Alderon currently has 1,300 litres of endor on hand, since the material is used in virtually all of the company's products. The last time endor was purchased, Alderon paid $10 per litre. However, the average price paid for the endor in stock was only $9.50. The market price for endor is quite volatile, with the current price at $11. If the special order is accepted, Alderon will have to place a new order next week to replace the 900 litres of endor used. By then the price is expected to reach $11.50 per litre.

   Using the cost terminology introduced in this chapter, comment on each of the cost figures mentioned in the preceding discussion. What is the real cost of endor if the special order is produced?

   b. The special order also would require 1,400 kilograms of tatooine, a material not normally required in any of Alderon's regular products. The company does happen to have 1,900 kilograms of tatooine on hand, since it formerly manufactured a ceramic product that used the material. Alderon recently received an offer of $28,000 from Solo Industries for its entire supply of tatooine. However, Solo Industries is not interested in buying any quantity less than Alderon's entire 1,900-kilogram stock. Alderon's management is unenthusiastic about Solo's offer, since Alderon paid $40,000 for the tatooine. Moreover, if the tatooine were purchased at today's market price, it would cost $22 per kilogram. Due to the volatility of tatooine, Alderon will need to get rid of its entire supply one way or another. If the material is not used in production or sold, Alderon will have to pay $2,000 for every 500 kilograms transported away and disposed of in a hazardous waste disposal site.

   Using the cost terminology introduced in this chapter, comment on each of the cost figures mentioned in the preceding discussion. What is the real cost of tatooine to be used in the special order?

2. FastQ Company, a specialist in printing, has established 500 convenience copying centres throughout the country. In order to upgrade its services, the company is considering three new models of laser copying machines for use in producing high-quality copies. These copies would be added to the growing list of products offered in the FastQ shops. The selling price to the customer for each laser copy would be the same, no matter which machine is installed in the shop. The three models of laser copying machines under consideration are 1500S, a small-volume model; 1500M, a medium-volume model; and 1500G, a large-volume model. The annual rental costs and the operating costs vary with the size of each machine. The machine capacities and costs are as follows:

	Copier Model		
	1500S	**1500M**	**1500G**
Annual capacity (copies)	80,000	300,000	600,000
Costs:			
Annual machine rental	$ 4,000	$ 5,500	$ 10,000
Direct material and direct labour	.010	.010	.010
Variable overhead costs	.060	.035	.015

   a. Calculate the volume level in copies where FastQ Company would be indifferent to acquiring either the small-volume model laser copier, 1500S, or the medium-volume model laser copier, 1500M.

   b. The management of FastQ Company is able to estimate the number of copies to be sold at each establishment. Present a decision rule that would enable FastQ Company to select the most profitable machine without having to make a separate cost calculation for each establishment. (*Hint:* To specify a decision rule, determine the volume at which FastQ would be indifferent between the small and medium copiers. Then determine the volume at which FastQ would be indifferent between the medium and large copiers.)

3. A local TV station has decided to produce a TV series on state-of-the-art manufacturing. The director of the TV series, Justin Tyme, is currently attempting to analyze some of the projected costs for the series. Tyme intends to take a TV production crew on location to shoot various manufacturing scenes as they occur. If the four-week series is shown in the 8:00–9:00 p.m. prime-time slot, the station will have to cancel a currently scheduled wildlife show. Management projects a 10 percent viewing audience for the wildlife show, and each 1 percent is expected to bring in advertising revenues of $20,000. In contrast, the manufacturing show is expected to be watched by 15 percent of the viewing audience. However, each 1 percent of the viewership will likely generate only $10,000 in advertising revenues. If the wildlife show is cancelled, it can be sold to network television for $50,000.

   Using the cost terminology introduced in this chapter, comment on each of the financial amounts mentioned in the preceding discussion. What are the relative merits of the two shows regarding the projected revenue to the station?

(CMA, adapted)

Chapter Three

Product Costing and Cost Accumulation

FOCUS COMPANY

Rocky Mountain Outfitters, a small manufacturer of canoes and small boats near Lake Claire, Alberta, uses job-order costing to accumulate the costs of each of its products. Job-order costing is well-suited to companies like Rocky Mountain Outfitters that manufacture relatively small numbers of distinct products. In a job-order costing system, direct material, direct labour, and manufacturing overhead are first assigned to each production job, such as a set number of canoes of a particular type. Then the cost of the production job is averaged across the number of units in the job.

IN CONTRAST

In contrast to the manufacturing setting of Rocky Mountain Outfitters, we explore job-order costing in a service industry environment. Metro Advertising Agency is a small firm in St. John's, Newfoundland. The ad agency has two managing partners, six artistic staff personnel, and an office support staff. Metro Advertising Agency calculates predetermined overhead rates based on two cost

drivers: partner direct professional labour and artistic staff direct professional labour. The ad agency's cost of completing the work for an advertising contract with Super Scoop Ice Cream Company includes direct material, direct professional labour for both partner and artistic staff time, and applied overhead.

After completing this chapter, you should be able to:

1 Discuss the role of product and service costing in manufacturing and nonmanufacturing firms.

2 Diagram and explain the flow of costs through the manufacturing accounts used in product costing.

3 Distinguish between job-order costing and process costing.

4 Compute a predetermined overhead rate and explain its use in job-order costing for job-shop and batch-production environments.

5 Prepare journal entries to record the costs of direct material, direct labour, and manufacturing overhead in a job-order costing system.

6 Prepare a schedule of cost of goods manufactured, a schedule of cost of goods sold, and an income statement for a manufacturer using a normal costing system.

7 Demonstrate the process of project costing used in service industry firms and nonprofit organizations.

8 Apply the two-stage allocation process used to compute departmental overhead rates (Appendix).

Product and Service Costing

A **product-costing system** accumulates the costs incurred in a production process and assigns those costs to the organization's final products. Product costs are needed for a variety of purposes in financial accounting, managerial accounting, and cost management.

Use in Financial Accounting   In financial accounting, product costs are needed to value inventory on the balance sheet and to compute cost-of-goods-sold expense on the income statement. Under generally accepted accounting principles, inventory is usually valued at its cost until it is sold. Then the cost of the inventory becomes an expense of the period in which it is sold.

Use in Managerial Accounting   In managerial accounting, product costs are needed to help managers with planning and to provide them with data for decision making. Decisions about product prices, the mix of products to be produced, and the quantity of output to be manufactured are among those for which product cost information is needed.

Use in Cost Management   It is hard to imagine how management can control or reduce production costs if management does not have a clear idea of how much it costs to make its product. Thus, product costs provide crucial data for a variety of cost management purposes. Many of the cost management uses of product-costing information will be covered throughout this book.

Use in Reporting to Interested Organizations   In addition to financial statement preparation and internal decision making, there is an ever-growing need for product cost information in relationships between firms and various outside organizations. Public utilities, such as electric and gas companies, record product costs to justify rate increases that must be approved by regulatory agencies. Hospitals keep track of the costs of medical procedures that are reimbursed by the provincial health authorities. Manufacturing firms often sign cost-plus contracts with the government, where the contract price depends on the cost of manufacturing the product.

"We recognized that our key competitors were overseas. We realized that in order to compete, we had to be extremely cost conscious." (3a)

**MiCRUS
(joint venture of IBM
and Cirrus Logic)**

Product Costing in Nonmanufacturing Firms

The need for product costs is not limited to manufacturing firms. Merchandising companies include the costs of buying and transporting merchandise in their product costs. Producers of inventoriable goods, such as mining products, petroleum, and agricultural products, also record the costs of producing their goods. The role of product costs in these companies is identical to that in manufacturing firms. For example, the pineapples grown and sold by Dole are inventoried at their product cost until they are sold. Then the product cost becomes cost-of-goods-sold expense.

Service Firms and Nonprofit Organizations   The production output of service firms and nonprofit organizations consists of services that are consumed as they are produced. Since services cannot be stored and sold later like manufactured goods, there are no inventoriable costs in service industry firms and nonprofit organizations. However, such organizations need information about the costs of producing services. Banks, insurance companies, restaurants, airlines, law firms, hospitals, and city governments all record the costs of producing various services for the purposes of planning, cost control, and decision making. For example, in making a decision about adding a flight from Toronto to Vancouver, Air Canada's management needs to know the cost

"The closer we get to the client physically, the more likely it is that we're going to have an opportunity to participate in what's going on in the business. The more remote you are from where the business decision makers are, the less likely they are to think about you." (3b)

Qwest

of flying the proposed route. Before building a new branch bank, BMO's management would want to know the cost of maintaining the branch, as well as the additional revenue to be generated. A Vancouver city manager can make a better decision as to whether the city government should begin a drug counselling program if the cost of providing similar, existing services is known.

Manufacturing Cost Flows

Manufacturing costs consist of direct material, direct labour, and manufacturing overhead. The product-costing systems used by manufacturing firms employ several manufacturing accounts. As production takes place, all manufacturing costs are added to the *Work-in-Process Inventory* account. Work in process is partially completed inventory. A debit to the account increases the cost-based valuation of the asset represented by the unfinished products. As soon as products are completed, their product costs are transferred from Work-in-Process Inventory to *Finished-Goods Inventory*. This is accomplished with a credit to Work in Process and a debit to Finished Goods. During the time period when products are sold, the product cost of the inventory sold is removed from Finished Goods and added to *Cost of Goods Sold*, which is an expense of the period in which the sale occurred. A credit to Finished Goods and a debit to Cost of Goods Sold completes this step. Cost of Goods Sold is closed into the Retained Earnings account at the end of the accounting period, along with all other expenses and revenues of the period. Exhibit 3–1 depicts the flow of costs through the manufacturing accounts.

Example of Manufacturing Cost Flows   Suppose that the Bradley Paper Company incurred the following manufacturing costs during 20x1.

Direct material	$30,000
Direct labour	20,000
Manufacturing overhead	40,000

During 20x1, products costing $60,000 were finished and products costing $25,000 were sold for $32,000. Exhibit 3–2 shows the flow of costs through the Bradley Paper Company's manufacturing accounts and the effect of the firm's product costs on its balance sheet and income statement.

Exhibit 3–1
Flow of Costs through
Manufacturing Accounts

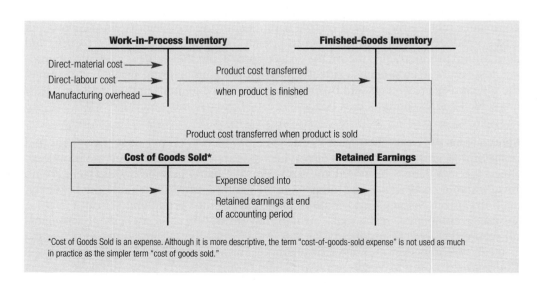

Work-in-Process Inventory

Direct-material cost ⟶
Direct-labour cost ⟶
Manufacturing overhead ⟶

Product cost transferred
when product is finished

Finished-Goods Inventory

Product cost transferred when product is sold

Cost of Goods Sold*

Expense closed into

Retained earnings at end
of accounting period

Retained Earnings

*Cost of Goods Sold is an expense. Although it is more descriptive, the term "cost-of-goods-sold expense" is not used as much in practice as the simpler term "cost of goods sold."

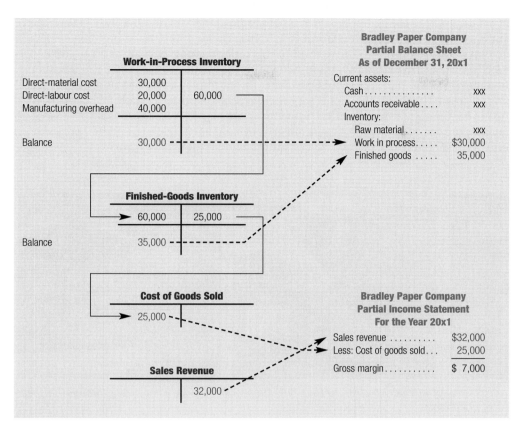

Exhibit 3–2
Example of Manufacturing
Cost Flows for Bradley Paper
Company

Product-Costing Systems

The detailed accounting procedures used in product-costing systems depend on the type of industry involved. Two basic sets of procedures are used: job-order costing and process costing.

Job-Order Costing Systems

Job-order costing is used by companies with *job-shop* operations or *batch-production* operations. In a job-shop environment, products are manufactured in very low volumes or one at a time. Examples of a job-shop environment include feature film production, custom house building, ship building, aircraft manufacture, and custom machining operations. In a batch-production environment, multiple products are produced in batches of relatively small quantity. Examples include furniture manufacture, printing, agricultural equipment, and pleasure boat production.

In **job-order costing**, each distinct batch of production is called a *job* or *job order*. The cost-accounting procedures are designed to assign costs to each job. Then the costs assigned to each job are averaged over the units of production in the job to obtain an average cost per unit. For example, suppose that AccuPrint worked on two printing jobs during October, and the following costs were incurred.

> **Learning Objective 3**
>
> Distinguish between job-order costing and process costing.

	Job A27 (1,000 campaign posters)	Job B39 (100 wedding invitations)
Direct material	$100	$ 36
Direct labour	250	40
Manufacturing overhead	150	24
Total manufacturing cost	$500	$100

The cost per campaign poster is $.50 per poster ($500 divided by 1,000 posters), and the cost per wedding invitation is $1 ($100 divided by 100 invitations).

Procedures similar to those used in job-order costing also are used in many service industry firms, although these firms have no work-in-process or finished-goods inventories. In a public accounting firm, for example, costs are assigned to audit engagements in much the same way they are assigned to a batch of products by a furniture manufacturer. Similar procedures are used to assign costs to "cases" in health-care facilities, to "programs" in government agencies, to research "projects" in universities, and to "contracts" in consulting and architectural firms.

"We have to be the best in cost throughout the world." (3c)

MiCRUS
(joint venture of IBM and Cirrus Logic)

The cost-accounting system keeps track of production costs as they flow from work-in-process inventory through finished-goods inventory and into cost of goods sold.

Process-Costing Systems

Process costing is used by companies that produce large numbers of identical units. Firms that produce chemicals, microchips, gasoline, beer, fertilizer, textiles, processed food, and electricity are among those using process costing. In these kinds of firms, there is no need to trace costs to specific batches of production, because the products in the different batches are identical. A **process-costing system** accumulates all the production costs for a large number of units of output, and then these costs are averaged over all of the units. For example, suppose the Silicon Valley Company produced 40,000 microchips during November. The following manufacturing costs were incurred in November.

Direct material	$1,000
Direct labour	2,000
Manufacturing overhead	3,000
Total manufacturing cost	$6,000

The cost per microchip is $.15 (total manufacturing cost of $6,000 ÷ 40,000 units produced).

Summary of Alternative Product-Costing Systems

The distinction between job-order and process costing hinges on the type of production process involved. Job-order costing systems assign costs to distinct production jobs that are significantly different. Then an average cost is computed for each unit of product in each job. Process-costing systems average costs over a large number of identical (or very similar) units of product. Exhibit 3–3 summarizes the differences between these two product-costing systems.

Job-Order Costing System	Process Costing System
Used for production of large, unique, high-cost items.	Used for production of small, identical, low-cost items.
Built to order rather than mass-produced.	Mass-produced in automated continuous production process.
• *Job-shop operations.* Products manufactured in very low volumes or one at a time.	
• *Batch-production operations.* Multiple products in batches of relatively small quantity.	
Many costs can be directly traced to each job.	Costs cannot be directly traced to each unit of product.
Typical applications are special-order printing, building construction, hospitals, law firms.	Typical applications are petrochemical refinery, paint manufacturer, paper mill.

Exhibit 3–3
Comparison of Product-Costing Systems

The remainder of this chapter examines the details of job-order costing. The next chapter covers process costing.

Cost Accumulation in a Job-Order Costing System

To illustrate job-order costing, we will focus on Rocky Mountain Outfitters, Inc. This small company, nestled near Lake Claire, Alberta, manufactures canoes and small boats.

In a job-order costing system, costs of direct material, direct labour, and manufacturing overhead are assigned to each production job. These costs comprise the *inputs* of the product-costing *system*. As costs are incurred, they are added to the Work-in-Process Inventory account in the ledger. To keep track of the manufacturing costs assigned to *each job*, a subsidiary ledger is maintained. The subsidiary ledger account assigned to each job is a document called a **job-cost record**.

Job-Cost Record

An example of a job-cost record is displayed in Exhibit 3–4. At this juncture, just focus on the major sections and headings, which are printed in blue. (For now just ignore the detailed entries, printed in black, which will be explained in due course.)

This job-cost record is for job F16 consisting of 80 deluxe aluminum fishing boats, which were produced during November 20x1. Three major sections on the job-cost record are used to accumulate the costs of direct material, direct labour, and manufacturing overhead assigned to the job. The other two sections are used to record the total cost and average unit cost for the job, and to keep track of units shipped to customers. A job-cost record may be a paper document upon which the entries for direct material, direct labour, and manufacturing overhead are written. Increasingly, it is a computer file where entries are made using a computer.

The procedures used to accumulate the costs of direct material, direct labour, and manufacturing overhead for a job constitute the *set of activities* performed by the job-order costing *system*. These procedures are discussed next.

Direct-Material Costs

As raw materials are needed for the production process, they are transferred from the warehouse to the production department. To authorize the release of materials, the production department supervisor completes a **material requisition form** and presents it to the warehouse supervisor. A copy of the material requisition form goes to the cost-accounting department. There it is used as the basis for transferring the cost of the requisitioned material from the Raw-Material Inventory account to the Work-in-Process Inventory account, and for entering the direct-material cost on the job-cost record for the production job in process. A document such as the material requisition

Exhibit 3–4

Job-Cost Record: Rocky
Mountain Outfitters, Inc.

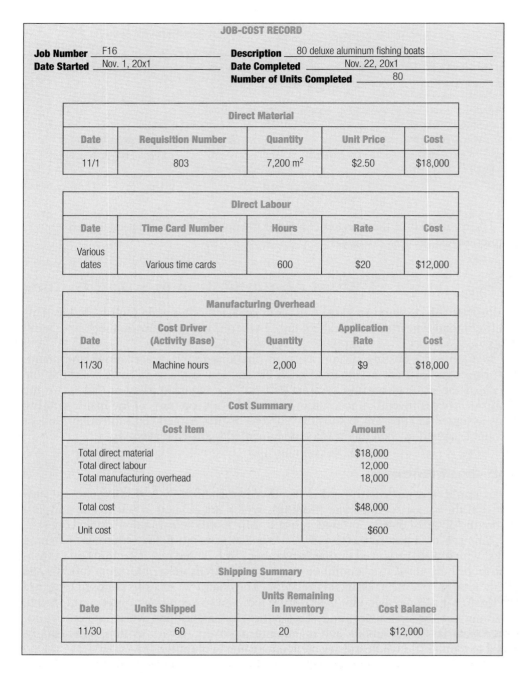

JOB-COST RECORD				
Job Number F16		**Description** 80 deluxe aluminum fishing boats		
Date Started Nov. 1, 20x1		**Date Completed** Nov. 22, 20x1		
		Number of Units Completed 80		

Direct Material

Date	Requisition Number	Quantity	Unit Price	Cost
11/1	803	7,200 m²	$2.50	$18,000

Direct Labour

Date	Time Card Number	Hours	Rate	Cost
Various dates	Various time cards	600	$20	$12,000

Manufacturing Overhead

Date	Cost Driver (Activity Base)	Quantity	Application Rate	Cost
11/30	Machine hours	2,000	$9	$18,000

Cost Summary

Cost Item	Amount
Total direct material	$18,000
Total direct labour	12,000
Total manufacturing overhead	18,000
Total cost	$48,000
Unit cost	$600

Shipping Summary

Date	Units Shipped	Units Remaining in Inventory	Cost Balance
11/30	60	20	$12,000

form, which is used as the basis for an accounting entry, is called a **source document**. Exhibit 3–5 shows an example of a material requisition form.

In many factories, material requisitions are entered directly into a computer by the production department supervisor. The requisition is automatically transmitted to computers in the warehouse and in the cost-accounting department. Such automation reduces the flow of paperwork, minimizes clerical errors, and speeds up the product-costing process.

Direct-Labour Costs

The assignment of direct-labour costs to jobs is based on time records filled out by employees. A **time record** is a form that records the amount of time an employee

Material-Requisition Number _352_		Date _1/28/x1_	
Job Number to Be Charged _J621_		Department _Painting_	
Department Supervisor _Timothy Williams_			

Item	Quantity	Unit Cost	Amount
White enamel paint	8 litres	$14	$112
Clear lacquer	2 litres	11	22

Exhibit 3–5
Material Requisition Form

ROCKY MOUNTAIN
OUTFITTERS

spends on each production job. The time record is the source document used in the cost-accounting department as the basis for adding direct-labour costs to Work-in-Process Inventory and to the job-cost records for the various jobs in process. In some factories, a computerized time-clock system may be used. Employees enter the time they begin and stop work on each job into the time clock. The time clock is connected to a computer, which records the time spent on various jobs and transmits the information to the accounting department.

Exhibit 3–6 displays an example of a time record. As the example shows, most of the employee's time was spent working on two different production jobs. In the accounting department, the time spent on each job will be multiplied by the employee's wage rate, and the cost will be recorded in Work-in-Process Inventory and on the appropriate job-cost records. The employee also spent one-half hour on shop cleanup duties. This time will be classified by the accounting department as indirect labour, and its cost will be included in manufacturing overhead.

Manufacturing Overhead Costs

It is relatively simple to trace direct-material and direct-labour costs to production jobs, but manufacturing overhead is not easily traced to jobs. By definition, manufacturing overhead is a heterogeneous pool of indirect production costs, such as indirect material, indirect labour, utility costs, and depreciation. These costs often bear no obvious relationship to individual jobs or units of product, but they must be incurred for production to take place. Therefore, it is necessary to assign manufacturing-overhead costs to jobs in order to have a complete picture of product costs. This process of assigning manufacturing-overhead costs to production jobs is called **overhead application** (or sometimes **overhead absorption**).

Overhead Application   For product-costing information to be useful, it must be provided to managers on a timely basis. Suppose the cost-accounting department waited until the end of an accounting period so that the *actual* costs of manufacturing

| Employee Name _Ron Bradley_ | | Date _12/19/x1_ | |
| Employee Number _12_ | | Department _Painting_ | |

Time Started	Time Stopped	Job Number
8:00	11:30	A267
11:30	12:00	Shop cleanup
1:00	5:00	J122

Exhibit 3–6
Time Record

ROCKY MOUNTAIN
OUTFITTERS

overhead could be determined before applying overhead costs to the firm's products. The result would be very accurate overhead application. However, the information might be useless because it was not available to managers for planning, control, and decision making during the period.

Learning Objective 4

Compute a predetermined overhead rate and explain its use in job-order costing for job-shop and batch-production environments.

Predetermined Overhead Rate   The solution to this problem is to apply overhead to products on the basis of estimates made at the beginning of the accounting period. The accounting department chooses some measure of productive activity to use as the basis for overhead application. In traditional product-costing systems, this measure is usually some **volume-based cost driver** (or **activity base**), such as direct-labour hours, direct-labour cost, or machine hours. An estimate is made of (1) the amount of manufacturing overhead that will be incurred during a specified period of time and (2) the amount of the cost driver (or activity base) that will be used or incurred during the same time period. Then a **predetermined overhead rate** is computed as follows:

$$\text{Predetermined overhead rate} = \frac{\text{Budgeted manufacturing-overhead cost}}{\text{Budgeted amount of cost driver (or activity base)}}$$

For example, Rocky Mountain Outfitters has chosen machine hours as its cost driver (or activity base). For the year 20x1, the firm estimates that overhead cost will amount to $360,000 and that total machine hours used will be 40,000 hours. The predetermined overhead rate is computed as follows:

$$\text{Predetermined overhead rate} = \frac{\$360,000}{40,000 \text{ hours}} = \$9 \text{ per machine hour}$$

In our discussion of the predetermined overhead rate, we have emphasized the term *cost driver*, because increasingly this term is replacing the more traditional term *activity base*. Furthermore, we have emphasized that *traditional* product-costing systems tend to rely on a *single, volume-based cost driver*. We will discuss more elaborate product-costing systems based on multiple cost drivers later in this chapter. This topic is examined in even greater detail in Chapter 5.

Applying Overhead Costs   The predetermined overhead rate is used to apply manufacturing overhead costs to production jobs. The quantity of the cost driver (or activity base) required by a particular job is multiplied by the predetermined overhead rate to determine the amount of overhead cost applied to the job. For example, suppose Rocky Mountain Outfitters' job number D22 requires 30 machine hours. The overhead applied to the job is computed as follows:

Predetermined overhead rate	$ 9
Machine hours required by job D22	× 30
Overhead applied to job D22	$270

The $270 of applied overhead will be added to Work-in-Process Inventory and recorded on the job-cost record for job D22. The accounting entries made to add manufacturing overhead to Work-in-Process Inventory may be made daily, weekly, or monthly, depending on the time required to process production jobs. Before the end of an accounting period, entries should be made to record all manufacturing costs incurred to date in Work-in-Process Inventory. This is necessary to properly value Work-in-Process Inventory on the balance sheet.

Job-Order Costing Illustrated

Now let's examine the accounting entries made by Rocky Mountain Outfitters, Inc. during November of 20x1. The company worked on two production jobs:

Job number C12   80 deluxe wooden canoes
Job number F16   80 deluxe aluminum fishing boats

The job numbers designate these as the 12th canoe production job and the 16th fishing boat production job undertaken during the year. The events of November are described below along with the associated accounting entries.

ROCKY MOUNTAIN
OUTFITTERS

Purchase of Material

Four thousand square metres of rolled aluminum sheet metal were purchased on account for $10,000. The purchase is recorded with the following journal entry.

(1)	Raw-Material Inventory	10,000	
	Accounts Payable		10,000

The postings of this and all subsequent journal entries to the ledger are shown in Exhibit 3–11, which appears on page 86.

Use of Direct Material

On November 1, the following material requisitions were submitted.

Requisition number 802
(for job number C12):   8,000 board metres of lumber, at $2 per board metre, for a total of $16,000

Requisition number 803
(for job number F16):   7,200 square metres of aluminum sheet metal, at $2.50 per square metre, for a total of $18,000

The following journal entry records the release of these raw materials to production.

(2)	Work-in-Process Inventory	34,000	
	Raw-Material Inventory		34,000

The associated ledger posting is shown in Exhibit 3–11. These direct-material costs are also recorded on the job-cost record for each job. The job-cost record for job number F16 is displayed in Exhibit 3–4 on page 74. Since the job-cost record for job number C12 is similar, it is not shown.

This small production facility records the cost of manufacturing canoes and other boats, which are manufactured in small batches. Direct material, direct labour, and manufacturing-overhead costs are tracked.

Use of Direct Labour

At the end of November, the cost-accounting department uses the labour time records filed during the month to determine the following direct-labour costs of each job.

Direct labour: Job number C12	$ 9,000
Direct labour: Job number F16	12,000
Total direct labour	$21,000

The journal entry made to record these costs is as follows:

(3)	Work-in-Process Inventory	21,000	
	Wages Payable		21,000

The associated ledger posting is shown in Exhibit 3–11. These direct-labour costs also are recorded on the job-cost record for each job. The job-cost record for job number F16 is displayed in Exhibit 3–4 on page 74. Only one direct-labour entry is shown on the job-cost record. In practice, there would be numerous entries made on different dates at a variety of wage rates for different employees.

Incurrence of Manufacturing Overhead Costs

The following information related to the incurrence of manufacturing overhead costs in the month of November.

Use of Indirect Material   On November 15, the following material requisition was submitted.

> Requisition number 804:   5 litres of bonding glue, at $10 per litre, for a total cost of $50

Small amounts of bonding glue are used in the production of all classes of boats manufactured by Rocky Mountain Outfitters. Since the cost incurred is small, no attempt is made to trace the cost of glue to specific jobs. Instead, glue is considered an indirect material, and its cost is included in manufacturing overhead. The company accumulates all manufacturing-overhead costs in the Manufacturing Overhead account. All actual overhead costs are recorded by debiting this account. The account is debited when indirect materials are requisitioned, when indirect-labour costs are incurred, when utility bills are paid, when depreciation is recorded on manufacturing equipment, and so forth. The journal entry made to record the usage of glue is as follows:

(4)	Manufacturing Overhead	50	
	Manufacturing Supplies Inventory		50

The posting of this journal entry to the ledger is shown in Exhibit 3–11. No entry is made on any job-cost record for the usage of glue, since its cost is not traced to individual production jobs.

Use of Indirect Labour   The analysis of labour time records undertaken on November 30 also revealed the following use of indirect labour:

> Indirect labour: Not charged to any particular job $14,000

This cost comprises the production supervisor's salary and the wages of various employees who spent some of their time on maintenance and general cleanup duties during November. The following journal entry is made to add indirect-labour costs to manufacturing overhead:

(5)	Manufacturing Overhead	14,000	
	Wages Payable		14,000

No entry is made on any job-cost record, since indirect-labour costs are not traceable to any particular job.

In addition to indirect materials and indirect labour, the following manufacturing-overhead costs were incurred during November.

Manufacturing overhead:	
Rent on factory building	$ 3,000
Depreciation on equipment	5,000
Utilities (electricity and natural gas)	4,000
Property taxes	2,000
Insurance	1,000
Total	$15,000

The following compound journal entry is made on November 30 to record these costs.

(6)	Manufacturing Overhead	15,000	
	Prepaid Rent		3,000
	Accumulated Depreciation—Equipment		5,000
	Accounts Payable (utilities and property taxes)		6,000
	Prepaid Insurance		1,000

The entry is posted in Exhibit 3–11. No entry is made on any job-cost record, since manufacturing-overhead costs are not traceable to any particular job.

Application of Manufacturing Overhead

Various manufacturing overhead costs were incurred during November, and these costs were accumulated by debiting the Manufacturing-Overhead account. However, no manufacturing overhead costs have yet been added to Work-in-Process Inventory or recorded on the job-cost records. The application of overhead to the firm's products is based on a predetermined overhead rate. This rate was computed by the accounting department at the beginning of 20x1 as follows:

$$\text{Predetermined overhead rate} = \frac{\text{Budgeted total manufacturing overhead for 20x1}}{\text{Budgeted total machine hours for 20x1}}$$

$$= \frac{\$360,000}{40,000} = \$9 \text{ per machine hour}$$

Factory records indicate the following usage of machine hours during November:

Machine hours used: Job number C12	1,200 hours
Machine hours used: Job number F16	2,000 hours
Total machine hours	3,200 hours

The total manufacturing overhead applied to Work-in-Process Inventory during November is calculated as follows:

	Machine Hours		Predetermined Overhead Rate		Manufacturing Overhead Applied
Job number C12	1,200	×	$9	=	$10,800
Job number F16	2,000	×	$9	=	18,000
Total manufacturing overhead applied					$28,800

The following journal entry is made to add **applied manufacturing overhead** to Work-in-Process Inventory.

(7)	Work-in-Process Inventory	28,800	
	Manufacturing Overhead		28,800

Exhibit 3–7
Manufacturing Overhead
Account

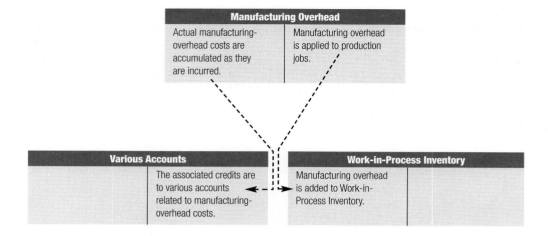

The entry is posted in Exhibit 3–11, and the manufacturing overhead applied to job number F16 is entered on the job-cost record in Exhibit 3–4 on page 74.

Summary of Accounting for Manufacturing Overhead

As the following time line shows, three concepts are used in accounting for overhead. Overhead is *budgeted* at the *beginning* of the accounting period, it is *applied during* the period, and *actual* overhead is measured at the *end* of the period.

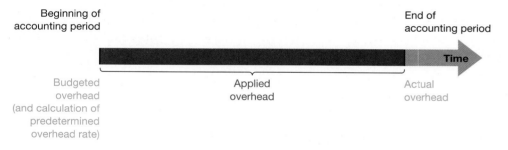

Exhibit 3–7 summarizes the accounting procedures used for manufacturing overhead. The left side of the Manufacturing Overhead account is used to accumulate **actual manufacturing overhead** costs as they are incurred throughout the accounting period. The actual costs incurred for indirect material, indirect labour, factory rental, equipment depreciation, utilities, property taxes, and insurance are recorded as debits to the account.

The right side of the Manufacturing Overhead account is used to record overhead *applied* to Work-in-Process Inventory. It is important to note that actual overhead costs are not charged to jobs and thus do not appear in the Work-in-Process account. Only the applied overhead costs, based on the predetermined overhead rate, appears in the Work-in-Process account.

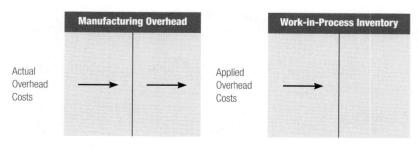

The Manufacturing Overhead account acts as a temporary (clearing) account. While the left side of the Manufacturing Overhead account accumulates *actual* overhead costs, the right side applies overhead costs using the predetermined overhead rate, based on *estimated* overhead costs. The estimates used to calculate the predetermined overhead rate will generally prove to be incorrect to some degree. Consequently, there will usually be a balance left in the Manufacturing Overhead account at the end of the year. This balance is usually relatively small, and its disposition is covered later in this illustration.

> "As production processes are becoming more automated, manufacturing overhead is becoming a greater and greater portion of total manufacturing costs. This is true of almost all manufacturing firms." (3d)
>
> **Chrysler**

Selling and Administrative Costs

During November, Rocky Mountain Outfitters incurred selling and administrative costs as follows:

Rental of sales and administrative offices	$ 1,500
Salaries of sales personnel	4,000
Salaries of management	8,000
Advertising	1,000
Office supplies used	300
Total	$14,800

Since these are not manufacturing costs, they are not added to Work-in-Process Inventory. Selling and administrative costs are **period costs**, not product costs. They are treated as expenses of the accounting period in which they are incurred. The following journal entry is made.

(8)	Selling and Administrative Expenses	14,800	
	Wages Payable		12,000
	Accounts Payable		1,000
	Prepaid Rent		1,500
	Offices Supplies Inventory		300

The entry is posted in Exhibit 3–11.

Completion of a Production Job

Job number F16 was completed during November, whereas job number C12 remained in process. As the job-cost record in Exhibit 3–4 (page 74) indicates, the total cost of job number F16 was $48,000. The following journal entry records the transfer of these job costs from Work-in-Process Inventory to Finished-Goods Inventory.

(9)	Finished-Goods Inventory	48,000	
	Work-in-Process Inventory		48,000

The entry is posted in Exhibit 3–11.

Sale of Goods

Sixty deluxe aluminum fishing boats manufactured in job number F16 were sold for $900 each during November. The cost of each unit sold was $600, as shown on the job-cost record in Exhibit 3–4. The following journal entries are made.

These entries are posted in Exhibit 3–11.

(10)	Accounts Receivable	54,000	
	Sales Revenue		54,000

| (11) | Cost of Goods Sold .... | 36,000 | |
| | Finished-Goods Inventory .... | | 36,000 |

The remainder of the manufacturing costs for job number F16 stays in Finished-Goods Inventory until some subsequent accounting period when the units are sold. Therefore, the cost balance for job number F16 remaining in inventory is $12,000 (20 units remaining times $600 per unit). This balance is shown on the job-cost record in Exhibit 3–4 (page 74).

Underapplied and Overapplied Overhead

During November, Rocky Mountain Outfitters incurred total *actual* manufacturing overhead costs of $29,050, but only $28,800 of overhead was *applied* to Work-in-Process Inventory. The amount by which actual overhead exceeds applied overhead, called **underapplied overhead**, is calculated below.

Actual manufacturing overhead*	$29,050
Applied manufacturing overhead†	28,800
Underapplied overhead	$ 250

*Sum of debit entries in the Manufacturing-Overhead account: $50 + $14,000 + $15,000 = $29,050. See Exhibit 3–11.
†Applied overhead: $9 per machine hour × 3,200 machine hours.

If actual overhead had been less than applied overhead, the difference would have been called **overapplied overhead**. Underapplied or overapplied overhead is caused by differences in the estimates of overhead and activity used to compute the predetermined overhead rate. In this illustration, Rocky Mountain Outfitters' predetermined rate was underestimated by a small amount.

Disposition of Underapplied or Overapplied Overhead   At the end of an accounting period, the managerial accountant has two alternatives for the disposition of underapplied or overapplied overhead. Under the most common alternative, the underapplied or overapplied overhead is closed into Cost of Goods Sold. This is the method used by Rocky Mountain Outfitters, and the required journal entry is shown below.

| (12) | Cost of Goods Sold .... | 250 | |
| | Manufacturing Overhead .... | | 250 |

This entry, which is posted in Exhibit 3–11, brings the balance in the Manufacturing Overhead account to zero. The account is then clear to accumulate manufacturing overhead costs incurred in the next accounting period. The Manufacturing Overhead account is a temporary (clearing) account containing costs or amounts that are to be transferred to another account.

Journal entry (12) has the effect of increasing cost-of-goods-sold expense. This reflects the fact that the cost of the units sold had been underestimated due to the slightly underestimated predetermined overhead rate. Most companies use this approach because it is simple and the amount of underapplied or overapplied overhead is usually small. Moreover, most firms wait until the end of the year to close underapplied or overapplied overhead into Cost of Goods Sold, rather than making the entry monthly as in this illustration.

Proration of Underapplied or Overapplied Overhead   Some companies use a more accurate procedure to dispose of underapplied or overapplied overhead. This approach recognizes that underestimation or overestimation of the predetermined overhead rate affects not only Cost of Goods Sold, but also Work-in-Process Inventory and

Finished-Goods Inventory. As the following diagram shows, applied overhead passes through all three of these accounts. Therefore, all three accounts are affected by any inaccuracy in the predetermined overhead rate.

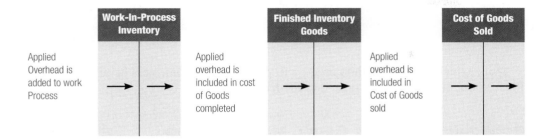

When underapplied or overapplied overhead is allocated among the three accounts shown above, the process is called **proration**. The amount of the current period's applied overhead remaining in each account is the basis for the proration procedure. In the Rocky Mountain Outfitters illustration, the amounts of applied overhead remaining in the three accounts on November 30 are determined as follows:

Applied Overhead Remaining in Each Account on November 30

Account	Explanation	Amount	Percentage*	Calculation of Percentages
Work in Process	Job C12 only	$10,800	37%	10,800 ÷ 28,800
Finished Goods	¼ of units in job F16	4,500	16%	4,500 ÷ 28,800
Cost of Goods Sold	¾ of units in job F16	13,500	47%	13,500 ÷ 28,800
Total overhead applied in November		$28,800	100%	

*Rounded.

Using the percentages calculated above, the proration of Rocky Mountain Outfitters' underapplied overhead is determined as follows:

Account	Underapplied Overhead	×	Percentage	=	Amount Added to Account
Work in Process	$250	×	37%	=	$ 92.50
Finished Goods	250	×	16%	=	40.00
Cost of Goods Sold	250	×	47%	=	117.50
Total underapplied overhead prorated					$250.00

If Rocky Mountain Outfitters had chosen to prorate underapplied overhead, the following journal entry would have been made.

Work-in-Process Inventory	92.50	
Finished-Goods Inventory	40.00	
Cost of Goods Sold	117.50	
Manufacturing Overhead		250.00

Since this is *not* the method used by Rocky Mountain Outfitters in our continuing illustration, this entry is *not* posted to the ledger in Exhibit 3–11.

Learning Objective 6

Prepare a schedule of cost of goods manufactured, a schedule of cost of goods sold, and an income statement for a manufacturer using a normal costing system.

Schedule of Cost of Goods Manufactured

Exhibit 3–8 displays the November **schedule of cost of goods manufactured** for Rocky Mountain Outfitters. The schedule details the costs of direct material, direct labour, and manufacturing overhead *applied* to work in process during November and shows the change in Work-in-Process Inventory. The **cost of goods manufactured**, shown in the last line of the schedule, is $48,000. This is the amount transferred from Work-in-Process Inventory to Finished-Goods Inventory during November, as recorded in journal entry number (9).

Exhibit 3–8
Schedule of Cost of Goods
Manufactured

ROCKY MOUNTAIN
OUTFITTERS

ROCKY MOUNTAIN OUTFITTERS, INC.
Schedule of Cost of Goods Manufactured
For the Month of November, 20x1

Direct material:		
Raw-material inventory, November 1	$30,000	
Add: November purchases of raw material	10,000	
Raw material available for use	40,000	
Deduct: Raw-material Inventory, November 30	6,000	
Raw material used		$34,000
Direct labour		21,000
Manufacturing overhead:		
Indirect material	$ 50	
Indirect labour	14,000	
Rent on factory building	3,000	
Depreciation on equipment	5,000	
Utilities	4,000	
Property taxes	2,000	
Insurance	1,000	
Total actual manufacturing overhead	29,050	
Deduct: Underapplied overhead*	250	
Overhead applied to work in process		28,800
Total manufacturing costs		83,800
Add: Work-in-process inventory, November 1		4,000
Subtotal		87,800
Deduct: Work-in-process inventory, November 30		39,800
Cost of goods manufactured		$48,000

*The schedule of cost of goods manufactured lists the manufacturing costs *applied* to work in process. Therefore, the underapplied overhead, $250, must be deducted from total actual overhead to arrive at the amount of overhead *applied* to work in process during November. If there had been overapplied overhead, the balance would have been *added* to total manufacturing overhead.

ROCKY MOUNTAIN OUTFITTERS, INC.
Schedule of Cost of Goods Sold
For the Month of November, 20x1

Finished-goods, inventory, November 1	$12,000
Add: Cost of goods manufactured*	48,000
Cost of goods available for sale	60,000
Deduct: Finished-goods inventory, November 30	24,000
Cost of goods sold	36,000
Add: Underapplied overhead†	250
Cost of goods sold (adjusted for underapplied overhead)	$36,250

*From the Schedule of Cost of Goods Manufactured in Exhibit 3–8.
†The company closes underapplied or overapplied overhead into cost of goods sold. Hence, the $250 balance in underapplied overhead is added to the cost of goods sold for the month.

Exhibit 3–9
Schedule of Cost of
Goods Sold

ROCKY MOUNTAIN OUTFITTERS, INC.
Income Statement
For the Month of November, 20x1

Sales revenue	$54,000
Less: Cost of goods sold*	36,250
Gross margin	17,750
Selling and administrative expenses	14,800
Income before taxes	2,950
Income tax expense	1,420
Net income	$ 1,530

*From the schedule of Cost of Goods Sold in Exhibit 3–9.

Exhibit 3–10
Income Statement

Schedule of Cost of Goods Sold

A **schedule of cost of goods sold** for Rocky Mountain Outfitters is displayed in Exhibit 3–9. This schedule shows the November cost of goods sold and details the changes in Finished-Goods Inventory during the month. Exhibit 3–10 displays the company's November income statement. As the income statement shows, income before taxes is $2,950, from which income tax expense of $1,420 is subtracted, yielding net income of $1,530.

Posting Journal Entries to the Ledger

All of the journal entries in the Rocky Mountain Outfitters illustration are posted to the ledger in Exhibit 3–11. An examination of these T-accounts provides a summary of the cost flows discussed throughout the illustration.

Further Aspects of Overhead Application

Actual and Normal Costing   Most firms use a predetermined overhead rate, based on overhead and activity estimates for a relatively long time period. When direct material and direct labour are added to Work-in-Process Inventory at their actual amounts, but overhead is applied to Work-in-Process Inventory using a *predetermined overhead rate*, the product-costing system is referred to as **normal costing**. This approach, which takes its name from the use of an overhead rate that is **normalized** over a fairly long period, is used in the Rocky Mountain Outfitters illustration.

> "We use an actual costing system for the costs incurred in producing a feature film." (3e)
> The Walt Disney Company

Exhibit 3–11
Ledger Accounts for Rocky
Mountain Outfitters
Illustration*

ROCKY MOUNTAIN
OUTFITTERS

Accounts Receivable		
Bal.	11,000	
(10)	54,000	

Accounts Payable		
	3,000	Bal.
	10,000	(1)
	6,000	(6)
	1,000	(8)

Prepaid Insurance		
Bal.	2,000	1,000	(6)

Wages Payable		
	10,000	Bal.
	21,000	(4)
	14,000	(5)
	12,000	(8)

Prepaid Rent		
Bal.	5,000		
		3,000	(6)
		1,500	(8)

Office Supplies Inventory		
Bal.	900	300	(8)

Manufacturing Supplies Inventory		
Bal.	750	50	(3)

Accumulated Depreciation: Equipment		
		105,000	Bal.
		5,000	(6)

Raw-Material Inventory		
Bal.	30,000	34,000	(2)
(1)	10,000		

Manufacturing Overhead			
(3)	50	28,800	(7)
(5)	14,000	250	(12)
(6)	15,000		

Work-in-Process Inventory		
Bal.	4,000	48,000	(9)
(2)	34,000		
(4)	21,000		
(7)	28,800		

Cost of Goods Sold		
(11)	36,000	
(12)	250	

Finished-Goods Inventory		
Bal.	12,000	36,000	(11)
(9)	48,000		

Selling and Administrative Expenses		
(8)	14,800	

Sales Revenue		
	54,000	(10)

*The numbers in parentheses relate T-account entries to the associated journal entries. The numbers in colour are the November 1 account balances.

A few companies use **actual costing**, a system in which direct material and direct labour are added to work in process at their actual amounts, and actual overhead is allocated to work in process using an **actual overhead rate** computed at the *end* of each accounting period. Note that even though an actual overhead rate is used, the amount of overhead assigned to each production job is still an allocated amount.

Overhead costs, which are by definition indirect costs, cannot be traced easily to individual production jobs. Actual and normal costing may be summarized as follows:

ACTUAL COSTING Work-in-Process Inventory		NORMAL COSTING Work-in-Process Inventory	
Actual direct- material costs Actual direct- labour costs Overhead allocated:		Actual direct- material costs Actual direct- labour costs Overhead applied:	
Actual overhead rate (computed at *end of* period)	Actual amount of × cost driver used (e.g., direct-labour hours)	*Predetermined* overhead rate (computed at *beginning* of period)	Actual amount of × cost driver used (e.g., direct-labour hours)

Choosing a Cost Driver for Overhead Application

Manufacturing overhead includes various indirect manufacturing costs that vary greatly in their relationship to the production process. If a single, volume-based cost driver (or activity base) is used in calculating the predetermined overhead rate, it should be some productive input that is common across all of the firm's products. If, for example, all of the firm's products require direct labour, but only some products require machine time, direct-labour hours would be a preferable activity base. If machine time were used as the base, products not requiring machine time would not be assigned any overhead cost.

In selecting a volume-based cost driver (or activity base), the goal is to choose an input that varies in a pattern that is most similar to the pattern with which overhead costs vary. Products that indirectly cause large amounts of overhead costs also should require large amounts of the cost driver, and vice versa. During periods when the cost driver is at a low level, the overhead costs incurred should be low. Thus, there should be a correlation between the incurrence of overhead costs and use of the cost driver.

Limitation of Direct Labour as a Cost Driver   In traditional product-costing systems, the most common volume-based cost drivers are direct-labour hours and direct-labour cost. However, there is a trend away from using direct labour as the overhead application base. Many production processes are becoming increasingly automated, through the use of robotics and computer-integrated manufacturing systems. Increased automation brings two results. First, manufacturing-overhead costs represent a larger proportion of total production costs. Second, direct labour decreases in importance as a factor of production. As direct labour declines in importance as a productive input, it becomes less appropriate as a cost driver. For this reason, some firms have switched to machine hours, process time, or throughput time as cost drivers that better reflect the pattern of overhead cost incurrence. **Throughput time** (or **cycle time**) is the average amount of time required to convert raw materials into finished goods ready to be shipped to customers. Throughput time includes the time required for material handling, production processing, inspection, and packaging.

> "As we continue to automate our production processes, direct labour is becoming less and less appropriate as a basis for the application of manufacturing overhead." (3f)
> **Chrysler**

Departmental Overhead Rates

In the Rocky Mountain Outfitters illustration presented earlier in this chapter, all of the firm's manufacturing overhead was combined into a single cost pool. Then the overhead was applied to products using a single predetermined overhead rate based on machine hours. Since only one overhead rate is used in Rocky Mountain Outfitters' entire factory, it is known as a **plantwide overhead rate**. In some production processes, the relationship between overhead costs and the firm's products differs substantially across production departments. In such cases, the firm may use **departmental overhead rates**, which differ across production departments. This usually results in a more accurate assignment of overhead costs to the firm's products. This process is described in the chapter's appendix. An even more detailed assignment of overhead costs can be achieved with *activity-based costing (ABC)*. ABC is covered extensively in Chapter 5.

Management
Accounting
Practice

General Motors and
Boeing

ARE LAYOFFS A GOOD WAY TO CUT COSTS DURING AN ECONOMIC DOWNTURN?

"At many companies, bolstering the bottom line by cutting jobs is the favored method for coping with a downturn. Yet layoffs often prove to be a flawed strategy. Companies that capriciously cut key employees often lose the talent they need to compete effectively. Those that cut too many positions may also end up paying hefty severance packages and then have to spend even more to find replacements once the recovery occurs. Rather than plan ahead in good times for what they will do if the economy slows, executives typically wait until they feel their backs are against the wall. Then they decide 'let's take out 2 percent or 5 percent of labor costs across divisions,' says David Kieffer, a principal at consultant William M. Mercer. 'They say this is the fairest way, but in taking this approach they focus only on the cost of labor rather than the value created by labor.'"[1]

As an example, consider the case of General Motors. The auto maker has recently announced a major cutback in capacity, which will entail closing several plants and idling thousands of workers. While such a move will save billions in cash in the short term, will it come back to haunt the company if demand for GM vehicles picks up again? Another example is Boeing, which announced a cut of 30,000 workers in its commercial aircraft division right after the September 11 terrorist attacks. Some wondered at the time if Boeing was moving too fast. Now it turns out that Boeing is rebounding quickly, largely because of introducing new aircraft models. Some are speculating that the new Boeing 787, built mostly of plastic composites, may remould the airline industry. Will Boeing have the skilled labour force it needs to carry off its bold new production program?[2]

Project Costing: Job-Order Costing in Nonmanufacturing Organizations

Learning Objective 7

Demonstrate the process of project costing used in service industry firms and nonprofit organizations.

METRO
ADVERTISING

Job-order costing also is used in service industry companies and other nonmanufacturing organizations. However, rather than referring to production "jobs," such organizations use terminology that reflects their operations. For example, hospitals such as the Vancouver Children's Hospital assign costs to "cases," and consulting firms like McKinsey track "contract" costs. Law firms assign costs to cases, while government agencies typically refer to "programs" or "missions." The need for cost accumulation exists in these and similar organizations for the same reasons found in manufacturing firms. For example, a mission to launch a commercial satellite by NASA or Arianespace is assigned a cost for the purposes of planning, cost control, and pricing of the launch service.

To illustrate the cost-accumulation system used in a service industry firm, let's turn our attention to Metro Advertising Agency in St. John's, Newfoundland. This small ad agency has two managing partners who pay themselves annual salaries of $100,000 each, and an artistic staff of six people who each earns $50,000 per year. Fringe benefits for these professionals average 40 percent of their compensation. So Metro Advertising Agency's direct professional labour budget is as follows:

Partner salaries..	$200,000
Partner benefits (40%)	80,000
Total partner compensation	$280,000
Artistic staff salaries	$300,000
Artistic staff benefits (40%)	120,000
Total artistic staff compensation	$420,000

The ad agency's annual overhead budget, which totals $756,000, appears in Exhibit 3–12. The overhead budget includes the costs of the support staff, artistic and

METRO ADVERTISING AGENCY Annual Overhead Budget For the Year 20x6	
Support staff:	
Receptionist..	$ 32,000
Secretarial...	70,000
Accounting...	40,000
Custodial...	29,000
Support staff benefits...	68,400
Artistic supplies..	160,000
Photographic supplies..	120,000
Office:	
Computer..	20,000
Photocopying..	15,000
Office supplies..	18,000
Postage..	2,100
Utilities:	
Electricity..	13,000
Heat/air conditioning...	16,000
Internet access...	1,500
Cable TV..	2,000
Telephone...	3,100
Trash collection...	2,400
Other..	2,500
Building rent...	50,000
Insurance...	15,000
Advertising...	20,000
Vehicle maintenance..	4,000
Depreciation:	
Equipment...	12,000
Vehicles..	20,000
Other...	20,000
Total overhead..	$756,000

Exhibit 3–12
Metro Advertising Agency:
Annual Overhead Budget

photographic supplies, office operation, utilities, rent, insurance, advertising, vehicle maintenance, and depreciation. Metro's accountant has estimated that one-third of the budgeted overhead cost is incurred to support the ad agency's two partners, and two-thirds of it goes to support the artistic staff. Thus, the following two overhead rates are calculated.

$$\frac{\text{Budgeted annual partner support overhead}}{\text{Budgeted annual partner compensation}} = \frac{\$756,000 \times \frac{1}{3}}{\$280,000} = 90\%$$

$$\frac{\text{Budgeted annual artistic staff support overhead}}{\text{Budgeted annual artistic staff compensation}} = \frac{\$756,000 \times \frac{2}{3}}{\$420,000} = 120\%$$

Overhead is assigned to each ad contract at the rate of 90 percent of partner direct professional labour plus 120 percent of artistic staff direct professional labour. During May, Metro Advertising Agency completed an advertising project for Super Scoop Ice Cream Company. The contract required $1,800 in direct material, $1,200 of partner direct professional labour, and $2,000 of artistic staff direct professional labour. The total cost of the contract is computed as follows:

Contract MJH0207: Advertising Program **for Super Scoop Ice Cream Company**	
Direct material	$1,800
Direct professional labour (partner)	1,200
Direct professional labour (artistic staff)......................	2,000
Applied overhead:	
Partner support ($1,200 × 90%)	1,080
Artistic staff support ($2,000 × 120%)	2,400
Total cost	$8,480

The total contract cost of $8,480 includes actual direct material and direct professional labour costs, and applied overhead based on the predetermined overhead rates for partner support costs and artistic staff support costs. The contract cost can be used by the firm in controlling costs, for planning cash flows and operations, and as one informational input in its contract-pricing decisions. In addition to the contract cost, the firm also should consider the demand for its advertising services and the prices charged by its competitors.

The discussion above provides only a brief overview of cost-accumulation procedures in service industry and nonprofit organizations. The main point is that job-order costing systems are used in a wide variety of organizations, and these systems provide important information to managers for planning, decision making, and control.

Changing Technology in Manufacturing Operations

The technology of manufacturing is changing rapidly. These technological changes often affect the managerial accounting procedures used to collect data and transmit information to the intended users. Three such technological changes are electronic data interchange (EDI), Extensible Markup Language (XML), and the use of bar codes.

Electronic Data Interchange

Electronic data interchange (EDI) is the direct exchange of data between organizations via a computer-to-computer interface. EDI is used to transmit such documents as purchase orders, shipping notices, receiving notices, invoices, and a host of other production-related data. This eliminates the need for paperwork, speeding up the flow of information and substantially reducing errors. EDI is now in widespread use. For example, Wal-Mart places most of its merchandise orders to its suppliers using this information technology.

A recently developed alternative to EDI is *Extensible Markup Language (XML)*, which is Web-based and less expensive to implement than EDI. Its purpose is to allow users to share structured data (e.g., product order lists or price data) via the Internet. XML allows its users to define "tags," which the computer then interprets as a particular type of information. For example, a tag might indicate a product's in-stock date or price. See www.xml.com for a primer on this rapidly growing Web-based data-sharing tool.

Management
Accounting
Practice

Wal-Mart, the U.S.
Department of Defense,
GlaxoSmithKline,
Bell Canada, and CN

RADIO FREQUENCY IDENTIFICATION SYSTEMS (RFID)

Bar codes are in some places being replaced by radio frequency identification systems (RFID). Unlike bar codes, which can be read by a scanner only when visible, the RFID system allows the information to be read from longer distances and without visibility. For example, a raw-material shipment that embeds the RFID system could be identified while still unpacked or in a delivery truck. Among the benefits attributed to RFID systems are reduced labour costs, fewer supply delays, and a reduction of waste in the supply chain.[3] Leading the move toward RFID systems are Wal-Mart and the U.S. Department of Defense. "Both organizations have mandated that their suppliers comply with their RFID guidelines." GlaxoSmithKline is putting RFID tags on bottles of some of its medications.[4] The Bell Canada RFID-enabled asset management solution allows CN, the Canadian National Railway Company, to accurately manage incoming and outgoing truck chassis wirelessly, resulting in an increase in supply chain efficiency, productivity, and cost savings.

Use of Bar Codes

We have all seen bar codes used to record inventory and sales information in retail stores. This efficient means of recording data also is becoming widely used in recording important events in manufacturing processes. Production employees can record the time they begin working on a particular job order by scanning the bar code on their employee ID badge and a bar code assigned to the production job order. When raw materials arrive at the production facility, their bar code is scanned and the event is recorded. Inventory records are updated automatically. Raw materials and partially completed components are assigned bar codes, and their movement throughout the production process is efficiently recorded. For example, raw materials may be requisitioned by a production employee simply by scanning the bar code assigned to the needed raw materials. When the materials are sent from the warehouse to the requisitioning production department, the bar code is scanned again. Inventory records are updated instantly. Bar codes represent one more instance where technology is changing both the production environment and the procedures used in accounting for production operations.

"Each production job, from beginning to end, can take several weeks. Bar code technology is used extensively. The container that carries the work in process is bar-coded, and we use that to track each job." (3h)
MiCRUS (joint venture of IBM and Cirrus Logic)

Focus on Ethics

DID BOEING EXPLOIT ACCOUNTING RULES TO CONCEAL COST OVERRUNS AND PRODUCTION SNAFUS?

Aircraft manufacturers use job-order costing to determine the cost of an airplane. Supply chain management and production controls are also important tools used by manufacturers to manage production costs. As *Business-Week* reports, however, things don't always go according to plan.

For three years, Boeing's top management had been seeking a merger with McDonnell-Douglas Corporation, whose board of directors was reluctant to approve the deal. Finally, the deal went through, and the world's largest aerospace company was born—"the first manufacturer ever with the ability to build everything that flies, from helicopters and fighter jets to space stations."

Unfortunately, "a disaster was quietly unfolding inside Boeing's sprawling factories—one that would ultimately wind up costing billions of dollars, cause several executives to lose their jobs, and lead to claims of accounting fraud. Facing an unprecedented surge in orders because of a booming economy, workers were toiling around the clock, pushing the assembly line to the breaking point. At the same time, the company was struggling to overhaul outdated production methods. These pressures were building up to what was, in essence, a manufacturing nervous breakdown. In the weeks after the merger announcement, parts shortages and overtime approached all-time highs. As costs went through the roof, the profitability of airliners such as the 777 swooned. A special team formed to study the crisis issued a report with a blunt conclusion: 'Our production system is broken.'"

Had investors "understood the scope of the problems, the stock would probably have tumbled and the McDonnell deal—a stock swap that hinged on Boeing's ability to maintain a lofty share price—would have been jeopardized."

In May of 2002, *BusinessWeek* reported the results of its three-month investigation, which "reconstructed this hidden chapter in the company's history—and analyzed its current implications." The *BusinessWeek* article alleges that "new details supplied by several inside witnesses indicate that Boeing did more than simply fail to tell investors about its production disaster. It also engaged in a wide variety of aggressive accounting techniques that papered over the mess. Critics say the company should have taken charges for the assembly-line disaster in the first half of 1997, even if it meant jeopardizing the McDonnell merger. They also claim that Boeing took advantage of the unusual flexibility provided by *program accounting*—a system that allows the huge upfront expense of building a plane to be spread out over several years—to cover up cost overruns and to book savings from efficiency initiatives that never panned out. 'Boeing managed its earnings to the point where it got caught,' says Debra A. Smith, a partner at Constraints Management, a Seattle-area manufacturing consultancy, and a former senior auditor at Deloitte & Touche who worked on the company's account during the early 1980s. 'Boeing basically decided in the short run that [managing earnings] was a lesser evil than losing the merger,' adds Smith. At a time when investors are asking themselves how far Corporate America can be trusted, the Boeing saga provides rich new evidence that companies have much greater leeway to manipulate their numbers than most people suspect."[5]

Boeing allegedly used program accounting to spread their huge cost overruns across several years, propping up earnings and the company's share price. After the merger, however, the truth came out in the form of much lower earnings.

What is your view of how Boeing handled its cost overruns, production problems, and the merger? Did the company's top executives act ethically? How about their accountants?

Chapter Summary

Product costing is the process of accumulating the costs of a production process and assigning them to the firm's products. Product costs are needed for three major purposes: (1) to value inventory and cost of goods sold in financial accounting; (2) to provide managerial accounting information to managers for planning, cost control, and decision making; and (3) to provide cost data to various organizations outside the firm, such as governmental agencies or insurance companies. Information about the costs of producing goods and services is needed in manufacturing companies, service industry firms, and nonprofit organizations.

Two types of product-costing systems are used, depending on the nature of product manufactured. Process costing is used by companies that produce large numbers of nearly identical products, such as canned dog food and motor oil. Job-order costing, the topic of this chapter, is used by firms that engage in either job-shop or batch-production operations. Such firms produce relatively small numbers of dissimilar products, such as feature films, custom furniture, and major kitchen appliances.

In a job-order costing system, the costs of direct material, direct labour, and manufacturing overhead are first entered into the Work-in-Process Inventory account. When goods are completed, the accumulated manufacturing costs are transferred from Work-in-Process Inventory to Finished-Goods Inventory. Finally, these product costs are transferred from Finished-Goods Inventory to Cost of Goods Sold when sales occur. Direct material and direct labour are traced easily to specific batches of production, called job orders. In contrast, manufacturing overhead is an indirect cost with respect to job orders or units of product. Therefore, overhead is applied to production jobs using a predetermined overhead rate, which is based on estimates of manufacturing overhead and the level of some cost driver (or activity base). The most commonly used volume-based cost drivers are direct-labour hours, direct-labour cost, and machine hours. Since these estimates will seldom be completely accurate, the amount of overhead applied during an accounting period to Work-in-Process Inventory will usually differ from the actual costs incurred for overhead items. The difference between actual overhead and applied overhead, called *overapplied* or *underapplied overhead*, may be closed out into Cost of Goods Sold or prorated among Work-in-Process Inventory, Finished-Goods Inventory, and Cost of Goods Sold.

The accuracy of product costs often can be increased by the use of departmental overhead rates instead of a single, plantwide overhead rate.

Job-order costing methods also are used in a variety of service industry firms and nonprofit organizations. Accumulating costs of projects, contracts, cases, programs, or missions provides important information to managers in such organizations as hospitals, law firms, and government agencies.

Review Problem on Job-Order Costing

Piedmont Paint Company uses a job-order costing system, and the company had two jobs in process at the beginning of the current year. Job JY65 currently has a cost of $134,400 assigned to it, and job DC66 currently has a cost of $85,600 assigned to it. The following additional information is available.

- The company applies manufacturing overhead on the basis of machine hours. Budgeted overhead and machine activity for the year were anticipated to be $1,344,000 and 16,000 hours, respectively.

- The company worked on four jobs during the first quarter. Direct materials used, direct labour incurred, and machine hours consumed were as follows:

Job No.	Direct Material	Direct Labour	Machine Hours
JY65	$33,600	$ 56,000	1,200
DC66	—	35,200	700
SG78	70,400	104,000	2,000
RG82	24,000	14,080	500

- Manufacturing overhead during the first quarter included charges for depreciation ($54,400), indirect labour ($96,000), indirect materials used ($8,000), and other factory costs ($223,200).

- Piedmont Paint Company completed job JY65 and job DC66. Job DC66 was sold on account, producing a profit of $55,520 for the firm.

Required:

1. Determine Piedmont Paint Company's predetermined overhead application rate.

2. Prepare journal entries as of March 31 to record the following. (*Note:* Use summary entries where appropriate by combining individual job data.)

    a.   The issuance of direct material to production and the direct labour incurred

    b.   The manufacturing overhead incurred during the quarter

    c.   The application of manufacturing overhead to production

    d.   The completion of jobs JY65 and DC66

    e.   The sale of job DC66

3. Determine the cost of the jobs still in production as of March 31

4. Did the finished-goods inventory increase or decrease during the first quarter? By how much?

5. Was manufacturing overhead under- or overapplied for the first quarter of the year? By how much?

Solution to Review Problem

1. Predetermined overhead rate = Budgeted overhead ÷ Budgeted machine hours
    = $1,344,000 ÷ 16,000 = $84 per machine hour

2. *(a)*   Work-in-Process Inventory 128,000*
    Raw-Material Inventory..   128,000

    Work-in-Process Inventory .... 209,280†
    Wages Payable..   209,280

    *$33,600 + $70,400 + $24,000 = $128,000

    †$56,000 + $35,200 + $104,000 + $14,080 = $209,280

    (b)   Manufacturing Overhead... 381,600
    Accumulated Depreciation   54,400
    Wages Payable...   96,000
    Manufacturing Supplies Inventory   8,000
    Miscellaneous Accounts   223,200

    (c)   Work-in-Process Inventory 369,600*
    Manufacturing Overhead...   369,600

    *(1,200 + 700 + 2,000 + 500) × $84 = $369,600.

    (d)   Finished-Goods Inventory 504,400*
    Work-in-Process Inventory...   504,400

    *Job JY65: $134,400 + $33,600 + $56,000 + (1,200 × $84) = $324,800
    Job DC66: $85,600 + $35,200 + (700 × $84) = $179,600
    $504,400 = $324,800 + $179,600

    (e)   Accounts Receivable 235,120*
    Sales Revenue...   235,120

    *$179,600 + $55,520 = $235,120.

    Cost of Goods Sold.. 179,600
    Finished-Goods Inventory   179,600

3. Job SG78 and RG82 are in production as of March 31:

    Job SG78: $70,400 + $104,000 + (2,000 × $84)........................ $342,400
    Job RG82: $24,000 + $14,080 + (500 × $84)   80,080
    Total... $422,480

4. Finished-goods inventory increased by $324,800 ($504,400 − $179,600).

5. The company's actual overhead amounted to $381,600, whereas applied overhead totalled $369,600. Thus, overhead was underapplied by $12,000.

Key Terms

For each term's definition refer to the indicated page, or turn to the glossary at the end of the text.

activity base, 76

actual costing, 86

actual manufacturing
    overhead, 80

actual overhead rate, 86

applied manufacturing
    overhead, 79

cost distribution (*or* cost
    allocation),* 95

cost of goods manufac-
    tured, 84

cycle time, 87

departmental overhead
    centres,* 95

departmental overhead
    rate, 88

job-cost record, 73

job-order costing, 71

material requisition form, 73

normal costing, 85

normalized overhead rate, 85

overapplied overhead, 82

overhead application (*or*
    absorption), 75

period costs, 81

plantwide overhead rate, 88

predetermined overhead
    rate, 76

process-costing system, 72

product-costing
    system, 69

proration, 83

schedule of cost of goods
    manufactured, 84

schedule of cost of goods
    sold, 85

service department cost
    allocation,* 95

service departments,* 95

source document, 74

throughput time, 87

time record, 74

two-stage cost
    allocation,* 95

underapplied
    overhead, 82

volume-based cost
    driver, 76

*Term appears in the Appendix to this chapter.

APPENDIX TO CHAPTER 3

Two-Stage Cost Allocation for Departmental Overhead Rates

When a company uses departmental overhead rates, the assignment of manufacturing-overhead costs to production jobs is accomplished in two stages, which make up what is called **two-stage cost allocation**. In the first stage, all manufacturing overhead costs are assigned to the production departments, such as machining and assembly. In the second stage, the overhead costs that have been assigned to each production department are applied to the production jobs that pass through the department. Let's examine this process in more detail.

- *Stage 1.* In the first stage, all manufacturing overhead costs are assigned to the firm's production departments. However, stage one often involves two different types of allocation processes. First, all manufacturing overhead costs are assigned to **departmental overhead centres**. This step is called **cost distribution** (or sometimes **cost allocation**). For example, the costs of heating a factory with natural gas would be distributed among all of the departments in the factory, possibly in proportion to the cubic metres of space in each department. In the cost distribution step, manufacturing overhead costs are assigned to *both* production departments and service departments. **Service departments**, such as equipment-maintenance and material-handling departments, are departments that do not work directly on the firm's products but are necessary for production to take place.

    Second, all service department costs are reassigned to the production departments through a process called **service department cost allocation**. In this step, an attempt is made to allocate service department costs on the basis of the relative proportion of each service department's output that is used by the various production departments. For example, production departments with more equipment would be allocated a larger share of the maintenance department's costs.

    At the conclusion of stage one, all manufacturing overhead costs have been assigned to the production departments.

Learning Objective 8

Apply the two-stage allocation process used to compute departmental overhead rates.

"We're going to have much more general knowledge of how the business works." (3i)

Boeing

Exhibit 3–13
Developing Departmental
Overhead Rates Using
Two-Stage Allocation

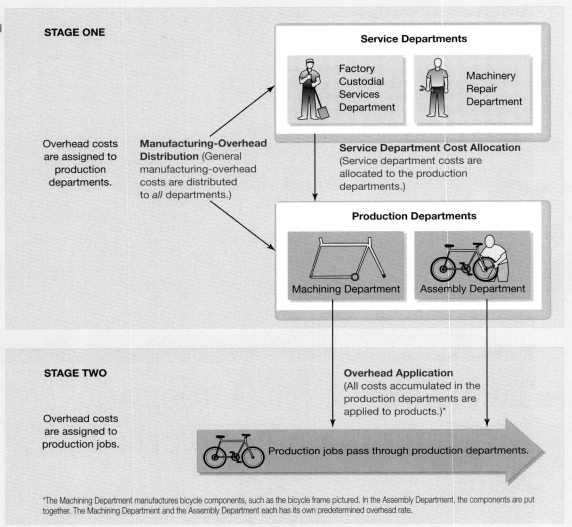

*The Machining Department manufactures bicycle components, such as the bicycle frame pictured. In the Assembly Department, the components are put together. The Machining Department and the Assembly Department each has its own predetermined overhead rate.

- *Stage 2.* In the second stage, all of the manufacturing overhead costs accumulated in each production department are assigned to the production jobs on which the department has worked. This process is called *overhead application* (or sometimes *overhead absorption*). In stage 2, each production department has its own predetermined overhead rate. These rates often are based on different cost drivers.

The two-stage process of assigning overhead costs to production jobs is portrayed in Exhibit 3–13. Notice the roles of cost distribution, service department cost allocation, and overhead application in the Exhibit. The techniques of overhead distribution and service department cost allocation will be covered later in the text. In this chapter, we are focusing primarily on the process of overhead application.[6]

Different Overhead Rates under Plantwide and Departmental Costing Systems

The accuracy of a product-costing system is affected by the number of cost drivers and overhead rates. A single, plantwide overhead rate based on only one volume-related cost driver generally is the least accurate. It is also the simplest system, however, and is the most commonly used method. A two-stage allocation process resulting in multiple departmental overhead rates typically will improve the accuracy of the product-costing system. This is particularly true when the production technology differs markedly among the departments. If, for example, one department relies chiefly on manual labour, while another department makes heavy use of machinery, departmental overhead rates with different cost drivers generally will increase product-costing accuracy.

Let's examine the effects of two alternative product-costing systems at Delta Controls Corporation, which manufactures two types of sophisticated control valves used in the food processing industry. Valve A has been Delta's main product for 15 years; it is used to control the flow of milk in various food processing operations, such as the production of cookies. Valve B, a more recently introduced product, is a specialty valve used to control the flow of thicker foods such as jelly and applesauce. The basic data for the illustration follow:

	Valve A	Valve B
Annual production and sales...	30,000 units	5,000 units
Direct material...	$ 140	$ 140
Direct labour:		
Machining Department...	30 (1.5 hrs. @ $20)	30 (1.5 hrs. @ $20)
Assembly Department..	30 (1.5 hrs. @ $20)	30 (1.5 hrs. @ $20)
Total prime costs	$ 200	$ 200
Machine time in Machining Department	1 h	3 h
Budgeted overhead costs:		
Machining Department...	$ 630,000	
Assembly Department..	315,000	
Total	$ 945,000	

Now let's compute the applied overhead cost per valve under two alternative product-costing systems.

Plantwide Overhead Rate

Using a single, plantwide overhead rate based on direct-labour hours (DLH), each product is assigned $27 of overhead per unit.

	Valve A	Valve B
Applied overhead per unit*	$27 (3 DLH @ $9 per DLH)	$27 (3 DLH @ $9 per DLH)

*Total budgeted DLH = (30,000 units of A)(3 DLH per unit) + (5,000 units of B)(3 DLH per unit) = 105,000 DLH.

$$\text{Predetermined overhead rate} = \frac{\text{Total budgeted overhead}}{\text{Total budgeted DLH}} = \frac{\$945,000}{105,000} = \$9 \text{ per DLH}$$

Adding the $200 of prime costs for each valve, we have product costs of $227 per unit for each type of valve.

Departmental Overhead Rates

Now suppose we use departmental overhead rates. The Machining Department rate is based on machine hours (MH), whereas the Assembly Department rate is based on direct-labour hours (DLH). This approach yields assigned overhead costs of $23 per unit of valve A and $51 per unit of valve B.

	Valve A	Valve B
Applied overhead per unit:		
Machining Department*	$14 (1 MH @ $14 per MH)	$42 (3 MH @ $14 per MH)
Assembly Department†	9 (1.5 DLH @ $6 per DLH)	9 (1.5 DLH @ $6 per DLH)
Total	$23	$51

*Total budgeted MH = (30,000 units of A)(1 MH per unit) + 5,000 units of B)(3 MH per unit) = 45,000 MH.

$$\text{Machining Department overhead rate} = \frac{\text{Machining Department overhead}}{\text{Budgeted MH}} = \frac{\$630,000}{45,000} = \$14 \text{ per MH}$$

†Total budgeted DLH in Assembly Department = (30,000 units of A)(1.5 DLH) + (5,000 units of B)(1.5 DLH) = 52,500 DLH.

$$\text{Assembly Department overhead rate} = \frac{\text{Assembly Department overhead}}{\text{Budgeted DLH}} = \frac{\$315,000}{52,500} = \$6 \text{ per DLH}$$

Adding the $200 of prime costs for each valve, we have product costs of $223 for each unit of valve A and $251 for each unit of valve B. Valve A, which spends considerably less time in the more costly Machining Department than valve B, is now assigned a lower product cost than it was when a plantwide overhead rate was used. In contrast, valve B's assigned product cost has increased.

Summary

The following table compares the total reported product costs of each product under the two alternative product-costing systems.

	Valve A	Valve B
Plantwide overhead rate	$227	$227
Departmental overhead rates	223	251

The use of departmental overhead rates yields a more accurate product cost for each valve. Notice that the use of a plantwide overhead rate overcosts the high-volume and relatively simple valve A, and undercosts the low-volume and complex valve B.

Review Questions

3–1. List and explain four purposes of product costing.

3–2. Explain the difference between job-order and process costing.

3–3. How is the concept of product costing applied in service industry firms?

3–4. What are the purposes of the following documents: (*a*) material requisition form, (*b*) labour time record, and (*c*) job-cost record.

3–5. Why is manufacturing overhead applied to products when product costs are used in making pricing decisions?

3–6. Explain the benefits of using a predetermined overhead rate instead of an actual overhead rate.

3–7. Describe one advantage and one disadvantage of pro-rating overapplied or underapplied overhead.

3–8. Describe an important cost-benefit issue involving accuracy versus timeliness in accounting for overhead.

3–9. Explain the difference between actual and normal costing.

3–10. When a single, volume-based cost driver (or activity base) is used to apply manufacturing overhead, what is the managerial accountant's primary objective in selecting the cost driver?

3–11. Describe how job-order costing concepts are used in hospitals.

3–12. What is meant by the term *cost driver*? What is a *volume-based cost driver*?

3–13. Describe the flow of costs through a product-costing system. What special accounts are involved, and how are they used?

3–14. Give an example of how a hospital might use job-order costing concepts.

3–15. Why are some manufacturing firms switching from direct-labour hours to machine hours or throughput time as the basis for overhead application?

3–16. What is the cause of overapplied or underapplied overhead?

3–17. Briefly describe two ways of closing out overapplied or underapplied overhead at the end of an accounting period.

3–18. (Appendix) Describe some costs and benefits of using multiple overhead rates instead of a plantwide overhead rate.

3–19. (Appendix) Describe the process of two-stage cost allocation in the development of departmental overhead rates.

3–20. (Appendix) Define each of the following terms, and explain the relationship among them: (*a*) overhead cost distribution, (*b*) service department cost allocation, and (*c*) overhead application.

Exercises

■ **Exercise 3–21**
Job-Order versus Process Costing
(LO 1, 3)

For each of the following companies, indicate whether job-order or process costing is more appropriate.

1. Manufacturer of household cleaning solutions
2. Manufacturer of custom hot tubs and spas
3. Architectural firm
4. Manufacturer of ceramic tile
5. Producer of yogurt

6. Manufacturer of custom tool sheds
7. Manufacturer of papers clips
8. Engineering consulting firm
9. Manufacturer of balloons
10. Manufacturer of custom sailboats

The controller for Tender Bird Poultry, Inc. estimates that the company's fixed overhead is $150,000 per year. She also has determined that the variable overhead is approximately $.15 per chicken raised and sold. Since the firm has a single product, overhead is applied on the basis of output units, chickens raised and sold.

Exercise 3–22
Fixed and Variable Costs; Overhead Rate; Agribusiness
(LO 1, 4)

Required:

1. Calculate the predetermined overhead rate under each of the following output predictions: 100,000 chickens, 200,000 chickens, and 300,000 chickens.
2. Does the predetermined overhead rate change in proportion to the change in predicted production? Why?

Dewitt Educational Products started and finished job number RM67 during June. The job required $5,100 of direct material and 40 hours of direct labour at $18 per hour. The predetermined overhead rate is $6 per direct-labour hour.

Exercise 3–23
Basic Journal Entries in Job-Order Costing
(LO 5)

Required: Prepare journal entries to record the incurrence of production costs and the completion of job number RM67.

Visit the Web site of a film producer, such as Disney, MGM, or Warner Brothers.

Walt Disney Studios   www.disney.com

MGM   www.mgm.com

Warner Brothers   www.warnerbros.com

Exercise 3–24
Job-Order Costing; Feature Film Production; Use of Internet
(LO 1, 3)

Required: Read about one of the company's recent (or upcoming) film releases. Then discuss why or why not job-order costing would be an appropriate costing method for feature film production. Would your answer be any different depending on the type of film being produced (e.g., animation in a studio versus filming on location in Timbuktu)?

Rexford Company manufactures finger splints for kids who get tendonitis from playing video games. The firm had the following inventories at the beginning and end of the month of January.

Exercise 3–25
Job-Order Costing Basics
(LO 2, 4, 6)

	January 1	January 31
Finished goods	$162,500	$152,100
Work in process	305,500	326,300
Raw material	174,200	161,200

The following additional data pertain to January operations.

Raw material purchased	$248,300
Direct labour	390,000
Actual manufacturing overhead	227,500
Actual selling and administrative expenses	230,000

Rexford Company applies manufacturing overhead at the rate of 70 percent of direct-labour cost. Any overapplied or underapplied manufacturing overhead is accumulated until the end of the year.

Required: Compute the following amounts.

1. The company's prime cost for January
2. The total manufacturing cost for January
3. The cost of goods manufactured for January

4.   The cost of goods sold for January
5.   The balance in the Manufacturing Overhead account on January 31. Debit or credit?

(CMA, adapted)

■ **Exercise 3–26**
Cost Relationships, Normal
Costing System
(LO 2, 6)

Cherry Hill Glass Company employs a normal costing system. The following information pertains to the year just ended.

- Total manufacturing costs were $1,250,000.
- Cost of goods manufactured was $1,212,500.
- Applied manufacturing overhead was 30 percent of total manufacturing costs.
- Manufacturing overhead was applied to production at a rate of 80 percent of direct-labour cost.
- Work-in-process inventory on January 1 was 75 percent of work-in-process inventory on December 31.

Required:

1.   Compute Cherry Hill's total direct-labour cost for the year.
2.   Calculate the total cost of direct material used during the year.
3.   Compute the value of the company's work-in-process inventory on December 31.

(CMA, adapted)

■ **Exercise 3–27**
Job-Cost Record
(LO 2, 3, 4)

Shawn Toy Company incurred the following costs to produce job number TB78, which consisted of 1,000 teddy bears that can walk, talk, and play cards.

Direct material:
   8/11/x0 Requisition number 201: 500 metres of fabric at $.90 per metre
   8/12/x0 Requisition number 208: 600 cubic metres of stuffing at $.40 per cubic metre
Direct labour:
   From employee time cards for 8/11/x0 through 8/15/x0: 550 hours at $14 per hour
Manufacturing overhead:
   Applied on the basis of direct-labour hours at $3 per hour.

Job number TB78 was finished on August 20. On August 30, 800 of the bears were shipped to a local toy store.

Required: Prepare a job-cost record using the information given above. (Use Exhibit 3–4 as a guide.)

■ **Exercise 3–28**
Schedule of Cost of Goods
Manufactured
(LO 2, 6)

Crunchem Cereal Company incurred the following actual costs during 20x4:

Direct material used	$412,500
Direct labour	180,000
Manufacturing overhead	378,000

The firm's predetermined overhead rate is 210 percent of direct-labour cost. The January 1 inventory balances were as follows:

Raw material	$45,000
Work in process	58,500
Finished goods	63,000

Each of these inventory balances was 10 percent higher at the end of the year.

Required:

1.   Prepare a schedule of cost of goods manufactured for 20x4.
2.   What was the cost of goods sold for the year?
3.   *Build a spreadsheet:* Construct an Excel spreadsheet to solve all of the preceding requirements. Show how the solution will change if the following data change: direct material used amounted to $409,000 and raw-material inventory on December 31 was $43,000.

Jay Sports Equipment Company, Inc. incurred the following costs during 20x2:

■ **Exercise 3–29**
Manufacturing Cost Flows
(LO 2, 5, 6)

Direct material used	$226,200
Direct labour..	421,200
Manufacturing overhead applied	234,000

During 20x2, products costing $156,000 were finished, and products costing $171,600 were sold on account for $253,500. There were no purchases of raw material during the year. The beginning balances in the firm's inventory accounts are as follows:

Raw material	$295,100
Work in process	23,400
Finished goods	39,000

Required:

1. Prepare T-accounts to show the flow of costs through the company's manufacturing accounts during 20x2.
2. Prepare a partial balance sheet and a partial income statement to reflect the information given above. (*Hint:* See Exhibit 3–2.)

Selected data concerning the past year's operations of the Yukon Manufacturing Company are as follows:

■ **Exercise 3–30**
Basic Manufacturing Cost
Flows
(LO 2, 6)

	Inventories	
	Beginning	**Ending**
Raw material	$142,000	$ 162,000
Work in process	160,000	60,000
Finished goods	180,000	220,000
Other data:		
Direct material used		$ 652,000
Total manufacturing costs charged to production during the year (includes direct material, direct labour, and manufacturing overhead applied at a rate of 60% of direct-labour cost)		1,372,000
Cost of goods available for sale		1,652,000
Selling and administrative expenses		63,000

Required:

1. What was the cost of raw materials purchased during the year?
2. What was the direct-labour cost charged to production during the year?
3. What was the cost of goods manufactured during the year?
4. What was the cost of goods sold during the year?

(CMA, adapted)

Happy Days Balloon Company incurred $167,000 of manufacturing overhead costs during the year just ended. However, only $145,000 of overhead was applied to production. At the conclusion of the year, the following amounts of the year's applied overhead remained in the various manufacturing accounts.

■ **Exercise 3–31**
Proration of Underapplied
Overhead
(LO 5)

	Applied Overhead Remaining in Account on December 31
Work-in-Process Inventory	$29,000
Finished-Goods Inventory	50,750
Cost of Goods Sold	65,250

Required: Prepare a journal entry to close out the balance in the Manufacturing Overhead account and prorate the balance to the three manufacturing accounts.

Exercise 3–32
Overapplied or Underapplied
Overhead
(LO 4, 5)

The following information pertains to Paramus Metal Works for the year just ended:

Budgeted direct-labour cost	77,000 hours at $17 per hour
Actual direct-labour cost	79,000 hours at $18 per hour
Budgeted manufacturing overhead	$993,300
Budgeted selling and administrative expenses	417,000
Actual manufacturing overhead:	
Depreciation	$225,000
Property taxes	19,000
Indirect labour	79,000
Supervisory salaries	210,000
Utilities	58,000
Insurance	32,000
Rental of space	295,000
Indirect material (see data below)	79,000
Indirect material:	
Beginning inventory, January 1	46,000
Purchases during the year	95,000
Ending inventory, December 31	62,000

Required:

1. Compute the firm's predetermined overhead rate, which is based on direct-labour hours.
2. Calculate the overapplied or underapplied overhead for the year.
3. Prepare a journal entry to close out the Manufacturing Overhead account into Cost of Goods Sold.
4. *Build a spreadsheet:* Construct an Excel spreadsheet to solve requirements (1) and (2) above. Show how the solution will change if the following data change: budgeted manufacturing overhead was $990,000, property taxes were $25,000, and purchases of indirect material amounted to $97,000.

Exercise 3–33
Predetermined Overhead
Rate; Various Cost Drivers
(LO 4)

The following data pertain to the Aquarius Hotel Supply Company for the year just ended:

Budgeted sales revenue	$945,000
Budgeted manufacturing overhead	650,000
Budgeted machine hours	20,000
Budgeted direct-labour hours	25,000
Budgeted direct-labour rate	$13
Actual manufacturing overhead	$690,000
Actual machine hours	22,000
Actual direct-labour hours	26,000
Actual direct-labour rate	$14

Required:

1. Compute the firm's predetermined overhead rate for the year using each of the following common cost drivers: (*a*) machine hours, (*b*) direct-labour hours, and (*c*) direct-labour dollars.
2. Calculate the overapplied or underapplied overhead for the year using each of the cost drivers listed above.

Exercise 3–34
Actual versus Normal Costing
(LO 4, 5)

Refer to the data for the preceding exercise for Aquarius Hotel Supply Company. Prepare a journal entry to add to work-in-process inventory the total manufacturing overhead cost for the year, assuming:

1. The firm uses actual costing.
2. The firm uses normal costing, with a predetermined overhead rate based on machine hours.

Contemporary Trends is an interior decorating firm in Munich. The following costs were incurred in the firm's contract to redecorate the mayor's offices:

Direct material used	4,100 euros
Direct professional labour	7,000 euros

The firm's budget for the year included the following estimates:

Budgeted overhead	510,000 euros
Budgeted direct professional labour	300,000 euros

Overhead is applied to contracts using a predetermined overhead rate calculated annually. The rate is based on direct professional labour cost.

Required: Calculate the total cost of the firm's contract to redecorate the mayor's offices. (Remember to express your answer in terms of euros.)

■ **Exercise 3–35**
Project Costing; Interior Decorating
(LO 1, 7)

e**X**cel

Suppose you are the controller for a company that produces handmade glassware.

1. Choose a volume-based cost driver upon which to base the application of overhead. Write a memo to the company president explaining your choice.
2. Now you have changed jobs. You are the controller of a microchip manufacturer that uses a highly automated production process. Repeat the same requirements stated above.

■ **Exercise 3–36**
Choice of a Cost Driver for Overhead Application
(LO 1, 4)

Rocky Mountain Leatherworks, which manufactures saddles and other leather goods, has three departments. The Assembly Department manufactures various leather products, such as belts, purses, and saddlebags, using an automated production process. The Saddle Department produces handmade saddles and uses very little machinery. The Tanning Department produces leather. The tanning process requires little in the way of labour or machinery, but it does require space and process time. Due to the different production processes in the three departments, the company uses three different cost drivers for the application of manufacturing overhead. The cost drivers and overhead rates are as follows:

■ **Exercise 3–37**
Cost Drivers; Different Production Methods
(LO 4, 5)

	Predetermined Cost Driver	Overhead Rate
Tanning Department	Square metres of leather	$4 per square metre
Assembly Department	Machine time	$11 per machine hour
Saddle Department	Direct-labour time	$5 per direct-labour hour

The company's deluxe saddle and accessory set consists of a handmade saddle, two saddlebags, a belt, and a vest, all coordinated to match. The entire set uses 110 square metres of leather from the Tanning Department, 4 machine hours in the Assembly Department, and 45 direct-labour hours in the Saddle Department.

Required: Job number DS-25 consisted of 25 deluxe saddle and accessory sets. Prepare journal entries to record applied manufacturing overhead in the Work-in-Process Inventory account for each department.

Refer to the illustration of overhead application in the Midtown Advertising Agency on pages 89–90. Suppose the firm used a single cost driver, total staff compensation, to apply overhead costs to each ad contract.

■ **Exercise 3–38**
Overhead Application in a Service Industry Firm
(LO 7)

Required:

1. Compute the total budgeted staff compensation: both partner and artistic staff compensation.
2. Compute Midtown's overhead rate on the basis of this single cost driver.
3. Recalculate the applied overhead for the Super Scoop Ice Cream Company contract.
4. Compare the applied overhead using the single cost driver with the applied overhead computed using the two cost drivers used in the text illustration.

■ **Exercise 3–39**
Two-Stage Allocation
(Appendix)
(LO 1, 8)

Refer to Exhibit 3–13, which portrays the three types of allocation procedures used in two-stage allocation. Give an example of each of these allocation procedures in a hospital setting. The ultimate cost object is a patient-day of hospital care. This is one day of care for one patient. (*Hint:* First think about the
various departments in a hospital. Which departments deal directly with patients? Which ones are service departments and do not deal directly with patients? What kinds of costs does a hospital incur that
should be distributed among all of the hospital's departments? Correct hospital terminology is not important here. Focus on the *concepts* of cost allocation portrayed in Exhibit 3–13.)

Problems

■ **Problem 3–40**
Schedule of Cost of Goods
Manufactured and Sold;
Income Statement
(LO 6)

1. Cost of goods manufactured:
$524,700
3. Selling and administrative
expenses: $69,600

The following data refer to Mister Munchie, Inc. for the year 20x4:

Work-in-process inventory, 12/31/x3	$ 24,300	Utilities for sales and administrative offices	7,500
Selling and administrative salaries	41,400	Other selling and administrative expenses	12,000
Insurance on factory and equipment	10,800	Indirect-labour cost incurred	87,000
Work-in-process inventory, 12/31/x4	24,900	Depreciation on factory building	11,400
Finished-goods inventory, 12/31/x3	42,000	Depreciation on cars used by sales personnel	3,600
Indirect material used	14,700	Direct-labour cost incurred	237,000
Depreciation on factory equipment	6,300	Raw-material inventory, 12/31/x4	33,000
Raw-material inventory, 12/31/x3	30,300	Rental for warehouse space to store raw material	9,300
Property taxes on factory	7,200	Rental of space for company president's office	5,100
Finished-goods inventory, 12/31/x4	46,200	Applied manufacturing overhead	174,000
Purchases of raw material in 20x4	117,000	Sales revenue	617,400
Utilities for factory	18,000	Income tax expense	15,300
Cash balance, 12/31/x4	7,500	Accounts receivable, 12/31/x4	5,100

Required:

1. Prepare Mister Munchie's schedule of cost of goods manufactured for 20x4.
2. Prepare the company's schedule of cost of goods sold for 20x4. The company closes overapplied
   or underapplied overhead into Cost of Goods Sold.
3. Prepare the company's income statement for 20x4.

■ **Problem 3–41**
Basic Job-Order Costing;
Journal Entries
(LO 4, 5)

1. Predetermined overhead
rate: $13 per hour

Burlington Clock Works manufactures fine handcrafted clocks. The firm uses a job-order costing system, and manufacturing overhead is applied on the basis of direct-labour hours. Estimated manufacturing overhead for the year is $260,000. The firm employs 10 master clockmakers, who constitute the
direct-labour force. Each of these employees is expected to work 2,000 hours during the year. The following events occurred during October:

a. The firm purchased 2,900 board metres of mahogany veneer at $12 per board metre.
b. Twenty brass counterweights were requisitioned for production. Each weight cost $27.
c. Five litres of glue were requisitioned for production. The glue cost $5 per litre. Glue is treated as
       an indirect material.
d. Depreciation on the clockworks building for October was $7,000.
e. A $300 utility bill was paid in cash.
f. Time cards showed the following usage of labour:

> Job number G60:   12 grandfather clocks, 950 hours of direct labour
> Job number C81:   15 cuckoo clocks, 500 hours of direct labour

The master clockmakers (direct-labour personnel) earn $22 per hour.
g. The October property tax bill for $890 was received but has not yet been paid in cash.
h. The firm employs labourers who perform various tasks such as material handling and shop
       cleanup. Their wages for October amounted to $3,100.
i. Job number G60, which was started in July, was finished in October. The total cost of the job was
       $15,100.
j. Nine of the grandfather clocks from job number G60 were sold in October for $1,600 each.

Required:

1. Calculate the firm's predetermined overhead rate for the year.
2. Prepare journal entries to record the events described above.

Dessert Delite Company produces frozen microwaveable desserts. The following accounts appeared in the ledger as of December 31.

■ **Problem 3–42**
Manufacturing Cost Flows;
Analysis of T-Accounts
(LO 2, 5)

Raw-Material Inventory

Bal. 1/1	29,400		
	?	?	
Bal. 12/31	50,400		

Accounts Payable

		3,500	Bal. 1/1
191,100		?	
		1,400	Bal. 12/31

Work-in-Process Inventory

Bal. 1/1	23,800		
Direct material	?	?	
Direct labour	?		
Manufacturing overhead	?		
Bal. 12/31	26,600		

Finished-Goods Inventory

Bal. 1/1	16,800		
	?	?	
Bal. 12/31	28,000		

Manufacturing Overhead

?	?

Cost of Goods Sold

994,000

Wages Payable

	2,800	Bal. 1/1	
205,800	?		
	7,000	Bal. 12/31	

Sales Revenue

?

Accounts Receivable

Bal. 1/1	15,400		
	?	1,128,400	
Bal. 12/31	21,000		

Additional information:

a. Accounts payable is used only for direct-material purchases.
b. Underapplied overhead of $3,500 for the year has not yet been closed into cost of goods sold.

Required: Complete the T-accounts by computing the amounts indicated by a question mark.

Stellar Sound, Inc., which uses a job-order costing system, had two jobs in process at the start of the year: job no. 101 ($168,000) and job no. 102 ($107,000). The following information is available:

■ **Problem 3–43**
Job-Order Costing; Journal
Entries
(LO 2, 5)

1. Predetermined overhead
rate: $52.50 per machine hour
4. Finished goods inventory
increase: $406,000

a. The company applies manufacturing overhead on the basis of machine hours. Budgeted overhead and machine activity for the year were anticipated to be $1,680,000, and 32,000 hours, respectively.
b. The company worked on four jobs during the first quarter. Direct materials used, direct labour incurred, and machine hours consumed were as follows:

Job No.	Direct Material	Direct Labour	Machine Hours
101	$42,000	$ 70,000	2,400
102	—	44,000	1,400
103	88,000	130,000	4,000
104	30,000	17,600	1,000

   c.   Manufacturing overhead during the first quarter included charges for depreciation ($68,000), indirect labour ($120,000), indirect materials used ($10,000), and other factory costs ($279,000).

   d.   Stellar Sound completed job no. 101 and job no. 102. Job no. 102 was sold on account, producing a profit of $69,400 for the firm.

Required:

1. Determine the company's predetermined overhead application rate.
2. Prepare journal entries for the first quarter to record the following. (*Note:* Use summary entries where appropriate by combining individual job data.)
   a.   The issuance of direct material to production and the direct labour incurred
   b.   The manufacturing overhead incurred during the quarter
   c.   The application of manufacturing overhead to production
   d.   The completion of jobs no. 101 and no. 102
   e.   The sale of job no. 102
3. Determine the cost of the jobs still in production as of March 31.
4. Did the finished-goods inventory increase or decrease during the first quarter? By how much?
5. Was manufacturing overhead under- or overapplied for the first quarter of the year? By how much?

■ **Problem 3–44**
Job-Order Costing; Focus on
Manufacturing Overhead
(LO 2, 4)

5. BBBC's applied overhead:
$2,827,500
6. Overapplied overhead:
$50,500

Burbany Bowling Ball Company (BBBC) uses a job-order costing system to accumulate manufacturing costs. The company's work-in-process on December 31, 20x3, consisted of one job (no. 3088), which was carried on the year-end balance sheet at $78,400. There was no finished-goods inventory on this date.

     BBBC applies manufacturing overhead to production on the basis of direct-labour cost. Budgeted totals for 20x4 for direct labour and manufacturing overhead are $2,100,000 and $2,730,000, respectively. Actual results for the year follow:

Direct material used	$2,800,000
Direct labour	2,175,000
Indirect material used	32,500
Indirect labour	1,430,000
Factory depreciation	870,000
Factory insurance	29,500
Factory utilities	415,000
Selling and administrative expenses	1,080,000
Total	$8,832,000

     Job no. 3088 was completed in January 20x4; there was no work in process at year-end. All jobs produced during 20x4 were sold with the exception of job no. 3154, which contained direct-material costs of $78,000 and direct-labour charges of $42,500. The company charges any under- or overapplied overhead to Cost of Goods Sold.

Required:

1. Determine the company's predetermined overhead application rate.
2. Determine the additions to the Work-in-Process Inventory account for direct material used, direct labour, and manufacturing overhead.
3. Compute the amount that the company would disclose as finished-goods inventory on the December 31, 20x4, balance sheet.
4. Prepare the journal entry needed to record the year's completed production.
5. Compute the amount of under- or overapplied overhead at year-end, and prepare the necessary journal entry to record its disposition.
6. Determine BBBC's 20x4 cost of goods sold.
7. Would it be appropriate to include selling and administrative expenses in either manufacturing overhead or cost of goods sold? Briefly explain.

JLR Enterprises provides consulting services throughout Quebec and uses a job-order costing system to accumulate the cost of client projects. Traceable costs are charged directly to individual clients; in contrast, other costs incurred by JLR, but not identifiable with specific clients, are charged to jobs by using a predetermined overhead application rate. Clients are billed for directly chargeable costs, overhead, and a markup.

JLR's director of cost management, Brent Dean, anticipates the following costs for the upcoming year:

■ **Problem 3–45**
Job-Order Costing in a
Consulting Firm
(LO 1, 2, 4, 7)

2. Predetermined overhead
rate: 28% of traceable costs
4. Overhead: $21,000

	Cost		Percentage of Cost Directly Traceable to Clients
Professional staff salaries	$3,750,000		80%
Administrative support staff	450,000		60%
Photocopying	75,000		90%
Travel	375,000		90%
Other operating costs	150,000		50%
Total	$4,800,000		

The firm's partners desire to make a $960,000 profit for the firm and plan to add a percentage markup on total cost to achieve that figure.

On March 10, JLR completed work on a project for Davis Manufacturing. The following costs were incurred: professional staff salaries, $61,500; administrative support staff, $3,900; photocopying, $750; travel, $6,750; and other operating costs, $2,100.

Required:

1. Determine JLR's total traceable costs for the upcoming year and the firm's total anticipated overhead.
2. Calculate the predetermined overhead rate. The rate is based on total costs traceable to client jobs.
3. What percentage of cost will JLR add to each job to achieve its profit target?
4. Determine the total cost of the Davis Manufacturing project. How much would Davis be billed for services performed?
5. Notice that only 50 percent of JLR's other operating cost is directly traceable to specific client projects. Cite several costs that would be included in this category and difficult to trace to clients.
6. Notice that 80 percent of the professional staff cost is directly traceable to specific client projects. Cite several reasons that would explain why this figure isn't 100 percent.

■ **Problem 3–46**
Job-Order Costing; Focus on
Overhead and Cost Drivers
(LO 2, 4, 8)

4. Overapplied overhead:
$64,500

Juarez, Inc. uses a job-order costing system for its products, which pass from the Machining Department, to the Assembly Department, to finished-goods inventory. The Machining Department is heavily automated; in contrast, the Assembly Department performs a number of manual-assembly activities. The company applies manufacturing overhead by the use of machine hours in the Machining Department and direct-labour cost in the Assembly Department. The following information relates to the year just ended:

	Machining Department	Assembly Department
Budgeted manufacturing overhead	$2,000,000	$1,540,000
Actual manufacturing overhead	2,130,000	1,525,000
Budgeted direct-labour cost	750,000	2,800,000
Actual direct-labour cost	725,000	2,890,000
Budgeted machine hours	200,000	50,000
Actual machine hours	212,500	55,000

The data that follow pertain to job no. DC66, the only job in production at year-end.

	Machining Department	Assembly Department
Direct material	$12,250	$ 3,350
Direct labour	13,950	29,300
Machine hours	180	75

Selling and administrative expense amounted to $2,325,000.

Required:

1. Assuming the use of normal costing, determine the predetermined overhead rates used in the Machining Department and the Assembly Department.
2. Compute the cost of the company's year-end work-in-process inventory.
3. Determine whether overhead was under- or overapplied during the year in the Machining Department.
4. Repeat requirement (3) for the Assembly Department.
5. If the company disposes of under- or overapplied overhead as an adjustment to Cost of Goods Sold, would the company's Cost of Goods Sold account increase or decrease? Explain.
6. How much overhead would have been charged to the company's Work-in-Process account during the year?
7. Comment on the appropriateness of the company's cost drivers (i.e., the use of machine hours in Machining and direct-labour cost in Assembly).

■ **Problem 3–47**
Journal Entries in Job-Order Costing
(LO 4, 5)

2. Applied manufacturing overhead: $143,000

Seaway, Inc. manufactures outboard motors and an assortment of other marine equipment. The company uses a job-order costing system. Normal costing is used, and manufacturing overhead is applied on the basis of machine hours. Estimated manufacturing overhead for the year is $1,520,200, and management expects that 69,100 machine hours will be used.

Required:

1. Calculate Seaway's predetermined overhead rate for the year.
2. Prepare journal entries to record the following events, which occurred during April.
    a. The firm purchased marine propellers from Peninsula Marine Corporation for $8,240 on account.
    b. A requisition was filed by the Gauge Department supervisor for 280 kilograms of clear plastic. The material cost $.70 per kilogram when it was purchased.
    c. The Motor Testing Department supervisor requisitioned 320 metres of electrical wire, which is considered an indirect material. The wire cost $.10 per metre when it was purchased.
    d. An electric utility bill of $900 was paid in cash.
    e. Direct-labour costs incurred in April were $73,500.
    f. April's insurance cost was $2,100 for insurance on the cars driven by sales personnel. The policy had been prepaid in March.
    g. Metal tubing costing $2,800 was purchased on account.
    h. A cash payment of $1,850 was made on outstanding accounts payable.
    i. Indirect-labour costs of $19,000 were incurred during April.
    j. Depreciation on equipment for April amounted to $8,500.
    k. Job number G22, consisting of 60 tachometers, was finished during April. The total cost of the job was $1,200.
    l. During April, 6,500 machine hours were used.
    m. Sales on account for April amounted to $181,000. The cost of goods sold in April was $142,500.

■ **Problem 3–48**
Schedules of Cost of Goods Manufactured and Sold; Income Statement
(LO 6)

1. Total actual manufacturing overhead: $435,000
2. Cost of goods available for sale: $1,355,625

The following data refers to Superior Metals Corporation for the year 20x4:

Raw-material inventory, 12/31/x3	$ 66,750	Depreciation on factory equipment	45,000
Purchases of raw material in 20x4	548,250	Insurance on factory and equipment	30,000
Raw-material inventory, 12/31/x4	44,250	Utilities for factory	52,500
Direct-labour cost incurred	355,500	Work-in-process inventory, 12/31/x3	–0–
Selling and administrative expenses	201,750	Work-in-process inventory, 12/31/x4	30,000
Indirect labour cost incurred	112,500	Finished-goods inventory, 12/31/x3	26,250
Property taxes on factory	67,500	Finished-goods inventory, 12/31/x4	30,000
Depreciation on factory building	93,750	Applied manufacturing overhead	433,125
Income tax expense	18,750	Sales revenue	1,578,750
Indirect material used	33,750		

Required:

1. Prepare Superior Metals' schedule of cost of goods manufactured for 20x4.

2. Prepare the company's schedule of cost of goods sold for 20x4. The company closes overapplied or underapplied overhead into Cost of Goods Sold.

3. Prepare the company's income statement for 20x4.

4. *Build a spreadsheet:* Construct an Excel spreadsheet to solve all of the preceding requirements. Show how the solution will change if the following data change: sales revenue was $1,580,000, applied manufacturing overhead was $430,000, and utilities amounted to $49,000.

Refer to the schedule of cost of goods manufactured prepared for Superior Metals Corporation in the preceding problem.

Required:

1. How much of the manufacturing costs incurred during 20x4 remained associated with work-in-process inventory on December 31, 20x4?

2. Suppose the company had increased its production in 20x4 by 30 percent. Would the direct-material cost shown on the schedule have been larger or the same? Why?

3. Answer the same question as in requirement (2) for depreciation on the factory building.

4. Suppose only half of the $45,000 in depreciation on equipment had been related to factory machinery, and the other half was related to selling and administrative equipment. How would this have changed the schedule of cost of goods manufactured?

■ **Problem 3–49**
Interpreting the Schedule of
Cost of Goods Manufactured
(LO 2, 6)

Marvellous Marshmallow Company's cost of goods sold for March was $690,000. January 31 work-in-process inventory was 90 percent of January 1 work-in-process inventory. Manufacturing overhead applied was 50 percent of direct-labour cost. Other information pertaining to the company's inventories and production for the month of January is as follows:

Beginning inventories, January 1:	
Raw material	$ 34,000
Work in process	80,000
Finished goods	204,000
Purchases of raw material during March	226,000
Ending inventories, January 31:	
Raw material	52,000
Work in process	?
Finished goods	210,000

Required:

1. Prepare a schedule of cost of goods manufactured for the month of January.

2. Prepare a schedule to compute the prime costs (direct material and direct labour) incurred during January.

3. Prepare a schedule to compute the conversion costs (direct labour and manufacturing overhead) charged to work in process during January.

(CMA, adapted)

■ **Problem 3–50**
Cost of Goods Manufactured;
Prime and Conversion Costs
(LO 2, 6)

1. Manufacturing overhead
applied: $160,000
2. Raw material available for
use: $260,000

Midnight Sun Apparel Company uses normal costing, and manufacturing overhead is applied to work-in-process on the basis of machine hours. On January 1 of the current year, there were no balances in work-in-process or finished-goods inventories. The following estimates were included in the current year's budget:

Total budgeted manufacturing overhead	$306,000
Total budgeted machine hours	51,000

■ **Problem 3–51**
Proration of Overapplied or
Underapplied Overhead
(LO 2, 4, 5)

2. Applied manufacturing
overhead: $36,000
5. Work-in-Process Inventory:
$10,800

During January, the firm began the following production jobs:

M07	1,200 machine hours
T28	3,000 machine hours
B19	1,800 machine hours

During January, job numbers M07 and T28 were completed, and job number B19 was sold. The actual manufacturing overhead incurred during January was $38,000.

Required:

1. Compute the company's predetermined overhead rate for the current year.
2. How much manufacturing overhead was applied to production during January?
3. Calculate the overapplied or underapplied overhead for January.
4. Prepare a journal entry to close the balance calculated in requirement (3) into Cost of Goods Sold.
5. Prepare a journal entry to prorate the balance calculated in requirement (3) among the Work-in-Process Inventory, Finished-Goods Inventory, and Cost of Goods Sold accounts.

■ **Problem 3–52**
Ethical Issues;
Underapplication of
Manufacturing Overhead
(LO 1, 2, 4, 6)

Marc Jackson has recently been hired as a cost accountant by Offset Press Company, a privately held company that produces a line of offset printing presses and lithograph machines. During his first few months on the job, Jackson discovered that Offset has been underapplying factory overhead to the Work-in-Process Inventory account, while overstating expenses through the General and Administrative Expense account. This practice has been going on since the start of the company, which is in its sixth year of operation. The effect in each year has been favourable, having a material impact on the company's tax position. No internal audit function exists at Offset, and the external auditors have not yet discovered the underapplied factory overhead.

Prior to the sixth-year audit, Jackson had pointed out the practice and its effect to Mary Brown, the corporate controller, and had asked her to let him make the necessary adjustments. Brown directed him not to make the adjustments, but to wait until the external auditors had completed their work and see what they uncovered.

The sixth-year audit has now been completed, and the external auditors have once again failed to discover the underapplication of factory overhead. Jackson again asked Brown if he could make the required adjustments and was again told not to make them. Jackson, however, believes that the adjustments should be made and that the external auditors should be informed of the situation.

Since there are no established policies at Offset Press Company for resolving ethical conflicts, Jackson is considering one of the following three alternative courses of action:

- Follow Brown's directive and do nothing further.
- Attempt to convince Brown to make the proper adjustments and to advise the external auditors of her actions.
- Tell the Audit Committee of the Board of Directors about the problem and give them the appropriate accounting data.

Required:

1. For each of the three alternative courses of action that Jackson is considering, explain whether the action is appropriate.
2. Independent of your answer to requirement (1), assume that Jackson again approaches Brown to make the necessary adjustments and is unsuccessful. Describe the steps that Jackson should take in proceeding to resolve this situation.

(CMA, adapted)

■ **Problem 3–53**
Predetermined Overhead Rate;
Different Time Periods; Pricing
(LO 4)

2. May, total cost: $1,140
5. February, total cost:
$1,117.80

Troy Electronics Company calculates its predetermined overhead rate on a quarterly basis. The following estimates were made for the current year.

	Estimated Manufacturing Overhead	Estimated Direct-Labour Hours	Quarterly Predetermined Overhead Rate (per direct-labour hour)
First quarter	$ 400,000	50,000	?
Second quarter	320,000	32,000	?
Third quarter	200,000	25,000	?
Fourth quarter	280,000	28,000	?
Total	$1,200,000	135,000	

The firm's main product, part number SC71, requires $600 of direct material and 20 hours of direct labour per unit. The labour rate is $17 per hour.

Required:

1. Calculate the firm's *quarterly* predetermined overhead rate for each quarter.
2. Determine the cost of one unit of part number SC71 if it is manufactured in February versus May.
3. Suppose the company's pricing policy calls for a 10 percent markup over cost. Calculate the price to be charged for a unit of part number SC71 if it is produced in February versus May.
4. Calculate the company's predetermined overhead rate for the year if the rate is calculated *annually*.
5. Based on your answer to requirement (4), what is the cost of a unit of part number SC71 if it is manufactured in February? In May?
6. What is the price of a unit of part SC71 if the predetermined overhead rate is calculated annually?

Tiana Shar, the controller for Bondi Furniture Company, is in the process of analyzing the overhead costs for the month of November. She has gathered the following data for the month:

Problem 3–54
Overhead Application Using a Predetermined Overhead Rate
(LO 2, 4, 6)

2. Job 57, applied manufacturing overhead: $35,000
6. November, applied manufacturing overhead: $85,000

Labour

Direct-labour hours:

Job 57	7,000
Job 58	6,000
Job 59	4,000

Labour costs:

Direct-labour wages	$408,000
Indirect-labour wages	30,000
Supervisory salaries	12,000

Material

Inventories, November 1:

Raw material and supplies	$ 21,000
Work in process (job 57)	108,000
Finished goods	125,000

Purchases of raw material and supplies:

Raw material	$270,000
Supplies (indirect material)	30,000

Direct material and supplies requisitioned for production:

Job 57	$ 90,000
Job 58	75,000
Job 59	51,000
Supplies (indirect material)	24,000
Total	$240,000

(continued)

(concluded)

Other

Building occupancy costs (heat, light, depreciation, etc.):

Factory facilities	$ 12,800
Sales offices	3,200
Administrative offices	2,000
Total	$ 18,000

Production equipment costs:

Power	$ 8,200
Repairs and maintenance	3,000
Depreciation	3,000
Other	2,000
Total	$ 16,200

The firm's job-order costing system uses direct-labour hours as the cost driver for overhead application. In December of the preceding year, Shar had prepared the following budget for direct-labour and manufacturing-overhead costs for the current year. The plant is capable of operating at 140,000 direct-labour hours per year. However, Shar estimates that the normal usage is 115,000 hours in a typical year.

Direct-Labour Hours	Manufacturing Overhead	
	Variable	**Fixed**
100,000	$300,000	$230,000
115,000	345,000	230,000
130,000	390,000	230,000

During November the following jobs were completed:

Job 57	Side chairs
Job 58	End tables

Required: Assist Shar by making the following calculations:

1. Calculate the predetermined overhead rate for the current year.
2. Calculate the total cost of job 57.
3. Compute the amount of manufacturing overhead applied to job 59 during November.
4. What was the total amount of manufacturing overhead applied during November?
5. Compute the actual manufacturing overhead incurred during November.
6. Calculate the overapplied or underapplied overhead for November.

(CMA, adapted)

■ **Problem 3–55**
Comprehensive Job-Order
Costing Problem
(LO 2, 4, 5, 6)

4. Total actual overhead:
$36,230
7. Gross margin: $12,165

Bandway Company manufactures brass musical instruments for use by secondary school students. The company uses a normal costing system, in which manufacturing overhead is applied on the basis of direct-labour hours. The company's budget for the current year included the following predictions:

Budgeted total manufacturing overhead	$462,000
Budgeted total direct-labour hours	21,000

During October, the firm worked on the following two production jobs:

     Job number T79, consisting of 76 trombones
     Job number C41, consisting of 110 cornets

The events of October are described as follows:

a. One thousand square metres of rolled brass sheet metal were purchased on account for $6,000.

b. Four hundred kilograms of brass tubing were purchased on account for $5,200.

c. The following requisitions were submitted on October 5:

Requisition number 112: 260 square metres of brass sheet metal at $5.50 per square metre (for job number T79)

Requisition number 113: 1,100 kilograms of brass tubing, at $9 per kilogram (for job number C41)

Requisition number 114: 10 litres of valve lubricant, at $12 per litre

All brass used in production is treated as direct material. Valve lubricant is an indirect material.

d. An analysis of labour time cards revealed the following labour usage for October.

Direct labour: Job number T79, 850 hours at $20 per hour

Direct labour: Job number C41, 950 hours at $20 per hour

Indirect labour: General factory cleanup, $4,500

Indirect labour: Factory supervisory salaries, $9,600

e. Depreciation of the factory building and equipment during October amounted to $13,000.

f. Rent paid in cash for warehouse space used during October was $1,340.

g. Utility costs incurred during October amounted to $2,400. The invoices for these costs were received, but the bills were not paid in October.

h. October property taxes on the factory were paid in cash, $2,370.

i. The insurance cost covering factory operations for the month of October was $2,900. The insurance policy had been prepaid.

j. The costs of salaries and fringe benefits for sales and administrative personnel paid in cash during October amounted to $7,500.

k. Depreciation on administrative office equipment and space amounted to $4,500.

l. Other selling and administrative expenses paid in cash during October amounted to $1,150.

m. Job number T79 was completed on October 20.

n. Half of the trombones in job number T79 were sold on account during October for $720 each.

The October 1 balances in selected accounts are as follows:

Cash	$ 11,000
Accounts Receivable	20,000
Prepaid Insurance	6,000
Raw-Material Inventory	150,000
Manufacturing Supplies Inventory	600
Work-in-Process Inventory	89,000
Finished-Goods Inventory	223,000
Accumulated Depreciation: Buildings and Equipment	99,000
Accounts Payable	14,500
Wages Payable	8,500

Required:

1. Calculate the company's predetermined overhead rate for the year.
2. Prepare journal entries to record the events of October.
3. Set up T-accounts, and post the journal entries made in requirement (2).
4. Calculate the overapplied or underapplied overhead for March. Prepare a journal entry to close this balance into Cost of Goods Sold.
5. Prepare a schedule of cost of goods manufactured for October.
6. Prepare a schedule of cost of goods sold for October.
7. Prepare an income statement for October.

■ **Problem 3–56**
Job-Cost Record; Continuation
of Preceding Problem
(LO 2, 4, 6)

Unit cost: $488.55 (rounded)

Refer to the preceding problem regarding Bandway Company. Complete the following job-cost record for job number T79. (Assume that all of the labour hours for job T79 occurred during the week of October 8 through October 12.)

JOB-COST RECORD

Job Number _____ T79 _____   Description _____
Date Started _____   Date Completed _____
                                                                    Number of Units Completed _____

Direct Material

Date	Requisition Number	Quantity	Unit Price	Cost

Direct Labour

Date	Time Card Number	Hours	Rate	Cost
10/8 to 10/12	10-08 through 10-12			

Manufacturing Overhead

Date	Cost Driver (Activity Base)	Quantity	Application Rate	Cost
10/8 to 10/12				

Cost Summary

Cost Item	Amount
Total direct material
Total direct labour
Total manufacturing overhead	
Total cost	
Unit cost	

Shipping Summary

Date	Units Shipped	Units Remaining in Inventory	Cost Balance

■ **Problem 3–57**
Flow of Manufacturing Costs;
Incomplete Data
(LO 2, 4, 5)

4. $114,000

Conundrum Corporation manufactures furniture. Due to a fire in the administrative offices, the accounting records for September of the current year were partially destroyed. You have been able to piece together the following information from the ledger.

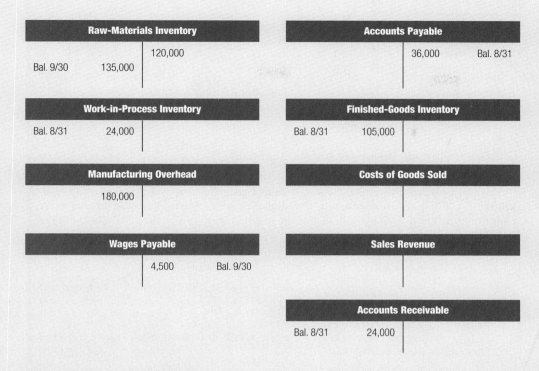

Upon examining various source documents and interviewing several employees, you were able to gather the following additional information.

a. Collections of accounts receivable during September amounted to $615,000.

b. Sales revenue in September was 120 percent of cost of goods sold. All sales are on account.

c. Overhead is applied using an annual predetermined overhead rate based on direct-labour hours.

d. The budgeted overhead for the current year is $2,160,000.

e. Budgeted direct-labour cost for the current year is $2,880,000. The direct-labour rate is $20 per hour.

f. The accounts payable balance on September 30 was $3,000. Only purchases of raw material are credited to accounts payable. A payment of $243,000 was made on September 15.

g. September's cost of goods sold amounted to $540,000.

h. The September 30 balance in finished-goods inventory was $15,000.

i. Payments of $238,500 were made to direct-labour employees during September. The August 31 balance in the Wages Payable account was $3,000.

j. The *actual* manufacturing overhead for September was $180,000.

k. An analysis of the furniture still in process on September 30 revealed that so far these items have required 1,500 hours of direct labour and $61,500 of direct material.

Required: Calculate the following amounts. Then complete the T-accounts given in the problem.

1. Sales revenue for September
2. September 30 balance in accounts receivable
3. Cost of raw material purchased during September
4. September 30 balance in work-in-process inventory
5. Direct labour added to work in process during September
6. Applied overhead for September
7. Cost of goods completed during September
8. Raw material used during September
9. August 31 balance in raw-material inventory
10. Overapplied or underapplied overhead for September

■ **Problem 3–58**
Plantwide versus Departmental
Overhead Rates; Product
Pricing (Appendix)
(LO 1, 8)

2. Advanced system,
price: $1,804
5. Basic system,
price: $1,243

ColourTech Corporation manufactures two different colour printers for the business market. Cost estimates for the two models for the current year are as follows:

	Basic System	Advanced System
Direct material	$ 450	$ 900
Direct labour (20 hours at $16 per hour)	320	320
Manufacturing overhead*...	420	420
Total	$1,190	$1,640

*The predetermined overhead rate is $21 per direct-labour hour.

Each model of printer requires 20 hours of direct labour. The basic system requires 5 hours in department A and 15 hours in department B. The advanced system requires 15 hours in department A and 5 hours in department B. The overhead costs budgeted in these two production departments are as follows:

	Department A	Department B
Variable cost	$17 per direct-labour hour	$5 per direct-labour hour
Fixed cost	$210,000	$210,000

The firm's management expects to operate at a level of 21,000 direct-labour hours in each production department during the current year.

Required:

1. Show how the company's predetermined overhead rate was determined.
2. If the firm prices each model of printer at 10 percent over its cost, what will be the price of each model?
3. Suppose the company were to use departmental predetermined overhead rates. Calculate the rate for each of the two production departments.
4. Compute the product cost of each model using the departmental overhead rates calculated in requirement (3).
5. Compute the price to be charged for each model, assuming the company continues to price each product at 10 percent above cost. Use the revised product costs calculated in requirement (4).
6. Write a memo to the president of ColourTech Corporation making a recommendation as to whether the firm should use a plantwide overhead rate or departmental rates. Consider the potential implications of the overhead rates and the firm's pricing policy. How might these considerations affect the firm's ability to compete in the marketplace?

Cases

■ **Case 3–59**
Interpreting Information from
a Job-Order Costing System
(LO 2, 3, 4, 6)

2. Manufacturing overhead
rate: $7.50 per hour
3. Value of finished-goods inventory on 12/31: $455,600

KidCo, Inc. is a manufacturer of furnishings for children. KidCo uses a job-order costing system. KidCo's work-in-process inventory on November 30 consisted of the following jobs:

Job No.	Description	Units	Accumulated Cost
CBS102	Cribs	20,000	$ 900,000
PLP086	Playpens	15,000	420,000
DRS114	Dressers	25,000	250,000
Total			$1,570,000

The company's November 30 finished-goods inventory, which is valued using the first-in, first-out (FIFO) method, consisted of five items:

Item	Quantity and Unit Cost	Accumulated Cost
Cribs	7,500 units @ $64 each	$ 480,000
Strollers	13,000 units @ $23 each	299,000
Carriages	11,200 units @ $102 each	1,142,400
Dressers	21,000 units @ $55 each	1,155,000
Playpens	19,400 units @ $35 each	679,000
Total		$3,755,400

KidCo applies manufacturing overhead on the basis of direct-labour hours. The company's overhead budget for the year totalled $4,500,000, and the company planned to use 600,000 direct-labour hours during this period. Through the first 11 months of the year, a total of 555,000 direct-labour hours were worked, and total overhead amounted to $4,273,500.

At the end of November, the balance in KidCo's Raw-Materials Inventory account, which includes both raw materials and purchased parts, was $668,000. Additions to and requisitions from the materials inventory during the month of December included the following:

Additions	Raw Materials	Purchased Parts
Additions	$242,000	$396,000
Requisitions:		
Job CBS102	51,000	104,000
Job PLP086	3,000	10,800
Job DRS114	124,000	87,000
Job STR077 (10,000 strollers)	62,000	81,000
Job CRG098 (5,000 carriages)	65,000	187,000

During December, KidCo's factory payroll consisted of the following:

CBS102	12,000 hrs.	$122,400
PLP086	4,400 hrs.	43,200
DRS114	19,500 hrs.	200,500
STR077	3,500 hrs.	30,000
CRG098	14,000 hrs.	138,000
Indirect labour		29,400
Supervision		57,600
Total		$621,100

The following list shows the jobs that were completed and the unit sales for December:

Production				Sales	
Job No.	Items	Quantity Completed		Items	Quantity Shipped
CBS102	Cribs	20,000		Cribs	17,500
PLP086	Playpens	15,000		Playpens	21,000
STR077	Strollers	10,000		Strollers	14,000
CRG098	Carriages	5,000		Dressers	18,000
				Carriages	6,000

Required:

1. Explain when it is appropriate for a company to use a job-order costing system.
2. Calculate the dollar balance in KidCo's Work-in-Process Inventory account as of December 31.
3. Calculate the dollar amount related to the playpens in KidCo's Finished-Goods Inventory as of December 31.

(CMA, adapted)

■ **Case 3–60**
Cost Flows in a Job-Order
Costing System; Schedule of
Cost of Goods Manufactured;
Automation
(LO 2, 4, 6)

3. Manufacturing overhead
applied in December:
$180,000
6. Total actual manufacturing
overhead: $2,392,000

Opticom, Inc., a manufacturer of fibre optic communications equipment, uses a job-order costing system. Since the production process is heavily automated, manufacturing overhead is applied on the basis of machine hours using a predetermined overhead rate. The current annual rate of $30 per machine hour is based on budgeted manufacturing overhead costs of $2,400,000 and a budgeted activity level of 80,000 machine hours. Operations for the year have been completed, and all of the accounting entries have been made for the year except the application of manufacturing overhead to the jobs worked on during December, the transfer of costs from Work in Process to Finished Goods for the jobs completed in December, and the transfer of costs from Finished Goods to Cost of Goods Sold for the jobs that have been sold during December. Summarized data as of November 30 and for the month of December are presented in the following table. Jobs T11-007, N11-013, and N11-015 were completed during December. All completed jobs except job N11-013 had been turned over to customers by the close of business on December 31.

Work-in-Process		December Activity		
Job No.	**Balance November 30**	**Direct Material**	**Direct Labour**	**Machine Hours**
T11-007	$ 174,000	$ 3,000	$ 9,000	300
N11-013	110,000	8,000	24,000	1,000
N11-015	–0–	51,200	53,400	1,400
D12-002	–0–	75,800	40,000	2,500
D12-003	–0–	52,000	33,600	800
Total	$284,000	$190,000	$160,000	6,000

Operating Activity	Activity through November 30	December Activity
Actual manufacturing overhead incurred:		
Indirect material	$ 250,000	$ 18,000
Indirect labour	690,000	60,000
Utilities	490,000	44,000
Depreciation	770,000	70,000
Total overhead	$2,200,000	$192,000
Other data:		
Raw-material purchases*	$1,930,000	$196,000
Direct-labour costs	$1,690,000	$160,000
Machine hours	73,000	6,000

Account Balances at Beginning of Year	January 1
Raw-material inventory*	$210,000
Work-in-process inventory	120,000
Finished-goods inventory	250,000

*Raw-material purchases and raw-material inventory consist of both direct and indirect materials. The balance of the Raw-Material Inventory account as of December 31 of the year just completed is $170,000.

Required:

1. Explain why manufacturers use a predetermined overhead rate to apply manufacturing overhead to their jobs.
2. How much manufacturing overhead would Opticom have applied to jobs through November 30 of the year just completed?
3. How much manufacturing overhead would have been applied to jobs during December of the year just completed?
4. Determine the amount by which manufacturing overhead is overapplied or underapplied as of December 31 of the year just completed.
5. Determine the balance in the Finished-Goods Inventory account on December 31 of the year just completed.
6. Prepare a Schedule of Cost of Goods Manufactured for Opticom, Inc. for the year just completed. (*Hint:* In computing the cost of direct material used, remember that Opticom includes both direct and indirect material in its Raw-Material Inventory account.)

(CMA, adapted)

Chapter Four

Process Costing and Hybrid Product-Costing Systems

FOCUS COMPANY

The MVP Sports Equipment Company's Alberta Division manufactures ski gloves in its Calgary plant. Each glove requires work in two departments, each of which engages in a production process.

The departments are the Cutting Department and the Stitching Department. MVP's Alberta Division uses a product-costing method called process costing. Under process costing, direct material and conversion costs (direct labour and manufacturing overhead) are first assigned to each of the processes (or departments) used in the manufacturing operation. Then, the costs of each process (or department) are assigned to the units worked on in the department. Process costing is used only by manufacturing companies that produce relatively large numbers of similar products.

After completing this chapter, you should be able to:

1. List and explain the similarities and important differences between job-order and process costing.

2. Prepare journal entries to record the flow of costs in a process-costing system with sequential production departments.

3. Prepare a table of equivalent units under weighted-average process costing.

4. Compute the cost per equivalent unit under the weighted-average method of process costing.

5. Analyze the total production costs for a department under the weighted-average method of process costing.

6. Prepare a departmental production report under weighted-average process costing.

IN CONTRAST

In contrast to the process-costing system used in MVP's Alberta Division, we explore a different product-costing system in the company's Ontario Division. This MVP division manufactures two types of basketballs in its Kingston plant. The professional basketballs are covered with genuine leather, whereas the scholastic basketballs are covered with imitation leather. Except for the different exterior material, though, each basketball requires the same production steps. MVP's Ontario Division uses a product-costing system called operation costing, which is well suited to its production environment. Operation costing is used only by manufacturing companies.

W̲e have seen that a product-costing system performs two primary functions:

1. Accumulating production costs
2. Assigning those production costs to the firm's products

Product costs are needed for the purposes of planning, cost management, decision making, and reporting to various outside organizations, such as governmental regulatory agencies.

Job-order costing was described in Chapter 3. This type of product-costing system is used when relatively small numbers of products are produced in distinct batches or job orders and these products differ significantly from each other. This chapter covers **process-costing systems**. Process costing is used in **repetitive production** environments, where large numbers of identical or very similar products are manufactured in a continuous flow. Industries using process costing include paper, petroleum, chemicals, textiles, food processing, lumber, and electronics.

Comparison of Job-Order Costing and Process Costing

> **Learning Objective 1**
>
> List and explain the similarities and important differences between job-order and process costing.

In many ways, job-order costing and process costing are similar. Both product-costing systems have the same ultimate purpose—assignment of production costs to units of output. Moreover, the flow of costs through the manufacturing accounts is the same in the two systems.

Flow of Costs

Exhibit 4–1 displays the flow of costs in two process-costing situations: one with a single production department and one with two production departments used in sequence. The same accounts are used in this process-costing illustration as were used in job-order costing in the preceding chapter. As the illustration shows, direct-material, direct-labour, and manufacturing-overhead costs are added to a Work-in-Process Inventory account. As goods are finished, costs are transferred to Finished-Goods Inventory. During the period when goods are sold, the product costs are transferred to Cost of Goods Sold. In the two-department case, when goods are finished in the first production department, costs accumulated in the Work-in-Process Inventory account for production department A are transferred to the Work-in-Process Inventory account for production department B.

> **Learning Objective 2**
>
> Prepare journal entries to record the flow of costs in a process-costing system with sequential production departments.

The journal entries for the case of two sequential production departments, as illustrated in Exhibit 4–1, are as follows. (The numbers used in the journal entries are assumed for the purpose of showing the form of the entries.)

1. As direct material and direct labour are used in production department A, these costs are added to the Work-in-Process Inventory account for department A. Overhead is applied using a predetermined overhead rate. The predetermined overhead rate is computed in the same way in job-order and process costing.

Work-in-Process Inventory: Production Department A	100,000	
Raw-Material Inventory		50,000
Wages Payable		20,000
Manufacturing Overhead		30,000

2. When production department A completes its work on some units of product, these units are transferred to production department B. The costs assigned to these goods are transferred from the Work-in-Process Inventory account for department A to the Work-in-Process Inventory account for

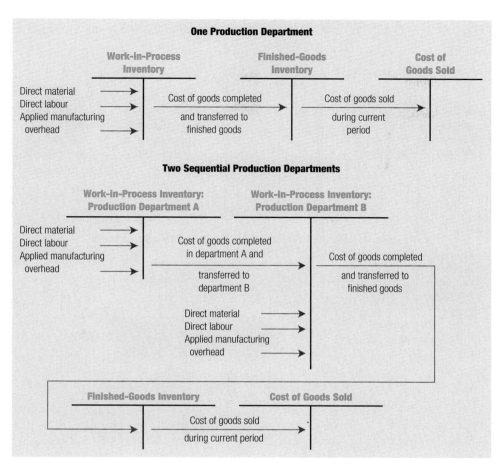

Exhibit 4–1
Flow of Costs in Process-Costing Systems

department B. In department B, the costs assigned to these partially completed products are called **transferred-in costs**.

Work-in-Process Inventory: Production Department B	80,000	
Work-in-Process Inventory: Production Department A		80,000

3.   Direct material and direct labour are used in production department B, and manufacturing overhead is applied using a predetermined overhead rate.

Work-in-Process Inventory: Production Department B	75,000	
Raw-Material Inventory		40,000
Wages Payable		15,000
Manufacturing Overhead		20,000

4.   Goods are completed in production department B and transferred to the finished-goods warehouse.

Finished-Goods Inventory	130,000	
Work-in-Process Inventory: Production Department B		130,000

5.   Goods are sold.

Cost of Goods Sold	125,000	
Finished-Goods Inventory		125,000

"Process-based costing provided our first opportunity to convert the functional budget into process costing. It allowed us to look at what drives the costs of the individual processes." (4a)

John Deere Health Care, Inc.

Exhibit 4–2
Comparison of Job-Order
and Process Costing

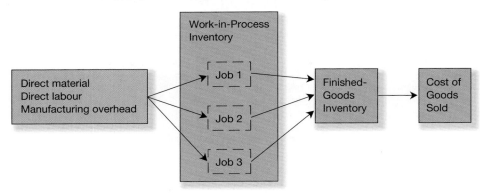

A. Job-Order Costing: Accumulates Costs by Job Order

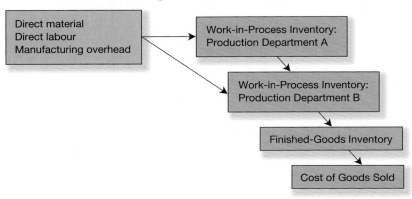

B. Process Costing: Accumulates Costs by Production Department

Differences between Job-Order and Process Costing

In job-order costing, *costs are accumulated by job order* and recorded on job-cost records. The cost of each unit in a particular job order is found by dividing the total cost of the job order by the number of units in the job.

In process costing, *costs are accumulated by department*, rather than by job order or batch. The cost per unit is found by averaging the total costs incurred over the units produced. Exhibit 4–2 summarizes this key difference between job-order and process costing.

Equivalent Units: A Key Concept

Learning Objective 3

Prepare a table of equivalent units under weighted-average process costing.

Material, labour, and overhead costs often are incurred at different rates in a production process. Direct material is usually placed into production at one or more discrete points in the process. In contrast, direct labour and manufacturing overhead, called *conversion costs*, are usually incurred continuously throughout the process. When an accounting period ends, the partially completed goods that remain in process generally are at different stages of completion with respect to material and conversion activity. For example, the in-process units may be 75 percent complete with respect to conversion, but they may already include all of their direct materials. This situation is portrayed in Exhibit 4–3.

Equivalent Units

The graphical illustration in Exhibit 4–3 supposes there are 1,000 physical units in process at the end of an accounting period. Each of the physical units is 75 percent complete with respect to conversion (direct labour and manufacturing overhead).

Exhibit 4–3
Direct Material and
Conversion Activity in a
Typical Production Process

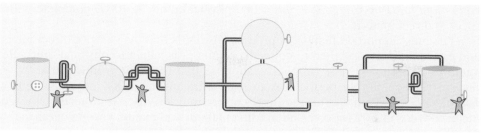

Production Process (e.g., chemical refining process)

Conversion activity (direct labour and manufacturing overhead) applied uniformly throughout the process

Direct material is placed
into production at the
beginning of the
production process.

When the accounting
period ends, the partially
completed goods are 75%
complete with respect to
conversion. The goods are
100% complete with
respect to direct material.

How much conversion activity has been applied to these partially completed units? Conversion activity occurs uniformly throughout the production process. Therefore, the amount of conversion activity required to do 75 percent of the conversion on 1,000 units is *equivalent* to the amount of conversion activity required to do all of the conversion on 750 units. This number is computed as follows:

$$\begin{array}{c} 1,000 \text{ partially completed} \\ \text{physical units in process} \end{array} \times \begin{array}{c} 75\% \text{ complete with} \\ \text{respect to conversion} \end{array} = 750 \text{ equivalent units}$$

The term **equivalent units** is used in process costing to refer to the amount of manufacturing activity that has been applied to a batch of physical units. The *1,000 physical units* in process represent *750 equivalent units* of conversion activity.

The term *equivalent units* also is used to measure the amount of direct materials represented by the partially completed goods. Since direct materials are incorporated at the beginning of the production process, the *1,000 physical units* represent *1,000*

Process costing is used in the timber industry. First, raw material (in this case, logs) are harvested and entered into production. Then conversion costs are incurred in the production process. At the end of the accounting period, partially completed units of building lumber often remain in process.

equivalent units of direct material (1,000 physical units × 100% complete with respect to direct materials).

The most important feature of process costing is that the costs of direct material and conversion are assigned to equivalent units rather than to physical units. Refer again to Exhibit 4–3. For simplicity, suppose that the only production activity of the current accounting period was to start work on the 1,000 physical units and complete 75 percent of the required conversion activity. Assume that the costs incurred were $1,500 for conversion (direct labour and manufacturing overhead) and $5,000 for direct material. These costs would then be assigned as follows:

$$\frac{\$1,500 \text{ conversion cost}}{750 \text{ equivalent units of conversion}} = \frac{\$2 \text{ per equivalent unit}}{\text{for conversion}}$$

$$\frac{\$5,000 \text{ direct-material cost}}{1,000 \text{ equivalent units of direct material}} = \frac{\$5 \text{ per equivalent unit}}{\text{for direct material}}$$

This is a highly simplified example because there is no work-in-process inventory at the beginning of the accounting period and no goods were completed during the period. Nevertheless, it illustrates the important concept that under process costing, costs are assigned to equivalent units rather than physical units.

Process Costing Illustrated

The key document in a typical process-costing system is the **departmental production report**, prepared for each production department at the end of every accounting period. This report replaces the job-cost record, which is used to accumulate costs by job in a job-order costing system. The departmental production report summarizes the flow of production quantities through the department, and it shows the amount of production cost transferred out of the department's Work-in-Process Inventory account during the period. The following four steps are used in preparing a departmental production report:

1. Analysis of physical flow of units
2. Calculation of equivalent units (for direct material and conversion activity)
3. Computation of unit costs (i.e., the cost per equivalent unit for direct material and conversion)
4. Analysis of total costs (determine the cost to be removed from work in process and transferred either to the next production department or to finished goods)

The method of process costing that we will focus on in this chapter is called the **weighted-average method**. *This method is almost always used in practice* by companies using process costing. There is another process-costing method called the *first-in, first-out, or FIFO, method*. This method is covered in some cost accounting courses, but it is rarely used in practice.[1]

Basic Data for Illustration

The Alberta Division of MVP Sports Equipment Company manufactures ski gloves in its Calgary plant. Two production departments are used in sequence: the Cutting Department and the Stitching Department. In the Cutting Department, direct material consisting of imitation leather is placed into production at the beginning of the process. Direct-labour and manufacturing overhead costs are incurred uniformly throughout the process. The material is rolled to make it softer and then cut into the pieces

Work in process, March 1—20,000 units		
Direct material: 100% complete, cost of*	$ 50,000	
Conversion: 10% complete, cost of*	7,200	
Balance in work in process, March 1*	$ 57,200	
Units started during March	30,000	units
Units completed during March and transferred out of the Cutting Department	40,000	units
Work in process, March 31	10,000	units
Direct material: 100% complete		
Conversion: 50% complete		
Costs incurred during March:		
Direct material	$ 90,000	
Conversion costs:		
Direct labour	$ 86,000	
Applied manufacturing overhead†	107,500	
Total conversion costs	$193,500	

*These costs were incurred during the prior month, February.
†(Predetermined overhead rate) × (Direct labour cost) = 125% × $86,000 = $107,500.

Exhibit 4–4
Basic Data for Illustration—
Cutting Department

needed to produce gloves. The predetermined overhead rate used in the Cutting Department is 125 percent of direct-labour *cost*.

The data in Exhibit 4–4 presents a summary of the activity and costs in the Cutting Department during March. The direct-material and conversion costs listed in Exhibit 4–4 for the March 1 work in process consist of costs that were incurred during February. These costs were assigned to the units remaining in process at the end of February.

Based on the data in Exhibit 4–4, the Cutting Department's Work-in-Process Inventory account has the following balance on March 1:

Work-in-Process Inventory: Cutting Department	
March 1 balance 57,200	

The following journal entry is made during March to add the costs of direct material, direct labour, and manufacturing overhead to Work-in-Process Inventory.

Work-in-Process Inventory: Cutting Department	283,500	
Raw-Material Inventory		90,000
Wages Payable		86,000
Manufacturing Overhead		107,500

Weighted-Average Method of Process Costing

We now present the four steps used to prepare a departmental production report using weighted-average process costing.

Management
Accounting
Practice

BRITISH COLUMBIA WINE INDUSTRY

British Columbia is the second-largest wine producer in Canada, after Ontario. Known as the "Napa Valley of the North," the Okanagan Valley in central B.C. boasts about 2,400 hectares of vineyards and over seven dozen wineries. Some of the most notable wineries are Mission Hill (the largest and most elaborate), Summerhill Pyramid Winery (with bottles aged inside a four-storey-high pyramid the most unique), Sumac Ridge, and Quails Gate Estate. B.C. wineries constitute the fastest-growing segment of the province's large tourism industry. Wine production provides an excellent example of process costing. The processes used in a typical Okanagan vineyard are as follows:[2]

- *Trimming.* At the end of a growing season, the vines are trimmed, which helps prepare them for the next harvest.
- *Tying.* The vines are tied onto wires to help protect them from the weather. (This also occurs at the end of the season.)
- *Hilling.* Dirt is piled up around the roots to further protect them.
- *Conditioning.* In the spring, dirt is levelled back from the roots.
- *Untying.* The vines are untied from the wires to allow them freedom to grow during the spring and summer months.
- *Chemical spraying.* The vines are sprayed in the spring to protect them from disease and insects.
- *Harvesting.* The highest-quality grapes are picked by hand to minimize damage.
- *Stemming and crushing.* Batches of grapes are loaded into a machine, which gently removes the stems and mildly crushes them.
- *Pressing.* After removal from the stemmer/crusher, the juice runs freely from the grapes.
- *Filtering.* The grapes are crushed mechanically to render more juice from them.
- *Fermentation.* This process varies, depending on the type of wine. For example, Riesling grape juice is placed in stainless-steel tanks for fermentation. Chardonnay grape juice undergoes a two-stage fermentation process in oak barrels.
- *Aging.* Again, this process varies. Riesling wines are aged in the stainless-steel tanks for approximately a year. Chardonnays are aged in the oak barrels for about two years.
- *Bottling.* A machine bottles the wine and corks the bottles.
- *Labelling.* Each bottle is labelled with the name of the vintner, vintage, and variety.
- *Packing.* The bottles are packed in 12-bottle cases.
- *Case labelling.* The cases are stamped with the same information as is on the bottles.
- *Shipping.* The wine is shipped to wine distributors and retailers.

Step 1: Analysis of Physical Flow of Units   The first step is to prepare a table summarizing the physical flow of production units during March. The table is shown in Exhibit 4–5 and reflects the following inventory formula.

$$\begin{pmatrix} \text{Physical units} \\ \text{in beginning} \\ \text{work in process} \end{pmatrix} + \begin{pmatrix} \text{Physical} \\ \text{units} \\ \text{started} \end{pmatrix} - \begin{pmatrix} \text{Physical units} \\ \text{completed and} \\ \text{transferred out} \end{pmatrix} = \begin{pmatrix} \text{Physical units} \\ \text{in ending work} \\ \text{in process} \end{pmatrix}$$

Step 2: Calculation of Equivalent Units   The second step in the process-costing procedure is to calculate the equivalent units of direct material and conversion activity. A table of

	Physical Units
Work in process, March 1	20,000
Units started during March	30,000
Total units to account for	**50,000**
Units completed and transferred out during March	40,000
Work in process, March 31	10,000
Total units accounted for	**50,000**

Exhibit 4–5

Step 1: Analysis of Physical Flow of Units— Cutting Department

equivalent units, displayed in Exhibit 4–6, is based on the table of physical flows prepared in step 1 (Exhibit 4–5). The 40,000 physical units that were completed and transferred out of the Cutting Department were 100 percent complete. Thus, they represent 40,000 equivalent units for both direct material and conversion. The 10,000 units in the ending work-in-process inventory are complete with respect to direct material, and they represent 10,000 equivalent units of direct material. However, they are only 50 percent complete with respect to conversion. Therefore, the ending work-in-process inventory represents 5,000 equivalent units of conversion activity (10,000 physical units × 50% complete).

As Exhibit 4–6 indicates, the total number of equivalent units is calculated:

$$\left(\begin{array}{c}\text{Equivalent units of}\\\text{activity in units completed}\\\text{and transferred out}\end{array}\right) + \left(\begin{array}{c}\text{Equivalent units of}\\\text{activity in ending}\\\text{work in process}\end{array}\right) + \left(\begin{array}{c}\text{Physical units}\\\text{completed and}\\\text{transformed out}\end{array}\right) = \left(\begin{array}{c}\text{Total}\\\text{equivalent units}\\\text{of activity}\end{array}\right)$$

	Physical Units (from Exhibit 4–5)	Percentage of Completion with Respect to Conversion	Equivalent Units	
			Direct Material	Conversion
Work in process, March 1	20,000	10%		
Units started during March	30,000			
Total units to account for	**50,000**			
Units completed and transferred out during March	40,000	100%	40,000	40,000
Work in process, March 31	10,000	50%	10,000	5,000
Total units accounted for	**50,000**			
Total equivalent units			**50,000**	**45,000**

Exhibit 4–6

Step 2: Calculation of Equivalent Units—Cutting Department (weighted-average method)

Note that the total equivalent units of activity, for both direct material and conversion, exceeds the activity accomplished in the current period alone. Since only 30,000 physical product units were started during March and direct material is added at the beginning of the process, only 30,000 equivalent units of direct material were actually placed into production during March. However, the total number of equivalent units of direct material used for weighted-average process costing is 50,000 (see Exhibit 4–6). The other 20,000 equivalent units of direct material were actually entered into production during the preceding month. *This is the key feature of the weighted-average method. The number of equivalent units of activity is calculated without making a distinction as to whether the activity occurred in the current accounting period or the preceding period.*

Step 3: Computation of Unit Costs The third step in the process-costing procedure, calculating the cost per equivalent unit for both direct material and conversion activity, is presented in Exhibit 4–7. The cost per equivalent unit for direct material is

Learning Objective 4

Compute the cost per equivalent unit under the weighted-average method of process costing.

Exhibit 4–7

Step 3: Computation of Unit
Costs—Cutting Department
(weighted-average method)

	Direct Material	Conversion	Total
Work in process, March 1 (from Exhibit 4–4)	$ 50,000	$ 7,200	$ 57,200
Costs incurred during March (from Exhibit 4–4)	90,000	193,500	283,500
Total costs to account for	$140,000	$200,700	$340,700
Equivalent units (from Exhibit 4–6)	50,000	45,000	
Costs per equivalent unit	$ 2.80	$ 4.46	$ 7.26
	$\dfrac{\$140{,}000}{50{,}000}$	$\dfrac{\$200{,}700}{45{,}000}$	$\$2.80 + \$4.46$

computed by dividing the total direct-material cost, including the cost of the beginning work in process *and* the cost incurred during March, by the total equivalent units (from step 2, Exhibit 4–6). A similar procedure is used for conversion costs.

Analyze the total production
costs for a department under
the weighted-average method
of process costing.

Step 4: Analysis of Total Costs   Now we can complete the process-costing procedure by determining the total cost to be transferred out of the Cutting Department's Work-in-Process Inventory account and into the Stitching Department's Work-in-Process Inventory account. Exhibit 4–8 provides the required calculations. For convenience, the computations in step 3 are repeated in Exhibit 4–8. At the bottom of Exhibit 4–8, a check is made to be sure that the total costs of $340,700 have been fully accounted for in the cost of goods completed and transferred out and the balance remaining in work-in-process inventory.

The calculations in Exhibit 4–8 are used as the basis for the following journal entry to transfer the cost of goods completed and transferred out to the Stitching Department.

Exhibit 4–8

Step 4: Analysis of Total
Costs—Cutting Department
(weighted-average method)

	Direct Material	Conversion	Total
Work in process, March 1 (from Exhibit 4–4)	$ 50,000	$ 7,200	$ 57,200
Costs incurred during March (from Exhibit 4–4)	90,000	193,500	283,500
Total costs to account for	$140,000	$200,700	$340,700
Equivalent units (from Exhibit 4–6)	50,000	45,000	
Costs per equivalent unit	$ 2.80	$ 4.46	$ 7.26
	$\dfrac{\$140{,}000}{50{,}000}$	$\dfrac{\$200{,}700}{45{,}000}$	$\$2.80 + \$4.46$

Cost of goods completed and transferred out of the Cutting Department during March:

$\left(\begin{array}{c}\text{Number of units}\\ \text{transferred out}\end{array}\right) \times \left(\begin{array}{c}\text{Total cost per}\\ \text{equivalent unit}\end{array}\right)$ $40{,}000 \times \$7.26$ **$290,400**

Cost remaining in March 31 work-in-process inventory in the Cutting Department:

Direct material:

$\left(\begin{array}{c}\text{Number of equivalent}\\ \text{units of direct material}\end{array}\right) \times \left(\begin{array}{c}\text{Cost per equivalent}\\ \text{unit of direct material}\end{array}\right)$ $10{,}000 \times \$2.80$ .... $ 28,000

Conversion:

$\left(\begin{array}{c}\text{Number of equivalent}\\ \text{units of conversion}\end{array}\right) \times \left(\begin{array}{c}\text{Cost per equivalent}\\ \text{unit of conversion}\end{array}\right)$ $5{,}000 \times \$4.46$ 22,300

Total cost of March 31 work in process	$ 50,300
Check: Cost of goods completed and transferred out	$290,400
Cost of March 31 work-in-process inventory	50,300
Total costs accounted for	$340,700

Work-in-Process Inventory: Stitching Department	290,400	
Work-in-Process Inventory: Cutting Department		290,400

On March 31, the Cutting Department's Work-in-Process Inventory account appears as follows. The March 31 balance in the account agrees with that calculated in Exhibit 4–8.

Work-in-Process Inventory: Cutting Department			
March 1 balance	57,200		
March cost of direct material, direct labour, and applied manufacturing overhead	283,500	290,400	Cost of goods completed and transferred to Stitching Department
March 31 balance	50,300		

Departmental Production Report We have now completed all four steps necessary to prepare a production report for the Cutting Department. The report, which is displayed in Exhibit 4–9, simply combines the tables presented in Exhibits 4–6 and 4–8. The report provides a convenient summary of all of the process-costing calculations made under the weighted-average method.

Why is this process-costing method called the *weighted-average* method? Because the cost per equivalent unit for March, for both direct material and conversion activity, is computed as a weighted average of the costs incurred during two different

Prepare a departmental production report under weighted-average process costing.

Exhibit 4–9

Production Report: Cutting Department (weighted-average method)

MVP SPORTS EQUIPMENT COMPANY
Production Report: Cutting Department

	Physical Units	Percentage of Completion with Respect to Conversion	Equivalent Units Direct Material	Conversion
Work in process, March 1	20,000	10%		
Units started during March	30,000			
Total units to account for	**50,000**			
Units completed and transferred out during March	40,000	100%	40,000	40,000
Work in process, March 31	10,000	50%	10,000	5,000
Total units accounted for	**50,000**			
Total equivalent units			50,000	45,000

(Steps 1 & 2)

	Direct Material	Conversion	Total
Work in process, March 1	$ 50,000	$ 7,200	$ 57,200
Costs incurred during March	90,000	193,500	283,500
Total costs to account for	**$140,000**	**$200,700**	**$340,700**
Equivalent units	50,000	45,000	
Costs per equivalent unit	$ 2.80	$ 4.46	$ 7.26

(Step 3)

Cost of goods completed and transferred out during March		$290,400
Cost in March 31 work-in-process inventory:		
Direct material		$ 28,000
Conversion		22,300
Total cost of March 31 work in process		$ 50,300
Total costs accounted for		**$340,700**

(Step 4)

accounting periods, February and March. To demonstrate this fact, we will focus on direct material. Since direct material is placed into production at the beginning of the process, the 20,000 physical units in the March 1 work in process already have their direct material. The direct-material cost per equivalent unit in the March 1 work in process is $2.50 ($50,000 ÷ 20,000, from Exhibit 4–4). This cost was actually incurred in *February*.

In March, 30,000 physical units were entered into work in process and received their direct material. The direct-material cost incurred in March was $90,000. Thus, the direct-material cost per equivalent unit experienced in *March* was $3 ($90,000 ÷ 30,000, from Exhibit 4–4).

Under the weighted-average method of process costing, the cost per equivalent unit for direct material was calculated in Exhibit 4–7 to be $2.80. *This $2.80 unit-cost figure is a weighted average*, as the following calculation shows.

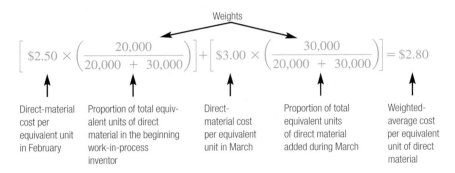

The point of this demonstration is that under weighted-average process costing, unit-cost figures are weighted averages of costs incurred over two or more accounting periods.

Other Issues in Process Costing

Several other issues related to process costing are worth discussing.

Actual versus Normal Costing

Our illustration of process costing assumed that *normal costing* was used. As explained in Chapter 3, in a normal-costing system, direct material and direct labour are applied to Work-in-Process Inventory at their *actual* amounts, but manufacturing overhead is applied to Work-in-Process Inventory using a predetermined overhead rate. In contrast, under an *actual-costing* system, the actual costs of direct material, direct labour, *and manufacturing overhead* are entered into Work-in-Process Inventory.

Either actual or normal costing may be used in conjunction with a process-costing system. Our illustration used normal costing since a predetermined overhead rate was used to compute applied manufacturing overhead in Exhibit 4–4. This resulted in applied overhead for March of $107,500 (125% × $86,000). If actual costing had been used, the manufacturing overhead cost for March would have been the actual overhead cost incurred instead of the applied overhead amount given in Exhibit 4–4. In all other ways, the process-costing procedures used under actual and normal costing are identical.

When normal costing is used, there may be overapplied or underapplied overhead at the end of the period. This amount is either closed into Cost of Goods Sold or prorated, as explained in Chapter 3.

Other Cost Drivers for Overhead Application

Our illustration used a predetermined overhead rate based on direct-labour cost. Since the application of manufacturing overhead was based on direct-labour cost, direct labour and manufacturing overhead were combined into the single cost element, *conversion costs*. This procedure is quite common in practice. If some cost driver (or activity base) other than direct labour had been used to apply manufacturing overhead, then overhead costs would be accounted for separately from direct-labour costs in the process-costing calculations.

Suppose, for example, that manufacturing overhead is applied on the basis of machine hours. A group of 100 physical units is 100 percent complete as to direct material, 60 percent complete as to direct labour, and 40 percent complete as to machine time. This situation could arise in a production process that is labour-intensive in its early stages but more automated in its later stages. In this case, the 100 physical units represent the following quantities of equivalent units:

	Equivalent Units		
Physical Units	**Direct Material**	**Direct Labour**	**Manufacturing Overhead**
100	100	60	40
	↑	↑	↑
	100 × 100%	100 × 60%	100 × 40%

Throughout the process-costing procedure, there will now be three cost elements (direct material, direct labour, and manufacturing overhead) instead of only two (direct material and conversion). In all other respects, the process-costing calculations will be identical to those illustrated earlier in the chapter.

Subsequent Production Departments

In our illustration, production requires two sequential production operations: cutting and stitching. Although the process-costing procedures for the second department are similar to those illustrated for the first, there is one additional complication. The cost of goods completed and transferred out of the Cutting Department must remain assigned to the partially completed product units as they undergo further processing in the Stitching Department. Process-costing procedures for subsequent production departments are covered in cost accounting texts.[3]

Hybrid Product-Costing Systems

Job-order and process costing represent the polar extremes of product-costing systems. But some production processes exhibit characteristics of both job-order and process-costing environments. Examples of such production processes include some clothing and food-processing operations. In these production processes, the conversion activities may be very similar or identical across all of the firm's product lines, even though the direct materials may differ significantly. Different clothing lines require significantly different direct materials, such as cotton, wool, or polyester. However, the conversion of these materials, involving direct labour and manufacturing overhead, may not differ much across product types. In the food industry, production of economy-grade or premium applesauce differs with regard to the quality and cost of the direct-material input, apples. However, the cooking, straining, and canning operations for these two product lines are similar.

The production processes described above often are referred to as **batch manufacturing** processes. Such processes are characterized by high-volume production of several product lines that differ in some important ways but are nearly identical in others. Since batch manufacturing operations have characteristics of both job-order costing and process-costing environments, a **hybrid product-costing system** is required. One common approach is called **operation costing**. This product-costing system is used when conversion activities are very similar across product lines, but the direct materials differ significantly. *Conversion costs* are accumulated by *department*, and process-costing methods are used to assign these costs to products. In contrast, *direct-material costs* are accumulated by *job order or batch*, and job-order costing is used to assign material costs to products.[4]

Chapter Summary

Process costing is used in production processes where relatively large numbers of nearly identical products are manufactured. The purpose of a process-costing system is the same as that of a job-order costing system—to accumulate costs and assign these costs to units of product. Product costs are needed for planning, cost management, decision making, and reporting to various outside organizations.

The flow of costs in process-costing systems and job-order costing systems is the same. Costs of direct material, direct labour, and manufacturing overhead are added to a Work-in-Process Inventory account. Direct labour and manufacturing overhead are often combined into a single cost category termed *conversion costs*. When products are completed, the costs assigned to them are transferred either to Finished-Goods Inventory or to the next production department's Work-in-Process Inventory account. In sequential production processes, the cost of the goods transferred from one production department to another is called transferred-in cost.

There are some important differences between job-order and process-costing systems. Chief among these is that job-order costing systems accumulate production costs by job or batch, whereas process-costing systems accumulate costs by department. Another important difference is the focus on equivalent units in process costing. An equivalent unit is a measure of the amount of productive input that has been applied to a fully or partially completed unit of product. In process costing, production costs per equivalent unit are calculated for direct-material and conversion costs.

The key document in a process-costing system is the departmental production report, rather than the job-cost record used in job-order costing. There are four steps in preparing a departmental production report: (1) analyze the physical flow of units, (2) calculate the equivalent units, (3) compute the cost per equivalent unit, and (4) analyze the total costs of the department.

In the weighted-average method of process costing, the cost per equivalent unit, for each cost category, is a weighted average of (1) the costs assigned to the beginning work-in-process inventory and (2) the costs incurred during the current period.

Job-order and process costing represent the polar extremes of product-costing systems. Operation costing is a hybrid of these two methods. It is designed for production processes in which the direct material differs significantly among product lines but the conversion activities are essentially the same. Direct-material costs are accumulated by batches of products using job-order costing methods. Conversion costs are accumulated by production departments and are assigned to product units by process-costing methods.

Review Problem on Process Costing

The following data have been compiled for MVP's Cutting Department for the month of June. Conversion activity occurs uniformly throughout the production process.

Work in process, June 1—25,000 units:	
Direct material: 100% complete, cost of	$ 73,750
Conversion: 40% complete, cost of	46,000
Balance in work in process, June 1	$119,750
Units started during June	40,000
Units completed during June and transferred out	60,000
Work in process, June 30:	
Direct material: 100% complete	
Conversion: 60% complete	
Costs incurred during June:	
Direct material	$121,250
Conversion costs: direct labour and applied manufacturing overhead	237,500

Required: Prepare the Cutting Department's June production report using weighted-average process costing. (*Hint:* Follow the format of Exhibit 4–9.)

Exhibit 4–10
June Production Report:
Cutting Department
(weighted-average method)

MVP SPORTS EQUIPMENT COMPANY
June Production Report: Cutting Department

	Physical Units	Percentage of Completion with Respect to Conversion	Equivalent Units	
			Direct Material	Conversion
Work in process, June 1	25,000	40%		
Units started during June	40,000			
Total units to account for	65,000			
Units completed and transferred out during June	60,000	100%	60,000	60,000
Work in process, June 30	5,000	60%	5,000	3,000
Total units accounted for	65,000			
Total equivalent units			65,000	63,000

	Direct Material	Conversion	Total
Work in process, June 1	$ 73,750	$ 46,000	$119,750
Costs incurred during June	121,250	237,500	358,750
Total costs to account for	$195,000	$283,500	$478,500
Equivalent units	65,000	63,000	
Costs per equivalent unit	$ 3.00	$ 4.50	$ 7.50
	↑	↑	↑
	$195,000 / 65,000	$283,500 / 63,000	$3.00 + $4.50

Cost of goods completed and transferred out of the Cutting Department during June:

$\left(\begin{array}{c}\text{Number of units}\\\text{transferred out}\end{array}\right) \times \left(\begin{array}{c}\text{Total cost per}\\\text{equivalent unit}\end{array}\right)$ ......   60,000 × $7.50 ....   **$450,000**

Cost remaining in June 30 work-in-process inventory in the Cutting Department:

Direct material:

$\left(\begin{array}{c}\text{Number of equivalent}\\\text{units of direct material}\end{array}\right) \times \left(\begin{array}{c}\text{Cost per equivalent}\\\text{unit of direct material}\end{array}\right)$ ....   5,000 × $3.00 .... $ 15,000

Conversion:

$\left(\begin{array}{c}\text{Number of equivalent}\\\text{units of conversion}\end{array}\right) \times \left(\begin{array}{c}\text{Cost per equivalent}\\\text{unit of conversion}\end{array}\right)$ ....   3,000 × $4.50   13,500

Total cost of June 30 work in process .... $ 28,500

Check: Cost of goods completed and transferred out $450,000
Cost of June 30 work-in-process inventory   28,500
Total costs accounted for $478,500

Solution to Review Problem

The Cutting Department's June production report is displayed in Exhibit 4–10.

Key Terms

For each term's definition refer to the indicated page, or turn to the glossary at the end of the text.

Review Questions

4–1. Explain the primary differences between job-order and process costing.

4–2. List five types of manufacturing in which process costing would be an appropriate product-costing system. What is the key characteristic of these products that makes process costing a good choice?

4–3. List three nonmanufacturing businesses in which process costing could be used. For example, a public accounting firm could use process costing to accumulate the costs of processing clients' tax returns.

4–4. What are the purposes of a product-costing system?

4–5. Define the term *equivalent unit* and explain how the concept is used in process costing.

4–6. List and briefly describe the purpose of each of the four process-costing steps.

4–7. Show how to prepare a journal entry to enter direct-material costs into the Work-in-Process Inventory account for the first department in a sequential production process. Show how to prepare the journal entry recording the transfer of goods from the first to the second department in the sequence.

4–8. What are transferred-in costs?

4–9. A food processing company has two sequential production departments: mixing and cooking. The cost of the January 1 work in process in the cooking department is detailed as follows:

Direct material	$ 79,000
Conversion	30,000
Transferred-in costs	182,000

During what time period and in what department were the $182,000 of costs listed above incurred? Explain your answer.

4–10. Explain the reasoning underlying the name of the weighted-average method.

4–11. How does process costing differ under normal or actual costing?

4–12. How would the process-costing computations differ from those illustrated in the chapter if overhead were applied on some activity base other than direct labour?

4–13. What is the purpose of a departmental production report prepared using process costing?

4–14. Explain the concept of *operation costing*. How does it differ from process or job-order costing? Why is operation costing well suited for batch manufacturing processes?

Exercises

■ Exercise 4–15
Physical Flow of Units
(LO 1, 3)

In each case below, fill in the missing amount.

1.
Work in Process, June 1	10,000 tonnes
Units started during June	?
Units completed during June	16,000 tonnes
Work in process, June 30	3,000 tonnes

2.
Work in process, April 1	12,000 metres
Units started during April	22,000 metres
Units completed during April	21,500 metres
Work in process, April 30	?

3.
Work in process, January 1	50,000 litres
Units started during the year	67,000 litres
Units completed during the year	?
Work in process, December 31	45,000 litres

■ Exercise 4–16
Process Costing; Use of Internet
(LO 1)

Use the Internet to access the Web site for Canfor (www.canfor.com), Domtar (www.domtar.com), or Boise Cascade (www.boisecascade.com).

Required: Skim over the information presented on the Web site about the company's products and operations. Then discuss why process costing is an appropriate product-costing method for this company.

■ Exercise 4–17
Equivalent Units; Weighted Average
(LO 3)

Andromeda Glass Company manufactures decorative glass products. The firm employs a process-costing system for its manufacturing operations. All direct materials are added at the beginning of the process, and conversion costs are incurred uniformly throughout the process. The company's production schedule for August follows.

	Units
Work in process on August 1 (60% complete as to conversion)	2,000
Units started during August	3,500
Total units to account for	5,500
Units from beginning work in process, which were completed and transferred out during August	2,000
Units started and completed during August	1,800
Work in process on August 31 (20% complete as to conversion)	1,700
Total units accounted for	5,500

Required: Calculate each of the following amounts using weighted-average process costing.

1. Equivalent units of direct material during August.
2. Equivalent units of conversion activity during August.

(CMA, adapted)

Exercise 4–18
Equivalent Units; Weighted Average
(LO 3)

PetroTech Company refines a variety of petrochemical products. The following data are from the firm's Fort McMurray plant.

Work in process, July 1	1,900,000 litres
Direct material...	100% complete
Conversion...	30% complete
Units started in process during July...	750,000 litres
Work in process, July 31	250,000 litres
Direct material...	100% complete
Conversion...	70% complete

Required: Compute the equivalent units of direct material and conversion for the month of July. Use the weighted-average method of process costing.

Exercise 4–19
Physical Flow and Equivalent Units; Weighted Average
(LO 3)

The Edmonton plant of Healthy Life Styles, Inc. produces low-fat salad dressing. The following data pertain to the year just ended.

		Percentage of Completion	
	Units	Direct Material	Conversion
Work in process, January 1	30,000 litres	70%	50%
Work in process, December 31.........................	25,000 litres	75%	20%

During the year, the company started 140,000 litres of material in production.

Required: Prepare a schedule analyzing the physical flow of units and computing the equivalent units of both direct material and conversion for the year. Use weighted-average process costing.

Exercise 4–20
Cost per Equivalent Unit; Weighted Average
(LO 3, 4)

BC Lumber Company grows, harvests, and processes timber for use in construction. The following data pertain to the firm's sawmill during June:

Work in process, June 1:	
Direct material...	$ 74,900
Conversion...	167,000
Costs incurred during June:	
Direct material...	$380,700
Conversion...	625,000

The equivalent units of activity for June were as follows: 6,700 equivalent units of direct material and 1,600 equivalent units of conversion activity.

Required: Calculate the cost per equivalent unit, for both direct material and conversion, during June. Use weighted-average process costing.

■ **Exercise 4–21**
Cost per Equivalent Unit;
Weighted Average
(LO 3, 4)

Duluth Glass Company manufactures window glass for automobiles. The following data pertain to the Plate Glass Department.

Work in process, February 1:	
Direct material	$ 43,200
Conversion	40,300
Costs incurred during February:	
Direct material	$135,000
Conversion	190,000

The equivalent units of activity for February were as follows: 16,500 equivalent units of direct material and 47,000 equivalent units of conversion activity.

Required: Calculate the cost per equivalent unit, for both direct material and conversion, during February. Use weighted-average process costing.

■ **Exercise 4–22**
Analysis of Total Costs;
Weighted Average
(LO 5)

Raleigh Textiles Company manufactures a variety of natural fabrics for the clothing industry. The following data pertain to the Weaving Department for the month of November:

Equivalent units of direct material (weighted-average method)	62,500
Equivalent units of conversion (weighted-average method)	49,000
Units completed and transferred out during November	47,000

The cost data for November are as follows:

Work in process, November 1:	
Direct material	$ 85,750
Conversion	16,900
Costs incurred during November:	
Direct material	$158,000
Conversion	267,300

There were 19,000 units in process in the Weaving Department on November 1 (100% complete as to direct material and 38% complete as to conversion).

Required: Compute each of the following amounts using weighted-average process costing:

1. Cost of goods completed and transferred out of the Weaving Department
2. Cost of the November 30 work-in-process inventory in the Weaving Department
3. *Build a spreadsheet.* Construct an Excel spreadsheet to solve all of the preceding requirements. Show how the solution will change if the following data change: the costs incurred in November were $160,000 for direct material and $270,000 for conversion.

■ **Exercise 4–23**
Analysis of Total Costs;
Weighted Average
(LO 5)

The following data pertain to Thomas Paperboard Company, a manufacturer of cardboard boxes:

Work in process, March 1	10,000 units*
Direct material	$ 10,900
Conversion	28,950
Costs incurred during March:	
Direct material	$112,700
Conversion	160,200

*Complete as to direct material; 35 percent complete as to conversion.

The equivalent units of activity for March were as follows:

Direct material (weighted-average method)	103,000
Conversion (weighted-average method)	97,000
Completed and transferred out	89,000

Required: Compute the following amounts using weighted-average process costing.

1. Cost of goods completed and transferred out during March
2. Cost of the March 31 work-in-process inventory

Problems

Jupiter Corporation manufactures home security devices. During 20x4, 1,000,000 units were completed and transferred to finished-goods inventory. On December 31, 20x4, there were 310,000 units in work in process. These units were 48 percent complete as to conversion and 100 percent complete as to direct material. Finished-goods inventory consisted of 250,000 units. Materials are added to production at the beginning of the manufacturing process, and overhead is applied to each product at the rate of 100 percent of direct-labour costs. There was no finished-goods inventory on January 1, 20x4. A review of the inventory cost records disclosed the following information:

	Costs		
	Units	**Materials**	**Labour**
Work in process, January 1, 20x4			
(83% complete as to conversion)	210,000	$ 300,000	$ 310,400
Units started in production	1,100,000		
Direct-material costs		$1,403,000	
Direct-labour costs			$1,700,000

Required: Prepare schedules as of December 31, 20x4, to compute the following:

1. Physical flow of units
2. Equivalent units of production using the weighted-average method
3. Costs per equivalent unit for material and conversion
4. Cost of the December 31, 20x4, finished-goods inventory and work-in-process inventory

(CMA, adapted)

Toronto Titanium Corporation manufactures a highly specialized titanium sheathing material that is used extensively in the aircraft industry. The following data have been compiled for the month of June. Conversion activity occurs uniformly throughout the production process:

Work in process, June 1—40,000 units:	
Direct material: 100% complete cost of	$110,500
Conversion: 38% complete, cost of	22,375
Balance in work in process, June 1	$132,875
Units started during June	190,000
Units completed during June and transferred out to finished-goods inventory	180,000
Work in process, June 30:	
Direct material: 100% complete	
Conversion: 55% complete	
Costs incurred during June:	
Direct material	$430,000
Conversion costs:	
Direct labour	$128,000
Applied manufacturing overhead	192,000
Total conversion costs	$320,000

Required: Prepare schedules to accomplish each of the following process-costing steps for the month of June. Use the weighted-average method of process costing.

1. Analysis of physical flow of units
2. Calculation of equivalent units

3. Computation of unit costs
4. Analysis of total costs

■ **Problem 4–26**
Missing Data; Production
Report; Weighted Average
(LO 4, 5, 6)

Costs incurred during
October, direct material:
$600,000
Cost per equivalent unit,
conversion: $11.85

The following data pertain to the Fantasia Flour Milling Company for the month of October.

Work in process, October 1 (in units)...	?
Units started during October...	70,000
Total units to account for...	80,000
Units completed and transferred out during October..	?
Work in process, October 31 (in units)...	5,000
Total equivalent units: Direct material...	80,000
Total equivalent units: Conversion	?
Work in process, October 1: Direct material..	$ 112,000
Work in process, October 1: Conversion	?
Costs incurred during October: Direct material..	?
Costs incurred during October: Conversion	900,000
Work in process, October 1: Total cost..	142,225
Total costs incurred during October...	1,500,000
Total costs to account for	1,642,225
Cost per equivalent unit: Direct material	8.90
Cost per equivalent unit: Conversion...	?
Total cost per equivalent unit	20.75
Cost of goods completed and transferred out during October..............................	?
Cost remaining in ending work-in-process inventory: Direct material.....................	?
Cost remaining in ending work-in-process inventory: Conversion	41,475
Total cost of October 31 work in process...	85,975

Additional Information:

a. Direct material is added at the beginning of the production process, and conversion activity occurs uniformly throughout the process.

b. The company uses weighted-average process costing.

c. The October 1 work in process was 15 percent complete as to conversion.

The October 31 work in process was 70 percent complete as to conversion.

Required: Compute the missing amounts, and prepare the firm's October production report.

■ **Problem 4–27**
Partial Production Report;
Journal Entries; Weighted-
Average Method
(LO 2, 3, 4, 5)

1a. Conversion, total equivalent units: 58,000
1b. Total cost per equivalent
unit: $54.50

Triangle Fastener Corporation accumulates costs for its single product using process costing. Direct material is added at the beginning of the production process, and conversion activity occurs uniformly throughout the process. A partially completed production report for the month of June follows.

Production Report
For the Month of June

	Physical Units	Percentage of Completion with Respect to Conversion	Direct Material	Conversion
			Equivalent Units	
Work in process, June 1	30,000	35%		
Units started during June	34,000			
Total units to account for	64,000			
Units completed and transferred out during June	40,000		40,000	40,000
Work in process, June 30	24,000	75%	24,000	18,000
Total units accounted for	64,000			

	Direct Material	Conversion	Total
Work in process, June 1	$147,600	$ 623,400	$ 771,000
Costs incurred during June	201,200	2,221,500	2,422,700
Total costs to account for	$348,800	$2,844,900	$3,193,700

Required:

1. Complete each of the following process-costing steps using the weighted-average method:
   a. Calculation of equivalent units
   b. Computation of unit costs
   c. Analysis of total costs
2. Prepare a journal entry to record the transfer of the cost of goods completed and transferred out during June.

■ **Problem 4–28**
Straightforward Weighted-Average Process Costing; Step-by-Step Approach
(LO 3, 4, 5)

2. Equivalent units, direct material: 110,000
3. Conversion, cost per equivalent unit: $1.81

Moravia Company processes and packages cream cheese. The following data have been compiled for the month of April. Conversion activity occurs uniformly throughout the production process.

Work in process, April 1—10,000 units:	
Direct material: 100% complete, cost of	$ 22,000
Conversion: 20% complete, cost of	4,500
Balance in work in process, April 1	$ 26,500
Units started during April	100,000
Units completed during April and transferred out to finished-goods inventory	80,000
Work in process, April 30:	
Direct material: 100% complete	
Conversion: 33 1/3% complete	
Costs incurred during April:	
Direct material	$198,000
Conversion costs:	
Direct labour	$ 52,800
Applied manufacturing overhead	105,600
Total conversion costs	$158,400

Required: Prepare schedules to accomplish each of the following process-costing steps for the month of April. Use the weighted-average method of process costing.

1. Analysis of physical flow of units
2. Calculation of equivalent units
3. Computation of unit costs
4. Analysis of total costs
5. *Build a spreadsheet:* Construct an Excel spreadsheet to solve all of the preceding requirements. Show how the solution will change if the following data change: the April 1 work-in-process costs were $27,000 for direct material and $5,000 for conversion.

■ **Problem 4–29**
Partial Production Report; Journal Entries; Weighted-Average Method
(LO 2, 3, 4, 5)

1. Equivalent units, direct material: 120,000
2. Conversion, cost per equivalent unit: $10.28

Taffy Company produces various kinds of candy, but saltwater taffy is by far its most important product. The company accumulates costs for its product using process costing. Direct material is added at the beginning of the production process, and conversion activity occurs uniformly throughout the process.

Production Report
For August 20x1

	Physical Units	Percentage of Completion with Respect to Conversion	Equivalent Units Direct Material	Conversion
Work in process, August 1	40,000	80%		
Units started during August	80,000			
Total units to account for	120,000			
Units completed and transferred out during August	100,000		100,000	100,000
Work in process, August 31	20,000	30%	20,000	6,000
Total units accounted for	120,000			

	Direct Material	Conversion	Total
Work in process, August 1	$ 42,000	$ 305,280	$ 347,280
Costs incurred during August	96,000	784,400	880,400
Total costs to account for	$138,000	$1,089,680	$1,227,680

Required: Use weighted-average process costing in completing the following requirements:

1. Prepare a schedule of equivalent units.
2. Compute the costs per equivalent unit.
3. Compute the cost of goods completed and transferred out during August.
4. Compute the cost remaining in the work-in-process inventory on August 31.
5. Prepare a journal entry to record the transfer of the cost of goods completed and transferred out.

■ **Problem 4–30**
Determination of Production Costs; Analysis of Equivalent Units
(LO 3, 4, 5)

1. Overhead applied: $441,186
2. Equivalent units, conversion: 27,800

Texarkana Corporation assembles various components used in the computer industry. The company's major product, a disk drive, is the result of assembling three parts: JR1163, JY1065, and DC0766. The following information relates to activities of April:

- Beginning work-in-process inventory: 3,000 units, 80 percent complete as to conversion; cost, $293,940 (direct materials, $230,000; conversion cost, $63,940)
- Production started: 27,000 units
- Production completed: 26,000 units
- Ending work-in-process inventory: 4,000 units, 45 percent complete as to conversion
- Direct materials used: JR1163, $225,000; JY1065, $710,000; DC0766, $455,000
- Hourly wage of direct labourers, $21; total direct-labour payroll, $134,274
- Overhead application rate: $69 per direct-labour hour

All parts are introduced at the beginning of the manufacturing process; conversion cost is incurred uniformly throughout production.

Required:

1. Calculate the total cost of direct material and conversion during April.
2. Determine the cost of goods completed during the month.
3. Determine the cost of the work-in-process inventory on April 30.
4. With regard to the ending work-in-process inventory on April 30:
   a. How much direct-material cost would be added to these units in May?
   b. What percentage of conversion would be performed on these units in May?
5. Assume that the disk drive required the addition of another part (TH55) at the 75 percent stage of completion. How many equivalent units with respect to part TH55 would be represented in April's ending work-in-process inventory?

Lawncraft, Inc. manufactures wooden lawn furniture using an assembly-line process. All direct materials are introduced at the start of the process, and conversion cost is incurred evenly throughout manufacturing. An examination of the company's Work-in-Process Inventory account for June revealed the following selected information:

Debit side:

    June 1 balance: 200 units, 25% complete as to conversion, cost $18,000*

    Production started: 800 units

    Direct material used during June: $43,000

    June conversion cost: $30,000

Credit side:

    Production completed: 600 units

    *Supplementary records revealed direct-material cost of $12,000 and conversion cost of $6,000.

Conversations with manufacturing personnel revealed that the ending work in process was 75 percent complete as to conversion.

Required:

1. Determine the number of units in the June 30 work-in-process inventory.
2. Calculate the cost of goods completed during June and prepare the appropriate journal entry to record completed production.
3. Determine the cost of the June 30 work-in-process inventory.
4. Briefly explain the meaning of equivalent units. Why are equivalent units needed to properly allocate costs between completed production and production in process?

The following data pertain to the Canandaigua Carpet Company for January:

Work in process, January 1 (in units)	25,000
Units started during January	?
Total units to account for	80,000
Units completed and transferred out during January	?
Work in process, January 31 (in units)	20,000
Total equivalent units: Direct material	80,000
Total equivalent units: Conversion	?
Work in process, January 1: Direct material	$ 232,000
Work in process, January 1: Conversion	?
Costs incurred during January: Direct material	?
Costs incurred during January: Conversion	820,000
Work in process, January 1: Total cost	342,000
Total costs incurred during January	1,220,000
Total costs to account for	1,562,600
Cost per equivalent unit: Direct material	7.90
Cost per equivalent unit: Conversion	?
Total cost per equivalent unit	22.00
Cost of goods completed and transferred out during January	?
Cost remaining in ending work-in-process inventory: Direct material	?
Cost remaining in ending work-in-process inventory: Conversion	84,600
Total cost of January 31 work in process	242,600

Additional Information:

a. Direct material is added at the beginning of the production process, and conversion activity occurs uniformly throughout the process.
b. Hercules uses weighted-average process costing.
c. The January 1 work in process was 25 percent complete as to conversion.
d. The January 31 work in process was 30 percent complete as to conversion.

Required: Compute the missing amounts, and prepare the firm's May production report.

■ **Problem 4–31**
Analysis of Work-in-Process
Inventory Account
(LO 3, 4, 5)

2. Conversion, total equivalent
units: 900
2. Direct material, cost per
equivalent unit: $55

■ **Problem 4–32**
Missing Data; Production
Report; Weighted Average
(LO 4, 5, 6)

Total equivalent units,
conversion: 66,000
Cost incurred during January,
direct material: $400,000

■ **Problem 4–33**
Process Costing in a Public
Accounting Firm
(LO 3, 4, 5)

1*a*. Equivalent units,
overhead: 1,100
1*b*. Overhead, cost per
equivalent unit: £50

Scrooge and Zilch, a public accounting firm in London, is engaged in the preparation of income tax returns for individuals. The firm uses the weighted-average method of process costing for internal reporting. The following information pertains to February. (£ denotes the British monetary unit, pounds sterling.)*

Returns in process, February 1	
(20% complete)	300
Returns started in February	900
Returns in process, February 28	
(75% complete)	400
Returns in process, February 1:	
Labour	£3,500
Overhead	4,000
Labour, February (4,500 hours)	90,000
Overhead, February	51,000

*Although the euro is used in most European markets, day-to-day business in the United Kingdom continues to be conducted in pounds sterling.

Required:

1. Compute the following amounts for labour and for overhead:
    a. Equivalent units of activity
    b. Cost per equivalent unit (remember to express your answer in terms of the British pound sterling, denoted by £)
2. Compute the cost of returns in process as of February 28.

(CMA, adapted)

■ **Problem 4–34**
Process Costing; Production
Report; Journal Entries;
Weighted-Average Method
(LO 2, 3, 4, 5, 6)

1. Direct material, total
equivalent units: 22,000
1. Conversion, cost per
equivalent unit: $14.90

GroFast Company manufactures a high-quality fertilizer, which is used primarily by commercial vegetable growers. Two departments are involved in the production process. In the Mixing Department, various chemicals are entered into production. After processing, the Mixing Department transfers a chemical called Chemgro to the Finishing Department. There the product is completed, packaged, and shipped under the brand name Vegegro.

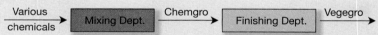

In the Mixing Department, the raw material is added at the beginning of the process. Labour and overhead are applied continuously throughout the process. All direct departmental overhead is traced to the departments, and plant overhead is allocated to the departments on the basis of direct labour. The plant overhead rate for 20x5 is $1.50 per direct-labour dollar.

The following information relates to production during November 20x5 in the Mixing Department:

a. Work in process, November 1 (5,000 kilograms, 70% complete as to conversion):

Raw material	$31,600
Direct labour	18,000
Departmental overhead	10,220
Allocated plant overhead	27,000

b. Raw material:

Inventory, November 1, 3,000 kilograms	16,000
Purchases, November 3, 9,000 kilograms	44,000
Purchases, November 18, 12,000 kilograms	60,000
Released to production during November, 17,000 kilograms	

c. Direct-labour cost, $70,000

d. Direct departmental overhead costs, $35,000

e. Transferred to Finishing Department, 16,000 kilograms

f. Work in process, November 30, 6,000 kilograms, 30 percent complete

The company uses weighted-average process costing to accumulate product costs. However, for raw-material inventories, the firm uses the FIFO inventory method.

Required:

1. Prepare a production report for the Mixing Department for November 20x5. The report should show:
   a. Equivalent units of production by cost factor (i.e., direct material and conversion)
   b. Cost per equivalent unit for each cost factor (round your answers to the nearest cent)
   c. Cost of Chemgro transferred to the Finishing Department
   d. Cost of the work-in-process inventory on November 30, 20x5, in the Mixing Department
2. Prepare journal entries to record the following events:
   a. Release of direct material to production during November
   b. Incurrence of direct-labour costs in November
   c. Application of overhead costs for the Mixing Department (direct departmental and allocated plant overhead costs)
   d. Transfer of Chemgro out of the Mixing Department

(CMA, adapted)

Case

Lycoming Leather Company manufactures high-quality leather goods in Manitoba. The company's profits have declined during the past nine months. In an attempt to isolate the causes of poor profit performance, management is investigating the manufacturing operations of each of its products.

One of the company's main products is leather belts. The belts are produced in a single, continuous process in the Winnipeg Plant. During the process, leather strips are sewn, punched, and dyed. The belts then enter a final finishing stage to conclude the process. Labour and overhead are applied continuously during the manufacturing process. All materials, leather strips, and buckles are introduced at the beginning of the process. The firm uses the weighted-average method to calculate its unit costs.

The leather belts produced at the Winnipeg Plant are sold wholesale for $22.95 each. Management wants to compare the current manufacturing costs per unit with the market prices for leather belts. Top management has asked the plant controller to submit data on the cost of manufacturing the leather belts for the month of October. These cost data will be used to determine whether modifications in the production process should be initiated or whether an increase in the selling price of the belts is justified. The cost per belt used for planning and control is $11.50.

The work-in-process inventory consisted of 500 partially completed units on October 1. The belts were 30 percent complete as to conversion. The costs included in the inventory on October 1 were as follows:

Leather strips	$1,650
Buckles	350
Conversion costs	2,500
Total	$4,500

During October 8,000 leather strips and buckles were put into production. A total of 8,100 leather belts were completed. The work-in-process inventory on October 31 consisted of 400 belts, which were 40 percent complete as to conversion.

The costs charged to production during October were as follows:

Leather strips	$ 41,000
Buckles	8,000
Conversion costs	55,320
Total	$104,320

Required:
In order to provide cost data regarding the manufacture of leather belts in the Winnipeg Plant to the top management of Lycoming Leather Company, compute the following amounts for the month of October:

1. The equivalent units for material and conversion
2. The cost per equivalent unit of material and conversion
3. The assignment of production costs to the October 31 work-in-process inventory and to goods transferred out

■ **Case 4–35**
Weighted-Average Process Costing; Ethics
(LO 3, 4, 5, 6)

Equivalent units, direct material: 8,500
Total cost per equivalent unit: $13

4. The weighted-average unit cost of leather belts completed and transferred to finished goods. Comment on the company's cost per belt used for planning and control.

5. Lycoming Leather Company's production manager, Jack Murray, has been under pressure from the company president to reduce the cost of conversion. In spite of several attempts to reduce conversion costs, they have remained more or less constant. Now Murray is faced with an upcoming meeting with the company president, at which he will have to explain why he has failed to reduce conversion costs. Murray has approached his friend, Jeff Daley, who is the corporate controller, with the following request: "Jeff, I'm under pressure to reduce costs in the production process. There is no way to reduce material cost, so I've got to get the conversion costs down. If I can show just a little progress in next week's meeting with the president, then I can buy a little time to try some other cost-cutting measures I've been considering. I want you to do me a favour. If we raise the estimate of the percentage of completion of October's inventory to 50 percent, that will increase the number of equivalent units. Then the unit conversion cost will be a little lower." By how much would Murray's suggested manipulation lower the unit conversion cost? What should Daley do? Discuss this situation, citing specific ethical standards for managerial accountants.

(CMA, adapted)

See the Online Learning Centre for supplements to this chapter: Supplement 4A: Process Costing: The First-In, First-Out Method; Supplement 4B: Process Costing in Sequential Production Departments; and Supplement 4C: Hybrid Product Costing Systems: Operation Costing in Batch Manufacturing Processes.

Chapter Five

Activity-Based Costing and Management

FOCUS COMPANY

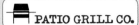 **PATIO GRILL CO.**

The Patio Grill Company manufactures high-end, gas barbeque grills in its Mississauga plant. The company has recently experienced intense competition in its two high-volume product lines, forcing management to drop these products' prices below their target levels. A careful study of this situation revealed that Patio Grill Company's traditional product-costing system distorted product costs by assigning too much cost to the high-volume gas-grill lines and not enough cost to the low-volume, complex line of grills. Management then implemented a new costing system, called activity-based costing (or ABC), which assigns product costs more accurately than traditional product-costing systems. With the cost insights from the ABC system, management was able to change its pricing structure to compete more effectively in the gas-grill market. Using ABC data, the Patio Grill Company has embraced activity-based management (or ABM).

IN CONTRAST

In contrast to the manufacturing setting of the Patio Grill Company, we explore the use of activity-based costing by the Toronto General Hospital's Ambulatory Cardiac Clinic. ABC is used in this health-care services setting to assign treatment costs to categories of patient visits, such as routine, extended, and complex visits, as well as new and continuing patients.

After completing this chapter, you should be able to:

1 Compute product costs under a traditional, volume-based product-costing system.

2 Explain how an activity-based costing system operates, including the use of a two-stage procedure for cost assignment, the identification of activity cost pools, and the selection of cost drivers.

3 Explain the concept of cost levels, including unit-level, batch-level, product-sustaining-level, and facility-level costs.

4 Compute product costs under an activity-based costing system.

5 Explain why traditional, volume-based costing systems tend to distort product costs.

6 Explain three criteria for selecting cost drivers.

7 Discuss several key issues in activity-based costing, including data collection, storyboarding, and indicators that an ABC system might be useful.

8 Explain the concept of activity-based management and two-dimensional ABC.

9 Explain and execute a customer-profitability analysis.

10 Understand and discuss how activity-based costing is used in service organizations.

11 List and explain eight important features of just-in-time inventory and production management systems (Appendix).

A revolution is transforming the world of business. Not since the mid-19th century have we seen changes as sweeping and dramatic. The growth of international competition, the breakneck pace of technological innovation, and startling advances in computerized systems have created a new playing field for manufacturers around the globe. Some manufacturers have emerged as world-class producers, while others have fallen by the wayside. World-class companies such as Caterpillar, Coca-Cola, Johnson & Johnson, and Pfizer are among the many manufacturers that have changed key business processes to compete effectively in the 21st century.

The service sector also is undergoing dramatic transformation. The growth of the Internet, the trend toward a service economy, and the willingness of businesses to outsource many critical service functions have caused many service organizations to reinvent the way they do business. Among the many service firms that have adapted most successfully to the changing business environment are American Express, TD Canada Trust, FedEx, Google, and WestJet Airlines.

PATIO GRILL CO.

What is the role of managerial accounting in this rapidly changing environment? To explore these issues, we will review recent events in the life of Patio Grill Company, a manufacturer of barbeque grills and accessories. The company's Mississauga plant manufactures three product lines, all high-end, gas barbeque grills. The plant's three gas grill lines are the Patio Standard (STD), the Deluxe (DEL), and the Ultimate (ULT).

Traditional, Volume-Based Product-Costing System

Learning Objective 1

Compute product costs under a traditional, volume-based product-costing system.

Until recently, Patio Grill Company used a job-order product-costing system similar to the one described in Chapter 3 for Rocky Mountain Outfitters. The cost of each product was the sum of its actual direct-material cost, actual direct-labour cost, and applied manufacturing overhead. Overhead was applied using a predetermined overhead rate based on direct-labour hours. Exhibit 5–1 provides the basic data upon which the traditional costing system was based.

The Excel spreadsheet in Exhibit 5–2 shows the calculation of the product cost for each of three gas grill lines (STD, DEL, and ULT). Overhead is applied to the products at the rate of $24 per direct-labour hour. Notice that all of the plant's budgeted manufacturing overhead costs are lumped together in a single cost pool. This total budgeted overhead amount ($4,896,000) then is divided by the total budgeted direct-labour hours (204,000 hours).

Patio Grill Company's labour-hour-based product-costing system is typical of many manufacturing companies. Labour hours are related closely to the volume of activity in the factory, which sometimes is referred to as *throughput*. Consequently, these traditional product-costing systems often are said to be **volume-based** (or **throughput-based**) **costing systems**.

Exhibit 5–1
Basic Production and Cost Data: Patio Grill Company

	Patio Standard Grill STD	**Deluxe Grill** DEL	**Ultimate Grill** ULT
Planned annual production:			
Volume in units......................	10,000	8,000	2,000
Production runs.....................	80 runs of 125 units each	80 runs of 100 units each	40 runs of 50 units each
Direct material...........................	$100	$120	$180
Direct labour (not including setup time)............	$180 (9 hours @ $20 per hour)	$220 (11 hours @ $20 per hour)	$260 (13 hours @ $20 per hour)
Machine hours (MH) per product unit.....................	10 MH	12 MH	17 MH
Total machine hours consumed by product line	100,000 (10 MH × 10,000 units)	96,000 (12 MH × 8,000 units)	34,000 (17 MH × 2,000 units)

	A	B	C	D	E	F	G	H
1			STD		DEL		ULT	
2								
3	Direct material		$100.00		$120.00		$180.00	
4	Direct labour							
5	(not including setup time)		180.00	(9 hr. @ $20)	220.00	(11 hr. @ $20)	260.00	(13 hr. @ $20)
6	Manufacturing overhead*		216.00	(9 hr. @ $24)	264.00	(11 hr. @ $24)	312.00	(13 hr. @ $24)
7	Total		$496.00		$604.00		$752.00	
8								
9								
10	*Calculation of predetermined-overhead rate:							
11								
12	Budgeted manufacturing overhead			$4,896,000				
13								
14	Direct labour, budgeted hours:							
15	STD: 10,000 units x 9 hours			90,000				
16	DEL: 8,000 units x 11 hours			88,000				
17	ULT: 2,000 units x 13 hours			26,000				
18	Total direct-labour hours			204,000	hours			
19								
20	Predetermined overhead rate:							
21	(Budgeted manufacturing overhead / Budgeted direct-labour hours) = $4,896,000 / 204,000 = $24 per hour							

Exhibit 5–2
Product Costs from Traditional, Volume-Based Product-Costing System: Patio Grill Company

PATIO GRILL CO.

Trouble in Mississauga

The profitability of Patio Grill Company's Mississauga operation has been faltering in recent years. The company's pricing policy has been to set a target price for each grill equal to 120 percent of the full product cost. Thus, the prices were determined as shown in Exhibit 5–3. Also shown are the actual prices that Patio Grill Company has been obtaining for its products.

Due to price competition from other grill manufacturers, Patio Standard (STD) grills were selling at $585, approximately $10 below their target price of $595.20. Moreover, Patio Grill Company's competition had forced management to reduce the price of the Deluxe grill (DEL) to $705, almost $20 below its target price of $724.80. Even at this lower price, the sales team was having difficulty getting orders for its planned volume of Deluxe grill production. Fortunately, the disappointing profitability of the Patio Standard and Deluxe model grills was partially offset by greater-than-expected profits on the Ultimate (ULT) line of grills. Patio Grill Company's sales personnel had discovered that the company was swamped with orders when the Ultimate grill's target price of $902.40 was charged. Consequently, management had raised the price on the Ultimate grills several times, and eventually the product was selling for $940. Even at this price, Patio Grill Company's customers did not seem to hesitate to place orders. Moreover, the company's competitors did not mount a challenge in the market for the Ultimate line of grills. Patio's management was pleased to have a niche for the Ultimate grill market, which appeared to be a highly profitable, low-volume specialty product. Nevertheless, concern continued to mount about the difficulty in the Patio Standard and Deluxe grill markets. After all, these were the Mississauga plant's bread-and-butter products, with projected annual sales of 10,000 Patio Standard grills and 8,000 Deluxe grills.

	Patio Standard Grill STD	Deluxe Grill DEL	Ultimate Grill ULT
Production cost under traditional, volume-based system (Exhibit 5–2)	$496.00	$604.00	$752.00
Target selling price (Cost × 120%)	595.20	724.80	902.40
Actual current selling price	585.00	705.00	940.00

Exhibit 5–3
Target and Actual Selling Prices: Patio Grill Company

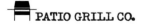
PATIO GRILL CO.

Activity-Based Costing System

Patio Grill Company's director of cost management, Hamilton Burger, had been thinking for some time about a refinement in the plant's product-costing system. He wondered if the traditional, volume-based system was providing management with accurate data about product costs. Burger had read about **activity-based costing (ABC) systems**, which follow a two-stage procedure to assign overhead costs to products. The first stage identifies significant activities in the production of the three products and assigns overhead costs to each activity in accordance with the cost of the organization's resources used by the activity. The overhead costs assigned to each activity make up an **activity-cost pool**.

After assigning overhead costs to activity cost pools in stage one, cost drivers appropriate for each cost pool are identified in stage two. Then, using **pool rates**, the overhead costs are allocated from each activity cost pool to each product line in proportion to the amount of the cost driver consumed by the product line.

The two-stage cost-assignment process of activity-based costing is depicted in Exhibit 5–4.

Burger discussed activity-based costing with Patty Cook, the assistant director of cost management. Together they met with all of Patio Grill Company's department supervisors to discuss development of an ABC system. After initial discussion, an ABC proposal was made to the company's top management. Approval was obtained, and an ABC project team was formed, which included Burger, Cook, and representatives of various functional departments. Through several months of painstaking data collection and analysis, the project team was able to gather the data necessary to implement an ABC system.

ABC Stage One

Patio Grill Company's ABC project team identified eight activity cost pools, which fall into four broad categories:

Exhibit 5–4
Activity-Based Costing System

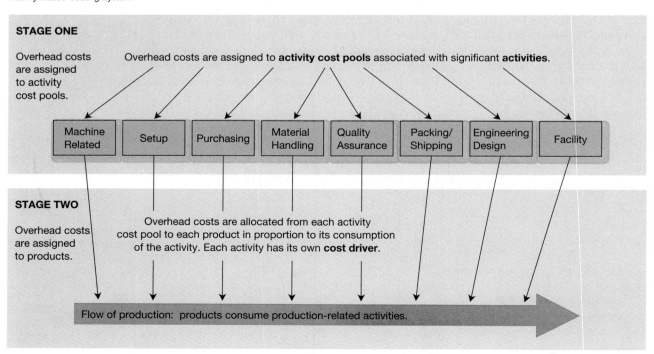

STAGE ONE

Overhead costs are assigned to activity cost pools.

Overhead costs are assigned to **activity cost pools** associated with significant **activities**.

| Machine Related | Setup | Purchasing | Material Handling | Quality Assurance | Packing/ Shipping | Engineering Design | Facility |

STAGE TWO

Overhead costs are assigned to products.

Overhead costs are allocated from each activity cost pool to each product in proportion to its consumption of the activity. Each activity has its own **cost driver**.

Flow of production: products consume production-related activities.

This forklift operator is engaged in material handling, which is usually a batch-level activity in an ABC system. The engineer using this computer-aided-design (CAD) system is engaged in the product-sustaining-level activity of product design.

- *Unit level.* This type of activity must be done for each unit of production. The machine-related activity cost pool represents a **unit-level activity** since every product unit requires machine time.
- *Batch level.* These activities must be performed for each batch of products, rather than each unit. Patio Grill Company's **batch-level activities** include the setup, purchasing, material handling, quality assurance, and packing/shipping activity cost pools.
- *Product-sustaining level.* This category includes activities that are needed to support an entire product line but are not performed every time a new unit or batch of products is produced. Patio Grill Company's project team identified engineering design costs as a **product-sustaining-level activity** cost pool.
- *Facility (or general operations) level.* **Facility-(or general-operations-) level activities** are required in order for the entire production process to occur. Examples of such activity costs include plant management salaries, plant depreciation, property taxes, plant maintenance, and insurance.

This classification of activities into unit-level, batch-level, product-sustaining-level, and facility-level activities is called a **cost hierarchy**.

Patio Grill Company's eight activity cost pools are depicted in Exhibit 5–5. Notice that the total overhead cost for all eight activity cost pools, $4,896,000, is shown at the top. This amount is the same as the total overhead cost shown in Exhibit 5–2, which shows the details of the product costs calculated under Patio Grill Company's traditional product-costing system.

ABC Stage Two

In stage two of the activity-based costing project, Burger and Cook identified cost drivers for each activity cost pool. Then they used a three-step process to compute unit activity costs for each of Patio Grill Company's three product lines, and for each of the eight activity cost pools. In the following sections, we will discuss in detail how stage two of the ABC project was carried out for the various activity cost pools identified in stage one. Then we will complete the ABC project by developing new product costs for each of the company's gas grill product lines.

Machine-Related Cost Pool Let's begin by focusing on only one of the eight activity cost pools. The machine-related cost pool, a unit-level activity, totals $1,242,000 and includes the costs of machine maintenance, depreciation, computer support, lubrication, electricity, and calibration. Burger and Cook selected machine hours for the cost driver, since a product that uses more machine hours should bear a larger share of machine-related costs. Exhibit 5–6 shows how machinery costs are assigned to products in stage two of the ABC analysis. Notice that the Exhibit includes just a portion of a larger spreadsheet that we will examine in due course. The spreadsheet rows

Learning Objective **4**

Compute product costs under an activity-based costing system.

Exhibit 5–5
Stage One of Activity-Based
Costing: Identification of
Activity Cost Pools

PATIO GRILL CO.

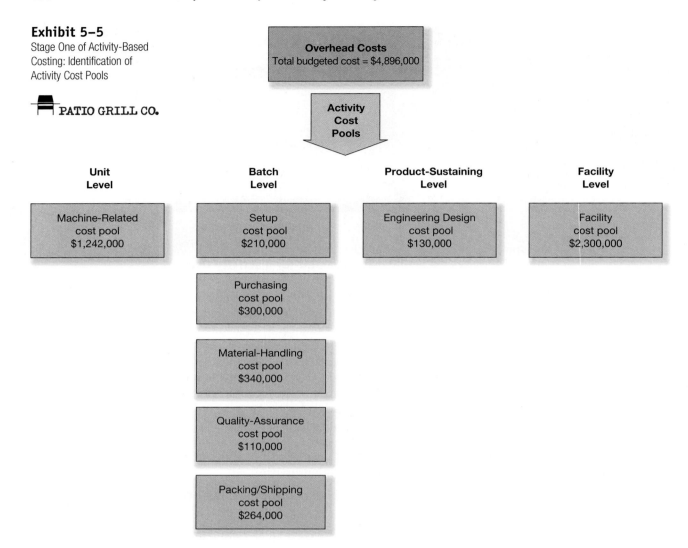

shown focus just on the machine-related activity cost pool. Most of the columns in the Exhibit contain ABC data that were collected by the ABC project team. We will learn more later in this chapter about how that information is collected. For now, though, let's just take this ABC information as a given. As noted in Exhibit 5–6, the following columns contain *data collected by the ABC project team.*

Data Collected by ABC Project Team (Exhibit 5–6)

Column A   Activity: Machine-related

Column B   Activity cost pool: $1,242,000 (from Exhibit 5–5)

Column C   Cost driver: Machine hours

Column D   Cost driver quantity: 230,000 machine hours (total of machine hours for the three products lines in column G)

Column F   Product lines: STD, DEL, ULT

Column G   Cost driver quantity for each product line (from Exhibit 5–1):
            STD 100,000 machine hours
            DEL 96,000 machine hours
            ULT 34,000 machine hours

Column I   Product line production volume (from Exhibit 5–1):
            STD 10,000 units
            DEL 8,000 units
            ULT 2,000 units

**INFORMATION SUPPLIED
BY ABC PROJECT TEAM**

Exhibit 5–6
ABC Data and Calculations for the Machine-Related Cost Pool: Patio Grill Company

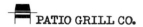 PATIO GRILL CO.

	A	B	C	D	E	F	G	H	I	J
1							Cost	Activity	Product	Activity
2		Activity		Cost			Driver	Cost for	Line	Cost
3		Cost	Cost	Driver	Pool	Product	Quantity for	Product	Production	per Unit
4	Activity	Pool	Driver	Quantity	Rate	Line	Product Line	Line	Volume	of Product
5										
6	Machine	$1,242,000	Machine	230,000	$5.40	STD	100,000	$540,000	10,000	$ 54.00
7	Related		Hours			DEL	96,000	518,400	8,000	64.80
8						ULT	34,000	183,600	2,000	91.80
9						Total	230,000	1,242,000		

ABC CALCULATIONS

1 Compute pool rate for machine-related activity

$$\frac{\text{Activity cost pool}}{\text{(Col. B)}} \div \frac{\text{Cost driver quantity}}{\text{(Col. D)}} = \frac{\text{Pool rate}}{\text{(Col. E)}}$$

$1,242,000 \div 230,000 = $5.40

2 Compute total activity cost for each product line

Product line (Col. F)	Pool rate (Col. E)	×	Cost driver quantity for each product line (Col. G)	=	Activity cost for each product line (Col. H)
STD	$5.40	×	100,000	=	$540,000
DEL	5.40	×	96,000	=	518,400
ULT	5.40	×	34,000	=	183,600

3 Compute product cost per unit for each product line

Product line (Col. F)	Activity cost for each product line (Col. H)	÷	Product line production volume (Col. I)	=	Activity cost per unit of product (Col. J)
STD	$540,000	÷	10,000	=	$54.00
DEL	518,400	÷	8,000	=	64.80
ULT	183,600	÷	2,000	=	91.80

Notice that only three columns in Exhibit 5–6 remain: columns E, H, and J. These columns contain the *amounts that are computed* during the ABC calculations, and they appear in red in Exhibit 5–6.

Amounts Computed during ABC Calculations (Exhibit 5–6)

Column E   Pool rate

Column H   Activity cost for each product line

Column J   Activity cost per unit of product for each product line

Exhibit 5–6, below the spreadsheet excerpt, shows in detail how each of these amounts (shown in red) is computed. Take time now to examine the Exhibit carefully, in order to understand how these amounts are computed in the ABC calculations.

Now we have seen the type of data that the ABC project team must supply for the machine-related cost pool. In addition, we have studied how the ABC calculations are carried out in order to determine the machine-related activity cost per unit of each type of product (STD, DEL, and ULT). The final conclusion of the ABC analysis *for the machine-related cost pool only* is given in column J of Exhibit 5–6. Thus, under activity-based costing, the following machine-related costs per product unit should be assigned to each of the three product lines.

Exhibit 5–7
Activity-Based Costing Data and Calculations: Patio Grill Company

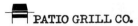 PATIO GRILL CO.

	A	B	C	D	E	F	G	H	I	J
	Activity	Activity Cost Pool	Cost Driver	Cost Driver Quantity	Pool Rate	Product Line	Cost Driver Quantity for Product Line	Activity Cost for Product Line	Product Line Production Volume	Activity Cost per Unit of Product
6	Machine	$ 1,242,000	Machine	230,000	$ 5.40	STD	100,000	$ 540,000	10,000	$ 54.00
7	Related		Hours			DEL	96,000	518,400	8,000	64.80
8						ULT	34,000	183,600	2,000	91.80
9						Total	230,000	1,242,000		
10	Setup	210,000	Production	200	1,050.00	STD	80	84,000	10,000	8.40
11			Runs			DEL	80	84,000	8,000	10.50
12						ULT	40	42,000	2,000	21.00
13						Total	200	210,000		
14	Purchasing	300,000	Purchase	600	500.00	STD	200	100,000	10,000	10.00
15			Orders			DEL	192	96,000	8,000	12.00
16						ULT	208	104,000	2,000	52.00
17						Total	600	300,000		
18	Material	340,000	Production	200	1,700.00	STD	80	136,000	10,000	13.60
19	Handling		Runs			DEL	80	136,000	8,000	17.00
20						ULT	40	68,000	2,000	34.00
21						Total	200	340,000		
22	Quality	110,000	Inspection	2,200	50.00	STD	800	40,000	10,000	4.00
23	Assurance		Hours			DEL	800	40,000	8,000	5.00
24						ULT	600	30,000	2,000	15.00
25						Total	2,200	110,000		
26	Packing/	264,000	Shipments	2,200	120.00	STD	1,000	120,000	10,000	12.00
27	Shipping					DEL	800	96,000	8,000	12.00
28						ULT	400	48,000	2,000	24.00
29						Total	2,200	264,000		
30	Engineering	130,000	Engineering	1,300	100.00	STD	500	50,000	10,000	5.00
31	Design		Hours			DEL	400	40,000	8,000	5.00
32						ULT	400	40,000	2,000	20.00
33						Total	1,300	130,000		
34	Facility	2,300,000	Machine	230,000	10.00	STD	100,000	1,000,000	10,000	100.00
35			Hours			DEL	96,000	960,000	8,000	120.00
36						ULT	34,000	340,000	2,000	170.00
37						Total	230,000	2,300,000		
39	Grand Total	$ 4,896,000				Grand Total		$ 4,896,000		

STD: $54.00 of machine-related cost per grill
DEL: $64.80 of machine-related cost per grill
ULT: $91.80 of machine-related cost per grill

Completing the ABC Calculations   Now that we have studied the ABC data requirements and calculations for the machine-related cost pool (Exhibit 5–6), we can complete the ABC calculations by including all eight of the activity cost pools. These eight cost pools were given in Exhibit 5–5. The entire Excel spreadsheet for Patio Grill Company's activity-based costing project is displayed in Exhibit 5–7. As the cliché goes, there is good news and bad news. The bad news is that the spreadsheet in Exhibit 5–7 contains eight times as many rows as the one we just examined in detail for the machine-related cost pool. The good news, though, is that the ABC data requirements and calculations are conceptually *identical* for each of the eight activity cost pools. In other words, the same type of ABC data is supplied for each activity cost pool, and the three steps of ABC computations are performed for each activity cost pool in exactly the same manner as they were for the machine-related cost pool. So if we understand the computations in Exhibit 5–6 (for the machine-related costs), then we will understand the computations in Exhibit 5–7 for all eight activity cost pools. (The amounts that are *computed* in Exhibit 5–7 are shown in red.)

Pause here and take a few moments to examine Exhibit 5–7. Select an activity other than the machine-related activity we studied earlier. Try to verify the computations of the pool rate in column E, the activity cost for each product line in column H, and the ABC overhead cost per unit of product in column J.

Now that we have the activity cost per unit of product for each activity cost pool and each product line, it is straightforward to compute the total unit product cost for each type of grill. To do so, we need only add the direct-material and direct-labour costs for each grill type (given in Exhibit 5–1) to the ABC activity costs calculated in Exhibit 5–7. We do this in the Excel spreadsheet displayed as Exhibit 5–8.

	A	B	C	D	E	F	G	H
1			STD		DEL		ULT	
2								
3	Direct material		$100.00		$120.00		$180.00	
4	Direct labour							
5	(not including setup time)		180.00	(9 hr. @ $20)	220.00	(11 hr. @ $20)	260.00	(13 hr. @ $20)
6	Total direct costs per unit		$280.00		$340.00		$440.00	
7								
8	Manufacturing overhead (based on ABC):*							
9	Machine-related		$ 54.00		$ 64.80		$ 91.80	
10	Setup		8.40		10.50		21.00	
11	Purchasing		10.00		12.00		52.00	
12	Material handling		13.60		17.00		34.00	
13	Quality assurance		4.00		5.00		15.00	
14	Packing/shipping		12.00		12.00		24.00	
15	Engineering design		5.00		5.00		20.00	
16	Facility		100.00		120.00		170.00	
17	Total ABC overhead cost per unit		$207.00		$246.30		$427.80	
18	Total product cost per unit		$487.00		$586.30		$867.80	
19								
20	*ABC overhead costs from Exhibit 5-7.							

Exhibit 5–8
Product Costs from Activity-Based Costing System: Patio Grill Company

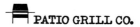 PATIO GRILL CO.

Interpreting the ABC Product Costs

Hamilton Burger was amazed to see the product costs reported under the activity-based costing system. Both the STD and the DEL grills exhibited lower product costs under the ABC system than under the traditional system. This might explain the price competition Patio Grill Company faced on its STD and DEL grills. Patio Grill Company's competitors might sell their comparable standard and deluxe grills at a lower price because they realized it cost less to produce these grills than Patio Grill Company's traditional costing system had indicated. However, as Burger scanned the new product costs shown in Exhibit 5–8, he was alarmed by the substantial increase in the reported cost of an ULT grill. The cost of an ULT grill had risen by more than $100 above the company's original estimate. The complexity of the ULT grills, and its impact on costs, was hidden by the traditional, volume-based costing system. To compare the results of the two alternative costing systems, Burger prepared Exhibit 5–9.

As shown in Exhibit 5–9, the STD grills emerged as a profitable product, selling for approximately 120 percent of their reported cost under the activity-based costing system ($585 ÷ $487). The DEL grills also were selling at approximately 120 percent of their new reported product cost ($705 ÷ $586.30). "No wonder we couldn't sell the deluxe grills at the old target price of $724.80," said Burger to Cook, as they looked over the data. "Our competitors probably knew their deluxe grills cost around $586, and they priced them accordingly." When he got to the ULT column in Exhibit 5–9, Burger was appalled. "We thought those ultimate grills were a winner," lamented Burger, "but we've been selling them at a price that is just about 8 percent over their

	STD	DEL	ULT
Reported unit *overhead* cost:			
Traditional, volume-based costing system (Exhibit 5–2)	$216.00	$264.00	$ 312.00
Activity-based costing system (Exhibit 5–8)	207.00	246.30	427.80
Reported unit *product* cost (direct material, direct labour, and overhead):			
Traditional, volume-based costing system (Exhibit 5–2)	496.00	604.00	752.00
Activity-based costing system (Exhibit 5–8)	487.00	586.30	867.80
Sales price data:			
Original target price (120% of product cost based on traditional, volume-based costing system (Exhibit 5–3)	595.20	724.80	902.40
New target price (120% of product cost based on activity-based costing system	584.40	703.56	1,041.36
Actual current selling price (Exhibit 5–3)	585.00	705.00	940.00

Exhibit 5–9
Comparison of Product Costs and Target Prices from Alternative Product-Costing Systems: Patio Grill Company

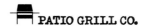 PATIO GRILL CO.

cost!" (Burger had made this calculation: actual current selling price of $940 ÷ ABC product cost of $867.80.) "And worse yet," Burger continued, "we've been selling the ultimate grills for $940, which is more than a hundred dollars below the new target price of $1,041.36." After looking over the data, Burger made a beeline for the president's office. "We've got to get this operation straightened out," he thought.

Burger also realized that the comparison of the two product-costing systems was even more striking when he focused on just the reported *overhead* costs. He commented to Cook, "The direct-material and direct-labour costs for each product line don't change under ABC. They're the same under both costing systems. Since these are direct costs, it's straightforward to trace these costs to each product with considerable accuracy. It's the overhead costs that cause the problem." To see what Burger was getting at, look again at Exhibit 5–9 and focus on the top two rows. The overhead cost of a STD grill dropped from the old reported cost of $216 to $207 under ABC. Similarly, the overhead cost of a DEL grill dropped from the old reported cost of $264 to $246.30 under ABC. Now look at the ULT column, though. Here the overhead cost rose from the old reported cost of $312 to $427.80 under ABC! This represents an increase of more than a third. ($427.80 ÷ $312.00 is a little over 137 percent, which yields an *increase* of over 37 percent.)

The Punch Line

Learning Objective 5

Explain why traditional, volume-based costing systems tend to distort product costs.

What has happened at Patio Grill Company's plant? The essence of the problem is that the traditional, volume-based costing system was overcosting the high-volume product lines (STD and DEL) and undercosting the complex, relatively low-volume product line (ULT). The high-volume products basically subsidized the low-volume line. The activity-based costing system revealed this problem by more accurately assigning overhead costs to the three product lines.

Exhibit 5–10 summarizes the effects of the cost distortion under the traditional product-costing system. Patio Grill Company's traditional system *overcosted* each STD grill by $9, for a total of $90,000 for the STD product line on a volume of 10,000 units. Each DEL grill was *overcosted* by $17.70, for a total of $141,600 on a volume of 8,000 units for the DEL product line. These excess costs had to come from somewhere, and that place was the ULT product line. Each ULT grill was *undercosted* by $115.80, for a total of $231,600 for the ULT product line on a volume of 2,000 units. Notice that the *total* amount by which the STD and DEL grill lines were overcosted equals the *total* amount by which the ULT grill line was undercosted.

Cost Distortions with Traditional, Volume-Based Costing Systems

Why did Patio Grill Company's traditional product-costing system distort its product costs? The answer lies in the use of a single, volume-based cost driver. The company's old costing system assigned overhead to products on the basis of their relative usage of direct labour. Since the STD and DEL grill lines use substantially more direct labour than the ULT grill line, *in total*, the traditional system assigned them more overhead costs.

The problem with this result is that for every one of Patio Grill Company's overhead activities, the proportion of the activity actually consumed by the ULT grill line is far greater than its low volume would suggest. The ULT grill line has a budgeted production volume of just 2,000 units, which is only 10 percent of Patio Grill Company's total budgeted production volume of 20,000 units. (20,000 units = 10,000 STD units + 8,000 DEL units + 2,000 ULT units.) Now examine the ABC calculations in Exhibit 5–7. Focus on column G, which details the consumption of the cost driver by each product line for each activity cost pool. Notice that for every one of the overhead activities, the ULT grill line consumes much more than a 10 percent share of the activity, even though

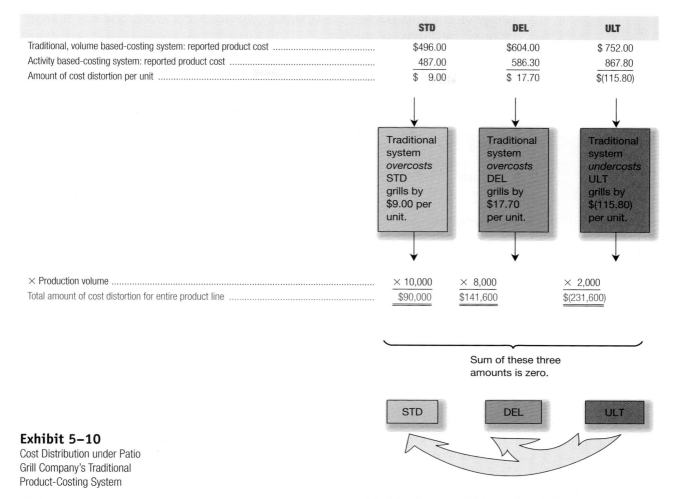

	STD	DEL	ULT
Traditional, volume based-costing system: reported product cost	$496.00	$604.00	$ 752.00
Activity based-costing system: reported product cost	487.00	586.30	867.80
Amount of cost distortion per unit	$ 9.00	$ 17.70	$(115.80)

	STD	DEL	ULT
	Traditional system *overcosts* STD grills by $9.00 per unit.	Traditional system *overcosts* DEL grills by $17.70 per unit.	Traditional system *undercosts* ULT grills by $(115.80) per unit.

	STD	DEL	ULT
× Production volume	× 10,000	× 8,000	× 2,000
Total amount of cost distortion for entire product line	$90,000	$141,600	$(231,600)

Sum of these three amounts is zero.

Exhibit 5–10
Cost Distribution under Patio
Grill Company's Traditional
Product-Costing System

PATIO GRILL CO.

Traditional system shifts costs from ULT product line to STD and DEL product lines.

the ULT line accounts for only 10 percent of budgeted production volume. The relatively heavy consumption of overhead activities by the ULT product line is due to its greater complexity and small production runs. We must conclude, therefore, that direct labour is not a suitable cost driver for Patio Grill Company's overhead costs. Usage of direct labour does not drive most overhead costs in this company.

There are actually two factors working against Patio Grill Company's old product-costing system. First, many of the activities that result in the company's overhead costs are *not unit-level activities*. Second, the company manufactures a *diverse set of products*.

Non-Unit-Level Overhead Costs   When Patio Grill Company's ABC project team designed the activity-based costing system, only the machine-related overhead cost pool was classified as a unit-level activity. All of the other activities were classified as batch-level, product-sustaining-level, or facility-level activities. This means that many of the company's overhead costs are not incurred every time a unit is produced. Instead, many of these overhead costs are related to starting new production batches, supporting an entire product line, or running the entire operation. Since direct labour is a unit-level cost driver, it fails to capture the forces that drive these other types of costs. In Patio Grill Company's new ABC system, cost drivers were chosen that were appropriate for each activity cost pool. For example, since setting up machinery for a new production run is a batch-level activity, the number of production runs is an appropriate batch-level cost driver.

Product Diversity   Patio Grill Company manufactures three different products. Although all three are gas barbeque grills, the three grills are quite different. The STD and DEL grills are high-volume, relatively simple products. The ULT grills constitute a considerably more complex, and relatively low-volume, product line. As a result of this *product line diversity*, Patio Grill Company's three product lines consume overhead activities in different proportions. For example, compare the *consumption ratios* for the purchasing and material-handling activity cost pools shown below. The **consumption ratio** is the proportion of an activity consumed by a particular product.

	Consumption Ratios*		
Activity Cost Pool	**STD**	**DEL**	**ULT**
Purchasing activity (cost driver is purchase orders, or POs)..	200 POs (33%)	192 POs (32%)	208 POs (35%)
Material-handling activity (cost driver is production runs)	80 runs (40%)	80 runs (40%)	40 runs (20%)

*The purchase order and production run data come from Exhibit 5–7.

These widely varying consumption ratios result from Patio Grill Company's product line diversity. A single cost driver will not capture the widely differing usage of these activities by the three products. The activity-based costing system uses two different cost drivers to assign these costs to the company's diverse products.

Two Key Points   To summarize, each of the following characteristics will undermine the ability of a volume-based product-costing system to assign overhead costs accurately.

- *A large proportion of non-unit-level activities.* A unit-level cost driver, such as direct labour, machine hours, or throughput, will not be able to assign the costs of non-unit-level activities accurately.
- *Product diversity.* When the consumption ratios differ widely between activities, no single cost driver will accurately assign the resulting overhead costs.

When either of these characteristics is present, a volume-based product-costing system is likely to distort product costs.

Does the sort of product-cost distortion experienced by Patio Grill Company occur in other companies? The answer is yes, as illustrated by the following examples from Rockwell International and DHL express transport service.[1]

Management
Accounting
Practice

Rockwell International

COST DISTORTION AT ROCKWELL INTERNATIONAL

When managers at Rockwell International noticed erratic sales in one of the company's lines of truck axles, they investigated. One of the company's best axle products was losing market share. A special cost study revealed that the firm's costing system, which applied costs to products in proportion to direct-labour costs, had resulted in major distortions. The reported product costs for high-volume axles were approximately 20 percent too high, and the low-volume axles were being undercosted by roughly 40 percent. The firm's practice of basing prices on reported product costs resulted in the overpricing of the high-volume axles. As a consequence, Rockwell's competitors entered the market for the high-volume axle business.[2]

COST DISTORTION AT DHL

DHL, the express transport company, ships a billion packages a year worldwide. Management at DHL found that its cost accounting system had distorted costs between the various types of express transport services the firm provided. Before implementation of a full activity-based costing system at DHL, express transport services provided to banks appeared to be unprofitable, whereas transport services provided to heavy manufacturers appeared to be highly profitable. "This was bad news because we [DHL] had a lot more banking customers than heavy manufacturing customers." After fully implementing ABC, however, management found that the previous costing system had used cost drivers that failed to account for package weights, thereby distorting costs between services to banks and services to heavy manufacturers. The ABC analysis revealed that express transport services to banks were actually quite profitable after all.[3]

Activity-Based Costing: Key Issues

Patio Grill Company's movement toward activity-based costing is typical of changes currently under way in many companies. Added domestic and foreign competition is forcing manufacturers to strive for a better understanding of their cost structures. Moreover, the cost structures of many manufacturers have changed significantly over the past decade. Years ago, a typical manufacturer produced a relatively small number of products that did not differ much in the amount and types of manufacturing support they required. Labour was the dominant element in such a firm's cost structure. Nowadays, it's a different ball game. Products are more numerous, are more complicated, and vary more in their production requirements. Perhaps most important, labour is becoming an ever-smaller component of total production costs. All these factors mean manufacturers must take a close look at their traditional, volume-based costing systems and consider a move toward activity-based costing. Among the many well-known manufacturers that have benefited from ABC are Caterpillar, Coca-Cola, Hewlett-Packard, Vale Inco, John Deere, Johnson & Johnson, Magna Automotive, Pennzoil, and Pfizer, to name only a few.

The service sector also has undergone dynamic change in recent years. Increasing competition, outsourcing of key business processes, and the growth of the Internet have changed many service companies' business models. As their business environment changes, many service organizations have made use of activity-based costing. Service companies benefiting from ABC include American Express, BC Hydro, FedEx, Gemico (GE Capital Mortgage Insurance Company), Purolator Courier Ltd., Sun Life Insurance, TELUS, and WestJet Airlines, among many others. Governmental units also have implemented activity-based costing. Among the governmental units that have benefited from ABC are such diverse organizations as the Canadian Navy, the Royal Canadian Mounted Police, BC Shared Services Agency, the City of Toronto, and several agencies of the federal government, including the Canadian Human Rights Commission, the Department of National Defence, Fisheries and Oceans Canada, Health Canada, and the Treasury Board of Canada.

An important factor in the move toward ABC systems is related to the information requirements of such systems. The data required for activity-based costing are more readily available than in the past. Increasing automation, coupled with sophisticated real-time information systems, provides the kind of data necessary to implement highly accurate product-costing systems. Some key issues related to activity-based costing systems are discussed in the following sections.

> "Before the industry really became wide open in long-distance competition [as the result of deregulation], you could get by with knowing less. You could get by with having price structures that were not based on the underlying activities and the costs associated with those activities, but were instead based on broad averages. It was okay. It worked. It's not good enough anymore. We have to get more precise in our costs. We have to deliver the kinds of prices to our customers that they're willing to pay." (5a)
>
> **TELUS**

Cost Drivers

A **cost driver** is a characteristic of an event or activity that results in the incurrence of costs. In activity-based costing systems, the most significant cost drivers are identified. Then a database is created, which shows how these cost drivers are distributed across products. Three factors are important in selecting appropriate cost drivers.

1. *Degree of correlation.* The central concept of an activity-based costing system is to assign the costs of each activity to product lines on the basis of how each product line consumes the cost driver identified for that activity. The idea is to *infer* how each product line consumes the activity by *observing* how each product line consumes the cost driver. Therefore, the accuracy of the resulting cost assignments depends on the *degree of correlation* between consumption of the activity and consumption of the cost driver.

   Say that inspection cost is selected as an activity cost pool. The objective of the ABC system is to assign inspection costs to product lines on the basis of their consumption of the inspection activity. Two potential cost drivers come to mind: number of inspections and hours of inspection time. If every inspection requires the same amount of time for all products, then the number of inspections on a product line will be highly correlated with the consumption of inspection activity by that product line. On the other hand, if inspections vary significantly in the time required, then simply recording the number of inspections will not adequately portray the consumption of inspection activity. In this case, hours of inspection time would be more highly correlated with the actual consumption of the inspection activity.

2. *Cost of measurement.* Designing any information system entails cost-benefit trade-offs. The more activity cost pools there are in an activity-based costing system, the greater will be the accuracy of the cost assignments. However, more activity cost pools also entail more cost drivers, which results in greater costs of implementing and maintaining the system.

   Similarly, the higher the correlation between a cost driver and the actual consumption of the associated activity, the greater the accuracy of the cost assignments. However, it also may be more costly to measure the more highly correlated cost driver. Returning to our example of the inspection activity, it may be that inspection hours make a more accurate cost driver than the number of inspections. It is likely, however, that inspection hours also will be more costly to measure and track over time.

3. *Behavioural effects.* Information systems have the potential not only to facilitate decisions but also to influence the behaviour of decision makers. This can be good or bad, depending on the behavioural effects. In identifying cost drivers, an ABC analyst should consider the possible behavioural consequences. For example, in a just-in-time (JIT) production environment, a key goal is to reduce inventories and material-handling activities to the absolute minimum level possible. The number of material moves may be the most accurate measure of the consumption of the material-handling activity for cost assignment purposes. It also may have a desirable behavioural effect of inducing managers to reduce the number of times materials are moved, thereby reducing material-handling costs.

   Dysfunctional behavioural effects are also possible. For example, the number of vendor contacts may be a cost driver for the purchasing activity of vendor selection. This could induce purchasing managers to contact fewer vendors, which might result in the failure to identify the lowest-cost or highest-quality vendor.

Collecting ABC Data

The output of an organization's various departments consists of the activities performed by personnel or machines in those departments. Activities usually result in paperwork or the generation of computer documents. For example, engineering departments typically deal with documents such as specification sheets and engineering change orders. Purchasing departments handle requisitions and orders, which may be either hard-copy or computer documents. In an ABC system, analysis of documents such as these can be used to assign the costs of activities to product lines on the basis of the amount of activity generated by each product.

Interviews and Paper Trails   The information used in Patio Grill Company's ABC system came initially from extensive interviews with key employees in each of the organization's support departments and a careful review of each department's records. In the engineering area, for example, ABC project team members interviewed each engineer to determine the breakdown of time spent on each of the three products. They also examined every engineering change order completed in the past two years. The team concluded that engineering costs were driven largely by engineering hours and that the breakdown was 500 hours for the STD grill line, 400 hours for the DEL grill line, and 400 hours for the ULT grill line.

Storyboarding   As Patio Grill Company's project team delved further into the ABC analysis, they made considerable use of another technique for collecting activity data. **Storyboarding** is a procedure used to develop a detailed process flowchart, which visually represents activities and the relationships among the activities. A storyboarding session involves all or most of the employees who participate in the activities oriented toward achieving a specific objective. A facilitator helps the employees identify the key activities involved in their jobs. These activities are written on small cards and placed on a large board in the order they are accomplished. Relationships among the activities are shown by the order and proximity of the cards. Other information about the activities is recorded on the cards, such as the amount of time and other resources that are expended on each activity and the events that trigger the activity. After several storyboarding sessions, a completed storyboard emerges, recording key activity information vital to the ABC project. Historically, storyboards have been

Learning Objective 7

Discuss several key issues in activity-based costing, including data collection, storyboarding, and indicators that an ABC system might be useful.

"We were negotiating fees, and the customer was under the impression that they were paying more than they should . . . . To make this customer comfortable with the pricing, we needed a [more accurate] costing system." (5d)

Dana Commercial Credit Corporation

Interviews with department personnel and storyboarding sessions are often used by activity-based costing project teams to accumulate the data needed for an ABC study. In the interview sessions, an ABC project team member asks department employees to detail their activities, as well as the time and other resources consumed by the activities. Storyboards, like the one shown here, depict the relationships between the activities performed in an organization.

used by Walt Disney and other film producers in the development of plots for animated films. More recently, storyboarding has been used by advertising agencies in developing event sequences for TV commercials.

Storyboarding provides a powerful tool for collecting and organizing the data needed in an ABC project. Patio Grill Company's ABC project team used storyboarding very effectively to study each of the firm's activity cost pools. The team concluded that purchasing costs were driven by the number of purchase orders. Material-handling costs were driven by the number of production runs. Quality-assurance costs were driven by the number of inspection hours devoted to each product line. Packaging and shipping costs were driven by the number of shipments made.

In summary, the ABC project team conducted a painstaking and lengthy analysis involving many employee interviews, the examination of hundreds of documents, and storyboarding sessions. The final result was the data used in the ABC calculations displayed in Exhibits 5–7 and 5–8. This in-depth analysis is normally conducted only at the implementation phase of a new ABC system; once implemented, data needed for ABC is captured by the product-costing system.

Multidisciplinary ABC Project Teams   In order to gather information from all facets of an organization's operations, it is essential to involve personnel from a variety of functional areas. A typical ABC project team includes accounting and finance people as well as engineers, marketing personnel, production and operations managers, and so forth. Hence, ABC should be seen as a company-wide initiative, not simply an accounting project. A multidisciplinary project team not only designs a better ABC system but also helps in gaining credibility for the new system throughout the organization. Senior management commitment and support is also crucial to the successful implementation of ABC.

Activity Dictionary and Bill of Activities

> "Having a plant-level activity dictionary allows the plant to manage its activities locally and serves as a standard reference that employees can use to see which activities roll up into which processes." (5e)
> **Navistar International Corporation**

Many organizations' ABC teams compile an **activity dictionary**, which is a complete listing of the activities identified and used in the ABC analysis. An activity dictionary helps in the implementation of activity-based costing across several divisions of an organization, because it provides for consistency in the ABC system terminology and the complexity of the ABC analyses in the various divisions.

A **bill of activities** is another commonly used element in an ABC analysis. A bill of activities for a product or service is a complete listing of the activities required for the product or service to be produced. As a familiar analogy, think about a recipe for chocolate chip cookies. The *bill of materials* for the cookies is the list of ingredients provided in the recipe. The *bill of activities* is the list of steps given in the recipe for making the cookies (e.g., combine ingredients in a bowl, stir in chocolate chips, place spoon-size globs of dough on greased cookie sheet, bake at 375° for 10 minutes or until done).

Indicators for ABC

The following signals often indicate that management should consider incurring the significant cost of updating their costing system and implementing ABC:[4]

- Line managers do not believe the product costs reported by the accounting department.
- Marketing personnel are unwilling to use reported product costs in making pricing decisions.
- Complex products that are difficult to manufacture are reported to be very profitable, although they are not priced at a premium.
- Product-line profit margins are difficult to explain.

- Sales are increasing, but profits are declining.
- Line managers suggest that apparently profitable products be dropped.
- Marketing or production managers are using "bootleg costing systems," which are informal systems they designed, often on a personal computer.
- Some products that have reported high profit margins are not sold by competitors.
- The firm seems to have captured a highly profitable product niche all for itself.
- Overhead rates are very high, and increasing over time.
- Product lines are diverse.
- Direct labour is a small percentage of total costs.
- The results of bids are difficult to explain.
- Competitors' high-volume products seem to be priced unrealistically low.
- The accounting department spends significant amounts of time on special costing projects to support bids or pricing decisions.

Activity-Based Management

Using activity-based costing (ABC) information to support organizational strategy, improve operations, and manage costs is called **activity-based management** or **ABM**. We have already caught a glimpse of activity-based management in the previous sections, where the management of Patio Grill Company used ABC information to better understand its product-pricing decisions. The company's management discovered through the ABC analysis that some products were overcosted and some products were undercosted by their traditional product-costing system. They realized that, as a result of this cost distortion, they were setting some product prices too high to be competitive, and other products were being priced too low. This important insight presented management with the opportunity to revise its product pricing in order to reflect the more accurate product costs provided by the ABC analysis. When management followed up on this product-pricing opportunity, it was engaging in activity-based management. However, ABM is a much broader concept than this. Activity-based management involves any use of ABC information to support the organization's strategy, improve operations, or manage activities and their resulting costs.

> **Learning Objective 8**
>
> Explain the concept of activity-based management and two-dimensional ABC.

Two-Dimensional ABC

One way of picturing the relationship between ABC and ABM is in terms of the **two-dimensional ABC model** depicted in Exhibit 5–11.[5] The vertical dimension of the model depicts the cost assignment view of an ABC system. From the *cost assignment viewpoint*, the ABC system uses two-stage cost allocation to *assign* the costs of resources to the firm's cost objects. These cost objects could be products manufactured, services produced, or customers served.

Now focus on the horizontal dimension of the model. Depicted here is the *process view* of an ABC system. The emphasis now is on the activities themselves, the various processes by which work is accomplished in the organization. The left-hand side of Exhibit 5–11 depicts **activity analysis**, which is the detailed identification and description of the activities conducted in the enterprise. Activity analysis entails identification not only of the activities but also of their *root causes*, the events that *trigger* activities, and the *linkages* among activities. The right-hand side of Exhibit 5–11 depicts the evaluation of activities through performance measures. It is these processes of *activity analysis and evaluation* that make up activity-based management. Notice that the *activities*, which appear in the centre of both dimensions in Exhibit 5–11, are the focal point of ABC and ABM.

Exhibit 5–11
Two-Dimensional ABC Model

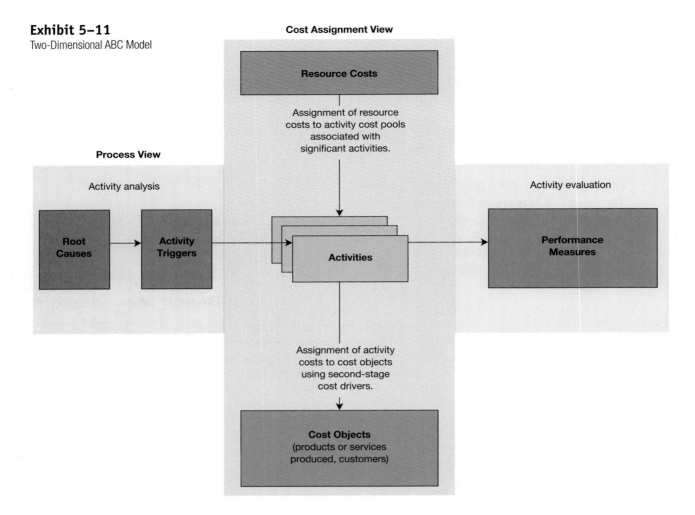

Using ABM to Identify Non-Value-Added Activities and Costs

An important goal of activity-based management is to identify and eliminate non-value-added activities and costs. **Non-value-added activities** are operations that are either (1) unnecessary and dispensable or (2) necessary, but inefficient and improvable.[6] **Non-value-added costs**, which result from such activities, are the costs of activities that can be eliminated without deterioration of product quality, performance, or perceived value. The following five steps provide a strategy for eliminating non-value-added costs in both manufacturing and service firms.

Identifying Activities   The first step is activity analysis, which identifies all of the organization's significant activities. The resulting activity list should be broken down to the most fundamental level practical. For example, rather than listing purchasing as an activity, the list should break down the purchasing operation into its component activities, such as obtaining part specifications, compiling vendor lists, selecting vendors, negotiating prices, ordering, and expediting.

Identifying Non-Value-Added Activities   Three criteria for determining whether an activity adds value are as follows:

- *Is the activity necessary?* If it's a duplicate or nonessential operation, it is non-value-added.

- *Is the activity efficiently performed?* In answering this question, it is helpful to compare the actual performance of the activity to a value-added baseline established using budgets, targets, or external benchmarks.
- *Is an activity sometimes value-added and sometimes non-value-added?* For example, it may be necessary to move work-in-process units between production operations, but unnecessary to move raw materials around while in storage.

Understanding Activity Linkages, Root Causes, and Triggers   In identifying non-value-added activities, it is critical to understand the ways in which activities are linked together. The following chain of activities provides an example:

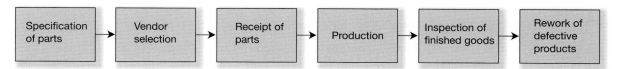

The rework of defective units is a non-value-added activity. The rework is *triggered* by the identification of defective products during inspection. The *root cause* of the rework, however, might lie in any one of a number of preceding activities. Perhaps the part specifications were in error. Possibly an unreliable vendor was selected. Maybe the wrong parts were received. Perhaps the production activity is to blame.

A set of linked activities (such as that depicted above) is called a **process**. Sometimes activity analysis is referred to as **process value analysis (PVA)**.

Establishing Performance Measures   By continually measuring the performance of all activities, and comparing performance with benchmarks, management's attention may be directed to unnecessary or inefficient activities. We will explore performance measurement extensively in Chapter 11.

Reporting Non-Value-Added Costs   Non-value-added costs should be highlighted in activity centre cost reports. By identifying non-value-added activities, and reporting their costs, management can strive toward the ongoing goals of process improvement and elimination of non-value-added costs.

One approach that cost-management analysts find helpful in identifying non-value-added activities is to categorize the ways in which time is spent in a production process. Let's return to our illustration of Patio Grill Company's Mississauga plant, where gas barbeque grills are manufactured. How is time spent in the plant between the arrival of raw material and shipment of a finished gas grill to a customer? As in most manufacturing operations, time is spent in the following five ways:

- *Process time.* The time during which a product is undergoing conversion activity
- *Inspection time.* The amount of time spent ensuring that the product is of high quality
- *Move time.* The time spent moving raw materials, work in process, or finished goods between operations
- *Waiting time.* The amount of time that raw materials or work in process spend waiting for the next operation
- *Storage time.* The time during which materials, partially completed products, or finished goods are held in stock before further processing or shipment to customers

Thinking about the production operation in these terms allows management to ask: "Does the time spent in all of these activities add value to the product? Will the customer pay for it? Can the time spent on inspection be reduced without diminishing product quality? Can production efficiency be improved by reducing the number of times materials, work-in-process, or finished goods are moved from one place to another? Can production be scheduled so that partially completed products spend less time just waiting for the next operation? Can storage time be reduced by ordering raw material and producing products only as they are needed?" If reductions can be made in any of these time-consuming activities, without diminishing product quality or functionality, management has a real opportunity to reduce non-value-added costs.

Customer-Profitability Analysis

Learning Objective 9

Explain and execute a customer-profitability analysis.

It is quite possible for a company to have profitable products and, at the same time, incur customer-related costs that make certain customer relationships unprofitable. **Customer-profitability analysis** uses activity-based costing to determine the activities, costs, and profit associated with serving particular customers. Suppose, for example, that customer X frequently changes its orders after they are placed, but customer Y typically does not. Then the costs incurred in updating sales orders for changes should be recorded in a manner that reflects the fact that customer X is more responsible for those activities and costs than is customer Y. An effective cost management system should allow managers to derive such cost details.

Many factors can result in some customers being more profitable than others. Customers that order in small quantities, order frequently, often change their orders, require special packaging or handling, demand faster delivery, or need special parts or engineering design generally are less profitable than customers who demand less in terms of customized services. If managers have a good understanding of which customers are generating the greatest profit, they can make more-informed decisions about customer service. Moreover, this allows customers to be educated as to the costs they are causing when demanding special services. In many cases, customers' behaviour can be changed in a way that reduces costs to the supplier. Then these cost savings can be shared by the supplier and the customer.

The task of assigning costs to customers is a challenge. A system must be in place that enables the company to identify which customers are using customer support services and how frequently they do so. How much time must the company spend on a customer to make the sale and to provide ongoing support services? These costs are in addition to the cost of manufacturing the product or initially providing a service for the customer.

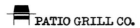

Customer-Profitability Analysis Illustrated

To illustrate customer-profitability analysis, let's focus again on Patio Grill Company. Two more years have passed, and the company has successfully implemented its activity-based costing system in its Mississauga plant. At a recent strategy meeting with her senior management team, Patio Grill Company's president and CEO expressed interest in assessing the profitability of the entire company's various customer relationships. She found support for the idea from the director of cost management, who had been reading about customer-profitability analysis in some of his professional journals. The company's marketing manager also expressed interest in customer-profitability analysis, since he was concerned about the profitability of a couple of Patio Grill Company's customers in particular. "We have a few customers who seem to want the moon and the stars when it comes to customer service," he complained. "I know the customer is always right and all, but you really have to wonder if we're making any money from a couple of these customers, what with all the extra design and packaging they demand. And some of our other customers seem to require an awful lot of extra attention in sales calls, order processing, and billing. If we had a better idea of each customer's profitability, it would help our marketing and sales staffs to focus their efforts."

The controller soon had his cost management staff attacking the customer-profitability analysis that the president had requested. The first step required an activity-based costing analysis of certain *customer-related costs* that could seriously affect a customer's profitability. Recall that ABC analysis relies on a cost hierarchy with cost levels, such as unit-level, batch-level, product-line-level, customer-level, and facility- or general-operations-level costs. In this use of activity-based costing, the cost management team is focusing on the customer-related costs. After an extensive analysis and several interviews with personnel throughout Patio Grill Company, the cost management team came up with the ABC analysis in Exhibit 5–12.[7]

Based on the activity-based costing information, the cost management team assessed the profitability of each of Patio Grill Company's customer relationships. Detailed information from that analysis for five of these customers appears in the Excel spreadsheet in Exhibit 5–13. These five customers were singled out because three of them are key customers (i.e., customers 106, 112, and 113), and two of them (107 and 119) were suspected by the marketing manager to be at best marginally profitable. As it turned out, suspicions about customers 107 and 119 were well founded. Both customers were found to be unprofitable; in fact, customer 119 had caused a loss of almost $120,000 during the year.

> "When we saw what some of our customers were costing us, we were quite surprised. We shared this information with them, and they were also surprised to see how much work went into servicing them. At this point, we negotiated with them to eliminate certain discounts they were receiving." (5g)
>
> **Pfizer**

Customer-Related Activities	Cost Driver Base	Cost Driver Rate
Order processing	Purchase orders	$ 150
Sales contacts (phone calls, faxes, etc.)	Contacts	100
Sales visits	Visits	1,000
Shipment processing	Shipments	200
Billing and collection	Invoices	160
Design/engineering change orders	Engineering/design changes	4,000
Special packaging	Units packaged	40
Special handling	Units handled	60

Exhibit 5–12
ABC Analysis for Customer-Related Costs: Patio Grill Company

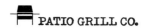
PATIO GRILL CO.

	A	B	C	D	E	F
1		Designated Customers (By 3-Digit Customer Code)				
2		Customer 106	Customer 107	Customer 112	Customer 113	Customer 119
3						
4	Sales revenue	$ 4,320,000	$ 3,480,000	$ 6,500,000	$ 4,490,000	$ 1,960,000
5	Cost of goods sold	3,220,000	2,810,000	4,890,000	3,380,000	1,480,000
6	Gross margin	$ 1,100,000	$ 670,000	$ 1,610,000	$ 1,110,000	$ 480,000
7	Selling and administrative costs:					
8	General selling costs	$ 362,000	$ 220,000	$ 530,000	$ 366,000	$ 160,000
9	General administrative costs	181,000	110,000	265,000	183,000	80,000
10	Customer-related costs					
11	Order processing	11,100	80,250	16,050	22,200	38,400
12	Sales contacts	22,000	13,400	32,000	24,100	28,800
13	Sales visits	44,000	20,000	47,000	38,000	32,000
14	Shipment processing	33,000	27,800	64,200	44,600	19,200
15	Billing and collection	33,600	14,000	80,480	22,400	9,600
16	Design/engineering changes	93,000	96,000	84,000	112,000	68,000
17	Special packaging	88,000	27,200	64,440	44,480	76,800
18	Special handling	33,000	80,400	48,300	33,300	86,400
19	Total selling and administrative cost	$ 900,700	$ 689,050	$ 1,231,470	$ 890,080	$ 599,200
20	Operating income	$ 199,300	$ (19,050)	$ 378,530	$ 219,920	$ (119,200)

Exhibit 5–13
Customer-Profitability Analysis for Five Designated Customers: Patio Grill Company

PATIO GRILL CO.

M anagement
A ccounting
P ractice

Bank One Corp

CUSTOMER PROFITABILITY ANALYSIS AT BANK ONE CORP.

The Wall Street Journal described how Bank One Corp. (now part of JPMorgan Chase Bank) has used customer-profitability analysis to guide decisions about customer service.

At Bank One Corp., at the time one of the largest banks, "the line in the sand between preferred and nonpreferred customers has become strikingly obvious." The bank is redesigning its 218 branches in Louisiana so its "Premier One" customers can be whisked away to a special teller window with no wait or to the desk of an appropriate bank officer. "Customers qualify by keeping at least $2,500 in a checking account or a total of $25,000 in a combination of certain bank accounts," or by paying a $17 monthly fee. "Management estimates that the extra attention will go only to the top 20 percent of its customers."[8]

> "Almost any person in any organization that implements ABM has some real surprises when they start seeing the data about customer profitability and product profitability." (5h)
> **Shiloh Industries, Inc.**

A complete customer-profitability analysis for all of Patio Grill Company's customers appears in the spreadsheet in Exhibit 5–14. This exhibit reveals several interesting aspects of the customer-profitability scenario. Seventeen of 20 customers are profitable. The three unprofitable customers (107, 134, and 119) resulted in losses of over $240,000 in operating income for Patio Grill Company in a single year! Notice that over 25 percent of the company's profit is generated by its top three customers. Almost half the company's profit comes from its top six customers, and fully three-quarters of its profit is generated by half its customers. This sort of customer-profitability scenario is quite typical for manufacturers. The lion's share of most companies' profits come from a handful of their customers. Such an insight is important for management as it determines where to devote the company's resources in serving customers.[9]

A graphical portrayal of Patio Grill Company's complete customer-profitability analysis is given in Exhibit 5–15. This graph is called a **customer-profitability profile**, and it is a common and useful way of presenting a customer-profitability analysis to management.

Exhibit 5–14

Customer-Profitability Analysis with Customers Ranked by Operating Income: Patio Grill Company

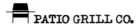
PATIO GRILL CO.

	A	B	C	D	E	F
1						Cumulative Operating
2	3-Digit	Customer	Customer	Customer	Cumulative	Income as a
3	Customer	Sales	Gross	Operating	Operating	Percentage of Total
4	Code	Revenue	Margin	Income	Income	Operating Income
5						
6	112	$ 6,500,000	$ 1,610,000	$ 378,530	$ 378,530	8.8%
7	108	6,964,000	1,570,000	370,000	748,530	17.3%
8	114	6,694,000	1,484,300	351,000	1,099,530	25.5%
9	116	5,846,000	1,461,600	340,000	1,439,530	33.4%
10	110	5,602,000	1,430,000	336,070	1,775,600	41.1%
11	121	5,400,000	1,413,000	331,000	2,106,600	48.8%
12	124	5,601,000	1,405,520	330,000	2,436,600	56.5%
13	127	5,090,000	1,280,020	300,000	2,736,600	63.4%
14	128	4,760,000	1,160,200	281,400	3,018,000	69.9%
15	125	5,000,200	1,181,000	276,000	3,294,000	76.3%
16	135	4,431,000	1,150,000	270,000	3,564,000	82.6%
17	133	4,008,000	1,059,800	251,400	3,815,400	88.4%
18	113	4,490,000	1,110,000	219,920	4,035,320	93.5%
19	111	4,200,000	875,220	205,000	4,240,320	98.2%
20	106	4,320,000	1,100,000	199,300	4,439,620	102.9%
21	136	1,920,000	351,200	82,000	4,521,620	104.8%
22	137	1,641,000	139,400	35,600	4,557,220	105.6%
23	107	3,480,000	670,000	(19,050)	4,538,170	105.1%
24	134	2,820,000	582,000	(102,600)	4,435,570	102.8%
25	119	1,960,000	480,000	(119,200)	4,316,370	100.0%

Cumulative Operating Income as a
Percentage of Total Operating Income

Exhibit 5–15

Customer-Profitability Profile in Terms of Cumulative Operating Income as a Percentage of Total Operating Income: Patio Grill Company

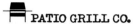

*Customers ranked by operating income.

CUSTOMER PROFITABILITY ANALYSIS AT BEST BUY

Best Buy, with over $27 billion in annual revenue, is a leading retailer of consumer electronics.[10] Best Buy's CEO "is embracing a heretical notion for a retailer. He wants to separate the best customers among the 1.5 million people who visit Best Buy's stores every day from the worst customers." Best Buy's preferred customers "boost profits at the consumer-electronics giant by snapping up high-definition televisions, portable electronics, and newly released DVDs without waiting for mark-downs or rebates."[11] The retailer's worst customers, on the other hand, "buy products, apply for rebates, return the purchases, and then buy them back at returned-merchandise discounts. They load up on loss-leaders, severely discounted merchandise designed to boost store traffic, then 'flip' the goods at a profit on eBay. They slap down rock-bottom price quotes from Web sites and demand that Best Buy make good on its lowest-price pledge." According to Best Buy's CEO, these customers "can wreak enormous economic havoc." The company estimates "that as many as 100 million of its 500 million customer visits each year are undesirable." And Best Buy's CEO "wants to be rid of these customers." The company's new approach "upends what has long been standard practice for mass merchants. Most chains use their advertising budgets chiefly to maximize customer traffic." Best Buy's new plan is to "rate its customers according to profitability, and then dump the up to 20 percent that are unprofitable." Best Buy is rolling out its new strategy in about 100 of its 670 stores. Best Buy "is examining its sales records and demographic data and sleuthing through computer databases to identify good and bad customers. To lure the high spenders, it is stocking more merchandise and providing more appealing service. To deter the undesirables, it is cutting back on promotions and sales tactics that tend to draw them, and culling them from marketing lists."[12]

Management
Accounting
Practice

Best Buy

Activity-Based Costing in the Service Sector

Learning Objective 10

Understand and discuss how activity-based costing is used in service organizations.

"BMO implemented new funds transfer pricing and cost methodologies. The new funds transfer pricing methodology is matched-maturity based, and the cost system is activity based. These enhancements provide more detailed profitability information." (5i)

BMO Financial Group

We conclude this chapter with the important point that activity-based costing has found widespread usage in the service sector as well as in manufacturing. There have been many ABC success stories in such diverse organizations as airlines, insurance companies, banks, hospitals, financial services firms, hotels, railroads, and government agencies. Among the service organizations that used activity-based costing are Air France, American Express, the BC Ministry of Health, the Canadian Forces, the Canadian National Railway Company, the City of Toronto, DHL, Ericsson Mobile Communications, FedEx, IKEA, the Royal Bank of Canada, TELUS, and WestJet Airlines.

The overall objectives of ABC in service firms are no different than they are in manufacturing companies. Managers want more accurate information about the cost of producing the services they are selling. Moreover, they want to use this information to improve operations and to better meet the needs of their customers in a more cost-effective manner. The general approach of identifying activities, activity cost pools, and cost drivers is used in the service sector as well as in manufacturing. The classification of activities into unit-level, batch-level, product-sustaining-level, and facility-level activities also applies in service settings. For example, a private insurance provider might use the following activity classifications in its ABC system:[13]

- *Unit level.* Entering initial claim data into the computer (for each claim received)
- *Batch level.* Moving a batch of claims from one processing step to the next
- *Product-sustaining level.* Maintenance of the medical-services provider network (i.e., maintaining relationships with physicians and hospitals providing medical care to claimants)
- *Facility (general operations) level.* General administration of the claims business unit

Activity-Based Costing at Toronto General Hospital's Ambulatory Cardiac Clinic

To see how management can use activity-based costing in a service setting, let's explore how ABC is used at Toronto General Hospital's Ambulatory Cardiac Clinic.[14] The TGH's Ambulatory Cardiac Clinic provides a variety of cardiac assessment, diagnosis, and management services to patients, and is made up of seven different clinics, with each clinic offering a specific cardiac service. The Ambulatory Cardiac Clinic's administration implemented activity-based costing in order to determine how much it costs to serve patients in various categories. The Ambulatory Cardiac Clinic classifies patient appointments as routine, extended, or complex, depending on the appointment length and complexity. In addition, each appointment is classified as either a new-patient appointment or a continuing-patient appointment. Thus, every patient appointment is one of the following six types:

	Routine	Extended	Complex
New patient	New patient; routine appointment	New patient; extended appointment	New patient; complex appointment
Continuing patient	Continuing patient; routine appointment	Continuing patient; extended appointment	Continuing patient; complex appointment

Every patient appointment involves a registered nurse (or RN), who takes vital signs and prepares the patient for the primary health-care professional. Then, every patient is seen by one primary health-care professional, which can be a physician, a nurse practitioner,[15] an intern, or a resident. No appointment involves more than one of these types of primary health-care professionals.

The Ambulatory Cardiac Clinic's ABC project team designated the following activities and cost drivers:

Activity	Cost Driver
Physician time	Physician minutes with patient
Nurse practitioner time	Nurse practitioner minutes with patient
Intern or resident time	Intern or resident minutes with patient
Registered nurse time	Registered nurse minutes with patient
Clerical time: New patients	New patient visits
Clerical time: Continuing patients	Continuing patient visits
Billing	Billing lines (i.e., number of line items on bill)
Facility	Patient visits (both new and continuing)

The activity-based costing analysis is displayed in the Excel spreadsheet in Exhibit 5–16. Notice that this ABC spreadsheet for the Ambulatory Cardiac Clinic has a format that is identical to the ABC spreadsheet prepared for Patio Grill Company (Exhibit 5–7 on page 152). The column headings are different, because the Ambulatory Cardiac Clinic provides medical services to patients, whereas Patio Grill Company manufactures barbeque grills. Conceptually and computationally, however, the two Excel spreadsheets are identical. *The ABC computations* are in columns E, H, and J and are shown in red.

	A Activity	B Activity Cost Pool	C Cost Driver	D Cost Driver Quantity	E Pool Rate	F Patient Visit Type	G Cost Driver Quantity for Patient Visit Type	H Activity Cost for Patient Type	I Patient Type Visit Volume	J Activity Cost per Patient of Each Type
6	Physician	$960,000	Physician	240,000	$4.00	Routine	80,000	$ 320,000	8,000	$ 40.00
7	Time		Minutes			Extended	100,000	400,000	5,000	80.00
8			with Patient			Complex	60,000	240,000	2,000	120.00
9						Total	240,000	960,000		
10	Nurse	90,000	NP	30,000	3.00	Routine	12,000	36,000	1,200	30.00
11	Practitioner		Minutes			Extended	10,000	30,000	500	60.00
12	(NP) Time		with Patient			Complex	8,000	24,000	320	75.00
13						Total	30,000	90,000		
14	Intern or	412,500	I/R	125,000	3.30	Routine	40,000	132,000	4,000	33.00
15	Resident		Minutes			Extended	50,000	165,000	2,500	66.00
16	(I/R) Time		with Patient			Complex	35,000	115,500	1,000	115.50
17						Total	125,000	412,500		
18	Registered	281,980	RN	245,200	1.15	Routine	132,000	151,800	13,200	11.50
19	Nurse		Minutes			Extended	80,000	92,000	8,000	11.50
20	(RN) Time		with Patient			Complex	33,200	38,180	3,320	11.50
21						Total	245,200	281,980		
22	Clerical Time:	135,300	New	12,300	11.00	Routine	7,200	79,200	7,200	11.00
23	New		Patient			Extended	3,000	33,000	3,000	11.00
24	Patients		Visits			Complex	2,100	23,100	2,100	11.00
25						Total	12,300	135,300		
26	Clerical Time:	61,100	Continuing	12,220	5.00	Routine	6,000	30,000	6,000	5.00
27	Continuing		Patient			Extended	5,000	25,000	5,000	5.00
28	Patients		Visits			Complex	1,220	6,100	1,220	5.00
29						Total	12,220	61,100		
30	Billing	38,480	Billing	76,960	0.50	Routine	26,400	13,200	13,200	1.00
31			Lines			Extended	24,000	12,000	8,000	1.50
32						Complex	26,560	13,280	3,320	4.00
33						Total	76,960	38,480		
34	Facility	245,200	Patient	24,520	10.00	Routine	13,200	132,000	13,200	10.00
35			Visits			Extended	8,000	80,000	8,000	10.00
36			(Both New &			Complex	3,320	33,200	3,320	10.00
37			Continuing)			Total	24,520	245,200		
38										
39	Grand Total	$2,224,560				Grand Total		$2,224,560		

Exhibit 5–16
Activity-Based Costing Analysis: Ambulatory Cardiac Clinic

Toronto ✚ General Hospital

Interpreting the Ambulatory Cardiac Clinic's ABC Information

The TGH's Ambulatory Cardiac Clinic's administration can use the ABC information in Exhibit 5–16 to determine the cost of each of the six types of patient appointments discussed earlier. Notice, though, that there is an important conceptual difference in the interpretation of the Ambulatory Cardiac Clinic's ABC data (Exhibit 5–16) versus the interpretation of Patio Grill Company's ABC data (Exhibit 5–7 on page 152). In the Patio Grill Company manufacturing illustration, *all eight of the activities* identified in the ABC analysis were required by each line of barbeque grills manufactured. However, that is not true in the Ambulatory Cardiac Clinic example. In this health-care services setting, each patient sees *either* a physician, *or* a nurse practitioner, *or* an intern, *or* a resident—not all four. Moreover, each patient is *either* a new patient *or* a continuing patient—not both. Therefore, to compute the cost of a particular type of appointment, we must *select only one of the primary health-care professionals*, which are highlighted by the red bar on the right-hand side of Exhibit 5–16. Moreover, we select *just one of the two categories for clerical time*, new patient or continuing patient, which are highlighted by the green bar on the right-hand side of Exhibit 5–16. Finally, since every patient appointment involves a registered nurse, *and* billing, *and* use of the Ambulatory Cardiac Clinic facility, *all* of these activities must be included in the cost calculation. (These activities are highlighted by the yellow bars on the right-hand side of Exhibit 5–16.)

Let's compute the cost of an extended appointment in which a new patient sees a nurse practitioner:

Activity	Cost (spreadsheet cell in Exhibit 5–16)
Nurse practitioner time	$60.00 (cell J11)
Registered nurse time	11.50 (cell J19)
Clerical time: New patients	11.00 (cell J23)
Billing	1.50 (cell J31)
Facility	10.00 (cell J35)
Total	$94.00

Now let's compute the cost of a routine appointment in which a continuing patient sees a physician:

Activity	Cost (spreadsheet cell in Exhibit 5–16)
Physician time	$40.00 (cell J6)
Registered nurse time	11.50 (cell J18)
Clerical time: Continuing patients	5.00 (cell J26)
Billing	1.00 (cell J30)
Facility	10.00 (cell J34)
Total	$67.50

With a good understanding of how much it costs the Ambulatory Cardiac Clinic to provide various types of patient appointments, the clinic's administration is in a much better position to make decisions. Determining appropriate charges for appointments, justifying third-party reimbursements from insurance companies and government agencies, and adding or discontinuing services are among the types of decisions that will be enhanced by the ABC information.

Focus on Ethics

ETHICAL ISSUES SURROUNDING ACTIVITY-BASED COSTING

Xavier Auto Parts, Inc. manufactures a wide range of auto parts, which it sells to auto manufacturers, primarily in the United States and Canada.[16] The company's Engine Parts Division operated three plants in South Carolina and specialized in engine parts. The division's Charlotte plant manufactured some 6,500 different parts.

Trouble Brewing

Both the Engine Parts Division and, in particular, the Charlotte plant had shown satisfactory profitability through the 1980s and 1990s. In 2000, however, the Charlotte plant's profitability took a sharp downward turn, in spite of rising sales. The trend continued through the next several years. Management at both the division and the plant level took note of the plant's declining profits and held several strategy meetings as a result.

Division Strategy

The Engine Parts Division had always positioned itself as the industry's full-line producer. If a customer wanted a product, the division would make it. Although occasionally very-low-volume products were discontinued due to lack of consistent orders, the division's product line remained a full line of engine parts. As part of its strategy review, division management did two things. First, an activity-based costing study was initiated in the Charlotte plant in order to give management a better picture of each product line's profitability. Second, a high-level review was undertaken to determine whether the full-line-producer strategy continued to make sense.

Activity-Based Costing

An ABC project team was formed, and a successful pilot study was conducted on two of the Charlotte plant's product lines. Then the ABC project was extended to the entire Charlotte operation. Management was astonished to find that fully a quarter of the plant's products were selling at a loss. Moreover, the ABC project highlighted the extent of the product-line proliferation at the Charlotte plant. It turned out that in many instances, unprofitable products had been dropped only to creep back into the product lineup after a customer requested it and a salesperson acquiesced. It became a joke around the plant that the only way to be sure a dropped product was really gone was to burn the engineering drawings and destroy the special tools required to make it.

ABC Team Recommendations

The ABC project team made sweeping recommendations to division management, which suggested that the Charlotte plant's product lines be pruned and that roughly 20 percent of its products be dropped. New emphasis would then be devoted to increasing the profitability of the remaining 80 percent of the Charlotte plant's products. Attention would be given to identifying inefficient processes, and process improvements would be evaluated.

Top Management Response

Top management balked at the recommendations of the ABC project team. Some did not believe the ABC results. It just seemed impossible to them that so many of the Charlotte plant's products were losers. Other members of the management team largely accepted the validity of the ABC study, but they, too, hesitated to drop so many products. To do so would most likely have meant massive layoffs and even the possibility of closing the Charlotte plant altogether, while shifting its remaining production to the division's other two plants. Some members of the ABC project team quietly speculated that some of the division's managers were more concerned about their own pay and perks than they were about the well-being of the division. In the final analysis, only a handful of products were dropped, and then only if they were suspected to be unprofitable before the ABC study was undertaken.

Aftermath

The Charlotte plant's profits continued to deteriorate, as did the Engine Parts Division's profitability. Eventually, Xavier's corporate management cut its losses by selling off the Engine Parts Division to a competitor at bargain-basement prices. The division's new owners closed the Charlotte plant and changed the division's focus to be a boutique producer of high-quality engine parts, which was more in line with its own corporate strategy.

What ethical issues do you see in this scenario? How would you resolve them?

Chapter Summary

Sweeping changes are revolutionizing the way business is conducted. Global competition coupled with rapid technological innovation are changing both the manufacturing and service sectors in a dramatic way. The role of managerial accounting is changing also. Many firms are moving from a traditional cost-accounting approach toward a more proactive cost management perspective.

As the business environment has changed, many managers have come to believe that traditional, volume-based product-costing systems do not accurately reflect product costs. Product-costing systems structured on single, volume-based cost drivers, such as direct labour or machine hours, often tend to overcost high-volume products and undercost low-volume or complex products. These distortions can have serious effects on pricing and other decisions. To alleviate the problems, more and more firms are adopting an activity-based costing system based on multiple cost drivers. Such costing systems provide better information for strategic management decisions.

Many organizations are implementing new cost management systems to better meet the needs of management in an economy that continually grows more competitive. One such cost management system is activity-based management, which is the use of activity-based costing information to improve operations and eliminate non-value-added costs. One way of depicting ABM is the two-dimensional ABC model. This model combines the cost assignment role of ABC with the process and activity evaluation view of an ABC system.

Customer profitability analysis is an application of ABM in which management determines the cost drivers for customer-related costs. The resulting ABC information is then used to assess the profitability of key customer relationships.

Activity-based costing also has found widespread successful implementation in the service sector.

Review Problem on Cost Drivers and Product-Cost Distortion

Edgeworth Box Corporation manufactures a variety of special packaging boxes used in the pharmaceutical industry. The company's plant is semiautomated, but the special nature of the boxes requires some manual labour. The controller has chosen the following activity cost pools, cost drivers, and pool rates for the plant's product-costing system.

Activity Cost Pool	Overhead Cost	Cost Driver	Budgeted Level for Cost Driver	Pool Rate
Purchasing, storage, and material handling	$ 200,000	Raw-material costs	$1,000,000	20% of material cost
Engineering and product design..............................	100,000	Hours in design department	5,000 hrs.	$20/hr.
Machine setup costs..............	70,000	Production runs	1,000 runs	$70/run
Machine depreciation and maintenance...............	300,000	Machine hours	100,000 hrs.	$3/hr.
Factory depreciation, taxes, insurance, and utilities	200,000	Machine hours	100,000 hrs.	$2/hr.
Other manufacturing-overhead costs..................	150,000	Machine hours	100,000 hrs.	$1.50/hr.
Total	$1,020,000			

Two recent production orders had the following requirements:

	20,000 Units of Box C52	10,000 Units of Box W29
Direct-labour hours...	42 hrs.	21 hrs.
Raw-material cost..	$40,000	$35,000
Hours in design department..	10	25
Production runs	2	4
Machine hours..	24	20

Required:

1. Compute the total overhead that should be assigned to each of the two production orders, C52 and W29.

2. Compute the overhead cost per box in each order.

3. Suppose the plant were to use a single predetermined overhead rate based on direct-labour hours. The direct-labour budget calls for 4,000 hours.

   a. Compute the predetermined overhead rate per direct-labour hour.

   b. Compute the total overhead cost that would be assigned to the order for box C52 and the order for box W29.

   c. Compute the overhead cost per box in each order.

4. Why do the two product-costing systems yield such widely differing overhead costs per box?

Solution to Review Problem

1.

	Box C52	Box W29
Purchasing, storage, and material handling	$8,000 (20% × $40,000)	$7,000 (20% × $35,000)
Engineering and product design	200 (10 × $20/hr.)	500 (25 × $20/hr.)
Machine setup costs	140 (2 × $70/run)	280 (4 × $70/run)
Machine depreciation and maintenance	72 (24 × $3/hr.)	60 (20 × $3/hr.)
Factory depreciation, taxes, insurance, and utilities	48 (24 × $2/hr.)	40 (20 × $2/hr.)
Other manufacturing overhead costs	36 (24 × $1.50/hr.)	30 (20 × $1.50/hr.)
Total overhead assigned to production order	$8,496	$7,910

2. Overhead cost per box: $.4248 per box $\left(\dfrac{\$8,496}{20,000}\right)$ $.791 per box $\left(\dfrac{\$7,910}{10,000}\right)$

3. Computations based on a single predetermined overhead rate based on direct-labour hours:

   a. $\dfrac{\text{Total budgeted overhead}}{\text{Total budgeted direct-labour hours}} = \dfrac{\$1,020,000}{4,000} = \$255$ per hour

   b. Total overhead assigned to each order:

   Box C52 order: 42 direct-labour hours × $255/hr. = $10,710

   Box W29 order: 21 direct-labour hours × $255/hr. = $5,355

   c. Overhead cost per box:

   Box C52: $10,710 ÷ 20,000 = $.5355 per box

   Box W29: $5,355 ÷ 10,000 = $.5355 per box

4. The widely differing overhead costs are assigned as a result of the inherent inaccuracy of the single, volume-based overhead rate. The relative usage of direct labour by the two production orders does not reflect their relative usage of other manufacturing support services.

Key Terms

For each term's definition refer to the indicated page, or turn to the glossary at the end of the text.

activity analysis, 161
activity-based costing (ABC) system, 148
activity-based management (ABM), 161
activity-cost pool, 148
activity dictionary, 160
batch-level activity, 149
bill of activities, 160
consumption ratio, 156
cost driver, 158

cost hierarchy, 149
customer-profitability analysis, 164
customer-profitability profile, 166
facility-(or general-operations-)level activity, 149
JIT purchasing,* 175
just-in-time (JIT) inventory and production management system,* 174

non-value-added activities, 162
non-value-added costs, 162
pool rate, 148
process, 163
process value analysis (PVA), 163
production Kanban,* 174
product-sustaining-level activity, 149
pull method,* 174

storyboarding, 159
total quality control (TQC),* 174
two-dimensional ABC model, 161
unit-level activity, 149
volume-based (or through-put-based) costing system, 146
withdrawal Kanban,* 174

*Term appears in the Appendix to this chapter.

Just-in-Time Inventory and Production Management

Learning Objective 11

List and explain eight important features of just-in-time inventory and production management systems.

A cost management tool that is widely used in manufacturing is the *just-in-time* (or JIT) system. A **just-in-time (JIT) inventory and production management system** is a comprehensive inventory and manufacturing control system in which no materials are purchased and no products are manufactured until they are needed. Raw materials and parts are purchased only as they are needed in some phase of the production process. Component parts and subassemblies are not manufactured in any stage of production until they are required in the next stage. Finished goods are manufactured only as they are needed to fill customer orders. A primary goal of a JIT production system is to reduce or eliminate inventories at every stage of production, from raw materials to finished goods. The JIT philosophy, made famous by Toyota, has been credited with the success of many of the world's leading manufacturers. Tremendous cost savings have been realized by many companies that have adopted the JIT approach.

How does a JIT system achieve its vast reductions in inventory and associated cost savings? A production-systems expert lists the following key features of the JIT approach:[17]

1. *A smooth, uniform production rate.* An important goal of a JIT system is to establish a smooth production flow, beginning with the arrival of materials from suppliers and ending with the delivery of goods to customers.

2. *A pull method of coordinating steps in the production process.* Most manufacturing processes occur in multiple stages. Under the **pull method**, goods are produced in each manufacturing stage only as they are needed at the next stage. This approach reduces or eliminates work-in-process inventory between production steps. The result is a reduction in waiting time and its associated non-value-added cost.

    The pull method of production begins at the last stage of the manufacturing process.[18] When additional materials and parts are needed for final assembly, a message is sent to the immediately preceding work centre to send the amount of materials and parts that will be needed over the next few hours. Often this message is in the form of a **withdrawal Kanban**, a card indicating the number and type of parts requested from the preceding work centre. The receipt of the withdrawal Kanban in the preceding work centre triggers the release of a **production Kanban**, which is another card specifying the number of parts to be manufactured in that work centre. Thus, the parts are "pulled" from a particular work centre by a need for parts in the subsequent work centre. This *pull approach* to production is repeated all the way back through the manufacturing sequence toward the beginning. Nothing is manufactured at any stage until its need is signalled from the subsequent process via a Kanban.[19]

3. *Purchase of materials and manufacture of subassemblies and products in small lot sizes.* This is an outgrowth of the pull method of production planning. Materials are purchased and goods are produced only as required, rather than for the sake of building up stocks.

4. *Quick and inexpensive setups of production machinery.* In order to produce in small lot sizes, a manufacturer must be able to set up production runs quickly. Advanced manufacturing technology aids in this process, as more and more machines are computer-controlled.

5. *High quality levels for raw material and finished products.* If raw materials and parts are to arrive "just in time" for production, they must be "just right" for their intended purpose. Otherwise, the production line will be shut down and significant non-value-added costs of waiting will result. Moreover, if very small stocks of finished goods are to be maintained, then finished products must be of uniform high quality. For this reason, a **total quality control (TQC)** program often accompanies a just-in-time production environment.

6. *Effective preventive maintenance of equipment.* If goods are to be manufactured just in time to meet customer orders, a manufacturer cannot afford significant production delays. By strictly adhering to routine maintenance schedules, the firm can avoid costly down time from machine breakdowns.

7. *An atmosphere of teamwork to improve the production system.* A company can maintain a competitive edge in today's worldwide market only if it is constantly seeking ways to improve its product or service, achieve more efficient operations, and eliminate non-value-added costs. Any coach will tell you that a team must improve from one week to the next. Otherwise the team will get worse, because it rarely will stay at the same level. So it goes in business as well. If a company's employees are not constantly seeking ways to improve the firm's performance, before long its competitors will pass it by.

8. *Multiskilled workers and flexible facilities.* To facilitate just-in-time production, manufacturing equipment must be flexible enough to produce a variety of components and products. Otherwise, if a particular production line can produce only one item, bottlenecks may result. A bottleneck can hold up production in subsequent manufacturing stages and result in the non-value-added costs associated with waiting time.

JIT Purchasing   Along with a JIT production approach, many companies implement *JIT purchasing*. Under this approach, materials and parts are purchased from outside vendors only as they are needed. This avoids the costly and wasteful buildup of raw-material inventories. The following are five key features of **JIT purchasing**.

1. *Only a few suppliers.* This results in less time spent on vendor relations. Only highly reliable vendors, who can invariably deliver high-quality goods on time, are used.

2. *Long-term contracts negotiated with suppliers.* This eliminates costly paperwork and negotiations with each individual transaction. The need for delivery can be communicated via a telephone call or computer message. The long-term contracts state the price, quality, and delivery terms of the goods.

3. *Materials and parts delivered in small lot sizes immediately before they are needed.* This is the essence of the just-in-time approach. Costly inventories are avoided by having supplies arrive "just-in-time" to be placed into production.

4. *Only minimal inspection of delivered materials and parts.* The long-term contracts clearly state the quality of material required. Vendors are selected on the basis of their reliability in meeting these stringent standards and in delivering the correct amount of materials on time.

5. *Grouped payments to each vendor.* Instead of paying for each delivery, payments are made for batches of deliveries according to the terms of the contract. This reduces costly paperwork for both the vendor and the purchaser.

JIT purchasing is widely used in a variety of organizations. In manufacturing firms, it goes hand in hand with JIT production. In retail and service industry firms, JIT purchasing reduces costly warehouse inventories and streamlines the purchasing function.

Review Questions

5-1. Briefly explain how a traditional, volume-based product-costing system operates.

5-2. Why was Patio Grill Company's management being misled by the traditional product-costing system? What mistakes were being made?

5-3. Explain how an activity-based costing system operates.

5-4. What are cost drivers? What is their role in an activity-based costing system?

5-5. List and briefly describe the four broad categories of activities identified in stage one of an activity-based costing system.

5-6. How can an activity-based costing system alleviate the problems Patio Grill Company's management was having under its traditional, volume-based product-costing system?

5-7. Why do product-costing systems based on a single, volume-based cost driver tend to overcost high-volume products? What undesirable strategic effects can such distortion of product costs have?

5-8. Explain the concept of a *pool rate* in activity-based costing. (Refer to Exhibit 5-6.)

5-9. Briefly explain two factors that tend to result in product cost distortion under traditional, volume-based product-costing systems.

5-10. List three factors that are important in selecting cost drivers for an ABC system.

5-11. What is the role of *activity dictionary* in an ABC project?

5-12. Explain why a new product-costing system may be needed when line managers suggest that an apparently profitable product be dropped.

5-13. Explain why a manufacturer with diverse product lines may benefit from an ABC system.

5–14. Are activity-based costing systems appropriate for the service sector? Explain.

5–15. Explain why the maintenance of a network is treated as a product-sustaining-level activity by a medical-services provider.

5–16. How could the administration at TGH's Ambulatory Cardiac Clinic use the activity-based costing information developed by the ABC project team?

5–17. Explain a key difference in the interpretation of the ABC data in Exhibit 5–7 (Patio Grill Company) and Exhibit 5–16 (TGH's Ambulatory Cardiac Clinic).

5–18. Explain the concept of *two-dimensional ABC*. Support your explanation with a diagram.

5–19. What is meant by the term *activity analysis*? Give three criteria for determining whether an activity adds value.

5–20. Distinguish between an activity's *trigger* and its *root cause*. Give an example of each.

5–21. What is meant by *customer-profitability analysis*? Give an example of an activity that might be performed more commonly for one customer than for another.

5–22. Explain the relationship between customer profitability analysis and activity-based costing.

5–23. What is a customer profitability profile?

5–24. (Appendix) Explain in words and then draw a diagram depicting the pull method of coordinating steps in a JIT system. (Refer to the JIT discussion in this chapter and to the JIT exhibit in Chapter 1.)

Exercises

■ **Exercise 5–25**
Volume-Based Cost Driver versus ABC
(LO 1, 2, 4)

Precision Company manufactures sophisticated lenses and mirrors used in large optical telescopes. The company is now preparing its annual profit plan. As part of its analysis of the profitability of individual products, the controller estimates the amount of overhead that should be allocated to the individual product lines from the following information.

	Lenses	Mirrors
Units produced	30	30
Material moves per product line	4	16
Direct-labour hours per unit	250	250

The total budgeted material-handling cost is $90,000.

Required:

1. Under a costing system that allocates overhead on the basis of direct-labour hours, the material-handling costs allocated to one lens would be what amount?

2. Answer the same question as in requirement (1), but for lenses.

3. Under activity-based costing (ABC), the material-handling costs allocated to one mirror would be what amount? The cost driver for the material-handling activity is the number of material moves.

4. Answer the same question as in requirement (3), but for lenses.

(CMA, adapted)

■ **Exercise 5–26**
Activity-Based Costing; Quality Control Costs
(LO 1, 2, 4, 5)

Rainbow Spray Paints, Inc. has used a traditional cost accounting system to apply quality-control costs uniformly to all products at a rate of 16 percent of direct-labour cost. Monthly direct-labour cost for the enamel paint line is $98,000. In an attempt to more equitably distribute quality-control costs, Rainbow is considering activity-based costing. The monthly data shown in the following chart have been gathered for the enamel paint line:

Activity Cost Pool	Cost Driver	Pool Rates	Quantity of Driver for Satin Sheen
Incoming material inspection	Type of material	$23 per type	24 types
In-process inspection	Number of units	.28 per unit	35,000 units
Product certification	Per order	144 per order	50 orders

Required:

1. Calculate the monthly quality-control cost to be assigned to the enamel paint line under each of the following product-costing systems.

   a. Traditional system, which assigns overhead on the basis of direct-labour cost

   b. Activity-based costing

2. Does the traditional product-costing system overcost or undercost the enamel paint line with respect to quality-control costs? By what amount?

(CMA, adapted)

Digitech, Ltd. manufactures various computer components in its Tokyo plant. The following costs are budgeted for January. (*Yen* is the Japanese monetary unit.)

Exercise 5–27
Cost Drivers; Activity Cost Pools
(LO 2, 3)

Raw materials and components	3,835,000 yen
Insurance, plant	780,000
Electricity, machinery	156,000
Electricity, light	78,000
Engineering design	793,000
Depreciation, plant	910,000
Depreciation, machinery	1,820,000
Custodial wages, plant	52,000
Equipment maintenance, wages	195,000
Equipment maintenance, parts	39,000
Setup wages	52,000
Inspection of finished goods	39,000
Property taxes	156,000
Natural gas, heating	39,000

Required: Divide these costs into activity cost pools, and identify a cost driver for assigning each pool of costs to products. Calculate the total cost in each activity cost pool.

Refer to the information given in the preceding exercise. For each of the activity cost pools identified, indicate whether it represents a unit-level, batch-level, product-sustaining-level, or facility-level activity.

Exercise 5–28
Categorizing Activity Cost Pools
(LO 2, 3)

Exercise 5–29
Activity-Based Costing in a Government Agency; Use of Internet
(LO 2, 8, 10)

Visit the Web site of a city or province of your choosing.

Required: Read about the services offered to the public by this governmental unit. Then discuss how activity-based costing could be used effectively by the governmental unit to determine the cost of providing these services.

Exercise 5–30
Distortion of Product Costs
(LO 2, 5)

Wheelco, Inc. manufactures automobile and truck wheels. The company produces four basic, high-volume wheels used by each of the large automobile and pickup truck manufacturers. Wheelco also has two specialty wheel lines. These are fancy, complicated wheels used in expensive sports cars.

Lately, Wheelco's profits have been declining. Foreign competitors have been undercutting Wheelco's prices in three of its bread-and-butter product lines, and Wheelco's sales volume and market share have declined. In contrast, Wheelco's specialty wheels have been selling steadily, although in relatively small numbers, in spite of three recent price increases. At a recent staff meeting, Wheelco's president made the following remarks: "Our profits are going down the tubes, folks. It costs us 31 dollars to manufacture our DC16 wheel. That's our best seller, with a volume last year of 19,000 units. But our chief competitor is selling basically the same wheel for 28 dollars. I don't see how they can do it. I think it's just one more example of foreign dumping. I'm going to write my MP about it! Thank goodness for our specialty wheels. I think we've got to get our salespeople to push those wheels more and more. Take the JY16 model, for example. It's a complicated thing to make, and we don't sell many. But look at the profit margin. Those wheels cost us 52 dollars to make, and we're selling them for 110 dollars each."

Required: What do you think is behind the problems faced by Wheelco? Comment on the president's remarks. Do you think his strategy is a good one? What do you recommend, and why?

Refer to the description given for Wheelco, Inc. in the preceding exercise. Suppose the firm's president has decided to implement an activity-based costing system.

Exercise 5–31
Key Features of Activity-Based Costing
(LO 2, 5, 8)

Required:

1. List and briefly describe the key features that Wheelco's new product-costing system should have.

2. What impact will the new system be likely to have on the company's situation?

3.   What strategic options would you expect to be suggested by the product-costing results from the new system?

■ Exercise 5–32
Winery; Classification of
Activities
(LO 2, 3)

Seneca Falls Winery is a small, family-run operation. The winery produces two varieties of wine; Riesling and Chardonnay. Among the activities engaged in by the winery are the following:

1. *Trimming.*	At the end of a growing season, the vines are trimmed, which helps prepare them for the next harvest.
2. *Tying.*	The vines are tied onto wires to help protect them from the cold. (This also occurs at the end of the season.)
3. *Hilling.*	Dirt is piled up around the roots to help protect them from frost.
4. *Conditioning.*	After the snow melts in the spring, dirt is levelled back from the roots.
5. *Untying.*	The vines are untied from the wires to allow them freedom to grow during the spring and summer months.
6. *Chemical spraying.*	The vines are sprayed in the spring to protect them from disease and insects.
7. *Harvesting.*	All of the grapes of both varieties are picked by hand to minimize damage.
8. *Stemming and crushing.*	Batches of grapes are hand-loaded into a machine, which gently removes the stems and mildly crushes them.
9. *Pressing.*	After removal from the stemmer/crusher, the juice runs freely from the grapes.
10. *Filtering.*	The grapes are crushed mechanically to render more juice from them.
11. *Fermentation.*	The Riesling grape juice is placed in stainless steel tanks for fermentation. The Chardonnay grape juice undergoes a two-stage fermentation process in oak barrels.
12. *Aging.*	The Riesling wines are aged in the stainless steel tanks for approximately a year. The chardonnays are aged in the oak barrels for about two years.
13. *Bottling.*	A machine bottles the wine and corks the bottles.
14. *Labelling.*	Each bottle is manually labelled with the name of the vintner, vintage, and variety.
15. *Packing.*	The bottles are manually packed in 12-bottle cases.
16. *Case labelling.*	The cases are hand-stamped with the same information that the bottles received.
17. *Shipping.*	The wine is shipped to wine distributors and retailers, mainly in central New York. Generally, about 100 cases are shipped at a time.
18. *Maintenance on buildings.*	This is done during the slow winter months.
19. *Maintenance on equipment.*	This is done when needed, and on a routine basis for preventive maintenance.

Required: Classify each of the activities listed as a unit-, batch-, product-sustaining-, or facility-level activity.

■ Exercise 5–33
United Technologies;
Classification of Activities
(LO 2, 3)

United Technologies Corporation is using activity-based costing in two of its subsidiaries: Otis Elevator Company and Carrier Corporation. The following table shows 27 activities and eight accounts identified at Carrier, along with the classification determined by the ABC project team.[20]

Name of Activity or Account	Classification by Activity Level	Name of Activity or Account	Classification by Activity Level
Acquiring material	Batch	Inspecting production processes	Batch
Inspecting incoming materials	Batch	Processing purchase orders	Batch
Moving materials	Batch	Building occupancy	Facility
Planning production	Batch	Depreciation	Facility
Processing special orders	Batch	General management	Facility
Processing supplier invoices	Batch	Maintaining facilities	Facility
Receiving material	Batch	Managing the environment	Facility
Scheduling production	Batch	Assuring quality	Sustaining

Name of Activity or Account	Classification by Activity Level	Name of Activity or Account	Classification by Activity Level
Expediting	Sustaining	Supervising production....................	Sustaining
Maintaining tools and dies...............	Sustaining	Sustaining accounting......................	Sustaining
Maintaining/improving production processes...................	Sustaining	Maintaining production equipment	Sustaining
		Direct-labour allowances.................	Unit
Managing human resources	Sustaining	Direct-labour fringes	Unit
Managing waste disposal	Sustaining	Utilities (equipment)	Unit
Processing payroll...........................	Sustaining	Overtime (hourly)	Unit
Processing production information	Sustaining	Rework	Unit
Providing product cost.....................	Sustaining	Shift differential	Unit
Setting manufacturing methods	Sustaining	Spoilage..	Unit

Required: Choose two activities or accounts from each of the four classifications and explain why you agree or disagree with the ABC project team's classification.

■ **Exercise 5–34**
ABC; Selling Costs
(LO 4)

Zodiac Model Rocketry Company sells model rocketry kits and supplies to retail outlets and through its catalogue. Some of the items are manufactured by Zodiac, while others are purchased for resale. For the products it manufactures, the company currently bases its selling prices on a product-costing system that accounts for direct material, direct labour, and the associated overhead costs. In addition to these product costs, Zodiac incurs substantial selling costs, and Jack Maxey, controller, has suggested that these selling costs should be included in the product pricing structure.

After studying the costs incurred over the past two years for one of its products, rocket motors, Maxey has selected four categories of selling costs and chosen cost drivers for each of these costs. The selling costs actually incurred during the past year and the cost drivers are as follows:

Cost Category	Amount	Cost Driver
Sales commissions	$ 675,000	Boxes of rocket motors sold to retail stores – ①
Catalogues..	295,400	Catalogues distributed ②
Cost of catalogue sales	105,000	Rocket motors sold through catalogue ③
Credit and collection	60,000	Number of retail orders ④
Total selling costs	$1,135,400	

The rocket motors are sold to retail outlets in boxes, each containing 12 motors. The sale of partial boxes is not permitted. Commissions are paid on sales to retail outlets but not on catalogue sales. The cost of catalogue sales includes telephone costs and the wages of personnel who take the catalogue orders. Maxey believes that the selling costs vary significantly with the size of the order. Order sizes are divided into three categories as follows:

Order Size	Catalogue Sales	Retail Sales
Small	1–10 rocket motors	1–10 boxes of motors
Medium	11–20 rocket motors	11–20 boxes of motors
Large...	Over 20 rocket motors	Over 20 boxes of motors

An analysis of the previous year's records produced the following statistics:

	Order Size				
	Small	Medium	Large	Total	
Retail sales in boxes (12 motors per box)....... ①	2,000	45,000	178,000	225,000	675/225 – $3
Catalogue sales in units (i.e., motors) ③	79,000	52,000	44,000	175,000	
Number of retail orders ... ④	485	2,415	3,100	6,000	
Catalogues distributed.... ②	254,300	211,300	125,200	590,800	

Required:

1. Prepare a schedule showing Zodiac Model Rocketry Company's total selling cost for each order size and the per-rocket motor selling cost within each order size.

2. Explain how the analysis of the selling costs for rocket motors is likely to impact future pricing and product decisions at Zodiac Model Rocketry Company.

(CMA, adapted)

■ **Exercise 5–35**
Non-Value-Added Costs
(LO 8)

Non-value-added costs occur in nonmanufacturing firms also.

Required: Identify four potential non-value-added costs in (1) an airline, (2) a bank, and (3) a hotel.

■ **Exercise 5–36**
Classification of Activities in a
University; Cost Drivers
(LO 2, 3, 6, 7, 10)

As a group, discuss the activities of your college or university (e.g., admission, registration, etc.). List as many activities as you can.

Required: Make a presentation to your class that includes the following:

1. Your list of activities
2. The classification of each activity (e.g., unit-level)
3. An appropriate cost driver for each activity

■ **Exercise 5–37**
Performance Measures in
Two-Dimensional ABC; ABM
(LO 8, 10)

List five activities performed by the employees of an airline *on the ground*. For each of these activities, suggest a performance measure that could be used in activity-based management.

■ **Exercise 5–38**
Activity Analysis; Non-Value-
Added Activities
(LO 8, 10)

Visit a restaurant for a meal or think carefully about a recent visit to a restaurant. List as many activities as you can think of that would be performed by the restaurant's employees for its customers.

Required: For each activity on your list, indicate the following:

1. Value-added or non-value-added.
2. The trigger of the activity.
3. The possible root causes of the activity.

■ **Exercise 5–39**
College Registration; Activity
Analysis
(LO 8, 10)

As a group, think carefully about the various activities and steps involved in the course registration process at your college or university.

Required:

1. List the steps in the registration process in the sequence in which they occur.
2. Prepare an activity analysis of the registration process. Discuss the activity linkages, triggers, and root causes.
3. Redesign your institution's course registration process with these goals in mind:
   a.   Improve the convenience and effectiveness of the process for the student registering.
   b.   Improve the effectiveness and cost efficiency of the process from the standpoint of the institution.

■ **Exercise 5–40**
Customer Profitability
Analysis; Customers Ranked
by Sales Revenue
(LO 9)

The customer-profitability analysis for Patio Grill Company, which is displayed in Exhibit 5–14, ranks customers by operating income. An alternative, often-used approach is to rank customers by sales revenue.

Required:

1. List the customer numbers in the left-hand column of Exhibit 5–14 by sales revenue, from highest to lowest. Is the ranking different from that in Exhibit 5–14?
2. Patio Grill Company's smallest customers, in terms of sales revenue, are last in the listing done for requirement (1). Are these customers the company's least profitable?
3. Would the customer-profitability profile in Exhibit 5–15 be different if the customers were ranked by sales revenue instead of operating income? Explain.
4. What factors could cause a larger customer (in terms of sales revenue) to be less profitable than a smaller customer?

■ **Exercise 5–41**
Customer-Profitability Graph
(LO 9)

Windy City Design Company specializes in designing commercial office space in Winnipeg. The firm's president recently reviewed the following income statement and noticed that operating profits were below her expectations. She had a hunch that certain customers were not profitable for the company and asked the controller to perform a customer-profitability analysis showing profitability by customer for the month of October.

WINDY CITY DESIGN COMPANY
Income Statement
For the Month Ended October 31

Sales revenue	$300,000
Cost of services billed	255,000
Gross margin	45,000
Marketing and administrative costs	30,000
Operating profit	$ 15,000

The controller provided the following customer-profitability graph:

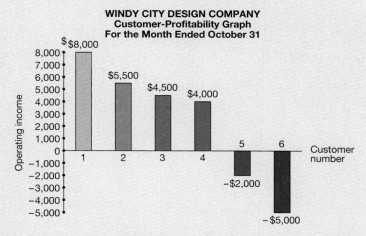

WINDY CITY DESIGN COMPANY
Customer-Profitability Graph
For the Month Ended October 31

Required: Put yourself in the position of Windy City's controller and write a memo to the president to accompany the customer-profitability graph. Comment on the implications of the customer-profitability analysis and raise four or more questions that should be addressed by the firm's management team.

Service-industry firms can make effective use of ABC systems as well as manufacturers. For each of the following businesses, list five key activities that are important in the provision of the firms's service. For each activity cost pool, suggest an appropriate cost driver to use in assigning costs from the activity cost pool to the services provided to customers.

Exercise 5–42
Activity-Based Costing
(LO 2, 3, 10)

1. Air Canada
2. Tim Hortons
3. Vancouver Health & Fitness Club
4. BMO branch
5. Four Seasons Hotel
6. Toronto General Hospital

Problems

Digital Light Corporation has just completed a major change in its quality control (QC) process. Previously, products had been reviewed by QC inspectors at the end of each major process, and the company's 10 QC inspectors were charged as direct labour to the operation or job. In an effort to improve efficiency and quality, a computerized video QC system was purchased for $250,000. The system consists of a minicomputer, 15 video cameras, other peripheral hardware, and software. The new system uses cameras stationed by QC engineers at key points in the production process. Each time an operation changes or there is a new operation, the cameras are moved, and a new master picture is loaded into the computer by a QC engineer. The camera takes pictures of the units in process, and the computer compares them to the picture of a "good" unit. Any differences are sent to a QC engineer, who removes the bad units and discusses the flaws with the production supervisors. The new system has replaced the 10 QC inspectors with two QC engineers.

Problem 5–43
Overhead Application;
Activity-Based Costing
(LO 1, 2, 7)

The operating costs of the new QC system, including the salaries of the QC engineers, have been included as factory overhead in calculating the company's plantwide manufacturing-overhead rate, which is based on direct-labour dollars. The company's president is confused. His vice-president of production has told him how efficient the new system is. Yet there is a large increase in the overhead rate. The computation of the rate before and after automation is as follows:

	Before	After
Budgeted manufacturing overhead	$3,800,000	$4,200,000
Budgeted direct-labour cost	2,000,000	1,400,000
Budgeted overhead rate	190%	300%

"Three hundred percent," lamented the president. "How can we compete with such a high overhead rate?"

Required:

1. *a.* Define "manufacturing overhead," and cite three examples of typical costs that would be included in manufacturing overhead.

   b. Explain why companies develop predetermined overhead rates.

2. Explain why the increase in the overhead rate should not have a negative financial impact on Borealis Manufacturing.

3. Explain how Borealis Manufacturing could change its overhead application system to eliminate confusion over product costs.

4. Discuss how an activity-based costing system might benefit Borealis Manufacturing.

(CMA, adapted)

■ **Problem 5–44**
Activity-Based Costing; Cost Analysis
(LO 1, 2, 4, 5, 7)

1. Predetermined overhead rate: $35.50 per direct-labour hour
2. Application rate, product inspection: $6 per inspection hour

Meditech manufactures two types of medical devices, Medform and Procel, and applies overhead on the basis of direct-labour hours. Anticipated overhead and direct-labour time for the upcoming accounting period are $710,000 and 20,000 hours, respectively. Information about the company's products follows.

Medform
   Estimated production volume, 2,500 units
   Direct-material cost, $30 per unit
   Direct labour per unit, 3 hours at $15 per hour
Procel
   Estimated production volume, 3,125 units
   Direct-material cost, $45 per unit
   Direct labour per unit, 4 hours at $15 per hour

Meditech's overhead of $710,000 can be identified with three major activities: order processing ($120,000), machine processing ($500,000), and product inspection ($90,000). These activities are driven by number of orders processed, machine hours worked, and inspection hours, respectively. Data relevant to these activities follow.

	Orders Processed	Machine Hours Worked	Inspection Hours
Medform	350	23,000	4,000
Procel	250	27,000	11,000
Total	600	50,000	15,000

Top management is very concerned about declining profitability despite a healthy increase in sales volume. The decrease in income is especially puzzling because the company recently undertook a massive plant renovation during which new, highly automated machinery was installed—machinery that was expected to produce significant operating efficiencies.

Required:

1. Assuming use of direct-labour hours to apply overhead to production, compute the unit manufacturing costs of the Medform and Procel products if the expected manufacturing volume is attained.

2. Assuming use of activity-based costing, compute the unit manufacturing costs of the Medform and Procel products if the expected manufacturing volume is attained.

3. Meditech's selling prices are based heavily on cost.

   a. By using direct-labour hours as an application base, which product is overcosted and which product is undercosted? Calculate the amount of the cost distortion for each product.

   b. Is it possible that overcosting and undercosting (i.e., cost distortion) and the subsequent determination of selling prices are contributing to the company's profit woes? Explain.

4. *Build a spreadsheet:* Construct an Excel spreadsheet to solve requirements 1, 2, and 3(*a*) above. Show how the solution will change if the following data change: the overhead associated with order processing is $125,000 and the overhead associated with product inspection is $95,000.

■ **Problem 5–45**
Straightforward ABC calculations
(LO 1, 2, 4, 5)
2. Machine-related costs for REG line: $135,000
3. Total cost per unit, under ABC, for GMT line: $663.90
5. Cost distortion per unit for ADV line: overcosted by $8.85

Kitchen King's Windsor plant manufactures three product lines, all multi-burner, ceramic cook tops. The plant's three product models are the Regular (REG), the Advanced (ADV), and the Gourmet (GMT). Until recently, the plant used a job-order product-costing system, with manufacturing overhead applied on the basis of direct-labour hours. The following table displays the basic data upon which the traditional costing system was based.

	REG	ADV	GMT
Planned annual production:			
Volume in units	5,000	4,000	1,000
Production runs	40 runs of 125 units	40 runs of 100 units	20 runs of 50 units
Direct material	$129	$151	$203
Direct labour (not including setup)	$171 (9 hrs. @ $19 per hr.)	$209 (11 hrs. @ $19 per hr.)	$247 (13 hrs. @ $19 per hr.)
Machine hours (MH) per product unit	10 MH	12 MH	17 MH
Total machine hours consumed by product line in a year	50,000 (10 MH × 5,000)	48,000 (12 MH × 4,000)	17,000 (17 MH × 1,000)

The annual budgeted overhead is $1,224,000, and the company's predetermined overhead rate is $12 per direct-labour hour. The product costs for the three product models, as reported under the plant's traditional costing system, are shown in the following table.

	REG	ADV	GMT
Direct material	$129.00	$151.00	$203.00
Direct labour (not including setup time)	171.00 (9 hrs. @ $19 per hr.)	209.00 (11 hrs. @ $19 per hr.)	247.00 (13 hrs. @ $19 per hr.)
Manufacturing overhead	108.00 (9 hrs. @ $12 per hr.)	132.00 (11 hrs. @ $12 per hr.)	156.00 (13 hrs. @ $12 per hr.)
Total	$408.00	$492.00	$606.00

Kitchen King's pricing policy is to set a target price for each product equal to 130 percent of the full product cost. Due to price competition from other appliance manufacturers, REG units were selling at $525, and ADV units were selling for $628. These prices were somewhat below the firm's target prices. However, these results were partially offset by greater-than-expected profits on the GMT product line. Management had raised the price on the GMT model to $800, which was higher than the original target price. Even at this price, Kitchen King's customers did not seem to hesitate to place orders. Moreover, the company's competitors did not mount a challenge in the market for the GMT product line. Nevertheless, concern continued to mount in Toledo about the difficulty in the REG and ADV markets. After all, these were the plant's bread-and-butter products, with projected annual sales of 5,000 REG units and 4,000 ADV units.

Kitchen King's director of cost management, Angela Ramirez, had been thinking for some time about a refinement in the Toledo plant's product-costing system. Ramirez wondered if the traditional, volume-based system was providing management with accurate data about product costs. She had read about activity-based costing, and wondered if ABC would be an improvement to the plant's product-costing system. After some discussion, an ABC proposal was made to the company's top management, and approval was obtained. The data collected for the new ABC system is displayed in the following table.

Activity	Activity Cost Pool	Cost Driver	Product Line	Cost Driver Quantity for Product Line
Machine-related	$310,500	Machine hours	REG	50,000
			ADV	48,000
			GMT	17,000
			Total	115,000
Material handling	$ 52,500	Production runs	REG	40
			ADV	40
			GMT	20
			Total	100
Purchasing	$ 75,000	Purchase orders	REG	100
			ADV	96
			GMT	104
			Total	300
Setup	$ 85,000	Production runs	REG	40
			ADV	40
			GMT	20
			Total	100
Inspection	$ 27,500	Inspection hours	REG	400
			ADV	400
			GMT	300
			Total	1,100
Shipping	$ 66,000	Shipments	REG	500
			ADV	400
			GMT	200
			Total	1,100
Engineering	$ 32,500	Engineering hours	REG	250
			ADV	200
			GMT	200
			Total	650
Facility	$575,000	Machine hours	REG	50,000
			ADV	48,000
			GMT	17,000
			Total	115,000

Required:

1.   Show how the company's overhead rate of $12 per direct-labour hour was calculated.
2.   Complete an activity-based costing analysis for Kitchen King's three product lines. Display the results of your ABC analysis in a table similar to Exhibit 5–7 in the text.
3.   Prepare a table similar to Exhibit 5–8, which computes the new product cost for each product line under ABC.
4.   Prepare a table similar to Exhibit 5–9, which compares the overhead cost, total product cost, and target price for each product line under the two alternative costing systems.
5.   Was each of Kitchen King's three product lines overcosted or undercosted? By how much per unit?
6.   *Build a spreadsheet:* Construct an Excel spreadsheet to solve requirement (2) above. Show how the solution would change if the machine-related cost pool was $621,000, and the facility cost pool was $1,150,000.

Refer to your solution to requirement (2) of the preceding problem.

Required: Prepare an exhibit similar to Exhibit 5–6 in the text to explain the ABC calculations for the material-handling activity. Use your exhibit to explain ABC to a friend who is not a business student.

Westminster Office Equipment manufactures two types of filing cabinets—Deluxe and Executive—and applies manufacturing overhead to all units at the rate of $80 per machine hour. Production information follows.

	Deluxe	Executive
Budgeted volume (units)	16,000	30,000
Direct-material cost	$40	$65
Direct-labour cost	25	25

The controller, who is studying the use of activity-based costing, has determined that the firm's overhead can be identified with three activities: manufacturing setups, machine processing, and product shipping. Data on the number of setups, machine hours, and outgoing shipments, which are the activities' three respective cost drivers, follow.

	Deluxe	Executive	Total
Setups	100	60	160
Machine hours	32,000	45,000	77,000
Outgoing shipments	200	150	350

The firm's total overhead of $6,160,000 is subdivided as follows: manufacturing setups, $1,344,000; machine processing, $3,696,000; and product shipping, $1,120,000.

Required:

1. Compute the unit manufacturing cost of Deluxe and Executive filing cabinets by using the company's current overhead costing procedures.
2. Compute the unit manufacturing cost of Deluxe and Executive filing cabinets by using activity-based costing.
3. Is the cost of the Deluxe filing cabinet overstated or understated (i.e., distorted) by the use of machine hours to allocate total manufacturing overhead to production? By how much?
4. Calculate the aggregate amount by which the Deluxe cabinet line is undercosted by the company's current traditional overhead costing procedures. Then calculate the aggregate amount by which the traditional system overcosts the Executive cabinet line.
5. Assume that the current selling price of a Deluxe filing cabinet is $270 and the marketing manager is contemplating a $30 discount to stimulate volume. Is this discount advisable? Briefly discuss.

Clark and Shiffer LPP performs a variety of activities related to information systems and e-commerce consulting in Vancouver. The firm, which bills $140 per hour for services performed, is in a very tight local labour market and is having difficulty finding quality help for its overworked professional staff. The cost per hour for professional staff time is $50. Selected information follows.

- Billable hours to clients for the year totalled 6,000, consisting of information systems services, 3,600; e-commerce consulting, 2,400.

- Administrative cost of $381,760 was (and continues to be) allocated to both services based on billable hours. These costs consist of staff support, $207,000; in-house computing, $145,000; and miscellaneous office charges, $29,760.

A recent analysis of staff support costs found a correlation with the number of clients served. In-house computing and miscellaneous office charges varied directly with the number of computer hours logged and number of client transactions, respectively. A tabulation revealed the following data:

	Information Systems Services	E-Commerce Consulting	Total
Number of clients	240	60	300
Number of computer hours	2,900	2,100	5,000
Number of client transactions	480	720	1,200

■ **Problem 5–46**
Continuation of Preceding Problem; Explaining ABC
(LO 2, 4)

Pool rate for material-handling activity: $525 per production run

■ **Problem 5–47**
Activity-Based Costing; Cost Distortion; Product Promotion
(LO 1, 2, 4, 5)

2. Application rate, product shipping: $3,200 per outgoing shipment
2. Deluxe, total cost per unit: $253.50

■ **Problem 5–48**
Activity-Based Costing; Analysis of Operations
(LO 1, 2, 4, 7, 10)

2. E-commerce consulting, billings: $336,000
3. Application rate, staff support: $690 per client

Required:

1. Activity-based costing (ABC) is said to result in improved costing accuracy when compared with traditional costing procedures. Briefly explain how this improved accuracy is attained.

2. Assume that the firm uses traditional costing procedures, allocating total costs on the basis of billable hours. Determine the profitability of the firm's information systems and e-commerce activities, expressing your answer both in dollars and as a percentage of activity revenue.

3. Repeat requirement (2), using activity-based costing.

4. Stephen Shiffer, one of the firm's partners, doesn't care where his professionals spend their time because, as he notes, "many clients have come to expect both services and we need both to stay in business. Also, information systems and e-commerce professionals are paid the same hourly rate." Should Shiffer's attitude change? Explain.

5. Is an aggressive expansion of either service currently desirable? Briefly discuss.

■ Problem 5–49
Activity Cost Pools; Cost Drivers; Pool Rates
(LO 1, 2, 5)

1. Assigned overhead cost, machine setups: $24,000
3. Predetermined overhead rate: $62.50 per machine hr.

Burnaby Radiology, Inc. manufactures chemicals used in radiological imaging systems. The controller has established the following activity cost pools and cost drivers.

Activity Cost Pool	Budgeted Overhead Cost	Cost Driver	Budgeted Level for Cost Driver	Pool Rate
Machine setups	$1,000,000	Number of setups	250	$4,000 per setup
Material handling	300,000	Weight of raw material	75,000 kg	$4 per kg
Hazardous waste control	100,000	Weight of hazardous chemicals used	10,000 kg	$10 per kg
Quality control	300,000	Number of inspections	2,000	$150 per inspection
Other overhead costs	800,000	Machine hours	40,000	$20 per machine hour
Total.....................................	$2,500,000			

An order for 1,000 boxes of radiological development chemicals has the following production requirements.

Machine setups	6
Raw material	9,000 kilograms
Hazardous materials	2,100 kilograms
Inspections..	8
Machine hours..	550 machine hours

Required:

1. Compute the total overhead that should be assigned to the development-chemical order.

2. What is the overhead cost per box of chemicals?

3. Suppose Burnaby Radiology, Inc. were to use a single predetermined overhead rate based on machine hours. Compute the rate per hour.

4. Under the approach in requirement (3), how much overhead would be assigned to the development-chemical order:

   a. In total?

   b. Per box of chemicals?

5. Explain why these two product-costing systems result in such widely differing costs. Which system do you recommend? Why?

6. *Build a spreadsheet:* Construct an Excel spreadsheet to solve requirements (1), (2), (3), and (4) above. Show how the solution will change if the following data change. The overhead associated with machine setups is $500,000, and there are 1,000 inspections budgeted.

■ Problem 5–50
Overhead Cost Drivers
(LO 4, 5)

Refer to the original data given in the preceding problem for Burnaby Radiology, Inc.

Required:

1. Calculate the unit cost of a production order for 100 specially coated plates used in radiological imaging. In addition to direct material costing $210 per plate and direct labour costing $60 per plate, the order requires the following:

Machine setups	4 raw material	800 kilograms
Hazardous materials	400 kilograms	
Inspections	4	
Machine hours	60	

2. *Build a spreadsheet:* Construct an Excel spreadsheet to solve the preceding requirement. (This will be an extension of the spreadsheet constructed for the preceding problem.) Show how the solution will change if the data *given in the preceding problem* change as follows: the overhead associated with machine setups is $500,000, and there are 1,000 inspections budgeted.

■ **Problem 5–51**
Activity-Based Costing;
Activity-Based Management
(LO 1, 2, 3, 4, 5)

2. Quality control: $15 per inspection
2. Novelle, total costs: $11,650,400

Queensland Electronics Company manufactures two large-screen television models: the Novelle, which has been produced for 10 years and sells for $910, and the Zodiac, a new model introduced in early 20x3, which sells for $1,160. Based on the following income statement for 20x4, a decision has been made to concentrate Queensland's marketing resources on the Zodiac model and to begin to phase out the Novelle model.

QUEENSLAND ELECTRONICS COMPANY
Income Statement
For the Year Ended December 31, 20x4

	Zodiac	Novelle	Total
Sales	$4,640,000	$20,020,000	$24,660,000
Cost of goods sold	3,232,000	13,024,000	16,256,000
Gross margin	1,408,000	6,996,000	8,404,000
Selling and administrative expense	980,000	5,700,000	6,680,000
Net income	$ 428,000	$ 1,296,000	$ 1,724,000
Units produced and sold	4,000	22,000	
Net income per unit sold	$107.00	$58.91*	

*Rounded

The standard unit costs for the Zodiac and Novelle models are as follows:

	Zodiac	Novelle
Direct material	$579	$211
Direct labour:		
Zodiac (3.5 hrs. × $14)	49	
Novelle (1.5 hrs. × $14)		21
Machine usage:		
Zodiac (4 hrs. × $19)	76	
Novelle (8 hrs. × $19)		152
Manufacturing overhead*	104	208
Standard cost	$808	$592

*Manufacturing overhead was applied on the basis of machine hours at a predetermined rate of $26 per hour.

Queensland Electronics Company's controller is advocating the use of activity-based costing and activity-based management and has gathered the following information about the company's manufacturing-overhead costs for 20x4.

		Number of Events		
Activity Centre (cost driver)	Traceable Costs	Zodiac	Novelle	Total
Soldering (number of solder joints)	$ 880,000	400,000	1,200,000	1,600,000
Shipments (number of shipments)	836,000	3,800	15,200	19,000
Quality control (number of inspections)	1,170,000	21,060	56,940	78,000
Purchase orders (number of orders)	1,110,000	105,450	79,550	185,000
Machine power (machine hours)	47,500	15,200	174,800	190,000
Machine setups (number of setups)	948,500	4,500	4,985	9,485
Total traceable costs	$4,992,000			

Required:

1. Briefly explain how an activity-based costing system operates.

2. Using activity-based costing, determine if Queensland Electronics should continue to emphasize the Zodiac model and phase out the Novelle model.

(CMA, adapted)

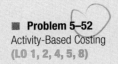

Ultratech, Inc. manufactures several different types of printed circuit boards; however, two of the boards account for the majority of the company's sales. The first of these boards, a television circuit board, has been a standard in the industry for several years. The market for this type of board is competitive and price-sensitive. Ultratech plans to sell 65,000 of the TV boards in 20x4 at a price of $300 per unit. The second high-volume product, a personal computer circuit board, is a recent addition to Ultratech's product line. Because the PC board incorporates the latest technology, it can be sold at a premium price. The 20x4 plans include the sale of 40,000 PC boards at $600 per unit.

Ultratech's management group is meeting to discuss how to spend the sales and promotion dollars for 20x4. The sales manager believes that the market share for the TV board could be expanded by concentrating Ultratech's promotional efforts in this area. In response to this suggestion, the production manager said, "Why don't you go after a bigger market for the PC board? The cost sheets that I get show that the contribution from the PC board is more than double the contribution from the TV board. I know we get a premium price for the PC board. Selling it should help overall profitability."

The cost-accounting system shows that the following costs apply to the PC and TV boards:

	PC Board	TV Board
Direct material	$280	$160
Direct labour	4 hrs.	1.5 hrs.
Machine time	1.5 hrs.	.5 hrs.

Variable manufacturing overhead is applied on the basis of direct-labour hours. For 20x4, variable overhead is budgeted at $2,240,000, and direct-labour hours are estimated at 280,000. The hourly rates for machine time and direct labour are $20 and $28, respectively. The company applies a material-handling charge at 10 percent of material cost. This material-handling charge is not included in variable manufacturing overhead. Total 20x4 expenditures for direct material are budgeted at $21,600,000.

Andrew Fulton, Ultratech's controller, believes that before the management group proceeds with the discussion about allocating sales and promotional dollars to individual products, it might be worthwhile to look at these products on the basis of the activities involved in their production. Fulton has prepared the following schedule to help the management group understand this concept.

"Using this information," Fulton explained, "we can calculate an activity-based cost for each TV board and each PC board and then compare it to the standard cost we have been using. The only cost that remains the same for both cost methods is the cost of direct material. The cost drivers will replace the direct labour, machine time, and overhead costs in the old standard cost figures."

	Budgeted Cost	Cost Driver	Budgeted Annual Activity for Cost Driver
Procurement	$ 800,000	Number of parts	4,000,000 parts
Production scheduling	440,000	Number of boards	110,000 boards
Packaging and shipping	880,000	Number of boards	110,000 boards
Total	$ 2,120,000		
Machine setup	$ 892,000	Number of setups	278,750 setups
Hazardous waste disposal	96,000	Kilograms of waste	16,000 kg
Quality control	1,120,000	Number of inspections	160,000 inspections
General supplies	132,000	Number of boards	110,000 boards
Total	$ 2,240,000		
Machine insertion	$ 2,400,000	Number of parts	3,000,000 parts
Manual insertion	8,000,000	Number of parts	1,000,000 parts
Wave-soldering	264,000	Number of boards	110,000 boards
Total	$10,664,000		

	Required per Unit	
	PC Board	**TV Board**
Parts:	55	26
Machine insertions...	36	25
Manual insertions	19	1
Machine setups...	3	2
Hazardous waste disposal	.40 kg	.03 kg
Inspections...	2	1

Required:

1. Identify at least four general advantages associated with activity-based costing.

2. On the basis of Ultratech's unit cost data given in the problem, calculate the total amount that each of the two product lines will contribute toward covering fixed costs and profit in 20x4. (In other words, for each product line, calculate the total sales revenue minus the total *variable* costs. This amount is often referred to as a product's total *contribution margin*.)

3. Repeat requirement (2) but now use the cost data from the activity-based costing system.

4. Explain how a comparison of the results of the two costing methods may impact the decisions made by Ultratech's management group.

(CMA, adapted)

Gourmet Specialty Coffee Company (GSCC) is a distributor and processor of different blends of coffee. The company buys coffee beans from around the world and roasts, blends, and packages them for resale. GSCC currently has 15 different coffees that it offers to gourmet shops in one-kilogram bags. The major cost is raw materials; however, there is a substantial amount of manufacturing overhead in the predominantly automated roasting and packing process. The company uses relatively little direct labour.

Some of the coffees are very popular and sell in large volumes, while a few of the newer blends have very low volumes. GSCC prices its coffee at full product cost, including allocated overhead, plus a markup of 30 percent. If prices for certain coffees are significantly higher than market, adjustments are made. The company competes primarily on the quality of its products, but customers are price-conscious as well.

Data for the 20x5 budget include manufacturing overhead of $12,000,000, which has been allocated on the basis of each product's direct-labour cost. The budgeted direct-labour cost for 20x5 totals $1,200,000. Based on the sales budget and raw-material budget, purchases and use of raw materials (mostly coffee beans) will total $5,800,000.

The expected prime costs for one-kilogram bags of two of the company's products are as follows:

	Jamaican	Colombian
Direct material...	$2.90	$3.90
Direct labour..	.40	.40

GSCC's controller believes the traditional product-costing system may be providing misleading cost information. She has developed an analysis of the 20x5 budgeted manufacturing-overhead costs shown in the following chart.

Activity	Cost Driver	Budgeted Activity	Budgeted Cost
Purchasing............................	Purchase orders	2,316.......................	$ 2,316,000
Material handling....................	Setups	3,600.......................	2,880,000
Quality control	Batches.................................	1,440.......................	576,000
Roasting...............................	Roasting hours	192,200.......................	3,844,000
Blending...............................	Blending hours	67,200.......................	1,344,000
Packaging	Packaging hours....................	52,000.......................	1,040,000
Total manufacturing-overhead cost			$12,000,000

Data regarding the 20x5 production of Jamaican and Colombian coffee are shown in the following table. There will be no raw-material inventory for either of these coffees at the beginning of the year.

■ **Problem 5–53**
Activity-Based Costing
(LO 1, 2, 4, 5, 7)

1*a*. Overhead rate: $10 per direct-labour dollar
2. New product cost: $11.06 per kilogram of Jamaican coffee

	Jamaican	Colombian
Budgeted sales..	2,000 kg	100,000 kg
Batch size	500 kg	20,000 kg
Setups	3 per batch	3 per batch
Purchase order size	500 kg	50,000 kg
Roasting time..	1 hr. per 200 kg	1 hr. per 200 kg
Blending time..	.5 hr. per 200 kg	.5 hr. per 200 kg
Packaging time..	.1 hr. per 200 kg	.1 hr. per 200 kg

Required:

1. Using GSCC's current product-costing system:
    a.   Determine the company's predetermined overhead rate using direct-labour cost as the single cost driver.
    b.   Determine the full product costs and selling prices of one kilogram of Jamaican coffee and one kilogram of Colombian coffee.
2. Develop a new product cost, using an activity-based costing approach, for one kilogram of Jamaican coffee and one kilogram of Colombian coffee.
3. What are the implications of the activity-based costing system with respect to:
    a.   The use of direct labour as a basis for applying overhead to products?
    b.   The use of the existing product-costing system as the basis for pricing?

(CMA, adapted)

■ **Problem 5–54**
Activity-Based Costing;
Activity Cost Pools; Pool
Rates; Calculation of Product
Costs; Cost Distortion
(LO 1, 2, 3, 4, 5)

2. II. Setup and inspection:
$9,000 per run
5. Odds, new target price:
$2,420.64

Knickknack, Inc. manufactures two products: odds and ends. The firm uses a single, plantwide overhead rate based on direct-labour hours. Production and product-costing data are as follows:

	Odds	Ends
Production quantity	1,000 units	5,000 units
Direct material	$160	$240
Direct labour (not including setup time)	120 (4 hrs. @ $30 per hr.)	180 (6 hrs. @ $30 per hr.)
Manufacturing overhead*	384 (4 hrs. @ $96 per hr.)	576 (6 hrs. @ $96 per hr.)
Total cost per unit	$664	$996

*Calculation of predetermined overhead rate:

Manufacturing overhead budget:

Machine-related costs...	$1,800,000
Setup and inspection..	720,000
Engineering...	360,000
Plant-related costs...	384,000
Total...	$3,264,000

Predetermined overhead rate:

$$\frac{\text{Budgeted manufacturing overhead}}{\text{Budgeted direct-labour hours}} = \frac{\$816,000}{(1,000)(2) + (5,000)(3)} = \$48 \text{ per direct-labour hour}$$

Knickknack, Inc. prices its products at 120 percent of cost, which yields target prices of $796.80 for odds and $1,195.20 for ends. Recently, however, Knickknack has been challenged in the market for ends by a European competitor, Bricabrac Corporation. A new entrant in this market, Bricabrac has been selling ends for $880 each. Knickknack's president is puzzled by Bricabrac's ability to sell ends at such a low cost. She has asked you (the controller) to look into the matter. You have decided that Knickknack's traditional, volume-based product-costing system may be causing cost distortion between the firm's two products. Ends are a high-volume, relatively simple product. Odds, on the other hand, are quite complex and exhibit a much lower volume. As a result, you have begun work on an activity-based costing system.

Required:

1. Let each of the overhead categories in the budget represent an activity cost pool. Categorize each in terms of the type of activity (e.g., unit-level activity).

2. The following cost drivers have been identified for the four activity cost pools:

Activity Cost Pool	Cost Driver	Budgeted Level of Cost Driver
Machine-related costs	Machine hours	18,000 hrs.
Setup and inspection	Number of production runs	80 runs
Engineering	Engineering change orders	200 change orders
Plant-related costs	Square metres of space	3,840 m²

You have gathered the following additional information:

- Each odd requires 8 machine hours, whereas each end requires 2 machine hour.
- Odds are manufactured in production runs of 25 units each. Ends are manufactured in 125-unit batches.
- Three-quarters of the engineering activity, as measured in terms of change orders, is related to odds.
- The plant has 3,840 square metres of space, 80 percent of which is used in the production of odds.

For each activity cost pool, compute a pool rate.

3. Determine the unit cost, for each activity cost pool, for odds and ends.
4. Compute the new product cost per unit for odds and ends, using the ABC system.
5. Using the same pricing policy as in the past, compute prices for odds and ends. Use the product costs determined by the ABC system.
6. Show that the ABC system fully assigns the total budgeted manufacturing overhead costs of $3,264,000.
7. Show how Knickknack's traditional, volume-based costing system distorted its product costs. (Refer to Exhibit 5–10 for guidance.)

■ **Problem 5–55**
Activity-Based Costing; Forecasting; Ethics
(LO 1, 2, 4, 5)

1. Material-handling rate: 10%
2a. Material-handling cost per purchase order: $1

Northwest Aircraft Industries (NAI) manufactures parts for small aircraft. Over the past decade, NAI's management has met its goal of reducing its reliance on government contract work to 50 percent of total sales. Thus, NAI's sales are now roughly evenly split between government and commercial sales.

Traditionally, the costs of the Material-Handling Department have been allocated to direct material as a percentage of direct-material dollar value. This was adequate when the majority of the manufacturing was homogeneous and related to government contracts. Recently, however, government auditors have rejected some proposals, stating that "the amount of Material-Handling Department costs allocated to these proposals is disproportionate to the total effort involved."

Kara Lindley, the newly hired cost-accounting manager, was asked by the manager of the Government Contracts Unit, Paul Anderson, to find a more equitable method of allocating Material-Handling Department costs to the user departments. Her review has revealed the following information:

- The majority of the direct-material purchases for government contracts are high-dollar, low-volume purchases, while commercial materials represent low-dollar, high-volume purchases.
- Administrative departments such as marketing, finance and administration, human resources, and maintenance also use the services of the Material-Handling Department on a limited basis but have never been charged in the past for material-handling costs.
- One purchasing agent with a direct phone line is assigned exclusively to purchasing high-dollar, low-volume material for government contracts at an annual salary of $54,000. Employee benefits are estimated to be 20 percent of the annual salary. The annual dedicated phone line costs are $4,200.

The components of the Material-Handling Department's budget for 20x4, as proposed by Lindley's predecessor, are as follows:

Payroll	$ 270,000
Employee benefits	54,000
Telephone	57,000
Other utilities	33,000
Materials and supplies	9,000
Depreciation	9,000
Direct-material budget:	
Government contracts	3,009,000
Commercial products	1,311,000

Lindley has estimated the number of purchase orders to be processed in 20x4 to be as follows:

Government contracts*	120,000
Commercial products	234,000
Marketing	2,700
Finance and administration	4,050
Human resources	750
Maintenance	1,500
Total	363,000

*Exclusive of high-dollar, low-volume materials.

Lindley recommended to Anderson that material-handling costs be allocated on a per-purchase-order basis. Anderson realizes and accepts that the company has been allocating to government contracts more material-handling costs than can be justified. However, the implication of Lindley's analysis could be a decrease in his unit's earnings and, consequently, a cut in his annual bonus. Anderson told Lindley to "adjust" her numbers and modify her recommendation so that the results will be more favourable to the Government Contracts Unit.

Being new in her position, Lindley is not sure how to proceed. She feels ambivalent about Anderson's instructions and suspects his motivation. To complicate matters for Lindley, Preston has asked her to prepare a three-year forecast of the Government Contracts Unit's results, and she believes that the newly recommended allocation method would provide the most accurate data. However, this would put her in direct opposition to Anderson's directives.

Lindley has assembled the following data to project the material-handling costs:

- Total direct-material costs increase 2.5 percent per year.
- Material-handling costs remain the same percentage of direct-material costs.
- Direct government costs (payroll, employee benefits, and direct phone line) remain constant.
- The number of purchase orders increases 5 percent per year.
- The ratio of government purchase orders to total purchase orders remains at 33 percent.
- In addition, she has assumed that government material in the future will be 70 percent of total material.

Required:

1. Calculate the material-handling rate that would have been used by Kara Lindley's predecessor at Northwest Aircraft Industries.

2. *a.* Calculate the revised material-handling costs to be allocated on a per-purchase-order basis.

   b. Discuss why purchase orders might be a more reliable cost driver than the dollar amount of direct material.

3. Calculate the difference due to the change to the new method of allocating material-handling costs to government contracts.

4. Prepare a forecast of the cumulative dollar impact over a three-year period from 20x4 through 20x6 of Kara Lindley's recommended change for allocating Material-Handling Department costs to the Government Contracts Unit. Round all calculations to the nearest whole number.

5. Referring to the standards of ethical conduct for management accountants:

   a. Discuss why Kara Lindley has an ethical conflict.

   b. Identify several steps that Lindley could take to resolve the ethical conflict.

(CMA, adapted)

■ **Problem 5–56**
Activity-Based Costing;
Production and Pricing
Decisions
(LO 1, 2, 3, 4, 5, 8)

1*a*. Total overhead:
$1,050,000
1*b*. Total budgeted direct-
labour hours: 1000,000

Scott Manufacturing produces two items in its Surrey Plant: Tuff Stuff and Ruff Stuff. Since inception, Scott has used only one manufacturing-overhead cost pool to accumulate costs. Overhead has been allocated to products based on direct-labour hours. Until recently, Scott was the sole producer of Ruff Stuff and was able to dictate the selling price. However, last year Marvella Products began marketing a comparable product at a price below the cost assigned by Scott. Market share has declined rapidly, and Scott must now decide whether to meet the competitive price or to discontinue the product line. Recognizing that discontinuing the product line would place an additional burden on its remaining product, Tuff Stuff, management is using activity-based costing to determine if it would show a different cost structure for the two products.

The two major indirect costs for manufacturing the products are power usage and setup costs. Most of the power is used in fabricating, while most of the setup costs are required in assembly. The setup costs are predominantly related to the Tuff Stuff product line.

A decision was made to separate the Manufacturing Department costs into two activity cost pools as follows:

Fabricating: Machine hours will be the cost driver.
Assembly: Number of setups will be the cost driver.

The controller has gathered the following information:

MANUFACTURING DEPARTMENT
Annual Budget before Separation of Overhead

	Total	Product Line	
		Tuff Stuff	Ruff Stuff
Number of units		20,000	20,000
Direct-labour hours*		2 hours per unit	3 hours per unit
Total direct-labour cost	$2,400,000		
Direct material		$15 per unit	$9 per unit
Budgeted overhead:			
Indirect labour	72,000		
Fringe benefits	15,000		
Indirect material	93,000		
Power	540,000		
Setup	225,000		
Quality assurance	30,000		
Other utilities	30,000		
Depreciation	45,000		

*Direct-labour hourly rate is the same in both departments.

MANUFACTURING DEPARTMENT
Cost Structure after Separation of Overhead into Activity Cost Pools

	Fabrication	Assembly
Direct-labour cost	74%	26%
Direct material (no change)	100%	0%
Indirect labour	76%	24%
Fringe benefits	80%	20%
Indirect material	$60,000	$33,000
Power	$480,000	$60,000
Setup	$15,000	$210,000
Quality assurance	80%	20%
Other utilities	50%	50%
Depreciation	78%	22%

	Product Line	
Cost driver:	Tuff Stuff	Ruff Stuff
Machine-hours per unit	4.4	6.0
Setups	1,000	272

Required:

1. Assigning overhead based on direct-labour hours, calculate the following:

   a.   Total budgeted cost of the Manufacturing Department
   b.   Unit cost of Tuff Stuff and Ruff Stuff

2. After separation of overhead into activity cost pools, compute the total budgeted cost of each department: fabricating and assembly.

3. Using activity-based costing, calculate the unit costs for each product. (In computing the pool rates for the fabricating and assembly activity cost pools, round to the nearest cent. Then, in computing unit product costs, round to the nearest cent.)

4.   Discuss how a decision regarding the production and pricing of Ruff Stuff will be affected by the results of your calculations in the preceding requirements.

(CMA, adapted)

Home Furnishings Corporation (HFC) manufactures a variety of housewares for the consumer market. The company's three major product lines are cooking utensils, tableware, and flatware. HFC implemented activity-based costing four years ago and now has a well-developed ABC system in place for determining product costs. Only recently, however, has the ABC system been systematically used for the purposes of activity-based management. As a pilot project, HFC's controller asked the ABC project team to do a detailed activity analysis of the purchasing activity. The following specific activities were identified:

1. Receipt of parts specifications from the Design Engineering Department
2. Follow-up with design engineers to answer any questions
3. Vendor (supplier) identification
4. Vendor consultations (by phone or in person)
5. Price negotiation
6. Vendor selection
7. Ordering (by phone or mail)
8. Order follow-up
9. Expediting (attempting to speed up delivery)
10. Order receiving
11. Inspection of parts
12. Return of parts not meeting specifications
13. Consultation with design engineers and production personnel if parts do not satisfy intended purpose
14. Further consultation and/or negotiation with vendor if necessary
15. Ship parts back to vendor if necessary
16. If satisfactory, move parts to storage

Required:

1. Draw a diagram to depict HFC's two-dimensional activity-based costing efforts. The diagram should include the following:
    a. The cost assignment role of ABC, with the cost pools, activities, and product lines represented
    b. The process view of ABC, with the purchasing activities displayed. Also indicated here will be the linkages among the activities. (To save space, indicate the activities by their numbers.)
    c. The activity evaluation phase of two-dimensional ABC
2. Identify the triggers for each of the following activities in HFC's purchasing activity analysis:
    Follow-up with design engineers (activity 2)
    Expediting (activity 9)
    Inspection of parts (activity 11)
    Return of parts (activity 12)
    Consultation with design engineers and production personnel (activity 13)
3. For each of the activities listed in requirement (2), identify the possible root causes.
4. Choose four activities in HFC's purchasing function, and suggest a performance measure for each of these activities.

Fibre Optics, Inc. manufactures fibre optic cables for the computer and telecommunications industries. At the request of the company vice-president of marketing, the cost management staff has recently completed a customer-profitability study. The following activity-based costing information was the basis for the analysis.

Customer-Related Activities	Cost Driver Base	Cost Driver Rate
Sales activity	Sales visits	$2,000
Order taking	Purchase orders	400
Special handling	Units handled	100
Special shipping	Shipments	1,000

Cost-driver data for two of Fibre Optics' customers for the most recent year are:

Customer-Related Activities	Trace Telecom	Caltex Computer
Sales activity	6 visits	8 visits
Order taking	20 orders	15 orders
Special handling	600 units handled	800 units handled
Special shipping	20 shipments	18 shipments

The following additional information has been compiled for Fibre Optics for two of its customers, Trace Telecom and Caltex Computer, for the most recent year:

	Trace Telecom	Caltex Computer
Sales revenue	$247,600	$380,000
Cost of goods sold	124,000	160,000
General selling costs	36,000	48,000
General administrative costs	32,000	38,000

Required:

1. Prepare a customer profitability analysis for Trace Telecom and Caltex Computer. (*Hint:* Refer to Exhibit 5–13 for guidance.)

2. *Build a spreadsheet:* Construct an Excel spreadsheet to solve requirement (1) above. Show how the solution will change if the following information changes: Trace Telecom's sales revenue was $250,000 and Caltex Computer's cost of goods sold was $155,000.

Refer to the information given in the preceding problem for Fibre Optics and two of its customers, Trace Telecom and Caltex Computer. Additional information for six of Fibre Optics' other customers for the most recent year follows:

Customer	Operating Income
Golden Gate Service Associates	$142,000
Tele-Install, Inc.	(36,000)
Graydon Computer Company	120,000
Atlantic Computing Company	84,000
Network-All, Inc.	186,000
The Ontario Group	12,000

Required:

1. Prepare Fibre Optics' customer profitability profile for the most recent year.

2. As Fibre Optics' director of cost management, write a memo to the company's vice-president of marketing that will accompany the customer profitability profile. Include a brief explanation of the methodology used and comment on the results.

■ **Problem 5–59**
Customer Profitability Profile;
Continuation of Preceding
Problem
(LO 9)

Cases

Madison Electric Pump Corporation manufactures electric pumps for commercial use. The company produces three models, designated as regular, advanced, and deluxe. The company uses a job-order cost-accounting system with manufacturing overhead applied on the basis of direct-labour hours. The system has been in place with little change for 25 years. Product costs and annual sales data are as follows:

■ **Case 5–60**
Traditional versus Activity-
Based Costing Systems
(LO 1, 2, 3, 4, 5, 8)

1. Regular model, target
price: $231
2. Advanced model, total unit
cost: $875.50

	Regular Model	Advanced Model	Deluxe Model
Annual sales (units)	20,000	1,000	10,000
Product costs:			
Raw material	$ 20	$ 50	$ 84
Direct labour	20 (1 hr. @ $20 per hr.)	40 (2 hrs. @ $20 per hr.)	40 (2 hrs. @ $20 per hr.)
Manufacturing overhead*	170 (1 hr. @ $170 per hr.)	340 (2 hrs. @ $170 per hr.)	340 (2 hrs. @ $170 per hr.)
Total product cost	$210	$430	$464

*Calculation of predetermined overhead rate:

Manufacturing-overhead budget:

Depreciation, machinery..	$2,960,000
Maintenance, machinery	240,000
Depreciation, taxes, and insurance for factory...	600,000
Engineering...	700,000
Purchasing, receiving and shipping...	500,000
Inspection and repair of defects..	750,000
Material handling...	800,000
Miscellaneous manufacturing overhead costs..	590,000
Total...	$7,140,000

Direct-labour budget:

Regular model	20,000 hours
Advanced model	2,000 hours
Deluxe model	20,000 hours
Total	42,000 hours

Predetermined overhead rate: $\dfrac{\text{Budgeted overhead}}{\text{Budgeted direct-labour hours}} = \dfrac{\$3,570,000}{21,000 \text{ hours}} = \$170 \text{ per hour}$

For the past 10 years, the company's pricing formula has been to set each product's target price at 110 percent of its full product cost. Recently, however, the regular-model motor has come under increasing price pressure from offshore competitors. The result was that the price on the regular model has been lowered to $220.

The company president recently asked the controller, "Why can't we compete with these other companies? They're selling pumps just like our regular model for $212. That's only two dollars more than our production cost. Are we really that inefficient? What gives?"

The controller responded by saying, "I think this is due to an outmoded product-costing system. As you may remember, I raised a red flag about our system when I came on board last year. But the decision was to keep our current system in place. In my judgment, our product-costing system is distorting our product costs. Let me run a few numbers to demonstrate what I mean."

Getting the president's go-ahead, the controller compiled the basic data needed to implement an activity-based costing system. These data are displayed in the following table. The percentages are the proportion of each cost driver consumed by each product line.

		Product Lines		
Activity Cost Pool	**Cost Driver**	**Regular Model**	**Advanced Model**	**Deluxe Model**
I: Depreciation, machinery	Machine time	39%	13%	48%
Maintenance, machinery				
II: Engineering	Engineering hours	47%	6%	47%
Inspection and repair of defects				
III: Purchasing, receiving, and shipping	Number of material orders	47%	8%	45%
Material handling				
IV: Depreciation, taxes, and insurance for factory	Factory space usage	42%	15%	43%
Miscellaneous manufacturing overhead				

Required:

1. Compute the target prices for the three models, based on the traditional, volume-based product-costing system.

2. Compute new product costs for the three products, based on the new data collected by the controller. Round to the nearest cent.

3. Calculate a new target price for the three products, based on the activity-based costing system. Compare the new target price with the current actual selling price for the regular model pump.

4. Write a memo to the company president explaining what has been happening as a result of the firm's traditional, volume-based product-costing system.

5. What strategic options does management have? What do you recommend, and why?

Refer to the product costs developed in requirement (2) of the preceding problem. Prepare a table showing how Madison Electric Pump Corporation's traditional, volume-based product-costing system distorts the product costs of the standard, deluxe, and heavy-duty models. (You might wish to refer to Exhibit 5–10 for guidance. Because of rounding in the calculation of the product costs, there will be a small rounding error in this cost distortion analysis as well.)

Case 5–61
Cost Distortion; Continuation of Preceding Case
(LO 2, 5)

Madison Electric Pump Corporation's controller, Erin Jackson, developed new product costs for the three pump models using activity-based costing. It was apparent that the firm's traditional product-costing system had been undercosting the advanced model electric pump by a significant amount. This was due largely to the low volume of the advanced model. Before she could report back to the president, Jackson received a phone call from her friend, Alan Tyler. He was the production manager for the advanced model electric motor. Tyler was upset, and he let Jackson know it. "Erin, I've gotten wind of your new product-cost analysis. There's no way the advanced model costs anywhere near what your numbers say. For years and years, this line has been highly profitable, and its reported product cost was low. Now you're telling us it costs more than twice what we thought. I just don't buy it."

Jackson briefly explained to her friend about the principles of activity-based costing and why it resulted in more accurate product costs. "Alan, the advanced model is really losing money. It simply has too low a volume to be manufactured efficiently."

Tyler was even more upset now. "Erin, if you report these new product costs to the president, he's going to discontinue the advanced model. My job's on the line, Erin! How about massaging those numbers a little bit. Who's going to know?"

"I'll know, Alan. And you'll know," responded Jackson. "Look, I'll go over my analysis again, just to make sure I haven't made an error."

Case 5–62
Ethical Issues Related to Product-Cost Distortion; Activity-Based Costing; Continuation of Cases 5–60 and 5–61
(LO 2, 5, 7)

Required: Discuss the ethical issues involved in this scenario:
1. Is the controller, Erin Jackson, acting ethically?
2. Is the production manager, Alan Tyler, acting ethically?
3. What are Jackson's ethical obligations? To the president? To her friend?

Stanley Cycle Company produces two subassemblies, JY-63 and RX-67, used in manufacturing motorcycles. The company is currently using an absorption costing system that applies overhead based on direct-labour hours. The budget for the current year ending December 31, 20x4 is as follows:

Case 5–63
Activity-Based Costing; Budgeted Operating Margin

2. Assembly: $40 per assembly hour
4. RX-67, gross margin: $(226,000)

eXcel

STANLEY CYCLE COMPANY
Budgeted Statement of Gross Margin for 20x4

	JY-63	RX-67	Total
Sales in units	5,000	5,000	10,000
Sales revenue	$ 3,400,000	$ 4,400,000	$ 7,800,000
Cost of goods manufactured and sold:			
Beginning finished-goods inventory	$ 480,000	$ 600,000	$ 1,080,000
Add: Direct material	2,000,000	3,500,000	5,500,000
Direct labour	370,370	185,186	555,556
Applied manufacturing overhead*	1,088,050	544,026	1,632,076
Cost of goods available for sale	3,938,420	4,829,212	8,767,632
Less: Ending finished-goods inventory	480,000	600,000	1,080,000
Cost of goods sold	3,458,420	4,229,212	7,687,632
Gross margin	$ (58,420)	$ 170,788	$ 112,368

*Applied on the basis of direct-labour hours:

Machining	$ 849,056
Assembly	433,962
Material handling	113,208
Inspection	235,850
Total	$1,632,076

Jay Rexford, Stanley Cycle's president, has been reading about a new type of costing method called activity-based costing. Rexford is convinced that activity-based costing will cast a new light on future profits. As a result, Jack Canfield, the company's director of cost management, has accumulated cost pool information for this year shown on the following chart. This information is based on a product mix of 5,000 units of JY-63 and 5,000 units of RX-67.

Cost Pool Information for 20x4

Cost Pool	Activity	JY-63	RX-67
Direct labour......................	Direct-labour hours (per product line)............	10,000	5,000
Material handling..............	Number of parts (per unit)............................	5	10
Inspection.........................	inspection hours (per product line)...............	5,000	7,500
Machining.........................	Machine hours (per product line)...................	15,000	30,000
Assembly..........................	Assembly hours (per product line).................	6,000	5,500

In addition, the following information is projected for the next calendar year, 20x5:

	JY-63	RX-67
Sales (in units)...	5,100	4,900
Beginning inventory, finished goods (in units)...	800	600
Ending inventory, finished goods (in units)..	700	700

On January 1, 20x5, Rexford is planning to increase the prices of JY-63 to $710 and RX-67 to $910. Material costs are not expected to increase in 20x5, but direct labour will increase by 8 percent, and all manufacturing overhead costs will increase by 6 percent. Due to the nature of the manufacturing process, the company does not have any beginning or ending work-in-process inventories.

Stanley Cycle Company has materials delivered to the production facility directly from the vendors. The raw-material inventory both at the beginning and the end of the month is immaterial and can be ignored for the purposes of a budgeted income statement. The company uses the first-in, first-out (FIFO) inventory method.

Required:

1. Explain how activity-based costing differs from traditional product-costing methods.
2. Using activity-based costing, calculate the total cost for 20x5 for the following activity cost pools: material handling, inspection, machining, and assembly. (For the total costs, round to the nearest dollar.) Then, calculate the pool rate per unit of the appropriate cost driver for each of the four activities.
3. Prepare a table showing for each product line the estimated 20x5 cost for each of the following cost elements: direct material, direct-labour, machining, assembly, material handling, and inspection. (Round to the nearest dollar.)
4. Prepare a budgeted statement showing the gross margin for Stanley Cycle Company for 20x5, using activity-based costing. The statement should show each product and a total for the company. Be sure to include detailed calculations for the cost of goods manufactured and sold. (Round each amount in the statement to the nearest dollar.)

(CMA, adapted)

Chapter Six

Activity Analysis, Cost Behaviour, and Cost Estimation

FOCUS COMPANY

Tasty Donuts, Inc. is a chain of 10 donut shops in Toronto. Using the Tasty Donuts illustration, we explore cost behaviour, cost estimation, and cost prediction. Cost behaviour refers to the

relationship between cost and activity. Variable and fixed costs, which we studied in Chapter 2, are two examples of the many types of cost behaviour. Cost estimation is the process of determining how a particular cost behaves, often relying on historical cost data. Cost prediction means using our knowledge of cost behaviour to forecast the cost to be incurred at a particular level of activity. Cost analysis helps Tasty Donuts' management plan for the costs to be incurred at various levels of donut sales activity.

IN CONTRAST

In contrast to the service-industry setting of Tasty Donuts, we turn to a manufacturing environment to explore the effect of the

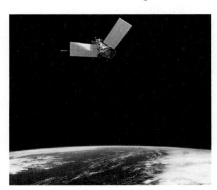

learning curve on cost behaviour. In many production processes, production efficiency increases with experience. As cumulative production output increases, the average labour time required per unit declines. As the labour time declines, labour cost declines as well. This phenomenon is called the *learning curve*. To illustrate the concept, we explore its use by Cosmos Communications Technology (CCT), a manufacturer of sophisticated communications satellites in Vancouver. CCT's management has found that the learning curve applies to the labour-intensive assembly operation for each new satellite design.

After completing this chapter, you should be able to:

1. Explain the relationships between cost estimation, cost behaviour, and cost prediction.

2. Define and describe the behaviour of the following types of costs: variable, step-variable, fixed, step-fixed, mixed, and curvilinear.

3. Explain the importance of the relevant range in using a cost behaviour pattern for cost prediction.

4. Describe and use the following cost-estimation methods: account classification, visual fit, high-low, and least-squares regression.

5. Describe the multiple regression and engineering approaches to cost estimation.

6. Describe some problems often encountered in collecting data for cost estimation.

7. Define and give examples of engineered costs, committed costs, and discretionary costs.

8. Describe the effect of learning on cost behaviour.

9. Perform and interpret a least-squares regression analysis with a single independent variable (Appendix).

Learning Objective **1**

Explain the relationships
between cost estimation, cost
behaviour, and cost prediction.

Managers in almost any organization want to know how costs will be affected by changes in the organization's activity. The relationship between cost and activity, called **cost behaviour**, is relevant to the management functions of planning, control, and decision making. In order to *plan* operations and prepare a budget, managers at Kellogg's need to predict the costs that will be incurred at different levels of production and sales. To *control* the costs of providing commercial-loan services at CIBC, executives need to have a feel for the costs that the bank should incur at various levels of commercial-loan activity. In *deciding* whether to add a new intensive care unit, a hospital's administrators need to predict the cost of operating the new unit at various levels of patient demand. In each of these situations, knowledge of *cost behaviour* will help the manager to make the desired **cost prediction**. A cost prediction is a forecast of cost at a particular level of activity. In the first half of this chapter, we will study cost behaviour patterns and their use in making cost predictions.

How does a managerial accountant determine the cost behaviour pattern for a particular cost item? The determination of cost behaviour, which is often called cost estimation, can be accomplished in a number of ways. One way is to analyze historical data concerning costs and activity levels. *Cost estimation* is covered in the second half of this chapter.

The following diagram summarizes the key points in the preceding discussion.

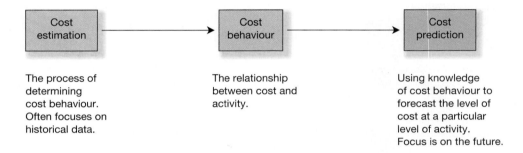

Cost estimation	→	Cost behaviour	→	Cost prediction
The process of determining cost behaviour. Often focuses on historical data.		The relationship between cost and activity.		Using knowledge of cost behaviour to forecast the level of cost at a particular level of activity. Focus is on the future.

Cost Behaviour Patterns

Our discussion of cost behaviour patterns, also called *cost functions,* will be set in the context of a restaurant business. Tasty Donuts, Inc. operates a chain of 10 donut shops in Toronto. Each shop sells a variety of donuts, muffins, and sweet rolls as well as various beverages. Beverages, such as coffee and fruit juices, are prepared in each donut shop, but all of the company's donuts and baked products are made in a centrally located bakery. The company leases several small delivery trucks to transport the bakery items to its restaurants. Use of a central bakery is more cost-efficient. Moreover, this approach allows the firm to smooth out fluctuations in demand for each type of product. For example, the demand for glazed donuts may change from day to day in each donut shop, but these fluctuations tend to cancel each other out when the total demand is aggregated across all 10 shops.

The corporate controller for Tasty Donuts has recently completed a study of the company's cost behaviour to use in preparing the firm's budget for the coming year. The controller studied the following costs:

- *Direct material:* Ingredients for donuts, muffins, and sweet rolls; beverages; paper products, such as napkins and disposable cups
- *Direct labour:* Wages and fringe benefits of bakers, restaurant sales personnel, and delivery-truck drivers
- *Overhead:*

  Facilities costs. Property taxes; depreciation on bakery building, donut shops, and equipment; salaries and fringe benefits of maintenance personnel

Indirect labour. Salaries and fringe benefits of managers and assistant managers for bakery and restaurants

Delivery trucks. Rental payments under lease contract; costs of gasoline, oil, tires, and maintenance

Utilities. Electricity, telephone, and trash collection

In studying the behaviour of each of these costs, the controller measured company *activity* in terms of *dozens of bakery items sold*. Thus, dozens of bakery items sold is the *cost driver* for each of the costs studied. A bakery item is one donut, muffin, or sweet roll. The costs to make each of these products are nearly identical. The number of bakery items sold each day is roughly the same as the number produced, since bakery goods are produced to keep pace with demand as reported by the company's restaurant managers.

> "Failure to understand costs would have left Portugal Telecom vulnerable to competition. Understanding the company's costs became essential to cost reduction efforts and to the company's long-term viability." (6a)
> **Accenture, regarding its client Portugal Telecom**

Variable Costs

Variable costs were discussed briefly in Chapter 2. We will summarize that discussion here in the context of the Tasty Donuts illustration. A **variable cost** changes *in total* in direct proportion to a change in the activity level (or cost driver). Tasty Donuts' direct-material cost is a variable cost. As the company sells more donuts, muffins, and sweet rolls, the total cost of the ingredients for these goods increases in direct proportion to the number of items sold. Moreover, the quantities of beverages sold and paper products used by customers also increase in direct proportion to the number of bakery items sold. As a result, the costs of beverages and paper products are also variable costs.

Panel A of Exhibit 6–1 displays a graph of Tasty Donuts' direct-material cost. As the graph shows, *total* variable cost increases in proportion to the activity

> **Learning Objective 2**
>
> Define and describe the behaviour of the following types of costs: variable, step-variable, fixed, step-fixed, mixed, and curvilinear.

A. Graph of Total Direct-Material Cost

Total direct-material cost
(food ingredients, beverages, paper products)

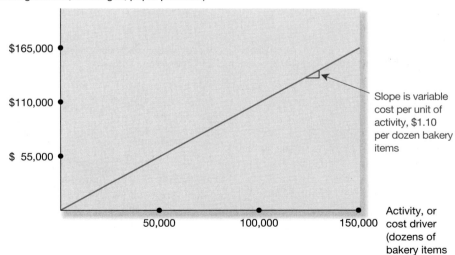

Slope is variable cost per unit of activity, $1.10 per dozen bakery items

Activity, or cost driver (dozens of bakery items sold)

Exhibit 6–1

Variable Cost: Direct-Material Cost, Tasty Donuts, Inc.

B. Tabulation of Direct-Material Cost

Activity (or cost driver)	Direct-Material Cost per Dozen Bakery Items Sold	Total Direct-Material Cost
50,000	$1.10	$ 55,000
100,000	1.10	110,000
150,000	1.10	165,000

level (or cost driver). When activity triples, for example, from 50,000 dozen items to 150,000 dozen items, total direct-material costs triple, from $55,000 to $165,000. However, the variable cost *per unit* remains the same as activity changes. The total direct-material cost incurred *per dozen* items sold is constant at $1.10 per dozen. The table in panel B of Exhibit 6–1 illustrates this point. The variable cost per unit also is represented in the graph in panel A of Exhibit 6–1 as the slope of the cost line.

To summarize, as activity changes, total variable cost increases in direct proportion to the change in activity level, but the variable cost per unit remains constant.

Step-Variable Costs

Some costs are nearly variable, but they increase in small steps instead of continuously. Such costs, called **step-variable costs**, usually include inputs that are purchased and used in relatively small increments. At Tasty Donuts, Inc. the direct-labour cost of bakers, restaurant counter-service personnel, and delivery-truck drivers is a step-variable cost. Many of these employees are part-time workers, called upon for relatively small increments of time, such as a few hours. On a typical day, for example, Tasty Donuts may have 35 employees at work in the bakery and the donut shops. If activity increases slightly, these employees can handle the extra work. However, if activity increases substantially, the bakery manager or various restaurant managers may call on additional help. Exhibit 6–2, a graph of Tasty Donuts' monthly direct-labour cost, shows that this cost remains constant within an activity range of about 5,000 dozen bakery items per month. When monthly activity increases beyond this narrow range, direct-labour costs increase.

Approximating a Step-Variable Cost   If the steps in a step-variable cost behaviour pattern are small, the step-variable cost function may be approximated by a variable cost function without much loss in accuracy. Exhibit 6–3 shows such an approximation for Tasty Donuts' direct-labour cost.

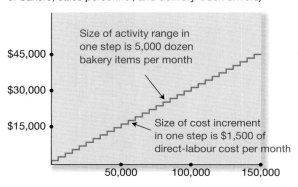

Total direct-labour cost (wages and fringe benefits of bakers, sales personnel, and delivery-truck drivers)

Exhibit 6–2
Step-Variable Cost: Direct-Labour Cost, Tasty Donuts

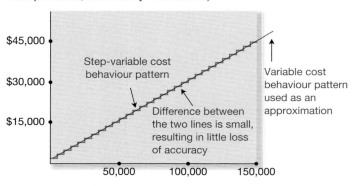

Total direct-labour cost (wages and fringe benefits of bakers, sales personnel, and delivery-truck drivers)

Exhibit 6–3
Approximating a Step-Variable Cost, Tasty Donuts

Fixed Costs

Fixed costs were covered briefly in Chapter 2. We will summarize that discussion here, using the Tasty Donuts illustration. A **fixed cost** remains unchanged *in total* as the activity level (or cost driver) varies. Facilities costs, which include property taxes, depreciation on buildings and equipment, and the salaries of maintenance personnel, are fixed costs for Tasty Donuts, Inc. These fixed costs are graphed in panel A of Exhibit 6–4. This graph shows that the *total* monthly cost of property taxes, depreciation, and maintenance personnel is $200,000 regardless of how many dozen bakery items are produced and sold during the month.

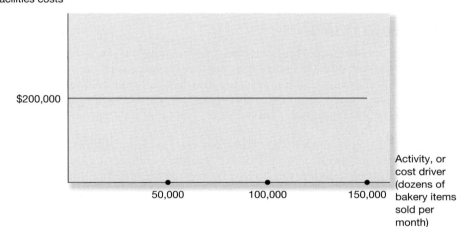

A. Graph of Total Monthly Fixed Costs: Facilities Costs

Total monthly fixed costs: facilities costs

$200,000

50,000   100,000   150,000   Activity, or cost driver (dozens of bakery items sold per month)

Exhibit 6–4

Fixed Cost: Facilities Costs, Tasty Donuts, Inc.

B. Tabulation of Monthly Fixed Costs: Facilities Costs

Activity (or cost driver)	Cost of Facilities per Dozen Bakery Items Sold	Total Monthly Cost of Facilities
50,000	$4.00	$200,000
100,000	2.00	200,000
150,000	1.33*	200,000

*Rounded.

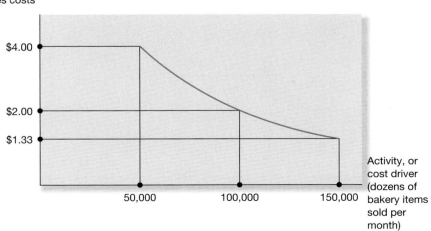

C. Graph of Unit Fixed Costs: Cost of Facilities per Dozen Bakery Items Sold

Unit fixed cost: facilities costs

$4.00

$2.00

$1.33

50,000   100,000   150,000   Activity, or cost driver (dozens of bakery items sold per month)

The fixed cost *per unit* does change as activity varies. Exhibit 6–4 (panel B) shows that the company's facilities cost per dozen bakery items is $4 when 50,000 dozen items are produced and sold. However, this unit cost declines to $2 when 100,000 dozen items are produced and sold. If activity increases to 150,000 dozen items, unit fixed cost will decline further, to about $1.33.

A graph provides another way of viewing the change in unit fixed cost as activity changes. Panel C of Exhibit 6–4 displays a graph of Tasty Donuts' cost of property taxes, depreciation, and maintenance personnel *per dozen bakery items*. As the graph shows, the fixed cost per dozen bakery items declines steadily as activity increases.

To summarize, as the activity level increases, total fixed cost does not change, but unit fixed cost declines. For this reason, it is preferable in any cost analysis to work with total fixed cost rather than fixed cost per unit.

Step-Fixed Costs

Some costs remain fixed over a wide range of activity but jump to a different amount for activity levels outside that range. Such costs are called step-fixed costs. Tasty Donuts' cost of indirect labour is a **step-fixed cost**. Indirect-labour cost consists of the salaries and fringe benefits for the managers and assistant managers of the company's bakery and restaurants. Tasty Donuts' monthly indirect-labour cost is graphed in Exhibit 6–5.

As Exhibit 6–5 shows, for activity in the range of 50,000 to 100,000 dozen bakery items per month, Tasty Donuts' monthly indirect-labour cost is $35,000. For this range of activity, the company employs a full-time manager and a full-time assistant manager in the bakery and in each restaurant. When monthly activity exceeds this range during the summer tourist season, the company employs additional part-time assistant managers in the bakery and in its busiest donut shops. The company hires college students who are majoring in hospitality management for these summer positions. Their salaries boost the monthly indirect-labour cost to $45,000. Tasty Donuts has not experienced demand of less than 50,000 dozen bakery items per month. However, the controller anticipates that if such a decrease in demand were to occur, the company would reduce the daily operating hours for its donut shops. This would allow the firm to operate each restaurant with only a

> "By understanding the costs and workload associated with the real business activities we undertake . . . we are better positioned to understand where value is created. . . . From this information, we can then make better decisions as to the management and direction of the business." (6b)
>
> **Transco**

Exhibit 6–5
Step-Fixed Cost: Indirect-Labour Cost, Tasty Donuts, Inc.

Total indirect-labour cost
(salaries and fringe benefits of bakery and donut shop management personnel)

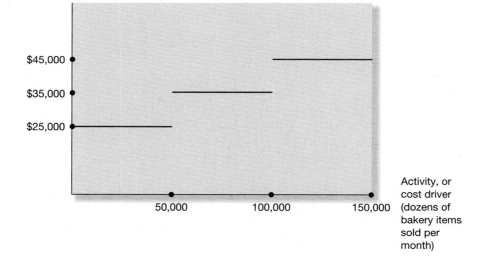

full-time manager and no assistant manager. As the graph in Exhibit 6–5 indicates, such a decrease in managerial personnel would reduce monthly indirect-labour cost to $25,000.

Mixed Costs

A **mixed cost** has both a fixed and a variable component. The cost of operating delivery trucks is a mixed cost for Tasty Donuts, Inc. These costs are graphed in Exhibit 6–6. As the graph shows, the company's delivery-truck costs have two components. The fixed-cost component is $3,000 per month, which is the monthly rental payment paid under the lease contract for the delivery trucks. The monthly rental payment is constant, regardless of the level of activity (or cost driver). The variable-cost component consists of the costs of gasoline, oil, routine maintenance, and tires. These costs vary with activity, since greater activity levels result in more deliveries. The distance between the fixed-cost line (dashed line) and the total-cost line in Exhibit 6–6 is the amount of variable cost. For example, at an activity level of 100,000 dozen bakery items, the total variable-cost component is $10,000.

The slope of the total-cost line is the variable cost per unit of activity. For Tasty Donuts, the variable cost of operating its delivery trucks is $.10 per dozen bakery items sold.

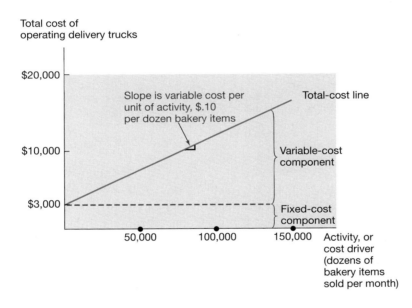

Exhibit 6–6
Mixed Cost: Cost of Operating Delivery Trucks, Tasty Donuts, Inc.

Curvilinear Cost

The graphs of all of the cost behaviour patterns examined so far consist of either straight lines or several straight-line sections. A **curvilinear cost** behaviour pattern has a curved graph. Tasty Donuts' utilities cost, depicted as the *solid curve* in Exhibit 6–7, is a curvilinear cost. For low levels of activity, this cost exhibits *decreasing marginal costs*. As the discussion in Chapter 2 indicated, a marginal cost is the cost of producing the next unit, in this case the next dozen bakery items. As the graph in Exhibit 6–7 shows, the marginal utilities cost of producing the next dozen bakery items declines as activity increases in the range zero to 100,000 dozen items per month. For activity greater than 100,000 dozen bakery items per month, the graph in Exhibit 6–7 exhibits *increasing marginal costs*.

Tasty Donuts' utilities cost includes electricity, telephone, and trash-collection costs. The utilities cost is curvilinear as a result of the company's pattern of electricity

Exhibit 6–7
Curvilinear Cost: Utilities
Cost, Tasty Donuts, Inc.

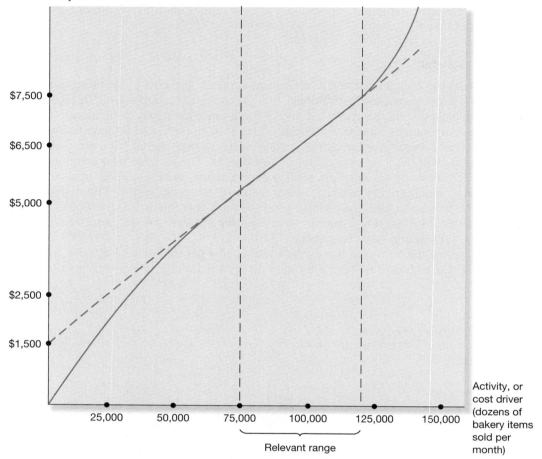

Total monthly cost of utilities

$7,500

$6,500

$5,000

$2,500

$1,500

25,000   50,000   75,000   100,000   125,000   150,000

Relevant range

Activity, or
cost driver
(dozens of
bakery items
sold per
month)

usage in the bakery. If the demand in a particular month is less than 100,000 dozen bakery items, the goods can be produced entirely in the modernized section of the bakery. This section uses recently purchased deep-fat fryers and ovens that are very energy-efficient. As long as the bakery operates only the modernized section, the utilities cost per dozen items declines as production increases.

During the summer tourist months, when Tasty Donuts' sales exceed 100,000 dozen items per month, the older section of the bakery also must be used. This section uses much older cooking equipment that is less energy-efficient. As a result, the marginal utilities cost per dozen bakery items rises as monthly activity increases in the range above 100,000 dozen items per month.

Learning Objective 3

Explain the importance of the relevant range in using a cost behaviour pattern for cost prediction.

Relevant Range The cost behaviour graphed in Exhibit 6–7 is very different at low activity levels (below 50,000) than it is at high activity levels (above 125,000). However, management need not concern itself with these extreme levels of activity if it is unlikely that Tasty Donuts, Inc. will operate at those activity levels. Management is interested in cost behaviour within the company's **relevant range**, the range of activity within which management expects the company to operate. Tasty Donuts' management believes the firm's relevant range to be 75,000 to 120,000 dozen bakery items per month. Based on past experience and sales projections, management does not expect the firm to operate outside that range of monthly activity. Tasty

IS DIRECT LABOUR A VARIABLE OR A FIXED COST?

Are direct-labour costs variable or fixed? The answer, as with many questions, is "It depends." What it depends on is the ability and willingness of a company's management to continually fine-tune the size of its workforce. If union labour contracts make it difficult to lay off workers during an economic downturn, or if top management adopts a policy of maintaining a stable workforce, direct-labour costs will tend to be largely fixed (or step-fixed). However, if management is able *and willing* to reduce the labour force when activity declines, then labour cost will be a variable (or step-variable) cost.

The current trend in many companies seems to be toward adjusting the workforce to conform to current needs. Here are several cases in point.

Nestlé

"Nestlé's prepared foods unit has built an in-house roster of part-time workers in Cherokee County, South Carolina, who stick by the telephone to hear if they should report on a given day to assemble frozen chicken dinners. The county job-placement office sends Nestlé lists of 'call-ins': people available to work when Nestlé phones them. The workers usually get a day's notice. Some agree to stay by the phone in the morning, in case the company is short for the afternoon shift. They typically work two to six days a week and earn slightly more than $11 an hour, which is considered good part-time pay in the area."

The head of human resources for the prepared-foods division says demand for its Lean Cuisine glazed-chicken entrees and Stouffers creamed-spinach side dishes is fairly steady. The company still hires some people full time. But the Nestlé executive says it is still hard to predict labour needs, because schedules for producing certain meals vary, and each product requires a different number of people to make. "'We don't need the same number of people every day,' he says. 'They work as we need them.'"[1]

General Motors

"One of the truly nefarious costs holding General Motors (and all the other domestic manufacturers) back is the UAW's job banks. Created in the mid-1980s, the Job Opportunity Bank Security system pays eligible workers as much as 95% of their salary plus all health and pension benefits until they are eligible to retire. According to the *Detroit Free Press*, GM had 5,223 workers in those job banks at the end of last year, costing GM up to US$679-million. GM also noted it has to set aside a further US$835-million for workers who will be idled as a result of all the plant closings it has recently instituted. Along with GM's 5,000-plus recipients and Delphi's 4,000, Ford has 1,275 employees in the job banks, while Chrysler has about 2,000. That is more than 12,000 people being paid top dollar not to work.

"What it has done is force domestic manufacturers to keep producing cars even when there has been little demand for them. Deep discounting and rebates are the result. Or, as John Novak, a Morningstar analyst, said recently in the *Chicago Tribune,* 'Essentially, what they are doing is making labour, which in most industries is a variable cost, into a fixed cost. In most businesses, when demand declines, you can downsize your workforce and your costs also shrink.' Even the UAW union can figure out that paying US$1.5-billion to people to not work is not a plan to turn around a very troubled company."[2]

Hilton Hotels

"Many employers, wary of losing valued workers altogether, are reducing the workweek rather than the workforce. Officials of Hilton Hotels Corp. in Beverly Hills, California, boast that they have laid off relatively few workers. However, Hilton says workweek reductions are widespread among its 77,000 workers."[3]

By relying more on part-time workers and daily call-ins, cross-training and frequently moving employees to new jobs, and shortening the workweek, Nestlé, Lincoln Electric, and Hilton Hotels are moving toward direct-labour costs that are much more variable than in the past. Other companies trending toward a "just-in-time workforce" are Wal-Mart, Taco Bell, Starbucks, and U-Haul, among others. This is "all part of the larger development in corporate America of transforming labor from a fixed to a more flexible cost."[4]

Donuts' relevant range is shown in Exhibit 6–7 as the section of the graph between the dashed lines.

Approximating a Curvilinear Cost within the Relevant Range   The straight, dashed line in Exhibit 6–7 may be used to approximate Tasty Donuts' utilities cost. Notice that the approximation is quite accurate for activity levels within the relevant range. However, as the activity level gets farther away from the boundary of the relevant range, the approximation declines in accuracy. For monthly activity levels of 25,000 or 150,000, for example, the approximation is very poor.

The straight, dashed line used to approximate Tasty Donuts' utilities cost *within the relevant range* represents a semi variable-cost behaviour pattern. This straight-line graph has a slope of $.05, which represents a unit variable-cost component of $.05 per dozen bakery items. The line intersects the vertical axis of the graph at $1,500, which represents a fixed-cost component of $1,500 per month. Managerial accountants often use a mixed-cost behaviour pattern to approximate a curvilinear cost. However, it is important to limit this approximation to the range of activity in which its accuracy is acceptable.

Using Cost Behaviour Patterns to Predict Costs

How can Tasty Donuts' corporate controller use the cost behaviour patterns identified in the cost study to help in the budgeting process? First, a sales forecast is made for each month during the budget year. Suppose management expects Tasty Donuts' activity level to be 110,000 dozen bakery items during the month of June. Second, a *cost prediction* is made for each of the firm's cost items. The following cost predictions are based on the cost behaviour patterns discussed earlier. (Try to verify these cost predictions by referring to the graphs in Exhibits 6–1 through 6–7.)

Cost Item	Cost Prediction for June (110,000 dozen bakery items per month)
Direct material	$121,000
Direct labour	33,000
Overhead:	
Facilities costs	200,000
Indirect labour	45,000
Delivery trucks	14,000
Utilities	7,000

The preparation of a complete budget involves much more analysis and detailed planning than is shown here.[5] The point is that cost prediction is an important part of the planning process. The cost behaviour patterns discussed in this chapter make those cost predictions possible.

Shifting Cost Structure in the Contemporary Manufacturing Environment

Fixed costs are becoming more prevalent in many industries. This is due to two factors. First, automation is replacing labour to an increasing extent. Second, labour unions have been increasingly successful in negotiating agreements that result in a relatively stable workforce. This makes management less flexible in adjusting a firm's workforce to the desired level of production.

In the advanced manufacturing environment that is emerging, many costs that once were largely variable have become fixed, most becoming committed fixed costs. Take the electronics industry, for example. Years ago, small electronic components were placed onto circuit boards, wired, and soldered by hand. Hundreds of employees performed these operations in "white rooms," which are sterile environments, in order to prevent the electronic units from being contaminated with dust or other foreign particles. Now much of the electronic industry is highly automated. Pick-and-place robots and auto-insertion machines place electronic components on circuit boards with incredible speed and precision. Wash and dry machines eliminate any contaminants, and wave-solder machines solder the connections. A large part of the manufacturing process is computerized. In the past, a major portion of the cost of electronics manufacturing was variable. The workforce could be adjusted as the economy grew rapidly or more slowly. In contrast, companies now spend hundreds of millions of dollars on computer-integrated manufacturing (CIM) systems and flexible manufacturing systems (FMS). Much of the manufacturing labour force consists of computer programmers and highly skilled operators of sophisticated production equipment. The depreciation, maintenance, and upgrades for the CIM systems constitute very large committed fixed costs. Moreover, the compensation costs for the highly skilled computer experts and equipment operators are largely committed fixed costs. Firms often cannot risk losing such highly trained personnel even during an economic downturn. Thus, the shifting cost structure we are observing in today's manufacturing environment has had a major impact on the nature of the cost behaviour to be estimated in CIM and FMS settings.

Operations-Based versus Volume-Based Cost Drivers Much of the discussion of cost behaviour in this chapter focuses on production volume as the cost driver. As Chapter 5 pointed out, however, production costs are affected by operations-based cost drivers as well. Product complexity, the configuration of the manufacturing process, and the number of production runs are among the many operational cost drivers that have been identified. In today's highly competitive environment, it is crucial that managers thoroughly understand the effects of both operations-based and volume-based cost drivers on the costs incurred in their organizations. For example, it will cost more to produce 10,000 radios in 10 production runs of 1,000 units than in 4 runs of 2,500 units. Increasing the number of production runs will drive setup costs up, even though the other costs of producing each radio may not vary.

> "Cost information about activities provides a benchmark to assess how we are doing against best-in-class and competitors." (6d)
> **BlueCross BlueShield of North Carolina**

Cost Behaviour in Other Industries

We have illustrated a variety of cost behaviour patterns for Tasty Donuts' restaurant business. The same cost behaviour patterns are used in other industries. The cost behaviour pattern appropriate for a particular cost item depends on the organization and the activity base (or cost driver). In manufacturing firms, production quantity, direct-labour hours, and machine hours are common cost drivers. Direct-material and direct-labour costs are usually considered variable costs. Other variable costs include some manufacturing-overhead costs, such as indirect material and indirect labour. Fixed manufacturing costs are generally the costs of creating production capacity. Examples include depreciation on plant and equipment, property taxes, and the plant manager's salary. Such overhead costs as utilities and equipment maintenance are usually mixed or curvilinear costs. A mixed-cost behaviour pattern is generally used to approximate a curvilinear cost within the relevant range. Supervisory salaries are usually step-fixed costs, since one person can supervise production over a range of activity. When activity increases beyond that range, such as when a new shift is added, an additional supervisor is added.

In merchandising firms, such as Chapters, the activity base (or cost driver) usually is sales revenue. The cost of merchandise sold is a variable cost. Most labour costs are fixed or step-fixed costs, since a particular number of sales and stock

> "In the management of a university, just like any other organization, you have to know your cost structure. We think very carefully about how student enrollment will affect faculty salary costs, computing costs, and lots of other costs students don't necessarily tend to think about." (6e)
> **Cornell University**

personnel can generally handle sales activity over a fairly wide range of sales. Store facility costs, such as rent, depreciation on buildings and furnishings, and property taxes, are fixed costs.

In some industries, the choice of the cost driver is not obvious, and the cost behaviour pattern can depend on the cost driver selected. At WestJet Airlines, for instance, the cost driver might be air miles flown, passengers flown, or passenger miles flown. A passenger mile is the transportation of one passenger for one mile. Fuel costs are variable with respect to air miles travelled, but are not necessarily variable with respect to passenger miles flown. An airplane uses more fuel in flying from Toronto to Vancouver than from Toronto to Montreal. However, a plane does not require significantly more fuel to fly 200 people from one city to another than to fly 190 people the same distance. In contrast, an airport landing fee is a fixed cost for a particular number of aircraft arrivals, regardless of how far the planes have flown or how many people were transported. The point of this discussion is that both the organization and the cost driver are crucial determinants of the cost behaviour for each cost item. Conclusions drawn about cost behaviour in one industry are not necessarily transferable to another industry.

Cost Estimation

Learning Objective 4

Describe and use the following cost-estimation methods: account classification, visual fit, high-low, and least-squares regression.

As the preceding discussion indicates, different costs exhibit a variety of cost behaviour patterns. **Cost estimation** is the process of determining how a particular cost behaves. Several methods are commonly used to estimate the relationship between cost and activity. Some of these methods are simple, while some are quite sophisticated. In some firms, managers use more than one method of cost estimation. The results of the different methods are then combined by the cost analyst on the basis of experience and judgment. We will examine five methods of cost estimation in the context of the Tasty Donuts illustration.

Account-Classification Method

The **account-classification method** of cost estimation, also called **account analysis**, involves a careful examination of the organization's ledger accounts. The cost analyst classifies each cost item in the ledger as a variable, fixed, or mixed cost. The classification is based on the analyst's knowledge of the organization's activities and experience with the organization's costs. For example, it may be obvious to the analyst going through the ledger that direct-material cost is variable, building depreciation is fixed, and utility costs are mixed.

Once the costs have been classified, the cost analyst estimates cost amounts by examining job-cost records, paid bills, labour time cards, or other source documents. A property-tax bill, for example, will provide the cost analyst with the information needed to estimate this fixed cost. This examination of historical source documents is combined with other knowledge that may affect costs in the future. For example, the municipal government may have recently enacted a 10 percent property-tax increase, which takes effect the following year.

For some costs, particularly those classified as mixed, the cost analyst may use one of several more systematic methods of incorporating historical data in the cost estimate. These methods are discussed next.

Visual-Fit Method

When a cost has been classified as mixed, or when the analyst has no clear idea about the behaviour of a cost item, it is helpful to use the **visual-fit method** to plot recent observations of the cost at various activity levels. The resulting **scatter diagram** helps the analyst to visualize the relationship between cost and the level of activity (or cost driver). To illustrate, suppose Tasty Donuts' controller has compiled the following historical data for the company's utility costs.

Month	Utility Cost for Month	Activity or Cost Driver (dozens of bakery items sold per month)
January	$5,100	75,000
February	5,300	78,000
March	5,650	80,000
April	6,300	92,000
May	6,400	98,000
June	6,700	108,000
July	7,035	118,000
August	7,000	112,000
September	6,200	95,000
October	6,100	90,000
November	5,600	85,000
December	5,900	90,000

The scatter diagram of these data is shown in Exhibit 6–8. The cost analyst can *visually fit a line* to these data by laying a ruler on the plotted points. The line is positioned so that a roughly equal number of plotted points lie above and below the line. Using this method, Tasty Donuts' controller visually fit the line shown in Exhibit 6–8.

Just a glance at the visually fit cost line reveals that Tasty Donuts' utilities cost is a mixed cost *within the relevant range*. The scatter diagram provides little or no information about the cost relationship outside the relevant range. Recall from the discussion of Tasty Donuts' utilities cost (see Exhibit 6–7) that the controller believes the cost behaviour pattern to be curvilinear over the *entire range* of activity. This judgment is based on the controller's knowledge of the firm's facilities and an understanding of electricity usage by the modern bakery equipment and the older bakery equipment. As Exhibit 6–7 shows, however, the curvilinear utilities cost can be approximated closely by a mixed cost *within the relevant range*. The data plotted in

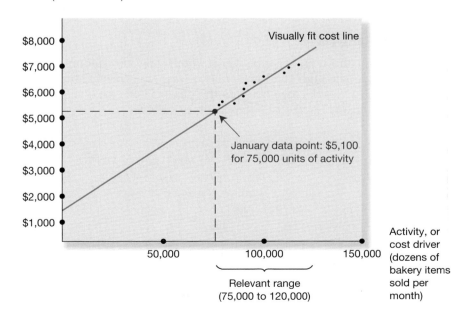

Exhibit 6–8
Scatter Diagram of Cost Data with Visually Fit Cost Line, Tasty Donuts, Inc.

the scatter diagram lie within the relevant range. Consequently, the data provide a sound basis for the mixed approximation that the controller has chosen to use.

The visually fit cost line in Exhibit 6–8 intercepts the vertical axis at $1,500. Thus, $1,500 is the estimate of the fixed-cost component in the mixed-cost approximation. To determine the variable cost per unit, subtract the fixed cost from the total cost at any activity level. The remainder is the total variable cost for that activity level. For example, the total variable cost for an activity level of 50,000 dozen items is $2,500 (total cost of $4,000 minus fixed cost of $1,500). This yields a variable cost of $.05 per dozen bakery items ($.05 = $2,500 ÷ 50,000).

These variable and fixed cost estimates were used for the mixed-cost approximation discussed earlier in the chapter (Exhibit 6–7). These estimates are valid only *within the relevant range*.

Evaluation of Visual-Fit Method   The scatter diagram and visually fit cost line provide a valuable first step in the analysis of any cost item suspected to be semivariable or curvilinear. The method is easy to use and to explain to others, and it provides a useful view of the overall cost behaviour pattern.

The visual-fit method also enables an experienced cost analyst to spot *outliers* in the data. An **outlier** is a data point that falls far away from the other points in the scatter diagram and is not representative of the data. Suppose, for example, that the data point for January had been $6,000 for 75,000 units of activity. Exhibit 6–8 reveals that such a data point would be way out of line with the rest of the data. The cost analyst would follow up on such a cost observation to discover the reasons behind it. The data point might be in error. Perhaps a utility bill was misread when the data were compiled, or possibly the billing itself was in error. Another possibility is that the cost observation is correct but due to unusual circumstances. Perhaps Toronto experienced a record cold wave during January that required the company's donut shops to use unusually high amounts of electric heat. Perhaps an oven in the bakery had a broken thermostat during January that caused the oven to overheat consistently until discovered and repaired. An outlier can result from many causes. If the outlier is due to an error or very unusual circumstances, the data point should be ignored in the cost analysis.

The primary drawback of the visual-fit method is its lack of objectivity. Two cost analysts may draw two different visually fit cost lines. This is not usually a serious problem, however, particularly if the visual-fit method is combined with other, more objective methods.

High-Low Method

In the **high-low method**, the mixed-cost approximation is computed using exactly two data points. The high and low *activity levels* are chosen from the available data set. These activity levels, together with their associated cost levels, are used to compute the variable and fixed cost components as follows:

$$\frac{\text{Variable cost per}}{\text{dozen bakery items}} = \frac{\text{Difference between the } \textit{costs} \text{ corresponding to the highest and lowest activity levels}}{\text{Difference between the highest and lowest } \textit{activity} \text{ levels}}$$

$$= \frac{\$7,035 - \$5,100}{118,000 - 75,000} = \frac{\$1,935}{43,000}$$

$$= \$.045 \text{ per dozen items}$$

Now we can compute the total variable cost at either the high or low activity level. At the low activity of 75,000 dozen items, the total variable cost is $3,375

Utilities cost (for one month)

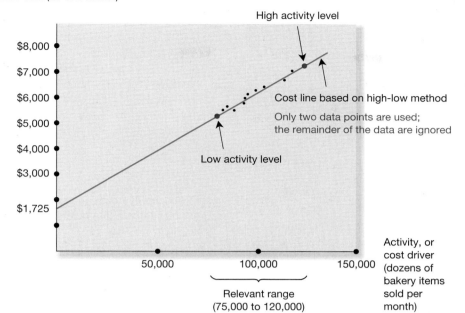

Exhibit 6–9
Graph of Utilities Cost Using High-Low Method, Tasty Donuts, Inc.

($.045 × 75,000). Subtracting the total variable cost from the total cost at the 75,000 dozen activity level, we obtain the fixed-cost estimate of $1,725 ($5,100 − $3,375). Notice that the high and low *activity* levels are used to choose the two data points. In general, these two points need not necessarily coincide with the high and low cost levels in the data set.

Exhibit 6–9 presents a graph of Tasty Donuts' utilities cost, which is based on the high-low method of cost estimation. As in any cost-estimation method, this estimate of the cost behaviour pattern should be *restricted to the relevant range*.

Evaluation of High-Low Method The high-low method is more objective than the visual-fit method, since it leaves no room for the cost analyst's judgment. However, the high-low method suffers from a major weakness. Only two data points are used to estimate the cost behaviour pattern; the remainder of the data points are ignored. In this regard, the visual-fit method is superior to the high-low method, since the former approach uses all of the available data.

Least-Squares Regression Method

Statistical techniques may be used to estimate objectively a cost behaviour pattern using all of the available data. The most common of these methods is called *least-squares regression*. To understand this method, examine Exhibit 6–10, which repeats the scatter diagram of Tasty Donuts' utilities cost data. The Exhibit also includes a cost line that has been drawn through the plotted data points. Since the data points do not lie along a perfectly straight line, any cost line drawn through this scatter diagram will miss some or most of the data points. The objective is to draw the cost line so as to make the deviations between the cost line and the data points as small as possible.

In the **least-squares regression method**, the cost line is positioned so as to *minimize* the sum of the *squared deviations* between the cost line and the data points. The inset to Exhibit 6–10 depicts this technique graphically. Note that the deviations between the cost line and the data points are measured vertically on the graph rather

Utilities cost (for one month)

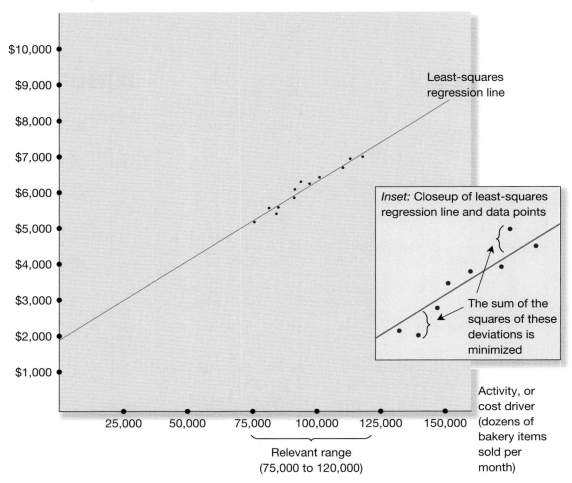

Exhibit 6–10
Graph of Utilities Cost Using
Least-Squares Regression
Method, Tasty Donuts, Inc.

than perpendicular to the line. The cost line fit to the data using least-squares regression is called a *least-squares regression line* (or simply a **regression line**). As always, the least-squares regression estimate of the cost behaviour pattern should be restricted to the relevant range.

Equation Form of Least-Squares Regression Line   The least-squares regression line shown in Exhibit 6–10 may be represented by the equation of a straight line. In the following equation, X denotes Tasty Donuts' activity level for a month, and Y denotes the estimated utilities cost for that level of activity. The intercept of the line on the vertical axis is denoted by a, and the slope of the line is denoted by b. *Within the relevant range*, a is interpreted as an estimate of the fixed-cost component, and b is interpreted as an estimate of the variable cost per unit of activity.

$$Y = a + bX \tag{1}$$

In regression analysis, X is referred to as the **independent variable**, since it is the variable upon which the estimate is based. Y is called the **dependent variable**, since its estimate depends on the independent variable.

The least-squares regression line for Tasty Donuts' utilities cost is shown below in equation form.

$$Y = 1{,}920 + .0448X$$

Estimated utilities cost for one month

Activity level for one month

Within the relevant range of activity, the regression estimate of the fixed-cost component is $1,920 per month, and the regression estimate of the variable-cost component is $.0448 per dozen bakery items. These estimates are derived in the appendix at the end of this chapter, which you may want to read now.

Evaluation of Least-Squares Regression Method   The least-squares regression is an objective method of cost estimation that makes use of all available data. Moreover, the regression line has desirable statistical properties for making cost predictions and drawing inferences about the relationship between cost and activity. The method does require considerably more computation than either the visual-fit or high-low method. However, computer programs are readily available to perform least-squares regression.

Evaluating a Particular Least-Squares Regression Line   We have seen the benefits of least-squares regression *in general*. How does a cost analyst evaluate a *particular* regression line based on a specific set of data? A number of criteria may be used, including *economic plausibility* and *goodness of fit*.

The cost analyst should always evaluate a regression line from the perspective of *economic plausibility*. Does the regression line make economic sense? Is it intuitively plausible to the cost analyst? If not, the analyst should reconsider using the regression line to make cost predictions. It may be that the chosen independent variable is not a good predictor of the cost behaviour being analyzed. Perhaps another independent variable should be considered. Alternatively, there may be errors in the data upon which the regression is based. Rechecking the data will resolve this issue. It could be that fundamental assumptions that underlie the regression method have been violated. In this case, the analyst may have to resort to some other method of cost estimation.

Another criterion commonly used to evaluate a particular regression line is to assess its **goodness of fit**. Statistical methods can be used to determine objectively how well a regression line fits the data upon which it is based. If a regression line fits the data well, a large proportion of the variation in the dependent variable will be explained by the variation in the independent variable. One frequently used measure of goodness of fit, called the *coefficient of determination* and commonly denoted R^2, is described in the appendix at the end of this chapter.

Multiple Regression

In each of the cost-estimation methods discussed so far, we have based the estimate on a single independent variable. Moreover, all of Tasty Donuts' cost behaviour patterns were specified with respect to a single activity (or cost driver), dozens of bakery items produced and sold. However, there may be two or more independent variables that are important predictors of cost behaviour.

To illustrate, we will continue our analysis of Tasty Donuts' utilities costs. The company uses electricity for two primary purposes: operating cooking equipment, such as deep-fat fryers and ovens, and heating the bakery and donut shops. The cost of electricity for food production is a function of the firm's activity, as measured in dozens of bakery items produced and sold. However, the cost of electricity for

Learning Objective 5

Describe the multiple regression and engineering approaches to cost estimation.

restaurant heating is related more closely to the number of customers than to the number of bakery items sold. A restaurant's heating costs go up each time the restaurant door is opened, resulting in loss of heat. Two customers purchasing half a dozen donuts each result in greater heating cost than one customer buying a dozen donuts.

Suppose Tasty Donuts' controller wants to estimate a cost behaviour pattern for utilities cost that is based on both units of sales and number of customers. The method of *multiple regression* may be used for this purpose. **Multiple regression** is a statistical method that estimates a linear (straight-line) relationship between one dependent variable and two or more independent variables. In Tasty Donuts' case, the following regression equation would be estimated.

$$Y = a + b_1 X_1 + b_2 X_2 \tag{2}$$

where Y denotes the dependent variable, utilities cost

X_1 denotes the first independent variable, dozens of bakery items sold

X_2 denotes the second independent variable, number of customers served

In regression equation (2), a denotes the regression estimate of the fixed-cost component, b_1 denotes the regression estimate of the variable utilities cost per dozen bakery items, and b_2 denotes the regression estimate of the variable utilities cost per customer served. The multiple-regression equation will likely enable Tasty Donuts' controller to make more accurate cost predictions than could be made with the *simple regression* discussed previously. A **simple regression** is based on a single independent variable. Multiple regression is covered more extensively in cost-accounting and statistics texts.

Engineering Method

All of the methods of cost estimation examined so far are based on historical data. Each method estimates the relationship between cost and activity by studying the relationship observed in the past. A completely different method of cost estimation is to study the process that results in cost incurrence. This approach is called the **engineering method**. In a manufacturing firm, for example, a detailed study is made of the production technology, materials, and labour used in the manufacturing process. Rather than asking what the cost of material was last period, the engineering approach is to ask how much material should be needed and how much it should cost. Industrial engineers sometimes perform *time and motion studies*, which determine the steps required for people to perform the manual tasks that are part of the production process. Cost behaviour patterns for various types of costs are then estimated on the basis of the engineering analysis. Engineering cost studies are time-consuming and expensive, but they often provide highly accurate estimates of cost behaviour. Moreover, in rapidly evolving, high-technology industries, there may not be any historical data on which to base cost estimates. Such industries as genetic engineering, superconductivity, and electronics are evolving so rapidly that historical data are often irrelevant in estimating costs.

Data Collection Problems

Learning Objective 6

Describe some problems often encountered in collecting data for cost estimation.

Regardless of the method used, the resulting cost estimation will be only as good as the data upon which it is based. The collection of data appropriate for cost estimation requires a skilled and experienced cost analyst. Six problems frequently complicate the process of data collection:

1. *Missing data.* Misplaced source documents or failure to record a transaction can result in missing data.
2. *Outliers.* We have discussed these extreme observations of cost-activity relationships. If outliers are determined to represent errors or highly unusual circumstances, they should be eliminated from the data set.

3. *Mismatched time periods.* The units of time for which the dependent and independent variables are measured may not match. For example, production activity may be recorded daily, but costs may be recorded monthly. A common solution is to aggregate the production data to get monthly totals.

4. *Trade-offs in choosing the time period.* In choosing the length of the time period for which data are collected, there are conflicting objectives. One objective is to obtain as many data points as possible, which implies a short time period. Another objective is to choose a long enough time period to ensure that the accounting system has accurately associated costs with time periods. If, for example, a cost that resulted from production activity in one period is recorded in a later period, the cost and activity data will not be matched properly. Longer time periods result in fewer recording lags in the data.

5. *Allocated and discretionary costs.* Fixed costs are often *allocated* on a per-unit-of-activity basis. For example, fixed manufacturing-overhead costs such as depreciation are allocated to units of production. As a result, such costs may appear to be variable in the cost records. *Discretionary costs* often are budgeted in a manner that makes them appear variable. A cost such as advertising, for example, may be fixed once management decides on the level of advertising. If management's policy is to budget advertising on the basis of sales dollars, however, the cost will appear to be variable to the cost analyst. An experienced analyst will be wary of such costs and take steps to learn how their amounts are determined.

6. *Inflation.* During periods of inflation, historical cost data may not reflect future cost behaviour. One solution is to choose historical data from a period of low inflation and then factor in the current inflation rate. Other, more sophisticated approaches are also available, and they are covered in cost-accounting texts.

Costs and Benefits of Information

We have discussed a variety of cost-estimation methods ranging from the simple visual-fit approach to sophisticated techniques such as regression. Which of these methods is best? In general, the more sophisticated methods will yield more accurate cost estimates than the simpler methods. However, even a sophisticated method still yields only an imperfect estimate of an unknown cost behaviour pattern.

All cost-estimation methods are based on simplifying assumptions. The two most important assumptions are as follows:

1. Except for the multiple-regression technique, all of the methods assume that cost behaviour depends on *one activity variable*. Even multiple regression uses only a small number of independent variables. In reality, however, costs are affected by a host of factors including the weather, the mood of the employees, and the quality of the raw materials used.

2. Another simplifying assumption usually made in cost estimation is that cost behaviour patterns are linear (straight lines) within the relevant range.

The cost analyst must consider on a case-by-case basis whether these assumptions are reasonable. The analyst also must decide when it is important to use a more sophisticated, and more costly, cost-estimation method and when it is acceptable to use a simpler approach. As in any choice among managerial accounting methods, the costs and benefits of the various cost-estimation techniques must be weighed.

Other Issues in Cost Behaviour and Cost Estimation

Engineered, Committed, and Discretionary Costs

Learning Objective 7

Define and give examples of engineered costs, committed costs, and discretionary costs.

In the process of budgeting costs, it is often useful for management to make a distinction between engineered, committed, and discretionary costs. An **engineered cost** bears a definitive physical relationship to the activity measure. Tasty Donuts' direct-material cost is an engineered cost. It is impossible to produce more donuts without incurring greater material cost for food ingredients.

A **committed cost** results from an organization's ownership or use of facilities and its basic organization structure. Property taxes, depreciation on buildings and equipment, costs of renting facilities or equipment, and the salaries of management personnel are examples of committed fixed costs. Tasty Donuts' facilities cost is a committed fixed cost.

A **discretionary cost** arises as a result of a *management decision* to spend a particular amount of money for some purpose. Examples of discretionary costs include amounts spent on research and development, advertising and promotion, management development programs, and contributions to charitable organizations. For example, suppose Tasty Donuts' management decided to spend $12,400 each month on promotion and advertising.

The distinction between committed and discretionary costs is an important one. Management can change committed costs only through relatively major decisions that have long-term implications. Decisions to build a new production facility, lease a fleet of vehicles, or add more management personnel to oversee a new division are examples of such decisions. These decisions will generally influence costs incurred over a long period of time. In contrast, discretionary costs can be changed in the short run much more easily. Management can be flexible about expenditures for advertising, promotion, employee training, or research and development. This does not imply that such programs are unimportant, but simply that management can alter them over time. For example, the management of a manufacturing firm may decide to spend $100,000 on research and development in the current year, but cut back to $60,000 in the next year because of an anticipated economic downturn.

Whether a particular type of cost is committed or discretionary sometimes differs between organizations. For example, one company's board of directors may view the salaries of top management as a committed cost. Even in an economic downturn, it is important for a firm to keep its basic organization structure intact and retain its key executives. In contrast, the tradition in another firm might be to ask its top-management personnel to accept a salary cut during difficult economic times, in order to cut expenses and set an example for other employees.

Effect of Learning on Cost Behaviour

Learning Objective 8

Describe the effect of learning on cost behaviour.

In many production processes, production efficiency increases with experience. As cumulative production output increases, the average labour time required per unit declines. As the labour time declines, labour cost declines as well. This phenomenon is called the **learning curve**. First documented by aeronautical engineer P. T. Wright in the 1930s, the learning curve concept was popularized by the Boston Consulting Group (BCG) in the 1970s. BCG broadened the learning-curve idea to include costs other than direct labour and named this phenomenon the **experience curve**. The learning-curve and experience-curve concepts have been applied primarily to complex, labour-intensive manufacturing operations, such as aircraft assembly and ship building. Boeing and Airbus, for example, make extensive use of the learning and experience curve concepts when budgeting the cost for a new aircraft design.

A. Graphical Presentation of Learning Curve

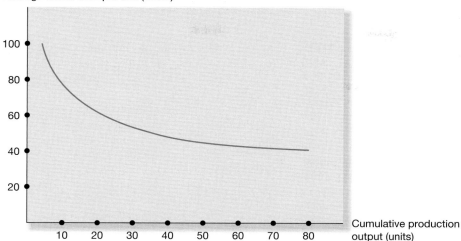

Exhibit 6–11
Learning Curve

B. Tabular Presentation of Learning Curve

Cumulative Output (in units)	Average Labour Time per Unit (hours)	Total Labour Time (hours)
5	100.00	500.0
10	80.00	800.0
20	64.00	1,280.0
40	51.20	2,048.0

However, the learning curve also has seen limited application in the health care services industry, mainly focusing on complex surgical procedures.

To illustrate the learning curve concept, let's explore its use by Cosmos Communications Technology (CCT), a manufacturer of sophisticated communications satellites in Vancouver. The company's satellites transmit voice and data communications around the world. CCT's management has found that the learning curve applies to the labour-intensive assembly operation for each new satellite design. A graphical portrayal of CCT's learning curve is shown in panel A of Exhibit 6–11. On this learning curve, when cumulative output doubles, the average labour time per unit declines by 20 percent. Panel B displays the total labour time and average labour time per unit for various levels of cumulative output. As cumulative output doubles from 5 to 10 units, for example, the average labour time per unit declines by 20 percent, from 100 hours per unit to 80 hours per unit. As CCT gains experience with a new satellite design, estimates of the cost of direct labour should be adjusted downward to take this learning effect into account.

When the learning-curve concept is applied to a broader set of costs than just labour costs, it is referred to as an *experience curve*. Suppose, for example, that all labour and variable overhead costs are observed to decline by 20 percent every time cumulative output doubles. Then we would change the vertical axis of Exhibit 6–11 to *labour and variable overhead costs*. The graph would then be called an *experience curve*.

Learning curves have been used extensively in such industries as aircraft production, ship building, and electronics to assist cost analysts in predicting labour costs. These cost predictions are then used in scheduling production, budgeting, setting product prices, and other managerial decisions.

Focus on Ethics

CISCO SYSTEMS, WAL-MART, TACO BELL, STARBUCKS, U-HAUL, GENERAL DYNAMICS, AND FARMER'S INSURANCE: IS DIRECT LABOUR A VARIABLE COST?[6]

The question as to whether direct labour is a variable cost is interesting from a cost-estimation perspective, but it also presents an interesting ethical issue.

Direct material is always a variable cost. At the other extreme, depreciation on fixed facilities and infrastructure typically is not. What about direct labour? Here it depends on the ability and willingness of management to adjust the labour force to current needs. If management is able *and willing* to hire workers as needed and lay them off when activity declines, direct labour would be a variable cost. The contemporary trend at many companies seems to be in this direction. "Companies are looking first to bring in contract workers that they can quickly tap and zap without paying any benefits or severance." In fact, the temps have recently been the fastest-growing sector of employment. "And they aren't accounted for as regular employees. This helps companies that use a lot of them, like Cisco Systems Inc., to drive up revenue per employee."

"The growing use of the *just-in-time workforce* is not the only means by which companies are priming the productivity pump. Workers complain that many employers are taking advantage of outdated labour laws by misclassifying them as salaried-exempt so they can skirt overtime pay. Wal-Mart, Taco Bell, Starbucks, and U-Haul, among others, have been slapped with class actions. In the case of General Dynamics Corp., this resulted in a $100 million award that is now on appeal. At Farmer's Insurance, employees got $90 million. Some employers are so worried about the issue that they are now doing wage-and-hour audits."

Is it ethical to "tap and zap" employees? What do you think? (For more on this issue, see the Management Accounting Practice box on page 207.)

Chapter Summary

Understanding an organization's cost behaviour enables managers to anticipate changes in cost when the organization's level of activity (or cost driver) changes. Cost predictions, which are based on cost behaviour patterns, facilitate planning, cost management, and decision making throughout the organization. These cost predictions should be confined to the relevant range, which is the range of activity expected for the organization.

A variety of cost behaviour patterns exist, ranging from simple variable and fixed costs to more complicated mixed and curvilinear costs. Several cost-estimation methods are used to determine which cost behaviour pattern is appropriate for a particular cost. The account-classification, visual-fit, high-low, and regression methods are all based on an analysis of historical cost data observed at a variety of activity levels. The engineering method of cost estimation is based on a detailed analysis of the process in which the costs are incurred. These methods are frequently used in combination to provide a more accurate cost estimate.

As in selecting any managerial-accounting technique, the choice of a cost-estimation method involves a trade-off of costs and benefits. More accurate estimation methods provide the benefits of better information, but they are often more costly to apply.

In many production processes, production efficiency increases with experience. As cumulative production output increases, the average labour time required per unit declines. As the labour time declines, labour cost declines as well. This phenomenon is called the *learning curve*.

Review Problems on Cost Behaviour and Estimation

Problem 1

Erie Hardware, Inc. operates a chain of four retail stores. Data on the company's maintenance costs for its store buildings and furnishings are as follows:

Month	Maintenance Cost	Sales
January	$53,000	$600,000
February	55,000	700,000
March	47,000	550,000
April	51,000	650,000
May	45,000	500,000
June	49,000	610,000

Using the high-low method, estimate and graph the cost behaviour for the firm's maintenance costs.

Problem 2

The *Keystone Sentinel* is a weekly newspaper. The following costs were incurred by its publisher during a week when circulation was 100,000 newspapers: total variable costs, $40,000; total fixed costs, $66,000. Fill in your predictions for the following cost amounts.

	Circulation	
	110,000 Newspapers	120,000 Newspapers
Total variable cost	_____	_____
Variable cost per unit	_____	_____
Total fixed cost	_____	_____
Fixed cost per unit	_____	_____

Solutions to Review Problems
Problem 1

	Sales	Cost
At high activity	$700,000	$55,000
At low activity	500,000	45,000
Difference	$200,000	$10,000

$$\text{Variable cost per sales dollar} = \frac{\$10,000}{\$200,000} = \$.05 \text{ per sales dollar}$$

Total cost at $700,000 of sales	$55,000
Total variable cost at $700,000 of sales (700,000 × $.05)	35,000
Difference is total fixed cost	$20,000

The company's maintenance cost may be expressed by the following equation:

Total maintenance cost = $20,000 + $.05 (sales dollars)

Alternatively, the maintenance cost can be expressed in the following graph:

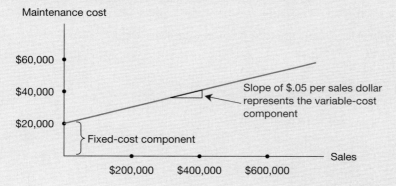

Problem 2

	Circulation	
	110,000 Newspapers	**120,000 Newspapers**
Total variable cost	$\$40,000 \times \left(\dfrac{110,000}{100,000} \right) = \$44,000$	$\$40,000 \times \left(\dfrac{120,000}{100,000} \right) = \$48,000$
Variable cost per unit	$\$44,000 \div 110,000 = \$.40$	$\$48,000 \div 120,000 = \$.40$
Total fixed cost	$66,000	$66,000
Fixed cost per unit	$\$66,000 \div 110,000 = \$.60$	$\$66,000 \div 120,000 = \$.55$

Key Terms

For each term's definition refer to the indicated page, or turn to the glossary at the end of the text.

account analysis, 210

account-classification method (*or* account analysis), 210

coefficient of determination,* 224

committed cost, 218

cost behaviour, 200

cost estimation, 210

cost prediction, 200

curvilinear cost, 205

dependent variable, 214

discretionary cost, 218

engineered cost, 218

engineering method, 216

experience curve, 218

fixed cost, 203

goodness of fit, 215

high-low method, 212

independent variable, 214

learning curve, 218

least-squares regression method, 213

mixed costs, 205

multiple regression, 216

outlier, 212

regression line, 214

relevant range, 206

scatter diagram, 210

simple regression, 216

step-fixed cost, 204

step-variable costs, 202

variable cost, 201

visual-fit method, 210

*Term appears in the Appendix to this chapter.

APPENDIX TO CHAPTER 6

Finding the Least-Squares Regression Estimates

The least-squares regression line, which is shown below in equation form, includes two estimates. These estimates, which are called parameters, are the intercept (denoted by a) and the slope coefficient (denoted by b).

$$Y = a + bX \tag{3}$$

where X denotes the independent variable (activity level for one month)

Y denotes the dependent variable (cost for one month)

Statistical theorists have shown that these parameters are defined by the following two equations:[7]

$$a = \frac{(\Sigma Y)(\Sigma X^2) - (\Sigma X)(\Sigma XY)}{n(\Sigma X^2) - (\Sigma X)(\Sigma X)} \tag{4}$$

$$b = \frac{n(\Sigma XY) - (\Sigma X)(\Sigma Y)}{n(\Sigma X^2) - (\Sigma X)(\Sigma X)} \tag{5}$$

where n denotes the number of data points

Σ denotes summation; for example, ΣY denotes the sum of the Y (cost) values in the data

Calculating the intercept (*a*) and the slope coefficient (*b*) would be very laborious to do manually. Fortunately, there are many statistical software programs available to do the regression calculations. Alternatively, Microsoft® Excel can calculate the regression estimates, as the next section demonstrates.

Using Microsoft® Excel to Calculate the Regression Parameters

A cost analyst can use commands in Microsoft® Excel to easily calculate the regression estimate for the intercept (*a*) and the slope (*b*). All the analyst needs to do is input the data in a spreadsheet. The spreadsheet in Exhibit 6–12 displays the data used to compute Tasty Donuts' utilities cost. The dependent variable (utilities cost) is in column B, and the independent variable (activity) is in column C. Then the Excel functions INTERCEPT and SLOPE are used to compute the parameters. To use each command, the analyst specifies the range of cells in the spreadsheet in which the values of the dependent variable reside and the range of cells in which the values of the independent variable reside. This is illustrated in the Excel worksheet in Exhibit 6–12 as follows:

Cell B24 contains the following formula: = INTERCEPT(B7:B18,C7:C18)

Cell B25 contains the following formula: = SLOPE(B7:B18,C7:C18)

In these formulas, B7:B18 specifies the range of cells where the values of the dependent variable reside, and C7:C18 specifies the range of cells where the values of the independent variable reside.

As the Excel calculations show in Exhibit 6–12, the regression estimates are as follows:

Intercept: $a = 1,920$

Slope: $b = .0448$

So the regression equation is the following:

$$Y = 1,920 + .0448X$$

↑ Estimated utilities cost for one month

↑ Activity level for one month

	A	B	C
1		Utility	
2	Month	Cost	Activity
3	of	for	during
4	Preceding	Month	Month
5	Year	Y	X
6			
7	January	5,100	75,000
8	February	5,300	78,000
9	March	5,650	80,000
10	April	6,300	92,000
11	May	6,400	98,000
12	June	6,700	108,000
13	July	7,035	118,000
14	August	7,000	112,000
15	September	6,200	95,000
16	October	6,100	90,000
17	November	5,600	85,000
18	December	5,900	90,000
19	Total	73,285	1,121,000
20			
21	Computation of Regression Parameters		
22	Using Spreadsheet Functions		
23			
24	Intercept	1,920	
25	Slope	0.0448	
26	R²	0.949	

Exhibit 6–12
Using Microsoft® Excel to Compute the Least-Squares Regression Estimates

Goodness of Fit

The goodness of fit for Tasty Donuts' regression line may be measured by the **coefficient of determination**, commonly denoted R^2. This measure is defined as the percentage of the variability of the dependent variable about its mean that is explained by the variability of the independent variable about its mean. The higher the R^2, the better the regression line fits the data. The interpretation for a high R^2 is that the independent variable is a good predictor of the behaviour of the dependent variable. In cost estimation, a high R^2 means that the cost analyst can be relatively confident in the cost predictions based on the estimated cost behaviour pattern.

Statistical theorists have shown that R^2 can be computed using the following formula:

$$R^2 = 1 - \frac{\Sigma(Y - Y')^2}{\Sigma(Y - \overline{Y})^2} \tag{6}$$

where Y denotes the observed value of the dependent variable (cost) at a particular activity level

Y' denotes the predicted value of the dependent variable (cost), based on the regression line, at a particular activity level

$\overline{Y}$ denotes the mean (average) observation of the dependent variable (cost)

Excel can be used once again to calculate the R^2. The analyst simply uses the RSQ command in Excel. As shown in cell B26 of the Excel worksheet in Exhibit 6–12, the R^2 is .949.

Cell B26 contains the following formula: = RSQ(B7:B18,C7:C18)

This is a high value for R^2, and Tasty Donuts' controller may be quite confident in the resulting cost predictions. As always, these predictions should be confined to the relevant range.

Review Questions

6–1. Describe the importance of cost behaviour patterns in planning, control, and decision making.

6–2. Define the following terms, and explain the relationship between them: (a) cost estimation, (b) cost behaviour, and (c) cost prediction.

6–3. Suggest an appropriate activity base (or cost driver) for each of the following organizations: (a) hotel, (b) hospital, (c) computer manufacturer, (d) computer sales store, (e) computer repair service, and (f) public accounting firm.

6–4. Draw a simple graph of each of the following types of cost behaviour patterns: *(a)* variable, *(b)* step-variable, *(c)* fixed, *(d)* step-fixed, *(e)* mixed, and *(f)* curvilinear.

6–5. Explain the impact of an increase in the level of activity (or cost driver) on (a) total fixed cost and (b) fixed cost per unit of activity.

6–6. Explain why a manufacturer's cost of supervising production might be a step-fixed cost.

6–7. Explain the impact of an increase in the level of activity (or cost driver) on (a) total variable cost and (b) variable cost per unit.

6–8. Using graphs, show how a mixed cost behaviour pattern can be used to approximate (a) a step-variable cost and (b) a curvilinear cost.

6–9. Indicate which of the following descriptions is most likely to describe each cost listed below.

Description	Costs
Engineered cost	Annual cost of maintaining a highway
Committed cost	Cost of ingredients in a breakfast cereal
Discretionary cost	Cost of advertising for a credit card company
	Depreciation on an insurance company's computer
	Cost of charitable donations that are budgeted as 1 percent of sales revenue
	Research and development costs, which have been budgeted at $45,000 per year

6–10. A cost analyst showed the company president a graph that portrayed the firm's utility cost as mixed. The president criticized the graph by saying, "This fixed-cost component doesn't look right to me. If we shut down the plant for six months, we wouldn't incur half of these costs." How should the cost analyst respond?

6–11. What is meant by a *learning curve*? Explain its role in cost estimation.

6–12. Suggest an appropriate independent variable to use in predicting the costs of the following tasks:
   a. Handling materials at a loading dock
   b. Registering vehicles at a provincial motor vehicle office
   c. Picking oranges
   d. Inspecting computer components in an electronics firm

6–13. What is an *outlier*? List some possible causes of outliers. How should outliers be handled in cost estimation?

6–14. Explain the cost-estimation problem caused by allocated and discretionary costs.

6–15. Describe the visual-fit method of cost estimation. What are the main strengths and weaknesses of this method?

6–16. What is the main drawback of the high-low method of cost estimation? What problem might an outlier cause if the high-low method were used?

6–17. Explain the meaning of the term *least squares* in the least-squares regression method of cost estimation.

6–18. Use an equation to express a least-squares regression line. Interpret each term in the equation.

6–19. Distinguish between simple regression and multiple regression.

6–20. List several possible cost drivers that could be used by a cruise line such as Carnival.

6–21. Briefly describe two methods that can be used to evaluate a particular least-squares regression line.

Exercises

Draw a graph of the cost behaviour for each of the following costs incurred by the Mountain Summit Hospital. The hospital measures monthly activity in patient days. Label both axes and the cost line in each graph.

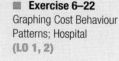

■ **Exercise 6–22**
Graphing Cost Behaviour Patterns; Hospital
(LO 1, 2)

1. The cost of food varies in proportion to the number of patient days of activity. In January, the hospital provided 2,800 patient days of care, and food costs amounted to $22,400.

2. The cost of salaries and fringe benefits for the administrative staff totals $13,000 per month.

3. The hospital's laboratory costs include two components: (*a*) $40,000 per month for compensation of personnel and depreciation on equipment and (*b*) $10 per patient day for chemicals and other materials used in performing the tests.

4. The cost of utilities depends on how many wards the hospital needs to use during a particular month. During months with activity under 2,000 patient days of care, two wards are used, resulting in utility costs of $9,000. During months with greater than 2,000 patient days of care, three wards are used, and utility costs total $14,000.

5. Many of the hospital's nurses are part-time employees. As a result, the hours of nursing care provided can be easily adjusted to the amount required at any particular time. The cost of wages and fringe benefits for nurses is approximately $2,500 for each block of 200 patient days of care provided during a month. For example, nursing costs total $2,500 for 1 to 200 patient days, $5,000 for 201 to 400 patient days, $7,500 for 401 to 600 patient days, and so forth.

The behaviour of the annual maintenance and repair cost in the Bus Transportation Department of the Coquitlam School District is shown by the solid line in the following graph. The dashed line depicts a mixed-cost approximation of the department's repair and maintenance cost.

■ **Exercise 6–23**
Approximating a Curvilinear Cost; School District
(LO 1, 2, 3)

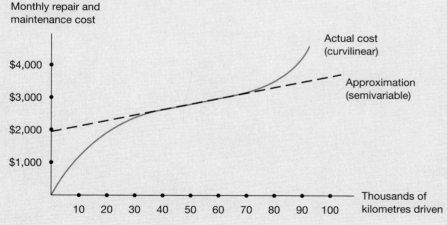

Required:

1. What is the actual (curvilinear) and estimated (mixed) cost shown by the graph for each of the following activity levels?

	Actual	Estimated
a. 20,000 kilometres		
b. 40,000 kilometres		
c. 60,000 kilometres		
d. 90,000 kilometres		

2.   How good an approximation does the mixed-cost pattern provide if the department's relevant range is 40,000 to 60,000 kilometres per month? What if the relevant range is 20,000 to 90,000 kilometres per month?

■ 'Exercise 6–24
Behaviour of Fixed and
Variable Costs; Television
Station
(LO 1, 2)

CMEJ is an independent local television station. The station's broadcast hours vary during the year. The station's production-crew and supervisory costs are as follows for August and October.

Cost Item	Cost Behaviour	Cost Amount	Broadcast Hours during Month
Production crew	Variable		
August		$5,330	410
October		8,840	680
Supervisory employees	Fixed		
August		6,000	410
October		6,000	680

Required:

1.   Compute the cost per broadcast hour during August and October for each of these cost items.
2.   What will be the total amount incurred for each of these costs during December, when the station's activity will be 440 broadcast hours?
3.   What will be the cost per broadcast hour in December for each of the cost items?

■ Exercise 6–25
Estimating Cost Behaviour;
High-Low Method
(LO 1, 2, 4)

Jonathan Macintosh is a highly successful apple grower who has formed his own company to produce and package applesauce. Apples can be stored for several months in cold storage, so applesauce production is relatively uniform throughout the year. The recently hired controller for the firm is about to apply the high-low method in estimating the company's energy cost behaviour. The following costs were incurred during the past 12 months:

Month	Pints of Applesauce Produced	Energy Cost
January	105,000	$70,200
February	63,000	66,300
March	66,000	66,000
April	72,000	67,350
May	90,000	68,700
June	96,000	70,050
July	120,000	84,000
August	90,000	68,400
September	90,000	69,000
October	84,000	68,100
November	123,000	72,300
December	117,000	74,850

Required:

1.   Use the high-low method to estimate the company's energy cost behaviour and express it in equation form.
2.   Predict the energy cost for a month in which 78,000 pints of applesauce are produced.

Refer to the data in the preceding exercise.

Required:

1. Draw a scatter diagram and graph the company's energy cost behaviour using the visual-fit method.
2. Predict the energy cost for a month in which 26,000 pints of applesauce are produced.
3. What peculiarity is apparent from the scatter diagram? What should the cost analyst do?

■ **Exercise 6–26**
Estimating Cost Behaviour;
Visual-Fit Method
(LO 1, 2, 4)

Visit the Web site of one of the following companies, or a different company of your choosing:

Boeing	www.boeing.com
Dell Inc.	www.dell.com
Ford	www.ford.com
General Electric	www.ge.com
Shaw	www.shaw.ca

Required: Read about the company's products and operations. Then list five costs that the company would incur and explain what type of cost behaviour you believe would be appropriate for each of these cost items.

■ **Exercise 6–27**
Cost Behaviour; Use of
Internet
(LO 2)

The West Vancouver Veterinary Laboratory performs a variety of diagnostic tests on commercial and domestic animals. The lab has incurred the following costs over the past year.

■ **Exercise 6–28**
Visual-Fit Method; Veterinary
Laboratory
(LO 1, 2, 4)

Month	Diagnostic Tests Completed	Cost
January	1,525	$30,100
February	2,250	36,500
March	3,550	50,000
April	3,100	47,800
May	2,350	37,400
June	2,950	44,000
July	3,000	45,500
August	3,050	45,000
September	2,650	43,500
October	2,450	38,300
November	2,400	39,050
December	2,525	40,100

Required:

1. Plot the data above in a scatter diagram. Assign cost to the vertical axis and the number of diagnostic tests to the horizontal axis. Visually fit a line to the plotted data.
2. Using the visually fit line, estimate the monthly fixed cost and the variable cost per diagnostic test.

Winnipeg Meat Company produces one of the best sausage products. The company's controller used the account-classification method to compile the following information.

■ **Exercise 6–29**
Account-Classification
Method; Food Processing
(LO 1, 2, 4)

a. Depreciation schedules revealed that monthly depreciation on buildings and equipment is $21,000.
b. Inspection of several invoices from meat packers indicated that meat costs the company $1.20 per pound of sausage produced.
c. Wage records showed that compensation for production employees costs $.85 per pound of sausage produced.
d. Payroll records showed that supervisory salaries total $11,000 per month.
e. Utility bills revealed that the company incurs utility costs of $5,000 per month plus $.25 per pound of sausage produced.

Required:

1. Classify each cost item as variable, fixed, or mixed.

2. Write a cost formula to express the cost behaviour of the firm's production costs. (Use the formula $Y = a + bX$, where Y denotes production cost and X denotes quantity of sausage produced.)

Exercise 6–30
High-Low Method; Tour
Company
(LO 1, 2, 4)

Rio Bus Tours has incurred the following bus maintenance costs during the recent tourist season. (The *real*, R\$, plural *reais*, is Brazil's national monetary unit. On the day this exercise was written, the real was equivalent in value to .5976 Canadian dollar.)

Month	Kilometres Travelled by Tour Buses	Cost (R\$)
November	12,750	17,100
December	15,900	17,400
January	19,050	17,550
February	22,500	18,000
March	30,000	18,750
April	12,000	16,500

Required:

1. Use the high-low method to estimate the variable cost per tour mile travelled and the fixed cost per month.
2. Develop a formula to express the cost behaviour exhibited by the company's maintenance cost.
3. Predict the level of maintenance cost that would be incurred during a month when 34,000 tour miles are driven. (Remember to express your answer in terms of the real.)
4. *Build a spreadsheet*: Construct an Excel spreadsheet to solve all of the preceding requirements. Show how the solution will change if the following information changes: in March there were 32,000 miles travelled and the cost was 20,000 real.

Exercise 6–31
Work Measurement;
Government Agency
(LO 2, 5)

The Canada Revenue Agency processes and audits income-tax returns for Canadian residents. The tax commissioner has recently begun a program of work measurement to help in estimating the costs of running the agency. The independent variable used in the program is the number of returns processed. The analysis revealed that the following variable costs are incurred in auditing a typical tax return.

> Time spent by clerical employees, 10 hours at \$12 per hour
> Time spent by tax professional, 20 hours at \$25 per hour
> Computer time, \$50 per audit
> Telephone charges, \$10 per audit
> Postage, \$2 per audit

In addition, the department incurs \$10,000 of fixed costs each month that are associated with the process of auditing returns.

Required: Draw a graph depicting the monthly costs of auditing tax returns. Label the horizontal axis "Tax returns audited."

Exercise 6–32
Learning Curve; High
Technology
(LO 1, 8)

Weathereye, Inc. manufactures weather satellites. The final assembly and testing of the satellites is a largely manual operation involving dozens of highly trained electronics technicians. The following learning curve has been estimated for the firm's newest satellite model, which is about to enter production.

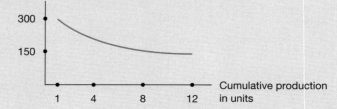

Assembly and Testing

Required:

1. What will be the average labour time required to assemble and test each satellite when the company has produced four satellites? Eight satellites?

2. What will be the total labour time required to assemble and test all satellites produced if the firm manufactures only four satellites? Eight satellites?

3. How can the learning curve be used in the company's budgeting process? In setting cost standards?

Recent monthly costs of providing on-board flight service incurred by Great Plains Airlines are shown in the following table.

■ Exercise 6–33
Airline; Least-Squares
Regression (Appendix)
(LO 1, 2, 4, 9)

Month	Number of Passengers	Cost of On-Board Flight Service
July	16,000	$54,000
August	17,000	54,000
September	16,000	57,000
October	18,000	60,000
November	15,000	54,000
December	17,000	57,000

Required:

1. *Build a spreadsheet:* Construct an Excel spreadsheet and use the Excel commands to perform a least-squares regression. Estimate the cost behaviour of the airline's on-board flight service. Express the cost behaviour in equation form.

2. Use Excel to calculate and interpret the R^2 value for the regression.

Easy Mart, a chain of convenience grocery stores, has store hours that fluctuate from month to month as the tourist trade in the community varies. The utility costs for one of the company's stores are listed below for the past six months.

■ Exercise 6–34
Estimating Cost Behaviour by
Multiple Methods (Appendix)
(LO 1, 2, 4, 9)

Month	Total Hours of Operation	Total Utility Cost
January	550	$3,240
February	600	3,400
March	700	3,800
April	500	3,200
May	450	2,700
June	400	2,600

Required:

1. Use the high-low method to estimate the cost behaviour for the store's utility costs. Express the cost behaviour in formula form ($Y = a + bX$). What is the variable utility cost per hour of operation?

2. Draw a scatter diagram of the store's utility costs. Visually fit a cost line to the plotted data. Estimate the variable utility cost per hour of operation.

3. *Build a spreadsheet:* Construct an Excel spreadsheet and use the Excel commands to perform a least-squares regression. Estimate the cost behaviour for the store's utility cost. Express the cost behaviour in formula form. What is the variable utility cost per hour of operation?

4. During July, the store will be open 300 hours. Predict the store's total utility cost for July using each of the cost-estimation methods employed in requirements (1), (2), and (3).

5. Use your Excel sheet from requirement (3) to calculate and interpret the R^2 value for the regression.

Problems

For each of the cost items described below, choose the graph here that best represents it.

■ Problem 6–35
Cost Behaviour Patterns in a
Variety of Settings;
International Issues
(LO 1, 2)

1. The cost of utilities at a university. For low student enrolments, utility costs increase with enrolment, but at a decreasing rate. For large student enrolments, utility costs increase at an increasing rate.

2. The cost of telephone service, which is based on the number of message units per month. The charge is $.79 per message unit, for up to 650 message units. Additional message units (above 650) are free.

3. The cost of outsourcing diagnostic blood testing by a hospital. The hospital pays an independent lab a fee of $1,000 per month plus $3 for each test done.

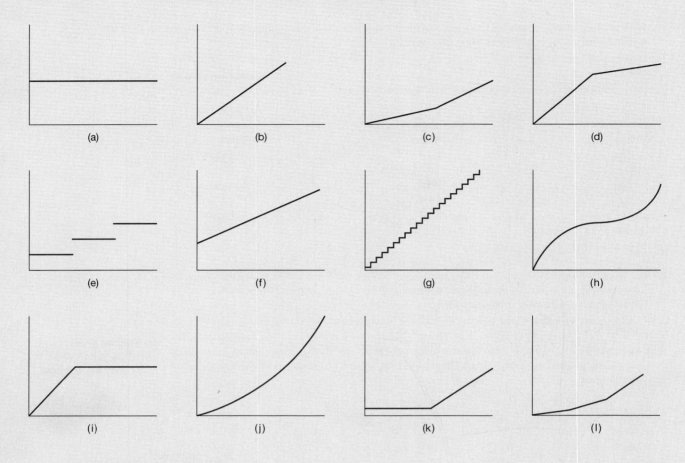

(a)   (b)   (c)   (d)

(e)   (f)   (g)   (h)

(i)   (j)   (k)   (l)

4. The salary costs of the shift supervisors at a truck depot. Each shift is eight hours. The depot operates with one, two, or three shifts at various times of the year.

5. The salaries of the security personnel at a factory. The security guards are on duty around the clock.

6. The wages of table-service personnel in a restaurant. The employees are part-time workers, who can be called upon for as little as two hours at a time.

7. The cost of electricity during peak-demand periods is based on the following schedule:

Up to 10,000 kilowatt-hours (kWh)	$.09/kWh
Above 10,000 kilowatt-hours	$.12/kWh

The price schedule is designed to discourage overuse of electricity during periods of peak demand.

8. The cost of sheet metal used to manufacture automobiles.

9. The cost of chartering a private airplane. The cost is $410 per hour for the first three hours of a flight. Then the charge drops to $305 per hour.

10. Under a licensing agreement with a South American import/export company, your firm has begun shipping machine tools to several countries. The terms of the agreement call for an annual licensing fee of $95,000 to be paid to the South American import company if total exports are under $4,500,000. For sales in excess of $4,500,000, an additional licensing fee of 9 percent of sales is due.

11. Your winery exports wine to several Pacific Rim countries. In one nation, you have to pay a tariff for every case of wine brought into the country. The tariff schedule is the following:

0 to 6,000 cases per year	$11 per case
6,001 to 12,000 cases per year	$14 per case
Above 12,000 cases per year.................................	$19 per case

The following selected data were taken from the accounting records of Manitoba Manufacturing Company. The company uses direct-labour hours as its cost driver for overhead costs.

Month	Direct-Labour Hours	Manufacturing Overhead
January	26,000	$749,250
February	25,000	720,000
March	28,000	772,500
April	23,000	681,000
May	30,000	775,500
June	34,000	879,000

Problem 6–36
Cost Behaviour and Analysis;
High-Low Method
(LO 2, 4)

2. Plant maintenance costs,
April: $555,000

June's costs consisted of machine supplies ($153,000), depreciation ($22,500), and plant maintenance ($703,500). These costs exhibit the following respective behaviour: variable, fixed, and mixed.

The manufacturing overhead figures presented in the preceding table do not include Metcalf's supervisory labour cost, which is step-fixed in nature. For volume levels of less than 15,000 hours, supervisory labour amounts to $67,500. The cost is $135,000 from 15,000 to 29,999 hours and $202,500 when activity reaches 30,000 hours or more.

Required:

1. Determine the machine supplies cost and depreciation for April.
2. Using the high-low method, analyze Metcalf's plant maintenance cost and calculate the monthly fixed portion and the variable cost per direct-labour hour.
3. Assume that present cost behaviour patterns continue into the latter half of the year. Estimate the *total* amount of manufacturing overhead the company can expect in November if 29,500 direct-labour hours are worked.
4. Briefly explain the difference between a fixed cost and a step-fixed cost.
5. Assume that a company has a step-fixed cost. Generally speaking, where on a step should the firm attempt to operate if it desires to achieve a maximum return on its investment?

Problem 6–37
Cost Behaviour and Analysis;
High-Low Method
(LO 2, 4)

2. Total cost for 1,700 tonnes:
$852,000

Lone Mountain Extraction, which mines ore in Alberta, uses a calendar year for both financial-reporting and tax purposes. The following selected costs were incurred in December, the low point of activity, when 1,400 tonnes of ore were extracted:

Straight-line depreciation	$30,000	Royalties	$140,000
Charitable contributions*	12,000	Trucking and hauling	280,000
Mining labour/fringe benefits	315,000		

*Incurred only in December.

Peak activity of 2,700 tonnes occurred in June, resulting in mining labour/fringe benefit costs of $607,500, royalties of $224,500, and trucking and hauling outlays of $360,000. The trucking and hauling outlays exhibit the following behaviour:

Less than 1,400 tonnes	$240,000
From 1,400 to 1,899 tonnes	280,000
From 1,900 to 2,399 tonnes	320,000
From 2,400 to 2,899 tonnes	360,000

Lone Mountain Extraction uses the high-low method to analyze costs.

Required:

1. Classify the five costs listed in terms of their behaviour: variable, step-variable, committed fixed, discretionary fixed, step-fixed, or mixed. Show calculations to support your answers for mining labour/fringe benefits and royalties.
2. Calculate the total cost for next February when 1,700 tonnes are expected to be extracted.
3. Comment on the cost-effectiveness of hauling 1,400 tonnes with respect to Lone Mountain's trucking/hauling cost behaviour. Can the company's effectiveness be improved? How?
4. Distinguish between committed and discretionary fixed costs. If the company were to experience severe economic difficulties, which of the two types of fixed costs should management try to cut? Why?
5. Speculate as to why the company's charitable contribution cost arises only in December.

■ **Problem 6–38**
High-Low Method; Fitness
Centres
(LO 1, 2, 4)

1. Fixed maintenance cost per
month: $510

Capital Fitness, Inc. operates a chain of fitness centres in the Ottawa area. The firm's controller is accumulating data to be used in preparing its annual profit plan for the coming year. The cost behaviour pattern of the firm's equipment maintenance costs must be determined. The accounting staff has suggested the use of an equation, in the form of $Y = a + bX$, for maintenance costs. Data regarding the maintenance hours and costs for last year are as follows:

Month	Hours of Maintenance Service	Maintenance Costs
January	525	$ 4,710
February	505	4,310
March	310	2,990
April	495	4,200
May	315	3,000
June	485	4,215
July	315	2,950
August	405	3,680
September	475	4,100
October	345	3,250
November	350	3,260
December	335	3,015
Total	4,860	$43,680
Average	405	$ 3,640

Required:

1. Using the high-low method of cost estimation, estimate the behaviour of the maintenance costs incurred by Capital Fitness, Inc. Express the cost behaviour pattern in equation form.
2. Using your answer to requirement (1), what is the variable component of the maintenance cost?
3. Compute the predicted maintenance cost at 600 hours of activity.
4. Compute the variable cost per hour and the fixed cost per hour at 610 hours of activity. Explain why the fixed cost per hour could be misleading.

(CMA, adapted)

■ **Problem 6–39**
Account-Classification
Method; Private School
(LO 1, 2, 4)

The Regina School of Music has hired you as a consultant to help in analyzing the behaviour of the school's costs. Use the account-classification method of cost estimation to classify each of the following costs as variable, fixed, or mixed. Before classifying the costs, choose an appropriate measure for the school's activity.

1. Cost of buying books, sheet music, and other academic materials that are supplied to the students by the school
2. Repairs on musical instruments. The school employs a full-time repair technician. Repair jobs beyond the technician's capability are taken to a local musical-instrument dealer for repairs.
3. Fee charged by a local public accounting firm to audit the school's accounting records
4. Salaries and fringe benefits of the school's full-time teachers
5. Salaries and fringe benefits of the school's full-time administrative staff
6. Wages of the school's part-time assistant recital instructors. These employees are hired on a temporary basis. For each student enrolled in the school's music programs, four hours of assistant instructor time are needed per week.
7. Depreciation on the school's musical instruments
8. Rent for the building in which the school operates
9. Electricity for the school. The school pays a fixed monthly charge plus $.10 per kilowatt-hour of electricity.

■ **Problem 6–40**
Approximating a Step-
Variable Cost; Visual-Fit
Method; Golf Course
(LO 1, 2, 4)

Rolling Hills Golf Association is a nonprofit, private organization that operates three 18-hole golf courses. The organization's financial director has just analyzed the course maintenance costs incurred by the golf association during recent summers. The courses are maintained by a full-time crew of four people, who are assisted by part-time employees. These employees are typically college students on their summer vacations. The course maintenance costs vary with the number of people using the course. Since a large part of the maintenance work is done by part-time employees, the maintenance crew size can easily be adjusted to reflect current needs. The financial director's analysis revealed that the course maintenance cost includes two components:

1. A fixed component of $13,000 per month (when the courses are open)
2. A step-variable cost component. For each additional 1 to 10 people teeing off in one day, $10 in costs are incurred. Thus, if 101 to 110 people tee off, $110 of additional cost will be incurred. If 111 to 120 people tee off, $120 of additional cost will be incurred.

Required:

1. Draw a graph of Rolling Hills Golf Association's course maintenance costs. Show on the graph the fixed-cost component and the step-variable cost component. Label each clearly.
2. Use a mixed-cost behaviour pattern to approximate the golf association's course maintenance cost behaviour. Visually fit the mixed cost line to your graph.
3. Using your graph, estimate the variable- and fixed-cost components included in your mixed approximation. Express this approximate cost behaviour pattern in equation form.
4. Fill in the following table of cost predictions.

	Predicted Course Maintenance Costs	
	Using Fixed Cost Coupled with Step-Variable Cost Behaviour Pattern	Using Mixed-Cost Approximation
150 people tee off	?	?
158 people tee off	?	?

(*Note:* Instructors who wish to cover all three cost-estimation methods with the same data set may assign this problem in conjunction with the next one.) Marine Supply is a wholesaler for a large variety of boating and fishing equipment. The company's controller, Alan Denney, has recently completed a cost study of the firm's material-handling department in which he used work measurement to quantify the department's activity. The control factor unit used in the work-measurement study was hundreds of kilograms of equipment unloaded or loaded at the company's loading dock. Denney compiled the following data.

■ Problem 6–41
Cost Estimation with Different Methods; Wholesaler
(LO 1, 2, 4, 5)

3. Variable cost per unit of activity: $1

Month	Units of Activity (hundreds of kilograms of equipment loaded or unloaded)	Material-Handling Department Costs
January	1,800	$11,700
February	1,600	11,300
March	1,300	11,250
April	1,000	10,200
May	2,200	11,100
June	2,400	12,550
July	2,000	12,000
August	1,800	11,400
September	2,600	12,120
October	1,100	11,050
November	1,200	11,350
December	1,400	11,350

Required:

1. Draw a scatter diagram of the cost data for the material-handling department.
2. Visually fit a cost line to the scatter diagram.
3. Estimate the variable and fixed components of the department's cost behaviour pattern using the visually fit cost line.
4. Using your estimate from requirement (3), specify an equation to express the department's cost behaviour.

5. Estimate the material-handling department's cost behaviour using the high-low method. Use an equation to express the results of this estimation method.

6. Write a brief memo to the company's president explaining why the cost estimates developed in requirements (4) and (5) differ.

7. Predict the company's material-handling costs for a month when 2,250 units of activity are recorded. Use each of your cost equations to make the prediction. Which prediction would you prefer to use? Why?

Problem 6–42

Continuation of Preceding Problem; Computing Least-Squares Regression Estimates; Comparing Multiple Methods (Appendix)
(LO 1, 2, 4, 5, 9)

1c. Monthly fixed cost: $9,943

Refer to the original data in the preceding problem for Marine Supply.

Required:

1. *Build a spreadsheet:* Construct an Excel spreadsheet and use the Excel commands to perform a least-squares regression. Estimate the variable- and fixed-cost components in the company's material-handling department costs.

2. Write the least-squares regression equation for the department's costs.

3. Predict the firm's material-handling department's costs for a month when 2,250 units of activity are recorded.

4. Why do the three cost predictions computed in this and the preceding problem differ? Which method do you recommend? Why?

5. Use your Excel spreadsheet from requirements (1) to compute the R^2 value for the regression. Interpret the R^2 value.

Problem 6–43

Cost Estimation Methods; Cost Analysis; E-Commerce
(LO 2, 4)

4.C $1,549,000

Shortly after being hired as an analyst with Global Airlines, Kim Williams was asked to prepare a report that focused on passenger ticketing cost. The airline writes most of its own tickets (largely through reservations personnel), makes little use of travel agents, and has seen an ever-increasing passenger interest in e-ticketing (i.e., electronic reservations and tickets handled over the Internet).

After some discussion, Williams thought it would be beneficial to begin her report with an overview of three different cost estimation tools: scatter diagrams, least-squares regression, and the high-low method. She would then present the results of her analysis of the past year's monthly ticketing cost, which was driven largely by the number of tickets written. These results would be presented in the form of algebraic equations that were derived by the three tools just cited. The equations follow. (C denotes ticketing cost, and PT denotes number of passenger tickets written.)

Least-squares regression: $C = \$300,000 + \$2.25PT$

Scatter diagram: $C = \$295,000 + \$2.20PT$

High-low method: $C = \$301,000 + \$2.40PT$

Williams had analyzed data over the past 12 months and built equations on these data, purposely including the slowest month of the year (February) and the busiest month (October) so that things would "tend to average out." She observed that October was especially busy because of Thanksgiving, passengers purchasing tickets for upcoming holiday travel in December, and the effects of a strike by National Airlines, Global's chief competitor. The lengthy strike resulted in many of National's passengers being rerouted on Global flights.

Required:

1. Prepare a bullet-point list suitable for use in Williams's report that describes the features of scatter diagrams, least-squares regression, and the high-low method. Determine which of the three tools will typically produce the most accurate results.

2. Will the three cost estimation tools normally result in different equations? Why?

3. Assuming the use of least-squares regression, explain what the $300,000 and $2.25 figures represent.

4. Assuming the use of a scatter diagram, predict the cost of an upcoming month when Global American expects to write 570,000 tickets.

5. Did Williams err in constructing the equations on data of the past 12 months? Briefly explain.

6. Assume that over the next few years, more of Global's passengers will take advantage of e-ticketing over the Internet. What will likely happen to the airline's cost structure in terms of variable and fixed cost incurred?

The controller of Mirabel Auto Cylinder believes that the identification of the variable and fixed components of the firm's costs will enable the firm to make better planning and control decisions. Among the costs the controller is concerned about is the behaviour of indirect-materials cost. She believes there is a correlation between machine hours and the amount of indirect materials used.

A member of the controller's staff has suggested that least-squares regression be used to determine the cost behaviour of indirect materials. The regression equation shown below was developed from 40 pairs of observations.

$$S = \$190 + \$5H$$

where S = Total monthly cost of indirect materials

   H = Machine hours per month

Required:

1. Explain the meaning of 190 and 5 in the regression equation $S = \$190 + \$5H$.
2. Calculate the estimated cost of indirect materials if 850 machine hours are to be used during a month (Assume that 850 falls within the relevant range for this cost equation).
3. To determine the validity of the cost estimate computed in requirement (2), what question would you ask the controller about the data used for the regression?
4. The high and low activity levels during the past four years, as measured by machine hours, occurred during April and August, respectively. Data concerning machine hours and indirect-material usage follow.

	April	August
Machine hours..	1,000	700
Indirect supplies:		
Beginning inventory..	$1,300	$1,000
Ending inventory..	1,350	3,000
Purchases...	5,900	6,200

Determine the cost of indirect materials used during April and August.

5. Use the high-low method to estimate the behaviour of the company's indirect-material cost. Express the cost behaviour pattern in equation form.
6. Which cost estimate would you recommend to the controller, the regression estimate or the high-low estimate? Why?

(CMA, adapted)

Randolph Dana owns a catering company that prepares banquets and parties for both individual and business functions throughout the year. Dana's business is seasonal, with a heavy schedule during the summer months and the year-end holidays and a light schedule at other times. During peak periods, there are extra costs; however, even during nonpeak periods Dana must work more to cover her expenses.

One of the major events Dana's customers request is a cocktail party. She offers a standard cocktail party and has developed the following cost structure on a per-person basis:

Food and beverages	$14.00
Labour (.6 hrs. @ $11 per hr.)	6.60
Overhead (.6 hrs. @ $14 per hr.)	8.40
Total cost per person	$29.00

When bidding on cocktail parties, Dana adds a 15 percent markup to this cost structure as a profit margin. Dana is quite certain about his estimates of the prime costs but is not as comfortable with the overhead estimate. This estimate was based on the actual data for the past 12 months presented in the following table. These data indicate that overhead expenses vary with the direct-labour hours expended. The $14 per hour overhead estimate was determined by dividing total overhead expended for the 12 months ($805,000) by total labour hours (57,600) and rounding to the nearest dollar.

■ **Problem 6–44**
Comparing Regression and
High-Low Estimates;
Manufacturer
(LO 1, 2, 4)

2. Estimated cost of indirect
material at 850 machine
hours: $4,440
5. Fixed cost: $350

■ **Problem 6–45**
Interpreting Regression
Analysis in Cost Estimation
(LO 2, 4)

2b. Absorption cost per
person: $29

Month	Labour Hours	Overhead Expenses
January	2,800	$59,000
February	2,500	55,000
March	3,000	60,000
April	4,500	67,000
May	4,200	64,000
June	6,500	74,000
July	5,500	71,000
August	7,000	75,000
September	7,500	77,000
October	4,500	68,000
November	3,100	62,000
December	6,500	73,000

Dana recently attended a meeting of the local chamber of commerce and heard a business consultant discuss regression analysis and its business applications. After the meeting, Dana decided to do a regression analysis of the overhead data she had collected. The following results were obtained.

Intercept (*a*)	48,000
Coefficient (*b*)	4

Required:

1. Explain the difference between the overhead rate originally estimated by Dana Rand and the overhead rate developed from the regression method.

2. Using data from the regression analysis, develop the following cost estimates per person for a cocktail party:
   a. Variable cost per person
   b. Absorption (full) cost per person (includes both variable and fixed cost per person)
   Assume that the level of activity remains within the relevant range.

3. Dana Rand has been asked to prepare a bid for a 250-person cocktail party to be given next month. Determine the minimum bid price that Dana should be willing to submit.

4. What other factors should Dana consider in developing the bid price for the cocktail party?

(CMA, adapted)

■ Problem 6–46
Computing Least-Squares
Regression Estimates; Airport
Costs (Appendix)
(LO 1, 2, 4, 9)

2*c.* Monthly fixed cost:
$11,796
5*c.* R^2: .58 (rounded)

Langley Airport handles several daily commuter flights and many private flights. The budget officer has compiled the following data regarding airport costs and activity over the past year.

Month	Flights Originating at Langley Airport	Airport Costs
January	1,200	$20,000
February	1,000	19,000
March	900	18,000
April	1,400	19,000
May	800	17,000
June	1,100	20,000
July	1,500	21,000
August	900	17,000
September	1,200	21,000
October	1,000	19,000
November	1,400	24,000
December	1,100	18,000

Required:

1. Draw a scatter diagram of the airport costs shown above.

2. *Build a spreadsheet:* Construct an Excel spreadsheet and use the Excel commands to perform a least-squares regression. Estimate the variable- and fixed-cost components in the airport's cost behaviour pattern.

3. Write the least-squares regression equation for the airport's costs.
4. Predict the airport's costs during a month when 1,500 flights originate at the airport.
5. Using the Excel spreadsheet prepared for requirement (2), compute the coefficient of determination (R^2) for the regression equation. Briefly interpret R^2.

Cases

Outside Environment, Inc. provides commercial landscaping services. Sasha Cairns, the firm's owner, wants to develop cost estimates that she can use to prepare bids on jobs. After analyzing the firm's costs, Cairns has developed the following preliminary cost estimates for each 1,000 square metre of landscaping:

Direct material	$390
Direct labour (5 direct-labour hours at $11 per hour)	55
Overhead (at $18 per direct-labour hour)	90
Total cost per 1,000 square metres	$535

Cairns is quite certain about the estimates for direct material and direct labour. However, she is not as comfortable with the overhead estimate. The estimate for overhead is based on the overhead costs that were incurred during the past 12 months as presented in the following schedule. The estimate of $18 per direct-labour hour was determined by dividing the total overhead costs for the 12-month period ($1,296,000) by the total direct-labour hours (72,000).

■ **Case 6–47**
Interpreting Least-Squares Regression; Landscaping Service; Activity-Based Costing
(LO 1, 2, 4)

2. Total variable cost per 1,000 square metres: $491.25
3. Overtime premium: $412.50

	Total Overhead	Regular Direct-Labour Hours	Overtime Direct-Labour Hours*	Total Direct-Labour Hours
January	$ 108,000	5,820	380	6,200
February	94,000	4,760	40	4,800
March	96,000	4,420	80	4,500
April	112,000	5,180	420	5,600
May	114,000	6,060	940	7,000
June	130,000	6,480	1,520	8,000
July	128,000	6,760	1,240	8,000
August	112,000	6,100	700	6,800
September	106,000	5,520	80	5,600
October	94,000	5,540	60	5,600
November	94,000	4,240	60	4,300
December	108,000	5,120	480	5,600
Total	$1,296,000	66,000	6,000	72,000

*The overtime premium is 50 percent of the direct-labour wage rate.

Cairns believes that overhead is affected by total monthly direct-labour hours. Cairns decided to perform a least-squares regression of overhead (OH) on total direct-labour hours (DLH). The following regression formula was obtained.

$$OH = \$52,400 + \$9.25\ DLH$$

Required:

1. The overhead rate developed from the least-squares regression is different from Cairns' preliminary estimate of $18 per direct-labour hour. Explain the difference in the two overhead rates.
2. Using the overhead formula that was derived from the least-squares regression, determine a total variable-cost estimate for each 1,000 square metres of landscaping.
3. Cairns has been asked to submit a bid on a landscaping project for the city government consisting of 50,000 square metres. Cairns estimates that 30 percent of the direct-labour hours required for the project will be on overtime. Calculate the incremental costs that should be included in any bid that Cairns would submit on this project. Use the overhead formula derived from the least-squares regression.
4. Should management rely on the overhead formula derived from the least-squares regression as the basis for the variable overhead component of its cost estimate? Explain your answer.

5. After attending a seminar on activity-based costing, Cairns decided to further analyze the company's activities and costs. She discovered that a more accurate portrayal of the firm's cost behaviour could be achieved by dividing overhead into three separate pools, each with its own cost driver. Separate regression equations were estimated for each of the cost pools, with the following results:

$OH_1 = \$20,000 + \$4.15DLH$,

where DLH denotes direct-labour hours

$OH_2 = \$18,200 + \$13.60SMS$,

where SMS denotes the number of square metres of turf seeded (in thousands)

$OH_3 = \$16,000 + \$5.90PL$,

where PL denotes the number of individual plantings (e.g., trees and shrubs)

Assume that five direct-labour hours will be needed to landscape each 1,000 square metres, regardless of the specific planting material used.

  a. Suppose the landscaping project for the city will involve seeding all 50,000 square metres of turf and planting 70 trees and shrubs. Calculate the incremental *variable overhead* cost that Cairns should include in the bid.

  b. Recompute the incremental variable overhead cost for the city's landscaping project assuming half of the 50,000-square-metre landscaping area will be seeded and there will be 230 individual plantings. The plantings will cover the entire 50,000-square-metre area.

  c. Briefly explain, using concepts from activity-based costing, why the incremental costs differ in requirements (*a*) and (*b*).

(CMA, adapted)

■ **Case 6–48**
Approximating a Curvilinear Cost; Visual-Fit Method; Paediatrics Clinic
(LO 1, 2, 4)

(*Note*: Instructors who wish to cover all three cost-estimation methods with the same data set may assign this case in conjunction with the following case.) "I don't understand this cost report at all," exclaimed Jeff Mahoney, the newly appointed administrator of Mountainview General Hospital. "Our administrative costs in the new paediatrics clinic are all over the map. One month the report shows $7,000, and the next month it's $13,900. What's going on?"

Mahoney's question was posed to Megan McDonough, the hospital's director of cost management. "The main problem is that the clinic has experienced some widely varying patient loads in its first year of operation. There seems to be some confusion in the public's mind about what services we offer in the clinic. When do they come to the clinic? When do they go to the emergency room? That sort of thing. As the patient load has varied, we've frequently changed our clinic administrative staffing."

Mahoney continued to puzzle over the report. "Could you pull some data together, Megan, so we can see how this cost behaves over a range of patient loads?"

"You'll have it this afternoon," McDonough responded. Later that morning, she gathered the following data:

Month	Patient Load	Administrative Cost
January	400	$ 6,000
February	500	7,000
March	1,400	13,900
April	900	9,200
May	1,300	11,900
June	1,000	10,000
July	700	9,400
August	300	4,100
September	1,100	10,200
October	1,500	16,100
November	600	8,300
December	1,200	11,100

McDonough does not believe the first year's widely fluctuating patient load will be experienced again in the future. She has estimated that the clinic's relevant range of monthly activity in the future will be 600 to 1,200 patients.

Required:

1. Draw a scatter diagram of the clinic's administrative costs during its first year of operation.
2. Visually fit a curvilinear cost line to the plotted data.
3. Mark the clinic's relevant range of activity on the scatter diagram.
4. Visually fit a mixed-cost line to approximate the curvilinear cost behaviour pattern within the clinic's relevant range.
5. Estimate the fixed- and variable-cost components of the visually fit mixed-cost line.
6. Use an equation to express the mixed-cost approximation of the clinic's administrative costs.
7. What is your prediction of the clinic's administrative cost during a month when 750 patients visit the clinic? When 350 patients visit? Which one of your visually fit cost lines did you use to make each of these predictions? Why?

Refer to the data and accompanying information in the preceding case.

Required:

1. Use the high-low method to estimate the cost behaviour for the clinic's administrative costs. Express the cost behaviour in formula form ($Y = a + bX$). What is the variable cost per patient?
2. *Build a spreadsheet:* Construct an Excel spreadsheet and use the Excel commands to perform a least-squares regression and estimate the administrative cost behaviour. Express the cost behaviour in formula form. What is the variable cost per patient? Computer and interpret the R^2 value for the regression.
3. Write a memo to the hospital administrator comparing the cost estimates using (*a*) least-squares regression, (*b*) the high-low method, and (*c*) the scatter diagram and visually fit mixed-cost line from the preceding case (requirements (4) and (5)). Make a recommendation as to which estimate should be used, and support your recommendation. Make any other suggestions you feel are appropriate.
4. After receiving the memo comparing the three cost estimates, Mahoney called McDonough to discuss the matter. The following exchange occurred.

    Mahoney: As you know, Megan, I was never in favour of this clinic. It's going to be a drag on our administrative staff, and we'd have been far better off keeping the paediatrics operation here in the hospital.

    McDonough: I was aware that you felt the clinic was a mistake. Of course, the board of trustees had other issues to consider. I believe the board felt the clinic should be built to make paediatric care more accessible to the economically depressed area on the other side of the city.

    Mahoney: That's true, but the board doesn't realize how difficult it's going to make life for us here in the hospital. In any case, I called to tell you that when you and I report to the board next week, I'm going to recommend that the clinic be shut down. I want you to support my recommendation with one of your cost estimates showing that administrative costs will soar at high activity levels.

    McDonough: But that estimate was based on the high-low method. It's not an appropriate method for this situation.

    Mahoney: It *is* an estimate, Megan, and it's based on a well-known estimation method. This is just the ammunition I need to make the board see things my way.

    McDonough: I don't know, Jeff. I just don't think I can go along with that.

    Mahoney: Be a team player, Megan. I've got a meeting now. Got to run.

How would you advise McDonough?

■ **Case 6–49**
Comparing Multiple Cost
Estimation Methods; Ethics
(Appendix)
(LO 1, 2, 4, 9)

1. Variable administrative cost per patient: $10

Chapter Seven

Cost-Volume-Profit Analysis

FOCUS COMPANY

The Toronto Contemporary Theatre, a nonprofit enterprise, was formed to bring contemporary drama to the Toronto area. It operates in a historic theatre building owned by the city, for which

it pays the city a fixed monthly rental charge and a portion of the price of each ticket sold. The Theatre has to cover its operating expenses with ticket revenue in order to break even. Using the Toronto Contemporary Theatre as an illustration, we will explore a technique called cost-volume-profit (or CVP) analysis, which the theatre's managing director and business manager use to better understand the relationships between the theatre's costs, ticket sales volume, and revenue.

IN CONTRAST

In contrast to the nonprofit, entertainment-service setting of the Toronto Contemporary Theatre, we explore the use of cost-volume-profit analysis by AccuTime Company. The management of this manufacturer of digital clocks uses CVP analysis to better understand the relationships between the company's costs, sales volume, and profit. The company's management also analyzes the firm's cost structure, which refers to the relative proportion of fixed and variable costs.

After completing this chapter, you should be able to:

1 Compute a break-even point using the contribution-margin approach and the equation approach.

2 Compute the contribution-margin ratio and use it to find the break-even point in sales dollars.

3 Prepare a cost-volume-profit (CVP) graph and explain how it is used.

4 Apply CVP analysis to determine the effect on profit of changes in fixed expenses, variable expenses, sales prices, and sales volume.

5 Compute the break-even point and prepare a profit-volume graph for a multiproduct enterprise.

6 List and discuss the key assumptions of CVP analysis.

7 Prepare and interpret a contribution income statement.

8 Explain the role of cost structure and operating leverage in CVP relationships.

9 Understand the implications of activity-based costing for CVP analysis.

10 Be aware of the effects of advanced manufacturing technology on CVP relationships.

11 Understand the effect of income taxes on CVP analysis (Appendix).

W hat effect on profit can WestJet Airlines expect if it adds a flight on the Vancouver to Toronto route? How will CBC's profit change if the ratings increase for its evening news program? How many patient days of care must Vancouver General Hospital provide to break even for the year? What happens to this break-even patient load if the hospital leases a new computerized system for patient records?

Each of these questions concerns the effects on costs and revenues when the organization's activity changes. The analytical technique used by managerial accountants to address these questions is called **cost-volume-profit analysis**, or **CVP analysis** for short. This technique summarizes the effects of changes in an organization's *volume* of activity on its *costs*, revenue, and *profit*. Cost-volume-profit analysis can be extended to cover the effects on profit of changes in selling prices, service fees, costs, income-tax rates, and the organization's mix of products or services. What will happen to profit, for example, if the Toronto Maple Leafs raise ticket prices for stadium seats? In short, CVP analysis provides management with a comprehensive overview of the effects on revenue and costs of all kinds of short-run financial changes.

Although the word *profit* appears in the term, cost-volume-profit analysis is not confined to profit-seeking enterprises. Managers in nonprofit organizations also routinely use CVP analysis to examine the effects of activity and other short-run changes on revenue and costs. For example, as the State of Florida gains nearly 1,000 people a day in population, the state's political leaders must analyze the effects of this change on sales-tax revenues and the cost of providing services, such as education, transportation, and police protection. Managers at such diverse nonprofit institutions as Vancouver General Hospital, Simon Fraser University, and the United Way all use CVP analysis as a routine operational tool.

Cost-Volume-Profit Analysis Illustrated

To illustrate the various analytical techniques used in cost-volume-profit analysis, we will focus on a performing arts organization. The Toronto Contemporary Theatre was recently formed as a nonprofit enterprise to bring contemporary drama to the Toronto area. The organization has a part-time, unpaid board of trustees comprising local professional people who are avid theatre fans. The board has hired the following full-time employees.

- *Managing director.* Responsibilities include overall management of the organization; direction of six plays per year.
- *Artistic director.* Responsibilities include hiring of actors and production crews for each play; direction of six plays per year.
- *Business manager and producer.* Responsibilities include managing the organization's business functions and ticket sales; direction of the production crews, who handle staging, lighting, costuming, and makeup.

The board of trustees has negotiated an agreement with the city of Toronto to hold performances in a historic theatre owned by the city. The theatre has not been used for 30 years, but the city has agreed to refurbish it and to provide lighting and sound equipment. In return, the city will receive a rental charge of $10,000 per month plus $8 for each theatre ticket sold.

"Accounting is changing. You're no longer sitting behind a desk just working on a computer, just crunching the numbers. You're actually getting to be a part of the day-to-day functions of the business." (7a)
Abbott Laboratories

Projected Expenses and Revenue

The theatre's business manager and producer, Andrew Lloyd, has made the following projections for the first few years of operation.

Fixed expenses per month:	
Theatre rental	$10,000
Employees' salaries and fringe benefits	8,000
Actors' wages	15,000
(to be supplemented with local volunteer talent)	
Production crew's wages	5,600
(to be supplemented with local volunteers)	
Playwrights' royalties for use of plays	5,000
Insurance	1,000
Utilities—fixed portion	1,400
Advertising and promotion	800
Administrative expenses	1,200
Total fixed expenses per month	$48,000
Variable expenses per ticket sold:	
City's charge per ticket for use of theatre	$ 8
Other, miscellaneous expenses (e.g., printing of playbills and tickets,	
variable portion of utilities)	2
Total variable cost per ticket sold	$10
Revenue:	
Price per ticket	$16

Importance of Cost Behaviour   Notice that the theatre's expenses have been categorized according to their cost behaviour: fixed or variable. Analyzing an organization's cost behaviour, the topic of Chapter 6, is a necessary first step in any cost-volume-profit analysis. As we proceed through this chapter, the data pertaining to Toronto Contemporary Theatre will be an important part of our cost-volume-profit analysis.

The Break-Even Point

Learning Objective 1

Compute a break-even point using the contribution-margin approach and the equation approach.

As the first step in the CVP analysis for Toronto Contemporary Theatre, we will find the **break-even point**. The break-even point is the volume of activity where the organization's revenues and expenses are equal. At this amount of sales, the organization has no profit or loss; it *breaks even*.

Whether running a small business or a worldwide enterprise, understanding cost-volume-profit relationships is crucial in managing any organization.

Suppose Toronto Contemporary Theatre sells 8,000 tickets during a play's one-month run. The following income statement shows that the profit for the month will be zero; thus, the theatre will break even.

Sales revenue (8,000 × $16)	$128,000
Less variable expenses (8,000 × 10)	80,000
Total contribution margin	$ 48,000
Less fixed expenses	48,000
Profit	$ 0

Notice that this income statement highlights the distinction between variable and fixed expenses. The statement also shows the **total contribution margin**, which is defined as total sales revenue minus total variable expenses. This is the amount of revenue that is available to *contribute* to covering fixed expenses after all variable expenses have been covered. The contribution income statement will be covered in more depth later in the chapter. At this juncture, it provides a useful way to think about the meaning of breaking even.

How could we compute Toronto Contemporary Theatre's break-even point if we did not already know it is 8,000 tickets per month? This is the question to which we turn our attention next.

Contribution-Margin Approach

Toronto Contemporary Theatre will break even when the organization's revenue from ticket sales is equal to its expenses. How many tickets must be sold during one month (one play's run) for the organization to break even?

Each ticket sells for $16, but $10 of this is used to cover the variable expense per ticket. This leaves $6 per ticket to *contribute* to covering the fixed expenses of $48,000. When enough tickets have been sold in one month so that these $6 contributions per ticket add up to $48,000, the organization will break even for the month. Thus, we may compute the break-even volume of tickets as follows:

$$\frac{\text{Fixed expenses}}{\text{Contribution of each ticket toward covering fixed expenses}} = \frac{\$48,000}{\$6} = 8,000$$

Toronto Contemporary Theatre must sell 8,000 tickets during a play's one-month run to break even for the month.

The $6 amount that remains of each ticket's price, after the variable expenses are covered, is called the **unit contribution margin**. The general formula for computing the break-even sales volume in units is given below.

$$\frac{\text{Fixed expenses}}{\text{Unit contribution margin}} = \text{Break-even point (in units)} \qquad (1)$$

Contribution-Margin Ratio   Sometimes management prefers that the break-even point be expressed in sales *dollars* rather than *units*. Toronto Contemporary Theatre's break-even point in sales dollars is computed as follows.

Break-even point in units (tickets)	8,000
Sales price per unit	× $16
Break-even point in sales dollars	$128,000

Learning Objective 2

Compute the contribution-margin ratio and use it to find the break-even point in sales dollars.

The following computation provides an alternative way to determine the break-even point in sales dollars.

$$\frac{\text{Fixed expenses}}{\frac{\text{Unit contribution margin}}{\text{Unit sales price}}} = \frac{\$48,000}{\frac{\$6}{\$16}} = \frac{\$48,000}{.375} = \$128,000$$

The unit contribution margin divided by the unit sales price is called the **contribution-margin ratio**. This ratio also can be expressed as a percentage, in which case it is called the *contribution-margin percentage*. Toronto Contemporary Theatre's contribution-margin ratio is .375 (in percentage form, 37.5%). Thus, the organization's break-even point in sales dollars may be found by dividing its fixed expenses by its contribution-margin ratio. The logic behind this approach is that 37.5 percent of each sales dollar is available to make a contribution toward covering fixed expenses. The general formula is given below.

$$\frac{\text{Fixed expenses}}{\text{Contribution-margin ratio}} = \text{Break-even point in sales dollars} \qquad (2)$$

Equation Approach

Learning Objective 1

Compute a break-even point using the contribution-margin approach and the equation approach.

An alternative approach to finding the break-even point is based on the profit equation. Income (or profit) is equal to sales revenue minus expenses. If expenses are separated into variable and fixed expenses, the essence of the income (profit) statement is captured by the following equation:

$$\text{Sales revenue} - \text{Variable expenses} - \text{Fixed expenses} = \text{Profit}$$

This equation can be restated as follows:

$$\left[\begin{pmatrix}\text{Unit} \\ \text{sales} \\ \text{price}\end{pmatrix} \times \begin{pmatrix}\text{Sales} \\ \text{volume} \\ \text{in units}\end{pmatrix}\right] - \left[\begin{pmatrix}\text{Unit} \\ \text{variable} \\ \text{expense}\end{pmatrix} \times \begin{pmatrix}\text{Sales} \\ \text{volume} \\ \text{in units}\end{pmatrix}\right] - \begin{pmatrix}\text{Fixed} \\ \text{expenses}\end{pmatrix} = \text{Profit} \qquad (3)$$

To find Toronto Contemporary Theatre's break-even volume of ticket sales per month, we define profit in equation (3) to be zero.

$$(\$16 \times X) - (\$10 \times X) - \$48{,}000 = 0$$

$$\left[\begin{pmatrix}\text{Unit} \\ \text{sales} \\ \text{price}\end{pmatrix} \times \begin{pmatrix}\text{Sales} \\ \text{volume} \\ \text{in units}\end{pmatrix}\right] - \left[\begin{pmatrix}\text{Unit} \\ \text{variable} \\ \text{expense}\end{pmatrix} \times \begin{pmatrix}\text{Sales} \\ \text{volume} \\ \text{in units}\end{pmatrix}\right] - \begin{pmatrix}\text{Fixed} \\ \text{expenses}\end{pmatrix} = \begin{matrix}\text{Break-even} \\ \text{profit (zero)}\end{matrix} \qquad (4)$$

where

X denotes the number of sales units (tickets) required to break even

Equation (4) can be solved for X as shown below.

$$\$16X - \$10X - \$48{,}000 = 0$$

$$\$6X = \$48{,}000$$

$$X = \frac{\$48{,}000}{\$6} = 8{,}000$$

Using the equation approach, we have arrived at the same general formula for computing the break-even sales volume [formula (1)].

The contribution-margin and equation approaches are two equivalent techniques for finding the break-even point. Both methods reach the same conclusion, and so personal preference dictates which approach should be used.

Graphing Cost-Volume-Profit Relationships

Learning Objective 3

Prepare a cost-volume-profit (CVP) graph and explain how it is used.

While the break-even point conveys useful information to management, it does not show how profit changes as activity changes. To capture the relationship between profit and volume of activity, a **cost-volume-profit (CVP) graph** is commonly used. The following steps are used to prepare a CVP graph for Toronto Contemporary Theatre. The graph is displayed in Exhibit 7–1. Notice that the graph shows the *relevant range,* which is the range of activity within which management expects the theatre to operate.

> **Step 1:** Draw the axes of the graph. Label the vertical axis in dollars and the horizontal axis in units of sales (tickets).
>
> **Step 2:** Draw the fixed-expense line. It is parallel to the horizontal axis, since fixed expenses do not change with activity.

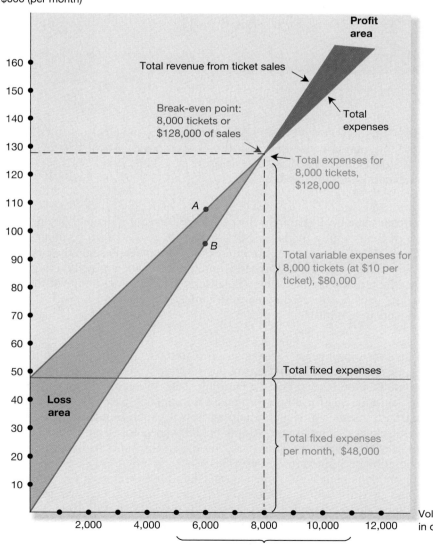

Exhibit 7–1

Cost-Volume-Profit Graph: Toronto Contemporary Theatre

> **Step 3:** Compute *total* expense at any convenient volume. For example, select a volume of 6,000 tickets.

Variable expenses (6,000 × $10 per ticket)	$ 60,000
Fixed expenses	48,000
Total expenses (at 6,000 tickets)	$108,000

> Plot this point ($108,000 at 6,000 tickets) on the graph. See point *A* on the graph in Exhibit 7–1.
>
> **Step 4:** Draw the total-expense line. This line passes through the point plotted in step 3 (point *A*) and the intercept of the fixed-expense line on the vertical axis ($48,000).
>
> **Step 5:** Compute total sales revenue at any convenient volume. We will choose 6,000 tickets again. Total revenue is $96,000 (6,000 × $16 per ticket). Plot this point ($96,000 at 6,000 tickets) on the graph. See point *B* on the graph in Exhibit 7–1.
>
> **Step 6:** Draw the total revenue line. This line passes through the point plotted in step 5 (point *B*) and the origin.
>
> **Step 7:** Label the graph as shown in Exhibit 7–1.

Interpreting the CVP Graph

Several conclusions can be drawn from the CVP graph in Exhibit 7–1.

Break-Even Point   The break-even point is determined by the intersection of the total-revenue line and the total-expense line. Toronto Contemporary Theatre breaks even for the month at 8,000 tickets, or $128,000 of ticket sales. This agrees with our calculations in the preceding section.

Profit and Loss Areas   The CVP graph discloses more information than the break-even calculation. From the graph, a manager can see the effects on profit of changes in volume. The vertical distance between the lines on the graph represents the profit or loss at a particular sales volume. If Toronto Contemporary Theatre sells fewer than 8,000 tickets in a month, the organization will suffer a loss. The magnitude of the loss increases as ticket sales decline. The theatre organization will have a profit if sales exceed 8,000 tickets in a month.

Implications of the Break-Even Point   The position of the break-even point within an organization's relevant range of activity provides important information to management. The Toronto Contemporary Theatre building seats 450 people. The agreement with the city of Toronto calls for 20 performances during each play's one-month run. Thus, the maximum number of tickets that can be sold each month is 9,000 (450 seats × 20 performances). The organization's break-even point is quite close to the maximum possible sales volume. This could be cause for concern in a nonprofit organization operating on limited resources.

What might management do to improve this situation? One possibility is to renegotiate with the city to schedule additional performances. However, this might not be feasible, because the actors need some rest each week. Also, additional performances would likely entail additional costs, such as increased theatre-rental expenses and increased compensation for the actors and production crew. Other possible solutions are to raise ticket prices or reduce costs. These kinds of issues will be explored later in the chapter.

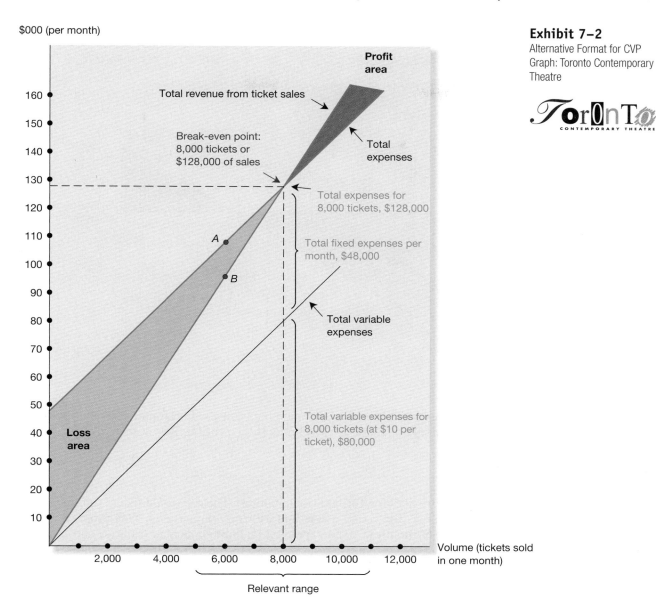

$000 (per month)

Exhibit 7–2
Alternative Format for CVP Graph: Toronto Contemporary Theatre

Profit area

Total revenue from ticket sales

Break-even point:
8,000 tickets or
$128,000 of sales

Total expenses

Total expenses for 8,000 tickets, $128,000

Total fixed expenses per month, $48,000

Total variable expenses

A

B

Loss area

Total variable expenses for 8,000 tickets (at $10 per ticket), $80,000

Volume (tickets sold in one month)

2,000   4,000   6,000   8,000   10,000   12,000

Relevant range

The CVP graph will not resolve this potential problem for the management of Toronto Contemporary Theatre. However, the graph will *direct management's attention* to the situation.

Alternative Format for the CVP Graph

An alternative format for the CVP graph, preferred by some managers, is displayed in Exhibit 7–2. The key difference is that fixed expenses are graphed above variable expenses, instead of the reverse as they were in Exhibit 7–1.

Profit-Volume Graph

Yet another approach to graphing cost-volume-profit relationships is displayed in Exhibit 7–3. This format is called a **profit-volume graph**, since it highlights the amount of profit or loss. Notice that the graph intercepts the vertical axis at the amount equal to fixed expenses at the zero activity level. The graph crosses the horizontal axis at the

Exhibit 7–3

Profit-Volume Graph: Toronto
Contemporary Theatre

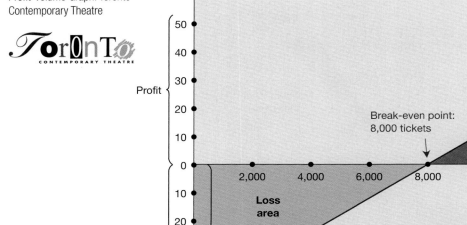

break-even point. The vertical distance between the horizontal axis and the profit
line, at a particular level of sales volume, is the profit or loss at that volume.

Target Net Profit

The board of trustees for Toronto Contemporary Theatre would like to run free work-
shops and classes for young actors and aspiring playwrights. This program would
cost $3,600 per month in fixed expenses, including teachers' salaries and rental of
space at a local college. No variable expenses would be incurred. If Toronto Contemporary Theatre could make a profit of $3,600 per month on its performances, the
Toronto Drama Workshop could be opened. The board has asked Andrew Lloyd, the
organization's business manager and producer, to determine how many theatre tickets
must be sold during each play's one-month run to make a profit of $3,600.

   The desired profit level of $3,600 is called a **target net profit** (or **income**). The
problem of computing the volume of sales required to earn a particular target net profit
is very similar to the problem of finding the break-even point. After all, the break-even
point is the number of units of sales required to earn a target net profit of zero.

Contribution-Margin Approach

Each ticket sold by Toronto Contemporary Theatre has a unit contribution margin of
$6 (sales price of $16 minus unit variable expense of $10). Eight thousand of these $6
contributions will contribute just enough to cover fixed expenses of $48,000. *Each
additional ticket sold will contribute $6 toward profit.* Thus, we can modify formula
(1) given earlier in the chapter as follows:

$$\frac{\text{Fixed expenses} + \text{Target net profit}}{\text{Unit contribution margin}} = \begin{matrix}\text{Number of sales units required} \\ \text{to earn target net profit}\end{matrix} \qquad (5)$$

$$\frac{\$48,000 + \$3,600}{\$6} = 8,600 \text{ tickets}$$

If Toronto Contemporary Theatre sells 8,600 tickets during each play's one-month run, the organization will make a monthly profit of $3,600 on its performances. This profit can be used to fund the Toronto Drama Workshop. The total dollar sales required to earn a target net profit is found by modifying formula (2) given previously.

$$\frac{\text{Fixed expenses} + \text{Target net profit}}{\text{Contribution-margin ratio}} = \frac{\text{Dollar sales required to earn}}{\text{target net profit}} \qquad (6)$$

$$\frac{\$48,000 + \$3,600}{.375} = \$137,600$$

where the contribution margin ratio $= \dfrac{\$6}{\$16} = .375$

This dollar sales figure also can be found by multiplying the required sales of 8,600 tickets by the ticket price of $16 (8,600 $\times$ $16 = $137,600).

Equation Approach

The equation approach also can be used to find the units of sales required to earn a target net profit. We can modify the profit equation given previously as follows:

$$\left[\left(\begin{array}{c}\text{Unit}\\\text{sales}\\\text{price}\end{array}\right) \times \left(\begin{array}{c}\text{Sales volume}\\\text{required to}\\\text{earn target}\\\text{net profit}\end{array}\right)\right] - \left[\left(\begin{array}{c}\text{Unit}\\\text{variable}\\\text{expense}\end{array}\right) \times \left(\begin{array}{c}\text{Sales volume}\\\text{required to}\\\text{earn target}\\\text{net profit}\end{array}\right)\right]$$

$$- \left(\begin{array}{c}\text{Fixed}\\\text{expenses}\end{array}\right) = \text{Target net profit}$$

Filling in the values for Toronto Contemporary Theatre, we have the following equation.

$$(\$16 \times X) - (\$10 \times X) - \$48,000 = \$3,600 \qquad (7)$$

where X denotes the sales volume required to earn the target net profit.

Equation (7) can be solved for X as follows:

$$\$16X - \$10X - \$48,000 = \$3,600$$

$$\$6X = \$51,600$$

$$X = \frac{\$51,600}{\$6} = 8,600$$

Graphical Approach

The profit-volume graph in Exhibit 7–3 also can be used to find the sales volume required to earn a target net profit. First, locate Toronto Contemporary Theatre's target net profit of $3,600 on the vertical axis. Then move horizontally until the profit line is reached. Finally, move down from the profit line to the horizontal axis to determine the required sales volume.

Applying CVP Analysis

The cost-volume-profit relationships that underlie break-even calculations and CVP graphs have wide-ranging applications in management. We will look at several common applications illustrated by Toronto Contemporary Theatre.

Safety Margin

The **safety margin** of an enterprise is the difference between the budgeted sales revenue and the break-even sales revenue. Suppose Toronto Contemporary Theatre's business manager expects every performance of each play to be sold out. Then budgeted monthly sales revenue is $144,000 (450 seats × 20 performances of each play × $16 per ticket). Since break-even sales revenue is $128,000, the organization's safety margin is $16,000 ($144,000 − $128,000). The safety margin gives management a feel for how close projected operations are to the organization's break-even point. We will further discuss the safety margin concept later in the chapter.

Changes in Fixed Expenses

What would happen to Toronto Contemporary Theatre's break-even point if fixed expenses change? Suppose the business manager is concerned that the estimate for fixed utilities expenses, $1,400 per month, is too low. What would happen to the break-even point if fixed utilities expenses prove to be $2,600 instead? The break-even calculations for both the original and the new estimate of fixed utilities expenses are as follows:

	Original Estimate	New Estimate
Fixed utilities expenses	$ 1,400	$ 2,600
Total fixed expenses	$48,000	$49,200
Break-even calculation	$48,000	$49,200
(Fixed expenses ÷ Unit contribution margin)	$6	$6
Break-even point (units)	8,000 tickets	8,200 tickets
Break-even point (dollars)	$128,000	$131,200

The estimate of fixed expenses has increased by 2.5 percent, since $1,200 is 2.5 percent of $48,000. Notice that the break-even point also increased by 2.5 percent (200 tickets is 2.5 percent of 8,000 tickets). This relationship will always exist.

$$\frac{\text{Fixed expenses}}{\text{Unit contribution margin}} = \text{Break-even point (in units)}$$

$$\frac{\text{Fixed expenses} \times 1.025}{\text{Unit contribution margin}} = (\text{Break-even point in units}) \times 1.025$$

Donations to Offset Fixed Expenses Nonprofit organizations often receive cash donations from people or organizations desiring to support a worthy cause. A donation is equivalent to a reduction in fixed expenses, and it reduces the organization's break-even point. In our original set of data, Toronto Contemporary Theatre's monthly fixed expenses total $48,000. Suppose that various people pledge donations amounting to $6,000 per month. The new break-even point is computed as follows:

$$\frac{\text{Fixed expenses} - \text{Donations}}{\text{Unit contribution margin}} = \text{Break-even point (in units)}$$

$$\frac{\$48,000 - \$6,000}{\$6} = 7,000 \text{ tickets}$$

Changes in the Unit Contribution Margin

What would happen to Toronto Contemporary Theatre's break-even point if miscellaneous variable expenses were $3 per ticket instead of $2? Alternatively, what would be the effect of raising the ticket price to $18?

Change in Unit Variable Expenses   If the theatre organization's miscellaneous variable expenses increase from $2 to $3 per ticket, the unit contribution margin will fall from $6 to $5. The original and new break-even points are computed as follows:

	Original Estimate	New Estimate
Miscellaneous variable expenses	$2 per ticket	$ 3 per ticket
Unit contribution margin	$6	$5
Break-even calculation	$48,000	$48,000
(Fixed expenses ÷ Unit contribution margin)	$6	$5
Break-even point (units)	8,000 tickets	9,600 tickets
Break-even point (dollars)	$128,000	$153,600

If this change in unit variable expenses actually occurs, it will no longer be possible for the organization to break even. Only 9,000 tickets are available for each play's one-month run (450 seats × 20 performances), but 9,600 tickets would have to be sold to break even. Once again, CVP analysis will not solve this problem for management, but it will direct management's attention to potentially serious difficulties.

Change in Sales Price   Changing the unit sales price will also alter the unit contribution margin. Suppose the ticket price is raised from $16 to $18. This change will raise the unit contribution margin from $6 to $8. The new break-even point will be 6,000 tickets ($48,000 ÷ $8).

A $2 increase in the ticket price will lower the break-even point from 8,000 tickets to 6,000 tickets. Is this change desirable? A lower break-even point decreases the risk of operating with a loss if sales are sluggish. However, the organization may be more likely to at least break even with a $16 ticket price than with an $18 ticket price. The reason is that the lower ticket price encourages more people to attend the theatre's performances. It could be that break-even sales of 8,000 tickets at $16 are more likely than break-even sales of 6,000 tickets at $18. Ultimately, the desirability of the ticket-price increase depends on management's assessment of the likely reaction by theatre patrons.

Management's decision about the ticket price increase also will reflect the fundamental goals of Toronto Contemporary Theatre. This nonprofit drama organization was formed to bring contemporary drama to the people of Toronto. The lower the ticket price, the more accessible the theatre's productions will be to people of all income levels.

The point of this discussion is that CVP analysis provides valuable information, but it is only one of several elements that influence management's decisions.

Predicting Profit Given Expected Volume

So far, we have focused on finding the required sales volume to break even or achieve a particular target net profit. Thus, we have asked the following question:

Given: $\begin{cases} \text{Fixed expenses} \\ \text{Unit contribution margin} \\ \text{Target net profit} \end{cases}$, Find: {Required sales volume}

We also can use CVP analysis to turn this question around and make the following query:

Given: $\begin{cases} \text{Fixed expenses} \\ \text{Unit contribution margin} \\ \text{Expected sales volume} \end{cases}$, Find: {Expected profit}

Suppose the management of Toronto Contemporary Theatre expects fixed monthly expenses of $48,000 and unit variable expenses of $10 per ticket. The organization's board of trustees is considering two different ticket prices, and the business manager has forecast monthly demand at each price.

Ticket Price	Forecast Monthly Demand
$16	9,000
$20	6,000

Expected profit may be calculated at each price as shown in the following table. In these profit calculations, the *total contribution margin* is the difference between *total* sales revenue and *total* variable expenses. This use of the term *contribution margin* is a "total" concept rather than the "per-unit" concept used earlier in the chapter. The *total contribution margin* is the *total* amount left to contribute to covering fixed expenses after *total* variable expenses have been covered.

	Ticket Price	
	$16	**$20**
Sales revenue:		
9,000 × $16	$144,000	
6,000 × $20		$120,000
Less variable expenses:		
9,000 × $10	90,000	
6,000 × $10		60,000
Total contribution margin	$ 54,000	$ 60,000
Less fixed expenses	48,000	48,000
Profit	$ 6,000	$ 12,000

The difference in expected profit at the two ticket prices is due to two factors:

1. A different *unit* contribution margin, defined previously as *unit* sales price minus *unit* variable expenses
2. A different sales volume

Incremental Approach   Rather than presenting the entire income statement under each ticket price alternative, we can use a simpler incremental approach. This analysis focuses only on the difference in the total contribution margin under the two prices. Thus, the combined effect of the change in unit contribution margin and the change in sales volume is as follows:

Expected *total* contribution margin at $20 ticket price:	
6.000 × ($20 − $10)	$60,000
Expected *total* contribution margin at $16 ticket price:	
9.000 × ($16 − $10)	54,000
Difference in *total* contribution margin	$ 6,000

The $6,000 difference in expected profit, at the two ticket prices, is due to a $6,000 difference in the total contribution margin. The board of trustees will consider these projected profits as it decides which ticket price is best. Even though Toronto Contemporary Theatre is a nonprofit organization, it may still have legitimate reasons for attempting to make a profit on its theatre performances. For example, the board might use these profits to fund a free drama workshop, provide scholarships for local young people to study drama in college, or produce a free outdoor play for Toronto's residents.

Interdependent Changes in Key Variables

Sometimes a change in one key variable will cause a change in another key variable. Suppose the board of trustees is choosing between ticket prices of $16 and $20, and the business manager has projected demand as shown in the preceding section. A famous retired actress who lives in Toronto has offered to donate $10,000 per month to Toronto Contemporary Theatre if the board will set the ticket price at $16. The actress is interested in making the theatre's performances affordable by as many people as possible. The facts are now as follows:

Ticket Price	Unit Contribution Margin	Forecast Monthly Demand	Net Fixed Expenses (after subtracting donation)
$16	$ 6	9,000	$38,000 ($48,000 − $10,000)
20	10	6,000	48,000

The organization's expected profit at each price is computed as follows:

	Ticket Price	
	$16	**$20**
Sales revenue:		
9,000 × $16	$144,000	
6,000 × $20		$120,000
Less variable expenses:		
9,000 × $10	90,000	
6,000 × $10		60,000
Total contribution margin	$ 54,000	$ 60,000
Less fixed expenses	38,000	48,000
Profit	$ 16,000	$ 12,000

Now the difference in expected profit at the two ticket prices is due to three factors:

1. A different *unit* contribution margin
2. A different sales volume
3. A difference in the *net* fixed expenses, after deducting the donation

Incremental Approach   The combined effect of these factors is shown in the following analysis, which focuses on the effects of the price alternatives on the total contribution margin and the net fixed expenses:

Expected *total* contribution margin at $20 ticket price:	
6,000 × ($20 − $10)	$60,000
Expected *total* contribution margin at $16 ticket price:	
9,000 × ($16 − $10)	54,000
Difference in *total* contribution margin (higher with $20 ticket price)	$ 6,000
Net fixed expenses at $20 ticket price	$48,000
Net fixed expenses at $16 ticket price	38,000
Difference in net fixed expenses (higher with $20 ticket price)	$10,000

The expected total contribution margin is $6,000 higher with the $20 ticket price, but net fixed expenses are $10,000 higher. Thus, Toronto Contemporary Theatre will make $4,000 more in profit at the $16 price ($10,000 − $6,000).

CVP Information in Annual Reports

Cost-volume-profit relationships are so important to understanding an organization's operations that some companies disclose CVP information in their published annual reports. The Management Accounting Practice item here is from the airline industry.

AIRLINES KEEP A CLOSE EYE ON BREAK-EVEN LOAD FACTORS

"Air France has been able to make up for cutting Dallas and Miami flights with more flights and larger planes to African cities. The airline has also recently expanded its service to many French-speaking former destinations in the Caribbean and the Indian Ocean. Together with Africa, the former colonies should account for almost the same amount of Air France's revenue this year as North America, analysts say. Still, the operating costs of flying to Africa are 50 percent higher for Air France than flying to the U.S., and the logistical problems are much more challenging."

In past years, "Sabena [the former Belgian Airlines operating as Brussels Airlines since 2006] lost at least 8 percent on its flights to the U.S., but had margins above 10 percent on routes to its former colonies Congo, Rwanda, and Burundi, according to an internal Sabena study. That kind of difference in profit margins is common. Across the busy North Atlantic, where competition and seasonal variation force heavy discounting, all airlines are lucky to break even with a plane 75 percent full. For Kinshasa and other parts of Africa, where traffic is steadier, European carriers can break even with their planes barely 60 percent full, and planes often fly 85 percent full."[1]

Airlines generally disclose their system-wide break-even load factors in their annual reports. British Airways, for example, listed its break-even load factor as 64 percent in a recent annual report. The large airlines, like British Airways, usually fill a smaller percentage of their seats than the upstart, discount airlines. JetBlue is a good example. "The low-fare, low-cost carrier now operates more than 100 flights a day to 18 cities in nine states. Its load factor, or percentage of seats filled, is an industry-leading 78 percent."[2]

CVP Analysis with Multiple Products

Our CVP illustration for Toronto Contemporary Theatre has assumed that the organization has only one product, a theatre seat at a dramatic performance. Most firms have a *sales mix* consisting of more than one product, and this adds some complexity to their CVP analyses.

As we have seen, Toronto Contemporary Theatre's monthly fixed expenses total $48,000, and the unit variable expense per ticket is $10. Now suppose that the city of Toronto has agreed to refurbish 10 theatre boxes in the historic theatre building. Each box has five seats, which are more comfortable and afford a better view of the stage than the theatre's general seating. The board of trustees has decided to charge $16 per ticket for general seating and $20 per ticket for box seats. These facts are summarized as follows:

Seat Type	Ticket Price	Unit Variable Expense	Unit Contribution Margin	Seats in Theatre	Seats Available per Month (20 performances)
Regular	$16	$10	$ 6	450	9,000
Box	20	10	10	50	1,000

Notice that 90 percent of the available seats are regular seats, and 10 percent are box seats. The business manager estimates that tickets for each type of seat will be sold in the same proportion as the number of seats available. If, for example, 5,000 tickets are sold during a month, sales will be as follows:

Regular seats:	90% × 5,000	4,500
Box seats:	10% × 5,000	500
Total		5,000

For any organization selling multiple products, the relative proportion of each type of product *sold* is called the **sales mix**. The business manager's estimate of Toronto Contemporary Theatre's *sales mix* is 90 percent regular seats and 10 percent box seats.

The sales mix is an important assumption in multiproduct CVP analysis. The sales mix is used to compute a **weighted-average unit contribution margin**. This is the *average* of the several products' *unit contribution margins*, *weighted* by the relative sales proportion of each product. Toronto Contemporary Theatre's weighted-average unit contribution margin is computed below.

$$\begin{array}{l}\text{Weighted-average unit} \\ \text{contribution margin}\end{array} = (\$6 \times 90\%) + (\$10 \times 10\%) = \$6.40$$

The organization's break-even point in units is computed using the following formula:

$$\text{Break-even point} = \frac{\text{Fixed expenses}}{\begin{array}{c}\text{Weighted-average unit contribution} \\ \text{margin}\end{array}} \qquad (8)$$

$$= \frac{\$48,000}{\$6.40} = 7,500 \text{ tickets}$$

The break-even point of 7,500 tickets must be interpreted in light of the sales mix. Toronto Contemporary Theatre will break even for the month if it sells 7,500 tickets as follows:

Break-even sales in units		
Regular seats: 7,500 × 90%		6,750 tickets
Box seats: 7,500 × 10%		750 tickets
Total		7,500 tickets

The following income calculation verifies the break-even point.

Sales revenue:		
Regular seats: 6,750 × $16		$108,000
Box seats: 750 × $20		15,000
Total Revenue: 7,500 seats in total		$123,000
Less variable expenses: 7,500 × $10		75,000
Total contribution margin		$ 48,000
Less fixed expenses		48,000
Profit		$ 0

The break-even point of 7,500 tickets per month is *valid only for the sales mix assumed* in computing the weighted-average unit contribution margin. If 7,500 tickets are sold in any other mix of regular and box seats, the organization will not break even.

Notice that break-even formula (8) is a modification of formula (1) given earlier in the chapter. The only difference is that formula (8) uses the weighted-average unit contribution margin.

Toronto Contemporary Theatre's business manager has constructed the profit-volume graph in Exhibit 7–4. The PV graph shows the organization's profit at any level of total monthly sales, assuming the sales mix of 90 percent regular seats and 10 percent box seats. For example, if 9,000 tickets are sold in total, at the assumed sales mix, the PV graph indicates that profit will be $9,600.

With multiproduct CVP analysis, a managerial accountant can investigate the impact on profit of changes in sales volume, prices, variable costs, fixed costs, or the sales mix itself. For example, what would be the effect on Toronto Contemporary Theatre's break-even point if the sales mix were 95 percent regular seats and 5 percent

Exhibit 7–4
Profit-Volume Graph with
Multiple Products: Toronto
Contemporary Theatre

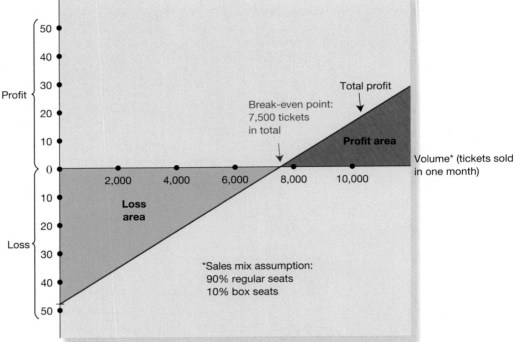

box seats? With this sales mix, the weighted-average unit contribution margin is computed as follows:

$$\text{Weighted-average unit contribution margin} = (\$6 \times 95\%) + (\$10 \times 5\%) = \$6.20$$

The break-even point increases from 7,500 tickets to approximately 7,742 tickets as a result of the lower proportion of expensive seats in the sales mix.

$$\text{Break-even point} = \frac{\text{Fixed expenses}}{\text{Weighted-average unit contribution margin}}$$

$$= \frac{\$48,000}{\$6.20} = 7,742 \text{ tickets*}$$

*Rounded.

Assumptions of CVP Analysis

For any cost-volume-profit analysis to be valid, the following important assumptions must be reasonably satisfied *within the relevant range*.

1. The behaviour of total revenue is linear (straight-line). This implies that the price of the product or service will not change as sales volume varies within the relevant range.
2. The behaviour of total expenses is linear (straight-line) over the relevant range. This implies the following more specific assumptions.
    a. Expenses can be categorized as fixed, variable, or mixed. *Total* fixed expenses remain constant as activity changes, and the *unit* variable expense remains unchanged as activity varies.
    b. The efficiency and productivity of the production process and workers remain constant.

3. In multiproduct organizations, the sales mix remains constant over the relevant range.

4. In manufacturing firms, the inventory levels at the beginning and end of the period are the same. This implies that the number of units produced during the period equals the number of units sold.

Cost-volume-profit analysis is based on the four general assumptions listed above as well as specific estimates of all the variables used in the analysis. Since these variables are rarely known with certainty, it is helpful to run a CVP analysis many times with different combinations of estimates. For example, Toronto Contemporary Theatre's business manager might do the CVP analysis using different estimates for the ticket prices, sales mix for regular and box seats, unit variable expenses, and fixed expenses. This approach is called **sensitivity analysis**, since it provides the analyst with a feel for how sensitive the analysis is to the estimates upon which it is based. The widespread availability of personal computers and electronic spreadsheet software has made sensitivity analysis relatively easy to do.

CVP Relationships and the Income Statement

The management functions of planning, control, and decision making all are facilitated by an understanding of cost-volume-profit relationships. These relationships are important enough to operating managers that some businesses prepare income statements in a way that highlights CVP issues. Before we examine this new income-statement format, we will review the more traditional income statement used in the preceding chapters.

Traditional Income Statement

An income statement for AccuTime Company, a manufacturer of digital clocks, is shown in Exhibit 7–5 (panel A). During 20x1 the firm manufactured and sold 20,000 clocks at a price of $25 each. This income statement is prepared in the traditional manner. *Cost of goods sold* includes both variable and fixed manufacturing costs, as measured by the firm's product-costing system. The *gross margin* is computed by subtracting cost of goods sold from sales. Selling and administrative expenses are then subtracted; each expense includes both variable and fixed costs. *The traditional income statement does not disclose the breakdown of each expense into its variable and fixed components.*

AccuTime

Contribution Income Statement

Many operating managers find the traditional income-statement format difficult to use, because it does not separate variable and fixed expenses. Instead they prefer the **contribution income statement**. A contribution income statement for AccuTime is shown in Exhibit 7–5 (panel B). *The contribution format highlights the distinction between variable and fixed expenses.* The variable manufacturing cost of each clock is $14, and the total fixed manufacturing cost is $100,000. On the contribution income statement, all variable expenses are subtracted from sales to obtain the *contribution margin*. For AccuTime, $200,000 remains from total sales revenue, after all variable costs have been covered, to contribute to covering fixed costs and making a profit. All fixed costs are then subtracted from the contribution margin to obtain net income.

Learning Objective **7**

Prepare and interpret a contribution income statement.

Comparison of Traditional and Contribution Income Statements

Operating managers frequently prefer the contribution income statement, because its separation of fixed and variable expenses highlights cost-volume-profit relationships. It is readily apparent from the contribution-format statement how income will be affected when sales volume changes by a given percentage. Suppose management projects that sales volume in 20x2 will be 20 percent greater

Exhibit 7–5
Income Statement: Traditional
and Contribution Formats

A. Traditional Format

ACCUTIME COMPANY
Income Statement
For the Year Ended December 31, 20x1

Sales		$500,000
Less: Cost of goods sold		380,000
Gross margin		$120,000
Less: Operating expenses:		
Selling expenses	$ 35,000	
Administrative expenses	35,000	70,000
Net income		$ 50,000

B. Contribution Format

ACCUTIME COMPANY
Income Statement
For the Year Ended December 31, 20x1

Sales		$500,000
Less: Variable expenses:		
Variable manufacturing	$280,000	
Variable selling	15,000	
Variable administrative	5,000	300,000
Contribution margin		$200,000
Less: Fixed expenses:		
Fixed manufacturing	$100,000	
Fixed selling	20,000	
Fixed administrative	30,000	150,000
Net income		$ 50,000

than in 20x1. No changes are anticipated in the sales price, variable cost per unit, or fixed costs. Examination of the contribution income statement shows that if sales volume increases by 20 percent, the following changes will occur. (Our discussion ignores income taxes, which are covered in the appendix at the end of this chapter.)

Income Statement Item	20x1 Amount	Change	20x2 Amount
Sales	$500,000	$100,000	$600,000
		(20% × $500,000)	
Total variable expenses	$300,000	$60,000	$360,000
		(20% × $300,000)	
Contribution margin	$200,000	$40,000	$240,000
		(20% × $200,000)	
Total fixed expenses	$150,000	–0–	$150,000
		(No change in fixed expenses when volume changes)	
Net income	$ 50,000	$40,000	$ 90,000
		(Income changes by the amount of the contribution-margin change)	

Notice that net income increases by the same amount as the increase in the contribution margin. Moreover, the contribution margin changes in direct proportion to the change in sales volume. These two facts enable us to calculate the increase in net income using the following shortcut. Recall that the *contribution-margin ratio* is the percentage of contribution margin to sales.

$$\left(\begin{array}{c}\text{Increase in}\\\text{sales revenue}\end{array}\right) \times \left(\begin{array}{c}\text{Contribution-margin}\\\text{ratio}\end{array}\right) = \left(\begin{array}{c}\text{Increase in}\\\text{net income}\end{array}\right)$$

$$\$100,000 \qquad \times \qquad .40 \qquad = \qquad \$40,000$$

$$\text{where} \qquad \left(\begin{array}{c}\text{Contribution-margin}\\\text{ratio}\end{array}\right) = \frac{\text{Contribution margin}}{\text{Sales revenue}}$$

$$.40 \qquad = \frac{\$200,000}{\$500,000}$$

The preceding analysis makes use of cost-volume-profit relationships that are disclosed in the contribution income statement. Such an analysis cannot be made with the information presented in the traditional income statement.

Cost Structure and Operating Leverage

The **cost structure** of an organization is the relative proportion of its fixed and variable costs. Cost structures differ widely among industries and among firms within an industry. A company using a computer-integrated manufacturing system has a large investment in plant and equipment, which results in a cost structure dominated by fixed costs. In contrast, a cleaning service firm's cost structure has a much higher proportion of variable costs. The highly automated manufacturing firm is capital-intensive, whereas the service firm is labour-intensive.

An organization's cost structure has a significant effect on the sensitivity of its profit to changes in volume. A convenient way to portray a firm's cost structure is shown in the Excel spreadsheet in Exhibit 7–6.[3] The data for AccuTime Company (company A) comes from the firm's 20X1 contribution income statement in Exhibit 7–5. For comparison purposes, two other firms' cost structures also are shown. Although these three firms have the same sales revenue ($500,000) and net income ($50,000), they have very different cost structures. Company B's production process is largely manual, and its cost structure is dominated by variable costs. It has a low contribution-margin ratio of only 20 percent. In contrast, company C employs a highly automated production process, and its cost structure is dominated by fixed costs. The firm's contribution-margin ratio is 90 percent. Company A falls between these two extremes with a contribution-margin ratio of 40 percent.

Suppose sales revenue increases by 10 percent, or $50,000, in each company. The resulting increase in each company's profit is calculated in Exhibit 7–7.

Notice that company B, with its high variable expenses and low contribution-margin ratio, shows a relatively low *percentage* increase in profit. In contrast, the high fixed expenses and large contribution-margin ratio of company C result in a relatively high *percentage* increase in profit. Company A falls in between these two extremes.

To summarize, the greater the proportion of fixed costs in a firm's cost structure, the greater the impact on profit will be from a given percentage change in sales revenue.

Learning Objective 8

Explain the role of cost structure and operating leverage in CVP relationships.

	A	B	C	D	E	F	G
1		Company A		Company B		Company C	
2		(AccuTime Company)		(Manual System)		(Automated System)	
3							
4		Amount	%	Amount	%	Amount	%
5							
6	Sales	$ 500,000	100	$ 500,000	100	$ 500,000	100
7	Variable expenses	300,000	60	400,000	80	50,000	10
8	Contribution margin	$ 200,000	40	$ 100,000	20	$ 450,000	90
9	Fixed expenses	150,000	30	50,000	10	400,000	80
10	Net income	$ 50,000	10	$ 50,000	10	$ 50,000	10

Exhibit 7–6

Comparison of Cost Structures

 AccuTime

Exhibit 7–7

Effect on Profit of Increase in Sales Revenue

 AccuTime

	$\left(\begin{array}{c}\text{Increase}\\\text{In Sales}\\\text{Revenue}\end{array}\right)$	$\times$	$\left(\begin{array}{c}\text{Contribution}\\\text{Margin}\\\text{Ratio}\end{array}\right)$	$=$	$\left(\begin{array}{c}\text{Increase}\\\text{In Net}\\\text{Income}\end{array}\right)$	Percentage Increase in Net Income
Company A (AccuTime)	$50,000	$\times$	40%	$=$	$20,000	40% ($20,000 ÷ $50,000)
Company B (high variable expenses) ...	$50,000	$\times$	20%	$=$	$10,000	20% ($10,000 ÷ $50,000)
Company C (high fixed expenses)	$50,000	$\times$	90%	$=$	$45,000	90% ($45,000 ÷ $50,000)

Operating Leverage

The extent to which an organization uses fixed costs in its cost structure is called **operating leverage**. The operating leverage is greatest in firms with a large proportion of fixed costs, low proportion of variable costs, and the resulting high contribution-margin ratio. Exhibit 7–6 shows that company B has low operating leverage, company C has high operating leverage, and company A falls in between. To a physical scientist, *leverage* refers to the ability of a small force to move a heavy weight. To the managerial accountant, *operating leverage* refers to the ability of the firm to generate an increase in net income when sales revenue increases.

Measuring Operating Leverage   The managerial accountant can measure a firm's operating leverage, *at a particular sales volume*, using the **operating leverage factor**:

$$\text{Operating leverage factor} = \frac{\text{Contribution margin}}{\text{Net income}}$$

Using the data in Exhibit 7–6, the operating leverage factors of companies A, B, and C are computed as follows:

	$\left(\begin{array}{c}\text{Contribution}\\\text{Margin}\end{array}\right)$	$\div$	$\left(\begin{array}{c}\text{Net}\\\text{Income}\end{array}\right)$	$=$	$\left(\begin{array}{c}\text{Operating}\\\text{Leverage}\\\text{Factor}\end{array}\right)$
Company A (AccuTime)	$200,000	$\div$	$50,000	$=$	4
Company B (high variable expenses)	$100,000	$\div$	$50,000	$=$	2
Company C (high fixed expenses)	$450,000	$\div$	$50,000	$=$	9

The operating leverage factor is a measure, at a particular level of sales, of the *percentage* impact on net income of a given *percentage* change in sales revenue. Multiplying the *percentage* change in sales revenue by the operating leverage factor yields the *percentage* change in net income.

	$\left(\begin{array}{c}\text{Percentage}\\\text{Increase in}\\\text{Sales Revenue}\end{array}\right)$	$\times$	$\left(\begin{array}{c}\text{Operating}\\\text{Leverage}\\\text{Factor}\end{array}\right)$	$=$	$\left(\begin{array}{c}\text{Percentage}\\\text{Change in}\\\text{Net Income}\end{array}\right)$
Company A (AccuTime)	10%	$\times$	4	$=$	40%
Company B (high variable expenses)	10%	$\times$	2	$=$	20%
Company C (high fixed expenses)	10%	$\times$	9	$=$	90%

The percentage change in net income shown above for each company may be verified by re-examining Exhibit 7–7.

Break-Even Point and Safety Margin   A firm's operating leverage also affects its break-even point. Since a firm with relatively high operating leverage has proportionally high fixed expenses, the firm's break-even point will be relatively high. This fact is illustrated using the data from Exhibit 7–6.

	$\left(\begin{array}{c}\text{Fixed}\\\text{Expenses}\end{array}\right)$	÷	$\left(\begin{array}{c}\text{Contribution}\\\text{Margin Ratio}\end{array}\right)$	=	$\left(\begin{array}{c}\text{Break-Even}\\\text{Sales Revenue}\end{array}\right)$
Company A (AccuTime)	$150,000	÷	40%	=	$375,000
Company B (high variable expenses)	$ 50,000	÷	20%	=	$250,000
Company C (high fixed expenses)	$400,000	÷	90%	=	$444,444*

*Rounded.

The safety margin also is affected by a firm's operating leverage. Suppose the budgeted sales revenue for each of the three companies is $500,000. Then the safety margin, defined as budgeted sales revenue minus break-even sales revenue, is calculated as follows:

	Budgeted Sales Revenue	Break-Even Sales Revenue	Safety Margin
Company A (AccuTime)	$500,000	$375,000	$125,000
Company B (high variable expenses)	500,000	250,000	250,000
Company C (high fixed expenses)	500,000	444,444	55,556

M anagement
A ccounting
P ractice

Expedia,
Hotels.com,
eBay,
and Overture Services

OPERATING LEVERAGE HELPS THESE WEB COMPANIES BECOME PROFITABLE

"Four Web companies made a recent ranking of the Info Tech One Hundred: search engine Overture Services, auctioneer eBay, discount-hotel broker Hotels.com, and travel site Expedia." That's up from only one, and all of them are profitable. "The leaders of the Web pack are starting to show that once they turn profitable, they can quickly become big moneymakers. The reason is operating leverage. That's accounting-speak for a simple concept: Once you invest enough to build a Web site and your basic operations, you don't need to spend much money as sales rise. After you cover your fixed costs, the expense of processing each sale is so little that profits grow faster than revenues. That philosophy made for big Internet losses early on." The payoff, however, is at hand.

"Online travel agency Expedia Inc. is a textbook example of leverage in action." In one quarter alone, "Expedia doubled its sales, to $116 million. Yet its overhead, including administrative and marketing costs, rose only 8 percent, to $63 million. One big reason is that the company already had paid for the computing gear it needed to handle the higher volume of ticket sales."

Just a few years after the boom in e-commerce IPOs, "a clear pecking order of profitability has emerged. The biggest moneymakers: online travel, software, and financial-services firms. "Why did these online companies turn profitable first? "Because software, financial services, and travel reservations are pure information products, without a physical widget to store or ship. Once overhead costs are covered, the expense in providing the service to one more customer is close to zero. Online retailers are making slower, yet tangible, progress toward profitability. What's holding Amazon.com Inc. and other e-tailers back is simple: Every time someone buys a book on Amazon, the company has to buy a new copy from the publisher. The upshot is that Amazon's gross margins are around 26 percent, compared with 70 percent at Expedia."

Every year, Web business writes a different story, "but now it's past the point where predictions of profitability are written in sand. Some Web businesses do work. The proof is in the black ink."[4]

Exhibit 7–8
Labour-Intensive Production
Processes versus Advanced
Manufacturing Systems

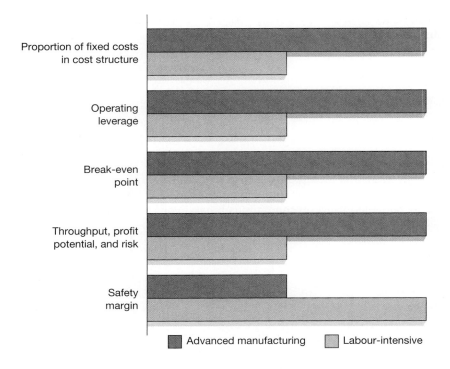

To summarize, company C's high fixed expenses result in a high break-even point and low safety margin. Company B displays the opposite characteristics, and company A falls in between the two extremes.

Labour-Intensive Production Processes versus Advanced Manufacturing Systems   The effects of labour-intensive (manual) production processes and highly automated, advanced manufacturing systems illustrated by companies A, B, and C are typical. As Exhibit 7–8 shows, a movement toward an advanced manufacturing environment often results in a higher break-even point, lower safety margin, and higher operating leverage. However, high-technology manufacturing systems generally have greater throughput, thus allowing greater potential for profitability. Along with the increased potential for profitability comes increased risk. In an economic recession, for example, a highly automated company with high fixed costs will be less able to adapt to lower consumer demand than will a firm with a more labour-intensive production process.

Indifference Analysis   We have seen that the use of CVP analysis as a tool for decisions regarding the profitability of individual products. CVP analysis is also useful in comparing the profitability of various products or methods of production. As we discussed in the previous section, a product manufactured in an environment with high fixed costs will result in a higher break-even point and require a higher sales activity level to generate a profit than will a product manufactured in an environment with low fixed costs and comparatively high variable costs. Hence, CVP analysis helps to compare alternative manufacturing environment with different cost structures.

To illustrate, we can use the information provided in Exhibit 7–6 and calculate the indifference point (denoted by Q) between using a labour intensive production system (company B) or a capital-intensive production system (company C). Let us assume that both companies sold 10,000 units during 20X1.

1. Determine the total costs (variable and fixed) of each alternative.
   Company B: ($400,000 ÷ 10,000 units)$Q$ + $50,000
   Company C: ($50,000 ÷ 10,000 units)$Q$ + $400,000

2. Set up an equation with each cost alternative on opposite sides of the equation and solve for Q.

$$\$40Q + \$50,000 = \$5Q + \$400,000$$
$$\$35Q = \$350,000$$
$$Q = 10,000 \text{ units}$$

Note that Q is indeed the indifference point since, as shown on Exhibit 7–6, both companies would have a profit of $50,000 for this activity sales level. At sales level below Q, profitability will be higher the labour-intensive production system (company B). Sales above Q will result in higher profitability for the capital-intensive production system (company C), because company C's contribution margin ratio (90%) is higher than company B's contribution margin ratio (20%).

Cost Structure and Operating Leverage: A Cost-Benefit Issue

An organization's cost structure plays an important role in determining its cost-volume-profit relationships. A firm with proportionately high fixed costs has relatively high operating leverage. The result of high operating leverage is that the firm can generate a large percentage increase in net income from a relatively small percentage increase in sales revenue. On the other hand, a firm with high operating leverage has a relatively high break-even point. This entails some risk to the firm.

The optimal cost structure for an organization involves a trade-off. Management must weigh the benefits of high operating leverage against the risks of large committed fixed costs and the associated high break-even point.

CVP Analysis, ABC, and Advanced Manufacturing Systems

Traditional CVP analysis focuses on the number of units sold as the only cost and revenue driver. Sales revenue is assumed to be linear in units sold. Moreover, costs are categorized as fixed or variable, with respect to the number of units sold, within the relevant range. This approach is consistent with traditional product-costing systems, in which cost assignment is based on a single, volume-related cost driver. In CVP analysis, as in product costing, the traditional approach can be misleading or provide less than adequate information for various management purposes. An ABC system can provide a much more complete picture of cost-volume-profit relationships and thus provide better information to managers.

To illustrate the potential impact of ABC on CVP analysis, we will use the following information from AccuTime Company, a manufacturer of digital clocks:

> **Learning Objective 9**
>
> Understand the implications of activity-based costing for CVP analysis.

 AccuTime

Sales volume	20,000 units
Sales price	$25
Unit variable costs:	
Variable manufacturing	$14
Variable selling and administrative	1
Total unit variable cost	$15
Unit contribution margin	$10
Fixed costs:	
Fixed manufacturing	$100,000
Fixed selling and administrative	50,000
Total fixed costs	$150,000

These data are adequate for a traditional CVP analysis of various questions management may ask. For example, the break-even point is easily calculated as 15,000 units, as the following analysis shows:

$$\text{Break-even point} = \frac{\text{Fixed costs}}{\text{Unit contribution margin}} = \frac{\$150,000}{\$10} = 15,000 \text{ units}$$

Alternatively, management may determine how many clocks must be sold to earn a target net profit of $200,000, as the following calculation demonstrates:

$$\frac{\text{Sales volume required to earn}}{\text{target net profit of \$200,000}} = \frac{\text{Fixed costs} + \text{Target net profit}}{\text{Unit contribution margin}}$$

$$= \frac{\$150,000 + \$200,000}{\$10} = 35,000 \text{ units}$$

What do these questions have in common? They both focus on *sales volume* as the sole revenue and cost driver. The CVP analysis depends on a distinction between costs that are fixed and costs that are variable *with respect to sales volume.*

Pictured here is a production cell in a flexible manufacturing system engaged in the production of disks for computer hard disk drives. In such a high-tech manufacturing environment, setups are quicker and more frequent, and production runs are smaller. An activity-based costing CVP analysis will give management a better understanding of cost-volume-profit relationships.

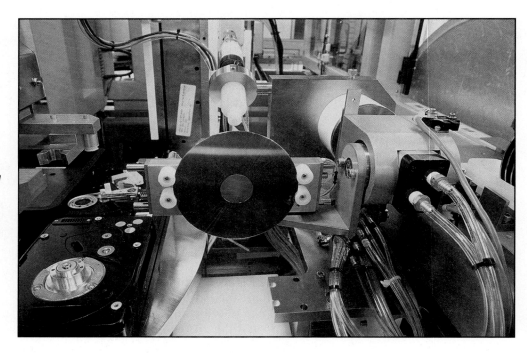

A Move toward JIT and Flexible Manufacturing

Learning Objective 10

Be aware of the effects of advanced manufacturing technology on CVP relationships.

Now let's examine another question AccuTime's management might face. Suppose management is considering the installation of a *flexible manufacturing system* and a move toward just-in-time (JIT) production. A flexible manufacturing system uses highly automated material-handling and production equipment to manufacture a variety of similar products. In the new production process, setups would be quicker and more frequent and production runs would be smaller. Fewer inspections would be required, due to the total quality control (TQC) philosophy that often accompanies JIT. Variable manufacturing costs would be lower, due to savings in direct labour. Finally, general factory overhead costs would increase, due to the greater depreciation charges on the new production equipment.

Suppose management wants to answer the same two questions addressed previously, under the assumption that the production process changes are adopted. To properly address this issue, we need a much more detailed understanding of the impact of other, *non-volume-based cost drivers* on AccuTime's costs. This type of detail is the hallmark of an activity-based costing system. Suppose AccuTime's controller

Sales price	$25
Unit variable costs:	
Variable manufacturing	$14
Variable selling and administrative	1
Total unit variable costs	$15
Unit contribution margin	$10
Fixed costs (fixed with respect to sales volume):	
General factory overhead (including depreciation on plant and equipment)	$ 60,000
Setup (52 setups at $100 per setup)*	5,200
Inspection (52 × 21 inspections at $20 per inspection)†	21,840
Material handling (1,080 hours at $12 per hour)	12,960
Total fixed manufacturing costs	$100,000
Fixed selling and administrative costs	50,000
Total fixed costs	$150,000

*One setup per week.

†Three inspections per day, seven days a week (52 weeks per year).

Exhibit 7–9

Activity-Based Costing Data under Current Production Process (20x1)

completes an ABC analysis of the company's 20x1 activity before the new equipment is installed. The results are shown in Exhibit 7–9.

There is a subtle but important point to realize about the cost behaviour depicted in Exhibit 7–9. Setup, inspection, and material handling are listed as fixed costs. *They are largely fixed with respect to sales volume.* However, they are *not* fixed with respect to *other cost drivers*, such as the number of setups, inspections, and hours of material handling. This is the fundamental distinction between a traditional CVP analysis and an activity-based costing CVP analysis. The traditional CVP analysis recognizes a single, volume-based cost driver, namely, sales volume. The activity-based costing CVP analysis recognizes multiple cost drivers. As a result, some costs viewed as fixed under the traditional analysis are considered variable (with respect to the appropriate cost drivers) under the ABC approach.

Now let's return to management's decision regarding the installation of a flexible manufacturing system and the adoption of the JIT and TQC philosophies. The ABC analysis of the proposed production technology is displayed in Exhibit 7–10. Due to the decreased use of direct labour, the unit variable manufacturing cost has declined from $14 to $9, thus bringing the total unit variable cost down to $10. This results in an increase in the unit contribution margin to $15. The installation of sophisticated

Sales price	$25
Unit variable costs:	
Variable manufacturing	$ 9
Variable selling and administrative	1
Total unit variable costs	$10
Unit contribution margin	$15
Fixed costs (fixed with respect to sales volume):	
General factory overhead (including depreciation on plant and equipment)	$184,000
Setup (365 setups at $30 per setup)	10,950
Inspection (365 inspections at $10 per inspection)	3,650
Material handling (100 hours at $14 per hour)	1,400
Total fixed manufacturing costs	$200,000
Fixed selling and administrative costs	50,000
Total fixed costs	$250,000

Exhibit 7–10

Activity-Based Costing Data under Proposed Production Technology

new manufacturing equipment has more than tripled general factory overhead, from $60,000 to $184,000. Under the proposed JIT approach, setups will be daily instead of weekly; each setup will be quicker and less expensive. As a result of the emphasis on total quality control, only one inspection per day will be necessary, instead of three as before. Moreover, each inspection will be less expensive. Finally, the amount of material-handling activity will decline dramatically, although there will be a slight increase in the cost per hour. This is due to the higher skill grade of labour required to operate the new automated material-handling system.

Using the ABC data in Exhibit 7–10, we can answer the two CVP questions posed by management. If the new production technology is adopted, the following CVP computations will be appropriate:

$$\text{Break-even point} = \frac{\text{Fixed costs}}{\text{Unit contribution margin}} = \frac{\$250,000}{\$15} = \frac{16,667 \text{ units}}{\text{(rounded)}}$$

$$\frac{\text{Sales volume required to earn}}{\text{target net profit of } \$200,000} = \frac{\text{Fixed costs} + \text{Target net profit}}{\text{Unit contribution margin}}$$

$$= \frac{\$250,000 + \$200,000}{\$15} = 30,000 \text{ units}$$

Notice that AccuTime's break-even point increased with the introduction of the advanced manufacturing system (from 15,000 to 16,667 units). However, the number of sales units required to earn a target net profit of $200,000 declined (from 35,000 to 30,000 units). These kinds of CVP changes are typical when firms install an advanced manufacturing system. Typically, the cost structure of an advanced manufacturing environment is characterized by a lower proportion of variable costs and a larger proportion of costs that are fixed (with respect to sales volume).

ABC Provides a Richer Understanding of Cost Behaviour and CVP Relationships   The important point in this section is that ABC provides a richer description of a company's cost behaviour. AccuTime's traditional costing system treated setup, inspection, and material handling as fixed costs. However, the ABC analysis showed that while these costs are largely fixed with respect to sales volume, they are not fixed with respect to other appropriate cost drivers. In analyzing the cost-volume-profit implications of the proposed changes in manufacturing technology, it was crucial to have an understanding of how these costs would change with respect to such cost drivers as the number of setups, number of inspections, and amount of material-handling activity.

Just as ABC can improve an organization's product-costing system, it also can facilitate a deeper understanding of cost behaviour and CVP relationships.

Chapter Summary

An understanding of cost-volume-profit relationships is necessary for the successful management of any enterprise. CVP analysis provides a sweeping overview of the effects on profit of all kinds of changes in sales volume, expenses, product mix, and sales prices. Calculation of the sales volume required to break even or earn a target net profit provides an organization's management with valuable information for planning and decision making.

An organization's cost structure has an important impact on its CVP relationships. The cost structure of an organization defines its operating leverage, which determines the impact on profit of changes in sales volume.

Activity-based costing can provide a richer description of an organization's cost behaviour and CVP relationships than is provided by a traditional costing system. An ABC cost-volume-profit analysis recognizes that some costs that are fixed with respect to sales volume may not be fixed with respect to other important cost drivers. In many cases, management can benefit substantially from such an improved understanding of cost behaviour and relationships.

Review Problem on Cost-Volume-Profit Analysis

Overlook Inn is a small bed-and-breakfast located on Vancouver island. The charge is $50 per person for one night's lodging and a full breakfast in the morning. The retired couple who own and manage the B&B estimate that the variable expense per person is $20. This includes such expenses as food, maid service, and utilities. The B&B's fixed expenses total $42,000 per year. The B&B can accommodate 10 guests each night.

Required: Compute the following:

1. Contribution margin per unit of service (a unit of service is one night's lodging for one guest)
2. Contribution-margin ratio
3. Annual break-even point in units of service and in dollars of service revenue
4. The number of units of service required to earn a target net profit of $60,000 for the year (ignore income taxes)

Solution to Review Problem

1. Contribution margin per unit of service = Nightly room charge − Variable expense per person

$$\$30 \qquad = \qquad \$50 \qquad - \qquad \$20$$

2. $\text{Contribution-margin ratio} = \dfrac{\text{Contribution margin per unit}}{\text{Nightly room charge}}$

$$.60 \qquad = \dfrac{\$30}{\$50}$$

3. $\dfrac{\text{Break-even point}}{\text{in units of service}} = \dfrac{\text{Fixed expenses}}{\text{Contribution margin per unit}}$

$$1,400 = \dfrac{\$42,000}{\$30}$$

$\dfrac{\text{Break-even point in}}{\text{dollars of revenue}} = \dfrac{\text{Fixed expenses}}{\text{Contribution-margin ratio}}$

$$\$70,000 \quad = \dfrac{\$42,000}{.60}$$

4. $\dfrac{\text{Number of units of service}}{\text{required to earn target net profit}} = \dfrac{\text{Fixed expenses} + \text{Target net profit}}{\text{Contribution margin per unit of service}}$

$$3,400 \qquad = \dfrac{\$42,000 + \$60,000}{\$30}$$

Key Terms

For each term's definition refer to the indicated page, or turn to the glossary at the end of the text.

after-tax net income,* 268
before-tax income,* 268
break-even point, 242
contribution income
  statement, 257
contribution-margin
  ratio, 244

cost structure, 259
cost-volume-profit (CVP)
  analysis, 241
cost-volume-profit (CVP)
  graph, 245
operating leverage, 260
operating leverage factor, 260

profit-volume graph, 247
safety margin, 250
sales mix, 255
sensitivity analysis, 257
target net profit (or income),
  248

total contribution margin,
  243
unit contribution margin, 243
weighted-average unit
  contribution margin, 255

*Term appears in the Appendix to this chapter.

APPENDIX TO CHAPTER 7

Effect of Income Taxes

Profit-seeking enterprises must pay income taxes on their profits. A firm's **after-tax net income**, the amount of income remaining after subtracting the firm's income-tax expense, is less than its **before-tax income**. This fact is expressed in the following formula:

$$(\text{After-tax net income}) = (\text{Before-tax income}) - t(\text{Before-tax income})$$

where t denotes the income-tax rate

Rearranging this equation yields the following formula:

$$(\text{After-tax net income}) = (\text{Before-tax income})(1 - t) \tag{9}$$

To illustrate this formula, suppose AccuTime Company must pay income taxes of 40 percent of its before-tax income. The company's contribution income statement for 20x1 appears below.

Sales, 20,000 units at $25 each	$500,000
Variable expenses, 20,000 units at $15 each*	300,000
Contribution margin	$200,000
Fixed expenses	150,000
Income before taxes	$ 50,000
Income-tax expense, .40 × $50,000	20,000
Net income, $50,000 × (1 − .40)	$ 30,000

*Variable cost per unit is $15: variable manufacturing cost of $14 plus variable selling and administrative costs of $1.

The requirement that companies pay income taxes affects their cost-volume-profit relationships. To earn a particular after-tax net income will require greater before-tax income than if there were no tax. For example, if AccuTime's target after-tax net income were $30,000, the company would have to earn before-tax income of $50,000. AccuTime's income statement shows this relationship.

How much before-tax income must be earned in order to achieve a particular target after-tax net income? Rearranging equation (9) above yields the following formula:

$$\begin{pmatrix} \text{Target} \\ \text{after-tax} \\ \text{net income} \end{pmatrix} = \begin{pmatrix} \text{Target} \\ \text{before-tax} \\ \text{income} \end{pmatrix}(1 - t)$$

Divide both sides by $(1 - t)$

$$\frac{\begin{pmatrix} \text{Target} \\ \text{after-tax} \\ \text{net income} \end{pmatrix}}{1 - t} = \begin{pmatrix} \text{Target} \\ \text{before-tax} \\ \text{income} \end{pmatrix}\frac{1 - t}{1 - t}$$

$$\frac{\begin{pmatrix} \text{Target} \\ \text{after-tax} \\ \text{net income} \end{pmatrix}}{1 - t} = \begin{matrix} \text{Target} \\ \text{before-tax} \\ \text{income} \end{matrix}$$

If AccuTime Company's target after-tax net income is $30,000, its target before-tax income is calculated as follows:

$$\frac{\begin{matrix}\text{Target after-tax}\\ \text{net income}\end{matrix}}{1 - t} = \frac{\$30,000}{1 - .40} = \$50,000 = \text{Target before-tax income}$$

Now we are in a position to compute the number of digital clocks that AccuTime must sell in order to achieve a particular after-tax net income. We begin with the following before-tax income equation:

$$\text{Sales} - \text{Variable expenses} - \text{Fixed expenses} = \text{Before-tax income}$$

Now we use our formula for before-tax income:

$$\text{Sales} - \text{Variable expenses} - \text{Fixed expenses} = \frac{\text{After-tax net income}}{1 - t}$$

$$\left[\binom{\text{Unit}}{\substack{\text{sales} \\ \text{price}}} \times \binom{\text{Sales}}{\substack{\text{volume} \\ \text{in units}}}\right] - \left[\binom{\text{Unit}}{\substack{\text{variable} \\ \text{expense}}} \times \binom{\text{Sales}}{\substack{\text{volume} \\ \text{in units}}}\right] - \binom{\text{Fixed}}{\text{expenses}} = \frac{\substack{\text{After-tax} \\ \text{net income}}}{1 - t}$$

Using the data for AccuTime Company, and assuming target after-tax net income of $30,000:

$$(\$25 \times X) - (\$15 \times X) - \$150,000 = \frac{\$30,000}{1 - .40}$$

where X denotes the number of units that must be sold to achieve the target after-tax net income

Now we solve for X as follows:

$$(\$25 - \$15) \times X = \$150,000 + \frac{\$30,000}{1 - .40}$$

$$\$10 \quad \times X = \$150,000 + \frac{\$30,000}{1 - .40}$$

$$X = \frac{\$150,000 + \dfrac{\$30,000}{1 - .40}}{\$10}$$

$$= 20,000 \text{ units}$$

In terms of sales revenue, AccuTime must achieve a sales volume of $500,000 (20,000 units $\times$ $25 sales price). We can verify these calculations by examining AccuTime's income statement given previously.

AccuTime Company

Exhibit 7–11
Cost-Volume-Profit Graph
(with income taxes)

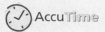

$000 (per year)

- Total revenue
- Break-even point: 15,000 units or $375,000 of sales
- Total expenses
- Total variable expenses for 20,000 units (at $15 per unit), $300,000
- Before-tax income for 20,000 units of sales, $50,000*
- Total fixed expenses per year, $150,000

Volume (digital clocks sold in one year): 5,000 · 10,000 · 15,000 · 20,000 · 25,000 · 30,000

Sales volume required to achieve after-tax net income of $30,000*

*(Before-tax income) $\times$ (1 − Tax rate) = After-tax income
$50,000 $\times$ (1 − .40) = $30,000

Notice in the calculations above that $10 is the unit contribution margin ($25 sales price minus $15 variable expense). Thus, the general formula illustrated above is the following:

$$\begin{array}{c}\text{Number of units of sales}\\\text{required to earn target}\\\text{after-tax net income}\end{array} = \frac{\text{Fixed expenses} + \dfrac{\text{Target after-tax net income}}{1 - t}}{\text{Unit contribution margin}}$$

where t denotes the income tax rate

A cost-volume-profit graph for AccuTime Company is displayed in Exhibit 7–11. As the graph shows, 20,000 units must be sold to achieve $30,000 in after-tax net income. The company's break-even point is 15,000 units. The break-even point is not affected by income taxes, because at the break-even point, there is no income.

Notice that AccuTime Company must sell 5,000 units *beyond the break-even point* in order to achieve after-tax net income of $30,000. Each unit sold beyond the break-even point contributes $10 toward *before-tax* income. However, of that $10 contribution margin, $4 will have to be paid in income taxes. This leaves an *after-tax contribution* of $6 toward after-tax net income. Thus, selling 5,000 units beyond the break-even point results in after-tax net income of $30,000 (5,000 units × $6 after-tax contribution per unit).

Review Questions

7–1. Briefly explain each of the following methods of computing a break-even point in units: (*a*) contribution-margin approach, (*b*) equation approach, and (*c*) graphical approach.

7–2. What is the meaning of the term *unit contribution margin*? Contribution to what?

7–3. What information is conveyed by a cost-volume-profit graph in addition to a company's break-even point?

7–4. What does the term *safety margin* mean?

7–5. Suppose the fixed expenses of a travel agency increase. What will happen to its break-even point, measured in number of clients served? Why?

7–6. Delmarva Oyster Company has been able to decrease its variable expenses per kilogram of oysters harvested. How will this affect the firm's break-even sales volume?

7–7. In a strategy meeting, a manufacturing company's president said, "If we raise the price of our product, the company's break-even point will be lower." The financial vice-president responded by saying, "Then we should raise our price. The company will be less likely to incur a loss." Do you agree with the president? Why? Do you agree with the vice-president? Why?

7–8. What will happen to a company's break-even point if the sales price and unit variable cost of its only product increase by the same dollar amount?

7–9. An art museum covers its operating expenses by charging a small admission fee. The objective of the non-profit organization is to break even. A local arts enthusiast has just pledged an annual donation of $10,000 to the museum. How will the donation affect the museum's break-even attendance level?

7–10. How can a profit-volume graph be used to predict a company's profit for a particular sales volume?

7–11. List the most important assumptions of cost-volume-profit analysis.

7–12. Why do many operating managers prefer a contribution income statement instead of a traditional income statement?

7–13. What is the difference between a manufacturing company's *gross margin* and its total *contribution margin*?

7–14. East Company manufactures DVDs using a completely automated production process. West Company also manufactures DVDs, but its products are assembled manually. How will these two firms' cost structures differ? Which company will have a higher operating leverage factor?

7–15. When sales volume increases, which company will experience a larger percentage increase in profit: company X, which has mostly fixed expenses, or company Y, which has mostly variable expenses?

7–16. What does the term *sales mix* mean? How is a *weighted-average unit contribution margin* computed?

7–17. A car rental agency rents subcompact, compact, and full-size automobiles. What assumptions would be made about the agency's sales mix for the purpose of a cost-volume-profit analysis?

7–18. How can a hotel's management use cost-volume-profit analysis to help in deciding on room rates?

7–19. How could cost-volume-profit analysis be used in budgeting? In making a decision about advertising?

7–20. Two companies have identical fixed expenses, unit variable expenses, and profits. Yet one company has set a much lower price for its product. Explain how this can happen.

7–21. A company with an advanced manufacturing environment typically will have a higher break-even point, greater operating leverage, and larger safety margin than a labour-intensive firm. True or false? Explain.

7–22. Explain briefly how activity-based costing (ABC) affects cost-volume-profit analysis.

Exercises

Fill in the missing data for each of the following independent cases. (Ignore income taxes.)

	Sales Revenue	Variable Expenses	Total Contribution Margin	Fixed Expenses	Net Income	Break-Even Sales Revenue
1.	?	$120,000	$240,000	?	$150,000	?
2.	$ 55,000	11,000	?	?	19,000	?
3.	?	80,000	?	$60,000	?	$ 80,000
4.	160,000	?	30,000	?	?	160,000

Exercise 7–23
Fill in Blanks; Basic CVP Relationships
(LO 1)

University Pizza delivers pizzas to the dormitories and apartments near a major university. The company's annual fixed expenses are $54,000. The sales price of a pizza is $10, and it costs the company $6 to make and deliver each pizza. (In the following requirements, ignore income taxes.)

Required:

1. Using the contribution-margin approach, compute the company's break-even point in units (pizzas).
2. What is the contribution-margin ratio?
3. Compute the break-even sales revenue. Use the contribution-margin ratio in your calculation.
4. How many pizzas must the company sell to earn a target net profit of $60,000? Use the equation method.

Exercise 7–24
Basic CVP Analysis; Pizza Delivery Business
(LO 1, 2, 4)

Rosario Company, which is located in Buenos Aires, Argentina, manufactures a component used in farm machinery. The firm's fixed costs are 2,000,000 p per year. The variable cost of each component is 1,000 p, and the components are sold for 1,500 p each. The company sold 7,000 components during the prior year. (p denotes the peso, Argentina's national currency. Several countries use the peso as their monetary unit. On the day this exercise was written, Argentina's peso was worth .314 Canadian dollar. In the following requirements, ignore income taxes.)

Required: Answer requirements (1) through (4) independently.

1. Compute the break-even point in units.
2. What will the new break-even point be if fixed costs increase by 5 percent?
3. What was the company's net income for the prior year?
4. The sales manager believes that a reduction in the sales price to 1,400 p will result in orders for 1,000 more components each year. What will the break-even point be if the price is changed?
5. Should the price change discussed in requirement (4) be made?

Exercise 7–25
Using CVP Analysis; Manufacturing
(LO 1, 4)

A minor-league hockey team plays their weekly games in a small stadium just outside Richmond. The stadium holds 6,000 people and tickets sell for $20 each. The franchise owner estimates that the team's annual fixed expenses are $360,000, and the variable expense per ticket sold is $2. (In the following requirements, ignore income taxes.)

Required:

1. Draw a cost-volume-profit graph for the sports franchise. Label the axes, break-even point, profit and loss areas, fixed expenses, variable expenses, total-expense line, and total-revenue line.
2. If the stadium is two-thirds full for each game, how many games must the team play to break even?

Exercise 7–26
CVP Graph; Sports Franchise
(LO 3, 4)

Refer to the data given in the preceding exercise. (Ignore income taxes.)

Required:

1. Prepare a fully labelled profit-volume graph for the hockey team.
2. What is the safety margin for the hockey franchise if the team plays a 10-game season and the team owner expects the stadium to be 45 percent full for each game?
3. If the team plays a 10-game season and the stadium is 40 percent half full for each game, what ticket price would the team have to charge in order to break even?

Exercise 7–27
Continuation of Preceding Exercise; Profit-Volume Graph; Safety Margin
(LO 3, 4)

■ **Exercise 7–28**
Contribution Income
Statement; Publishing
(LO 7, 8)

Pacific Rim Publications, Inc. specializes in reference books that keep abreast of the rapidly changing political and economic issues in the Pacific Rim countries. The results of the company's operations during the prior year are given in the following table. All units produced during the year were sold. (Ignore income taxes.)

Sales revenue	$1,000,000
Manufacturing costs:	
Fixed	250,000
Variable	500,000
Selling costs:	
Fixed	25,000
Variable	50,000
Administrative costs:	
Fixed	60,000
Variable	15,000

Required:

1. Prepare a traditional income statement and a contribution income statement for the company.
2. What is the firm's operating leverage for the sales volume generated during the prior year?
3. Suppose sales revenue increases by 12 percent. What will be the percentage increase in net income?
4. Which income statement would an operating manager use to answer requirement (3)? Why?

■ **Exercise 7–29**
CVP Analysis with Multiple
Products; Retail
(LO 1, 5)

Michael's Bicycle Shop sells 21-speed bicycles. For purposes of a cost-volume-profit analysis, the shop owner has divided sales into two categories, as follows:

Product Type	Sales Price	Invoice Cost	Sales Commission
High-quality	$1,000	$550	$50
Medium-quality	600	270	30

    Seventy percent of the shop's sales are medium-quality bikes. The shop's annual fixed expenses are $148,500. (In the following requirements, ignore income taxes.)

Required:

1. Compute the unit contribution margin for each product type.
2. What is the shop's sales mix?
3. Compute the weighted-average unit contribution margin, assuming a constant sales mix.
4. What is the shop's break-even sales volume in dollars? Assume a constant sales mix.
5. How many bicycles of each type must be sold to earn a target net income of $99,000? Assume a constant sales mix.

■ **Exercise 7–30**
Cost-Volume-Profit Analysis in
an Airline; Use of Internet
(LO 4)

Use the Internet to access the Web site of one of these airlines, or a different airline of your choosing:

Air Canada	www.aircanada.com
American Airlines	www.aa.com
British Airways	www.britishairways.com
Delta Air Lines	www.delta.com
Northwest Airlines	www.nwa.com
WestJet Airlines	www.westjet.com

Required: Find the company's most recent annual report. Does the management discussion in the report disclose the airline's break-even load factor? If so, what is it for the most recent year reported?

A contribution income statement for the Nantucket Hotel is shown below. (Ignore income taxes.)

■ **Exercise 7–31**
Cost Structure and Operating
Leverage; Hotel and Restaurant
(LO 8)

Revenue	$1,500,000
Less: Variable expenses	900,000
Contribution margin	$600,000
Less: Fixed expenses	450,000
Net income	$ 150,000

Required:

1. Show the hotel's cost structure by indicating the percentage of the hotel's revenue represented by each item on the income statement.
2. Suppose the hotel's revenue declines by 20 percent. Use the contribution-margin percentage to calculate the resulting decrease in net income.
3. What is the hotel's operating leverage factor when revenue is $1,500,000?
4. Use the operating leverage factor to calculate the increase in net income resulting from a 25 percent increase in sales revenue.

Refer to the income statement given in the preceding exercise. Prepare a new contribution income statement for the Nantucket Inn in each of the following independent situations. (Ignore income taxes.)

■ **Exercise 7–32**
Continuation of Preceding
Exercise
(LO 7)

1. The hotel's volume of activity increases by 25 percent, and fixed expenses increase by 50 percent.
2. The ratio of variable expenses to revenue doubles. There is no change in the hotel's volume of activity. Fixed expenses decline by $100,000.

Power Grid Engineering Associates, Inc. provides consulting services to commercial electric utilities. The consulting firm's contribution-margin ratio is 25 percent, and its annual fixed expenses are $200,000. The firm's income-tax rate is 40 percent.

■ **Exercise 7–33**
CVP Analysis with Income
Taxes; Consulting Firm
(Appendix)
(LO 1, 4, 11)

Required:

1. Calculate the firm's break-even volume of service revenue.
2. How much before-tax income must the firm earn to make an after-tax net income of $120,000?
3. What level of revenue for consulting services must the firm generate to earn an after-tax net income of $120,000?
4. Suppose the firm's income-tax rate rises to 35 percent. What will happen to the break-even level of consulting service revenue?

Problems

Disk City, Inc. is a retailer for DVDs. The projected net income for the current year is $600,000 based on a sales volume of 400,000 DVDs. Disk City has been selling the DVDs for $24 each. The variable costs consist of the $15 unit purchase price of the DVDs and a handling cost of $3 per DVD. Disk City's annual fixed costs are $1,800,000.

   Management is planning for the coming year, when it expects that the unit purchase price of the DVDs will increase 30 percent. (Ignore income taxes.)

■ **Problem 7–34**
Basic CVP Relationships;
Retailer
(LO 1, 2, 4)

2. New projected sales volume:
440,000 units

Required:

1. Calculate Disk City's break-even point for the *current year* in number of DVDs.
2. What will be the company's net income for the *current year* if there is a 10 percent increase in projected unit sales volume?
3. What volume of sales (in dollars) must Disk City achieve in the *coming year* to maintain the same net income as projected for the current year if the unit selling price remains at $24, but the unit purchase price of the DVDs increases by 30 percent as expected?
4. In order to cover a 30 percent increase in the DVD's purchase price for the *coming year* and still maintain the current contribution-margin ratio, what selling price per DVD must Disk City establish for the coming year?
5. *Build a spreadsheet:* Construct an Excel spreadsheet to solve requirements (1), (2), and (3) above. Show how the solution will change if the following information changes: the selling price is $25 and the annual fixed costs are $1,700,000.

(CMA, adapted)

■ **Problem 7–35**
Basic CVP Computations
(LO 1, 2, 4)

1. Break-even point:
$1,890,000
4. Selling price: $32

CollegePak Company produced and sold 70,000 backpacks during the year just ended at an average price of $30 per unit. Variable manufacturing costs were $12 per unit, and variable marketing costs were $6 per unit sold. Fixed costs amounted to $540,000 for manufacturing and $216,000 for marketing. There was no year-end work-in-process inventory. (Ignore income taxes.)

Required:

1. Compute CollegePak's break-even point in sales dollars for the year.
2. Compute the number of sales units required to earn a net income of $540,000 during the year.
3. CollegePak's variable manufacturing costs are expected to increase by 10 percent in the coming year. Compute the firm's break-even point in sales dollars for the coming year.
4. If CollegePak's variable manufacturing costs do increase by 10 percent, compute the selling price that would yield the same contribution-margin ratio in the coming year.

(CMA, adapted)

■ **Problem 7–36**
CVP Relationships;
Indifference Point
(LO 1, 4)

1. Break-even point:
88,000 units

Corrigan Enterprises is studying the acquisition of two electrical component insertion systems for producing its sole product, the universal gismo. Data relevant to the systems follow.

> Model A:
>   Variable costs, $8 per unit
>   Annual fixed costs, $1,971,200
> Model B:
>   Variable costs, $6.40 per unit
>   Annual fixed costs, $2,227,200

Corrigan's selling price is $32 per unit for the universal gismo, which is subject to a 5 percent sales commission. (In the following requirements, ignore income taxes.)

Required:

1. How many units must the company sell to break even if Model A is selected?
2. Which of the two systems would be more profitable if sales and production are expected to average 184,000 units per year?
3. Assume Model B requires the purchase of additional equipment that is not reflected in the preceding figures. The equipment will cost $900,000 and will be depreciated over a five-year life by the straight-line method. How many units must Corrigan sell to earn $1,912,800 of income if Model B is selected?
4. Ignoring the information presented in requirement (3), at what volume level will management be indifferent between the acquisition of Model A and Model B? In other words, at what volume level will the annual total cost of each system be equal?

■ **Problem 7–37**
CVP Analysis; Impact of
Operating Changes
(LO 1, 4)

2. Break-even point:
32,000 units

CompTronics manufactures audio speakers for desktop computers. The following data relate to the period just ended when the company produced and sold 42,000 speaker sets:

Sales	$4,032,000
Variable costs	1,008,000
Fixed costs	2,736,000

Management is considering relocating its manufacturing facilities to Mexico to reduce costs. Variable costs are expected to average $21.60 per set; annual fixed costs are anticipated to be $2,380,800. (In the following requirements, ignore income taxes.)

Required:

1. Calculate the company's current income and determine the level of dollar sales needed to double that figure, assuming that manufacturing operations remain in Canada.
2. Determine the break-even point in speaker sets if operations are shifted to Mexico.
3. Assume that management desires to achieve the Mexican break-even point; however, operations will remain locally.

a. If variable costs remain constant, what must management do to fixed costs? By how much must fixed costs change?

b. If fixed costs remain constant, what must management do to the variable cost per unit? By how much must unit variable cost change?

4. Determine the impact (increase, decrease, or no effect) of the following operating changes.

a. Effect of an increase in direct material costs on the break-even point

b. Effect of an increase in fixed administrative costs on the unit contribution margin

c. Effect of an increase in the unit contribution margin on net income

d. Effect of a decrease in the number of units sold on the break-even point

Premier Corporation sells two models of home ice cream makers, Mister Ice Cream and Cold King. Current sales total 60,000 units, consisting of 21,000 Mister Ice Cream units and 39,000 Cold King units. Selling price and variable cost information follow.

	Mister Ice Cream	Cold King
Selling price	$37.00	$43.00
Variable cost	20.50	32.50

Salespeople currently receive flat salaries that total $200,000. Management is contemplating a change to a compensation plan that is based on commissions in an effort to boost the company's presence in the marketplace. Two plans are under consideration:

Plan A: 10% commission computed on gross dollar sales. Mister Ice Cream sales are expected to total 19,500 units; Cold King sales are anticipated to be 45,500 units.

Plan B: 30% commission computed on the basis of production contribution margins. Mister Ice Cream sales are anticipated to be 39,000 units; Cold King sales are expected to total 26,000 units.

Required:

1. Define the term *sales mix*.

2. Comparing Plan A to the current compensation arrangement:

a. Will Plan A achieve management's objective of an increased presence in the marketplace? Briefly explain.

b. From a sales-mix perspective, will the salespeople be promoting the product that one would logically expect? Briefly discuss.

c. Will the sales force likely be satisfied with the results of Plan A? Why?

d. Will Premier likely be satisfied with the resulting impact of Plan A on company profitability? Why?

3. Assume that Plan B is under consideration.

a. Compare Plan A and Plan B with respect to total units sold and the sales mix. Comment on the results.

b. In comparison with flat salaries, is Plan B more attractive to the sales force? To the company? Show calculations to support your answers.

PneumoTech, Inc. is studying the addition of a new valve to its product line. The valve would be used by manufacturers of pneumatic equipment. The company anticipates starting with a relatively low sales volume and then boosting demand over the next several years. A new salesperson must be hired because PneumoTech's current sales force is working at capacity. Two compensation plans are under consideration:

Plan A: An annual salary of $33,000 plus a 10% commission based on gross dollar sales.

Plan B: An annual salary of $99,000 and no commission.

PneumoTech, Inc. will purchase the valve for $75 and sell it for $120. Anticipated demand during the first year is 6,000 units. (In the following requirements, ignore income taxes.)

Required:

1. Compute the break-even point for Plan A and Plan B.

2. What is meant by the term *operating leverage*?

■ **Problem 7–38**
Sales Mix and Employee Compensation; Operating Changes
(LO 4, 5)

2c. Commissions: $267,800
3b. Plan B, net income: $641,550

■ **Problem 7–39**
Leverage; Analysis of Operating Change
(LO 4, 8)

1. Plan B break-even point: 2,200 units

3. Analyze the cost structures of both plans at the anticipated demand of 6,000 units. Which of the two plans is more highly leveraged? Why

4. Assume that a general economic downturn occurred during year 2, with product demand falling from 6,000 to 5,000 units. Determine the percentage decrease in company net income if Consolidated had adopted Plan A.

5. Repeat requirement (4) for Plan B. Compare Plan A and Plan B, and explain a major factor that underlies any resulting differences.

6. Briefly discuss the likely profitability impact of an economic recession for highly automated manufacturers. What can you say about the risk associated with these firms?

Problem 7–40
Basic CVP Relationships
(LO 1, 2, 4)

2. Break-even point:
$3,375,000
4. Margin of safety: $125,000

Surreal Sound, Inc. manufactures and sells CDs. Price and cost data are as follows:

Selling price per unit (package of two CDs)	$25.00
Variable costs per unit:	
Direct material	$ 8.20
Direct labour	4.00
Manufacturing overhead	6.00
Selling expenses	1.60
Total variable costs per unit	$19.80
Annual fixed costs:	
Manufacturing overhead	$ 288,000
Selling and administrative	414,000
Total fixed costs	$ 702,000
Forecasted annual sales volume (140,000 units)	$3,500,000

In the following requirements, ignore income taxes.

Required:

1. What is Surreal Sound's break-even point in units?
2. What is the company's break-even point in sales dollars?
3. How many units would Surreal Sound have to sell in order to earn $390,000?
4. What is the firm's margin of safety?
5. Management estimates that direct-labour costs will increase by 10 percent next year. How many units will the company have to sell next year to reach its break-even point?
6. If the company's direct-labour costs do increase by 10 percent, what selling price per unit of product must it charge to maintain the same contribution-margin ratio?

(CMA, adapted)

Problem 7–41
CVP Graph; Cost Structure;
Operating Leverage
(LO 3, 4, 8)

2. Break-even point:
$8,000,000

SkiCo, Inc. manufactures ski boots. The company's projected income for the coming year, based on sales of 160,000 units, is as follows:

Sales		$16,000,000
Operating expenses:		
Variable expenses	$4,000,000	
Fixed expenses	6,000,000	
Total expenses		10,000,000
Net income		$ 6,000,000

Required: In completing the following requirements, ignore income taxes.

1. Prepare a CVP graph for SkiCo, Inc. for the coming year.
2. Calculate the firm's break-even point for the year in sales dollars.
3. What is the company's margin of safety for the year?

4. Compute SkiCo's operating leverage factor, based on the budgeted sales volume for the year.

5. Compute SkiCo's required sales in dollars in order to earn income of $9,000,000 in the coming year.

6. Describe the firm's cost structure. Calculate the percentage relationships between variable and fixed expenses and sales revenue.

(CMA, adapted)

The Asian Division of Worldwide Reference Corporation produces a pocket dictionary containing popular phrases in six Asian languages. Annual budget data for the coming year follow. Projected sales are 100,000 books.

	Variable	Fixed	
Sales			$2,000,000
Costs:	**Variable**	**Fixed**	
Direct material	$ 600,000	–0–	
Direct labour	400,000	–0–	
Manufacturing overhead	300,000	200,000	
Selling and administrative	100,000	220,000	
Total costs	$1,400,000	$420,000	1,820,000
Budgeted operating income			$ 180,000

Required:

1. Calculate the break-even point in units and in sales dollars.

2. If the Asian Division is subject to an income-tax rate of 40 percent, compute the number of units the company would have to sell to earn an after-tax profit of $180,000.

3. If fixed costs increased $63,000 with no other cost or revenue factor changing, compute the firm's break-even sales in units.

4. Assuming the original data, prepare a profit-volume graph for the Asian Division.

5. Due to an unstable political situation in the country in which the Asian Division is located, management believes the country may split into two independent nations. If this happens, the tax rate could rise to 50 percent. Assuming all other data as in the original problem, how many pocket dictionaries must be sold to earn $180,000 after taxes?

6. *Build a spreadsheet:* Construct an Excel spreadsheet to solve requirements (1), (2), (3), and (5) above. Show how the solution will change if the following information changes: sales amounted to $2,100,000 and fixed manufacturing overhead was $220,000.

(CMA, adapted)

Terry Smith and two of his colleagues are considering opening a law office in a large metropolitan area that would make inexpensive legal services available to those who could not otherwise afford services. The intent is to provide easy access for their clients by having the office open 360 days per year, 16 hours each day from 7:00 a.m. to 11:00 p.m. The office would be staffed by a lawyer, paralegal, legal secretary, and clerk-receptionist for each of the two eight-hour shifts.

In order to determine the feasibility of the project, Smith hired a marketing consultant to assist with market projections. The results of this study show that if the firm spends $980,000 on advertising the first year, the number of new clients expected each day will be 50. Smith and his associates believe this number is reasonable and are prepared to spend the $980,000 on advertising. Other pertinent information about the operation of the office follows:

• The only charge to each new client would be $60 for the initial consultation. All cases that warrant further legal work will be accepted on a contingency basis with the firm earning 30 percent of any favourable settlements or judgments. Smith estimates that 20 percent of new client consultations will result in favourable settlements or judgments averaging $4,000 each. It is not expected that there will be repeat clients during the first year of operations.

• The hourly wages of the staff are projected to be $50 for the lawyer, $40 for the paralegal, $30 for the legal secretary, and $20 for the clerk-receptionist. Fringe benefit expense will be 40 percent of

■ **Problem 7–42**
Break-Even Point; After-Tax Net Income; Profit-Volume Graph; International Issues (Appendix)
(LO 1, 3, 4, 11)

1*b*. Break-even point: $1,400,000
3. Break-even point: 80,500 units

■ **Problem 7–43**
Break-Even Point; Safety Margin; Law Firm
(LO 1, 4)

1. Total fixed expenses: $2,983,960
2. Break-even number of clients: 10,220 (rounded)

the wages paid. A total of 400 hours of overtime is expected for the year; this will be divided equally between the legal secretary and the clerk-receptionist positions. Overtime will be paid at one and one-half times the regular wage, and the fringe benefit expense will apply to the full wage.

* Smith has located 6,000 square metres of suitable office space that rents for $56 per square metre annually. Associated expenses will be $54,000 for property insurance and $74,000 for utilities.

* It will be necessary for the group to purchase malpractice insurance, which is expected to cost $360,000 annually.

* The initial investment in the office equipment will be $120,000. This equipment has an estimated useful life of four years.

* The cost of office supplies has been estimated to be $8 per expected new client consultation.

Required:

1. Determine how many new clients must visit the law office being considered by Terry Smith and his colleagues in order for the venture to break even during its first year of operations.

2. Compute the law firm's safety margin.

(CMA, adapted)

■ **Problem 7–44**
Break-Even Analysis;
Operating Leverage; New
Manufacturing Environment
(LO 1, 8, 10)

1. Computer-assisted, contribution margin per unit: $21

Zodiac Company has decided to introduce a new product, which can be manufactured by either a computer-assisted manufacturing system or a labour-intensive production system. The manufacturing method will not affect the quality of the product. The estimated manufacturing costs by the two methods are as follows:

	Computer-Assisted Manufacturing System		Labour-Intensive Production System	
Direct material		$7.50		$8.40
Direct labour (DLH denotes direct-labour hours)	.5DLH @ $18	9.00	.8DLH @ $13.50	10.80
Variable overhead	.5DLH @ $9	4.50	.8DLH @ $9	7.20
Fixed overhead*		$3,660,000		$1,980,000

*These costs are directly traceable to the new product line. They would not be incurred if the new product were not produced.

The company's marketing research department has recommended an introductory unit sales price of $45. Selling expenses are estimated to be $750,000 annually plus $3 for each unit sold. (Ignore income taxes.)

Required:

1. Calculate the estimated break-even point in annual unit sales of the new product if the company uses the (*a*) labour-intensive production system; (*b*) computer-assisted manufacturing system

2. Determine the annual unit sales volume at which the firm would be indifferent between the two manufacturing methods.

3. Management must decide which manufacturing method to employ. One factor it should consider is operating leverage. Explain the concept of operating leverage. How is this concept related to Zodiac's decision?

4. Describe the circumstances under which the firm should employ each of the two manufacturing methods.

5. Identify some business factors other than operating leverage that management should consider before selecting the manufacturing method.

(CMA, adapted)

■ **Problem 7–45**
Break-Even Analysis;
Profit-Volume Graph; Movie
Theatres
(LO 1, 3, 4)

1. Break-even sales volume, standard: 25,000 tubs

Silver Screen, Inc. owns and operates a nationwide chain of movie theatres. The 450 properties in the Silver Screen chain vary from low-volume, small-town, single-screen theatres to high-volume, urban, multiscreen theatres. The firm's management is considering installing popcorn machines, which would allow the theatres to sell freshly popped corn rather than pre-popped corn. This new feature would be advertised to increase patronage at the company's theatres. The fresh popcorn will be sold for $3.50 per tub. The annual rental costs and the operating costs vary with the size of the popcorn machines. The machine capacities and costs are shown below. (Ignore income taxes.)

	Popper Model		
	Standard	**Super**	**Giant**
Annual capacity	40,000 tubs	80,000 tubs	120,000 tubs
Costs:			
Annual machine rental	$16,000	$22,000	$40,000
Popcorn cost per tub	.26	.26	.26
Other costs per tub	2.44	2.28	2.10
Cost of each tub...	.16	.16	.16

Required:

1. Calculate each theatre's break-even sales volume (measured in tubs of popcorn) for each model of popcorn popper.
2. Prepare a profit-volume graph for one theatre, assuming that the Giant Popper is purchased.
3. Calculate the volume (in tubs) at which the Standard Popper and the Super Popper earn the same profit or loss in each movie theatre.

(CMA, adapted)

Saturn Game Company manufactures pocket electronic games. Last year Jupiter sold 25,000 games at $50 each. Total costs amounted to $1,050,000, of which $300,000 were considered fixed.

In an attempt to improve its product, the company is considering replacing a component part that has a cost of $5 with a new and better part costing $9 per unit in the coming year. A new machine also would be needed to increase plant capacity. The machine would cost $36,000 with a useful life of six years and no salvage value. The company uses straight-line depreciation on all plant assets. (Ignore income taxes.)

Required:

1. What was Saturn's break-even point in number of units last year?
2. How many units of product would the company have had to sell in the last year to earn $280,000?
3. If management holds the sales price constant and makes the suggested changes, how many units of product must be sold in the coming year to break even?
4. If the firm holds the sales price constant and makes the suggested changes, how many units of product will the company have to sell to make the same net income as last year?
5. If Saturn Game Company wishes to maintain the same contribution-margin ratio, what selling price per unit of product must it charge next year to cover the increased direct-material cost?

(CMA, adapted)

■ **Problem 7–46**
CVP Analysis of Changes in Sales Prices and Costs
(LO 1, 4)

1. Unit contribution margin: $20
3. New break-even point: 19,125 units

Refer to the original data given for Saturn Game Company in the preceding problem. An activity-based costing study has revealed that Saturn's $300,000 of fixed costs include the following components:

Setup (40 setups at $800 per setup)	$32,000
Engineering (500 hours at $50 per hour)	25,000
Inspection (1,000 inspections at $60 per inspection)	60,000
General factory overhead	123,000
Total	$240,000
Fixed selling and administrative costs	60,000
Total fixed costs	$300,000

■ **Problem 7–47**
Continuation of Preceding Problem; Activity-Based Costing; Advanced Manufacturing Systems; Ethical Issues
(LO 4, 9, 10)

2. Unit contribution margin: $28
3. Number of sales units required to earn target net profit: 27,000 units

Management is considering the installation of new, highly automated manufacturing equipment that would significantly alter the production process. In addition, management plans a move toward just-in-time inventory and production management. If the new equipment is installed, setups will be quicker and less expensive. Under the proposed JIT approach, there would be 300 setups per year at $100 per setup. Since a total quality control program would accompany the move toward JIT, only 100 inspections would be anticipated annually, at a cost of $90 each. After the installation of the new production system, 800 hours of engineering would be required at a cost of $56 per hour. General factory overhead would increase to $332,200. However, the automated equipment would allow Jupiter to cut its unit variable cost by 20 percent. Moreover, the more consistent product quality anticipated would allow management to raise the price of electronic games to $52 per unit. (Ignore income taxes.)

Required:

1. Upon seeing the ABC analysis given in the problem, Saturn's vice-president for manufacturing exclaimed to the controller, "I thought you told me this $300,000 cost was fixed. These don't look like fixed costs at all. What you're telling me now is that setup costs us $800 every time we set up a production run. What gives?"

   As Saturn's controller, write a short memo explaining to the vice-president what is going on.

2. Compute Saturn's new break-even point if the proposed automated equipment is installed.

3. Determine how many units Saturn will have to sell to show a profit of $280,000, assuming the new technology is adopted.

4. If Saturn adopts the new manufacturing technology, will its break-even point be higher or lower? Will the number of sales units required to earn a profit of $280,000 be higher or lower? (Refer to your answers for the first two requirements of the preceding problem.) Are the results in this case consistent with what you would typically expect to find? Explain.

5. The decision as to whether to purchase the automated manufacturing equipment will be made by Saturn's board of directors. In order to support the proposed acquisition, the vice-president for manufacturing asked the controller to prepare a report on the financial implications of the decision. As part of the report, the vice-president asked the controller to compute the new break-even point, assuming the installation of the equipment. The controller complied, as in requirement (2) of this problem.

   When the vice-president for manufacturing saw that the break-even point would increase, he asked the controller to delete the break-even analysis from the report. What should the controller do? Which ethical standards for managerial accountants are involved here?

Problem 7–48
CVP Relationships; Retail
(LO 1, 4)

1. Total decrease in operating income: $(32,400)

Boundaries, a chain of retail stores, sells books and music CDs. Condensed monthly income data are presented in the following table for November 20x4. (Ignore income taxes.)

	Mall Store	Downtown Store	Total
Sales	$ 360,000	$240,000	$600,000
Less: Variable expenses	252,000	96,000	348,000
Contribution margin	$ 108,000	$144,000	$252,000
Less: Fixed expenses	120,000	60,000	180,000
Operating income	$ (12,000)	$ 84,000	$ 72,000

Additional Information:

- Management estimates that closing the mall store would result in a 10 percent decrease in downtown store sales, while closing the downtown store would not affect mall store sales.
- One-fourth of each store's fixed expenses would continue through December 31, 20x5, if either store were closed.
- The operating results for November 20x4 are representative of all months.

Required:

1. Calculate the increase or decrease in Boundaries' monthly operating income during 20x5 if the mall store is closed.

2. The management of Boundaries is considering a promotional campaign at the mall store that would not affect the downtown store. Annual promotional expenses at the mall store would be increased by $180,000 in order to increase mall store sales by 10 percent. What would be the effect of this promotional campaign on the company's monthly operating income during 20x5?

3. One-half of the mall store's dollar sales are from items sold at their variable cost to attract customers to the store. Boundaries' management is considering the deletion of these items, a move that would reduce the mall store's direct fixed expenses by 15 percent and result in the loss of 20 percent of the remaining mall store's sales volume. This change would not affect the downtown store. What would be the effect on Boundaries' monthly operating income if the items sold at their variable cost are eliminated?

4. *Build a spreadsheet:* Construct an Excel spreadsheet to solve all of the preceding requirements. Show how the solution will change if the following information changes: the downtown store's sales amounted to $235,000 and its variable expenses were $90,000.

(CMA, adapted)

Coquitlam Tool Company (CTC) manufactures a line of electric garden tools that are sold in general hardware stores. The company's controller, Will Fulton, has just received the sales forecast for the coming year for CTC's three products: hedge clippers, line trimmers, and leaf blowers. CTC has experienced considerable variations in sales volumes and variable costs over the past two years, and Fulton believes the forecast should be carefully evaluated from a cost-volume-profit viewpoint. The preliminary budget information for 20x4 follows:

Problem 7–49
CVP; Multiple Products;
Changes in Costs and
Sales Mix
(LO 4, 5)

2. Weighted-average unit
contribution margin: $48
3. Total unit sales to break
even: 200,000 units

	Hedge Clippers	Line Trimmers	Leaf Blowers
Unit sales	50,000	50,000	100,000
Unit selling price	$84	$108	$144
Variable manufacturing cost per unit	39	36	75
Variable selling cost per unit	15	12	18

For 20x4, CTC's fixed manufacturing overhead is budgeted at $6,000,000, and the company's fixed selling and administrative expenses are forecasted to be $1,800,000. CTC has a tax rate of 40 percent.

Required:

1. Determine CTC's budgeted net income for 20x4.
2. Assuming the sales mix remains as budgeted, determine how many units of each product CTC must sell in order to break even in 20x4.
3. After preparing the original estimates, management determined that its variable manufacturing cost of leaf blowers would increase by 20 percent, and the variable selling cost of line trimmers could be expected to increase by $3 per unit. However, management has decided not to change the selling price of either product. In addition, management has learned that its leaf blower has been perceived as the best value on the market, and it can expect to sell three times as many leaf blowers as each of its other products. Under these circumstances, determine how many units of each product CTC would have to sell in order to break even in 20x4.

(CMA, adapted)

The Limestone Company produces thin limestone sheets used for cosmetic facing on buildings. The following income statement represents the operating results for the year just ended. The company had sales of 1,800 tonnes during the year. The manufacturing capacity of the firm's facilities is 3,000 tonnes per year. (Ignore income taxes.)

Problem 7–50
CVP Relationships; International Business; Automation
(LO 1, 4, 10)

1. Break-even volume in
tonnes: 1,100
5. Break-even point in tonnes:
1,224

THE LIMESTONE COMPANY
Income Statement
For the Year Ended December 31, 20x4

Sales	$1,800,000
Variable costs:	
Manufacturing	630,000
Selling costs	360,000
Total variable costs	990,000
Contribution margin	810,000
Fixed costs:	
Manufacturing	200,000
Selling	215,000
Administrative	80,000
Total fixed costs	495,000
Net income	$ 315,000

Required:

1. Calculate the company's break-even volume in tonnes for 20x4.

2. If the sales volume is estimated to be 2,100 tonnes in the next year, and if the prices and costs stay at the same levels and amounts, what is the net income that management can expect for 20x5?

3. Limestone has been trying for years to get a foothold in the European market. The company has a potential German customer that has offered to buy 1,500 tonnes at $900 per tonne. Assume that all of the firm's costs would be at the same levels and rates as in 20x4. What net income would the firm earn if it took this order and rejected some business from regular customers so as not to exceed capacity?

4. Limestone plans to market its product in a new territory. Management estimates that an advertising and promotion program costing $123,000 annually would be needed for the next two or three years. In addition, a $50 per tonne sales commission to the sales force in the new territory, over and above the current commission, would be required. How many tonnes would have to be sold in the new territory to maintain the firm's current net income? Assume that sales and costs will continue as in 20x4 in the firm's established territories.

5. Management is considering replacing its labour-intensive process with an automated production system. This would result in an increase of $117,000 annually in fixed manufacturing costs. The variable manufacturing costs would decrease by $50 per tonne. Compute the new break-even volume in tonnes and in sales dollars.

6. Ignore the facts presented in requirement (5). Assume that management estimates that the selling price per tonne would decline by 10 percent next year. Variable costs would increase by $80 per tonne, and fixed costs would not change. What sales volume in dollars would be required to earn a net income of $189,000 next year?

(CMA, adapted)

■ **Problem 7–51**
Cost-Volume-Profit Analysis
with Income Taxes and
Multiple Products
(Appendix)
(LO 1, 2, 4, 5, 11)

1. Contribution margin
ratio: .34
4. New break-even point:
10,729 units (rounded)

Great Northern Ski Company recently expanded its manufacturing capacity. The firm will now be able to produce up to 15,000 pairs of cross-country skis of either the mountaineering model or the touring model. The sales department assures management that it can sell between 9,000 and 13,000 units of either product this year. Because the models are very similar, the company will produce only one of the two models.

The following information was compiled by the accounting department:

	Model	
	Mountaineering	**Touring**
Selling price per unit	$120.00	$132.00
Variable costs per unit	79.20	79.20

Fixed costs will total $554,400 if the touring model is produced but will be only $475,200 if the mountaineering model is produced. Great Northern Ski Company is subject to a 40 percent income tax rate. (Round each answer to the nearest whole number.)

Required:

1. Compute the contribution-margin ratio for the mountaineering model.

2. If Great Northern Ski Company desires an after-tax net income of $33,120, how many pairs of mountaineering skis will the company have to sell?

3. How much would the variable cost per unit of the mountaineering model have to change before it had the same break-even point in units as the touring model?

4. Suppose the variable cost per unit of mountaineering skis decreases by 10 percent, and the total fixed cost of mountaineering skis increases by 10 percent. Compute the new break-even point.

5. Suppose management decided to produce both products. If the two models are sold in equal proportions, and total fixed costs amount to $514,800, what is the firm's break-even point in units?

(CMA, adapted)

■ **Problem 7–52**
CVP Analysis; Marketing
Decisions; Income Taxes
(Appendix)
(LO 1, 4, 11)

1a. Contribution margin
ratio: .40
2. Required sales dollars to
break even: $29,538,462
(rounded)

Seattle Telecom, Inc. manufactures telecommunications equipment. The company has always been production-oriented and sells its products through agents. Agents are paid a commission of 15 percent of the selling price. Seattle Telecom's budgeted income statement for 20x5 follows:

SEATTLE TELECOM, INC.
Budgeted Income Statement
For the Year Ended December 31, 20x5
(in thousands)

Sales		$24,000
Manufacturing costs:		
Variable	$10,800	
Fixed overhead	3,510	14,310
Gross margin		$ 9,690
Selling and administrative expenses:		
Commissions	$3,600	
Fixed marketing expenses	210	
Fixed administrative expenses	2,670	6,480
Net operating income		$ 3,210
Less fixed interest expense		810
Income before income taxes		$ 2,400
Less income taxes (30%)		720
Net income		$ 1,680

After the profit plan was completed for the coming year, Seattle Telecom's sales agents demanded that the commissions be increased to 22½ percent of the selling price. This demand was the latest in a series of actions that Vinnie McGraw, the company's president, believed had gone too far. He asked Maureen Elliott, the most sales-oriented officer in his production-oriented company, to estimate the cost to Seattle Telecom of employing its own sales force. Elliott's estimate of the additional annual cost of employing its own sales force, exclusive of commissions, follows. Sales personnel would receive a commission of 10 percent of the selling price in addition to their salary.

Estimated Annual Cost of
Employing a Company Sales Force
(in thousands)

Salaries:	
Sales manager	$ 150
Sales personnel	1,500
Travel and entertainment	600
Fixed marketing costs	1,350
Total	$3,600

Required:

1. Calculate Seattle Telecom's estimated break-even point in sales dollars for 20x5.
   a. If the events that are represented in the budgeted income statement take place.
   b. If the company employs its own sales force.
2. If Seattle Telecom continues to sell through agents and pays the increased commission of 22½ percent of the selling price, determine the estimated volume in sales dollars for 20x5 that would be required to generate the same net income as projected in the budgeted income statement.
3. Determine the estimated volume in sales dollars that would result in equal net income for 20x5 regardless of whether the company continues to sell through agents and pays a commission of 22½ percent of the selling price or employs its own sales force.

(CMA, adapted)

I ignore

■ **Problem 7–53**
CVP Analysis with Production and Marketing Decisions; Taxes (Appendix)
(LO 1, 4, 11)

1a. Break-even point: 500 units

Windsor Canopy Company manufactures and sells adjustable canopies that attach to motor homes and trailers. The market covers both new units as well as replacement canopies. Windsor developed its 20x4 business plan based on the assumption that canopies would sell at a price of $800 each. The variable cost of each canopy is projected at $400, and the annual fixed costs are budgeted at $200,000. Windsor's after-tax profit objective is $480,000; the company's tax rate is 40 percent.

While Windsor's sales usually rise during the second quarter, the May financial statements reported that sales were not meeting expectations. For the first five months of the year, only 350 units had been sold at the established price, with variable costs as planned. It was clear the 20x4 after-tax profit projection would not be reached unless some actions were taken. Windsor's president, Melanie Grand, assigned a management committee to analyze the situation and develop several alternative courses of action. The following mutually exclusive alternatives were presented to the president:

- Reduce the sales price by $80. The sales organization forecasts that with the significantly reduced sales price, 2,700 units can be sold during the remainder of the year. Total fixed and variable unit costs will stay as budgeted.
- Lower variable costs per unit by $50 through the use of less expensive raw materials and slightly modified manufacturing techniques. The sales price also would be reduced by $60, and sales of 2,200 units for the remainder of the year are forecast.
- Cut fixed costs by $20,000 and lower the sales price by 5 percent. Variable costs per unit will be unchanged. Sales of 2,000 units are expected for the remainder of the year.

Required:

1. If no changes are made to the selling price or cost structure, determine the number of units that Windsor Canopy Company must sell:
   a. In order to break even
   b. To achieve its after-tax profit objective
2. Determine which one of the alternatives Windsor Canopy Company should select to achieve its annual after-tax profit objective.

(CMA, adapted)

Cases

Case 7–54
Break-Even Analysis; Hospital
CVP Relationships
(LO 1,4)

1. Contribution margin per patient day: $240
2. Fixed charges by medical centre: $1,160,000

Manitoba Medical Centre operates a general hospital. The medical centre also rents space and beds to separately owned entities rendering specialized services, such as Paediatrics and Psychiatric Care. Manitoba Medical Centre charges each separate entity for common services, such as patients' meals and laundry, and for administrative services, such as billings and collections. Space and bed rentals are fixed charges for the year, based on bed capacity rented to each entity. Manitoba Medical Centre charged the following costs to Paediatrics for the year ended June 30, 20x5:

	Patient Days (variable)	Bed Capacity (fixed)
Dietary	$ 720,000	—
Janitorial	—	$ 84,000
Laundry	360,000	—
Laboratory	540,000	—
Pharmacy	420,000	—
Repairs and maintenance	—	36,000
General and administrative	—	1,560,000
Rent	—	1,800,000
Billings and collections	360,000	—
Total	$2,400,000	$3,480,000

During the year ended June 30, 20x5, Paediatrics charged each patient an average of $360 per day, had a capacity of 60 beds, and had revenue of $7.2 million for 365 days. In addition, Paediatrics directly employed personnel with the following annual salary costs per employee: supervising nurses, $30,000; nurses, $24,000; and aides, $10,800.

Manitoba Medical Centre has the following minimum departmental personnel requirements, based on total annual patient days:

Annual Patient Days	Aides	Nurses	Supervising Nurse
Up to 22,000	20	10	4
22,001 to 26,000	25	14	5
26,001 to 29,200	31	16	5

Paediatrics always employs only the minimum number of required personnel. Salaries of supervising nurses, nurses, and aides are therefore fixed within ranges of annual patient days.

Paediatrics operated at 100 percent capacity on 90 days during the year ended June 30, 20x5. Administrators estimate that on these 90 days, Paediatrics could have filled another 20 beds above capacity. Manitoba Medical Centre has an additional 20 beds available for rent for the year ending June 30, 20x6. Such additional rental would increase Paediatrics' fixed charges based on bed capacity. (In the following requirements, ignore income taxes.)

Required:

1. Calculate the minimum number of patient days required for Paediatrics to break even for the year ending June 30, 20x6, if the additional 20 beds are not rented. Patient demand is unknown, but assume that revenue per patient day, cost per patient day, cost per bed, and salary rates will remain the same as for the year ended June 30, 20x5.

2. Assume that patient demand, revenue per patient day, cost per patient day, cost per bed, and salary rates for the year ending June 30, 20x6, remain the same as for the year ended June 30, 20x5. Prepare a schedule of Paediatrics' increase in revenue and increase in costs for the year ending June 30, 20x6. Determine the net increase or decrease in Paediatrics' earnings from the additional 20 beds if Paediatrics rents this extra capacity from Manitoba Medical Centre.

(CPA, adapted)

Niagara Falls Sporting Goods Company, a wholesale supply company, engages independent sales agents to market the company's products throughout New York and Ontario. These agents currently receive a commission of 20 percent of sales, but they are demanding an increase to 25 percent of sales made during the year ending December 31, 20x4. The controller already prepared the 20x4 budget before learning of the agents' demand for an increase in commissions. The budgeted 20x4 income statement is shown below. Assume that cost of goods sold is 100 percent variable cost.

■ Case 7–55
Sales Commissions in a
Wholesale Firm; Income Taxes
(Appendix)
(LO 1, 2, 4, 11)

1. Break-even point: $750,000
3. Contribution-margin ratio: .15

<table>
<tr><td colspan="3" align="center">**NIAGARA FALLS SPORTING GOODS COMPANY**
Budgeted Income Statement
For the Year Ended December 31, 20x4</td></tr>
<tr><td>Sales</td><td></td><td>$15,000,000</td></tr>
<tr><td>Cost of goods sold</td><td></td><td>9,000,000</td></tr>
<tr><td>Gross margin</td><td></td><td>$ 6,000,000</td></tr>
<tr><td>Selling and administrative expenses:</td><td></td><td></td></tr>
<tr><td>Commissions</td><td>$3,000,000</td><td></td></tr>
<tr><td>All other expenses (fixed)</td><td>150,000</td><td>3,150,000</td></tr>
<tr><td>Income before taxes</td><td></td><td>$ 2,850,000</td></tr>
<tr><td>Income tax (30%)</td><td></td><td>855,000</td></tr>
<tr><td>Net income</td><td></td><td>$ 1,995,000</td></tr>
</table>

The company's management is considering the possibility of employing full-time sales personnel. Three individuals would be required, at an estimated annual salary of $45,000 each, plus commissions of 5 percent of sales. In addition, a sales manager would be employed at a fixed annual salary of $120,000. All other fixed costs, as well as the variable cost percentages, would remain the same as the estimates in the 20x4 budgeted income statement.

Required:

1. Compute Niagara Falls Sporting Goods' estimated break-even point in sales dollars for the year ending December 31, 20x4, based on the budgeted income statement prepared by the controller.

2. Compute the estimated break-even point in sales dollars for the year ending December 31, 20x4, if the company employs its own sales personnel.

3. Compute the estimated volume in sales dollars that would be required for the year ending December 31, 20x4, to yield the same net income as projected in the budgeted income statement, if management continues to use the independent sales agents and agrees to their demand for a 25 percent sales commission.

4. Compute the estimated volume in sales dollars that would generate an identical net income for the year ending December 31, 20x4, regardless of whether Niagara Falls Sporting Goods Company employs its own sales personnel or continues to use the independent sales agents and pays them a 25 percent commission.

(CPA, adapted)

Chapter Eight

Absorption and Variable Costing

Quikmath.com

Quikmath.com is a manufacturer of hand-held calculators, pagers, and other electronic gadgetry. Quikmath specializes in the school-age market, and virtually all of its sales are Web-based. In this chapter, we explore two product-costing systems called *absorption costing* and *variable costing*. Under absorption costing, all manufacturing costs, including fixed manufacturing overhead, are assigned as product costs and stored in inventory until the products are sold. Under variable costing, fixed manufacturing overhead is not included in inventory as a product cost; instead, fixed manufacturing overhead is treated as a period cost, and it is expensed during the period it is incurred. The choice between absorption and variable costing arises only in manufacturing firms.

After completing this chapter, you should be able to:

1 Explain the accounting treatment of fixed manufacturing overhead under absorption and variable costing.

2 Prepare an income statement under absorption costing.

3 Prepare an income statement under variable costing.

4 Reconcile reported income under absorption and variable costing.

5 Explain the implications of absorption and variable costing for cost-volume-profit analysis.

6 Evaluate absorption and variable costing.

7 Explain the rationale behind throughput costing.

8 Prepare an income statement under throughput costing.

IN CONTRAST

In contrast to the absorption and variable costing systems discussed in the first part of the chapter, we explore yet another product-costing method called *throughput costing*. We continue our illustration with Quikmath.com to explain how this product-costing method works. Throughput costing assigns only the unit-level spending for direct costs as the cost of a product. A unit-level cost is one that is incurred every time a unit is manufactured.

Income is one of many important measures used to evaluate the performance of companies and segments of companies. There are two commonly used methods for determining product costs and reporting income in a manufacturing firm, depending on the accounting treatment of fixed manufacturing overhead. In this chapter, we will examine these two income-reporting alternatives, called *absorption costing* and *variable costing*. In addition, we will study a third alternative for product costing and income reporting, which is called *throughput costing*.

Product Costs

In the product-costing systems we have studied so far, manufacturing overhead is applied to Work-in-Process Inventory as a product cost along with direct material and direct labour. When the manufactured goods are finished, these product costs flow from Work-in-Process inventory into Finished-Goods Inventory. Finally, during the accounting period when the goods are sold, the product costs flow from Finished-Goods Inventory into Cost of Goods Sold, an expense account. The following diagram summarizes this flow of costs.

Fixed Manufacturing Overhead: The Key   In our study of product-costing systems, we have included both variable and fixed manufacturing overhead in the product costs that flow through the manufacturing accounts. This approach to product costing is called **absorption costing** (or **full costing**), because *all* manufacturing-overhead costs are applied to (or absorbed by) manufactured goods. An alternative approach to product costing is called **variable costing** (or **direct costing**), in which *only variable* manufacturing overhead is applied to Work-in-Process Inventory as a product cost.

The distinction between absorption and variable costing is summarized in Exhibit 8–1. Notice that the distinction involves the *timing* with which fixed manufacturing

Learning Objective 1

Explain the accounting treatment of fixed manufacturing overhead under absorption and variable costing.

Exhibit 8–1
Absorption versus Variable Costing

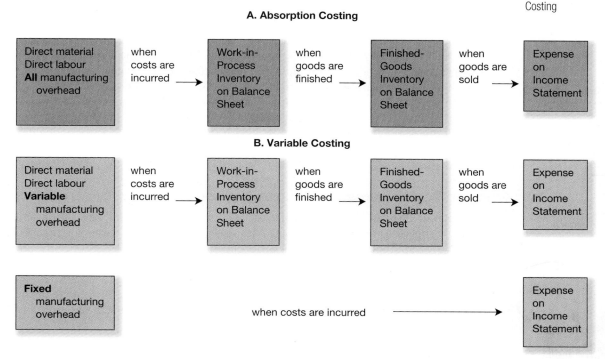

overhead becomes an expense. Eventually, fixed overhead is expensed under both product-costing systems. Under variable costing, however, fixed overhead is expensed *immediately*, as it is incurred. Under absorption costing, fixed overhead is *inventoried* until the accounting period during which the manufactured goods are sold.

Absorption and Variable Costing Illustrated

Quikmath.com

Quikmath.com began operations on January 1, 20x0, to manufacture hand-held electronic calculators. Cost, production, and sales data for the first three years of Quikmath's operations are given in Exhibit 8–2. Comparative income statements for 20x0, 20x1, and 20x2 are presented in Exhibit 8–3, using both absorption and variable costing.

Absorption-Costing Income Statements

Examine the absorption-costing income statements in the upper half of Exhibit 8–3. Two features of these income statements are highlighted in the left-hand margin. First,

The fixed costs of operating this truck manufacturing plant include such costs as the depreciation on plant and equipment, property taxes, insurance, and the salary of the plant manager. Fixed manufacturing costs are incurred in order to generate production capacity. Under absorption costing, these costs are treated as product costs and included in the cost of inventory. Under variable costing, they are expensed during the period in which they are incurred.

notice that the Cost of Goods Sold expense for each year is determined by multiplying the year's sales by the absorption manufacturing cost per unit, $9. Included in the $9 cost per unit is the predetermined fixed manufacturing-overhead cost of $3 per unit. Second, notice that on Quikmath's absorption-costing income statements, the only period expenses are the selling and administrative expenses. There is no deduction of fixed-overhead costs as a lump-sum period expense at the bottom of each income statement. As mentioned above, fixed manufacturing-overhead costs are included in Cost of Goods Sold on these absorption-costing income statements.

Variable-Costing Income Statements

Now examine the income statements based on variable costing in the lower half of Exhibit 8–3. Notice that the format of the statements is different from the format used in the absorption-costing statements. In the variable-costing statements, the contribution format is used to highlight the separation of variable and fixed costs. Let's focus on the same two aspects of the variable-costing statements that we discussed for the absorption-costing statements. First, the manufacturing expenses subtracted from sales revenue each year include only the variable costs, which amount to $6 per unit. Second, fixed manufacturing overhead is subtracted as a lump-sum period expense at the bottom of each year's income statement.

Reconciling Income under Absorption and Variable Costing

Examination of Exhibit 8–3 reveals that the income reported under absorption and variable costing is sometimes different. Although income is the same for the two product-costing methods in 20x0, it is different in 20x1 and 20x2. Let's figure out why these results occur.

No Change in Inventory In 20x0 there is no change in inventory over the course of the year. Beginning and ending inventory are the same, because actual production and

	20x0	20x1	20x2
Production and Inventory Data			
Planned production (in units)	50,000	50,000	50,000
Finished-goods inventory (in units), January 1	–0–	–0–	15,000
Actual production (in units)	50,000	50,000	50,000
Sales (in units)	50,000	35,000	65,000
Finished-goods inventory (in units), December 31	–0–	15,000	–0–
Revenue and Cost Data, All Three Years			
Sales price per unit			$12
Manufacturing costs per unit:			
Direct material			$ 3
Direct labour			2
Variable manufacturing overhead			1
Total variable cost per unit			$ 6
Used only under absorption costing { Fixed manufacturing overhead: Budgeted annual fixed overhead / Planned annual production = $150,000 / 50,000			3
Total absorption cost per unit			$ 9
Variable selling and administrative cost per unit			$ 1
Fixed selling and administrative cost per year			$25,000

Exhibit 8–2
Data for Illustration

Quíkmath.com

QUIKMATH.COM
Absorption-Costing Income Statement

	20x0	20x1	20x2
Sales revenue (at $12 per unit)	$600,000	$420,000	$780,000
Less: Cost of goods sold (at absorption cost of $9 per unit)	450,000	315,000	585,000
Gross margin	$150,000	$105,000	$195,000
Less: Selling and administrative expenses:			
Variable (at $1 per unit)	50,000	35,000	65,000
Fixed	25,000	25,000	25,000
Net income	$ 75,000	$ 45,000	$105,000

QUIKMATH.COM
Variable-Costing Income Statement

	20x0	20x1	20x2
Sales revenue (at $12 per unit)	$600,000	$420,000	$780,000
Less: Variable expenses:			
Variable manufacturing costs (at variable cost of $6 per unit)	300,000	210,000	390,000
Variable selling and administrative costs (at $1 per unit)	50,000	35,000	65,000
Contribution margin	$250,000	$175,000	$325,000
Less: Fixed expenses:			
Fixed manufacturing overhead	150,000	150,000	150,000
Fixed selling and administrative expenses	25,000	25,000	25,000
Net income	$ 75,000	$ 0	$150,000

Exhibit 8–3
Income Statements under Absorption and Variable Costing

Quíkmath.com

Exhibit 8–4
Reconciliation of Income
under Absorption and Variable
Costing: Quikmath.com

Quikmath.com

		20x0	20x1	20x2
1	Cost of goods sold under absorption costing	$450,000	$315,000	$585,000
	Variable manufacturing costs under variable costing	300,000	210,000	390,000
	Subtotal	$150,000	$105,000	$195,000
2	Fixed manufacturing overhead as period expense under variable costing	150,000	150,000	150,000
	Total	$ 0	$ (45,000)	$ 45,000
	Net income under variable costing	$ 75,000	$ 0	$150,000
	Net income under absorption costing	75,000	45,000	105,000
	Difference in net income	$ 0	$ (45,000)	$ 45,000

sales are the same. Think about the implications of the stable inventory level for the treatment of fixed manufacturing overhead. On the variable-costing statement, the $150,000 of fixed manufacturing overhead incurred during 20x0 is an expense in 20x0. Under absorption costing, however, fixed manufacturing overhead was applied to production at the predetermined rate of $3 per unit. Since all of the units produced in 20x0 also were sold in 20x0, all of the fixed manufacturing-overhead cost flowed through into Cost of Goods Sold. Thus, $150,000 of fixed manufacturing overhead was expensed in 20x0 under absorption costing also.

The 20x0 column of Exhibit 8–4 reconciles the 20x0 net income reported under absorption and variable costing. The reconciliation focuses on the two places in the income statements where differences occur between absorption and variable costing. The numbers in the left-hand margin of Exhibit 8–4 correspond to the numbers in the left-hand margin of the income statements in Exhibit 8–3.

Increase in Inventory   In 20x1 inventory increased from zero on January 1 to 15,000 units on December 31. The increase in inventory was the result of production exceeding sales. Under variable costing, the $150,000 of fixed overhead cost incurred in 20x1 is expensed, just as it was in 20x0. Under absorption costing, however, only a portion of the 20x1 fixed manufacturing overhead is expensed in 20x1. Since the fixed overhead is inventoried under absorption costing, some of this cost *remains in inventory* at the end of 20x1.

The 20x1 column of Exhibit 8–4 reconciles the 20x1 net income reported under absorption and variable costing. As before, the reconciliation focuses on the two places in the income statements where differences occur between absorption and variable costing.

> "The operational managers' bonuses are based on profitability, so they are keenly interested in the financial management reports' results." (8a)
>
> John Deere Health Care, Inc.

Decrease in Inventory   In 20x2 inventory decreased from 15,000 units to zero. Sales during the year exceeded production. As in 20x0 and 20x1, under variable costing, the $150,000 of fixed manufacturing overhead incurred in 20x2 is expensed in 20x2. Under absorption costing, however, *more than* $150,000 of fixed overhead is expensed in 20x2. Why? Because some of the fixed overhead incurred during the prior year, which was inventoried then, is now expensed in 20x2 as the goods are sold.

The 20x2 column of Exhibit 8–4 reconciles the 20x2 income under absorption and variable costing. Once again, the numbers on the left-hand side of Exhibit 8–4 correspond to those on the left-hand side of the income statements in Exhibit 8–3.

A Shortcut to Reconciling Income   When inventory increases or decreases during the year, reported income differs under absorption and variable costing. This results from the fixed overhead that is inventoried under absorption costing but expensed immediately under variable costing. The following formula may be used to compute the difference in the amount of fixed overhead expensed in a given time period under the two product-costing methods:

$$\begin{pmatrix} \text{Difference in fixed overhead} \\ \text{expensed under absorption} \\ \text{and variable costing} \end{pmatrix} = \begin{pmatrix} \text{Change in} \\ \text{inventory,} \\ \text{in units} \end{pmatrix} \times \begin{pmatrix} \text{Predetermined} \\ \text{fixed-overhead} \\ \text{rate per unit} \end{pmatrix}$$

As the following table shows, this difference in the amount of fixed overhead expensed explains the difference in reported income under absorption and variable costing:

Year	Change in Inventory (in units)		Predetermined Fixed-Overhead Rate		Difference in Fixed Overhead Expensed		Absorption-Costing Income Minus Variable-Costing Income
20x0	–0–	×	$3	=	–0–	=	–0–
20x1	15,000 increase	×	$3	=	$45,000	=	$45,000
20x2	15,000 decrease	×	$3	=	$(45,000)	=	$(45,000)

Length of Time Period The discrepancies between absorption-costing and variable costing income in Exhibit 8–3 occur because of the changes in inventory levels during 20x1 and 20x2. It is common for production and sales to differ over the course of a week, month, or year. Therefore, the income measured for those time periods often will differ between absorption and variable costing. This discrepancy is likely to be smaller over longer time periods. Over the course of a decade, for example, Quikmath.com cannot sell much more or less than it produces. Thus, the income amounts under the two product-costing methods, when added together over a lengthy time period, will be approximately equal under absorption and variable costing.

Notice in Exhibit 8–3 that Quikmath.com's total income over the three-year period is $225,000 under *both* absorption and variable costing. This results from the fact that the company produced and sold the same total amount over the three-year period.

Cost-Volume-Profit Analysis

Quikmath.com's break-even point in units can be computed as follows:

Learning Objective 5

Explain the implications of absorption and variable costing for cost-volume-profit analysis.

$$\text{Break-even point} = \frac{\text{Fixed costs}}{\text{Unit contribution margin}} = \frac{\$150,000 + \$25,000}{\$12 - \$6 - \$1}$$

$$= \frac{\$175,000}{\$5} = 35,000 \text{ units}$$

If Quikmath.com sells 35,000 calculators, net income should be zero, as Exhibit 8–5 confirms.

Now return to Exhibit 8–3 and examine the 20x1 income statements under absorption and variable costing. In 20x1 Quikmath.com sold 35,000 units, the break-even volume.

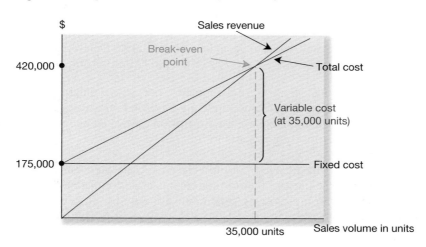

Exhibit 8–5
Break-Even Graph: Quikmath.com

Quikmath.com

This fact is confirmed on the variable-costing income statement, since net income is zero. On the absorption-costing income statement, however, the 20x1 net income is $45,000. What has happened here?

The answer to this inconsistency lies in the different treatment of fixed manufacturing overhead under absorption and variable costing. Variable costing highlights the separation between fixed and variable costs, as do CVP analysis and break-even calculations. Both of these techniques account for fixed manufacturing overhead as a lump sum. In contrast, *absorption costing is inconsistent with CVP analysis*, because fixed overhead is applied to goods as a product cost on a per-unit basis.

Evaluation of Absorption and Variable Costing

Learning Objective 6

Evaluate absorption and variable costing.

Some managers find the inconsistency between absorption costing and CVP analysis troubling enough to warrant using variable costing for internal income reporting. Variable costing dovetails much more closely than absorption costing with any operational analyses that require a separation between fixed and variable costs.

Pricing Decisions   Many managers prefer to use absorption-costing data in cost-based pricing decisions. They argue that fixed manufacturing overhead is a necessary cost incurred in the production process. To exclude this fixed cost from the inventoried cost of a product, as is done under variable costing, is to understate the cost of the product. For this reason, most companies that use cost-based pricing set up their prices on absorption-costing data.

Proponents of variable costing argue that a product's variable cost provides a better basis for the pricing decision. They point out that any price above a product's variable cost makes a positive contribution to covering fixed cost and profit.

Definition of an Asset   Another controversy about absorption and variable costing hinges on the definition of an asset. An *asset* is a thing of value owned by the organization with future service potential. By accounting convention, assets are valued at their cost. Since fixed costs make up part of the cost of production, advocates of absorption costing argue that inventory (an asset) should be valued at its full (absorption) cost of production. Moreover, they argue that these costs have future service potential since the inventory can be sold in the future to generate sales revenue.

Proponents of variable costing argue that the fixed-cost component of a product's absorption-costing value has no future service potential. Their reasoning is that the fixed manufacturing-overhead costs during the current period will not prevent these costs from having to be incurred again next period. Fixed-overhead costs will be incurred every period, regardless of production levels. In contrast, the incurrence of variable costs in manufacturing a product does allow the firm to avoid incurring these costs again.

To illustrate, Quikmath.com produced 15,000 more calculators in 20x1 than it sold. These units will be carried in inventory until they are sold in some future year. Quikmath.com will never again have to incur the costs of direct material, direct labour, and variable overhead incurred in 20x1 to produce those calculators. Yet Quikmath.com will have to incur approximately $150,000 of fixed-overhead costs every year, even though the firm has the 15,000 units from 20x1 in inventory.

External Reporting   For external reporting purposes, generally accepted accounting principles require that income reporting be based on absorption costing. Federal tax laws allow either direct costing or absorption costing as acceptable methods of inventory costing in reporting income for tax purposes.[1]

Why Not Both?   In the age of computerized accounting systems, it is straightforward for a company to prepare income statements under both absorption and variable costing. Since absorption-costing statements are required for external reporting, managers will want to keep an eye on the effects of their decisions on financial reports to outsiders. Yet the superiority of variable-costing income reporting as a method for dovetailing with operational analyses cannot be denied. Preparation of both absorption costing and variable-costing data is perhaps the best solution to the controversy.

JIT Manufacturing Environment   In a just-in-time inventory and production management system, all inventories are kept very low. Since finished-goods inventories are minimal, there is little change in inventory from period to period. Thus, in a JIT environment, the income differences under absorption and variable costing generally will be insignificant.

Throughput Costing

Some managers advocate *throughput costing* as an alternative to either absorption or variable costing for product costing and income reporting. **Throughput costing** assigns *only* the unit-level *spending* for direct costs as the cost of products or services. A unit-level cost is one that is incurred every time a unit of product is manufactured and that will *not* be incurred if another unit is not manufactured.[2] Advocates of throughput costing argue that classifying any other past or committed cost as a product cost creates an incentive to drive down the average cost per unit simply by manufacturing more units on nonbottleneck processes.

> **Learning Objective 7**
>
> Explain the rationale behind throughput costing.

Throughput-Costing Income Statements

Suppose Quikmath.com's management team decided that only direct material qualified as a throughput cost. This implies that Quikmath.com's management has *committed*, at least for the time being, to provide *all* other resources (i.e., direct labour and all manufacturing support costs included in manufacturing overhead) regardless of how many calculators and other devices Quikmath.com produces. Under throughput costing, then, Quikmath.com's income statements for the three years in our illustration would appear as in the Excel spreadsheet shown in Exhibit 8–6. Notice that all costs other than the throughput cost (only direct material in this hypothetical illustration) are considered to be operating costs of the period.

> **Learning Objective 8**
>
> Prepare an income statement under throughput costing.

	A	B	C	D	E
1	QUIKMATH.COM				
2	Throughput-Costing Income Statement				
3					
4			20x0	20x1	20x2
5					
6	Sales revenue (at $12 per unit)		$ 600,000	$ 420,000	$ 780,000
7	Less: Cost of goods sold (at throughput cost:				
8	standard direct-material cost)[a]		150,000	105,000	195,000
9	Gross margin		$ 450,000	$ 315,000	$ 585,000
10	Less: Operating costs:				
11	Direct labour[b]		$ 100,000	$ 100,000	$ 100,000
12	Variable manufacturing overhead[c]		50,000	50,000	50,000
13	Fixed manufacturing overhead[c]		150,000	150,000	150,000
14	Variable selling and administrative costs[d]		50,000	35,000	65,000
15	Fixed selling and administrative costs[d]		25,000	25,000	25,000
16	Total operating costs		$ 375,000	$ 360,000	$ 390,000
17	Net income		$ 75,000	$ (45,000)	$ 195,000
18					
19	[a]Standard direct-material cost per unit of $3 multiplied by sales volume in units.				
20					
21	[b]Assumes management has committed to direct labour sufficient to produce the planned annual production				
22	volume of 50,000; direct-labour cost is used at a rate of $2 per unit produced.				
23					
24	[c]Assumes management has committed to support resources sufficient to produce the planned annual				
25	production volume of 50,000 units; variable-overhead cost is used at a rate of $1 per unit produced. Fixed				
26	overhead is $150,000 per year.				
27					
28	[d]Variable selling and administrative costs used amount to $1 per unit sold. Fixed selling and				
29	administrative costs are $25,000 per year.				

Exhibit 8–6

Income Statements under Throughput Costing

Q**uikmath**.com

A comparison of the reported income under throughput costing (Exhibit 8–6) with the reported income under either variable or absorption costing (Exhibit 8–3) reveals substantial differences in the "bottom line" under the three methods for each year. Proponents of throughput costing argue that this method alone eliminates the incentive to produce excess inventory simply to reduce unit costs by spreading *committed* resource costs (i.e., direct labour and variable and fixed manufacturing overhead) across more units. The incentive for such overproduction disappears under throughput costing, because all nonthroughput costs (direct labour and manufacturing overhead in our illustration) will be expensed as period costs regardless of how many units are produced.

Focus on Ethics

INCENTIVE TO OVERPRODUCE INVENTORY

This classic case is based on an actual company's experience.[3] Brandolino Company uses an actual cost system to apply all production costs to units produced. The plant has a maximum production capacity of 40 million units but produced and sold only 10 million units during year 1. There were no beginning or ending inventories. The company's absorption-costing income statement for year 1 follows:

BRANDOLINO COMPANY
Income Statement
For Year 1

Sales (10,000,000 units at $6)		$ 60,000,000
Cost of goods sold:		
Direct costs (material and labour)		
(10,000,000 at $2)	$20,000,000	
Manufacturing overhead	48,000,000	68,000,000
Gross margin		(8,000,000)
Selling and administrative costs		10,000,000
Operating profit (loss)		$(18,000,000)

The board of directors is upset about the $18 million loss. A consultant approached the board with the following offer: "I agree to become president for no fixed salary. But I insist on a year-end bonus of 10 percent of operating profit (before considering the bonus)." The board of directors agreed to these terms and hired the consultant as Brandolino's new president. The new president promptly stepped up production to an annual rate of 30 million units. Sales for year 2 remained at 10 million units. The resulting absorption-costing income statement for year 2 is displayed in the right-hand column.

The day after the year 2 statement was verified, the president took his cheque for $1,400,000 and resigned to take a job with another corporation. He remarked, "I enjoy challenges. Now that Brandolino Company is in the black,

I'd prefer tackling another challenging situation." (His contract with his new employer is similar to the one he had with Brandolino Company.)

BRANDOLINO COMPANY
Income Statement
For Year 2

Sales (10,000,000 units at $6)		$60,000,000
Cost of goods sold:		
Costs of goods manufactured:		
Direct costs (material and labour)		
(30,000,000 at $2)	$ 60,000,000	
Manufacturing overhead	48,000,000	
Total cost of goods		
manufactured	108,000,000	
Less: Ending inventory:		
Direct costs (material and labour)		
(20,000,000 at $2)	40,000,000	
Manufacturing overhead		
(20/30 × $48,000,000)	32,000,000	
Total ending inventory costs	72,000,000	
Cost of goods sold		36,000,000
Gross margin		24,000,000
Selling and administrative costs		10,000,000
Operating profit before bonus		14,000,000
Bonus		1,400,000
Operating profit after bonus		$12,600,000

What do you think is going on here? How would you evaluate the company's year 2 performance? Using variable costing, what would operating profit be for year 1? For year 2? (Assume that all selling and administrative costs are committed and unchanged.) Compare those results with the absorption-costing statements. Comment on the ethical issues in this scenario.

Chapter Summary

Absorption and variable costing are two alternative product-costing systems that differ in their treatment of fixed manufacturing overhead. Under absorption (or full) costing, fixed overhead is applied to manufactured goods as a product cost. The fixed-overhead cost remains in inventory until the goods are sold. Under variable (or direct) costing, fixed overhead is a period cost expensed during the period when it is incurred. Absorption costing is required for external reporting, and either variable or absorption costing are acceptable for tax purposes. However, variable costing is more consistent with operational decision analyses, which require a separation of fixed and variable costs.

One of the tools used by managers to plan and control business operations is cost-volume-profit analysis. Variable costing highlights the separation between fixed and variable costs, as do CVP analysis and break-even calculations. Both of these techniques account for fixed manufacturing overhead as a lump sum. In contrast, absorption costing is inconsistent with CVP analysis, because fixed overhead is applied to goods as a product cost on a per-unit basis. Some managers find the inconsistency between absorption costing and CVP analysis troubling enough to warrant using variable costing for internal income reporting. Variable costing dovetails much more closely than absorption costing with any operational analyses that require a separation between fixed and variable costs.

Some accountants and managers advocate throughput costing, in which only throughput costs are inventoried as product costs. They argue that throughput costing reduces the incentive for management to produce excess inventory simply for the purpose of spreading committed (nonthroughput) costs across a larger number of units produced.

Review Problem on Absorption and Variable Costing

ScholasticPak Company manufactures backpacks used by students. A typical backpack has the following price and variable costs:

Sales price	$45
Direct material	15
Direct labour	6
Variable overhead	9

Budgeted fixed overhead in the company's first year of operations, was $900,000. Actual production was 150,000 units, of which 125,000 were sold. ScholasticPak incurred the following selling and administrative expenses.

Fixed	$150,000 for the year
Variable	$3 per unit sold

Required:

1. Compute the product cost per backpack under (*a*) variable costing and (*b*) absorption costing.
2. Prepare income statements for the year using (*a*) variable costing and (*b*) absorption costing.
3. Reconcile the income reported under the two methods by analyzing the two key places where the income statements differ.

Solution to Review Problem

1. Predetermined fixed overhead rate $= \dfrac{\text{Budgeted fixed overhead}}{\text{Budgeted production}}$

$$= \frac{\$900,000}{150,000} = \$6 \text{ per unit}$$

Product Cost per Unit

Direct material	$15
Direct labour	6
Variable overhead	9
a. Cost per unit under variable costing	$30
Fixed overhead per unit under absorption costing	6
b. Cost per unit under absorption costing	$36

2. *a.*   **Variable-Costing Income Statement**

Sales revenue (125,000 units sold at $45 per unit)	$5,625,000
Less: Variable expenses:	
Variable manufacturing costs (at variable cost of $30 per unit)	3,750,000
Variable selling and administrative costs (at $3 per unit × 125,000 units sold)	375,000
Contribution margin	1,500,000
Less: Fixed expenses:	
Fixed manufacturing overhead	900,000
Fixed selling and administrative expenses	150,000
Net income	$ 450,000

b.   **Absorption-Costing Income Statement**

Sales revenue (125,000 units sold at $45 per unit)..	$5,625,000
Less: Cost of goods sold	
(at absorption cost of $36 per unit)	4,500,000
Gross margin	1,125,000
Less: Selling and administrative expenses:	
Variable (at $3 per unit × 125,000 units sold)	375,000
Fixed	150,000
Net income	$ 600,000

3.

Cost of goods sold under absorption costing	$4,500,000
Less: Variable manufacturing costs under variable costing	3,750,000
Subtotal	750,000
Less: Fixed manufacturing overhead as period expense	
under variable costing	900,000
Total	$ (150,000)
Net income under variable costing	$ 450,000
Less: Net income under absorption costing	600,000
Difference in net income	$ (150,000)

Key Terms

For each term's definition refer to the indicated page, or turn to the glossary at the end of the text.

absorption (*or* full) costing, 287	throughput costing, 293	variable (*or* direct) costing, 287

Review Questions

8–1. Briefly explain the difference between absorption costing and variable costing.

8–2. Timing is the key in distinguishing between absorption and variable costing. Explain this statement.

8–3. "The term *direct costing* is a misnomer. *Variable costing* is a better term for the product-costing method." Do you agree or disagree? Why?

8–4. When inventory increases, will absorption-costing or variable-costing income be greater? Why?

8–5. Why do many managers prefer variable costing over absorption costing?

8–6. Explain how throughput costing differs from absorption and variable costing.

8–7. Explain why some management accountants believe that absorption costing may provide an incentive for managers to overproduce inventory. How does throughput costing avoid this problem?

8–8. Will variable and absorption costing result in significantly different income measures in a JIT setting? Why?

8–9. Why do proponents of absorption costing argue that absorption costing is preferable as the basis for pricing decisions?

8–10. Why do proponents of variable costing prefer variable costing when making pricing decisions?

8–11. Which is more consistent with cost-volume-profit analysis, variable costing or absorption costing? Why?

8–12. Explain how the accounting definition of an asset is related to the choice between absorption and variable costing.

Exercises

Dolphin Company manufactures two-person sailboats with a variable cost of $1,000. The sailboats sell for $1,750 each. Budgeted fixed manufacturing overhead for the most recent year was $11,000,000. Planned and actual production for the year were the same.

Required: Under each of the following conditions, state (*a*) whether income is higher under variable or absorption costing and (*b*) the amount of the difference in reported income under the two methods. Treat each condition as an independent case.

1.	Production	22,000 units
	Sales	25,000 units
2.	Production	10,600 units
	Sales	10,600 units
3.	Production	11,000 units
	Sales	9,800 units

■ **Exercise 8–13**
Difference in Income under Absorption and Variable Costing
(LO 1, 4)

Refer to the data given in the preceding exercise for Dolphin Company.

Required:

1. Prepare a cost-volume-profit graph for the company. (Scale the vertical axis in millions of dollars, and draw the CVP graph up through 15,000 units on the horizontal axis.)
2. Calculate Dolphin Company's break-even point in units, and show the break-even point on the CVP graph.
3. Explain why variable costing is more compatible with your CVP graph than absorption costing would be.

■ **Exercise 8–14**
Variable Costing and Cost-Volume-Profit Analysis
(LO 5)

Easton Pump Company's planned production for the year just ended was 20,000 units. This production level was achieved, and 21,000 units were sold. Other data follow:

Direct material used	$300,000
Direct labour incurred	150,000
Fixed manufacturing overhead	210,000
Variable manufacturing overhead	100,000
Fixed selling and administrative expenses	175,000
Variable selling and administrative expenses	52,500
Finished-goods inventory, January 1	2,000 units

■ **Exercise 8–15**
Absorption and Variable Costing
(LO 1, 4)

   The cost per unit remained the same in the current year as in the previous year. There were no work-in-process inventories at the beginning or end of the year.

Required:

1. What would be Easton Pump Company's finished-goods inventory cost on December 31 under the variable-costing method?
2. Which costing method, absorption or variable costing, would show a higher operating income for the year? By what amount?

(CMA, adapted)

Manta Ray Company manufactures diving masks with a standard variable cost of $12.50. The masks sell for $17. Budgeted fixed manufacturing overhead for the most recent year was $396,000. Actual production was equal to planned production.

■ **Exercise 8–16**
Difference in Income under Absorption and Variable Costing
(LO 1, 4)

Required: Under each of the following conditions, state (*a*) whether income is higher under variable or absorption costing and (*b*) the amount of the difference in reported income under the two methods. Treat each condition as an independent case.

1.	Production	110,000 units
	Sales	107,000 units
2.	Production	88,000 units
	Sales	93,000 units
3.	Production	80,100 units
	Sales	80,100 units

Exercise 8–17
Absorption versus Variable Costing
(LO 1)

Information taken from Allied Pipe Company's records for the most recent year is as follows:

Direct material used	$272,000
Direct labour	128,000
Variable manufacturing overhead	60,000
Fixed manufacturing overhead	100,000
Variable selling and administrative costs	56,000
Fixed selling and administrative costs	29,600

Required:

1. Assuming Allied Pipe Company uses absorption costing, compute the inventoriable costs for the year.
2. Compute the year's inventoriable costs using variable costing.

(CMA, adapted)

Exercise 8–18
Absorption, Variable, and Throughput Costing; Use of Internet
(LO 1, 7)

Visit the Web site for one of the following companies, or a different company of your choosing.

Bombardier	www.bombardier.com
Corby Distilleries Limited	www.corby.ca
Goodyear Canada	www.goodyear.ca
Magna International	www.magna.com
Research In Motion	www.rim.com
Xerox Corporation	www.xerox.com

Required: Read about the company's products and operations. Discuss the pros and cons of absorption, variable, and throughput costing as the basis for product costing if the firm uses cost-based pricing.

Exercise 8–19
Absorption, Variable, and Throughput Costing
(LO 1, 4, 7)

Pandora Pillow Company's planned production for the year just ended was 10,000 units. This production level was achieved, but only 9,000 units were sold. Other data follow:

Direct material used	$80,000
Direct labour incurred	40,000
Fixed manufacturing overhead	50,000
Variable manufacturing overhead	24,000
Fixed selling and administrative expenses	60,000
Variable selling and administrative expenses	9,000
Finished-goods inventory, January 1	None

There were no work-in-process inventories at the beginning or end of the year.

Required:

1. What would be Pandora Pillow Company's finished-goods inventory cost on December 31 under the variable-costing method?
2. Which costing method, absorption or variable costing, would show a higher operating income for the year? By what amount?
3. Suppose Pandora Pillow Company uses throughput costing, and direct material is its only unit-level cost. What would be Pandora's finished-goods inventory on December 31?

(CMA, adapted)

Information taken from Tuscarora Paper Company's records for the most recent year is as follows:

Direct material used	$203,000
Direct labour	70,000
Variable manufacturing overhead	35,000
Fixed manufacturing overhead	56,000
Variable selling and administrative costs	28,000
Fixed selling and administrative costs	14,000

Exercise 8–20
Absorption, Variable, and
Throughput Costing
(LO 1, 7)

Required:

1. Assuming Tuscarora Paper Company uses variable costing, compute the inventoriable costs for the year.
2. Compute the year's inventoriable costs using absorption costing.
3. Now assume that Tuscarora Paper Company uses throughput costing, and the company has committed to spending for direct labour, variable overhead, and fixed overhead in the amounts given in the problem. Under this scenario, compute the company's inventoriable costs for the year.

(CMA, adapted)

Problems

Algonquin Can Company manufactures metal cans used in the food-processing industry. A case of cans sells for $25. The variable costs of production for one case of cans are as follows:

Direct material	$ 7.50
Direct labour	2.50
Variable manufacturing overhead	6.00
Total variable manufacturing cost per case	$16.00

Problem 8–21
Variable-Costing and
Absorption Costing Income
Statements; Reconciling
Reported Income
(LO 2, 3, 4)

1. Standard absorption cost
per case: $21

Variable selling and administrative costs amount to $.50 per case. Budgeted fixed manufacturing overhead is $400,000 per year, and fixed selling and administrative cost is $37,500 per year. The following data pertain to the company's first three years of operation.

	Year 1	Year 2	Year 3
Planned production (in units)	80,000	80,000	80,000
Finished-goods inventory (in units), January 1	0	0	20,000
Actual production (in units)	80,000	80,000	80,000
Sales (in units)	80,000	60,000	90,000
Finished-goods inventory (in units), December 31	0	20,000	10,000

There were no variances during Algonquin's first three years of operation. Actual costs were the same as the budgeted costs.

Required:

1. Prepare operating income statements for Algonquin Can Company for its first three years of operations using:
   a. Absorption costing
   b. Variable costing
2. Reconcile Algonquin Can Company's operating income reported under absorption and variable costing for each of its first three years of operation. Use the shortcut method.
3. Suppose that during Algonquin's fourth year of operation actual production equals planned production, actual costs are equal to budgeted or standard costs, and the company ends the year with no inventory on hand.
   a. What will be the difference between absorption-costing income and variable-costing income in year 4?
   b. What will be the relationship between total operating income for the four-year period as reported under absorption and variable costing? Explain.

Problem 8–22
Throughput Costing
(LO 7, 8)

Gross margin, year 1:
$1,400,000

Refer to the information in the preceding problem for Algonquin Can Company. Assume that direct material is the *only unit-level* manufacturing cost.

Required: Prepare income statements for all three years using throughput costing.

Problem 8–23
Absorption and Variable
Costing; CVP Analysis
(LO 4, 5)

1. Fixed overhead: $200,000

Yellowstone Company began operations on January 1 to produce a single product. It used an absorption costing system with a planned production volume of 100,000 units. During its first year of operations, there were no fixed selling or administrative expenses. Inventory on December 31 was 20,000 units, and net income for the year was $480,000.

Required:

1. If Yellowstone Company had used variable costing, its net income would have been $440,000. Compute the break-even point in units under variable costing.
2. Draw a profit-volume graph for Yellowstone Company. (Use variable costing.)

Problem 8–24
Straightforward Problem on
Absorption versus Variable
Costing
(LO 2, 3, 4, 6)

1. Predetermined fixed
overhead rate: $4 per unit
2a. Gross margin: $750,000

Skinny Dippers, Inc. produces nonfat frozen yogurt. The product is sold at wholesale in 10-litre commercial containers, which have the following price and variable costs.

Sales price	$30
Direct material	10
Direct labour	4
Variable overhead	6

Budgeted fixed overhead in 20x4, the company's first year of operations, was $600,000. Actual production was 150,000 10-litre containers, of which 125,000 were sold. Skinny Dippers, Inc. incurred the following selling and administrative expenses.

Fixed	$100,000 for the year
Variable	$2 per container sold

Required:

1. Compute the product cost per container of frozen yogurt under (*a*) variable costing and (*b*) absorption costing.
2. Prepare income statements for 20x4 using (*a*) absorption costing and (*b*) variable costing.
3. Reconcile the income reported under the two methods by listing the two key places where the income statements differ.
4. Reconcile the income reported under the two methods using the shortcut method.
5. *Build a spreadsheet:* Construct an Excel spreadsheet to solve all of the preceding requirements. Show how the solution will change if the following information changes: the selling price and direct-material cost per unit are $32 and $9, respectively.

Problem 8–25
Straightforward Problem on
Throughput Costing
(LO 7, 8)

2. Gross margin: $2,500,000

Refer to the information given in the preceding problem for Skinny Dippers, Inc. Assume that the company has committed spending for direct labour and manufacturing overhead; direct material is the only unit-level production cost.

Required:

1. Compute the cost of Skinny Dippers' year-end finished-goods inventory using throughput costing.
2. Prepare an income statement for 20x1 using throughput costing.
3. Briefly explain the difference between gross margin computed under absorption costing and gross margin computed under throughput costing.
4. *Build a spreadsheet:* Construct an Excel spreadsheet to solve requirement (2) above. Show how the solution will change if the following information changes: the selling price and direct-material cost per unit are $32 and $9, respectively.

Outback Corporation manufactures rechargeable flashlights in Melbourne, Australia. The firm uses an absorption costing system for internal reporting purposes; however, the company is considering using variable costing. Data regarding Outback's planned and actual operations for 20x4 follow:

	Budgeted Costs		
	Per Unit	**Total**	**Actual Costs**
Direct material	$ 6.00	$ 840,000	$ 780,000
Direct labour	4.50	630,000	585,000
Variable manufacturing overhead	2.00	280,000	260,000
Fixed manufacturing overhead	2.50	350,000	357,500
Variable selling expenses	4.00	560,000	500,000
Fixed selling expenses	3.50	490,000	490,000
Variable administrative expenses	1.00	140,000	125,000
Fixed administrative expenses	1.50	210,000	212,500
Total	$25.00	$3,500,000	$3,310,000

	Planned Activity	**Actual Activity**
Beginning finished-goods inventory in units	35,000	35,000
Sales in units	140,000	125,000
Production in units	140,000	130,000

The budgeted per-unit cost figures were based on Outback producing and selling 140,000 units in 20x4. Outback uses a predetermined overhead rate for applying manufacturing overhead to its product. A total manufacturing overhead rate of $4.50 per unit was employed for absorption costing purposes in 20x4. Any overapplied or underapplied manufacturing overhead is closed to the Cost of Goods Sold account at the end of the year. The 20x4 beginning finished-goods inventory for absorption costing purposes was valued at the 20x3 budgeted unit manufacturing cost, which was the same as the 20x4 budgeted unit manufacturing cost. There are no work-in-process inventories at either the beginning or the end of the year. The planned and actual unit selling price for 20x4 was $35 per unit.

Required: Was Outback's 20x4 income higher under absorption costing or variable costing? Why? Compute the following amounts.

1. The value of Outback Corporation's 20x4 ending finished-goods inventory under absorption costing.
2. The value of Outback Corporation's 20x4 ending finished-goods inventory under variable costing.
3. The difference between Outback Corporation's 20x4 reported income calculated under absorption costing and calculated under variable costing.
4. Suppose Outback Corporation had introduced a JIT production and inventory management system at the beginning of 20x4.
   a. What would likely be different about the scenario as described in the problem?
   b. Would reported income under variable and absorption costing differ by the magnitude you found in requirement (3)? Explain.

(CMA, adapted)

Emerson Corporation, which uses throughput costing, just completed its first year of operations. Planned and actual production equalled 10,000 units, and sales totalled 9,600 units at $216 per unit. Cost data for the year are as follows:

Direct material (per unit)	$36
Conversion cost:	
Direct labour	135,000
Variable manufacturing overhead	195,000
Fixed manufacturing overhead	660,000
Selling and administrative costs:	
Variable (per unit)	24
Fixed	354,000

The company classifies only direct material as a throughput cost.

Problem 8–26
Variable versus Absorption
Costing; JIT
(LO 1, 4)

1. Total budgeted manufacturing costs: $2,100,000
2. Budgeted variable manufacturing costs: $12.50 per unit

Problem 8–27
Throughput Costing,
Absorption Costing, and
Variable Costing
(LO 1, 2, 3, 7, 8)

2. Year-end inventory: 400 units
4. Net income: $153,600

Required:

1. Compute the company's total cost for the year assuming that variable manufacturing costs are driven by the number of units produced, and variable selling and administrative costs are driven by the number of units sold.
2. How much of this cost would be held in year-end inventory under (*a*) absorption costing, (*b*) variable costing, and (*c*) throughput costing?
3. How much of the company's total cost for the year would be included as an expense on the period's income statement under (*a*) absorption costing, (*b*) variable costing, and (*c*) throughput costing?
4. Prepare Emerson's throughput-costing income statement.
5. ***Build a spreadsheet:*** Construct an Excel spreadsheet to solve requirements (1) and (2) above. Show how the solution will change if the following information changes: the direct-material cost is $35 per unit, and the total direct-labour cost is $130,000.

■ **Problem 8–28**
Variable and Absorption
Costing
(LO 4, 6)

2*a*. Contribution margin per
unit: $33

Victoria Lighting Company had net income for the first 10 months of the current year of $300,000. One hundred thousand units were manufactured during this period, and 100,000 units were sold. Fixed manufacturing overhead was $3,000,000 over the 10-month period (i.e., $300,000 per month). There are no selling and administrative expenses for Victoria Lighting Company. Both variable and fixed costs are expected to continue at the same rates for the balance of the year (i.e., fixed costs at $300,000 per month and variable costs at the same variable cost per unit). There were 10,000 units in inventory on October 31. Twenty thousand units are to be produced and 19,000 units are to be sold in total over the last two months of the current year. Assume the unit variable cost is the same in the current year as in the previous year. (*Hint:* You cannot calculate revenue or cost of goods sold; you must work directly with contribution margin or gross margin.)

Required:

1. If operations proceed as described, will net income be higher under variable or absorption costing for the current year in total? Why?
2. If operations proceed as described, what will net income for the year in total be under (*a*) variable costing and (*b*) absorption costing? (Ignore income taxes.)
3. Discuss the advantages and disadvantages of absorption and variable costing.

■ **Problem 8–29**
Variable-Costing and
Absorption-Costing Income
Statements; FMS; JIT
(LO 2, 3, 4)

1. Total variable cost:
$78 per unit
2*a*. Absorption costing,
net income: $688,000

Great Outdoze, Inc. manufactures high-quality sleeping bags, which sell for $130 each. The variable costs of production are as follows:

Direct material	$40
Direct labour	22
Variable manufacturing overhead	16

Budgeted fixed overhead in 20x4 was $400,000 and budgeted production was 25,000 sleeping bags. The year's actual production was 25,000 units, of which 22,000 were sold. Variable selling and administrative costs were $2 per unit sold; fixed selling and administrative costs were $60,000.

Required:

1. Calculate the product cost per sleeping bag under (*a*) absorption costing and (*b*) variable costing.
2. Prepare income statements for the year using (*a*) absorption costing and (*b*) variable costing.
3. Reconcile reported income under the two methods using the shortcut method.
4. Suppose that Great Outdoze, Inc. implemented a JIT inventory and production management system at the beginning of 20x4. In addition, the firm installed a flexible manufacturing system. Would you expect reported income under variable and absorption costing to be different by as great a magnitude as you found in requirement (3)? Explain.

■ **Problem 8–30**
Throughput Costing
(LO 7, 8)

2. Throughput costing, gross
margin: $1,980,000

Refer to the information given in the preceding problem for Great Outdoze, Inc. Assume that direct material is the only unit-level manufacturing cost. The company has committed its spending for direct labour and overhead (variable and fixed).

Required:

1. Calculate the product cost per sleeping bag under throughput costing.
2. Prepare an income statement for the year 20x4 using throughput costing.
3. Give an argument for and against throughput costing.

Cases

Huron Chalk Company manufactures blackboard chalk for educational uses. The company's product is sold by the box at $25 per unit. Huron uses an actual costing system, which means that the actual costs of direct material, direct labour, and manufacturing overhead are entered into work-in-process inventory. The actual application rate for manufacturing overhead is computed each year; actual manufacturing overhead is divided by actual production (in units) to compute the application rate. Information for Huron's first two years of operation is as follows:

	Year 1	Year 2
Sales (in units)	2,500	2,500
Production (in units)	3,000	2,000
Production costs:		
Variable manufacturing costs	$10,500	$ 7,000
Fixed manufacturing overhead	21,000	21,000
Selling and administrative costs:		
Variable	12,500	12,500
Fixed	10,000	10,000

Required: Huron Chalk Company had no beginning or ending work-in-process inventories for either year.

1. Prepare operating income statements for both years based on absorption costing.
2. Prepare operating income statements for both years based on variable costing.
3. Prepare a numerical reconciliation of the difference in income reported under the two costing methods used in requirements (1) and (2).

Refer to the information given in the preceding problem for Huron Chalk Company.

Required:

1. Reconcile Huron's income reported under absorption and variable costing, during each year, by comparing the following two amounts on each income statement:
   - Cost of goods sold
   - Fixed cost (expensed as a period expense)
2. What was Huron's total income across both years under absorption costing and under variable costing?
3. What was the total sales revenue across both years under absorption costing and under variable costing?
4. What was the total of all costs expensed on the income statements across both years under absorption costing and under variable costing?
5. Subtract the total costs expensed across both years (requirement (4)) from the total sales revenue across both years (requirement (3)): (*a*) under absorption costing and (*b*) under variable costing.
6. Comment on the results obtained in requirements (1), (2), (3), and (4) in light of the following assertion: *Timing is the key in distinguishing between absorption and variable costing.*

■ **Case 8–31**
Comparison of Absorption and Variable Costing; Actual Costing
(LO 2, 3, 4)

1. Operating income, year 1: $13,750
2. Contribution margin, year 2: $41,250

■ **Case 8–32**
Analysis of Differences in Absorption-Costing and Variable-Costing Income Statements; Continuation of Preceding Problem
(LO 1, 4)

1. Year 1, absorption costing income: $13,750
4. Total of all costs expensed across both years: $104,500

Refer to the information given in Case 8–31 for Huron Chalk Company. Selected information from Huron's year-end balance sheets for its first two years of operation is as follows:

HURON CHALK COMPANY		
Selected Balance Sheet Information		
Based on Absorption Costing	**End of Year 1**	**End of Year 2**
Finished-goods inventory	$5,250	$ 0
Retained earnings	8,250	12,300
Based on Variable Costing	**End of Year 1**	**End of Year 2**
Finished-goods inventory	$1,750	$ 0
Retained earnings.	4,750	12,300

Required:

1. Why is the year 1 ending balance in finished-goods inventory higher if absorption costing is used than if variable costing is used?

2. Why is the year 2 ending balance in finished-goods inventory the same under absorption and variable costing?

3. Notice that the ending balance of finished-goods inventory under absorption costing is greater than or equal to the ending finished-goods inventory balance under variable costing *for both years 1 and 2.* Will this relationship always hold true at any balance sheet date? Explain.

4. Compute the amount by which the year-end balance in finished-goods inventory declined during year 2 (i.e., between December 31 of year 1 and December 31 of year 2):
    *   Using the data from the balance sheet prepared under absorption costing
    *   Using the data from the balance sheet prepared under variable costing

5. Refer to your calculations from requirement (4). Compute the difference in the amount by which the year-end balances in finished-goods inventory declined under absorption versus variable costing. Then compare the amount of this difference with the difference in the company's reported income for year 2 under absorption versus variable costing. (Refer to the income statements prepared in Case 8–31.)

6. Notice that the retained earnings balance at the end of both years 1 and 2 on the balance sheet prepared under absorption costing is greater than or equal to the corresponding retained earnings balance on the statement prepared under variable costing. Will this relationship hold true at any balance sheet date? Explain.

Chapter Nine

Profit Planning and Activity-Based Budgeting

cozycamp.ca

FOCUS COMPANY

This chapter's Focus is on CozyCamp Company, a manufacturer of backpacking tents. CozyCamp uses a highly automated manufacturing process to produce its tents, and 75 percent of its sales are made through its Web site, CozyCamp.ca. In this chapter, we will explore how CozyCamp.ca goes about developing its annual budget. A budget is a detailed plan, expressed in quantitative terms, that specifies how resources will be acquired and used during a specific period of time. CozyCamp.ca's management uses the budget for many purposes, including planning, communication, resource allocation, control of operations, evaluation of performance, and provision of incentives.

IN CONTRAST

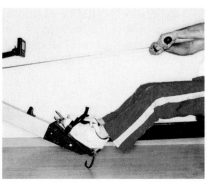

In contrast to the manufacturing setting of CozyCamp.ca, we explore budgeting at Canadian Fitness Cooperative. As the name suggests, this service organization operates as a cooperative. The members elect a board of directors who hire a manager and assistant manager to run the fitness club. The Cooperative does not seek to make a profit. Every year, membership fees are adjusted with the intention of bringing in just enough revenue to cover projected expenses. The club's budget is an important part of that process.

After completing this chapter, you should be able to:

1 List and explain five purposes of budgeting systems.

2 Describe the similarities and differences in the operational budgets prepared by manufacturers, service industry firms, merchandisers, and nonprofit organizations.

3 Explain the concept of activity-based budgeting and the benefits it brings to the budgeting process.

4 Prepare each of the budget schedules that make up the master budget.

5 Discuss the role of assumptions and predictions in budgeting.

6 Describe a typical organization's process of budget administration.

7 Understand the importance of budgeting product life-cycle costs.

8 Discuss the behavioural implications of budgetary slack and participative budgeting.

Developing a budget is a critical step in planning any economic activity. This is true for businesses, for governmental agencies, and for individuals. We all have to budget our money to meet day-to-day expenses and to plan for major expenditures, such as buying a car or paying for college tuition. Similarly, businesses of all types and governmental units at every level have to make financial plans to carry out routine operations, plan for major expenditures, and help in making financial decisions.

Purposes of Budgeting Systems

Learning Objective 1

List and explain five purposes of budgeting systems.

A **budget** is a detailed plan, expressed in quantitative terms, that specifies how resources will be acquired and used during a specified period of time. The procedures used to develop a budget constitute a **budgeting system**. Budgeting systems have five primary purposes:

Planning   The most obvious purpose of a budget is to quantify a plan of action. The budgeting process forces the individuals who make up an organization to plan ahead. The development of a quarterly budget for Fairmont Hotel, for example, forces the hotel manager, the reservation manager, and the food and beverage manager to plan for the staffing and supplies needed to meet anticipated demand for the hotel's services.

Facilitating Communication and Coordination   For any organization to be effective, every manager in the organization must be aware of the plans made by other managers. In order to plan reservations and ticket sales effectively, the reservations manager for WestJet Airlines must know the flight schedules developed by the airline's route manager. The budgeting process pulls together the plans of each manager in an organization.

Allocating Resources   Generally, an organization's resources are limited, and budgets provide one means of allocating resources among competing uses. The city of Port Moody, for example, must allocate its revenue among basic life services (such as police and fire protection), maintenance of property and equipment (such as city streets, parks, and vehicles), and other community services (such as child-care services and programs to prevent alcohol and drug abuse).

Controlling Profit and Operations   A budget is a plan, and plans are subject to change. Nevertheless, a budget serves as a useful benchmark with which actual results can be compared. For example, Manulife Insurance Company can compare its actual sales of insurance policies for a year against its budgeted sales. Such a comparison can help managers evaluate the firm's effectiveness in selling insurance. The next chapter examines the control purpose of budgets in more depth.

"Budgeting is used extensively for cost control. Each plant manager develops a plant budget, and then each department supervisor is responsible for his or her own cost center. . . . There are budgets for every department in the company." (9a)
Best Foods (a subsidiary of Unilever)

Evaluating Performance and Providing Incentives   Comparing actual results with budgeted results also helps managers to evaluate the performance of individuals, departments, divisions, or entire companies. Since budgets are used to evaluate performance, they also can be used to provide incentives for people to perform well. For example, General Motors Corporation, like many other companies, provides incentives for managers to improve profits by awarding bonuses to managers who meet or exceed their budgeted profit goals.

Types of Budgets

Different types of budgets serve different purposes. A **profit plan**, or **master budget**, is a comprehensive set of budgets covering all phases of an organization's operations for a specified period of time. We will examine a master budget in detail later in this chapter.

Diverse organizations use budgets for a variety of reasons. A cruise line, such as Carnival, uses budgets to plan for meeting the payroll and operating expenses and to coordinate operations by matching staffing with projected cruise demand. Carnival also uses its budgeting process to allocate capital improvement funds among competing projects, such as expanding its fleet or improving landside facilities.

Budgeted financial statements, often called **pro forma financial statements**, show how the organization's financial statements will appear at a specified time if operations proceed according to plan. Budgeted financial statements include a *budgeted income statement*, *a budgeted balance sheet*, and *a budgeted statement of cash flows*.

A **capital budget** is a plan for the acquisition of capital assets, such as buildings and equipment. Capital budgeting is covered in depth later in the text. A **financial budget** is a plan that shows how the organization will acquire its financial resources, such as through the issuance of stock or incurrence of debt.

Budgets are developed for specific time periods. *Short-range budgets* cover a year, a quarter, or a month, whereas *long-range budgets* cover periods longer than a year. **Rolling budgets** are continually updated by periodically adding a new incremental time period, such as a quarter, and dropping the period just completed. Rolling budgets are also called **revolving budgets** or **continuous budgets**.

The Master Budget: A Planning Tool

The master budget, the principal output of a budgeting system, is a comprehensive profit plan that ties together all phases of an organization's operations. The master budget comprises many separate budgets, or schedules, that are interdependent. Exhibit 9–1 portrays these interrelationships in a flowchart.

Sales of Services or Goods

The starting point for any master budget is a sales revenue budget based on a sales forecast for services or goods. Airlines forecast the number of passengers on each of their routes. Financial institutions forecast the number and dollar amount of consumer loans and home mortgages to be provided. Hotels forecast the number of rooms that will be occupied during various seasons. Manufacturing and merchandising companies forecast sales of their goods. Some companies sell both goods and services. For example, Canadian Tire is a large merchandising company, but its Auto Service Centres provide the firm with substantial service revenue.

Sales Forecasting

All companies have two things in common when it comes to forecasting sales of services or goods. **Sales forecasting** is a critical step in the budgeting process, and it is very difficult to do accurately.

Sales Budget

Operational Budgets

Budgeted Financial Statements

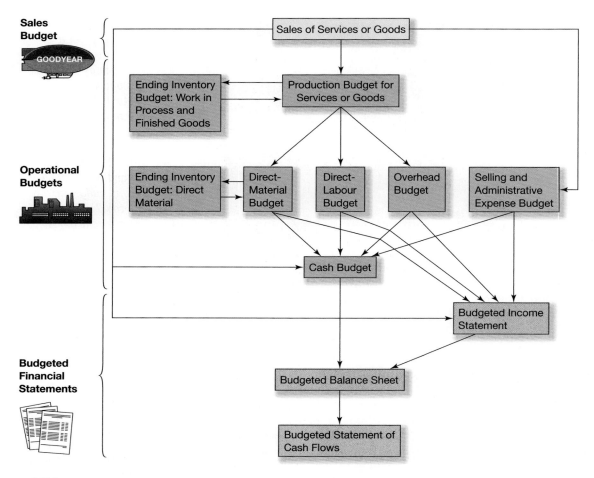

Exhibit 9–1
Components of a Master Budget

Various procedures are used in sales forecasting, and the final forecast usually combines information from many different sources. Many firms have a top-management-level market research staff whose job is to coordinate the company's sales forecasting efforts. Typically, everyone from key executives to the firm's sales personnel will be asked to contribute sales projections.

Major factors considered when forecasting sales include the following:

1. Past sales levels and trends:
   a.   For the firm developing the forecast (e.g., Petro-Canada)
   b.   For the entire industry (e.g., the petroleum industry)
2. General economic trends. (Is the economy growing? How fast? Is a recession or economic slowdown expected?)
3. Economic trends in the company's industry. (In the petroleum industry, for example, is personal travel likely to increase, thereby implying increased demand for gasoline?)
4. Other factors expected to affect sales in the industry. (Is an unusually cold winter expected, which would result in increased demand for home heating oil?)
5. Political and legal events. (E.g., is any legislation pending that would affect the demand for petroleum, such as tax incentives to use alternative energy sources?)

"Sales forecasting is difficult in every industry, but it's especially difficult in a highly competitive industry such as ours. Sales forecasting relies on several areas for input—market research, sales and marketing. We forecast the size of the market for each product, and then we forecast our share of that market." (9b)
Best Foods
(a subsidiary of Unilever)

6. The intended pricing policy of the company
7. Planned advertising and product promotion
8. Expected actions of competitors
9. New products contemplated by the company or other firms (E.g., automobile manufacturers are continuing to develop hybrids, which run on a combination of gasoline and battery power, thereby reducing the demand for gasoline.)
10. Market research studies

The starting point in the sales forecasting process is generally the sales level of the prior year. Then the market research staff considers the information discussed above along with input from key executives and sales personnel. In many firms, elaborate *econometric models* are built to incorporate all the available information systematically. (*Econometric* means economic measurement.) Statistical methods, such as regression analysis and probability distributions for sales, are often used. All in all, a great deal of effort generally goes into the sales forecast, since it is such a critical step in the budgeting process. Making a sales forecast is like shooting an arrow. If the archer's aim is off by only a fraction of an inch, the arrow will go further and further astray and miss the bull's-eye by a wide margin. Similarly, a slightly inaccurate sales forecast, coming at the very beginning of the budgeting process, will throw off all of the other schedules comprised by the master budget.

> "I see more and more forecasting and less time spent on what has happened." (9c)
> **Caterpillar**

Operational Budgets

Based on the sales budget, a company develops a set of **operational budgets** that specify how its operations will be carried out to meet the demand for its goods or services. The budgets constituting this operational portion of the master budget are depicted in the middle portion of Exhibit 9–1.

> **Learning Objective 2**
>
> Describe the similarities and differences in the operational budgets prepared by manufacturers, service industry firms, merchandisers, and nonprofit organizations.

Manufacturing Firms   A manufacturing company develops a production budget, which shows the number of product units to be manufactured. Coupled with the production budget are ending-inventory budgets for raw material, work in process, and finished goods. Manufacturers plan to have some inventory on hand at all times to meet peak demand while keeping production at a stable level. From the production budget, a manufacturer develops budgets for the direct materials, direct labour, and overhead that will be required in the production process. A budget for selling and administrative expenses also is prepared.

Merchandising Firms   The operational portion of the master budget is similar in a merchandising firm, but instead of a production budget for goods, a merchandiser develops a budget for merchandise purchases. A merchandising firm will not have a budget for direct material, because it does not engage in production. However, the merchandiser will develop budgets for labour (or personnel), overhead, and selling and administrative expenses.

Service Industry Firms   Based on the sales budget for its services, a service industry firm develops a set of budgets that show how the demand for those services will be met. An airline, for example, prepares the following operational budgets: a budget of planned air miles to be flown; material budgets for spare aircraft parts, aircraft fuel, and in-flight food; labour budgets for flight crews and maintenance personnel; and an overhead budget.

Cash Budget   Every business prepares a cash budget. This budget shows expected cash receipts, as a result of selling goods or services, and planned cash disbursements, to pay the bills incurred by the firm.

Summary of Operational Budgets   Operational budgets differ since they are adapted to the operations of individual companies in various industries. However, operational budgets are also similar in important ways. In each firm, they encompass a detailed plan for using the basic factors of production—material, labour, and overhead—to produce a product or provide a service.

Budgeted Financial Statements

The final portion of the master budget, depicted in Exhibit 9–1, includes a budgeted income statement, a budgeted balance sheet, and a budgeted statement of cash flows. These budgeted financial statements show the overall financial results of the organization's planned operations for the budget period.

Nonprofit Organizations

The master budget for a nonprofit organization includes many of the components shown in Exhibit 9–1. However, there are important differences. Many nonprofit organizations provide services free of charge. Hence, there is no sales budget as shown in Exhibit 9–1. However, such organizations do begin their budgeting process with a budget that shows the level of services to be provided. For example, the budget for the city of Toronto would show the planned levels of various public services, such as the hours of operation for libraries and parks.

Nonprofit organizations also prepare budgets showing their anticipated funding. The City of Toronto budgets for such revenue sources as city taxes, and provincial and federal revenue sharing.

In summary, all organizations begin the budgeting process with plans for (1) the goods or services to be provided and (2) the revenue to be available, whether from sales or from other funding sources.

Activity-Based Budgeting

The process of constructing a master budget can be significantly enhanced if the concepts of activity-based costing are applied.[1] Activity-based costing uses a two-stage cost-assignment process. In stage I, overhead costs are assigned to cost pools that represent the most significant *activities* constituting the production process. The activities identified vary across manufacturers, but such activities as engineering design, material handling, machine setup, production scheduling, inspection, quality control, and purchasing provide examples.

After assigning costs to the activity cost pools in stage I, cost drivers are identified that are appropriate for each cost pool. Then, in stage II, the overhead costs are allocated from each activity cost pool to cost objects (e.g., products, services, and customers) in proportion to the amount of activity consumed.

Exhibit 9–2 portrays the two-stage allocation process used in activity-based costing systems.

Applying ABC concepts to the budgeting process yields **activity-based budgeting (ABB)**.[2] Under ABB, the first step is to specify the products or services to be produced and the customers to be served. Then the activities that are necessary to produce these products and services are determined. Finally, the resources necessary to perform the specified activities are quantified. Conceptually, ABB takes the ABC model and reverses the flow of the analysis, as depicted in Exhibit 9–3. As portrayed in the diagram, ABC assigns resource costs to activities, and then it assigns activity costs to products and services produced and customers served. ABB, on the other hand, begins by forecasting the demand for products and

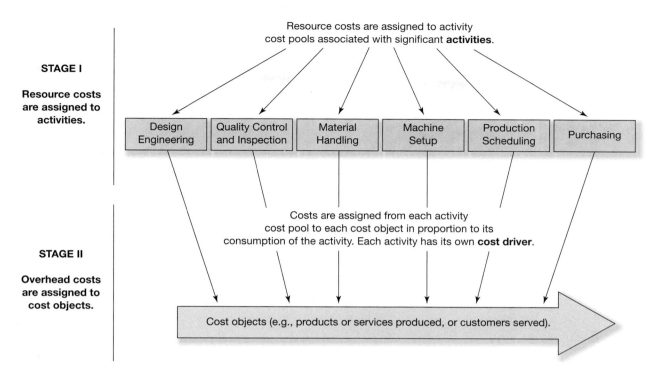

STAGE I

Resource costs are assigned to activities.

Resource costs are assigned to activity cost pools associated with significant **activities**.

Design Engineering | Quality Control and Inspection | Material Handling | Machine Setup | Production Scheduling | Purchasing

STAGE II

Overhead costs are assigned to cost objects.

Costs are assigned from each activity cost pool to each cost object in proportion to its consumption of the activity. Each activity has its own **cost driver**.

Cost objects (e.g., products or services produced, or customers served).

Exhibit 9–2
Activity-Based Costing System

services as well as the customers to be served. These forecasts are then used to plan the activities for the budget period and budget the resources necessary to carry out the activities.

In the next section of this chapter, we will illustrate the process of constructing a master budget. Notice how the conceptual activity-based budgeting model is employed in the budgeting process. In the context of the master-budget illustration, we will explore the benefits and implications of the ABB approach.

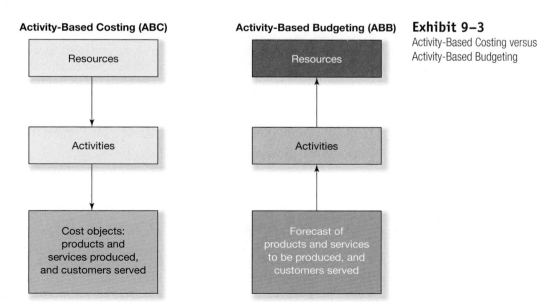

Activity-Based Costing (ABC)

Resources

Activities

Cost objects: products and services produced, and customers served

Activity-Based Budgeting (ABB)

Resources

Activities

Forecast of products and services to be produced, and customers served

Exhibit 9–3
Activity-Based Costing versus Activity-Based Budgeting

Source: Robert S. Kaplan and Robin Cooper, *Cost and Effect* (Boston: Harvard Business School Press, 1998), p. 303.

Management
Accounting
Practice

American Express, AT&T
Paradyne

ACTIVITY-BASED BUDGETING (ABB) AT AMERICAN EXPRESS AND AT&T PARADYNE

American Express has successfully used ABB for its travel-related services in its New York operations. This relatively new system has been used to identify and implement cost reduction and process improvement initiatives. Then, an activity-by-activity analysis of each department has allowed process improvement savings to be factored into the forecasted costs for each department in the next budget cycle.[3]

AT&T Paradyne designs and produces medium- and high-speed data communications equipment, which provides an interface between telephone networks and computers. The company's activity-based costing project ultimately led to activity-based budgeting. As ABM and ABB matured at AT&T Paradyne, the company began to experience a culture change. A key lesson learned in this case was that linking activity-based costing to the budgeting process and performance evaluation led to the integration of ABC into the management of the company.[4]

Preparing the Master Budget

Learning Objective 4

Prepare each of the budget schedules that make up the master budget.

cozycamp.ca

To illustrate the steps in developing a master budget, or profit plan, we will focus on CozyCamp.ca, a manufacturer of backpacking tents. The company is wholly owned by Mary Edwards, who started the company in her basement 15 years ago. After a difficult two to three years, success came quickly for the company, and Edwards eventually built a production facility. The manufacturing process is highly automated, using several machines to cut out pieces of tent fabric and sew them together to form a lightweight but durable backpacking tent. Production of the aluminum tent poles is outsourced to a company nearby, and the poles are purchased on a just-in-time basis so they can be packaged with the finished tents just before they are shipped. Initially, Edwards called her firm CozyCamp Company, and its sales were made to regional retailers in Western Canada using a traditional sales approach. Three years ago, however, Edwards changed the company's name to CozyCamp.ca and made a major foray into the world of Internet sales. Now almost 75 percent of CozyCamp.ca's sales are made through the company's Web site. Although CozyCamp.ca retained several of its sales personnel to handle the traditional sales to area retailers, new personnel had to be hired to handle the company's Internet sales environment. Tents are shipped to Internet customers via UPS, FedEx, and other express delivery services.

The 20x2 master budget for CozyCamp.ca has just been completed. It contains the following schedules, which are displayed and explained in the following pages:

Schedule	Title of Schedule
1	Sales Budget
2	Cash Receipts Budget
3	Production Budget
4	Direct-Material Budget
5	Direct-Labour Budget
6	Manufacturing Overhead Budget
7	Selling, General, and Administrative Expense Budget
8	Cash Disbursements Budget
9	Cash Budget

Schedule	Title of Schedule
10	Budgeted Schedule of Cost of Goods Manufactured and Sold
11	Budgeted Income Statement
12	Budgeted Statement of Cash Flows
13	Budgeted Balance Sheet

Sales Budget

The first step in developing CozyCamp.ca's 20x2 master budget is to prepare the **sales budget**, which is displayed as schedule 1. This budget displays the projected sales in units for each quarter and then multiplies the unit sales by the sales price to determine sales revenue. Notice that there is a significant seasonal pattern in the sales forecast, with the bulk of the sales coming in the spring and summer.

Schedule 1

cozycamp.ca

COZYCAMP.CA
Sales Budget
For the Year Ending December 31, 20x2

	Quarter				
	1st	2nd	3rd	4th	Year
Sales in units	5,000	15,000	20,000	10,000	50,000
Unit sales price	× $225	× $225	× $225	× $225	× $225
Total sales revenue	$1,125,000	$3,375,000	$4,500,000	$2,250,000	$11,250,000

Cash Receipts Budget

The **cash receipts budget** details the expected cash collections during a budget period. CozyCamp.ca's cash receipts budget is displayed as schedule 2. The firm collects 80 percent of its billings during the same quarter in which the sale is made, and another 18 percent in the following quarter. Two percent of each quarter's sales are expected to be uncollectible accounts.

Schedule 2

cozycamp.ca

COZYCAMP.CA
Cash Receipts Budget
For the Year Ending December 31, 20x2

	Quarter				
	1st	2nd	3rd	4th	Year
Sales revenue (from schedule 1)	$1,125,000	$3,375,000	$4,500,000	$2,250,000	$11,250,000
Collections in quarter of sale (80% of revenue)	$ 900,000	$2,700,000	$3,600,000	$1,800,000	$ 9,000,000
Collections in quarter following sale (18% of prior quarter's revenue)*	405,000†	202,500	607,500	810,000	2,025,000
Total cash receipts	$1,305,000	$2,902,500	$4,207,500	$2,610,000	$11,025,000

*Two percent of each quarter's sales are expected to be uncollectible, as follows:

	Quarter				
	1st	2nd	3rd	4th	Year
Uncollectible accounts	$22,500	$67,500	$90,000	$45,000	$225,000

†The revenue in the prior quarter (i.e., the 4th quarter of 20x1) is assumed to be $2,250,000. Therefore, the $405,000 is 18% of $2,250,000.

How to Budget Cash Receipts   To understand how the cash receipts budget is prepared, let's focus again on the second quarter column, which is shaded. The $3,375,000 of total revenue comes directly from schedule 1, the sales budget (second column, last row). Since most of CozyCamp.ca's sales are on account, not all of the second quarter's revenue will be collected during the second quarter. The cash that the firm will collect during the second quarter comprises two components, as depicted in the following diagram.

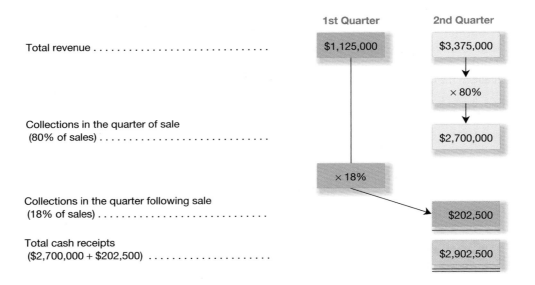

The second quarter's total cash receipts are the sum of $2,700,000 (80 percent of second quarter sales) and $202,500 (18 percent of first quarter sales).

One final point to notice is that 2 percent of each quarter's sales are not expected to be collected. Thus, the $67,500 of second quarter uncollectible accounts amounts to 2 percent of the second quarter's revenue ($67,500 = 2% × $3,375,000). Almost all of CozyCamp.ca's uncollectible accounts relate to the company's traditional sales.

Production Budget

The **production budget** shows the number of units of services or goods that are to be produced during a budget period. CozyCamp.ca's production budget, displayed as schedule 3, determines the number of tents to be produced each quarter based on the quarterly sales projections in the sales budget. Schedule 3 is based on the following formula:

$$\text{Sales in units} + \text{Desired ending inventory of finished goods} = \text{Total units required}$$

$$\text{Total units required} - \text{Expected beginning inventory of finished goods} = \text{Units to be produced}$$

Focus on the second-quarter column in schedule 3, which is shaded. Expected sales are 15,000 tents, and Edwards desires to have 2,000 finished units on hand at the end of the quarter. This is 10 percent of the expected sales for the third quarter.

However, 1,500 tents are expected to be in inventory at the beginning of the second quarter. Thus, only 15,500 tents need to be produced.

Schedule 3

cozycamp.ca

COZYCAMP.CA Production Budget For the Year Ending December 31, 20x2					
	Quarter				
	1st	**2nd**	**3rd**	**4th**	**Year**
Sales in units (from schedule 1)	5,000	15,000	20,000	10,000	50,000
Add desired ending inventory of finished goods*	1,500	2,000	1,000	500[†]	500
Total units required	6,500	17,000	21,000	10,500	50,500
Less expected beginning inventory of finished goods	500	1,500	2,000	1,000	500
Units to be produced.	6,000	15,500	19,000	9,500	50,000

*Ten percent of the next quarter's expected sales.

[†]Ten percent of the expected sales for the 1st quarter of the next year,20x3, which is predicted to be 5,000 units.

Direct-Material Budget

The **direct-material budget** shows the number of units and the cost of material to be purchased and used during a budget period. CozyCamp.ca's direct-material budget, which is displayed as schedule 4, has two sections: one for tent fabric and one for tent poles. As is true for almost all manufacturers, CozyCamp.ca's direct-material cost is a unit-level cost.[5] Each tent requires 12 metres of fabric and one tent pole kit. The tent poles required for each tent are prepackaged in a kit by the outside vendor and delivered to CozyCamp.ca on a just-in-time basis.[6] The top section of CozyCamp.ca's direct-material budget shows the total amount of tent fabric needed to make tents during each quarter. The shaded portion of schedule 4 computes the amount of tent fabric to be purchased each quarter. This part of the schedule is based on the following formula.

$$\begin{array}{c}\text{Raw} \\ \text{material} \\ \text{required} \\ \text{for} \\ \text{production}\end{array} + \begin{array}{c}\text{Desired} \\ \text{ending} \\ \text{inventory} \\ \text{of raw} \\ \text{material}\end{array} = \begin{array}{c}\text{Total raw} \\ \text{material} \\ \text{required}\end{array}$$

$$\begin{array}{c}\text{Total raw} \\ \text{material} \\ \text{required}\end{array} - \begin{array}{c}\text{Expected beginning} \\ \text{inventory of} \\ \text{raw material}\end{array} = \begin{array}{c}\text{Raw material} \\ \text{to be} \\ \text{purchased}\end{array}$$

The shaded portion of schedule 4 also computes the cost of each quarter's tent fabric purchases. (This information also will be needed later in the budgeting process, in schedule 10.)

The lower unshaded section of schedule 4 calculates the quantity and cost of tent pole kits to be purchased each quarter.

Finally, the last row of schedule 4 totals the cost of tent fabric and tent pole kits to yield the total cost of raw material to be purchased each quarter.

Schedule 4

cozycamp.ca

	Quarter				
COZYCAMP.CA Direct-Material Budget For the Year Ending December 31, 20x2					
	1st	2nd	3rd	4th	Year
Tent fabric:					
Tents to be produced (from schedule 3)	6,000	15,500	19,000	9,500	50,000
Raw material required per unit (metres of fabric)	× 12	× 12	× 12	× 12	× 12
Raw material required for production (metres)	72,000	186,000	228,000	114,000	600,000
Add desired ending inventory of raw material (metres)*	18,600	22,800	11,400	7,200†	7,200
Total raw material required	90,600	208,800	239,400	121,200	607,200
Less expected beginning inventory of raw material (metres).	7,200	18,600	22,800	11,400	7,200
Raw material to be purchased (metres)	83,400	190,200	216,600	109,800	600,000
Cost per metre	× $9	× $9	× $9	× $9	× $9
Total cost of tent fabric purchases	$750,600	$1,711,800	$1,949,400	$ 988,200	$5,400,000
Tent poles:					
Tents to be produced (from schedule 3)	6,000	15,500	19,000	9,500	50,000
Tent pole kits required per tent	× 1	× 1	× 1	× 1	× 1
Tent pole kits to be purchased‡	6,000	15,500	19,000	9,500	50,000
Cost per tent pole kit	× $20	× $20	× $20	× $20	× $20
Total cost of tent pole kit purchases	$120,000	$ 310,000	$ 380,000	$ 190,000	$1,000,000
Total cost of raw material purchases (fabric and poles)	$870,600	$2,021,800	$2,329,400	$1,178,200	$6,400,000

*Ten percent of the next quarter's expected raw material requirements.

†Ten percent of the expected raw material requirements for the 1st quarter of the next year, 20x3, which is assumed to be 72,000 metres. (Sales, and therefore production, is predicted to be the same in each quarter of 20x3 as in the corresponding quarter of 20x2.)

‡Since the tent pole kits are prepackaged by the vendor and delivered on a just-in-time basis, there is no need for buffer inventory stocks. Thus, the number of tent pole kits purchased each quarter is the same as the number needed each quarter.

Production and Purchasing: An Important Link   Notice the important link between planned production and purchases of raw material. This link is apparent in schedule 4, and it is also emphasized in the formula preceding the schedule. Let's focus on the second quarter. Since 15,500 tents are to be produced, 186,000 metres of tent material will be needed (15,500 tents times 12 metres per unit). In addition, Edwards desires to have 22,800 metres of material in inventory at the end of the quarter.[7] Thus, total needs are 208,800 metres. Does CozyCamp.ca need to purchase this much raw material? No, it does not, because 18,600 metres will be in inventory at the beginning of the quarter. Therefore, the firm needs to purchase only 190,200 metres of material during the quarter (208,800 metres less 18,600 metres in the beginning inventory).

Inventory Management   The linkage between planned production and raw material purchases is a particularly critical one in manufacturing firms. Thus, considerable effort is devoted to careful inventory planning and management. How did Edwards decide how much raw material to have in inventory at the end of each quarter? Examination of schedule 4 reveals that each quarter's desired ending inventory of raw material is 10 percent of the *material needed for production* in the next quarter. For example, 22,800 metres of raw material will be in inventory at the end of the second quarter, because 228,000 metres will be needed for production in the third quarter (22,800 = 10% × 228,000). The effect of this approach is to have a larger ending inventory when the next quarter's planned production is greater. Inventories are drawn down when the subsequent quarter's planned production is lower.[8]

Direct-Labour Budget

The **direct-labour budget** shows the number of hours and the cost of the direct labour to be used during the budget period. CozyCamp.ca's direct-labour budget is displayed as schedule 5. Based on each quarter's planned production, this schedule computes the amount of direct labour needed each quarter and the cost of the required labour. CozyCamp.ca is a relatively small company, and owner Mary Edwards hires all of her direct-labour production employees on a part-time basis only. This allows CozyCamp.ca to meet the labour demands of a given time period, which vary significantly with the seasonal pattern of demand and production. Thus, CozyCamp.ca's direct labour may be adjusted up or down to meet short-term needs. As a result, direct labour for this company is a unit-level cost. As schedule 5 shows, each tent manufactured requires half an hour of direct labour.

A Note on Direct Labour and the Cost Hierarchy   It is important to note that where direct labour belongs in the cost hierarchy depends on management's ability to adjust the organization's labour force to match short-term requirements, as well as management's attitude about making such adjustments.[9] Either for strategic business reasons or due to ethical concerns, many companies strive to maintain a relatively stable labour force. If production employees are retained when production declines, then direct labour will not be a unit-level cost. In the extreme case, where employees are virtually never laid off, direct labour becomes a facility- or general-operations-level cost. CozyCamp.ca's ability to easily adjust the total hours of its part-time workforce results in a unit-level designation for direct-labour cost in this situation.

Schedule 5

cozycamp.ca

	Quarter				
	1st	2nd	3rd	4th	Year
Units to be produced (from schedule 3)	6,000	15,500	19,000	9,500	50,000
Direct-labour required per unit (hours)..........	× .5	× .5	× .5	× .5	× .5
Total direct-labour hours required	3,000	7,750	9,500	4,750	25,000
Direct-labour cost per hour.........................	× $15	× $15	× $15	× $15	× $15
Total direct-labour cost.............................	$45,000	$116,250	$142,500	$71,250	$375,000

COZYCAMP.CA
Direct-Labour Budget
For the Year Ending December 31, 20x2

Manufacturing-Overhead Budget

The **manufacturing-overhead budget** shows the cost of overhead expected to be incurred in the production process during the budget period. CozyCamp.ca's manufacturing overhead budget, displayed as schedule 6, lists the expected cost of each overhead item by quarter. At the bottom of the schedule, the total budgeted overhead for each quarter is shown. Then each quarter's depreciation is subtracted to determine the total cash disbursements to be expected for overhead during each quarter. This cash disbursement information will be needed later in the budgeting process when the cash disbursements budget is constructed (schedule 8).

Activity-Based Budgeting and the Cost Hierarchy   CozyCamp.ca uses an activity-based budgeting (ABB) approach in the construction of the manufacturing-overhead budget. This budget explicitly uses activity-based costing information in that the budgeted costs for various overhead items are based on the expected quantity of the appropriate cost driver. For example, the cost driver used to budget setup costs is the number of production runs.

In CozyCamp.ca's cost hierarchy, unit-level costs include indirect material and electricity used to run the production machinery.[10] Batch-level costs include machine setup, purchasing and material handling, and quality control and inspection. The cost driver for these costs is the number of production runs. A run typically produces 500 tents. CozyCamp.ca's only product-level cost is design engineering. The company typically develops one new tent design each quarter. Each new design costs $1,200. The remaining overhead costs in schedule 6 are costs incurred at the facility, or general-operations, level.

Benefits of ABB   Proponents of ABB believe that real, sustainable payoffs from activity-based costing and activity-based management will not be forthcoming until an organization's budgeting process embraces the ABM approach. Utilizing ABC information in the budgeting process provides solid reasoning for budgeting costs at particular levels, since the underlying ABC information is based explicitly on the relationships among cost drivers, activities, and resources consumed. Moreover, the resulting budget is more useful to management, because it reveals how cost levels will change if the predicted quantities of the cost drivers change. For example, what will happen to CozyCamp.ca's setup costs in the 1st quarter if the quantity produced is 6,000 units as reflected in the budget (see schedule 6), but 15 production runs are used to produce these 6,000 units instead of 12 runs as specified in the budget? According to schedule 6, setup cost is $400 per production run ($4,800/12 runs). Therefore, 15 runs would result in $6,000 of setup cost in the 1st quarter, instead of $4,800 as forecast in the budget. This will be true even if 6,000 units are produced as forecast in the budget.[11]

Traditional budgeting processes, which do not embrace the ABB approach, often classify such costs as setup, purchasing and material handling, quality control and inspection, or design engineering as *fixed* costs, since they do not vary with the number of units produced. The ABB approach, however, recognizes that these costs are really *variable* if the budget analyst is careful to identify the appropriate cost driver with which each of these costs varies.

Selling, General, and Administrative (SG&A) Expense Budget

The **selling, general, and administrative (SG&A) expense budget** shows the planned amounts of expenditures for selling, general, and administrative expenses

Schedule 6

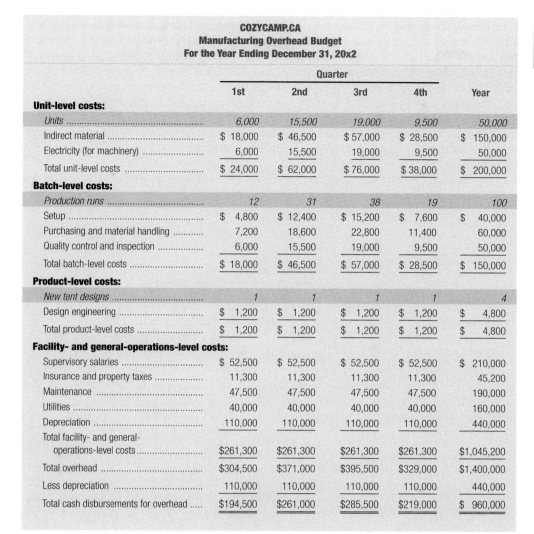

cozycamp.ca

	\multicolumn{5}{c}{COZYCAMP.CA Manufacturing Overhead Budget For the Year Ending December 31, 20x2}
	\multicolumn{4}{c}{Quarter}	
	1st	2nd	3rd	4th	Year
Unit-level costs:					
Units	6,000	15,500	19,000	9,500	50,000
Indirect material	$ 18,000	$ 46,500	$ 57,000	$ 28,500	$ 150,000
Electricity (for machinery)	6,000	15,500	19,000	9,500	50,000
Total unit-level costs	$ 24,000	$ 62,000	$ 76,000	$ 38,000	$ 200,000
Batch-level costs:					
Production runs	12	31	38	19	100
Setup	$ 4,800	$ 12,400	$ 15,200	$ 7,600	$ 40,000
Purchasing and material handling	7,200	18,600	22,800	11,400	60,000
Quality control and inspection	6,000	15,500	19,000	9,500	50,000
Total batch-level costs	$ 18,000	$ 46,500	$ 57,000	$ 28,500	$ 150,000
Product-level costs:					
New tent designs	1	1	1	1	4
Design engineering	$ 1,200	$ 1,200	$ 1,200	$ 1,200	$ 4,800
Total product-level costs	$ 1,200	$ 1,200	$ 1,200	$ 1,200	$ 4,800
Facility- and general-operations-level costs:					
Supervisory salaries	$ 52,500	$ 52,500	$ 52,500	$ 52,500	$ 210,000
Insurance and property taxes	11,300	11,300	11,300	11,300	45,200
Maintenance	47,500	47,500	47,500	47,500	190,000
Utilities	40,000	40,000	40,000	40,000	160,000
Depreciation	110,000	110,000	110,000	110,000	440,000
Total facility- and general-operations-level costs	$261,300	$261,300	$261,300	$261,300	$1,045,200
Total overhead	$304,500	$371,000	$395,500	$329,000	$1,400,000
Less depreciation	110,000	110,000	110,000	110,000	440,000
Total cash disbursements for overhead	$194,500	$261,000	$285,500	$219,000	$ 960,000

during the budget period. CozyCamp.ca's selling, general, and administrative expense budget is displayed as schedule 7. This budget lists the expenses of administering the firm and selling its product.

Activity-Based Budgeting and the Cost Hierarchy   Similarly to the manufacturing-overhead budget, CozyCamp.ca's SG&A expense budget reflects the activity-based budgeting (ABB) approach. Activity-based costing information was used to develop this budget. For example, the cost driver used to budget sales commissions (for sales in the firm's traditional market) is the number of units sold.

In CozyCamp.ca's cost hierarchy, the only unit-level marketing expenses consist of sales commissions.[12] For CozyCamp's traditional sales through regional retail outlets, sales personnel are paid commissions based on the number of units sold. The SG&A budget reflects a $5 commission paid on each tent sold through traditional outlets, which account for 25 percent of CozyCamp.ca's sales. In the second quarter, for example, sales commissions are predicted to be $18,750 (15,000 tents × 25% traditional sales × $5).

The customer-level expenses incurred by CozyCamp.ca are the sales personnel salaries, which differ depending on whether the customers are traditional regional retailers or Web shoppers. In order to sell its tents in the traditional marketplace, CozyCamp.ca employs sales personnel who travel to the retailers in the area and personally take orders. These sales personnel receive both a salary and sales commissions. (The sales commissions are unit-level expenses, as noted above.) To serve its Internet customers, CozyCamp.ca employs computer operators to update the company's Web site and a couple of telephone operators to provide customer service over the phone. For example, some Internet customers are hesitant to give their credit card numbers to CozyCamp.ca online, so they place their orders online and then phone in to an authorized telephone number to submit their credit card information.

The remainder of CozyCamp.ca's selling, general, and administrative expenses are incurred at the facility or general-operations level.

Schedule 7

cozycamp.ca

COZYCAMP.CA
Selling, General, and Administrative Expense Budget
For the Year Ending December 31, 20x2

	1st	2nd	3rd	4th	Year
Unit-level expenses:					
Units	5,000	15,000	20,000	10,000	50,000
Sales commissions (traditional market) ...	$ 6,250	$ 18,750	$ 25,000	$ 12,500	$ 62,500
Total unit-level expenses	$ 6,250	$ 18,750	$ 25,000	$ 12,500	$ 62,500
Customer-level expenses:					
Sales personnel salaries (traditional market)	$ 16,000	$ 16,000	$ 16,000	$ 16,000	$ 64,000
Computer operator salaries	18,000	18,000	18,000	18,000	72,000
Telephone operator salaries	6,000	6,000	6,000	6,000	24,000
Total customer-level expenses	$ 40,000	$ 40,000	$ 40,000	$ 40,000	$ 160,000
Facility- and general-operations-level expenses:					
Sales manager's salary	$ 15,000	$ 15,000	$ 15,000	$ 15,000	$ 60,000
Media advertising	61,000	61,000	61,000	61,000	244,000
Administrative salaries	220,000	220,000	220,000	220,000	880,000
Total facility- and general-operations-level expenses	$296,000	$296,000	$296,000	$296,000	$1,184,000
Total expenses	$342,250	$354,750	$361,000	$348,500	$1,406,500

Quarter headers: 1st, 2nd, 3rd, 4th, Year

Cash Disbursements Budget

The **cash disbursements budget** details the expected cash payments during a budget period. Schedule 8 displays CozyCamp.ca's cash disbursements budget. The shaded top portion shows the schedule of cash payments for raw material purchases, which are made on account. The company pays for 60 percent of its purchases on account during the quarter in which the purchase is made. The remaining 40 percent of each quarter's purchases are paid for during the quarter following the purchase.

The unshaded lower portion of schedule 8 shows all of CozyCamp.ca's direct-labour, manufacturing overhead, and selling, general, and administrative expenditures.

Schedule 8

cozycamp.ca

	Quarter				
COZYCAMP.CA **Cash Disbursements Budget** **For the Year Ending December 31, 20x2**	**1st**	**2nd**	**3rd**	**4th**	**Year**
Cost of raw material purchases (from schedule 4)	$ 870,600	$2,021,800	$2,329,400	$1,178,200	$6,400,000
Cash payments for purchases made during the quarter (60% of current quarter's purchases)	$ 522,360	$1,213,080	$1,397,640	$ 706,920	$3,840,000
Cash payments for prior quarter's purchases (40% of prior quarter's purchases)	471,280*	348,240	808,720	931,760	2,560,000
Total cash payments for raw material purchases	$ 993,640	$1,561,320	$2,206,360	$1,638,680	$6,400,000
Other cash disbursements:					
Direct labour (schedule 5)	$ 45,000	$ 116,250	$ 142,500	$ 71,250	$ 375,000
Indirect material (schedule 6)	18,000	46,500	57,000	28,500	150,000
Electricity (schedule 6)	6,000	15,500	19,000	9,500	50,000
Setup (schedule 6)	4,800	12,400	15,200	7,600	40,000
Purchasing and material handling (schedule 6)	7,200	18,600	22,800	11,400	60,000
Quality control and inspection (schedule 6)	6,000	15,500	19,000	9,500	50,000
Design engineering (schedule 6)	1,200	1,200	1,200	1,200	4,800
Supervisory salaries (schedule 6)	52,500	52,500	52,500	52,500	210,000
Insurance and property taxes (schedule 6)	11,300	11,300	11,300	11,300	45,200
Maintenance (schedule 6)	47,500	47,500	47,500	47,500	190,000
Utilities (schedule 6)	40,000	40,000	40,000	40,000	160,000
Sales commissions (schedule 7)	6,250	18,750	25,000	12,500	62,500
Sales personnel (schedule 7)	16,000	16,000	16,000	16,000	64,000
Computer operators (schedule 7)	18,000	18,000	18,000	18,000	72,000
Telephone operators (schedule 7)	6,000	6,000	6,000	6,000	24,000
Sales manager (schedule 7)	15,000	15,000	15,000	15,000	60,000
Media advertising (schedule 7)	61,000	61,000	61,000	61,000	244,000
Administration (schedule 7)	220,000	220,000	220,000	220,000	880,000
Total of other cash disbursements	$ 581,750	$ 732,000	$ 789,000	$ 638,750	$2,741,500
Total cash disbursements	$1,575,390	$2,293,320	$2,995,360	$2,277,430	$9,141,500

*Forty percent of the purchases in the 4th quarter of the prior year, 20x1, which is assumed to be $1,178,200.

How to Budget Cash Disbursements   CozyCamp.ca purchases raw material, direct labour, and various services. The raw-material purchases are made on account, which means payment is not made in cash at the time of the purchase. The shaded top portion of schedule 8 shows the purchases on account. Let's focus on the second quarter column. The second quarter's raw material purchases on account amount to $2,021,800. Does the company pay for all of the $2,021,800 purchases on account during the same quarter? No, it does not. As the following diagram shows, the second quarter's actual cash payment for purchases made on account comprises two components.

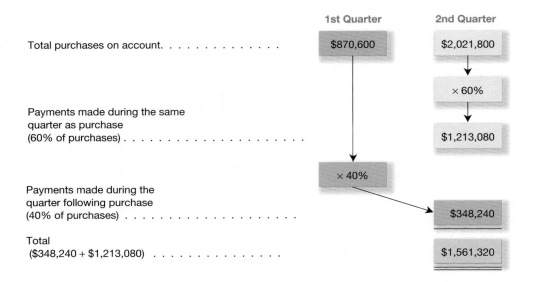

	1st Quarter	2nd Quarter
Total purchases on account.	$870,600	$2,021,800
		× 60%
Payments made during the same quarter as purchase (60% of purchases)		$1,213,080
	× 40%	
Payments made during the quarter following purchase (40% of purchases)		$348,240
Total ($348,240 + $1,213,080)		$1,561,320

The second quarter's total cash payments *for purchases made on account* are the sum of $1,213,080 (which relates to second-quarter purchases on account) and $348,240 (which relates to first-quarter purchases on account).

We are not finished with the second quarter's cash disbursements yet, because CozyCamp.ca *also pays for some of its purchases in cash at the time of purchase*. These cash expenditures are detailed in the unshaded lower portion of schedule 8. The amounts are drawn from schedules 5, 6, and 7, which detail expenditures for direct-labour, manufacturing-overhead, and selling, general, and administrative expenses, respectively. For example, schedule 5 lists $116,250 for direct labour in the second quarter; schedule 6 lists $261,000 for cash expenditures on manufacturing-overhead costs; and schedule 7 lists $354,750 for selling, general, and administrative expenditures.

Finally, the last row in the cash disbursements budget (schedule 8) shows the total cash disbursements during each quarter. Thus, the $2,293,320 total payment in the second quarter is the sum of $1,561,320 (for raw material purchases on account) and $732,000 for other purchases made in cash.

Cash Budget: Combining Receipts and Disbursements

The **cash budget** details the expected cash receipts and disbursements during a budget period. CozyCamp.ca's completed cash budget is displayed as schedule 9. The shaded top portion pulls together the cash receipts and cash disbursements detailed in schedules 2 and 8. The lower portion of schedule 9 discloses the company's plans to take out a short-term bank loan on January 2, 20x2, for the purpose of building an addition to its production facility. The pattern of construction payments reflects high outlays early in the year as the major construction takes place. The high payment in the fourth quarter is due to the costs of reconfiguring the production line after the addition is finished. The company will repay the loan (with interest) in four equal instalments on the last day of each quarter in 20x2. The funds for this repayment will come from excess cash generated from operations during 20x2.

Also shown in schedule 9 are the interest payments on the short-term bank loan.

Budgeted Schedule of Cost of Goods Manufactured and Sold

The **budgeted schedule of cost of goods manufactured and sold** details the direct material, direct-labour, and manufacturing-overhead costs to be incurred, and shows the cost of the goods to be sold during the budget period. Schedule 10 shows

Schedule 9

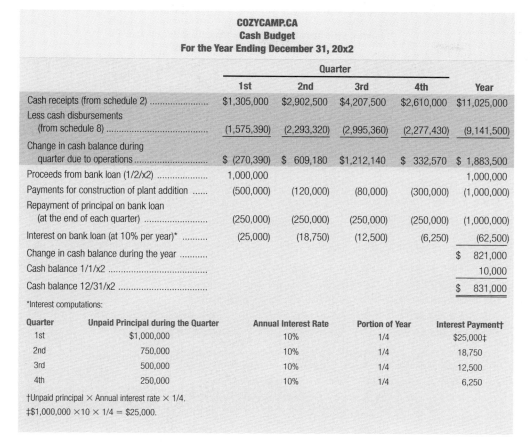

COZYCAMP.CA
Cash Budget
For the Year Ending December 31, 20x2

	Quarter				
	1st	2nd	3rd	4th	Year
Cash receipts (from schedule 2)	$1,305,000	$2,902,500	$4,207,500	$2,610,000	$11,025,000
Less cash disbursements (from schedule 8)	(1,575,390)	(2,293,320)	(2,995,360)	(2,277,430)	(9,141,500)
Change in cash balance during quarter due to operations	$ (270,390)	$ 609,180	$1,212,140	$ 332,570	$ 1,883,500
Proceeds from bank loan (1/2/x2)	1,000,000				1,000,000
Payments for construction of plant addition	(500,000)	(120,000)	(80,000)	(300,000)	(1,000,000)
Repayment of principal on bank loan (at the end of each quarter)	(250,000)	(250,000)	(250,000)	(250,000)	(1,000,000)
Interest on bank loan (at 10% per year)*	(25,000)	(18,750)	(12,500)	(6,250)	(62,500)
Change in cash balance during the year					$ 821,000
Cash balance 1/1/x2					10,000
Cash balance 12/31/x2					$ 831,000

*Interest computations:

Quarter	Unpaid Principal during the Quarter	Annual Interest Rate	Portion of Year	Interest Payment†
1st	$1,000,000	10%	1/4	$25,000‡
2nd	750,000	10%	1/4	18,750
3rd	500,000	10%	1/4	12,500
4th	250,000	10%	1/4	6,250

†Unpaid principal × Annual interest rate × 1/4.
‡$1,000,000 ×10 × 1/4 = $25,000.

cozycamp.ca

CozyCamp.ca's budgeted schedule of cost of goods manufactured and sold. The following Excel spreadsheet shows how the cost of the beginning and ending inventories of finished goods in schedule 10 are determined. From schedule 3, we see that the expected beginning and ending inventories of finished goods for 20x2 consist of 500 units. The absorption manufacturing cost for one unit of product is $163.50. The direct-material cost per unit is $128 ($108 + $20) (schedule 4), and the unit direct-labour cost is $7.50 (schedule 5). Recall that the *absorption* cost includes the direct-material and direct-labour costs and an allocation of all manufacturing overhead costs (i.e., overhead at the unit, batch, product, and facility, or general-operations, levels). The overhead cost data come from schedule 6.

	A	B
1	Type of Manufacturing Cost	Amount
2		
3	Direct material, tent fabric (12 metres x $9 per metre)	$108.000
4	Direct material, tent poles (1 tent pole kit x $20 per kit)	20.000
5	Direct labour (.5 hour x $15 per hour)	7.500
6	Unit-level manufacturing overhead ($200,000/50,000 units)	4.000
7	Batch-level manufacturing overhead ($150,000/50,000 units)	3.000
8	Product-level manufacturing overhead ($4,800/50,000 units)	0.096
9	Facility-level manufacturing overhead ($1,045,200/50,000 units)	20.904
10		
11	Total absorption cost per unit	$163.500

Schedule 10

cozycamp.ca

COZYCAMP.CA
Budgeted Schedule of Cost of Goods Manufactured and Sold
For the Year Ending December 31, 20x2

Direct material (see schedule 4 for details):

Raw-material inventory, January 1	$ 64,800*	
Add: Purchases of raw material	6,400,000†	
Raw material available for use	6,464,800	
Deduct: Raw-material inventory, December 31	64,800*	
Direct material used		$6,400,000
Direct labour (see schedule 5 for details).		375,000
Manufacturing overhead (see schedule 6 for details)		1,400,000
Total manufacturing costs		8,175,000
Add: Work-in-process inventory, January 1		0‡
Subtotal		8,175,000
Deduct: Work-in-process inventory, December 31		0‡
Cost of goods manufactured		8,175,000
Add: Finished-goods inventory, January 1		81,750ǁ
Cost of goods available for sale		8,256,750
Deduct: Finished-goods inventory, December 31		81,750ǁ
Cost of goods sold		$8,175,000

*From schedule 4: 7,200 metres of tent fabric × $9 per metre, and zero inventory of tent pole kits.

†From schedule 4: $5,400,000 for tent fabric + $1,000,000 for tent pole kits.

‡The company's production cycle is short enough that there is no work-in-process inventory at any time.

ǁFrom schedule 3: 500 units × $163.50 per unit, which is the absorption manufacturing cost per unit.

Budgeted Income Statement

The **budgeted income statement** shows the expected revenue and expenses for the budget period, assuming that planned operations are carried out. CozyCamp.ca's budgeted income statement is displayed as schedule 11.

Schedule 11

cozycamp.ca

COZYCAMP.CA
Budgeted Income Statement
For the Year Ending December 31, 20x2

Sales revenue (from schedule 1)		$11,250,000
Less: Cost of goods sold (from schedule 10)		8,175,000
Gross margin		3,075,000
Other expenses:		
Selling, general, and administrative expenses (from schedule 7)	$1,406,500	
Uncollectible accounts expense (from schedule 2: 2% × $11,250,000)*	225,000	
Interest expense (from schedule 9)*	62,500	
Total other expenses		1,694,000
Net income		$ 1,381,000

*Usually these two expenses would be included in selling, general, and administrative expenses. They are listed separately in our illustration because they were determined after the selling, general, and administrative expense budget had already been explained.

Budgeted Statement of Cash Flows

The **budgeted statement of cash flows** provides information about the expected sources and uses of cash for operating activities, investing activities, and financing activities during a particular period of time. CozyCamp.ca's budgeted statement of cash flows for 20x2 is displayed as schedule 12. Notice that the format used in the budgeted statement of cash flows follows that specified under the *direct method* of preparing the statement, which is recommended by Canadian Accounting Standards and International Financial Reporting Standards (IFRS).[13] The format used in the statement of cash flows, which is a statement prepared by companies for *external* reporting purposes, generally differs from the format used in the cash receipts and cash disbursements budgets, which are prepared for *internal* use by management. Notice the differences in the format of schedule 12 when compared with schedules 2, 8, and 9. Notice also the greater detail in schedules 2, 8, and 9, which are designed for internal managerial use.

Schedule 12

cozycamp.ca

COZYCAMP.CA		
Budgeted Statement of Cash Flows		
For the Year Ending December 31, 20x2		
Cash flows from operating activities:		
Cash receipts from customers (from schedule 2)		$11,025,000
Cash payments:		
To suppliers of raw material (from schedule 8)	$6,400,000	
For direct labour (from schedule 5)	375,000	
For manufacturing-overhead expenditures (from schedule 6)	960,000	
For selling, general, and administrative expenses (from schedule 7)	1,406,500	
For interest (from schedule 9)	62,500	
Total cash payments		9,204,000
Net cash flow from operating activities		$ 1,821,000
Cash flows from investing activities:		
Construction of building addition (from schedule 9)	(1,000,000)	
Net cash used by investing activities		(1,000,000)
Cash flows from financing activities:		
Principal of bank loan (from schedule 9)	$1,000,000	
Repayment of bank loan (from schedule 9)	(1,000,000)	
Net cash provided by financing activities		0
Net increase in cash and cash equivalents		$ 821,000
Balance in cash and cash equivalents, beginning of year		10,000
Balance in cash and cash equivalents, end of year		$ 831,000

Budgeted Balance Sheet

The **budgeted balance sheet** shows the expected end-of-period balances for the company's assets, liabilities, and owner's equity, assuming that planned operations are carried out. CozyCamp.ca's budgeted balance sheet for December 31,

Exhibit 9–4
Balance Sheet for
December 31, 20x1

cozycamp.ca

COZYCAMP.CA
Balance Sheet
December 31, 20x1

Assets

Current assets:

Cash		$ 10,000
Accounts receivable (net of allowance for uncollectible accounts)		405,000
Inventory:		
Raw material	$ 64,800	
Finished goods	81,750	
Supplies	42,000	
Total inventory		188,550
Total current assets		603,550
Long-lived assets:		
Building	$8,200,000	
Equipment	2,280,000	
Less accumulated depreciation on building and equipment	(1,883,550)	
Building and equipment, net of accumulated depreciation		8,596,450
Total assets		$9,200,000

Liabilities and Owner's Equity

Current liabilities:

Accounts payable	$ 471,280
Total current liabilities	471,280
Long-term liabilities:	
Note payable (non-interest-bearing; due on December 31, 20x4)	4,100,000
Total liabilities	4,571,280
Owner's equity	4,628,720
Total liabilities and owner's equity	$9,200,000

20x2, is displayed as schedule 13. To construct this budgeted balance sheet, we start with the firm's balance sheet projected for the *beginning* of the budget year (Exhibit 9–4) and adjust each account balance for the changes expected during 20x2. These expected changes are reflected in the various 20x2 budget schedules.

Balance sheet December 31, 20x1 (Exhibit 9–4)	→ Expected changes in account balances during 20x2	Balance sheet December 31, 20x2 (schedule 13)

Explanations for the account balances on the budgeted balance sheet for December 31, 20x2, are given in the second half of schedule 13. Examine these explanations carefully. Notice how the budgeted balance sheet pulls together information from most of the schedules constituting the master budget.

Schedule 13

cozycamp.ca

COZYCAMP.CA
Budgeted Balance Sheet
December 31, 20x2

Assets

Current assets:

Cash (from schedule 9) .... $ 831,000

Accounts receivable (net of allowance for uncollectible accounts) 405,000*

Inventory:

Raw material (from schedule 10) .... $ 64,800

Finished goods (from schedule 10) 81,750

Supplies 42,000

Total inventory 188,550

Total current assets 1,424,550

Long-lived assets:

Building .... $9,200,000†

Equipment 2,280,000

Less accumulated depreciation on building and equipment .... (2,323,550)‡

Building and equipment, net of accumulated depreciation 9,156,450

Total assets $10,581,000

Liabilities and Owner's Equity

Current liabilities:

Accounts payable .... $ 471,280∥

Total current liabilities 471,280

Long-term liabilities:

Note payable (non-interest-bearing; due on December 31, 20x4) 4,100,000

Total liabilities 4,571,280

Owner's equity 6,009,720**

Total liabilities and owner's equity $10,581,000

*From schedule 2: 4th quarter sales of $2,250,000 times 18% amounts to $405,000.

†Balance in the Building account on the December 31, 20x1, balance sheet, plus the $1,000,000 cost of the building construction project in 20x2 (schedule 9).

‡Balance in the Accumulated Depreciation account on the December 31, 20x1, balance sheet, plus the $440,000 in depreciation during 20x2 (schedule 6).

∥From schedule 8: 4th quarter raw-material purchases of $1,178,200 times 40% amounts to $471,280.

**Balance in Owner's Equity on the December 31, 20x1, balance sheet, plus the 20x2 budgeted net income of $1,381,000 (schedule 11).

Assumptions and Predictions Underlying the Master Budget

A master budget is based on many assumptions and estimates of unknown parameters. Some estimates tend to be quite accurate, while other predictions are much more difficult to make accurately.

To explore the role of assumptions and predictions in the budgeting process, let's turn our attention away from the manufacturing environment of CozyCamp.ca and consider the budget prepared for Canadian Fitness Cooperative. This service organization operates as a cooperative. The members elect a board of directors who hire a manager and assistant manager to run the club. Canadian Fitness Cooperative does

Learning Objective 5

Discuss the role of assumptions and predictions in budgeting.

CANADIAN *FITNESS* CO-OP

Exhibit 9–5

Annual Budget: Canadian
Fitness Cooperative

CANADIAN
FITNESS
CO-OP

	A	B	C	D	E	F
1		CANADIAN FITNESS COOPERATIVE				
2		ANNUAL BUDGET				
3		For the Year 20x6				
4						
5						
6		1st Quarter	2nd Quarter	3rd Quarter	4th Quarter	Year
7						
8	Revenue:					
9	Membership revenue:					
10	Individual adult memberships					
11	Monthly	$ 52,200	$ 36,000	$ 14,400	$ 52,200	$ 154,800
12	Annual	30,000	30,000	30,000	30,000	120,000
13	Family memberships					
14	Monthly	22,500	18,000	3,000	22,500	66,000
15	Annual	48,750	48,750	48,750	48,750	195,000
16	Youth/student memberships	9,000	8,100	900	9,000	27,000
17	Fees for professional space:					
18	Massage therapists	5,460	5,460	1,820	5,460	18,200
19	Nutritionists	3,640	3,640	1,300	3,640	12,220
20	Total revenue	$ 171,550	$ 149,950	$ 100,170	$ 171,550	$ 593,220
21						
22	Operating expenses:					
23	Salaries and wages:					
24	Administration	$ 20,000	$ 20,000	$ 20,000	$ 20,000	$ 80,000
25	Yoga/pilates instruction	14,700	13,200	4,200	14,700	46,800
26	Aerobics instruction	14,700	13,200	4,200	14,700	46,800
27	Weight training/fitness instruction	9,600	6,400	2,200	9,600	27,800
28	Personal trainers	6,400	4,200	1,200	6,400	18,200
29	Other instruction (e.g., racquetball)	5,400	3,400	800	5,400	15,000
30	Reception/cashier	13,650	13,650	7,800	13,650	48,750
31	Maintenance/custodial	13,000	13,000	13,000	13,000	52,000
32	Employee fringe benefits	29,235	26,115	16,020	29,235	100,605
33	Utilities:					
34	Electricity	3,000	3,000	1,800	3,000	10,800
35	Heat/air conditioning	2,500	2,500	2,500	2,500	10,000
36	Telephone	600	600	600	600	2,400
37	Satellite TV	450	450	450	450	1,800
38	Trash collection	200	200	200	200	800
39	Other	1,000	1,000	1,000	1,000	4,000
40	Insurance	3,200	3,200	3,200	3,200	12,800
41	Supplies	900	700	450	900	2,950
42	Administrative	800	800	800	800	3,200
43	Maintenance/repair	2,500	2,500	4,000	2,500	11,500
44	Property taxes	9,000	9,000	9,000	9,000	36,000
45	Advertising	1,100	1,100	500	1,100	3,800
46	Depreciation:					
47	Building	10,000	10,000	10,000	10,000	40,000
48	Equipment	2,500	2,500	2,500	2,500	10,000
49	Other	1,300	1,300	1,300	1,300	5,200
50	Total operating expenses	$ 165,735	$ 152,015	$ 107,720	$ 165,735	$ 591,205
51						
52	Revenue less operating expenses	$ 5,815	$ (2,065)	$ (7,550)	$ 5,815	$ 2,015

not seek to make a profit. Each year the membership fees are adjusted with the intention of bringing in just enough revenue to cover projected expenses. The budget is an important part of that process.

Canadian Fitness Cooperative's annual budget is displayed in Exhibit 9–5. The cooperative sells individual adult, family, and youth/student memberships. The individual adult and family memberships can be monthly or annual, with a significant price break offered on the annual memberships. The fitness cooperative also allows licensed massage therapists and nutritional counsellors to meet clients in the club's facilities and charges a fee to the professional offering the service. The staff includes a manager and assistant manager to administer the operation;

various part-time instructors who teach classes such as yoga, pilates, aerobic exercise, weight training, and proper use of the fitness equipment; reception and cashier personnel; and custodians. Other operating expenses include such items as utilities, insurance, supplies, maintenance, property taxes, advertising, and depreciation.

Notice the differences and similarities between the budgets for CozyCamp.ca and Canadian Fitness Cooperative. CozyCamp.ca's budgeted income statement (schedule 11 on page 324) subtracts cost of goods sold expense from sales revenue to calculate the gross margin. In contrast, Canadian Fitness Cooperative does not show cost of goods sold, because the fitness cooperative does not sell a physical product. Nor does it show a gross margin. The Canadian Fitness Cooperative budget shows revenue from membership dues and rental of space to licensed massage therapists and nutritional counsellors, and operating expenses. While CozyCamp.ca's budget shows net income, the Canadian Fitness Cooperative's budget refers to revenue less operating expenses. This emphasizes the Fitness Cooperative's status as a nonprofit enterprise.

There are also similarities between these two budgets. For example, both businesses experience significant seasonality in activity. CozyCamp.ca sells more tents in the second and third quarters than in the first and fourth quarters. Canadian Fitness Cooperative sells more monthly memberships in the cold months (first and fourth quarters) than in the warmer months (second and third quarters). During quarters with increased sales activity, both businesses show correspondingly higher expenses.

Now let's briefly discuss some of the assumptions and predictions that are reflected in Canadian Fitness Cooperative's budget. First, the fitness club's managers have assumed that people will continue to use the club more in the colder months of the year than in the warmer months as they have in the past. Second, the managers have assumed that the split between monthly and annual memberships for both individuals and families will be about the same as in the past. Based on these assumptions, the managers have predicted membership sales for each quarter. For example, the budget reflects the following predictions for memberships and prices in the first and second quarters. Notice that the monthly memberships decline in the second quarter, whereas the annual memberships are constant across the entire year.

Membership Type	1st Quarter	2nd Quarter
Individual adult, monthly	290 @ $60 per month	200 @ $60 per month
Individual adult, annual	200 @ $600 per year	200 @ $600 per year
Family, monthly	50 @ $150 per month	40 @ $150 per month
Family, annual	130 @ $1,500 per year	130 @ $1,500 per year
Youth/student	100 @ $30 per month	90 @ $30 per month

The Canadian Fitness Cooperative reflects many other predictions, such as salaries, wage rates, electric and other utility rates, insurance and property tax rates, and so forth. Some of these predictions—property tax rates, for example—would likely be quite accurate. Other predictions would be more difficult, as, for example, the cost of natural gas for heating purposes due to its dependence on the weather.

Financial Planning Models

Managers have to make assumptions and predictions in preparing budgets, because organizations operate in a world of uncertainty. One way of coping with that uncertainty is to supplement the budgeting process with a *financial planning model*.

A **financial planning model** is a set of mathematical relationships that express the interactions among the various operational, financial, and environmental events, which determine the overall results of an organization's activities. A financial planning model is a mathematical expression of all the relationships expressed in the flowchart of Exhibit 9–1.

To illustrate this concept, focus on the following equation, which is used to budget Canadian Fitness Cooperative's employee fringe benefits:

$$(\text{Employee fringe benefits}) = .30 \times (\text{Total salaries and wages})$$

However, suppose the cooperative's managers are uncertain about this 30 percent estimate. A financial planning model might include the following equation instead:

$$(\text{Employee fringe benefits}) = p \times (\text{Total salaries and wages})$$

$$\text{where } 0 \leq p \leq 1.0$$

The budget staff can run the financial planning model as many times as desired on a computer, using a different value for p each time. Perhaps the following values would be tried: 29, 30, and 31. Now management can answer the question, What if employee fringe benefits cost 29 percent of salaries and wages? In a fully developed financial planning model, all of the key estimates and assumptions are expressed as general mathematical relationships. Then the model is run on a computer many times to determine the impact of different combinations of these unknown variables. "What if" questions can be answered about such unknown variables as inflation, interest rates, the value of the dollar, demand, competitors' actions, union demands in forthcoming wage negotiations, and a host of other factors. The widespread availability of personal computers and electronic-spreadsheet software has made financial planning models a more and more common management tool.

Budget Administration

In small organizations, the procedures used to gather information and construct a master budget are usually informal. In contrast, larger organizations use a formal process to collect data and prepare the master budget. Such organizations usually designate a **budget director** or **chief budget officer**. This is often the organization's controller. The budget director specifies the process by which budget data will be gathered, collects the information, and prepares the master budget. To communicate budget procedures and deadlines to employees throughout the organization, the budget director often develops and disseminates a **budget manual**. The budget manual states who is responsible for providing various types of information, when the information is required, and what form the information is to take. For example, the budget manual for a manufacturing firm might specify that each regional sales director is to send an estimate of the following year's sales, by product line, to the budget director by September 1. The budget manual also states who should receive each schedule when the master budget is complete.

A **budget committee**, consisting of key senior executives, is often appointed to advise the budget director during the preparation of the budget. The authority to give final approval to the master budget usually belongs to the board of directors, or a board of trustees in many nonprofit organizations. Usually the board has a subcommittee whose task is to examine the proposed budget carefully and recommend approval or any changes deemed necessary. By exercising its authority to make changes in the budget and grant final approval, the board of directors, or trustees, can wield considerable influence on the overall direction the organization takes.

M anagement
A ccounting
P ractice

Simon Fraser University

BUDGET ADMINISTRATION AT SIMON FRASER UNIVERSITY

Simon Fraser University's annual budget covers the period from April 1 through the following March 31. The budgeting process begins in October, when the university president consults with the academic community at all levels. The deans and vice-presidents have meetings to discuss the programs the university will conduct during the following budget year. The university's priorities in educational, research, and public service programs are established during these meetings. In early October, a set of assumptions to be used during the remainder of the budgeting process is distributed to the vice presidents. These assumptions include such key forecasts as the next year's inflation rate, interest rates, and tuition levels. Based on these assumptions, the dean of each of SFU's faculties must develop a detailed budget for salaries and general expenses. These detailed budgets are prepared during November and December by the financial staff in each faculty. In February, the university president reviews these budgets with the vice-presidents. After any needed revisions have been made, the budgets for the faculties are consolidated by the university's budget office into a master budget. This budget is presented to the university's board of governors in March for final approval.

As more and more companies operate globally, the Internet is playing an ever-greater role in the budgeting process. E-budgeting is an increasingly popular, Internet-based budgeting tool that can help streamline and speed up an organization's budgeting process. The *e* in **e-budgeting** stands for both *electronic* and *enterprisewide*; employees throughout an organization, at all levels and around the globe, can submit and retrieve budget information electronically via the Internet. Budgeting software is utilized and made available on the Web, so that budget information electronically submitted from any location is in a consistent company-wide format. Managers in organizations using e-budgeting have found that it greatly streamlines the entire budgeting process. In the past, these organizations have compiled their master budgets on hundreds of spreadsheets, which had to be collected and integrated by the corporate controller's office. One result of this cumbersome approach was that a disproportionate amount of time was spent compiling and verifying data from multiple sources. Under e-budgeting, both the submission of budget information and its compilation are accomplished electronically by the Web-based budgeting software. Thus, e-budgeting is just one more area where the Internet has transformed how the workplace operates in the era of e-business.[14]

International Aspects of Budgeting

As the economies and cultures of countries throughout the world become intertwined, more and more companies are becoming multinational in their operations. Firms with international operations face a variety of additional challenges in preparing their budgets. First, a multinational firm's budget must reflect the translation of foreign currencies into the local currency. Since almost all the world's other currencies fluctuate in their values relative to the local currency, this makes budgeting for those translations difficult. Although multinationals have sophisticated financial ways of hedging against such currency fluctuations, the budgeting task is still more challenging. Second, it is difficult to prepare budgets when inflation is high or unpredictable. While Canada has experienced

As this photo from Rome, Italy shows, United Parcel Service (UPS) operates throughout the world. Multinational companies face special challenges in preparing their budgets.

periods of inflation, some foreign countries have experienced hyperinflation, sometimes with annual inflation rates well over 100 percent. Predicting such high inflation rates is difficult and further complicates a multinational's budgeting process. Finally, the economies of all countries fluctuate in terms of consumer demand, availability of skilled labour, laws affecting commerce, and so forth. Companies with overseas operations face the task of anticipating such changing conditions in their budgeting processes.

Budgeting Product Life-Cycle Costs

Learning Objective 7

Understand the importance of budgeting product life-cycle costs.

A relatively recent focus of the budgeting process is to plan for all of the costs that will be incurred throughout a product's life cycle, before a commitment is made to the product.[15] Product life-cycle costs encompass the following five phases in a product's life cycle:

- Product planning and concept design
- Preliminary design
- Detailed design and testing
- Production
- Distribution and customer service

In order to justify a product's introduction, the sales revenues it will generate over its lifetime have to cover all these costs. Thus, planning these life-cycle costs is a crucial step in making a decision about the introduction of a new product. This is particularly true for firms with very short product life cycles, such as some products in the computer and electronics industries. When product life cycles are as short as a year or two, the firm does not have time to adjust its pricing strategy or production methods to ensure that the product turns a profit. Management must be fairly certain before a commitment is made to the product that its life-cycle costs will be covered. As Exhibit 9–6 shows, most of a product's life-cycle costs are committed rather early in the product's life. By the time the planning, design, and testing phases are complete,

Exhibit 9–6
Product Life-Cycle Costs and Cost Commitment for a Typical Product

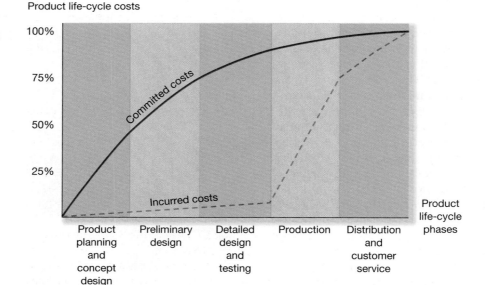

	Year				
Life-Cycle Phase	**20x5**	**20x6**	**20x7**	**20x8**	**20x9**
Product planning and concept design	$300,000				
Preliminary design	100,000				
Detail design and testing		$600,000			
Production		300,000	$2,000,000	$2,700,000	$1,200,000
Distribution and customer service		50,000	750,000	1,000,000	1,000,000

Exhibit 9–7
Product Life-Cycle Cost Budget

roughly 85 percent of this product's life-cycle costs have been committed, while only about 5 percent actually have been incurred.

Given the early commitment that must be made to significant downstream costs in a product's life cycle, it is crucial to budget these costs as early as possible. Exhibit 9–7 displays a product life-cycle cost budget for an ancillary computer device with an anticipated five-year life cycle.

Behavioural Impact of Budgets

One of the underlying themes stressed in this text is the behavioural impact of managerial accounting practices. There is no other area where the behavioural implications are more important than in the budgeting area. A budget affects virtually everyone in an organization: those who prepare the budget, those who use the budget to facilitate decision making, and those who are evaluated using the budget. The human reactions to the budgeting process can have considerable influence on an organization's overall effectiveness.

A great deal of study has been devoted to the behavioural effects of budgets. Here we will barely scratch the surface by briefly considering two issues: budgetary slack and participative budgeting.

Learning Objective 8

Discuss the behavioural implications of budgetary slack and participative budgeting.

Budgetary Slack: Padding the Budget

The information upon which a budget is based comes largely from people throughout an organization. For example, the sales forecast relies on market research and analysis by market research staff but also incorporates the projections of sales personnel. If a territorial sales manager's performance is evaluated on the basis of whether the sales budget for the territory is exceeded, what is the incentive for the sales manager in projecting sales? The incentive is to give a conservative, or cautiously low, sales estimate. The sales manager's performance will look much better in the eyes of top management when a conservative estimate is exceeded than when an ambitious estimate is not met. At least that is the *perception* of many sales managers, and, in the behavioural area, perceptions are what count most.

When a supervisor provides a departmental cost projection for budgetary purposes, there is an incentive to overestimate costs. When the actual cost incurred in the department proves to be less than the inflated cost projection, the supervisor appears to have managed in a cost-effective way.

These illustrations are examples of **padding the budget**. Budget padding means underestimating revenue or overestimating costs. The difference between the revenue or cost projection that a person provides and a realistic estimate of the revenue or cost is called **budgetary slack**. For example, if a manager believes the annual utilities cost will be $18,000, but gives a budgetary projection of $20,000, the manager has built $2,000 of slack into the budget.

Why do people pad budgets with budgetary slack? There are three primary reasons. First, people often *perceive* that their performance will look better in their superiors' eyes if they can "beat the budget." Second, budgetary slack often is used to cope with uncertainty. A departmental supervisor may feel confident in the cost projections for 10 cost items. However, the supervisor also may feel that some unforeseen event during the budgetary period could result in unanticipated costs. For example, an unexpected machine breakdown could occur. One way of dealing with that unforeseen event is to pad the budget. If nothing goes wrong, the supervisor can beat the cost budget. If some negative event does occur, the supervisor can use the budgetary slack to absorb the impact of the event and still meet the cost budget.

The third reason why cost budgets are padded is that budgetary cost projections are often cut in the resource-allocation process. Thus, we have a vicious circle. Budgetary projections are padded because they will likely be cut, and they are cut because they are likely to have been padded.

How does an organization solve the problem of budgetary slack? First, it can avoid relying on the budget as a negative evaluation tool. If a departmental supervisor is harassed by the budget director or some other top manager every time a budgetary cost projection is exceeded, the likely behavioural response will be to pad the budget. In contrast, if the supervisor is allowed some managerial discretion to exceed the budget when necessary, there will be less tendency toward budgetary padding. Second, managers can be given incentives not only to achieve budgetary projections but also to *provide accurate projections*. This can be accomplished by asking managers to justify all or some of their projections and by rewarding managers who consistently provide accurate estimates.

Participative Budgeting

Most people will perform better and make greater attempts to achieve a goal if they have been consulted in setting the goal. The idea of **participative budgeting** is to

Focus on Ethics

IS PADDING THE BUDGET UNETHICAL?

A departmental or divisional budget often is used as the basis for evaluating a manager's performance. Actual results are compared with budgeted performance levels, and those who outperform the budget often are rewarded with promotions or salary increases. In many cases, bonuses are tied explicitly to performance relative to a budget. For example, the top-management personnel of a division may receive a bonus if divisional profit exceeds budgeted profit by a certain percentage.

Serious ethical issues can arise in situations where a budget is the basis for rewarding managers. For example, suppose a division's top-management personnel will split a bonus equal to 10 percent of the amount by which actual divisional profit exceeds the budget. This may create an incentive for the divisional budget officer, or other managers supplying data, to pad the divisional profit budget. Such padding would make the budget easier to achieve, thus increasing the chance of a bonus. Alternatively, there may be an incentive to manipulate the actual divisional results in

order to maximize management's bonus. For example, year-end sales could be shifted between years to increase reported revenue in a particular year. Budget personnel could have such incentives for either of two reasons: (1) they might share in the bonus or (2) they might feel pressure from the managers who would share in the bonus.

Put yourself in the position of the division controller. Your bonus, and that of your boss, the division vice-president, will be determined in part by the division's income in comparison to the budget. When your division has submitted budgets in the past, the corporate management has usually cut your budgeted expenses, thereby increasing the division's budgeted profit. This, of course, makes it more difficult for your division to achieve the budgeted profit. Moreover, it makes it less likely that you and your divisional colleagues will earn a bonus.

Now your boss is pressuring you to pad the expense budget, because "The budgeted expenses will just be cut anyway at the corporate level." Is padding the budget ethical under these circumstances? What do you think?

involve employees throughout an organization in the budgetary process. Such participation can give employees the feeling that "This is our budget," rather than the all-too-common feeling that "This is the budget you imposed on us."

While participative budgeting can be very effective, it also can have shortcomings. Too much participation and discussion can lead to vacillation and delay. Also, when those involved in the budgeting process disagree in significant and irreconcilable ways, the process of participation can accentuate those differences. Finally, the problem of budget padding can be severe unless incentives for accurate projections are provided.

Chapter Summary

The budget is a key tool for planning, control, and decision making in virtually every organization. Budgeting systems are used to force planning, to facilitate communication and coordination, to allocate resources, to control profit and operations, and to evaluate performance and provide incentives. Various types of budgets are used to accomplish these objectives.

The comprehensive set of budgets that covers all phases of an organization's operations is called a master budget. The first step in preparing a master budget is to forecast sales of the organization's services or goods. Based on the sales forecast, operational budgets are prepared to plan production of services or goods and to outline the acquisition and use of material, labour, and other resources. Finally, a set of budgeted financial statements is prepared to show what the organization's overall financial condition will be if planned operations are carried out.

The application of activity-based costing (ABC) concepts to the budgeting process yields activity-based budgeting (ABB). Utilizing ABC information in the budgeting process through activity-based budgeting provides sound information for budgeting costs, because the underlying ABC information is based explicitly on the relationships among cost drivers, activities, and resources consumed.

E-budgeting means electronic and enterprisewide budgeting by making use of the Internet. Employees throughout an organization, at all levels and around the world, can submit and retrieve budget information via the Internet.

Since budgets affect almost everyone in an organization, they can have significant behavioural implications and can raise difficult ethical issues. One common problem in budgeting is the tendency of people to pad budgets. The resulting budgetary slack makes the budget less useful because the padded budget does not present an accurate picture of expected revenue and expenses.

A relatively recent focus of the budgeting process is to plan for product life-cycle costs. A large portion of these costs often are committed early in a product's life cycle. It is important for management to be fairly certain that the revenue to be generated by a product will cover all of its life-cycle costs.

Participative budgeting is the process of allowing employees throughout the organization to have a significant role in developing the budget. Participative budgeting can result in greater commitment to meet the budget by those who participated in the process.

Review Problem on Preparing Master Budget Schedules

SolarTech, Inc. manufactures a special ceramic tile used as a component in residential solar energy systems. Sales are seasonal due to the seasonality in the home-building industry.

- The expected pattern of sales for the next year (20x8) is as follows:

	Quarter				
	1st	2nd	3rd	4th	Year
Sales in units	2,000	6,000	8,000	4,000	20,000

- Each tile sells for $25. All sales are on account, and SolarTech's experience with cash collections is that 60 percent of each quarter's sales are collected during the same quarter as the sale. The remaining 40 percent of sales is collected in the quarter after the sale. SolarTech experiences negligible bad debts, and so this is ignored in the budgeting process. Sales in the 4th quarter of 20x7 are expected to be $100,000 (4,000 units).

- SolarTech desires to have 10 percent of the following quarter's sales needs in finished-goods inventory at the end of each quarter. (On December 31, 20x7, SolarTech expects to have 200 units in inventory.)
- Each tile requires two kilograms of raw material. SolarTech desires to have 10 percent of the next quarter's raw material in inventory at the end of each quarter. (On December 31, 20x7, SolarTech expects to have 480 kilograms of raw material in inventory.)
- The raw material price is $5 per kilogram. The company buys its raw material on account and pays 70 percent of the resulting accounts payable during the quarter of the purchase. The remaining 30 percent is paid during the following quarter. (The raw-material purchases in the 4th quarter of 20x7 are expected to be $36,600.)

Required: Prepare the following budget schedules for 20x8. Include a column for each quarter and for the year.

1. Sales budget (in units and dollars)
2. Cash receipts budget
3. Production budget
4. Direct material budget (*Hint:* The desired ending inventory in the 4th quarter is 480 kilograms.)
5. Cash disbursements budget for raw material purchases

Solution to Review Problem

1. Sales budget for 20x8:

	Quarter				
	1st	2nd	3rd	4th	Year
Sales in units	2,000	6,000	8,000	4,000	20,000
Unit sales price	$ 25	$ 25	$ 25	$ 25	$ 25
Total sales revenue	$50,000	$150,000	$200,000	$100,000	$500,000

2. Cash receipts budget for 20x8:

	Quarter				
	1st	2nd	3rd	4th	Year
Sales revenue (from sales budget)	$50,000	$150,000	$200,000	$100,000	$500,000
Collections in quarter of sale (60% of revenue)	$30,000	$ 90,000	$120,000	$ 60,000	$300,000
Collections in quarter after sale (40% of prior quarter's revenue)*	40,000*	20,000	60,000	80,000	200,000
Total cash receipts	$70,000	$110,000	$180,000	$140,000	$500,000

*Forty percent of sales revenue from the 4th quarter of 20x7, which was given at $100,000.

3. Production budget for 20x8:

	Quarter				
	1st	2nd	3rd	4th	Year
Sales in units (from sales budget)	2,000	6,000	8,000	4,000	20,000
Add desired ending inventory of finished goods*	600	800	400	200†	2,000
Total units required	2,600	6,800	8,400	4,200	22,000
Less expected beginning inventory of finished goods	200	600	800	400	2,000
Units to be produced	2,400	6,200	7,600	3,800	20,000

*Ten percent of the next quarter's expected sales.
†Ten percent of the expected sales for the 1st quarter of the next year 20x9, which is predicted to be 2,000 units.

4. Direct-material budget for 20x8:

	Quarter				
	1st	**2nd**	**3rd**	**4th**	**Year**
Units to be produced (from production budget)	2,400	6,200	7,600	3,800	20,000
Raw material required per unit (kilograms)	× 2	× 2	× 2	× 2	× 2
Raw material required for production (kilograms)	4,800	12,400	15,200	7,600	40,000
Add desired ending inventory of raw material (kilograms)*	1,240	1,520	760	480†	4,000
Total raw material required	6,040	13,920	15,960	8,080	44,000
Less expected beginning inventory of raw material (kilograms)	480‡	1,240	1,520	760	4,000
Raw material to be purchased (kilograms)	5,560	12,680	14,440	7,320	40,000
Cost per pound	× $5	× $5	× $5	× $5	× $5
Total cost of raw material purchases	$27,800	$63,400	$72,200	$36,600	$200,000

*Ten percent of the next quarter's raw material requirements.

†The desired ending raw material inventory for the 4th quarter of 20x8 is given at 480 kilograms. However, it can also be computed independently by noting that the expected sales pattern for 20x9 is the same as that for 20x8. Therefore, the 1st quarter budgets for 20x9 will be the same as those for the 1st quarter of 20x8. So the desired ending raw-material inventory for the 4th quarter of 20x8 is 480 kilograms (10% × 4,800 kilograms required for production in the 1st quarter of 20x9).

‡Given in problem.

5. Cash disbursements budget for raw material purchases for 20x8:

	Quarter				
	1st	**2nd**	**3rd**	**4th**	**Year**
Cost of raw material purchases (from direct-material budget)	$27,800	$63,400	$72,200	$36,600	$200,000
Cash payments for purchases made during the quarter (70% of current quarter's purchases)	$19,460	$44,380	$50,540	$25,620	$140,000
Cash payments for prior quarter's purchases (30% of prior quarter's purchases)	10,980*	8,340	19,020	21,660	60,000
Total cash payments for raw material purchases	$30,440	$52,720	$69,560	$47,280	$200,000

*Purchases in the 4th quarter of 20x7 were given at $36,600.

Key Terms

For each term's definition refer to the indicated page, or turn to the glossary at the end of the text.

Review Questions

9–1. Explain how a budget facilitates communication and coordination.

9–2. Use an example to explain how a budget could be used to allocate resources in a university.

9–3. Explain what a master *budget* is, and list five of its parts.

9–4. Draw a flowchart similar to the one in Exhibit 9–1 for a service station. The service station provides automotive maintenance services in addition to selling gasoline and related products.

9–5. Give an example of how general economic trends would affect sales forecasting in the airline industry.

9–6. What is meant by the term *operational budgets*? List three operational budgets that would be prepared by a hospital.

9–7. How does activity-based budgeting differ from more traditional budgeting methods?

9–8. How does e-budgeting make use of the Internet?

9–9. Give three examples of how a city could use a budget for planning purposes.

9–10. Describe the role of a *budget director*.

9–11. What is the purpose of a *budget manual*?

9–12. How can a company's board of directors use the budget to influence the future direction of the firm?

9–13. Discuss the importance of predictions and assumptions in the budgeting process.

9–14. Define the term *budgetary slack*, and briefly describe a problem it can cause.

9–15. How can an organization help to reduce the problems caused by budgetary slack?

9–16. Why is participative budgeting often an effective management tool?

9–17. Discuss this comment by a small business owner: "Budgeting is a waste of time. I've been running this business for 40 years. I don't need to plan."

9–18. List the steps you would go through in developing a budget to meet your college expenses.

9–19. Briefly describe three issues that create special challenges for multinational firms in preparing their budgets.

9–20. List five phases in a product's *life cycle*, and explain why it is important to budget the costs in each of these phases.

Exercises

■ **Exercise 9–21**
Missing Amounts; Various
Types of Budgets
(LO 2, 4)

Fill in the missing amounts in the following schedules:

	July	August	September
1. Sales*	$240,000	$180,000	$?
Cash receipts:			
From cash sales	$?	$?	$135,000
From sales on account†	?	102,000	?
Total cash receipts	$?	$?	$?

2. Accounts payable, 12/31/x0		$ 600,000
Purchase of goods and services on account during 20x1		2,400,000
Payments of accounts payable during 20x1		?
Accounts payable, 12/31/x1		800,000
3. Accounts receivable, 12/31/x0		$1,700,000
Sales on account during 20x1		4,500,000
Collections of accounts receivable during 20x1		3,900,000
Accounts receivable, 12/31/x1		?
4. Accumulated depreciation, 12/31/x0		$ 405,000
Depreciation expense during 20x1		75,000
Accumulated depreciation, 12/31/x1		?
5. Retained earnings, 12/31/x0		$1,537,500
Net income for 20x1		300,000
Dividends paid in 20x1		–0–
Retained earnings, 12/31/x1		?

*Half of each month's sales are on account. June sales amounted to $180,000.

†60% of credit sales is collected in the month of sale; 40% is collected in the following month.

Choose a city or province, and use the Internet to explore the annual budget of the governmental unit you selected. For example, you could check out the budget for Vancouver at www.city.vancouver.bc.ca/corpsvcs/financial/index.htm.

Required: List three items in the budget that you found surprising or particularly interesting, and explain why.

■ **Exercise 9–22**
City or Provincial Budget;
Use of Internet
(LO 1, 2)

Alder Company budgets on an annual basis. The following beginning and ending inventory levels (in units) are planned for the year 20x1. Two units of raw material are required to produce each unit of finished product.

■ **Exercise 9–23**
Budgeting Production and
Direct-Material Purchases
(LO 2, 4)

Demo

	January 1	December 31
Raw material	245,000	315,000
Work in process	84,000	84,000
Finished goods	560,000	350,000

Required:

1. If Alder Company plans to sell 3,360,000 units during the year, compute the number of units the firm would have to manufacture during the year.
2. If 3,500,000 finished units were to be manufactured by Alder Company during the year, determine the amount of raw material to be purchased.

(CMA, adapted)

Coyote Loco, Inc., a manufacturer of salsa, has the following historical collection pattern for its credit sales:

■ **Exercise 9–24**
Cash Collections
(LO 2, 4)

+ Calculate the balance of net A/L @ Dec 31

- 70 percent collected in the month of sale
- 15 percent collected in the first month after sale
- 10 percent collected in the second month after sale
- 4 percent collected in the third month after sale
- 1 percent uncollectible

The sales on account have been budgeted for the last seven months as follows:

GOOD PROBLEM, SEE CHANGES

June	$122,500
July	150,000
August	175,000
September	200,000
October	225,000
November	250,000
December	212,500

Required:

1. Compute the estimated total cash collections during October from credit sales.
2. Compute the estimated total cash collections during the fourth quarter ~~from sales made on account during the fourth quarter~~.
3. *Build a spreadsheet:* Construct an Excel spreadsheet to solve both of the preceding requirements. Show how the solution will change if the following information changes: sales in June and July were $100,000 and $130,000, respectively.

(CMA, adapted)

Greener Grass Fertilizer Company plans to sell 40,000 units of finished product in July and anticipates a growth rate in sales of 5 percent per month. The desired monthly ending inventory in units of finished product is 80 percent of the next month's estimated sales. There are 32,000 finished units in inventory on June 30. Each unit of finished product requires four kilograms of raw material at a cost of $1.40 per kilogram. There are 140,000 kilograms of raw material in inventory on June 30.

■ **Exercise 9–25**
Budgeting Production and
Raw-Material Purchases
(LO 2, 4)

Required:

1. Compute the company's total required production in units of finished product for the entire three-month period ending September 30.

2. Independent of your answer to requirement (1), assume the company plans to produce 120,000 units of finished product in the three-month period ending September 30, and to have raw-material inventory on hand at the end of the three-month period equal to 25 percent of the use in that period. Compute the total estimated cost of raw-material purchases for the entire three-month period ending September 30.

(CMA, adapted)

Exercise 9–26
Cash Budgeting
(LO 2, 4)

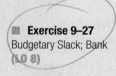

The following information is from White Mountain Furniture Company's financial records.

Month	Sales	Purchases
July	$180,000	$105,000
August	165,000	120,000
September	150,000	90,000
October	195,000	135,000

Collections from customers are normally 70 percent in the month of sale, 20 percent in the month following the sale, and 9 percent in the second month following the sale. The balance is expected to be uncollectible. All purchases are on account. Management takes full advantage of the 2 percent discount allowed on purchases paid for by the tenth of the following month. Purchases for November are budgeted at $150,000, and sales for November are forecasted at $165,000. Cash disbursements for expenses are expected to be $36,000 for the month of November. The company's cash balance on November 1 was $55,000.

Required: Prepare the following schedules:

1. Expected cash collections during November
2. Expected cash disbursements during November
3. Expected cash balance on November 30

Exercise 9–27
Budgetary Slack; Bank
(LO 8)

Tanya Williams is the bank's new accounts manager at Coast Mountain Bank. She has just been asked to project how many new bank accounts she will generate during 20x5. The economy of the region in which the bank operates has been growing, and the bank has experienced a 10 percent increase in its number of bank accounts over each of the past five years. In 20x4, the bank had 10,000 accounts.

The new accounts manager is paid a salary plus a bonus of $45 for every new account she generates above the budgeted amount. Thus, if the annual budget calls for 500 new accounts, and 540 new accounts are obtained, Williams's bonus will be $1,800 (40 × $45).

Williams believes the economy of the region will continue to grow at the same rate in 20x5 as it has in recent years. She has decided to submit a budgetary projection of 800 new accounts for 20x5.

Required: Your consulting firm has been hired by the bank president to make recommendations for improving its operations. Write a memorandum to the president defining and explaining the negative consequences of budgetary slack. Also discuss the bank's bonus system for the new accounts manager and how the bonus program tends to encourage budgetary slack.

Exercise 9–28
Using Budgets for Financial Planning
(LO 1, 4, 5)

Sound Investments, Inc. is a large retailer of stereo equipment. The controller is about to prepare the budget for the first quarter of 20x5. Past experience has indicated that 75 percent of the store's sales are cash sales. The collection experience for the sales on account is as follows:

*   80 percent during month of sale
*   15 percent during month following sale
*   5 percent uncollectible

The total sales for December 20x4 are expected to be $380,000. The controller feels that sales in January 20x5 could range from $200,000 to $320,000.

Required:

1. Demonstrate how financial planning can be used to project cash receipts in January of 20x5 for three different levels of January sales. Use the following columnar format:

	Total Sales in January 20x5		
	$200,000	$260,000	$320,000
Cash receipts in January 20x5:			
From December sales on account	$	$	$
From January cash sales			
From January sales on account			
Total cash receipts	$	$	$

2. How could the controller of Sound Investments, Inc. use this financial planning approach to help in planning operations for January?

■ **Exercise 9–29**
Budgeted Financial
Statements; Retailer
(LO 2, 4)

Village Hardware is a retail hardware store. Information about the store's operations follows.

- November 20x4 sales amounted to $400,000.
- Sales are budgeted at $440,000 for December 20x4 and $400,000 for January 20x5.
- Collections are expected to be 60 percent in the month of sale and 38 percent in the month following the sale. Two percent of sales are expected to be uncollectible. Bad debts expense is recognized monthly.
- The store's gross margin is 25 percent of its sales revenue.
- A total of 80 percent of the merchandise for resale is purchased in the month prior to the month of sale, and 20 percent is purchased in the month of sale. Payment for merchandise is made in the month following the purchase.
- Other monthly expenses paid in cash amount to $45,200.
- Annual depreciation is $432,000.

The company's balance sheet as of November 30, 20x4, is as follows:

VILLAGE HARDWARE, INC.
Balance Sheet
November 30, 20x4

ASSETS

Cash	$ 44,000
Accounts receivable (net of $7,000 allowance for uncollectible accounts)	152,000
Inventory	280,000
Property, plant, and equipment (net of $1,180,000 accumulated depreciation)	1,724,000
Total assets	$2,200,000

LIABILITIES AND STOCKHOLDERS' EQUITY

Accounts payable	$ 324,000
Common stock	1,590,000
Retained earnings..	286,000
Total liabilities and stockholders' equity	$2,200,000

Required: Compute the following amounts:

1. The budgeted cash collections for December 20x4
2. The budgeted income (loss) before income taxes for December 20x4
3. The projected balance in accounts payable on December 31, 20x4

(CMA, adapted)

Metropolitan Dental Associates is a large dental practice. The firm's controller is preparing the budget for the next year. The controller projects a total of 48,000 office visits, to be evenly distributed throughout the year. Eighty percent of the visits will be half-hour appointments, and the remainder will be one-hour visits. The average rates for professional dental services are $60 for half-hour appointments and $105 for one-hour office visits. Ninety percent of each month's professional service revenue is collected during the month when services are rendered, and the remainder is collected the month following service. Uncollectible billings are negligible. Metropolitan's dental associates earn $90 per hour.

Metropolitan uses activity-based budgeting to budget office overhead and administrative expenses. Two cost drivers are used: office visits and direct professional labour. The cost-driver rates are as follows:

Patient registration and records	$3.00 per office visit (of any length)
All other overhead and administrative expenses	$7.50 per direct professional labour hour

Required: Prepare the following budget schedules:

1. Direct-professional-labour budget for the month of June
2. Cash collections during June for professional services rendered during May and June
3. Overhead and administrative expense budget for the month of June
4. *Build a spreadsheet:* Construct an Excel spreadsheet to solve all of the preceding requirements. Show how the solution will change if the following information changes: a total of 54,000 office visits are expected for the year and 70 percent of the office visits are half-hour appointments.

Problems

Shady Shades Corporation manufactures artistic frames for sunglasses. Talia Demarest, controller, is responsible for preparing the company's master budget. In compiling the budget data for 20x1, Demarest has learned that new automated production equipment will be installed on March 1. This will reduce the direct labour per frame from 1 hour to .75 hour.

Labour-related costs include pension contributions of $.50 per hour, workers' compensation insurance of $.20 per hour, employee medical insurance of $.80 per hour, and other benefits equal to 7 percent of direct-labour wages. The cost of employee benefits paid by the company on its employees is treated as a direct-labour cost. Spiffy Shades Corporation has a labour contract that calls for a wage increase to $18 per hour on April 1, 20x1. Management expects to have 32,000 frames on hand at December 31, 20x0, and has a policy of carrying an end-of-month inventory of 100 percent of the following month's sales plus 50 percent of the second following month's sales.

These and other data compiled by Demarest are summarized in the following table:

	January	February	March	April	May
Direct-labour hours per unit	1.0	1.0	.75	.75	.75
Wage per direct-labour hour................	$16.00	$16.00	$16.00	$18.00	$18.00
Estimated unit sales	20,000	24,000	16,000	18,000	18,000
Sales price per unit	$50.00	$47.50	$47.50	$47.50	$47.50
Manufacturing overhead:					
Shipping and handling (per unit sold)	$3.00	$3.00	$3.00	$3.00	$3.00
Purchasing, material handling, and inspection (per unit produced)	$4.50	$4.50	$4.50	$4.50	$4.50
Other manufacturing overhead (per direct-labour hour)	$10.50	$10.50	$10.50	$10.50	$10.50

Required:

1. Prepare a production budget and a direct-labour budget for Shady Shades Corporation by month and for the first quarter of 20x1. Both budgets may be combined in one schedule. The direct-labour budget should include direct-labour hours and show the detail for each direct-labour cost category.

2. For each item used in the firm's production budget and direct-labour budget, identify the other components of the master budget that also would use these data.

3. Prepare a manufacturing overhead budget for each month and for the first quarter.

(CMA, adapted)

Western University (WU) is preparing its master budget for the upcoming academic year. Currently, 12,000 students are enrolled on campus; however, the admissions office is forecasting a 5 percent growth in the student body despite a tuition hike to $75 per credit hour. The following additional information has been gathered from an examination of university records and conversations with university officials:

- WU is planning to award 180 tuition-free scholarships.
- The average class has 25 students, and the typical student takes 15 credit hours each semester. Each class is three credit hours. WU operates two semesters per year and has no summer term.
- WU's faculty members are evaluated on the basis of teaching, research, and university and community service. Each faculty member teaches five classes during the academic year.

■ **Problem 9–32**
Revenue and Labour
Budgeting for a University;
Budget Linkages
(LO 4, 5, 6)

2. Total student class enrolments to be covered:
126,000

Required:

1. Prepare a tuition revenue budget for the upcoming academic year.
2. Determine the number of faculty members needed to cover classes.
3. Assume there is a shortage of full-time faculty members. List at least five actions that WU might take to accommodate the growing student body.
4. You have been requested by the university's administrative vice-president (AVP) to construct budgets for other areas of operation (e.g., the library, grounds, dormitories, and maintenance). The AVP noted: "The most important resource of the university is its faculty. Now that you know the number of faculty needed, you can prepare the other budgets. Faculty members are indeed the key driver—without them we don't operate." Does the administrative vice-president really understand the linkages within the budgeting process? Explain.

Mary and Kay, Inc., a distributor of cosmetics, is in the process of assembling a cash budget for the first quarter of 20x1. The following information has been extracted from the company's accounting records:

■ **Problem 9–33**
Cash budgeting
(LO 2, 4)

2. Total cash disbursements
in February: $363,000

- All sales are on account. Sixty percent of customer accounts are collected in the month of sale; 35 percent are collected in the following month. Uncollectibles amounting to 5 percent of sales are anticipated, and management believes that only 20 percent of the accounts outstanding on December 31, 20x0, will be recovered and that the recovery will be in January 20x1.
- Seventy percent of the merchandise purchases are paid for in the month of purchase; the remaining 30 percent are paid for in the month after acquisition.
- The December 31, 20x0, balance sheet disclosed the following selected figures: cash, $60,000; accounts receivable, $165,000; and accounts payable, $66,000.
- Mary and Kay, Inc. maintains a $60,000 minimum cash balance at all times. Financing is available (and retired) in $1,000 multiples at an 8 percent interest rate, with borrowings taking place at the beginning of the month and repayments occurring at the end of the month. Interest is paid at the time of repaying principal and computed on the portion of principal repaid at that time.

Additional data:

	January	February	March
Sales revenue	$450,000	$540,000	$555,000
Merchandise purchases	270,000	300,000	420,000
Cash operating costs	93,000	72,000	135,000
Proceeds from sale of equipment	—	—	15,000

Required:

1. Prepare a schedule that discloses the firm's total cash collections for January through March.
2. Prepare a schedule that discloses the firm's total cash disbursements for January through March.

3. Prepare a schedule that discloses the firm's cash needs, if any, for January through March. The schedule should present the following information in the order cited: beginning cash balance, total receipts (from requirement (1)), total payments (from requirement (2)), the cash excess (deficiency) before financing, borrowing needed to maintain minimum balance, loan principal repaid, loan interest paid, and ending cash balance.

■ Problem 9–34
Relationships of the Master-Budget Components
(LO 2, 4)

3. February sales: $196,000
5. January sales: $190,000

Badlands, Inc. manufactures a household fan that sells for $20 per unit. All sales are on account, with 40 percent of sales collected in the month of sale and 60 percent collected in the following month. The data that follow were extracted from the company's accounting records.

- Badlands maintains a minimum cash balance of $15,000. Total payments in January 20x1 are budgeted at $195,000.
- A schedule of cash collections for January and February of 20x1 revealed the following receipts for the period:

	Cash Receipts	
	January	**February**
From December 31 accounts receivable	$108,000	
From January sales	76,000	$114,000
From February sales		78,400

- March 20x1 sales are expected to total 10,000 units.
- Finished-goods inventories are maintained at 20 percent of the following month's sales.
- The December 31, 20x0, balance sheet revealed the following selected figures: cash, $22,500; accounts receivable, $108,000; and finished goods, $22,350.

Required:

1. Determine the number of units that Badlands sold in December 20x0.
2. Compute the sales revenue for March 20x1.
3. Compute the total sales revenue to be reported on Badlands' budgeted income statement for the first quarter of 20x1.
4. Determine the accounts receivable balance to be reported on the March 31, 20x1, budgeted balance sheet.
5. Calculate the number of units in the December 31, 20x0, finished-goods inventory.
6. Calculate the number of units of finished goods to be manufactured in January 20x1.
7. Calculate the financing required in January, if any, to maintain the firm's minimum cash balance.

■ Problem 9–35
Completion of Budget Schedules
(LO 2, 4)

2. Planned production, September: 7,500 sets
4. Planned direct-labour cost, August: $198,450

Scholastic Furniture, Inc. manufactures a variety of desks, chairs, tables, and shelf units that are sold to public school districts. The controller of the company's Desk Division is currently preparing a budget for the second quarter of the year. The following sales forecast has been made by the division's sales manager:

July	5,000 desk-and-chair sets
August	6,000 desk-and-chair sets
September	7,500 desk-and-chair sets

Each desk-and-chair set requires 10 board metres of pine planks and 1.5 hours of direct labour. Each set sells for $60. Pine planks cost $.60 per board metre, and the division ends each month with enough wood to cover 10 percent of the next month's production requirements. The division incurs a cost of $21 per hour for direct-labour wages and fringe benefits. The division ends each month with enough finished-goods inventory to cover 20 percent of the next month's sales.

Required: Complete the following budget schedules.

(handwritten note: Do TOTALS FOR QTR)

1. Sales budget:

	July	August	September
Sales (in sets)	5,000		
Sales price per set	× $60		
Sales revenue	$300,000		

2. Production budget (in sets):

	July	August	September
Sales	5,000		
Add: Desired ending inventory	1,200		1,500
Total requirements	6,200		
Less: Projected beginning inventory	1,000		
Planned production	5,200		

3. Raw-material purchases:

	July	August	September
Planned production (sets)	5,200		
Raw material required per set (board metres)	× 10		
Raw material required for production (board metres)	52,000		
Add: Desired ending inventory of raw material, in board metres (10% of next month's requirement)	6,300		8,000
Total requirements	58,300		
Less: Projected beginning inventory of raw material, in board metres (10% of current month's requirement)	5,200		
Planned purchases of raw material (board metres)	53,100		
Cost per board metre	× $.60		
Planned purchases of raw material (dollars)	$31,860		

4. Direct-labour budget:

	July	August	September
Planned production (sets)	5,200		
Direct-labour hours per set	× 1.5		
Direct-labour hours required	7,800		
Cost per hour	× $21		
Planned direct-labour cost	$163,800		

5. *Build a spreadsheet:* Construct an Excel spreadsheet to solve all of the preceding requirements. Show how the solution will change if the following information changes: each set sells for $62 and direct-labour cost per hour is $22.

Niagara Chemical Company produces three products using three different continuous processes. The products are Yarex, Darol, and Norex. Projected sales in litres for the three products for the years 20x2 and 20x3 are as follows:

■ **Problem 9–36**
Production and Materials Budgets
(LO 2, 4)

2. Conversion hours required, Norex: 8,128
4. Increase in cost of raw material: $201,640

	20x2	20x3
Yarex	120,000	130,000
Darol	80,000	70,000
Norex	50,000	60,000

- Inventories are planned for each product so that the projected finished-goods inventory at the beginning of each year is equal to 8 percent of that year's projected sales.
- Because of the continuous nature of Niagara's processes, work-in-process inventory for each of the products remains constant throughout the year.
- The conversion requirements in hours per litre for the three products are Yarex, .07 hours; Darol, .10 hours; and Norex, .16 hours. The conversion cost of $20 per hour is considered 100 percent variable.
- The raw-material requirements of the three products are shown in the following chart:

Raw Material	Units	Unit Price	Yarex	Darol	Norex
Gamma	Kilograms	$ 8	.2	.4	—
Murad	Kilograms	6	.4	—	.5
Islin	Litres	5	1.0	.7	.5
Tarden	Litres	10	—	.3	.5

- Raw-material inventories are planned so that each raw material's projected inventory at the beginning of a year is equal to 10 percent of the previous year's usage of that raw material.

Required:

1. Determine Niagara Chemical Company's production budget (in litres) for the three products for 20x2.
2. Determine Niagara Chemical Company's conversion cost budget for 20x2.
3. Assuming the 20x1 usage of Islin is 200,000 litres, determine the company's raw-material purchases budget (in dollars) for Islin for 20x2.
4. Assume that for 20x2 production, Niagara Chemical Company could replace the raw material Islin with the raw material Philin. The usage of Philin would be the same as the usage of Islin. However, Philin would cost 20 percent more than Islin and would cut production times on all three products by 10 percent. Determine whether management should use Philin or Islin for the 20x2 production, supporting your decision with appropriate calculations. For this requirement, ignore any impact of beginning and ending inventory balances.

(CMA, adapted)

■ **Problem 9–37**
Sales, Production, and
Purchases Budgets; Activity-
Based Overhead Budget
(LO 2, 3, 4)

2. Production required (units),
light coils: 65,000
4. Total raw-material
purchases: $10,316,000

Vista Electronics, Inc. manufactures two different types of coils used in electric motors. In the fall of the current year, the controller compiled the following data.

- Sales forecast for 20x3 (all units to be shipped in 20x3):

Product	Units	Price
Light coil	60,000	$130
Heavy coil	40,000	190

- Raw-material prices and inventory levels:

Raw Material	Expected Inventories, January 1, 20x3	Desired Inventories, December 31, 20x3	Anticipated Purchase Price
Sheet metal	32,000 kilograms	36,000 kilograms	$16
Copper wire	29,000 kilograms	32,000 kilograms	10
Platform	6,000 units	7,000 units	6

- Use of raw material:

Raw Material	Amount Used per Unit	
	Light Coil	Heavy Coil
Sheet metal	4 kilograms	5 kilograms
Copper wire	2 kilograms	3 kilograms
Platform		1 unit

- Direct-labour requirements and rates:

Product	Hours per Unit	Rate per Hour
Light coil	4	$15
Heavy coil	6	20

- Finished-goods inventories (in units):

Product	Expected January 1, 20x3	Desired December 31, 20x3
Light coil	20,000	25,000
Heavy coil	8,000	9,000

- Manufacturing overhead:

Overhead Cost Item	Activity-Based Budget Rate
Purchasing and material handling	$ .50 per kilogram of sheet metal and copper wire purchased
Depreciation, utilities, and inspection	$8.00 per coil produced (either type)
Shipping	$2.00 per coil shipped (either type)
General manufacturing overhead	$6.00 per direct-labour hour

Required: Prepare the following budgets for 20x3:

1. Sales budget (in dollars)
2. Production budget (in units)
3. Raw-material purchases budget (in quantities)
4. Raw-material purchases budget (in dollars)
5. Direct-labour budget (in dollars)
6. Manufacturing-overhead budget (in dollars)

(CPA, adapted)

United Security Systems, Inc. (USSI) manufactures and sells security systems. The company started by installing photoelectric security systems in offices and has expanded into the private-home market. USSI has a basic security system that has been developed into three standard products, each of which can be adapted to meet the specific needs of customers. The manufacturing operation is moderate in size, as the bulk of the component manufacturing is completed by independent contractors. The security systems are approximately 75 percent complete when received from contractors and require only final assembly in the USSI plant. Each product passes through at least one of three assembly operations.

USSI operates in a rapidly growing community. There is evidence that a great deal of new commercial construction will take place in the near future, and management has decided to pursue this new market. In order to be competitive, the firm will have to expand its operations.

In view of the expected increase in business, Sandra Feldman, the controller, believes that USSI should implement a complete budgeting system. Feldman has decided to make a formal presentation to the company's president explaining the benefits of a budgeting system and outlining the budget schedules and reports that would be necessary.

■ Problem 9–38
Interrelationships Between Components of Master Budget
(LO 1, 2, 4, 6)

Required:

1. Explain the benefits that USSI would gain from implementing a budgeting system.
2. If Sandra Feldman develops a master budget:
   a. Identify, in order, the schedules that will have to be prepared.
   b. Identify the subsequent schedules that would be based on the schedules identified above. Use the following format for your answer.

Schedule	Subsequent Schedule

(CMA, adapted)

■ Problem 9–39
Revised Operating Budget;
Consulting Firm
(LO 1, 4, 5)

1. Operating income: $359,200
Management consulting, total
compensation: $490,000

Vancouver Consulting Associates, a division of Maple Leaf Services Corporation, offers management and computer consulting services to clients throughout Canada and the northwestern United States. The division specializes in Web site development and other Internet applications. The corporate management at Maple Leaf Services is pleased with the performance of Vancouver Consulting Associates for the first nine months of the current year and has recommended that the division manager, Richard Howell, submit a revised forecast for the remaining quarter, as the division has exceeded the annual plan year-to-date by 20 percent of operating income. An unexpected increase in billed hour volume over the original plan is the main reason for this increase in income. The original operating budget for the first three quarters for Vancouver Consulting Associates follows.

VANCOUVER CONSULTING ASSOCIATES
20X4 OPERATING BUDGET

	1st Quarter	2nd Quarter	3rd Quarter	Total for First Three Quarters
Revenue:				
Consulting fees:				
Computer system consulting	$ 843,750	$ 843,750	$ 843,750	$2,531,250
Management consulting	630,000	630,000	630,000	1,890,000
Total consulting fees	1,473,750	1,473,750	1,473,750	4,421,250
Other revenue	20,000	20,000	20,000	60,000
Total revenue	1,493,750	1,493,750	1,493,750	4,481,250
Expenses:				
Consultant salary expenses	773,500	773,500	773,500	2,320,500
Travel and related expenses	91,250	91,250	91,250	273,750
General and administrative expenses	200,000	200,000	200,000	600,000
Depreciation expense	80,000	80,000	80,000	240,000
Corporate expense allocation	100,000	100,000	100,000	300,000
Total expenses	1,244,750	1,244,750	1,244,750	3,734,250
Operating income	$ 249,000	$ 249,000	$ 249,000	$ 747,000

Howell will reflect the following information in his revised forecast for the fourth quarter.

• Vancouver Consulting Associates currently has 25 consultants on staff, 10 for management consulting and 15 for computer systems consulting. Three additional management consultants have been hired to start work at the beginning of the fourth quarter in order to meet the increased client demand.

• The hourly billing rate for consulting revenue will remain at $180 per hour for each management consultant and $150 per hour for each computer consultant. However, due to the favourable increase in billing hour volume when compared to the plan, the hours for each consultant will be increased by 50 hours per quarter.

• The budgeted annual salaries and actual annual salaries, paid monthly, are the same: $100,000 for a management consultant and $92,000 for a computer consultant. Corporate management has approved a merit increase of 10 percent at the beginning of the fourth quarter for all 25 existing consultants, while the new consultants will be compensated at the planned rate.

• The planned salary expense includes a provision for employee fringe benefits amounting to 30 percent of the annual salaries. However, the improvement of some corporatewide employee programs will increase the fringe benefits to 40 percent.

• The original plan assumes a fixed hourly rate for travel and other related expenses for each billing hour of consulting. These are expenses that are not reimbursed by the client, and the previously determined hourly rate has proven to be adequate to cover these costs.

- Other revenue is derived from temporary rentals and interest income and remains unchanged for the fourth quarter.
- General and administrative expenses have been favourable at 7 percent below the plan; this 7 percent savings on fourth quarter expenses will be reflected in the revised plan.
- Depreciation of office equipment and personal computers will stay constant at the projected straight-line rate.
- Due to the favourable experience for the first three quarters and the division's increased ability to absorb costs, the corporate management at Maple Leaf Services has increased the corporate expense allocation by 50 percent.

Required:

1. Prepare a revised operating budget for the fourth quarter for Vancouver Consulting Associates that Richard Howell will present to corporate management.
2. Discuss the reasons why an organization would prepare a revised operating budget.

(CMA, adapted)

Edgeworth Box Corporation manufactures two types of cardboard boxes used in shipping canned food, fruit, and vegetables. The canned food box (type C) and the perishable food box (type P) have the following material and labour requirements.

	Type of Box	
	C	**P**
Direct material required per 100 boxes:		
Paperboard ($.30 per kilogram)	30 kilograms	70 kilograms
Corrugating medium ($.15 per kilogram)	20 kilograms	30 kilograms
Direct labour required per 100 boxes ($18 per hour)	.25 hour	.50 hour

The following manufacturing-overhead costs are anticipated for the next year. The predetermined overhead rate is based on a production volume of 495,000 units for each type of box. Manufacturing overhead is applied on the basis of direct-labour hours.

Indirect material	$ 15,750
Indirect labour	75,000
Utilities	37,500
Property taxes	27,000
Insurance	24,000
Depreciation	43,500
Total	$ 222,750

The following selling and administrative expenses are anticipated for the next year:

Salaries and fringe benefits of sales personnel	$ 112,500
Advertising	22,500
Management salaries and fringe benefits	135,000
Clerical wages and fringe benefits	39,000
Miscellaneous administrative expenses	6,000
Total	$315,000

Problem 9–40
Preparation of Master Budget
(LO 2, 4)

1. Total sales revenue: $1,650,000
4. Total direct-labour cost: $66,825

The sales forecast for the next year is as follows:

	Sales Volume	Sales Price
Box type C	500,000 boxes	$135 per hundred boxes
Box type P	500,000 boxes	195 per hundred boxes

The following inventory information is available for the next year:

	Expected Inventory, January 1	Desired Ending Inventory, December 31
Finished goods:		
Box type C	10,000 boxes	5,000 boxes
Box type P	20,000 boxes	15,000 boxes
Raw material:		
Paperboard	15,000 kilograms	5,000 kilograms
Corrugating medium	5,000 kilograms	10,000 kilograms

Required: Prepare a master budget for Edgeworth Box Corporation for the next year. Assume an income tax rate of 35 percent. Include the following schedules:

1. Sales budget
2. Production budget
3. Direct-material budget
4. Direct-labour budget
5. Manufacturing-overhead budget
6. Selling and administrative expense budget
7. Budgeted income statement (*Hint:* To determine cost of goods sold, first compute the manufacturing cost per unit for each type of box. Include applied manufacturing overhead in the cost. Carry these calculations to three decimal places.)

 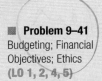

Problem 9–41
Budgeting; Financial
Objectives; Ethics
(LO 1, 2, 4, 5)

2. Increase in sales: 11.5%

Fit-for-Life Foods Inc., a manufacturer of breakfast cereals and snack bars, has experienced several years of steady growth in sales, profits, and dividends while maintaining a relatively low level of debt. The board of directors has adopted a long-run strategy to maximize the value of the shareholders' investment. In order to achieve this goal, the board of directors established the following five-year financial objectives:

- Increase sales by 12 percent per year.
- Increase income before taxes by 15 percent per year.
- Maintain long-term debt at a maximum of 16 percent of assets.

These financial objectives have been attained for the past three years. At the beginning of last year, the president of Fit-for-Life Foods, Andrea Donis, added a fourth financial objective of maintaining cost of goods sold at a maximum of 70 percent of sales. This goal also was attained last year.

The company's budgeting process is to be directed toward attaining these goals for the forthcoming year, a difficult task with the economy in a prolonged recession. In addition, the increased emphasis on eating healthful foods has driven up the price of ingredients used by the company significantly faster than the expected rate of inflation. John Winslow, cost accountant at Fit-for-Life Foods, has responsibility for preparation of the profit plan for next year. Winslow assured Donis that he could present a budget that achieved all of the financial objectives. Winslow believed that he could overestimate the ending inventory and reclassify fruit and grain inspection costs as administrative rather than manufacturing costs to attain the desired objective. The actual statements for 20x4 and the budgeted statements for 20x5 that Winslow prepared are as follows:

FIT-FOR-LIFE FOODS INC.
Income Statement

	20x4 Actual	20x5 Budgeted
Sales	$1,700,000	$1,895,500
Less: Variable costs:		
Cost of goods sold	1,020,000	1,149,450
Selling and administrative	180,000	175,000
Contribution margin	500,000	571,050
Less: Fixed costs:		
Manufacturing	170,000	189,550
Selling and administrative	120,000	140,000
Income before taxes	$ 210,000	$ 241,500

FIT-FOR-LIFE FOODS INC.
Balance Sheet

	20x4 Actual	20x5 Budgeted
Assets:		
Cash	$ 20,000	$ 34,000
Accounts receivable	120,000	136,000
Inventory	600,000	730,000
Plant and equipment (net of accumulated depreciation)	3,260,000	3,200,000
Total	$4,000,000	$4,100,000
Liabilities:		
Accounts payable	$ 220,000	$ 244,000
Long-term debt	640,000	616,000
Shareholders' equity:		
Common stock	800,000	800,000
Retained earnings	2,340,000	2,440,000
Total	$4,000,000	$4,100,000

The company paid dividends of $55,440 in 20x4, and the expected tax rate for 20x5 is 34 percent.

Required:

1. Describe the role of budgeting in a firm's strategic planning.

2. For each of the financial objectives established by the board of directors and the president of Fit-for-Life Foods Inc., determine whether John Winslow's budget attains these objectives. Support your conclusion in each case by presenting appropriate calculations, and use the following format for your answer.

Objective	Attained/Not Attained	Calculations

3. Explain why the adjustments contemplated by John Winslow are unethical, citing specific standards of ethical conduct for management accountants.

(CMA, adapted)

■ **Problem 9–42**
Comprehensive Master
Budget; Borrowing;
Acquisition of Automated
Material-Handling System
(LO 1, 2, 4)

1. Sales on account, first
quarter: $2,184,600
3. Purchases, first quarter:
$2,103,640
5. Cash receipts, first quarter:
$2,734,060
7. Net income: $321,312

"We really need to get this new material-handling equipment in operation just after the new year begins. I hope we can finance it largely with cash and marketable securities, but if necessary we can get a short-term loan down at Metro Bank." This statement by Beth Davies-Lowry, president of Global Electronics Company, concluded a meeting she had called with the firm's top management. Global is a small, rapidly growing wholesaler of consumer electronic products. The firm's main product lines are small kitchen appliances and power tools. Marcia Wilcox, Global Electronics' general manager of marketing, has recently completed a sales forecast. She believes the company's sales during the first quarter of 20x1 will increase by 10 percent each month over the previous month's sales. Then Wilcox expects sales to remain constant for several months. Global's projected balance sheet as of December 31, 20x0, is as follows:

Cash	$ 70,000
Accounts receivable	540,000
Marketable securities	30,000
Inventory	308,000
Buildings and equipment (net of accumulated depreciation)	1,252,000
Total assets	$2,200,000
Accounts payable	$ 352,800
Bond interest payable	25,000
Property taxes payable	7,200
Bonds payable (10%; due in 20x6)	600,000
Common stock	1,000,000
Retained earnings	215,000
Total liabilities and stockholders' equity	$2,200,000

Jack Hanson, the assistant controller, is now preparing a monthly budget for the first quarter of 20x1. In the process, the following information has been accumulated:

1. Projected sales for December of 20x0 are $800,000. Credit sales typically are 75 percent of total sales. Global's credit experience indicates that 10 percent of the credit sales are collected during the month of sale, and the remainder are collected during the following month.

2. Global Electronics' cost of goods sold generally runs at 70 percent of sales. Inventory is purchased on account, and 40 percent of each month's purchases are paid during the month of purchase. The remainder is paid during the following month. In order to have adequate stocks of inventory on hand, the firm attempts to have inventory at the end of each month equal to half of the next month's projected cost of goods sold.

3. Hanson has estimated that Global's other monthly expenses will be as follows:

Sales salaries	$42,000
Advertising and promotion	32,000
Administrative salaries	42,000
Depreciation	50,000
Interest on bonds	5,000
Property taxes	1,800

In addition, sales commissions run at the rate of 1 percent of sales.

4. Global Electronics' president, Davies-Lowry, has indicated that the firm should invest $250,000 in an automated inventory-handling system to control the movement of inventory in the firm's warehouse just after the new year begins. These equipment purchases will be financed primarily from the firm's cash and marketable securities. However, Davies-Lowry believes that the company needs to keep a minimum cash balance of $50,000. If necessary, the remainder of the equipment purchases will be financed using short-term credit from a local bank. The minimum period for such a loan is three months. Hanson believes short-term interest rates will be 10 percent per year at the time of the equipment purchases. If a loan is necessary, Davies-Lowry has decided it should be paid off by the end of the first quarter if possible.

5. Global Electronics' board of directors has indicated an intention to declare and pay dividends of $100,000 on the last day of each quarter.

6. The interest on any short-term borrowing will be paid when the loan is repaid. Interest on Global Electronics' bonds is paid semiannually on January 31 and July 31 for the preceding six-month period.

7. Property taxes are paid semiannually on February 28 and August 31 for the preceding six-month period.

Required: Prepare Global Electronics Company's master budget for the first quarter of 20x1 by completing the following schedules and statements:

1. Sales budget:

	20x0		20x1		
	December	**January**	**February**	**March**	**1st Quarter**
Total sales					
Cash sales					
Sales on account					

2. Cash receipts budget:

	20x1			
	January	**February**	**March**	**1st Quarter**
Cash sales				
Cash collections from credit sales made during current month..................				
Cash collections from credit sales made during preceding month...............				
Total cash receipts....................................				

3. Purchases budget:

	20x0		20x1		
	December	**January**	**February**	**March**	**1st Quarter**
Budgeted cost of goods sold					
Add: Desired ending inventory.........					
Total goods needed.........					
Less: Expected beginning inventory.....					
Purchases					

4. Cash disbursements budget:

	20x1			
	January	**February**	**March**	**1st Quarter**
Inventory purchases:				
Cash payments for purchases during the current month*..............				
Cash payments for purchases during the preceding month†				
Total cash payments for inventory purchases				
Other expenses:				
Sales salaries				
Advertising and promotion.................				
Administrative salaries				
Interest on bonds‡				
Property taxes‡				
Sales commissions				
Total cash payments for other expenses				
Total cash disbursements				

*40% of the current month's purchases (schedule 3).

†60% of the prior month's purchases (schedule 3).

‡Bond interest is paid every six months, on January 31 and July 31. Property taxes also are paid every six months, on February 28 and August 31.

5. Complete the first three lines of the following summary cash budget. Then do the analysis of short-term financing needs in requirement (6). Then finish requirement (5).

	20x1			
	January	**February**	**March**	**1st Quarter**
Cash receipts (from schedule 2)....................				
Less: Cash disbursements (from schedule 4)				
Change in cash balance during period due to operations				
Sale of marketable securities (1/2/x1)				
Proceeds from bank loan (1/2/x1).................				
Purchase of equipment				
Repayment of bank loan (3/31/x1)				
Interest on bank loan....................................				
Payment of dividends....................................				
Change in cash balance during first quarter...				
Cash balance, 1/1/x1				
Cash balance, 3/31/x1				

6. Analysis of short-term financing needs:

Projected cash balance as of December 31, 20x0..	$
Less: Minimum cash balance..	
Cash available for equipment purchases...	$
Projected proceeds from sale of marketable securities	
Cash available	$
Less: Cost of investment in equipment	
Required short-term borrowing	$

7. Prepare Global Electronics' budgeted income statement for the first quarter of 20x1. (Ignore income taxes.)

8. Prepare Global Electronics' budgeted statement of retained earnings for the first quarter of 20x1.

9. Prepare Global Electronics' budgeted balance sheet as of March 31, 20x1. (*Hint:* On March 31, 20x1, Bond Interest Payable is $10,000 and Property Taxes Payable is $1,800.)

Cases

■ Case 9–43
Using Budgets to Evaluate
Business Decisions
(LO 1, 2, 5)

City Racquetball Club (CRC) offers racquetball and other physical fitness facilities to its members. There are four of these clubs in the metropolitan area. Each club has between 1,700 and 2,500 members. Revenue is derived from annual membership fees and hourly court fees. The annual membership fees are as follows:

Individual...	$ 45
Student...	30
Family...	100

The hourly court fees vary from $8 to $12 depending upon the season and the time of day (prime-time versus non-prime-time).

The peak racquetball season is considered to run from September through April. During this period, court usage averages 90 to 100 percent of capacity during prime time (5:00–9:00 p.m.) and 50 to 60 percent of capacity during the remaining hours. Daily court usage during the off-season (i.e., summer) averages only 20 to 40 percent of capacity.

Most of CRC's memberships have September expirations. A substantial amount of the cash receipts are collected during the early part of the racquetball season due to the renewal of the annual membership fees and heavy court usage. However, cash receipts are not as large in the spring and drop significantly in the summer months.

CRC is considering changing its membership and fee structure in an attempt to change its cash receipts. Under the new membership plan, only an annual membership fee would be charged, rather than a membership fee plus hourly court fees. There would be two classes of membership as follows:

Individual...	$300
Family..	500

The annual fee would be collected in advance at the time the membership application is completed. Members would be allowed to use the racquetball courts as often as they wish during the year under the new plan.

All future memberships would be sold under these new terms. Current memberships would be honoured on the old basis until they expired. However, a special promotional campaign would be instituted to attract new members and to encourage current members to convert to the new membership plan immediately.

The annual fees for individual and family memberships would be reduced to $250 and $450, respectively, during the two-month promotional campaign. In addition, all memberships sold or renewed during this period would be for 15 months rather than the normal one-year period. Current members also would be given a credit toward the annual fee for the unexpired portion of their membership fee, and for all prepaid hourly court fees for league play that have not yet been used.

CRC's management estimates that 60 to 70 percent of the present membership would continue with the club. The most active members (45 percent of the present membership) would convert immediately to the new plan, while the remaining members who continue would wait until their current memberships expire. Those members who would not continue are not considered active (i.e., they play five or less times during the year). Management estimates that the loss of members would be offset fully by new members within six months of instituting the new plan. Furthermore, many of the new members would be individuals who would play during nonprime time. Management estimates that adequate court time will be available for all members under the new plan.

If the new membership plan is adopted, it would be instituted on February 1, well before the summer season. The special promotional campaign would be conducted during March and April. Once the plan is implemented, annual renewal of memberships and payment of fees would take place as each individual or family membership expires.

Required:　Your consulting firm has been hired to help CRC evaluate its new fee structure. Write a letter to the club's president answering the following questions:

1.　Will City Racquetball Club's new membership plan and fee structure improve its ability to plan its cash receipts? Explain your answer.

2.　City Racquetball Club should evaluate the new membership plan and fee structure completely before it decides to adopt or reject it.

　a.　Identify the key factors that CRC should consider in its evaluation.

　b.　Explain what type of financial analyses CRC should prepare in order to make a complete evaluation.

3.　Explain how City Racquetball Club's cash management would differ from the present if the new membership plan and fee structure were adopted.

(CMA, adapted)

■ **Case 9–44**
Participative Budgeting
(LO 1, 2, 8)

Patricia Eklund, controller in the division of social services for the province, recognizes the importance of the budgetary process for planning, control, and motivational purposes. She believes that a properly implemented participative budgetary process for planning purposes and an evaluation procedure will motivate the managers to improve productivity within their particular departments. Based upon this philosophy, Eklund has implemented the following budgetary procedures:

- An appropriation target figure is given to each department manager. This amount is the maximum funding that each department can expect to receive in the next year.

- Department managers develop their individual budgets within the following spending constraints as directed by the controller's staff:

  - Expenditure requests cannot exceed the appropriation target.

  - All fixed expenditures should be included in the budget. Fixed expenditures would include such items as contracts and salaries at current levels.

  - All government projects directed by higher authority should be included in the budget in their entirety.

- The controller's staff consolidates the budget requests from the various departments into a master budget submission for the entire division.
- Upon final budget approval by the legislature, the controller's staff allocates the appropriation to the various departments on instructions from the division manager. However, a specified percentage of each department's appropriation is held back in anticipation of potential budget cuts and special funding needs. The amount and use of this contingency fund is left to the discretion of the division manager.
- Each department is allowed to adjust its budget when necessary to operate within the reduced appropriation level. However, as stated in the original directive, specific projects authorized by higher authority must remain intact.
- The final budget is used as the basis of control. Excessive expenditures by account for each department are highlighted on a monthly basis. Department managers are expected to account for all expenditures over budget. Fiscal responsibility is an important factor in the overall performance evaluation of department managers.

Eklund believes her policy of allowing the department managers to participate in the budgetary process and then holding them accountable for their performance is essential, especially during times of limited resources. She further believes that the department managers will be positively motivated to increase the efficiency and effectiveness of their departments because they have provided input into the initial budgetary process and are required to justify any unfavourable performances.

Required:

1. Describe several operational and behavioural benefits that are generally attributed to a participative budgetary process.
2. Identify at least four deficiencies in Patricia Eklund's participative policy for planning and performance evaluation purposes. For each deficiency identified, recommend how it can be corrected.

(CMA, adapted)

■ Case 9–45
Comprehensive Master
Budget; Short-Term
Financing; Acquisition of
Robotic Equipment
(LO 2, 4)

1. Total sales revenue, 4th
quarter: $1,600,000
7. Cost of goods sold:
$3,850,000
8. Gross margin: $1,800,000

Jeffrey Vaughn, president of Frame-It Company, was just concluding a budget meeting with his senior staff. It was November of 20x4, and the group was discussing preparation of the firm's master budget for 20x5. "I've decided to go ahead and purchase the industrial robot we've been talking about. We'll make the acquisition on January 2 of next year, and I expect it will take most of the year to train the personnel and reorganize the production process to take full advantage of the new equipment."

In response to a question about financing the acquisition, Vaughn replied as follows: "The robot will cost $950,000. There will also be an additional $50,000 in ancillary equipment to be purchased. We'll finance these purchases with a one-year $1,000,000 loan from Shark Bank and Trust Company. I've negotiated a repayment schedule of four equal instalments on the last day of each quarter. The interest rate will be 10 percent, and interest payments will be quarterly as well." With that the meeting broke up, and the budget process was on.

Frame-It Company is a manufacturer of metal picture frames. The firm's two product lines are designated as S (small frames) and L (large frames). The primary raw materials are flexible metal strips and glass sheets. Each S frame requires two metal strips; an L frame requires three strips. Allowing for normal breakage and scrap glass, Frame-It can get either four S frames or two L frames out of a glass sheet. Other raw materials, such as cardboard backing, are insignificant in cost and are treated as indirect materials. Emily Jackson, Frame-It's controller, is in charge of preparing the master budget for 20x5. She has gathered the following information:

1. Sales in the fourth quarter of 20x4 are expected to be 50,000 S frames and 40,000 L frames. The sales manager predicts that over the next two years, sales in each product line will grow by 5,000 units

each quarter over the previous quarter. For example, S frame sales in the first quarter of 20x5 are expected to be 55,000 units.

2. Frame-It's sales history indicates that 60 percent of all sales are on credit, with the remainder of the sales in cash. The company's collection experience shows that 80 percent of the credit sales are collected during the quarter in which the sale is made, while the remaining 20 percent is collected in the following quarter. (For simplicity, assume the company is able to collect 100 percent of its accounts receivable.)

3. The S frame sells for $10, and the L frame sells for $15. These prices are expected to hold constant throughout 20x5.

4. Frame-It's production manager attempts to end each quarter with enough finished-goods inventory in each product line to cover 20 percent of the following quarter's sales. Moreover, an attempt is made to end each quarter with 20 percent of the glass sheets needed for the following quarter's production. Since metal strips are purchased locally, Frame-It's buys them on a just-in-time basis; inventory is negligible.

5. All of Frame-It's direct-material purchases are made on account, and 80 percent of each quarter's purchases are paid in cash during the same quarter as the purchase. The other 20 percent is paid in the next quarter.

6. Indirect materials are purchased as needed and paid for in cash. Work-in-process inventory is negligible.

7. Projected manufacturing costs in 20x5 are as follows:

	S Frame	L Frame
Direct material:		
Metal strips:		
S: 2 @ $1 per strip	$2	
L: 3 @ $1 per strip		$ 3
Glass sheets:		
S: ¼ sheet @ $8 per sheet	2	
L: ½ sheet @ $8 per sheet		4
Direct labour:		
.1 hour @ $20 per hour	2	2
Manufacturing overhead:		
.1 direct-labour hour × $10 per hour	1	1
Total manufacturing cost per unit	$7	$10

8. The predetermined overhead rate is $10 per direct-labour hour. The following manufacturing overhead costs are budgeted for 20x5:

	1st Quarter	2nd Quarter	3rd Quarter	4th Quarter	Entire Year
Indirect material	$ 10,200	$ 11,200	$ 12,200	$ 13,200	$ 46,800
Indirect labour	40,800	44,800	48,800	52,800	187,200
Other overhead	31,000	36,000	41,000	46,000	154,000
Depreciation	20,000	20,000	20,000	20,000	80,000
Total overhead	$102,000	$112,000	$122,000	$132,000	$468,000

All of these costs will be paid in cash during the quarter incurred except for the depreciation charges.

9. Frame-It's quarterly selling and administrative expenses are $100,000, paid in cash.

10. Jackson anticipates that dividends of $50,000 will be declared and paid in cash each quarter.

11. Frame-It's projected balance sheet as of December 31, 20x4, follows:

Cash	$ 95,000
Accounts receivable	132,000
Inventory:	
Raw material	59,200
Finished goods	167,000
Plant and equipment (net of accumulated depreciation)	8,000,000
Total assets	$8,453,200
Accounts payable	$ 99,400
Common stock	5,000,000
Retained earnings	3,353,800
Total liabilities and stockholders' equity	$8,453,200

Required: Prepare Frame-It Company's master budget for 20x5 by completing the following schedules and statements.

1. Sales budget:

	20x4	20x5				
	4th Quarter	1st Quarter	2nd Quarter	3rd Quarter	4th Quarter	Entire Year
S frame unit sales						
× S sales price						
S frame sales revenue						
L frame unit sales						
× L sales price						
L frame sales revenue						
Total sales revenue						
Cash sales*						
Sales on account†						

*40% of total sales.
†60% of total sales.

2. Cash receipts budget:

	20x5				
	1st Quarter	2nd Quarter	3rd Quarter	4th Quarter	Entire Year
Cash sales					
Cash collections from credit sales made during current quarter*					
Cash collections from credit sales made during previous quarter†					
Total cash receipts					

*80% of current quarter's credit sales.
†20% of previous quarter's credit sales.

3. Production budget:

	20x4	20x5				
	4th Quarter	1st Quarter	2nd Quarter	3rd Quarter	4th Quarter	Entire Year
S frames:						
Sales (in units)						
Add: Desired ending inventory						
Total units needed						
Less: Expected beginning inventory						
Units to be produced						
L frames:						
Sales (in units)						
Add: Desired ending inventory						
Total units needed........................						
Less: Expected beginning inventory						
Units to be produced						

4. Direct-material budget:

	20x4	20x5				
	4th Quarter	1st Quarter	2nd Quarter	3rd Quarter	4th Quarter	Entire Year
Metal strips:						
S frames to be produced						
$\times$ Metal strips per unit						
Needed for S frame production						
L frames to be produced						
$\times$ Metal strips per unit						
Needed for L frame production						
Total metal strips needed for production; to be purchased						
$\times$ Price per strip						
Cost of metal strips to be purchased						
Glass sheets:						
S frames to be produced (sheets)						
$\times$ Glass quantity per unit						
Needed for S frame production						
L frames to be produced (sheets)........						
$\times$ Glass quantity per unit						
Needed for L frame production						
Total glass needed for production (sheets)						
Add: Desired ending inventory						10,400	10,400
Total glass needs						
Less: Expected beginning inventory...........................						
Glass to be purchased...........................						
$\times$ Price per glass sheet						
Cost of glass to be purchased						
Total raw-material purchases (metal and glass)						

5. Cash disbursements budget:

	20x5				
	1st Quarter	2nd Quarter	3rd Quarter	4th Quarter	Entire Year
Raw-material purchases:					
Cash payments for purchases during the current quarter					
Cash payments for purchases during the preceding quarter					
Total cash payments for raw-material purchases					
Direct labour:					
Frames produced (S and L)					
Direct-labour hours per frame					
Direct-labour hours to be used					
Rate per direct-labour hour					
Total cash payments for direct labour					
Manufacturing overhead:					
Indirect material					
Indirect labour					
Other					
Total cash payments for manufacturing overhead					
Cash payments for selling and administrative expenses					
Total cash disbursements					

6. Summary cash budget:

	20x5				
	1st Quarter	2nd Quarter	3rd Quarter	4th Quarter	Entire Year
Cash receipts (from schedule 2)					
Less: Cash disbursements (from schedule 5)					
Change in cash balance due to operations					
Payment of dividends					
Proceeds from bank loan (1/2/x5)					
Purchase of equipment					
Quarterly instalment on loan principal					
Quarterly interest payment					
Change in cash balance during the period					
Cash balance, beginning of period					
Cash balance, end of period					

7. Prepare a budgeted schedule of cost of goods manufactured and sold for the year 20x5. (*Hint:* In the budget, actual and applied overhead will be equal.)

8. Prepare Frame-It's budgeted income statement for 20x5. (Ignore income taxes.)

9. Prepare Frame-It's budgeted statement of retained earnings for 20x5.

10. Prepare Frame-It's budgeted balance sheet as of December 31, 20x5.

Chapter Ten

Standard Costing and Flexible Budgeting

FOCUS COMPANY

This chapter's Focus Company is DCdesserts.com, which supplies fancy desserts to a variety of restaurants, caterers, and upscale food stores. The company's order-taking system is entirely Web-based. Every day, DCdesserts.com posts its dessert menu on its Web site, and orders are accepted via the Internet. In this chapter, we explore DCdesserts.com's use of standard costing. A standard-costing system sets predetermined (or standard) costs for each of a product's inputs, such as direct material and direct labour. Then the actual costs to produce the product are compared with the standard costs that should have been incurred. DCdesserts.com's man-agement uses a standard costing system to help control the company's production costs. We also explore DCdesserts.com's use of flexible budgeting to plan for and control overhead costs. A flexible budget allows for a variety of levels of activity. As activity increases, the costs in the flexible budget rise as well. This tool enables management to compare the actual overhead costs incurred with the costs that should have been incurred, given the actual level of production activity.

After completing this chapter, you should be able to:

1 Explain how standard costing is used to help manage costs and describe ways to set standards.

2 Compute and interpret the direct-material and direct-labour variances.

3 Distinguish between static and flexible budgets, and explain the advantages of a flexible overhead budget.

4 Prepare a flexible overhead budget and explain how over-head is applied to Work-in-Process Inventory.

5 Explain some important issues in choosing an activity measure for overhead budgeting and application.

6 Compute and interpret the variable-overhead and fixed-overhead variances.

7 Prepare an overhead cost per-formance report.

8 Explain how an activity-based flexible budget differs from a conventional flexible budget.

9 Explain methods for determining the significance of cost variances.

10 Describe some behavioural effects of standard costing.

11 Explain how standard costs are used in product costing and summarize some advan-tages of standard costing.

12 Prepare journal entries to record manufacturing overhead under standard costing (Appendix A).

13 Compute and interpret the sales-price and sales-volume variances (Appendix B).

IN CONTRAST

In contrast to the food-processing setting of DCdesserts.com, we will turn our attention to flexible budgeting in the service industry. Tri-Cities Auto Rentals is a small automobile rental company in Coquitlam, Port Coquitlam, and Port Moody. The company has four rental locations in the Tri-Cities area and specializes in short-term car rentals, primarily for local use when a customer's car is in the repair shop. Tri-Cities Auto Rentals' flexible budget uses two cost drivers: the number of miles driven by its rental cars and the number of customer contracts.

A budget provides a plan for managers to follow in making decisions and directing an organization's activities. At the end of a budget period, the budget serves another useful purpose. At that time, managers use the budget as a benchmark against which to compare the results of actual operations. Did the company make as much profit as anticipated in the budget? Were costs greater or less than expected? These questions involve issues of cost management and control. In this chapter, we will study one of the tools used by managerial accountants to assist managers in controlling an organization's operations and costs.

Managing Costs

Learning Objective 1

Explain how standard costing is used to help manage costs and describe ways to set standards.

How can managers use a control system as a cost management tool? Any control system has three basic parts: a predetermined or *standard* performance level, a measure of *actual* performance, and a *comparison* between standard and actual performance. A thermostat is a control system with which we are all familiar. First, a thermostat has a predetermined or standard temperature, which can be set at any desired level. If you want the temperature in a room to be 68 degrees, you set the thermostat at the *standard* of 68 degrees. Second, the thermostat has a thermometer, which measures the *actual* temperature in the room. Third, the thermostat *compares* the preset or standard temperature with the actual room temperature. If the actual temperature falls below the preset or standard temperature, the thermostat activates a heating device. The three features of a control system are depicted in Exhibit 10–1.

A managerial accountant's budgetary-control system works like a thermostat. First, a predetermined or **standard cost** is set. In essence, a standard cost is a budget for the production of one unit of product or service. It is the cost chosen by the

Exhibit 10–1
Control System: A Thermostat

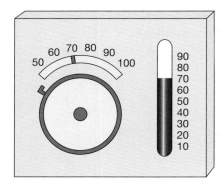

1. **Predetermined or standard performance** (The thermostat is set to a standard temperature.)

2. **Measure of actual performance** (The thermometer measures the actual room temperature.)

3. **Comparison of actual and standard performance** (The thermostat compares the preset or standard temperature with the actual temperature.)

managerial accountant to serve as the benchmark in the budgetary-control system. When the firm produces many units, the managerial accountant uses the standard unit cost to determine the total standard or budgeted cost of production. For example, suppose the standard direct-material cost for one unit of product is $5 and 100 units are manufactured. The total standard or budgeted direct-material cost, given an actual output of 100 units, is $500 ($5 × 100).

Second, the managerial accountant measures the actual cost incurred in the production process.

Third, the managerial accountant compares the actual cost with the budgeted or standard cost. Any difference between the two is called a **cost variance**. Cost variances then are used in controlling costs.

Management by Exception

Managers are busy people. They do not have time to look into the causes of every variance between actual and standard costs. However, they do take the time to investigate the causes of significant cost variances. This process of following up on only significant cost variances is called **management by exception**. When operations are going along as planned, actual costs and profit will typically be close to the budgeted amounts. However, if there are significant departures from planned operations, such effects will show up as significant cost variances. Managers investigate these variances to determine their causes, if possible, and take corrective action when indicated.

What constitutes a significant variance? No precise answer can be given to this question, since it depends on the size and type of the organization and its production process. We will consider this issue later in the chapter when we discuss common methods for determining the significance of cost variances. First, however, we will turn our attention to the process of setting standards.

Setting Standards

Methods for Setting Standards

Managerial accountants typically use two methods for setting cost standards: analysis of historical data and task analysis.

Analysis of Historical Data One indicator of future costs is historical cost data. In a mature production process, where the firm has a lot of production experience, historical costs can provide a good basis for predicting future costs. The methods for analyzing cost behaviour that we studied in Chapter 6 are used in making cost predictions. The managerial accountant often will need to adjust these predictions to reflect movements in price levels or technological changes in the production process. For example, the amount of rubber required to manufacture a particular type of tire will likely be the same this year as last year, unless there has been a significant change in the process used to manufacture tires. However, the price of rubber is likely to be different this year than last, and this fact must be reflected in the new standard cost of a tire.

Despite the relevance of historical cost data in setting cost standards, managerial accountants must guard against relying on them excessively. Even a seemingly minor change in the way a product is manufactured may make historical data almost totally irrelevant. Moreover, new products also require new cost standards. For new products, such as genetically engineered medicines, there are no historical cost data upon which to base standards. In such cases, the managerial accountant must turn to another approach.

Task Analysis Another way to set cost standards is to analyze the process of manufacturing a product to determine what it *should* cost. The emphasis shifts from what the product *did* cost in the past to what it *should* cost in the future. In using **task analysis**, the managerial accountant typically works with engineers who are intimately familiar with the production process. Together they conduct studies to determine exactly how much direct material should be required and how machinery should be used in the production process. Time and motion studies are conducted to determine how long each step performed should take.

A Combined Approach   Managerial accountants often apply both historical cost analysis and task analysis in setting cost standards. It may be, for example, that the technology has changed for only one step in the production process. In such a case, the managerial accountant would work with engineers to set cost standards for the technologically changed part of the production process. However, the accountant would likely rely on the less expensive method of analyzing historical cost data to update the cost standards for the remainder of the production process.

Participation in Setting Standards

Standards should not be determined by the managerial accountant alone. People generally will be more committed to meeting standards if they are allowed to participate in setting them. For example, production supervisors should have a role in setting production cost standards, and sales managers should be involved in setting targets for sales prices and volume. In addition, knowledgeable staff personnel should participate in the standard-setting process. For example, task analysis should be carried out by a team consisting of production engineers, production supervisors, and managerial accountants.

Perfection versus Practical Standards: A Behavioural Issue

How difficult should it be to attain standard costs? Should standards be set so that actual costs rarely exceed standard costs? Or should it be so hard to attain standards that actual costs frequently exceed them? The answers to these questions depend on the purpose for which standards will be used and how standards affect behaviour.

Perfection Standards   A **perfection** (or **ideal**) **standard** is one that can be attained only under nearly perfect operating conditions. Such standards assume peak efficiency, the lowest possible input prices, the best-quality materials obtainable, and no disruptions in production due to such causes as machine breakdowns or power failures. Some managers believe that perfection standards motivate employees to achieve the lowest cost possible. They claim that since the standard is theoretically attainable, employees will have an incentive to come as close as possible to achieving it.

Other managers and many behavioural scientists disagree. They feel that perfection standards discourage employees, since they are so unlikely to be attained. Moreover, setting unrealistically difficult standards may encourage employees to sacrifice product quality to achieve lower costs. By skimping on raw-material quality or the attention given manual production tasks, employees may be able to lower the production cost. However, this lower cost may come at the expense of a higher rate of defective units. Thus, the firm ultimately may incur higher costs than necessary as defective products are returned by customers or scrapped upon inspection.

Practical Standards   Standards that are as tight as practical, but still are expected to be attained, are called **practical** (or **attainable**) **standards**. Such standards assume a production process that is as efficient as practical under normal operating conditions. Practical standards allow for such occurrences as occasional machine breakdowns and normal amounts of raw-material waste. Attaining a practical standard keeps employees on their toes, without demanding miracles. Most behavioural theorists believe that practical standards encourage more positive and productive employee attitudes than do perfection standards.

Use of Standards by Service Organizations

Many service industry firms, nonprofit organizations, and governmental units make use of standards. For example, FedEx allows its crews 18 minutes to unload the 9 to 12 containers of packages from a Boeing 727. A delay of over a minute must be explained at a daily 5:00 a.m. meeting. Burger King sets a standard for the amount of meat in a hamburger. Airlines such as WestJet or Air Canada set standards for fuel and maintenance costs. Insurance companies such as Manulife or Pacific Blue Cross set standards for the amount of time to process an insurance application. Even a provincial licensing office may have a standard for the number of days required to process and return an application for licence. These and similar organizations use standards in budgeting and cost control in much the same way that manufacturers use standards.

Cost Variance Analysis: Direct Material and Direct Labour

To illustrate the use of standards in managing costs, we will focus on a producer of fancy desserts. DCdesserts.com supplies fresh and frozen desserts to a variety of restaurants, caterers, and upscale food stores. The company's order-taking system is entirely Web-based. DCdesserts.com posts its menu of fresh fancy dessert products for each day on its Web site four days in advance of the delivery date. Orders are accepted via the Internet three days in advance of delivery. For example, the menu of desserts to be available for delivery on Friday afternoon is posted to DCdesserts.com's Web site on Monday, and orders are accepted up to midnight on Tuesday. The company places orders for ingredients on Wednesday and accepts delivery on Thursday. DCdesserts.com's ordering is also done largely via the Internet. Production then takes place throughout the day on Friday, and the desserts are delivered Friday afternoon. DCdesserts.com uses independent delivery services to deliver its dessert products.

DCdesserts.com also produces frozen dessert products for upscale grocery stores. Unlike the fresh desserts, which vary daily, the frozen desserts are stock items that are varied less frequently. Like the fresh desserts, however, the frozen dessert menu is posted to DCdesserts.com's Web site, and orders are accepted entirely via the Internet. DCdesserts.com produces its fresh fancy desserts and frozen desserts in two different production facilities.

The production process for the fresh fancy desserts involves a combination of semiautomated equipment and manual labour. Even in this era of widespread automation, making fancy desserts still involves considerable direct labour. In the words of DCdesserts.com's founder and owner, "making a Black Forest cake or a linzer torte is not the same as making your basic pumpkin pie. There's a lot of touch labour by skilled people in doing these fancy desserts." The basic steps in the production process are much as you might expect. These steps include selecting ingredients, mixing, baking, cooling, and finishing. The finishing work, of course, involves the most skilled direct labour. In making a six-layer chocolate raspberry cake, for example, each individual cake layer must be sliced into two pieces, and then fillings and icings are applied to each layer. The cake's top is finished artistically, and any additional toppings are carefully applied.

DCdesserts.com's director of cost management has set standards for direct material and direct labour as follows for a category of dessert products generically referred to as multilayer fancy cakes.

> Learning Objective 2
>
> Compute and interpret the direct-material and direct-labour variances.

Direct-Material Standards

The standard quantity and price of ingredients for one multilayer fancy cake, such as a Black Forest cake, are shown in the following table:

Standard quantity:	
Ingredients in finished product	4.75 kilograms
Allowance for normal waste	.25 kilogram
Total standard quantity required per multilayer fancy cake	5.00 kilograms
Standard price:	
Purchase price per kilogram of ingredients (net of purchase discounts)	$1.30
Transportation cost per kilogram	.10
Total standard price per kilogram of ingredients	$1.40

The standard quantity of ingredients needed to produce one cake is 5 kilograms, even though only 4.75 kilograms actually remain in the finished product. One-quarter kilogram of ingredients is wasted as a normal result of the production process. Therefore, the entire amount of ingredients needed to produce a fancy cake is included in the standard quantity of material.

The standard price of ingredients reflects all of the costs incurred to acquire the material and transport it to the plant. Notice that the cost of transportation is added to the purchase price. Any purchase discounts would be subtracted out from the purchase price to obtain a net price.

To summarize, the **standard direct-material quantity** is the total amount of direct material normally required to produce a finished product, including allowances for normal waste or inefficiency. The **standard direct-material price** is the total delivered cost, after subtracting any purchase discounts.

Direct-Labour Standards

The standard quantity and rate for direct labour for the production of one multilayer fancy cake are:

Standard quantity:	
Direct labour required per multilayer fancy cake	.5 hour
Standard rate:	
Hourly wage rate	$16
Fringe benefits (25% of wages)	4
Total standard rate per hour	$20

The **standard direct-labour quantity** is the number of direct-labour hours normally needed to manufacture one unit of product. The **standard direct-labour rate** is the total hourly cost of compensation, including fringe benefits.

Standard Costs Given Actual Output

During September, DCdesserts.com produced 2,000 multilayer fancy cakes. The total standard or budgeted costs for direct material and direct labour are computed as follows:

Direct material:	
Standard direct-material cost per cake (5 kilograms × $1.40 per kilogram)	$ 7
Actual output	× 2,000
Total standard direct-material cost	$14,000
Direct labour:	
Direct-labour cost per cake (.5 hour × $20 per hour)	$ 10
Actual output	× 2,000
Total standard direct-labour cost	$20,000

Notice that the total standard cost for the direct-material and direct-labour inputs is based on DCdesserts.com's actual *output*. The company should incur costs of $34,000 for direct material and direct labour, *given that it produced 2,000 multilayer fancy cakes*. The total standard costs for direct material and direct labour serve as the managerial accountant's benchmarks against which to compare actual costs. This comparison then serves as the basis for controlling direct-material and direct-labour costs.

Analysis of Cost Variances

During September, DCdesserts.com incurred the following actual costs for direct material and direct labour in the production of multilayer fancy cakes:

Direct material purchased: Actual cost 12,500 kilograms at $1.42 per kilogram	$17,750
Direct material used: Actual cost 10,250 kilograms at $1.42 per kilogram	$14,555
Direct labour: Actual cost 980 hours at $21 per hour	$20,580

Compare these actual expenditures with the total standard costs for the production of 2,000 multilayer fancy cakes. DCdesserts.com spent more than the budgeted amount for both direct material and direct labour. But why were these excess costs incurred? Is there any further analysis the managerial accountant can provide to help answer this question?

Direct-Material Variances

What caused DCdesserts.com to spend more than the anticipated amount on direct material? First, the company purchased ingredients at a higher price ($1.42 per kilogram) than the standard price ($1.40 per kilogram). Second, the company used more ingredients than the standard amount. The amount actually used was 10,250 kilograms instead of the standard amount of 10,000 kilograms, which is based on actual output of 2,000 multilayer fancy cakes. The managerial accountant can show both of these deviations from standards by computing a **direct-material price variance** (or **purchase price variance**) and a **direct-material quantity variance**. The computation of these variances is depicted in Exhibit 10–2.

Exhibit 10–2
Direct-Material Price and Quantity Variances

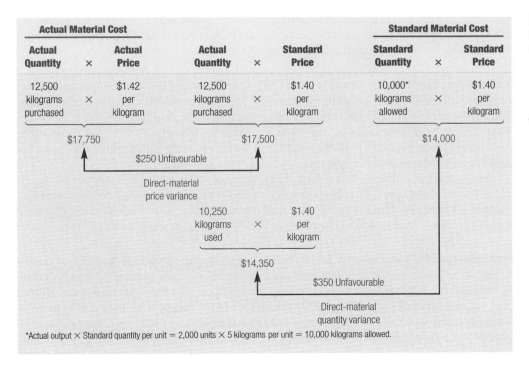

The formula for the direct-material price variance is as follows:

$$\text{Direct-material price variance} = (PQ \times AP) - (PQ \times SP) = PQ(AP - SP)$$

where

PQ = Actual quantity purchased
AP = Actual price
SP = Standard price

DCdesserts.com's direct-material price variance for September's production of multilayer fancy cakes is computed as follows:

$$\begin{aligned}\text{Direct-material price variance} &= PQ(AP - SP) \\ &= 12{,}500(\$1.42 - \$1.40) \\ &= \$250 \text{ Unfavourable}\end{aligned}$$

This variance is unfavourable, because the actual purchase price exceeded the standard price. Notice that the price variance is based on the actual quantity of material *purchased* (PQ), not the quantity actually used in production.

As Exhibit 10–2 shows, the following formula defines the direct-material quantity variance:

$$\text{Direct-material quantity variance} = (AQ \times SP) - (SQ \times SP) = SP(AQ - SQ)$$

where

AQ = Actual quantity used
SQ = Standard quantity allowed

DCdesserts.com's direct-material quantity variance for September's production of multilayer fancy cakes is computed as follows:

$$\begin{aligned}\text{Direct-material price variance} &= SP(AQ_p - SQ) \\ &= \$1.40(10{,}250 - 10{,}000) \\ &= \$350 \text{ Unfavourable}\end{aligned}$$

This variance is unfavourable, because the actual quantity of direct material used in September exceeded the standard quantity allowed, *given actual September output* of 2,000 multilayer fancy cakes. The quantity variance is based on the quantity of material actually *used* in production (AQ).

Quantity Purchased versus Quantity Used   As stated above, the direct-material price variance is based on the quantity purchased (PQ). This makes sense, because deviations between the actual and standard price, which are highlighted by the price variance, relate to the *purchasing* function in the firm. Timely action to follow up a significant price variance will be facilitated by calculating this variance as soon as possible after the material is *purchased*.

In contrast, the direct-material quantity variance is based on the amount of material *used* in production (AQ). The quantity variance highlights deviations between the quantity of material actually used (AQ) and the standard quantity allowed (SQ). Thus, it makes sense to compute this variance at the time the material is *used* in production.

Basing the Quantity Variance on Actual Output   Notice that the standard quantity of material must be based on the actual production output in order for the quantity variance to be meaningful. It would not make any sense to compare standard or budgeted material usage at one level of output (say 1,000 multilayer fancy cakes) with the actual material usage at a *different* level of output (say 2,000 multilayer fancy cakes). Everyone would expect more direct material to be used in the production of 2,000 cakes than in the production of 1,000 cakes. For the direct-material quantity variance to provide helpful information for management, the standard or budgeted quantity must be based on *actual output*. Then the quantity variance compares the following two quantities.

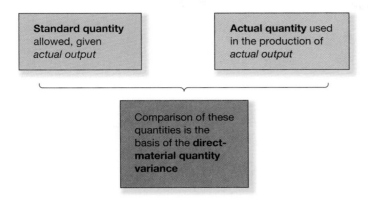

Direct-Labour Variances

Why did DCdesserts.com spend more than the anticipated amount on direct labour during September? First, the division incurred a cost of $21 per hour for direct labour instead of the standard amount of $20 per hour. Second, the division used only 980 hours of direct labour, which is less than the standard quantity of 1,000 hours, given actual output of 2,000 multilayer fancy cakes. The managerial accountant analyzes direct-labour costs by computing a **direct-labour rate variance** and a **direct-labour efficiency variance**. Exhibit 10–3 depicts the computation of these variances.

The formula for the direct-labour rate variance is shown below.

$$\text{Direct-labour rate variance} = (AH \times AR) - (AH \times SR) = AH(AR - SR)$$

where

AH = Actual hours used
AR = Actual rate per hour
SR = Standard rate per hour

DCdesserts.com's direct-labour rate variance for September's production of multilayer fancy cakes is computed as follows:

$$\text{Direct-labour rate variance} = AH(AR - SR)$$
$$= 980(\$21 - \$20) = \$980 \text{ Unfavourable}$$

This variance is unfavourable because the actual rate exceeded the standard rate during September.

As Exhibit 10–3 shows, the formula for the direct-labour efficiency variance is as follows:

$$\text{Direct-labour efficiency variance} = (AH \times SR) - (SH \times SR) = SR(AH - SH)$$

where

SH = Standard hours allowed

DCdesserts.com's direct-labour efficiency variance for September is computed as follows:

$$\text{Direct-labour efficiency variance} = SR(AH - SH)$$
$$= \$20(980 - 1,000)$$
$$= \$400 \text{ Favourable}$$

Exhibit 10–3
Direct-Labour Rate and
Efficiency Variances

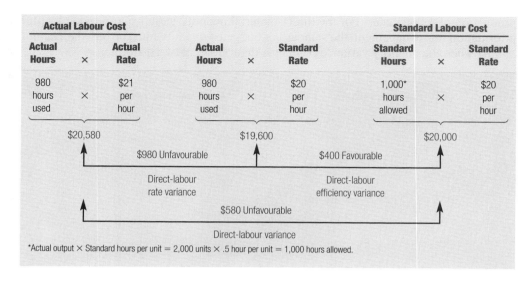

Actual Labour Cost					Standard Labour Cost		
Actual Hours	×	**Actual Rate**	**Actual Hours**	×	**Standard Rate**	**Standard Hours**	×	**Standard Rate**

| 980 hours used | × | $21 per hour | 980 hours used | × | $20 per hour | 1,000* hours allowed | × | $20 per hour |

$20,580 $19,600 $20,000

$980 Unfavourable $400 Favourable

Direct-labour   Direct-labour
rate variance   efficiency variance

$580 Unfavourable

Direct-labour variance

*Actual output × Standard hours per unit = 2,000 units × .5 hour per unit = 1,000 hours allowed.

This variance is favourable because the actual direct-labour hours used in September were less than the standard hours allowed, *given actual September output of 2,000 multilayer fancy cakes.*

Notice that the direct-labour rate and efficiency variances add up to the total direct-labour variance. However, the rate and efficiency variances have opposite signs, since one variance is unfavourable and the other favourable.

Direct-labour rate variance	$980 Unfavourable	Different signs of variances cancel just as plus
Direct-labour efficiency variance	400 Favourable	and minus signs cancel in arithmetic.
Direct-labour variance	$580 Unfavourable	

Basing the Efficiency Variance on Actual Output   The number of standard hours of direct labour allowed is based on the *actual* production output. It would not be meaningful to compare standard or budgeted labour usage at one level of output with the actual hours used at a different level of output.

Multiple Types of Direct Material or Direct Labour

Manufacturing processes usually involve several types of direct material. In such cases, direct-material price and quantity variances are computed for each type of material. Then these variances are added to obtain a total price variance and a total quantity variance, as follows:

	Price Variance	Quantity Variance
Direct material A	$1,000 F	$1,600 U
Direct material B	2,500 U	200 U
Direct material C	800 U	500 F
Total variance	$2,300 U	$1,300 U

Similarly, if a production process involves several types of direct labour, rate and efficiency variances are computed for each labour type. Then they are added to obtain a total rate variance and a total efficiency variance.

Allowing for Spoilage or Defects

In some manufacturing processes, a certain amount of spoilage or defective production is normal. This must be taken into account when the standard quantity of material is computed. To illustrate, suppose that 100 litres of chemicals are normally required in

PARKER HANNIFIN CORPORATION'S BRASS PRODUCTS DIVISION

Parker Hannifin's Brass Products Division, a world-class manufacturer of brass fittings, valves, and tubing, is a standard-costing success story.[1] "Parker Brass uses its standard-costing system and variance analyses as important business tools to target problem areas so it can develop solutions for continuous improvement. Variances are reported for each product line, and if any production variance exceeds 5 percent of product-line sales, the product-line manager is required to provide an explanation. Also required is a plan to correct the problems underlying any unfavourable variances. Variance reports, which are generated within one day of the completion of a job order, are distributed to managers and production schedulers. A variance database is kept, which can be accessed by product-line managers, to provide variance data by part number, by job-order number, or by dollar amount."

From the perspective of Parker Brass's management, the division has modified its standard-costing system to provide disaggregated and timely cost information to enable timely corrective action in a rapidly changing business environment.

a chemical process in order to obtain 80 litres of good output. If total good output in January is 500 litres, what is the standard allowed quantity of input?

$$\text{Good output quantity} = 80\% \times \text{Input quantity}$$

Dividing both sides of the equation by 80%
$$\frac{\text{Good output quantity}}{80\%} = \text{Input quantity allowed}$$

Using the numbers in the illustration
$$\frac{500 \text{ gallons of good output}}{80\%} = 625 \text{ litres of input allowed}$$

The total standard allowed input is 625 litres, given 500 litres of good output.

Overhead Budgets

How do service industry companies, such as Manulife, Pizza Hut, Budget Rent-a-Car, TD Canada Trust, Holiday Inn, and WestJet Airlines, control the overhead costs they incur in producing their services? Similarly, how do manufacturing firms such as General Motors, Hewlett-Packard, and Whirlpool control the many overhead costs incurred in their production processes? Unlike direct material and direct labour, overhead costs are not traceable to individual products. Moreover, overhead is a pool of many different kinds of costs. Indirect material, indirect labour, and other indirect production costs often exhibit different relationships to productive activity. Some overhead costs are variable, and some are fixed. Moreover, different individuals in an organization are responsible for different types of overhead costs. Considering all of these issues together, controlling overhead presents a challenge for managerial accountants.

Since direct material and direct labour are traceable to products, it is straightforward to determine standard costs for these inputs. If a table requires 20 board metres of oak lumber at $4 per board metre, the standard direct-material cost for the table is $80. But how much electricity does it take to produce a table? How much supervisory time, equipment depreciation, or machinery repair services does the table require? Since all of these overhead costs are indirect costs of production, we cannot set overhead cost standards for the oak table. If standard costs do not provide the answer to controlling overhead, what does?

> **Learning Objective 3**
>
> Distinguish between static and flexible budgets, and explain the advantages of a flexible overhead budget.

Flexible Budgets

The tool used by most companies to control overhead costs is called a **flexible budget**. A flexible budget resembles the budgets we studied in Chapter 9, with one important difference: *a flexible budget is not based on only one level of activity*. Instead, it covers a range of activity within which the firm may operate. A *flexible overhead budget* is defined as a detailed plan for controlling overhead costs that is valid in the firm's relevant range of activity. In contrast, a **static budget** is based on a particular planned level of activity.

At DCdesserts.com, the measure of activity used for flexible budgeting purposes is process time. The process time for a dessert is the total amount of time the product is in process, including selecting ingredients, mixing, baking, cooling, assembly and finishing, and packaging. DCdesserts.com's director of cost management estimates that the average process time required for fancy desserts is three hours.

To illustrate the flexible budgeting concept, suppose DCdesserts.com's director of cost management has determined that electricity is a variable cost, incurred at the rate of $.50 per hour of process time. Two different budgets for electricity cost are shown in Exhibit 10–4. The static budget is based on management's predicted level of activity for September—7,500 hours of process time. This estimate is based on planned production of 2,500 multilayer fancy cakes, in which each cake requires three hours of total process time. The flexible budget includes three different production activity levels within the relevant range: 6,000, 7,500, and 9,000 hours of process time.

Advantages of Flexible Budgets

Why is the distinction between static and flexible budgets so important? Suppose DCdesserts.com produced 2,000 multilayer fancy cakes during September, used 6,000 hours of process time, and incurred electricity costs of $3,200. Does this constitute good control or poor control of electricity costs? Which budget in Exhibit 10–4 is more useful in answering this question?

A manager using the static budget makes the following comparison:

Actual Electricity Cost	Budgeted Electricity Cost (static budget)	Cost Variance
$3,200	$3,750	550 Favourable

This comparison suggests that operating personnel maintained excellent control over electricity costs during September, generating a favourable variance of $550. Is this a valid analysis and conclusion?

The fault with this analysis is that the manager is comparing the electricity cost incurred at the *actual* activity level, 2,000 multilayer fancy cakes, with the budgeted electricity cost at the *planned* activity level, 2,500 multilayer fancy cakes. Since these activity levels are different, we should expect the electricity cost to be different.

Exhibit 10–4
Static Budget versus
Flexible Budget

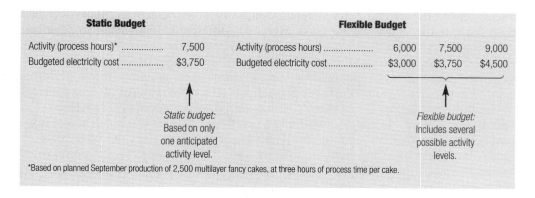

Static Budget		Flexible Budget			
Activity (process hours)*	7,500	Activity (process hours)	6,000	7,500	9,000
Budgeted electricity cost	$3,750	Budgeted electricity cost	$3,000	$3,750	$4,500

Static budget:
Based on only
one anticipated
activity level.

Flexible budget:
Includes several
possible activity
levels.

*Based on planned September production of 2,500 multilayer fancy cakes, at three hours of process time per cake.

A more sensible approach is to compare the actual electricity cost incurred with the cost that should be incurred when 2,000 multilayer fancy cakes are produced. At this production level, 6,000 process hours should be used (3 per cake). The flexible budget in Exhibit 10–4 shows that the manager should expect $3,000 of electricity cost at the 6,000 process-hour level of activity. Therefore, an analysis based on the flexible budget gives the following comparison:

Actual Electricity Cost	Budgeted Electricity Cost (flexible budget)	Cost Variance
$3,200	$3,000	.... $200 Unfavourable

Now the manager's conclusion is different; the revised analysis indicates an unfavourable variance. Electricity cost was greater than it should have been, given the actual level of output. The flexible budget provides the correct basis for comparison between actual and expected costs, given actual activity.

The Activity Measure

Notice that the flexible budget for electricity cost in Exhibit 10–4 is based on hours of process time, which is an input in the production process. The process-hour activity levels shown in the flexible budget are the standard allowed process hours given various levels of output. If 2,000 multilayer fancy cakes are produced, and the standard allowance per cake is 3 process hours, then the standard allowed number of process hours is 6,000.

Why are the activity levels in the flexible budget based on process hours, an *input* measure, instead of the number of multilayer fancy cakes produced, an *output* measure? When only a single product is manufactured, it makes no difference whether the flexible budget is based on input or output. In our illustration, either of the flexible budgets shown in Exhibit 10–5 could be used.

Now suppose that during August, DCdesserts.com produced three different products: 1,000 multilayer fancy cakes, 1,500 single-layer sheet cakes, and 600 specialty cakes (such as wedding cakes). The following standards have been assigned to these products:

Product	Standard Process Hours per Unit
Multilayer fancy cakes	3
Single-layer sheet cakes	2
Specialty cakes	6

During August, the company's production output was 3,100 cakes. Is 3,100 cakes a meaningful output measure? Adding numbers of multilayer fancy cakes, sheet cakes, and specialty cakes, which require different amounts of productive inputs, is like adding apples and oranges. It would not make sense to base a flexible budget for electricity cost on units of output when the output consists of different products with

> "I will give you an example of when we were supporting budgets. We would have to go out to the person and say, 'What is going on in your budget? I don't understand why you are overspending or underspending.' Now a person looks at their budget and comes to accounting and will say, 'Can you help me with this problem?'" (10c)
> **Abbott Laboratories**

Exhibit 10–5
Flexible Budgets: Input versus Output

DC desserts

	Flexible Budget (based on input)			
3 standard allowed process hours per multilayer fancy cake	Activity: Standard allowed process hours	6,000	7,500	9,000
	Budgeted electricity cost	$3,000	$3,750	$4,500
	Flexible Budget (based on output)			
	Activity: Multilayer fancy cakes produced	2,000	2,500	3,000
	Budgeted electricity cost	$3,000	$3,750	$4,500

different electricity requirements. In this case, the flexible budget must be based on an *input* measure. The standard allowed number of process hours for the August production is computed as follows:

Product	Units Produced	Standard Process Hours per Unit	Total Standard Allowed Process Hours
Multilayer fancy cakes	1,000	3	3,000
Single-layer sheet cakes	1,500	2	3,000
Specialty cakes	600	6	3,600
Total			9,600

Recall that the controller estimates electricity cost at $.50 per process hour. Thus, the flexible-budget cost of electricity during August is computed as follows:

Standard allowed process hours given August output	9,600
Electricity cost per process hour	$.50
Flexible budget for electricity cost	$4,800

The important point is that *units of output* usually is not a meaningful measure in a multiproduct firm, because it would require us to add numbers of unlike products. To avoid this problem, output is measured in terms of the *standard allowed input, given actual output*. The flexible overhead budget is then based on this standard input measure.

Flexible Overhead Budget Illustrated

Learning Objective 4

Prepare a flexible overhead budget and explain how overhead is applied to Work-in-Process Inventory.

DCdesserts.com's monthly flexible overhead budget is shown in the Excel spreadsheet in Exhibit 10–6. The overhead costs on the flexible budget are divided into variable and fixed costs. The total budgeted variable cost increases proportionately with increases in the activity. Thus, when the number of process hours increases by 50 percent, from 6,000 hours to 9,000 hours, the total budgeted variable overhead cost also increases by 50 percent, from $30,000 to $45,000. In contrast, the total budgeted fixed overhead does not change with increases in activity; it remains constant at $15,000 per month.

When overhead costs can be divided into variable and fixed categories, we can express the flexible overhead budget differently. The format used in Exhibit 10–6 is called a *columnar flexible budget*. The budgeted overhead cost for each overhead item is listed in a column under a particular activity level. Notice that the columnar format allows for only a limited number of activity levels. DCdesserts.com's flexible budget shows only three.

A more general format for expressing a flexible budget is called a *formula flexible budget*. In this format, the managerial accountant expresses the relationship between activity and total budgeted overhead cost by the following formula:

$$\text{Total budgeted monthly overhead cost} = \left(\begin{array}{c} \text{Budgeted variable} \\ \text{overhead cost per} \times \text{activity} \\ \text{activity unit} \quad \text{units} \end{array} \right) + \begin{array}{c} \text{Budgeted fixed} \\ \text{overhead cost} \\ \text{per month} \end{array}$$

To use this formula for DCdesserts.com, we first need to compute the budgeted variable-overhead cost per process hour. Dividing total budgeted variable-overhead cost by the associated activity level yields a budgeted variable-overhead rate of $5 per process hour. Notice that we can use any activity level in Exhibit 10–6 to compute this rate.

$$\frac{\$30,000}{6,000} = \frac{\$37,500}{7,500} = \frac{\$45,000}{9,000} = \$5 \text{ per process hour}$$

	A	B	C	D	E	F	G
1				DCdesserts.com			
2			Monthly Flexible Overhead Budget				
3							
4					Process Hours		
5							
6					6,000	7,500	9,000
7	Budgeted costs:						
8							
9	Variable costs:						
10	Indirect material:						
11	Nonstick cooking spray				$ 12,000	$ 15,000	$ 18,000
12	Waxed paper				2,000	2,500	3,000
13	Other paper products				2,000	2,500	3,000
14	Miscellaneous supplies				6,000	7,500	9,000
15	Indirect labour: maintenance				4,000	5,000	6,000
16	Utilities						
17	Electricity				3,000	3,750	4,500
18	Natural gas				1,000	1,250	1,500
19	Total variable cost				$ 30,000	$ 37,500	$ 45,000
20							
21							
22	Fixed costs:						
23	Indirect labour:						
24	Inspection				$ 2,200	$ 2,200	$ 2,200
25	Production supervisors				6,000	6,000	6,000
26	Setup				3,000	3,000	3,000
27	Material handling				2,000	2,000	2,000
28	Depreciation: Plant and equipment				500	500	500
29	Insurance and property taxes				100	100	100
30	Test kitchen				1,200	1,200	1,200
31	Total fixed cost				$ 15,000	$ 15,000	$ 15,000
32	Total overhead cost				$ 45,000	$ 52,500	$ 60,000

Exhibit 10–6

Flexible Overhead Budget

DCdesserts.com's formula flexible overhead budget is shown below.

$$\text{Total budgeted monthly overhead cost} = (\$5 \times \text{Total process hours}) + \$15,000$$

To check the accuracy of the formula, compute the total budgeted overhead cost at each of the activity levels shown in Exhibit 10–6.

Activity (process hours)	Formula Flexible Overhead Budget		Budgeted Monthly Overhead Cost
6,000	$5 × 6,000 + $15,000	=	$45,000
7,500	$5 × 7,500 + $15,000	=	$52,500
9,000	$5 × 9,000 + $15,000	=	$60,000

The budgeted monthly overhead cost computed above is the same as that shown in Exhibit 10–6 for each activity level.

The formula flexible budget is more general than the columnar flexible budget, because the formula allows the managerial accountant to compute budgeted overhead costs at any activity level. Then the flexible-budgeted overhead cost can be used at the end of the period as a benchmark against which to compare the actual overhead costs incurred.

"It's critical to understand variable and fixed overhead costs. When activity levels change, what costs will change and how?" (10d)

A. T. Kearney

Overhead Application in a Standard-Costing System

Recall that *overhead application* refers to the addition of overhead cost to the Work-in-Process Inventory account as a product cost. In the normal-costing system, described in Chapter 3, overhead is applied as shown in the top panel of Exhibit 10–7. Overhead application is based on *actual* hours. In a standard-costing system, overhead application is based on standard hours allowed, given actual output. This system is depicted in the bottom panel of Exhibit 10–7. Notice that the difference between normal costing and standard costing, insofar as overhead is concerned, lies in the quantity of hours used.

Both normal- and standard-costing systems use a predetermined overhead rate. In a standard-costing system, the predetermined overhead rate also is referred to as the *standard overhead rate*. DCdesserts.com calculates its predetermined or standard overhead rate annually. The rate for the current year, computed in Exhibit 10–8, is based on *planned* activity of 7,500 process hours per month. Notice that DCdesserts.com breaks its predetermined overhead rate into a variable rate and a fixed rate.

Exhibit 10–7
Overhead Application

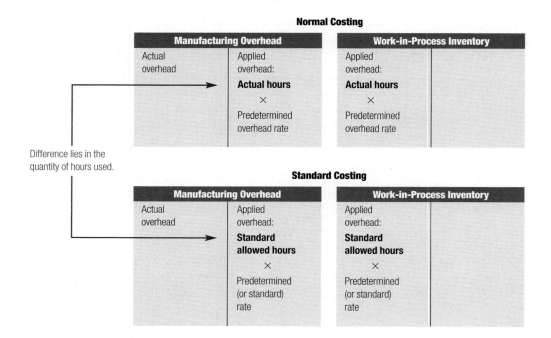

Exhibit 10–8
Predetermined Overhead Rate: DCdesserts.com

	Budgeted Overhead	Planned Monthly Activity	Predetermined Overhead Rate
Variable	$37,500*	7,500 process hours	$5.00 per process hour
Fixed	15,000*	7,500 process hours	2.00 per process hour
Total	$52,500	7,500 process hours	$7.00 per process hour

*From the flexible budget (Exhibit 10–6) for planned monthly activity of 7,500 process hours.

Choice of Activity Measure

DCdesserts.com's flexible overhead budget is based on process hours. A variety of activity measures are used in practice. Machine hours, direct-labour hours, direct-labour cost, total process time, and direct-material cost are among the most common measures. Choosing the appropriate activity measure for the flexible overhead budget is important, because the flexible budget is the chief tool for managing overhead costs.

As manufacturing has become increasingly automated, direct labour is becoming less appropriate as an activity measure in flexible budgeting. Moreover, computer-integrated manufacturing entails a shift in the cost structure away from direct-labour costs and toward greater overhead costs. Left, pouring molten steel into casts is a labour-intensive process for these steel workers. Right, automated equipment like that used in producing these silicon wafers is commonplace in high-tech manufacturing.

Criteria for Choosing the Activity Measure

How should the managerial accountant select the activity measure for the flexible budget? The activity measure should be one that varies in a similar pattern to the way that variable overhead varies. As productive activity increases, both variable-overhead cost and the activity measure should increase in roughly the same proportion. As productive activity declines, both variable-overhead cost and the activity measure should decline in roughly the same proportion. In short, variable-overhead cost and the activity measure should *move together* as overall productive activity changes.

Changing Manufacturing Technology: Computer-Integrated Manufacturing Direct labour time has traditionally been the most popular activity measure in manufacturing firms. However, as automation increases, more and more firms are switching to such measures as machine hours or process time for their flexible overhead budgets. Machine hours and process time are linked more closely than direct-labour hours to the robotic technology and computer-integrated manufacturing (CIM) systems common in today's manufacturing environment.

Cost Drivers As we discussed in Chapter 5, some companies have refined their cost management systems even further. *Cost drivers* are identified as the most significant factors affecting overhead costs. Then multiple overhead rates based on these cost drivers are used to compute product costs and control overhead expenditures. A relentless search for *non-value-added* costs is an integral part of such a cost management system. We will discuss the role of *activity-based costing* in flexible budgeting later in the chapter.

Beware of Dollar Measures Dollar measures, such as direct-labour or raw-material costs, often are used as the basis for flexible overhead budgeting. However, such measures have significant drawbacks, and they should be avoided. Dollar measures are subject to price-level changes and fluctuate more than physical measures. For example, the direct-labour *hours* required to produce a fancy dessert will be relatively stable over time. However, the direct-labour *cost* will vary as wage levels and fringe benefit costs change with inflation and conditions in the labour market.

Cost Variance Analysis: Manufacturing Overhead Costs

The flexible overhead budget is one of the managerial accountant's primary tools for the control of manufacturing-overhead costs. At the end of each accounting period, the managerial accountant uses the flexible overhead budget to determine the level of overhead cost that should have been incurred, given the actual level of activity. Then the accountant compares the overhead cost in the flexible budget

> **Learning Objective 6**
>
> Compute and interpret the variable-overhead and fixed-overhead variances.

with the actual overhead cost incurred. The managerial accountant then computes four separate overhead variances, each of which conveys information useful in controlling overhead costs.

To illustrate overhead variance analysis, we will continue our illustration for DCdesserts.com.

Flexible Budget   DCdesserts.com's monthly flexible overhead budget, displayed in Exhibit 10–6, shows budgeted variable and fixed manufacturing-overhead costs at three levels of production activity. During September, DCdesserts.com produced 2,000 multilayered fancy cakes. Since production standards allow three process hours per cake, the total standard allowed number of process hours is 6,000 hours.

Actual production output	2,000 multilayered fancy cakes
Standard allowed process hours per multilayered fancy cake	× 3
Total standard allowed process hours	6,000 process hours

From the 6,000 process-hour column in Exhibit 10–6, the budgeted overhead cost for September is as follows:

	Budgeted Overhead Cost for September
Variable overhead	$30,000
Fixed overhead	15,000

From the cost-accounting records, DCdesserts.com's director of cost management determined that the following overhead costs were actually incurred during September.

	Actual Cost for September
Variable overhead	$34,650
Fixed overhead	16,100
Total overhead	$50,750

The production supervisor's records indicate that the actual total process time in September was as follows:

Actual process hours for September	6,300

Notice that the actual number of process hours used (6,300) exceeds the standard allowed number of process hours, given actual production output (6,000).

We now have assembled all of the information necessary to compute DCdesserts.com's overhead variances for September.

Variable Overhead

DCdesserts.com's total variable-overhead variance for September is computed below.

Actual variable overhead	$34,650
Budgeted variable overhead	30,000
Total variable-overhead variance	$ 4,650 Unfavourable

What caused the company to spend $4,650 more than the budgeted amount on variable overhead? To discover the reasons behind this performance, the managerial accountant computes a **variable-overhead spending variance** and a **variable-overhead efficiency variance**. The computation of these variances is depicted in Exhibit 10–9.

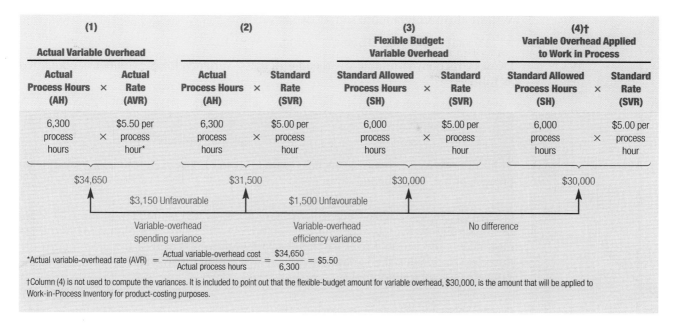

(1) **Actual Variable Overhead**		(2)		(3) **Flexible Budget:** **Variable Overhead**		(4)† **Variable Overhead Applied** **to Work in Process**	
Actual **Process Hours** × **(AH)**	**Actual** **Rate** **(AVR)**	**Actual** **Process Hours** × **(AH)**	**Standard** **Rate** **(SVR)**	**Standard Allowed** **Process Hours** × **(SH)**	**Standard** **Rate** **(SVR)**	**Standard Allowed** **Process Hours** × **(SH)**	**Standard** **Rate** **(SVR)**
6,300 process hours ×	$5.50 per process hour*	6,300 process hours ×	$5.00 per process hour	6,000 process hours ×	$5.00 per process hour	6,000 process hours ×	$5.00 per process hour
$34,650		$31,500		$30,000		$30,000	

$3,150 Unfavourable $1,500 Unfavourable   No difference

Variable-overhead   Variable-overhead
spending variance   efficiency variance

*Actual variable-overhead rate (AVR) $= \dfrac{\text{Actual variable-overhead cost}}{\text{Actual process hours}} = \dfrac{\$34,650}{6,300} = \$5.50$

†Column (4) is not used to compute the variances. It is included to point out that the flexible-budget amount for variable overhead, $30,000, is the amount that will be applied to Work-in-Process Inventory for product-costing purposes.

Exhibit 10–9
Variable-Overhead Spending
and Efficiency Variances

Two equivalent formulas for the variable-overhead spending variance are shown below.

1. $\dfrac{\text{Variable-overhead}}{\text{spending variance}}$ = Actual variable overhead − (AH × SVR), or

2. $\dfrac{\text{Variable-overhead}}{\text{spending variance}}$ = (AH × AVR) − (AH × SVR)

where   AH denotes actual process hours
         AVR denotes actual variable-overhead rate
            (Actual variable overhead ÷ AH)
         SVR denotes standard variable-overhead rate

These two formulas are equivalent because actual variable overhead is equal to actual hours times the actual variable overhead rate (AH × AVR). Formula 2 above can be simplified:

3. Variable-overhead spending variance = AH(AVR − SVR)

DCdesserts.com's variable-overhead spending variance for September is computed as follows (using formula 1):

$$\begin{aligned}\frac{\text{Variable-overhead}}{\text{spending variance}} &= \text{Actual variable overhead} \ -\ (\text{AH} \times \text{SVR}), \\ &= \qquad \$34,650 \qquad\quad -\ (6,300 \times \$5) \\ &= \$3,150\ \text{Unfavourable}\end{aligned}$$

This variance is unfavourable because the actual variable-overhead cost exceeded the expected amount, after adjusting that expectation for the actual number of process hours used.

As Exhibit 10–9 shows, the following formula defines the variable-overhead efficiency variance:

Variable-overhead efficiency variance = (AH × SVR) − (SH × SVR)

where   SH denotes standard process hours

Writing this formula more simply, we have:

$$\text{Variable-overhead efficiency variance} = \text{SVR(AH} - \text{SH)}$$

DCdesserts.com's variable-overhead efficiency variance for September is computed as follows:

$$\text{Variable-overhead efficiency variance} = \text{SVR(AH} - \text{SH)}$$
$$= \$5(6{,}300 - 6{,}000)$$
$$= \$1{,}500 \text{ Unfavourable}$$

This variance is unfavourable because actual process hours exceeded standard allowed process hours, given actual output.

Product Costing versus Cost Management   Columns (1), (2), and (3) in Exhibit 10–9 are used to compute the variances for *cost-management purposes*. Column (4) in the exhibit shows the variable overhead applied to work in process for the *product-costing purpose*. Notice that the variable-overhead cost on the flexible budget, $30,000, is the same as the amount applied to work in process.

Graphing Variable-Overhead Variances   Exhibit 10–10 provides a graphical analysis of DCdesserts.com's variable-overhead variances for September. The graph shows the variable-overhead rate per process hour on the vertical axis. The standard rate is $5 per process hour, while the actual rate is $5.50 per process hour (actual variable-overhead cost of $34,650 divided by actual process hours of 6,300). Process hours are shown on the horizontal axis.

The green area on the graph represents the flexible-budget amount for variable overhead, given actual September output of 2,000 multilayered fancy cakes. The large area on the graph enclosed by coloured lines on the top and right sides represents actual variable-overhead cost. The coloured area in between, representing the total variable overhead variance, is divided into the spending and efficiency variances.

Managerial Interpretation of Variable-Overhead Variances   What do the variable-overhead variances mean? What information do they convey to management? The formulas for

Exhibit 10–10
Graphical Analysis of Variable-
Overhead Variances

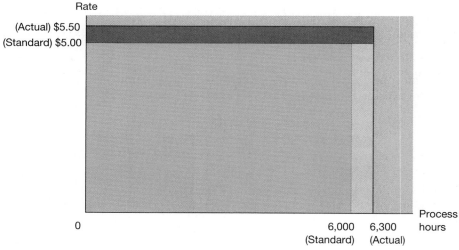

Key:
Total variable-overhead variance: blue areas
Variable-overhead spending variance: dark blue area
Variable-overhead efficiency variance: light blue area

computing the variable-overhead variances resemble those used to compute the direct-labour variances. To see this, compare Exhibit 10–9 (variable overhead) with Exhibit 10–3 (direct labour).

Despite the similar formulas, the interpretation of the variable-overhead variances is quite different from that applicable to the direct-labour variances.

Spending Variance   An unfavourable direct-labour rate variance is straightforward to interpret; the actual labour rate *per hour* exceeds the standard rate. Although the formula for computing the variable-overhead spending variance is similar to that for the direct-labour rate variance, its interpretation is quite different.

An unfavourable spending variance simply means that the total actual cost of variable overhead is greater than expected, after adjusting for the actual quantity of process hours used. An unfavourable spending variance could result from paying a higher-than expected price per unit for variable-overhead items. Or the variance could result from using more of the variable-overhead items than expected.

Suppose, for example, that electricity were the only variable-overhead cost item. An unfavourable variable-overhead spending variance could result from paying a higher than-expected price per kilowatt-hour for electricity, from using more than the expected amount of electricity, or from both.

Efficiency Variance   Recall that an unfavourable direct-labour efficiency variance results when more direct labour is used than the standard allowed quantity. Thus, direct labour has been used inefficiently, relative to the standard. However, that is not the proper interpretation of an unfavourable variable-overhead efficiency variance. DCdesserts.com's variable-overhead efficiency variance did *not* result from using more of the variable-overhead items, such as electricity and indirect material, than the standard allowed amount. Instead, this variance resulted when the division used *more process hours* than the standard quantity, given actual output. Recall that the company's director of cost management has found that variable-overhead cost varies in a pattern similar to that with which process hours vary. Since 300 more process hours were used than the standard quantity, the division's management should expect that variable-overhead costs will be greater. Thus, the variable-overhead efficiency variance has nothing to do with efficient or inefficient usage of electricity, indirect material, and other variable-overhead items. This variance simply reflects an adjustment in the managerial accountant's expectation about variable-overhead cost, because the division used more than the standard quantity of process hours.

What is the important difference between direct labour and variable overhead that causes this different interpretation of the efficiency variance? Direct labour is a traceable cost and is budgeted on the basis of direct-labour hours. Variable overhead, on the other hand, is a pool of *indirect* costs that are budgeted on the basis of *process hours*. The indirect nature of variable-overhead costs causes the different interpretation.

Management of Variable Overhead Costs   Since the variable-overhead efficiency variance says nothing about efficient or inefficient usage of variable overhead, the spending variance is the real control variance for variable overhead. Managers can use the spending variance to alert them if variable-overhead costs are out of line with expectations.

Fixed Overhead

To analyze performance with regard to fixed overhead, the managerial accountant calculates two fixed-overhead variances.

Fixed-Overhead Budget Variance   The variance used by managers to control fixed overhead is called the **fixed-overhead budget variance**. It is defined as follows:

$$\text{Fixed-overhead budget variance} = \text{Actual fixed overhead} - \text{Budgeted fixed overhead}$$

DCdesserts.com's fixed-overhead budget variance for September is as follows:

$$
\begin{aligned}
\text{Fixed-overhead budget variance} &= \text{Actual fixed overhead} - \text{Budgeted fixed overhead} \\
&= \qquad \$16,100 \qquad - \qquad \$15,000* \\
&= \$1,100 \text{ Unfavourable}
\end{aligned}
$$

*From the flexible budget (Exhibit 10–6).

The fixed-overhead budget variance is unfavourable, because the company spent more than the budgeted amount on fixed overhead. Notice that we need not specify an activity level to determine budgeted fixed overhead. All three columns in the flexible budget (Exhibit 10–6) specify $15,000 as budgeted fixed overhead.

Fixed-Overhead Volume Variance   The **fixed-overhead volume variance** is defined as follows:

$$\text{Fixed-overhead volume variance} = \text{Budgeted fixed overhead} - \text{Applied fixed overhead}$$

DCdesserts.com's applied fixed overhead for September is $12,000:

$$
\begin{aligned}
\text{Applied fixed overhead} &= \text{Predetermined fixed overhead rate} \times \text{Standard allowed hours} \\
&= \$2 \text{ per process hour} \times 6,000 \text{ process hours} \\
&= \$12,000
\end{aligned}
$$

The $2 predetermined fixed-overhead rate was calculated in Exhibit 10–8. The 6,000 standard allowed process hours is based on actual September production of 2,000 multilayered fancy cakes, each with a standard allowance of three process hours. DCdesserts.com's fixed-overhead volume variance is calculated below.

$$
\begin{aligned}
\text{Fixed-overhead volume variance} &= \text{Budgeted fixed overhead} - \text{Applied fixed overhead} \\
&= \qquad \$15,000 \qquad - \qquad \$12,000 \\
&= \$3,000 \text{ Unfavourable}
\end{aligned}
$$

Managerial Interpretation of Fixed-Overhead Variances   Exhibit 10–11 shows DCdesserts.com's two fixed-overhead variances for September. The budget variance is the real control variance for fixed overhead, because it compares actual expenditures with budgeted fixed-overhead costs.

The volume variance provides a way of reconciling two different purposes of the cost management system. For the *control purpose*, the system recognizes that fixed overhead does not change as production activity varies. Hence, budgeted fixed overhead is the same at all activity levels in the flexible budget. (Review Exhibit 10–6 to verify this.) Budgeted fixed overhead is the basis for controlling fixed overhead, because it provides the benchmark against which actual expenditures are compared.

For the *product-costing purpose* of the system, budgeted fixed overhead is divided by planned activity to obtain a predetermined (or standard) fixed-overhead rate. For DCdesserts.com, this rate is $2 per process hour (budgeted fixed overhead of $15,000 divided by planned activity of 7,500 process hours). This predetermined rate is then used to apply fixed overhead to Work-in-Process Inventory. During any period in which the standard allowed number of process hours, given actual output, differs from the planned level of process hours, the budgeted fixed overhead differs from applied fixed overhead.

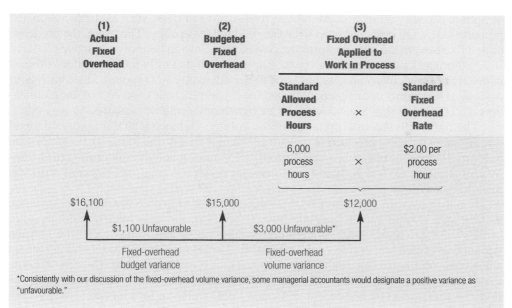

Exhibit 10–11
Fixed-Overhead Budget and
Volume Variances

Table columns:

(1) Actual Fixed Overhead | (2) Budgeted Fixed Overhead | (3) Fixed Overhead Applied to Work in Process

Standard Allowed Process Hours × Standard Fixed Overhead Rate

6,000 process hours × $2.00 per process hour

$16,100 .... $15,000 .... $12,000

$1,100 Unfavourable — Fixed-overhead budget variance

$3,000 Unfavourable* — Fixed-overhead volume variance

*Consistently with our discussion of the fixed-overhead volume variance, some managerial accountants would designate a positive variance as "unfavourable."

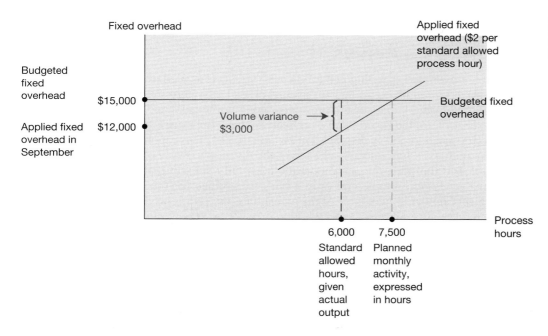

Exhibit 10–12
Budgeted versus Applied
Fixed Overhead

Fixed overhead. Applied fixed overhead ($2 per standard allowed process hour). Budgeted fixed overhead $15,000. Applied fixed overhead in September $12,000. Volume variance $3,000. Budgeted fixed overhead. Process hours: 6,000 Standard allowed hours, given actual output; 7,500 Planned monthly activity, expressed in hours.

Exhibit 10–12 illustrates this point graphically. Budgeted fixed overhead is constant at $15,000 for all levels of activity. However, applied fixed overhead increases with activity, since fixed overhead is applied to Work-in-Process Inventory at the rate of $2 per standard allowed process hour. Notice that budgeted and applied fixed overhead are equal *only* if the number of standard allowed hours equals the planned activity level of 7,500 process hours. When this happens, there is no fixed-overhead volume variance. DCdesserts.com has a $3,000 volume variance in September because the standard allowed hours and planned hours are different.

Capacity Utilization   A common, but faulty, interpretation of a positive volume variance is that it measures the cost of underutilizing productive capacity. Some firms even designate a positive volume variance as unfavourable. The reasoning behind this view is that the planned activity level used to compute the predetermined fixed overhead rate is a measure of normal capacity utilization. Moreover, fixed-overhead costs, such as depreciation and property taxes, are costs incurred to create productive capacity. Therefore, the predetermined fixed-overhead rate measures the cost of providing an hour of productive capacity. If 7,500 process hours are planned, but output is such that only 6,000 standard process hours are allowed, then capacity has been underutilized by 1,500 hours. Since each hour costs $2 (DCdesserts.com's predetermined fixed-overhead rate), the cost of underutilization is $3,000 (1,500 × $2), which is DCdesserts.com's volume variance.

The fault with this interpretation of the volume variance is that it ignores the real cost of underutilizing productive capacity. The real cost is due to the lost contribution margins of the products that are not produced when capacity is underutilized. Moreover, this interpretation fails to recognize that underutilizing capacity and reducing inventory may be a wise managerial response to slackening demand.

For this reason, many managerial accountants interpret the volume variance merely as a way of reconciling the two purposes of the cost management system. Moreover, these managerial accountants would choose not to designate the volume variance as either favourable or unfavourable. However, some accountants designate a positive volume variance as *unfavourable*. Their reasoning is that when the volume variance is closed into Cost of Goods Sold expense at the end of the accounting period, the effect is to increase Cost of Goods Sold, which in turn has an *unfavourable* effect on income.[2] In contrast, other accountants argue that no sign (favourable or unfavourable) should be assigned to the fixed-overhead volume variance.

Overhead Cost Performance Report

The variable-overhead spending and efficiency variances, as well as the fixed-overhead budget variance, can be computed for each overhead cost item in the flexible budget. When these itemized variances are presented along with actual and budgeted costs for each overhead item, the result is an **overhead cost performance report**. DCdesserts.com's performance report is displayed in Exhibit 10–13. This report would be used by management to exercise control over each of the division's overhead costs.

Notice that the performance report includes only spending and efficiency variances for the variable items, and only a budget variance for the fixed items. Upon receiving this report, a manager might investigate the relatively large variances for indirect maintenance labour, electricity, and production supervisory labour.

M anagement
A ccounting
P ractice

Stihl, Inc.

COST MANAGEMENT SYSTEMS IN GERMANY

Throughout the world, flexible budgeting is found in cost management systems as a means of controlling overhead costs. In Germany, for example, *grenzplankostenrechnung* (or "flexible standard costing") exhibits many of the features illustrated in this chapter. Under the German approach, "each cost center distinguishes between variable costs (e.g., energy) and fixed costs (e.g., a manager's salary)." The number of machine hours is a common activity measure. "For purposes of cost planning and control, companies budget each cost center's expenses and then distribute the expenses to each month of the budget year. The budgeted costs are standards for efficient resource consumption. . . ." The cost and performance information "allows for effective discussions about productivity improvement" among department managers, management accountants, and plant managers.

Among the companies using the flexible standard costing system is Stihl, a well-known German manufacturer of chain saws and other landscaping equipment.[3]

	(1) Flexible Budget (for 6,000 process hr.)	(2) Standard Rate per Process Hr. [variable costs only; col. (1) ÷ 6,000 process hr.]	(3) 6,300 Actual Process Hr. × Standard Rate	(4) Actual Cost	(5) Spending Variance [col. (4) − col. (3)]	(6) Efficiency Variance [col. (3) − col. (1)]	(7) Budget Variance [col. (4) − col. (1)]
Variable costs:							
Indirect material:							
Nonstick cooking spray	$12,000	$2.00	$12,600	$12,700	$ 100 U	$ 600 U	
Waxed paper	2,000	.33	2,079	2,090	11 U	79 U	
Other paper products	2,000	.33	2,079	2,000	(79) F	79 U	
Miscellaneous supplies	6,000	1.00	6,300	6,500	200 U	300 U	
Indirect labour:							
Maintenance	4,000	.67	4,221	6,400	2,179 U	221 U	
Utilities:							
Electricity	3,000	.50	3,150	4,050	900 U	150 U	
Natural gas	1,000	.17	1,071	910	(161) F	71 U	
Total variable cost	$30,000	$5.00	$31,500	$34,650	$3,150 U	$1,500 U	
Fixed costs:							
Indirect labour:							
Inspection	$ 2,200			$ 2,210			$ 10 U
Production supervisors	6,000			7,000			1,000 U
Setup	3,000			3,000			–0–
Material handling	2,000			2,000			–0–
Depreciation:							
Plant and equipment	500			500			–0–
Insurance and property taxes	100			100			–0–
Test kitchen	1,200			1,290			90 U
Total fixed cost	$15,000			$16,100			$1,100 U
Total overhead cost	$45,000			$50,750			$1,100 U
Total variance between actual overhead cost and flexible budget		$5,750 U	Sum of spending, efficiency, and budget variances				$5,750 U

DC desserts

Exhibit 10–13
Overhead Cost Performance
Report: DCdesserts.com

Activity-Based Flexible Budget

The flexible budget shown in Exhibit 10–6, which underlies our variance analysis for DCdesserts.com, is based on a single cost driver. Overhead costs that vary with respect to *process hours* are categorized as variable; all other overhead costs are treated as fixed. This approach is consistent with traditional, volume-based product-costing systems.

Under the more accurate product-costing method called activity-based costing, several cost drivers are identified.[4] Costs that may appear fixed with respect to a single volume-based cost driver, such as process hours, may be variable with respect to some other cost driver. The activity-based costing approach also can be used as the basis for a flexible budget for planning and cost management purposes. Exhibit 10–14 displays an **activity-based flexible budget** for DCdesserts.com, using the same data as Exhibit 10–6.

Learning Objective 8

Explain how an activity-based flexible budget differs from a conventional flexible budget.

Exhibit 10–14

Activity-Based Flexible
Budget: DCdesserts.com

DCDESSERTS.COM Monthly Flexible Overhead Budget			
Budgeted Cost	**Level of Activity**		
Cost Pool I (cost driver: process hours)	**6,000**	**7,500**	**9,000**
Indirect material:			
Nonstick cooking spray	$ 12,000	$ 15,000	$ 18,000
Waxed paper	2,000	2,500	3,000
Other paper products	2,000	2,500	3,000
Miscellaneous supplies	6,000	7,500	9,000
Indirect labour: maintenance	4,000	5,000	6,000
Utilities:			
Electricity	3,000	3,750	4,500
Natural gas	1,000	1,250	1,500
Total of cost pool I	$ 30,000	$ 37,500	$ 45,000
Cost Pool II (cost driver: production runs)	**8**	**12**	**16**
Indirect labour:			
Inspection	$ 2,200	$ 3,300	$ 4,400
Setup	3,000	4,500	6,000
Total of cost pool II	$ 5,200	$ 7,800	$ 10,400
Cost Pool III (cost driver: new products tested)	**20**	**30**	**40**
Test kitchen	$ 1,200	$ 1,800	$ 2,400
Total of cost pool III	$ 1,200	$ 1,800	$ 2,400
Cost Pool IV (cost driver: pounds of material handled)	**20,000**	**30,000**	**40,000**
Material handling	$ 2,000	$ 3,000	$ 4,000
Total of cost pool IV	$ 2,000	$ 3,000	$ 4,000
Cost Pool V (facility level costs)			
Indirect labour: production supervisors	$ 6,000	$ 6,000	$ 6,000
Depreciation: plant and equipment	500	500	500
Insurance and property taxes	100	100	100
Total of cost pool V	$ 6,600	$ 6,600	$ 6,600
Total overhead cost	**$45,000**	**$56,700**	**$68,400**

Compare the conventional flexible budget (Exhibit 10–6) and the activity-based flexible budget (Exhibit 10–14). The key difference lies in the costs that were categorized as fixed on the conventional flexible budget. These costs are fixed with respect to process hours but are not fixed with respect to other more appropriate cost drivers. For example, cost pool II includes inspection and setup costs, which vary with respect to the number of production runs.

Effect on Performance Reporting   The activity-based flexible budget provides a more accurate prediction (and benchmark) of overhead costs. For example, suppose that activity in December is as follows:

December activity		
	Process hours	6,000
	Production runs	12
	New products tested	40
	Direct material handled (kilograms)	30,000

The following table compares the budgeted cost levels for several overhead items on the conventional and activity-based flexible budgets:

Overhead Cost Item	Conventional Flexible Budget	Activity-Based Flexible Budget
Electricity	$3,000	$3,000
Inspection	2,200	3,300
Setup	3,000	4,500
Test kitchen	1,200	2,400
Material handling	2,000	3,000
Insurance and property taxes	100	100

The budgeted electricity cost is the same on both budgets, because both use the same cost driver (process hours). Insurance and property taxes are also the same, because both budgets recognize these as facility-level fixed costs. However, the other overhead costs are budgeted at different levels, because the conventional and activity-based flexible budgets use *different cost drivers* for these items. While the conventional budget treats inspection, setup, test kitchen, and material-handling costs as fixed, the activity-based flexible budget shows that they are all variable with respect to the appropriate cost driver.

These differences are important for performance reporting. The activity-based flexible budget provides a more accurate benchmark against which to compare actual costs. Suppose the actual inspection cost in December is $3,000. Using the conventional flexible budget would result in an unfavourable variance of $800 ($3,000 − $2,200). However, the activity-based flexible budget yields a favourable variance of $300 ($3,000 − $3,300).

To summarize, activity-based flexible budgeting provides a richer view of cost behaviour and the underlying cost drivers, and it provides a valuable tool for cost management.

> "ABC has enhanced our clients' ability to manage overhead costs through flexible budgeting systems." (10g)
>
> A. T. Kearney

Flexible Budgeting in the Service Industry

All kinds of organizations benefit from the concept of a flexible budget. Like manufacturing firms, service industry organizations incur overhead costs that vary with appropriately chosen cost drivers. At York University, for example, the cost of operating the admissions department depends in part on the number of applicants. At Pacific Blue Cross Insurance Company, the cost of administering the claims department depends in part on the number of claims. At Vancouver General Hospital, the cost of operating the patient records department depends in part on the number of patients.

Let's briefly turn our attention to Tri-Cities Auto Rentals, a small automobile rental company in Coquitlam, Port Coquitlam, and Port Moody. The company has four rental locations in the Tri-Cities area and specializes in short-term car rentals, primarily for local use when a customer's car is in the repair shop. Tri-Cities Auto Rentals' flexible budget is displayed in Exhibit 10–15. Notice that unlike DCdesserts. com's flexible overhead budget, Tri-Cities Auto Rentals' flexible budget lists its operating expenses. All of this service industry firm's costs are operating expenses. Tri-Cities Auto Rentals' management has chosen two cost drivers for its activity-based flexible budget: the number of miles driven and the number of customer contracts.

An activity-based flexible budget is based on many cost drivers. Think about the costs that are incurred at your college. The cost of staffing the college's faculty, for example, depends on factors such as the number of students enrolled, the number of courses offered, and the average class size. The cost of operating the admissions department would depend in part on the number of applicants.[5]

Some operating expenses (cost pool I in the flexible budget) vary with the number of miles driven by the rental cars. Automobile maintenance and tire replacement expenses increase as the cars drive more miles. Similarly, such operating expenses as insurance and leasing costs increase with the number of miles driven, because the company needs more cars on hand. Other operating expenses (cost pool II) vary with the number of customer contracts, regardless of how many miles each customer drives

Exhibit 10–15

Flexible Budget: Tri-Cities
Auto Rentals

	A	B	C	D
1	TRI– CITIES AUTO RENTALS			
2	Annual Flexible Budget: Operating Expenses			
3				
4	Budgeted Operating Expenses		Level of Activity	
5				
6	Cost Pool I (cost driver: miles driven)	750,000	1,000,000	1,250,000
7	Automobile maintenance	$ 240,000	$ 320,000	$ 400,000
8	Tire replacement	6,000	8,000	10,000
9	Automobile insurance	27,000	36,000	45,000
10	New York State registration and inspection	900	1,200	1,500
11	Leasing costs	36,000	48,000	60,000
12	Total of cost pool I	$ 309,900	$ 413,200	$ 516,500
13				
14	Cost Pool II (cost driver: customer contracts)	3,000	6,000	9,000
15	Reservations	$ 16,000	$ 32,000	$ 48,000
16	Registration of contract information	18,000	36,000	54,000
17	Inspection of vehicle by employee/customer	8,000	16,000	24,000
18	Employee commissions	20,000	40,000	60,000
19	Cleaning/washing automobile	17,000	34,000	51,000
20	Total of cost pool II	$ 79,000	$ 158,000	$ 237,000
21				
22	Cost Pool III (overall organization: fixed costs)			
23	Office managers' salaries	240,000	240,000	240,000
24	Rent: Buildings	36,000	36,000	36,000
25	Utilities: Buildings	13,000	13,000	13,000
26	Liability insurance: Rental offices	12,000	12,000	12,000
27	Depreciation: Equipment	11,000	11,000	11,000
28	Total of cost pool III	$ 312,000	$ 312,000	$ 312,000
29				
30	Total operating expenses	$ 700,900	$ 883,200	$1,065,500

a rental car. Such expenses as rental reservations, filling out contracts, and cleaning up a rental car upon return depend on the number of times the cars are rented. Finally, some fixed operating expenses (cost pool III), such as the office managers' salaries and rental charges on the office locations, do not vary with any cost driver.

Tri-Cities Auto Rentals' management can use this flexible budget to predict operating expenses at varying levels of activity, as measured by the two cost drivers.

Focus on Ethics

MISSTATED STANDARDS AFFECT ACCURACY OF REPORTS

The scenario described here, while placed in the context of a fictitious enterprise, is based on an actual situation that occurred at NuTone Housing Group, which at the time was a subsidiary of Scoville, Inc.[6]

To set the stage, consider these facts about the standard costing system in place at Shrood Division, a subsidiary of Gigantic Enterprises, Inc. Shrood Division manufactures a wide range of electric household products, such as lighting, fans, water pumps, and security systems. The division manufactures approximately 10,000 products, made from over 70,000 components. Tom Cleverly has run the division in what he calls a hands-on manner for over a

quarter-century. When Shrood was acquired by Gigantic a decade ago, Cleverly was at first unhappy with the merger, but it soon became apparent that Gigantic's top management would let him run the business the way he was used to running it. Three aspects of Cleverly's management style are noteworthy. First, he insists on being involved in all major pricing decisions; he's not a delegator. Second, he has developed a second-level management that is loyal and supportive of his approach. Third, he has refused to lower the direct-labour time standards for years, even though many productivity improvements have been made. At present, the actual direct-labour times are on average only about a third of the standard times. Moreover, since manufacturing overhead is applied on the basis of direct labour, both the standard direct labour and the standard overhead costs are inflated relative to actual costs.

The implications of this practice are that huge favourable variances are experienced all year long in both direct labour and overhead. Cleverly has used these favourable variances to "manage the quarterly earnings" reported by Shrood Division to corporate. Cleverly has instructed his manager of accounting, Evan Twixt, to release just enough of the favourable variances into Cost of Goods Sold (CGS) on a quarterly basis to ensure that Shrood Division just meets its earnings target in the budget. Then, at the end of the year, the remainder of this large favourable variance is released into CGS, with the result that Shrood ends each year with fourth-quarter earnings far in excess of the target. Like a knight in shining white armour, Shrood Division saves the day for Gigantic Enterprises year after year. Shrood has come to be known in corporate circles as "the jewel in the crown of Gigantic."

Now for the conflict. Gigantic has hired a new corporate controller, Jeffrey Fixit, whose charge is to introduce more consistency in the reporting methods of Gigantic's various divisions. When Fixit visited Shrood Division and discovered what was going on, he tried to get Tom Cleverly to instruct Evan Twixt to correct the direct-labour standards to reflect attainable results (i.e., reality). Cleverly has refused, though, and Fixit doesn't have the power to force him to do so. Meanwhile, poor Twixt is caught in the middle.

Here is what each of them had to say about the situation.

Cleverly (division manager): I've been running this business for 25 years. And you know what?

We've been profitable for 25 years! The high labour standards help me make sure that neither I nor my salespeople shave prices too much. It's like setting the clock 10 minutes ahead to make sure you're not late. We always make budget. We always report the highest profits in the company. And we are, in fact, the "jewel in the crown."

Fixit (corporate controller): This is a really bad situation. Shrood is reporting fictitious numbers to corporate on a quarterly basis, which then get rolled up into Gigantic's quarterly results. Then these numbers get published to the shareholders. We're misleading them. I don't have the authority to get Tom Cleverly to fix the problem. I can, however, go to the board of directors and explain to them that they need to get Cleverly to do what needs to be done.

Twixt (Shrood's accounting manager): I'm caught in the middle. We basically have two sets of books: the ones based on Mr. Cleverly's labour standards, and the ones based on the more accurate results that Mr. Fixit wants. I can report either set of results. I feel like I'm serving two gods—and so far I'm getting away with it.

What do you make of this situation? Can a company that keeps two sets of books be well managed? What ethical issues do you see here? What actions should Cleverly, Twixt, and Fixit take?

Significance of Cost Variances

Managers do not have time to investigate the causes of every cost variance. Management by exception enables managers to look into the causes of only significant variances. But what constitutes an exception? How does the manager know when to follow up on a cost variance and when to ignore it?

These questions are difficult to answer, because to some extent the answers are part of the art of management. A manager applies judgment and experience in making guesses, pursuing hunches, and relying on intuition to determine when a variance should be investigated. Nevertheless, there are guidelines and rules of thumb that managers often apply.

Learning Objective 9

Explain methods for determining the significance of cost variances.

Size of Variances The absolute size of a variance is one consideration. Managers are more likely to follow up on large variances than on small ones. The relative size of the variance is probably even more important. A manager is more likely to investigate a $20,000 material quantity variance that is 20 percent of the standard direct-material cost of $100,000 than a $50,000 labour efficiency variance that is only 2 percent of the standard direct-labour cost of $2,500,000. The *relative* magnitude of the $20,000

Exhibit 10–16
Cost Variance Report for
September: DCdesserts.com

	Amount		Percentage of Standard Cost
Direct material			
Standard cost, given actual output	$14,000		
Direct-material price variance..	250	Unfavourable	1.79%
Direct-material quantity variance	350	Unfavourable	2.50%
Direct labour			
Standard cost, given actual output	$20,000		
Direct-labour rate variance	980	Unfavourable	4.9%
Direct-labour efficiency variance	400	Favourable	(2.0%)

material quantity variance (20%) is greater than the *relative* magnitude of the $50,000 labour efficiency variance (2%). For this reason, managerial accountants often show the relative magnitude of variances in their cost-variance reports. For example, the September cost-variance report for DCdesserts.com's production of multilayer fancy cakes is shown in Exhibit 10–16.

Managers often apply a rule of thumb that takes into account both the absolute and the relative magnitudes of a variance. An example of such a rule is the following: Investigate variances that are either greater than $10,000 or greater than 10 percent of standard cost.

Recurring Variances   Another consideration in deciding when to investigate a variance is whether the variance occurs repeatedly or only infrequently. Suppose a manager uses the rule of thumb stated above and direct-material quantity variances occur as shown in the following Excel spreadsheet:

	A	B	C	D	E
1		Standard	Direct-Material		Percentage
2		Direct-Material	Quantity		of Standard
3	Month	Cost	Variance		Cost
4					
5	January	$ 50,000	$ 3,000	F*	6.0%
6	February	50,000	3,200	F	6.4%
7	March	50,000	1,800	F	3.6%
8	April	50,000	3,100	F	6.2%
9					
10	*F denotes a favourable variance.				

A strict adherence to the rule of thumb indicates no investigation, since none of the monthly variances is greater than $10,000 or 10 percent of standard cost. Nevertheless, the manager might investigate this variance in April, since it has *recurred* at a reasonably high level for several consecutive months. In this case, the consistency of the variance triggers an investigation, not its absolute or relative magnitude.

Trends   A trend in a variance also may call for investigation. Suppose a manager observes the direct-labour efficiency variances shown in the following Excel spreadsheet.

None of these variances is large enough to trigger an investigation if the manager uses the "$10,000 or 10 percent" rule of thumb. However, the four-month *trend* is worrisome. An alert manager will likely follow up on this unfavourable trend to determine its causes before costs get out of hand.

	A	B	C	D	E
1		Standard	Direct-Labour		Percentage
2		Direct-Labour	Efficiency		of Standard
3	Month	Cost	Variance		Cost
4					
5	January	$ 100,000	$ 100	U*	0.10%
6	February	100,000	550	U	0.55%
7	March	100,000	3,000	U	3.00%
8	April	100,000	9,100	U	9.10%
9					
10	*U denotes an unfavourable variance.				

Controllability Another important consideration in deciding when to look into the causes of a variance is the manager's view of the **controllability** of the cost item. A manager is more likely to investigate the variance for a cost that is controllable by someone in the organization than one that is not. For example, there may be little point to investigating a material price variance if the organization has no control over the price. This could happen, for example, if the firm has a long-term contract with a supplier of the material at a price determined on the international market. In contrast, the manager is likely to follow up on a variance that should be controllable, such as a direct-labour efficiency variance or a direct-material quantity variance.

Favourable Variances It is just as important to investigate significant favourable variances as significant unfavourable variances. For example, a favourable direct-labour efficiency variance may indicate that employees have developed a more efficient way of performing a production task. By investigating the variance, management can learn about the improved method. It may be possible to use a similar approach elsewhere in the organization.

Costs and Benefits of Investigation The decision whether to investigate a cost variance is a cost-benefit decision. The costs of investigation include the time spent by the investigating manager and the employees in the department where the investigation occurs. Other potential costs include disruption of the production process as the investigation is conducted, and corrective actions taken to eliminate the cause of a variance. The benefits of a variance investigation include reduced future production costs if the cause of an unfavourable variance is eliminated. Another potential benefit is the cost saving associated with the lowering of cost standards when the cause of a favourable variance is discovered.

Weighing these considerations takes the judgment of skilful and experienced managers. Key to this judgment is an intimate understanding of the organization's production process and day-to-day contact with its operations.

Behavioural Impact of Standard Costing

Standard costs and variance analysis are useful in diagnosing organizational performance. These tools help managers discern "the story behind the story"—the details of operations that underlie reported cost and profit numbers. Standard costs, budgets, and variances are also used to evaluate the performance of individuals and departments. The performance of individuals, relative to standards or budgets, often is used to help determine salary increases, bonuses, and promotions. When standards and variances affect employee reward structures, they can profoundly influence behaviour.

For example, suppose the manager of a hotel's Food and Beverage Department earns a bonus when food and beverage costs are below the budgeted amount, given actual sales. This reward structure will provide a concrete incentive for the manager to keep food and beverage costs under control. But such an incentive can have either positive or negative effects. The bonus may induce the manager to seek the most economical food suppliers

Learning Objective 10

Describe some behavioural effects of standard costing.

and to watch more carefully for employee theft and waste. However, the bonus also could persuade the manager to buy cheaper but less tender steaks for the restaurant. This could ultimately result in lost patronage for the restaurant and the hotel. One aspect of skilful management is knowing how to use standards, budgets, and variances to get the most out of an organization's employees. Unfortunately, there are no simple answers or formulas for success in this area. Despite such difficulties, standards, budgets, and variances are used in the executive compensation schemes of many well-known companies.

Controllability of Variances

> "We designate variances as controllable or uncontrollable. Plant managers are held accountable for the controllable variances." (10h)
> **Best Foods (a subsidiary of Unilever)**

Cost control is accomplished through the efforts of individual managers in an organization. By determining which managers are in the best position to influence each cost variance, the managerial accountant can assist managers in deriving the greatest benefit from cost variance analysis.

Who is responsible for the direct-material price and quantity variances? The direct-labour rate and efficiency variances? Answering these questions is often difficult, because it is rare that any one person completely controls any event. Nevertheless, it is often possible to identify the manager who is *most able to influence* a particular variance, even if he or she does not exercise complete control over the outcome.

Direct-Material Price Variance   The purchasing manager is generally in the best position to influence material price variances. Through skilful purchasing practices, an expert purchasing manager can get the best prices available for purchased goods and services. To achieve this goal, the purchasing manager uses such practices as buying in quantity, negotiating purchase contracts, comparing prices among vendors, and global sourcing.

Despite these purchasing skills, the purchasing manager is not in complete control of prices. The need to purchase component parts with precise engineering specifications, the all-too-frequent rush requests from the production department, and worldwide shortages of critical materials all contribute to the challenges faced by the purchasing manager.

Direct-Material Quantity Variance   The production supervisor is usually in the best position to influence material quantity variances. Skilful supervision and motivation of production employees, coupled with the careful use and handling of materials, contribute to minimal waste. Production engineers are also partially responsible for material quantity variances, since they determine the grade and technical specifications of materials and component parts. In some cases, using a low-grade material may result in greater waste than using a high-grade material.

Direct-Labour Rate Variance   Direct-labour rate variances generally result from using a different mix of employees than that anticipated when the standards were set. Wage rates differ among employees due to their skill levels and their seniority with the organization. Using a higher proportion of more senior or more highly skilled employees than a task requires can result in unfavourable direct-labour rate variances. The production supervisor is generally in the best position to influence the work schedules of employees.

Direct-Labour Efficiency Variance   Once again, the production supervisor is usually most responsible for the efficient use of employee time. Through motivation toward production goals and effective work schedules, the efficiency of employees can be maximized.

Interaction among Variances

Interactions among variances often occur, making it even more difficult to determine the responsibility for a particular variance. To illustrate, consider the following anecdote from a manufacturer of brass musical instruments. The purchasing manager obtained a special price on brass alloy from a new supplier. When the material was placed into production, it turned out to be a lower grade of material than the production employees were used to. The alloy was of a slightly different composition, which made the material bend less easily during the formation of brass instruments. The company could have returned the material to the supplier, but that would have interrupted production and kept the division from filling its orders on time. Since using the off-standard material would not affect the quality of the company's finished products, the division manager decided to keep the material and make the best of the situation.

The ultimate result was that the company incurred four interrelated variances during May. The material was less expensive than normal, so the direct-material price variance was favourable. However, the employees had difficulty using the material, which resulted in more waste than expected. Hence, the division incurred an unfavourable direct-material quantity variance.

What were the labour implications of the off-standard material? Due to the difficulty in working with the metal alloy, the employees required more than the standard amount of time to form the instruments. This resulted in an unfavourable direct-labour efficiency variance. Finally, the production supervisor had to use his most senior employees to work with the off-standard material. Since these people earned relatively high wages, the direct-labour rate variance was also unfavourable.

To summarize, the purchase of off-standard material resulted in the following interrelated variances:

Purchase of off-standard material $\longrightarrow$
$\begin{cases} \text{Favourable direct-material price variance} \\ \text{Unfavourable direct-material quantity variance} \\ \text{Unfavourable direct-labour rate variance} \\ \text{Unfavourable direct-labour efficiency variance} \end{cases}$

Such interactions of variances make it more difficult to assign responsibility for any particular variance.

Trade-Offs among Variances   Does the incident described above mean that the decision to buy and use the off-standard material was a poor one? Not necessarily. Perhaps these variances were anticipated, and a conscious decision was made to buy the material anyway. How could this be a wise decision? Suppose the amounts of the variances were as follows:

$(8,500)	Favourable direct-material price variance
1,000	Unfavourable direct-material quantity variance
2,000	Unfavourable direct-labour rate variance
1,500	Unfavourable direct-labour efficiency variance
$(4,000)	Favourable net overall variance

The company saved money overall on the decision to use a different grade of brass alloy. Given that the quality of the final product was not affected, the company's management acted wisely.

Standard Costs and Product Costing

Our discussion of standard costing has focused on its use in controlling costs. But firms that use standard costs for control also use them for product costing. Recall from Chapter 3 that *product costing* is the process of accumulating the costs of a production process and assigning them to the completed products. Product costs are used for various purposes in both financial and managerial accounting.

As production takes place, product costs are added to the Work-in-Process Inventory account. The flow of product costs through a firm's manufacturing accounts is depicted in Exhibit 10–17.

Different types of product-costing systems are distinguished by the type of costs that are entered into Work-in-Process Inventory. In Chapter 3, we studied *actual-* and

> **Learning Objective 11**
>
> Explain how standard costs are used in product costing and summarize some advantages of standard costing.

Exhibit 10–17
Flow of Product Costs through
Manufacturing Accounts

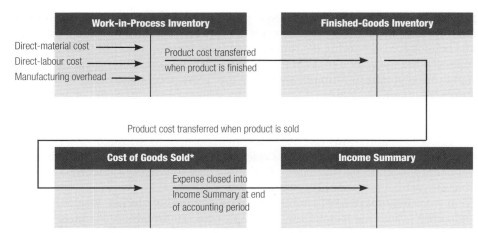

*Cost of Goods Sold is an expense. Although it is more descriptive, the term *cost-of-goods-sold expense* is not used as much in practice as the simpler term *cost of goods sold*.

normal-costing systems. In these product-costing systems, the *actual* costs of direct material and direct labour are charged to Work-in-Process Inventory. In a **standard-costing system**, the *standard* costs of direct material and direct labour are entered into Work-in-Process Inventory.[7]

Evaluation of Standard Costing

Standard costing has been the predominant accounting system in manufacturing companies, for both cost control and product-costing purposes, for several decades. This remains true today, and the use of standard costing is spreading to nonmanufacturing firms as well. The widespread use of standard costing over such a long time period suggests that it has traditionally been perceived as offering several advantages. However, today's manufacturing environment is changing dramatically. Some managers are calling into question the usefulness of the traditional standard-costing approach. They argue that the role of standard-costing systems must change.

Advantages of Standard Costing

Some advantages traditionally attributed to standard costing include the following:

- Standard costs provide a basis for *sensible cost comparisons*. As we discussed earlier, it would make no sense to compare budgeted costs at one (planned) activity level with actual costs incurred at a different (actual) activity level. Standard costs enable the managerial accountant to compute the standard allowed cost, given actual output, which then serves as a sensible benchmark to compare with the actual cost.
- Computation of standard costs and cost variances enables managers to employ *management by exception*. This approach conserves valuable management time.
- Variances provide a means of *performance evaluation* and rewards for employees.
- Since the variances are used in performance evaluation, they provide *motivation* for employees to adhere to standards.
- Use of standard costs in product costing results in *more stable product costs* than if actual production costs are used. Actual costs often fluctuate erratically, whereas standard costs are changed only periodically.
- A standard-costing system is usually *less expensive* than an actual or normal product-costing system.

Like any tool, a standard-costing system can be misused. When employees are criticized for every cost variance, the positive motivational effects will quickly vanish. Moreover, if standards are not revised often enough, they will become outdated. Then the benefits of cost benchmarks and product costing will disappear.

Criticisms of Standard Costing

Listed below are several drawbacks attributed to standard costing in an advanced manufacturing setting.[8]

- Some accountants argue that traditional standard costing is out of step with the philosophy of *activity-based management*. A production process comprises many activities, which result in costs. By focusing on the activities that cause costs to be incurred, by eliminating non-value-added activities, and by continually improving performance in value-added activities, costs will be minimized and profit maximized.[9]

M anagement
A ccounting
P ractice

Texas Instruments, Northrop, and Black & Decker

COST OF OWNERSHIP

Texas Instruments has developed a supplier rating system referred to as CETRAQ, which stands for cost, environmental responsibility, technology, responsiveness, assurance of supply, and quality. The company's vendors are regularly measured on these six criteria.

Northrop Aircraft Division tracks various elements of the total cost of ownership (TCO)* through its cost-based Supplier Performance Rating System (SPRS). Among the cost factors measured by the SPRS are the costs Northrop incurs due to suppliers' hardware, paperwork, or delivery deficiencies. Any "non-conformance event is assigned a standard cost based on industrial engineering studies of the hours required to resolve the problem."

At a Spennymore, England plant owned by Black & Decker, the company "has integrated the cost-of-ownership concept into its activity-based costing system." Among the

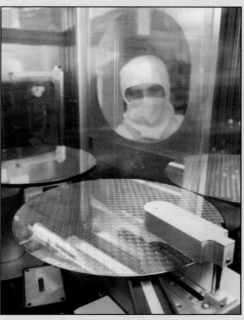

This Texas Instruments manufacturing facility relies on its suppliers for high-quality raw materials delivered on a timely basis. Texas Instruments, like many other companies, employs a sophisticated supplier rating system to measure the performance of its vendors.

TCO issues included are quality, delivery, flexibility, and customer service. Also considered is a supplier's billing reliability. One Spennymore manager noted, "You can be dealing with the best company in the world in terms of quality, but if they can't get their invoices right, you're going to have trouble doing business with them."

*The total cost of ownership includes all costs incurred in order to have materials in place and ready for use in production, including the purchase price; transportation cost; and costs of ordering, receiving, inspecting, and storing the materials."[10]

- Traditional cost variances are also too aggregate in the sense that they are not tied to specific product lines or production batches. The aggregate nature of the variances makes it difficult for managers to determine their cause.
- Traditional standard-costing systems focus too much on the cost and efficiency of direct labour, which is rapidly becoming a relatively unimportant factor of production.
- An important condition for the successful use of standard costing is a stable production process. Yet the introduction of flexible manufacturing systems has reduced this stability, with frequent switching among products on the same production line.
- Traditional standard costs are not defined broadly enough to capture various important aspects of performance. For example, the standard direct-material price does not capture all of the *costs of ownership*. In addition to the purchase price and transportation costs, the *cost of ownership* includes the costs of ordering, paying bills, scheduling delivery, receiving, inspecting, handling and storing, and any production-line disruptions resulting from untimely or incorrect delivery.[11]
- Traditional standard-costing systems tend to focus too much on cost minimization, rather than increasing product quality or customer service. For example, buying the least expensive materials of a given quality, in order to avoid a material price variance, may result in using a vendor whose delivery capabilities are not consistent with JIT requirements.

Focus on Ethics

SACRIFICING QUALITY TO CUT STANDARD COSTS

Pressures to control costs, coupled with bonus systems based on adherence to standards, can present the opportunity to engage in ethical lapses. The following hypothetical scenario describes such a situation.

Keystone Company manufactures small wooden household items such as cutting boards and knife racks. Keystone's controller, Marc Rigas, recently completed the installation of a new standard-costing system, which has been in place now for six months. Jack Smith, the purchasing manager, is about to place an order for wood to be used in Keystone's cutting boards. Smith has found a supplier that will furnish the necessary wood at $2 per board metre, rather than the standard cost of $3. This is very appealing to Smith, since his annual bonus is influenced by any favourable price variances he is able to obtain. Smith is due to be transferred at the end of the year to Keystone's Allentown Division, which manufactures metal kitchen utensils. The transfer is a promotion for Smith.

After further discussions with the potential supplier, Smith realized that the wood being offered would not be well suited for cutting boards. Although the wood would seem fine in the manufacturing process, and it would result in an attractive product, it would not hold up well. After repeated cycles of getting wet and drying out, it

would tend to crack. Smith figured that it might take about a year for the boards to deteriorate, and then Keystone Company would be beset with customer complaints.

Smith mulled over the situation for a while and then decided to accept the new supplier's offer. The $2 price would help him get a nice annual bonus, which he could use to help with the down payment on a new home. By the time the boards cracked and customers started to complain, he would be long gone. Someone else could worry about it then, he reasoned. After all, he thought, people shouldn't expect a cutting board to last forever.

Several weeks later, when the invoice for the first shipment of wood came through, Rigas noticed the large, favourable price variance. When he ran into Smith on the golf course, Rigas congratulated Smith on the purchase. The following conversation resulted:

Rigas: "That was quite a price break on that wood, Jack. How'd you swing it?"

Smith: "Hard-ball negotiating, Marc. It's as simple as that."

Rigas: "Is it good wood? And how about the supplier, Jack? Will they deliver on time?"

Smith: "This supplier is very timely in their deliveries. I made sure of that."

Rigas: "How about the quality, Jack? Did you check into that?"

Smith: "Sure I did, Marc. Hey, what is this? An interrogation? I thought we were here to play golf."

Rigas was left feeling puzzled and disconcerted by Smith's evasiveness. The next day, Rigas talked to the production manager, Amy Wilcox, about his concerns. Later that day, Wilcox raised the issue with Smith. After

a lengthy and sometimes heated exchange, the story came out.

Discuss the ethical issues involved in this scenario. Did the purchasing manager, Jack Smith, act ethically? Did the controller, Marc Rigas, act ethically when he asked Smith about the quality of the wood? Did Rigas act ethically when he went to the production manager with his concerns? What should the controller do now?

Chapter Summary

A standard-costing system serves two purposes: cost control and product costing. The managerial accountant works with others in the organization to set standard costs for direct material, direct labour, and manufacturing overhead through either historical cost analysis or task analysis. The accountant then uses the standard cost as a benchmark against which to compare actual costs incurred. Managers use management by exception to determine the causes of significant cost variances. This control purpose of the standard-costing system is accomplished by computing a direct-material price variance, a direct-material quantity variance, a direct-labour rate variance, and a direct-labour efficiency variance. Overhead is a heterogeneous pool of indirect costs. Since overhead costs cannot be traced easily to products or services, a flexible budget is used to budget overhead costs at various levels of activity. A columnar flexible budget is based on several distinct activity levels, while a formula flexible budget is valid for a continuous range of activity. The flexible overhead budget is based on some activity measure that varies in a pattern similar to that of variable overhead. Machine hours, process time, and direct-labour hours are common activity bases.

In a standard-costing system, the flexible budget is used to control overhead costs. The managerial accountant uses the amount of overhead cost specified by the flexible budget as a benchmark against which to compare actual overhead costs. The accountant computes four overhead variances: the variable-overhead spending and efficiency variances and the fixed-overhead budget and volume variances. These variances help management to control overhead costs.

The managerial accountant also uses the standard or predetermined overhead rate as the basis for product costing in a standard-costing system. The amount of overhead cost entered into Work-in-Process Inventory is equal to the standard overhead rate multiplied by the standard allowed amount of the activity base, given actual output.

When an activity-based costing system is in use, an activity-based flexible budget may be developed. Such a flexible budget is more accurate than conventional budgets, because multiple cost drivers are identified to explain the behaviour of overhead costs.

Managers determine the significance of cost variances through judgment and rules of thumb. The absolute and relative sizes of variances, recurrence of variances, variance trends, and controllability of variances are all considered in deciding whether variances warrant investigation. The managerial accountant achieves the product-costing purpose of the standard-costing system by entering the standard cost of production into Work-in-Process Inventory as a product cost. Standard-costing systems offer an organization many benefits. However, these benefits will be obtained only if the standard-costing system is used properly.

Review Problem on Standard Costing

In November, DCdesserts.com produced 3,000 multilayered fancy cakes, used 9,100 hours of process time, and incurred the following actual costs for direct material, direct labour, and manufacturing overhead:

Purchased 16,500 kilograms of ingredients at $1.44 per kilogram.

Used 15,500 kilograms of ingredients at $1.44 per kilogram.

Used 1,520 hours of direct labour at $22 per hour.

Variable overhead $45,955

Fixed overhead $15,800

The standard costs for production of multilayer fancy cakes were the same in November as those given in Exhibit 10–6.

Compute DCdesserts.com's direct-material and direct-labour variances for November using the format shown in Exhibits 10–2 and 10–3, and the variable-overhead and fixed-overhead variances using the format shown in Exhibits 10–9 and 10–11.

Solutions to Review Problem

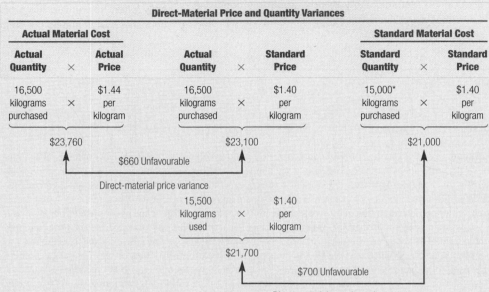

Direct-Material Price and Quantity Variances

Actual Material Cost				Standard Material Cost	
Actual Quantity ×	**Actual Price**	**Actual Quantity** ×	**Standard Price**	**Standard Quantity** ×	**Standard Price**
16,500 kilograms purchased ×	$1.44 per kilogram	16,500 kilograms purchased ×	$1.40 per kilogram	15,000* kilograms purchased ×	$1.40 per kilogram
$23,760		$23,100		$21,000	

$660 Unfavourable
Direct-material price variance

15,500 kilograms used × $1.40 per kilogram

$21,700

$700 Unfavourable
Direct-material quantity variance

*Actual output × Standard quantity per unit = 3,000 units × 5 kilograms per unit = 15,000 kilograms allowed.

Using Formulas

$$\text{Direct-material price variance} = \text{PQ}(\text{AP} - \text{SP})$$
$$= 16{,}500(\$1.44 - \$1.40)$$
$$= \$660 \text{ Unfavourable}$$
$$\text{Direct-material quantity variance} = \text{SP}(\text{AQ} - \text{SQ})$$
$$= \$1.40(\$15{,}500 - 15{,}000)$$
$$= \$700 \text{ Unfavourable}$$

Direct-Labour Rate and Efficiency Variances

Actual Labour Cost				Standard Labour Cost	
Actual Hours ×	**Actual Rate**	**Actual Hours** ×	**Standard Rate**	**Standard Hours** ×	**Standard Rate**
1,520 hours used ×	$22 per hour	1,520 hours used ×	$20 per hour	1,500* hours used ×	$20 per hour
$33,440		$30,400		$30,000	

$3,040 Unfavourable
Direct-labour rate variance

$400 Unfavourable
Direct-labour efficiency variance

*Actual output × Standard quantity per unit = 3,000 units × .5 hour per unit = 1,500 hours allowed.

Using Formulas

$$\text{Direct-labour rate variance} = \text{AH(AR} - \text{SR)}$$
$$= 1{,}520(\$22 - \$20)$$
$$= \$3{,}040 \text{ Unfavourable}$$
$$\text{Direct-labour efficiency variance} = \text{SR(AH} - \text{SH)}$$
$$= \$20(1{,}520 - 1{,}500)$$
$$= \$400 \text{ Unfavourable}$$

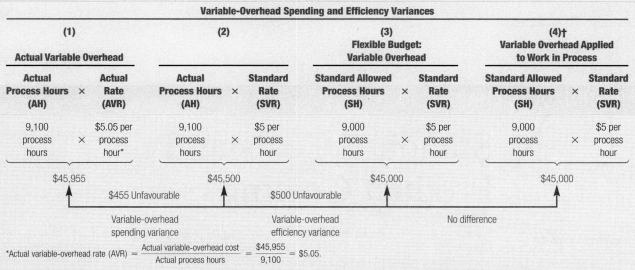

Variable-Overhead Spending and Efficiency Variances

(1) Actual Variable Overhead		(2)		(3) Flexible Budget: Variable Overhead		(4)† Variable Overhead Applied to Work in Process	
Actual Process Hours (AH) ×	Actual Rate (AVR)	Actual Process Hours (AH) ×	Standard Rate (SVR)	Standard Allowed Process Hours (SH) ×	Standard Rate (SVR)	Standard Allowed Process Hours (SH) ×	Standard Rate (SVR)
9,100 process hours ×	$5.05 per process hour*	9,100 process hours ×	$5 per process hour	9,000 process hours ×	$5 per process hour	9,000 process hours ×	$5 per process hour
$45,955		$45,500		$45,000		$45,000	

$455 Unfavourable → Variable-overhead spending variance

$500 Unfavourable → Variable-overhead efficiency variance

No difference

*Actual variable-overhead rate (AVR) = $\dfrac{\text{Actual variable-overhead cost}}{\text{Actual process hours}} = \dfrac{\$45{,}955}{9{,}100} = \$5.05.$

†Column (4) is not used to compute the variances. It is included to point out that the flexible-budget amount for variable overhead, $45,000, is the amount that will be applied to Work-in-Process Inventory for product-costing purposes.

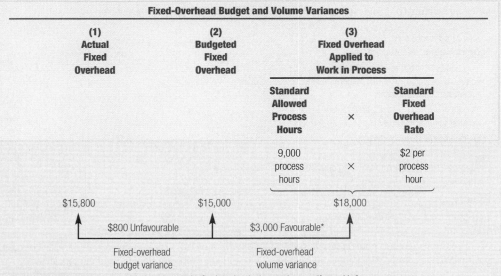

Fixed-Overhead Budget and Volume Variances

(1) Actual Fixed Overhead	(2) Budgeted Fixed Overhead	(3) Fixed Overhead Applied to Work in Process	
		Standard Allowed Process Hours ×	Standard Fixed Overhead Rate
		9,000 process hours ×	$2 per process hour
$15,800	$15,000	$18,000	

$800 Unfavourable → Fixed-overhead budget variance

$3,000 Favourable* → Fixed-overhead volume variance

*Some managerial accountants would designate a negative fixed-overhead volume variance as "favourable."

Key Terms

For each term's definition refer to the indicated page, or turn to the glossary at the end of the text.

activity-based flexible budget, 385

controllability, 391

cost variance, 363

direct-labour efficiency variance, 369

direct-labour rate variance, 369

direct-material price variance (*or* purchase price variance), 367

*Term appears in Appendix B.

APPENDIX A TO CHAPTER 10

Standard Costs and Product Costing

Learning Objective 12

Prepare journal entries to record manufacturing overhead under standard costing.

In a standard-costing system, the standard costs are used for product costing as well as for cost control. The costs of direct material, direct labour, and manufacturing overhead are all entered into Work-in-Process Inventory at their standard costs. (Review Exhibit 10–7.)

Journal Entries under Standard Costing   To illustrate the use of standard costs in product costing, we will continue our illustration of DCdesserts.com. The following journal entries record the information shown on Exhibit 10–2 and isolate the direct-material price and quantity variances.

Raw-Material Inventory	17,500	
Direct-Material Price Variance	250	
Accounts Payable		17,750
To record the purchase of raw material and the incurrence of an unfavourable price variance.		

Work-in-Process Inventory	14,000	
Direct-Material Quantity Variance	350	
Raw-Material Inventory		14,350
To record the use of direct material in production and the incurrence of an unfavourable quantity variance.		

Notice that the material purchase is recorded in the Raw-Material Inventory account at its standard price ($17,500 = 12,500 pounds purchased × $1.40 per pound). The $14,000 debit entry to Work-in-Process Inventory adds only the standard cost of the material to Work-in-Process Inventory as a product cost ($14,000 = 10,000 pounds purchased × $1.40 per pound). The two variances are isolated in their own variance accounts. Since they are both unfavourable, they are represented by debit entries.

The following journal entry records the actual September cost of direct labour, as an addition to Wages Payable. The entry also adds the standard cost of direct labour to Work-in-Process Inventory and isolates the direct-labour variances, shown on Exhibit 10–3.

Work-in-Process Inventory	20,000	
Direct-Labour Rate Variance	980	
Direct-Labour Efficiency Variance		400
Wages Payable		20,580
To record the usage of direct labour and the direct-labour variances for September.		

Since the direct-labour efficiency variance is favourable, it is recorded as a credit entry.

For September's production of multiplayer fancy cakes, the company incurred actual manufacturing-overhead costs of $50,750, which includes $34,650 of variable overhead and $16,100 of fixed overhead. A summary journal entry to record these actual expenditures follows.

Manufacturing Overhead	50,750	
Indirect-Material Inventory		23,290*
Wages Payable		20,610*
Utilities Payable		4,960
Accumulated Depreciation		500
Prepaid Insurance and Property Taxes		100
Test Kitchen Salaries Payable		1,290

*The credit amounts can be verified in column (4) of Exhibit 10–13. For example, indirect-material costs amounted to $23,290 ($12,700 + $2,090 + $2,000 + $6,500). The credit to Wages Payable is for indirect-labour costs, which amounted to $20,610 ($6,400 + $2,210 + $7,000 + $3,000 + $2,000).

The application of manufacturing overhead to Work-in-Process Inventory is based on a predetermined overhead rate of $7 per process hour (the total of the variable and the fixed rates) and 6,000 standard allowed process hours, given an actual output of 2,000 multilayered fancy cakes. The summary journal entry is as follows:

Work-in-Process Inventory	42,000	
Manufacturing Overhead		42,000*

*Applied overhead = $7 × 6,000 = $42,000.

Now the Manufacturing Overhead account appears as follows:

Manufacturing Overhead			
Actual	$50,750	$42,000	Applied

The *underapplied overhead* for September is $8,750 ($50,750 – $42,000). This means that the overhead applied to Work-in-Process Inventory in September was $8,750 less than the actual overhead cost incurred. Notice that the underapplied overhead is equal to the sum of the four overhead variances for September, shown on Exhibits 10–9 and 10–11. The total of the four overhead variances will always be equal to the overapplied or underapplied overhead for the accounting period.

Variable-Overhead Spending Variance	$3,150 Unfavourable
Variable-Overhead Efficiency Variance	$1,500 Unfavourable
Fixed-Overhead Budget Variance	$1,100 Unfavourable
Fixed-Overhead Volume Variance	$3,000 Unfavourable
Underapplied Overhead	$8,750

Disposition of Variances   Variances are temporary accounts and most companies close them directly into Cost of Goods Sold at the end of each accounting period. The journal entry required to close out the September variances is as follows:

Cost of Goods Sold	9,930	
Direct-Labour Efficiency Variance	400	
Direct-Material Price Variance		250
Direct-Material Quantity Variance		350
Direct-Labour Rate Variance		980
Manufacturing Overhead		8,750

The journal entry to dispose of the variances and close out underapplied or overapplied overhead typically is made annually, rather than monthly.

An alternative accounting treatment is to prorate the variances and the underapplied or overapplied overhead among Work-in-Process Inventory, Finished-Goods Inventory, and Cost of Goods Sold.

Cost Flow under Standard Costing   In a standard-costing system, since standard costs are entered into Work-in-Process Inventory, all of the product costs flowing through the accounts are standard costs. To illustrate, suppose DCdesserts.com produced 2,000 multilayer fancy cakes in September and sold all 2,000 of them. The journal entries to record the flow of standard costs are shown below.

Finished-Goods Inventory	76,000*	
Work-in-Process Inventory		76,000

*Total standard cost of direct material, direct labour, and variable and fixed overhead: $76,000 = $14,000 + $20,000 + $30,000 + $12,000.

Cost of Goods Sold	76,000*	
Finished-Goods Inventory		76,000

*All 2,000 multilayer fancy cakes were sold.

A Note on Perishable Products and JIT Production Management Systems   Traditional manufacturing systems typically exhibit the cost flows explained in this section. Direct-material, direct-labour, and manufacturing-overhead costs are entered in Work-in-Process Inventory, from which they flow into Finished-Goods Inventory when the goods are finished, and then on into Cost of Goods Sold. Since DCdesserts.com produces perishable goods, which are produced and sold on the same day, a simpler procedure might be used. In DCdesserts.com's case, the *standard* costs of direct material, direct labour, and manufacturing overhead might be entered directly into Cost of Goods Sold as they are incurred. This simplification is feasible because the production process is very short and the goods are sold immediately, and thus there is never any work-in-process inventory or finished-goods inventory on hand. Such situations are common with producers of perishable goods.

     An analogous situation occurs with manufacturers that employ a just-in-time (JIT) production and inventory control system. In such an environment, raw materials are delivered just in time to be entered into production, and parts or components are manufactured in each stage of the production process just in time for the next stage. Thus, as in the case of perishable goods, there is little or no work-in-process or finished-goods inventory at any given time. For this reason, many manufacturers that employ the JIT approach make use of highly simplified cost accounting procedures similar to those just explained for DCdesserts.com.

APPENDIX B TO CHAPTER 10

Sales Variances

The variances discussed in this chapter focus on production costs. Managerial accountants also compute variances to help management analyze the firm's sales performance. To illustrate two commonly used sales variances, we will continue our discussion of DCdesserts.com. The expected sales price and standard variable cost for a multilayered fancy cake are as follows:

Budgeted sales price	$38
Standard variable costs:	
Direct material (1.4 kilograms × $5 per kilogram)..	$ 7
Direct labour (.5 hour × $20 per hour)...	10
Variable overhead (3 process hours at $5 per hour)	15
Total unit variable cost	$32

     During October, management expects to sell 1,500 multilayered fancy cakes. Based on this sales forecast, the controller computed the following budgeted **total contribution margin**.

Budgeted sales revenue (1,500 multilayered fancy cakes × $38)	$57,000
Budgeted variable costs (1,500 multilayered fancy cakes × $32)	48,000
Budgeted total contribution margin (1,500 multilayered fancy cakes × $6)	$ 9,000

The *actual* results for October were as follows:

Actual sales volume	1,600 cakes
Actual sales price	$37
Actual unit variable cost	$32

Using these actual results, the actual total contribution margin for October is as follows:

Actual sales revenue (1,600 multilayered fancy cakes × $37)	$59,200
Actual variable costs (1,600 multilayered fancy cakes × $32)	51,200
Actual total contribution margin (1,600 multilayered fancy cakes × $5)	$ 8,000

DCdesserts' actual and budgeted results for October are summarized in the following table. Notice that actual sales revenue exceeded budgeted sales revenue by $2,200. However, this favourable variance was more than offset by the additional $3,200 in variable costs resulting from actual sales volume exceeding budgeted sales volume. So the actual total contribution margin was $1,000 less than the budgeted total contribution margin, as this table shows:

	Budget	**Actual**	**Variance**
Revenue	$57,000	$59,200	$2,200 F
Variable costs	48,000	51,200	3,200 U
Contribution margin	$ 9,000	$ 8,000	$1,000 U

The managerial accountant computes two sales variances to explain the $2,200 favourable variance in sales revenue. These variances are defined and computed as follows:

$$\text{Sales-price variance} = \left(\begin{array}{c} \text{Actual} \\ \text{sales} \\ \text{price} \end{array} - \begin{array}{c} \text{Budgeted} \\ \text{sales} \\ \text{price} \end{array} \right) \times \text{Actual sales volume}$$

$$= (\$37 - \$38) \times 1,600$$

$$= \$1,600 \text{ Unfavourable}$$

$$\text{Sales-volume variance} = \left(\begin{array}{c} \text{Actual} \\ \text{sales} \\ \text{volume} \end{array} - \begin{array}{c} \text{Budgeted} \\ \text{sales} \\ \text{volume} \end{array} \right) \times \text{Budgeted sales price}$$

$$= (1,600 - 1,500) \times \$38$$

$$= \$3,800 \text{ Favourable}$$

Together, the **sales-price** and **sales-volume variances** explain the $2,200 favourable variance between actual and budgeted sales revenue.

Sales-price variance	$1,600 Unfavourable
Sales-volume variance	3,800 Favourable
Variance between actual and budgeted sales revenue	$2,200 Favourable

Review Questions

10–1. List the three parts of a control system, and explain how such a system works.

10–2. What is meant by the phrase management by exception?

10–3. Describe two methods of setting standards.

10–4. Distinguish between perfection and practical standards. Which type of standard is likely to produce the best motivational effects?

10–5. Explain how standard material prices and quantities are set.

10–6. What is the interpretation of the direct-material price variance? What manager is usually in the best position to influence the direct-material price variance?

10–7. What is the interpretation of the direct-material quantity variance? What manager is usually in the best position to influence the direct-material quantity variance?

10–8. Explain why the quantity purchased (PQ) is used in computing the direct-material price variance, but the actual quantity consumed (AQ) is used in computing the direct-material quantity variance.

10–9. What is the interpretation of the direct-labour rate variance? What are some possible causes? What manager is generally in the best position to influence the direct-labour rate variance?

10–10. What is the interpretation of the direct-labour efficiency variance? What manager is generally in the best position to influence the direct-labour efficiency variance?

10–11. Distinguish between static and flexible budgets. Explain the advantage of using a flexible budget.

10–12. Why are flexible overhead budgets based on an activity measure, such as hours of process time, machine time, or direct-labour hours?

10–13. What is the interpretation of the variable-overhead spending variance?

10–14. Jeffries Company's only variable-overhead cost is electricity. Does an unfavourable variable-overhead spending variance imply that the company paid more than the anticipated rate per kilowatt-hour?

10–15. What is the interpretation of the variable-overhead efficiency variance? Distinguish between the interpretations of the direct labour and variable-overhead efficiency variances.

10–16. What is the fixed-overhead budget variance? What is the correct interpretation of the fixed-overhead volume variance?

10–17. Describe a common but misleading interpretation of the fixed-overhead volume variance. Why is this interpretation misleading?

10–18. What types of organizations use flexible budgets?

10–19. Distinguish between the control purpose and the product-costing purpose of standard costing and flexible budgeting.

10–20. Why are fixed-overhead costs sometimes called capacity-producing costs?

10–21. Give one example of a plausible activity base to use in flexible budgeting for each of the following organizations: an insurance company, an express delivery service, a restaurant, and CRA.

10–22. Explain how an activity-based flexible budget differs from a conventional flexible budget.

Exercises

■ **Exercise 10–23**
Straightforward Computation of Variances
(LO 2)

Saskatchewan Can Company manufactures recyclable soft-drink cans. A unit of production is a case of 12 dozen cans. The following standards have been set by the production-engineering staff and the controller:

Direct labour:
 Quantity, .25 hour
 Rate, $12 per hour

Direct material:
 Quantity, 4 kilograms
 Price, $.60 per kilogram

Actual material purchases amounted to 240,000 kilograms at $.62 per kilogram. Actual costs incurred in the production of 50,000 units were as follows:

Direct labour $158,600 for 13,000 hours
Direct material $130,200 for 210,000 kilograms

Required:

1. Use the variance formulas to compute the direct-material price and quantity variances and the direct-labour rate and efficiency variances. Indicate whether each variance is favourable or unfavourable.

2. *Build a spreadsheet:* Construct an Excel spreadsheet to solve the preceding requirement. Show how the solution will change if the following information changes: the standard direct-labour rate is $14 per hour, and the standard direct-material price is $.59 per kilogram.

■ **Exercise 10–24**
Determination of Variances Using Diagrams
(LO 2)

Refer to the data in the preceding exercise. Use diagrams similar to those in Exhibits 10–2 and 10–3 to determine the direct-material and direct-labour variances. Indicate whether each variance is favourable or unfavourable.

■ **Exercise 10–25**
Developing Standards for New Products; Use of Internet
(LO 1)

Choose one of the following manufacturers (or any manufacturer of your choosing), and use the Internet to gather information about any new products the company has recently introduced or plans to introduce.

Boeing	www.boeing.com	Kodak	www.kodak.com
Caterpillar	www.caterpillar.com	Pfizer	www.pfizer.com
Ford	www.ford.com	Xerox	www.xerox.com

Required: Discuss the steps you think the company would go through in establishing standard costs for its new product.

Cayuga Hardwoods produces handcrafted jewellery boxes. A standard-size box requires 7 board metres of hardwood in the finished product. In addition, 1.5 board metres of scrap lumber are normally left from the production of one box. Hardwood costs $5 per board metre, plus $1.20 in transportation charges per board metre.

Required: Compute the standard direct-material cost of a jewellery box.

■ **Exercise 10–26**
Computing Standard Direct-Material Cost
(LO 1)

Choose a city or province, and use the Internet to explore the annual budget for the governmental unit you selected.

Required:

1. Select three items in the budget and explain how these items would be treated if the budget were converted to an activity-based flexible budget.
2. What would be appropriate cost drivers for the budgetary items you selected?

■ **Exercise 10–27**
City or Provincial Budget; Activity-Based Flexible Budget; Cost Drivers; Use of Internet
(LO 5, 8)

The following data are the actual results for Marvellous Marshmallow Company for August:

Actual output	13,500 cases
Actual variable overhead	$607,500
Actual fixed overhead	$183,000
Actual machine time	60,750 machine hours

■ **Exercise 10–28**
Straightforward Computation of Overhead Variances
(LO 6)

Standard cost and budget information for Marvellous Marshmallow Company follows:

Standard variable-overhead rate	$9 per machine hour
Standard quantity of machine hours	4 hours per case of marshmallows
Budgeted fixed overhead	$180,000 per month
Budgeted output	15,000 cases per month

Required:

1. Use any of the methods explained in the chapter to compute the following variances. Indicate whether each variance is favourable or unfavourable, where appropriate.
   a. Variable-overhead spending variance
   b. Variable-overhead efficiency variance
   c. Fixed-overhead budget variance
   d. Fixed-overhead volume variance
2. *Build a spreadsheet:* Construct an Excel spreadsheet to solve the preceding requirement. Show how the solution will change if the following information changes: actual output was 13,350 cases, and actual variable overhead was $609,000.

Outdoor Optics Company produces binoculars of two quality levels: field and professional. The field model requires four direct-labour hours, while the professional binoculars require six hours. The firm uses direct labour hours for flexible budgeting.

■ **Exercise 10–29**
Standard Hours Allowed; Flexible Budgeting; Multiple Products
(LO 3, 4)

Required:

1. How many standard hours are allowed in May, when 300 field models and 400 professional binoculars are manufactured?
2. Suppose the company based its flexible overhead budget for May on the number of binoculars manufactured, which is 700. What difficulties would this approach cause?

The controller for Rainbow Children's Hospital, located in Munich, Germany, estimates that the hospital uses 25 kilowatt-hours of electricity per patient-day, and that the electric rate will be .13 Euro per kilowatt-hour. The hospital also pays a fixed monthly charge of 2,000 Euros to the electric utility to rent emergency backup electric generators.

■ **Exercise 10–30**
Construct a Flexible Overhead Budget; Hospital
(LO 3, 4)

Required: Construct a flexible budget for the hospital's electricity costs using each of the following techniques:

1. Formula flexible budget.
2. Columnar flexible budget for 30,000, 40,000 and 50,000 patient-days of activity. List variable and fixed electricity costs separately.

Exercise 10–31
Interpretation of Variable-Overhead Efficiency Variance
(LO 6)

You recently received the following note from the production supervisor of the company where you serve as controller. "I don't understand these crazy variable-overhead efficiency variances. My employees are very careful in their use of electricity and manufacturing supplies, and we use very little indirect labour. What are we supposed to do?" Write a brief memo responding to the production supervisor's concern.

Exercise 10–32
Reconstruct Missing Information from Partial Data
(LO 3, 6)

You brought your work home one evening, and your nephew spilled his chocolate milk shake on the variance report you were preparing. Fortunately, you were able to reconstruct the obliterated information from the remaining data. Fill in the missing numbers below. (*Hint:* It is helpful to solve for the unknowns in the order indicated by the letters in the following table.)

Budgeted fixed overhead	$25,000
Actual fixed overhead	a
Budgeted production in units	12,500
Actual production in units	c
Standard machine hours per unit of output	4 hours
Standard variable-overhead rate per machine hour	$8
Actual variable-overhead rate per machine hour	b
Actual machine hours per unit of output	d
Variable-overhead spending variance	$ 36,000 U
Variable-overhead efficiency variance	$ 96,000 F
Fixed-overhead budget variance	$ 7,500 U
Fixed-overhead volume variance	g
Total actual overhead	$356,500
Total budgeted overhead (flexible budget)	e
Total budgeted overhead (static budget)	f
Total applied overhead	$408,000

Exercise 10–33
Activity-Based Flexible Budget
(LO 8)

Refer to DCdesserts.com's activity-based flexible budget in Exhibit 10–14. Suppose that the company's activity in June is described as follows:

Process hours	9,000
Production runs	12
New products tested	40
Direct material handled (kilograms)	30,000

Required:

1. Determine the flexible budgeted cost for each of the following:
   - a. Indirect material
   - b. Utilities
   - c. Inspection
   - d. Test kitchen
   - e. Material handling
   - f. Total overhead cost
2. Compute the variance for setup cost during the month, assuming that the actual setup cost was $3,500:
   - a. Using the activity-based flexible budget.
   - b. Using DCdesserts.com's conventional flexible budget (Exhibit 10–6).

Exercise 10–34
Overhead Variances
(LO 6)

Montoursville Control Company, which manufactures electrical switches, uses a standard-costing system. The standard manufacturing overhead costs per switch are based on direct-labour hours and are as follows:

Variable overhead (5 hrs. @ $12 per hr.)	$ 60
Fixed overhead (5 hrs. @ $18 per hr.)*	90
Total overhead	$150

*Based on capacity of 300,000 direct-labour hours per month.

Required:

1. Compute Wolfe's direct-material variances of each type of fertilizer.
2. Compute the direct-labour variances.
3. Compute the actual cost of the client applications. (*Note:* Exclude any fertilizer in inventory, as remaining fertilizer can be used next year.) Was the new service a financial success? Explain.
4. Analyze the variances that you computed in requirements (1) and (2).
   a. Was the new service a success from an overall cost-control perspective? Briefly discuss.
   b. What seems to have happened that would give rise to customer complaints?
5. In view of the complaints, should the fertilizer service be continued next year? Why?

SolarPrime, Inc. uses a standard-costing system to assist in the evaluation of operations. The company has had considerable trouble in recent months with suppliers and employees, so much so that management hired a new production supervisor, Frank Schmidt. The new supervisor has been on the job for five months and has seemingly brought order to an otherwise chaotic situation.

The vice-president of manufacturing recently commented that "Schmidt has really done the trick. The change to a new direct-material supplier and Schmidt's team-building/morale-boosting training exercises have truly brought things under control." The VP's comments were based on both a plant tour, where he observed a contented workforce, and a review of a performance report. Included in the report were the following variances: direct material, $4,620 favourable; and direct labour, $6,175 favourable. These variances are especially outstanding, given that the amounts are favourable and small. (SolarPrime's budgeted material and labour costs generally each average about $350,000 for similar periods.) Additional data follow.

- The company purchased and consumed 45,000 kilograms of direct materials at $7.70 per kilogram, and paid $16.25 per hour for 20,900 direct-labour hours of activity. Total completed production amounted to 9,500 units.
- A review of the firm's standard cost records found that each completed unit requires 4.2 kilograms of direct material at $8.80 per kilogram and 2.6 direct-labour hours at $14 per hour.

Required:

1. On the basis of the information contained in the performance report, should SolarPrime's management be concerned about its variances? Why?
2. Calculate the company's direct-material variances and direct-labour variances.
3. On the basis of your answers to requirement (2), should SolarPrime's management be concerned about its variances? Why?
4. Are things going as smoothly as the vice-president believes? Evaluate the company's variances and determine whether the change to a new supplier and Schmidt's team-building/morale-boosting training exercises appear to be working. Explain.
5. Is it possible that some of the company's current problems lie outside Schmidt's area of responsibility? Explain.

The director of cost management for Portland Instrument Corporation compares each month's actual results with a monthly plan. The standard direct-labour rates for the year just ended and the standard hours allowed, given the actual output in April, are shown in the following schedule:

	Standard Direct-Labour Rate per Hour	Standard Direct-Labour Hours Allowed, Given April Output
Labour class III	$24.00	1,000
Labour class II	21.00	1,000
Labour class I	15.00	1,000

A new union contract negotiated in March resulted in actual wage rates that differed from the standard rates. The actual direct-labour hours worked and the actual direct-labour rates per hour experienced for the month of April were as follows:

	Actual Direct-Labour Rate per Hour	Actual Direct-Labour Hours
Labour class III	$25.80	1,100
Labour class II	22.50	1,300
Labour class I	16.20	750

■ **Problem 10–41**
Analysis of Performance and Responsibility; Computing Variances
(LO 1, 2, 10)

2. Standard quantity allowed: 39,900 kilograms
2. Standard hours allowed: 24,700 hours

■ **Problem 10–42**
Direct-Labour Variances
(LO 1, 2, 10)

1. Direct-labour rate variance, labour class III: $1,980 U

Required:

1. Compute the following variances for April. Indicate whether each is favourable or unfavourable.

    a.   Direct-labour rate variance for *each* labour class

    b.   Direct-labour efficiency variance for *each* labour class

2. Discuss the advantages and disadvantages of a standard-costing system in which the standard direct-labour rates are not changed during the year to reflect such events as a new labour contract.

3. *Build a spreadsheet:* Construct an Excel spreadsheet to solve requirement (1) above. Show how the solution will change if the following information changes: the actual labour rates were $27, $22.90, and $17 for labour classes III, II, and I, respectively.

(CMA, adapted)

■ **Problem 10–43**
Development of Standard
Costs; Ethics
(LO 1, 10)

Ogwood Company's Johnstown Division is a small manufacturer of wooden household items. Al Rivkin, division controller, plans to implement a standard-costing system. Rivkin has collected information from several co-workers that will assist him in developing standards. One of the Johnstown Division's products is a wooden cutting board. Each cutting board requires 1.25 board metres of lumber and 12 minutes of direct-labour time to prepare and cut the lumber. The cutting boards are inspected after they are cut. Because the cutting boards are made of a natural material that has imperfections, one board is normally rejected for each five that are accepted. Four rubber foot pads are attached to each good cutting board. A total of 15 minutes of direct-labour time is required to attach all four foot pads and finish each cutting board. The lumber for the cutting boards cost $4 per board metre, and each foot pad costs $.10. Direct labour is paid at the rate of $8 per hour.

Required:

1. Develop the standard cost for direct material and direct labour of a cutting board.

2. Explain the role of each of the following people in developing standards:

    a.   Purchasing manager

    b.   Industrial engineer

    c.   Managerial accountant

3. The production manager complained that the standards are unrealistic, stifle motivation by concentrating only on unfavourable variances, and are out of date too quickly. He noted that his recent switch to cherry for the cutting boards has resulted in higher material costs but decreased labour hours. The net result was no increase in the total cost to produce the product. The monthly reports continue to show an unfavourable material variance and a favourable labour variance despite indications that the workers are slowing down.

    a.   Explain why a standard-costing system can strengthen cost management.

    b.   Give at least two reasons to explain why a standard-costing system could negatively impact the motivation of production employees.

■ **Problem 10–44**
Determining Standard
Costs; Ethics
(LO 1)

1. Standard cost per 10-gallon
batch, blending labour: $3.60

Concord Farms, located central California, produces items made from local farm products that are distributed to supermarkets. For many years, Concord's products have had strong regional sales on the basis of brand recognition; however, other companies have begun marketing similar products in the area, and price competition has become increasingly important. Doug Gilbert, the company's controller, is planning to implement a standard cost system for Concord and has gathered considerable information from his co-workers on production and material requirements for Concord's products. Gilbert believes that the use of standard costing will allow Concord to improve cost control and make better pricing decisions.

Concord's most popular product is strawberry jam. The jam is produced in 10-gallon batches, and each batch requires six quarts of good strawberries (1 gallon is approximately 3.8 litres and there are 4 quarts in a gallon). The fresh strawberries are sorted by hand before entering the production process. Because of imperfections in the strawberries and normal spoilage, one quart of berries is discarded for every four quarts of acceptable berries. Three minutes is the standard direct-labour time for sorting required to obtain one quart of acceptable strawberries. The acceptable strawberries are then blended with the other ingredients. Blending requires 12 minutes of direct-labour time per batch. After blending, the jam is packaged in quart containers. Gilbert has gathered the following information from Joe Adams, Concord's cost accountant:

- Concord purchases strawberries at a cost of $1.60 per quart. All other ingredients cost a total of $.90 per gallon.
- Direct labour is paid at the rate of $18 per hour.
- The total cost of material and labour required to package the jam is $.76 per quart.

Adams has a friend who owns a strawberry farm that has been losing money in recent years. Because of good crops, there has been an oversupply of strawberries, and prices have dropped to $1 per quart. Adams has arranged for Concord to purchase strawberries from his friend and hopes that $1.60 per quart will help his friend's farm become profitable again.

Required:

1. Develop the standard cost for the direct-cost components of a 10-gallon batch of strawberry jam. The standard cost should identify the following amounts for each direct-cost component of a batch of strawberry jam: (*a*) standard quantity, (*b*) standard price or rate, and (*c*) standard cost per batch.

2. Citing the specific ethical standards of competence, confidentiality, integrity, and credibility for management accountants, explain why Joe Adams' behaviour regarding the cost information provided to Doug Gilbert is unethical.

3. As part of the implementation of a standard-costing system at Concord Farms, Doug Gilbert plans to train those responsible for maintaining the standards in the use of variance analysis. Gilbert is particularly concerned with the causes of unfavourable variances. Discuss the possible causes of the following unfavourable variances and identify the individual(s) who should be held responsible: (*a*) direct-material price variance and (*b*) direct-labour efficiency variance.

(CMA, adapted)

■ **Problem 10–45**
Straightforward Overhead Variances
(LO 6)

Actual variable-overhead rate: $6.20 per hour
Budgeted fixed overhead: $900,000

Manitoba Paper Company produces paper for photocopiers. The company has developed standard overhead rates based on a monthly capacity of 90,000 direct-labour hours as follows:
Standard costs per unit (one box of paper):

Variable overhead (2 hrs. @ $6 per hr.)	$12
Fixed overhead (2 hrs. @ $10 per hr.)	20
Total	$32

During April, 45,000 units were scheduled for production; however, only 40,000 units were actually produced. The following data relate to June.

1. Actual direct-labour cost incurred was $1,567,500 for 82,500 actual hours of work.
2. Actual overhead incurred totalled $1,371,500, of which $511,500 was variable and $860,000 was fixed.

Required: Prepare two Exhibits similar to Exhibits 10–9 and 10–11 in the chapter, which show the following variances. State whether each variance is favourable or unfavourable, where appropriate.

1. Variable-overhead spending variance
2. Variable-overhead efficiency variance
3. Fixed-overhead budget variance
4. Fixed-overhead volume variance

(CMA, adapted)

■ **Problem 10–46**
Standard Hours Allowed; Flexible Budget; Multiple Products; Insurance Company
(LO 3, 4, 5)

1. Total standard hours allowed: 3,825

Rock Solid Insurance Company uses a flexible overhead budget for its application-processing department. The firm offers five types of policies, with the following standard hours allowed for clerical processing:

Automobile	1 hour
Renter's	1.5 hours
Homeowner's	2 hours
Health	2 hours
Life	5 hours

The following numbers of insurance applications were processed during May:

Automobile	375
Renter's	300
Homeowner's	150
Health	600
Life	300

The controller estimates that the variable-overhead rate in the application-processing department is $5 per hour, and that fixed-overhead costs will amount to $3,000 per month.

Required:

1. How many standard clerical hours are allowed in May, given actual application activity?
2. Why would it not be sensible to base the company's flexible budget on the number of applications processed instead of the number of clerical hours allowed?
3. Construct a formula flexible overhead budget for the company.
4. What is the flexible budget for total overhead cost in May?

■ **Problem 10–47**
Graphing Budgeted and
Applied Overhead;
Recording Studio
(LO 3, 4)

Countrytime Studios is a recording studio in Nashville. The studio budgets and applies overhead costs on the basis of production time. Countrytime's controller anticipates 10,000 hours of production time to be available during the year. The following overhead amounts have been budgeted for the year:

Variable overhead	$80,000
Fixed overhead	90,000

Required:

1. Draw two graphs, one for variable overhead and one for fixed overhead. The variable on the horizontal axis of each graph should be production time, in hours, ranging from 5,000 to 15,000 hours. The variable on the vertical axis of each graph should be overhead cost (variable or fixed). Each graph should include two lines, one for the flexible-budget amount of overhead and one for applied overhead.
2. Write a brief memo to Countrytime Studio's general manager, explaining the graph so that she will understand the concepts of budgeted and applied overhead.

■ **Problem 10–48**
Overhead Variances
(LO 6)

1*a*. Applied overhead costs:
$792,000

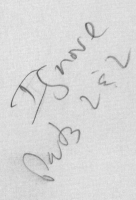

Wilmington Composites, Inc. developed its overhead application rate from the annual budget. The budget is based on an expected total output of 720,000 units requiring 3,600,000 machine hours. The company is able to schedule production uniformly throughout the year.

A total of 66,000 units requiring 315,000 machine hours were produced during March. Actual overhead costs for March amounted to $750,000. The actual costs, as compared to the annual budget and to one-twelfth of the annual budget, are as follows:

WILMINGTON COMPOSITES, INC. Annual Budget					
	Total Amount	Per Unit	Per Machine Hour	Monthly Budget	Actual Costs for May
Variable overhead:					
Indirect material	$2,448,000	$ 3.40	$ .68	$204,000	$222,000
Indirect labour	1,800,000	2.50	.50	150,000	150,000
Fixed overhead:					
Supervision	1,296,000	1.80	.36	108,000	102,000
Utilities	1,080,000	1.50	.30	90,000	108,000
Depreciation	2,016,000	2.80	.56	168,000	168,000
Total	$8,640,000	$12.00	$2.40	$720,000	$750,000

Required:

1. Prepare a schedule showing the following amounts for Wilmington Composites, Inc. for March:
   a. Applied overhead costs
   b. Variable-overhead spending variance

c. Fixed-overhead budget variance

d. Variable-overhead efficiency variance

e. Fixed-overhead volume variance

Where appropriate, be sure to indicate whether each variance is favourable or unfavourable.

2. Draw a graph similar to Exhibit 10–10 to depict the variable-overhead variances.

3. Why does your graph differ from Exhibit 10–10, other than the fact that the numbers differ?

(CMA, adapted)

Johnson Electrical produces industrial ventilation fans. The company plans to manufacture 72,000 fans evenly over the next quarter at the following costs: direct material, $2,880,000; direct labour, $720,000; variable manufacturing overhead, $900,000; and fixed manufacturing overhead, $1,800,000. The last amount includes $144,000 of straight-line depreciation and $216,000 of supervisory salaries.

Shortly after the conclusion of the quarter's first month, Johnson reported the following costs:

Direct material	$ 865,000
Direct labour	221,200
Variable manufacturing overhead	304,000
Depreciation	48,000
Supervisory salaries	75,600
Other fixed manufacturing overhead	478,000
Total	$1,991,800

Dave Kellerman and his crews turned out 20,000 fans during the month—a remarkable feat given that the firm's manufacturing plant was closed for several days because of storm damage and flooding.

Kellerman was especially pleased with the fact that overall financial performance for the period was favourable when compared with the budget. His pleasure, however, was very short-lived, as Johnson's general manager issued a stern warning that performance must improve, and improve quickly, if Kellerman had any hopes of keeping his job.

Required:

1. Explain the difference between a static budget and a flexible budget.

2. Which of the two budgets would be more useful when planning the company's cash needs over a range of activity?

3. Prepare a performance report that compares budgeted and actual costs for the period just ended (i.e., the report that Kellerman likely used when assessing his performance).

4. Prepare a performance report that compares budgeted and actual costs for the period just ended (i.e., the report that the general manager likely used when assessing Kellerman's performance).

5. Which of the two reports is preferred? Should Kellerman be praised for outstanding performance or is the general manager's warning appropriate? Explain, citing any apparent problems for the firm.

Valley View Hospital has an outpatient clinic. Jeffrey Harper, the hospital's chief administrator, is very concerned about cost control and has asked that performance reports be prepared that compare budgeted and actual amounts for medical assistants, clinic supplies, and lab tests. Past financial studies have shown that the cost of clinic supplies used is driven by the number of medical assistant labour hours worked, whereas lab tests are highly correlated with the number of patients served.
The following information is available for June:

- *Medical assistants.* Valley View's standard wage rate is $14 per hour, and each assistant is expected to spend 30 minutes with a patient. Assistants totalled 420 hours in helping the 790 patients seen, at an average pay rate of $15.50 per hour.

- *Clinic supplies.* The cost of clinic supplies used is budgeted at $12 per labour hour, and the actual cost of supplies used was $4,575.

- *Lab tests.* Actual lab tests for June cost $159,027 and averaged 3.3 per patient. Each patient is anticipated to have three lab tests, at an average budgeted cost of $65 per test.

Required:

1. Prepare a report that shows budgeted and actual costs for the 790 patients served during June. Compute the differences (variances) between these amounts and label them as favourable or unfavourable.

■ Problem 10–49
Budgets and Performance Evaluation
(LO 3, 7)

3. Direct material used: $40 per unit
4. Total variance: $141,800 U

■ Problem 10–50
Linkages between the Flexible Budget and Variances
(LO 3, 4, 6)

1. Lab tests, variance: $4,977 U
3. Variable-overhead efficiency variance: $15,405 U

2. On the basis of your answer to requirement (1), determine whether Valley View Hospital has any significant problems with respect to clinic supplies and lab tests. Briefly discuss your findings.

3. By performing a detailed analysis, determine the spending and efficiency variances for lab tests. Does it appear that Valley View Hospital has any significant problems with the cost of its lab tests? Briefly explain. (*Hint:* In applying the overhead variance formulas, think of the number of tests as analogous to the number of hours, and think of the cost per test as analogous to the variable overhead rate.)

4. Compare the lab test variance computed in requirement (1), a flexible-budget variance, with the sum of the variances in requirement (3). Discuss your findings and explain the relationship of flexible budget variances and standard cost variances for variable overhead.

■ **Problem 10–51**
Overhead Calculations;
Variance Interpretation
(LO 6)

3. Standard hours allowed:
5,350 hours
5. Applied overhead: $40,125

Maxwell Company uses a standard cost accounting system and applies manufacturing overhead to products on the basis of machine hours. The following information is available for the year just ended:

Actual variable overhead	$166,320
Actual total overhead	$467,700
Actual machine hours worked	23,100
Standard variable overhead rate per hour	$7.50
Standard fixed overhead rate per hour	$12
Planned activity during the period	20,000 machine hours
Actual production	10,700 finished units
Machine-hour standard	Two completed units per machine hour

Required:

1. Calculate the budgeted fixed overhead for the year.
2. Compute the variable-overhead spending variance.
3. Calculate the company's fixed-overhead volume variance.
4. Did the company spend more or less than anticipated for fixed overhead? How much?
5. Was variable overhead underapplied or overapplied during the year? By how much?
6. On the basis of the data presented, does it appear that the company suffered a lengthy strike during the year by its production workers? Briefly explain.

■ **Problem 10–52**
Flexible Budget; Performance
Report
(LO 3, 7)

2. Variance, total expenses:
$18,400 F

EduSoft Corporation's president, Mark Fletcher, was looking forward to seeing the performance reports for October because he knew the company's sales for the month had exceeded budget by a considerable margin. EduSoft, a distributor of educational software packages, had been growing steadily for approximately two years. Fletcher's biggest challenge at this point was to ensure that the company did not lose control of expenses during this growth period. When Fletcher received the October reports, he was dismayed to see the large unfavourable variance in the company's Monthly Selling Expense Report that follows.

EDUSOFT CORPORATION **Monthly Selling Expense Report** **For the Month of October**				
	Annual Budget	**October Budget**	**October Actual**	**October Variance**
Dollar sales	$160,000,000	$22,400,000	$24,800,000	$2,400,000
Unit sales	2,000,000	280,000	310,000	30,000
Orders processed	54,000	6,500	5,800	(700)
Sales personnel per month	90	90	96	(6)
Advertising	$39,600,000	$ 3,300,000	$ 3,320,000	$ 20,000 U
Staff salaries	3,000,000	250,000	250,000	—
Sales salaries	2,592,000	216,000	230,800	14,800 U
Commissions	6,400,000	896,000	992,000	96,000 U
Per diem expense	3,564,000	297,000	325,200	28,200 U
Office expenses	8,160,000	760,000	716,800	43,200 F
Shipping expenses	13,500,000	1,805,000	1,953,000	148,000 U
Total expenses	$76,816,000	$ 7,524,000	$ 7,787,800	$ 263,800 U

Fletcher called in the company's new controller, Susan Porter, to discuss the implications of the variances reported for October and to plan a strategy for improving performance. Porter suggested that the company's reporting format might not be giving Fletcher a true picture of the company's operations. She proposed that EduSoft implement flexible budgeting. Porter offered to redo the Monthly Selling Expense Report for October using flexible budgeting so that Fletcher could compare the two reports and see the advantages of flexible budgeting.

Porter discovered the following information about the behaviour of EduSoft's selling expenses:

- The total compensation paid to the sales force consists of a monthly base salary and a commission; the commission varies with sales dollars.
- Sales office expense is a mixed cost with the variable portion related to the number of orders processed. The fixed portion of office expense is $6,000,000 annually and is incurred uniformly throughout the year.
- Subsequent to the adoption of the annual budget for the current year, EduSoft decided to open a new sales territory. As a consequence, approval was given to hire six additional salespeople effective October 1. Porter decided that these additional six people should be recognized in her revised report.
- Per diem reimbursement to the sales force, while a fixed amount per day, is variable with the number of sales personnel and the number of days spent travelling. EduSoft's original budget was based on an average sales force of 90 people throughout the year with each salesperson travelling 15 days per month.
- The company's shipping expense is a mixed cost with the variable portion, $6 per unit, dependent on the number of units sold. The fixed portion is incurred uniformly throughout the year.

Required:

1. Citing the benefits of flexible budgeting, explain why Susan Porter would propose that EduSoft use flexible budgeting in this situation.
2. Prepare a revised Monthly Selling Expense Report for October that would permit Mark Fletcher to more clearly evaluate EduSoft's control over selling expenses. The report should have a line for each selling expense item showing the appropriate budgeted amount, the actual selling expense, and the monthly dollar variance.

(CMA, adapted)

LakeMaster Company manufactures outboard motors that are sold throughout Canada and the United States. The company uses a comprehensive budgeting process and compares actual results to budgeted amounts on a monthly basis. Each month, LakeMaster's accounting department prepares a variance analysis and distributes the report to all responsible parties. Al Richmond, production manager, is upset about the results for June. Richmond, who is responsible for the cost of goods manufactured, has implemented several cost cutting measures in the manufacturing area and is discouraged by the unfavourable variance in variable costs.

■ Problem 10–53
Flexible Budgeting; Variances; Impact on Behaviour
(LO 3, 4, 6)

1. Flexible budget, operating income: $183,600
2. Flexible-budget variance, operating income: $68,000 U

LAKEMASTER COMPANY Operating Results For the Month of June			
	Master Budget	Actual	Variance
Units sold	5,000	4,800	200 U
Revenue	$1,800,000	$1,728,000	72,000 U
Variable cost	1,140,000	1,170,000	30,000 U
Contribution margin	$ 660,000	558,000	102,000 U
Fixed overhead	270,000	270,000	—
Fixed general and administrative cost	180,000	172,500	7,500 F
Operating income	$ 210,000	$ 115,500	$94,500 U

When the master budget was prepared, LakeMaster's cost accountant, Joan Ballard, supplied the following unit costs: direct material, $90; direct labour, $66; variable overhead, $54; and variable selling, $18.

The total variable costs of $1,170,000 for June include $480,000 for direct material, $288,000 for direct labour, $264,000 for variable overhead, and $138,000 for variable selling expenses. Ballard believes that LakeMaster's monthly reports would be more meaningful to everyone if the company adopted flexible budgeting and prepared more detailed analyses.

Required:

1. Prepare a flexible budget for LakeMaster Company for the month of June that includes separate variable-cost budgets for each type of cost (direct material, etc.).

2. Determine the variance between the flexible budget and actual cost for each cost item.

3. Discuss how the revised budget and variance data are likely to impact the behaviour of Al Richmond, the production manager.

4. *Build a spreadsheet:* Construct an Excel spreadsheet to solve requirements (1) and (2) above. Show how the solution will change if the following information changes: actual sales amounted to 4,700 units, and actual fixed overhead was $272,000.

(CMA, adapted)

■ **Problem 10–54**

Finding Missing Data; Overhead Accounting

(LO 3, 6)

Case A(2), standard fixed overhead rate: $21 per hour
Case B(2), standard fixed overhead rate: $9 per hour

For each of the following independent cases, fill in the missing information. The company budgets and applies manufacturing-overhead costs on the basis of direct-labour hours. (U denotes *unfavourable variance*; F denotes *favourable variance*.)

	Case A	Case B
1. Standard variable-overhead rate	$7.50 per hour	? per hour
2. Standard fixed-overhead rate	? per hour	? per hour
3. Total standard overhead rate	? per hour	$13 per hour
4. Flexible budget for variable overhead	$270,000	?
5. Flexible budget for fixed overhead	$630,000	?
6. Actual variable overhead	?	?
7. Actual fixed overhead	$621,000	?
8. Variable-overhead spending variance	$16,650 U	$8,000 U
9. Variable-overhead efficiency variance	?	$1,600 F
10. Fixed-overhead budget variance	?	$4,320 U
11. Fixed-overhead volume variance	?	$14,400 U (positive sign)
12. Under- (or over-) applied variable overhead	?	?
13. Under- (or over-) applied fixed overhead	?	?
14. Budgeted production (in units)	5,000 units	?
15. Standard direct-labour hours per unit	6 hours per unit	8 hours per unit
16. Actual production (in units)	?	?
17. Standard direct-labour hours allowed, given actual production	36,000 hours	6,400 hours
18. Actual direct-labour hours	37,000 hours	6,000 hours
19. Applied variable overhead	?	?
20. Applied fixed overhead	?	?

■ **Problem 10–55**

Preparing and Using a Columnar Flexible Budget; Tour Company; Ethical Issues

(LO 3, 4, 7)

1. Activity level (32,000 air miles), total expenses: $306,600
4. Variance, total expenses: $3,600 U

Foliage Sky Tours is a small sightseeing tour company in Quebec. The firm specializes in aerial tours of the countryside during September and October, when the fall colour is at its peak. Until recently, the company had not had an accounting department. Routine bookkeeping tasks, such as billing, had been handled by an individual who had little formal training in accounting. As the business began to grow, however, the owner recognized the need for more formal accounting procedures. Jacqueline Frost has recently been hired as the new controller, and she will have the authority to hire an assistant.

During her first week on the job, Frost was given the following performance report. The report was prepared by Red Leif, the company's manager of aircraft operations, who was planning to present it to the owner the next morning. "Look at these favourable variances for fuel and so forth," Leif pointed out, as he showed the report to Frost. "My operations people are really doing a great job." Later that day, Frost looked at the performance report more carefully. She immediately realized that it was improperly prepared and would be misleading to the company's owner.

	FOLIAGE SKY TOURS Performance Report For the Month of September			
	Formula Flexible Budget (per air mile)	**Actual (32,000 air miles)**	**Static Budget (35,000 air miles)**	**Variance**
Passenger revenue..............................	$10.50	$336,000	$367,500	$31,500 U
Less: Variable expenses:				
Fuel...	1.50	51,000	52,500	1,500 F
Aircraft maintenance.........................	2.25	70,500	78,750	8,250 F
Flight crew salaries..........................	1.20	39,300	42,000	2,700 F
Selling and administrative	2.40	74,700	84,000	9,300 F
Total variable expenses	7.35	235,500	257,250	21,750 F
Contribution margin	$ 3.15	100,500	110,250	9,750 U
Less: Fixed expenses:	**Per Month**			
Depreciation on aircraft....................	$ 8,700	8,700	8,700	$0
Landing fees	2,700	3,000	2,700	300 U
Supervisory salaries.........................	27,000	25,800	27,000	1,200 F
Selling and administrative	33,000	37,200	33,000	4,200 U
Total fixed expenses	$71,400	74,700	71,400	3,300 U
Net income.......................................		$ 25,800	$ 38,850	$13,050 U

Required:

1. Prepare a columnar flexible budget for Foliage Sky Tours' expenses, based on the following activity levels: 32,000 air miles, 35,000 air miles, and 38,000 air miles.

2. In spite of several favourable expense variances shown on the report above, the company's September net income was only about two-thirds of the expected level. Why?

3. Write a brief memo to the manager of aircraft operations explaining why the original variance report is misleading.

4. Prepare a revised expense variance report for September, which is based on the flexible budget prepared in requirement (1).

5. Jacqueline Frost presented the revised expense report to Leif along with the memo explaining why the original performance report was misleading. Leif did not take it well. He complained of Frost's "interference" and pointed out that the company had been doing just fine without her. "I'm taking my report to the owner tomorrow," Leif insisted. "Yours just makes us look bad." What are Frost's ethical obligations in this matter? What should she do?

Western Auto Parts Company manufactures replacement parts for automobile repair. The company recently installed a flexible manufacturing system (FMS), which has significantly changed the production process. The installation of the new FMS was not anticipated when the current year's budget and cost structure were developed. The installation of the new equipment was hastened by several major breakdowns in the company's old production machinery.

The new equipment was very expensive, but management expects it to cut the labour time required by a substantial amount. Management also expects the new equipment to allow a reduction in direct material waste. On the negative side, the FMS requires a more highly skilled labour force to operate it than the company's old equipment.

The following cost variance report was prepared for the month of May, the first full month after the equipment was installed:

Problem 10–56
Interactions between Variances; Flexible Manufacturing System

(LO 6)

WESTERN AUTO PARTS COMPANY Cost Variance Report For the Month of May	
Direct material:	
Standard cost	$301,225
Actual cost	299,350
Direct-material price variance	75 U*
Direct-material quantity variance	1,950 F
Direct labour:	
Standard cost	196,500
Actual cost	191,900
Direct-labour rate variance	2,400 U
Direct-labour efficiency variance	7,000 F
Manufacturing overhead:	
Applied to work in process	200,000
Actual cost	204,000
Variable-overhead spending variance	4,000 U
Variable-overhead efficiency variance	5,000 F
Fixed-overhead budget variance	15,000 U
Fixed-overhead volume variance	(10,000)†

*F denotes favourable variance; U denotes unfavourable variance.

†The sign of the volume variance is negative; applied fixed overhead exceeded budgeted fixed overhead.

Required: Comment on the possible interactions between the variances listed in the report. Which ones are likely to have been caused by the purchase of the new production equipment? The company budgets and applies manufacturing overhead on the basis of direct-labour hours.

■ **Problem 10–57**
Flexible Budget; Improved
Performance Report;
Behavioural Issues
(LO 3, 7)

WoodCrafts, Inc. is a manufacturer of furniture for specialty shops and has an annual sales volume of $24 million. The company has four major product lines: bookcases, magazine racks, end tables, and barstools. Each line is managed by a production manager. Since production is spread fairly evenly over the 12 months of operation, Sara McKinley, WoodCrafts' controller, has prepared an annual budget divided into 12 periods for monthly reporting purposes.

WoodCrafts uses a standard-costing system and applies variable overhead on the basis of process hours. Fixed production cost is allocated on the basis of square metre occupied using a predetermined plantwide rate; the size of the space occupied varies considerably across the product lines. All other costs are assigned on the basis of revenue dollars earned. At the monthly meeting to review November performance, Steve Clark, manager of the bookcase line, received the following report:

WOODCRAFTS, INC. Bookcase Production Performance Report For the Month of November			
	Actual	**Budget**	**Variance**
Units	3,000	2,500	500 F
Revenue	$483,000	$412,500	$70,500 F
Variable production costs:			
Direct material	69,300	60,000	9,300 U
Direct labour	54,900	45,000	9,900 U
Machine time	57,600	48,750	8,850 U
Manufacturing overhead	123,000	105,000	18,000 U
Fixed production costs:			
Indirect labour	28,200	18,000	10,200 U
Depreciation	16,500	16,500	—
Property taxes	7,200	6,900	300 U
Insurance	13,500	13,500	—
Administrative expenses	36,000	27,000	9,000 U
Marketing expenses	24,900	21,000	3,900 U
Research and development	18,000	13,500	4,500 U
Total expenses	449,100	375,150	73,950 U
Operating income	$ 33,900	$ 37,350	$ 3,450 U

While distributing the monthly reports at the meeting, McKinley remarked to Clark, "We need to talk about getting your division back on track. Be sure to see me after the meeting."

Clark had been so convinced that his division did well in November that McKinley's remark was a real surprise. He spent the balance of the meeting avoiding the looks of his fellow managers and trying to figure out what could have gone wrong. The monthly performance report was no help.

Required:

1. *a.* Identify three weaknesses in WoodCrafts, Inc.'s monthly Bookcase Production Performance Report.
   b. Discuss the behavioural implications of Sara McKinley's remarks to Steve Clark during the meeting.
2. WoodCrafts, Inc. could do a better job of reporting monthly performance to the production managers.
   a. Recommend how the report could be improved to eliminate weaknesses, and revise it accordingly.
   b. Discuss how the recommended changes in reporting are likely to affect Steve Clark's behaviour.

(CMA, adapted)

Williamsport Wheel and Axle, Inc. has an automated production process, and production activity is quantified in terms of process hours. A standard-costing system is used. The annual static budget for 20x4 called for 6,000 units to be produced, requiring 30,000 machine hours. The standard overhead rate for the year was computed using this planned level of production. The 20x4 manufacturing cost report follows.

■ **Problem 10–58**
Using a Flexible Budget
(LO 3, 4, 6)

7. Actual variable overhead: $618,000
11. Standard allowed machine hours: 30,250

	Static Budget	Flexible Budget		
WILLIAMSPORT WHEEL AND AXLE, INC. Manufacturing Cost Report for 20x4 (in thousands of dollars)				
Cost Item	30,000 Machine Hours	31,000 Machine Hours	32,000 Machine Hours	Actual Cost
Direct material:				
A42 aluminum..	$ 504.0	$ 520.8	$ 537.6	$ 540.0
S18 steel alloy......................................	156.0	161.2	166.4	166.0
Direct labour:				
Assembler...	546.0	564.2	582.4	574.0
Grinder	468.0	483.6	499.2	500.0
Manufacturing overhead:				
Maintenance	48.0	49.6	51.2	50.0
Supplies..	258.0	266.6	275.2	260.0
Supervision	160.0	164.0	168.0	162.0
Inspection	288.0	294.0	300.0	294.0
Insurance..	100.0	100.0	100.0	100.0
Depreciation...	400.0	400.0	400.0	400.0
Total cost	$2,928.0	$3,004.0	$3,080.0	$3,046.0

Williamsport develops flexible budgets for different levels of activity for use in evaluating performance. A total of 6,200 units was produced during 20x4, requiring 32,000 machine hours. The preceding manufacturing cost report compares the company's actual cost for the year with the static budget and the flexible budget for two different activity levels.

Required: Compute the following amounts. For variances, indicate whether favourable or unfavourable where appropriate. Answers should be rounded to two decimal places when necessary.

1. The standard number of machine hours allowed to produce one unit of product

2. The actual cost of direct material used in one unit of product

3. The cost of material that should be processed per machine hour

4. The standard direct-labour cost for each unit produced

5. The variable-overhead rate per machine hour in a flexible-budget formula (*Hint:* Use the high-low method to estimate cost behaviour.)

6. The standard fixed-overhead rate per machine hour used for product costing

7. The variable-overhead spending variance (Assume management has determined that the actual fixed overhead cost in 20x4 amounted to $648,000.)

8. The variable-overhead efficiency variance

9. The fixed-overhead budget variance

10. The fixed-overhead volume variance. [Make the same assumption as in requirement (7).]

11. The total budgeted manufacturing cost (in thousands of dollars) for an output of 6,050 units. (*Hint:* Use the flexible-budget formula.)

(CMA, adapted)

■ **Problem 10–59**
Complete Analysis of Cost Variances
(LO 6)

1. Standard quantity: 14,500 kilograms
1. Standard hours: 3,625 hrs.

Ice Box Gourmet, Inc. produces containers of frozen food. During April, Ice Box produced 725 cases of food and incurred the following actual costs:

Variable overhead	$ 5,500
Fixed overhead	13,000
Actual labour cost (4,000 direct-labour hours)	75,600
Actual material cost (15,000 kilograms purchased and used)	33,000

Standard cost and annual budget information are as follows:

Standard Costs per Case

Direct labour (5 hrs. @ $18 per hr.)	$ 90.00
Direct material (20 kg @ $2 per kg)	40.00
Variable overhead (5 hrs. @ $1.50 per hr.)	7.50
Fixed overhead (5 hrs. @ $3 per hr.)	15.00
Total	$152.50

Annual Budget Information

Variable overhead	$75,000
Fixed overhead	$150,000
Planned activity for year	50,000 direct-labour hours

Required:

1. Prepare as complete an analysis of cost variances as is possible from the available data.

2. *Build a spreadsheet:* Construct an Excel spreadsheet to solve the preceding requirement. Show how the solution will change if the following information changes: the standard rates were $17.50 per hour for direct labour, and $1.60 per direct-labour hour for variable overhead.

■ **Problem 10–60**
Investigating Cost Variances
(LO 9)

McKeag Corporation manufactures agricultural machinery. At a recent staff meeting, the following direct-labour variance report for the year just ended was presented by the controller:

McKEAG CORPORATION				
Direct-Labour Variance Report				
	Direct-Labour Rate Variance		Direct-Labour Efficiency Variance	
	Amount	Standard Cost, %	Amount	Standard Cost, %
January	$ 1,600 F	.16%	$ 10,000 U	1.00%
February	9,800 F	.98%	15,000 U	1.50%
March	200 U	.02%	19,400 U	1.94%
April	4,000 U	.40%	25,600 U	2.56%
May	7,600 F	.76%	40,200 U	4.02%
June	7,800 F	.78%	34,000 U	3.40%
July	8,400 F	.84%	57,000 U	5.70%
August	10,200 F	1.02%	76,000 U	7.60%
September	9,600 F	.96%	74,000 U	7.40%
October	11,400 F	1.14%	84,000 U	8.40%
November	8,400 F	.84%	120,000 U	12.00%
December	8,600 F	.86%	104,000 U	10.40%

McKeag's controller uses the following rule of thumb: Investigate all variances equal to or greater than $60,000, which is 6 percent of standard cost.

Required:

1. Which variances would have been investigated during the year? (Indicate month and type of variance.)

2. What characteristics of the variance pattern shown in the report should draw the controller's attention, regardless of the usual investigation rule? Explain. Given these considerations, which variances would you have investigated? Why?

3. Is it important to follow up on favourable variances, such as those shown in the report? Why?

McCartney Company manufactures guitars. The company uses a standard, job-order cost-accounting system in two production departments. In the Construction Department, the wooden guitars are built by highly skilled craftsmen and coated with several layers of lacquer. Then the units are transferred to the Finishing Department, where the bridge of the guitar is attached and the strings are installed. The guitars are also tuned and inspected in the Finishing Department. The diagram below depicts the production process.

■ **Problem 10–61**
Comprehensive Problem on Variance Analysis
(LO 1, 2)

1. Construction, total standard cost of direct material: $72,000
3. Finishing, direct-labour rate variance: $2,355 U

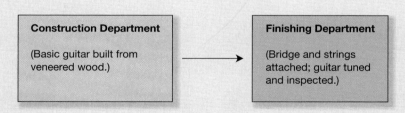

Each finished guitar contains seven kilograms of veneered wood. In addition, one kilogram of wood is typically wasted in the production process. The veneered wood used in the guitars has a standard price of $12 per kilogram. The other parts needed to complete each guitar, such as the bridge and strings, cost $15 per guitar. The labour standards for McCartney's two production departments are as follows:

Construction Department	6 hours of direct labour at $20 per hour
Finishing Department	3 hours of direct labour at $15 per hour

The following pertains to the month of July:

1. There were no beginning or ending work-in-process inventories in either production department.

2. There was no beginning finished-goods inventory.

3. Actual production was 750 guitars, and 450 guitars were sold on account for $390 each.

4. The company purchased 9,000 kilograms of veneered wood at a price of $12.50 per kilogram.
5. Actual usage of veneered wood was 6,750 kilograms.
6. Enough parts (bridges and strings) to finish 900 guitars were purchased at a cost of $13,500.
7. The Construction Department used 4,275 direct-labour hours. The total direct-labour cost in the Construction Department was $81,225.
8. The Finishing Department used 2,355 direct-labour hours. The total direct-labour cost in that department was $37,680.
9. There were no direct-material variances in the Finishing Department.

Required:

1. Prepare a schedule that computes the standard costs of direct material and direct labour in each production department and in total for the month of July.
2. Prepare three exhibits that compute the July direct-material and direct-labour variances in the Construction Department and the July direct-labour variances in the Finishing Department. (Refer to Exhibits 10–2 and 10–3 for guidance.)
3. Prepare a cost variance report for July similar to that shown in Exhibit 10–16.

Cases

■ **Case 10–62**
Missing Data; Variances
(LO 1, 2)

2a. Standard quantity per drum, material B: 5 L.
3g. Rate variance, labour class II: $615 F

MacGyver Corporation manufactures a product called Miracle Goo, which comes in handy for just about anything. The thick, tarry substance is sold in six-litre drums. Two raw materials are used, referred to as "A" and "B" by people in the business. Two types of labour are required also: "mixers" (labour class I) and "packers" (labour class II). You were recently hired by the company president, Pete Thorn, to be the controller. You soon learned that MacGyver uses a standard-costing system. Variances are computed and closed into Cost of Goods Sold monthly. After your first month on the job, you gathered the necessary data to compute the month's variances for direct material and direct labour. You finished everything up by 5:00 p.m. on the 31st, including the credit to Cost of Goods Sold for the sum of the variances. You decided to take all your notes home to review them prior to your formal presentation to Thorn first thing in the morning. As an afterthought, you grabbed a drum of Miracle Goo as well, thinking it could prove useful in some unanticipated way.

You spent the evening boning up on the data for your report and were ready to call it a night. As luck would have it, though, you knocked over the Miracle Goo as you rose from the kitchen table. The stuff splattered everywhere, and, most unfortunately, obliterated most of your notes. All that remained legible was the following information:

Direct Material A: Quantity Variance		Direct Material B: Price Variance	
3,750		1,800	

Direct Labour I: Rate Variance		Direct Labour II: Efficiency Variance	
900		1,800	

Cost of Goods Sold		Accounts Payable		
214,500			2,250	Beg. bal.
	2,265	105,000	109,800	
			7,050	End. bal.

Other assorted data gleaned from your notes:

- The standards for each drum of Miracle Goo include 10 kilograms of material A at a standard price of $5 per kilogram.

- The standard cost of material B is $15 for each drum of Miracle Goo.
- Purchases of material A were 18,000 kilograms at $4.50 per kilogram.
- Given the actual output for the month, the standard allowed quantity of material A was 15,000 kilograms. The standard allowed quantity of material B was 7,500 litres.
- Although 9,000 litres of B were purchased, only 7,200 litres were used.
- The standard wage rate for mixers is $15 per hour. The standard labour cost per drum of product for mixers is $30 per drum.
- The standards allow 4 hours of direct labour II (packers) per drum of Miracle Goo. The standard labour cost per drum of product for packers is $48 per drum.
- Packers were paid $11.90 per hour during the month.

You happened to remember two additional facts. There were no beginning or ending inventories of either work in process or finished goods for the month. The increase in accounts payable relates to direct-material purchases only.

Required: Now you've got a major problem. Somehow you've got to reconstruct all the missing data in order to be ready for your meeting with the president. You start by making the following list of the facts you want to use in your presentation. Before getting down to business, you need a brief walk to clear your head. Out to the trash you go, and toss the remaining Miracle Goo.

Fill in the missing amounts in this list, using the available facts:

1. Actual output (in drums): _____
2. Direct material:

	A	B
a. Standard quantity per drum	_____	_____
b. Standard price	_____	_____
c. Standard cost per drum	_____	_____
d. Standard quantity allowed, given actual output	_____	_____
e. Actual quantity purchased	_____	_____
f. Actual price	_____	_____
g. Actual quantity used	_____	_____
h. Price variance	_____	_____
i. Quantity variance	_____	_____

3. Direct labour:

	I (mixers)	II (packers)
a. Standard hours per drum	_____	_____
b. Standard rate per hour	_____	_____
c. Standard cost per drum	_____	_____
d. Standard quantity allowed, given actual output	_____	_____
e. Actual rate per hour	_____	_____
f. Actual hours	_____	_____
g. Rate variance	_____	_____
h. Efficiency variance	_____	_____

4. Total of all variances for the month: _____

Your next-door neighbour recently began a new job as assistant controller for Conundrum Corporation. As her first assignment, she prepared a performance report for March. She was scheduled to present the report to management the next morning, so she brought it home to review. Unfortunately, her dog thought the report was an object to be fetched. The pup made a flying leap and got a firm grip on the report. After chasing the dog around the house, she managed to wrest the report from its teeth. Needless to say, it was torn to bits. Only certain data are legible on the report. This information follows:

■ Case 10–63
Integrative; Drawing
Conclusion from Missing Data
(LO 3, 4, 6)

5. Direct-labour rate variance: $13,200 U
8. Direct-material quantity variance: $9,000 U

CONUNDRUM CORPORATION
Performance Report for the Month of March

	Direct Material	Direct Labour	Variable Overhead	Fixed Overhead
Standard allowed cost given actual output	?	?		
	(? kilograms at $18 per kilogram)	(2 hours at $21 per hour)		
Flexible overhead budget...................................			?	$60,000
Actual cost	$283,500	?	?	?
	(14,000 kilograms at $20.25 per kilogram)	(8,800 hours at ? per hour)		
Direct-material price variance	?			
Direct-material quantity variance........................	$9,000 U			
Direct-labour rate variance		$13,200 U		
Direct-labour efficiency variance		4,200 F		
Variable-overhead spending variance			$3,960 U	
Variable-overhead efficiency variance			1,800 F	
Fixed-overhead budget variance				$4,875 U
Fixed-overhead volume variance				?

In addition to the fragmentary data still legible on the performance report, she happened to remember the following facts:

- Planned production of Conundrum's sole product was 500 units more than the actual production.
- All of the direct material purchased in January was used in production.
- There were no beginning or ending inventories.
- Variable and fixed overhead are applied on the basis of direct-labour hours. The fixed overhead rate is $6 per hour.

Required: She needs to reconstruct the following facts, which will be necessary for her presentation:

1. Planned production (in units)
2. Actual production (in units)
3. Actual fixed overhead
4. Total standard allowed direct-labour hours
5. Actual direct-labour rate
6. Standard variable-overhead rate
7. Actual variable-overhead rate
8. Standard direct-material quantity per unit
9. Direct-material price variance
10. Applied fixed overhead
11. Fixed-overhead volume variance

Chapter Eleven

Cost Management Tools

FOCUS COMPANY

 CANADIAN PACIFIC BANK

This chapter's Focus Company is Canadian Pacific Bank (CPB), a chartered bank headquartered in Vancouver with principal operations in western Canada. CPB's use of the balanced scorecard helps management and employees focus on the customer, internal operations, and learning and growth areas of the business, so that ultimately the bank's long-term financial goals will be attained.

IN CONTRAST

In contrast to the financial-services industry of Canadian Pacific Bank, we will turn to a manufacturing company to explore the

management of product quality and environmental costs. Handico manufactures cordless telephones. Using the Handico illustration, we will explore various types of quality-related costs incurred in manufacturing companies. We also will discuss how companies try to identify and manage a variety of environmental costs.

After completing this chapter, you should be able to:

1   Describe the balanced scorecard concept and explain the reasoning behind it.

2   Describe the operational performance measures appropriate for today's manufacturing environment.

3   Define and give an example of target costing.

4   Explain the concept of kaizen costing and prepare a kaizen costing chart.

5   Briefly explain the concepts of benchmarking, reengineering, and the theory of constraints.

6   Prepare a quality cost report.

7   Discuss the traditional and contemporary views of the optimal level of product quality.

8   Understand the different types of environmental costs and discuss environmental cost management.

Managers of the most successful organizations do not rely on either financial or nonfinancial performance measures alone. They recognize that financial performance measures summarize the results of past actions. These measures are important to a firm's owners, creditors, employees, and so forth. Thus, they must be watched carefully by management as well. Nonfinancial performance measures concentrate on *current* activities, which will be the drivers of *future* financial performance. Thus, effective management requires a balanced perspective on performance measurement, a viewpoint that some call the *balanced scorecard* perspective.

In the new manufacturing environment, operational measures are also being developed to control key aspects of the production process. A JIT philosophy demands adherence to strict quality standards for raw materials, manufactured components, and finished products. Nonfinancial data are vital for assessing a manufacturer's effectiveness in maintaining product quality.

Learning Objective 1

Describe the balanced scorecard concept and explain the reasoning behind it.

The Balanced Scorecard

The **balanced scorecard** is a model of business performance evaluation that balances measures of financial performance, internal operations, innovation and learning, and customer satisfaction.[1]

Management **A**ccounting **P**ractice

United Parcel Service (UPS)

THE BALANCED SCORECARD

For many companies, the balanced scorecard plays a key role in formulating strategy. According to a survey by Bain & Company, approximately 50 percent of Fortune 1000 companies in North America and roughly 40 percent in Europe use some version of the balanced scorecard (often abbreviated BSC). Among them are both manufacturers and service industry companies.[2]

Managers at United Parcel Service (UPS) believe that its balanced scorecard has played a critical strategic role in moving the organization forward. The company's scorecard was widely accepted by its employees, who felt that the BSC helped them link their jobs to the big picture of overall company success. UPS includes the following key measures in the four perspectives of its balanced scorecard.[3]

Financial

- Profit
- Revenue
- Cost
- Volume

Internal Operations

- Quality (e.g., timeliness of delivery, care in handling parcels)
- Operations (i.e., operational efficiency)

Customer

- Customer claims (e.g., lost parcels)
- Customer concerns
- Data integrity (e.g., accuracy of the parcel tracking process)

Learning and Growth*

- Employee injuries
- Employee retention
- Employee relation index

*The heading used on the UPS scorecard is "People."

"The balanced scorecard is a communication, information, and learning system. Building a scorecard helps managers link today's actions with the achievement of today's priorities." (11a)

City of Charlotte, North Carolina

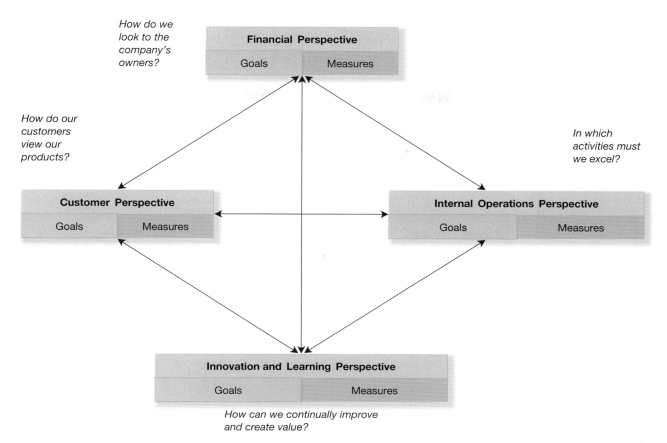

How do we look to the company's owners?

How do our customers view our products?

In which activities must we excel?

How can we continually improve and create value?

Exhibit 11–1
Hypothetical Balanced Scorecard

If an organization is to remain viable in a changing and ever more competitive business environment, its managers need to continually ask the questions emphasized in the balanced scorecard. A management team has to be concerned with the cost-effectiveness of their company's business processes as well as its products and/or services. Management has to continually monitor the needs of its customers and assess their level of satisfaction with the products sold and/or services provided. The company's overall financial strength also has to be prominent in management's thinking. Finally, are the company's products keeping up with the times in terms of popular culture and technology? Are the company's employees providing the innovation critical to the company's future success?

Let's think about the goals and measures that top management might consider for the balanced scorecard depicted in Exhibit 11–1. According to its Web site, the company's "primary financial goals are to maximize earnings and cash flow, and to allocate capital profitably toward growth initiatives that will drive long-term shareholder value." So the company's *financial perspective* would include such measures as earnings, earnings per share, and cash flow.

Now the question is, For the company to achieve its *financial goals* in *the future*, what does it need to be doing *now* in the balanced scorecard's *other three perspectives*? For its *customer perspective*, the company might use surveys to access customer satisfaction with its products, as well as collect more objective data such as the number of customer claims or product returns. For the *learning and growth perspective*, the company might focus on the percentage of sales obtained from new products and services, and the average time from initial design to production. For its *internal operations perspective*, the company might focus on measures such as the percentage reduction in scraps/waste, the percentage improvement

"[We are] a partner with all of the other functions in the business here. We are an equal partner with our product groups, with the engineering and manufacturing cohorts in making sure this business is a success."
(11b)
                    Caterpillar

How do we look to the firm's owners?

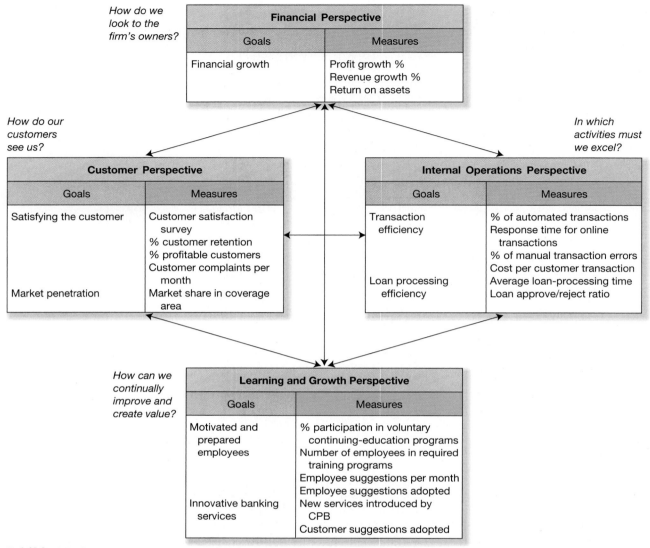

Exhibit 11–2
Balanced Scorecard:
Canadian Pacific Bank

in labour productivity, the number of defects and number of items reworked, and so forth. The key point of the balanced scorecard concept is that by focusing on measures of performance *now* in these three key perspectives, the company can achieve its financial goals in the *future*.

To illustrate the balanced scorecard, we will explore its use by Canadian Pacific Bank (CPB). The bank's balanced scorecard, depicted in Exhibit 11–2, integrates performance measures in four key areas: financial, internal operations, customer, and learning and growth.[4] What is the rationale behind CPB's scorecard? The bank's overarching, long-term goal is financial growth. This goal will be assessed by the following financial measures: profit growth percentage, revenue growth percentage, and return on assets.

This raises the question, though, of what CPB has to be doing right now to ensure its long-term financial goals are met. Management has decided on several key goals that have to be achieved in the near term for this to happen.

Let's first look at the customer perspective in the balanced scorecard. The question for CPB's management is "How do the bank's customers see us?" Management has expressed its customer-perspective goal as "satisfying the customer." How, then, can management measure progress on this short-term, day-to-day objective? Management has chosen five measures:

1. A customer satisfaction survey is conducted annually among all the bank's customers. Moreover, a more detailed customer satisfaction survey is aimed at the bank's key customers, which account for about 20 percent of the customer base.

2. CPB's management keeps track of the percentage of its customers that it retains from one year to the next. The assumption is that a customer who stays with CPB is largely satisfied with the service.

3. Not all of CPB's customers are profitable. (This is true of almost all banks.) For example, customers that keep low account balances, pay off their credit cards each month, and avoid service charges tend to be unprofitable. Therefore, the percentage of profitable customers is a very important measure. A trend in the wrong direction here would almost certainly spell trouble for the bank's financial goals in the future.

4. CPB's management has found that a particularly sensitive customer-satisfaction measure is the number of complaints received in a month. If something is going awry in CPB's customer interface, customers are not shy about letting the bank know about it—and quickly.

5. Finally, CPB's market share in its coverage area is a key measure of market penetration. Increasing this key measure would most likely translate into revenue and profit growth in the future.

What about Canadian Pacific Bank's internal operations? In what business processes must CPB excel in order to achieve its long-term financial goals? Management has decided to focus on two important goals: completing routine bank transactions efficiently and processing loan applications efficiently. For routine bank transactions (e.g., making deposits, withdrawals, or loan payments), CPB's management focuses on three key measures:

1. Customers can complete automated transactions in three ways. They can bank online, use an ATM, or use a touch-tone telephone to make phone-automated inquiries. CPB's management believes that the greater the percentage of automated transactions, as opposed to transactions involving a bank teller, the more efficient will be the bank's transaction operations.

2. Another measure of transaction efficiency is the average time that it takes a customer to complete an online transaction. The smaller this time interval is, CPB's management believes, the more likely customers will be to use online banking.

3. As far as manual, teller-assisted transactions go, CPB's management keeps track of the percentage of these transactions that exhibit errors.

On the loan side of CPB's internal operations, management tracks two measures of loan-processing efficiency:

1. The average time to process a loan application is a key indicator of how smoothly this aspect of the bank's operations is running.

2. CPB's management also believes that the higher the ratio of approved to rejected loans, the more successful the bank has been in communicating its loan criteria to the bank's customer base.

Finally, let's look at the learning and growth perspective in Canadian Pacific Bank's balanced scorecard. Management has highlighted two goals: motivated and prepared employees and innovative banking services. To assess the goal of

> "The overall big picture reason we designed the balanced scorecard for performance management at CIBC was to facilitate the deployment of strategic goals through the organization, and we needed a common framework to do this. It was important that every employee had ownership for the goals that they were expected to achieve, and understood what their contribution was to the goals of the overall business." (11c)
>
> **CIBC**

motivated and prepared employees, CPB's management has established three measures:

1. The bank's human resource management team believes that the percentage of employees participating in voluntary continuing-education programs is an indicator of both employee motivation and preparation.

2. On the other hand, the number of employees in required training programs speaks to both the company's training program offerings as well as employee preparation.

3. The number of employee suggestions per month, as well as the number of those suggestions adopted, also speaks to both employee motivation and preparation. A motivated employee is more likely to submit a suggestion, and a well-prepared employee is more likely to make an adoptable suggestion.

The second goal under innovation and learning on CPB's scorecard involves innovative banking services.

1. The number of new banking services first offered by CPB in its coverage area, as opposed to those first offered by competing banks, is a measure of just how innovative CPB's management is.

2. When the bank is able to act positively on a customer suggestion, this too speaks to CPB's ability to learn from its customer base.

All in all, CPB's management team believes that if the bank meets its current goals for its customer, internal operations, and learning and growth perspectives, the bank will ultimately be successful in achieving its long-term goal of financial growth.

Lead and Lag Measures: The Key to the Balanced Scorecard

Key to understanding the balanced scorecard is the distinction between lead and lag indicators of performance. *Lead indicators* of performance are measures of nonfinancial and financial outcomes that guide management in making current decisions that will result in desirable results in the future. In other words, lead indicators guide management to take actions *now* that will have positive effects on enterprise performance *later*. For example, Canadian Pacific Bank's scorecard includes the bank's market share in its coverage area as an indicator of future market growth, which will ultimately translate into growth of the bank's profitability. By including this key lead indicator in

Rockwater, which is now owned by Halliburton, is a global undersea oil services company headquartered in Aberdeen, Scotland. Doing the undersea engineering and construction for drilling rigs such as the one pictured here requires diverse technical operations, both on- and offshore. Rockwater's management found the balanced scorecard to be an invaluable tool in clarifying the company's goals and communicating them to the employees. Among the measures in Rockwater's balanced scorecard are the following: cash flow and project profitability (financial); safety index and hours spent with customers on new work (internal); project pricing and customer satisfaction (customer); percentage of revenue from new services; and number of employee suggestions (innovation and learning).[5]

Exhibit 11–3
Selected Performance
Measures Used in Balanced
Scorecards

Financial Perspective

Earnings	Cash flow
Earnings per share	Cash flow from operations

Customer Perspective

Customer contacts	Customer satisfaction (surveyed)
Repeat customers	Customer complaints
New customers	Market share

Learning and Growth Perspective

Employee training hours	New processes
Employee promotion rate	Employee suggestions
New products or services	Employee retention

Internal Operations Perspective

Product quality/defect rates	Finished products per day per employee
Number of vendors	Floor space per finished product
Cycle time	Cost of inventories held
Throughput	Number of common parts
Machine downtime	Number of part numbers

its scorecard, management is directed to take actions now that will increase the bank's market share.

Lag indicators are measures of the final outcomes of earlier management decisions. Examples of lag indicators are a company's profit and cash flow. These key financial measures, while important, only improve in later time periods, well after management has taken important actions to affect key operational results.

The whole idea of the balanced scorecard is to *use lead indicators to communicate with, motivate, and evaluate individuals* with the expectation that their current actions will result in improvements in the company's important lag measures (e.g., profitability) in the future. Exhibit 11–3 gives examples of several key lead and lag measures used in a variety of organizations' balanced scorecards.

Many companies, in all types of industries, have developed a balanced scorecard to help management and employees understand the important lead indicators of performance that will ultimately bring success on the company's key long-term goals. Among the many service-industry firms that have developed a balanced scorecard are CIBC, Toronto's Hospital for Sick Children, Rogers Wireless Communications, Scotia Bank, and UPS. Retailers too have made use of the balanced scorecard. Among them are Best Buy, The Gap, and IKEA.

Among the well-known manufacturers making use of the balanced-scorecard concept are Apple Computer, Caterpillar, Cisco Systems, General Motors, Microsoft, Motorola, Nissan Canada, and Phillips Electronics. Finally, governmental units have benefited from a balanced scorecard, among them Canada's Air Force, the Ontario Ministry of Health and Long-Term Care, and Vancouver Coastal Health.

> "Because of the balanced scorecard, the nature of the monthly financial meetings changed from a focus on the things Pitney Bowes is doing well to the three things we need to improve, with the emphasis on an appropriate action plan." (11d)
> **Pitney Bowes**

Linking the Balanced Scorecard to Organizational Strategy

A key to making successful use of the balanced scorecard is linking the scorecard's lead and lag measures to the organization's strategy. As depicted in the diagram in Exhibit 11–4, the organization's vision and strategy drive the specification of both goals and metrics in the scorecard's financial, customer, internal operations, and learning and growth perspectives.[6]

Exhibit 11–4
Linkage between the
Balanced Scorecard and
Organizational Strategy

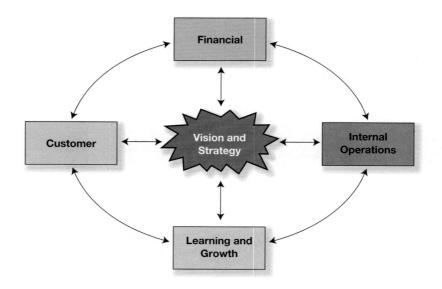

The precise form of the linkage between strategy and the goals and measures in the balanced scorecard will, of course, depend on the nature of the organization and its strategy. The following case in point explores this linkage for Dell Computer Corporation. (See also the Management Accounting Practice box on page 33 in Chapter 2.)

M anagement
A ccounting
P ractice

Dell Computer

LINKING THE BALANCED SCORECARD TO ORGANIZATIONAL STRATEGY

Key to successfully using the balanced scorecard is linking the scorecard's lead and lag measures to the organization's strategy. According to Dell Computer's Web site, the company's strategy is "to be the most successful computer company in the world at delivering the best customer experience in markets we serve."[7]

As the following diagram shows, Dell's strategy of using its direct-sales model to provide unparalleled customer service drives through each of the perspectives that make up a balanced scorecard.

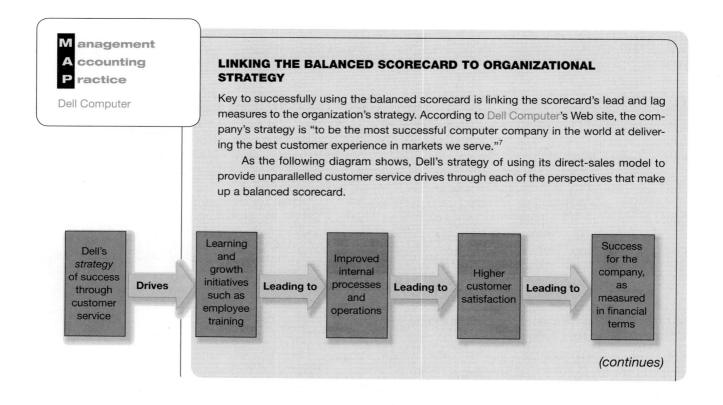

(continues)

The following selected balanced scorecard measures are among those relevant for Dell Computer to successfully implement its strategy. Notice the frequency of the words *customer* and *sales* in these measures. Dell's strategy and its relevant balanced scorecard measures are dominated by its customer-focused direct-sales business model.

Financial
Profit (in relation to assets invested)
Cash flow
Revenue growth by customer segment
Gross margin by customer segment

Customer
Customer perception of value (i.e., product quality relative to cost)
Customer retention
Customer perception of ease of interacting with Dell
Customer perception of customer response by Dell

Internal processes and operations
Defect rate within Dell's manufacturing operations
Defect rate by Dell's suppliers
Order-to-delivery cycle time
Time spent in contact with customers
Number of customer-focused process innovations

Learning and growth
Training expenditures per full-time employees
Number of customer-initiated product innovations
Number of patents that improve Dell's direct-sales business model
Number of emerging technologies evaluated

Dell's vision and strategy

Operational Performance Measures in Today's Manufacturing Environment

Learning Objective 2

Describe the operational performance measures appropriate for today's manufacturing environment.

In today's advanced manufacturing environment, operational performance measures are taking on ever-greater importance.[8] Under the philosophy of *activity-based management*, the goal is to focus on continually improving each activity. As a result, the emerging operational control measures focus on the key *activities* in which the organization engages. Exhibit 11–5 lists some commonly used operational performance measures. The list is representative, but not exhaustive, of those used in practice. In using these measures to control operations, management emphasizes trends over time. The goal is to continually improve all aspects of the plant's operations.

Raw Material and Scrap   Raw material continues to be a significant cost element in any manufacturing process, whether labour-intensive or highly automated. Worldwide material sourcing and international competition have resulted in the purchasing function taking on greater importance in many firms. As a result, purchasing performance has become an important area of measurement; criteria include total raw-material cost,

Exhibit 11–5
Operational Performance Measures for an Advanced Manufacturing Environment

Raw Material and Scrap

Number of vendors
Number of unique parts
Number of common parts
Raw material as a percentage of total cost
Lead time for material delivery
Percentage of orders received on time
Total raw-material cost
Deviations between actual and budgeted raw-material prices
Scrap as a percentage of raw-material cost
Cost of scrap
Quality of raw material

Inventory

Average value of inventory
Average amount of time various inventory items are held
Ratio of inventory value to sales revenue
Number of inventoried parts

Machinery

Hours of machine downtime
Percentage of machine downtime
Percentage of machine availability
Bottleneck machine downtime
Percentage of bottleneck machine downtime
Percentage of bottleneck machine availability
Detailed maintenance records
Percentage of on-time routine maintenance procedures
Setup time
Machine flexibility:
    Product switchover times in an FMS cell
    Number of different products manufactured in an FMS cell

Product Quality

Customer acceptance measures:
    Number of customer complaints
    Number of warranty claims
    Number of products returned
    Cost of repairing returned products
In-process quality measures:
    Number of defects found
    Cost of rework
Quality costs

Production and Delivery

Manufacturing cycle time
Velocity
Manufacturing cycle efficiency
Percentage of on-time deliveries
Percentage of orders filled
Delivery cycle time

Productivity

Financial measures:
    Aggregate or total productivity (Output in dollars ÷ Total input in dollars)
    Partial or component productivity (Output in dollars ÷ A particular input in dollars)
Operational (physical) measures:
    Partial or component productivity measures. These measures express relationships between inputs and outputs, in physical terms. For example:
        Finished products produced per day per employee
        Square metres of floor space required per finished product per day
        Electricity required per finished product

Innovation and Learning

New products:
    Percentage of sales from new products
    New products introduced by this firm versus introductions by competitors
Process improvements:
    Number of process improvements made
    Cost savings from process improvements

deviations between actual and budgeted material prices, the quality of raw materials, and the delivery performance of vendors.

The cost of scrap is highlighted as a separate item, rather than being included in the standard direct-material cost as a normal production cost. The objective is to reduce scrap to the absolute minimum.

Inventory   The essence of the just-in-time production environment is low inventories at every stage of production. Thus, inventory control is of paramount importance in achieving the benefits of the JIT philosophy. Inventory control measures include the average value of inventory, the average amount of time various inventory items are held, and other inventory turnover measures, such as the ratio of inventory value to sales revenue.

Machinery   If inventories are to be kept low, as the JIT philosophy demands, then the production process must be capable of producing goods quickly. This goal requires that production machinery must work when it is needed, which means that routine maintenance schedules must be adhered to scrupulously. Performance controls in this area include measures of machine downtime and machine availability, and detailed maintenance records. Some manufacturers make a distinction between *bottleneck machinery* and non-bottleneck machinery. A bottleneck operation is one that limits the production capacity of the entire facility. It is vital that the machinery in bottleneck operations be available 100 percent of the time, excluding time for routine required maintenance. In an advanced manufacturing environment, based on JIT and FMS, the investment in machinery is extremely large. To obtain the anticipated return from this investment, through the benefits of JIT and FMS, the machinery has to be kept running. This emphasis on bottleneck operations is consistent with the management philosophy known as the *theory of constraints*. This approach stresses the importance of identifying and easing the organization's constraints, which are the phenomena that limit the organization's productive capacity.[9]

Setup time also is highlighted as a machinery performance measure, and the objective in a JIT/FMS setting is to minimize this non-value-added activity. Machine flexibility measures emphasize the value of producing many different products in the same FMS cell.

Product Quality   A JIT philosophy demands adherence to strict quality standards for raw materials, manufactured components, and finished products. Various nonfinancial data are vital for assessing a manufacturer's effectiveness in maintaining product quality. **Customer-acceptance measures** focus on the extent to which a firm's customers perceive its product to be of high quality. Typical performance measures include the number of customer complaints, the number of warranty claims, the number of products returned, and the cost of repairing returned products. **In-process quality controls** refer to procedures designed to assess product quality before production is completed. For example, in a *quality audit program*, partially completed products are randomly inspected at various stages of production. Defect rates are measured, and corrective actions are suggested. A third area of quality measurement relates to *raw-material quality*. Suppliers are rated on the basis of the quality of their materials as well as customer service.

Some companies routinely prepare a *quality cost report*, which details the costs incurred in assuring product quality. We will discuss quality costs in a later section.

Production and Delivery   A company will achieve little success if it manufactures a great product but delivers it to the customer a week late. World-class manufacturers are striving toward a goal of filling 100 percent of their orders on time. Common measures of product delivery performance include the percentage of on-time deliveries and the percentage of orders filled. Another measure is **delivery cycle time**, the average time between the receipt of a customer order and delivery of the goods.

Delivering goods on time requires that they be produced on time. Various operational performance measures have been developed to assess the timeliness of the

"We have to be the best in cost throughout the world. And cycle time is also very important." (11e)
MiCRUS (joint venture of IBM and Cirrus Logic)

production process. **Manufacturing cycle time** is the total amount of production time (or throughput time) required per unit. It can be computed by dividing the total time required to produce a batch by the number of units in the batch. **Velocity** is defined as the number of units produced in a given time period. Perhaps an even more important operational measure is the **manufacturing cycle efficiency (MCE)**, defined as follows:

$$\text{Manufacturing cycle efficiency} = \frac{\text{Processing time}}{\text{Processing time} + \text{Inspection time} + \text{Waiting time} + \text{Move time}}$$

The value of the MCE measure lies in its comparison between value-added time (processing) and non-value-added time (inspection, waiting, and moving). In many manufacturing companies, MCE is less than 10 percent. Firms with advanced manufacturing systems strive for as high an MCE measure as possible.

Productivity   Global competitiveness has forced virtually all manufacturers to strive for greater productivity. One *financial* productivity measure is **aggregate** (or **total**) **productivity**, defined as total output divided by total input. A firm's total output is measured as the sum, across all of the goods and services produced, of those products and services times their sales prices. Total input is the sum of the direct-material, direct-labour, and overhead costs incurred in production. Another financial measure is a **partial** (or **component**) **productivity** measure, in which total output (in dollars) is divided by the cost of a particular input.

A preferable approach to productivity measurement is to record multiple physical measures that capture the most important determinants of a company's productivity. These *operational* (or *physical*) measures are also partial productivity measures, since each one focuses on a particular input. For example, a large automobile manufacturer routinely records the following data for one of its plants: the number of engines produced per day per employee and the number of square metres of floor space required per engine produced in a day. A large chemical company keeps track of the amount of energy (in British thermal units, Btu, or about 1,055 joules) required to convert a kilogram of raw chemicals into a kilogram of finished product. Data such as these convey more information to management than a summary financial measure such as aggregate productivity.

Innovation and Learning   Global competition requires that companies continually improve and innovate. New products must be developed and introduced to replace those that become obsolete. New processes must continually be developed to make production more efficient. In a world-class manufacturer or service firm, the one thing that is most constant is change.

To summarize, nonfinancial measures are being used increasingly. These operational performance measures assist management in its goal of continuous process improvement. To be most effective, operational controls should be tied to the strategic objectives of the organization. Specific improvement targets can be set for various measures to provide motivation for improvement in the areas deemed most important by management.

Gain-Sharing Plans

One widely used method of providing incentives to employees to improve their performance on various operational control measures is gain sharing. A **gain-sharing plan** is an incentive system that specifies a formula by which cost or productivity gains achieved by a company are shared with the workers who helped accomplish the improvements. For example, suppose an electronics manufacturer reduced its defect rate in the Manual Insertion Department by 2 percent for a savings of $100,000. A gain-sharing formula might call for 25 percent of the savings to be shared with the employees in that department.

Other Management Tools

To remain competitive in today's global market, businesses must continually improve. Moreover, this continuous improvement needs to apply across the spectrum of business activity: from product design and quality, through production operations and cost management, to customer service. **Continuous improvement** may be defined as the constant effort to eliminate waste, reduce response time, simplify the design of both products and processes, and improve quality and customer service. One compelling reason for the need for continuous improvement is the *price down/cost down concept*. This refers to the tendency of prices to fall over the life cycle of a newly introduced product. Think, for example, about the prices of hand-held calculators, DVD players, personal listening devices, and HDTVs. When each of these products was first introduced, prices were quite high. However, as manufacturers gained experience in producing them, prices fell and the products became accessible to a much wider customer pool. However, if prices are to fall over time, manufacturers have to continually reduce costs as well.

> "The idea of continuous improvement is just paramount. People have a sense of purpose. They have a real sense of 'I'm adding value to the company by reducing this waste.'" (11f)
> **Caterpillar**

Two approaches to continuous improvement (i.e., reduction) in production costs are now in widespread use. These techniques are called *target costing* and *kaizen costing*.

Target Costing

> **Learning Objective 3**
>
> Define and give an example of target costing.

Target costing refers to the design of a product, and the processes used to produce it, so that ultimately the product can be manufactured at a cost that will enable the firm to make a profit when the product is sold at an estimated market-driven price. This estimated price is called the *target price*, the desired profit margin is called the *target profit*, and the cost at which the product must be manufactured is called the *target cost*.

To illustrate, suppose the design engineers of the Patio Grill Company we have seen in Chapter 5 have designed a new built-in poolside barbeque grill to be sold under the brand name Poolside Grill. The company's management estimates that after a few years on the market, assuming the firm's competitors come out with comparable products, the Poolside Grill will sell for approximately $2,100. Moreover, management desires a target profit on its new Poolside Grill of $250. The target cost, then, for the manufacture of a Poolside Grill is $1,850 ($2,100 − $250). The task faced by Patio Grill Company's design engineers now is to refine the Poolside Grill's product design, and the processes that will be used to manufacture it, so that ultimately it will cost no more than $1,850 to produce.

Since target costing is closely related to the pricing process, it is explored more extensively in Chapter 14, which covers pricing decisions.

Kaizen Costing

> **Learning Objective 4**
>
> Explain the concept of kaizen costing and prepare a kaizen costing chart.

Target costing applies to the *design* of a new product or model and the *design* of its production process. In contrast, **kaizen costing** is the process of cost reduction during the manufacturing phase of an existing product. The Japanese word *kaizen* refers to continual and gradual improvement through small betterment activities, rather than large or radical improvement made through innovation or large investments in technology. The idea is simple. Improvement is the goal and responsibility of every worker, from the CEO to the manual labourers, in every activity, every day, all the time! Through the small but continual efforts of everyone, significant reductions in costs can be attained over time.

To help achieve the continuous cost reduction implied by the kaizen costing concept, an annual (or monthly) *kaizen cost goal* is established. Then, actual costs are tracked over time and compared to the kaizen goal. A kaizen costing chart used by Daihatsu (a Japanese auto manufacturer owned in part by Toyota) is shown in Exhibit 11–6.[10] Notice that the cost base or reference point is the actual cost performance at

Exhibit 11–6

Kaizen Costing Chart Used by
Daihatsu Motor Company
(Osaka. Japan)

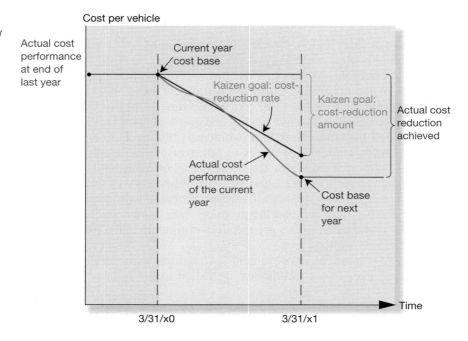

the end of the prior year. A kaizen goal is established for the cost-reduction rate and amount during the current year. Actual cost performance throughout the year is compared with the kaizen goal. At the end of the current year, the current actual cost becomes the cost base or reference point for the next year. Then, a new (lower) kaizen goal is established, and the cost-reduction effort continues.

How are kaizen costing goals met? The continual and relentless reduction of non-value-added activities and costs, the elimination of waste, and improvements in manufacturing cycle time all contribute to the effort. In addition, the improvement suggestions and kaizen efforts of all employees are taken seriously and implemented when appropriate. The result is a continually more efficient and cost-effective production process.

A good example of the successful use of both target costing and kaizen costing in bringing about continuous improvement is provided by Toyota, as the next section illustrates.

Toyota: Target Costing and Kaizen Costing in Action

Toyota Motor Corporation, the world's largest auto maker, uses both target costing and kaizen costing to maintain its strong competitive position. "Cost planning at Toyota is mainly an effort to reduce cost at the design stage. Toyota sets goals for cost reduction, and then seeks to achieve those goals through design changes. To correctly assess the gains made, the exact amount of cost reduction through redesign is measured. Setting goals and assessing the results based on cost differences between old and new models constitute the essence of cost control at Toyota."[11]

Toyota also has achieved significant cost reduction through the redesign of production processes. For example, "over a five-year period, Toyota reduced the setup time for its 800-ton (1 ton = 0.90718474 tonnes) stamping presses from more than one hour to under 12 minutes."[12] Time savings such as this significantly reduce costs.

In addition to the cost savings realized in the design phase, Toyota aggressively pursues kaizen costing to reduce costs in the manufacturing phase. "In July and January, plant managers submit six-month plans for attaining their kaizen goals. Methods for achieving these goals include cutting material costs per unit and improvements in standard operating procedures. These are pursued based on employee suggestions.

For improvements involving industrial engineering or value engineering, employees often receive support from the technical staff. To draw up a kaizen plan after kaizen goals have been set by top management, employees look for ways to contribute to kaizen in their daily work. About two million suggestions were received from Toyota employees in one recent year alone (roughly 35 suggestions per employee). Ninety-seven percent of them were adopted."[13] This is a prime example of the concept of **employee empowerment**, in which workers are encouraged to take the initiative in improving operations, reducing costs, and improving product quality and customer service.

Benchmarking

Learning Objective 5

Briefly explain the concepts of benchmarking, reengineering, and the theory of constraints.

Benchmarking is the continual search for the most effective method of accomplishing a task, by comparing existing methods and performance levels with those of other organizations or with other subunits within the same organization. The most effective methods of accomplishing various tasks in a particular industry, often discovered through benchmarking, are referred to as **best practices**. Xerox Corporation is often credited with originating the benchmarking concept, but now the idea is widely used by organizations throughout the world. **Benchmarking** (also called **competitive benchmarking**) provides one more tool for companies to use in identifying non-value-added activities and pursuing continuous improvement.

Reengineering

In contrast to the concept of kaizen, which involves small, incremental steps toward gradual improvement, reengineering involves a giant leap. **Reengineering** is the complete redesign of a process, with an emphasis on finding creative new ways to accomplish an objective. Reengineering has sometimes been described as taking a blank piece of paper and starting from scratch to redesign a business process. Rather than searching continually for minute improvements, reengineering involves a radical shift in thinking about how an objective should be met. In the words of one reengineering consultant: "Reengineering prescribes radical, quick and significant change. Admittedly, this can entail high risks, but it can also bring big rewards. These benefits are most dramatic when new models are discovered for conducting business."[14]

Theory of Constraints

The theory of constraints (or TOC) is another contemporary management tool that supports continuous improvement and cost management programs. The **theory of constraints** is a management approach that seeks to maximize long-run profit through proper management of organizational bottlenecks or constrained resources.[15] The key idea in TOC is to identify the constraints in a system that are preventing the organization from achieving a higher level of success, then to seek to relieve or relax those constraints. Moreover, TOC recommends subordinating all other management goals to the objective of solving the constraint problems. For example, if limited capacity in a particular machining operation is increasing cycle time, reducing throughput, and reducing profits, then management would concentrate much of its efforts on expanding the capacity of that bottleneck operation.

Total Quality Management

For many companies, quality is at the forefront of the areas in which nonfinancial performance is critically important. The quality of the product or service that an organization provides can spell the difference between future profitability and disaster. Quality is equally important in the service and manufacturing industries. For Canadian Pacific Bank, the quality of service includes the convenience of branch locations, the customer support provided for online banking, the expediency of loans approvals, the friendliness of the bank tellers, and so forth. Bank customers are ever more discriminating as they assess the overall quality of service and then select their banks accordingly. Similar comments apply to the airlines, long-distance telecommunications companies, hotels, car rental firms, and financial investment firms.

In the manufacturing industry, product quality has become a key factor in determining a firm's success or failure in the global marketplace. Advanced, highly reliable manufacturing methods have made it possible to achieve very high standards of product quality. As a result, more and more firms are making product quality a keystone of their competitive strategy.

Measuring and Reporting Quality Costs

Recognizing the importance of maintaining high product quality, companies often measure and report the costs of doing so. Before we examine the costs that companies incur to maintain high product quality, let's consider what product quality means.

Product Quality   What is meant by a high-quality product? There are two concepts of quality that determine a product's degree of excellence or the product's ultimate fitness for its intended use. A product's **grade** refers to the extent of its capability in performing its intended purpose, in relation to other products with the same functional use. For example, a computer monitor that displays 65,536 colours is of a higher grade than a monitor that displays only 256 colours. A product's **quality of design** refers to how well it is conceived or designed for its intended use. For example, a coffee mug designed with a handle that is too small for the user's fingers is a poorly designed mug. The **quality of conformance** refers to the extent to which a product meets the specifications of its design. A coffee mug with an appropriately sized handle might be well designed, but if the handle breaks off due to shoddy manufacturing, it will be useless. This mug fails to conform to its design specifications. Both quality of design and quality of conformance are required in order to achieve a high-quality finished product.

Learning Objective 6

Prepare a quality cost report.

Handic◎

Costs of Quality   Due to the increasing importance of maintaining high product quality, many companies routinely measure and report the costs of ensuring high quality. Four types of costs are monitored.

First are **prevention costs**, the costs of preventing defects. Second are **appraisal costs**, the costs of determining whether defects exist. The third type of costs are **internal failure costs**, those costs of repairing defects found prior to product sale. The last type of costs are **external failure costs**, those costs incurred when defective products have been sold.

Exhibit 11–7 shows a quality-cost report prepared by Handico, Inc., a manufacturer of cordless telephones.[16] As is always true in cost monitoring, quality-cost reporting is most useful when cost trends are examined over a period of time. Through trend analysis, management can see where improvement is occurring and where difficulties exist. Goals can be set to achieve a particular cost target in an area of concern. For example, Handico's management might strive to reduce warranty costs to zero by a certain date.

Observable versus Hidden Quality Costs   The quality costs discussed in the preceding section are *observable*. They can be measured and reported, often on the basis of

	Current Month's Cost	Percent of Total
Prevention costs		
Quality training	$ 2,000	1.3
Reliability engineering	10,000	6.5
Pilot studies	5,000	3.3
Systems development	8,000	5.2
Total prevention costs	$ 25,000	16.3
Appraisal costs		
Materials inspection	$ 6,000	3.9
Supplies inspection	3,000	2.0
Reliability testing	5,000	3.3
Metallurgical laboratory	25,000	16.3
Total appraisal costs	$ 39,000	25.5
Internal failure costs		
Scrap	$ 15,000	9.8
Repair	18,000	11.8
Rework	12,000	7.8
Downtime	6,000	3.9
Total internal failure costs	$ 51,000	33.3
External failure costs		
Warranty costs	$ 14,000	9.2
Out-of-warranty repairs and replacement	6,000	3.9
Customer complaints	3,000	2.0
Product liability	10,000	6.5
Transportation losses	5,000	3.3
Total external failure costs	$ 38,000	24.9
Total quality costs	$ 153,000	100.0

Exhibit 11–7
Quality-Cost Report: Handico

Handico

information in the accounting records. In addition to these observable quality costs, however, companies incur *hidden* quality costs. When products of inferior quality make it to market, customers are dissatisfied. Their dissatisfaction can result in decreased sales and a tarnished reputation for the company. Not only does the company experience lost sales for the inferior products but it will also likely experience lost sales in its other product lines. The opportunity cost of these lost sales and decreased market share can represent a significant hidden cost. Such hidden costs are difficult to estimate or report.

Changing Views of Optimal Product Quality

One way to express product quality is in the percentage of products that fail to conform to their specifications, that is, the percentage of defects. Given this perspective, what is the optimal level of product quality?[17]

Traditional Perspective The traditional viewpoint holds that finding the optimal level of product quality is a balancing act between incurring costs of prevention and appraisal on one hand and incurring costs of failure on the other. Panel A of Exhibit 11–8 depicts this trade-off. As the percentage of defective products decreases, the costs of prevention and appraisal increase. However, the costs of internal and

Learning Objective 7

Discuss the traditional and contemporary views of the optimal level of product quality.

Exhibit 11–8
Quality Costs and the Optimal
Level of Product Quality

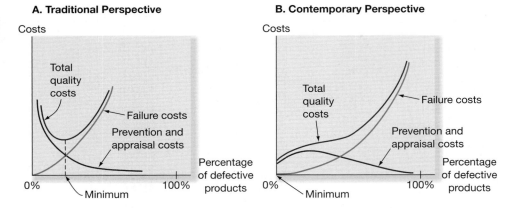

external failure decrease. Adding the costs of prevention, appraisal, and internal and external failure yields total quality costs. The optimal product quality level is the point that minimizes total quality costs.

Contemporary Perspective   Due largely to the influence of Japanese product quality expert Genichi Taguchi, the contemporary viewpoint of optimal product quality differs from the traditional perspective. The contemporary view is that if both observable and hidden costs of quality are considered, *any* deviation from a product's target specifications results in the incurrence of increasing quality costs. Under the contemporary viewpoint, as depicted in panel B of Exhibit 11–8, the optimal level of product quality occurs at the *zero-defect level*. As panel B shows, the observable and hidden costs of internal and external failure increase as the percentage of defective products increases. The observable and hidden costs of prevention and appraisal increase slightly and then decrease as the percentage of defects increases. The most important point, though, is that the total costs of quality are minimized at the zero-defect level.

Whether the traditional or contemporary view of optimal product quality is most accurate is still being debated by quality-control experts. Moreover, the exact shape of the cost functions in Exhibit 11–8 is largely an empirical question, and the cost functions probably differ across industries and product types. One thing is certain, though. To compete successfully in today's global market, any company must pay very close attention to achieving a very high level of product quality.

Total Quality Management   Monitoring product quality coupled with measuring and reporting quality costs helps companies maintain programs of **total quality management**, or **TQM**. This refers to the broad set of management and control processes designed to focus the entire organization and all of its employees on providing products or services that do the best possible job of satisfying the customer. Among the tools used in total quality management is the **Six Sigma** program, an analytical method that aims at achieving near-perfect results in a production process. (See the Management Accounting Practice illustration here for details.)

Identifying Quality-Control Problems   An effective TQM program includes methods for identifying quality-control problems. One method of identifying quality

Management
Accounting
Practice

Motorola, General
Electric, Dell Computer,
Wal-Mart, Dow
Chemical, Allied Signal,
and Honeywell

SIX SIGMA FOR QUALITY MANAGEMENT AND COST REDUCTION

"Originally conceived by Motorola Inc. as a quality-improvement device" two decades ago, "Six Sigma soon morphed into a cost-cutting utensil for manufacturers of all stripes. Now, it's fast becoming the Swiss army knife of the business world. Goods producers still make up the bulk of users, who typically rely on statistics to uncover and then reduce product variance in order to boost quality and efficiency. But increasingly, manufacturers are applying Six Sigma to functions as varied as accounts receivable, sales, and research and development. And their success in these nonfactory domains has inspired Six Sigma projects at financial institutions, retailers, health-care concerns, and in other areas of the service sector."

Six Sigma is "an analytical method aimed at achieving *near-perfect results* in a production process. In statistics, the Greek letter *sigma* denotes variation in a standard bell curve. One sigma equals 690,000 defects per 1 million. Most companies do no better than three sigma, or 66,000 errors per million. Six Sigma reduces that count to *3.4 defects per million*. That saves money by preventing waste."

Six Sigma "achieves results by reducing subjective errors in the assessment of problems. First, auditors *define* a process where results are subpar. Then they *measure* the process to determine current performance, *analyze* this information to pinpoint where things are going wrong, and *improve* the process and eliminate the error. Last, *controls* are set up to prevent future bugs."

"In the world of manufacturing, Six Sigma has become something akin to a religion." When General Electric's former chairman Jack Welch embraced Six Sigma, for example, "he quickly assembled an unprecedented army of employees to pinpoint and fix problems throughout GE" using their Six Sigma training. "The results were awesome: In three years alone, these troops saved the company $8 billion, according to GE." Now "GE is sending out its Six Sigma squads to customers such as Dell Computer and Wal-Mart stores to help them root out what GE estimates to be more than $1 billion in inefficiencies and waste—and help GE win more business."[18]

Dow Chemical has initiated several Six Sigma projects, each of which has saved an average of a half million dollars in its first year alone.[19] Allied Signal, which uses activity-based costing in conjunction with its Six Sigma program, saved over $500 million in the program's first year.[20] Honeywell is using the Six Sigma approach, in conjunction with other productivity improvements, with a goal of over a billion dollars in cost savings.[21]

"Employees charged with Six Sigma duties generally have what's called a *black belt*." At Allied Signal, for example, "it's awarded to those employees who complete four separate weeks of classroom study. In between those weeks of class, black-belt candidates must use what they've learned to focus on a project within the company and show some cost savings achieved by using Six Sigma."[22]

problems is the *cause-and-effect diagram* (also called an *Ishikawa* or *fishbone diagram*). Exhibit 11–9 displays such a diagram used by Xerox Corporation to identify the causes of errors in its customer billing process. As can be seen, the quality improvement team has identified a wide range of possible causes for billing errors. After identifying possible causes for billing errors, the Xerox team, nicknamed the Billing Bloopers Team, might take systematic steps to eliminate the root causes of the errors.

"Six Sigma might be the maturation of everything we've learned over the past 100 years about quality." (11g)

President, American Society for Quality

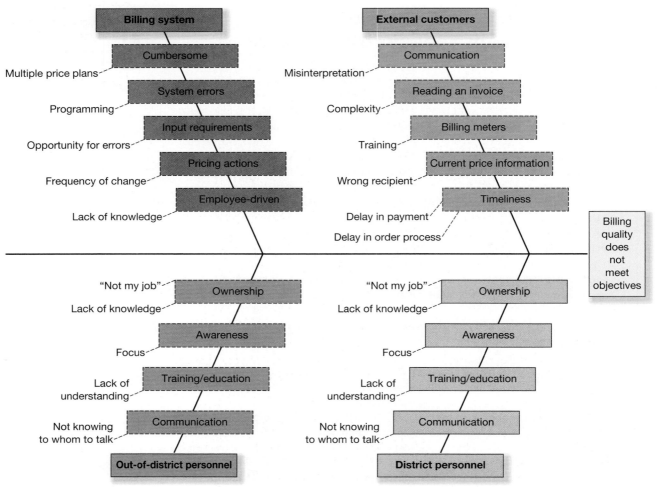

Source: David M. Buehlman and Donald Stover, "How Xerox Solves Quality Problems," *Management Accounting* 75, no. 3 (September 1993), pp. 33–36.

Exhibit 11–9

Cause-and-Effect Diagram: Billing Quality at Xerox Corporation

Another helpful tool in quality improvement programs is the *Pareto diagram*, depicted in Exhibit 11–10. This one shows graphically the frequency with which various quality-control problems are observed for a particular model of cordless telephone. The diagram helps the TQM team visualize and communicate to others what the most serious types of defects are. Steps can then be taken to attack the most serious and most frequent problems first.

ISO 9000 Standards

A key factor in determining the quality of a company's products is its quality-control system. The organizational structure, personnel, procedures, and policies that are in place to monitor product quality will greatly affect a firm's ability to achieve high quality standards. In 1987, the International Organization for Standardization (ISO), based in Geneva, Switzerland, issued a set of quality-control standards for companies selling products in Europe. The ISO 9000 standards, as they have come to be known, focus on a manufacturer's quality-control system. The ISO 9000 standards basically require that a manufacturer have a well-defined quality-control system in place, and that the target level of product quality be maintained consistently. Moreover, the ISO 9000 standards require a manufacturer to prepare extensive documentation of all aspects of the quality-control system. The first standard, ISO 9000, lists three objectives:

- The company should sustain the quality of its product or service at a level that continually meets the purchaser's stated or implied needs.

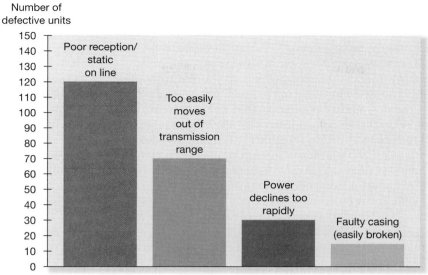

Number of
defective units

Type of product defect

Handico

- The quality-control system should be sufficient to give the supplier's own management confidence that the intended quality is being maintained.
- The supplying company should give the purchaser confidence that the intended quality is consistently achieved in the delivered product or service.

The ISO 9000 standards have been adopted in Canada as well. In fact, as early as 1972, Canada held a seat on the International Organization for Standardization (ISO)'s governing Council and the Standards Council of Canada (SCC) manages Canada's participation in the ISO. The Canadian government and many large companies are more and more inclined to require their suppliers to have ISO 9000 certification.

The ISO 9000 standards consist of five major parts. ISO 9000 states the objectives of the standards, defines a quality-related vocabulary, and provides a guide to the other standards in the series. ISO 9001 provides a model for quality assurance in design, development, production, installation, and servicing. ISO 9002 focuses more narrowly on quality assurance in production and installation. ISO 9003 addresses quality assurance in final inspection and testing. Finally, ISO 9004 provides guidelines for the design of a quality management system.

Implications for Managerial Accounting   The ISO 9000 standards have several implications for managerial accountants. First, the standards require extensive documentation of the quality-control system. This task often falls to the controller's office. In fact, several of the largest public accounting firms are offering assurance services in helping companies meet the ISO documentation requirements. Second, the ISO standards require that the costs and benefits of the quality-control system be measured and documented. This means that management accountants will be responsible for measuring and reporting product life-cycle costs, quality costs, and the effectiveness of efforts at continuous improvement.

To summarize, the ISO 9000 standards are having a global impact on the way companies approach their quality assurance objectives. The standards will affect virtually every area within a firm subject to its guidelines. Management accountants will be integrally involved in the informational and documentation aspects of the ISO 9000 program.[23]

Environmental Cost Management

As the world's population grows, business activity expands, and the globe seemingly shrinks, millions of people the world over are ever-more aware of the critical need to preserve our environment for ourselves and our posterity. Issues like air and water quality, hidden carcinogens, global warming, and the overconsumption of nonrenewable energy sources are in the headlines every day. Business leaders have come to talk of the desirability of **sustainable development**, which means business activity that produces the goods and services needed in the present without limiting the ability of future generations to meet their needs. Many companies are striving for greater *eco-efficiency*, which means increasing their production of goods and services while at the same time decreasing the deleterious effects on the environment of that production. Unfortunately, not all companies are striving equally hard toward these desirable goals. To force companies to pay attention to environmental issues, in Canada we have environmental laws, such as the *Canadian Environmental Protection Act, 1999* and the *Canadian Environmental Assessment Act*, as well as a federal agency, Environment Canada, which uses regulations to place strict controls on areas governed by these acts. On a global scale, there are environmental initiatives as well, such as the Kyoto Protocol, which seeks to reduce emissions of greenhouse gases that many scientists believe contribute to climate change.

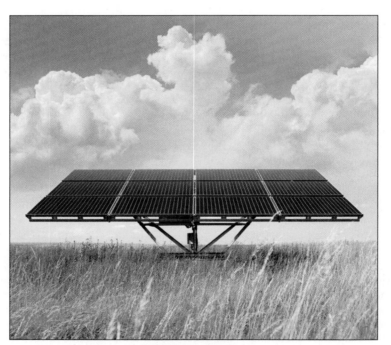

The Ontario government is proposing a solar farm similar to the one in Amstein, Germany. The massive solar "farm" near Sarnia will blanket an area larger than all three Toronto islands with hundreds of thousands of sun-soaking panels. The Ontario plant, the largest solar power station in North America, will be able to supply enough electricity to power up to 15,000 homes on sunny days, and will be the most expansive in the world to use photovoltaic cells that produce electricity when exposed to sunlight.

So, besides being a very important issue to all of us due to the clear health and quality-of-life implications, what does any of this have to do with managerial accounting? The answer is that the *costs* of dealing with environmental issues in one way or another are enormous. These **environmental costs** take many forms, such as installing scrubbers on a smokestack to comply with environmental regulations, improving a production process to reduce or eliminate certain pollutants, or cleaning up a contaminated river. In the next section, we will systematically explore these costs with the goal of having a better understanding of how to manage them.

Classifying Environmental Costs

There are many types of environmental costs.

Learning Objective 8

Understand the different types of environmental costs and discuss environmental cost management.

Private versus Social Environmental Costs   One important distinction is between private costs and social (or public) costs. *Private environmental costs* are those borne by a company or individual. Examples would be costs incurred by a company to comply with environmental regulations or to clean up a polluted lake. *Social environmental costs* are those borne by the public at large. Examples of these include costs borne by the taxpayers to staff Environment Canada; costs borne by the taxpayers to clean up a polluted lake or river; costs borne by individuals, insurance companies, and Medicare due to health problems caused by pollutants; and the unquantifiable quality-of-life costs we all bear from a degraded environment. While these social environmental costs are of great importance to all of us, we will focus our attention here on **environmental cost management**, which is the systematic attempt to measure and control or reduce the private environmental costs borne by a company or other organization.[24]

Visible versus Hidden Environmental Costs   Both social and private environmental costs can be *visible* or *hidden*. *Visible social environmental costs* are those that are known and clearly identified as tied to environmental issues, such as the taxpayers' costs of staffing Environment Canada or cleaning up a polluted lake. *Hidden social environmental costs* include those that are caused by environmental issues but have not been so identified, such as the costs borne by individuals, insurance companies, or Medicare due to cancers caused by pollutants but not clearly identified as such. For example, is melanoma (a serious type of skin cancer) caused by a familial tendency, failure to use sun block, or a thinning of the ozone layer resulting from industrial emissions of chlorofluorocarbons? No one knows for sure.

Managing Private Environmental Costs

Let's focus our attention now on environmental cost management, or the measuring and control or reduction of private environmental costs.

Visible versus Hidden Private Environmental Costs   Once again, we need to distinguish between visible and hidden costs. *Visible private environmental costs* are those that are measurable and have been clearly identified as tied to environmental issues. *Hidden private environmental costs* are those that are caused by environmental issues but have not been so identified by the accounting system.[25] Exhibit 11–11 provides examples of both visible and hidden private environmental costs.[26] Notice that the visible and the hidden costs listed in Exhibit 11–11 are further classified as follows:

- *Monitoring costs.* Costs of monitoring the production process to determine if pollution is being generated (e.g., costs of testing wastewater for contaminants)
- *Abatement costs.* Costs incurred to reduce or eliminate pollution (e.g., changing a product's design to use more expensive materials that do not result in environmental contamination)
- *Remediation costs.* (Cleanup costs)
- *On-site remediation.* Costs of reducing or preventing the discharge into the environment of pollutants that have been generated in the production process (e.g., cost of installing scrubbers on a smokestack to remove certain air pollutants in the smoke)

Exhibit 11–11
Private Environmental Costs

	Visible Costs	Hidden Costs*
Monitoring	Inspecting products for contamination	Inspection of products
	Measuring contamination of processes or machinery	Incremental costs of procurement staff to ensure vendor compliance with environmental standards
	Verifying vendor compliance with environmental standards	
Abatement	Qualifying vendors for environmental compliance	Incremental material costs incurred to use less-polluting materials
	Recycling materials, containers, or water	Incremental direct-labour costs incurred to perform duties related to reducing pollution
	Designing products and processes to reduce or eliminate negative environmental impacts	Incremental costs of more expensive processes installed all or in part to reduce pollution
	Doing environmental impact analyses	Incremental costs of purchasing hybrid (electric and gasoline-powered) vehicles to reduce air pollution
Remediation		
On-site	Installing pollution reduction or elimination devices	Incremental direct-labour costs incurred to maintain remediation equipment
	Disposing of toxic waste in an environmentally sound manner	Incremental energy or other overhead costs incurred to operate remediation equipment
	Treating toxic waste	
Off-site	Cleaning up polluted sites (e.g., water, soil, or buildings)	Incremental direct-labour costs for workers used to perform environmental cleanup tasks
	Defending or settling environmental lawsuits	
	Paying regulatory fines	Forgone contribution margins on lost sales due to an unfavourable environmental record or reputation

*Each of the costs listed in the *hidden costs* column is included under the assumption that although these costs are caused by environmental concerns, the accounting system has not identified them as such. A study by Joshi et al. provides evidence for the plausibility of this assumption. See Satish Joshi, Ranjani Krishnan, and Lester Lave, "Estimating the Hidden Costs of Environmental Regulation," *The Accounting Review* 76, no. 2 (April 2001), pp. 171–98.

- *Off-site remediation.* Costs of reducing or eliminating pollutants from the environment after they have been discharged (e.g., cost of cleaning up a river polluted by a company's operations)

The distinction between the visible and hidden costs listed in Exhibit 11–11 is an important but subtle one. Consider, for example, the incremental cost of using a more expensive material because it causes less (or no) negative environmental impact. Is this a visible or a hidden cost? The answer is *it depends* on whether the accounting system has measured this cost and identified it as an environmental cost. Studies show that many environmental costs are hidden, because the accounting system does not measure and identify them as environmental costs. "Most accounting systems accumulate visible costs into environmental cost pools, separate from other overhead cost pools. . . . For example, many steel mills compile separate cost pools for waste-water treatment, remediation, hazardous waste disposal, pollution-abatement capital expenditures, and depreciation on pollution abatement equipment."[27] However, a steel mill's incremental material costs caused by changing from sinters to less-polluting pellets in response to more stringent environmental regulations is typically not separately reported by the accounting system as an environmental cost.[28] Hence, it remains a *hidden* environmental cost.

Why is this point about visible versus hidden costs so important? Because many observers believe that the visible costs reported by most accounting systems may be only a small proportion of the hidden costs. A steel-industry study, for example, concluded that the hidden costs were nearly 10 times the visible costs!

Environmental Cost Strategies

We have only scratched the surface in our discussion of environmental costs, and it is an area certain to receive much greater attention in the future—both in practice and in academia. Let's conclude our discussion with a brief mention of three strategies for managing environmental costs.[29]

1. *End-of-pipe strategy.* Under this approach, companies produce the waste or pollutant, and then clean it up before it is discharged into the environment. Smokestack scrubbers, wastewater treatment, and carbon air filters are examples of end-of-pipe strategies.

2. *Process improvement strategy.* Under this approach, companies modify products and production processes to produce little or no pollutants, or find ways to recycle wastes internally.

3. *Prevention strategy.* "The ultimate strategy for maximizing the value of pollution-related activities involves . . . not producing any pollutants in the first place. With this strategy, companies avoid all problems with regulatory authorities and, in many cases, generate significant profit improvements."[30]

ISO 14000 Standards

The ISO 14000 standards address "environmental management." This means what the organization does to minimize harmful effects on the environment caused by its activities, and to achieve continual improvement of its environmental performance. The very first two standards deal with environmental management systems (EMS). ISO 14001 provides the requirements for an EMS and ISO 14004 gives general EMS guidelines. The other standards and guidelines address specific environmental aspects, including: labelling, performance evaluation, life cycle analysis, communication and auditing.

An ISO 14001-based EMS is a management tool enabling an organization of any size or type to:

- Identify and control the *environmental impact* of its activities, products or services
- *Improve* its environmental performance continually
- Implement a *systematic approach* to setting environmental objectives and targets, to achieving these and to demonstrating that they have been achieved

The Standards Council of Canada accredits certification bodies that assess and certify environmental management systems to the international standard ISO 14001. In addition, SCC manages various sector programs. For example, the use of forestry standards by Canadian producers enables them to move towards sustainable practices and ensure a renewable supply of raw materials. The Canadian national standard, *CAN/CSA Z809-2002 Sustainable Forest Management* and the *Sustainable Forestry Initiative (SFI) 2005–2009 standard*, outline the principal requirements of conformance. These standards support continued marketplace acceptance, both domestically and internationally, of forestry products by environmentally-conscious consumers. Certification to ISO 14001, CAN/CSA Z809 and SFI 2005–2009 provide significant contributions to the verification of sustainable forestry management practices. Organizations that achieve this certification from a body accredited by the SCC are showing their dedication to corporate social responsibility and continuous improvement.

Chapter Summary

The balanced scorecard is an important tool designed to focus management's attention on key current goals, which, if achieved, will facilitate the attainment of the organization's long-term goals. By achieving current goals in the customer, internal operations, and learning and growth perspectives, the company will ultimately achieve its long-term financial goals.

The current manufacturing environment is rapidly changing, due to the influences of worldwide competition, JIT, FMS, and an emphasis on product quality and customer service. As a result, many manufacturers are adapting to reflect these aspects of the new manufacturing environment. Moreover, nonfinancial measures of operational performance are widely used to augment the control information provided by standard costing. These measures typically focus on raw material and scrap, inventory, machinery, product quality, production and delivery, productivity, and innovation and learning.

In today's competitive environment, a company must continually improve in order to remain successful. A continuous improvement program is a constant effort to eliminate waste, reduce response time, simplify the design of both products and processes, and improve quality and customer service. Consistent with continuous improvement are the concepts of target costing and kaizen costing. Both of these methods seek to improve a product and its production process and, in so doing, reduce costs. Target costing focuses on the design phase, while kaizen costing concentrates on the manufacturing phase. Other management tools that are consistent with continuous improvement efforts include value engineering, benchmarking, reengineering, and the theory of constraints.

Product and service quality has become a key factor in determining a firm's success or failure in the global marketplace. As product quality becomes ever more important, many firms are beginning to carefully monitor the costs of maintaining product quality. Quality costs often are categorized as follows: prevention costs, appraisal costs, internal failure costs, and external failure costs. In addition to observable quality costs, companies experience hidden quality costs, such as the opportunity cost associated with lost market share. The contemporary perspective on product quality holds that if both observable and hidden costs of product quality are considered, the optimal level of product quality occurs at the zero-defect level.

Monitoring product quality coupled with measuring and reporting quality costs helps companies maintain programs of total quality management, or TQM. This refers to the broad set of management and control processes designed to focus the entire organization and all of its employees on providing products or services that do the best possible job of satisfying the customer.

Environmental issues have come to the forefront in many ways. Companies incur a variety of environmental costs, some visible and some hidden, in dealing with environmental issues. Companies are pursuing several different strategies to manage these environmental costs.

Review Problem on Operational Performance Measures

Tuscarora Door Company manufactures high-quality wooden doors used in home construction. The following information pertains to operations during April.

Processing time (average per batch)	6 hours
Inspection time (average per batch)	1 hour
Waiting time (average per batch)	4 hours
Move time (average per batch)	5 hours
Units per batch	40 units

Compute the following operational measures: (1) average value-added time per batch; (2) average non-value-added time per batch; (3) manufacturing cycle efficiency; (4) manufacturing cycle time; (5) velocity.

Solutions to Review Problem

1. Average value-added time per batch = Processing time = 6 hours
2. Average non-value-added time per batch = Inspection time + Waiting time + Move time
    = 10 hours
3. Manufacturing cycle efficiency = $\dfrac{\text{Processing time}}{\text{Processing time} + \text{Inspection time} + \text{Waiting time} + \text{Move time}}$

    $= \dfrac{6 \text{ hours}}{6 \text{ hours} + 1 \text{ hour} + 4 \text{ hours} + 5 \text{ hours}} = 37.5\%$

4. Manufacturing cycle time $= \dfrac{\text{Total production time per batch}}{\text{Units per batch}}$

$= \dfrac{16 \text{ hours}}{40 \text{ units per batch}} = .4 \text{ hour (or 24 minutes) per unit}$

5. Velocity $= \dfrac{\text{Units per batch}}{\text{Total production time per batch}}$

$= \dfrac{40 \text{ units}}{16 \text{ hours}} = 2.5 \text{ units per hour}$

Key Terms

For each term's definition refer to the indicated page, or turn to the glossary at the end of the text.

aggregate (*or* total) productivity, 436

appraisal costs, 440

balanced scorecard, 426

benchmarking (*or* competitive benchmarking), 439

best practices, 439

continuous improvement, 437

customer-acceptance measures, 435

delivery cycle time, 435

employee empowerment, 439

environmental cost management, 447

environmental costs, 446

external failure costs, 440

gain-sharing plan, 436

grade, 440

internal failure costs, 440

in-process quality controls, 435

kaizen costing, 437

manufacturing cycle efficiency (MCE), 436

manufacturing cycle time, 436

partial (*or* component) productivity, 436

prevention costs, 440

quality of conformance, 440

quality of design, 440

reengineering, 439

Six Sigma, 442

sustainable development, 446

target costing, 437

theory of constraints, 439

total quality management (TQM), 442

velocity, 436

Review Questions

11–1. Suggest two performance measures in each of the four balanced scorecard categories for a service industry firm of your choosing. Using these measures as examples, explain the difference between lead and lag measures.

11–2. List seven areas in which nonfinancial, operational performance measures are receiving increased emphasis in today's manufacturing environment.

11–3. Define the term *manufacturing cycle efficiency*.

11–4. List four examples of customer acceptance measures.

11–5. What is meant by *aggregate productivity*, and what are its limitations?

11–6. Give an example of a gain-sharing plan that could be implemented by an airline.

11–7. What is meant by the following terms: continuous improvement, price down/cost down concept, target costing, target price, target cost, target profit, value engineering, and kaizen costing?

11–8. Which of the following terms is most consistent with the old saying "Slow and steady wins the race": target costing, kaizen costing, or reengineering? Explain.

11–9. What is meant by employee empowerment, benchmarking, best practices, and reengineering?

11–10. Explain how the concepts of *continuous improvement* and the *theory of constraints* are related.

11–11. Elimination of production bottleneck activities is an example of what management concept?

11–12. List and define four types of product quality costs.

11–13. Explain the difference between observable and hidden quality costs.

11–14. Distinguish between a product's quality of design and its quality of conformance.

11–15. What is meant by a product's *grade*, as a characteristic of quality? Give an example in the service industry.

11–16. "An ounce of prevention is worth a pound of cure." Interpret this old saying in the light of Exhibit 11–7.

11–17. Briefly explain the purpose of a cause-and-effect (or fishbone) diagram.

11–18. Define the following types of environmental costs: private, social, visible, hidden, monitoring, abatement, and both on-site and off-site remediation.

11–19. Explain three strategies of environmental cost management.

Exercises

Exercise 11–20
Balanced Scorecard; Higher Education
(LO 1)

Think carefully about the overall mission and goals of your college or university.

Required:

1. How does the task of building a balanced scorecard for an educational institution differ from that for a profit-seeking enterprise?
2. Design a simple balanced scorecard for your institution, with a minimum of two measures in each of the scorecard's perspectives.

Exercise 11–21
Operational Performance Measures
(LO 2)

Hiawatha Hydrant Company manufactures fire hydrants in London, Ontario. The following information pertains to operations during May.

Processing time (average per batch)	4.25 hours
Inspection time (average per batch)	.25 hour
Waiting time (average per batch)	.25 hour
Move time (average per batch)	.25 hour
Units per batch	20 units

Required: Compute the following operational measures: (1) manufacturing cycle efficiency; (2) manufacturing cycle time; (3) velocity.

Exercise 11–22
Performance Measures for Production and Delivery
(LO 2)

Data Screen Corporation is a highly automated manufacturing firm. The vice-president of finance has decided that traditional standards are inappropriate for performance measures in an automated environment. Labour is insignificant in terms of the total cost of production and tends to be fixed, material quality is considered more important than minimizing material cost, and customer satisfaction is the number-one priority. As a result, production and delivery performance measures have been chosen to evaluate performance. The following information is considered typical of the time involved to complete and ship orders.

Waiting time:	
From order being placed to start of production	16 days
From start of production to completion	14 days
Inspection time	3 days
Processing time	6 days
Move time	5 days

Required:

1. Calculate the manufacturing cycle efficiency.
2. Calculate the delivery cycle time.

(CMA, adapted)

Exercise 11–23
Productivity Measurement
(LO 2)

Managerial accounting procedures developed for the manufacturing industry often are applied in non-manufacturing settings also. Ontario Bank and Trust Company's total output of financial services during the year just ended was valued at $11 million. The total cost of the firm's inputs, primarily direct labour and overhead, was $10 million.

Required:

1. Compute Ontario's aggregate (or total) productivity for the year.
2. Do you believe this is a useful measure? Why? Suggest an alternative approach that Ontario Bank and Trust might use to measure productivity.

Exercise 11–24
Target Costing
(LO 3)

Suppose you have just started a business to manufacture your newest invention, the photon gismo. Let's say you believe that after a few years on the market, photon gismos will sell for about $125. This allows for the introduction of similar devices by your competitors. Furthermore, let's say you want to make a profit of $25 on each gismo sold.

Required:

1. What is the target cost for the photon gismo?
2. What is the target profit?
3. What is the target price?
4. Suppose your engineers and cost accountants conclude that your design of the photon gismo will result in a unit cost of $115. How can you use the concept of target costing to help achieve your objective?

The continual search for the most effective method of accomplishing a task through comparison of existing methods and performance levels with those of other organizations or with other subunits within the same organization is called *benchmarking*. Sometimes organizations benchmark their operations against similar organizations, including their competitors. In other cases, organizations benchmark against a completely different type of organization. For example, a telecommunications company benchmarked its customer service operations against a NASCAR pit crew. The idea was to see how the telecommunications company's customer service unit could improve its response time by learning from the NASCAR crew. The pit crew, of course, had honed its procedures meticulously to get the necessary service accomplished in the least time possible. This type of benchmarking study is sometimes referred to as benchmarking "outside the box."

Exercise 11–25
Benchmarking
(LO 5)

Required:

1. How could your college or university benefit from benchmarking against a similar institution of higher education? What departments, operations, or procedures might be appropriate for the focus of such a benchmarking study?
2. How could your college or university benefit from benchmarking outside the box? What departments, operations, or procedures might benefit from such a study? What noneducational organizations might be chosen for the benchmarking study?

The following costs were incurred by Akasaka Metals Company to maintain the quality of its products. (*Yen* is the national currency of Japan.)

Exercise 11–26
Quality Costs
(LO 6)

1. Operating an X-ray machine to detect faulty welds, 99,000 yen
2. Repairs of products sold last year, 103,000 yen
3. Cost of rewelding faulty joints, 19,000 yen
4. Cost of sending machine operators to a three-week training program so they could learn to use new production equipment with a lower defect rate, 17,900 yen

Required: Classify each of these costs as a prevention, appraisal, internal failure, or external failure cost.

Coquitlam Circuitry manufactures electrical instruments for a variety of purposes. The following costs related to maintaining product quality were incurred in May.

Exercise 11–27
Quality-Cost Report
(LO 6)

Training of quality-control inspectors	$31,500
Tests of instruments before sale	45,000
Inspection of electrical components purchased from outside suppliers	18,000
Costs of rework on faulty instruments	13,500
Replaement of instruments already sold, which were still covered by warranty	24,750
Costs of defective parts that cannot be salvaged	9,150

Required: Prepare a quality-cost report similar to the report shown in Exhibit 11–7.

List three observable and three hidden quality costs that could occur in the airline industry related to the quality of service provided.

Exercise 11–28
Costs of Quality; Airline
(LO 6)

Visit the Web site of TransAlta, Inc. at www.transalta.com. Then go to the part of the site about the company's efforts toward sustainable development (the Corporate Responsibility section).

Exercise 11–29
Environmental Cost
Management; Internet
(LO 8)

Required: What are TransAlta's products? Describe the company's efforts toward sustainable development.

Problems

■ **Problem 11–30**
Balanced Scorecard; Banking;
Use of Internet
(LO 1)

Visit the Web site of a major bank, for example, TD Bank at www.td.com. Explore the site to learn about the bank's services and operations.

Required:

1. What do you think the bank's overall, long-term goals are?
2. Develop a balanced scorecard for the bank. Include two to five measures in each of the scorecard's perspectives.
3. How would the balanced scorecard affect the way managers develop the bank's strategy?
4. Explain the concept of lead and lag measures in the context of the scorecard you have developed.

■ **Problem 11–31**
Manufacturing Performance
Measurement
(LO 2)

Diagnostic Technology, Inc. manufactures diagnostic testing equipment used in hospitals. The company practises just-in-time inventory management and has a state-of-the-art manufacturing system. The following nonfinancial data were collected biweekly in the Surrey plant during the first quarter of the current year.

Biweekly Measurement Period

	1	2	3	4	5	6
Cycle time (days)	1.7	1.5	1.5	1.4	1.4	1.3
Number of defective finished products	3	3	2	3	2	2
Manufacturing-cycle efficiency	95%	94%	96%	96%	97%	96%
Customer complaints	5	6	5	4	6	7
Unresolved complaints	2	1	0	0	0	0
Products returned	3	3	2	2	1	1
Warranty claims	2	2	2	0	1	0
In-process products rejected	5	5	7	9	10	10
Aggregate productivity	1.5	1.5	1.5	1.5	1.4	1.5
Number of units produced per day per employee	410	405	412	415	415	420
Percentage of on-time deliveries	94%	95%	95%	97%	100%	100%
Percentage of orders filled	100%	100%	100%	98%	100%	100%
Inventory value/sales revenue	2%	2%	2%	1.5%	2%	1.5%
Machine downtime (minutes)	80	80	120	80	70	75
Bottleneck machine downtime (minutes)	25	20	15	0	60	10
Overtime (minutes) per employee	20	0	0	10	20	10
Average setup time (minutes)	119	119	114	111	107	100

Required:

1. For each nonfinancial performance measure, indicate which of the following areas of manufacturing performance is involved: (*a*) production processing, (*b*) product quality, (*c*) customer acceptance, (*d*) in-process quality control, (*e*) productivity, (*f*) delivery performance, (*g*) raw material and scrap, (*h*) inventory, (*i*) machine maintenance. Some measures may relate to more than one area.
2. Write a memo to management commenting on the performance data collected for the Surrey plant. Be sure to note any trends or other important results you see in the data. Evaluate the Surrey plant in each of the areas listed in requirement (1).

■ **Problem 11–32**
Production Efficiency Report;
Operational Performance
Measures
(LO 2)

Montreal Plastics Corporation manufactures a range of moulded plastic products, such as kitchen utensils and desk accessories. The production process in the Mirabel plant uses a just-in-time inventory and production management system. Every month, the controller prepares a production efficiency report, which is sent to corporate headquarters. The data compiled in these reports, for the first six months of the year, are as follows:

PRODUCTION EFFICIENCY REPORT MONTREAL PLASTICS CORPORATION Mirabel Plant January through June							
	Jan.	Feb.	Mar.	Apr.	May	June	Average
Overtime hours	59	69	74	79	84	104	78.2
Total setup time	69	69	64	63	61	61	64.5
Cycle time (average in hours)	19	19	18	17	18	16	17.8
Manufacturing-cycle efficiency	95%	94%	96%	90%	89%	90%	92.3%
Percentage of orders filled	100%	100%	100%	100%	100%	100%	100%
Percentage of on-time deliveries	99%	98%	99%	100%	96%	94%	97.7%
Inventory value/sales revenue	5%	5%	5%	4%	5%	5%	4.8%
Number of defective units, finished goods	80	82	75	40	25	22	54
Number of defective units, in process	9	29	34	39	59	59	38.2
Number of raw-material shipments with defective materials	3	3	2	0	0	0	1.3
Number of products returned	0	0	0	0	0	0	0
Aggregate productivity	1.3	1.3	1.2	1.25	1.2	1.15	1.23
Power consumption (thousands of kilowatt-hours)	800	795	802	801	800	800	799.7
Machine downtime (hours)	30	25	25	20	20	10	21.7
Bottleneck machine downtime	0	0	2	0	15	2	3.2
Number of unscheduled machine maintenance calls	0	0	1	0	2	3	1

Required:

1. Write a memo to the company president evaluating the Mirabel plant's performance. Structure your report by dividing it into the following parts: (*a*) production processing and productivity; (*b*) product quality and customer acceptance; (*c*) delivery performance; (*d*) raw material, scrap, and inventory; and (*e*) machine maintenance.

2. If you identify any areas of concern in your memo, indicate an appropriate action for management.

CommLine Equipment Corporation specializes in the manufacture of communication equipment, a field that has become increasingly competitive. Approximately two years ago, Ben Harrington, president of CommLine, became concerned that the company's bonus plan, which focused on division profitability, was not helping CommLine remain competitive. Harrington decided to implement a gain-sharing plan that would encourage employees to focus on operational areas that were important to customers and that added value without increasing cost. In addition to a profitability incentive, the revised plan also includes incentives for reduced rework costs, reduced sales returns, and on-time deliveries. Bonuses are calculated and awarded semiannually on the following basis. The bonuses are distributed among the relevant employees according to a formula developed by the division manager.

- *Profitability.* Two percent of operating income.
- *Rework.* Costs in excess of 2 percent of operating income are deducted from the bonus amount.
- *On-time delivery.* $10,000 if over 98 percent of deliveries are on time, $4,000 if 96 to 98 percent of deliveries are on time, and no increment if on-time deliveries are below 96 percent.
- *Sales returns.* $6,000 if returns are less than 1.5 percent of sales. Fifty percent of any amount in excess of 1.5 percent of sales is deducted from the bonus amount.
- If the calculation of the bonus results in a negative amount for a particular period, there is no bonus, and the negative amount is not carried forward to the next period.

■ **Problem 11–33**
Gain-Sharing; Operational Performance Measures
(LO 2)

1*a.* Second semiannual bonus awarded: $13,200
2*a.* Second semiannual bonus awarded: $22,240

The revised bonus plan was implemented on January 1, 20x1. Presented in the following table are the results for CommLine's Cloverdale and Vernon Divisions, for the first year under the new bonus plan. Both of these divisions had similar sales and operating income results for the prior year, when the old bonus plan was in effect. Based on the 20x0 results, the employees of the Cloverdale Division earned a bonus of $54,120 while the employees of the Vernon Division earned $44,880.

	Cloverdale Division		Vernon Division	
	January 20x1– June 20x1	July 20x1– December 20x1	January 20x1– June 20x1	July 20x1– December 20x1
Sales	$8,400,000	$8,800,000	$5,700,000	$5,800,000
Operating income	$924,000	$880,000	$684,000	$812,000
On-time delivery	95.4%	97.3%	98.2%	94.6%
Rework costs	$23,000	$22,000	$12,000	$16,000
Sales returns	$168,000	$140,000	$89,500	$85,000

Required:

1. For the Cloverdale Division:
    a. Compute the semiannual instalments and total bonus awarded for 20x1.
    b. Discuss the likely behaviour of the Cloverdale Division employees under the revised bonus plan.

2. For the Vernon Division:
    a. Compute the semiannual instalments and total bonus awarded for 20x1.
    b. Discuss the likely behaviour of the Vernon Division employees under the revised bonus plan.

3. Citing specific examples, evaluate whether Harrington's revisions to the bonus plan at CommLine Equipment Corporation have achieved the desired results, and recommend any changes that might improve the plan.

(CMA, adapted)

■ **Problem 11–34**
Kaizen Costing Chart
(LO 4)

Queensland Television Corporation (QTC) manufactures TV sets in Australia, largely for the domestic market. QTC has recently implemented a kaizen costing program, with the goal of reducing the manufacturing cost per television set by 10 percent during 20x1, the first year of the kaizen effort. The cost per TV set at the end of 20x0 was $500. The following table shows the average cost per television set estimated during each month of 20x1. (The day this problem was written, the Australian dollar was valued at $.74 in Canadian dollars.)

Month	Cost per Set	Month	Cost per Set
January	$500	July	$485
February	500	August	470
March	495	September	460
April	492	October	460
May	490	November	450
June	485	December	440

Required: Prepare a kaizen costing chart for 20x1 to show the results of Queensland Television Corporation's first year of kaizen costing. In developing the chart, use the following steps:

1. Draw and label the axes of the kaizen costing chart.
2. Indicate the current year cost base and the kaizen goal (cost reduction rate) on the chart.
3. Tick-mark the horizontal axis with the months of 20x1, and the vertical axis with dollar amounts in the appropriate range.
4. Plot the 12 monthly estimates of the average cost per TV set. Then draw a line connecting the cost points that were plotted.
5. Complete the chart with any further labelling necessary.
6. Briefly explain the purpose of kaizen costing. How could a continuous-quality-improvement program, coupled with the kaizen costing effort implemented by Queensland Television Corporation, help the firm begin competing in the worldwide market?

Industrial Technologies, Inc. (ITI) produces two compression machines that are popular with manufacturers of plastics: no. 165 and no. 172. Machine no. 165 has an average selling price of $30,000, whereas no. 172 typically sells for approximately $27,500. The company is very concerned about quality and has provided the following information:

	No. 165	No. 172
Number of machines produced and sold	160	200
Warranty costs:		
Average repair cost per unit	$900	$350
Percentage of units needing repair	70%	10%
Reliability engineering at $150 per hour	1,600 hours	2,000 hours
Rework at ITI's manufacturing plant:		
Average rework cost per unit	$1,900	$1,600
Percentage of units needing rework	35%	25%
Manufacturing inspection at $50 per hour	300 hours	500 hours
Transportation costs to customer sites to fix problems	$29,500	$15,000
Quality training for employees	$35,000	$50,000

Required:

1. Classify the preceding costs as prevention, appraisal, internal failure, or external failure.
2. Using the classifications in requirement (1), compute ITI's quality costs for machine no. 165 in dollars and ˙as a percentage of sales revenues. Also calculate prevention, appraisal, internal failure, and external failure costs as a percentage of total quality costs.
3. Repeat requirement (2) for machine no. 172.
4. Comment on your findings, noting whether the company is "investing" its quality expenditures differently for the two machines.
5. Quality costs can be classified as observable or hidden. What are hidden quality costs, and how do these costs differ from observable costs?

News Technology, Inc. manufactures computerized laser printing equipment used by newspaper publishers throughout North America. In recent years, the company's market share has been eroded by stiff competition from Asian and European competitors. Price and product quality are the two key areas in which companies compete in this market.

Ben McDonough, News Technology's president, decided to devote more resources to the improvement of product quality after learning that his company's products had been ranked fourth in product quality in a recent survey of newspaper publishers. He believed that the company could no longer afford to ignore the importance of product quality. McDonough set up a task force that he headed to implement a formal quality-improvement program. Included on the task force were representatives from engineering, sales, customer service, production, and accounting, as McDonough believed this was a companywide program and all employees should share the responsibility for its success.

After the first meeting of the task force, Sheila Hayes, manager of sales, asked Tony Reese, the production manager, what he thought of the proposed program. Reese replied, "I have reservations. Quality is too abstract to be attaching costs to it and then to be holding you and me responsible for cost improvements. I like to work with goals that I can see and count! I don't like my annual income to be based on a decrease in quality costs; there are too many variables that we have no control over!"

News Technology's quality-improvement program has now been in operation for 18 months, and the following quality cost report has recently been issued. As they were reviewing the report, Hayes asked Reese what he thought of the quality program now. "The work is really moving through the Production Department," replied Reese. "We used to spend time helping the Customer Service Department solve their problems, but they are leaving us alone these days. I have no complaints so far. I'll be anxious to see how much the program increases our bonuses."

NEWS TECHNOLOGY, INC.
Cost of Quality Report
(in thousands)

	6/30/x3	9/30/x3	12/31/x3	3/31/x4	6/30/x4	9/30/x4
			Quarter Ended:			
Prevention costs:						
Design review	$ 19	$ 101	$ 110	$ 99	$ 103	$ 94
Machine maintenance	215	215	202	190	170	160
Training suppliers	6	46	26	21	21	16
Total	$ 240	$ 362	$ 338	$ 310	$ 294	$ 270
Appraisal costs:						
Incoming inspection	$ 45	$ 53	$ 57	$ 36	$ 34	$ 22
Final testing	160	160	154	140	115	94
Total	$ 205	$ 213	$ 211	$ 176	$ 149	$ 116
Internal failure costs:						
Rework	$ 120	$ 106	$ 114	$ 88	$ 78	$ 62
Scrap	68	64	53	42	40	40
Total	$ 188	$ 170	$ 167	$ 130	$ 118	$ 102
External failure costs:						
Warranty repairs	$ 69	$ 31	$ 24	$ 25	$ 23	$ 23
Customer returns	262	251	122	116	87	80
Total	$ 331	$ 282	$ 146	$ 141	$ 110	$ 103
Total quality cost	$ 964	$1,027	$ 862	$ 757	$ 671	$ 591
Total production cost	$4,120	$4,540	$4,380	$4,650	$4,580	$4,510

Required:

1. Identify at least three factors that should be present for an organization to successfully implement a quality improvement program.
2. By analyzing the cost of quality report presented, determine if News Technology's quality improvement program has been successful. List specific evidence to support your answer.
3. Discuss why Tony Reese's current reaction to the quality improvement program is more favourable than his initial reaction.
4. News Technology's president believed that the quality improvement program was essential and that the firm could no longer afford to ignore the importance of product quality. Discuss how the company could measure the opportunity cost of not implementing the quality-improvement program.

(CMA, adapted)

■ **Problem 11–37**
Environmental Cost
Management
(LO 8)

As a group, take a walking tour of your campus and the surrounding community. Make a list of all of the environmental costs of which you see evidence.

Required: Make a presentation to the class about your findings. List and categorize the environmental costs you noted either for your college/university or for businesses in the community. (You might consider writing a letter to your campus newspaper regarding these environmental issues and their costs.)

Chapter Twelve

Responsibility Accounting, Investment Centres, and Transfer Pricing

FOCUS COMPANY

This chapter's Focus Company is Aloha Hotels and Resorts, a chain of luxury hotels and resorts in Hawaii. Here we will explore this hospitality company's responsibility accounting system. Responsibility accounting refers to the various concepts and tools used to measure the performance of both people and departments in an organization. The management of Aloha Hotels and Resorts uses detailed performance reports about the company's divisions, hotels, and departments to help ensure that everyone in the organization is working toward the same overall corporate goals.

IN CONTRAST

In contrast to the hospitality-services setting of Aloha Hotels and Resorts, we will turn to Suncoast Food Centres, a chain of retail grocery stores on the Sunshine Coast of British Columbia. The company has three divisions. The Lower Sunshine Coast and Upper Sun-

shine Coast Divisions operate individual grocery stores in six coastal cities. The Food Processing Division operates dairy plants, bakeries, and meat-processing facilities in order to supply the grocery stores with fresh food products. We will explore how companies evaluate the

After completing this chapter, you should be able to:

1 Explain the role of responsibility accounting in fostering goal congruence.

2 Define and give an example of a cost centre, a revenue centre, a profit centre, and an investment centre.

3 Prepare a performance report and explain the relationships between the performance reports for various responsibility centres.

4 Use a cost allocation base to allocate costs.

5 Prepare a segmented income statement.

6 Compute an investment centre's return on investment (ROI), residual income (RI), and economic value added (EVA).

7 Explain how a manager can improve ROI.

8 Describe some advantages and disadvantages of both ROI and residual income as divisional performance measures.

9 Explain how to measure a division's income and invested capital.

10 Use the general economic rule to set an optimal transfer price.

11 Explain how to base a transfer price on market prices, costs, or negotiations.

performance of investment centres, such as Suncoast's three divisions. In addition to the evaluation of investment centre performance, we will also discuss transfer pricing, the amount charged when one division of a company sells products or services to another division. In our illustration of Suncoast Food Centres, the Food Processing Division sells their dairy, bakery, and meat products to the Suncoast grocery stores at a transfer price. We will explore different ways to set such transfer prices.

Suncoast
FOOD CENTRES

Most large organizations are decentralized, which means that they are divided into smaller units, each of which is assigned particular responsibilities. These units are called by various names, including divisions, segments, business units, and departments. Managers throughout these organizations are given autonomy to make decisions for their subunits. Decentralization takes advantage of the specialized knowledge and skills of managers, permits an organization to respond quickly to events, and relieves top management of the need to direct the organization's day-to-day activities.

The managers of an organization should ensure that the people in each department are striving toward the same overall goals. The biggest challenge in making a decentralized organization function effectively is to obtain goal congruence among the organization's autonomous managers.

Learning Objective 1

Explain the role of responsibility accounting in fostering goal congruence.

Obtaining Goal Congruence: A Behavioural Challenge

Goal congruence is obtained when the managers of subunits throughout an organization strive to achieve the goals set by top management. This desirable state of affairs is difficult to achieve for a variety of reasons. Managers often are unaware of the effects of their decisions on the organization's other subunits. Also, it is only human for people to be more concerned with the performance of their own subunit than with the effectiveness of the entire organization. The behavioural challenge in designing any management control system is to come as close as possible to obtaining goal congruence.

To obtain goal congruence, the behaviour of managers throughout an organization must be directed toward top management's goals. Successful managers not only have their sights set on these organizational goals, but also have been given positive incentives to achieve them.

How can an organization's managerial-accounting system promote goal congruence? **Responsibility accounting** refers to the various concepts and tools used by managerial accountants to measure the performance of people and departments in order to foster goal congruence. *The managerial accountant's objective* in designing a responsibility-accounting system is to provide these incentives to the organization's subunit managers. *The key factor in deciding how well the responsibility-accounting system works is the extent to which it directs managers' efforts toward organizational goals.*

Management by Objectives (MBO)   An emphasis on obtaining goal congruence is consistent with a broad managerial approach called **management by objectives**, or **MBO**. Under the MBO philosophy, managers participate in setting goals that they then strive to achieve. The goals usually are expressed in financial or other quantitative terms, and the responsibility-accounting system is used to evaluate performance in achieving them.

Adaptation of Management Control Systems

When an organization begins its operations, it is usually small and decision making generally is centralized. The chief executive can control operations without a formal responsibility-accounting system. It is relatively easy in a small organization for managers to keep in touch with routine operations through face-to-face contact with employees.

As an organization grows, however, its managers need more formal information systems, including managerial-accounting information, in order to maintain control. Accounting systems are established to record events and provide the framework for internal and external financial reports. Budgets become necessary to plan the organization's activity. As the organization gains experience in producing its goods or services, cost standards and flexible budgets often are established to help control operations. As the organization continues to grow, some delegation of decision making becomes necessary. Decentralization is often the result of this tendency toward delegation. Ultimately, a fully developed responsibility-accounting system emerges. Managerial accountants designate cost centres, revenue centres, profit centres, and investment centres, and develop appropriate performance measures for each subunit.

Thus, an organization's accounting and managerial control systems usually adapt and become more complex as the organization grows and changes.

Responsibility Centres

The basis of a responsibility-accounting system is the designation of each subunit in the organization as a particular type of *responsibility centre*. A **responsibility centre** is a subunit in an organization whose manager is held accountable for specified financial results of the subunit's activities. There are four common types of responsibility centres.

> **Learning Objective 2**
>
> Define and give an example of a cost centre, a revenue centre, a profit centre, and an investment centre.

Cost Centre   A **cost centre** is an organizational subunit, such as a department or division, whose manager is held accountable for the costs incurred in the subunit. The Painting Department in an automobile plant is an example of a cost centre.

Revenue Centre   The manager of a **revenue centre** is held accountable for the revenue attributed to the subunit. The Reservations Department of an airline and the Sales Department of a manufacturer are revenue centres.

Profit Centre   A **profit centre** is an organizational subunit whose manager is held accountable for profit. Since profit is equal to revenue minus expenses, profit-centre managers are held accountable for both the revenue and expenses attributed to their subunits. An example of a profit centre is a company-owned restaurant in a fast-food chain.

Investment Centre   The manager of an **investment centre** is held accountable for the subunit's profit *and the invested capital* used by the subunit to generate its profit. A division of a large corporation is typically designated as an investment centre.[1]

Responsibility Accounting Illustrated

To illustrate the concepts used in responsibility accounting, we will focus on a hotel chain. Aloha Hotels and Resorts operates luxury hotels in the state of Hawaii. The company is divided into the Maui Division, which operates seven hotels on the island of Maui, and the Oahu Division, with three properties on the island of Oahu. Exhibit 12–1 shows the company's organization chart, and Exhibit 12–2 depicts the responsibility-accounting system.

Exhibit 12–1
Organization Chart: Aloha
Hotels and Resorts

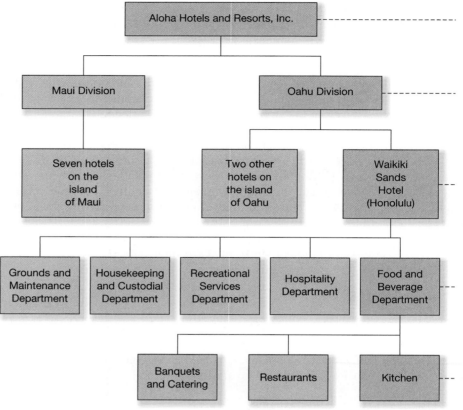

Exhibit 12–2
Responsibility Accounting
System: Aloha Hotels and
Resorts

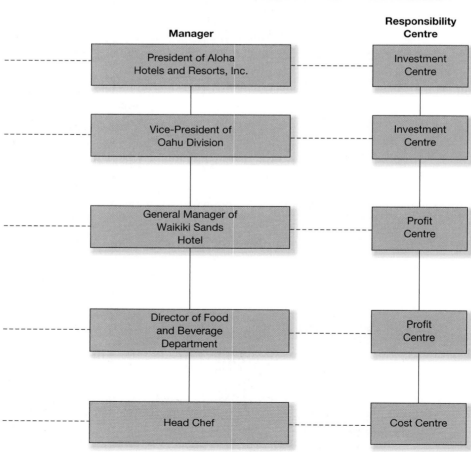

This engine assembly department is a cost centre. The telemarketing operation shown here is a revenue centre. This Starbucks coffee shop is a profit centre. The oil refinery pictured is an investment centre. What sort of responsibility centre designation would be appropriate for your local car wash, hair salon, and laundromat?

Corporate Level The chief executive officer (CEO) of Aloha Hotels and Resorts, Inc. is the company's president. The president, who is responsible to the company's stock-holders, is accountable for corporate profit in relation to the capital (assets) invested in the company. Therefore, the entire company is an *investment centre*. The president has the autonomy to make significant decisions that affect the company's profit and invested capital. For example, the final decision to add a new luxury tower to any of the company's resort properties would be made by the president.

Division Level The vice-president of the Oahu Division is accountable for the profit earned by the three resort hotels on Oahu in relation to the capital invested in those properties. Hence, the Oahu Division is also an *investment centre*. The vice-president has the authority to make major investment decisions regarding the properties on Oahu, up to a limit of $300,000. For example, he or she might decide to install a new swimming pool at one of the Oahu resort hotels, but could not decide to add a new wing.

Hotel Level The Waikiki Sands Hotel, in Honolulu, is one of the properties in the Oahu Division. The general manager of the Waikiki Sands Hotel is accountable for the profit earned by the hotel. The general manager does not have the authority to make major investment decisions, but is responsible for operational decisions. For example, the general manager hires all of the hotel's departmental managers, sets wage rates, determines procedures and standards for operations, approves decorating decisions, and generally oversees the hotel's operation. Since the hotel's general manager has no authority to make major investment decisions, she is held accountable only for the hotel's profit, not the capital invested in the property. Thus, the Waikiki Sands Hotel is a *profit centre*.

Departmental Level The Waikiki Sands Hotel has five departments, as shown in Exhibit 12–1. The Grounds and Maintenance Department includes landscaping, building and equipment maintenance, and hotel security. The Housekeeping and Custodial Services Department covers laundry and janitorial services. These two departments are called service departments, since they provide services to the hotel's other departments but do not deal directly with hotel guests. The Recreational Services Department operates the hotel's swimming pools, saunas, video arcade, and tennis courts. The Hospitality Department includes the hotel's reservations desk, rooms, bell staff, and shopping facilities. Finally, the Food and Beverage Department operates the resort's restaurants, coffee shop, lounges, poolside snack bar, banquet operations, and catering service.

The director of the Food and Beverage Department is accountable for the profit earned on all food and beverage operations. Therefore, this department is a *profit centre*. The director has the authority to approve the menu, set food and beverage prices, hire the wait staff, schedule entertainers, and generally oversee all food and beverage operations.

Kitchen Level The Food and Beverage Department is divided further into subunits responsible for Banquets and Catering, Restaurants, and the Kitchen.

The head chef manages the kitchen and is accountable for the costs incurred there. Thus, the Kitchen is a *cost centre*. The head chef hires the kitchen staff, orders food supplies, and oversees all food preparation. The head chef is responsible for providing high-quality food at the lowest possible cost.

Performance Reporting

The performance of each responsibility centre is summarized periodically on a *performance report*. A **performance report** shows the budgeted and actual amounts, and the variances between these amounts, of key financial results appropriate for the type of responsibility centre involved. For example, a cost centre's performance report concentrates on budgeted and actual amounts for various cost items attributable to the cost centre. Performance reports also typically show the variance between budgeted and actual amounts for the financial results conveyed in the report. The data

	A	B	C	D	E	F	G	H	I
1		Flexible Budget		Actual Results		Variance*			
2		February	Year to Date	February	Year to Date	February		Year to Date	
3									
4	Kitchen staff wages	$ 80,000	$ 168,000	$ 78,000	$ 169,000	$ 2,000	F	$ 1,000	U
5	Food	675,000	1,420,000	678,000	1,421,000	3,000	U	1,000	U
6	Paper products	120,000	250,000	115,000	248,000	5,000	F	2,000	F
7	Variable overhead	70,000	150,000	71,000	154,000	1,000	U	4,000	U
8	Fixed overhead	85,000	180,000	83,000	181,000	2,000	F	1,000	U
9	Total expense	$ 1,030,000	$ 2,168,000	$ 1,025,000	$ 2,173,000	$ 5,000	F	$ 5,000	U
10									
11	*F denotes favourable variance, U denotes unfavourable variance.								

in a performance report help managers use *management by exception* to control an organization's operations effectively.

The performance report for the kitchen of the Waikiki Sands Hotel for February is shown in the Excel spreadsheet in Exhibit 12–3.

As the organization chart in Exhibit 12–1 shows, Aloha Hotels and Resorts is a *hierarchy*. Each subunit manager reports to one higher-level manager, from the head chef all the way up to the president. In such an organization, there is also a hierarchy of performance reports, since the performance of each subunit constitutes part of the performance of the next higher-level subunit. For example, the cost performance in the kitchen of the Waikiki Sands Hotel constitutes part of the profit performance of the hotel's Food and Beverage Department.

Exhibit 12–4 shows the relationships between the February performance reports for several subunits of Aloha Hotels and Resorts. Notice that the numbers for the Grounds and Maintenance Department, the Housekeeping and Custodial Department, and the Kitchen are in parentheses. These subunits are cost centres, so the numbers shown are expenses. All of the other subunits shown in Exhibit 12–4 are either profit centres or investment centres. The numbers shown for these subunits are profits, so they are not enclosed in parentheses. In addition to the profit figures shown, the performance reports for the investment centres should include data about invested capital. The Maui Division, the Oahu Division, and the company as a whole are investment centres. Performance evaluation in investment centres is covered in the next chapter.

Notice the relationships between the performance reports in Exhibit 12–4. The kitchen is the lowest-level subunit shown, and its performance report is the same as that displayed in Exhibit 12–3. The *total expense* line from the kitchen performance report is included as one line in the performance report for the Food and Beverage Department. Also included are the total profit figures for the department's other two subunits: Banquets and Catering, and Restaurants. How is the *total profit* line for the Food and Beverage Department used in the performance report for the Waikiki Sands Hotel? Follow the relationships emphasized with arrows in Exhibit 12–4.

The hierarchy of performance reports starts at the bottom and builds toward the top, just like the organization structure depicted in Exhibit 12–1 builds from the bottom upward. Each manager in the organization receives the performance report for his or her own subunit in addition to the performance reports for the major subunits in the next lower level. For example, the general manager of the Waikiki Sands Hotel receives the reports for the hotel, and each of its departments: Grounds and Maintenance, Housekeeping and Custodial, Recreational Services, Hospitality, and Food and Beverage. With these reports, the hotel's general manager can evaluate her subordinates as well as her own performance. This will help the general manager in improving the hotel's performance, motivating employees, and planning future operations.

Exhibit 12–3
Performance Report for February: Kitchen, Waikiki Sands Hotel

"It is real important for accountants or finance people, when you get into the numbers, to be able to take a spreadsheet that has a zillion numbers on it and then turn around and present that to somebody at a high enough level in a meaningful manner that they can understand. I think probably in the last five years that is what I spend most of my time on—working on communications." (12c)

Caterpillar

	Flexible Budget*		Actual Results*		Variance†	
	February	Year to Date	February	Year to Date	February	Year to Date
Company	$30,660	$64,567	$ 30,716	$64,570	$56 F	$ 3 F
Maui Division	$18,400	$38,620	$ 18,470	$38,630	$70 F	$10 F
Oahu Division	12,260	25,947	12,246	25,940	14 U	7 U
Total profit	$ 30,660	$64,567	$ 30,716	$64,570	$56 F	$ 3 F
Oahu Division						
Waimea Beach Resort	$ 6,050	$12,700	$ 6,060	$12,740	$10 F	$40 F
Diamond Head Lodge	2,100	4,500	2,050	4,430	50 U	70 U
Waikiki Sands Hotel	4,110	8,747	4,136	8,770	26 F	23 F
Total profit	$12,260	$25,947	$ 12,246	$25,940	$14 U	$ 7 U
Waikiki Sands Hotel						
Grounds and Maintenance	$ (45)	$ (90)	$ (44)	$ (90)	$ 1 F	—
Housekeeping and Custodial	(40)	(90)	(41)	(90)	1 U	—
Recreational Services	40	85	41	88	1 F	$ 3 F
Hospitality	2,800	6,000	2,840	6,030	40 F	30 F
Food and Beverage	1,355	2,842	1,340	2,832	15 U	10 U
Total profit	$ 4,110	$ 8,747	$ 4,136	$ 8,770	$26 F	$23 F
Food and Beverage Department						
Banquets and Catering	$ 600	$ 1,260	$ 605	$ 1,265	$ 5 F	$ 5 F
Restaurants	1,785	3,750	1,760	3,740	25 U	10 U
Kitchen	(1,030)	(2,168)	(1,025)	(2,173)	5 F	5 U
Total profit	$ 1,355	$ 2,842	$ 1,340	$ 2,832	$15 U	$10 U
Kitchen						
Kitchen staff wages	$ (80)	$ (168)	$ (78)	$ (169)	$ 2 F	$ 1 U
Food	(675)	(1,420)	(678)	(1,421)	3 U	1 U
Paper products	(120)	(250)	(115)	(248)	5 F	2 F
Variable overhead	(70)	(150)	(71)	(154)	1 U	4 U
Fixed overhead	(85)	(180)	(83)	(181)	2 F	1 U
Total expense	$ (1,030)	$ (2,168)	$ (1,025)	$ (2,173)	$ 5 F	$ 5 U

*Numbers without parentheses denote profit; numbers with parentheses denote expenses; numbers in thousands.

†F denotes favourable variance; U denotes unfavourable variance.

Exhibit 12–4

Performance Reports for February: Selected Subunits of Aloha Hotels and Resorts

Budgets, Variance Analysis, and Responsibility Accounting

Notice that the performance reports in Exhibit 12–4 make heavy use of budgets and variance analysis. Thus, the topics of budgeting, variance analysis, and responsibility accounting are closely interrelated. The flexible budget provides the benchmark against which actual revenues, expenses, and profits are compared. As you saw in Chapter 10, it is important to use a flexible budget so that appropriate comparisons can be made. It would make no sense, for example, to compare the actual costs incurred in the kitchen at Waikiki Sands Hotel with budgeted costs established for a different level of hotel occupancy.

The performance reports in Exhibit 12–4 also show variances between budgeted and actual performance. These variances are often broken down into smaller components to help management pinpoint responsibility and diagnose performance. Variance analysis, which was discussed in detail in Chapter 10, is an important tool in a responsibility-accounting system.

Cost Allocation and Allocation Bases

Learning Objective 4

Use a cost allocation base to allocate costs.

Many costs incurred by an organization are the joint result of several subunits' activities. For example, the property taxes and utility costs incurred by Aloha Hotels and Resorts for the Waikiki Sands Hotel are the joint result of all of the hotel's activities. One function of a responsibility-accounting system is to assign all of an organization's costs to the subunits that cause them to be incurred.

A collection of costs to be assigned is called a **cost pool**. At the Waikiki Sands Hotel, for example, all utility costs are combined into a *utility cost pool*, which includes the costs of electricity, water, sewer, trash collection, television cable, and telephone. The responsibility centres, products, or services to which costs are to be assigned are called **cost objects**. The Waikiki Sands' cost objects are its major departments. (See the organization chart in Exhibit 12–1.) The process of assigning the costs in the *cost pool* to the *cost objects* is called **cost allocation** or **cost distribution**.

Allocation Bases and Budgets

To distribute (or allocate) costs to responsibility centres, the managerial accountant chooses an *allocation base* for each cost pool. An **allocation base** is a measure of activity, physical characteristic, or economic characteristic that is associated with the responsibility centres, which are the cost objects in the allocation process. The allocation base chosen for a cost pool should reflect some characteristic of the various responsibility centres that is related to the incurrence of costs. An allocation base also may be referred to as a *cost driver*.

Exhibit 12–5 shows the Waikiki Sands Hotel's February cost distribution for selected cost pools. Each cost pool is distributed to each responsibility centre in proportion to that centre's relative amount of the allocation base. For example, the Food and Beverage Department receives 30 percent of the total administrative costs, $25,000, because that department's 36 employees constitute 30 percent of the hotel's employees. Notice that no marketing costs are allocated to either the Grounds and Maintenance

Exhibit 12–5

Cost Distribution to Responsibility Centres: Waikiki Sands Hotel

Cost Pool	Responsibility Centre	Allocation Base	Percentage of Total	Costs Distributed
Administration	Grounds and Maintenance	12 employees	10.0%	$ 2,500
	Housekeeping and Custodial	24 employees	20.0	5,000
	Recreational Services	12 employees	10.0	2,500
	Hospitality	36 employees	30.0	7,500
	Food and Beverage	36 employees	30.0	7,500
	Total	120 employees	100.0%	$25,000
Facilities	Grounds and Maintenance	2,000 m²	1.0%	$ 300
	Housekeeping and Custodial	2,000 m²	1.0	300
	Recreational Services	5,000 m²	2.5	750
	Hospitality	175,000 m²	87.5	26,250
	Food and Beverage	16,000 m²	8.0	2,400
	Total	200,000 m²	100.0%	$30,000
Marketing	Grounds and Maintenance	—	—	—
	Housekeeping and Custodial	—	—	—
	Recreational Services	$ 20,000 of sales	4.0%	$ 2,000
	Hospitality	400,000 of sales	80.0	40,000
	Food and Beverage	80,000 of sales	16.0	8,000
	Total	$500,000 of sales	100.0%	$50,000

Exhibit 12–6
Cost Distribution: Budgeted versus Actual Allocation Bases

Responsibility Centre	Budgeted Sales Revenue	Actual Sales Revenue	Marketing Cost Distribution	
			Based on Budget	Based on Actual
Recreational Services	$ 20,000 (4%)*	$ 4,500 (1%)*	$ 2,000	$ 500
Hospitality	400,000 (80%)	405,000 (90%)	40,000	45,000
Food and Beverage	80,000 (16%)	40,500 (9%)	8,000	4,500
Total	$ 500,000	$450,000	$50,000	$50,000

*Percentage of column total.

Department or the Housekeeping and Custodial Department. Neither of these responsibility centres generates any sales revenue.

At the Waikiki Sands Hotel, administrative and marketing costs are distributed on the basis of *budgeted* amounts of the relevant allocation bases, rather than *actual* amounts. The managerial accountant should design an allocation procedure so that the behaviour of one responsibility centre does not affect the costs allocated to other responsibility centres.

Suppose, for example, that the budgeted and actual February sales revenues for the hotel were as shown in Exhibit 12–6. Notice that the Hospitality Department's actual sales revenue is close to the budget. However, the actual sales of the Recreational Services Department and the Food and Beverage Department are substantially below the budget. If the distribution of marketing costs is based on actual sales, instead of budgeted sales, then the cost distributed to the Hospitality Department jumps from $40,000 to $45,000, an increase of 12.5 percent. Why does this happen? As a result of a sales performance substantially below the budget for the *other two departments*, the Hospitality Department is penalized with a hefty increase in its cost distribution. This is misleading and unfair to the Hospitality Department manager. A preferable cost distribution procedure is to use budgeted sales revenue as the allocation base, rather than actual sales revenue. Then the marketing costs distributed to each department do not depend on the performance in the other two departments.

Activity-Based Responsibility Accounting

Traditional responsibility-accounting systems tend to focus on the financial performance measures of cost, revenue, and profit for the *subunits* of an organization. Contemporary cost management systems, however, are beginning to focus more and more on *activities*. Costs are incurred in organizations and their subunits because of activities. *Activity-based costing (ABC)* systems associate costs with the activities that drive those costs. The database created by an ABC system, coupled with nonfinancial measures of operational performance for each activity, enables management to employ **activity-based responsibility accounting**. Under this approach, management's attention is directed not only to the cost incurred in an activity but also to the activity itself. Is the activity necessary? Does it add value to the organization's product or service? Can the activity be improved? By seeking answers to these questions, managers can eliminate non-value-added activities and increase the cost-effectiveness of the activities that do add value.[2]

Behavioural Effects of Responsibility Accounting

Responsibility-accounting systems can influence behaviour significantly. Whether the behavioural effects are positive or negative, however, depends on how responsibility accounting is implemented.

Information versus Blame

The proper focus of a responsibility-accounting system is *information*. The system should identify the individual in the organization who is in the best position to explain each particular event or financial result. The emphasis should be on providing that individual and higher-level managers with information to help them understand the reasons behind the organization's performance. When properly used, a responsibility-accounting system *does not emphasize blame*. If managers feel they are beaten over the head with criticism and rebukes when unfavourable variances occur, they are unlikely to respond in a positive way. Instead, they will tend to undermine the system and view it with skepticism. But when the responsibility-accounting system emphasizes its informational role, managers tend to react constructively, and strive for improved performance.

Controllability

Some organizations use performance reports that distinguish between controllable and uncontrollable costs or revenues. For example, the head chef at the Waikiki Sands Hotel can influence the hours and efficiency of the kitchen staff, but he probably cannot change the wage rates. A performance report that distinguishes between the financial results influenced by the head chef and those he does not influence has the advantage of providing complete information to the head chef. Yet the report recognizes that certain results are beyond his control.

"Distinguishing between controllable and uncontrollable costs can increase the effectiveness of a cost management system, if it's done from the perspective of helping a client department understand where the opportunities for cost reduction are." (12d)
American Management Systems

Identifying costs as controllable or uncontrollable is not always easy. Many cost items are influenced by more than one person. The time frame also may be important in determining controllability. Some costs are controllable over a long time frame, but not within a short time period. To illustrate, suppose the Waikiki Sands' head chef has signed a one-year contract with a local seafood supplier. The cost of seafood can be influenced by the head chef if the time period is a year or more, but the cost cannot be controlled on a weekly basis.

Motivating Desired Behaviour

Managerial accountants often use the responsibility-accounting system to motivate actions considered desirable by upper-level management. Sometimes the responsibility-accounting system can solve behavioural problems as well. As a case in point, consider the problem of rush orders. To accept or reject a rush order is a cost-benefit decision:

Costs of Accepting Rush Order	**Benefits of Accepting Rush Order**
Disrupted production	Satisfied customers
More setups	Greater future sales
Higher costs	

The following real-world example involving rush orders provides a case in point.

The production scheduler in a manufacturing firm was frequently asked to interrupt production of one product with a rush order for another product. Rush orders typically resulted in greater costs because more product setups were required. Since the production scheduler was evaluated on the basis of costs, he was reluctant to accept rush orders. The sales manager, on the other hand, was evaluated on the basis of sales revenue. By agreeing to customers' demands for rush orders, the sales manager satisfied his customers. This resulted in more future sales and favourable performance ratings for the sales manager.

As the rush orders became more and more frequent, the production manager began to object. The sales manager responded by asking if the production scheduler wanted to take the responsibility for losing a customer by refusing a rush order. The production scheduler did not want to be blamed for lost sales, so he grudgingly accepted the rush orders. However, considerable ill will developed between the sales manager and production scheduler.

The company's managerial accountant came to the rescue by redesigning the responsibility-accounting system. The system was modified to accumulate the extra costs associated with rush orders and charge them to the sales manager's responsibility centre, rather than the production scheduler's centre. The ultimate result was that the sales manager chose more carefully which rush-order requests to make, and the production manager accepted them gracefully.

The problem described in the preceding illustration developed because two different managers were considering the costs and benefits of the rush-order decision. The production manager was looking only at the costs, while the sales manager was looking only at the benefits. The modified responsibility-accounting system made the sales manager look at *both the costs and the benefits* associated with each rush order. Then the sales manager could make the necessary trade-off between costs and benefits in considering each rush order. Some rush orders were rejected, because the sales manager decided the costs exceeded the benefits. Other rush orders were accepted, when the importance of the customer and potential future sales justified it.

This example illustrates how a well-designed responsibility-accounting system can make an organization run more smoothly and achieve higher performance.

Segmented Reporting

Subunits of an organization are often called *segments*. *Segmented reporting* refers to the preparation of accounting reports by segment and for the organization as a whole. Many organizations prepare **segmented income statements**, which show the income for major segments and for the entire enterprise.

In preparing segmented income statements, the managerial accountant must decide how to treat costs that are incurred to benefit more than one segment. Such costs are called **common costs**. The salary of the president of Aloha Hotels and Resorts is a common cost. The president manages the entire company. Some of her time is spent on matters related specifically to the Maui Division or the Oahu Division, but much of it is spent on tasks that are not traced easily to either division. The president works with the company's board of directors, develops strategic plans for the company, and helps set policy and goals for the entire enterprise. Thus, her compensation is a common cost, not easily related to any particular segment's activities.

Many managerial accountants believe that it is misleading to allocate common costs to an organization's segments. Since these costs are not traceable to the activities of segments, they can be allocated to segments only on the basis of some highly arbitrary allocation. Consider the salary of Aloha Hotels and Resorts' president. What allocation base would you choose to reflect the contribution of the president's managerial efforts to the company's two divisions? The possible allocation bases include budgeted divisional sales revenue, the number of hotels or employees in each division, or some measure of divisional size, such as total assets. However, all of these allocation bases would yield arbitrary cost allocations and possibly misleading segment profit information. For this reason, many organizations choose not to allocate common costs on segmented income statements.

Exhibit 12–7 shows February's segmented income statement (on a budgeted basis) for Aloha Hotels and Resorts. Each segment's income statement is presented in the *contribution format* discussed in Chapter 8. Notice that Exhibit 12–7 shows income statements for the following segments: ·

Aloha Hotels and Resorts ⎰ Maui Division ⎱ Oahu Division ⎰ Waimea Beach Resort ⎱ Diamond Head Lodge | Waikiki Sands Hotel

	Segment of Company			Segment of Oahu Division			
	Aloha Hotels and Resorts	Maui Division	Oahu Division	Waimea Beach Resort	Diamond Head Lodge	Waikiki Sands Hotel	Not Allocated
Sales revenue	$2,500,000	$1,600,000	$900,000	$450,000	$150,000	$300,000	—
Variable operating expenses:							
Personnel	820,900	510,400	310,500	155,500	50,000	105,000	—
Food, beverages, and supplies	738,000	458,600	279,400	139,700	46,400	93,300	—
Other	83,000	58,000	25,000	12,500	4,000	8,500	—
Total	1,641,900	1,027,000	614,900	307,700	100,400	206,800	—
Segment contribution margin	858,100	573,000	285,100	142,300	49,600	93,200	—
Less: Fixed expenses controllable by segment manager	30,000	21,000	9,000	4,000	1,000	3,000	$ 1,000
Profit margin controllable by segment manager	828,100	552,000	276,100	138,300	48,600	90,200	(1,000)
Less: Fixed expenses, traceable to segment, but controllable by others	750,000	500,000	250,000	26,000	8,000	16,000	200,000
Segment profit margin	78,100	$ 52,000	$ 26,100	$112,300	$ 40,600	$ 74,200	$(201,000)
Less: Common fixed expenses	10,000						
Income before taxes	68,100						
Less: Income tax expense	37,440						
Net income	$ 30,660						

Exhibit 12–7

Segmented Income Statements: Aloha Hotels and Resorts (in thousands)

Three numbers in Exhibit 12–7 require special emphasis. First, the $10,000,000 of common fixed expenses in the left-hand column is not allocated to the company's two divisions. Included in this figure are such costs as the company president's salary. These costs cannot be allocated to the divisions, except in some arbitrary manner.

Second, $1,000,000 of controllable fixed expense in the right-hand column constitutes part of the Oahu Division's $9,000,000 of controllable fixed expense. All $9,000,000 of expense is controllable by the vice-president of the Oahu Division. However, $1,000,000 of these expenses cannot be traced to the division's three hotels, except on an arbitrary basis. For example, this $1,000,000 of expense includes the salary of the Oahu Division's vice-president. Therefore, the $1,000,000 of expense is *not allocated* among the division's three hotels. This procedure illustrates an important point. Costs that are traceable to segments at one level in an organization may become common costs at a lower level in the organization. The vice-president's salary is traceable to the Oahu Division, but it cannot be allocated among the division's three hotels except arbitrarily. Thus, the vice-president's salary is a traceable cost at the divisional level, but it becomes a common cost at the hotel level.

Third, the $200,000,000 of fixed expenses controllable by others in the right-hand column constitutes part of the Oahu Division's $250,000,000 of fixed expenses controllable by others. However, the $200,000,000 portion cannot be allocated among the division's three hotels, except arbitrarily.

Segments versus Segment Managers

One advantage of segmented reports like the one in Exhibit 12–7 is that they make a distinction between segments and segment managers. Some costs that are traceable to a segment may be completely beyond the influence of the segment manager. Property taxes on the Waikiki Sands Hotel, for example, are traceable to the hotel, but the hotel's general manager cannot influence them. To properly evaluate the *Waikiki Sands Hotel as an investment* of the company's resources, the property taxes should be included in the hotel's costs. However, in evaluating the general manager's performance, the property-tax cost should be *excluded*, since the manager has no control over it.

Key Features of Segmented Reporting

To summarize, Exhibit 12–7 illustrates three important characteristics of segmented reporting:

1. *Contribution format.* These income statements use the contribution format. The statements subtract variable expenses from sales revenue to obtain the *contribution margin.*
2. *Controllable versus uncontrollable expenses.* The income statements in Exhibit 12–7 highlight the costs that can be controlled, or heavily influenced, by each segment manager. This approach is consistent with *responsibility accounting.*
3. *Segmented income statement. Segmented reporting* shows income statements for the company as a whole and for its major segments.

Performance Evaluation

How do the top managers of large companies such as General Electric and Procter & Gamble evaluate their divisions and other major subunits? The largest subunits within these and similar organizations usually are designated as investment centres. The manager of this type of *responsibility centre* is held accountable not only for the investment centre's *profit* but also for the *capital invested* to earn that profit. Invested capital refers to assets, such as buildings and equipment, used in a subunit's operations.

Measuring Performance in Investment Centres

In our study of investment-centre performance evaluation, we will focus on Suncoast Food Centres. This chain of retail grocery stores has three divisions, as depicted by the organization chart in Exhibit 12–8.

The Lower Sunshine Coast and Upper Sunshine Coast divisions consist of individual grocery stores located in six coastal cities. The company's Food Processing Division operates dairy plants, bakeries, and meat-processing plants in Gibsons and Powell River. These facilities provide all Suncoast Food Centres with milk, ice

Exhibit 12–8

Organization Chart: Suncoast Food Centres

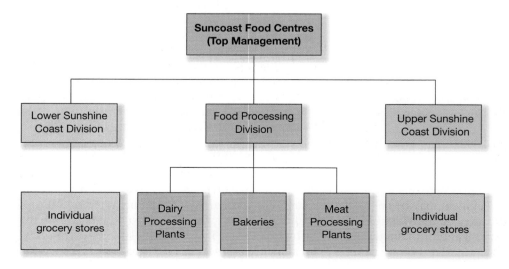

cream, yogurt, cheese, breads and desserts, and packaged meat. These Suncoast-brand food products are transferred to the company's Lower Sunshine Coast and Upper Sunshine Coast divisions at transfer prices established by the corporate controller's office.

Suncoast Food Centres' three divisions are investment centres. This responsibility-centre designation is appropriate, because each division manager has the authority to make decisions that affect both profit and invested capital. For example, the Lower Sunshine Coast Division manager approves the overall pricing policies in the Lower Sunshine Coast Division's stores, and also has the autonomy to sign contracts to buy food and other products for resale. These actions influence the division's profit. In addition, the Lower Sunshine Coast Division manager has the authority to build new Suncoast Food Centres, rent space in shopping centres, or close existing stores. These decisions affect the amount of capital invested in the division.

The primary goals of any profit-making enterprise include maximizing its profitability and using its invested capital as effectively as possible. Managerial accountants use three different measures to evaluate the performance of investment centres: return on investment (ROI), residual income (RI), and economic value added (EVA®). (EVA® is a registered trademark of Stern Stewart & Co.) We will illustrate each of these measures for Suncoast Food Centres.

> "Accounting is changing. You're no longer sitting behind a desk just working on a computer, just crunching the numbers. You're actually getting to be a part of the day to day functions of the business." (12f)
> **Abbott Laboratories**

Return on Investment

The most common investment-centre performance measure is **return on investment**, or **ROI**, which is defined as follows:

$$\text{Return on investment (ROI)} = \frac{\text{Income}}{\text{Invested capital}}$$

The most recent year's ROI calculations for Suncoast Food Centres' three divisions are:

	$\dfrac{\text{Income}}{\text{Invested capital}}$ =	Return on investment (ROI)
Lower Sunshine Coast Division	$\dfrac{\$3,000,000}{\$20,000,000}$ =	15%
Food Processing Division	$\dfrac{\$3,600,000}{\$18,000,000}$ =	20%
Upper Sunshine Coast Division	$\dfrac{\$6,750,000}{\$45,000,000}$ =	15%

Notice how the ROI calculation for each division takes into account *both divisional income and the capital invested* in the division. Why is this important? Suppose each division were evaluated only on the basis of its divisional profit. The Upper Sunshine Coast Division reported a higher divisional profit than the Lower Sunshine Coast Division. Does this mean the Upper Sunshine Coast Division performed better than the Lower Sunshine Coast Division? The answer is no. Although the Upper Sunshine Coast Division's profit exceeded the Lower Sunshine Coast Division's profit, the Upper Sunshine Coast Division used a much larger amount of invested capital to earn its profit. The Upper Sunshine Coast Division's assets are more than two times the assets of the Lower Sunshine Coast Division.

Considering the relative size of the two divisions, we should expect the Upper Sunshine Coast Division to earn a larger profit than the Lower Sunshine Coast Division. The important question is not how much profit each division earned, but rather how effectively each division used its invested capital to earn a profit.

Factors Underlying ROI   We can rewrite the ROI formula as follows:

$$\text{Return on investment} = \frac{\text{Income}}{\text{Invested capital}} = \frac{\text{Income}}{\text{Sales revenue}} \times \frac{\text{Sales revenue}}{\text{Invested capital}}$$

Notice that the *sales revenue* term cancels out in the denominator and numerator when the two right-hand fractions are multiplied.

Writing the ROI formula in this way highlights the factors that determine a division's return on investment. Income divided by sales revenue is called the **sales margin**. This term measures the percentage of each sales dollar that remains as profit after all expenses are covered. Sales revenue divided by invested capital is called the **capital turnover**. This term focuses on the number of sales dollars generated by every dollar of invested capital. The sales margin and capital turnover for Suncoast Food Centres' three divisions are calculated below for the most recent year.

	Sales margin	×	Capital turnover	= ROI
	$\dfrac{\text{Income}}{\text{Sales revenue}}$	×	$\dfrac{\text{Sales revenue}}{\text{Invested capital}}$	= ROI
Lower Sunshine Coast Division	$\dfrac{\$3,000,000}{\$60,000,000}$	×	$\dfrac{\$60,000,000}{\$20,000,000}$	= 15%
Food Processing Division	$\dfrac{\$3,600,000}{\$9,000,000}$	×	$\dfrac{\$9,000,000}{\$18,000,000}$	= 20%
Upper Sunshine Coast Division	$\dfrac{\$6,750,000}{\$135,000,000}$	×	$\dfrac{\$135,000,000}{\$45,000,000}$	= 15%

The Lower Sunshine Coast Division's sales margin is 5 percent ($3,000,000 of profit ÷ $60,000,000 of sales revenue). Thus, each dollar of divisional sales resulted in a five-cent profit. The division's capital turnover was 3 ($60,000,000 of sales revenue ÷ $20,000,000 of invested capital). Thus, three dollars of sales revenue were generated by each dollar of capital invested in the division's assets, such as store buildings, display shelves, checkout equipment, and inventory.

Improving ROI   How could the Lower Sunshine Coast Division manager improve the division's return on investment? Since ROI is the product of the sales margin and the capital turnover, ROI can be improved by increasing either or both of its components. For example, if the Lower Sunshine Coast Division manager increased the division's sales margin to 6 percent while holding the capital turnover constant at 3, the division's ROI would climb from 15 percent to 18 percent, as follows:

$$\begin{array}{ccc}
\text{Lower Sunshine Coast} & & \\
\text{Division's} & = & \text{Improved} \times \text{Same} \\
\text{improved ROI} & & \text{sales margin} \quad \text{capital turnover} \\
& = & 6\% \quad \times \quad 3 \qquad = 18\%
\end{array}$$

To bring about the improved sales margin, the Lower Sunshine Coast Division manager would need to increase divisional profit to $3,600,000 on sales of $60,000,000 ($3,600,000 ÷ $60,000,000 = 6%). How could profit be increased without changing total sales revenue? There are two possibilities: increase sales prices while selling less quantity or decrease expenses. Neither of these is necessarily easy to do. In increasing sales prices, the division manager must be careful not to lose sales to the extent that total sales revenue declines. Similarly, reducing the expenses must not diminish product quality, customer service, or overall store atmosphere. Any of these changes could also result in lost sales revenue.

An alternative way of increasing the Lower Sunshine Coast Division's ROI would be to increase its capital turnover. Suppose the Lower Sunshine Coast Division manager increased the division's capital turnover to 4 while holding the sales margin constant at 5 percent. The division's ROI would climb from 15 percent to 20 percent:

$$
\begin{array}{c}
\text{Lower Sunshine Coast} \\
\text{Division's} \\
\text{improved ROI}
\end{array}
=
\begin{array}{c}
\text{Same} \\
\text{sales margin}
\end{array}
\times
\begin{array}{c}
\text{Improved} \\
\text{capital turnover}
\end{array}
$$

$$
= \quad 5\% \quad \times \quad 4 \quad = 20\%
$$

To obtain the improved capital turnover, the Lower Sunshine Division manager would need to either increase sales revenue or reduce the division's invested capital. For example, the improved ROI could be achieved by reducing invested capital to $15,000,000 while maintaining sales revenue of $60,000,000. This would be a very tall order. The division manager can lower invested capital somewhat by reducing inventories and can increase sales revenue by using store space more effectively. But reducing inventories may lead to stockouts and lost sales, and crowded aisles may drive customers away.

Improving ROI is a balancing act that requires all the skills of an effective manager. The ROI analysis above merely shows the arena in which the balancing act is performed.

Residual Income

Although ROI is the most popular investment-centre performance measure, it has one major drawback. To illustrate, suppose Suncoast's Food Processing Division manager can buy a new food processing machine for $500,000, which will save $80,000 in operating expenses and thereby raise divisional profit by $80,000. The return on this investment in new equipment is 16 percent:

$$
\begin{array}{c}
\text{Return on investment} \\
\text{in new equipment}
\end{array}
=
\frac{\text{Increase in divisional profit}}{\text{Increase in invested capital}}
=
\frac{\$80,000}{\$500,000}
= 16\%
$$

Now suppose it costs Suncoast Food Centres 12 cents of interest for each dollar of capital borrowed to invest in operational assets. What is the optimal decision for the Food Processing Division manager to make, *viewed from the perspective of the company as a whole*? Since it costs Suncoast Food Centres 12 percent for every dollar of capital borrowed, and the return on investment in new equipment is 16 percent, the equipment should be purchased. For goal congruence, the autonomous division manager should decide to buy the new equipment.

Now consider what is likely to happen. The Food Processing Division manager's performance is evaluated on the basis of his division's ROI. Without the new equipment, the divisional ROI is 20 percent ($3,600,000 of divisional profit ÷ $18,000,000 of invested capital). If he purchases the new equipment, his divisional ROI will decline:

Food Processing Division's Return on Investment

Without Investment in New Equipment	With Investment in New Equipment
$\dfrac{\$3,600,000}{\$18,000,000} = 20\%$	$\dfrac{\$3,600,000\ +\ \$80,000}{\$18,000,000\ +\ \$500,000} < 20\%$

Why did this happen? Even though the investment in new equipment earns a return of 16 percent, which is greater than the company's cost of raising capital (12 percent), the return is less than the division's ROI without the equipment (20 percent). Averaging the new investment with those already in place in the Food Processing Division merely reduces the division's ROI. Since the division manager is evaluated using ROI, he will be reluctant to decide in favour of acquiring the new equipment.

The problem is that the ROI measure leaves out an important piece of information: it ignores the firm's cost of raising investment capital. For this reason, many managers prefer to use a different investment-centre performance measure instead of ROI.

Learning Objective 8

Describe some advantages and disadvantages of both ROI and residual income as divisional performance measures.

Computing Residual Income   An investment centre's **residual income** is defined as follows:

$$\text{Residual income} = \text{Investment centre's profit} - \left(\text{Investment centre's invested capital} \times \text{Imputed interest rate} \right)$$

where the imputed interest rate is the firm's cost of acquiring investment capital.

Residual income is a dollar amount, not a ratio like ROI. It is the amount of an investment centre's profit that remains (as a residual) after subtracting an imputed interest charge. The term imputed means that the interest charge is estimated. This charge reflects the firm's minimum required rate of return on invested capital. In some firms, the imputed interest rate depends on the riskiness of the investment for which the funds will be used. Thus, divisions that have different levels of risk sometimes are assigned different *imputed* interest rates.

ROI and residual income are common performance measures for investment centres. Both measures relate the profit earned from selling the final product to the capital required to carry out production operations. Here the product is orange juice, and this bottling equipment represents the capital investment.

The residual income of Suncoast's Food Processing Division is computed below, both with and without the investment in the new equipment. The imputed interest rate is 12 percent.

	Food Processing Division's Residual Income			
	Without Investment in New Equipment		**With Investment in New Equipment**	
Divisional profit		$3,600,000		$3,680,000
Less imputed interest charge:				
Invested capital	$18,000,000		$18,500,000	
× Imputed interest rate	× .12		× .12	
Imputed interest charge	⟶	2,160,000	⟶	2,220,000
Residual income		$1,440,000		$1,460,000

Investment in new equipment raises residual income by $20,000.

Notice that the Food Processing Division's residual income will *increase* if the new equipment is purchased. What will be the division manager's incentive if he is evaluated on the basis of residual income instead of ROI? He will want to make the investment because that decision will increase his division's residual income. Thus, goal congruence is achieved when the managerial accountant uses residual income to measure divisional performance.

Why does residual income facilitate goal congruence while ROI does not? Because the residual-income formula incorporates an important piece of data that is excluded from the ROI formula: the firm's minimum required rate of return on invested capital. To summarize, ROI and residual income are compared as follows:

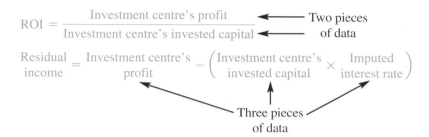

Unfortunately, residual income also has a serious drawback: It should not be used to compare the performance of different-sized investment centres because it incorporates a bias in favour of the larger investment centre. To illustrate, the following table compares the residual income of Suncoast Food Centres' Lower Sunshine Coast and Upper Sunshine Coast divisions. Notice that the Upper Sunshine Coast Division's residual income is considerably higher than the Lower Sunshine Coast Division's. This is entirely due to the much greater size of the Upper Sunshine Coast Division, as evidenced by its far greater invested capital.

	Comparison of Residual Income: Two Divisions	
	Lower Sunshine Coast Division	**Upper Sunshine Coast Division**
Divisional profit	$3,000,000	$6,750,000
Less imputed interest charge:		
Invested capital	$20,000,000	$45,000,000
× Imputed interest rate	× .12	× .12
Imputed interest charge	2,400,000	5,400,000
Residual income	$ 600,000	$1,350,000

The Upper Sunshine Coast Division's residual income is much higher simply because it is larger than the Lower Sunshine Coast Division.

In short, neither ROI nor residual income provides a perfect measure of investment-centre performance. ROI can undermine goal congruence. Residual income distorts comparisons between investment centres of different sizes. As a result, some companies routinely use both measures for divisional performance evaluation.

Shareholder Value Analysis   Some companies apply the residual income concept to individual product lines. **Shareholder value analysis** calculates the residual income for a major product line, with the objective of determining how the product line affects the firm's value to the shareholders. Suppose, for example, that Suncoast Food Centres offers in-store, one-hour film development in selected stores. Let's say that the company's investment in this service is $200,000 and the annual profit is $40,000. Then the residual income on one-hour film development is $16,000 [$40,000 − ($200,000 × 12%)].

Economic Value Added

The most contemporary measure of investment centre performance is **economic value added (EVA)**, which is defined as follows:

$$
\begin{array}{c}
\text{Economic} \\
\text{value} \\
\text{added}
\end{array}
=
\begin{array}{c}
\text{Investment} \\
\text{centre's after-tax} \\
\text{operating income}
\end{array}
-
\left[
\left(
\begin{array}{c}
\text{Investment} \\
\text{centre's} \\
\text{total assets}
\end{array}
-
\begin{array}{c}
\text{Investment} \\
\text{centre's current} \\
\text{liabilities}
\end{array}
\right)
\times
\begin{array}{c}
\text{Weighted-} \\
\text{average cost} \\
\text{of capital}
\end{array}
\right]
$$

Like residual income, the economic value added is a dollar amount. However, it differs from residual income in two important ways. First, an investment centre's current liabilities are subtracted from its total assets. Second, the weighted-average cost of capital is used in the calculation.

Weighted-Average Cost of Capital   Suncoast Food Centres has two sources of long-term capital: debt and equity. The cost to Suncoast of issuing debt is the after-tax cost of the interest payments on the debt, taking account of the fact that the interest payments are tax-deductible. The cost of Suncoast's equity capital is the investment opportunity rate of Suncoast Food Centres' investors, that is, the rate they could earn on investments of similar risk to that of investing in Suncoast Food Centres. The **weighted-average cost of capital (WACC)** is defined as follows:

$$
\begin{array}{c}
\text{Weighted-average} \\
\text{cost of capital}
\end{array}
=
\frac{
\left(
\begin{array}{c}
\text{After-tax cost} \\
\text{of debt} \\
\text{capital}
\end{array}
\right)
\left(
\begin{array}{c}
\text{Market} \\
\text{value} \\
\text{of debt}
\end{array}
\right)
+
\left(
\begin{array}{c}
\text{Cost of} \\
\text{equity} \\
\text{capital}
\end{array}
\right)
\left(
\begin{array}{c}
\text{Market} \\
\text{value} \\
\text{of equity}
\end{array}
\right)
}{
\begin{array}{c}
\text{Market} \\
\text{value} \\
\text{of debt}
\end{array}
+
\begin{array}{c}
\text{Market} \\
\text{value} \\
\text{of equity}
\end{array}
}
$$

The interest rate on Suncoast Food Centres' $40 million of debt is 9 percent, and the company's tax rate is 30 percent. Therefore, Suncoast's after-tax cost of debt is 6.3 percent [9% $\times$ (1 $-$ 30%)]. Let's assume that the cost of Suncoast's equity capital is 12 percent. Moreover, the market value of the company's equity is $60 million.[3] The following calculation shows that Suncoast Food Centres' WACC is 9.72 percent:

$$
\begin{array}{c}
\text{Weighted-average} \\
\text{cost of capital}
\end{array}
=
\frac{(.063)(\$40,000,000) + (.12)(\$60,000,000)}{\$40,000,000 + \$60,000,000}
= .0972
$$

Finally, Suncoast Food Centres had an average balance of $2 million in current liabilities, distributed as follows:

Division	Current Liabilities
Lower Sunshine Coast Division	$ 400,000
Food Processing Division	1,000,000
Upper Sunshine Coast Division	600,000

Now we can compute the economic value added (or EVA) for each of Suncoast's three divisions.

Division	After-tax operating income (in millions)		Total assets (in millions)		Current liabilities (in millions)				Economic value added
Lower Sunshine Coast	$3.00 $\times$ (1 $-$ .30) $-$		[($20	$-$	$ .4)	$\times$ .0972]		=	$194,880
Food Processing	$3.60 $\times$ (1 $-$ .30) $-$		[($18	$-$	$1.0)	$\times$ .0972]		=	867,600
Upper Sunshine Coast	$6.75 $\times$ (1 $-$ .30) $-$		[($45	$-$	$ .6)	$\times$ .0972]		=	409,320

PAY FOR PERFORMANCE BASED ON EVA

In the wake of the excesses in top management compensation over the past few years, at many companies pay for performance is back in vogue. Top executives earn hefty bonuses when times are good, but are expected to share in the pain during a decline in business.

Siemens, a global electronics firm, links the compensation of its top 500 managers to their business units' economic value added (EVA) measure. Similarly, the Royal Bank of Canada, upon observing that its lower-level managers were not acting in accordance with the bank's overall strategy, began linking their compensation to the bank's EVA and revenue growth.[4]

> **M**anagement
> **A**ccounting
> **P**ractice
>
> Siemens, Royal Bank of Canada

The EVA analysis reveals that all three of Suncoast Food Centres' divisions are contributing substantially to the company's economic value.

What does an EVA analysis tell us? EVA indicates how much shareholder wealth is being created, as Roberto Goizueta, Coca-Cola's former CEO, explained: "We raise capital to make concentrate and sell it at an operating profit. Then we pay the cost of that capital. Shareholders pocket the difference (EVA amount)."

Measuring Income and Invested Capital

The ROI, residual-income, and economic value added (EVA) measures of investment-centre performance all use profit and invested capital in their formulas. This raises the question of how to measure divisional profit and invested capital. This section will illustrate various approaches to resolving these measurement issues.

> **Learning Objective 9**
>
> Explain how to measure a division's income and invested capital.

Invested Capital

We will focus on Suncoast Food Centres' Food Processing Division to illustrate several alternative approaches to measuring an investment centre's capital. Exhibit 12–9 lists the assets and liabilities associated with the Food Processing Division. Notice that Exhibit 12–9 does not constitute a complete balance sheet. First, there are no long-term liabilities, such as bonds payable, associated with the Food Processing Division. Although Suncoast Food Centres may have such long-term debt, it would not be meaningful to assign portions of that debt to the company's individual divisions.

Assets*		
Current assets (cash, accounts receivable, inventories, etc.)		$ 2,000,000
Long-lived assets (land, buildings, equipment, vehicles, etc.):		
Gross book value (acquisition cost)	$19,000,000	
Less: Accumulated depreciation	4,000,000	
Net book value		15,000,000
Plant under construction		1,000,000
Total assets		$18,000,000
Liabilities		
Current liabilities (accounts payable, salaries payable, etc.)		$ 1,000,000

*This is not a balance sheet, but rather a listing of certain assets and liabilities associated with the Food Processing Division.

Exhibit 12–9

Assets and Liabilities Associated with Food Processing Division

Suncoast
FOOD CENTRES

Second, there is no stockholders' equity associated with the Food Processing Division. The owners of the company own stock in Suncoast Food Centres, not in its individual divisions.

Average Balances   ROI, residual income, and EVA are computed for a period of time, such as a year or a month. Asset balances, on the other hand, are measured at a point in time, such as December 31. Since divisional asset balances generally will change over time, we use average balances in calculating ROI, residual income, and EVA. For example, if the Food Processing Division's balance in invested capital was $19,000,000 on January 1 and $17,000,000 on December 31, we would use the year's average invested capital of $18,000,000 in the ROI, residual income, and EVA calculations.

Should Total Assets Be Used?   Exhibit 12–9 shows that the Food Processing Division had average balances during the year of $2,000,000 in current assets, $15,000,000 in long-lived assets, and $1,000,000 tied up in a plant under construction. (Suncoast Food Centres is building a new high-tech dairy plant in Gibsons to produce its innovative zero-calorie ice cream.) In addition, Exhibit 12–9 discloses that the Food Processing Division's average balance of current liabilities was $1,000,000.

What is the division's invested capital? Several possibilities exist:

1. *Total assets.* The management of Suncoast Food Centres has decided to use *average total assets* for the year in measuring each division's invested capital. Thus, $18,000,000 is the amount used in the ROI, residual-income, and EVA calculations discussed earlier in this chapter. This measure of invested capital is appropriate if the division manager has considerable authority in making decisions about *all* of the division's assets, *including nonproductive assets*. In this case, the Food Processing Division's partially completed dairy plant is a nonproductive asset. Since the division manager had considerable influence in deciding to build the new plant and he is responsible for overseeing the project, average total assets provides an appropriate measure.

2. *Total productive assets.* In other companies, division managers are directed by top management to keep nonproductive assets, such as vacant land or construction in progress. In such cases, it is appropriate to exclude nonproductive assets from the measure of invested capital. Then *average total productive assets* is used to measure invested capital. If Suncoast Food Centres had chosen this alternative, $17,000,000 would have been used in the ROI, residual-income, and EVA calculations (total assets of $18,000,000 less $1,000,000 for the plant under construction).

3. *Total assets less current liabilities.* Some companies allow division managers to secure short-term bank loans and other short-term credit. In such cases, invested capital often is measured by *average total assets less average current liabilities*. This approach encourages investment-centre managers to minimize resources tied up in assets and maximize the use of short-term credit to finance operations. If this approach had been used by Suncoast Food Centres, the Food Processing Division's invested capital would have been $17,000,000, total assets of $18,000,000 less current liabilities of $1,000,000. (Note that current liabilities are always subtracted from total assets for the measure of invested capital used in the EVA measure.)

Gross or Net Book Value   Another decision to make in choosing a measure of invested capital is whether to use the *gross book value (acquisition cost)* or the *net book value* of long-lived assets. (Net book value is the acquisition cost less accumulated depreciation.) Suncoast Food Centres' management has decided to use the average net book value of $15,000,000 to value the Food Processing Division's long-lived assets. If gross book value had been used instead, the division's measure of invested capital would have been $22,000,000, as the following calculation shows:

Current assets	$ 2,000,000
Long-lived assets (at gross book value)	19,000,000
Plant under construction	1,000,000
Total assets (at gross book value)	$22,000,000

There are advantages and disadvantages associated with both gross and net book value as a measure of invested capital:

1. Using net book value maintains consistency with the balance sheet prepared for external reporting purposes. This allows for more meaningful comparisons of return-on-investment measures across different companies.

2. Using net book value to measure invested capital is also more consistent with the definition of income, which is the numerator in ROI calculations. In computing income, the current period's depreciation on long-lived assets is deducted as an expense.

Advantages of Net Book Value; Disadvantages of Gross Book Value

1. The usual methods of computing depreciation, such as the straight-line and the declining-balance methods, are arbitrary. Hence, they should not be allowed to affect ROI, residual-income, or EVA calculations.

2. When long-lived assets are depreciated, their net book value declines over time. This results in a misleading increase in ROI, residual income, and EVA across time. Exhibit 12–10 provides an illustration of this phenomenon for the ROI calculated on an equipment purchase under consideration by the Food Processing Division manager. Notice that the ROI rises steadily across the five-year horizon if invested capital is measured by net book value. However, using gross book value eliminates this problem. If an accelerated depreciation method were used instead of the straight-line method, the increasing trend in ROI would be even more pronounced.

Advantages of Gross Book Value; Disadvantages of Net Book Value

Acquisition cost of equipment	$500,000
Useful life	5 years
Salvage value at end of useful life	0
Annual straight-line depreciation	$100,000
Annual income generated by asset (before deducting depreciation)	$150,000

Year	Income before Depreciation	Annual Depreciation	Income Net of Depreciation	Average Net Book Value*	ROI Based on Net Book Value†	Average Gross Book Value	ROI Based on Gross Book Value
1	$150,000	$100,000	$50,000	$450,000	11.1%	$500,000	10%
2	150,000	100,000	50,000	350,000	14.3	500,000	10
3	150,000	100,000	50,000	250,000	20.0	500,000	10
4	150,000	100,000	50,000	150,000	33.3	500,000	10
5	150,000	100,000	50,000	50,000	100.0	500,000	10

*Average net book value is the average of the beginning and ending balances for the year in net book value. In year 1, for example, the average net book value is:

$$\frac{\$500,000 + \$400,000}{2}$$

†ROI rounded to nearest tenth of 1 percent.

Exhibit 12–10

Increase in ROI over Time (when net book value is used)

Suncoast
FOOD CENTRES

A Behavioural Problem   The tendency for net book value to produce a misleading increase in ROI over time can have a serious effect on the incentives of investment centre managers. Investment centres with old assets will show much higher ROIs than investment centres with relatively new assets. This can discourage investment-centre managers from investing in new equipment. If this behavioural tendency persists, a division's assets can become obsolete, making the division uncompetitive.

Allocating Assets to Investment Centres   Some companies control certain assets centrally, although these assets are needed to carry on operations in the divisions. Common examples are cash and accounts receivable. Divisions need cash in order to operate, but many companies control cash balances centrally in order to minimize their total cash holdings. Some large retail firms manage accounts receivable centrally. A credit customer of some national department-store chains can make a payment either at the local store or by mailing the payment to corporate headquarters.

     When certain assets are controlled centrally, some allocation basis generally is chosen to allocate these asset balances to investment centres, for the purpose of measuring invested capital. For example, cash may be allocated based on the budgeted cash needs in each division or on the basis of divisional sales. Accounts receivable usually are allocated on the basis of divisional sales. Divisions with less stringent credit terms are allocated proportionately larger balances of accounts receivable.

Measuring Investment-Centre Income

Learning Objective 9

Explain how to measure a division's income and invested capital.

In addition to choosing a measure of investment-centre capital, an accountant must also decide how to measure a centre's income. The key issue is controllability; the choice involves the extent to which uncontrollable items are allowed to influence the income measure. The spreadsheet in Exhibit 12–11 illustrates several different possibilities for measuring the income of Suncoast Food Centres' Food Processing Division.

     Suncoast Food Centres' top management uses the *profit margin controllable by division manager*, $3,600,000, to evaluate the Food Processing Division manager. This profit measure is used in calculating ROI, residual income, or EVA. Some fixed costs traceable to the division have not been deducted from this $3,600,000 amount, but the division manager cannot control or significantly influence these costs. Hence they are excluded from the ROI calculation in evaluating the division manager. In calculating EVA, the $3,600,000 profit-margin amount is converted to an after-tax basis by multiplying by 1 minus the tax rate of 30 percent.

Pay for Performance   Some companies reward investment-centre managers with **cash bonuses** if they meet a predetermined target on a specified performance criterion,

Exhibit 12–11

Divisional Income Statement:
Food Processing Division

Suncoast
FOOD CENTRES

	A	B	C	D	E	F	G	H
1				FOOD PROCESSING DIVISION				
2				Divisional Income Statement				
3								
4		Sales revenue						$9,000,000
5		Variable expenses						3,800,000
6	(1)	Divisional contribution margin						$5,200,000
7		Fixed expenses controllable by division manager						1,600,000
8	(2)	Profit margin controllable by division manager						$3,600,000
9		Fixed expenses, traceable to division, but controlled by others						1,200,000
10	(3)	Profit margin traceable to division						$2,400,000
11		Common fixed expenses, allocated from corporate headquarters						400,000
12	(4)	Divisional income before interest and taxes						$2,000,000
13		Interest expense allocated from corporate headquarters						250,000
14	(5)	Divisional income before taxes						$1,750,000
15		Income taxes allocated from corporate headquarters						525,000
16	(6)	Divisional net income						$1,225,000

such as residual income, ROI, or EVA. Such payments often are referred to as **pay for performance**, **merit pay**, or **incentive compensation**. These cash bonuses generally are single payments, independent of a manager's base salary.

Managers versus Investment Centres   It is important to make a distinction between an investment centre and its manager. In evaluating the *manager's* performance, only revenues and costs that the manager can control or significantly influence should be included in the profit measure. Remember that the overall objective of the performance measure is to provide incentives for goal-congruent behaviour. No performance measure can motivate a manager to make decisions about costs he or she cannot control. This explains why Suncoast Food Centres' top management relies on the profit margin controllable by division manager to compute the manager's ROI performance measure.

Evaluating the Food Processing Division as a viable economic investment is a different matter altogether. In this evaluation, traceability of costs, rather than controllability, is the issue. For this purpose, Suncoast Food Centres' top management uses the profit margin traceable to division to compute the divisional ROI, residual income, or EVA. As Exhibit 12–11 shows, this amount is $2,400,000.

Other Profit Measures   The other measures of divisional profit shown in Exhibit 12–11 (4, 5, and 6) also are used by some companies. The rationale behind these divisional income measures is that all corporate costs have to be covered by the operations of the divisions. Allocating corporate costs, interest, and income taxes to the divisions makes division managers aware of these costs.

Transfer Pricing

In many organizations, one subunit manufactures a product or produces a service that is then transferred to another subunit in the same organization. For example, automobile parts manufactured in one division of General Motors are then transferred to another GM division that assembles vehicles.

The price at which products or services are transferred between two subunits in an organization is called a **transfer price**. Since a transfer price affects the profit of both the buying and selling divisions, the transfer price affects the performance evaluation of these responsibility centres. A high transfer price results in high profit for the selling division and low profit for the buying division. A low transfer price has the opposite effect. Consequently, the transfer-pricing policy *can* affect the *incentives* of autonomous division managers as they decide whether to make the transfer. Exhibit 12–12 depicts this scenario.

Transfer pricing is widely used in all kinds of businesses. When the chassis for this Ford Mustang convertible was transferred from the manufacturing division to the assembly division, a transfer price was specified.

Exhibit 12–12
The Transfer-Pricing Scenario

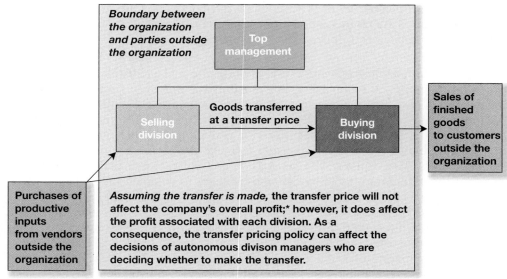

Boundary between the organization and parties outside the organization

Top management

Goods transferred at a transfer price

Selling division

Buying division

Sales of finished goods to customers outside the organization

Purchases of productive inputs from vendors outside the organization

Assuming the transfer is made, the transfer price will not affect the company's overall profit;* however, it does affect the profit associated with each division. As a consequence, the transfer pricing policy can affect the decisions of autonomous divison managers who are deciding whether to make the transfer.

*Assumes no tax complexities involving multinational companies. This issue is addressed later in the chapter.

Goal Congruence

What should be management's goal in setting transfer prices for internally transferred goods or services? In a decentralized organization, the managers of profit centres and investment centres often have considerable autonomy in deciding whether to accept or reject orders and whether to buy inputs from inside the organization or from outside. For example, a large manufacturer of farm equipment allows its Assembly Division managers to buy parts either from another division of the company or from independent manufacturers. The goal in setting transfer prices is to establish incentives for autonomous division managers to make decisions that support the overall goals of the organization.

Suppose it is in the best interests of Suncoast Food Centres for the baked goods produced by the Food Processing Division's Gibsons Bakery to be transferred to the Lower Sunshine Coast Division's stores in the Sechelt Bay area. Thus, if the firm were centralized, bakery products would be transferred from the Food Processing Division to the Lower Sunshine Coast Division. However, Suncoast Food Centres is a decentralized company, and the Lower Sunshine Coast Division manager is free to buy baked goods either from the Food Processing Division or from an outside bakery company. Similarly, the Food Processing Division manager is free to accept or reject an order for baked goods, at any given price, from the Lower Sunshine Coast Division. The goal of the company's controller in setting the transfer price is to provide incentives for each of these division managers to act in the company's best interests. The transfer price should be chosen so that each division manager, when striving to maximize his or her own division's profit, makes the decision that maximizes the company's profit.

General Transfer-Pricing Rule

Learning Objective 10

Use the general economic rule to set an optimal transfer price.

Management's objective in setting a transfer price is to encourage goal congruence among the division managers involved in the transfer. A general rule that will ensure goal congruence is given below.

$$\text{Transfer price} = \begin{array}{c}\text{Additional } \textit{outlay cost} \\ \text{per unit incurred because} \\ \text{goods are transferred}\end{array} + \begin{array}{c}\textit{Opportunity cost} \text{ per unit} \\ \text{to the organization} \\ \text{because of the transfer}\end{array}$$

The general rule specifies the transfer price as the sum of two cost components. The first component is the outlay cost incurred by the division that produces the goods or services to be transferred. Outlay costs will include the direct variable costs of the product or service and any other outlay costs that are incurred only as a result of the transfer. The second component in the general transfer-pricing rule is the opportunity cost incurred by the organization as a whole because of the transfer. Recall from Chapter 2 that an *opportunity cost* is a benefit that is forgone as a result of taking a particular action.

We will illustrate the general transfer-pricing rule for Suncoast Food Centres. The company's Food Processing Division produces bread in its Gibsons Bakery. The division transfers some of its products to the company's Lower Sunshine Coast and Lower Sunshine Coast divisions, and sells some of its products to other companies in the *external market* under different labels.

Bread is transported to stores in racks containing one dozen loaves of packaged bread. In the Gibsons bakery, the following variable costs are incurred to produce bread and transport it to a buyer:

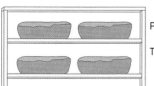

Production:
    Standard variable cost per rack (including packaging)....... $7.00
Transportation:
    Standard variable cost per rack to transport bread........... .25

In applying the general transfer-pricing rule, we will distinguish between two different scenarios.

Scenario I: No Excess Capacity   Suppose the Food Processing Division can sell all the bread it can produce to outside buyers at a market price of $11 per rack. Since the division can sell all of its production, it has *no excess capacity. Excess capacity* exists only when more goods can be produced than the producer is able to sell, due to low demand for the product.

What transfer price does the general rule yield under this scenario of no excess capacity? The transfer price is determined as follows:

Outlay cost:

Standard variable cost of production	$ 7.00 per rack
Standard variable cost of transportation	.25 per rack
Total outlay cost	$ 7.25 per rack

Opportunity cost:

Selling price per unit in external market	$11.00 per rack
Less: Variable cost of production and transportation	7.25 per rack
Opportunity cost (forgone contribution margin)	$ 3.75 per rack

General transfer-pricing rule:

Transfer price	=	Outlay cost	+	Opportunity cost
$11.00	=	$7.25	+	$3.75

The *outlay cost* incurred by the Food Processing Division in order to transfer a rack of bread includes the standard variable production cost of $7 and the standard variable transportation cost of $.25. The *opportunity cost* incurred by Suncoast Food Centres when its Food Processing Division transfers a rack of bread to the Lower Sunshine Coast Division instead of selling it in the external market is the forgone contribution margin from the lost sale, equal to $3.75. Why does the company lose a sale in the external market for every rack of bread transferred to the Lower Sunshine Coast Division? The sale is lost because there is *no excess capacity* in the Food Processing Division. Every rack of bread transferred to another company division results in one less rack of bread sold in the external market.

How does the general transfer-pricing rule promote goal congruence? Suppose the Lower Sunshine Coast Division's grocery stores can sell a loaf of bread for $1.50, or $18 for a rack of 12 loaves ($18 = 12 × $1.50). What is the best way for Suncoast Food Centres to use the limited production capacity in the Food Processing Division's Gibsons bakery? The answer is determined as follows:

Contribution to Suncoast Food Centres from Sale in External Market		Contribution to Suncoast Food Centres from Transfer to Lower Sunshine Coast Division	
Wholesale selling price per rack......................	$11.00	Retail selling price per rack	$18.00
Less: Variable costs	7.25	Less: Variable costs	7.25
Contribution margin	$ 3.75	Contribution margin	$10.75

The best use of the bakery's limited production capacity is to produce bread for transfer to the Lower Sunshine Coast Division. If the transfer price is set at $11, as the general rule specifies, goal congruence is maintained. The Food Processing Division manager is willing to transfer bread to the Lower Sunshine Coast Division, because the transfer price of $11 is equal to the external market price. The Lower Sunshine Coast Division manager is willing to buy the bread, because her division will have a contribution margin of $7 on each rack of bread transferred ($18 sales price minus the $11 transfer price).

Now consider a different situation. Suppose a local organization makes a special offer to the Lower Sunshine Coast Division manager to buy several hundred loaves of bread to sell in a promotional campaign. The organization offers to pay $.80 per loaf, which is $9.60 per rack of a dozen loaves. What will the Lower Sunshine Coast Division manager do? She must pay a transfer price of $11 per rack, so the Lower Sunshine Coast Division would lose $1.40 per rack if the special offer were accepted ($11 − $9.60 = $1.40). The Lower Sunshine Coast Division manager will decline the special offer. Is this decision in the best interests of Suncoast Food Centres as a whole? If the offer were accepted, the company as a whole would make a positive contribution of $2.35 per rack, as shown below.

Contribution to Suncoast Food Centers If Special Offer Is Accepted	
Special price per rack	$9.60 per rack
Less: Variable cost to company	7.25 per rack
Contribution to company, per rack..	$2.35 per rack

However, the company can make even more if its Food Processing Division sells bread directly in its external market. Then the contribution to the company is $3.75, as we have just seen. (The external market price of $11 per rack minus a variable cost of $7.25 per rack equals $3.75 per rack.) Thus, Suncoast Food Centres is better off, as a whole, if the Lower Sunshine Coast Division's special offer is rejected. Once again, the general transfer-pricing rule results in goal-congruent decision making.

Scenario II: Excess Capacity   Now let's change our basic assumption, and suppose the Food Processing Division's Gibsons bakery has excess production capacity. This means that the total demand for its bread from all sources, including the Lower Sunshine Coast and Upper Sunshine Coast divisions and the external market, is less than the bakery's production capacity. Under this scenario of excess capacity, what does the general rule specify for a transfer price?

$$\text{Transfer price} = \text{Outlay cost} + \text{Opportunity cost}$$
$$\$7.25 \quad = \quad \$7.25 \quad + \quad 0$$

The *outlay cost* in the Food Processing Division's Gibsons bakery is still $7.25, since it does not depend on whether there is idle capacity or not. The *opportunity cost*, however, is now zero. There is no opportunity cost to the company when a rack of bread is transferred to the Lower Sunshine Coast Division, because the

Food Processing Division can still satisfy all of its external demand for bread. Thus, the general rule specifies a transfer price of $7.25, the total standard variable cost of production and transportation.

Let's reconsider what will happen when the Lower Sunshine Coast Division manager receives the local organization's special offer to buy bread at $9.60 per rack. The Lower Sunshine Coast Division will now show a positive contribution of $2.35 per rack on the special order.

Special price per rack	$9.60 per rack
Less: Transfer price paid by Lower Sunshine Coast Division	7.25 per rack
Contribution to Lower Sunshine Coast Division	$2.35 per rack

The Lower Sunshine Coast Division manager will accept the special offer. This decision is also in the best interests of Suncoast Food Centres. The company, as a whole, also will make a contribution of $2.35 per rack on every rack transferred to the Lower Sunshine Coast Division to satisfy the special order. Once again, the general transfer-pricing rule maintains goal-congruent decision-making behaviour.

Notice that the general rule yields a transfer price that leaves the Food Processing Division manager indifferent as to whether the transfer will be made. At a transfer price of $7.25, the contribution to the Food Processing Division will be zero (transfer price of $7.25 less variable cost of $7.25). To avoid this problem, we can view the general rule as providing a lower bound on the transfer price. Some companies allow the producing division to add a markup to this lower bound in order to provide a positive contribution margin. This in turn provides a positive incentive to make the transfer.

Difficulty in Implementing the General Rule The general transfer-pricing rule will always promote goal-congruent decision making *if the rule can be implemented*. However, the rule is often difficult or impossible to implement due to the difficulty of measuring opportunity costs. Such a cost-measurement problem can arise for a number of reasons. One reason is that the external market may not be perfectly competitive. Under **perfect competition**, the market price does not depend on the quantity sold by any one producer. Under **imperfect competition**, a single producer or group of producers can affect the market price by varying the amount of product available in the market. In such cases, the external market price depends on the production decisions of the producer. This in turn means that the opportunity cost incurred by the company as a result of internal transfers depends on the quantity sold externally. These interactions may make it impossible to measure accurately the opportunity cost caused by a product transfer.

Other reasons for difficulty in measuring the opportunity cost associated with a product transfer include uniqueness of the transferred goods or services, a need for the producing division to invest in special equipment in order to produce the transferred goods, and interdependencies among several transferred products or services. For example, the producing division may provide design services as well as production of the goods for a buying division. What is the opportunity cost associated with each of these related outputs of the producing division? In many such cases, it is difficult to sort out the opportunity costs.

The general transfer-pricing rule provides a good conceptual model for the managerial accountant to use in setting transfer prices. Moreover, in many cases, it can be implemented. When the general rule cannot be implemented, organizations turn to other transfer-pricing methods, as we shall see next.

Transfers Based on the External Market Price

A common approach is to set the transfer price equal to the price in the external market. In the Suncoast Food Centres illustration, the Food Processing Division would set the transfer price for bread at $11 per rack, since that is the price the division can obtain in its external market. When the producing division has no excess capacity and perfect competition prevails, where no single producer can affect the market price,

> "It is difficult for people 'doing the business' to stop and consult about the transfer pricing implications of their moves, but they have to." (12i)
>
> **Respondent, Ernst & Young survey**

Transfe
483-48

Learning Objective 11

Explain how to base a transfer price on market prices, costs, or negotiations.

the general transfer-pricing rule and the external market price yield the same transfer price. This fact is illustrated for Suncoast Food Centres as follows:

General Transfer-Pricing Rule

$$\text{Transfer price} = \text{Outlay cost} + \text{Opportunity cost}$$

$$= \begin{array}{c}\text{Variable cost of}\\ \text{production and}\\ \text{transportation}\end{array} + \begin{array}{c}\text{Forgone contribution}\\ \text{margin of an external}\\ \text{sale}\end{array}$$

$$= \$7.25 + (\$11 - \$7.25) = \$11$$

Market Price

$$\text{Transfer price} = \text{External market price} = \$11$$

If the producing division has excess capacity or the external market is imperfectly competitive, the general rule and the external market price will not yield the same transfer price.

If the transfer price is set at the market price, the producing division should have the option of either producing goods for internal transfer or selling in the external market. The buying division should be required to purchase goods from inside its organization if the producing division's goods meet the product specifications. Otherwise, the buying division should have the autonomy to buy from a supplier outside its own organization. To handle pricing disputes that may arise, an arbitration process should be established.

Transfer prices based on market prices are consistent with the responsibility-accounting concepts of profit centres and investment centres. In addition to encouraging division managers to focus on divisional profitability, market-based transfer prices help to show the contribution of each division to overall company profit. Suppose the Food Processing Division of Suncoast Food Centres transfers bread to the Lower Sunshine Coast Division at a market-based transfer price of $11 per rack. The following contribution margins will be earned by the two divisions and the company as a whole:

Food Processing Division		Lower Sunshine Coast Division	
Transfer price	$11.00 per rack	Retail sales price	$18.00 per rack
Less: Variable costs	7.25 per rack	Less: Transfer price	11.00 per rack
Contribution margin	$ 3.75 per rack	Contribution margin	$ 7.00 per rack

Suncoast Food Centres

Retail sales price	$18.00 per rack
Less: Variable costs	7.25 per rack
Contribution margin	$10.75 per rack

When aggregate divisional profits are determined for the year, and ROI and residual income are computed, the use of a market-based transfer price helps to assess the contributions of each division to overall corporate profits.

Distress Market Prices

Occasionally an industry will experience a period of significant excess capacity and extremely low prices. For example, when gasoline prices soared, the market prices for recreational vehicles and power boats fell temporarily to very low levels.

Under such extreme conditions, basing transfer prices on market prices can lead to decisions that are not in the best interests of the overall company. Basing transfer prices on artificially *low distress market prices* could lead the producing division to sell or close the productive resources devoted to producing the product for transfer. Under distress market prices, the producing division manager might prefer to move the division into a more profitable product line. While such a decision might improve the division's profit in the short run, it could be contrary to the best interests of the company overall. It might be better for the company as a whole to avoid divesting itself of any productive resources and to ride out the period of market distress. To encourage an autonomous division manager to act in this fashion, some companies set the transfer price equal to the long-run average external market price, rather than the current (possibly depressed) market price.

Negotiated Transfer Prices

Many companies use negotiated transfer prices. Division managers or their representatives actually negotiate the price at which transfers will be made. Sometimes they start with the external market price and then make adjustments for various reasons. For example, the producing division may enjoy some cost savings on internal transfers that are not obtained on external sales. Commissions may not have to be paid to sales personnel on internally transferred products. In such cases, a negotiated transfer price may split the cost savings between the producing and buying divisions.

In other instances, a negotiated transfer price may be used because no external market exists for the transferred product.

Two drawbacks sometimes characterize negotiated transfer prices. First, negotiations can lead to divisiveness and competition between participating division managers. This can undermine the spirit of cooperation and unity that is desirable throughout an organization. Second, although negotiating skill is a valuable managerial talent, it should not be the sole or dominant factor in evaluating a division manager. If, for example, the producing division's manager is a better negotiator than the buying division's manager, then the producing division's profit may look better than it should, simply because of its manager's superior negotiating ability.

Cost-Based Transfer Prices

Organizations that do not base prices on market prices or negotiations often turn to a cost-based transfer-pricing approach.

Variable Cost   One approach is to set the transfer price equal to the standard variable cost. The problem with this approach is that even when the producing division has excess capacity, it is not allowed to show any contribution margin on the transferred products or services. To illustrate, suppose the Food Processing Division has excess capacity and the transfer price is set at the standard variable cost of $7.25 per rack of bread. There is no positive incentive for the division to produce and transfer bread to the Lower Sunshine Coast Division. The Food Processing Division's contribution margin from a transfer will be zero (transfer price of $7.25 minus variable costs of $7.25 equals zero). Some companies avoid this problem by setting the transfer price at standard variable cost plus a markup to allow the producing division a positive contribution margin.

Full Cost   An alternative is to set the transfer price equal to the *full cost* of the transferred product or service. **Full** (or **absorption**) cost is equal to the product's variable cost plus an allocated portion of fixed overhead.

Suppose the Food Processing Division's Gibsons bakery has budgeted annual fixed overhead of $500,000 and budgeted annual production of 200,000 racks of bread. The full cost of the bakery's product is computed as follows:

$$\text{Full cost} = \text{Variable cost} + \text{Allocated fixed overhead}$$

$$= \$7.25 \text{ per rack} + \frac{\$500,000 \text{ budgeted fixed overhead}}{200,000 \text{ budgeted racks of bread}}$$

$$= \quad \$7.25 \quad + \quad \$2.50$$

$$= \$9.75 \text{ per rack}$$

Under this approach, the transfer price is set at $9.75 per rack of bread.

Dysfunctional Decision-Making Behaviour Basing transfer prices on full cost entails a serious risk of causing dysfunctional decision-making behaviour. Full-cost-based transfer prices lead the buying division to view costs that are fixed for the company as a whole as variable costs to the buying division. This can cause faulty decision making.

To illustrate, suppose the Food Processing Division has excess capacity, and the transfer price of bread is equal to the full cost of $9.75 per rack. What will happen if the Lower Sunshine Coast Division receives the special offer discussed previously, where it can sell bread to a local organization at a special price of $9.60 per rack? The Lower Sunshine Coast Division manager will reject the special order, since otherwise her division would incur a loss of $.15 per rack.

Special price per rack	$9.60 per rack
Less: Transfer price based on full cost	9.75 per rack
Loss	$ .15 per rack

What is in the best interests of the company as a whole? Suncoast Food Centres would make a positive contribution of $2.35 per rack on the bread sold in the special order.

Special price per rack	$9.60 per rack
Less: Variable cost in Food Processing Division	7.25 per rack
Contribution to company as a whole	$2.35 per rack

What has happened here? Setting the transfer price equal to the full cost of $9.75 has turned a cost that is fixed in the Food Processing Division, and hence is fixed for the company as a whole, into a variable cost from the viewpoint of the Lower Sunshine Coast Division manager. The manager would tend to reject the special offer, even though accepting it would benefit the company as a whole.

Although the practice is common, transfer prices should not be based on full cost. The risk is too great that the cost behaviour in the producing division will be obscured. This can all too easily result in poor decisions in the buying division.

Standard versus Actual Costs

Throughout our discussion of transfer prices, we have used standard costs rather than actual costs. This was true in our discussion of the general transfer-pricing rule as well as for cost-based transfer prices. Transfer prices should not be based on actual costs, because such a practice would allow an inefficient producing division to pass its excess production costs on to the buying division in the transfer price. When standard costs are used in transfer-pricing formulas, the buying division is not forced to pick up the tab for the producer's inefficiency. Moreover, the producing division is given an incentive to control its costs, since any costs of inefficiency cannot be passed on.

Undermining Divisional Autonomy

Suppose the manager of Suncoast Food Centres' Food Processing Division has excess capacity but insists on a transfer price of $9.75, based on full cost. The Lower Sunshine Coast Division manager is faced with the special offer for bread at $9.60 per rack. She regrets that she will have to decline the offer because it would cause her division's profit to decline, even though the company's interests would be best served by accepting the special order. The Lower Sunshine Coast Division manager calls the company president and explains the situation. She asks the president to intervene and force the Food Processing Division manager to lower his transfer price.

As the company president, what would you do? If you stay out of the controversy, your company will lose the contribution on the special order. If you intervene, you will run the risk of undermining the autonomy of your division managers. You established a decentralized organization structure for Suncoast Centres and hired competent managers because you believed in the benefits of decentralized decision making.

"[Transfer pricing] affects nearly every aspect of multinational operations—R&D, manufacturing, marketing and distribution, after-sale services." (12j)

Ernst & Young

There is no obvious answer to this dilemma. In practice, central managers are reluctant to intervene in such disputes unless the negative financial consequences to the organization are quite large. Most managers believe the benefits of decentralized decision making are important to protect, even if it means an occasional dysfunctional decision.

An International Perspective

Two international issues arise in the case of multinational firms setting transfer prices between divisions in different countries.

Income-Tax Rates   Multinational companies often consider domestic and foreign income-tax rates when setting transfer prices. For example, suppose a company based in Europe also has a division in Asia. A European division produces a subassembly, which is transferred to the Asian division for assembly and sale of the final product. Suppose also that the income-tax rate for the company's European division is higher than the rate in the Asian division's country. How would these different tax rates affect the transfer price for the subassembly?

The company's management has an incentive to set a low transfer price for the subassembly. This will result in relatively low profits for the company's European division and a relatively high income for the Asian division. Since the tax rate is lower in the Asian country, the overall company will save on income tax. By setting a low transfer price, the company will shift a portion of its income to a country with a lower tax rate. Tax laws vary among countries with regard to flexibility in setting transfer prices. Some countries' tax laws prohibit the behaviour described in our example, while other countries' laws permit it.

Management
Accounting
Practice

Ernst & Young, CRA

TRANSFER PRICING AND TAX ISSUES

According to a survey by Ernst & Young LLP, "transfer pricing is the top tax issue facing multinational corporations." Of the international tax directors at 582 multinational organizations polled in the survey, 75 percent expect their company to face a transfer-pricing audit within the next two years. Respondents cited related-party transactions (including the intercompany transfer of goods, services, properties, loans, and leases) involving administrative and management services as the most likely to be audited. Moreover, there has been an increase in transfer pricing audit activity in recent years.[5]

"The Canada Revenue Agency (CRA) is concerned that companies could use transfer prices to shift profits between related entities through cost of goods sold. Thus, transfer pricing manipulation could be used by taxpayers to shift income from high tax jurisdictions like Canada to low tax jurisdictions. The right price from the CRA's perspective is the market value price. Because it's difficult to prove that the transfer price was equal to the market price, companies often find themselves in disputes with the CRA. But now there's help. The CRA's Advanced Pricing Agreement Program provides companies an opportunity to avoid costly audits and litigation by allowing them to negotiate a prospective agreement with the CRA regarding the facts, the transfer pricing methodology, and an acceptable range of results. The program is aimed at multinational corporations interested in avoiding penalties, managing risk, and determining their tax liability with certainty."[6]

Import Duties Another international issue that can affect a firm's transfer pricing policy is the imposition of import duties, or tariffs. These are fees charged to an importer, generally on the basis of the reported value of the goods being imported. Consider again the example of a firm with divisions in Europe and Asia. If the Asian country imposes an import duty on goods transferred in from the European division, the company has an incentive to set a relatively low transfer price on the transferred goods. This will minimize the duty to be paid and maximize the overall profit for the company as a whole. As in the case of taxation, countries sometimes pass laws to limit a multinational firm's flexibility in setting transfer prices for the purpose of minimizing import duties.

Transfer Pricing in the Service Industry

Service industry firms and nonprofit organizations also use transfer pricing when services are transferred between responsibility centres. In banks, for example, the interest rate at which depositors' funds are transferred to the loan department is a form of transfer price. At some universities, if, for example, a student in the law school takes a course in the business school, a transfer price is charged to the law school for the credit hours of instruction provided to the law student by the business school. Since the transfer price is based on tuition charges, it is a market-price-based transfer price.

Behavioural Issues: Risk Aversion and Incentives

The designer of a performance-evaluation system for responsibility-centre managers has to consider many factors. Trade-offs often have to be made between competing objectives. The overall objective is to achieve goal congruence by providing *incentives* for managers to act in the best interests of the organization as a whole. Financial performance measures such as divisional income, ROI, and residual income go a long way toward achieving this objective. However, these measures do have the disadvantage of imposing *risk* on a manager, because the measures also are affected by factors beyond

Transfer prices are used in the service industry as well as in manufacturing. Simon Fraser University, for example, charges an accessory instruction fee to a campus unit when one of its students enrols in a course offered in a different unit.

the manager's control. For example, the income of an orange-growing division of an agricultural company will be affected not only by the manager's diligence and ability, but also by the weather and insect infestations.

Since most people exhibit *risk aversion*, managers must be compensated for the risk they must bear. This compensation comes in the form of higher salaries or bonuses. Thus, the design of a managerial performance evaluation and reward system involves a trade-off between the following two factors:

Evaluation of a manager on the basis of financial performance measures, which provide incentives for the manager to act in the organization's interests	Imposition of risk on a manager who exhibits risk aversion, because financial performance measures are controllable only partially by the manager

Trade-offs in designing
managerial performance
evaluation and reward system

Achieving the optimal trade-off between risk and incentives is a delicate balancing act that requires the skill and experience of top management.

Chapter Summary

Responsibility-accounting systems are designed to foster goal congruence among the managers in decentralized organizations. Each subunit in an organization is designated as a cost centre, revenue centre, profit centre, or investment centre. The managerial accountant prepares a performance report for each responsibility centre. These reports show the performance of the responsibility centre and its manager for a specified time period.

To use responsibility accounting effectively, the emphasis must be on information rather than blame. The intent should be to provide managers with information to help them better manage their subunits. Responsibility-accounting systems can bring about desired behaviour, such as reducing the number of rush orders in a manufacturing company.

Segmented income statements often are included in a responsibility-accounting system, to show the performance of the organization and its various segments. To be most effective, such reports should distinguish between the performance of segments and segment managers.

The primary criterion for judging the effectiveness of performance measures for responsibility-centre managers is the extent to which the measures promote goal congruence. The three most common measures of investment-centre performance are return on investment (ROI), residual income (RI), and economic value added (EVA). Each of these performance measures relates an investment centre's income to the capital invested to earn it. Residual income and EVA have the additional advantage of incorporating the organization's cost of acquiring capital in the performance measure. An investment centre's ROI may be improved by increasing either the sales margin or capital turnover. ROI, residual income, and EVA all require the measurement of a division's income and invested capital, and the methods for making the measurements vary in practice.

When products or services are transferred between divisions in the same organization, divisional performance is affected by the transfer price. A general rule states that the transfer price should be equal to the outlay cost incurred to make the transfer plus the organization's opportunity cost associated with the transfer. Due to difficulties in implementing the rule, most companies base transfer prices on external market prices, costs, or negotiations. In some cases, these practical transfer-pricing methods may result in dysfunctional decisions. Top management then must weigh the benefits of intervening to prevent suboptimal decisions against the costs of undermining divisional autonomy.

Review Problems on Responsibility Accounting, Investment Centres, and Transfer Pricing

Problem 1

The North Shore Credit Union has a division for each of the two cities in which it operates, North Vancouver and West Vancouver. Each divisional vice-president is held accountable for both profit and invested capital. Each division consists of two branches. Each branch manager is responsible for that bank's profit. The North Vancouver Division's Deep Cove Branch has a Deposit Department, a Loan Department, and an Administrative Services Department. The department supervisors of the Loan and Deposit Departments are accountable for departmental revenues; the Administrative Services Department supervisor is accountable for costs.

All of the North Shore Credit Union's advertising and promotion is done centrally. The advertising and promotion cost pool for the year just ended, which amounted to $40,000, is allocated across the four branches on the basis of budgeted branch revenue. Budgeted revenue for the year is shown below.

North Vancouver Division:	Londsdale Branch	$400,000
	Deep Cove Branch	200,000
West Vancouver Division:	Howe Sound Branch	250,000
	Capilano Branch	150,000

Required:

1. Draw an organization chart for the North Shore Credit Union that shows each subunit described above, its manager's title, and its designation as a responsibility centre.

2. Distribute (allocate) the bank's advertising cost pool to the four branches.

Problem 2

Stellar Systems Company manufactures guidance systems for rockets used to launch commercial satellites. The company's Software Division reported the following results for 20x7.

Income	$ 300,000
Sales revenue	2,000,000
Invested capital (total assets)	3,000,000
Average balance in current liabilities	20,000

Stellar Systems' weighted-average cost of capital (WACC) is 9 percent, and the company's tax rate is 40 percent. Moreover, the company's required rate of return on invested capital is 9 percent.

Required:

1. Compute the Software Division's sales margin, capital turnover, return on investment (ROI), residual income, and economic value added (EVA) for 20x7.

2. If income and sales remain the same in 20x8, but the division's capital turnover improves to 80 percent, compute the following for 20x8: (*a*) invested capital and (*b*) ROI.

Problem 3

Stellar Systems Company's Microprocessor Division sells a computer module to the company's Guidance Assembly Division, which assembles completed guidance systems. The Microprocessor Division has no excess capacity. The computer module costs $10,000 to manufacture, and it can be sold in the external market to companies in the computer industry for $13,500.

Required: Compute the transfer price for the computer module using the general transfer-pricing rule.

Solution to Review Problems

Problem 1

1. Organization chart (subunits, managers, responsibility centre designation) is shown below.

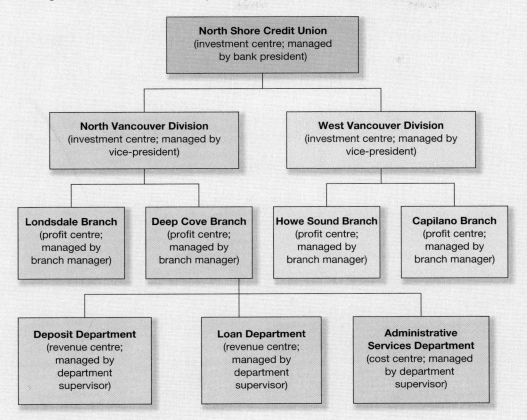

2. Cost distribution (or allocation):

Cost Pool	Responsibility Centre	Allocation Base: Revenue	Percentage of Total*	Costs Distributed
Advertising	North Vancouver, Londsdale Branch	$ 400,000	40%	$16,000
and	North Vancouver, Deep Cove Branch.........	200,000	20	8,000
promotion	West Vancouver, Howe Sound Branch.......	250,000	25	10,000
costs	West Vancouver, Capilano Branch	150,000	15	6,000
	Total	$1,000,000	100%	$40,000

*Branch revenue as a percentage of total revenue, $1,000,000.

Problem 2

1.
$$\text{Sales margin} = \frac{\text{Income}}{\text{Sales revenue}} = \frac{\$300,000}{\$2,000,000} = 15\%$$

$$\text{Capital turnover} = \frac{\text{Sales revenue}}{\text{Invested capital}} = \frac{\$2,000,000}{\$3,000,000} = 67\%$$

$$\text{Return on investment} = \frac{\text{Income}}{\text{Invested capital}} = \frac{\$300,000}{\$3,000,000} = 10\%$$

Residual income:

Divisional income $300,000

Less: Imputed interest charge:

Invested capital $3,000,000

$\times$ Imputed interest rate $\times$ .09

Imputed interest charge   270,000

Residual income.. $ 30,000

Economic value added (EVA):

$$EVA = \begin{bmatrix} \text{Investment centre's} \\ \text{after-tax} \\ \text{operating income} \end{bmatrix} - \left[\left(\begin{matrix} \text{Investment centre's} \\ \text{total assets} \end{matrix} - \begin{matrix} \text{Investment centre's} \\ \text{current liabilities} \end{matrix} \right) \times \begin{matrix} \text{Weighted-average} \\ \text{cost of capital} \end{matrix} \right]$$

$$= \$300,000 \ (1 - .40) \ - [(\quad \$3,000,000 \quad - \quad \$20,000 \quad) \times \quad .09 \quad]$$

$$= \$(88,200)$$

2.   *a.*   Capital turnover $= \dfrac{\text{Sales revenue}}{\text{Invested capital}} = \dfrac{\$2,000,000}{?} = 80\%$

Therefore: Invested capital $= \dfrac{\$2,000,000}{.80} = \$2,500,000$

b.   New ROI $= 15\% \times 80\% = 12\%$

Problem 3

Transfer price = Outlay cost + Opportunity cost

$$= \$10,000 \quad + (\$13,500 - \$10,000)$$

$$= \$13,500$$

The $3,500 opportunity cost of a transfer is the contribution margin that will be forgone if a computer module is transferred instead of sold in the external market.

Key Terms

For each term's definition refer to the indicated page, or turn to the glossary at the end of the text.

activity-based responsibility accounting, 468
allocation base, 467
capital turnover, 474
cash bonus, 482
common costs, 470
cost allocation (*or* distribution), 467
cost centre, 461
cost objects, 467

cost pool, 467
economic value added (EVA), 478
full (*or* absorption) cost, 489
goal congruence, 460
imperfect competition, 487
incentive compensation, 483
investment centre, 461
management by objectives (MBO), 460

merit pay, 483
pay for performance, 483
perfect competition, 487
performance report, 464
profit centre, 461
residual income, 476
responsibility accounting, 460
responsibility centre, 461
return on investment (ROI), 473

revenue centre, 461
sales margin, 474
segmented income statement, 470
shareholder value analysis, 477
transfer price, 483
weighted-average cost of capital (WACC), 478

Review Questions

12–1.   Why is goal congruence important to an organization's success? How does a responsibility-accounting system foster goal congruence?

12–2.   Define and give examples of the following terms: cost centre, revenue centre, profit centre, and investment centre.

12–3.   Under what circumstances would it be appropriate to change the Waikiki Sands Hotel from a profit centre to an investment centre?

12–4.   Explain the relationship between performance reports and flexible budgeting.

12–5. What is the key feature of activity-based responsibility accounting? Briefly explain.

12–6. Explain how to get positive behavioural effects from a responsibility-accounting system.

12–7. "Performance reports based on controllability are impossible. Nobody really *controls* anything in an organization!" Do you agree or disagree? Explain your answer.

12–8. Explain how and why cost allocation might be used to assign the costs of a mainframe computer system used for research purposes in a university.

12–9. Define the term *cost allocation base*. What would be a sensible allocation base for assigning advertising costs to the various components of a large theme park?

12–10. Referring to Exhibit 12–5, why are marketing costs distributed to the Waikiki Sands Hotel's departments on the basis of *budgeted* sales dollars?

12–11. Explain what is meant by a *segmented income statement*.

12–12. Why do some managerial accountants choose not to allocate common costs in segmented reports?

12–13. Why is it important in responsibility accounting to distinguish between segments and segment managers?

12–14. List and explain three key features of the segmented income statement shown in Exhibit 12–7.

12–15. Can a common cost for one segment be a traceable cost for another segment? Explain your answer.

12–16. Describe the managerial approach known as *management by objectives* or MBO.

12–17. Write the formula for ROI, showing sales margin and capital turnover as its components.

12–18. Explain how the manager of the Automobile Division of an insurance company could improve her division's ROI.

12–19. Make up an example showing how residual income is calculated. What information is used in computing residual income that is not used in computing ROI?

12–20. What is the main disadvantage of ROI as an investment-centre performance measure? How does the residual income measure eliminate this disadvantage?

12–21. Define the term *economic value added*. How does it differ from residual income?

12–22. Distinguish between the following measures of invested capital, and briefly explain when each should be used: *(a)* total assets, *(b)* total productive assets, and *(c)* total assets less current liabilities.

12–23. Why do some companies use gross book value instead of net book value to measure a division's invested capital?

12–24. Explain why it is important in performance evaluation to distinguish between investment centres and their managers.

12–25. How do organizations use pay for performance to motivate managers?

12–26. Describe an alternative to using ROI or residual income to measure investment-centre performance.

12–27. Identify and explain the managerial accountant's primary objective in choosing a transfer-pricing policy.

12–28. Describe four methods by which transfer prices may be set.

12–29. Explain the significance of excess capacity in the transferring division when transfer prices are set using the general transfer-pricing rule.

12–30. Why might income-tax laws affect the transfer-pricing policies of multinational companies?

12–31. Explain the role of import duties, or tariffs, in affecting the transfer-pricing policies of multinational companies.

Exercises

Oradell Electronics Company manufactures complex circuit boards for the aerospace industry. Demand for the company's products has fallen in recent months, and the firm has cut its production significantly. Many unskilled workers have been temporarily laid off. Top management has made a decision, however, not to lay off any highly skilled employees, such as inspectors and machinery operators. Management was concerned that these highly skilled employees would easily find new jobs elsewhere and not return when production returned to normal levels.

To occupy the skilled employees during the production cutback, they have been reassigned temporarily to the Maintenance Department. Here they are performing general maintenance tasks, such as repainting the interior of the factory, repairing the loading dock, and building wooden storage racks for the warehouse. The skilled employees continued to receive their normal wages, which average $19 per hour. However, the normal wages for Maintenance Department employees average $11 per hour.

The supervisor of the Maintenance Department recently received the March performance report, which indicated that his department's labour cost exceeded the budget by $21,230. The department's actual labour cost was approximately 85 percent over the budget. The department supervisor complained to the controller.

Required: As the controller, how would you respond? Would you make any modification in Oradell's responsibility-accounting system? If so, list the changes you would make. Explain your reasoning.

For each of the following organizational subunits, indicate the type of responsibility centre that is most appropriate:

1. An orange juice factory operated by a large orange grower
2. The Faculty of Engineering at a large state university

■ **Exercise 12–32**
Assigning Responsibility for Skilled Employees' Wages
(LO 1)

■ **Exercise 12–33**
Designating Responsibility Centres
(LO 2)

3. The European Division of a multinational manufacturing company
4. The outpatient clinic in a hospital
5. The Mayor's Office in a large city
6. A movie theatre in a company that operates a chain of theatres
7. A radio station owned by a large broadcasting network
8. The claims department in an insurance company
9. The ticket sales division of a major airline
10. A bottling plant of a soft drink company

■ Exercise 12–34
Responsibility Accounting;
Equipment Breakdown
(LO 1, 2)

How should a responsibility-accounting system handle each of the following scenarios?

1. Department A manufactures a component, which is then used by Department B. Department A recently experienced a machine breakdown that held up production of the component. As a result, Department B was forced to curtail its own production, thereby incurring large costs of idle time. An investigation revealed that Department A's machinery had not been properly maintained.

2. Refer to the scenario above, but suppose the investigation revealed the machinery in Department A had been properly maintained.

■ Exercise 12–35
Responsibility-Accounting
Centres; Xerox Corporation
(LO 1, 2)

Xerox Corporation has been an innovator in its responsibility-accounting system. In one initiative, management changed the responsibility-centre orientation of its Logistics and Distribution Department from a cost centre to a profit centre. The department manages the inventories and provides other logistical services to the company's Business Systems Group. Formerly, the manager of the Logistics and Distribution Department was held accountable for adherence to an operating expense budget. Now the department "sells" its services to the company's other segments, and the department's manager is evaluated partially on the basis of the department's profit. Xerox Corporation's management feels that the change has been beneficial. The change has resulted in more innovative thinking in the department and has moved decision making down to lower levels in the company.

Required: Comment on the new responsibility-centre designation for the Logistics and Distribution Department.

■ Exercise 12–36
Performance Report; Hotel
(LO 3)

The following data pertain to the Waikiki Sands Hotel for the month of March:

	Flexible Budget for March (in thousands)*	Actual Results for March (in thousands)*
Banquets and catering	$ 650	$ 658
Restaurants	1,800	1,794
Kitchen staff wages	(85)	(86)
Food	(690)	(690)
Paper products	(125)	(122)
Variable overhead	(75)	(78)
Fixed overhead	(90)	(93)

*Numbers without parentheses denote profit; numbers with parentheses denote expenses.

Required: Prepare a March performance report similar to the lower portion of Exhibit 12–4. The report should have six numerical columns with headings analogous to those in Exhibit 12–4. Your performance report should cover only the Food and Beverage Department and the Kitchen. Draw arrows to show the relationships between the numbers in the report. Refer to Exhibit 12–4 for guidance. For the year-to-date columns in your report, use the data given in Exhibit 12–4. You will need to update those figures using the March data given above.

■ Exercise 12–37
Cost Allocation in a College
(LO 4)

Vancouver Community College has three divisions: Liberal Arts, Sciences, and Business Administration. The college's controller is trying to decide how to allocate the costs of the Admissions Department, the Registrar's Department, and the Computer Services Department. The controller has compiled the following data for the year just ended:

Department	Annual Cost
Admissions	$117,000
Registrar	195,000
Computer Services	416,000

Division	Budgeted Enrollment	Budgeted Credit Hours	Planned Courses Requiring Computer Work
Liberal Arts	1,000	30,000	12
Sciences	800	28,000	24
Business Administration	700	22,000	24

Required:

1. For each department, choose an allocation base and distribute the departmental costs to the college's three divisions. Justify your choice of an allocation base.

2. Would you have preferred a different allocation base than those available using the data compiled by the controller? Why?

3. *Build a spreadsheet:* Construct an Excel spreadsheet to solve requirement (1) above. Show how the solution will change if the following information changes: the costs incurred by the departments were $120,000, $200,000, and $420,000, for Admissions, Registrar, and Computer Services, respectively.

Tri-Cities Cable Services, Inc. is organized with three segments: Metro, Suburban, and Outlying. Data for these segments for the year just ended follow.

Exercise 12–38
Segmented Income Statement; TV Cable Company
(LO 5)

	Metro	Suburban	Outlying
Service revenue	$950,000	$750,000	$350,000
Variable expenses	150,000	100,000	50,000
Controllable fixed expenses	350,000	270,000	100,000
Fixed expenses controllable by others	180,000	150,000	40,000

In addition to the expenses listed above, the company has $45,000 of common fixed expenses. Income-tax expense for the year is $245,000.

Required:

1. Prepare a segmented income statement for Tri-Cities Cable Services, Inc. Use the contribution format.

2. *Build a spreadsheet:* Construct an Excel spreadsheet to solve the preceding requirement. Show how the solution will change if the following information changes: the sales revenues were $960,000 and $780,000 for Metro and Suburban, respectively.

Visit the Web site for one of the following companies, or a different company of your choosing:

Exercise 12–39
Responsibility Accounting; Use of Internet
(LO 1, 2)

Marriott Hotels	www.marriott.com	Pizza Hut	www.pizzahut.com
McDonald's Corporation	www.mcdonalds.com	Xerox Corporation	www.xerox.com

Required: Read about the company's activities and operations. Then do as good a job as you can in preparing an organization chart for the firm. For each subunit in the organization chart, indicate what type of responsibility accounting centre designation you believe would be most appropriate. (Refer to Exhibits 12–1 and 12–2 for guidance.)

The following data pertain to Heritage Division's most recent year of operations:

Exercise 12–40
Components of ROI
(LO 6)

Income	$ 10,000,000
Sales revenue	125,000,000
Average invested capital	50,000,000

Required: Compute Heritage Division's sales margin, capital turnover, and return on investment for the year.

Exercise 12–41
Improving ROI
(LO 7)

Refer to the preceding exercise.

Required: Demonstrate two ways Heritage Division's manager could improve the division's ROI to 25 percent.

Exercise 12–42
Residual Income
(LO 6)

Refer to the data for Exercise 12–40. Assume that the company's minimum desired rate of return on invested capital is 11 percent.

Required: Compute Heritage Division's residual income for the year.

Exercise 12–43
Calculate Weighted-Average
Cost of Capital for EVA
(LO 6)

Coquitlam Construction Associates, a real estate developer and building contractor, has two sources of long-term capital: debt and equity. The cost to the company of issuing debt is the after-tax cost of the interest payments on the debt, taking into account the fact that the interest payments are tax-deductible. The cost of the company's equity capital is the investment opportunity rate of the company's investors, that is, the rate they could earn on investments of similar risk to that of investing in Coquitlam Construction Associates. The interest rate on the company's $90 million of long-term debt is 10 percent, and the company's tax rate is 40 percent. The cost of the company's equity capital is 15 percent. Moreover, the market value (and book value) of the company's equity is $135 million.

Required: Calculate Coquitlam Construction Associates' weighted-average cost of capital.

Exercise 12–44
Economic Value Added (EVA);
Continuation of Preceding
Exercise
(LO 6)

Refer to the data in the preceding exercise for Coquitlam Construction Associates. The company has two divisions: the real estate division and the construction division. The divisions' total assets, current liabilities, and before-tax operating income for the most recent year are as follows:

Division	Total Assets	Current Liabilities	Before-Tax Operating Income
Real estate	$150,000,000	$9,000,000	$30,000,000
Construction	90,000,000	6,000,000	27,000,000

Required: Calculate the economic value added (EVA) for each of Coquitlam Construction Associates' divisions. (You will need to use the weighted-average cost of capital, which was computed in the preceding exercise.)

Exercise 12–45
ROI; Residual Income
(LO 6)

Suburban Lifestyles, Inc. has manufactured prefabricated houses for over 20 years. The houses are constructed in sections to be assembled on customers' lots. Suburban Lifestyles expanded into the precut housing market when it acquired Fairmont Company, one of its suppliers. In this market, various types of lumber are precut into the appropriate lengths, banded into packages, and shipped to customers' lots for assembly. Suburban Lifestyles designated the Fairmont Division as an investment centre. Suburban Lifestyles uses return on investment (ROI) as a performance measure with investment defined as average productive assets. Management bonuses are based in part on ROI. All investments are expected to earn a minimum return of 15 percent before income taxes. Fairmont's ROI has ranged from 19.3 to 22.1 percent since it was acquired. Fairmont had an investment opportunity in 20x1 that had an estimated ROI of 18 percent. Fairmont's management decided against the investment, because it believed the investment would decrease the division's overall ROI. The 20x1 income statement for Fairmont Division follows. The division's productive assets were $25,200,000 at the end of 20x1, a 5 percent increase over the balance at the beginning of the year.

FAIRMONT DIVISION
Income Statement
For the Year Ended December 31, 20x1
(in thousands)

Sales revenue		$48,000
Cost of goods sold		31,600
Gross margin		16,400
Operating expenses:		
Administrative	$4,280	
Selling	7,200	11,480
Income from operations before income taxes		$ 4,920

Required:

1. Calculate the following performance measures for 20x1 for the Fairmont Division:
   a. Return on investment (ROI)
   b. Residual income

2. Would the management of Fairmont Division have been more likely to accept the investment opportunity it had in 20x1 if residual income were used as a performance measure instead of ROI? Explain your answer.

3. *Build a spreadsheet:* Construct an Excel spreadsheet to solve requirement (1) above. Show how the solution will change if income from operations was $5,400,000.

(CMA, adapted)

Select one of the following companies (or any company of your choosing) and use the Internet to explore the company's most recent annual report.

Air Canada	www.aircanada.com
Deere and Company	www.deere.com
IBM	www.ibm.com
Pizza Hut	www.pizzahut.com
Ramada Inn	www.ramada.com
Wal-Mart	www.wal-mart.com

■ Exercise 12–46
ROI and Residual Income; Annual Reports; Use of Internet
(LO 6)

Required:

1. Calculate the company's overall return on investment (ROI). Also, calculate the company's overall residual income. (Assume an imputed interest rate of 10 percent.) List and explain any assumptions you make.

2. Does the company include a calculation of ROI in its online annual report? If it does, do your calculations agree with those of the company? If not, what would be some possible explanations?

Refer to Exhibit 12–10. Assume that you are a consultant who has been hired by Suncoast Food Centres.

Required: Write a memorandum to the company president explaining why the ROI based on net book value (in Exhibit 12–10) behaves as it does over the five-year time horizon.

■ Exercise 12–47
Increasing ROI over Time
(LO 6, 8, 9)

The following data pertain to British Isles Aggregates Company, a producer of sand, gravel, and cement, for the year just ended. (£ denotes the British pound sterling, the national monetary unit of Great Britain.)

■ Exercise 12–48
Improving ROI
(LO 6, 7)

Sales revenue	£6,000,000
Cost of goods sold	3,300,000
Operating expenses	2,400,000
Average invested capital	3,000,000

Required:

1. Compute the company's sales margin, capital turnover, and ROI.

2. If the sales and average invested capital remain the same during the next year, to what level would total expenses have to be reduced in order to improve the firm's ROI to 15 percent?

3. Assume expenses are reduced, as calculated in requirement (2). Compute the firm's new sales margin. Show how the new sales margin and the old capital turnover together result in a new ROI of 15 percent.

Metallurgy Corporation has two divisions. The Fabrication Division transfers partially completed components to the Assembly Division at a predetermined transfer price. The Fabrication Division's standard variable production cost per unit is $450. The division has no excess capacity, and it could sell all of its components to outside buyers at $570 per unit in a perfectly competitive market.

■ Exercise 12–49
General Transfer-Pricing Rule
(LO 10)

Required:

1. Determine a transfer price using the general rule.
2. How would the transfer price change if the Fabrication Division had excess capacity?

Exercise 12–50
Cost-Based Transfer Pricing
(LO 11)

Refer to the preceding exercise. The Fabrication Division's full (absorption) cost of a component is $510, which includes $60 of applied fixed-overhead costs. The transfer price has been set at $561, which is the Fabrication Division's full cost plus a 10 percent markup.

   The Assembly Division has a special offer for its product of $700. The Assembly Division incurs variable costs of $150 in addition to the transfer price for the Fabrication Division's components. Both divisions currently have excess production capacity.

Required:

1. What is the Assembly Division's manager likely to do regarding acceptance or rejection of the special offer? Why?
2. Is this decision in the best interests of the company as a whole? Why?
3. How could the situation be remedied using the transfer price?

Problems

Problem 12–51
Create an Organization
(LO 1, 2)

Here is your chance to be a tycoon. Create your own company. You will be the president and chief executive officer. It can be a manufacturer, retailer, or service industry firm, but *not* a hotel or bank. Draw an organization chart for your company, similar to the one in Exhibit 12–1. Identify divisions and departments at all levels in the organization. Then prepare a companion chart similar to the one in Exhibit 12–2. This chart should designate the title of the manager of a subunit at each level in the organization. It also should designate the type of responsibility centre appropriate for each of these subunits. Finally, write a letter to your company's stockholders summarizing the major responsibilities of each of the managers you identified in your chart. For guidance, refer to the discussion of Exhibits 12–1 and 12–2 in the chapter. (Have fun, and be creative.)

Problem 12–52
Design Performance Reports;
Continuation of Preceding
Problem
(LO 3)

After designing your company, design a set of performance reports for the subunits you identified in your chart. Make up numbers for the performance reports, and show the relationship between the reports. Refer to Exhibit 12–4 for guidance.

Problem 12–53
Designating Responsibility
Centres; Hotel
(LO 2)

The following partial organization chart is an extension of Exhibit 12–1 for Aloha Hotels and Resorts.

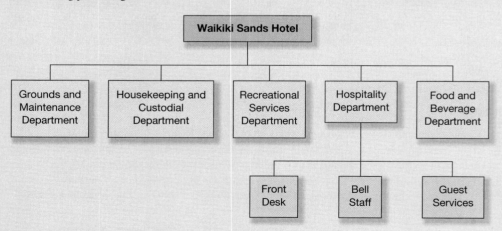

Each of the hotel's five main departments is managed by a director (e.g., director of hospitality). The Front Desk subunit, which is supervised by the front desk manager, handles the hotel's reservations, room assignments, guest payments, and key control. The Bell Staff, managed by the bell captain, is responsible for greeting guests, front door service, assisting guests with their luggage, and delivering room-service orders. The Guest Services subunit, supervised by the manager of Guest Services, is responsible for assisting guests with local transportation arrangements, advising guests on tourist attractions, and such conveniences as valet and floral services.

Required: As an outside consultant, write a memo to the hotel's general manager suggesting a responsibility-centre designation for each of the subunits shown in the organization chart above. Justify your choices.

Canadian Rockies General Hospital serves three counties in Alberta. The hospital is a nonprofit organization that is supported by government funding, patient billings, and private donations. The hospital's organization is shown in the following chart:

■ **Problem 12–54**
Preparation of Performance Reports; Hospital
(LO 3)

1. Flexible budget, August, Cafeteria, total cost: $32,400

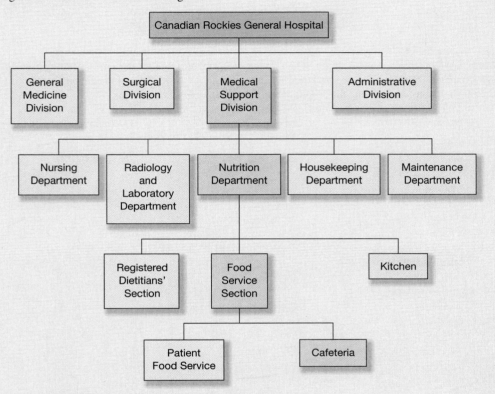

The following cost information has been compiled for August:

	Budget		Actual	
	August	**Year to Date**	**August**	**Year to Date**
Cafeteria:				
Food servers' wages	$ 16,000	$ 128,000	$ 18,000	$ 144,000
Paper products	9,000	72,000	8,800	72,400
Utilities	2,000	16,000	2,100	16,200
Maintenance	800	6,400	200	2,200
Custodial	2,200	17,600	2,200	17,200
Supplies	2,400	19,200	1,800	19,200
Patient Food Service	34,000	272,000	37,000	274,000
Registered Dietitians' Section	15,000	120,000	15,000	120,000
Kitchen	62,000	496,000	58,800	492,000
Nursing Department	140,000	1,120,000	150,000	1,160,000
Radiology and Laboratory Department	36,000	288,000	36,200	288,000
Housekeeping Department	20,000	160,000	23,200	172,000
Maintenance Department	26,000	208,000	12,000	154,000
General Medicine Division	420,000	3,360,000	408,000	3,341,800
Surgical Division	280,000	2,240,000	282,000	2,231,600
Administrative Division	100,000	800,000	107,000	812,000

Required:

1. Prepare a set of cost performance reports similar to Exhibit 12–4. The report should have six columns, as in Exhibit 12–4. The first four columns will have the same headings as those used above. The last two columns will have the following headings: Variance—August and Variance—Year to Date.

   Since all of the information in the performance reports for Canadian Rockies General Hospital is cost information, you do not need to show these data in parentheses. Use F or U to denote whether each variance in the reports is favourable or unfavourable.

2. Using arrows, show the relationships between the numbers in your performance reports for Canadian Rockies General Hospital. Refer to Exhibit 12–4 for guidance.

3. Put yourself in the place of the hospital's administrator. Which variances in the performance reports would you want to investigate further? Why?

Problem 12–55
Cost Distribution Using
Allocation Bases; Hospital
(LO 4)

1. Facilities cost distributed to
General Medicine: $142,500

Refer to the organization chart for Canadian Rockies General Hospital given in the preceding problem. Ignore the rest of the data in that problem. The following table shows the cost allocation bases used to distribute various costs among the hospital's divisions:

Cost Pool	Cost Allocation Base	Annual Cost
Facilities:		
Building depreciation	Square metres of space	$380,0000
Equipment depreciation		
Insurance		
Utilities:		
Electricity	Cubic metres of space	48,000
Waste disposal		
Water and sewer		
Cable TV and phone		
Heat		
General administration:		
Administrator	Budgeted number of employees	440,000
Administrative staff		
Office supplies		
Community outreach:		
Public education	Budgeted dollars of patient billings	80,000
School physical exams		

Shown below are the amounts of each cost allocation base associated with each division.

	Square Metres	Cubic Metres	Number of Employees	Patient Billings
General Medicine Division	15,000	135,000	30	$ 4,000,000
Surgical Division	8,000	100,000	20	2,500,000
Medical Support Division	9,000	90,000	20	1,500,000
Administrative Division	8,000	75,000	30	0
Total	40,000	400,000	100	$ 8,000,000

Required:

1. Prepare a table similar to Exhibit 12–5 that distributes each of the costs listed in the preceding table to the hospital's divisions.

2. Comment on the appropriateness of patient billings as the basis for distributing community outreach costs to the hospital's divisions. Can you suggest a better allocation base?

3. Is there any use in allocating utilities costs to the divisions? What purposes could such an allocation process serve?

4. *Build a spreadsheet:* Construct an Excel spreadsheet to solve requirement (1) above. Show how the solution will change if the following information changes: the costs incurred were $400,000, $50,000, $400,000, and $90,000, for facilities, utilities, general administration, and community outreach, respectively.

Show-Off, Inc. sells merchandise through three retail outlets—in Vancouver, Toronto, and Montreal—and operates a general corporate headquarters in Toronto. A review of the company's income statement indicates a record year in terms of sales and profits. Management, though, desires additional insights about the individual stores and has asked that Judson Wyatt, a newly hired intern, prepare a segmented income statement. The following information has been extracted from Show-Off's accounting records:

- The sales volume, sales price, and purchase price data are:

	Vancouver	Toronto	Montreal
Sales volume	37,000 units	41,000 units	46,000 units
Unit selling price	$18.00	$16.50	$14.25
Unit purchase price	8.25	8.25	9.00

- The following expenses were incurred for sales commissions, local advertising, property taxes, management salaries, and other noncontrollable (but traceable) costs:

	Vancouver	Toronto	Montreal
Sales commissions	6%	6%	6%
Local advertising	$16,500	$33,000	$72,000
Local property taxes	6,750	3,000	9,000
Sales manager salary	—	—	48,000
Store manager salaries	46,500	58,500	57,000
Other noncontrollable costs	8,700	6,900	26,700

Local advertising decisions are made at the store manager level. The sales manager's salary in Montreal is determined by the Montreal store manager; in contrast, store manager salaries are set by Show-Off's vice-president.

- Nontraceable fixed corporate expenses total $288,450.
- The company uses a responsibility accounting system.

Required:

1. Assume the role of Judson Wyatt and prepare a segmented income statement for Show-Off.
2. Determine the weakest-performing store and present an analysis of the probable causes of poor performance.
3. Assume that an opening has arisen at the Toronto corporate headquarters and the company's chief executive officer (CEO) desires to promote one of the three existing store managers. In evaluating the store managers' performance, should the CEO use a store's segment contribution margin, the profit margin controllable by the store manager, or a store's segment profit margin? Justify your answer.

Buckeye Department Stores, Inc. operates a chain of department stores in British Columbia. The company's organization chart appears below. Operating data for 20x5 follow.

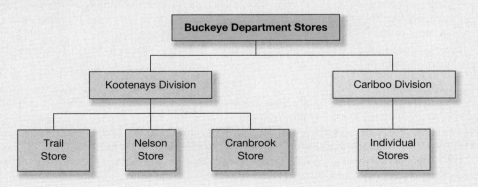

■ **Problem 12–56**
Segmented Income Statement; Responsibility Accounting
(LO 3, 5)

1. Segment contribution margin, Show-Off: $820,620

■ **Problem 12–57**
Prepare Segmented Income Statement; Contribution-Margin Format; Retail
(LO 5)

1. Profit margin traceable to segment, Cariboo Division: $10,950,000
1. Profit margin traceable to segment, Nelson store: $(1,320,000)

BUCKEYE DEPARTMENT STORES, INC.
Operating Data for 20x5
(in thousands)

	Kootenays Division			Cariboo Division (total for all stores)
	Trail Store	Nelson Store	Cranbrook Store	
Sales revenue	$15,000	$7,200	$33,000	$63,000
Variable expenses:				
Cost of merchandise sold	9,000	6,000	18,000	36,000
Sales personnel—salaries	1,200	900	2,250	4,800
Sales commissions	150	120	270	600
Utilities	240	180	450	900
Other	180	105	360	750
Fixed expenses:				
Depreciation—buildings	360	270	750	1,410
Depreciation—furnishings	240	150	420	870
Computing and billing	120	90	225	480
Warehouse	210	180	600	1,350
Insurance	120	75	270	600
Property taxes	105	60	240	510
Supervisory salaries	450	300	1,200	2,700
Security	90	90	240	630

The following fixed expenses are controllable at the divisional level: depreciation—furnishings, computing and billing, warehouse, insurance, and security. In addition to these expenses, each division annually incurs $150,000 of computing costs, which are not allocated to individual stores.

The following fixed expenses are controllable only at the company level: depreciation—building, property taxes, and supervisory salaries. In addition to these expenses, each division incurs costs for supervisory salaries of $300,000, which are not allocated to individual stores.

Buckeye Department Stores incurs common fixed expenses of $360,000, which are not allocated to the two divisions. Income-tax expense for 20x5 is $5,850,000.

Required:

1. Prepare a segmented income statement similar to Exhibit 12–7 for Buckeye Department Stores, Inc. The statement should have the following columns:

Buckeye Department Stores, Inc.	Segments of Company		Segments of Kootenays Division		
	Cariboo Division	Kootenays Division	Trail Store	Nelson Store	Cranbrook Store Not Allocated

Prepare the statement in the contribution format, and indicate the controllability of expenses. Subtract all variable expenses, including cost of merchandise sold, from sales revenue to obtain the contribution margin.

2. How would the segmented income statement help the president of Buckeye Department Stores manage the company?

■ **Problem 12–58**
Responsibility Accounting;
Participation; Behavioural
Issues
(LO 1, 2, 3)

Building Services, Co. (BSC) was started a number of years ago by Jim and Joan Forge to provide cleaning services to both large and small businesses in their home city. Over the years, as local businesses reduced underutilized building maintenance staffs, more and more cleaning services were subcontracted to BSC. BSC also expanded into other building services such as painting and local moving.

BSC maintains a pool of skilled workers who are contracted to perform the noncleaning services because these services do not recur on a day-to-day basis for the individual buildings. Many of BSC's full-time employees have been with the firm for a number of years. Five zone managers are each responsible for furnishing recurring nightly cleaning services to several businesses. In addition, the zone manager sells and schedules noncleaning service jobs for the company's central pool of skilled employees. Informal meetings are held periodically to discuss BSC's performance, personnel allocations, and scheduling problems. BSC's budgeting and planning have been done by the Forges, who also manage variations from budgets.

The Forges recently decided to retire and sold the business to Commercial Maintenance Inc. (CMI), which provides similar services in a number of metropolitan locations that surround BSC's business area. After news of the sale, several of BSC's long-term employees appeared resentful of the change in ownership and did not know what to expect.

CMI's senior management met with BSC's managers and announced that George Fowler would become president of BSC and that BSC would continue to operate as a separate subsidiary of CMI. Furthermore, in accordance with CMI's management philosophy, a responsibility-accounting system is to be implemented at BSC. Also, in line with other CMI subsidiaries, a participatory budgeting process is being considered. However, no decision will be made until an evaluation of BSC's existing policies, operational culture, and management is completed. In view of the significant change in management philosophy, CMI has taken considerable time in explaining how each system operates and assuring BSC's managers that they are expected and encouraged to participate in both the planning and implementation of any of the systems that are to be adopted.

Required: Two new systems are being considered at Building Services Co.:

- Responsibility-accounting system
- Participatory budgeting system

For each of these systems:

1. Identify at least two behavioural advantages that might arise.
2. Identify at least two potential problems that might arise.
3. Discuss the likelihood that the system will contribute to the alignment of organizational and personal goals.

(CMA, adapted)

Warriner Equipment Company, which is located in Ontario, manufactures heavy construction equipment. The company's primary product, an especially powerful bulldozer, is among the best produced in North America. The company operates in a very price-competitive industry, so it has little control over the price of its products. It must meet the market price. To do so, the firm has to keep production costs in check by operating as efficiently as possible. Mathew Basler, the company's president, has stated that, to be successful, the company must provide a very high-quality product and meet its delivery commitments to customers on time. Warriner Equipment Company is organized as shown below.

Problem 12–59
Designing a Responsibility-Accounting System
(LO 1, 2)

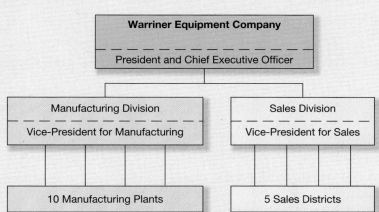

There is currently a disagreement between the company's two vice-presidents regarding the responsibility-accounting system. The vice-president for manufacturing claims that the 10 plants should be cost centres. He recently expressed the following sentiment: "The plants should be cost centres because the plant managers do not control the sales of our products. Designating the plants as profit centres would result in holding the plant managers responsible for something they can't control." A contrary view is held by the vice-president for marketing. He recently made the following remarks: "The plants should be profit centres. The plant managers are in the best position to affect the company's overall profit."

Required: As the company's new controller, you have been asked to make a recommendation to Mathew Basler, the company president, regarding the responsibility centre issue. Write a memo to the president making a recommendation and explaining the reasoning behind it. In your memo, address the following points.

1. Assuming that Warriner Equipment Company's overall goal is profitability, what are the company's critical success factors? A *critical success factor* is a variable that meets these two criteria: It is largely under the company's control and the company must succeed in this area in order to reach its overall goal of profitability.
2. Which responsibility-accounting arrangement is most consistent with achieving success on the company's critical success factors?
3. What responsibility-centre designation is most appropriate for the company's sales districts?
4. As a specific example, consider the rush-order problem illustrated in the chapter. Suppose that Warriner Equipment Company often experiences rush orders from its customers. Which of the two proposed responsibility-accounting arrangements is best suited to making good decisions about accepting or rejecting rush orders? Specifically, should the plants be cost centres or profit centres?

■ **Problem 12–60**
Comparing the Performance of Two Divisions
(LO 6, 8)

Imputed interest rate of 10%, Division I, residual income: $900,000

Long Beach Pharmaceutical Company has two divisions, which reported the following results for the most recent year:

	Division I	Division II
Income	$ 2,700,000	$ 600,000
Average invested capital	$18,000,000	$3,000,000
ROI	15%	20%

Required: Which was the more successful division during the year? Think carefully about this, and explain your answer.

■ **Problem 12–61**
ROI and Residual Income; Missing Data
(LO 6)

Division I, capital turnover: 4

The following data pertain to three divisions of Aggregates, Inc. The company's required rate of return on invested capital is 8 percent.

	Division I	Division II	Division III
Sales revenue	$40,000,000	?	?
Income	$8,000,000	$1,600,000	?
Average investment	$10,000,000	?	?
Sales margin	?	20%	25%
Capital turnover	?	1	?
ROI	?	?	20%
Residual income	?	?	$480,000

Required: Fill in the blanks above.

■ **Problem 12–62**
Improving ROI
(LO 6, 7)

Refer to the preceding problem about Aggregates, Inc.

Required:

1. Explain three ways the Division I manager could improve her division's ROI. Use numbers to illustrate these possibilities.
2. Suppose Division II's sales margin increased to 25 percent, while its capital turnover remained constant. Compute the division's new ROI.

■ **Problem 12–63**
Residual Income
(LO 6, 8)

2. Imputed interest rate of 15%, Division I, residual income: $0

Refer to the data for Problem 12–60 regarding Long Beach Pharmaceutical Company.

Required: Compute each division's residual income for the year under each of the following assumptions about the firm's cost of acquiring capital:

1. 12 percent
2. 15 percent
3. 18 percent

Which division was more successful? Explain your answer.

Refer to Exhibit 12–10. Prepare a similar table of the changing ROI assuming the following accelerated depreciation schedule. Assume the same income before depreciation as shown in Exhibit 12–10. (If there is a loss, leave the ROI column blank.)

Year	Depreciation
1	$200,000
2	120,000
3	72,000
4	54,000
5	54,000
Total	$500,000

Required:

1. How does your table differ from the one in Exhibit 12–10? Why?
2. What are the implications of the ROI pattern in your table?

■ **Problem 12–64**
Increasing ROI over Time;
Accelerated Depreciation
(LO 6, 8, 9)

Refer to Exhibit 12–10. Prepare a table similar to Exhibit 12–10, which focuses on residual income. Use a 10 percent rate to compute the imputed interest charge. The table should show the residual income on the investment during each year in its five-year life. Assume the same income before depreciation and the same depreciation schedule as shown in Exhibit 12–10.

■ **Problem 12–65**
Increasing Residual Income
over Time
(LO 6, 8, 9)

Megatronics Corporation, a massive retailer of electronic products, is organized in four separate divisions. The four divisional managers are evaluated at year-end, and bonuses are awarded based on ROI. Last year, the company as a whole produced a 13 percent return on its investment.

During the past week, management of the company's Western Division was approached about the possibility of buying a competitor that had decided to redirect its retail activities. (If the competitor is acquired, it will be acquired at its book value.) The data that follow relate to recent performance of the Western Division and the competitor:

■ **Problem 12–66**
ROI and Residual Income;
Investment Evaluation
(LO 6, 8)

1. Western Division, income:
$185,000
3. Variable costs: $1,690,000

	Western Division	Competitor
Sales	$4,200,000	$2,600,000
Variable costs	70% of sales	65% of sales
Fixed costs	$1,075,000	$835,000
Invested capital	$925,000	$312,500

Management has determined that in order to upgrade the competitor to Megatronics' standards, an additional $187,500 of invested capital would be needed.

Required: As a group, complete the following requirements:

1. Compute the current ROI of the Western Division and the division's ROI if the competitor is acquired.
2. What is the likely reaction of divisional management toward the acquisition? Why?
3. What is the likely reaction of Megatronics' corporate management toward the acquisition? Why?
4. Would the division be better off if it didn't upgrade the competitor to Megatronics' standards? Show computations to support your answer.
5. Assume that Megatronics uses residual income to evaluate performance and desires a 12 percent minimum return on invested capital. Compute the current residual income of the Western Division and the division's residual income if the competitor is acquired. Will divisional management be likely to change its attitude toward the acquisition? Why?

Hoosier Industries manufactures a variety of household products. Kenneth Washburn, head of the company's Hardware Division, has just completed a miserable nine months. "If it could have gone wrong, it did. Sales are down, income is down, inventories are bloated, and quite frankly, I'm beginning to worry about my job," he moaned. Washburn is evaluated on the basis of ROI. Selected figures for the past nine months follow.

■ **Problem 12–67**
ROI and Performance
Evaluations
(LO 6, 8)

1. Capital turnover: 80%

Sales	$7,200,000
Operating income	540,000
Invested capital	9,000,000

In an effort to make something out of nothing and to salvage the current year's performance, Washburn was contemplating implementation of some or all of the following four strategies:

a. Write off and discard $90,000 of obsolete inventory. The company will take a loss on the disposal.

b. Accelerate the collection of $120,000 of overdue customer accounts receivable.

c. Stop advertising through year-end and drastically reduce outlays for repairs and maintenance. These actions are expected to save the division $225,000 of expenses and will conserve cash resources.

d. Acquire two competitors that are expected to have the following financial characteristics:

	Projected Sales	Projected Operating Expenses	Projected Invested Capital
Anderson Manufacturing	$4,500,000	$3,600,000	$7,500,000
Palm Beach Enterprises	6,750,000	6,180,000	7,125,000

Required:

1. Briefly define sales margin, capital turnover, and return on investment and then compute these amounts for the Hardware Division over the past nine months.

2. Evaluate each of the first two strategies listed, with respect to its effect on the division's last nine months' performance, and make a recommendation to Washburn regarding which, if any, to adopt.

3. Are there possible long-term problems associated with strategy **c**? Briefly explain.

4. Determine the ROI of the investment in Anderson Manufacturing and do the same for the investment in Palm Beach Enterprises. Should Washburn reject both acquisitions, acquire one company, or acquire both companies? Assume that sufficient capital is available to fund investments in both organizations.

Problem 12–68
Weighted-Average Cost of Capital; Economic Value Added (EVA)
(LO 6)

2. Economic value added, Food Service: $4.3128 million

Lobster Shacks, Inc. (LS) is a seafood restaurant chain. The company has two sources of long-term capital: debt and equity. The cost to LS of issuing debt is the after-tax cost of the interest payments on the debt, taking into account the fact that the interest payments are tax-deductible. The cost of LS's equity capital is the investment opportunity rate of LS's investors, that is, the rate they could earn on investments of similar risk to that of investing in Lobster Shacks, Inc. The interest rate on LS's $120 million of long-term debt is 9 percent, and the company's tax rate is 40 percent. The cost of LS's equity capital is 14 percent. Moreover, the market value (and book value) of LS's equity is $180 million.

Lobster Shacks, Inc. consists of two divisions, the properties division and the food service division. The divisions' total assets, current liabilities, and before-tax operating income for the most recent year are as follows:

Division	Total Assets	Current Liabilities	Before-Tax Operating Income
Properties	$217,500,000	$4,500,000	$43,500,000
Food Service	96,000,000	9,000,000	22,500,000

Required:

1. Calculate the weighted-average cost of capital for Lobster Shacks, Inc.

2. Calculate the economic value added (EVA) for each of LS's divisions.

3. *Build a spreadsheet:* Construct an Excel spreadsheet to solve both of the preceding requirements. Show how the solution will change if the following information changes: before-tax operating income was $45,000,000 and $21,000,000 for Properties and Food Service, respectively.

Problem 12–69
Weighted-Average Cost of Capital; Economic Value Added (EVA)
(LO 6)

2. Weighted-average cost of capital: .0972

Maple Leaf Industries, headquartered in Toronto, is a multiproduct company with three divisions: Pacific Division, Plains Division, and Atlantic Division. The company has two sources of long-term capital: debt and equity. The interest rate on Maple Leaf's $400 million debt is 9 percent, and the company's tax rate is 30 percent. The cost of Maple Leaf's equity capital is 12 percent. Moreover, the market value of the company's equity is $600 million. (The *book value* of Maple Leaf's equity is $430 million, but that amount does not reflect the current value of the company's assets or the value of intangible assets.)

The following data (in millions) pertain to Maple Leaf's three divisions:

Division	Operating Income	Current Liabilities	Total Assets
Pacific	$14	$6	$ 70
Plains	45	5	300
Atlantic	48	9	480

Required:

1. Compute Maple Leaf's weighted-average cost of capital (WACC).
2. Compute the economic value added (or EVA) for each of the company's three divisions.
3. What conclusions can you draw from the EVA analysis?

Weathermaster Window Company manufactures windows for the home-building industry. The window frames are produced in the Frame Division. The frames are then transferred to the Glass Division, where the glass and hardware are installed. The company's best-selling product is a three-by-four, double-paned operable window.

The Frame Division also can sell frames directly to custom home builders, who install the glass and hardware. The sales price for a frame is $160. The Glass Division sells its finished windows for $380. The markets for both frames and finished windows exhibit perfect competition.

The standard variable cost of the window is detailed as follows:

	Frame Division	Glass Division
Direct material	$ 30	$ 60*
Direct labour	40	30
Variable overhead	60	60
Total	$130	$150

*Not including the transfer price for the frame.

Required:

1. Assume that there is no excess capacity in the Frame Division.
   a. Use the general rule to compute the transfer price for window frames.
   b. Calculate the transfer price if it is based on standard variable cost with a 10 percent markup.
2. Assume that there is excess capacity in the Frame Division.
   a. Use the general rule to compute the transfer price for window frames.
   b. Explain why your answers to requirements (1a) and (2a) differ.
   c. Suppose the predetermined fixed-overhead rate in the Frame Division is 125 percent of direct-labour cost. Calculate the transfer price if it is based on standard full cost plus a 10 percent markup.
   d. Assume the transfer price established in requirement (2c) is used. The Glass Division has been approached by the Canadian Forces with a special order for 1,000 windows at $310. From the perspective of Clearview Window Company as a whole, should the special order be accepted or rejected? Why?
   e. Assume the same facts as in requirement (2d). Will an autonomous Glass Division manager accept or reject the special order? Why?
   f. Comment on any ethical issues you see in the questions raised in requirements (2d) and (2e).
3. Comment on the use of full cost as the basis for setting transfer prices.

Mitachlordion Technology, Inc. (MTI) has two divisions: Surrey and Burnaby. Surrey currently sells a diode reducer to manufacturers of aircraft navigation systems for $1,550 per unit. Variable costs amount to $1,000, and demand for this product currently exceeds the division's ability to supply the marketplace.

Despite this situation, MTI is considering another use for the diode reducer, namely, integration into a satellite positioning system that would be made by Burnaby. The positioning system has an anticipated selling price of $2,800 and requires an additional $1,340 of variable manufacturing costs. A transfer price of $1,500 has been established for the diode reducer.

Problem 12-70
Comprehensive Transfer-Pricing Problem; Ethics
(LO 10, 11)

2a. Opportunity cost: 0
2d. Total variable (incremental) cost: $280 per unit

Problem 12-71
Transfer Pricing; Negotiation
(LO 11)

4. Produce diode, sell externally, contribution margin: $550

Top management is anxious to introduce the positioning system; however, unless the transfer is made, an introduction will not be possible because of the difficulty of obtaining needed diode reducers. Surrey and Burnaby are in the process of recovering from previous financial problems, and neither division can afford any future losses. The company uses responsibility accounting and ROI in measuring divisional performance, and awards bonuses to divisional management.

Required:

1. How would Surrey's divisional manager likely react to the decision to transfer diode reducers to Burnaby? Show computations to support your answer.

2. How would Burnaby's divisional management likely react to the $1,500 transfer price? Show computations to support your answer.

3. Assume that a lower transfer price is desired. Should top management lower the price or should the price be lowered by another means? Explain.

4. From a contribution margin perspective, does MTI benefit more if it sells the diode reducers externally or transfers the reducers to Burnaby? By how much?

Delta Telecom, Inc., which produces telecommunications equipment in Canada, has a very strong local market for its circuit board. The variable production cost is $390, and the company can sell its entire supply domestically for $510. The Canadian tax rate is 40 percent.

Alternatively, Delta can ship the circuit board to its division in Germany, to be used in a product that the German division will distribute throughout Europe. Information about the German product and the division's operating environment follows.

Selling price of final product	$1,080
Shipping fees to import circuit board	$ 60
Labour, overhead, and additional material costs of final product	$ 345
Import duties levied on circuit board (to be paid by the German division)	10% of transfer price
German tax rate	60%

Assume that Canadian and German tax authorities allow a transfer price for the circuit board set at either Canadian variable manufacturing cost or the Canadian market price. Delta's management is in the process of exploring which transfer price is better for the firm as a whole.

Required:

1. Compute overall company profitability per unit if all units are transferred and Canadian variable manufacturing cost is used as the transfer price. Show separate calculations for the Canadian operation and the German division.

2. Repeat requirement (1), assuming the use of the Canadian market price as the transfer price. Which of the two transfer prices is better for the firm?

3. Assume that the German division can obtain the circuit board in Germany for $465.
    a. If you were the head of the German division, would you rather do business with your Canadian division or buy the circuit board locally? Why?
    b. Rather than proceed with the transfer, is it in the best interest of Delta to sell its goods domestically and allow the German division to acquire the circuit board in Germany? Why? Show computations to support your answer.

4. Generally speaking, when tax rates differ between countries, what strategy should a company use in setting its transfer prices?

5. *Build a spreadsheet:* Construct an Excel spreadsheet to solve requirements (1) and (2) above. Show how the solution will change if the following information changes: the Canadian tax rate is 35 percent, the German tax rate is 55 percent, and the import duties are 8 percent of the transfer price.

Redstone Industrial Resources Company (RIRC) has several divisions. However, only two divisions transfer products to other divisions. The Mining Division refines toldine, which is then transferred to the Metals Division. The toldine is processed into an alloy by the Metals Division, and the alloy is sold to customers at a price of $450 per unit. The Mining division is currently required by RIRC to transfer its total yearly output of 400,000 units of toldine to the Metals Division at total actual manufacturing cost plus 10 percent. Unlimited quantities of toldine can be purchased and sold on the open market at $270 per unit. While the Mining Division could sell all the toldine it produces at $270 per unit on the open market, it would incur a variable selling cost of $15 per unit.

Brian Jones, manager of the Mining Division, is unhappy with having to transfer the entire output of toldine to the Metals Division at 110 percent of cost. In a meeting with the management of Provo, he said, "Why should my division be required to sell toldine to the Metals Division at less than market price? For the year just ended in May, Metals' contribution margin was over $57 million on sales of 400,000 units, while Mining's contribution was just over $15 million on the transfer of the same number of units. My division is subsidizing the profitability of the Metals Division. We should be allowed to charge the market price for toldine when transferring to the Metals Division."

The following table shows the detailed unit cost structure for both the Mining and Metals divisions during the most recent year:

	Mining Division	Metals Division
Transfer price from Mining Division	—	$198
Direct material	$ 36	18
Direct labour	48	60
Manufacturing overhead	96*	75†
Total cost per unit	$180	$351

*Manufacturing-overhead cost in the Mining Division is 25 percent fixed and 75 percent variable.
†Manufacturing-overhead cost in the Metals Division is 60 percent fixed and 40 percent variable.

Required:

1. Explain why transfer prices based on total actual costs are not appropriate as the basis for divisional performance measurement.

2. Using the market price as the transfer price, determine the contribution margin for both the Mining Division and the Metals Division.

3. If Redstone Industrial Resources Company were to institute the use of negotiated transfer prices and allow divisions to buy and sell on the open market, determine the price range for toldine that would be acceptable to both the Mining Division and the Metals Division. Explain your answer.

4. Use the general transfer-pricing rule to compute the lowest transfer price that would be acceptable to the Mining Division. Is your answer consistent with your conclusion in requirement (3)? Explain.

5. Identify which one of the three types of transfer prices (cost-based, market-based, or negotiated) is most likely to elicit desirable management behaviour at RIRC. Explain your answer.

(CMA, adapted)

Cases

Elite Classic Clothes is a retailer that sells to professional women. The firm leases space for stores in upscale shopping centres, and the organizational structure consists of regions, districts, and stores. Each region consists of two or more districts; each district consists of three or more stores. Each store, district, and region has been established as a profit centre. At all levels, the company uses a responsibility-accounting system focusing on information and knowledge rather than blame and control. Every year, managers, in consultation with their supervisors, establish financial and nonfinancial goals, and these goals are integrated into the budget. Actual performance is measured each month.

The British Columbia Region consists of the Lower Mainland and the Inland District. The Lower Mainland District includes the Vancouver, Victoria, and Surrey stores. The Lower Mainland District's performance has not been up to expectations in the past. For the month of May, the district manager has set performance goals with the managers of the Vancouver and Victoria stores, who will receive bonuses if certain performance measures are exceeded. The manager in Surrey decided not to participate in the bonus scheme. Since the district manager is unsure what type of bonus will encourage better performance, the Vancouver manager will receive a bonus based on sales in excess of budgeted sales of $1,140,000, while the Victoria manager will receive a bonus based on net income in excess of budgeted net income. The company's net income goal for each store is 12 percent of sales. The budgeted sales revenue for the Victoria store is $1,060,000.

■ **Case 12–74**
Segmented Income Statement; Responsibility Accounting; Bonuses; Motivation; Ethics
(LO 1, 2, 5)

1. Gross margin, Lower Mainland District: $1,732,500
1. Net income, Lower Mainland District: $312,300

Other pertinent data for May are as follows:

- Lower Mainland District sales revenue was $3,000,000, and its cost of goods sold amounted to $1,267,500.
- The Lower Mainland District spent $150,000 on advertising.
- General and administrative expenses for the Lower Mainland District amounted to $360,000.
- At the Vancouver store, sales were 40 percent of Lower Mainland District sales, while sales at the Victoria store were 35 percent of district sales. The cost of goods sold in both Vancouver and Victoria was 42 percent of sales.
- Variable selling expenses (sales commissions) were 6 percent of sales for all stores, districts, and regions.
- Variable administrative expenses were 2.5 percent of sales for all stores, districts, and regions.
- Maintenance cost includes janitorial and repair services and is a direct cost for each store. The store manager has complete control over this outlay. Maintenance costs were incurred as follows: Vancouver, $15,000; Victoria, $1,200; and Surrey, $9,000.
- Advertising is considered a direct cost for each store and is completely under the control of the store manager. The Vancouver store spent two-thirds of the Lower Mainland District total outlay for advertising, which was 10 times the amount spent in Victoria on advertising.
- Lower Mainland District rental expense amounted to $300,000.
- The rental expenses at the Vancouver store were 40 percent of the Lower Mainland District's total, while the Victoria store incurred 30 percent of the district total.
- District expenses were allocated to the stores based on sales.
- British Columbia Region general and administrative expenses of $330,000 were allocated to the Lower Mainland District. These expenses were, in turn, allocated equally to the district's three stores.

Required:

1. Prepare the May segmented income statement for the Lower Mainland District and for the Vancouver and Victoria stores.
2. Compute the Surrey store's net income for May.
3. Discuss the impact of the responsibility-accounting system and bonus structure on the managers' behaviour and the effect of their behaviour on the financial results for the Vancouver store and the Victoria store.
4. The assistant controller for the British Columbia Region, Jack Isner, has been a close friend of the Vancouver store manager for over 20 years. When Isner saw the segmented income statement (as prepared in requirement (1)), he realized that the Vancouver store manager had really gone overboard on advertising expenditures. To make his friend look better to the regional management, he reclassified $50,000 of the advertising expenditures as miscellaneous expenses, and buried them in rent and other costs. Comment on the ethical issues in the assistant controller's actions. (Refer to specific ethical standards for managerial accountants which were given in Chapter 1.)

(CMA, adapted)

■ **Case 12–75**
Segmented Income
Statement; International
Operations
(LO 1, 5)

1. Total unit sales, Asia:
106,000
1. Operating income, United
States: $488,600

Pacific Rim Industries is a diversified company whose products are marketed both domestically and internationally. The company's major product lines are furniture, sports equipment, and household appliances. At a recent meeting of Pacific Rim's board of directors, there was a lengthy discussion on ways to improve overall corporate profitability. The members of the board decided that they required additional financial information about individual corporate operations in order to target areas for improvement.

Danielle Murphy, the controller, has been asked to provide additional data that would assist the board in its investigation. Murphy believes that income statements, prepared along both product lines and geographic areas, would provide the directors with the required insight into corporate operations. Murphy had several discussions with the division managers for each product line and compiled the following information from these meetings:

	Product Lines			
	Furniture	Sports	Appliances	Total
Production and sales in units	80,000	90,000	80,000	250,000
Average selling price per unit	$16.00	$40.00	$30.00	
Average variable manufacturing cost per unit	8.00	19.00	$16.50	
Average variable selling expense per unit	4.00	5.00	$4.50	
Fixed manufacturing overhead, excluding depreciation				$ 500,000
Depreciation of plant and equipment				400,000
Administrative and selling expense				1,160,000

1. The division managers concluded that Murphy should allocate fixed manufacturing overhead to both product lines and geographic areas on the basis of the ratio of the variable costs expended to total variable costs.

2. Each of the division managers agreed that a reasonable basis for the allocation of depreciation on plant and equipment would be the ratio of units produced per product line (or per geographical area) to the total number of units produced.

3. There was little agreement on the allocation of administrative and selling expenses, so Murphy decided to allocate only those expenses that were traceable directly to a segment. For example, manufacturing staff salaries would be allocated to product lines, and sales staff salaries would be allocated to geographic areas. Murphy used the following data for this allocation:

Manufacturing Staff		Sales Staff	
Furniture	$120,000	United States	$ 60,000
Sports	140,000	Canada	100,000
Appliances	80,000	Asia	250,000

4. The division managers were able to provide reliable sales percentages for their product lines by geographical area:

	Percentage of Unit Sales		
	United States	Canada	Asia
Furniture	40%	10%	50%
Sports	40%	40%	20%
Appliances	20%	20%	60%

Murphy prepared the following product-line income statement based on the data presented above:

PACIFIC RIM INDUSTRIES
Segmented Income Statement by Product Line
For the Fiscal Year Ended April 30, 20x4

	Product Line				
	Furniture	Sports	Appliances	Unallocated	Total
Sales in units	80,000	90,000	80,000		
Sales	$1,280,000	$3,600,000	$2,400,000	—	$7,280,000
Variable manufacturing and selling costs ...	960,000	2,160,000	1,680,000	—	4,800,000
Contribution margin	$ 320,000	$1,440,000	$ 720,000	—	$2,480,000
Fixed costs:					
Fixed manufacturing overhead	$ 100,000	$ 225,000	$ 175,000	$ —	$ 500,000
Depreciation	128,000	144,000	128,000	—	400,000
Administrative and selling expenses ...	120,000	140,000	80,000	820,000	1,160,000
Total fixed costs	$ 348,000	$ 509,000	$ 383,000	$ 820,000	$2,060,000
Operating income (loss)	$ (28,000)	$ 931,000	$ 337,000	$(820,000)	$ 420,000

Required:

1. Prepare a segmented income statement for Pacific Rim Industries based on the company's geographical areas. The statement should show the operating income for each segment.

2. As a result of the information disclosed by both segmented income statements (by product line and by geographic area), recommend areas where Pacific Rim Industries should focus its attention in order to improve corporate profitability.

■ **Case 12–76**
ROI versus Residual Income;
Incentive Effects
(LO 1, 6, 8)

2. Residual income, combined
operations: $460,000

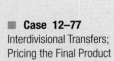

Fun Times Entertainment Corporation (FTEC), a subsidiary of New Age Industries, manufactures go-carts and other recreational vehicles. Family recreational centres that feature not only go-cart tracks but miniature golf, batting cages, and arcade games as well have increased in popularity. As a result, FTEC has been receiving some pressure from New Age's management to diversify into some of these other recreational areas. Recreational Leasing, Inc. (RLI), one of the largest firms that leases arcade games to family recreational centres, is looking for a friendly buyer. New Age's top management believes that RLI's assets could be acquired for an investment of $1.6 million and has strongly urged Bill Grieco, division manager of FTEC, to consider acquiring RLI.

Grieco has reviewed RLI's financial statements with his controller, Marie Donnelly, and they believe the acquisition may not be in the best interest of FTEC. "If we decide not to do this, the New Age people are not going to be happy," said Grieco. "If we could convince them to base our bonuses on something other than return on investment, maybe this acquisition would look more attractive. How would we do if the bonuses were based on residual income, using the company's 15 percent cost of capital?"

New Age Industries traditionally has evaluated all of its divisions on the basis of return on investment. The desired rate of return for each division is 20 percent. The management team of any division reporting an annual increase in the ROI is automatically eligible for a bonus. The management of divisions reporting a decline in the ROI must provide convincing explanations for the decline in order to be eligible for a bonus. Moreover, this bonus is limited to 50 percent of the bonus paid to divisions reporting an increase in ROI.

In the following table are condensed financial statements for both FTEC and RLI for the most recent year:

	RLI	FTEC
Sales revenue	—	$4,750,000
Leasing revenue	$1,550,000	—
Variable expenses	(650,000)	(3,000,000)
Fixed expenses	(600,000)	(750,000)
Operating income	$ 300,000	$1,000,000
Current assets	$ 950,000	$1,150,000
Long-lived assets	550,000	2,850,000
Total assets	$1,500,000	$4,000,000
Current liabilities	$ 425,000	$ 700,000
Long-term liabilities	600,000	1,900,000
Stockholders' equity	475,000	1,400,000
Total liabilities and stockholders' equity	$1,500,000	$4,000,000

Required:

1. If New Age Industries continues to use ROI as the sole measure of divisional performance, explain why FTEC would be reluctant to acquire Recreational Leasing, Inc.

2. If New Age Industries could be persuaded to use residual income to measure the performance of FTEC, explain why FTEC would be more willing to acquire RLI.

3. Discuss how the behaviour of division managers is likely to be affected by the use of the following performance measures: (*a*) return on investment and (*b*) residual income.

(CMA, adapted)

■ **Case 12–77**
Interdivisional Transfers;
Pricing the Final Product
(LO 10, 11)

1. Contribution margin per
unit, before 5% price
reduction: $400
2. Contribution margin per
unit, Air Comfort sales: $43

InterGlobal Industries is a diversified corporation with separate operating divisions. Each division's performance is evaluated on the basis of profit and return on investment.

The Air Comfort Division manufactures and sells air-conditioner units. The coming year's budgeted income statement, which follows, is based upon a sales volume of 15,000 units.

AIR COMFORT DIVISION
Budgeted Income Statement
(in thousands)

	Per Unit	Total
Sales revenue	$800	$12,000
Manufacturing costs:		
Compressor	140	2,100
Other direct material	74	1,110
Direct labour	60	900
Variable overhead	90	1,350
Fixed overhead	64	960
Total manufacturing costs	428	6,420
Gross margin	372	5,580
Operating expenses:		
Variable selling	36	540
Fixed selling	38	570
Fixed administrative	76	1,140
Total operating expenses	150	2,250
Net income before taxes	$222	$ 3,330

Air Comfort's division manager believes sales can be increased if the price of the air conditioners is reduced. A market research study by an independent firm indicates that a 5 percent reduction in the selling price would increase sales volume 16 percent, or 2,400 units. The division has sufficient production capacity to manage this increased volume with no increase in fixed costs.

The Air Comfort Division uses a compressor in its units, which it purchases from an outside supplier at a cost of $140 per compressor. The Air Comfort Division manager has asked the manager of the Compressor Division about selling compressor units to Air Comfort. The Compressor Division currently manufactures and sells a unit to outside firms that is similar to the unit used by the Air Comfort Division. The specifications of the Air Comfort Division compressor are slightly different, which would reduce the Compressor Division's direct material cost by $3 per unit. In addition, the Compressor Division would not incur any variable selling costs in the units sold to the Air Comfort Division. The manager of the Air Comfort Division wants all of the compressors it uses to come from one supplier and has offered to pay $100 for each compressor unit.

The Compressor Division has the capacity to produce 75,000 units. Its budgeted income statement for the coming year, which follows, is based on a sales volume of 64,000 units without considering Air Comfort's proposal.

COMPRESSOR DIVISION
Budgeted Income Statement
(in thousands)

	Per Unit	Total
Sales revenue	$200	$12,800
Manufacturing costs:		
Direct material	24	1,536
Direct labour	16	1,024
Variable overhead	20	1,280
Fixed overhead	22	1,408
Total manufacturing costs	82	5,248
Gross margin	118	7,552
Operating expenses:		
Variable selling	12	768
Fixed selling	8	512
Fixed administrative	14	896
Total operating expenses	34	2,176
Net income before taxes	$ 84	$ 5,376

Required:

1. Should the Air Comfort Division institute the 5 percent price reduction on its air-conditioner units even if it cannot acquire the compressors internally for $100 each? Support your conclusion with appropriate calculations.

2. Independently of your answer to requirement (1), assume the Air Comfort Division needs 17,400 units. Should the Compressor Division be willing to supply the compressor units for $100 each? Support your conclusions with appropriate calculations.

3. Independently of your answer to requirement (1), assume Air Comfort needs 17,400 units. Suppose InterGlobal's top management has specified a transfer price of $100. Would it be in the best interest of InterGlobal Industries for the Compressor Division to supply the compressor units at $100 each to the Air Comfort Division? Support your conclusions with appropriate calculations.

4. Is $100 a goal-congruent transfer price? (Refer to your answers for requirements (2) and (3).)

(CMA, adapted)

■ Case 12–78
Minimum and Maximum
Acceptable Transfer Prices;
Multinational
(LO 10)

2. Unit contribution margin,
LDP: $6

2. Unit contribution margin,
TCH-320 using imported
control pack: $47

General Instrumentation Company manufactures dashboard instruments for heavy construction equipment. The firm is based in Baltimore, but operates several divisions in the United States, Canada, and Europe. The Hudson Bay Division manufactures complex electrical panels that are used in a variety of the firm's instruments. There are two basic types of panels. The high-density panel (HDP) is capable of many functions and is used in the most sophisticated instruments, such as tachometers and pressure gauges. The low-density panel (LDP) is much simpler and is used in less-complicated instruments. Although there are minor differences among the different high-density panels, the basic manufacturing process and production costs are the same. The high-density panels require considerably more skilled labour than the low-density panels, but the unskilled labour needs are about the same. Moreover, the direct materials in the high-density panel run substantially more than the cost of materials in the low-density panels. Production costs are summarized as follows:

	LDP	HDP
Unskilled labour (5 hrs. @ $10)	$ 5	$ 5
Skilled labour:		
LDP (25 hrs. @ $20)	5	
HDP (15 hrs. @ $20)		30
Raw material	3	8
Purchased components	4	12
Variable overhead	5	15
Total variable cost	$22	$70

The annual fixed overhead in the Hudson Bay Division is $1,000,000. There is a limited supply of skilled labour available in the area, and the division must constrain its production to 40,000 hours of skilled labour each year. This has been a troublesome problem for Jacqueline Ducharme, the division manager. Ducharme has successfully increased demand for the LDP line to the point where it is essentially unlimited. Each LDP sells for $28. Business also has increased in recent years for the HDP, and Ducharme estimates the division could now sell anywhere up to 6,000 units per year at a price of $115.

On the other side of the Atlantic, General Instrumentation operates its Volkmar Tachometer Division in Berlin. A recent acquisition of General Instrumentation, the division was formerly a German company known as Volkmar Construction Instruments. The division's main product is a sophisticated tachometer used in heavy-duty cranes, bulldozers, and backhoes. The instrument, designated as a TCH-320, has the following production costs.

TCH–320

Unskilled labour (.5 hr. @ $9)	$ 4.50
Skilled labour (3 hrs. @ $17)	51.00
Raw material	10.50
Purchased components	150.00
Variable overhead	12.00
Total variable cost	$228.00

The cost of purchased components includes a $145 control pack currently imported from Japan. Fixed overhead in the Volkmar Tachometer Division runs about $800,000 per year. Both skilled and unskilled labour are in abundant supply. The TCH-320 sells for $275.

Bertram Mueller, the division manager of the Volkmar Tachometer Division, recently attended a high-level corporate meeting in Baltimore. In a conversation with Jacqueline Ducharme, it was apparent that Hudson Bay's high-density panel might be a viable substitute for the control pack currently imported from Japan and used in Volkmar's TCH-320. Upon returning to Berlin, Mueller asked his chief engineer to look into the matter. Hans Schmidt obtained several HDP units from Hudson Bay, and a minor R&D project was mounted to determine if the HDP could replace the Japanese control pack. Several weeks later, the following conversation occurred in Mueller's office:

Schmidt: There's no question that Hudson Bay's HDP unit will work in our TCH-320. In fact, it could save us some money.

Mueller: That's good news. If we can buy our components within the company, we'll help Baltimore's bottom line without hurting ours. Also, it will look good to the brass at corporate if they see us working hard to integrate our division into General Instrumentation's overall production program.

Schmidt: I've also been worried about the reliability of supply of the control pack. I don't like being dependent on such a critical supplier that way.

Mueller: I agree. Let's look at your figures on the HDP replacement.

Schmidt: I got together with the controller's people, and we worked up some numbers. If we replace the control pack with the HDP from Canada, we'll avoid the $145 control pack cost we're now incurring. In addition, I figure we'll save $5.50 on the basic raw materials. There is one catch, though. The HDP will require some adjustments in order to use it in the TCH-320. We can make the adjustments here in Berlin. I'm guessing it will require an additional two hours of skilled labour to make the necessary modifications. I don't think variable overhead would be any different. Then there is the cost of transporting the HDPs to Berlin. Let's figure on $4.50 per unit.

Mueller: Sounds good. I'll give Jacqueline Ducharme a call and talk this over. We can use up to 10,000 of the HDP units per year given the demand for the TCH-320. I wonder what kind of a transfer price Hudson Bay will want.

Required:

1. Draw a simple diagram depicting the two divisions and their products. Also show the two alternatives that the Volkmar Tachometer Division has in the production of its TCH-320.

2. From the perspective of General Instrumentation's top management, should any of the TCH-320 units be produced using the high-density panel? If so, how many?

3. Suppose Hudson Bay transfers 10,000 HDP units per year to Volkmar. From the perspective of General Instrumentation's top management, what effect will the transfer price have on the company's income?

4. What is the minimum transfer price that the Hudson Bay Division would find acceptable for the HDP?

5. What is the maximum transfer price that the Volkmar Tachometer Division would find acceptable for the HDP?

6. As the corporate controller for General Instrumentation, recommend a transfer price.

Chapter Thirteen

Decision Making: Relevant Costs and Benefits

FOCUS COMPANY

Worldwide Airways

This chapter's Focus Company is Worldwide Airways, an international airline. Using this service-industry company for our illustration, we will explore a variety of decisions that managers make routinely. Examples of such decisions are whether to accept or reject a special offer for the company's services, outsourcing a service, and adding or dropping a service or department. We will find in this chapter that different kinds of cost information are relevant, depending on the type of decision to be made.

IN CONTRAST

In contrast to the transportation-services setting of Worldwide Airways, we will explore certain types of decisions that most often arise in a manufacturing setting. Our illustration will be

based on International Chocolate Company, which produces a variety of chocolate products. In addition to producing chocolate candy, the company processes cocoa beans into cocoa powder and cocoa butter. The cocoa powder can then be processed further into instant cocoa mix. We will explore a variety of decisions faced by International Chocolate Company's management.

After completing this chapter, you should be able to:

1 Describe six steps in the decision-making process and the managerial accountant's role in that process.

2 Explain the relationship between quantitative and qualitative analyses in decision making.

3 List and explain two criteria that must be satisfied by relevant information.

4 Identify relevant costs and benefits, giving proper treatment to sunk costs, opportunity costs, and unit costs.

5 Prepare analyses of various special decisions, properly identifying the relevant costs and benefits.

6 Analyze manufacturing decisions involving joint products and limited resources.

7 Explain the impact of an advanced manufacturing environment and activity-based costing on a relevant-cost analysis.

8 Formulate a linear program to solve a product-mix problem with multiple constraints (Appendix).

D ecision making is a fundamental part of management. Decisions about the acquisition of equipment, mix of products, methods of production, and pricing of products and services confront managers in all types of organizations. This chapter covers the role of managerial accounting information in a variety of common decisions. The next chapter examines pricing decisions.

The Managerial Accountant's Role in Decision Making

Managerial accountants are increasingly playing important roles as full-fledged members of cross-functional management teams. These management teams face a broad array of decisions, including production, marketing, financial, and other decisions. All managers and management teams need information pertinent to their decisions. In support of the decision-making process, managerial accountants play a specific role in providing relevant information. Thus, the managerial accountant must have a good understanding of the decisions faced by managers throughout the organization.

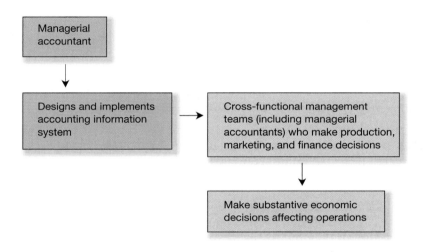

Steps in the Decision-Making Process

Six steps characterize the decision-making process:

1. *Clarify the decision problem.* Sometimes the decision to be made is clear. For example, if a company receives a special order for its product at a price below the usual price, the decision problem is to accept or reject the order. But the decision problem is seldom so clear and unambiguous. Perhaps demand for a company's most popular product is declining. What exactly is causing this problem? Increasing competition? Declining quality control? A new alternative product on the market? Before a decision can be made, the problem needs to be clarified and defined in more specific terms. Considerable managerial skill is required to define a decision problem in terms that can be addressed effectively.

2. *Specify the criterion.* Once a decision problem has been clarified, the manager should specify the criterion upon which a decision will be made. Is the objective to maximize profit, increase market share, minimize cost, or improve public service? Sometimes the objectives are in conflict, as in a decision problem where production cost is to be

minimized but product quality must be maintained. In such cases, one objective is specified as the decision criterion—for example, cost minimization. The other objective is established as a constraint—for example, product quality must not be worse than one defective part in 1,000 manufactured units.

3. *Identify the alternatives.* A decision involves selecting between two or more alternatives. If a machine breaks down, what are the alternative courses of action? The machine can be repaired or replaced, or a replacement can be leased. But perhaps repair will turn out to be more costly than replacement. Determining the possible alternatives is a critical step in the decision process.

4. *Develop a decision model.* A *decision model* is a simplified representation of the choice problem. Unnecessary details are stripped away, and the most important elements of the problem are highlighted. Thus, the decision model brings together the elements listed above: the criterion, the constraints, and the alternatives.

5. *Collect the data.* Although the managerial accountant often is involved in steps 1 through 4, he or she is chiefly responsible for step 5. Selecting data pertinent to decisions is one of the managerial accountant's most important roles in an organization.

6. *Select an alternative.* Once the decision model is formulated and the pertinent data are collected, the appropriate manager makes a decision.

Quantitative versus Qualitative Analysis

Learning Objective 2

Explain the relationship between quantitative and qualitative analyses in decision making.

Decision problems involving accounting data typically are specified in quantitative terms. The criteria in such problems usually include objectives such as profit maximization or cost minimization. When a manager makes a final decision, however, the qualitative characteristics of the alternatives can be just as important as the quantitative measures. **Qualitative characteristics** are the factors in a decision problem that cannot be expressed effectively in numerical terms. To illustrate, suppose Worldwide Airways' top management is considering the elimination of its hub operation in London. Airlines establish hubs at airports where many of their routes intersect. Hub operations include facilities for in-flight food preparation, aircraft maintenance and storage, and administrative offices. A careful quantitative analysis indicates that Worldwide Airway's profit-maximizing alternative is to eliminate the London hub. In making its decision, however, the company's managers will consider such qualitative issues as the effect of the closing on its London employees and on the morale of its remaining employees in the airline's Paris, Atlanta, and Tokyo hubs.

To clarify what is at stake in such qualitative analyses, quantitative analysis can allow the decision maker to put a "price" on the sum total of the qualitative characteristics. For example, suppose Worldwide Airways' controller gives top management a quantitative analysis showing that elimination of the London hub will increase annual profits by $2,000,000. However, the qualitative considerations favour the option of continuing the London operation. How important are these qualitative considerations to the top managers? If they decide to continue the London operation, the qualitative considerations must be worth at least $2,000,000 to them. Weighing the quantitative and qualitative considerations in making decisions is the essence of management. The skill, experience, judgment, and ethical standards of managers all come to bear on such difficult choices.

Exhibit 13–1 depicts the six steps in the decision process, and the relationship between quantitative and qualitative analysis.

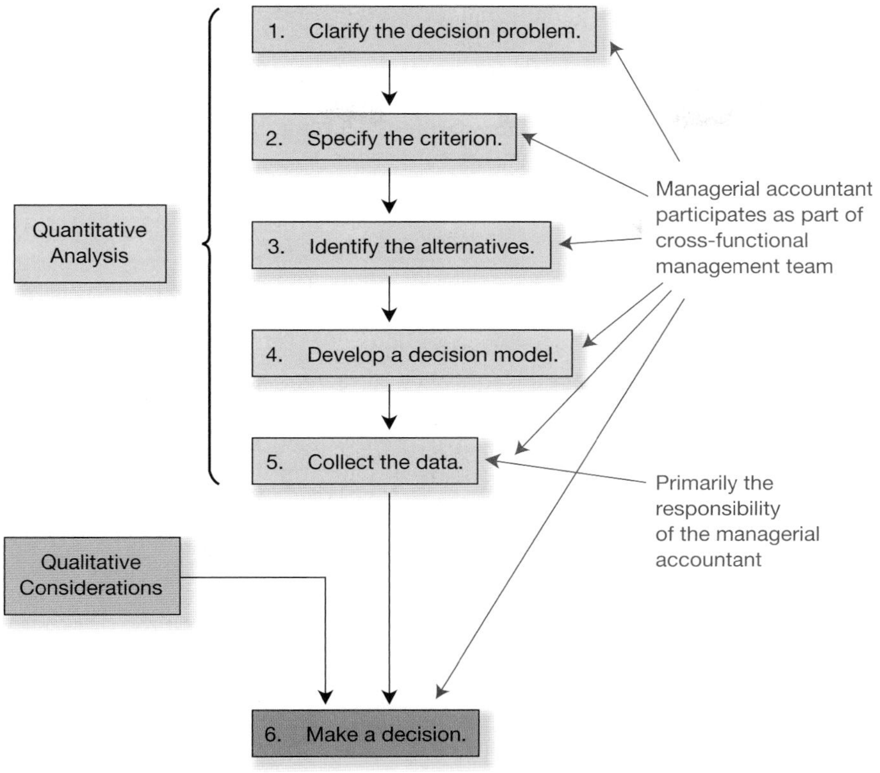

Exhibit 13–1
The Decision-Making Process

```
                  ┌──────────────────────────────────┐
                  │  1.  Clarify the decision problem.│
                  └──────────────────────────────────┘
                                 │
                                 ▼
                  ┌──────────────────────────────────┐
                  │  2.  Specify the criterion.       │
                  └──────────────────────────────────┘
                                 │
                                 ▼
   ┌──────────────┐ ┌──────────────────────────────────┐
   │ Quantitative │ │  3.  Identify the alternatives.   │
   │   Analysis   │ └──────────────────────────────────┘
   └──────────────┘                │
                                 ▼
                  ┌──────────────────────────────────┐
                  │  4.  Develop a decision model.    │
                  └──────────────────────────────────┘
                                 │
                                 ▼
                  ┌──────────────────────────────────┐
                  │  5.  Collect the data.            │
                  └──────────────────────────────────┘

   ┌──────────────┐
   │  Qualitative │
   │Considerations│
   └──────────────┘
                                 │
                                 ▼
                  ┌──────────────────────────────────┐
                  │  6.  Make a decision.             │
                  └──────────────────────────────────┘
```

Managerial accountant participates as part of cross-functional management team

Primarily the responsibility of the managerial accountant

Criteria of Useful Information: Relevance, Accuracy, and Timeliness

What criteria should the managerial accountant use in designing the accounting information system that supplies data for decision making? Three characteristics of information determine its usefulness.

Relevance   Information is **relevant** if it is *pertinent* to a decision problem. Different decisions typically will require different data. The primary theme of this chapter is how to decide what information is relevant to various common decision problems.

Accuracy   Information relevant to a decision problem must also be **accurate information**, or it will be of little use. This means the information must be precise. For example, the cost incurred by Worldwide Airways to rent facilities at London's Heathrow Airport is relevant to a decision about eliminating the airline's London hub. However, if the rental cost data are imprecise, due to incomplete or misplaced records, the usefulness of the information will be diminished.

Timeliness   Relevant and accurate data are useful only if they are **timely information**, that is, available in time for a decision. Thus, timeliness is the third important characteristic for determining the usefulness of information. Some situations involve a trade-off between the accuracy and the timeliness of information. More accurate information may take longer to produce. Therefore, as accuracy improves, timeliness suffers, and vice versa.

To summarize, the managerial accountant's primary role in the decision-making process is twofold:

1. Decide what information is *relevant* to each decision problem.
2. Provide *accurate* and *timely* data, keeping in mind the proper balance between these often-conflicting criteria.

Relevant Information

Learning Objective 3

List and explain two criteria that must be satisfied by relevant information.

What makes information relevant to a decision problem? Two criteria are important.

Bearing on the Future   The consequences of decisions are borne in the future, not the past. To be relevant to a decision, cost or benefit information must involve a future event. **Sunk costs** are costs that have already been incurred. They do not affect any future cost and cannot be changed by any current or future action. Sunk costs are irrelevant to decisions.

The cost information relevant to Worldwide Airways' decision concerning its London operations involves the costs that *will be incurred in the future* under the airline's two alternatives. Costs incurred in the past in the airline's London operations will not change regardless of management's decision, and they are irrelevant to the decision at hand.

Since relevant information involves future events, the managerial accountant must predict the amounts of the relevant costs and benefits. In making these predictions, the accountant often will use estimates of cost behaviour based on historical data. There is an important and subtle issue here. *Relevant* information must involve costs and benefits to be realized in the *future*. However, the accountant's *predictions* of those costs and benefits often are based on data from the *past*.

"You have to try to summarize numbers. You can't just give numbers. People in marketing are going to make decisions based on your numbers. They have to understand what those numbers mean." (13b)
Abbott Laboratories

Different under Competing Alternatives   Relevant information must involve costs or benefits that *differ among the alternatives*. Costs or benefits that are the same across all the available alternatives have no bearing on the decision. A **differential cost** is thus the difference in a cost item under two decision alternatives. The computation of differential costs is a convenient way of summarizing the relative advantage of one alternative over the other.

For example, suppose Worldwide Airways' management decides to keep its reservations and ticketing office in London regardless of whether its London hub is eliminated. Then the costs of the reservations and ticketing office will not differ between the two alternatives regarding elimination of the London hub. Hence, those costs are irrelevant to that decision.

A specific type of relevant costs is **opportunity cost**, which is the potential benefit given up when the choice of one action precludes a different action. Although people tend to overlook or underestimate the importance of opportunity costs, they are just as relevant as out-of-pocket costs in evaluating decision alternatives.

Repetitive versus Unique Decisions

Repetitive decisions are made over and over again. For example, Worldwide Airways makes route-scheduling decisions every six months. Cost predictions relevant to repetitive decisions typically can draw on a large amount of historical data. Since the decisions have been made repeatedly in the past, the data from those decisions should be readily available.

In contrast, *unique decisions* arise infrequently. Worldwide Airways' decision regarding its London hub is an example. The relevant information often will be found in many diverse places in the organization's overall information system. Information relevant to unique decisions is harder to generate. The managerial accountant typically will have to give more thought to deciding which data are relevant, and will have less historical data available upon which to base predictions.

Importance of Identifying Relevant Costs and Benefits

Why is it important for the managerial accountant to isolate the relevant costs and benefits in a decision analysis? First, generating information is a costly process. The relevant data must be sought, and this requires time and effort. By focusing on only the relevant information, the managerial accountant can simplify and shorten the data-gathering process.

Second, people can effectively use only a limited amount of information. Beyond this, they experience **information overload**, and their decision-making effectiveness declines. By routinely providing only information about relevant costs and benefits, the managerial accountant can reduce the likelihood of information overload.

Identifying Relevant Costs and Benefits

To illustrate how managerial accountants determine relevant costs and benefits, we will consider several decisions faced by the management of Worldwide Airways. The airline flies routes between North America and Europe, between various cities in Europe, and between the North America and several Asian cities.

Learning Objective 4

Identify relevant costs and benefits, giving proper treatment to sunk costs, opportunity costs, and unit costs.

Equipment Replacement

At Charles de Gaulle Airport in Paris, Worldwide Airways has a three-year-old loader truck used to load in-flight meals onto airplanes. The box on the truck can be lifted hydraulically to the level of a jumbo jet's side doors. The *book value* of this loader, defined as the asset's acquisition cost less the accumulated depreciation to date, is computed as follows:

Acquisition cost of old loader	$100,000
Less: Accumulated depreciation	75,000
Book value	$ 25,000

The loader has one year of useful life remaining, after which its salvage value will be zero. However, it could be sold now for $5,000. In addition to the annual depreciation of $25,000, Worldwide Airways annually incurs $80,000 in variable costs to operate the loader. These include the costs of operator labour, gasoline, and maintenance.

Jean Orville, Worldwide Airways' ramp manager at Charles de Gaulle Airport, faces a decision about replacement of the loader. A new kind of loader uses a conveyor belt to move meals into an airplane. The new loader is much cheaper than the old hydraulic loader and costs less to operate. However, the new loader would be operable for only one year before it would need to be replaced. Pertinent data about the new loader are as follows:

Acquisition cost of new loader	$15,000
Useful life	1 year
Salvage value after one year	0
Annual depreciation	$15,000
Annual operating costs	$45,000

Orville's initial inclination is to continue using the old loader for another year. He exclaims, "We can't dump that equipment now. We paid $100,000 for it, and we've

Exhibit 13–2

Equipment Replacement
Decision: Worldwide Airways

		Costs of Two Alternatives		
		(a) **Do Not Replace** **Old Loader***	**(b)** **Replace** **Old Loader***	**(c)** **Differential** **Cost: (a) − (b)**
Sunk cost	(1) Depreciation of old loader	$ 25,000		
	OR			−0−
	(2) Write-off of old loader's book value		$25,000	
Relevant data	(3) Proceeds from disposal of old loader	−0−	(5,000)†	$ 5,000
	(4) Depreciation (cost) of new loader	−0−	15,000	(15,000)
	(5) Operating costs	80,000	45,000	35,000
	Total cost	$105,000	$80,000	$25,000

*Since costs are the focus of the analysis in this Exhibit, costs are shown in columns (a) and (b) without parentheses.
†Parentheses denote a cash inflow in this case.

only used it three years. If we get rid of that loader now, we'll lose $20,000 on the disposal." Orville reasons that the old loader's book value of $25,000, less its current salvage value of $5,000, amounts to a loss of $20,000.

Michelle Imbert, the managerial accountant in the company's Charles de Gaulle Airport administrative offices, points out to Orville that the book value of the old loader is a *sunk cost*. It cannot affect any future cost the company might incur. To convince Orville that she is right, Imbert prepares the analysis shown in Exhibit 13–2.

Regardless of which alternative is selected, the $25,000 book value of the old loader will be an expense or loss in the next year. If the old loader is kept in service, the $25,000 will be recognized as depreciation expense; otherwise, the $25,000 cost will be incurred by the company as a write-off of the asset's book value. Thus, the current book value of the old loader is a *sunk cost* and irrelevant to the replacement decision.

Exhibit 13–2 includes a column entitled *Differential Cost*. Jean Orville can make a correct equipment replacement decision in either of two ways: (1) by comparing the total cost of the two alternatives, shown in columns (a) and (b); or (2) by focusing on the total *differential cost*, shown in column (c), which favours the "replacement" option.

Notice that the *relevant* data in the equipment replacement decision are items (3), (4), and (5). Each of these items meets the two tests of relevant information:

1. The costs or benefits relate to the future
2. The costs or benefits differ between the alternatives

The proceeds from selling the old loader, item (3), will be received in the future only under the "replace" alternative. Similarly, the acquisition cost (depreciation) of the new loader, item (4), is a future cost incurred only under the "replace" alternative. The operating cost, item (5), is also a future cost that differs between the two alternatives.

Obsolete Inventory The inventory of spare aircraft parts held by Worldwide Airways at Charles de Gaulle includes some obsolete parts originally costing $20,000. The company no longer uses the planes for which the parts were purchased. The obsolete parts include spare passenger seats, luggage racks, and galley equipment. The spare parts might be sold to another airline for $17,000. However, with some modifications, the obsolete parts might still be used in the company's current fleet of aircraft. Using the modified parts would save Worldwide Airways the cost of purchasing new parts for its airplanes.

		Costs of Two Alternatives		
		(a) **Modify and Use Parts***	(b) **Dispose of Parts***	(c) **Differential Cost: (a) − (b)**
Sunk cost	Book value of parts inventory: Asset value written off whether parts are used or not	$20,000	$20,000	$ –0–
Relevant data	Proceeds from disposal of parts	–0–	(17,000)†	17,000
	Cost to modify parts	12,000	–0–	12,000
	Cost incurred to buy new parts for current aircraft fleet	–0–	26,000	(26,000)
	Total cost	$32,000	$29,000	$ 3,000

*Since costs are the focus of the analysis in this Exhibit, costs are shown in columns (a) and (b) without parentheses.
†Parentheses denote a cash inflow in this case.

Exhibit 13–3
Obsolete Inventory Decision: Worldwide Airways

Jean Orville decides not to dispose of the obsolete parts, because doing so would entail a loss of $3,000. Orville reasons that the $20,000 book value of the parts, less the $17,000 proceeds from disposal, would result in a $3,000 loss on disposal. Michelle Imbert, the managerial accountant, comes to the rescue again, demonstrating that the right decision is to dispose of the parts. Imbert's analysis is shown in Exhibit 13–3.

Notice that the book value of the obsolete inventory is a *sunk cost*. If the parts are modified, the $20,000 book value will be an expense during the period when the parts are used. Otherwise, the $20,000 book value of the asset will be written off when the parts are sold. As a sunk cost, the book value of the obsolete inventory will not affect any future cash flow of the company.

As the managerial accountant's analysis reveals, the relevant data include the $17,000 proceeds from disposal, the $12,000 cost to modify the parts, and the $26,000 cost to buy new parts. All of these data meet the two tests of relevance: they affect future cash flows and they differ between the two alternatives. As Michelle Imbert's analysis shows, Worldwide Airways' cost will be $3,000 less if the obsolete parts are sold and new parts are purchased.

Flight-Route

At Worldwide Airways' headquarters, Amy Earhart, manager of flight scheduling, is in the midst of making a decision about the Atlanta to Honolulu route. The flight is currently nonstop, but she is considering a stop in San Francisco. She feels that the route would attract additional passengers if the stop is made, but there also would be additional variable costs. Her analysis appears in Exhibit 13–4.

The analysis indicates that the preferable alternative is the route that includes a stop in San Francisco. Notice that the cargo revenue, item (2), and the aircraft maintenance cost, item (8), are irrelevant to the flight-route decision. Although these data do affect future cash flows, they *do not differ between the two alternatives*. All of the other data in Exhibit 13–4 are relevant to the decision, because they do differ between the two alternatives. The analysis in Exhibit 13–4 could have ignored the irrelevant data; the same decision would have been reached.

Add Flights

Another decision confronting Amy Earhart is whether to add two daily round-trip flights between New York and Montreal. Her initial analysis of the relevant costs and benefits indicates that the additional revenue from the flights will exceed their costs

Exhibit 13–4

Flight-Route Decision:
Worldwide Airways

Relevant or Irrelevant		Revenues and Costs under Two Alternatives		
		(a) Nonstop Route*	(b) With Stop in San Francisco*	(c) Differential Amount:† (a) − (b)
Relevant	(1) Passenger revenue	$240,000	$258,000	$(18,000)
Irrelevant	(2) Cargo revenue	80,000	80,000	–0–
Relevant	(3) Landing fee in San Francisco	–0–	(5,000)	5,000
Relevant	(4) Use of airport gate facilities	–0–	(3,000)	3,000
Relevant	(5) Flight crew cost	(2,000)	(2,500)	500
Relevant	(6) Fuel	(21,000)	(24,000)	3,000
Relevant	(7) Meals and services	(4,000)	(4,600)	600
Irrelevant	(8) Aircraft maintenance	(1,000)	(1,000)	–0–
	Total revenue less costs	$292,000	$297,900	$ (5,900)

*In columns (a) and (b), parentheses denote costs and numbers without parentheses are revenues.

†In column (c), parentheses denote differential items favouring option (b).

by $30,000 per month. Hence, she is ready to add the flights to the schedule. However, Chuck Lindbergh, Worldwide Airways' hangar manager in New York, points out that Earhart has overlooked an important consideration.

Worldwide Airways currently has excess space in its hangar. A commuter airline has offered to rent the hangar space for $40,000 per month. However, if the New York–Montreal flights are added to the schedule, the additional aircraft needed in New York will require the excess hangar space.

If Worldwide Airways adds the New York–Montreal flights, it will forgo the opportunity to rent the excess hangar space for $40,000 per month. Thus, the $40,000 in rent forgone is an *opportunity cost* of the alternative to add the new flights. In Worldwide Airways' case, the best action is to rent the excess warehouse space to the commuter airline, rather than adding the new flights. The analysis in Exhibit 13–5 supports this conclusion.

It is a common mistake for people to overlook or underweight opportunity costs. The $40,000 hangar rental, which will be forgone if the new flights are added, is an *opportunity cost* of the option to add the flights. It is a *relevant cost* of the decision, and it is just as important as any out-of-pocket expenditure.

Summary

Relevant costs and benefits satisfy the following two criteria:

1. They affect the future.
2. They differ between alternatives.

Exhibit 13–5

Decision to Add Flights:
Worldwide Airways

	(a) Add Flights	(b) Do Not Add Flights	(c) Differential Amount: (a) − (b)
Additional revenue from new flights less additional costs	$30,000	–0–	$ 30,000
Rental of excess hangar space	–0–	$40,000	(40,000)*
Total	$30,000	$40,000	$(10,000)

*Parentheses denote that differential benefit favours option (b).

Sunk costs are not relevant costs, because they do not affect the future. An example of a sunk cost is the book value of an asset, either equipment or inventory. *Future costs or benefits that are identical across all decision alternatives are not relevant.* They can be ignored when making a decision. *Opportunity costs are relevant costs.* Such costs deserve particular attention because many people tend to overlook them when making decisions.

> "I would say that they [line managers] view us as business partners." (13d)
> **Boeing**

Analysis of Special Decisions

What are the relevant costs and benefits when a manager must decide whether to add or drop a product or service? What data are relevant when deciding whether to produce or buy a service or component? These decisions and certain other nonroutine decisions merit special attention in our discussion of relevant costs and benefits.

> **Learning Objective 5**
>
> Prepare analyses of various special decisions, properly identifying the relevant costs and benefits.

Accept or Reject a Special Offer

Jim Wright, Worldwide Airways' vice-president for operations, has been approached by a Japanese tourist agency about flying chartered tourist flights from Japan to Hawaii. The tourist agency has offered Worldwide Airways $150,000 per round-trip flight on a jumbo jet. Given the airline's usual occupancy rate and air fares, a round-trip jumbo-jet flight between Japan and Hawaii typically brings in revenue of $250,000. Thus, the tourist agency's specially priced offer requires a special analysis by Jim Wright.

Wright knows that Worldwide Airways has two jumbo jets that are not currently being used. The airline has just eliminated several unprofitable routes, freeing these aircraft for other uses. The airline was not currently planning to add any new routes, and therefore the two jets were idle. To help in making his decision, Wright asks for cost data from the controller's office. The controller provides the information in Exhibit 13–6, which pertains to a typical round-trip jumbo-jet flight between Japan and Hawaii.

The variable costs cover aircraft fuel and maintenance, flight-crew costs, in-flight meals and services, and landing fees. The fixed costs allocated to each flight cover Worldwide Airways' fixed costs, such as aircraft depreciation, maintenance and depreciation of facilities, and fixed administrative costs.

Revenue:		
Passenger	$250,000	
Cargo	30,000	
Total revenue		$280,000
Expenses:		
Variable expenses of flight	$ 90,000	
Fixed expenses allocated to each flight	100,000	
Total expenses		190,000
Profit		$ 90,000

Exhibit 13–6

Data for Typical Flight between Japan and Hawaii: Worldwide Airways

If Jim Wright had not understood managerial accounting, he might have done the following *incorrect analysis*:

Special price for charter	$150,000
Total cost per flight	190,000
Loss on charter flight	$ (40,000)

This calculation suggests that the special charter offer should be declined. What is the error in this analysis? The mistake is the inclusion of allocated fixed costs in the cost per flight. This is an error, because the *fixed costs will not increase in total* if the charter flight is added. Since the fixed costs will not change under either of the alternate choices, they are irrelevant.

Fortunately, Jim Wright does not make this mistake. He knows that only the variable costs of the proposed charter are relevant. Moreover, Wright determines that the variable cost of the charter would be lower than that of a typical flight, because Worldwide Airways would not incur the variable costs of reservations and ticketing. These variable expenses amount to $5,000 for a scheduled flight. Thus, Wright's analysis of the charter offer is as:

Assumes excess capacity (idle aircraft)

Special price for charter...		$150,000
Variable cost per routine flight	$90,000	
Less: Savings on reservations and ticketing	5,000	
Variable cost of charter		85,000
Contribution from charter		$ 65,000

Wright's analysis shows that the special charter flight will contribute $65,000 toward covering the airline's fixed costs and profit. Since the airline has excess flight capacity, due to the existence of idle aircraft, the optimal decision is to accept the special charter offer.

No Excess Capacity   Now let's consider how Wright's analysis would appear if Worldwide Airways had no idle aircraft. Suppose that in order to fly the charter between Japan and Hawaii, the airline would have to cancel its least profitable route, which is between Japan and Hong Kong. This route contributes $80,000 toward covering the airline's fixed costs and profit. Thus, if the charter offer is accepted, the airline will incur an opportunity cost of $80,000 from the forgone contribution of the Japan–Hong Kong route. Now Wright's analysis should appear as:

Assumes no excess capacity

Special price for charter		$150,000
Variable cost per routine flight	$90,000	
Less: Savings on reservations and ticketing (no idle aircraft)	5,000	
Variable cost of charter	85,000	
Add: Opportunity cost, forgone contribution on cancelled Japan–Hong Kong route.................................	80,000	165,000
Loss from charter..		$ (15,000)

Thus, if Worldwide Airways has no excess flight capacity, Jim Wright should reject the special charter offer.

Summary   The decision to accept or reject a specially priced order is common in both service industry and manufacturing firms. Manufacturers often are faced with decisions about selling products in a special order at less than full price. The correct analysis of such decisions focuses on the relevant costs and benefits. Fixed costs, which often are allocated to individual units of product or service, are usually irrelevant. Fixed costs typically will not change in total, whether the order is accepted or rejected.

When excess capacity exists, the only relevant costs usually will be the variable costs associated with the special order. When there is no excess capacity, the opportunity cost of using the firm's facilities for the special order is also relevant to the decision.

Outsource a Product or Service

Ellie Bishop is Worldwide Airways' manager of in-flight services. She supervises the airline's flight attendants and all of the firm's food and beverage operations. Bishop currently faces a decision regarding the preparation of in-flight dinners at the airline's Atlanta hub. In the Atlanta flight kitchen, full-course dinners are prepared and packaged for long flights that pass through Atlanta. In the past, all of the desserts were baked and packaged in the flight kitchen. However, Bishop has received an offer from an Atlanta bakery to bake the airline's desserts. Thus, her decision is whether to *outsource* the dessert portion of the in-flight dinners. An **outsourcing decision**, also called a **make-or-buy decision**, entails a choice between producing a product or service in-house or purchasing it from an outside supplier. To help guide her decision, Bishop has assembled the cost information in Exhibit 13–7, which shows a total cost per dessert of 25 cents.

	Cost per Dessert
Variable costs:	
Direct material (food and packaging)	$.06
Direct labour	.04
Variable overhead	.04
Fixed costs (allocated to products):	
Supervisory salaries	.04
Depreciation of flight-kitchen equipment	.07
Total cost per dessert	$.25

Exhibit 13–7
Cost of In-Flight Desserts: Worldwide Airways

The Atlanta bakery has offered to supply the desserts for 21 cents each. Bishop's initial inclination is to accept the bakery's offer, since it appears that the airline would save 4 cents per dessert. However, the controller reminds Bishop that not all of the costs listed in Exhibit 13–7 are relevant to the outsourcing decision. The controller modifies Bishop's analysis as shown in Exhibit 13–8.

If Worldwide Airways stops making desserts, it will save all of the variable costs but only 1 cent of fixed costs. The 1-cent saving in supervisory salaries would result because the airline could get along with two fewer kitchen supervisors. The remainder of the fixed costs would be incurred even if the desserts were purchased. These remaining fixed costs of supervision and depreciation would have to be reallocated to

	Cost per Dessert	Costs Saved by Purchasing Desserts
Variable costs:		
Direct material	$ .06	$ .06
Direct labour	.04	.04
Variable overhead	.04	.04
Fixed costs (allocated to products):		
Supervisory salaries	.04	.01
Depreciation of flight-kitchen equipment	.07	–0–
Total cost per dessert	$ .25	$ .15
Cost of purchasing desserts (per dessert)		$ .21
Loss per dessert if desserts are purchased (savings per dessert minus purchase cost per dessert, or $.15 − $.21)		$(.06)

Exhibit 13–8
Cost Savings from Buying In-Flight Desserts: Worldwide Airways

M anagement
A ccounting
P ractice

Northwest, Air Canada,
Apple, Hewlett-Packard,
Motorola, and Nokia

OUTSOURCING

Outsourcing is widely used in a variety of businesses. The management at Northwest Airlines, for example, has decided to outsource some of its flight attendants in order to reduce the cost of filling the most expensive of these positions. According to *The Wall Street Journal*, it's a sign "that Northwest, which has filed for bankruptcy protection, wants to become a 'virtual airline,' with all sorts of jobs previously claimed by organized labour outsourced to cheaper workers, some overseas."

Other airlines are outsourcing key maintenance operations. For example, Air Canada outsources full-service maintenance, repair and overhaul of airframes and engines to facilities in El Salvador. "The agreement offers Air Canada a customized, flexible maintenance program with advantageous fixed price guarantees." After any required maintenance is performed, the jets will fly back to Canada. "Northwest Airlines flies its wide-body jets to Singapore and Hong Kong for service by outside contractors."

BusinessWeek reports that many technology manufacturers are outsourcing research and development and product design to outside contractors in Taiwan and other countries. Among the companies outsourcing some of these key design functions are computer manufacturers Apple and Hewlett-Packard, and wireless phone manufacturers Motorola and Nokia.[1]

the flight kitchen's other products. In light of the controller's revised analysis, Bishop realizes that the airline should continue to make its own desserts. To outsource the desserts would require an expenditure of 21 cents per dessert, but only 15 cents per dessert would be saved.

To clarify her decision further, Bishop asks the controller to prepare an analysis of the *total costs* per month of making or buying desserts. The controller's report, displayed in Exhibit 13–9, shows the total cost of producing 1,000,000 desserts, the flight kitchen's average monthly volume.

The total-cost analysis confirmed Bishop's decision to continue making desserts in the airline's flight kitchen.

Exhibit 13–9
Total-Cost Analysis of
Outsourcing Decision:
Worldwide Airways

	Cost per Month	Costs Saved by Purchasing Desserts
Variable costs:		
Direct material	$ 60,000	$ 60,000
Direct labour	40,000	40,000
Variable overhead	40,000	40,000
Fixed costs (allocated to products):		
Supervisory salaries	40,000	10,000*
Depreciation of flight-kitchen equipment	70,000	–0–
Total cost per month	$250,000	$150,000
Cost of purchasing desserts (per month)		$210,000
Total loss if desserts are purchased (total savings minus total cost of purchasing, or $150,000 − $210,000)		$ (60,000)

*Cost of monthly compensation for two kitchen supervisors, who will not be needed if desserts are purchased.

In today's global economy, more and more companies are outsourcing significant products and services. Gallo Winery, for example, buys a significant portion of its grapes from other vintners. Kodak outsources its entire data processing operation. Cummins Engine outsources many of its pistons, and Intel Corporation buys microchips. Chase Bank outsources its cafeteria and legal services. Many pharmaceutical companies, such as Japan's Yamanouchi Pharmaceutical, have outsourced much of their production to cut costs.[2] Pictured here are grape harvesting and pharmaceutical production.

Beware of Unit-Cost Data   Fixed costs often are allocated to individual units of product or service for product-costing purposes. For decision-making purposes, however, unitized fixed costs can be misleading. As the total-cost analysis above shows, only $10,000 in fixed monthly cost will be saved if the desserts are purchased. The remaining $100,000 in monthly fixed cost will continue whether the desserts are made or purchased. Bishop's initial cost analysis in Exhibit 13–7 implies that each dessert costs the airline 25 cents, but that 25-cent cost includes 11 cents of unitized fixed costs. Most of these costs will remain unchanged regardless of the outsourcing decision. By allocating fixed costs to individual products or services, they are made to appear variable even though they are not.

Add or Eliminate a Service, Product, or Department

Worldwide Airways offers its passengers the opportunity to join its World Express Club. Club membership entitles a traveller to use the club facilities at the airport in Toronto. Club privileges include a private lounge and restaurant, discounts on meals and beverages, and use of a small health spa.

Jayne Wing, the president of Worldwide Airways, is worried that the World Express Club might not be profitable. Her concern is caused by the statement of monthly operating income shown in the Excel spreadsheet in Exhibit 13–10.

In her weekly staff meeting, Wing states her concern about the World Express Club's profitability. The controller responds by pointing out that not all of the costs

Exhibit 13–10

World Express Club Monthly
Operating Income Statement:
Worldwide Airways

Worldwide
Airways

	A	B	C	D	E	F	G
1	WORLDWIDE AIRWAYS: WORLD EXPRESS CLUB						
2	Monthly Operating Income Statement						
3							
4	Sales revenue					$ 200,000	
5	Less: Variable expenses:						
6	Food and beverages				$ 70,000		
7	Personnel				40,000		
8	Variable overhead				25,000	135,000	
9	Contribution margin					$ 65,000	
10	Less: Fixed expenses:						
11	Depreciation				$ 30,000		
12	Supervisory salaries				20,000		
13	Insurance				10,000		
14	Airport fees				5,000		
15	General overhead (allocated)				10,000	75,000	
16	Loss					$ (10,000)	

on the club's income statement would be eliminated if the club were discontinued. The vice-president for sales adds that the club helps Worldwide Airways attract passengers who it might otherwise lose to a competitor. As the meeting adjourns, Wing asks the controller to prepare an analysis of the relevant costs and benefits associated with the World Express Club. The controller's analysis is displayed in Exhibit 13–11.

The controller's report contains two parts. Part I focuses on the relevant costs and benefits of the World Express Club only, while ignoring any impact of the club on other airline operations. In column (a), the controller has listed the club's revenues and expenses from the income statement given previously (Exhibit 13–10). Column (b) lists the expenses that will continue if the club is eliminated. These expenses are called **unavoidable expenses**. In contrast, the expenses appearing in column (a) but not column (b) are **avoidable expenses**. The airline will no longer incur these expenses if the club is eliminated.

Notice that all of the club's variable expenses are avoidable. The depreciation expense, $30,000, is an allocated portion of the depreciation on a Worldwide Airways building, part of which is used by the World Express Club. If the Club is discontinued, the airline will continue to own and use the building, and the depreciation expense will continue. Thus, it is an unavoidable expense. The fixed supervisory salaries are avoidable, since these employees will no longer be needed if the club is eliminated. The fixed insurance expense of $10,000 is not avoidable; the $5,000 fee paid to the airport for the privilege of operating the club is avoidable. Finally, the club's allocated portion of general overhead expenses, $10,000, is not avoidable. Worldwide Airways will incur these expenses regardless of its decision about the World Express Club.

The conclusion shown by Part I of the controller's report is that the club should not be eliminated. If the club is closed, the airline will lose more in contribution margin, $65,000, than it saves in avoidable fixed expenses, $25,000. Thus, the club's $65,000 contribution margin is enough to cover the avoidable fixed expenses of $25,000 and still contribute $40,000 toward covering the overall airline's fixed expenses.

World Express Club's contribution margin	$65,000
Avoidable fixed expenses	25,000
Contribution of club toward covering overall airline's fixed expenses	$40,000

	(a) **Keep Club**	(b) **Eliminate Club**	(c) **Differential Amount: (a) − (b)**
Part I:			
Sales revenue	$200,000	–0–	$200,000
Less: Variable expenses:			
Food and beverages	(70,000)	–0–	(70,000)
Personnel	(40,000)	–0–	(40,000)
Variable overhead	(25,000)	–0–	(25,000)
Contribution margin	65,000	–0–	65,000
Less: Fixed expenses:			
Depreciation	(30,000)	(30,000)	–0–
Supervisory salaries	(20,000)	–0–	(20,000)
Insurance	(10,000)	(10,000)	–0–
Airport fees	(5,000)	–0–	(5,000)
General overhead (allocated)	(10,000)	(10,000)	–0–
Total fixed expenses	(75,000)	(50,000)	(25,000)
Profit (loss)	$ (10,000)	$(50,000)	$ 40,000*
		Expenses in the column above are **unavoidable** expenses	Expenses in the column above are **avoidable** expenses
Part II:			
Contribution margin from general airline operations that will be forgone if club is eliminated	$ 60,000	–0–	$ 60,000

*The *positive* $40,000 differential amount reflects the fact that the company is $40,000 *better off* by keeping the club.

Exhibit 13–11
Relevant Costs and Benefits
of World Express Club:
Worldwide Airways

ADDING A SERVICE

Changing business conditions can cause a company to rethink its business model and add new services. Federal Express, for example, found that a sizable portion of its overnight letter delivery business had been eliminated by e-mail. Customers no longer needed to ship a hard-copy document overnight, when the same document could be sent instantaneously via e-mail. FedEx also found a decline in the need for overnight repair parts shipments. Many customers' improved supply-chain systems resulted in better spare-parts preparedness and less need for last-minute overnight shipments. FedEx responded by adding slower ground shipment services to compete more directly with UPS and the U.S. Postal Service. While FedEx still excels when an overnight shipment is needed, its ground transport business is becoming an increasing part of its operations. FedEx also is adding new technology-based services that give customers greater ability to track shipments in transit.

   Caterpillar has added heavy equipment overhaul services to its already successful manufacturing operations. The company uses available capacity in its manufacturing plants to disassemble and rebuild heavy diesel engines, after cleaning, inspecting, and repairing them. This new service component of Caterpillar's operations has become the company's fastest-growing business unit, with annual revenue topping $1 billion.[3]

M anagement
A ccounting
P ractice

FedEx and Caterpillar

Now consider Part II of the controller's analysis in Exhibit 13–11. As the vice-president for sales pointed out, the World Express Club is an attractive feature to many travellers. The controller estimates that if the club were discontinued, the airline would lose $60,000 each month in forgone contribution margin from general airline operations. This loss in contribution margin would result from losing to a competing airline current passengers who are attracted to Worldwide Airways by its World Express Club. This $60,000 in forgone contribution margin is an *opportunity cost* of the option to close down the club.

Considering both Parts I and II of the controller's analysis, Worldwide Airways' monthly profit will be greater by $100,000 if the club is kept open. Recognition of two issues is key to this conclusion:

1. Only the avoidable expenses of the club will be saved if it is discontinued.
2. Closing the club will adversely affect the airline's other operations.

Special Decisions in Manufacturing Firms

Learning Objective 6

Analyze manufacturing decisions involving joint products and limited resources.

Some types of decisions are more likely to arise in manufacturing companies than in service industry firms. We will examine two of these decisions.

Joint Products: Sell or Process Further

A **joint production process** results in two or more products, called joint products. An example is the processing of cocoa beans into cocoa powder and cocoa butter. Cocoa beans constitute the input to the joint production process, and the two joint products are cocoa powder and cocoa butter. The point in the production process where the joint products are identifiable as separate products is called the **split-off point**. Other examples of joint production processes include the processing of animals for various cuts of meat and of petroleum into various products, such as kerosene and gasoline.

Manufacturers with joint production processes sometimes must decide whether a joint product should be sold at the split-off point or processed further before being sold. Such a decision recently confronted Bill Candee, the president of International Chocolate Company. Candee's firm imports cocoa beans and processes them into cocoa powder and cocoa butter. Only a portion of the cocoa powder is used by International Chocolate Company in the production of chocolate candy. The remainder of the cocoa powder is sold to an ice cream producer. Candee is considering the possibility of processing his remaining cocoa powder into an instant cocoa mix to be marketed under the brand name ChocoTime. Data pertaining to Candee's decision are displayed in Exhibit 13–12.

Notice from the diagram that cocoa beans are processed in one-tonne batches. The total cost of the cocoa beans and the joint processing is $1,100. This is called the **joint cost**. The output of the joint process is 1,500 kilograms of cocoa butter and 500 kilograms of cocoa powder.

How should Bill Candee approach the decision about processing the cocoa powder into instant cocoa mix? What are the relevant costs and benefits? First, let's consider the joint cost of $1,100. Is this a relevant cost in the decision at hand? *The joint cost is not a relevant cost*, because it will not change regardless of the decision Candee makes.

Suppose the $1,100 joint cost had been allocated to the two joint products for product-costing purposes. A common method of allocating a joint cost is the **relative-sales-value method**, in which the joint cost is allocated between the joint products in proportion to their sales value at the split-off point. International Chocolate Company would make the following joint cost allocation.

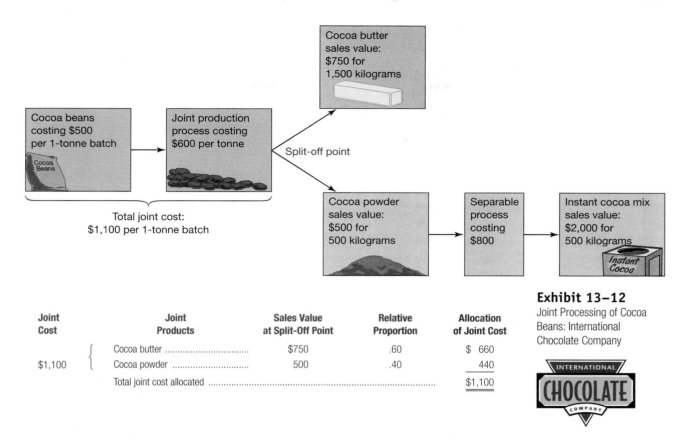

Exhibit 13–12
Joint Processing of Cocoa
Beans: International
Chocolate Company

Joint Cost	Joint Products	Sales Value at Split-Off Point	Relative Proportion	Allocation of Joint Cost
	Cocoa butter	$750	.60	$ 660
$1,100	Cocoa powder	500	.40	440
	Total joint cost allocated			$1,100

Does this allocation of the $1,100 joint cost make it relevant to the decision about processing cocoa powder into instant cocoa mix? The answer is no. *The $1,100 joint cost still does not change in total*, whether the cocoa powder is processed further or not. The joint cost is irrelevant to the decision at hand.

The only costs and benefits relevant to Candee's decision are those that differ between the two alternatives. The proper analysis is shown in Exhibit 13–13.

There is a shortcut method that arrives at the same conclusion as Exhibit 13–13. In this approach, the incremental revenue from the further processing of cocoa powder

Exhibit 13–13
Decision to Sell or Process
Further: International
Chocolate Company

Relevant or Irrelevant		(a) Process Cocoa Powder into Instant Cocoa Mix	(b) Sell Cocoa Powder at Split-Off Point	(c) Differential Amount: (a) − (b)
	Sales revenue:			
Irrelevant	Cocoa butter	$ 750	$ 750	–0–
Relevant	Instant cocoa mix	2,000		
Relevant	Cocoa powder		500	$1,500
	Less: Costs:			
Irrelevant	Joint cost	(1,100)	(1,100)	–0–
Relevant	Incremental cost of processing cocoa powder into instant cocoa mix	(800)	–0–	(800)
	Total	$ 850	$ 150	$ 700

is compared with the **incremental processing cost**, which is the cost incurred after the split-off point, as follows:

Sales value of instant cocoa mix	$2,000
Sales value of cocoa powder	500
Incremental revenue from further processing	$1,500
Less: Incremental processing cost	(800)
Net benefit from further processing	$ 700

Both analyses indicate that Bill Candee should process his excess cocoa powder into instant cocoa mix. The same conclusion is reached if the analysis is done on a per-unit basis rather than a total basis:

Sales value of instant cocoa mix ($2,000 ÷ 500 kilograms)	$4.00 per kilogram
Sales value of cocoa powder ($500 ÷ 500 kilograms)	1.00 per kilogram
Incremental revenue from further processing	$3.00 per kilogram
Less: Incremental processing cost ($800 ÷ 500 kilograms)	(1.60) per kilogram
Net benefit from further processing	$1.40 per kilogram

Once again, the analysis shows that Bill Candee should decide to process the cocoa powder into instant cocoa mix.

Decisions Involving Limited Resources

Organizations typically have limited resources. Limitations on floor space, machine time, labour hours, or raw materials are common. Operating with limited resources, a firm often has to choose between sales orders, deciding which orders to fill and which to decline. In making such decisions, managers have to decide which product or service is the most profitable.

To illustrate, suppose International Chocolate Company's plant makes two candy-bar products, Chewies and Chompo Bars. The contribution margin for a case of each of these products is computed in Exhibit 13–14.

A glance at the contribution-margin data suggests that Chompo Bars are more profitable than Chewies. It is true that a case of Chompo Bars contributes more toward covering the company's fixed cost and profit. However, an important consideration has been ignored in the analysis so far. The plant's capacity is limited by its available machine time. Only 700 machine hours are available in the plant each month. International Chocolate Company can sell as many cases of either candy bar as it can produce, so production is limited only by the constraint on machine time.

Exhibit 13–14
Contribution Margin per Case: International Chocolate Company

	Chewies	Chompo Bars
Sales price	$10.00	$14.00
Less: Variable costs:		
Direct material	3.00	3.75
Direct labour	2.00	2.50
Variable overhead	3.00	3.75
Variable selling and administrative costs	1.00	2.00
Total variable costs	9.00	12.00
Contribution margin per case	$ 1.00	$ 2.00

		Chewies	Chompo Bars
(a)	Contribution margin per case	$1.00	$2.00
(b)	Machine hours required per case	.02	.05
(a) ÷ (b)	Contribution margin per machine hour	$50	$40

Exhibit 13–15
Contribution Margin per Machine Hour: International Chocolate Company

	Chewies	Chompo Bars
Contribution margin per case	$1.00	$2.00
Number of cases produced in 100 hours of machine time	× 5,000*	× 2,000†
Total contribution toward covering fixed cost and profit	$5,000	$4,000

*Chewies: 100 hours ÷ .02 hour per case = 5,000 cases.

†Chompo Bars: 100 hours ÷ .05 hour per case = 2,000 cases.

Exhibit 13–16
Total Contribution from 100 Machine Hours: International Chocolate Company

To maximize the plant's total contribution toward covering fixed cost and profit, management should strive to use each machine hour as effectively as possible. This realization alters the analysis of product profitability. The relevant question is *not* "Which candy bar has the highest contribution margin *per case*?" but "Which product has the highest contribution margin *per machine hour*?" This question is answered in the calculation of Exhibit 13–15.

A machine hour spent in the production of Chewies will contribute $50 toward covering fixed cost and profit, while a machine hour devoted to Chompo Bars contributes only $40. Hence, the plant's most profitable product is Chewies, when the plant's scarce resource is taken into account.

Suppose International Chocolate Company's plant manager, Candace Barr, is faced with a choice between two sales orders, only one of which can be accepted. Only 100 hours of unscheduled machine time remains in the month, and it can be used to produce either Chewies or Chompos. The analysis in Exhibit 13–16 shows that Barr should devote the 100-hour block of machine time to filling the order for Chewies.

As Exhibit 13–16 demonstrates, a decision about the best use of a limited resource should be made on the basis of the *contribution margin per unit of the scarce resource*.

Multiple Scarce Resources   Suppose the plant had a limited amount of *both* machine hours *and* labour hours. Now the analysis of product profitability is more complicated. The choice as to which product is most profitable typically will involve a trade-off between the two scarce resources. Solving such a problem requires a powerful mathematical tool called *linear programming*, which is covered in the appendix to this chapter.

Theory of Constraints   As the previous analysis suggests, a binding constraint can limit a company's profitability. For example, a manufacturing company may have a *bottleneck operation*, through which every unit of a product must pass before moving on to other operations. The *theory of constraints (TOC)* calls for identifying such limiting constraints and seeking ways to relax them. Also referred to as *managing constraints*, this management approach can significantly improve an organization's level of goal

Exhibit 13–17
Sensitivity Analysis:
International Chocolate
Company

		Chewies	Chompo Bars
Original Analysis			
(a)	Contribution margin per case predicted	$1.00	$2.00
(b)	Machine hours required per case	.02	.05
(a) ÷ (b)	Contribution per machine hour	$50.00	$40.00
Sensitivity Analysis			
(c)	Contribution margin per case hypothesized in sensitivity analysis	$.80	
(d)	Machine hours required per case	.02	Same
(c) ÷ (d)	Contribution per machine hour	$40.00	

attainment. Among the ways that management can relax a constraint by expanding the capacity of a bottleneck operation are the following:

- *Outsourcing* (subcontracting) all or part of the bottleneck operation
- Investing in additional production equipment and employing *parallel processing*, in which multiple product units undergo the same production operation simultaneously
- Working *overtime* at the bottleneck operation
- *Retraining* employees and shifting them to the bottleneck
- Eliminating any *non-value-added activities* at the bottleneck operation

Uncertainty

Our analyses of the decisions in this chapter assumed that all relevant data were known with certainty. In practice, of course, decision makers are rarely so fortunate. One common technique for addressing the impact of uncertainty is *sensitivity analysis*. **Sensitivity analysis** is a technique for determining what would happen in a decision analysis if a key prediction or assumption proved to be wrong.

To illustrate, let's return to Candace Barr's decision about how to use the remaining 100 hours of machine time in International Chocolate Company's plant. The calculation in Exhibit 13–15 showed that Chewies have the higher contribution margin per machine hour. Suppose Barr is uncertain about the contribution margin per case of Chewies. A sensitivity analysis shows how sensitive her decision is to the value of this uncertain parameter. As Exhibit 13–17 shows, the Chewies contribution margin could decline to $.80 per case before Barr's decision would change. As long as the contribution margin per case of Chewies exceeds $.80 per case, the 100 hours of available machine time should be devoted to Chewies.

Sensitivity analysis can help the managerial accountant decide which parameters in an analysis are most critical to estimate accurately. In this case, the managerial accountant knows that the contribution margin per case of Chewies could be as much as 20 percent lower than the original $1 prediction without changing the outcome of the analysis.

Expected Values   Another approach to dealing explicitly with uncertainty is to base the decision on expected values. The **expected value** of a random variable is equal to the sum of the possible values for the variable, each weighted by its probability. To illustrate, suppose the contribution margins per case for Chewies and Chompos are uncertain, as shown in Exhibit 13–18. As the Exhibit shows, the choice as to which product to produce with excess machine time may be based on the *expected value* of the contribution per machine hour. Statisticians have developed many other methods

Chewies		Chompo Bars	
Possible Values of Contribution Margin	**Probability**	**Possible Values of Contribution Margin**	**Probability**
$ .75	.5	$1.50	.3
1.25	.5	2.00	.4
		2.50	.3
Expected value	(.5)($.75) + (.5)($1.25) = $1.00	(.3)($1.50) + (.4)($2.00) + (.3)($2.50) = $2.00	
Machine hours required per case	.02		.05
Expected value of contribution per machine hour	$50	>	$40

Exhibit 13–18
Use of Expected Values:
International Chocolate
Company

for dealing with uncertainty in decision making. These techniques are covered in statistics and decision analysis courses.

Activity-Based Costing and Today's Advanced Manufacturing Environment

In this chapter we have explored how to identify the relevant costs and benefits in various types of decisions. How will the relevant-costing approach change in a manufacturing environment, characterized by JIT production methods and flexible manufacturing systems (FMS)? How would a relevant-costing analysis change if a company uses an activity-based costing (ABC) system?[4]

> **Learning Objective 7**
>
> Explain the impact of an advanced manufacturing environment and activity-based costing on a relevant-cost analysis.

The *concepts* underlying a relevant-costing analysis continue to be completely valid in an advanced manufacturing setting and in a situation in which activity-based costing is used. The objective of the decision analysis is to determine the costs and benefits that are relevant to the decision. As we found earlier in this chapter, relevant costs and benefits *have a bearing on the future and differ among the decision alternatives.*

What *will* be different in a setting where activity-based costing is used is the decision maker's ability to determine what costs are relevant to a decision. Under ABC, the decision maker typically can associate costs with the activities that drive them much more accurately than under a conventional product-costing system. Let's explore these issues with an illustration.

Conventional Outsourcing (Make-or-Buy) Analysis

International Chocolate Company makes fine chocolates in its Richmond plant. The chocolates are packaged in two-kilogram and five-kilogram gift boxes. The company also manufactures the gift boxes in the plant. The plant manager was approached recently by a packaging company with an offer to supply the gift boxes at a price of $.45 each. She concluded that the offer should be rejected on the basis of the relevant-costing analysis in Exhibit 13–19. International Chocolate Company's traditional, volume-based product-costing system showed a unit product cost of $.80 per box. However, she realized that not all of the costs would be avoided. She reasoned that all of the direct material, direct labour, and variable overhead would be avoided, but only a small part of the assigned fixed overhead would be saved. She concluded that $60,000 of supervisory salaries and $20,000 of machinery depreciation could be traced directly to gift package production. These costs would be avoided, she felt, but the remaining fixed costs would not. Barr concluded that only $430,000 of costs would be avoided by purchasing, while $450,000 would be spent to buy the boxes. The decision was clear; the supplier's offer should be rejected.

Exhibit 13–19
Conventional Product-Costing
Data and Outsourcing
Analysis: International
Chocolate Company

A. Manufacturing Overhead Budget for Savannah Plant

Variable overhead:

Electricity	$ 700,000
Oil and lubricants	120,000
Equipment maintenance	180,000
Total variable overhead	$1,000,000

Variable overhead rate: $1,000,000 ÷ 100,000 direct-labour hours = $10 per hour

Fixed overhead:

Plant depreciation	$1,650,000
Product development	300,000
Supervisory salaries	600,000
Material handling	800,000
Purchasing	250,000
Inspection	300,000
Setup	400,000
Machinery depreciation	200,000
Total fixed overhead	$4,500,000

Fixed overhead rate: $4,500,000 ÷ 100,000 direct-labour hours = $45 per hour

B. Conventional Product-Costing Data: Gift Boxes

Direct material	$ 100,000
Direct labour (10,000 hr. at $15 per hr.)	150,000
Variable overhead ($10 per direct-labour hr.)	100,000
Fixed overhead ($45 per direct-labour hr.)	450,000
Total cost	$ 800,000

Unit cost: $800,000 ÷ 1,000,000 boxes = $.80 per box

C. Conventional Outsourcing Analysis: Gift Boxes

Relevant costs (costs that will be avoided if the gift boxes are purchased):

Direct material	$ 100,000
Direct labour	150,000
Variable overhead	100,000
Fixed overhead:	
Supervision	60,000
Machinery depreciation	20,000
Total costs to be avoided by purchasing	$ 430,000
Total cost of purchasing (1,000,000 boxes × $.45 per box)	$ 450,000

ABC Analysis of the Outsourcing Decision

At a staff meeting, the plant manager mentioned her tentative decision to Dave Mint, the plant controller. Mint then explained to the plant manager that he was completing a pilot project using activity-based costing. Mint offered to analyze the outsourcing decision using the new ABC database. The plant manager agreed, and Mint proceeded to do the ABC analysis shown in Exhibit 13–20.

In stage one of the ABC analysis, Mint had designated 11 activity cost pools corresponding to the major items in the plant's overhead budget. These activity cost pools were categorized as facility-level, product-sustaining level, batch-level, or unit-level activities. In stage two of the ABC project, cost drivers were identified and pool rates were computed. The ABC analysis showed that $243,000 of overhead should be assigned to the gift boxes, rather than $550,000 as the conventional product costing system had indicated.

Using the ABC database, Mint completed a new relevant-costing analysis of the outsourcing decision. Mint felt that all of the overhead costs assigned to the gift box

A. Activity Cost Pools and Pool Rates

Activity Cost Pools	Budgeted Cost	Pool Rate and Cost Driver	Cost Assigned to Gift Boxes		
Facility level:					
Plant depreciation	$1,650,000	—			
Product-sustaining level:					
Product development	300,000	$600 per product spec	$600 ×	5* =	$ 3,000
Supervisory salaries	600,000	$40 per supervisory hour	$40 ×	1,500 =	60,000
Batch level:					
Material handling	800,000	$8 per material-handling hour	$8 ×	5,000 =	40,000
Purchasing	250,000	$250 per purchase order	$250 ×	40 =	10,000
Inspection	300,000	$300 per inspection	$300 ×	20 =	6,000
Setup	400,000	$400 per setup	$400 ×	10 =	4,000
Unit level:					
Electricity	700,000	$1.40 per machine hour	$1.40 × 50,000 =		70,000
Oil and lubrication	120,000	$.24 per machine hour	$.24 × 50,000 =		12,000
Equipment maintenance	180,000	$.36 per machine hour	$.36 × 50,000 =		18,000
Machinery depreciation	200,000	$.40 per machine hour	$.40 × 50,000 =		20,000
Total overhead for Savannah plant	$5,500,000				
Total overhead assigned to gift box production					$243,000

*The numbers in this column are the quantities of each cost driver required for gift box production.

B. ABC Outsourcing Analysis: Gift Boxes

Relevant costs (costs that will be avoided if the gift boxes are purchased):	
Direct material	$100,000
Direct labour	150,000
Overhead (from ABC analysis in panel A, above)	243,000
Total costs to be avoided by purchasing	$493,000
Total cost of purchasing (1,000,000 boxes × $.45 per box)	$450,000

Exhibit 13–20
Activity-Based Costing Analysis of Outsourcing Decision: International Chocolate Company

operation could be avoided if the boxes were purchased. Notice that none of the facility-level costs are relevant to the analysis. They will not be avoided by purchasing the gift boxes. Mint's ABC analysis showed that a total of $493,000 of costs could be avoided by purchasing the boxes at a cost of $450,000. This would result in a net saving of $43,000.

Mint showed the ABC relevant-costing analysis to the plant manager. After some discussion, they agreed that various qualitative issues needed to be explored before a final decision was made. For example, would the new supplier be reliable, and would the gift boxes be of good quality? Nevertheless, Barr and Mint agreed that the ABC data cast an entirely different light on the decision.

The Key Point What has happened here? Why did the conventional and ABC analyses of this decision reach different conclusions? Is the relevant-costing concept faulty?

The answer is no; both analyses sought to identify the relevant costs as those that would be avoided by purchasing the gift boxes. That approach is valid. The difference in the analyses lies in the superior ability of the ABC data to properly identify what the avoidable costs are. This is the key point. The conventional analysis relied on a traditional, volume-based product-costing system. That system lumps all of the fixed overhead costs together and assigns them using a single, unit-based cost driver (i.e., direct-labour hours). That analysis simply failed to note that many of the so-called fixed costs are *not* really fixed with respect to the appropriate cost driver. The more accurate ABC system correctly showed this fact, and identified additional costs that could be avoided by purchasing.

To summarize, under activity-based costing, the concepts underlying relevant costing analysis remain valid. However, the ABC system does enable the decision maker to apply the relevant-costing decision model more accurately.

Other Issues in Decision Making

Incentives for Decision Makers

In this chapter, we studied how managers should make decisions by focusing on the relevant costs and benefits. In previous chapters, we covered accounting procedures for evaluating managerial performance. There is an important link between *decision making* and *managerial performance evaluation*. Managers typically will make decisions that maximize their perceived performance evaluations and rewards. This is human nature. If we want managers to make optimal decisions by properly evaluating the relevant costs and benefits, then the performance evaluation system and reward structure had better be consistent with that perspective.

The proper treatment of sunk costs in decision making illustrates this issue. Earlier in this chapter, we saw that sunk costs should be ignored as irrelevant. For example, the book value of an outdated machine is irrelevant in making an equipment-replacement decision. Suppose, however, that a manager correctly ignores an old machine's book value and decides on early replacement of the machine he purchased a few years ago. Now suppose the hapless manager is criticized by his superior for "taking a loss" on the old machine, or for "buying a piece of junk" in the first place. What is our manager likely to do the next time he faces a similar decision? If he is like many people, he will tend to keep the old machine in order to justify his prior decision to purchase it. In so doing, he will be compounding his error. However, he also may be avoiding criticism from a superior who does not understand the importance of goal congruence.

The point is simply that if we want managers to make optimal decisions, we must give them incentives to do so. This requires that managerial performance be judged on the same factors that should be considered in making correct decisions.

Short-Run versus Long-Run Decisions

The decisions we have examined in this chapter were treated as short-run decisions. *Short-run decisions* affect only a short time period, typically a year or less. In reality, many of these decisions would have longer-term implications. For example, managers usually make a decision involving the addition or deletion of a product or service with a relatively long time frame in mind. The process of identifying relevant costs and benefits is largely the same whether the decision is viewed from a short-run or long-run perspective. One important factor that does change in a long-run analysis, however, is the *time value of money*. When several time periods are involved in a decision, the analyst should account for the fact that a $1 cash flow today is different from a $1 cash flow in five years. A dollar received today can be invested to earn interest, while the dollar received in five years cannot be invested over the intervening time period. The analysis of long-run decisions requires a tool called *capital budgeting*.

Pitfalls to Avoid

Identification of the relevant costs and benefits is an important step in making any economic decision. Nonetheless, analysts often overlook relevant costs or incorrectly include irrelevant data. In this section, we review four common mistakes to avoid in decision making:

1. *Sunk costs.* The book value of an asset, defined as its acquisition cost less the accumulated depreciation, is a sunk cost. Sunk costs cannot be changed by any current or future course of action, so they are irrelevant in decision making. Nevertheless, a common behavioural tendency is to give undue importance to book values in decisions that involve replacing an asset or disposing of obsolete inventory. People often seek to justify their past decisions by refusing to dispose of an asset, even if a better alternative has been identified. *Conclusion: Ignore sunk costs.*

2. *Unitized fixed costs.* For product-costing purposes, fixed costs often are divided by some activity measure and assigned to individual units of product. The result is to make a fixed cost appear variable. While there are legitimate reasons for this practice, from a *product-costing* perspective, it can create havoc in decision making. Therefore, in a decision analysis, it is usually wise to include a fixed cost in its total amount, rather than as a per-unit cost. *Conclusion: Beware of unitized fixed costs in decision making.*

3. *Allocated fixed costs.* It is also common to allocate fixed costs across divisions, departments, or product lines. A possible result is that a product or department may appear unprofitable when in reality it does make a contribution toward covering fixed costs and profit. Before deciding to eliminate a department, be sure to ask which costs will be *avoided* if a particular alternative is selected. A fixed cost that has been allocated to a department may continue, in total or in part, even after the department has been eliminated. *Conclusion: Beware of allocated fixed costs; identify the avoidable costs.*

4. *Opportunity costs.* People tend to overlook opportunity costs, or to treat such costs as less important than out-of-pocket costs. Yet opportunity costs are just as real and important to making a correct decision as are out-of-pocket costs. *Conclusion: Pay special attention to identifying and including opportunity costs in a decision analysis.*

Focus on Ethics

EFFECTS OF DECISION TO CLOSE A DEPARTMENT AND OUTSOURCE

Outsourcing has become a common way of reducing costs in many organizations. Such decisions, though, often have repercussions that may not be captured "by the numbers." Employee morale, product quality, and vendor reliability are some of the issues that should be considered. Let's revisit the scenario described earlier at the International Chocolate Company. Recall that the plant manager, Candace Barr, was considering outsourcing the production of gift boxes for the company's fine chocolates. A conventional analysis of the decision pointed toward keeping the production operation in-house. Now let's change the scenario a bit, and consider the following conversation between Dave Mint, plant controller (C), and Jack Edgeworth, supervisor of the gift box production

department (SG). The conversation takes place after the two friends' weekly tennis game.

Mint (C): Well, you took me again, Jack. I'm starting to feel old.

Edgeworth (SG): It was a close match, Dave. Always is. Fortunately, it looks like we'll be able to keep our matches up, too.

Mint (C): What do you mean?

Edgeworth (SG): I'm talking about the outsourcing decision that is being considered. Fortunately, the analysis showed that we should keep making our own gift boxes. So my department stays in business. And I won't have to consider a transfer. My wife's very happy about that, with the twins in middle school and all.

Mint (C): Uh, Jack, I think there's something you need to know about.

Edgeworth (SG): What's that?

Mint (C): I've been doing some preliminary studies using a technique called activity-based costing. I think it could improve our decision making in a lot of areas.

Edgeworth (SG): So?

Mint (C): That outsourcing decision is one of the areas in which I tried out the new ABC approach. I just finished the analysis yesterday. I was going to schedule an appointment with you next week to discuss it.

Edgeworth (SG): I'm getting queasy about where this is going, Jack. What did your analysis show?

Mint (C): It changes the conclusion—pretty dramatically, in fact. The ABC study shows that we'd save over $40,000 each year by outsourcing.

Edgeworth (SG): Is that really all that much, Dave? Among friends, I mean?

Mint (C): It's not a trivial amount, Jack.

Edgeworth (SG): Look, Dave, I don't think I've ever asked anything of you before. But can't you bury this one for me? Our family really doesn't need another move. And I've got people working for me who will probably lose their jobs.

We've done a good job for the company. Our product is top-notch. Nobody's ever complained about a thing.

Mint (C): I don't see how I can withhold the analysis, Jack. Candace has a right to all the information I have.

Edgeworth (SG): But you said you were just doing preliminary studies, Dave. Candace doesn't know anything about this one does she?

Mint (C): Not yet, Jack, but I've got a professional obligation to show it to her.

Edgeworth (SG): You're opening a Pandora's box, Dave. What about employee morale if you close my department? And what about product quality, and reliability of the supply?

Mint (C): Those are valid issues, Jack. But they need to be addressed on their own merits, in a full and open discussion.

Edgeworth (SG): Could you at least share this so-called ABC study with me before you show it to Candace? Maybe I'll see something you've missed.

Mint (C): I don't see why not, Jack. Come by my office tomorrow morning—say about 10:00.

Identify any ethical issues you see in this scenario. How would you resolve them? What should the controller do?

Chapter Summary

The managerial accountant's key role in the decision-making process is to provide data relevant to the decision. Managers can then use these data in preparing a quantitative analysis of the decision. Qualitative factors also are considered in making the final decision.

In order to be relevant to a decision, a cost or benefit must (1) bear on the future and (2) differ under the various decision alternatives. Sunk costs, such as the book value of equipment or inventory, are not relevant in decisions. Such costs do not have any bearing on the future. Opportunity costs are frequently relevant to decisions, but often overlooked by decision makers. To analyze any special decision, the proper approach is to determine all of the costs and benefits that will differ among the alternatives.

Since decisions often are made under uncertainty, sensitivity analysis should be used to determine if the decision will change if various predictions prove to be wrong.

The concepts underlying a relevant-cost analysis remain valid in an advanced manufacturing environment and in situations where activity-based costing is used. However, an ABC system typically enables a decision maker to estimate the relevant costs in a decision problem more accurately.

Review Problem on Relevant Costs

Lansing Camera Company has received a special order for photographic equipment it does not normally produce. The company has excess capacity, and the order could be manufactured without reducing production of the firm's regular products. Discuss the relevance of each of the following items in computing the cost of the special order.

1. Equipment to be used in producing the order has a book value of $2,000. The equipment has no other use for Lansing Camera Company. If the order is not accepted, the equipment will be sold for $1,500. If the equipment is used in producing the order, it can be sold in three months for $800.

2. If the special order is accepted, the operation will require some of the storage space in the company's plant. If the space is used for this purpose, the company will rent storage space temporarily in a nearby warehouse at a cost of $18,000. The building depreciation allocated to the storage space to be used in producing the special order is $12,000.

3. If the special order is accepted, it will require a subassembly. Lansing Camera can purchase the subassembly for $24 per unit from an outside supplier or make it for $30 per unit. The $30 cost per unit was determined as follows:

Direct material	$10
Direct labour	6
Variable overhead	6
Allocated fixed overhead	8
Total unit cost of subassembly	$30

Should Lansing Camera purchase or make the Subassembly?

Solution to Review Problem

1. The book value of the equipment is a sunk cost, irrelevant to the decision. The relevant cost of the equipment is $700, determined as follows:

Sales value of equipment now	$1,500
Sales value after producing special order	800
Differential cost	$ 700

2. The $12,000 portion of building depreciation allocated to the storage space to be used for the special order is irrelevant. First, it is a sunk cost. Second, any costs relating to the company's factory building will continue whether the special order is accepted or not. The relevant cost is the $18,000 rent that will be incurred only if the special order is accepted.

3. Lansing Camera should make the subassembly. The subassembly's relevant cost is $22 per unit.

Relevant Cost of Making Subassembly (per unit)		Relevant Cost of Purchasing Subassembly (per unit)	
Direct material	$10	Purchase price	$24
Direct labour	6		
Variable overhead	6		
Total	$22		

Notice that the unitized fixed overhead, $8, is not a relevant cost of the subassembly. Lansing Camera Company's *total* fixed cost will not change, whether the special order is accepted or not.

Key Terms

For each term's definition refer to the indicated page, or turn to the glossary at the end of the text.

accurate information, 523

avoidable expenses, 534

constraints,* 548

decision variables,* 548

differential cost, 524

expected value, 540

feasible region,* 548

incremental processing cost, 538

information overload, 525

joint cost, 536

joint production process, 536

make-or-buy decision, 531

objective function,* 548

opportunity cost, 524

outsourcing decision, 531

qualitative characteristics, 522

relative-sales-value method, 536

relevant information, 523

sensitivity analysis, 540

split-off point, 536

sunk costs, 524

timely information, 523

unavoidable expenses, 534

---

*Term appears in the Appendix to this chapter.

Linear Programming

When a firm produces multiple products, management has to decide how much of each output to produce. In most cases, the firm is limited in the total amount it can produce, due to constraints on resources such as machine time, direct labour, or raw materials. This situation is known as a *product-mix problem.*

To illustrate, we will use International Chocolate Company's plant, which produces Chewies and Chompo Bars. Exhibit 13–21 provides data pertinent to the problem.

Linear programming is a powerful mathematical tool, well suited to solving International Chocolate Company's product-mix problem. The steps in constructing the linear program are as follows:

1. Identify the **decision variables**, which are the variables about which a decision must be made. International Chocolate's decision variables are as follows:

Decision	X = Number of cases of Chewies to produce each month
variables	Y = Number of cases of Chompo Bars to produce each month

2. Write the **objective function**, which is an algebraic expression of the firm's goal. International Chocolate's goal is to maximize its total contribution margin. Since Chewies bring a contribution margin of $1 per case, and Chompos result in a contribution margin of $2 per case, the firm's objective function is the following:

    Objective function Maximize $Z = X + 2Y$

3. Write the **constraints**, which are algebraic expressions of the limitations faced by the firm, such as those limiting its productive resources. International Chocolate has a constraint for machine time and a constraint for direct labour.

    Machine-time constraint $.02X + .05Y = 700$
    Labour-time constraint $.20X + .25Y = 5,000$

Suppose, for example, that management decided to produce 20,000 cases of Chewies and 6,000 cases of Chompos. The machine-time constraint would appear as follows:

$$(.02)(20,000) + (.05)(6,000) = 700$$

Thus, at these production levels, the machine-time constraint would just be satisfied, with no machine hours to spare.

Graphical Solution

To understand how the linear program described above will help International Chocolate's management solve its product-mix problem, examine the graphs in Exhibit 13–22. The two coloured lines in panel A represent the constraints. The coloured arrows indicate that the production quantities, X and Y, must lie on or below these lines. Since the production quantities must be nonnegative, coloured arrows also appear on the graphs' axes. Together, the axes and constraints form an area called the **feasible region**, in which the solution to the linear program must lie.

Exhibit 13–21
Data for Product-Mix Problem: International Chocolate Company

	Chewies	Chompo Bars
Contribution margin per case	$1.00	$2.00
Machine hours per case	.02	.05
Direct-labour hours per case	.20	.25
	Machine Hours	**Direct-Labour Hours**
Limited resources: Hours available per month	700	5,000

A. Constraints, Feasible Region, and Objective Function

Exhibit 13–22
Product-Mix Problem
Expressed as Linear
Program: International
Chocolate Company

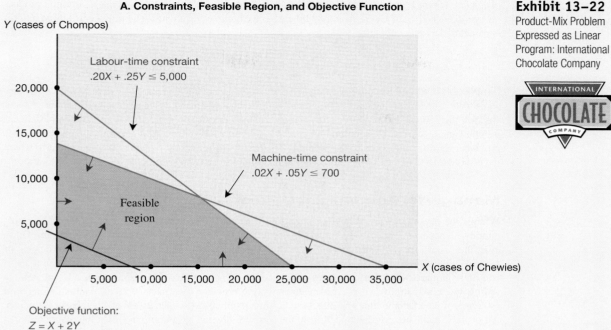

Y (cases of Chompos)

Labour-time constraint
.20X + .25Y ≤ 5,000

Machine-time constraint
.02X + .05Y ≤ 700

Feasible region

X (cases of Chewies)

Objective function:
Z = X + 2Y

B. Solution of Linear Program

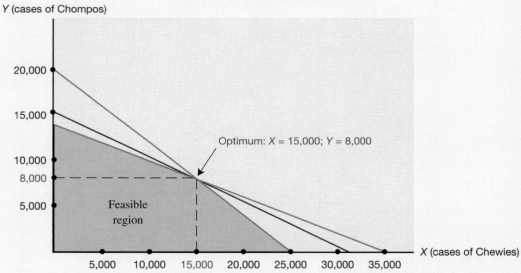

Y (cases of Chompos)

Optimum: X = 15,000; Y = 8,000

Feasible region

X (cases of Chewies)

The purple slanted line in panel A represents the objective function. Rearrange the objective function equation as follows:

$$Z = X + 2Y \longrightarrow Y = \frac{Z}{2} - \frac{1}{2}X$$

This form of the objective function shows that the slope of the equation is –½, which is the slope of the objective-function line in the Exhibit. Management's goal is to maximize total contribution margin, denoted by Z. To achieve the maximum, the objective-function line must be moved as far outward and upward in the feasible region as possible, while maintaining the same slope. This goal is represented in panel A by the arrow that points outward from the objective-function line.

Solution The result of moving the objective-function line as far as possible in the indicated direction is shown in panel B of the exhibit. The objective-function line intersects the feasible region at exactly one point, where *X* equals 15,000 and *Y* equals 8,000. Thus, International Chocolate's optimal product mix is 15,000 cases of Chewies and 8,000 cases of Chompos per month. The total contribution margin is calculated as shown below.

$$\text{Total contribution margin} = (15,000)(\$1) + (8,000)(\$2) + \$31,000$$

Simplex Method and Sensitivity Analysis   Although the graphical method is instructive, it is a cumbersome technique for solving a linear program. Fortunately, mathematicians have developed a more efficient solution method called the *simplex algorithm*. A computer can apply the algorithm to a complex linear program and determine the solution in seconds. In addition, most linear programming computer packages provide a sensitivity analysis of the problem. This analysis shows the decision maker the extent to which the estimates used in the objective function and constraints can change without changing the solution.

Managerial Accountant's Role

What is the managerial accountant's role in International Chocolate's product-mix decision? The production manager in the company's plant makes this decision, with the help of a linear program. However, the linear program uses *information supplied by the managerial accountant*. The coefficients of *X* and *Y* in the objective function are unit contribution margins. Exhibit 13–14 shows that calculating these contribution margins requires estimates of direct-material, direct-labour, variable-overhead, and variable selling and administrative costs. These estimates were provided by a managerial accountant, along with estimates of the machine time and direct-labour time required to produce a case of Chewies or Chompos. All of these estimates were obtained from the standard-costing system, upon which the plant's product costs are based. Thus, the managerial accountant makes the product-mix decision possible by providing the relevant cost data.

Linear programming is widely used in business decision making. Among the applications are blending in the petroleum and chemical industries; scheduling of personnel, railroad cars, and aircraft; and the mixing of ingredients in the food industry. In all of these applications, managerial accountants provide information crucial to the analysis.

Review Questions

13–1. List the six steps in the decision-making process.

13–2. Describe the managerial accountant's role in the decision-making process.

13–3. Distinguish between qualitative and quantitative decision analyses.

13–4. Explain what is meant by the term *decision model*.

13–5. A quantitative analysis enables a decision maker to put a "price" on the sum total of the qualitative characteristics in a decision situation. Explain this statement, and give an example.

13–6. What is meant by each of the following potential characteristics of information: relevant, accurate, and timely? Is objective information always relevant? Accurate?

13–7. List and explain two important criteria that must be satisfied in order for information to be relevant.

13–8. Explain why the book value of equipment is not a relevant cost.

13–9. Is the book value of inventory on hand a relevant cost? Why?

13–10. Why might a manager exhibit a behavioural tendency to inappropriately consider sunk costs in making a decision?

13–11. Give an example of an irrelevant future cost. Why is it irrelevant?

13–12. Define the term *opportunity cost*, and give an example of one.

13–13. What behavioural tendency do people often exhibit with regard to opportunity costs?

13–14. How does the existence of excess production capacity affect the decision to accept or reject a special order?

13–15. What is meant by the term *differential cost analysis*?

13–16. Briefly describe the proper approach for making a decision about adding or dropping a product line.

13–17. What is a *joint production process*? Describe a special decision that commonly arises in the context of a joint production process. Briefly describe the proper approach for making this type of decision.

13–18. Are allocated joint processing costs relevant when making a decision to sell a joint product at the split-off point or process it further? Why?

13–19. Briefly describe the proper approach to making a production decision when limited resources are involved.

13–20. What is meant by the term *contribution margin per unit of scarce resource*?

13–21. How is sensitivity analysis used to cope with uncertainty in decision making?

13–22. There is an important link between *decision making* and *managerial performance evaluation*. Explain.

13–23. List four potential pitfalls in decision making, which represent common errors.

13–24. Why can unitized fixed costs cause errors in decision making?

13–25. Give two examples of sunk costs, and explain why they are irrelevant in decision making.

13–26. "Accounting systems should produce only relevant data and forget about the irrelevant data. Then I'd know what was relevant and what wasn't!" Comment on this remark by a company president.

13–27. Are the concepts underlying a relevant-cost analysis still valid in an advanced manufacturing environment? Are these concepts valid when activity-based costing is used? Explain.

13–28. List five ways in which management can seek to relax a constraint by expanding the capacity of a bottleneck operation.

Exercises

Choose an organization and a particular decision situation. Then give examples, using that decision context, of each step illustrated in Exhibit 13–1. For example, you might choose a decision that would be made by a retailer, such as Best Buy or Chapters. Or you might focus on a service provider, such as Hertz car rentals or Marriott Hotels. Alternatively, select a manufacturer, such as Nike or Nokia. Or consider a decision to be made by your college or home city.

■ **Exercise 13–29**
Steps in Decision-Making Process
(LO 1)

Redo Exhibit 13–4 without the irrelevant data.

■ **Exercise 13–30**
Irrelevant Future Costs and Benefits
(LO 3, 4)

Day Street Deli's owner is disturbed by the poor profit performance of his ice cream counter. He has prepared the following profit analysis for the year just ended:

■ **Exercise 13–31**
Drop Product Line
(LO 4, 5)

Sales		$67,500
Less: Cost of food		30,000
Gross profit		37,500
Less: Operating expenses:		
Wages of counter personnel	$18,000	
Paper products (e.g., napkins)	6,000	
Utilities (allocated)	4,350	
Depreciation of counter equipment and furnishings	3,750	
Depreciation of building (allocated)	6,000	
Deli manager's salary (allocated)	4,500	
Total		42,600
Loss on ice cream counter		$ (5,100)

Required: Evaluate the owner's analysis and restate as necessary.

Toon Town Toy Company is considering the elimination of its Packaging Department. Management has received an offer from an outside firm to supply all Toon Town's packaging needs. To help her in making the decision, Toon Town's president has asked the controller for an analysis of the cost of running Toon Town's Packaging Department. Included in that analysis is $11,100 of rent, which represents the Packaging Department's allocation of the rent on Toon Town's factory building. If the Packaging Department is eliminated, the space it used will be converted to storage space. Currently Toon Town rents storage space in a nearby warehouse for $13,000 per year. The warehouse rental would no longer be necessary if the Packaging Department were eliminated.

■ **Exercise 13–32**
Closing a Department
(LO 4, 5)

Required:

1. Discuss each of the figures given in the exercise with regard to its relevance in the department-closing decision.

2. What type of cost is the $13,000 warehouse rental, from the viewpoint of the costs of the Packaging Department?

■ **Exercise 13–33**
Continuation of Preceding
Exercise
(LO 4, 5)

If Toon Town Toy Company closes its Packaging Department, the department manager will be appointed manager of the Cutting Department with a similar salary. The Packaging Department manager makes $51,000 per year. To hire a new Cutting Department manager will cost Toon Town $66,000 per year.

Required: Discuss the relevance of each of these salary figures to the department-closing decision.

■ **Exercise 13–34**
Machine Replacement
(LO 4, 5)

College Town Pizza's owner bought his current pizza oven two years ago for $10,500, and it has one more year of life remaining. He is using straight-line depreciation for the oven. He could purchase a new oven for $2,200, but it would last only one year. The owner figures the new oven would save him $3,000 in annual operating expenses compared to operating the old one. Consequently, he has decided against buying the new oven, since doing so would result in a "loss" of $500 over the next year.

Required:

1. How do you suppose the owner came up with $500 as the loss for the next year if the new pizza oven were purchased? Explain.
2. Criticize the owner's analysis and decision.
3. Prepare a correct analysis of the owner's decision.

■ **Exercise 13–35**
Outsourcing Decision; Use of
Internet
(LO 1, 2, 5)

Visit the Web site of one of the following companies, or a different company of your choosing:

Tim Hortons	www.timhortons.com
Compaq	www.compaq.com
Corning	www.corning.com
Hudson's Bay Company	www.hbc.com
Kodak	www.kodak.com
CBC	www.cbc.ca

Required: Read about the company's activities and operations. Choose an activity that is necessary for the company's operations and then discuss the pros and cons of outsourcing that activity.

■ **Exercise 13–36**
Obsolete Inventory
(LO 4, 5)

Armstrong Corporation manufactures bicycle parts. The company currently has a $19,500 inventory of parts that have become obsolete due to changes in design specifications. The parts could be sold for $7,000, or modified for $10,000 and sold for $20,300.

Required:

1. Which of the data above are relevant to the decision about the obsolete parts?
2. Prepare an analysis of the decision.

■ **Exercise 13–37**
Joint Products
(LO 4, 6)

Thorpe Industries produces chemicals for the swimming pool industry. In one joint process, 10,000 litres of GSX are processed into 7,000 litres of xenolite and 3,000 litres of banolide. The cost of the joint process, including the GSX, is $17,500. The firm allocates $11,800 of the joint cost to the xenolite and $5,700 of the cost to the banolide. The 3,000 litres of banolide can be sold at the split-off point for $3,500, or be processed further into a product called kitrocide. The sales value of 3,000 litres of kitrocide is $11,000, and the additional processing cost is $7,900.

Required: Thorpe's president has asked your consulting firm to make a recommendation as to whether the banolide should be sold at the split-off point or processed further. Write a letter providing an analysis and a recommendation.

■ **Exercise 13–38**
Joint Products; Relevant
Costs; Cost-Volume-Profit
Analysis
(LO 4, 6)

Zytel Corporation produces cleaning compounds and solutions for industrial and household use. While most of its products are processed independently, a few are related. Grit 337, a coarse cleaning powder with many industrial uses, costs $3.20 a kilogram to make and sells for $4 a kilogram. A small portion of the annual production of this product is retained for further processing in the Mixing Department, where it is combined with several other ingredients to form a paste, which is marketed as a silver polish selling for $8 per jar. This further processing requires ¼ kilogram of Grit 337 per jar. Costs of other ingredients, labour, and variable overhead associated with this further processing amount to $5 per jar. Variable selling costs are $.60 per jar. If the decision were made to cease production of the silver polish, $11,200 of Mixing Department fixed costs could be avoided. Zytel has limited production capacity for Grit 337, but unlimited demand for the cleaning powder.

Required: Calculate the minimum number of jars of silver polish that would have to be sold to justify further processing of Grit 337.

Exercise 13–39
Special Order
(LO 4, 5)

Global Chemical Company, located in Buenos Aires, Argentina, recently received an order for a product it does not normally produce. Since the company has excess production capacity, management is considering accepting the order. In analyzing the decision, the assistant controller is compiling the relevant costs of producing the order. Production of the special order would require 8,000 kilograms of theolite. Intercontinental does not use theolite for its regular product, but the firm has 8,000 kilograms of the chemical on hand from the days when it used theolite regularly. The theolite could be sold to a chemical wholesaler for 21,750 p. The book value of the theolite is 3 p per kilogram. Global could buy theolite for 3.60 p per kilogram. (*p* denotes the peso, Argentina's national monetary unit. Many countries use the peso as their unit of currency. On the day this exercise was written, Argentina's peso was worth C$.3459.)

Required:

1. What is the relevant cost of theolite for the purpose of analyzing the special-order decision? (Remember to express your answer in terms of Argentina's peso.)
2. Discuss each of the numbers given in the exercise with regard to its relevance in making the decision.

Exercise 13–40
Continuation of Preceding Exercise
(LO 4, 5)

Global's special order also requires 1,000 kilograms of genatope, a solid chemical regularly used in the company's products. The current stock of genatope is 8,000 kilograms at a book value of 12.15 p per kilogram. If the special order is accepted, the firm will be forced to restock genatope earlier than expected, at a predicted cost of 13.05 p per kilogram. Without the special order, the purchasing manager predicts that the price will be 12.45 p when normal restocking takes place. Any order of genatope must be in the amount of 5,000 kilograms.

Required:

1. What is the relevant cost of genatope?
2. Discuss each of the figures in the exercise in terms of its relevance to the decision.

(CMA, adapted)

Exercise 13–41
Limited Resource
(LO 6)

Plato Corporation manufactures two products, Alpha and Beta. Contribution margin data follow.

	Alpha	Beta
Unit sales price	$39.00	$93.00
Less variable cost:		
Direct material	21.00	15.00
Direct labour	3.00	18.00
Variable overhead	3.75	22.50
Variable selling and administrative cost	2.25	1.50
Total variable cost	30.00	57.00
Unit contribution margin	$ 9.00	$36.00

Plato Corporation's production process uses highly skilled labour, which is in short supply. The same employees work on both products and earn the same wage rate.

Required: Which of Plato Corporation's products is most profitable? Explain.

■ **Exercise 13–42**
Linear Programming
(Appendix)
(LO 6, 8)

Refer to the data given in the preceding exercise for Plato Corporation. Assume that the direct-labour rate is $12 per hour, and 11,000 labour hours are available per year. In addition, the company has a short supply of machine time. Only 9,000 hours are available each year. Alpha requires one machine hour per unit, and Beta requires two machine hours per unit.

Required: Formulate the production planning problem as a linear program. Specifically identify (1) the decision variables, (2) the objective function, and (3) the constraints.

■ **Exercise 13–43**
Linear Programming;
Formulate and Solve
Graphically (Appendix)
(LO 8)

Southern Alberta Chemical Company manufactures two industrial chemical products, called zanide and kreolite. Two machines are used in the process, and each machine has 24 hours of capacity per day. The following data are available:

	Zanide	Kreolite
Selling price per drum	$108	$126
Variable cost per drum	$ 84	$ 84
Hours required per drum on machine I	2 hrs.	2 hrs.
Hours required per drum on machine II	1 hr.	3 hrs.

The company can produce and sell partially full drums of each chemical. For example, a half drum of zanide sells for $54.

Required:

1. Formulate the product-mix problem as a linear program.
2. Solve the problem graphically.
3. What is the value of the objective function at the optimal solution?

Problems

■ **Problem 13–44**
Closing an Unprofitable
Department
(LO 5, 6)

1. Contribution margin,
carpeting: $69,000

Contemporary Trends sells paint and paint supplies, carpet, and wallpaper at a single-store location in suburban Calgary. Although the company has been very profitable over the years, management has seen a significant decline in wallpaper sales and earnings. Much of this decline is attributable to the Internet and to companies that advertise deeply discounted prices in magazines and offer customers free shipping and toll-free telephone numbers. Recent figures follow.

	Paint and Supplies	Carpeting	Wallpaper
Sales	$190,000	$230,000	$70,000
Variable costs	114,000	161,000	56,000
Fixed costs	28,000	37,500	22,500
Total costs	142,000	198,500	78,500
Operating income (loss)	$ 48,000	$ 31,500	$ (8,500)

Management is studying whether to drop wallpaper because of the changing market and accompanying loss. If the line is dropped, the following changes are expected to occur:

• The vacated space will be remodelled at a cost of $6,200 and will be devoted to an expanded line of high-end carpet. Sales of carpet are expected to increase by $60,000, and the line's overall contribution margin ratio will rise by five percentage points.
• Contemporary Trends can cut wallpaper's fixed costs by 40 percent. Remaining fixed costs will continue to be incurred.
• Customers who purchased wallpaper often bought paint and paint supplies. Sales of paint and paint supplies are expected to fall by 20 percent.
• The firm will increase advertising expenditures by $12,500 to promote the expanded carpet line.

Required:

1. Should Contemporary Trends close its wallpaper operation? Show computations to support your answer.

2. Assume that Contemporary Trends' wallpaper inventory at the time of the closure decision amounted to $11,850. How would you have treated this additional information in making the decision?

3. What advantages might Internet- and magazine-based firms have over Contemporary Trends that would allow these organizations to offer deeply discounted prices—prices far below what Contemporary Trends can offer?

4. *Build a spreadsheet:* Construct an Excel spreadsheet to solve requirement (1) above. Show how the solution will change if the following information changes: sales were $200,000, $225,000, and $65,000, for paint and supplies, carpeting, and wallpaper, respectively.

■ Problem 13–45
Add a Product Line
(LO 4, 5)

1. Total incremental
contribution margin: $68,712

Montreal Fashions, Inc., a high-fashion dress manufacturer, is planning to market a new cocktail dress for the coming season. Montreal Fashions supplies retailers in Quebec and Ontario.

Four metres of material are required to lay out the dress pattern. Some material remains after cutting, which can be sold as remnants. The leftover material also could be used to manufacture a matching handbag and an accessory cape to be worn about the shoulders. However, if the leftover material is to be used for the cape and handbag, more care will be required in the cutting operation, which will increase the cutting costs.

The company expects to sell 1,250 dresses. Market research reveals that dress sales will be 20 percent higher if a matching cape and handbag are available. The market research indicates that the cape and handbag will be saleable only as accessories with the dress. The combination of dresses, capes, and handbags expected to be sold by retailers are as follows:

	Percent of Total
Complete sets of dress, accessory cape, and handbag..................	70%
Dress and accessory cape...	6
Dress and handbag..	15
Dress only	9
Total	100%

The material used in the dress costs $20 a metre, or $80 for each dress. The cost of cutting the dress if the cape and handbag are not manufactured is estimated at $32 a dress, and the resulting remnants can be sold for $8 per dress. If the cape and handbag are manufactured, the cutting costs will be increased by $14.40 per dress and there will be no saleable remnants. The selling prices and the costs to complete the three items once they are cut are as follows:

	Selling Price per Unit	Unit Cost to Complete (excludes costs of material and cutting operation)
Dress	$320.00	$128.00
Cape	44.00	31.20
Handbag	15.20	10.40

Required:

1. Calculate Montreal Fashions' incremental profit or loss from manufacturing the accessory capes and handbags in conjunction with the dresses.

2. Identify any qualitative factors that could influence the company's management in its decision to manufacture accessory capes and handbags to match the dresses.

(CMA, adapted)

Chef Gourmet, Inc. has assembled the following data pertaining to its two most popular products:

	Blender	Food Processor
Direct material	$18	$ 33
Direct labour	12	27
Manufacturing overhead @ $48 per machine hour	48	96
Cost if purchased from an outside supplier	60	114
Annual demand (units)	20,000	28,000

Past experience has shown that the fixed manufacturing overhead component included in the cost per machine hour averages $30. Kitchen Magician's management has a policy of filling all sales orders, even if it means purchasing units from outside suppliers.

Required:

1. If 50,000 machine hours are available, and management desires to follow an optimal strategy, how many units of each product should the firm manufacture? How many units of each product should be purchased?
2. With all other things constant, if management is able to reduce the direct material for a food processor to $18 per unit, how many units of each product should be manufactured? Purchased?
3. *Build a spreadsheet:* Construct an Excel spreadsheet to solve requirement (1) above. Show how the solution will change if the following information changes: the unit cost if purchased from an outside supplier is $66 for the blender and $120 for the food processor.

(CMA, adapted)

Dentech, Inc. uses 10 units of part RM67 every month in the production of dentistry equipment. The cost of manufacturing one unit of RM67 is the following:

Direct material	$ 3,000
Material handling (20% of direct-material cost)	600
Direct labour	24,000
Manufacturing overhead (150% of direct labour)	36,000
Total manufacturing cost	$63,600

Material handling represents the direct variable costs of the Receiving Department that are applied to direct materials and purchased components on the basis of their cost. This is a separate charge in addition to manufacturing overhead. Dentech's annual manufacturing overhead budget is one-third variable and two-thirds fixed. Scott Supply, one of Dentech's reliable vendors, has offered to supply part number RM67 at a unit price of $45,000.

Required:

1. If Dentech purchases the RM67 units from Scott, the capacity Dentech used to manufacture these parts would be idle. Should Dentech decide to purchase the parts from Scott, the unit cost of RM67 would increase (or decrease) by what amount?
2. Assume Dentech is able to rent out all its idle capacity for $75,000 per month. If Dentech decides to purchase the 10 units from Scott Supply, Dentech's monthly cost for RM67 would increase (or decrease) by what amount?
3. Assume that Dentech does not wish to commit to a rental agreement but could use its idle capacity to manufacture another product that would contribute $156,000 per month. If Dentech's management elects to manufacture RM67 in order to maintain quality control, what is the net amount of Dentech's cost from using the space to manufacture part RM67?

(CMA, adapted)

Casting Technology Resources (CTR) has purchased 10,000 pumps annually from Kobec, Inc. Because the price keeps increasing and reached $102 per unit last year, CTR's management has asked for an estimate of the cost of manufacturing the pump in CTR's facilities. CTR makes stampings and castings and has little experience with products requiring assembly.

The engineering, manufacturing, and accounting departments have prepared a report for management that includes the following estimate for an assembly run of 10,000 pumps. Additional production employees would be hired to manufacture the pumps but no additional equipment, space, or supervision would be needed.

The report states that total costs for 10,000 units are estimated at $1,435,500, or $143.55 per unit. The current purchase price is $102 per unit, so the report recommends continued purchase of the product.

Components (outside purchases)	$ 180,000
Assembly labour*	450,000
Manufacturing overhead†	675,000
General and administrative overhead‡	130,500
Total costs	$1,435,500

*Assembly labour consists of hourly production workers.

†Manufacturing overhead is applied to products on a direct-labour-dollar basis. Variable-overhead costs vary closely with direct-labour dollars.

Fixed overhead	50% of direct-labour dollars
Variable overhead	100% of direct-labour dollars
Manufacturing-overhead rate	150% of direct-labour dollars

‡General and administrative overhead is applied at 10 percent of the total cost of material (or components), assembly labour, and manufacturing overhead.

Required: Was the analysis prepared by Casting Technology Resources' engineering, manufacturing, and accounting departments and their recommendation to continue purchasing the pumps correct? Explain your answer and include any supporting calculations you consider necessary.

(CMA, adapted)

■ **Problem 13–49**
Introducing a New Product
(LO 4, 5)

1. Unit contribution margin,
Enhanced: $300
3. Income, Basic: $2,175,000

Johnson, Inc. is a small firm involved in the production and sale of electronic business products. The company is well known for its attention to quality and innovation.

During the past 15 months, a new product has been under development that allows users handheld access to e-mail and video images. Johnson code-named the product the Wireless Wizard and has been quietly designing two models: Basic and Enhanced. Development costs have amounted to $181,500 and $262,500, respectively. The total market demand for each model is expected to be 40,000 units, and management anticipates being able to obtain the following market shares: Basic, 25 percent; Enhanced, 20 percent. Forecasted data follow.

	Basic	Enhanced
Projected selling price	$375.00	$495.00
Per-unit production costs:		
Direct material	42.00	67.50
Direct labour	22.50	30.00
Variable overhead	36.00	48.00
Marketing and advertising	195,000	300,000
Sales salaries	85,500	85,500
Sales commissions*	10%	10%

*Computed on the basis of sales dollars.

Since the start of development work on the Wireless Wizard, advances in technology have altered the market somewhat, and management now believes that the company can introduce only one of the two models. Consultants confirmed this fact not too long ago, with Johnson paying $34,500 for an in-depth market study. The total fixed overhead is expected to be the same, regardless of which product is manufactured.

Required:

1. Compute the per-unit contribution margin for both models.
2. Which of the data in the table above should be ignored in making the product-introduction decision? For what reason?
3. Prepare a financial analysis and determine which of the two models should be introduced.
4. What other factors should Johnson, Inc. consider before a final decision is made?

■ **Problem 13–50**
Excess Production Capacity
(LO 5, 6)

1. Contribution margin,
Deluxe: $36 per unit

Carpenter's Mate, Inc. manufactures electric carpentry tools. The Production Department has met all production requirements for the current month and has an opportunity to produce additional units of product with its excess capacity. Unit selling prices and unit costs for three different drill models are as follows:

	Basic Model	Deluxe Model	Pro Model
Selling price	$116	$130	$160
Direct material	32	40	38
Direct labour ($10 per hour)	20	30	40
Variable overhead	16	24	32
Fixed overhead	32	10	30

Variable overhead is applied on the basis of direct-labour dollars, while fixed overhead is applied on the basis of machine hours. There is sufficient demand for the additional production of any model in the product line.

Required:

1. If the company has excess machine capacity and can add more labour as needed (i.e., neither machine capacity nor labour is a constraint), the excess production capacity should be devoted to producing which product? (Assume that the excess capacity will be used for a single product line.)
2. If the company has excess machine capacity but a limited amount of labour time, the excess production capacity should be devoted to producing which product or products?

(CMA, adapted)

■ **Problem 13–51**
Special Order; Financial and
Production Considerations
(LO 4, 5)

1. Total contribution margin:
$80,300
2. Planned machine hours:
15,000

Mercury Skateboard Company manufactures skateboards. Several weeks ago, the firm received a special-order inquiry from Venus, Inc. Venus desires to market a skateboard similar to one of Mercury's and has offered to purchase 11,000 units if the order can be completed in three months. The cost data for Mercury's Champion model skateboard follow.

Direct material	$16.40
Direct labour: .25 hr. @ $18	4.50
Total manufacturing overhead:	
.5 hr. @ $40	20.00
Total	$40.90

Additional data:

- The normal selling price of the Champion model is $53; however, Venus has offered Mercury only $31.50 because of the large quantity it is willing to purchase.
- Venus requires a modification of the design that will allow a $4.20 reduction in direct-material cost.
- Mercury's production supervisor notes that the company will incur $7,400 in additional setup costs and will have to purchase a $4,800 special device to manufacture these units. The device will be discarded once the special order is completed.
- Total manufacturing overhead costs are applied to production at the rate of $40 per machine hour. This figure is based, in part, on budgeted yearly fixed overhead of $1,500,000 and planned production activity of 60,000 machine hours (5,000 per month).
- Mercury will allocate $3,600 of existing fixed administrative costs to the order as "part of the cost of doing business."

Required:

1. Assume that present sales will not be affected. Should the order be accepted from a financial point of view (i.e., is it profitable)? Why? Show calculations.

2. Assume that Mercury's current production activity consumes 70 percent of planned machine-hour activity. Can the company accept the order and meet Venus' deadline?

3. What options might Mercury consider if management truly wanted to do business with Venus in hopes of building a long-term relationship with the firm?

Winner's Circle, Inc. manufactures medals for winners of athletic events and other contests. Its manufacturing plant has the capacity to produce 2,500 medals each month. Current monthly production is 1,875 medals. The company normally charges $525 per medal. Variable costs and fixed costs for the current activity level of 75 percent of capacity are as follows:

■ **Problem 13–52**
Special Order; Ethics
(LO 3, 5)

2. Total variable costs, combined production: $778,125

2. Average unit cost, combined production: $446.25

Production Costs (at 75% of capacity)

Variable costs:	
Manufacturing:	
Direct labour	$281,250
Direct material	196,875
Marketing	140,625
Total variable costs	618,750
Fixed costs:	
Manufacturing	206,250
Marketing	131,250
Total fixed costs	337,500
Total costs	$956,250
Variable cost per unit	$330
Fixed cost per unit	180
Average unit cost	$510

Winner's Circle has just received a special one-time order for 625 medals at $300 per medal. For this particular order, no variable marketing costs will be incurred. Samantha Peters, the assistant controller, has been assigned the task of analyzing this order and recommending whether the company should accept or reject it. After examining the costs, Peters suggested to her supervisor, Katie Maas, who is the controller, that they request competitive bids from vendors for the raw material as the current quote seems high. Maas insisted that the prices are in line with those of other vendors, and told her that she was not to discuss her observations with anyone else. Peters later discovered that Maas is the sister-in-law of the owner of the current raw-material supply vendor.

Required:

1. Identify and explain the costs that will be relevant to Peters' analysis of the special order being considered by Winner's Circle, Inc.

2. Determine if Winner's Circle should accept the special order. In explaining your answer, compute both the new average unit cost and the incremental unit cost for the special order.

3. Discuss any other considerations that Peters should include in her analysis of the special order.

4. What steps might Peters take to resolve the ethical conflict arising out of the controller's insistence that the company avoid competitive bidding?

5. *Build a spreadsheet:* Construct an Excel spreadsheet to solve requirements (1) and (2) above. Show how the solution will change if the sales price is $535 per medal.

(CMA, adapted)

■ **Problem 13–53**
Outsourcing Decision;
Relevant Costs; Ethics
(LO 3, 4, 5)

1a. Total cost to make JY-65:
$287,520

The Atlantic Division of the Paibec Corporation manufactures subassemblies that are used in the corporation's final products. Lynn Hardt of Atlantic's Profit Planning Department has been assigned the task of determining whether a component, JY-65, should continue to be manufactured by the Atlantic Division or purchased from Marley Company, an outside supplier. JY-65 is part of a subassembly manufactured by the Atlantic Division.

Marley has submitted a bid to manufacture and supply the 32,000 units of JY-65 that Paibec will need for 20x1 at a unit price of $8.65. Marley has assured Paibec that the units will be delivered according to Paibec's production specifications and needs. While the contract price of $8.65 is only applicable in 20x1, Marley is interested in entering into a long-term arrangement beyond 20x1.

Hardt has gathered the following information regarding Atlantic's cost to manufacture JY-65 in 20x0. These annual costs will be incurred to manufacture 30,000 units.

Direct material	$ 97,500
Direct labour	60,000
Factory space rental	42,000
Equipment leasing costs	18,000
Other manufacturing overhead	112,500
Total manufacturing costs	$330,000

Hardt has collected the following additional information related to manufacturing JY-65.

- Direct materials used in the production of JY-65 are expected to increase 8 percent in 20x1.
- Atlantic's direct-labour contract calls for a 5 percent increase in 20x1.
- The facilities used to manufacture JY-65 are rented under a month-to-month rental agreement. Thus, Atlantic can withdraw from the rental agreement without any penalty. Atlantic will have no need for this space if JY-65 is not manufactured.
- Equipment leasing costs represent special equipment that is used in the manufacture of JY-65. This lease can be terminated by paying the equivalent of one month's lease payment for each year left on the lease agreement. Atlantic has two years left on the lease agreement, through the end of the year 20x2.
- Forty percent of the other manufacturing overhead is considered variable. Variable overhead changes with the number of units produced, and this rate per unit is not expected to change in 20x1. The fixed manufacturing overhead costs are not expected to change regardless of whether JY–65 is manufactured. Equipment other than the leased equipment can be used in Atlantic's other manufacturing operations.

John Porter, divisional manager of Atlantic, stopped by Hardt's office to voice his concern regarding the outsourcing of JY-65. Porter commented, "I am really concerned about outsourcing JY-65. I have a son-in-law and a nephew, not to mention a member of our bowling team, who work on JY-65. They could lose their jobs if we buy that component from Marley. I really would appreciate anything you can do to make sure the cost analysis comes out right to show we should continue making JY-65. Corporate is not aware of the material increases and maybe you can leave out some of those fixed costs. I just think we should continue making JY-65!"

Required:

1. *a.* Prepare an analysis of relevant costs that shows whether or not the Atlantic Division of Paibec Corporation should make JY-65 or purchase it from Marley Company for 20x1.

    b. Based solely on the financial results, recommend whether the 32,000 units of JY-65 for 20x1 should be made by Atlantic or purchased from Marley.

2. Identify and briefly discuss three qualitative factors that the Atlantic Division and Paibec Corporation should consider before agreeing to purchase JY-65 from Marley Company.

3. By referring to the standards of ethical conduct for managerial accountants given in Chapter 1, explain why Lynn Hardt would consider the request of John Porter to be unethical.

(CMA, adapted)

Island Mechanical, Inc. has been producing two bearings, components T79 and B81, for use in production. Data regarding these two components follow.

	T79	B81
Machine hours required per unit	2.5	3.0
Standard cost per unit:		
Direct material	$ 6.75	$11.25
Direct labour	12.00	13.50
Manufacturing overhead		
Variable*	6.00	6.75
Fixed†	11.25	13.50
Total	$36.00	$45.00

*Variable manufacturing overhead is applied on the basis of direct-labour hours.
†Fixed manufacturing overhead is applied on the basis of machine hours.

Island Mechanical's annual requirement for these components is 8,000 units of T79 and 11,000 units of B81. Recently, management decided to devote additional machine time to other product lines, leaving only 41,000 machine hours per year for producing the bearings. An outside company has offered to sell Island Mechanical its annual supply of bearings at prices of $33.75 for T79 and $40.50 for B81. Management wants to schedule the otherwise idle 41,000 machine hours to produce bearings so that the firm can minimize costs (maximize net benefits).

Required:

1. Compute the net benefit (loss) per machine hour that would result if Island Mechanical accepts the supplier's offer of $40.50 per unit for component B81.

2. Choose the correct answer. Island Mechanical will maximize its net benefits by:

   a. Purchasing 4,800 units of T79 and manufacturing the remaining bearings

   b. Purchasing 8,000 units of T79 and manufacturing 11,000 units of B81

   c. Purchasing 11,000 units of B81 and manufacturing 8,000 units of T79

   d. Purchasing 4,000 units of B81 and manufacturing the remaining bearings

   e. Purchasing and manufacturing some amounts other than those given above

3. Suppose management has decided to drop product T79. Independently of requirements (1) and (2), assume that the company's idle capacity of 41,000 machine hours has a traceable, avoidable annual fixed cost of $132,000, which will be incurred only if the capacity is used. Calculate the maximum price Island Mechanical should pay a supplier for component B81.

(CMA, adapted)

Problem 13–54
Outsourcing Decision
(LO 4, 5)

1. Total variable cost per unit, B81: $31.50
2. Total variable cost per unit, T79: $24.75

Mainland Specialty Chemical Company (MSCC) is a diversified chemical processing company. The firm manufactures swimming pool chemicals, chemicals for metal processing, specialized chemical compounds, and pesticides.

Currently, the Noorwood plant is producing two derivatives, RNA-1 and RNA-2, from the chemical compound VDB developed by the company's research labs. Each week, 1,200,000 kilograms of VDB are processed at a cost of $393,600 into 800,000 kilograms of RNA-1 and 400,000 kilograms of RNA-2. The proportion of these two outputs cannot be altered, because this is a joint process. RNA-1 has no market value until it is converted into a pesticide with the trade name Fastkil. Processing RNA-1 into Fastkil costs $384,000. Fastkil wholesales at $80 per 100 kilograms.

RNA-2 is sold as is for $128 per hundred kilograms. However, management has discovered that RNA-2 can be converted into two new products by adding 400,000 kilograms of compound LST to the 400,000 kilograms of RNA-2. This joint process would yield 400,000 kilograms each of DMZ-3 and Pestrol, the two new products. The additional direct-material and related processing costs of this joint process would be $192,000. DMZ-3 and Pestrol would each be sold for $92 per 100 kilograms. The company's management has decided not to process RNA-2 further based on the analysis presented in the following schedule.

Problem 13–55
Joint Products; Sell or Process Further
(LO 6)

Total revenue from further processing: $736,000

	Sold as Is	Process Further		
	RNA–2	DMZ–3	Pestrol	Total
Production in kilograms	400,000	400,000	400,000	
Revenue	$512,000	$368,000	$368,000	$736,000
Costs:				
VDB costs	131,200*	98,400	98,400	196,800†
Additional direct materials (LST) and processing of RNA-2	—	96,000	96,000	192,000
Total costs	131,200	194,400	194,400	388,800
Weekly gross profit	$380,800	$173,600	$173,600	$347,200

*$313,200 is one-third of the $393,600 cost of processing VDB. When RNA-2 is not processed further, one-third of the final output is RNA-2 (400,000 out of a total of 1,200,000 kilograms).

†$196,800 is one-half of the $393,600 cost of processing VDB. When RNA-2 is processed further, one-half of the final output consists of DMZ-3 and Pestrol. The final products then are: 800,000 kilograms of RNA-1; 400,000 kilograms of DMZ-3; and 400,000 kilograms of Pestrol.

Required: Evaluate Mainland Chemical Company's analysis, and make any revisions that are necessary. Your critique and analysis should indicate:

a.   Whether management made the correct decision

b.   The gross savings or loss per week resulting from the decision not to process RNA-2 further, if different from management's analysis

(CMA, adapted)

■ **Problem 13–56**
Conventional versus Activity-Based-Costing Analyses; Relevant Costs
(LO 5, 7)

2. Costs to be avoided by purchasing, material handling: $48,000

In addition to fine chocolate, International Chocolate Company also produces chocolate-covered pretzels in its plant. This product is sold in five-kilogram metal canisters, which also are manufactured at the facility. The plant manager, Marsha Mello, was recently approached by Catawba Canister Company with an offer to supply the canisters at a price of $.95 each. International Chocolate's traditional product-costing system assigns the following costs to canister production:

Direct material	$ 288,000
Direct labour (12,000 hrs. @ $16 per hr.)	192,000
Variable overhead ($10 per direct-labour hr.)	120,000
Fixed overhead ($45 per direct-labour hr.)	540,000
Total cost	$1,140,000

Unit costs: $1,140,000 ÷ 760,000 canisters = $1.50 per canister

Mello's conventional make-or-buy analysis indicated that Catawba's offer should be rejected, since only $708,000 of costs would be avoided (including $80,000 of supervisory salaries and $28,000 of machinery depreciation). In contrast, the firm would spend $722,000 buying the canisters. The controller, Dave Mint, came to the rescue with an activity-based costing analysis of the decision. Mint concluded that the cost driver levels associated with canister production are as follows:

10 product specs	30 inspections
2,000 supervisory hours	15 setups
6,000 material-handling hours	70,000 machine hours
55 purchase orders	

Additional conventional and ABC data from the plant are given in Exhibits 13–19 and 13–20.

Required:

1. Show how Mello arrived at the $708,000 of cost savings in her conventional make-or-buy analysis.
2. Determine the costs that will be saved by purchasing canisters, using Mint's ABC data.
3. Complete the ABC relevant-costing analysis of the make-or-buy decision. Should the firm buy from Catawba?
4. If the conventional and ABC analyses yield different conclusions, briefly explain why.

Excalibur, Inc. received an order for a piece of special machinery from Rex Company. Just as Excalibur completed the machine, Rex Company declared bankruptcy, defaulted on the order, and forfeited the 10 percent deposit paid on the selling price of $217,500.

Excalibur's manufacturing manager identified the costs already incurred in the production of the special machinery for Rex Company as follows:

Direct material		$ 49,800
Direct labour...		64,200
Manufacturing overhead applied:		
Variable	$32,100	
Fixed	16,050	48,150
Fixed selling and administrative costs...		16,215
Total		$178,365

■ **Problem 13–57**
Analysis of Special Order
(LO 4, 5)

1. Net contribution, if sell to Kaytell as special order: $161,544
2. Contribution with reduced price to Kaytell: $156,600

eXcel

Another company, Kaytell Corporation, will buy the special machinery if it is reworked to Kaytell's specifications. Excalibur, Inc. offered to sell the reworked machinery to Kaytell as a special order for $205,200. Kaytell agreed to pay the price when it takes delivery in two months. The additional identifiable costs to rework the machinery to Kaytell's specifications are as follows:

Direct materials	$18,600
Direct labour	12,600
Total	$31,200

A second alternative available to Excalibur's management is to convert the special machinery to the standard model, which sells for $187,500. The additional identifiable costs for this conversion are as follows:

Direct materials	$ 8,550
Direct labour	9,900
Total	$18,450

A third alternative for Excalibur, Inc. is to sell the machine as is for a price of $156,000. However, the potential buyer of the unmodified machine does not want it for 60 days. This buyer has offered a $21,000 down payment, with the remainder due upon delivery.

The following additional information is available regarding Excalibur's operations:

- The sales commission rate on sales of standard models is 2 percent, while the rate on special orders is 3 percent.
- Normal credit terms for sales of standard models are 2/10, net/30. This means that a customer receives a 2 percent discount if payment is made within 10 days, and payment is due no later than 30 days after billing. Most customers take the 2 percent discount. Credit terms for a special order are negotiated with the customer.
- The allocation rates for manufacturing overhead and fixed selling and administrative costs are as follows:

Manufacturing costs:	
Variable	50% of direct-labour cost
Fixed	25% of direct-labour cost
Fixed selling and administrative costs	10% of the total of direct-material, direct-labour, and manufacturing-overhead costs

- Normal time required for rework is one month.

Required:

1. Determine the dollar contribution each of the three alternatives will add to Excalibur's before-tax profit.
2. If Kaytell makes Excalibur a counteroffer, what is the lowest price Exacalibur should accept for the reworked machinery from Kaytell? Explain your answer.
3. Discuss the influence fixed manufacturing-overhead cost should have on the sales price quoted by Excalibur, Inc. for special orders.

(CMA, adapted)

■ **Problem 13–58**
Production Planning
(LO 5, 6)

1. Direct labour requirements,
Department 1, M50: 1,000
2. Contribution margin, T79:
$200 per unit

Oceana Corporation manufactures and sells three products, which are manufactured in a factory with four departments. Both labour and machine time are applied to the products as they pass through each department. The machines and labour skills required in each department are so specialized that neither machines nor labour can be switched from one department to another.

Inventory levels are satisfactory and need not be increased or decreased during the next six months. Unit price and cost data that will be valid for the next six months are as follows:

	Product		
	M50	**T79**	**B81**
Unit costs:			
Direct material	$ 28	$ 52	$ 68
Direct labour:			
Department 1	48	24	48
Department 2	84	56	56
Department 3	96	—	64
Department 4	36	72	36
Variable overhead	108	80	100
Fixed overhead	60	40	128
Variable selling expenses	12	8	16
Unit selling price	784	492	668

Oceana Corporation' management is planning its production schedule for the next few months. The planning is complicated, because there are labour shortages in the community and some machines will be down several months for repairs.

The sales department believes that the monthly demand for the next six months will be as follows:

Product	Monthly Unit Sales
M50	500
T79	400
B81	1,000

Management has assembled the following information regarding available machine and labour time by department and the machine hours and direct-labour hours required per unit of product. These data should be valid for the next six months.

	Department			
Monthly Capacity Availability	**1**	**2**	**3**	**4**
Normal machine capacity in machine hours	3,500	3,500	3,000	3,500
Capacity of machines being repaired in machine hours	(500)	(400)	(300)	(200)
Available machine capacity in machine hours	3,000	3,100	2,700	3,300
Available labour in direct-labour hours	3,700	4,500	2,750	2,600

Labour and Machine Specifications per Unit of Product

Product	Labour and Machine Time				
M50	Direct-labour hours	2	3	3	1
	Machine hours	1	1	2	2
T79	Direct-labour hours	1	2	—	2
	Machine hours	1	1	—	2
B81	Direct-labour hours	2	2	2	1
	Machine hours	2	2	1	1

Required:

1. Calculate the monthly requirement for machine hours and direct-labour hours for the production of products M50, T79, and B81 to determine whether the monthly sales demand for the three products can be met by the factory.

2. What monthly production schedule should Oceana Corporation select in order to maximize its dollar profits? Explain how you selected this production schedule, and present a schedule of the contribution to profit that would be generated by your production schedule.

3. Identify the alternatives Oceana Corporation might consider so it can supply its customers with all the product they demand.

(CMA, adapted)

Problem 13–59
Linear Programming
(Appendix)
(LO 8)

1. Objective function:
Maximize 60P + 45H
3. Contribution margin at optimal solution: $2,250

Time Saver Meals, Inc. offers monthly service plans providing prepared meals that are delivered to the customers' homes. The target market for these meal plans includes double-income families with no children and retired couples in upper income brackets. The firm offers two monthly plans: Premier Cuisine and Haute Cuisine. The Premier Cuisine plan provides frozen meals that are delivered twice each month; this plan generates a contribution margin of $60 for each monthly plan sold. The Haute Cuisine plan provides freshly prepared meals delivered on a daily basis and generates a contribution margin of $45 for each monthly plan sold. The company's reputation provides a market that will purchase all the meals that can be prepared. All meals go through food preparation and cooking steps in the company's kitchens. After these steps, the Premier Cuisine meals are flash-frozen. The time requirements per monthly meal plan and hours available per month are as follows:

	Preparation	Cooking	Freezing
Hours required:			
Premier Cuisine	2	2	1
Haute Cuisine	1	3	0
Hours available	60	120	45

For planning purposes, management uses linear programming to determine the most profitable number of Premier Cuisine and Haute Cuisine monthly meal plans to produce.

Required:

1. Using the notation P for Premier Cuisine and H for Haute Cuisine, state the objective function and the constraints that management should use to maximize the total contribution margin generated by the monthly meal plans.

2. Graph the constraints on the meal preparation process. Be sure to clearly label the graph.

3. Using the graph prepared in requirement (2), determine the optimal solution to the company's production planning problem in terms of the number of each type of meal plan to produce.

4. Calculate the value of the objective function at the optimal solution.

5. If the constraint on preparation time could be eliminated, determine the revised optimal solution.

(CMA, adapted)

Problem 13–60
Linear Programming;
Formulate and Solve
Graphically (Appendix)
(LO 8)

3. Total contribution margin:
$110,000

Galaxy Candy Company manufactures two popular candy bars, the Eclipse bar and the Nova bar. Both candy bars go through a mixing operation where the various ingredients are combined, and the Coating Department where the bars from the Mixing Department are coated with chocolate. The Eclipse bar is coated with both white and dark chocolate to produce a swirled effect. A material shortage of an ingredient in the Nova bar limits production to 300 batches per day. Production and sales data are presented in the following table. Both candy bars are produced in batches of 200 bars.

		Use of Capacity in Hours per Batch of Product	
Department	Available Daily Capacity in Hours	Eclipse	Nova
Mixing	525	1.5	1.5
Coating	500	2.0	1.0

Management believes that Galaxy Candy can sell all of its daily production of both the Eclipse and Nova bars. Other data follow.

	Eclipse	Nova
Selling price per batch	$ 600	$ 700
Variable cost per batch	200	450
Monthly fixed costs (allocated evenly between both products)	750,000	750,000

Required:

1. Formulate the objective function and all of the constraints in order to maximize contribution margin. Be sure to define the variables.

2. How many batches of each type of candy bar (Eclipse and Nova) should be produced to maximize the total contribution margin?

3. Calculate the contribution margin at the optimal solution.

(CMA, adapted)

■ **Problem 13–61**
Linear Programming;
Formulate and Discuss
(Appendix)
(LO 8)

2. Contribution margin,
Regular model in Labour
Assembly: $20.60 per unit

CoffeeTime, Inc. manufactures two types of electric coffeemakers, Regular and Deluxe. The major difference between the two appliances is capacity. Both are considered top-quality units and sell for premium prices. Both coffeemakers pass through two manufacturing departments: Plating and Assembly. The company has two assembly operations, one automated and one manual. The Automated Assembly Department has been in operation for one year and was intended to replace the Labour Assembly Department. However, business has expanded rapidly in recent months, and both assembly operations are still being used. Workers have been trained for both operations and can be used in either department. The only difference between the two departments is the proportion of machine time versus direct labour used. Data regarding the two coffeemakers are presented in the following schedule:

Machine Hour Data

	Plating	Labour Assembly	Automated Assembly
Machine hours required per unit	.15	.02	.05
Machine hours available per month	25,000	1,500	5,000
Annual machine hours available	300,000	18,000	60,000

Unit Variable Manufacturing Costs

	Plating Department		Labour Assembly	Automated Assembly
	Regular	Deluxe		
Raw material:				
Casing	$15.50	$29.00	—	—
Heating element	12.00	12.00	—	—
Other	16.50	16.50	—	—
Direct labour:				
@ $20 per hr.	4.00	4.00	—	—
@ $24 per hr.	—	—	$6.00	$1.20
Manufacturing overhead:				
Supplies	2.50	2.50	3.00	3.00
Power	2.40	2.40	1.50	3.60

Sales Data

	Regular	Deluxe
Selling price per unit	$ 90.00	$ 120.00
Variable selling cost per unit	6.00	6.00
Annual allocated fixed overhead	1,800,000	1,800,000

CoffeeTime produced and sold 600,000 Deluxe coffeemakers and 900,000 Regular coffeemakers last year. Management estimates that total unit sales could increase by 20 percent or more if the units can be produced. CoffeeTime already has contracts to produce and sell 35,000 units of each model each month. CoffeeTime has a monthly maximum labour capacity of 30,000 direct-labour hours in the Plating Department and 40,000 direct-labour hours for the assembly operation (Automated Assembly and Labour Assembly, combined). Sales, production, and costs occur uniformly throughout the year.

Required:

1. CoffeeTime's management believes that linear programming could be used to determine the optimum mix of Regular and Deluxe coffeemakers to produce and sell. Explain why linear programming is appropriate to use in this situation.
2. Management has decided to use linear programming to determine the optimal product mix. Formulate and label the following:
   a. Objective function
   b. Constraints
   Be sure to define your variables.

(CMA, adapted)

Cases

Ontario Pump Company, a small manufacturing company in Toronto, manufactures three types of pumps used in a variety of machinery. For many years the company has been profitable and has operated at capacity. However, in the last two years, prices on all gauges were reduced and selling expenses increased to meet competition and keep the plant operating at capacity. Second-quarter results for the current year, which follow, typify recent experience.

■ **Case 13–62**
Drop a Product Line
(LO 4, 5)

2a. Unit contribution margin, F-Pump: $57
2c. Contribution per direct-labour dollar, R-Pump: $1.85

ONTARIO PUMP COMPANY
Income Statement
Second Quarter
(in thousands)

	R-Pump	F-Pump	S-Pump	Total
Sales	$4,800	$2,700	$2,700	$10,200
Cost of goods sold	3,144	2,310	2,850	8,304
Gross margin	$1,656	$ 390	$ (150)	$ 1,896
Selling and administrative expenses	1,110	555	405	2,070
Income before taxes	$ 546	$ (165)	$ (555)	$ (174)

Maria Carlo, the company's president, is concerned about the results of the pricing, selling, and production prices. After reviewing the second-quarter results, she asked her management staff to consider the following three suggestions:

- Discontinue the S-Pump line immediately. S-Pumps would not be returned to the product line unless the problems with the gauge can be identified and resolved.
- Increase quarterly sales promotion by $300,000 on the R-Pump product line in order to increase sales volume by 15 percent.
- Cut production on the F-Pump line by 50 percent, and cut the traceable advertising and promotion for this line to $60,000 each quarter.

Justin Sperry, the controller, suggested a more careful study of the financial relationships to determine the possible effects on the company's operating results of the president's proposed course of action. The president agreed and assigned JoAnn Brower, the assistant controller, to prepare an analysis. Brower has gathered the following information:

- The unit sales prices for the three products are:

  R-Pump $600
  F-Pump 270
  S-Pump 540

- The company is manufacturing at capacity and is selling all the gauges it produces.
- All three gauges are manufactured with common equipment and facilities.
- The selling and administrative expense is allocated to the three gauge lines based on average sales volume over the past three years.
- Special selling expenses (primarily advertising, promotion, and shipping) are incurred for each gauge as follows:

	Quarterly Advertising and Promotion	Shipping Expenses
R-Pump	$630,000	$30 per unit
F-Pump	300,000	12 per unit
S-Pump	120,000	30 per unit

- The unit manufacturing costs for the three products are as follows:

	R-Pump	F-Pump	S-Pump
Direct material	$ 93	$ 51	$150
Direct labour	120	60	180
Variable manufacturing overhead	135	90	180
Fixed manufacturing overhead	45	30	60
Total	$393	$231	$570

Required:

1. JoAnn Brower says that Ontario Pump Company's product-line income statement for the second quarter is not suitable for analyzing proposals and making decisions such as the ones suggested by Maria Carlo. Write a memo to Ontario Pump's president that addresses the following points:

   a. Explain why the product-line income statement as presented is not suitable for analysis and decision making.

   b. Describe an alternative income-statement format that would be more suitable for analysis and decision making, and explain why it is better.

2. Use the operating data presented for Ontario Pump Company and assume that the president's proposed course of action had been implemented at the beginning of the second quarter. Then evaluate the president's proposal by specifically responding to the following points:

   a. Are each of the three suggestions cost-effective? Support your discussion with an analysis that shows the net impact on income before taxes for each of the three suggestions.

   b. Was the president correct in proposing that the S-Pump line be eliminated? Explain your answer.

   c. Was the president correct in promoting the R-Pump line rather than the F-Pump line? Explain your answer.

   d. Does the proposed course of action make effective use of the company's capacity? Explain your answer.

3. Are there any qualitative factors that Ontario Pump Company's management should consider before it drops the S-Pump line? Explain your answer.

(CMA, adapted)

All Sports Company's production manager, Chris Adler, had requested to have lunch with the company president. Adler wanted to put forward his suggestion to add a new product line. As they finished lunch, Meg Thomas, the company president, said, "I'll give your proposal some serious thought, Chris. I think you're right about the increasing demand for skateboards. What I'm not sure about is whether the skateboard line will be better for us than our tackle boxes. Those have been our bread and butter the past few years."

Adler responded with, "Let me get together with one of the controller's people. We'll run a few numbers on this skateboard idea that I think will demonstrate the line's potential."

All Sports is a wholesale distributor supplying a wide range of moderately priced sports equipment to large chain stores. About 60 percent of All Sports' products are purchased from other companies while the remainder of the products are manufactured by All Sports. The company has a Plastics Department that is currently manufacturing moulded fishing tackle boxes. All Sports is able to manufacture and sell 8,000 tackle boxes annually, making full use of its direct-labour capacity at available work stations. The selling price and costs associated with All Sports' tackle boxes are as follows:

Selling price per box		$91.00
Costs per box:		
Moulded plastic	$13.00	
Hinges, latches, handle	9.00	
Direct labour ($15 per hr.)	18.75	
Manufacturing overhead	12.50	
Selling and administrative cost	17.00	70.25
Profit per box		$20.75

Because All Sports' sales manager believes the firm could sell 12,000 tackle boxes if it had sufficient manufacturing capacity, the company has looked into the possibility of purchasing the tackle boxes for distribution. Maple Products, a steady supplier of quality products, would be able to provide up to 9,000 tackle boxes per year at a price of $73 per box delivered to All Sports' facility.

All Sports' production manager, has come to the conclusion that the company could make better use of its Plastics Department by manufacturing skateboards. Vonderweidt has a market study that indicates an expanding market for skateboards and a need for additional suppliers. Adler believes that All Sports could expect to sell 17,500 skateboards annually at a price of $50 per skateboard.

After his lunch with the company president, Adler worked out the following estimates with the assistant controller.

Selling price per skateboard		$50.00
Costs per skateboard:		
Moulded plastic	$10.50	
Wheels, hardware	7.00	
Direct labour ($15 per hr.)	7.50	
Manufacturing overhead	5.00	
Selling and administrative cost	9.00	39.00
Profit per skateboard		$11.00

In the Plastics Department, All Sports uses direct-labour hours as the application base for manufacturing overhead. Included in the manufacturing overhead for the current year is $50,000 of factorywide, fixed manufacturing overhead that has been allocated to the Plastics Department. For each unit of product that All Sports sells, regardless of whether the product has been purchased or is manufactured by All Sports, there is an allocated $6 fixed overhead cost per unit for distribution that is included in the selling and administrative cost for all products. Total selling and administrative costs for the purchased tackle boxes would be $10 per unit.

■ **Case 13–63**
Adding a Product Line
(LO 4, 5)

1. Unit contribution margin, purchased tackle boxes: $14
2. Contribution from manufacturing 8,000 boxes: $264,000

Required: In order to maximize the company's profitability, prepare an analysis that will show which product or products All Sports Corporation should manufacture or purchase.

1. First determine which of All Sports' options makes the best use of its scarce resources. How many skateboards and tackle boxes should be manufactured? How many tackle boxes should be purchased?

2. Calculate the improvement in All Sports' total contribution margin if it adopts the optimal strategy rather than continuing with the status quo.

(CMA, adapted)

Chapter Fourteen

Target Costing and Cost Analysis for Pricing Decisions

FOCUS COMPANY

The Focus Company for this chapter is Sydney Sailing Supplies, a manufacturer of sailing supplies and equipment in Sydney, Australia. One of the company's most popular products is the Wave Darter, a two-person sailboat. In this chapter, we will explore a variety of issues surrounding how Sydney Sailing Supplies' management could set a price for the Wave Darter. We also will study a pricing method called *target costing*. Under this approach, management determines what consumers are willing to pay for a particular product. Then management has to find a way to produce that product at a low enough cost to justify the price the consumers are willing to pay.

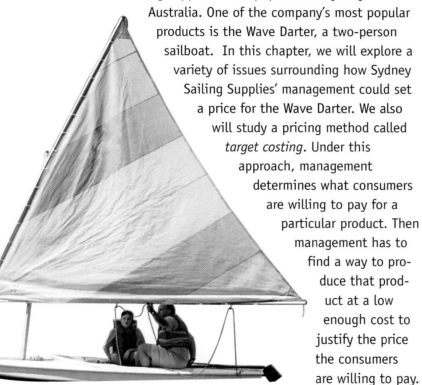

After completing this chapter, you should be able to:

1   List and describe the four major factors of pricing decisions.

2   Explain and use the economic, profit-maximizing pricing model.

3   Set prices using cost-plus pricing formulas.

4   List and discuss the key principles of target costing.

5   Explain the role of activity-based costing in setting a target cost.

6   Explain the process of value engineering and its role in target costing.

7   Determine prices using the time and material pricing approach.

8   Set prices in competitive-bidding situations.

9   Describe the legal restrictions on setting prices.

IN CONTRAST

In contrast to the product-pricing setting explored in the first part of the chapter, we turn our attention to competitive bidding on projects, services, or products. In a competitive-bidding situation, two or more companies submit sealed bids for a job, and the buyer selects from among the bids. We will explore competitive bidding in the context of Sydney Sailing Supplies' Marine Services Division. The company's Marine Services Division specializes in marina maintenance and construction, and its management is preparing a bid to build a new marina in Sydney Harbour.

Setting the price for an organization's product or service is one of the most important decisions a manager faces. It is also one of the most difficult, due to the number and variety of factors that must be considered. The pricing decision arises in virtually all types of organizations. Manufacturers set prices for the products they manufacture; merchandising companies set prices for their goods; service firms set prices for such services as insurance policies, train tickets, theme park admissions, and bank loans. Nonprofit organizations often set prices also. For example, governmental units price vehicle registrations, park-use fees, and utility services. The optimal approach to pricing often depends on the situation. Pricing a mature product or service that a firm has sold for a long time may be quite different from pricing a new product or service. Public utilities and telephone companies face political considerations in pricing their products and services, since their prices often must be approved by a governmental commission.

In this chapter, we will study pricing decisions, with an emphasis on the role of managerial accounting information. The setting for our discussion is Sydney Sailing Supplies, a manufacturer of sailing supplies and equipment located in Sydney, Australia.

Major Influences on Pricing Decisions

Learning Objective 1

List and describe the four major factors of pricing decisions.

Four major factors influence the prices set by Sydney Sailing Supplies:

1. Customer demand
2. Actions of competitors
3. Costs
4. Political, legal, and image-related issues

Customer Demand

The demands of customers are of paramount importance in all phases of business operations, from the design of a product to the setting of its price. Product-design issues and pricing considerations are interrelated, so they must be examined simultaneously. For example, if customers want a high-quality sailboat, this will entail greater production time and more expensive raw materials. The result almost certainly will be a higher price. On the other hand, management must be careful not to price its product out of the market. Discerning customer demand is a critically important and continuous process. Companies routinely obtain information from market research, such as customer surveys and test-marketing campaigns, and through feedback from sales personnel. To be successful, Sydney Sailing Supplies must provide the products its customers want at a price they perceive to be appropriate.

Actions of Competitors

Although Sydney Sailing Supplies' managers would like the company to have the sailing market to itself, they are not so fortunate. Domestic and foreign competitors are striving to sell their products to the same customers. Thus, as Sydney Sailing Supplies' management designs products and sets prices, it must keep a watchful eye on the firm's competitors. If a competitor reduces its price on sailboats of a particular type, Sydney Sailing Supplies may have to follow suit to avoid losing its market share. Yet the company cannot follow its competitors blindly either. Predicting competitive reactions to its product-design and pricing strategy is a difficult but important task for Sydney Sailing Supplies' management.

In considering the reactions of customers and competitors, management must be careful to properly define its product. Should Sydney Sailing Supplies' management define its product narrowly as sailing supplies, or more broadly as boating supplies? For example, if the company raises the price of its two-person sailboat, will this encourage potential customers to switch to canoes, rowboats, and small motorboats? Or will most potential sailboat customers react to a price increase only by price-shopping among competing sailboat manufacturers? The way in which Sydney Sailing Supplies' management answers these questions can profoundly affect its marketing and pricing strategies.

Costs

The role of costs in price setting varies widely among industries. In some industries, prices are determined almost entirely by market forces. An example is the agricultural industry, where grain and meat prices are market-driven. Farmers must meet the market price. To make a profit, they must produce at a cost below the market price. This is not always possible, so some periods of loss inevitably result. In other industries, managers set prices at least partially on the basis of production costs. For example, cost-based pricing is used in the aircraft, household appliance, and gasoline industries. Prices are set by adding a markup to production costs. Managers have some latitude in determining the markup, so market forces influence prices as well. In public utilities, such as electricity and natural gas companies, prices generally are set by a regulatory agency. Production costs are of prime importance in justifying utility rates. Typically, a public utility will make a request to a Provincial Utility Commission or Board for a rate increase on the basis of its current and projected production costs.

Balance of Market Forces and Cost-Based Pricing In most industries, both market forces and cost considerations heavily influence prices. No organization or industry can price its products below their production costs (i.e., the floor price) indefinitely. And no company's management can set prices blindly at cost plus a markup without keeping an eye on the market (i.e., the ceiling price). In most cases, pricing can be viewed in either of the following ways.

How Are Prices Set?

Prices are determined by the market, subject to the constraint that costs must be covered in the long run.

Prices are based on costs, subject to the constraint that the reactions of customers and competitors must be heeded.

In our illustration of Sydney Sailing Supplies' pricing policies, we will assume the company responds to both market forces and costs.

Political, Legal, and Image-Related Issues

Beyond the important effects on prices of market forces and costs are a range of environmental considerations. In the *legal* area, managers must adhere to certain laws. The law generally prohibits companies from discriminating among their customers in setting prices. Also prohibited is collusion in price setting, where the major firms in an industry all agree to set their prices at high levels. The *Competition Act* (Canada) is a federal law which is intended to, among other things, "maintain and

> "You're looked to for business expertise. You're looked to also [for] business perspective, pricing strategies, manufacturing strategies, to see if they make sense financially." (14a)
>
> **Caterpillar**

encourage competition in Canada" and "provide consumers with competitive prices and product choices."

Political considerations also can be relevant. For example, if the firms in an industry are *perceived* by the public as reaping unfairly large profits, there may be political pressure on legislators to tax those profits differentially or to intervene in some way to regulate prices.

Companies also consider their *public image* in the price-setting process. A firm with a reputation for very-high-quality products may set the price of a new product high to be consistent with its image. As we have all discovered, the same brand-name product may be available in a discount store at half the price charged in a more exclusive store.

Setting prices requires a balance between cost considerations and market forces. A good example is provided by the airlines, which keep a close eye on the fares of their competitors, while striving to cover operating costs. Large airlines, such as Air Canada, are increasingly finding it necessary to cut fares to compete with discounters such as WestJet.

Economic Profit-Maximizing Pricing

Learning Objective 2

Explain and use the economic, profit-maximizing pricing model.

Companies are sometimes **price takers**, which means their products' prices are determined totally by the market. Some agricultural commodities and precious metals are examples of such products. In most cases, however, firms have some flexibility in setting prices. Generally speaking, as the price of a product or service is increased, the quantity demanded declines, and vice versa.

Price, Quantity, and Total Revenue

The trade-off between a higher price and a higher sales quantity is shown in Exhibit 14–1. Sydney Sailing Supplies' total revenue for its two-person sailboat, the Wave Darter, increases with larger quantity of units sold, but the rate of increase in revenue declines as monthly sales quantity increases, the reason being that more goods can only be sold at lower prices. To see this, notice that the increase in total revenue when the sales quantity increases from 10 to 20 units is greater than the increase in total revenue when the sales quantity increases from 20 units to 30 units.

A good understanding of the relationships shown in Exhibit 14–1 will lead to better decisions. Before we can fully use the revenue data, however, we must examine the cost side of Sydney Sailing Supplies' business.

Quantity Sold per Month	Unit Sales Price	Total Revenue per Month		Changes in Total Revenue
10	$1,000	$10,000		
				$9,500
20	975	19,500		
				9,000
30	950	28,500		
				8,500
40	925	37,000		
				8,000
50	900	45,000		
				7,500
60	875	52,500		

Exhibit 14–1

Price, Quantity, and Total Revenue

Total Cost and Quantity

Understanding cost behaviour is important in many business decisions, and pricing is no exception. How does total cost behave as the number of Wave Darters produced and sold by Sydney Sailing Supplies changes? Exhibit 14–2 displays the firm's total cost and quantity data.[1] Total cost increases with larger quantities sold, but the rate of increase in cost declines as quantity increases, because of economies achieved by production in larger quantities. To verify this, notice that the increase in total costs when quantity increases from 10 to 20 units is greater than the increase in total costs when quantity increases from 20 units to 30 units.

Quantity Produced and Sold per Month	Average Cost per Unit	Total Cost per Month		Changes in Total Cost
10	$1,920	$19,200		
				$ 5,600
20	1,240	24,800		
				4,300
30	970	29,100		
				2,900
40	800	32,000		
				9,000
50	820	41,000		
				15,400
60	940	56,400		

Exhibit 14–2

Total Cost and Quantity

The rate of increase in total costs increases as quantity increases from 40 units upward, because of diseconomies that set in when the organization approaches the limits of its capacity, meaning that additional output gets harder and harder to achieve. To verify this, notice that the increase in total costs as quantity increases from 40 units to 50 units is less than the increase in total costs as quantity increases from 50 units to 60 units.

Profit-Maximizing Price and Quantity

Now we can determine the profit-maximizing price and quantity. In Exhibit 14–3, we combine the revenue and cost data presented in Exhibits 14–1 and 14–2. Notice that

	Quantity Produced and Sold per Month	Unit Sales Price	Total Revenue per Month	Total Cost per Month	Profit (Loss) per Month
	10	$1,000	$10,000	$19,200	$(9,200)
	20	975	19,500	24,800	(5,300)
Profit-	30	950	28,500	29,100	(600)
maximizing	40	925	37,000	32,000	5,000
quantity and price	50	900	45,000	41,000	4,000
	60	875	52,500	56,400	(3,900)

Exhibit 14–3

Determining the Profit Maximizing Price and Quantity

monthly profit is maximized when the price is set at $925 and 40 Wave Darters are produced and sold each month.

Price Elasticity

The impact of price changes on sales volume is called the **price elasticity**. Demand is *elastic* if a price increase has a large negative impact on sales volume, and vice versa. Demand is *inelastic* if price changes have little or no impact on sales quantity. **Cross-elasticity** refers to the extent to which a change in a product's price affects the demand for other *substitute products*. For example, if Sydney Sailing Supplies raises the price of its two-person sailboat, there may be an increase in demand for substitute recreational craft, such as small powerboats, canoes, or windsurfers.

Measuring price elasticity and cross-elasticity is an important objective of market research. Having a good understanding of these economic concepts helps managers to determine the profit-maximizing price.

Limitations of the Profit-Maximizing Model

The economic model of the pricing decision serves as a useful framework for approaching a pricing problem. However, it does have several limitations. First, the firm's price elasticity and cross-elasticity are difficult to determined with precision. Although market research is designed to gather data about product demand, it rarely enables management to predict completely the effects of price changes on the quantity demanded. Many other factors affect product demand in addition to price. Product design and quality, advertising and promotion, and company reputation also significantly influence consumer demand for a product.

Second, the simple economic pricing model is not valid for all forms of market organization. In an **oligopolistic market**, where a small number of sellers compete among themselves, such as the automobile industry, the reactions of competitors to a firm's pricing policies must be taken into account. While economists have studied oligopolistic pricing, the state of the theory is not sufficient to provide a thorough understanding of the impact of prices on demand.

The third limitation of the economic pricing model involves the difficulty of measuring the changes in cost. Cost-accounting systems are not designed to measure the changes in cost incurred as production and sales increase unit by unit. To measure changes in cost would entail a very costly information system. Most managers believe that any improvements in pricing decisions made possible by changes-in-cost data would not be sufficient to defray the cost of obtaining the information. For this reason, most managers make pricing decisions on the basis of a combination of economic considerations and accounting product-cost information.

In spite of its limitations, the economic pricing model serves as a useful conceptual framework for the pricing decision. Within this overall framework, managers typically rely heavily on a cost-based pricing approach, as we shall see next.

Role of Accounting Product Costs in Pricing

"Today we spend more of our time analyzing and understanding . . . our margins, understanding our prices, understanding the markets in which we do business." (14b)
Caterpillar

Most managers base prices on accounting product costs, at least to some extent. There are several reasons for this. First, most companies sell many products or services. There simply is not time enough to do an economic pricing analysis for every product or service. Managers must rely on a quick and straightforward method for setting prices, and cost-based pricing formulas provide it. Second, even though market considerations ultimately may determine the final product price, a cost-based pricing formula gives the manager a place to start. Finally, and most importantly, the cost of a product or service provides a floor below which the price cannot be set in the long-run. Although a product may be "given away" initially, at a price below cost, a product's price ultimately must cover its costs in order for the firm to remain in business. Even a nonprofit organization, unless it is heavily subsidized, cannot forever price products or services below their costs.

Cost-Plus Pricing

Cost-based pricing formulas typically have the following general form:

$$\text{Price} = \text{Cost} + (\text{Markup percentage} \times \text{Cost})$$

Such a pricing approach often is called **cost-plus pricing**, because the price is equal to *cost plus a markup*. Depending on how cost is defined, the markup percentage may differ. Several different definitions of cost, each combined with a different markup percentage, can result in the same price for a product or service.

Exhibit 14–4 illustrates how Sydney Sailing Supplies' management could use several different cost-plus pricing formulas and arrive at a price of $925 for the Wave Darter. Cost-plus formula (1) is based on variable manufacturing cost. Formula (2) is based on absorption (or full) manufacturing cost, which includes an allocated portion of fixed manufacturing costs. Formula (3) is based on all costs: both variable and fixed costs of the manufacturing, selling, and administrative functions. Formula (4) is based on all variable costs, including variable manufacturing, selling, and administrative costs. Notice that all four formulas are based on a linear representation of the cost function, in which all costs are categorized as fixed or variable.

As Sydney Sailing Supplies includes more costs in the cost base of the pricing formula, the required markup percentage declines. This reflects the fact that, one way or another, the price must cover all costs as well as a normal profit margin. If only variable manufacturing costs are included explicitly in the cost base, as in formula (1), then all of the other costs (and the firm's profit) must be covered by the markup. However, if the cost base used in the pricing formula includes all costs, as in formula (3), the markup can be much lower, since it need cover only the firm's normal profit margin.

Exhibit 14–4
Alternative Cost-Plus Pricing Formulas

Each of the following cost-plus pricing formulas yields the same $925 price for the Wave Darter.

Price and Cost Data			Cost-Plus Pricing Formulas
Variable manufacturing cost	$400	1	$925 = \$400 + (131.25\% \times \$400) = \text{Variable manufacturing cost} + \left(\text{Markup percentage} \times \text{Variable manufacturing cost} \right)$
Applied fixed manufacturing cost	250*		
Absorption manufacturing cost	650	2	$925 = \$650 + (42.3\%\dagger \times \$650) = \text{Absorption manufacturing cost} + \left(\text{Markup percentage} \times \text{Absorption manufacturing cost} \right)$
Variable selling and administrative cost	50		
Allocated fixed selling and administrative cost	100*		
Total cost	$800	3	$925 = \$800 + (15.63\%\dagger \times \$800) = \text{Total cost} + \left(\text{Markup percentage} \times \text{Total cost} \right)$
Variable manufacturing cost	$400		
Variable selling and administrative cost	50		
Total variable cost	$450	4	$925 = \$450 + (105.56\%\dagger \times \$450) = \text{Total variable cost} + \left(\text{Markup percentage} \times \text{Total variable cost} \right)$

*Based on planned monthly production of 40 units (or 480 units per year).
†Rounded.

A company typically uses only one of the four cost-plus pricing formulas illustrated in Exhibit 14–4. Which formula is best? Let's examine the advantages and disadvantages of each approach.

Absorption-Cost Pricing Formulas

Most companies that use cost-plus pricing use either absorption manufacturing cost or total cost as the basis for pricing products or services. (See formulas (2) and (3) in Exhibit 14–4.) The reasons generally given for this tendency are as follows:

1. In the long run, the price must cover all costs and a normal profit margin. Basing the cost-plus formula on only variable costs might encourage managers to set too low a price in order to boost sales. This will not happen if managers understand that a variable cost-plus pricing formula requires a higher markup to cover fixed costs and profit. Nevertheless, many managers argue that people tend to view the cost base in a cost-plus pricing formula as the floor for setting prices. If prices are set too close to variable manufacturing cost, the firm will fail to cover its fixed costs. Ultimately, such a practice could result in the failure of the business.

2. Absorption-cost or total-cost pricing formulas provide a justifiable price that tends to be perceived as equitable by all parties. Consumers generally understand that a company must make a profit on its product or service in order to remain in business. Justifying a price as the total cost of production, sales, and administrative activities, plus a reasonable profit margin, seems reasonable to buyers.

3. When a company's competitors have similar operations and cost structures, cost-plus pricing based on full costs gives management an idea of how competitors may set prices.

4. Absorption-cost information is provided by a firm's cost-accounting system, because it is required for external financial reporting under generally accepted accounting principles. Since absorption-cost information already exists, it is cost-effective to use it for pricing. The alternative would involve preparing special product-cost data specifically for the pricing decision. In a firm with hundreds of products, such data could be expensive to produce.

> "An indemnity [insurance] company prices products by looking at existing costs and at what the trends have been. The company then predicts, or forecasts, costs for the next year and uses this information to set the price." (14c)
>
> **BlueCross**

The primary disadvantage of absorption-cost or total-cost pricing formulas is that they obscure the cost behaviour pattern of the firm. Since absorption-cost and total-cost data include allocated fixed costs, it is not clear from these data how the firm's total costs will change as volume changes. Another way of stating this criticism is that absorption-cost data are not consistent with cost-volume-profit analysis. CVP analysis emphasizes the distinction between fixed and variable costs. This approach enables managers to predict the effects of changes in prices and sales volume on profit. Absorption-cost and total cost information obscures the distinction between variable and fixed costs.

Variable-Cost Pricing Formulas

To avoid blurring the effects of cost behaviour on profit, some managers prefer to use cost-plus pricing formulas based on either variable manufacturing costs or total variable costs. (See formulas (1) and (4) in Exhibit 14–4.) Three advantages are attributed to this pricing approach:

1. Variable-cost data do not obscure the cost behaviour pattern by unitizing fixed costs and making them appear variable. Thus, variable-cost information is more consistent with cost-volume-profit analysis often used by managers to see the profit implications of changes in price and volume.

2. Variable-cost data do not require allocation of common fixed costs to individual product lines. For example, the annual salary of Sydney Sailing Supplies' vice-president of sales is a cost that must be borne by all of the company's product lines. Arbitrarily allocating a portion of her salary to the Wave Darter product line is not meaningful.

3. Variable-cost data are exactly the type of information managers need when facing certain decisions, such as whether to accept a special order. This decision, examined in detail in the preceding chapter, often requires an analysis that separates fixed and variable costs.

The primary disadvantage of the variable-cost pricing formula was described earlier. If managers perceive the variable cost of a product or service as the floor for the price, they might tend to set the price too low for the firm to cover its fixed costs. Eventually this can spell disaster. Therefore, if variable-cost data are used as the basis for cost-plus pricing, managers must understand the need for higher markups to ensure that all costs are covered.

Determining the Markup

Regardless of which cost-plus formula is used, Sydney Sailing Supplies must determine its markup on the Wave Darter. If management uses a variable-cost pricing formula, the markup must cover all fixed costs and a reasonable profit. If management uses an absorption-costing formula, the markup still must be sufficient to cover the firm's profit on the Wave Darter product line. What constitutes a reasonable or normal profit margin?

Return-on-Investment Pricing   A common approach to determining the profit margin in cost-plus pricing is to base profit on the firm's target return on investment (ROI). To illustrate **return-on-investment pricing**, suppose Sydney Sailing Supplies' production plan calls for 480 Wave Darters to be manufactured during the year. Based on the cost data shown in Exhibit 14–4, this production plan will result in the following total costs:

Variable costs:		
Manufacturing	$192,000	
Selling and administrative	24,000	
Total variable costs		$216,000
Fixed costs:		
Manufacturing	$120,000	
Selling and administrative	48,000	
Total fixed costs		168,000
Total costs		$384,000

Suppose the year's average amount of capital invested in the Wave Darter product line is $300,000. If Sydney Sailing Supplies' target return on investment for the Wave Darter line is 20 percent, the required annual profit is computed as follows:

$$\text{Average invested capital} \times \text{Target ROI} = \text{Target profit}$$
$$\$300,000 \times 20\% = \$60,000$$

The markup percentage required to earn Sydney Sailing Supplies a $60,000 profit on the Wave Darter line depends on the cost-plus formula used. We will compute the markup percentage for two cost-plus formulas.

1. *Cost-plus pricing based on total costs.* The total cost of a Wave Darter is $800 per unit (Exhibit 14–4). To earn a profit of $60,000 on annual sales of 480 sailboats, the company must make a profit of $125 per boat ($125 = $60,000 ÷ 480). This entails a markup percentage of 15.63 percent above total cost of $800.

$$15.63\% = \frac{\$925}{\$800} - 100\%$$

A shortcut to the same conclusion uses the following formula:

$$\frac{\text{Markup percentage}}{\text{on total cost}} = \frac{\text{Target profit}}{\text{Annual volume} \times \text{Total cost per unit}}$$

$$15.63\% = \frac{\$60,000}{480 \times \$800}$$

2. *Cost-plus pricing based on total variable costs.* The total variable cost of a Wave Darter is $450 per unit (Exhibit 14–4). The markup percentage applied to variable cost must be sufficient to cover *both* annual profit of $60,000 *and* total annual fixed costs of $168,000. The required markup percentage is computed as follows:

$$\frac{\text{Markup percentage}}{\text{on total variable cost}} = \frac{\text{Target profit} + \text{Total annual fixed cost}}{\text{Annual volume} \times \text{Total variable cost per unit}}$$

$$105.56\% = \frac{\$60,000 + \$168,000}{480 \times \$450}$$

General Formula   The general formula for computing the markup percentage in cost-plus pricing to achieve a target ROI is as follows:

$$\frac{\text{Markup percentage}}{\substack{\text{applied to cost base in}\\ \text{cost-plus pricing formula}}} = \frac{\substack{\text{Profit required to}\\ \text{achieve target ROI}} + \substack{\text{Total annual costs } \textit{not}\\ \text{included in cost base}}}{\substack{\text{Annual}\\ \text{volume}} \times \substack{\text{Cost base per unit}\\ \text{used in cost-plus}\\ \text{pricing formula}}}$$

Strategic Pricing of New Products

Pricing a new product is an especially challenging decision problem. The newer the concept of the product, the more difficult the pricing decision. For example, if Sydney Sailing Supplies comes out with a new two-person sailboat, its pricing problem is far easier than the pricing problem of a company that first markets products using a radically new technology. Genetic engineering, superconductivity, artificial hearts, and space-grown crystals are all examples of such frontier technologies. Pricing a new product is harder than pricing a mature product because of the magnitude of the uncertainties involved—for example, obstacles encountered in manufacturing the product and costs of production.

In addition to the production uncertainties, new products pose another sort of challenge. A manufacturer of a new product can adopt either of two widely differing strategies. One is **skimming pricing**, in which the price is set high, and short-term profits are reaped on the new product. The initial market will be small, due in part to the high initial price. This pricing approach often is used for unique products, where there are people who "must have it" whatever the price. An example of a product for which skimming pricing was used is the high-definition televisions.

The other initial pricing strategy is **penetration pricing**, in which the price is set relatively low. By setting a low price for a new product, management hopes to penetrate a new market deeply, quickly gaining a large market share. This pricing approach often is used for products that are of good quality, but do not stand out as vastly better than competing products.

The decision between skimming and penetration pricing depends on the type of product and involves trade-offs of price versus volume. Skimming pricing results in much slower acceptance of a new product, but higher unit profits. Penetration pricing results in greater initial sales volume, but lower unit profits.

Regardless of the pricing strategy used, companies must closely monitor and manage costs to remain price-competitive.

Cost-Plus Pricing: Summary and Evaluation

We have examined two different approaches to setting prices: (1) the economic, profit-maximizing approach and (2) cost-plus pricing. Although the techniques involved in these methods are quite different, the methods complement each other. In setting prices, managers cannot ignore the market (i.e., the ceiling price), nor can they ignore costs (i.e., the floor price). Cost-plus pricing is used widely in practice to establish a starting point in the process of determining a price. Cost-plus formulas are simple; they can be applied mechanically without taking the time of top management. They make it possible for a company with hundreds of products or services to cope with the tasks of updating prices for existing products and setting initial prices for new products.

Cost-plus pricing formulas can be used effectively with a variety of cost definitions, but the markup percentage has to be appropriate for the type of cost used. It is imperative that price-setting managers understand that ultimately the price must cover all costs and a normal profit margin. Absorption-cost-plus or total-cost-plus pricing has the advantage of keeping the manager's attention focused on covering total costs. The variable-cost-plus formulas have the advantage of not obscuring important information about cost behaviour.

M anagement
A ccounting
P ractice

Rogers Communications, Bell Canada, TELUS, Fido, General Motors, and Toyota

PRICE COMPETITION AND COST MANAGEMENT

Intense price competition, sometimes referred to as a *price war*, can occur in just about any industry. Rogers Communications, Bell Canada, and TELUS are among the telecom carriers currently being forced to lower their rates. In order to survive in a price war, though, a company must aggressively manage its costs. Fido, for example, is relaunching its discount brand with new plans and doing away with the much-hated system access fees, forcing telecom giants to follow suit.[2]

BusinessWeek reports that the auto insurance industry is entering such a period of price competition. Price competition is always intense in the auto industry. According to *The Wall Street Journal*, "In an attempt to rewrite pricing rules in the highly competitive U.S. auto market, General Motors will slash the price on most of its new vehicles. The move is the auto maker's latest attempt to settle on a pricing strategy that is both profitable for the company and compelling for customers." In order to cut prices, though, GM will have to aggressively manage its production costs.[3]

Toyota's response to increased price competition is an aggressive cost-cutting campaign. In recent years, Toyota has reduced its procurement costs by nearly a third. The auto maker's next move is to reduce the average "number of steel parts in cars from 610 to 500 to deal with the soaring cost of steel."[4]

Meeting competitive prices and effectively managing costs go hand-in-hand in any business.

Cost-plus pricing formulas establish a starting point in setting prices. Then the price setter must weigh market conditions, likely actions of competitors, and general business conditions. Thus, effective price setting requires a constant interplay of market considerations and cost awareness.

Target Costing

Learning Objective 4

List and discuss the key principles of target costing.

Earlier in this chapter, we described product pricing as a process whereby the cost of the product is determined, and then an appropriate price is chosen. Increasingly, the opposite approach is being taken. The company first uses market research to determine the price at which a new product can be sold. Given the likely sales price, management

Management **A**ccounting **P**ractice

Amazon

PRICING ON THE INTERNET BY "E-TAILERS"

One of the most difficult issues in building an online retail business has proven to be pricing. "Many Internet merchants are still struggling to find ways to set prices to attract as many customers as possible, while fattening up their razor-thin profit margins. What these retailers do know is what *hasn't* worked."

As the dot-com industry struggles, flawed pricing strategies have taken much of the blame. "Too many merchants raced for the bottom with deep discounts that made profits all but impossible to achieve—especially when the stock market bottomed out and funding for dot-coms froze. Others have felt the consumer backlash to so-called price discrimination, as the Internet has given shoppers the ability to better detect price discrepancies and bargains. The survivors must now figure out if it is even possible to take advantage of the Internet's unique capabilities to set dynamic prices, which would better reflect a customer's willingness to pay more under different circumstances. 'Before the Internet existed, retail was a very competitive, difficult, low-margin business,' says economist Austan Goolsbee. 'With the advent of Internet retailers, there was a brief moment in which they and others believed they had broken the iron chain of low margins and high competition in retail by introducing the Internet. Now, retail online is starting to look like retail offline—very competitive, with squeezed profit margins. In all, a very tough place to be.'"

Pricing on the Internet "was expected to offer retailers a number of advantages." First, "it would be far easier to raise or lower prices in response to demand, without the need of a clerk running through a store with a pricing gun. Online prices could be changed in far smaller increments—even by just a penny or two—as frequently as a merchant desired, making it possible to fine-tune pricing strategies."

The real payoff, though, "was supposed to be better information on exactly how price-conscious customers are. For instance, knowing that customer A doesn't care whether the 'Gladiator' DVD in her shopping basket costs $21.95 or $25.95 would leave an enterprising merchant free to charge the higher price on the spot. By contrast, knowing that customer B is going to put author John le Carré's latest thriller back on the shelf unless it's priced at $20, instead of $28, would open an opportunity for a bookseller to make the sale by cutting the price in real time." However, putting this concept "into practice online has turned out to be exceptionally difficult, in part because the Internet also has empowered consumers to compare prices to find out if other merchants are offering a better deal or if other consumers are getting a bigger break." It has also made it easier for consumers to register a complaint. For example, "Amazon raised a furor . . . when customers learned they were paying different prices for the same DVD movies, the result of a marketing test in which the retailer varied prices to gauge the effect on demand." After receiving many complaints from irate consumers, "Amazon announced it would refund the difference between the highest and lowest prices in the test."[5]

computes the cost for which the product must be manufactured in order to provide the firm with an acceptable profit margin. Finally, engineers and cost analysts work together to design a product that can be manufactured for the allowable cost. This process, called **target costing**, is used widely by companies in the development stages of new products. A new product's **target cost** is the projected long-run cost that will enable a firm to enter and remain in the market for the product and compete successfully with the firm's competitors.

A Strategic Profit and Cost Management Process

Target costing can be a critical tool for management as it seeks to strategically manage the company's costs and profits. By ensuring that products are designed so that they can be produced at a low enough cost to be priced competitively, management can achieve and maintain a sustainable competitive position in the market.

Key Principles of Target Costing   Target costing involves seven key principles:[6]

- *Price-led costing.* Target costing sets the target cost by *first* determining the price at which a product can be sold in the marketplace. Subtracting the *target profit margin* from this *target price* yields the *target cost*, that is, the cost at which the product must be manufactured. This simple, but strategically important, relationship can be expressed in the following equation:

  Target cost = Target price − Target profit

  Notice that in a target costing approach, the price is set *first*, and *then* the target product cost is determined. This is opposite from the order in which the product cost and selling price are determined under traditional cost-plus pricing.

- *Focus on the customer.* To be successful at target costing, management must listen to the company's customers. What products do they want? What features are important? How much are they willing to pay for a certain level of product quality? Management needs to aggressively seek customer feedback, and then products must be designed to satisfy customer demand and be sold at a price they are willing to pay. In short, the target costing approach is market-driven.

- *Focus on product design.* Design engineering is a key element in target costing. Engineers must design a product from the ground up so that it can be produced at its target cost. This design activity includes specifying the raw materials and components to be used as well as the labour, machinery, and other elements of the production process. In short, a product must be designed for manufacturability.

Design engineers play a crucial role in target costing by designing a product that can be manufactured as its target cost and sold at its target price.

- *Focus on process design.* As indicated in the preceding point, every aspect of the production process must be examined to make sure that the product is produced as efficiently as possible. The use of touch labour, technology, global sourcing in procurement, and every aspect of the production process must be designed with the product's target cost in mind.

- *Cross-functional teams.* Manufacturing a product at or below its target cost requires the involvement of people from many different functions in an organization: market research, sales, design engineering, procurement, production engineering, production scheduling, material handling, and cost management. Individuals from all these diverse areas of expertise can make key contributions to the target costing process. Moreover, "a cross-functional team is not a set of specialists who contribute their expertise and then leave; they are responsible for the entire product."[7]

- *Life-cycle costs.* In specifying a product's target cost, analysts must be careful to incorporate all of the product's *life-cycle costs.* These include the costs of product planning and concept design, preliminary design, detailed design and testing, production, distribution, and customer service. Traditional cost-accounting systems have tended to focus only on the production phase and have not paid enough attention to the product's other life-cycle costs.

- *Value-chain orientation.* Sometimes the projected cost of a new product is above the target cost. Then efforts are made to eliminate *non-value-added costs* to bring the projected cost down. In some cases, a close look at the company's entire value chain can help managers identify opportunities for cost reduction. For example, Procter & Gamble placed order-entry computers in Wal-Mart stores. This resulted in substantial savings in order-processing costs for both companies.[8]

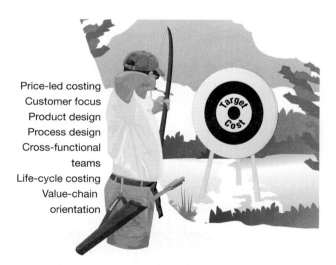

Price-led costing
Customer focus
Product design
Process design
Cross-functional teams
Life-cycle costing
Value-chain orientation

Activity-Based Costing and Target Costing

An activity-based costing (ABC) system can be particularly helpful as product design engineers try to achieve a product's target cost. ABC enables designers to break down the production process for a new product into its component activities. Then designers can attempt cost improvement in particular activities to bring a new product's projected cost in line with its target cost.

To illustrate, Sydney Sailing Supplies' Marine Instruments Division, located in Perth, Australia, wants to introduce a new depth finder. Target costing studies indicate that a target cost of $340 must be met in order to successfully compete in this market.

Learning Objective 5

Explain the role of activity-based costing in setting a target cost.

A. Activity-Based Costing System

Activity Cost Pool	Cost Driver	Pool Rate
Purchasing	Number of parts	$1 per part
Material handling	Dollar value of parts	$.20 per direct-material dollar
Inspection	Inspection hours	$28 per inspection hour

B. Cost Projections for a New Product: Depth Finder

	Original Cost Projection	Improved Cost Projection
Direct material	$200	$190
Direct labour	100	70
Purchasing:		
$1 per part (45 parts)	45	
$1 per part (32 parts)		32
Material handling:		
$.20 per direct-material dollar ($200)	40	
$.20 per direct-material dollar ($190)		38
Inspection:		
$28 per inspection hour (.5 hour)	14	
$28 per inspection hour (.25 hour)		7
Total projected cost	$399	$337
Target cost	$340	

Exhibit 14–5
Target Costing and Cost Improvement for a New Product

Exhibit 14–5 shows how ABC was used to bring the depth finder's initial cost estimate of $399 down to $337, just below the target cost. The company's design engineers were able to focus on key activities in the production process, such as material handling and inspection, and reduce the projected costs.

Product-Cost Distortion and Pricing: The Role of Activity-Based Costing   Use of a traditional, volume-based product-costing system may result in significant cost distortion among product lines. In many cases, high-volume and relatively simple products are overcosted while low-volume and complex products are undercosted. This results from the fact that high-volume and relatively simple products require proportionately less activity per unit for various manufacturing-support activities than do low-volume and complex products. Yet a traditional product-costing system, in which all overhead is assigned on the basis of a single unit-level activity like direct-labour hours, fails to capture the cost implications of product diversity. In contrast, an activity-based costing (ABC) system does measure the extent to which each product line drives costs in the key production-support activities.

   Managers should be aware that cost distortion can result in overpricing high-volume and relatively simple products, while low-volume and complex products are undercosted. This can undermine any effort to set prices competitively, even under the target-costing approach. The competitive implications of such strategic pricing errors can be disastrous.

Computer-Integrated Manufacturing   When a computer-integrated manufacturing (CIM) system is used, the process of target costing sometimes is computerized. A manufacturer's computer-aided design and cost-accounting software are interconnected.

> "A key Honda philosophy is that 'cost is a result.' To get better results, you must manage the cost drivers." (14e)
>
> Honda

An engineer can try out many different design features and immediately see the product-cost implications, without ever leaving the computer terminal.

Value Engineering and Target Costing

Target costing is an outgrowth of the concept of **value engineering**, which is a cost-reduction and process-improvement technique that utilizes information collected about a product's design and production processes and then examines various attributes of the design and processes to identify candidates for improvement efforts. The attributes examined include such characteristics as part diversity and process complexity. Examples of value engineering in the area of direct materials include changing the quality or grade of materials, reducing the number of bolts in a part, using a component common to other products instead of a unique or specialized component, and changing the method of painting.

Much of the historical development of the target-costing approach has taken place in Japanese industry, where "more than 80 percent of all assembly industries in Japan use target costing. Some of the best practitioners of target costing are leading Japanese companies."[9] In recent years, however, many other companies, including Caterpillar, Chrysler, Boeing, and Kodak, have made significant contributions to target costing theory and practice.

Isuzu Motors, Ltd. is a leading Japanese manufacturer of automobiles, buses, and both light and heavy-duty trucks. "At Isuzu, value engineering (VE) has been developed to cover all stages of product design and manufacture. Indeed, three different stages of VE—zeroth, first, and second 'looks'—are used in the design phase to increase the functionality of new products."[10]

- *Zeroth-look VE* is applied at the earliest stages of new product design—"the concept proposal stage, when the basic concept of the product is developed and its preliminary quality, cost, and investment targets are established."

- *First-look VE* is applied during the last half of the concept proposal stage and throughout the product planning phase. During this stage, a product's quality, functionality, and selling price are determined; a design plan is submitted; and target costs are determined for each of the new vehicle's major functions (e.g., engine and transmission). Also, the degree of component commonality is set. "First look VE is used at this stage to increase the value of the product by increasing its functionality without increasing its cost."

- *Second-look VE* is applied during the last half of the product planning stage and the first half of the product development and preparation stage. "The components of the vehicle's major functions are identified, and hand-made prototypes are assembled. At this stage, VE works to improve the value and functionality of existing components, not to create new ones."

In addition, various *tear-down methods* are used by Isuzu, and many other companies, "to analyze competitive products in terms of materials they contain, parts they use, ways they function, and ways they are manufactured." At Isuzu, for example, dynamic tear-down focuses on reducing the number of vehicle assembly operations or the time required to perform them. *Cost tear-down* examines ways to reduce the cost of the components used in a vehicle. *Material tear-down* compares the materials and surface treatments of the components used by Isuzu with those of its competitors. *Static tear-down* disassembles a competitor's product into its components to enable Isuzu's engineers to compare Isuzu's components with those used in the competitor's product.

Although the Isuzu approach is illustrative of target costing methods, many different approaches are used by the thousands of companies now engaged in target costing programs. However, the Isuzu target costing and value-engineering process is indicative of the seriousness with which companies approach the problem of reducing costs in order to meet a product's target cost and remain competitive in an ever more difficult market.

Time and Material Pricing

Another cost-based approach to pricing is called **time and material pricing**. Under this approach, the company determines one charge for the labour used on a job and another charge for the materials. The labour typically includes the direct cost of the employee's time and a charge to cover various overhead costs. The material charge generally includes the direct cost of the materials used in a job plus a charge for material handling and storage. Time and material pricing is used widely by construction companies, printers, repair shops, and professional firms, such as engineering, law, and public accounting firms.

> **Learning Objective 7**
>
> Determine prices using the time and material pricing approach.

To illustrate, we will examine a special job undertaken by Sydney Sailing Supplies. The company's vice-president for sales, Richard Moby, was approached by a successful local physician about refurbishing her yacht. She wanted an engine overhaul, complete refurbishment and redecoration of the cabin facilities, and stripping and repainting of the hull and deck. The work would be done in the Repair Department of the company's Yacht Division, located in Melbourne, Australia.

Data regarding the operations of the Repair Department are as follows:

Labour rate, including fringe benefits	$18 per hour
Hourly charge to cover profit margin	$7 per hour
Annual labour hours	10,000 hours
Annual overhead costs:	
Material handling and storage	$40,000
Other overhead costs (supervision, utilities, insurance, and depreciation)	$200,000
Annual cost of materials used in Repair Department	$1,000,000

Based on these data, the Repair Department computed its time and material prices as follows:

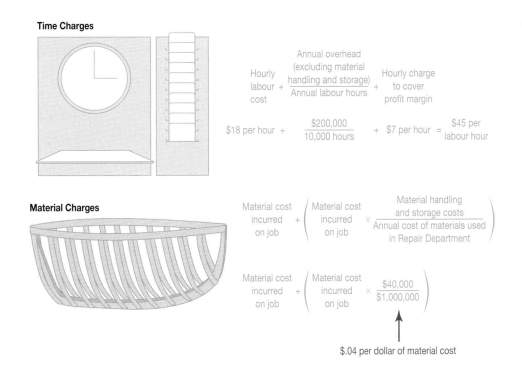

Time Charges

$$\text{Hourly labour cost} + \frac{\text{Annual overhead (excluding material handling and storage)}}{\text{Annual labour hours}} + \text{Hourly charge to cover profit margin}$$

$$\$18 \text{ per hour} + \frac{\$200,000}{10,000 \text{ hours}} + \$7 \text{ per hour} = \frac{\$45 \text{ per}}{\text{labour hour}}$$

Material Charges

$$\text{Material cost incurred on job} + \left(\text{Material cost incurred on job} \times \frac{\text{Material handling and storage costs}}{\text{Annual cost of materials used in Repair Department}} \right)$$

$$\text{Material cost incurred on job} + \left(\text{Material cost incurred on job} \times \frac{\$40,000}{\$1,000,000} \right)$$

↑
$.04 per dollar of material cost

The effect of the material-charge formula is to include a charge for the costs incurred in the handling and storage of materials.

Exhibit 14–6
Time and Material Pricing

	A	B	C	D	E	F	G	H
1			SYDNEY SAILING SUPPLIES					
2			Price Quotation					
3			Yacht Division: Repair Department					
4								
5	Time charges	Labour time					200	hours
6		x Rate				x	$ 45	per hour
7		Total					$ 9,000	
8								
9	Material charges	Cost of materials for job					$ 8,000	
10		+ Charge for material handling and storage*					320	
11		Total					$ 8,320	
12								
13	Total price of job	Time					$ 9,000	
14		Material					8,320	
15		Total					$ 17,320	
16								
17	*Charge for material handling and storage:							
18	($8,000 material cost) x ($.04 per dollar of material cost) = $320							

Richard Moby estimates that the yacht refurbishment job will require 200 hours of labour and $8,000 in materials. Moby's price quotation for the job is shown in the Excel spreadsheet in Exhibit 14–6.

Included in the $17,320 price quotation for the yacht refurbishment are charges for labour costs, overhead, material costs, material handling and storage costs, and a normal profit margin. Some companies also charge an additional markup on the materials used in a job in order to earn a profit on that component of their services. Sydney Sailing Supplies' practice is to charge a high enough profit charge on its labour to earn an appropriate profit for the Repair Department.

Competitive Bidding

Learning Objective 8

Set prices in competitive-bidding situations.

In a **competitive bidding** situation, two or more companies submit sealed bids (or prices) for a project, service, or product to a potential buyer. The buyer selects one of the companies for the job on the basis of the bid price and the design specifications for the job. Competitive bidding complicates a manager's pricing problem, because now the manager is in direct competition with one or more competitors. If all of the companies submitting bids offer a roughly equivalent product or service, the bid price becomes the sole criterion for selecting the contractor. The higher the price that is bid, the greater will be the profit on the job, if the firm gets the contract. However, a higher price also lowers the probability of obtaining the contract to perform the job. Thus, there is a trade-off between bidding high, to make a good profit, and bidding low, to land the contract. Some say there is a "winner's curse" in competitive bidding, meaning that the company bidding low enough to beat out its competitors probably bid too low to make an acceptable profit on the job. Despite the winner's curse, competitive bidding is a common form of selecting contractors in many types of business.

Richard Moby was approached recently by the city of Sydney about building a new marina for moderate-sized sailing vessels. Moby decided that his company's Marine Services Division should submit a bid on the job. The Marine Services Division specializes in marina maintenance and construction. The city announced that three other firms also would be submitting bids. Since all four companies were equally capable of building the marina to the city's specifications, Moby assumed that the bid price would be the deciding factor in selecting the contractor.

Moby consulted with the controller and chief engineer of the Marine Services Division, and the following data were compiled:

Estimated direct-labour requirements, 1,500 hrs. @ $12 per hr.	$18,000
Estimated direct-material requirements	30,000
Estimated variable overhead (allocated on the basis of direct labour), 1,500 direct-labour hrs. @ $5 per hr.	7,500
Total estimated variable costs	55,500
Estimated fixed overhead (allocated on the basis of direct labour), 1,500 direct-labour hrs. @ $8 per hr.	12,000
Estimated total cost	$67,500

The Marine Services Division allocates variable-overhead costs to jobs on the basis of direct-labour hours. These costs consist of indirect-labour costs, such as the wages of equipment-repair personnel, gasoline and lubricants, and incidental supplies such as rope, chains, and drill bits. Fixed-overhead costs, also allocated to jobs on the basis of direct-labour hours, include such costs as workers' compensation insurance, depreciation on vehicles and construction equipment, depreciation of the division's buildings, and supervisory salaries.

It was up to Richard Moby to decide on the bid price for the marina. In his meeting with the divisional controller and the chief engineer, Moby argued that the marina job was important to the company for two reasons. First, the Marine Services Division had been operating well below capacity for several months. The marina job would not preclude the firm from taking on any other construction work, so it would not entail an opportunity cost. Second, the marina job would be good advertising for Sydney Sailing Supplies. City residents would see the firm's name on the project, and this would promote sales of the company's boats and sailing supplies.

Based on these arguments, Moby pressed for a bid price that just covered the firm's variable costs and allowed for a modest contribution margin. The chief engineer was obstinate, however, and argued for a higher bid price that would give the division a good profit on the job. "My employees work hard to do an outstanding job, and their work is worth a premium to the city," was the engineer's final comment on the issue. After the threesome tossed the problem around all morning, the controller agreed with Moby. A bid price of $60,000 was finally agreed upon.

This is a typical approach to setting prices for competitively bid contracts. When a firm has excess capacity, a price that covers the incremental costs incurred because of the job will contribute toward covering the company's fixed cost and profit. None of the Marine Services Division's fixed costs will increase as a result of taking on the marina job. Thus, a bid price of $60,000 will cover the $55,500 of variable costs on the job and contribute $4,500 toward covering the division's fixed costs.

Bid price	$60,000
Variable costs of marina job (incremental costs incurred only if job is done)	55,500
Contribution from marina job (contribution to covering the division's fixed costs)	$ 4,500

Naturally, Sydney Sailing Supplies' management would like to make a larger profit on the marina job, but bidding a higher price means running a substantial risk of losing the job to a competitor.

If the Marine Services Division has no excess capacity, it would be appropriate to focus on the estimated full cost of the marina job, $67,500, which includes an allocation of the division's fixed capacity-producing costs. However, as Richard Moby pointed out, there will be valuable promotional benefits to Sydney Sailing Supplies if its Marine Services Division builds the marina. This is a qualitative factor, because these potential benefits are difficult to quantify. Moby will have to make a judgment

Exhibit 14–7

Summary of Competitive-Bidding Analysis

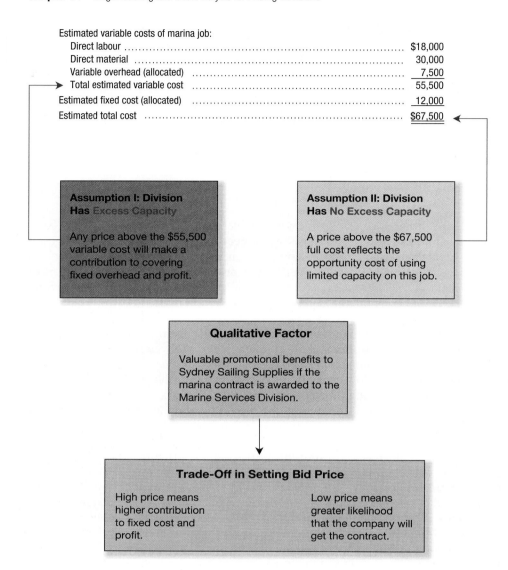

Estimated variable costs of marina job:

Direct labour	$18,000
Direct material	30,000
Variable overhead (allocated)	7,500
Total estimated variable cost	55,500
Estimated fixed cost (allocated)	12,000
Estimated total cost	$67,500

Assumption I: Division Has Excess Capacity

Any price above the $55,500 variable cost will make a contribution to covering fixed overhead and profit.

Assumption II: Division Has No Excess Capacity

A price above the $67,500 full cost reflects the opportunity cost of using limited capacity on this job.

Qualitative Factor

Valuable promotional benefits to Sydney Sailing Supplies if the marina contract is awarded to the Marine Services Division.

Trade-Off in Setting Bid Price

High price means higher contribution to fixed cost and profit.

Low price means greater likelihood that the company will get the contract.

regarding just how important the marina job is to the company. The greater the perceived qualitative benefits, the lower the bid price should be set to maximize the likelihood that the company will be awarded the contract.

Summary of Competitive-Bidding Analysis   The Marine Services Division's pricing problem is summarized in Exhibit 14–7. As you can see, the final pricing decision requires managerial judgment to fully consider the quantitative cost data, the qualitative promotional benefits, and the trade-off between a higher profit and a greater likelihood of getting the marina contract.

Effect of Regulations on Pricing

Learning Objective 9

Describe the legal restrictions on setting prices.

Businesses are not free to set any price they wish for their products or services. The Canadian *Competition Act*—enacted in 1889, one year before the U.S.'s *Sherman Act*, making it the oldest antitrust statute in the Western world—restricts certain types of pricing behaviour. These laws prohibit **price discrimination**, which means quoting different prices to different customers for the same product or service. Such price differences are unlawful unless they can be clearly justified by differences in the costs incurred to produce, sell, or deliver the product or service. Managers should keep careful records justifying such cost differences when they exist, because the records may be vital to a legal defense if price differences are challenged in court.

Another pricing practice prohibited by law is **predatory pricing**. This practice involves temporarily cutting a price to broaden demand for a product with the intention of later restricting the supply and raising the price again. In determining whether a price is predatory, the courts examine a business's cost records. If the product is sold below cost, the pricing is deemed to be predatory. The laws and court cases are ambiguous as to the appropriate definition of cost. However, various court decisions make it harder to prove predatory pricing. Nevertheless, this is one area where a price-setting decision maker is well advised to have an accountant on the left and a lawyer on the right before setting prices that could be deemed predatory.

Chapter Summary

Pricing of products and services is one of the most challenging decisions faced by management. Many influences affect pricing decisions. Chief among these are customer demand, the actions of competitors, and the costs of the products or services. Other factors such as political, legal, and image-related issues also affect pricing decisions.

The economic pricing model can be used under certain assumptions to determine the profit-maximizing price and quantity. While the economic model serves as a useful conceptual framework for the pricing decision, it is limited by its assumptions and the informational demands it implies.

Most companies set prices, at least to some extent, on the basis of costs. Cost-plus pricing formulas add a markup to some version of cost, typically either total variable cost or total absorption cost. Markups often are set to earn the company a target profit on its products, based on a target rate of return on investment. Strategic pricing of new products is an especially challenging problem for management. Various pricing approaches, such as skimming pricing or penetration pricing, may be appropriate depending on the product.

Target costing often is used to design a new product that can be produced at a cost that will enable the firm to sell it at a competitive price. Value engineering and activity-based costing are valuable tools used in the target costing process.

In industries such as construction, repair, printing, and professional services, time and material pricing is used. Under this approach, the price is determined as the sum of a labour-cost component and a material-cost component. Either or both of these components may include a markup to ensure that the company earns a profit on its services.

Determining competitive bid prices entail an analysis of the relevant costs to be incurred in completing the job, which should incorporate the existence of excess capacity or the lack of it.

Review Problem on Cost-Plus Pricing

Kitchenware Corporation manufactures high-quality copper pots and pans. Greta Cooke, one of the company's price analysts, is involved in setting a price for the company's new Starter Set. This set consists of seven of the most commonly used pots and pans. During the next year, the company plans to produce 10,000 Starter Sets, and the controller has provided Cooke with the following cost data:

	Predicted Costs of 10,000 Starter Sets
Direct material per set	$60
Direct labour per set, 2 hrs. @ $10 per hr.	20
Variable selling cost per set	5
Total	$85
Variable-overhead rate	$8 per direct-labour hour
Fixed-overhead rate	$12 per direct-labour hour

In addition, the controller indicated that the Accounting Department would allocate $20,000 of fixed administrative expenses to the Starter Set product line.

Required:

1. Compute the cost of a Starter Set using each of the four cost definitions commonly used in cost-plus pricing formulas.

2. Determine the markup percentage required for the Starter Set product line to earn a target profit of $317,500 before taxes during the next year. Use the total cost as the cost definition in the cost-plus formula.

Solution to Review Problem

1.

Variable manufacturing cost*	$ 96	1
Applied fixed-overhead cost†	24	
Absorption manufacturing cost	120	2
Variable selling cost	5	
Allocated fixed administrative cost‡	2	
Total cost	$127	3
Variable manufacturing cost	$ 96	
Variable selling cost	5	
Total variable cost	$101	4

*Direct material	$ 60	
Direct labour	20	
Variable overhead	16	(2 × $8 per hr.)
Total variable manufacturing cost	$ 96	

†Applied fixed overhead cost, $24 (2 × $12 per hr.).
‡Allocated fixed administrative cost, $2 ($20,000 ÷ 10,000 sets).

2. Markup percentage on total cost $= \dfrac{\$317,500}{10,000 \times \$127} = 25\%$

Proof
Price = Total cost + (.25 × Total cost) = $127 + (.25)($127) = $158.75

Income Statement

Sales revenue (10,000 × $158.75)		$1,587,500
Less: Variable costs:		
Direct material	$600,000	
Direct labour	200,000	
Variable overhead	160,000	
Variable selling cost	50,000	
Total variable costs		1,010,000
Contribution margin		577,500
Less: Fixed costs:		
Manufacturing overhead	$240,000	
Administrative cost	20,000	
Total fixed costs		260,000
Profit		$ 317,500

Key Terms

For each term's definition refer to the indicated page, or turn to the glossary at the end of the text.

competitive bidding, 588	penetration pricing, 581	price taker, 574	target cost, 583
cost-plus pricing, 577	predatory pricing, 591	return-on-investment	target costing, 583
cross-elasticity, 576	price discrimination,	pricing, 579	time and material
oligopolistic	590	skimming	pricing, 587
market, 576	price elasticity, 576	pricing, 580	value engineering, 586

Review Questions

14–1. Comment on the following remark made by a bank president: "The prices of our banking services are determined by the financial-services market. Costs are irrelevant."

14–2. "All this stuff about economic pricing model is just theory. Prices are determined by production costs." Evaluate this assertion.

14–3. List and briefly describe four major influences on pricing decisions.

14–4. Explain what is meant by the following statement: "In considering the reactions of competitors, it is crucial to define your product."

14–5. Explain the following assertion: "Price setting generally requires a balance between market forces and cost considerations."

14–6. Define the following terms: total revenue, price elasticity, and cross-elasticity.

14–7. Describe three limitations of the economic, profit-maximizing model of pricing.

14–8. Determining the best approach to pricing requires a cost-benefit trade-off. Explain.

14–9. Write the general formula for cost-plus pricing, and briefly explain its use.

14–10. List the four common cost bases used in cost-plus pricing. How can they all result in the same price?

14–11. List four reasons often cited for the widespread use of absorption cost as the cost base in cost-plus pricing formulas.

14–12. What is the primary disadvantage of basing the cost-plus pricing formula on absorption cost?

14–13. List three advantages of pricing based on variable cost.

14–14. Explain the behavioural problem that can result when cost-plus prices are based on variable cost.

14–15. Briefly explain the concept of *return-on-investment pricing*.

14–16. Explain the phrase *price-led costing*.

14–17. Why is a focus on the customer such a key principle of target costing?

14–18. Explain the role of value engineering in target costing.

14–19. Can *tear-down* methods be used effectively for target pricing in a service-industry company, such as a hotel or an airline? Explain.

14–20. Briefly describe the *time-and-material pricing approach*.

14–21. Explain the importance of the excess-capacity issue in setting a competitive bid price.

14–22. Describe the following approaches to pricing new products: skimming pricing, penetration pricing, and target costing.

14–23. Explain what is meant by unlawful price discrimination and predatory pricing.

Exercises

Spectrum Sound, Inc. manufactures DVD players with unusual features in its Mississauga Division. The divisional sales manager has estimated the following demand-curve data:

■ **Exercise 14–24**
Demand and Revenue Data
(LO 1, 2)

Quantity Sold per Month	Unit Sales Price
20	500
40	475
60	450
80	425
100	400

Required:

1. Prepare a table similar to the one of Exhibit 14–1 summarizing Spectrum Sound's price, quantity, and revenue data.

2. Draw a graph similar to the one of Exhibit 14–1 reflecting the data tabulated in requirement (1).

Exercise 14–25
Continuation of Preceding
Exercise; Cost Data
(LO 1, 2)

Refer to the preceding exercise. The divisional controller at Spectrum Sound's Mississauga Division has estimated the following cost data for the division's DVD players. (Assume there are no fixed costs.)

Quantity Produced and Sold per Month	Average Cost per Unit
20	$450
40	425
60	410
80	430
100	445

Required:

1. Prepare a table similar to the one of Exhibit 14–2 summarizing Spectrum Sound's cost relationships.
2. Draw a graph similar to the one of Exhibit 14–2 reflecting the data tabulated in requirement (1).

Exercise 14–26
Continuation of Preceding
Two Exercises; Profit-
Maximizing Price
(LO 1, 2)

Refer to the data given in the preceding two exercises.

Required:

1. Prepare a table of Spectrum Sound's revenue, cost, and profit relationships. For guidance, refer to Exhibit 14–3.
2. Draw a graph similar to the one of Exhibit 15–3 reflecting the data tabulated in requirement (1).
3. To narrow down the pricing decision, the Mississauga Division's sales manager has decided to price the DVD player at one of the following prices: $400, $425, $450, or $500. Which price do you recommend? Why?

Exercise 14–27
Cost-Plus Pricing Formulas;
Missing Data
(LO 1, 3)

The following data pertain to Lawn Master Corporation's top-of-the-line lawn mower.

Variable manufacturing cost	$275
Applied fixed manufacturing cost	55
Variable selling and administrative cost	66
Allocated fixed selling and administrative cost	?

To achieve a target price of $495 per lawn mower, the markup percentage is 12.5 percent on total unit cost.

Required:

1. What is the fixed selling and administrative cost allocated to each unit of Lawn Master's top-of-the-line mower?
2. For each of the following cost bases, develop a cost-plus pricing formula that will result in a target price of $495 per mower: (*a*) variable manufacturing cost, (*b*) absorption manufacturing cost, and (*c*) total variable cost.

Exercise 14–28
Cost-Plus Pricing Formulas
(LO 1, 3)

The following data pertain to Royal Lighting Company's oak-clad, contemporary chandelier:

Variable manufacturing cost	$300
Applied fixed manufacturing cost	105
Variable selling and administrative cost	45
Allocated fixed selling and administrative cost	75

Required: For each of the following cost bases, develop a cost-plus pricing formula that will result in a price of $600 for the oak chandelier.

- *a.* Variable manufacturing cost
- *b.* Absorption manufacturing cost
- *c.* Total cost
- *d.* Total variable cost

Refer to the cost and production data for the Wave Darter in Exhibit 14–4. The target profit is $60,000.

Required: Use the general formula for determining a markup percentage to compute the required markup percentages with the following two cost-plus formulas:

1. Variable manufacturing costs [formula (1) in Exhibit 14–4].
2. Absorption manufacturing cost [formula (2) in Exhibit 14–4].

■ **Exercise 14–29**
Determining Markup
Percentage; Target ROI
(LO 1, 3)

Visit the Web site of one of the following companies, or a different company of your choosing:

Research In Motion (RIM)	www.rim.com
Procter & Gamble	www.pg.com
Carnival Cruise Lines	www.carnival.com
TD Bank	www.td.com
General Electric Company	www.ge.com
Hewlett-Packard	www.hp.com
Intel Corporation	www.intel.com

Required: Read about a new product or service to be offered by the company. Then explain how the firm might use target costing to price the new product or service.

■ **Exercise 14–30**
Target Costing for a New
Product; Use of Internet
(LO 3, 4, 6)

Refer to Exhibit 14–6. Suppose the Repair Department of Sydney Sailing Supplies adds a markup of 5 percent on the material charges of a job (including the cost of material handling and storage).

Required:

1. Rewrite the material component of the time and material pricing formula to reflect the markup on material cost.
2. Compute the new price to be quoted on the yacht refurbishment described in Exhibit 14–6.

■ **Exercise 14–31**
Time and Material Pricing
(LO 7)

✓

Corrientes Company produces a single product in its Buenos Aires plant that currently sells for 7.5 p per unit. Fixed costs are expected to amount to 90,000 p for the year, and all variable manufacturing and administrative costs are expected to be incurred at a rate of 4.50 p per unit. Corrientes has two salespeople who are paid strictly on a commission basis. Their commission is 10 percent of the sales revenue they generate. (Ignore income taxes.) (*p* denotes the peso, Argentina's national currency. Many countries use the peso as their national currency. On the day this exercise was written, Argentina's peso was worth C$.3459.)

■ **Exercise 14–32**
Pricing, Advertising, and Bid
Decisions
(LO 8)

✓

Required:

1. Suppose management alters its current plans by spending an additional amount of 7,500 p on advertising and increases the selling price to 9 p per unit. Calculate the profit on 60,000 units.
2. Corrientes is bidding on a government contract for the sale of 10,000 units. These units would not be sold by the sales personnel, and, therefore, no commission would have to be paid. What is the price per unit Corrientes would have to bid in order to earn additional profit of 30,000 p?

(CMA, adapted)

Problems

For many years, Leigh Corporation has used a straightforward cost-plus pricing system, marking its goods up approximately 25 percent of total cost. The company has been profitable; however, it has recently lost considerable business to foreign competitors that have become very aggressive in the marketplace. These firms appear to be using target costing. An example of Leigh's problem is typified by item DC66, which has the following unit-cost characteristics:

■ **Problem 14–33**
Cost-Plus Pricing versus
Target Costing
(LO 3, 4, 5, 6)

2. Markup: $135

✓

Direct material	$ 90
Direct labour	225
Manufacturing overhead	150
Selling and administrative expenses	75

The going market price for an identical product of comparable quality is $585, which is significantly below what Leigh is charging.

Required:

1. Contrast cost-plus pricing and target costing. Which of the two approaches could be aptly labelled price-led costing? Why?

2. What is Leigh's current selling price of item DC66?

3. If Leigh used target costing for item DC66, by how much must costs change if the company desires to meet the market price and maintain its current rate of profit *on sales*?

4. Would the identification of value-added and non-value-added costs assist Leigh in this situation? Briefly explain.

5. Suppose that by previous cost-cutting drives, costs had already been "pared to the bone" on item DC66. What might Leigh be forced to do with its markup on cost to remain competitive? By how much must the markup change?

6. Early in this chapter, it was noted that, in many industries, prices are the result of an interaction between market forces and costs. Explain what is meant by this statement.

7. *Build a spreadsheet:* Construct an Excel spreadsheet to solve requirements (2) and (3) above. Show how the solution will change if the following information changes: the direct material and direct labour per unit are $85 and $220, respectively.

Problem 14–34

Target Costing
(LO 4, 5, 6)

3. Revenue per hour: $276
4. Target profit: $3,780,000

Maritime Services Corporation (MSC) will soon enter a very competitive marketplace in which it will have limited influence over the prices that are charged. Management and consultants are currently working to fine-tune the company's sole service, which hopefully will generate a 12 percent first-year return (profit) on the firm's $27,000,000 asset investment. Although the normal return in MSC's industry is 14 percent, executives are willing to accept the lower figure because of various startup inefficiencies. The following information is available for first-year operations:

Hours of service to be provided	25,000
Anticipated variable cost per service hour	$33
Anticipated fixed cost	$2,850,000 per year

Required:

1. Assume that management is contemplating what price to charge in the first year of operation. The company can take its cost and add a markup to achieve a 12 percent return; alternatively, it can use target costing. Given MSC's marketplace, which approach is probably more appropriate? Why?

2. How much profit must MSC generate in the first year to achieve a 12 percent return?

3. Calculate the revenue per hour that MSC must generate in the first year to achieve a 12 percent return.

4. Assume that prior to the start of business in year 1, management conducted a planning exercise to determine if MSC could attain a 14 percent return in year 2. Can the company achieve this return if (*a*) competitive pressures dictate a maximum selling price of $265 per hour and (*b*) service hours and the variable cost per service hour are the same as the amounts anticipated in year 1? Show calculations.

5. If your answer to requirement (4) is no, suggest and briefly describe a procedure that MSC might use to achieve the desired results.

Problem 14–35

Target Costing; Selection of Product Features
(LO 4, 5, 6)

3*b*. Cost of additional features: $36

Danish Interiors, Ltd. manufactures easy-to-assemble wooden furniture for home and office. The firm is considering modification of a table to make it more attractive to individuals and businesses that buy products through outlets such as Office Depot and Staples stores. The table is small, can be used to hold a computer printer or fax machine, and has several shelves for storage.

The company's marketing department surveyed potential buyers of the table regarding five proposed modifications. The 200 survey participants were asked to evaluate the modifications by using a five-point scale that ranged from 1 (strongly disagree) to 5 (strongly agree). Their responses, along with DF's related unit costs for the modifications, follow.

	1 Strongly Disagree	2 Disagree	3 Neutral	4 Agree	5 Strongly Agree
Add cabinet doors in storage area ($18)	10	20	30	60	80
Expand storage area ($7.50)	10	40	70	50	30
Add security lock to storage area ($4.95)	30	60	50	40	20
Give table top a more rich, marble appearance ($12.75) ...	10	20	50	60	60
Extend warranty to five years ($15.30)	40	70	30	35	25

The table currently costs $192 to produce and distribute, and Danish Interiors' selling price for this unit averages $240. An analysis of competitive tables in the marketplace revealed a variety of features, with some models having all of the features that management is considering and other models having only a few. The current manufacturers' selling prices for these tables averages $285.

Required:

1. Why is there a need in target costing to (*a*) focus on the customer and (*b*) have a marketing team become involved with product design?

2. Danish Interiors' marketing team will evaluate the survey responses by computing a weighted-average rating of each of the modifications. This will be accomplished by weighting (multiplying) the point values (1, 2, etc.) by the frequency of responses, summing the results, and dividing by 200. Rank the popularity of the five modifications using this approach.

3. Management desires to earn approximately the same rate of profit on sales that is being earned with the current design.

   a. If Danish Interiors uses target costing and desires to meet the current competitive selling price, what is the maximum cost of the modified table?

   b. Which of the modifications should management consider?

4. Assume that Danish Interiors wanted to add a modification or two that you excluded in your answer to requirement (3*b*). What process might management adopt to allow the company to make its target profit for the table? Briefly explain.

■ **Problem 14–36**
Target Costing; Value Engineering; ABC; JIT
(LO 4, 5, 6)

4. Total cost, current: $630
4. Total cost, revised: $532

Alexis Kunselman, president of Panorama Electronics (PE), is concerned about the prospects of one of its major products. The president has been reviewing a marketing report with Jeff Keller, marketing product manager, for their top-of-the-line stereo amplifier. The report indicates another price reduction is needed to meet anticipated competitors' reductions in sales prices. The current selling price for PE's amplifier is $700 per unit. It is expected that within three months PE's two major competitors will be selling their comparable amplifiers for $600 per unit. This concerns Kunselman because PE's current cost of producing the amplifiers is $630, which yields a $70 profit on each unit sold.

The situation is especially disturbing because PE had implemented an activity-based costing (ABC) system about two years ago. The ABC system helped them better identify costs, cost pools, cost drivers, and cost-reduction opportunities. Changes made when adopting ABC reduced costs on this product by approximately 15 percent during the last two years. Now it appears that costs will need to be reduced considerably more to remain competitive and to earn a profit on the amplifier. Total costs to produce, sell, and service the amplifiers are as follows:

Amplifier

		Per Unit
Material	Purchased components	$215
	All other material	85
Labour	Manufacturing, direct	130
	Setups	18
	Material handling	36
	Inspection	46
Machining	Cutting, shaping, and drilling	42
	Bending and finishing	28
Other	Finished-goods warehousing	10
	Warranty	20
	Total unit cost	$630

Kunselman has decided to hire Donald Collins, a consultant, to help decide how to proceed. After two weeks of review, discussion, and value-engineering analysis, Collins suggested that PE adopt a just-in-time (JIT) cell-manufacturing process to help reduce costs. He also suggested that using target costing would help in meeting the new target price.

By changing to a JIT cell-manufacturing system, PE expects that manufacturing direct labour will increase by $30 per finished unit. However, setup, material handling, inspection, and finished-goods warehousing will all be eliminated. Machine costs will be reduced from $70 to $60 per unit, and warranty costs are expected to be reduced by 40 percent.

Required:

1. Define target costing.
2. Define value engineering.
3. Determine Panorama Electronics' unit target cost at the $600 competitive sales price while maintaining the same percentage of profit on sales as is earned on the current $700 sales price.
4. If the just-in-time cell manufacturing process is implemented with the changes in costs noted, will Panorama Electronics meet the unit target cost you determined in requirement (3)? Prepare a schedule detailing cost reductions and the unit cost under the proposed JIT cell-manufacturing process.

(CMA, adapted)

■ Problem 14–37
Time and Material Pricing
(LO 7)

2. Material charges: $82,500
3. Markup on total material costs: $8,250

Tri-Cities Heating, Inc. installs heating systems in new homes built in Metro Vancouver. Jobs are priced using the time and materials method. The following predictions pertain to the company's operations for the next year:

Labour rate, including fringe benefits	$20 per hour
Annual labour hours	12,000 hours
Annual overhead costs:	
Material handling and storage	$31,250
Other overhead costs	$135,000
Annual cost of materials used	$312,500

The president of Tri-Cities Heating, B. T. Ewing, is pricing a job involving the heating systems for six houses to be built by a local developer. He has made the following estimates:

Material cost	$75,000
Labour hours	400

Required: Tri-Cities Heating adds a markup of $5 per hour on its time charges, but there is no markup on material costs.

1. Develop formulas for the company's (*a*) time charges and (*b*) material charges.
2. Compute the price for the job described above.
3. What would be the price of the job if Tri-Cities Heating also added a markup of 10 percent on all material charges (including material handling and storage costs)?

■ Problem 14–38
Cost-Plus Pricing; Bidding
(LO 3, 8)

1. Total traceable out-of-pocket costs: $16,000
2. Variable overhead: $6,000

North American Pharmaceuticals, Inc. specializes in packaging bulk drugs in standard dosages for local hospitals. Vancouver General Hospital (VGH) has asked North American Pharmaceuticals to bid on the packaging of one million doses of medication at total cost plus a return on total cost of no more than 15 percent. VGH defines total cost as including all variable costs of performing the service, a reasonable amount of fixed overhead, and reasonable administrative costs. The hospital will supply all packaging materials and ingredients. VGH's administrator has indicated that any bid over $.03 per dose will be rejected. The controller for North American Pharmaceuticals has accumulated the following information prior to the preparation of the bid:

Direct labour	$16 per direct-labour hour (DLH)
Variable overhead	$12 per DLH
Fixed overhead	$20 per DLH
Incremental administrative costs	$2,000 for the order
Production rate	2,000 doses per DLH

Required:

1. Calculate the minimum price per dose that North American Pharmaceuticals could bid for the VGH job that would not reduce the pharmaceutical company's income.

2. Calculate the bid price per dose using total cost and the maximum allowable return specified by VGH.

3. Independent of your answer to requirement (2), suppose that the price per dose that North American Pharmaceuticals, Inc. calculated using the cost-plus criterion specified by VGH is greater than the maximum bid of $.03 per dose allowed by VGH. Discuss the factors that the pharmaceutical company's management should consider before deciding whether or not to submit a bid at the maximum price of $.03 per dose that VGH allows.

(CMA, adapted)

Badger Valve and Fitting Company, located in southern Ontario, manufactures a variety of industrial valves and pipe fittings. Currently, the company is operating at about 70 percent capacity. Management is interested in bidding for a government contract that requires 120,000 units of a pressure valve. The contract specifies that the 120,000 valves are needed over the next four months. The contract states that the maximum price to be paid is $28.50 each for the valves. Badger's total product cost for the pressure valve is $30, calculated as follows:

Direct material	$ 7.50
Direct labour	9.00
Manufacturing overhead	13.50
Total product cost	$30.00

Problem 14–39
Bidding
(LO 8)

2. Total incremental revenue: $3,420,000
2. Total incremental costs: $2,592,000

Manufacturing overhead is applied to production at the rate of $27 per direct-labour hour. This overhead rate is made up of the following components:

Variable manufacturing overhead	$ 9.00
Fixed manufacturing overhead (traceable)	12.00
Fixed manufacturing overhead (allocated)	6.00
Applied manufacturing overhead rate	$27.00

Additional costs incurred in connection with sales of the pressure valve include sales commissions of 5 percent and freight expense of $1.50 per unit. However, the company does not pay sales commissions on orders that come directly to management. In determining selling prices, Badger adds a 40 percent markup to total product cost. This provides a $42 suggested selling price for the pressure valve. The Marketing Department, however, has set the current selling price at $40.50 in order to maintain market share. Production management believes that it can handle the government contract without disrupting its scheduled production. The government contract would, however, require additional fixed factory overhead of $18,000 per month in the form of supervision and clerical costs. If management wins the bid, 30,000 pressure valves will be manufactured and shipped to the government each month for the next four months. The contract specifies that shipping charges for the valves will be paid by the government.

Required:

1. Determine how many direct-labour hours would be required each month to fill the government contract.

2. Prepare an analysis showing the impact of winning the bid.

3. Calculate the minimum unit price that Badger Valve and Fitting Company's management could bid without reducing net income.

4. Identify the factors, other than price, that Badger's management should consider before bidding on the government contract.

5. *Build a spreadsheet:* Construct an Excel spreadsheet to solve requirements (2) and (3) above. Show how the solution will change if the following information changes: the direct material and direct labour per unit are $6.90 and $9.10, respectively.

(CMA, adapted)

■ **Problem 14–40**
Pricing of a Bid
(LO 8)
1. Income before taxes:
$23,250
2. Total manufacturing costs:
$51,000

Graydon, Inc. manufactures food blending machinery according to customer specifications. The company operated at 75 percent of practical capacity during the year just ended, with the following results (in thousands):

Sales revenue	$12,500
Less: Sales commissions (10%)	1,250
Net sales	11,250
Expenses:	
Direct material	3,000
Direct labour	3,750
Manufacturing overhead—variable	1,125
Manufacturing overhead—fixed	750
Corporate administration—fixed	375
Total costs	9,000
Income before taxes	2,250
Income taxes (40%)	900
Net income	$ 1,350

Graydon, which expects continued operations at 75 percent of capacity, recently submitted a bid of $82,500 on some custom-designed machinery for Premier Foods, Inc. Graydon used a pricing formula in deriving the bid amount, the formula being based on last year's operating results. The formula follows.

Estimated direct material	$14,600
Estimated direct labour	28,000
Estimated manufacturing overhead at 50% of direct labour	14,000
Estimated corporate overhead at 10% of direct labour	2,800
Estimated total costs excluding sales commissions	59,400
Add 25% for profit and taxes	14,850
Suggested price (with profit) before sales commissions	$74,250
Suggested total price: $74,250 ÷ .9 to adjust for 10% commission	$82,500

Required:

1. Calculate the impact the order would have on Graydon's net income if the $82,500 bid were accepted by Premier Foods, Inc.

2. Assume that Premier has rejected Graydon's bid but has stated it is willing to pay $63,500 for the machinery. Should Graydon manufacture the machinery for the counteroffer of $63,500? Explain your answer and show calculations.

3. At what bid price will Graydon break even on the order?

4. Explain how the profit performance in the coming year would be affected if Graydon accepted all of its work at prices similar to Premier's $63,500 counteroffer described in requirement (2).

5. *Build a spreadsheet:* Construct an Excel spreadsheet to solve requirements (1) and (2) above. Show how the solution will change if the following information changes: the direct material and direct labour for the year just ended were $2,900,000 and $3,800,000, respectively; and sales commissions were 8 percent.

(CMA, adapted)

■ **Problem 14–41**
Bidding on a Special Order
(LO 8)
1. Variable overhead: $1.50
2. Fixed overhead: $4

Surrey Synthetic Fibres Inc. specializes in the manufacture of synthetic fibres that the company uses in many products such as blankets, coats, and uniforms for police and firefighters. The company applies overhead on the basis of direct-labour hours. Management has recently received a request to bid on the manufacture of 800,000 blankets scheduled for delivery to several military bases. The bid must be stated at full cost per unit plus a return on full cost of no more than 15 percent before income taxes. Full cost has been defined as including all variable costs of manufacturing the product, a reasonable amount of fixed overhead, and reasonable incremental administrative costs associated with the manufacture and sale of the product. The contractor has indicated that bids in excess of $50 per blanket are not likely to be considered.

In order to prepare the bid for the 800,000 blankets, Andrea Lightner, director of cost management, has gathered the following information about the costs associated with the production of the blankets:

Direct material	$3 per kilogram of fibres
Direct labour	$14 per hour
Direct machine costs*	$20 per blanket
Variable overhead	$6 per direct-labour hour
Fixed overhead	$16 per direct-labour hour
Incremental administrative costs	$5,000 per 1,000 blankets
Special fee†	$1 per blanket
Material usage	6 kilograms per blanket
Production rate	4 blankets per direct-labour hour

*Direct machine costs consist of items such as special lubricants, replacement of needles used in stitching, and maintenance costs. These costs are not included in the normal overhead rates.

†Surrey Synthetic Fibres recently developed a new blanket fibre at a cost of $1,500,000. In an effort to recover this cost, management has instituted a policy of adding a $1 fee to the cost of each blanket using the new fibre. To date, the company has recovered $250,000. Lightner knows that this fee does not fit within the definition of full cost as it is not a cost of manufacturing the product.

Required:

1. Calculate the minimum price per blanket that Surrey Synthetic Fibres Inc. could bid without reducing the company's net income.

2. Using the full cost criteria and the maximum allowable return specified, calculate Surrey Synthetic Fibres Inc.'s bid price per blanket.

3. Independently of your answer to requirement (2), assume that the price per blanket that Surrey Synthetic Fibres Inc. calculated using the cost-plus criteria specified is greater than the maximum bid of $50 per blanket allowed. Discuss the factors that management should consider before deciding whether to submit a bid at the maximum acceptable price of $50 per blanket.

(CMA, adapted)

Cases

Handy Household Products, Inc. is a multiproduct company with several manufacturing plants. The Richmond Plant manufactures and distributes two household cleaning and polishing compounds, standard and commercial, under the Clean & Bright label. The operating results forecast for the first six months of the current year, when 100,000 cases of each compound are expected to be manufactured and sold, are presented in the following statement.

■ **Case 14–42**
Pricing in a Tight Market; Possible Plant Closing
(LO 8)
2. Contribution margin, standard: $700

CLEAN & BRIGHT COMPOUNDS—RICHMOND PLANT			
Forecasted Results of Operations			
For the Six-Month Period Ending June 30			
(in thousands)			
	Standard	Commercial	Total
Sales	$4,000	$6,000	$10,000
Cost of goods sold	3,200	3,800	7,000
Gross profit	800	2,200	3,000
Selling and administrative expenses:			
Variable	800	1,400	2,200
Fixed*	480	720	1,200
Total selling and administrative expenses	1,280	2,120	3,400
Income (loss) before taxes	$ (480)	$ 80	$ (400)

*The fixed selling and administrative expenses are allocated between the two products on the basis of dollar sales volume.

The standard compound sold for $40 a case and the commercial compound sold for $60 a case during the first six months of the year. The manufacturing costs, by case of product, are presented in the schedule below. Each product is manufactured on a separate production line. Annual normal manufacturing capacity is 200,000 cases of each product. However, the plant is capable of producing 250,000 cases of standard compound and 350,000 cases of commercial compound annually.

	Cost per Case	
	Standard	**Commercial**
Direct material	$14	$16
Direct labour	8	8
Variable manufacturing overhead	2	4
Fixed manufacturing overhead*	8	10
Total manufacturing cost	$32	$38
Variable selling and administrative costs	$ 8	$14

*Depreciation charges are 50 percent of the fixed manufacturing overhead of each line.

The following schedule reflects the consensus of top management regarding the price-volume alternatives for the Clean & Bright products for the last six months of the current year. These are essentially the same alternatives management had during the first six months of the year.

Standard Compound		Commercial Compound	
Alternative Prices (per case)	**Sales Volume (in cases)**	**Alternative Prices (per case)**	**Sales Volume (in cases)**
$38	120,000	$52	175,000
40	100,000	54	140,000
42	90,000	60	100,000
44	80,000	64	55,000
46	50,000	70	35,000

Handy Household Products' top management believes the loss for the first six months reflects a tight profit margin caused by intense competition. Management also believes that many companies will leave this market by next year and profit should improve.

Required:

1. What unit selling price should management select for each of the Clean & Bright compounds for the remaining six months of the year? Support your selection with appropriate calculations.

2. Independently of your answer to requirement (1), assume the optimum alternatives for the last six months were as follows: a selling price of $46 and volume of 50,000 cases for the standard compound, and a selling price of $70 and volume of 35,000 cases for the commercial compound.

   a. Should management consider closing down its operations until January 1 of the next year in order to minimize its losses? Support your answer with appropriate calculations.

   b. Identify and discuss the qualitative factors that should be considered in deciding whether the Richmond Plant should be closed down during the last six months of the current year.

(CMA, adapted)

Case 14–43
Bidding on a Special Order;
Ethics
(LO 8)
1. Manufacturing overhead:
$118,800
2. Direct material: $307,200

Bair Company is a manufacturer of standard and custom-designed bottling equipment. Early in December 20x0, Lyan Company asked Bair to quote a price for a custom-designed bottling machine to be delivered in April. Lyan intends to make a decision on the purchase of such a machine by January 1, so Bair would have the entire first quarter of 20x1 to build the equipment.

Bair's pricing policy for custom-designed equipment is 50 percent markup on absorption manufacturing cost. Lyan's specifications for the equipment have been reviewed by Bair's Engineering and Cost Management Departments, which made the following estimates for direct material and direct labour:

Direct material	$307,200
Direct labour (11,000 hours @ $18)	198,000

Manufacturing overhead is applied on the basis of direct-labour hours. Bair normally plans to run its plant at a level of 15,000 direct-labour hours per month and assigns overhead on the basis of 180,000 direct-labour hours per year. The overhead application rate for 20x1 of $10.80 per hour is based on the following budgeted manufacturing overhead costs for 20x1:

Variable manufacturing overhead	$1,166,400
Fixed manufacturing overhead	777,600
Total manufacturing overhead	$1,944,000

Bair's production schedule calls for 12,000 direct-labour hours per month during the first quarter. If Bair is awarded the contract for the Lyan equipment, production of one of its standard products would have to be reduced. This is necessary because production levels can only be increased to 15,000 direct-labour hours each month on short notice. Furthermore, Bair's employees are unwilling to work overtime.

Sales of the standard product equal to the reduced production would be lost, but there would be no permanent loss of future sales or customers. The standard product for which the production schedule would be reduced has a unit sales price of $14,400 and the following cost structure:

Direct material	$ 3,000
Direct labour (250 hours @ $18)	4,500
Manufacturing overhead (250 hours @ $10.80)	2,700
Total cost	$10,200

Lyan needs the custom-designed equipment to increase its bottle-making capacity so that it will not have to buy bottles from an outside supplier. Lyan Company requires 5,000,000 bottles annually. Its present equipment has a maximum capacity of 4,500,000 bottles with a directly traceable cash outlay cost of 18 cents per bottle. Thus, Lyan has had to purchase 500,000 bottles from a supplier at 48 cents each. The new equipment would allow Lyan to manufacture its entire annual demand for bottles at a direct-material cost savings of 1.2 cents per bottle. Bair estimates that Lyan's annual bottle demand will continue to be 5,000,000 bottles over the next five years, the estimated life of the special-purpose equipment.

Required: Bair Industries plans to submit a bid to Lyan Company for the manufacture of the special-purpose bottling equipment.

1. Calculate the bid Bair would submit if it follows its standard pricing policy for special-purpose equipment.
2. Calculate the minimum bid Bair would be willing to submit on the Lyan equipment that would result in the same total contribution margin as planned for the first quarter of 20x1.
3. Suppose Bair Industries has submitted a bid slightly above the minimum calculated in requirement (2). Upon receiving Bair's bid, Lyan's assistant purchasing manager telephoned his friend at Tygar Corporation: "Hey Joe, we just got a bid from Bair Industries on some customized equipment. I think Tygar would stand a good chance of beating it. Stop by the house this evening, and I'll show you the details of Bair's bid and the specifications on the machine."
   Is Lyan Company's assistant purchasing manager acting ethically? Explain.

(CMA, adapted)

Appendix I

Inventory Management

A key decision in manufacturing, retail, and some service industry firms is how much inventory to keep on hand. Once inventory levels are established, they become an important input to the budgeting system. Inventory decisions involve a delicate balance between three classes of costs: ordering costs, holding costs, and shortage costs. Examples of costs in each of these categories are given in Exhibit I–1.

The following illustration emphasizes the benefits of a sound inventory policy.

Economic Order Quantity

CozyCamp.ca, a camping equipment manufacturer, has recently expanded its product line into winter sports equipment. The company's newest product is a fibreglass snowboard. One of the raw materials is a special resin used to bind the fibreglass in the moulding phase of production. The production manager, Hi Mogul, uses an **economic order quantity (EOQ)** decision model to determine the size and frequency with which resin is ordered. The EOQ model is a mathematical tool for determining the order quantity that minimizes the costs of ordering and holding inventory.

Resin is purchased in 50-litre drums, and 9,600 drums are used each year. Each drum costs $400. The controller estimates that the cost of placing and receiving a typical resin order is $225. The controller's estimate of the annual cost of carrying resin in inventory is $3 per drum.

After completing this appendix, you should be able to:

1 Calculate the economic order quantity (EOQ) using the EOQ decision model.

2 Understand the differences between the economic-order-quantity and just-in-time approaches to inventory management.

Learning Objective 1

Calculate the economic order quantity (EOQ) using the EOQ decision model.

cozycamp.ca

Exhibit I–1
Inventory Ordering, Holding, and Shortage Costs

Ordering Costs

Clerical costs of preparing purchase orders

Time spent finding suppliers and expediting orders

Transportation costs

Receiving costs (e.g., unloading and inspection)

Holding Costs

Costs of storage space (e.g., warehouse depreciation)

Security

Insurance

Forgone interest on working capital tied up in inventory

Deterioration, theft, spoilage, or obsolescence

Shortage Costs

Disrupted production when raw materials are unavailable:

   Idle workers

   Extra machinery setups

Lost sales resulting in dissatisfied customers

Loss of quantity discounts on purchases

Tabular Approach   Suppose Mogul orders 800 drums of resin in each order placed during the year. The total annual cost of ordering and holding resin in inventory is calculated as follows:

$$\frac{\text{Annual requirement}}{\text{Quantity per order}} = \frac{9,600}{800} = 12 = \text{Number of orders}$$

$$\text{Annual ordering cost} = 12 \text{ orders} \times \$225 \text{ per order} = \$2,700$$

$$\text{Average quantity in inventory} = \frac{\text{Quantity per order}}{2} = \frac{800}{2} = 400 \text{ drums}$$

$$\text{Annual holding cost} = (\text{Average quantity in inventory}) \times (\text{Annual carrying cost per drum})$$
$$= 400 \times \$3 = \$1,200$$

$$\frac{\text{Total annual cost}}{\text{of inventory policy}} = \text{Ordering cost} + \text{Holding cost} = \$2,700 + \$1,200 = \$3,900$$

Notice that the $3,900 cost does not include the purchase cost of the resin at $400 per drum. We are focusing only on the costs of *ordering* and *holding* resin inventory.

Can Mogul do any better than $3,900 for the annual cost of his resin inventory policy? Exhibit I–2, which tabulates the inventory costs for various order quantities, indicates that Mogul can lower the costs of ordering and holding resin inventory. Of the five order quantities listed, the 1,200-drum order quantity yields the lowest total annual cost. Unfortunately, this tabular method for finding the least-cost order quantity is cumbersome. Moreover, it does not necessarily result in the optimal order quantity. It is possible that some order quantity other than those listed in Exhibit I–2 is the least-cost order quantity.

Equation Approach   The total annual cost of ordering and holding inventory is given by the following equation:

$$\text{Total annual cost} = \left(\frac{\text{Annual requirement}}{\text{Order quantity}}\right)\left(\begin{array}{c}\text{Cost per}\\\text{order}\end{array}\right)$$

$$+ \left(\frac{\text{Order quantity}}{2}\right)\left(\begin{array}{c}\text{Annual holding}\\\text{cost per unit}\end{array}\right)$$

Order size	800	960	1,200	1,600	2,400
Number of orders (9,600 ÷ Order size)	12	10	8	6	4
Ordering costs ($225 × Number of orders)	$2,700	$2,250	$1,800	$1,350	$ 900
Average inventory (Order size ÷ 2)	400	480	600	800	1,200
Holding costs ($3 × Average inventory)	$1,200	$1,440	$1,800	$2,400	$3,600
Total annual cost (Ordering cost + Holding cost)	$3,900	$3,690	$3,600	$3,750	$4,500

Minimum

Exhibit I–2
Tabulation of Inventory
Ordering and Holding Costs

cozycamp.ca

The following formula for the least-cost order quantity, called the economic order quantity (or EOQ), has been developed using calculus.

$$\text{Economic order quantity} = \sqrt{\frac{(2)(\text{Annual requirement})(\text{Cost per order})}{(\text{Annual holding cost per unit})}}$$

The EOQ formula in CozyCamp.ca's problem yields the following EOQ for resin:

$$\text{EOQ} = \sqrt{\frac{(2)(9,600)(225)}{3}} = 1,200$$

Graphical Approach   Another method for solving the EOQ problem is the graphical method, which is presented in Exhibit I–3. Notice that the ordering-cost line slants down to the right. This indicates a decline in these costs as the order size increases and the order frequency decreases. However, as the order size increases, so does the average inventory on hand. This results in an increase in holding costs, as indicated by the positive slope of the holding-cost line. The EOQ falls at 1,200 units, where the best balance is struck between these two costs. Total costs are minimized at $3,600.

Timing of Orders

The EOQ model helps management decide how much to order at a time. Another important decision is when to order. This decision depends on the **lead time**, which is the length of time it takes for the material to be received after an order is placed. Suppose the lead time for resin is one month. Since Cozycamp.com uses 9,600 drums

Exhibit I–3
Graphical Solution to Economic Order Quantity Decision

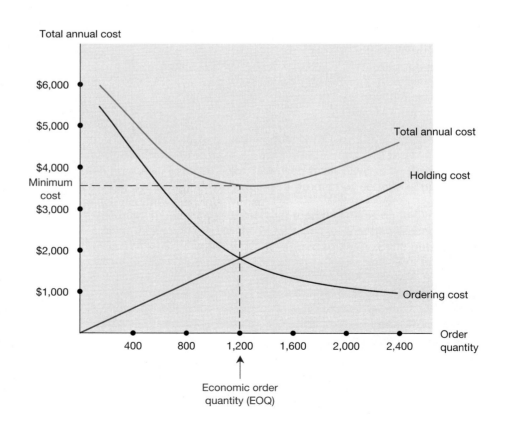

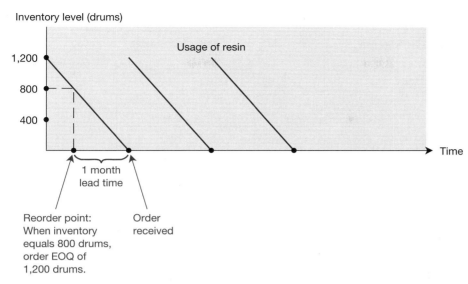

Inventory level (drums)

Usage of resin

1,200

800

400

Time

1 month
lead time

Reorder point:
When inventory
equals 800 drums,
order EOQ of
1,200 drums.

Order
received

of resin per year, and the production rate is constant throughout the year, this implies that 800 drums are used each month. Production manager Mogul should order resin, in the economic order quantity of 1,200 drums, when the inventory falls to 800 drums. By the time the new order arrives, one month later, the 800 drums in inventory will have been used in production. Exhibit I–4 depicts this pattern of ordering and using inventory. By placing an order early enough to avoid a stockout, management takes into account the potential costs of shortages.

Safety Stock   Our example assumed that the usage of resin is constant at 800 drums per month. Suppose instead that monthly usage fluctuates between 600 and 1,000 drums. Although average monthly usage still is 800 drums, there is the potential for an excess usage of 200 drums in any particular month. In light of this uncertainty, management may wish to keep a safety stock of resin equal to the potential excess monthly usage of 200 drums. With a safety stock of 200 drums, the reorder point is 1,000 drums. Thus, Mogul should order the EOQ of 1,200 drums whenever resin inventory falls to 1,000 drums. During the one-month lead time, another 600 to 1,000 drums of resin will be consumed in production. Although a safety stock will increase inventory holding costs, it will minimize the potential costs caused by shortages.

JIT Inventory Management: Implications for EOQ

The EOQ model minimizes the total cost of ordering and holding purchased inventory. Thus, this inventory management approach seeks to balance the cost of ordering against the cost of storing inventory. Under the JIT philosophy, the goal is to keep *all* inventories as low as possible. *Any* inventory holding costs are seen as inefficient and wasteful. Moreover, under JIT purchasing, ordering costs are minimized by reducing the number of vendors, negotiating long-term supply agreements, making less frequent payments, and eliminating inspections. The implication of the JIT philosophy is that inventories should be minimized by more frequent deliveries in smaller quantities. This result can be demonstrated using the EOQ formula, as shown in Exhibit I–5. As the cost of holding inventory increases, the EOQ decreases. Moreover, as the cost of placing an order declines, the EOQ decreases.

Learning Objective 2

Understand the differences between the economic-order-quantity and just-in-time approaches to inventory management.

Exhibit I–5

Economic Order Quantity
with Different Ordering
and Holding Costs

cozycamp.ca

Holding Costs per Unit	Ordering Costs per Order				
	$225	**$150**	**$100**	**$50**	
$3	1,200*	980	800	566	EOQ declines
4	1,039	849	693	490	
5	930	759	620	438	
6	849	693	566	400	
	EOQ declines				

*The annual requirement is assumed to be 9,600 units for each case in this table. This was the annual requirement for drums of resin in the CozyCamp.ca illustration. (Several of the EOQs in the table are rounded.)

The economics underlying the EOQ model support the JIT viewpoint that inventory should be purchased or produced in small quantities, and inventories should be kept to an absolute minimum. However, the basic philosophies of JIT and EOQ are quite different. The EOQ approach takes the view that some inventory is necessary, and the goal is to optimize the order quantity in order to balance the cost of ordering against the cost of holding inventory. In contrast, the JIT philosophy argues that holding costs tend to be higher than is apparent because of the inefficiency and waste of storing inventory. Thus, inventory should be minimized, or even eliminated completely if possible. Moreover, under the JIT approach, orders will typically vary in size, depending on needs. The EOQ model, in contrast, results in a constant order quantity.

Key Terms

For each term's definition refer to the indicated page, or turn to the glossary at the end of the text.

economic order quantity
 (EOQ), I-1

lead time, I-3

Review Questions

I–1. Define and give examples of *inventory ordering*, *holding*, and *shortage costs*.

I–2. Explain the differences in the basic philosophies underlying the JIT and EOQ approaches to inventory management.

Exercises

■ **Exercise I–3**
Economic Order Quantity
(LO 1)

For each of the following independent cases, use the equation method to compute the economic order quantity.

	Case A	Case B	Case C
Annual requirement (in units)	13,230	1,681	560
Cost per order	$250	$40	$10
Annual holding cost per unit	6	20	7

Andrew and Fulton, Inc. uses 780 tonnes of a chemical bonding agent each year. Monthly demand fluctuates between 50 and 80 tonnes. The lead time for each order is one month, and the economic order quantity is 130 tonnes.

■ **Exercise I–4**
Lead Time and Safety Stock
(LO 1)

Required:

1. Determine the safety stock appropriate for the chemical bonding agent.
2. At what order point, in terms of tonnes remaining in inventory, should Andrew and Fulton, Inc. order the bonding agent?

■ **Exercise I–5**
Economic Order Quantity;
Equation Approach; JIT
Purchasing
(LO 1, 2)

Fibre Technology, Inc. manufactures glass fibres used in the communications industry. The company's materials and parts manager is currently revising the inventory policy for XL-20, one of the chemicals used in the production process. The chemical is purchased in 10-kilogram canisters for $95 each. The firm uses 4,800 canisters per year. The controller estimates that it costs $150 to place and receive a typical order of XL-20. The annual cost of storing XL-20 is $4 per canister.

Required:

1. Write the formula for the total annual cost of ordering and storing XL-20.
2. Use the EOQ formula to determine the optimal order quantity.
3. What is the total annual cost of ordering and storing XL-20 at the economic order quantity?
4. How many orders will be placed per year?
5. Fibre Technology's controller, Jay Turnbull, recently attended a seminar on JIT purchasing. Afterward he analyzed the cost of storing XL-20, including the costs of wasted space and inefficiency. He was shocked when he concluded that the real annual holding cost was $19.20 per canister. Turnbull then met with Doug Kaplan, Fibre Technology's purchasing manager. Together they contacted Reno Industries, the supplier of XL-20, about a JIT purchasing arrangement. After some discussion and negotiation, Kaplan concluded that the cost of placing an order for XL-20 could be reduced to just $20. Using these new cost estimates, Turnbull computed the new EOQ for XL-20.
   a. Use the equation approach to compute the new EOQ.
   b. How many orders will be placed per year?

■ **Exercise I–6**
Economic Order Quantity;
Tabular Approach
(LO 1)

Refer to the *original* data given in the preceding exercise for Fibre Technology, Inc.

Required:

1. Prepare a table showing the total annual cost of ordering and storing XL-20 for each of the following order quantities: 400, 600, and 800 canisters.
2. What are the weaknesses in the tabular approach?

■ **Exercise I–7**
Economic Order Quantity;
Graphical Approach
(LO 1)

Refer to the *original* data given in Exercise I–5 for Fibre Technology, Inc.

Required: Prepare a graphical analysis of the economic order quantity decision for XL-20.

■ **Exercise I–8**
Economic Order Quantity;
Lead Time and Safety Stock
(LO 1)

Refer to the *original* data given in Exercise I–5 for Fibre Technology, Inc. The lead time required to receive an order of XL-20 is one month.

Required:

1. Assuming stable usage of XL-20 each month, determine the reorder point for XL-20.
2. Draw a graph showing the usage, lead time, and reorder point for XL-20.
3. Suppose that monthly usage of XL-20 fluctuates between 300 and 500 canisters, although annual demand remains constant at 4,800 canisters. What level of safety stock should the materials and parts manager keep on hand for XL-20? What is the new reorder point for the chemical?

Photo Credits

Chapter One

Page 1: © Mike Clark/AFP/Getty Images; **page 2:** © Syracuse Newspapers/Suzanne Dunn/The Image Works; **page 7 (left):** © PhotoLink/Getty Images/DIL; **page 7 (right):** © Susan Van Etten/PhotoEdit; **page 17 (top left):** © Kent Knudson/PhotoLink/Getty Images/DIL; **page 17 (top middle):** © Royalty-Free/CORBIS/DIL; **page 17 (bottom left):** © JG Photography/Alamy/DIL; **page 17 (bottom middle):** © Bill Aaron/PhotoEdit; **page 17 (bottom right):** © The McGraw-Hill Companies, Inc./Andrew Resek, photographer/DIL.

Chapter Two

Page 26 (top): © Ingram Publishing/Alamy; **page 26 (bottom):** © Collin Young Wolff/PhotoEdit; **page 32 (top):** © Buena Vista Pictures/Courtesy Everett Collection; **page 32 (top middle):** © Michael Abramson/Woodfin Camp & Associates; **page 32 (middle):** Royalty-Free/CORBIS; **page 32 (bottom middle):** © The McGraw-Hill Companies, Inc./Jimm Braaten, photographer; **page 32 (bottom):** © Malcolm Fife/Getty Images; **page 39:** © PhotoLink/Getty Images/DIL; **page 47:** © Sonja Sommerfeld/Daemmrich Associate.

Chapter Three

Page 68 (top): © Bill Curtsinger/Getty Images; **page 68 (bottom):** © Paul Barton/CORBIS; **page 72 (left):** © Robert Holmgren/Peter Arnold, Inc.; **page 72 (middle):** © Justin Sullivan/Getty Images; **page 72 (right):** © Michael Newman/PhotoEdit; **page 77:** © Dean Abramson/Stock Boston.

Chapter Four

Page 119 (top): © Erin Riley/Getty Images; **page 119 (bottom):** © Rim Light/PhotoLink/Getty Images; **page 123 (left):** © Royalty-Free/CORBIS/DIL; **page 123 (right):** © Russell Illig/Getty Images/DIL.

Chapter Five

Page 145 (top): © Russell Illig/Getty Images; **page 145 (bottom):** © Blend Images; **page 149 (left):** © Kim Steele/Getty Images/DIL; **page 149 (right):** © Royalty-Free/CORBIS/DIL; **page 159 (left):** © Flying Colours Ltd./Getty Images/DIL; **page 159 (right):** © Ronald W. Hilton.

Chapter Six

Page 199 (top): © PhotoDisc/PunchStock; **page 199 (bottom):** © Photo Disc/Getty Images.

Chapter Seven

Page 240 (top): © Siri Stafford/Getty Images; **page 240 (bottom):** © JupiterImages/Brand X/CORBIS; **page 242 (left):** © Erica Simone Leeds; **page 242 (right):** © The McGraw-Hill Companies, Inc./Andrew Resek, photographer; **page 254:** © Royalty-Free/CORBIS; **page 264:** Lonnie Duka/Getty Images.

Chapter Eight

Page 286 (top): © StockDisc/PunchStock; **page 286 (bottom):** © Royalty-Free/CORBIS; **page 288:** © Royalty-Free/CORBIS.

Chapter Nine

Page 305 (top): © Brand X Pictures; **page 305 (bottom):** © Stockbyte/PunchStock; **page 307:** © Royalty-Free/CORBIS; **page 331:** © Susan Van Etten/PhotoEdit.

Chapter Ten

Page 361: © Brand X Pictures/PunchStock; **page 362:** © Royalty-Free/CORBIS; **page 377 (left):** © Digital Vision/PunchStock; **page 377 (right):** © Royalty-Free/CORBIS; **page 387:** © BananaStock/JupiterImages; **page 395:** Courtesy of Texas Instruments.

Chapter Eleven

Page 425 (top): Ryan McVay/Getty Images; **page 425 (bottom):** © Royalty-Free/CORBIS; **page 430:** © Digital Vision/PunchStock; **page 446:** © Grafissimo/iStockphoto.

Chapter Twelve

Page 459 (top): © Chris Caldicott/Getty Images; **page 459 (bottom):** © Royalty-Free/CORBIS; **page 463 (top left):** © Robert Gumpert/Alamy; **page 463 (bottom left):** © PhotoLink/Getty Images; **page 463 (top right):** © The McGraw-Hill Companies, Inc./John Flournoy, photographer/DIL; **page 463 (bottom right):** © Digital Vision/PunchStock/DIL; **page 476:** © Royalty-Free/CORBIS/DIL; **page 483:** © J. Emilio Flores/Getty Images; **page 492:** www.sfu.ca.

Chapter Thirteen

Page 520 (top): © Royalty-Free/CORBIS; **page 520 (bottom):** © Banana Stock/PunchStock; **page 533 (left):** © PhotoLink/Getty Images; **page 533 (right):** © Royalty-Free/CORBIS.

Chapter Fourteen

Page 571 (top): © Jeff Greenberg/The Image Works; **page 571 (bottom):** © Richard Klune/CORBIS; **page 574:** Stockbyte/PunchStock Image; **page 583:** © Kevin Horan/Stone/Getty Images.

Chapter Fifteen (Online)

Page 1 (top): © Royalty-Free/CORBIS; **page 1 (bottom):** © Brand X Pictures/PunchStock; **page 12:** © Royalty-Free/CORBIS; **page 22:** © The McGraw-Hill Companies, Inc./John Flournoy, photographer/DIL.

Chapter Sixteen (Online)

Page 1 (top): © Mark Thornton/Getty Images; **page 1 (bottom):** © Rick Barrentine/CORBIS; **page 13:** © Lester Lefkowitz/CORBIS.

End Notes

Chapter One

1. Throughout the text, you will find these quotes from both practising managers and management accountants. Collectively they portray the important role managerial accounting plays in today's dynamic business environment. The references for these quotes appear at the end of the text, beginning on page R-1. The references are organized by chapter; thus, reference (1a) relates to the first quote in Chapter 1, and so forth.
2. Gary Siegel, "The Image of Corporate Accountants," *Strategic Finance* 82, no. 2 (August 2000), p. 71.
3. Although The Walt Disney Company, discussed in this chapter, is a real company, the subsequent focus organizations around which chapters are built are fictitious. But they also offer realistic settings in which to discuss business and managerial accounting issues, and in most cases are based on real organizations. Similarly, each chapter includes a discussion of a contrast company. Some of these, such as clothing retailer Gap, Inc. in this chapter, are real companies. Others are fictitious ones based on real organizations. These realistic illustrations and scenarios are intended to help students connect the business and managerial accounting issues discussed in this book to everyday life.
4. Ravi Kalakota and Andrew B. Whinston, *Electronic Commerce: A Manager's Guide* (Reading, MA: Addison-Wesley, 1997), p. 287.
5. Ravi Kalakota and Marcia Robinson, *E-Business: Road Map for Success* (Reading, MA: Addison-Wesley, 1999), p. 4.
6. The information and quotations for Canadian Direct Insurance, London Drugs, Viewtrak Technologies, and PropertyGuys.com in this inset are from Michael Favere-Marchesi and the respective companies' Web sites.
7. Excel® is a registered trademark of Microsoft Corporation.
8. Allan Sloan, "Laying Enron to Rest," *Newsweek* 147, no. 23 (June 5, 2006), pp. 25–30.
9. John Hodowanitz and Steven A. Solieri, "Guarding the Guardians," *Strategic Finance* 87, no. 2 (August 2005), pp. 47–53; and Andrew J. Felo and Steven A. Solieri, "New Laws, New Challenges: Implications of Sarbanes-Oxley," *Strategic Finance* 84, no. 8 (February 2003), pp. 31–34.

Chapter Two

1. Based on the well-known and widely used Hayes-Wheelwright production process matrix, with the exception of mass customization, which postdates the Hayes-Wheelwright formulation. See Robert H. Hayes and Steven C. Wheelwright, *Restoring Our Competitive Edge* (New York: John Wiley and Sons, 1984), p. 209.
2. Thaddeus Herrick, "Dell's Profit Soars," *The Wall Street Journal*, February 17, 2006, p. A3; Louise Lee and Spencer Ante, "Can the PC King Excel in Services: Dell Is on a Tear, but Maintaining That Clip Could Be Tough," *BusinessWeek*, May 30, 2005, pp. 70–73; and Andy Serwer, "Dell Does Domination," *Fortune*, January 21, 2002, pp. 70–75.
3. "The Best Little Factory in Texas," *Forbes*, June 10, 2002, p. 110.
4. Louise Lee and Emily Thornton, "Hanging Up on Dell: Gripes about Tech Support Are on the Rise, and the PC King Is Scrambling to Upgrade," *BusinessWeek*, October 10, 2005, pp. 80–81; and Steve Lohr, "On a Roll, Dell Enters Uncharted Territory," *The New York Times*, August 25, 2002, section 3, p. 1.
5. As mentioned at the beginning of Chapter 1, the focus organizations around which Chapters 2 through 16 are built are not real organizations. They are, however, realistic settings in which to discuss business and managerial accounting issues, and in most cases they are based on real organizations. These illustrations are intended to help students connect the business and managerial accounting issues discussed in this book to everyday life.
6. The description of the manufacturing process is based on that used by Dell Inc.
7. Such cost driver teams have been established by many companies. For descriptions of such efforts at Deere and Company and Hewlett-Packard Corporation, see the management cases John Deere Component Works and Hewlett-Packard Queensferry Telecommunications Division (Harvard Business School).
8. Christopher Conkey, "Airports May Boost Runway Fees in Peak Hours," *The Wall Street Journal*, January 15, 2008, p. A33; and Melanie Trottman and Scott McCartney, "The Age of Wal-Mart Airlines Crunches the Biggest Carriers," *The Wall Street Journal*, June 18, 2002, pp. A1, A8. See also Alan Cowell, "Low-Cost Airlines Grow and Compete in Europe," *The New York Times*, July 28, 2002, p. 3.
9. The outsourcing decision, as well as several other common management decisions, is covered in detail in Chapter 13.
10. In professional American football, the Super Bowl is the championship game of the National Football League (NFL) in the United States.
11. The details of the outsourcing decision, including its relevant costs and the role of opportunity costs, are covered in Chapter 13.
12. Marginal cost of 101st laptop computer is $995 (from Exhibit 2–11). Average cost per unit when 101 laptops are produced is $1,495 ($150,995 ÷ 101).
13. Recent Midas, Inc. annual reports and the company's Web site.
14. Jared Sandberg, Rebecca Blumenstein, and Shawn Young, "WorldCom Admits $3.8 Billion Error in Its Accounting—Firm Ousts Financial Chief and Struggles for Survival; SEC Probe Likely to Widen," *The Wall Street Journal*, June 26, 2002, p. A1; Jared Sandberg, Deborah Solomon, and Rebecca Blumenstein, "Disconnected: Inside WorldCom's Unearthing of a Vast Accounting Scandal," *The Wall Street Journal*, June 27, 2002, p. A1; and Jared Sandberg, "Leading the News: Was Ebbers Aware of Accounting Move at His WorldCom?," *The Wall Street Journal*, July 1, 2002, p. A3.
15. Devlin Barrett, "Ex-WorldCom Exec Pleads Guilty," Associated Press, September 27, 2002 (as it appeared in the *Ithaca Journal*). See also Kurt Eichenwald and Simon Romero, "Plea Deals Are Seen for Three WorldCom Executives," *The New York Times*, August 29, 2002, pp. C1, C4.
16. T. Richardson, "Worldcom CFO Lied, He Admits in Court," *The Register*, February 17, 2005, www.theregister.co.uk.
17. A. Latour, S. Young, and L. Yuan, "Ebbers Is Convicted in Massive Fraud," *The Wall Street Journal*, March 16, 2005, p. A1.

Chapter Three

1. Carol Hymowitz, "Using Layoffs to Battle Downturns Often Costs More Than It Saves," *The Wall Street Journal*, July 24, 2001, p. B1.
2. David Welch and David Henry, "Can GM Stop Blowing Cash?" *BusinessWeek*, November 21, 2005, pp. 50–52; Stanley Holmes, "A Plastic Dream Machine," *BusinessWeek*, June 20, 2005, pp. 32–35; and Stanley Holmes, "Is Boeing Cutting Too Close to the Bone?" *BusinessWeek*, November 26, 2001, pp. 108, 109.
3. An organization's supply chain refers to the flow of all goods, services, and information into and out of the organization.
4. Ariel Markelevich and Ronal Bell, "RFID: The Changes It Will Bring," *Strategic Finance* 88, no. 2 (August 2006), pp. 46–49.
5. Stanley Holmes and Mike France, "Boeing's Secret: Did the Aircraft Giant Exploit Accounting Rules to Conceal a Huge Factory Snafu?" *BusinessWeek*, May 20, 2002, pp. 110–120. Also see Andy Pasztor and Anne Soueo, "Boeing Could Pay Large Penalty to Settle Probes, Avoid Prosecution," *The Wall Street Journal*, September 17, 2005, pp. A1, A8.

6. One might legitimately ask why this is called "two-stage" cost alloca-tion, when there are three types of allocation involved, but the term is entrenched in the literature and in practice. It stems from the fact that there are two *cost objects*, or entities to which costs are assigned: production *departments* in stage 1 and production *jobs* in stage 2.

Chapter Four

1. The FIFO method of process costing is also covered in a supplement to this text titled *Process Costing: The First-In, First-Out Method*. This supplement is available to students on the text Web site at www.mcgrawhill.ca/olc/hilton and to instructors on the Instructor's Resource CD-ROM.

2. Based on the R. W. Hilton's research.

3. Sequential production operations are also covered in a supplement to this textbook titled *Process Costing in Sequential Production Depart-ments*. This supplement is available to students on the text Web site at www.mcgrawhill.ca/olc/hilton and to instructors on the Instructor's Resource CD-ROM.

4. Operation Costing is covered in a supplement to this text titled *Hybrid Product-Costing Systems: Operation Costing in Batch Manufactur-ing Processes*. This supplement is available to students on the text Web site at www.mcgrawhill.ca/olc/hilton and to instructors on the Instructor's Resource CD-ROM.

Chapter Five

1. For another example of cost distortion, see S. L. Mintz, "Compaq's Secret Weapon," *CFO* 10, no. 10, pp. 93–97.

2. Ford S. Worthy, "Accounting Bores You? Wake Up," *Fortune* 116, no. 8 (October 12, 1987), pp. 43–53.

3. S. Kranz, "Sitting Pretty in Prague: DHL's Tech Triumph," *Busi-nessWeek*, December 12, 2005, p. 56; and S. Player and C. Cobble, *Cornerstones of Decision Making: Profiles of Enterprise ABM* (Greensboro, NC: Oakhill Press, 1999), pp. 131–144.

4. Robin Cooper, "Does Your Company Need a New Cost System?," *Journal of Cost Management* 1, no. 1 (Spring 1987), pp. 45–49, and Robin Cooper, "You Need a New Costing System When…," *Har-vard Business Review* 67, no. 1 (1989), pp. 77–82. See also Peter B. B. Turney, *Common Cents: The ABC Performance Breakthrough* (Hillsboro, OR: Cost Technology, 1991).

5. This section draws on Lewis J. Soloway, "Using Activity-Based Management in Aerospace and Defense Companies," *Journal of Cost Management* 6, no. 4 (Winter 1993), pp. 56–66, and Peter B. B. Tur-ney, "What an Activity-Based Cost Model Looks Like," *Journal of Cost Management* 5, no. 4 (Winter 1992), pp. 54–60.

6. This definition, as well as other material in this section, is drawn from James A. Brimson, "Improvement and Elimination of Non-Value-Added Costs," *Journal of Cost Management* 2, no. 2 (Summer 1988), pp. 62–65.

7. An important point that could be overlooked here is that activity-based costing analysis can be used in a very specific, targeted manner to address a particular management problem. In this case, the ABC focus is customer-profitability analysis. This is the essence of activity-based management, using the results of an ABC analysis to manage an enterprise more effectively.

8. "Alienating Customers Isn't Always a Bad Idea, Many Firms Dis-cover," *The Wall Street Journal*, January 7, 1999.

9. In a conversation with a vice-president from a large consumer-products manufacturer, one of the authors was struck by the executive's statement "You can bet we pay a lot of attention to the needs and desires of the 'Mart Brothers,' K and Wal."

10. Recent Best Buy annual reports.

11. G. McWilliams, "Analyzing Customers, Best Buy Decides Not All Are Welcome," *The Wall Street Journal*, November 8, 2004.

12. Ibid.

13. Angela Norkiewicz, "Nine Steps to Implementing ABC," *Manage-ment Accounting* 75, no. 10 (April 1994), pp. 28–33.

14. For a more elaborate example of activity-based costing in a hospital's primary-care unit, see V. G. Narayanan, R. Moore, and L. Brem, "Cambridge Hospital Community Health Care Network—The Pri-mary Care Unit" (Boston: The President and Fellows of Harvard College, 2000). In this case, minutes of time with a health-care pro-fessional is a key cost driver.

15. Nurse practitioners are working in emergency departments and hospi-tal clinics such as heart function clinics and disease management clin-ics to provide ongoing care, monitoring, follow-up, and education to patients. Nurse practitioners in hospital-based clinics manage health care for many patients who do not have a family physician. They are expert nurses with additional education and skills that enable them to provide front-line primary health care.

16. The scenario described here, while fictitious, is based on several real-world events described in the ABC literature. Anecdotes in various ABC cases and other sources, as well as personal research, form the basis for the events described. A key source is the well-known "Schrader-Bellows" case, by R. Cooper (Boston: President and Fellows of Harvard College), which remains a classic describing issues surrounding activity-based costing.

17. James B. Dilworth, *Production and Operations Management*, 3rd ed. (New York: Random House, 1996), pp. 354–61.

18. You might find it helpful to review Exhibit 1–3, which depicts the pull method of the JIT system.

19. Toyota's groundbreaking JIT system originally was referred to as *Kanban*, a Japanese word meaning "signboard." See Takeo Tanaka, "Kaizen Budgeting: Toyota's Cost Control System under TQC," *Journal of Cost Management* 8, no. 3 (Fall 1994), p. 57.

20. Robert Adams and Ray Carter, "United Technologies' Activity-Based Accounting Is a Catalyst for Success," *As Easy as ABC* 18, p. 4. United Technologies uses the term "*structural*-level activity," instead of "*facility*-level activity" as we have done in the chapter and in the table presented here.

Chapter Six

1. Clare Ansberry, "In the New Workplace, Jobs Morph to Suit Rapid Change of Pace," *The Wall Street Journal*, March 3, 2002, pp. A1, A7.

2. David Booth, "Fixed-Cost Labour Killing Domestic Automakers," *National Post*, February 3, 2006.

3. Jonathan Eig, "Do Part-Time Workers Hold Key to When the Reces-sion Breaks?" *The Wall Street Journal*, January 3, 2002, p. A1.

4. Michelle Conlin, "The Big Squeeze on Workers," *BusinessWeek*, May 13, 2002, pp. 96–98; and Michelle Conlin, "The Software Says You're Just Average," *BusinessWeek*, February 25, 2002, p. 126.

5. The budgeting process is covered in Chapter 9.

6. The information and quotations in this inset are from Michelle Conlin, "The Big Squeeze on Workers," *BusinessWeek*, May 13, 2002, pp. 96, 97.

7. The derivation of these equations, which requires calculus, is covered in any introductory statistics text.

Chapter Seven

1. Daniel Michaels, "Kinshasa Is Poor, Scary, and a Boon for Air France," *The Wall Street Journal*, April 30, 2002, pp. A1, A8. Also see "The Importance of Breaking Even," *Business Line Inter-net Edition*, January 19, 2006, at www.blonnet.com/2006/01/19/stories/2006011900981000.htm.

2. Susan Carey, "JetBlue, One of the Few U.S. Airlines to Buck the Downturn, Files for $125 Million IPO," *The Wall Street Journal*, February 13, 2002, p. B4.

3. This form of income statement, in which each item on the statement is expressed as a percentage of sales revenue, is often called a *common-size income statement*.

4. Timothy J. Mullaney and Robert D. Hof, "Finally, the Pot of Gold," *BusinessWeek*, June 24, 2002, p. 106.

Chapter Eight

1. "Section 12: Inventory Valuation," *Income Tax Interpretation Bulletin IT-473R*.
2. See Chapter 5 for a thorough discussion of the concept of unit-level costs and cost hierarchies in the context of an activity-based-costing system.
3. This scenario is based on the case "I Enjoy Challenges," originally written by Michael W. Maher. It is used here with permission.

Chapter Nine

1. Activity-based costing (ABC) is covered in depth in Chapter 5.
2. This section is based on the following references: James A. Brimson and John Antos, *Driving Value Using Activity-Based Budgeting* (New York: John Wiley & Sons, 1999); Sofia Börjesson, "A Case Study on Activity-Based Budgeting," *Journal of Cost Management* 10, no. 4 (Winter 1997), pp. 7–18; and Robert S. Kaplan and Robin Cooper, *Cost and Effect* (Boston: Harvard Business School Press, 1998), pp. 301–315.
3. David M. Aldea and David E. Bullinger, "Using ABC for Shared Services, Charge-Outs, Activity-Based Budgeting, and Benchmarking," in *Activity-Based Management: Arthur Andersen's Lessons from the ABM Battlefield*, ed. Steve Player and David E. Keys (New York: John Wiley & Sons, 1999), pp. 138–145.
4. Jay Collins, "Advanced Use of ABM: Using ABC for Target Costing, Activity-Based Budgeting, and Benchmarking," in *Activity-Based Management: Arthur Andersen's Lessons from the ABM Battlefield*, ed. Steve Player and David E. Keys (New York: John Wiley & Sons, 1999), pp. 152–158.
5. A unit-level cost is one that must be incurred each time a unit is produced.
6. Just-in-time production and inventory control systems are covered in Chapter 5.
7. It is often desirable to have a buffer inventory just before a bottleneck manufacturing operation.
8. Further discussion of inventory management can be found in a supplement to this text titled *Inventory Management*. This supplement is available to students on the text Web site, which is at www.mcgrawhill.ca/olc/hilton, and to instructors on the Instructor's Resource CD-ROM.
9. A typical cost hierarchy includes costs incurred at the unit level, batch level, product-sustaining level, customer level, and facility or general-operations level. Cost hierarchies are discussed in detail in Chapter 5.
10. A typical cost hierarchy includes costs incurred at the unit level, batch level, product-sustaining level, customer level, and facility or general-operations level. Cost hierarchies are discussed in detail in Chapter 5.
11. These management consulting firms specialize in ABC, ABM, ABB, and cost management systems.
12. A typical cost hierarchy includes costs incurred at the unit level, batch level, product-sustaining level, customer level, and facility, or general-operations, level. Cost hierarchies are discussed in detail in Chapter 5.
13. The direct and indirect methods of preparing the statement of cash flows are covered in financial accounting texts. They also are covered in the supplement to this text entitled *The Statement of Cash Flows and Financial Statement Analysis*, which is available from the publisher. This supplement is *not* needed in order to understand the preparation of the budget, as explained in this chapter.
14. Steve Hornyak, "Budgeting Made Easy," *Management Accounting* 80, no. 4 (October 1998), pp. 18–23.
15. This section draws on Norm Raffish, "How Much Does That Product Really Cost?" in *Readings in Management Accounting*, 3rd ed., ed. S. Mark Young (Upper Saddle River, NJ: Prentice Hall, 2001), pp. 61, 62; Callie Berliner and James A. Brimson, eds., *Cost Management for Today's Advanced Manufacturing* (Boston: Harvard Business School Press, 1988).

Chapter Ten

1. David Johnsen and Parvez Sopariwala, "Standard Costing Is Alive and Well at Parker Brass," *Management Accounting Quarterly* 1, no. 2 (Winter 2000), pp. 12–20.
2. The journal entries to record and close out cost variances are illustrated in a supplement to this text titled *Use of Standard Costs for Product Costing*. This supplement is available to students on the text Web site at www.mcgrawhill.ca/olc/hilton and to instructors on the Instructor's Resource CD-ROM.
3. Kip R. Krumwiede, "Rewards and Realities of German Cost Accounting," *Strategic Finance* 86, no. 10 (April 2005), pp. 27–34; Carl S. Smith, "Going for GPK," *Strategic Finance* 86, no. 10 (April 2005), pp. 36–39; and Bernd Gaiser, "German Cost Management Systems," *Journal of Cost Management* 11, no. 5 (September/October 1997), pp. 35–41.
4. Activity-based costing is explored in detail in Chapter 5.
5. Key cost drivers used in activity-based flexible budgeting at Simon Fraser University include the number of students enrolled and the number of student credit hours. For further reading on activity-based budgeting, see Jay Collins, "Advanced Use of ABM: Using ABC for Target Costing, Activity-Based Budgeting, and Benchmarking," in *Activity-Based Management: Arthur Andersen's Lessons from the ABM Battlefield*, ed. Steve Player and David E. Keys (New York: John Wiley & Sons, 1999), pp. 152–158.
6. "Scoville: NuTone Housing Group" (a management accounting case) (Boston: President and Fellows of Harvard College).
7. The journal entries to record and close out cost variances are illustrated in a supplement to this text titled *Use of Standard Costs for Product Costing*. This supplement is available to students on the text Web site at www.mcgrawhill.ca/olc/hilton and to instructors on the Instructor's Resource CD-ROM.
8. The sources for this material are Robert S. Kaplan, "Limitations of Cost Accounting in Advanced Manufacturing Environments," in *Measures for Manufacturing Excellence*, ed. Robert S. Kaplan (Boston: Harvard Business School Press, 1990), pp. 1–14; H. Thomas Johnson, "Performance Measurement for Competitive Excellence," in *Measures for Manufacturing Excellence*, ed. Robert S. Kaplan (Boston: Harvard Business School Press, 1990), pp. 63–90; Robert A. Bonsack, "Does Activity-Based Costing Replace Standard Costing?" *Journal of Cost Management* 4, no. 4 (Winter 1991), pp. 46, 47; and Michiharu Sukurai, "The Influence of Factory Automation on Management Accounting Practices: A Study of Japanese Companies," in *Measures for Manufacturing Excellence*, ed. Robert S. Kaplan (Boston: Harvard Business School Press, 1990), pp. 39–62.
9. Activity-based management and the elimination of non-value-added costs are covered in Chapters 5.
10. L. Carr and C. Ittner. "Measuring the Cost of Ownership," *Journal of Cost Management* 6, no. 3 (Fall 1992), pp. 42–51.
11. Some companies have developed cost of ownership reporting systems. Among them are Northrop Aircraft Division, Texas Instruments, and Black & Decker. See L. Carr and C. Ittner, "Measuring the Cost of Ownership," *Journal of Cost Management* 6, no. 3 (Fall 1992), pp. 42–51. The information about Texas Instruments is based on R. W. Hilton's research.

Chapter Eleven

1. The balanced scorecard concept was developed by Robert S. Kaplan and David D. Norton. See Robert S. Kaplan and David D. Norton, *The Strategy-Focused Organization: How Balanced Scorecard Companies Thrive in the New Business Environment* (Boston: Harvard Business School Press, 2001).
2. Thomas Wunder, "New Strategy Alignment in Multinational Corporations," *Strategic Finance* 87, no. 5 (November 2005), pp. 35–41; and Andra Gumbus and Bridget Lyons, "The Balanced Scorecard at Philips Electronics," *Strategic Finance* 84, no. 5 (November 2002), pp. 45–49.

3. Robert S. Kaplan and David D. Norton, *The Strategy-Focused Organization: How Balanced Scorecard Companies Thrive in the New Business Environment* (Boston: Harvard Business School Press, 2001).

4. Many banking institutions have developed a balanced scorecard. This one is an amalgamation of bank scorecards from a number of sources, including the author's research and the following resources: Robert S. Kaplan and David P. Norton, *The Strategy-Focused Organization: How Balanced Scorecard Companies Thrive in the New Business Environment* (Boston: Harvard Business School Press, 2001); Robert S. Kaplan, "Wells Fargo Online Financial Services," an HBS management case (Boston: President and Fellows of Harvard College, 1998); and Norman Klein and Robert S. Kaplan, "Chemical Bank: Implementing the Balanced Scorecard," an HBS management case (Boston: President and Fellows of Harvard College, 1995).

5. Robert S. Kaplan and David P. Norton, *The Strategy-Focused Organization: How Balanced Scorecard Companies Thrive in the New Business Environment* (Boston: Harvard Business School Press, 2001).

6. Ibid.

7. This material is based on "Putting Strategy into the Balanced Scorecard," *Strategic Finance* 83, no. 7 (January 2002), pp. 44–52, and Robert S. Kaplan and David P. Norton, *The Strategy-Focused Organization: How Balanced Scorecard Companies Thrive in the New Business Environment* (Boston: Harvard Business School Press, 2001).

8. This section draws on Howard M. Armitage and Anthony A. Atkinson, "The Choice of Productivity Measures in Organizations," in *Measures for Manufacturing Excellence*, ed. Robert S. Kaplan (Boston: Harvard Business School Press, 1990), pp. 91–128; and Robert S. Kaplan and David P. Norton, *The Strategy-Focused Organization: How Balanced-Scorecard Companies Thrive in the New Business Environment* (Boston: Harvard Business School Press, 2001).

9. Eliyahu M. Goldratt, *Theory of Constraints* (Croton-on-Hudson, NY: North River Press, 1990).

10. Yasuhiro Monden and John Lee, "How a Japanese Auto Maker Reduces Costs," *Management Accounting* 75, no. 2 (August 1993), p. 24.

11. Takao Tanaka, "Target Costing at Toyota," *Journal of Cost Management* 7, no. 1 (Spring 1993), p. 4.

12. Peter B. B. Turney and James M. Reeve, "The Impact of Continuous Improvement on the Design of Activity-Based Cost Systems," *Journal of Cost Management* 4, no. 2 (Summer 1990), p. 44.

13. Takao Tanaka, "Kaizen Budgeting: Toyota's Cost Control System under TQC," *Journal of Cost Management* 8, no. 3 (Fall 1994), p. 62.

14. C. Kevin Cherry, "Re-engineering: Harnessing Creativity and Innovation," *Journal of Cost Management* 8, no. 2 (Summer 1994), p. 49.

15. John B. MacArthur, "Theory of Constraints and Activity-Based Costing: Friends or Foes?" *Journal of Cost Management* 7, no. 2 (Summer 1993), p. 51.

16. For further information on cost of quality, see Zafar U. Khan, "Cost of Quality," in Barry J. Brinker, ed., *Guide to Cost Management* (New York: John Wiley & Sons, 2000), pp. 319–344. For examples of quality cost reporting, see Lawrence Carr, "Cost of Quality: Making It Work," *Journal of Cost Management* 9, no. 1 (Spring 1995), pp. 61–65, and S. Brinkman and M. Applebaum, "The Quality Cost Report: It's Alive and Well," *Management Accounting* 76, no. 3 (September 1994), pp. 61–65.

17. This discussion is based on the following sources: Wayne J. Morse, Harold P. Roth, and Kay M. Poston, *Measuring, Planning and Controlling Quality Costs* (Montvale, NJ: National Association of Accountants, 1987); Jack Campanella, ed., *Principles of Quality Costs* (Milwaukee, WI: ASQC Quality Press, 1990); and Alahassane Diallo, Zafar V. Kahn, and Curtis F. Vail, "Cost of Quality in the New Manufacturing Environment," *Management Accounting* 77, no. 2 (August 1993), pp. 20–25.

18. R. Crockett, C. Edwards, and S. Ante, "How Motorola Got Its Groove Back," *BusinessWeek*, August 8, 2005, pp. 68–70; and M. Arndt, "Quality Isn't Just for Widgets," *BusinessWeek*, July 22, 2002, pp. 72, 73.

19. M. Arndt, "Quality Isn't Just for Widgets," *BusinessWeek*, July 22, 2002, pp. 72, 73.

20. Tad Leahy, "In Search of Perfection with Six Sigma," *Business Finance* 5, no. 1 (January 2000), pp. 73–76.

21. Amy Barrett and Diane Brady, "At Honeywell, It's Larry the Knife," *BusinessWeek*, November 26, 2001, pp. 98–100.

22. Tad Leahy, "In Search of Perfection with Six Sigma," *Business Finance* 5, no. 1 (January 2000), pp. 73–76. See also Gregory T. Lucier and Sridhar Seshadri, "GE Takes Six Sigma beyond the Bottom Line," *Strategic Finance* 82, no. 11 (May 2001), pp. 41–46.

23. The ISO standards are available on the Internet at www.iso.org.

24. Based on the discussion in German Böer, Margaret Curtin, and Louis Hoyt, "Environmental Cost Management," *Management Accounting* 80, no. 3 (September 1998), pp. 28–38. See also Ramona Dzinkowski, "Saving the Environment," *Strategic Finance* 89, no. 1 (July 2007), pp. 51–53.

25. Based on Satish Joshi, Ranjani Krishnan, and Lester Lave, "Estimating the Hidden Costs of Environmental Regulation," *The Accounting Review* 76, no. 2 (April 2001), pp. 171–198. See also Kathryn Kranhold, "GE's Environmental Push Hits Business Realities," *The Wall Street Journal*, September 14, 2007, p. A1.

26. Ibid.

27. Ibid.

28. Ibid.

29. German Böer, Margaret Curtin, and Louis Hoyt, "Environmental Cost Management," *Management Accounting* 80, no. 3 (September 1998), pp. 28–38.

30. Ibid.

Chapter Twelve

1. Although there is an important conceptual difference between profit centres and investment centres, the latter term is not always used in practice. Some managers use the term *profit centre* to refer to both types of responsibility centres. Hence, when businesspeople use the term *profit centre*, they may be referring to a true profit centre (as defined in this chapter) or to an investment centre.

2. Activity-based costing and the elimination of non-value-added activities are covered in Chapter 5.

3. The *book value* of Suncoast Food Centres' equity is $41 million, but that amount does not reflect the current value of the company's assets or the value of intangible assets such as the Suncoast Food Centres name.

4. Karra Seannell and Joann Lublin, "SEC Unhappy with Answers on Executive Pay," *The Wall Street Journal*, January 29, 2008, p. 31; Louis Lavelle, "The Gravy Train Just Got Derailed—'Pay for Performance' Is Back in Vogue," *BusinessWeek*, November 19, 2001; and Tad Leahy, "All the Right Moves," *Business Finance* 6, no. 1 (April 2000), p. 32.

5. Maheudra Gujarathi, "GlaxoSmithkline Plc.: International Transfer Pricing and Taxation," *Issues in Accounting Education* 22, no. 4 (November 2007), pp. 749–759; and Eric Krell, "Scrutiny of Transfer Pricing Grows," *Business Finance* 6, no. 4 (August 2000), p. 12.

6. Steven C. Wrappe, Ken Milani, and Julie Joy, "The Transfer Price Is Right," *Strategic Finance* 81, no. 1 (July 1999), p. 40.

Chapter Thirteen

1. The sources for these anecdotes are S. Carey, "Northwest Targets Flight Attendants for Outsourcing," *The Wall Street Journal*, October, 26, 2005, pp. A1, A8; S. Carey and A. Frangos, "Airlines, Facing Cost Pressure, Outsource Crucial Safety Tasks," *The Wall Street Journal*, January 21, 2005, pp. A1, A5; and P. Engardio and B. Einhorn, "Outsourcing Innovation," *BusinessWeek*, March 21, 2005, pp. 82–94.

2. Peter Landers, "Japan's Local Drug Makers to Outsource to Suppliers," *The Wall Street Journal*, March 26, 2002, p. A20.

3. "Delivering the Goods at FedEx," *BusinessWeek*, June 13, 2005, pp. 60–62; D. Foust, "The Ground War at FedEx," *BusinessWeek*, November 28, 2005, pp. 42, 43; "Overnight, Everything Changed for FedEx; Can It Reinvent Itself?" *The Wall Street Journal*, November 4, 1999, p. A1; and M. Arndt, "Cat Sinks Its Claws into Services," *BusinessWeek*, December 5, 2005, pp. 56–59.

4. Activity-based costing (ABC) is thoroughly explored in Chapter 5. This section can be studied most effectively after completing Chapter 5.

Chapter Fourteen

1. We will assume for simplicity that Sydney Sailing Supplies' monthly sales and production quantities are the same. This assumption tends to be true in the pleasure boat industry.

2. P. Nowak, "Goodbye to Cellphone System Access Fees?" *CBCNews.ca*, November 4, 2008.

3. L. Hawkins, "GM Cuts Prices on Most Vehicles: Latest Bid to Restore Profits May Spark Price War," *The Wall Street Journal*, January 11, 2006, pp. D1, D3.

4. C. Dawson, "A China Price for Toyota," *BusinessWeek*, February 21, 2005, pp. 50, 51.

5. David P. Hamilton, "The Price Isn't Right: Internet Pricing Has Turned Out to Be a Lot Trickier Than Retailers Expected," *The Wall Street Journal*, February 12, 2001, p. R8.

6. This section is based on Shahid L. Ansari, Jan E. Bell, and the CAM-I Target Cost Core Group, *Target Costing: The Next Frontier in Strategic Cost Management* (Burr Ridge, IL: Irwin, 1997).

7. Ibid., p. 15.

8. J. Shank and V. Govindarajan, "Strategic Cost Management and the Value Chain," *Journal of Cost Management* 5, no. 4 (Winter 1992), p. 10. See also T. Tanaka, "Target Costing at Toyota," *Journal of Cost Management* 7, no. 1 (Spring 1993), pp. 4–12.

9. Shahid L. Ansari, Jan E. Bell, and the CAM-I Target Cost Core Group, *Target Costing: The Next Frontier in Strategic Cost Management* (Burr Ridge, IL: Irwin, 1997). See also Y. Kato, "Target Costing Support Systems: Lessons from Leading Japanese Companies," *Management Accounting Research* 4 (1992), pp. 33–47; and T. Tani, H.

Okano, N. Shimizu, Y. Iwabuchi, J. Fukuda, and S. Cooray, "Target Cost Management in Japanese Companies: Current State of the Art," *Management Accounting Research* 6 (1994), pp. 67–81.

10. This description of Isuzu's target costing and value-engineering methods is drawn from Robin Cooper, *When Lean Enterprises Collide* (Boston, MA: Harvard Business School Press, 1995), pp. 165–83.

Chapter Fifteen (Online)

1. Based on S. Hensley, R. Winslow, and W. Mathews, "FDA Approves Pfizer Drug for Two Cancers," *The Wall Street Journal*, January 27, 2006, pp. 31, 34; J. Carey and A. Barrett, "Drug Prices: What's Fair," *BusinessWeek*, December 10, 2001, pp. 61–70; and the author's discussions with pharmaceutical company personnel.

2. This section is based on discussions in R. Kaplan, "Must CIM Be Justified by Faith Alone?" *Harvard Business Review* 64, no. 2 (March 1986), pp. 87–95; Callie Berliner and James A. Brimson, eds., *Cost Management for Today's Advanced Manufacturing* (Boston: Harvard Business School Press, 1988), pp. 16–18, 36–38, 150; and Jean L. Noble, "A New Approach for Justifying Computer-Integrated Manufacturing," *Journal of Cost Management* 3, no. 4 (Winter 1990), pp. 14–19.

3. Using formula (1): $F = \$800 (1 + .12)^{10}$. From Table I, $(1 + .12)^{10} = 3.106$. (Note that the values in Table I are rounded.) Thus, the future value of the investment is $(\$800)(3.106) = \$2,484.80$. Compound interest will more than triple the original $800 investment in 10 years.

4. Using formula (1): $F = \$18,000 (1 + .12)^{10}$. From Table III, $(1 + .08)^4 = .735$. (Note that the values in Table III are rounded.) Thus, the future value of the investment is $(\$18,000)(.735) = \$13,230$. An investment of $13,230 made now, earning annual interest at 8 percent, will accumulate to $18,000 at the end of four years.

Chapter Sixteen (Online)

1. A tie occurs when two or more service departments serve the same number of other service departments. Then the sequence among the tied service departments usually is an arbitrary choice.

2. Simultaneous equations are more quickly solved by computers than by people. Numerous software packages are available for this purpose.

Glossary

ABB See **activity-based budgeting**.

ABC See **activity-based costing (ABC) system**.

ABM See **activity-based management**.

absorption See **overhead application**.

absorption cost See **full (or absorption) cost**.

absorption costing (or full costing) A method of product costing in which both variable and fixed manufacturing overhead are included in the product costs that flow through the manufacturing accounts (i.e., Work-in-Process Inventory, Finished-Goods Inventory, and Cost of Goods Sold).

acceptance-or-rejection decision A decision on whether a particular capital investment proposal should be accepted.

account analysis See **account-classification method**.

account-classification method (or account analysis) A cost-estimation method involving a careful examination of the ledger accounts for the purpose of classifying each cost as variable, fixed, or semivariable.

accounting rate of return A percentage formed by taking a project's average incremental revenue minus its average incremental expenses (including depreciation and income taxes) and dividing by the project's initial investment.

accumulation factor The value of $(1 + r)^n$, in a future value calculation, where r denotes the interest rate per year and n denotes the number of years.

accurate information Precise and correct data.

activity A measure of an organization's output of goods or services.

activity accounting The collection of financial or operational performance information about significant activities in an enterprise.

activity analysis The detailed identification and description of the activities conducted in an enterprise.

activity base A measure of an organization's activity that is used as a basis for specifying cost behaviour. The activity base also is used to compute a predetermined overhead rate. The current trend is to refer to the activity base as a volume-based cost driver. See also **volume-based cost driver**.

activity dictionary A complete listing of the activities included in an organization's ABC analysis.

activity-based budgeting (ABB) The process of developing a master budget using information obtained from an activity-based costing (ABC) analysis.

activity-based costing (ABC) system A two-stage procedure used to assign overhead costs to products or services produced. In the first stage, significant activities are identified, and overhead costs are assigned to activity cost pools in accordance with the way resources are consumed by the activities. In the second stage, the overhead costs are allocated from each activity cost pool to each product line in proportion to the amount of the cost driver consumed by the product line.

activity-based flexible budget A flexible budget based on several cost drivers rather than on a single, volume-based cost driver.

activity-based management (ABM) Using an activity-based costing system to improve the operations of an organization.

activity-based responsibility accounting A system for measuring the performance of an organization's people and subunits, which focuses not only on the cost of performing activities but on the activities themselves.

activity-cost pool A grouping of overhead costs assigned to various similar activities identified in an activity-based costing system.

actual costing A product-costing system in which actual direct-material, direct-labour, and *actual* manufacturing-overhead costs are added to Work-in-Process Inventory.

actual manufacturing overhead The actual costs incurred during an accounting period for manufacturing overhead. Includes actual indirect material, indirect labour, and other manufacturing costs.

actual overhead rate The rate at which overhead costs are actually incurred during an accounting period. Calculated as follows: Actual manufacturing overhead ÷ Actual cost driver (or activity base).

after-tax cash flow The cash flow expected after all tax implications have been taken into account.

after-tax net income An organization's net income after its income-tax expense is subtracted.

aggregate (or total) productivity Total output divided by total input.

allocation base A measure of activity, physical characteristic, or economic characteristic that is associated with the responsibility centres that are the cost objects in an allocation process.

annuity A series of equivalent cash flows.

applied manufacturing overhead The amount of manufacturing-overhead costs added to Work-in-Process Inventory during an accounting period.

appraisal costs Costs of determining whether defective products exist.

attainable standard See **practical (or attainable) standard**.

attention-directing function The function of managerial-accounting information in pointing out to managers issues that need their attention.

average cost per unit The total cost of producing a particular quantity of product divided by the number of units produced.

avoidable expenses Expenses that will no longer be incurred if a particular action is taken.

balanced scorecard A model of business performance evaluation that balances measures of financial performance, internal operations, innovation and learning, and customer satisfaction.

batch manufacturing High-volume production of several product lines that differ in some important ways but are nearly identical in others.

batch-level activity An activity that must be accomplished for each batch of products rather than for each unit.

before-tax income   An organization's income before its income tax expense is subtracted.

benchmarking (or **competitive benchmarking**)   The continual search for the most effective method of accomplishing a task, by comparing existing methods and performance levels with those of other organizations or with other subunits within the same organization.

best practices   The most effective methods of accomplishing various tasks in a particular industry, often discovered through benchmarking.

bill of activities (for a product or service)   A complete listing of the activities required for that product or service to be produced.

break-even point   The volume of activity at which an organization's revenues and expenses are equal. May be measured either in units or in sales dollars.

budget   A detailed plan, expressed in quantitative terms, that specify how resources will be acquired and used during a specified period of time.

budget committee   A group of top-management personnel who advise the budget director during the preparation of the budget.

budget director (or **chief budget officer**)   The individual in charge of preparing an organization's budget.

budget manual   A set of written instructions that specify who will provide budgetary data, when and in what form the data will be provided, how the master budget will be prepared and approved, and who should receive the various schedules constituting the budget.

budgetary slack   The difference between the budgetary projection provided by an individual and his or her best estimate of the item being projected. (E.g., the difference between a supervisor's expected departmental utility cost and his or her budgetary projection for utilities.)

budgeted balance sheet   Shows the expected end-of-period balances for the company's assets, liabilities, and owners' equity.

budgeted financial statements (or **pro forma financial statements**)   A set of planned financial statements showing what an organization's overall financial condition is expected to be at the end of the budget period if planned operations are carried out.

budgeted income statement   Shows the expected revenue and expenses for a budget period, assuming that planned operations are carried out.

budgeted schedule of cost of goods manufactured and sold   Details the direct material, direct labour, and manufacturing overhead costs to be incurred and shows the cost of the goods to be sold during a budget period.

budgeted statement of cash flows   A budget schedule providing information about the expected sources and uses of cash for operating activities, investing activities, and financing activities during a particular period of time.

budgeting system   The set of procedures used to develop a budget.

by-product   A joint product with very little value relative to the other joint products.

CAD   See **computer-aided design (CAD) system**.

CAD/CIM system   See **computer-aided design** and **computer-integrated manufacturing**.

capital budget   A long-term budget that shows planned acquisition and disposal of capital assets, such as land, buildings, and equipment.

capital cost allowance (CCA)   A tax deduction that Canadian tax laws allow a business to claim for the loss in value of capital assets due to wear and tear or obsolescence.

capital turnover   Sales revenue divided by invested capital.

capital-budgeting decision   A decision involving cash flows beyond the current year.

capital-rationing decision   A decision in which management chooses which of several investment proposals to accept to make the best use of limited investment funds.

cash bonus   See **pay for performance**.

cash budget   Details the expected cash receipts and disbursements during a budget period.

cash disbursements budget   A schedule detailing expected cash payments during a budget period.

cash equivalents   Short-term, highly liquid investments that are treated as equivalent to cash in the preparation of a statement of cash flows.

cash receipts budget   A schedule detailing the expected cash collections during the budget period.

CCA   See **capital cost allowance (CCA)**.

CCA tax shield   The reduction in taxes payable due to CCA.

certified management accountant (CMA)   An accountant who has earned professional certification in managerial accounting.

CFO   See **chief financial officer**.

chief budget officer   See **budget director**.

chief financial officer (CFO)   An organization's top managerial and financial accountant. (Also see **controller**.)

CIM   See **computer-integrated manufacturing (CIM) system**.

CMA   See **certified management accountant**.

CMS   See **cost management system**.

coefficient of determination   A statistical measure of goodness of fit; a measure of how closely a regression line fits the data on which it is based.

committed cost   A cost that results from an organization's ownership or use of facilities and its basic organization structure.

common costs   Costs incurred to benefit more than one organizational segment.

competitive benchmarking   See **benchmarking**.

competitive benchmarking   See **benchmarking**.

competitive bidding   A situation where two or more companies submit bids (prices) for a product, service, or project to a potential buyer.

component productivity   See **partial** (or **component**) **productivity**.

compound interest   The interest earned on prior periods' interest.

comptroller   See **controller**.

computer-aided design (CAD) system   Computer software used by engineers in the design of a product.

computer-integrated manufacturing (CIM) system   The most advanced form of automated manufacturing, in which virtually all parts of the production process are accomplished by computer-controlled machines and automated material-handling equipment.

constraints Algebraic expressions of limitations faced by a firm, such as those limiting its productive resources.

consumption ratio The proportion of an activity consumed by a particular product.

continuous budget See **rolling** (or **revolving** or **continuous**) **budget**.

continuous improvement The constant effort to eliminate waste, reduce response time, simplify the design of both products and processes, and improve quality and customer service.

contribution income statement An income statement on which fixed and variable expenses are separated.

contribution margin per unit The difference between the unit sales price and the unit variable expense. The amount that each unit contributes to covering fixed expenses and profit.

contribution margin Sales revenue minus variable expenses. The amount of sales revenue, which is left to cover fixed expenses and profit after paying variable expenses.

contribution-margin ratio The unit contribution margin divided by the sales price per unit. Also may be expressed in percentage form; then it is called the contribution-margin percentage.

controllability The extent to which managers are able to control or influence a cost or cost variance.

controllable cost A cost subject to the control or substantial influence of a particular individual.

controller (or **comptroller**) The top managerial and financial accountant in an organization. Supervises the accounting department and assists management at all levels in interpreting and using managerial-accounting information. (Also, see **chief financial officer**.)

controlling Ensuring that an organization operates in the intended manner and achieves its goals.

conversion costs Direct-labour cost plus manufacturing-overhead cost.

cost The sacrifice made, usually measured by the resources given up, to achieve a particular purpose.

cost accounting system Part of the basic accounting system that accumulates cost for use in both managerial and financial accounting.

cost allocation The process of assigning costs in a cost pool to the appropriate cost objects. See also **cost distribution**.

cost behaviour The relationship between cost and activity.

cost centre A responsibility centre whose manager is accountable for its costs.

cost distribution The first step in assigning manufacturing-overhead costs. Overhead costs are assigned to all departmental overhead centres. See also **cost allocation**.

cost driver A characteristic of an activity or event that results in the incurrence of costs by that activity or event.

cost estimation The process of determining how a particular cost behaves.

cost hierarchy The classification of activities into levels, such as unit-level, batch-level, product-sustaining level, and facility-level activities.

cost management system (CMS) A management planning and controlling system that measures the cost of significant activities, identifies non-value-added costs, and identifies activities that will improve organizational performance.

cost objects Responsibility centres, products, or services to which costs are assigned.

cost of capital The cost of acquiring resources for an organization, either through debt or through the issuance of stock.

cost of goods manufactured The total cost of direct material, direct labour, and manufacturing overhead transferred from Work-in-Process Inventory to Finished-Goods Inventory during an accounting period.

cost of goods sold The expense measured by the cost of the finished goods sold during a period of time.

cost-plus pricing A pricing approach in which the price is equal to cost plus a markup.

cost pool A collection of costs to be assigned to a set of cost objects.

cost prediction Forecast of cost at a particular level of activity.

cost structure The relative proportions of an organization's fixed and variable costs.

cost variance The difference between actual and standard cost.

cost-volume-profit (CVP) analysis A study of the relationships between sales volume, expenses, revenue, and profit.

cost-volume-profit (CVP) graph A graphical expression of the relationships between sales volume, expenses, revenue, and profit.

cross-elasticity The extent to which a change in a product's price affects the demand for substitute products.

curvilinear cost A cost with a curved line for its graph.

customer-acceptance measures The extent to which a firm's customers perceive its product to be of high quality.

customer-profitability analysis Using the concepts of activity-based costing to determine the activities, costs, and profit associated with serving particular customers.

customer-profitability profile A graphical portrayal of a company's customer profitability analysis.

CVP See **cost-volume-profit**.

cycle time See **throughput time**.

decentralization A form of organization in which subunit managers are given authority to make substantive decisions.

decision making Choosing between alternatives.

decision variables The variables in a linear program about which a decision is made.

delivery cycle time The average time between the receipt of a customer order and delivery of the goods.

departmental overhead centre Any department to which overhead costs are assigned via overhead cost distribution.

departmental overhead rate An overhead rate calculated for a single production department.

departmental production report The key document in a process-costing system. This report summarizes the physical flow of units, equivalent units of production, cost per equivalent unit, and analysis of total departmental costs.

dependent variable A variable whose value depends on other variables, called *independent variables*.

differential cost The difference in a cost item under two decision alternatives.

direct cost A cost that can be traced to a particular department or other subunit of an organization.

direct costing See **variable costing**.

direct-exchange (or **noncash**) **transaction** A significant investing or financing transaction involving accounts other than cash, such as a transaction where land is obtained in exchange for the issuance of capital stock.

direct labour The costs of compensating employees who work directly on a firm's product. Should include wages, salary, and associated fringe benefits.

direct material Raw material that is physically incorporated in the finished product.

direct method (of preparing the statement of cash flows) A method of preparing the operating activities section of a statement of cash flows. A cash-basis income statement is constructed in which operating cash disbursements are subtracted from operating cash receipts.

direct method (of service department cost allocation) A method of service department cost allocation in which service department costs are allocated directly to the production departments.

directing operational activities Running an organization on a day-to-day basis.

direct-labour budget A schedule showing the number of hours and cost of direct labour to be used in production of services or goods during a budget period.

direct-labour cost The cost of salaries, wages, and fringe benefits for personnel who work directly on the manufactured products.

direct-labour efficiency variance The difference between actual and standard hours of direct labour multiplied by the standard hourly labour rate.

direct-labour rate variance The difference between actual and standard hourly labour rate multiplied by the actual hours of direct labour used.

direct-material budget A schedule showing the number of units and the cost of material to be purchased during a budget period.

direct-material price variance (or **purchase price variance**) The difference between actual and standard price multiplied by the actual quantity of material purchased.

direct-material quantity variance The difference between actual and standard quantity of materials allowed, given actual output, multiplied by the standard price.

discount rate The interest rate used in computing the present value of a cash flow.

discounted-cash-flow analysis An analysis of an investment proposal that takes into account the time value of money.

discretionary cost A cost that results from a discretionary management decision to spend a particular amount of money.

distribution cost The cost of storing and transporting finished goods for sale.

dual cost allocation An approach to service department cost allocation in which variable costs are allocated in proportion to short-term usage and fixed costs are allocated in proportion to long-term usage.

e-budgeting An electronic and enterprisewide budgeting process in which employees throughout the organization can submit and retrieve budget information electronically via the Internet.

economic order quantity (EOQ) The order size that minimizes inventory ordering and holding costs.

economic value added (EVA) An investment centre's after-tax operating income minus the investment centre's total assets (net of its current liabilities) times the company's weighted-average cost of capital.

EDI See **electronic data interchange**.

electronic data interchange (EDI) The direct exchange between organizations of data via a computer-to-computer interface.

employee empowerment The concept of encouraging and authorizing workers to take the initiative to improve operations, reduce costs, and improve product quality and customer service.

empowerment The concept of encouraging and authorizing workers to take the initiative to improve operations, reduce costs, and improve product quality and customer service.

engineered cost A cost that results from a definitive physical relationship with the activity measure.

engineering method A cost-estimation method in which a detailed study is made of the process that results in cost incurrence.

environmental cost management Strategies for reducing, eliminating, or otherwise controlling environmental costs.

environmental costs Costs incurred in dealing with environmental issues.

EOQ See **economic order quantity**.

equivalent unit A measure of the amount of production effort applied to a physical unit of production. For example, a physical unit that is 50 percent completed represents one-half of an equivalent unit.

estimated manufacturing overhead The amount of manufacturing-overhead cost expected for a specified period of time. Used as the numerator in computing the predetermined overhead rate.

EVA See **economic value added**.

excess present value index See **profitability index**.

expected value The sum of the possible values for a random variable, each weighted by its probability.

expense The consumption of assets for the purpose of generating revenue.

experience curve A graph (or other mathematical representation) that shows how a broad set of costs decline as cumulative production output increases.

external failure costs Costs incurred because defective products have been sold.

facility-(or general-operations-)level activity An activity that is required for an entire production process to occur.

feasible region The possible values for decision variables that are not ruled out by constraints.

FIFO (first-in, first-out) method A method of process costing in which the cost assigned to the beginning work-in-process inventory is not added to current-period production costs. The cost per equivalent unit calculated under FIFO relates to the current period only.

financial accounting   The use of accounting information for reporting to parties outside the organization.

financial budget   A schedule that outlines how an organization will acquire financial resources during the budget period (e.g., through borrowing or sale of capital stock).

financial leverage   The concept that a relatively small increase in income can provide a proportionately much larger increase in return to the common stockholders.

financial planning model   A set of mathematical relationships that express the interactions among the various operational, financial, and environmental events that determine the overall results of an organization's activities.

financing activities   Transactions involving a company's debt or equity capital.

finished goods   Completed products awaiting sale.

first-in, first-out method   See **FIFO (first-in, first-out) method**.

fixed cost   A cost that does not change in total as activity changes.

fixed-overhead budget variance   The difference between actual and budgeted fixed overhead.

fixed-overhead volume variance   The difference between budgeted and applied fixed overhead.

flexible budget   A budget that is valid for a range of activity.

flexible manufacturing system (FMS)   A series of manufacturing machines, controlled and integrated by a computer, which is designed to perform a series of manufacturing operations automatically.

FMS cell   A group of machines and personnel within a flexible manufacturing system (FMS).

FMS   See **flexible manufacturing system**.

full (or absorption) cost   A product's variable cost plus an allocated portion of fixed overhead.

full costing   See **absorption costing**.

functional layout   See **process (or functional) layout**.

future value   The amount to which invested funds accumulate over a specified period of time.

gain-sharing plan   An incentive system that specifies a formula by which the cost savings from productivity gains achieved by a company are shared with the workers who helped accomplish the improvements.

general-operations-level activity   See **facility-(or general-operations-)level activity**.

goal congruence   A meshing of objectives, where managers throughout an organization strive to achieve the goals set by top management.

goodness of fit   The closeness with which a regression line fits the data upon which it is based.

grade   The extent of a product's capability in performing its intended purpose, viewed in relation to other products with the same functional use.

high-low method   A cost-estimation method in which a cost line is fit using exactly two data points—the high and low activity levels.

homogeneous cost pool   A grouping of overhead costs in which each cost component is consumed in roughly the same proportion by each product line.

hurdle rate   The minimum desired rate of return used in a discounted-cash-flow analysis.

hybrid product-costing system   A system that incorporates features from two or more alternative product-costing systems, such as job-order and process costing.

ideal standard   See **perfection (or ideal) standard**.

idle time   Unproductive time spent by employees due to factors beyond their control, such as power outages and machine breakdowns.

imperfect competition   A market in which a single producer or group of producers can affect the market price.

incentive compensation   See **pay for performance**.

incremental cost   The increase in cost from one alternative to another.

incremental processing cost   Cost incurred on a joint product after the split-off point of a joint production process.

independent variable   The variable upon which an estimate is based in least-squares regression analysis.

indirect cost   A cost that cannot be traced to a particular department.

indirect labour   All costs of compensating employees who do not work directly on the firm's product but who are necessary for production to occur.

indirect materials   Materials that either are required for the production process to occur but do not become an integral part of the finished product, or are consumed in production but are insignificant in cost.

indirect method (or reconciliation method)   A method of preparing the operating activities section of a statement of cash flows, in which the analyst begins with net income. Then adjustments are made to convert from an accrual-basis income statement to a cash-basis income statement.

indirect-labour budget   A schedule showing the amount and cost of indirect labour to be used during a budget period.

information overload   The provision of so much information that, due to human limitations in processing information, managers cannot effectively use it.

in-process quality controls   Procedures designed to assess product quality before production is completed.

inspection time   The time spent on quality inspections of raw materials, partially completed products, or finished goods.

internal auditor   An accountant who reviews the accounting procedures, records, and reports in both the controller's and treasurer's areas of responsibility.

internal failure costs   Costs of correcting defects found prior to product sale.

internal rate of return   The discount rate required for an investment's net present value to be zero; also known as the *time-adjusted rate of return*.

inventoriable cost   Cost incurred to purchase or manufacture goods. Also see **product cost**.

inventoriable goods   Goods that can be stored before sale, such as durable goods, mining products, and some agricultural products.

inventory budgets   Schedules that detail the amount and cost of finished-goods, work-in-process, and direct-material inventories expected at the end of a budget period.

investing activities   Transactions involving the extension or collection of loans, acquisition or disposal of investments, and purchase or sale of productive, long-lived assets.

investment centre   A responsibility centre whose manager is accountable for its profit and for the capital invested to generate that profit.

investment opportunity rate   The rate of return an organization can earn on its best alternative investments that are of equivalent risk.

JIT   See **just-in-time**.

JIT purchasing   An approach to purchasing management in which materials and parts are purchased only as they are needed.

job-cost record   A document that records the costs of direct material, direct labour, and manufacturing overhead for a particular production job or batch. The job-cost record is a subsidiary ledger account for the Work-in-Process Inventory account in the general ledger.

job-order costing system   A product-costing system in which costs are assigned to batches or job orders of production. Used by firms that produce relatively small numbers of dissimilar products.

joint cost   The cost incurred in a joint production process before the joint products become identifiable as separate products.

joint production process   A production process that results in two or more joint products.

joint products   The outputs of a joint production process.

just-in-time (JIT) inventory and production management system   A comprehensive inventory and manufacturing control system in which no materials are purchased and no products are manufactured until they are needed.

just-in-time (JIT) production system   A comprehensive inventory and manufacturing control system in which no materials are purchased and no products are manufactured until they are needed.

just-in-time (JIT) purchasing   An approach to purchasing management in which materials and parts are purchased only as they are needed.

kaizen costing   The process of cost reduction during the manufacturing phase of a product. Refers to continual and gradual improvement through small betterment activities.

labour-intensive   A production process accomplished largely by manual labour.

lag indicators   Measures of the final outcomes of earlier management decisions.

lead indicators   Performance measures that identify future non-financial and financial outcomes to guide management decision making.

lead time   The time required to receive inventory after it has been ordered.

learning curve   A graphical expression of the decline in the average labour time required per unit as cumulative output increases.

least-squares regression method   A cost-estimation method in which the cost line is fit to the data by statistical analysis. The method minimizes the sum of the squared deviations between the cost line and the data points.

line positions   Positions held by managers who are directly involved in providing the goods or services that constitute an organization's primary goals.

make-or-buy decision   See **outsourcing** (or **make-or-buy**) **decision**.

management by exception   A managerial technique in which only significant deviations from expected performance are investigated.

management by objectives (MBO)   The process of designating the objectives of each subunit in an organization and planning for the achievement of these objectives. Managers at all levels participate in setting goals, which they then will strive to achieve.

managerial accounting   The process of identifying, measuring, analyzing, interpreting, and communicating information in pursuit of an organization's goals.

manufacturing   The process of converting raw materials into finished products.

manufacturing costs   Costs incurred in a manufacturing process, which consist of direct material, direct labour, and manufacturing overhead.

manufacturing cycle efficiency (MCE)   The ratio of process time to the sum of processing time, inspection time, waiting time, and move time.

manufacturing cycle time   The total amount of production time (or throughput time) required per unit.

manufacturing overhead   All manufacturing costs other than direct-material and direct-labour costs.

manufacturing-overhead budget   Shows the cost of overhead expected to be incurred in the production process during the budget period.

manufacturing-overhead variance   The difference between actual overhead cost and the amount specified in the flexible budget.

marginal cost   The extra cost incurred in producing one additional unit of output.

marketing cost   The cost incurred in selling goods or services. Includes order-getting costs and order-filling or distribution costs.

mass customization   A manufacturing environment in which many standardized components are combined to produce custom-made products to customer order.

master budget   See **profit plan**.

material requisition form   A document used by the production department supervisor to request the release of raw materials for production.

MBO   See **management by objectives**.

MCE   See **manufacturing cycle efficiency**.

merchandise cost   The cost of acquiring goods for resale. Includes purchasing and transportation costs.

merchandising   The business of acquiring finished goods for resale, either in a wholesale or a retail operation.

merit pay   See **pay for performance**.

mixed cost   A cost with both a fixed and a variable component.

move time   The time spent moving raw materials, subassemblies, or finished products from one production operation to another.

multiple regression A statistical method in which a linear (straight-line) relationship is estimated between a dependent variable and two or more independent variables.

multistage cost allocation The three-step process in which costs are assigned to products or services: (1) cost distribution (or allocation), (2) service department cost allocation, and (3) cost application.

net present value The present value of a project's future cash flows less the cost of the initial investment.

net realizable value A joint product's final sales value less any separable costs incurred after the split-off point.

net-realizable-value method A method in which joint costs are allocated to the joint products in proportion to the net realizable value of each joint product.

non-value-added activities Operations that are either (1) unnecessary and dispensable or (2) necessary, but inefficient and improvable.

non-value-added costs The costs of activities that can be eliminated without deterioration of product quality, performance, or perceived value.

normal costing A product-costing system in which actual direct-materials, actual direct-labour, and applied manufacturing-overhead costs are added to Work-in-Process Inventory.

normal equations The equations used to solve for the parameters of a regression equation.

normalized overhead rate An overhead rate calculated over a relatively long time period.

objective function An algebraic expression of the firm's goal.

oligopolistic market (or **oligopoly**) A market with a small number of sellers competing among themselves.

operating activities All activities that are not investing or financing activities. Generally speaking, operating activities include all cash transactions that are involved in the determination of net income.

operating expenses The costs incurred to produce and sell services, such as transportation, repair, financial, or medical services.

operating leverage The extent to which an organization uses fixed costs in its cost structure. The greater the proportion of fixed costs, the greater the operating leverage.

operating leverage factor A measure of operating leverage at a particular sales volume. Computed by dividing an organization's total contribution margin by its net income.

operation costing A hybrid of job-order and process costing. Direct material is accumulated by batch of products using job-order costing methods. Conversion costs are accumulated by department and assigned to product units by process-costing methods.

operational budgets A set of budgets that specify how operations will be carried out to produce an organization's services or goods.

opportunity cost The potential benefit given up when the choice of one action precludes selection of a different action.

organizational culture The mindset of employees, including their shared beliefs, values, and goals.

outlier A data point that falls far away from the other points in a scatter diagram and is not representative of the data.

out-of-pocket costs Costs incurred that require the expenditure of cash or other assets.

outsourcing (or **make-or-buy**) **decision** A decision as to whether a product or service should be produced in-house or purchased from an outside supplier.

overapplied overhead The amount by which the period's applied manufacturing overhead exceeds actual manufacturing overhead.

overhead application (or **absorption**) The third step in assigning manufacturing-overhead costs. All costs associated with each production department are assigned to the product units on which a department has worked.

overhead budget A schedule showing the cost of overhead expected to be incurred in the production of services or goods during a budget period.

overhead cost performance report A report showing the actual and flexible-budget cost levels for each overhead item, together with variable-overhead spending and efficiency variances and fixed-overhead budget variances.

overtime premium The extra compensation paid to an employee who works beyond the normal period of time.

padding the budget The process of building budgetary slack into a budget by overestimating expenses and underestimating revenue.

partial (or **component**) **productivity** Total output (in dollars) divided by the cost of a particular input.

participative budgeting The process of involving people throughout an organization in the budgeting process.

pay for performance A one-time cash payment to an investment-centre manager as a reward for meeting a predetermined criterion on a specified performance measure.

payback period The amount of time required for a project's after-tax cash inflows to accumulate to an amount that covers the initial investment.

penetration pricing Setting a low initial price for a new product in order to penetrate the market deeply and gain a large and broad market share.

percentage of completion The extent to which a physical unit of production has been finished with respect to direct material or conversion activity.

perfect competition A market in which the price does not depend on the quantity sold by any one producer.

perfection (or **ideal**) **standard** The cost expected under perfect or ideal operating conditions.

performance report A report showing the budgeted and actual amounts, and the variances between these amounts, of key financial results for a person or subunit.

period costs Costs that are expensed during the time period in which they are incurred.

physical unit An actual item of production, fully or partially completed.

physical-units method A method in which joint costs are allocated to the joint products in proportion to their physical quantities.

planning Developing a detailed financial and operational description of anticipated operations.

plantwide overhead rate   An overhead rate calculated by averaging manufacturing-overhead costs for the entire production facility.

pool rate   The cost per unit of the cost driver for a particular activity cost pool.

postaudit (or **reappraisal**)   A systematic follow-up of a capital-budgeting decision to see how the project turned out.

practical (or **attainable**) **standard**   The cost expected under normal operating conditions.

predatory pricing   An illegal practice in which the price of a product is set low temporarily to broaden demand. Then the product's supply is restricted and the price is raised.

predetermined overhead rate   The rate used to apply manufacturing overhead to Work-in-Process Inventory, calculated as: Estimated manufacturing overhead cost ÷ Estimated amount of cost driver (or activity base).

present value   The economic value now of a cash flow that will occur in the future.

prevention costs   Costs of preventing defective products.

price discrimination   The illegal practice of quoting different prices for the same product or service to different buyers, when the price differences are not justified by cost differences.

price elasticity   The impact of price changes on sales volume.

price takers   Firms whose products or services are determined totally by the market.

prime costs   The costs of direct material and direct labour.

principal   The amount originally invested, not including any interest earned.

pro forma financial statements   See **budgeted financial statements**.

process   A set of linked activities.

process-costing system   A product-costing system in which production costs are averaged over a large number of product units. Used by firms that produce large numbers of nearly identical products.

process (or **functional**) **layout**   A method of organizing the elements of a production process, in which similar processes and functions are grouped together.

process time   The amount of time during which a product is actually undergoing conversion activity.

process value analysis (PVA)   Another term for *activity analysis*, which is the detailed identification and description of the activities conducted in an enterprise.

product cost   Cost associated with goods for sale until the time period during which the products are sold, at which time the costs become expenses. See also **inventoriable cost**.

product life-cycle costing   The accumulation of costs that occur over the entire life cycle of a product.

product-costing system   The process of accumulating the costs of a production process and assigning them to the products that constitute the organization's output.

product-sustaining-level activity   An activity that is needed to support an entire product line but is not always performed every time a new unit or batch of products is produced.

production budget   A schedule showing the number of units of services or goods that are to be produced during a budget period.

production department   A department in which work is done directly on a firm's products.

production Kanban   A card specifying the number of parts to be manufactured in a particular work centre.

profit centre   A responsibility centre whose manager is accountable for its profit.

profit plan (or **master budget**)   A comprehensive set of budgets that cover all phases of an organization's operations during a specified period of time.

profitability index (or **excess present value index**)   The present value of a project's future cash flows (exclusive of the initial investment), divided by the initial investment.

profit-volume graph   A graphical expression of the relationship between profit and sales volume.

project costing   The process of assigning costs to projects, cases, contracts, programs, or missions in non manufacturing organizations.

proration   The process of allocating underapplied or overapplied overhead to Work-in-Process Inventory, Finished-Goods Inventory, and Cost of Goods Sold.

pull method   A method of coordinating stages in a production process. Goods are produced in each stage of manufacturing only as they are needed in the next stage.

purchase price variance   See **direct-material price variance**.

PVA   See **process value analysis**.

qualitative characteristics   Factors in a decision analysis that cannot be expressed easily in numerical terms.

quality of conformance   The extent to which a product meets the specifications of its design.

quality of design   The extent to which a product is designed to perform well in its intended use.

quick assets   Cash, marketable securities, accounts receivable, and current notes receivable. Excludes inventories and prepaid expenses, which are current assets but not quick assets.

R&D costs   See **research and development (R&D) costs**.

raw material   Material entered into a manufacturing process.

reappraisal   See **postaudit**.

reciprocal service   The mutual provision of service by two service departments to each other.

reciprocal-services method   A method of service department cost allocation that accounts for the mutual provision of reciprocal services among all service departments.

reconciliation method   See **indirect method**.

reengineering   The complete redesign of a process, with an emphasis on finding creative new ways to accomplish an objective.

regression line   A line fit to a set of data points using least-squares regression.

relative-sales-value method   A method in which joint costs are allocated to the joint products in proportion to their total sales values at the split-off point.

relevant information   Data that are pertinent to a decision.

relevant range   The range of activity within which management expects the organization to operate.

repetitive production   The manufacture of large numbers of identical or very similar products in a continuous flow.

research and development (R&D) costs   Costs incurred to develop and test new products or services.

residual income   Profit minus an imputed interest charge, which is equal to the invested capital times an imputed interest rate.

responsibility accounting   Tools and concepts used by managerial accountants to measure the performance of an organization's people and subunits.

responsibility centre   A subunit in an organization whose manager is held accountable for specified financial results of its activities.

return on investment (ROI)   Income divided by invested capital.

return-on-investment pricing   A cost-plus pricing method in which the markup is determined by the amount necessary for the company to earn a target rate of return on investment.

revenue centre   A responsibility centre whose manager is accountable for its revenue.

revolving budget   See **rolling** (or **revolving** or **continuous**) **budget**.

ROI   See **return on investment**.

rolling (or **revolving** or **continuous**) **budget**   A budget that is continually updated by adding another incremental time period and dropping the most recently completed period.

safety margin   Difference between budgeted sales revenue and break-even sales revenue.

safety stock   Extra inventory consumed during periods of above-average usage in a setting with fluctuating demand.

sales budget   A schedule that shows the expected sales of services or goods during a budget period, expressed in both monetary terms and units.

sales forecasting   The process of predicting sales of services or goods. The initial step in preparing a master budget.

sales margin   Income divided by sales revenue.

sales mix   Relative proportion of sales of each of an organization's multiple products.

sales-price variance   The difference between actual and expected unit sales price multiplied by the actual quantity of units sold.

sales-volume variance   The difference between actual sales volume and budgeted sales volume multiplied by the budgeted unit contribution margin.

scatter diagram   A set of plotted cost observations at various activity levels.

schedule of cost of goods manufactured   A detailed schedule showing the manufacturing costs incurred during an accounting period and the change in work-in-process inventory.

schedule of cost of goods sold   A detailed schedule showing the cost of goods sold and the change in finished-goods inventory during an accounting period.

segmented income statement   A financial statement showing the income for an organization and its major segments (subunits).

selling costs   Costs of obtaining and filling sales orders, such as advertising costs, compensation of sales personnel, and product promotion costs.

selling, general, and administrative (SG&A) expense budget   A schedule showing the planned amounts of selling, general, and administrative expenses during a budget period.

sensitivity analysis   A technique for determining what would happen in a decision analysis if a key prediction or assumption proves to be wrong.

sequential production process   A manufacturing operation in which partially completed products pass in sequence through two or more production departments.

service (or **support**) **departments**   Subunits in an organization that are not involved directly in producing the organization's output of goods or services.

service department cost allocation   The second step in assigning manufacturing-overhead costs. All costs associated with a service department are assigned to the departments that use the services it produces.

SG&A expense budget   See **selling, general, and administrative (SG&A) expense budget**.

shareholder value analysis   Calculation of the residual income associated with a major product line, with the objective of determining how the product line affects a firm's value to its shareholders.

simple regression   A regression analysis based on a single independent variable.

Six Sigma   An analytical method that aims at achieving near perfect results in a production process.

skimming pricing   Setting a high initial price for a new product in order to reap short-run profits. Over time, the price is reduced gradually.

source document   A document that is used as the basis for an accounting entry. Examples include material requisition forms and direct-labour time tickets.

split-off point   The point in a joint production process at which the joint products become identifiable as separate products.

staff positions   Positions held by managers who are only indirectly involved in producing an organization's product or service.

standard cost   A predetermined cost for the production of goods or services that serves as a benchmark against which to compare the actual cost.

standard-costing system   A cost-control and product-costing system in which cost variances are computed and production costs are entered into work-in-process inventory at their standard amounts.

standard direct-labour quantity   The number of labour hours normally needed to manufacture one unit of product.

standard direct-labour rate   Total hourly cost of compensation, including fringe benefits.

standard direct-material price   The total delivered cost, after subtracting any purchase discounts taken.

standard direct-material quantity   The total amount of material normally required to produce a finished product, including allowances for normal waste and inefficiency.

standard quantity allowed   The standard quantity per unit of output multiplied by the number of units of actual output.

statement of cash flows   A major financial statement that shows the change in an organization's total cash and cash equivalents and explains that change in terms of the organization's operating, investing, and financing activities during a period.

static budget   A budget that is valid for only one planned activity level.

step-down method   A method of service department cost allocation in which service department costs are allocated first to service departments and then to production departments.

step-fixed cost   A cost that remains fixed over wide ranges of activity, but jumps to a different amount for activity levels outside that range.

step-variable cost   A cost that is nearly variable, but increases in small steps instead of continuously.

storage time   The time during which raw materials or finished products are stored in stock.

storyboarding   A procedure used to develop a detailed process flowchart, which visually represents activities and the relationships among the activities.

strategic cost analysis   A broad-based managerial-accounting analysis that supports strategic management decisions.

strategic cost management   Overall recognition of the cost relationships among the activities in the value chain, and the process of managing those cost relationships to a firm's advantage.

summary cash budget   A combination of the cash receipts and cash disbursements budgets.

sunk costs   Costs that were incurred in the past and cannot be altered by any current or future decision.

supply chain   The flow of all goods, services, and information into and out of an organization.

support departments   See **service** (or **support**) **departments**.

sustainable development   Business activity that produces the goods and services needed in the present without limiting the ability of future generations to meet their needs.

target cost   The projected long-run product cost that will enable a firm to enter and remain in the market for the product and compete successfully with the firm's competitors.

target costing   The design of a product, and the processes used to produce it, so that ultimately the product can be manufactured at a cost that will enable a firm to make a profit when the product is sold at an estimated market-driven price. This estimated price is called the *target price*, the desired profit margin is called the *target profit*, and the cost at which the product must be manufactured is called the *target cost*.

target net income   See **target net profit** (or **income**).

target net profit (or **income**)   The profit level set as management's objective.

task analysis   Setting standards by analyzing the production process.

theory of constraints   A management approach that focuses on identifying and relaxing the constraints that limit an organization's ability to reach a higher level of goal attainment.

throughput-based costing system   See **volume-based** (or **throughput-based**) **costing system**.

throughput costing   A product-costing system that assigns only the unit-level spending for direct costs as the cost of products or services.

throughput time   The average amount of time required to convert raw materials into finished goods ready to be shipped to customers.

time and material pricing   A cost-plus pricing approach that includes components for labour cost and material cost, plus markups on either or both of these cost components.

time record   A document that records the amount of time an employee spends on each production job.

timely information   Data that are available in time for use in a decision analysis.

total contribution margin   Total sales revenue less total variable expenses.

total cost curve   Graphs the relationship between total cost and total quantity produced and sold.

total quality control (TQC)   A product-quality program in which the objective is complete elimination of product defects.

total quality management (TQM)   The broad set of management and control processes designed to focus an entire organization and all of its employees on providing products or services that do the best possible job of satisfying the customer.

total revenue curve   Graphs the relationship between total sales revenue and quantity sold.

TQC   See **total quality control**.

TQM   See **total quality management**.

transfer price   The price at which products or services are transferred between two divisions in an organization.

transferred-in costs   Costs assigned to partially completed products that are transferred into one production department from a prior department.

treasurer   An accountant in a staff position who is responsible for managing an organization's relationships with investors and creditors and maintaining custody of the organization's cash, investments, and other assets.

trend analysis   A comparison across time of three or more observations of a particular financial item, such as net income.

two-dimensional ABC model   A combination of the cost assignment view of the role of activity-based costing with its process analysis and evaluation role. Two-dimensional ABC is one way of depicting activity-based management.

two-stage cost allocation   A two-step procedure for assigning overhead costs to products or services produced. In the first stage, all production costs are assigned to the production departments. In the second stage, the costs that have been assigned to each production department are applied to the products or services produced in those departments.

unavoidable expenses   Expenses that will continue to be incurred even if a subunit or activity is eliminated.

underapplied overhead   The amount by which the period's actual manufacturing overhead exceeds applied manufacturing overhead.

unit contribution margin   Sales price minus the unit variable cost.

unit-level activity   An activity that must be done for each unit of production.

value analysis   See **value engineering**.

value chain   An organization's set of linked, value-creating activities, ranging from securing basic raw materials and energy to the ultimate delivery of products and services.

value engineering (or **value analysis**) A cost-reduction and process improvement technique that utilizes information collected about a product's design and production processes and then examines various attributes of the design and processes to identify candidates for improvement efforts.

variable cost A cost that changes in total in direct proportion to a change in an organization's activity.

variable costing (or **direct costing**) A method of product costing in which only variable manufacturing overhead is included as a product cost that flows through the manufacturing accounts (i.e., Work-in-Process Inventory, Finished-Goods Inventory, and Cost of Goods Sold). Fixed manufacturing overhead is treated as a period cost.

variable-overhead efficiency variance The difference between actual and standard hours of an activity base (e.g., machine hours) multiplied by the standard variable-overhead rate.

variable-overhead spending variance The difference between actual variable-overhead cost and the product of the standard variable-overhead rate and actual hours of an activity base (e.g., machine hours).

velocity The number of units produced in a given time period.

vertical analysis An analysis of the relationships among various financial items on a particular financial statement. Generally presented in terms of common-size financial statements.

visual-fit method A method of cost estimation in which a cost line is drawn through a scatter diagram according to the visual perception of the analyst.

volume-based cost driver (or **activity base**) A cost driver that is closely associated with production volume, such as direct-labour hours or machine hours.

volume-based (or **throughput-based**) **costing system** A product-costing system in which costs are assigned to products on the basis of a single activity base related to volume (e.g., direct-labour hours or machine hours).

WACC See **weighted-average cost of capital**.

waiting time The time during which partially completed products wait for the next phase of production.

weighted-average cost of capital (WACC) A weighted average of the after-tax cost of debt capital and the cost of equity capital.

weighted-average method A method of process costing in which the cost assigned to beginning work-in-process inventory is added to the current-period production costs. The cost per equivalent unit calculated under this process-costing method is a weighted average of the costs in the beginning work in process and the costs of the current period.

weighted-average unit contribution margin Average of a firm's several products' unit contribution margins, weighted by the relative sales proportion of each product.

withdrawal Kanban A card sent to the preceding work centre indicating the number and type of parts requested from that work centre by the next work centre.

work in process Partially completed products that are not yet ready for sale.

working capital Current assets minus current liabilities.

zero-base budgeting A budgeting approach in which the initial budget for each activity in an organization is set to zero. To be allocated resources, an activity's continuing existence must be justified by the appropriate management personnel.

References for "In Their Own Words"*

Chapter One

(1a) Gary Siegel and James E. Sorensen, principal investigators for the Gary Siegel Organization, *Counting More, Counting Less: Transformations in the Management Accounting Profession* (Montvale, NJ: Institute of Management Accountants, 1999).

(1b) Ibid.

(1c) Ibid.

(1d) Ibid.

(1e) Ibid.

(1f) Ibid.

(1g) Ibid.

(1h) Ibid.

(1i) Ibid.

Chapter Two

(2a) Gary Siegel and James E. Sorensen, principal investigators for the Gary Siegel Organization, *Counting More, Counting Less: Transformations in the Management Accounting Profession* (Montvale, NJ: Institute of Management Accountants, 1999).

(2b) Gary Siegel, project director, *The Practice Analysis of Management Accounting* (Montvale, NJ: Institute of Management Accountants, 1996), pp. 17, 18.

(2c) Ibid., p. 14.

(2d) Ibid., p. 19.

(2e) *Activity-Based Management: Part I*, a management education video (Boston: President and Fellows of Harvard College, 1993).

(2f) Gary Siegel, project director, *The Practice Analysis of Management Accounting* (Montvale, NJ: Institute of Management Accountants, 1996), p. 18.

(2g) Interview with a Delta Air Lines accountant conducted during research by Ronald W. Hilton.

(2h) Gary Siegel and James E. Sorensen, principal investigators for the Gary Siegel Organization, *Counting More, Counting Less: Transformations in the Management Accounting Profession* (Montvale, NJ: Institute of Management Accountants, 1999).

Chapter Three

(3a) *The Management Accounting Video*, a management education video (New York: McGraw-Hill, 1997). *Note:* Since this video was made, MiCRUS was sold to Philips.

(3b) Gary Siegel and James E. Sorensen, principal investigators for the Gary Siegel Organization, *Counting More, Counting Less: Transformations in the Management Accounting Profession* (Montvale, NJ: Institute of Management Accountants, 1999).

(3c) *The Management Accounting Video*, a management education video (New York: McGraw-Hill, 1997). *Note:* Since this video was made, MiCRUS was sold to Phillips.

(3d) Interview with a Chrysler accountant conducted during research by Ronald W. Hilton.

(3e) Interview with an accountant for The Walt Disney Company conducted during research by Ronald W. Hilton.

(3f) Interview with a Chrysler accountant conducted during research by Ronald W. Hilton.

(3g) Office of Research Services, Simon Fraser University, *Guidelines for Indirect Cost (Overhead)*.

(3h) *The Management Accounting Video*, a management education video (New York: McGraw-Hill, 1997).

(3i) Gary Siegel, project director, *The Practice Analysis of Management Accounting* (Montvale, NJ: Institute of Management Accountants, 1996), p. 17.

Chapter Four

(4a) Steve Player and Carol Cobble, *Cornerstones of Decision Making: Profiles of Enterprise ABM* (Greensboro, NC: Oakhill Press, 1999), p. 161.

(4b) Ibid., p. 12.

(4c) Ibid., p. 168.

Chapter Five

(5a) *Activity-Based Management: Part I*, a management education video (Boston: The President and Fellows of Harvard College, 1993).

(5b) Joyce R. Ochs and Kenneth L. Parkinson, "Moving to Activity-Based Cost Analysis," *Business Finance* 5, no. 11 (November 1999), p. 101.

(5c) Steve Player and Carol Cobble, *Cornerstones of Decision Making: Profiles of Enterprise ABM* (Greensboro, NC: Oakhill Press, 1999), p. 167.

(5d) Ibid., p. 119.

(5e) Tad Leahy, "The A to Z of ABC Dictionaries," *Business Finance* 5, no. 12 (December 1999), p. 82.

(5f) Steve Player and Carol Cobble, *Cornerstones of Decision Making: Profiles of Enterprise ABM* (Greensboro, NC: Oakhill Press, 1999), p. 151.

(5g) Ibid., p. 226.

(5h) Scott Smith, in Steve Player and Carol Cobble, *Cornerstones of Decision Making: Profiles of Enterprise ABM* (Greensboro, NC: Oakhill Press, 1999), p. 187.

(5i) BMO Financial Group, *Review of Operating Groups Performance, 1st Quarter of 2005*.

Chapter Six

(6a) Paulo Salgado, Margarida Bajanca, and Nuno Belo, in Steve Player and Carol Cobble, *Cornerstones of Decision Making: Profiles of Enterprise ABM* (Greensboro, NC: Oakhill Press, 1999), p. 172.

(6b) Steve Player and Carol Cobble, *Cornerstones of Decision Making: Profiles of Enterprise ABM* (Greensboro, NC: Oakhill Press, 1999), p. 214.

(6c) Interview with a Ford Motor Company accountant conducted during research by Ronald W. Hilton.

(6d) Steve Player and Carol Cobble, *Cornerstones of Decision Making: Profiles of Enterprise ABM* (Greensboro, NC: Oakhill Press, 1999), p. 78.

(6e) Interview with a Cornell University administrator conducted during research by Ronald W. Hilton.

---

*The references are organized by chapter. Thus, reference (1a) relates to the first quote in Chapter 1, and so forth.

Chapter Seven

(7a) Gary Siegel and James E. Sorensen, principal investigators for the Gary Siegel Organization, *Counting More, Counting Less: Transformations in the Management Accounting Profession* (Montvale, NJ: Institute of Management Accountants, 1999).

(7b) Interview with a Cornell University accountant conducted during research by Ronald W. Hilton.

(7c) Interview with a Delta Air Lines accountant conducted during research by Ronald W. Hilton.

(7d) Gary Siegel and James E. Sorensen, principal investigators for the Gary Siegel Organization, *Counting More, Counting Less: Transformations in the Management Accounting Profession* (Montvale, NJ: Institute of Management Accountants, 1999).

(7e) Steve Player and Carol Cobble, *Cornerstones of Decision Making: Profiles of Enterprise ABM* (Greensboro, NC: Oakhill Press, 1999), p. 78.

Chapter Eight

(8a) Steve Player and Carol Cobble, *Cornerstones of Decision Making: Profiles of Enterprise ABM* (Greensboro, NC: Oakhill Press, 1999), p. 168.

Chapter Nine

(9a) *The Management Accounting Video*, a management education video (New York: McGraw-Hill, 1997). Best Foods introduced several well-known brands, such as Skippy peanut butter, Hellmann's mayonnaise, and Thomas' English Muffins. Best Foods has been acquired by Unilever.

(9b) Ibid.

(9c) Gary Siegel and James E. Sorensen, principal investigators for the Gary Siegel Organization, *Counting More, Counting Less: Transformations in the Management Accounting Profession* (Montvale, NJ: Institute of Management Accountants, 1999).

(9d) Jay Collins, "Advanced Use of ABM: Using ABC for Target Costing, Activity-Based Budgeting, and Benchmarking," in *Activity-Based Management: Arthur Andersen's Lessons from the ABM Battlefield,* ed. Steve Player and David E. Keys (New York: John Wiley & Sons, 1999), p. 153.

(9e) James A. Brimson and John Antos, *Driving Value Using Activity-Based Budgeting* (New York: John Wiley & Sons, 1999), p. 10.

(9f) Steve Hornyak, "Budgeting Made Easy," *Management Accounting* 80, no. 4 (October 1998), pp. 18–23.

Chapter Ten

(10a) *The Management Accounting Video,* a management education video (New York: McGraw-Hill, 1997).

(10b) Gary Siegel and James E. Sorensen, principal investigators for the Gary Siegel Organization, *Counting More, Counting Less: Transformations in the Management Accounting Profession* (Montvale, NJ: Institute of Management Accountants, 1999).

(10c) Ibid.

(10d) Interview with an A. T. Kearney consultant conducted during research by Ronald W. Hilton.

(10e) Steve Player and Carol Cobble, Cornerstones of Decision Making: Profiles of Enterprise ABM (Greensboro, NC: Oakhill Press, 1999), p. 79.

(10f) Cynthia Beier Greeson and Mehmet C. Kocakulah, "Implementing an ABC Pilot at Whirlpool," *Journal of Cost Management* 11, no. 2 (March/April 1997), pp. 16–21.

(10g) Interview with an A. T. Kearney consultant conducted during research by Ronald W. Hilton.

(10h) *The Management Accounting Video*, a management education video (New York: McGraw-Hill, 1997).

Chapter Eleven

(11a) Robert S. Kaplan, *City of Charlotte*, a management case (Boston: The President and Fellows of Harvard College, 1998).

(11b) Gary Siegel and James E. Sorensen, principal investigators for the Gary Siegel Organization, *Counting More, Counting Less: Transformations in the Management Accounting Profession* (Montvale, NJ: Institute of Management Accountants, 1999).

(11c) Susan Savage and Peter Neufeld, *Case Study: From Business Strategy to the Front Line at CIBC*, Balanced Scorecard for HR conference, Toronto, April 19–21, 2004.

(11d) Mark Green, Jeanine Garrity, Andra Gumbus, and Bridget Lyons, "Pitney Bowes Calls for New Metrics," *Strategic Finance* 83, no. 11 (May 2002), p. 34.

(11e) *The Management Accounting Video*, a management education video (New York: McGraw-Hill, 1997).

(11f) Gary Siegel and James E. Sorensen, principal investigators for the Gary Siegel Organization, *Counting More, Counting Less: Transformations in the Management Accounting Profession* (Montvale, NJ: Institute of Management Accountants, 1999).

(11g) Michael Arndt, "Quality Isn't Just for Widgets," *BusinessWeek*, July 22, 2002, p. 72.

Chapter Twelve

(12a) Interview with a Chrysler accountant conducted during research by Ronald W. Hilton.

(12b) Gary Siegel and James E. Sorensen, principal investigators for the Gary Siegel Organization, *Counting More, Counting Less: Transformations in the Management Accounting Profession* (Montvale, NJ: Institute of Management Accountants, 1999).

(12c) Ibid.

(12d) Interview with an American Management Systems consultant conducted during research by Ronald W. Hilton.

(12e) Gary Siegel and James E. Sorensen, principal investigators for the Gary Siegel Organization, *Counting More, Counting Less: Transformations in the Management Accounting Profession* (Montvale, NJ: Institute of Management Accountants, 1999).

(12f) Ibid.

(12g) Thomas P. Kunes, "Environmental Cost Management," *Strategic Finance*, February 2001, p. 83.

(12h) *Current Practices, Perceptions and Trends: Transfer Pricing—1997 Global Survey* (Chicago: Ernst & Young, 1997), p. 1.

(12i) Ibid., p. 4.

(12j) Ibid., p. 11.

(12k) Ibid., p. 11.

Chapter Thirteen

(13a) Gary Siegel and James E. Sorensen, principal investigators for the Gary Siegel Organization, *Counting More, Counting Less: Transformations in the Management Accounting Profession* (Montvale, NJ: Institute of Management Accountants, 1999).

(13b) Ibid.

(13c) Ibid.

(13d) Ibid.

(13e) Ibid.

Chapter Fourteen

(14a) Gary Siegel and James E. Sorensen, principal investigators for the Gary Siegel Organization, *Counting More, Counting Less: Transformations in the Management Accounting Profession* (Montvale, NJ: Institute of Management Accountants, 1999).

(14b) Ibid.

(14c) Steve Player and Carol Cobble, *Cornerstones of Decision Making: Profiles of Enterprise ABM* (Greensboro, NC: Oakhill Press, 1999), p. 80.

(14d) Presentation by U.S. Navy Acquisition Center, *The Second Annual International Conference on Target Costing*, sponsored by the Consortium for Advanced Manufacturing—International, Arthur Andersen, Ernst & Young, and the University of Akron (Washington, DC: CAM-I, 1998).

(14e) Presentation by Honda of America, *The Second Annual International Conference on Target Costing*, sponsored by the Consortium for Advanced Manufacturing—International, Arthur Andersen, Ernst & Young, and the University of Akron (Washington, DC: CAM-I, 1998).

(14f) Ibid.

Chapter Fifteen (Online)

(15a) Interview with a Ford Motor Company accountant conducted during research by Ronald W. Hilton.

(15b) Interview with a Hewlett-Packard accountant conducted during research by Ronald W. Hilton.

(15c) Letter from Cheryl Wenezenki-Yolland, Comptroller General for the Province of British Columbia to the International Federation of Accountants (IFAC), commenting on the *International Management Accounting Statement Exposure Draft: Project Appraisal Using Discounted Cash Flow*, September 2007.

(15d) Interview with a Boeing Company accountant conducted during research by Ronald W. Hilton.

(15e) Interview with an A. T. Kearney consultant conducted during research by Ronald W. Hilton.

Chapter Sixteen (Online)

(16a) Interview with a Chrysler accountant conducted during research by Ronald W. Hilton.

(16b) Interview with a Cornell University accountant conducted during research by Ronald W. Hilton.

(16c) Interview with an A. T. Kearney consultant conducted during research by Ronald W. Hilton.

Index of Companies and Organizations

Index of Subjects